THE COOKS' CATALOGUE

A critical selection of the best, the necessary and the special in kitchen equipment and utensils. Over 4000 items including 200 extraordinary recipes plus cooking folklore and 1700 illustrations produced with the assistance of the world's leading food authorities. Introduction by James Beard.

Edited by

James Beard, Milton Glaser, Burton Wolf

Barbara Poses Kafka, Helen S. Witty

and Associates of the Good Cooking School

Paperback Edition Editor: Florence Fabricant

CAUTION

Retail prices given are intended as general guide lines and for comparative purposes only. They should not be relied on for purchasing. Prices will change in time and may also vary according to the outlet through which the item is purchased.

MAIL ORDER

All objects marked with ▲ are available by mail order through Beard Glaser Wolf Ltd. See the last page of this book for a mail order form and instructions.

AVON
PUBLISHERS OF BARD, CAMELOT, DISCUS, EQUINOX AND FLARE BOOKS

Acknowledgments

The editors of this work are indebted to hundreds of people who have been involved with this book during the past three years, and we sincerely appreciate the cooperation and assistance that we have been fortunate enough to receive. However, we would like to express our deepest and special appreciation to the following:

Barbara Poses Kafka, who devoted three years to testing and selecting the equipment and developing the text.

Helen S. Witty, who edited and nurtured every paragraph of this work...a monumental task.

Elizabeth David, who patiently introduced us to the European products and enlightened us as to the habits of manufacturers.

Elizabeth Benson, Philip Brown, Grace Zia Chu, John Clancy, Carol Cutler, Julie Dannenbaum, Edward Giobbi, Carl Jerome, Leon Lianides, Helen McCully, Perla Meyers, Maurice Moore-Betty, Elisabeth Ortiz, Jacques Pépin, Felipe Rojas-Lombardi, Raymond Sokolov, Alfredo Viazzi, and Karen Zehring, who shared their infinite knowledge with our editors.

Paul Bocuse, Michael Guérard, the Messrs. Haeberlin, Guy Legay, Raymond Oliver, Louis Outhier, Raymond Thuilier, the Messrs. Troisgros, and Roger Vergé, who showed us their special equipment and discussed their criteria for the batterie de cuisine.

Ivan Nataf, who guided us through the kitchens of France.

Lois Bloom, Susan Lipke, and Susan Ceci, who catalogued our collection, dealt with manufacturers, and "controlled the pots" for two years.

Irene Sax, who was the major writer of the text, and a daily source of inspiration.

George Lang, whose amazing and detailed knowledge of the culinary art and its history was constantly available to us.

Marta Hallett, production manager, who managed to manage the unmanageable.

Eugene Stuttman. He taught us printing technology; we taught him a good pâte à choux.

Peter Mayer and Judy Weber, who deserve a Nobel in mathematics and literary sainthood for their patience and understanding.

Guy Naggar and Allan Clore, whose faith in our staff and our project led them to invest the necessary funds to make this work possible.

Joseph Baum, who directed us in the pursuit of excellence.

James Udell, who designed this book.

Jerry Darvin, who photographed the thousands of individual objects.

And:

George Adolf, *at J. A. Henckels,* Emily Aronson, Charles Bernard, Albert Bonnier, Irene Borger, Herman Bosboom and Laszlo Roth, *at H. Roth,* Pia Bregulla, Ken Brozen, Pauline P. Cable, *at Nambé Mills,* Virginia Chapman, *at Porcelaine de Paris,* J. R. Chesneau, *at Pillivuyt,* Jim Chichester, *at La Cuisinière,* Elizabeth Susan Colchie, Billie Marie Colton, *at Schiller & Asmus,* Stephen Crosby, John D'Alimonte, Pierre de Charmant, Diane Einhorn, Toby and Bernard Feinstein, Alvaro Font, *at Nordiska,* Lee Friedlander, Ellie Giobbi, Art Gordon, Madeline Greenberg, Carol Guber, Lily Guhl, Herb Haber, O. W. Hardin, *at Lockwood,* Marvin Hoffman, William Holloran, Judith Jones, Ron M. Kasperzak, *at Commercial Aluminum,* Edwin Kasin, Louis Kaster, George Kelly, Ron Kitaj, Stephen Koplan, Jay Leary, Fred Levine, Arthur Lipper, Sterling Lord, Judy McBee, *at Farberware,* Homer McCall, *at Wearever,* Thomas Meltzer, Ray Merritt, Al Namen, Hassan Romeo Nasr, Gloria Pépin, Maurice Piot, Fran and Jeffrey Powell, Maxwell Powell, Carl Heinz Quack, Mill Roseman, George Roth, Hermine Rudolph, Heinrich Gustof Schlieper, Carl Sontheimer, *at Cuisinarts,* Harry Stern, *at H. Friedman,* Michael Tong, Maurice Tuchman, Robert van Lydegraph, Chuck Williams, *at Williams-Sonoma,* Robert Wolf, *at Rowoco,* Rose and Edward Wolf

And for the Paperback Edition: John Anderson, Naomi Cutner, Leo Fuller, Verne Moberg, Myra Meyer-Oertel.

Contents

The Staff of The Cooks' Catalogue

James Beard   Milton Glaser   Burton Wolf

Executive Editor: *Senior Editor:*
Barbara Poses Kafka   *Helen S. Witty*

Production Manager:
Marta Hallett

Production Consultant:
Eugene Stuttman

Art Directors:
Rochelle and James Udell

Associate Editors:
Lois Bloom, Susan Lipke, Irene Sax

Consultants and Editors:
Joseph Baum, Elizabeth Benson, Alexis Bespaloff,
Paul Bocuse, Philip Brown, Grace Zia Chu, John Clancy,
Elizabeth S. Colchie, Carol Cutler, Julie Dannenbaum,
Elizabeth David, Florence Fabricant, Edward Giobbi,
Carol Guber, Michel Guérard, the Messrs. Haeberlin,
Madhur Jaffrey, Carl Jerome, Marjorie P. Katz,
George Lang, Guy Legay, Leon Lianides,
Eleanor Lowenstein, Helen McCully, Perla Meyers,
Maurice Moore-Betty, Raymond Oliver,
Elizabeth Lambert Ortiz, Louis Outhier, Jacques Pépin,
William Rice, Felipe Rojas-Lombardi, Raymond Sokolov,
Raymond Thuilier, the Messrs. Troisgros, Roger Vergé,
Alfredo Viazzi, Cynthia Walsh, Karen Zehring

Photographer:
Jerry Darvin

Editorial Staff:
Barbara Acosta, Emily Aronson, Irene Borger, Susan Ceci,
Jamie Hamlin, Frances Jalet, George Kelly, Maurice Piot,
Beryl Tannenbaum, Dorothy Thompson, Joan Wan

Paperback Edition Staff

Editor: Florence Fabricant
Production: Hannelore Oxman, Vivien Fauerbach
Associate Editor: Susan Lipke
Photographer: Ed Fitzgerald

Introduction

I grew up in the Iron Age of American cookery. We had a cast-iron wood stove at home in Portland, Oregon, and another at the beach at Gearhart. For stove top cooking we used iron skillets, iron Dutch ovens, and an iron stew pot. Iron against iron worked with great efficiency, I must say. And for the oven, we used sheet-iron bread pans and iron baking sheets. Of course we also depended on earthenware, tin, some copper, and the ghastly enameled pots known as graniteware. But iron was king. Now, many decades later, after having cooked here and there around the world with every kind of stove and utensil imaginable, I find myself enjoying smooth-surface electric cooking. Its principle takes me back to the old wood stove of the Iron Age.

A good deal has happened in American kitchens in the years between iron and smooth-surface cooking and especially since World War II. We have become a country of dedicated cooks, with a taste for fine food and wine and a ravenous need for all the tools of the trade. The classic implements of the world's cuisines are part of every serious cook's *batterie,* and manufacturers keep up a flow of new products. The number of stores specializing in kitchenware—what I like to call "pot shops"—have proliferated across the land. In place of iron (still available and still excellent for many uses) and the horrid graniteware, one may choose from pans of handsome copper lined with tin or stainless steel, sturdy cast aluminum, or exquisitely made stainless steel. There are also Corning Ware and Magnalite; and for baking, fine earthenware and wonderfully delicate glass. We are inundated by the choice of utterly basic utensils, like knives, spatulas, cutters, shears, food mills, graters, mashers, racks, sifters, wire whips, pastry tins and thermometers. And if one wants to invest more heavily there are dazzling electric appliances—food processors, mixers, blenders, broilers, skillets, rotisseries, and ice-cream makers. In addition each national cuisine requires its own special equipment.

Until now the cook has had little help in finding his way through this opulence—no single source of information on the best equipment available. I was discussing the problem one day over lunch with Milton Glaser and Burton Wolf, both highly knowledgeable food people, when the idea for this book came into being. Burton has been its principal architect, aided by the meticulous management of Barbara Kafka and a distinguished roster of consultants in this country and in Europe. The project, started to answer a simple need, evolved into a gargantuan international operation. I continue to be impressed by the statistics.

It all began with questionnaires to the commercial attachés of 138 countries, who were asked for information on any manufacturers of equipment associated with food and drink, no matter how small. This yielded a list of 30,000, including individual craftsmen, who were invited to submit catalogs. From the catalogs, 500,000 items were evaluated, and 10,000 items were ordered for testing. It took a warehouse to contain the colossal inventory. In addition, scouts combed trade shows and supply houses in Europe and the United States for any new developments.

Then began a three-year job of evaluation by a team of chefs, restaurateurs, purveyors of food equipment, and food writers, as well as Beard Glaser Wolf's own staff. The number of eligible items was reduced to 4,000. The standards were rigorous. Every item had to be functional, durable, and well designed. The selection was not intended to be comprehensive, so don't complain that your favorite little knife isn't here. It is, better yet, a definitive compilation of the best in cooking equipment. Each entry is explained and rated, and there is accompanying information on cooking techniques, fascinating bits of history and food lore, and many recipes and photographs. There is no other book like it, to my knowledge. It should revolutionize the task of stocking a kitchen for years to come.

When I see the wealth presented here, I cannot help but recall an episode in my cooking career when I had nothing to work with but my wits. It was in the days when I was doing one-night stands, lecturing and demonstrating in small cities in the South, using the most primitive equipment. One night I arrived for a demonstration where I was scheduled to prepare a steak au poivre and flambéed crêpes, among other items. The tools on hand were one battered saucepan, a skillet made of something like sheet iron, and an electric burner normally used for warming. I needed high heat.

Thank God for the American drugstore. I rushed out and bought a somewhat fragile aluminum skillet, an equally lightweight saucepan, and two electric irons. The irons, upended and supported, provided the heat I needed, and very good they were for the job. The pans at least held up through the performance. Nowadays I carry a few accessories with me in a suitcase to be safe. But if you ever get caught without a stove, remember that an electric iron will do many things besides press your clothes. It is perhaps the only piece of equipment the compilers of this superlative guide failed to consider.

James A. Beard

About Using This Book

The Cooks' Catalogue offers a cook's tour of the vast world of equipment for preparing food, a world that stretches from the shelves of the neighborhood housewares store to the inventory of the restaurant supplier, from the French quincaillerie to the Oriental bazaar. We provide professional tour guides: master chefs and culinary experts, historians and testers who have evaluated thousands of objects to aid you, the cook, in selecting the implements of your craft. Our sole purpose has been to reduce the dilemma of choosing or rejecting, by showing you our selections and providing you with the criteria for making your own. This is an encyclopedia of cookware.

With the help of this book, for the first time a home kitchen can be outfitted on a more solid basis than just a manufacturer's advertisement, a friend's recommendation, trial and error, or dumb luck. We give you the information you need to make an intelligent decision and avoid anguish in the marketplace or in kitchen. We tell you about particular brands, models, and sizes. We have tested blenders priced at from twenty to four hundred dollars; how many could you have tried out? In every category of cookware the examples we show are analyzed in terms of efficiency, design, materials, economics, aesthetics. We give you current prices, too, not in the expectation that they will remain unchanged but as a basis for making intelligent comparisons between alternatives.

Just as function determines form, so are the procedures of food preparation the essential considerations when examining various implements. *The Cooks' Catalogue* has therefore been organized according to the logic of the kitchen, starting in Chapter 1 with everything you need beyond the shopping cart.

In each chapter and section the function the equipment must perform is set forth, the culinary science is explained, the particular art of cuisine related to that equipment is described. For example: Stock is a rich, long-simmered amalgam of flavors, at the heart of many dishes. You might instantly recognize the classic stockpot by its shape—stockpots, however large, must be proportionately tall and narrow. Why? The *Catalogue* tells you: the narrowness exposes only a small surface to evaporation and so conserves the savory broth, while the height permits the liquid to bubble up through layers of meat and bones and vegetables, its flavor building, blending, and becoming enriched as the stock simmers.

Next—we're still with the stockpots—you are introduced to eleven chosen pots, made of materials ranging from aluminum to stainless steel to copper lined with tin, in size going upwards from the five-quart little ones to behemoths holding more than a hundred quarts. Each is fully described in the text, its good points and drawbacks, if any, discussed; there is a photograph—sometimes more than one—accompanied by detailed specifications, sizes, and price information. In all this material on stockpots comparisons are made—and while our predisposition toward one or the other pot may emerge, we caution that it is relative to the use the pot will receive in a particular kitchen; when you have read our criteria and considered your own needs, you will know which choice will suit you best.

This approach is followed throughout—for bread pans or wooden spoons just as thoroughly as for stockpots or near-priceless copper saucepans. Having begun the section on each category of equipment with information about what it is designed to accomplish, we try always to inform you reliably about materials—why, for example, so many professionals prefer tin-lined copper pans, and why you would be wasting money if you should buy such ware for certain purposes. You will learn how to discern the difference between fine tinned copper, say, and throwaway chic. You will consider with our experts countless useful details about equipment—handling, comfort, safety, practicality, storage, cleaning, construction, durability, and multiplicity of use. Aesthetics are important, and they have not been neglected. Using beautiful tools will not guarantee the results, but it will certainly enhance the pleasure of preparing and serving food. Sleek and contemporary designs and honest handcrafts alike—not to mention some worthy old-fashioned survivals—are explained and evaluated.

Prices are another important consideration in both absolute and relative terms. Those given for the things we show you were verified in the spring of 1976. We can assure the reader they will, in complete defiance of Newton's Law of Gravity, continue to rise. But while the price of a stainless-steel frying pan may in time be leavened from $22.00 to $25.00, its cost of now still offers a useful comparison with that of the elegant copper sauteuse at $90.00. There is a splendidly serviceable corkscrew priced at $2.50 and the ultimate corkscrew, its functional twin at $125.00. The informed cook can balance the merits of each.

This detailed information has been liberally seasoned with historical and literary anecdotes and interleaved with etchings and engravings, both entertaining and informative, to deepen the reader's culinary perspective. As additional illustration of the points made by the text we have provided recipes, more than 200 of them, to demonstrate the specific uses to which the utensils and equipment may be put. A description of a soapstone griddle can only be enhanced by the proximity of James Beard's recipe for Girdle Scones; a daubière is in excellent company with Elizabeth David's Daube de Boeuf Provençale.

Exploring *The Cooks' Catalogue*, you will discover innumerable items, large and small, which you never knew existed or with which you may never have bothered but which can transform certain tasks from abominable tedium to sheer delight. There is a lemon squeezer for $1.30 that you insert right into the lemon and leave stored there to provide juice by the drop as you need it, without slippery seeds or a board or a knife or a reamer. A $225 machine will make pâte à chou or fresh-ground nut butter an everyday occurrence rather than a special event. The most expensive or esoteric equipment we show is often mandated by its uniqueness or its specificity—the $300 cheese grater, or the best tomato-juicing machine we've ever seen. Items of devastating simplicity or functional overkill have been included—and we always tell you why—yet the book is devoted largely to the well-made but commonplace kitchen tools, to helping you learn how to recognize them and use them with enjoyment.

This catalogue really covers all equipment you might need for preparing what has by now become the good cook's repertoire of dishes. We would have liked to include selections from the utensils used in various parts of the world to prepare very special, ethnic foods, but this book, large as it is, simply did not have the space. In the near future we will bring you a book devoted entirely to this exotic and fascinating equipment. Until then, we believe that you can prepare any dish from any cuisine with the collections of implements shown here.

Now that you have picked your whisk or your electric mixer, where can you buy it? Look in the Availability Index at the back of this book—there we give the name and address of the manufacturer, supplier, or importer of every object in the *Catalogue*. This information is up to date in all details as we go to press.

This book is not, however, a mail-order catalogue; instead it is a comprehensive evaluation of products that are available through normal retail channels, regardless of whether they are intended for professional or home use.

Manufacturers are constantly changing their lines, modifying their inventories, announcing a new space-age wonder or faithfully reproducing a time-honored classic. What is here today may be gone tomorrow. Yet the basic elements of design and material, as *The Cooks' Catalogue* explains them, will always apply. Whether you are setting up your first kitchen or the perfect kitchen you have dreamed of for years, or whether you have finally decided to invest in an electric mixer or another multipurpose kitchen machine or in some special piece of equipment to turn out tours de force to delight connoisseurs, with this book at your side you can determine the right equipment for you—not someone else—to have.

When we talk about cooking, eventually the questions will always become the same: How much? How hot? For how long? Take a few carrots —How many? Add some stock—How much? Cook it over a low flame— For how long? To the extent that cooking is chemistry, a life-enhancing science, it imposes on us a degree of precision. Saucemaking and baking are intimidatingly precise, oppressing the insecure while at the same time giving him something to lean on. The oven must be preheated to a precise temperature before the soufflé goes in, and a given number of eggs will be able to absorb only a certain amount of butter when we make a Hollandaise. Water hotter than a certain temperature will kill yeast, while water cooler than another given temperature will paralyze it with cold. It is when we leave the disciplines of baking and saucemaking that the question of measurement becomes more subjective, and when individual taste and judgment and the vagaries of ingredients come into the equation. The bride cannot understand that her grandmother simply does not *know* how long it will take for a pot roast to become tender, while the expert becomes irritated at the student's persistent questions: What does he mean, "how much sugar?" But the saying that "anyone who can read can cook" relies for its validity on a commonly accepted system of measurements.

What do we measure? We measure volume, weight, temperature, density, and time. All these are of ancient provenance, and hints of their great age remain in the terminology to remind us of the fact. When an Englishman weighs himself or his dog or his wife by *stones,* he is harking back to the time when stones were placed on a balance with gold in ancient Egypt. And *grain,* a term still in use for quantities of precious metals and pharmaceuticals, comes from the Babylonian practice of counting gold with seeds of grain. Even the division of hours into 60 minutes, of minutes into 60 seconds, comes from the fact that 60 was the Babylonian unit of counting. From these rough beginnings in earliest history we have evolved more or less precise standards of measurement, standards on which most of the world can agree. Of course, England, Canada, and the United States are on one system of measurement—with variations among themselves—while the rest of the world is on the metric system. And the measurements which we as laymen consider sufficiently precise are looked on as the grossest approximations by scientists and engineers, who are used to making distinctions which are hundreds or thousands of times more exact than anything the rest of us can distinguish.

But at bottom, measuring is simply an agreement among civilized people about certain standards. So that a gallon, which we consider an absolute, is in fact simply a formula we have made up for 231 cubic inches; and what we call a five-degree rise in temperature is really the change in heat which is necessary to make a column of liquid in a tube change its length to a given degree. For those who look for absolutes, take heart in the fact that in the National Bureau of Standards, somewhere in Washington, there is a prototype kilogram, an exact copy of an International prototype kilogram which resides in Sèvres. It indicates our future—the metric system will, within a few years, become

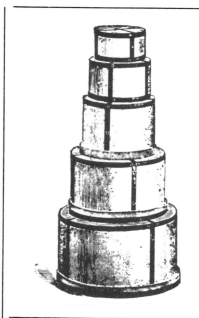

VØRTERKAKE

A very special Norwegian sweet bread baked in round loaves, *vørterkake* takes its name from *vørterøl,* or brewer's wort, one of the ingredients, which is a non-alcoholic beer very popular in Norway. *Vørterøl* used to be imported into this country, but since it is no longer available, dark beer can be substituted in its place. The bread is densely textured and has a highly interesting, spicy flavor, but I will tell you at the outset that the dough is difficult to work with. Therefore it is best to prepare it for the special occasions when you want a showoff loaf. It keeps extremely well, and is different enough from run-of-the-mill bread to warrant your mastering it. Serve it thinly sliced and well buttered, along with marmalade or jam.

The recipe comes from the Norwegian Government School for Domestic Science Teachers.

2 free-form loaves

2 packages active dry yeast
1¼ cups lukewarm milk
4 cups all-purpose flour
4 cups rye flour
⅔ cup lukewarm golden syrup or corn syrup
1¾ cups *vørterøl* (brewer's wort) or dark beer
¾ teaspoon ground cloves
¾ teaspoon freshly ground pepper
1 tablespoon salt
½ cup granulated sugar
½ cup raisins

Proof the yeast in the lukewarm milk. Add 2 cups flour and stir to make a soft dough. Put in a warm place for 35 to 40 minutes, until the dough has started to ferment and shows some signs of rising. At this point add the lukewarm syrup and the *vørterøl* or beer, which has been mixed with the spices, salt, and sugar. Add the remaining flour, 1 cup at a time, until the dough becomes supple, but just firm enough to hold its shape. (This step is crucial, because too firm a dough will not rise well, and too soft a dough cannot be formed into stable loaves.) Cover and place in a warm, draft-free spot and let rise until doubled in bulk.

Punch the dough down, turn out on a floured board, fold in the raisins, and knead for a few moments. Then form into two round loaves. Place on a buttered and floured baking sheet, cover, and let rise until about doubled in bulk. Brush with hot water and prick rather lightly. Bake in a preheated 375° oven for about 45 minutes, until the crusts have become quite shiny (because of the syrup) and the loaves sound hollow when rapped on the top and bottom. Cool thoroughly before slicing, and keep refrigerated until ready to use.

NOTE: If the loaves are brushed with a thin paste made with about 2 tablespoons potato flour and a little water, just before they are taken out of the oven, they will acquire a fine, even shinier crust.

VARIATION: For an interesting variation, use finely cut oatmeal for a third of the all-purpose and rye flours in the recipe.

(From BEARD ON BREAD, by James A. Beard, illustrated by Karl Stuecklen. Copyright © 1973 by James A. Beard. Reprinted by permission of Alfred A. Knopf, Inc.)

A finely calibrated pastry-making scale from a book published in 1886.

that of the United States. Already, you will notice, some domestic utensils—see the Pyrex measuring pitchers farther along—are already available with markings in both systems. In the meanwhile, as the wave of the metric future still approaches, we often need to translate quantities from British or Continental cookbooks. Until the time when all systems are unified, cooks in this country will find help in the conversion tables being included in good cookbooks.

So, in the kitchen we measure volume, weight, density, time, and temperature. And surely the most common of these is volume, the answer to the constant question: How much? We think of cups and teaspoonfuls, but in fact the basic unit of this standard is the cube, a more or less imaginary cubic inch of air. On this structure have been built all of the formulas which we use to illustrate capacity. A dry pint, for example, is 33.6 cubic inches, while a liquid pint is 28.875 cubic inches. And cups and half-cups and teaspoonfuls all have been devised to express a relationship to this cubic inch of air.

THE OTHER SYSTEMS

Which seems very straightforward, but that's not the end of the story, as any army wife who has moved to Europe with her cookbooks but not her measuring cups can testify. Because in addition to the standard American system there is the Imperial system of Great Britain, in which a pint of liquid measures a quarter again as much as an American pint, in which the gallon measures 277.420 cubic inches rather 231 cubic inches, and where they are both counted in gills (5/8 of a U.S. cup, or 5 ounces) rather than ounces. Further, small dry measurements in Great Britain are on a different basis—a British teaspoon equals 1¼ U.S. teaspoons, and a British tablespoon equals 4 (British) teaspoons, while three U.S. teaspoons equal one U.S. tablespoon—the more to add to the confusion. On the Continent, if dry measurement by volume is done at all, it is likely to be according to the volume measures of the metric system; but most likely, all dry measurements will be according to weight (again, according to the metric system), a far more precise and sensible affair in which we do not have to allow for such matters as the settling of flour or sugar in the cup, which make dry measurements variable, to say the least.

Still and all, there is no question that things are better than they used to be, when directions were given according to such measures as different sizes of wine glasses, or tea cups, or coffee cups. The only vestige of that system here is the teaspoon-tablespoon nomenclature, and these measures are now standardized in the United States at ⅙ and ½ of a fluid ounce. Imagine trying to follow an old recipe in which you are told to "add butter the size of a hazelnut," or "as much as a walnut"; you would have to possess a pretty good spatial memory.

THE AMERICAN WAY

Today in the United States we use volume measurements for both dry and liquid ingredients. Dry measurement is done in containers which

Continued from preceding page

hold exactly the amount wanted, whether a cupful or half a teaspoonful. You take the back of your knife and scrape it across the top of the cup or spoon to remove the excess flour or baking powder, and there you are. For liquid measurement we use containers that are marked to hold various quantities. Glass or plastic measuring pitchers are best, so that you may easily check the level of the liquid at eye level with the marking.

What do you need for measuring? Here is an area in which you might as well be profligate. Nothing costs very much, and enough good measuring equipment is worth the extra expense if only for those moments when, because you have extra measures, you will not have to wash the honey out of the cup before measuring the flour in it, or the vanilla extract out of the teaspoon before dipping it into the baking powder. Buy a few sets of measuring cups and a few bunches of spoons, hanging on their rings like a medieval housewife's keys. Then a few pitcher-shaped glass cups for liquid measure. Buy the most attractive ones you can find, or buy them from the five-and ten: in this case, cost brings no improvement in function. Keep them close at hand, on a pegboard over your stove or in that chock-full drawer right below your mixing area. And be sure that everything is totally washable.

Foley Stainless-Steel Measuring Cups 1.1

Stainless steel; set of 6 with rack; capacities of ⅛, ¼, ⅓, ½, 1, and 2 cups.
$7.98

We can't in all honesty recommend any single set of measuring cups. All we can do is to show you one or two that we like, tell you why we like them, and then let you use them as a standard when you go out to choose your own. This dry-measuring set from Foley, for example: in it you get six lightweight cups of stainless steel, each with a long handle. And on each handle there is a clear marking of the capacity of the measure: ⅛, ¼, ⅓, ½, 1, or 2 cups. There are ridges on the interiors to show fractional markings within the larger cups, useful to have in

case you simply must use them for liquid measure. And there is a rack provided for storage. Why do we like this set? It is well made and sturdy, strong enough so that it could, in a pinch, be used for measuring syrup or butter and warming it over the pilot light of your stove. It will be a simple matter to keep it clean. And the two-cup measure, while far from essential, will be a great convenience if you are a breadmaker and find yourself scooping six or eight cups of flour into your bowl. This is a good set; there are others which are just as good.

Measuring Cups and Spoons from Foley 1.2

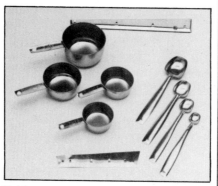

Stainless steel; set of 4 cups, 4 spoons, with 2 racks; spoon capacities ¼ tsp., ½ tsp., 1 tsp., 1 tbsp.; cup capacities ¼, ⅓, ½, and 1 cup.
$9.00 ▲

Another set from Foley, which we show you to illustrate the fact that you can get by with fewer than the six cups provided in the preceding set. Here you have the basics, the bare necessities: measures that hold ¼, ⅓, ½, and 1 cup. In addition, you get a set of four long-handled measuring spoons holding from ¼ teaspoon to 1 tablespoon. Both cups and spoons are clearly marked and made of an exceptionally good weight of stainless steel. When we tested this set, we were able to bend the bowl of one of the spoons all of the way back until it touched the handle, and it never snapped. We like the set because it is easy to care for, it's easy to distinguish among the various sizes, and because it can be stored close at hand on its own two racks or on your pegboard.

Metal Measuring Spoons from West Germany 1.3

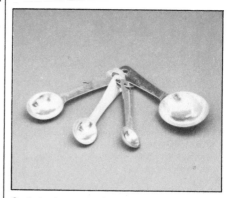

Cast aluminum; set of 4; capacities of ¼ tsp., ½ tsp., 1 tsp., and 1 tbsp.
$2.00 ▲

You can buy beautiful china measuring spoons, which will probably break. Or cheap plastic ones, which will eventually get left too close to the stove and will melt. Or you can start right out with a set like this one from Germany, a ringful of solidly made cast-aluminum spoons holding ¼ teaspoon, ½ teaspoon, 1 teaspoon, and 1 tablespoon. The maker apparently considers the sizes so familiar to the eye that, like the Coke bottle or Frank Sinatra, they need no identification, so he has not bothered to put markings on them. Do you know, by the way, how to measure ⅛ teaspoon? You dip the ¼ teaspoon measure into your cloves or baking powder, and then level it off. Now stick the point of your knife into the bowl so that it forms a diameter, and flick half of the contents back into the tin. We like this set very much because it

Foley Stainless-Steel Measuring Cups
Measuring Cups and Spoons from Foley
Metal Measuring Spoons from
West Germany

Measuring Spoon with Slide
All-in-One Plastic Slide Measure
Plastic Cup for Weight and Volume

is sturdy and easy to clean; buy more than one set for quick measuring without repeated washing of spoons—choose either this one or another set as sturdy.

"Where I find the American measurement system messy, unreliable and time-wasting is when it comes to cramming sticky things like butter or fat into a cup . . . and I have never been very successful in measuring cooked ingredients such as chopped meat or diced potatoes in cups. Do you cram the stuff down? Do you give it a good rattle so that it settles—or alternatively flies all over the place? Just press lightly, my American colleagues tell me. How light is lightly? And how much does it matter?"

Elizabeth David, Spices, Salts and Aromatics in the English Kitchen, *Penguin Books, 1973*

Measuring Spoon with Slide   1.4

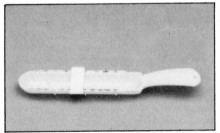

Plastic; 6¼″ long; measures any quantity from ¼ tsp. to 1 tbsp.
$.60 ▲

Now forget what a measuring spoon looks like; empty your mind of all of those clusters of tiny spoons on rings; and consider this very new, very sensible means of measurement. It is a long, narrow plastic scoop into which has been set a sliding barrier that works rather like a dam. Along either edge of the scoop is a rulerlike scale of measures: on one side they are in quarter-teaspoons and on the other they are in thirds of a teaspoon, to a maximum of 3 teaspoons (1 tablespoon). You set the slide for the quantity you want—say, ¾ teaspoon—and dip the tip of the scoop into your allspice or your cinnamon. Then you level it off with the back of a knife, and you've got it. If you can rid yourself of your preconceptions, you will see that this works; and more than that, it is sensible, nicely funny-looking, and wonderful for children who are learning their way around the kitchen. Think of the instructional value of seeing on a single gauge the relationship between ½ and

¾! And of having in concrete form a demonstration that 3 teaspoons equal 1 tablespoon! We really love it, having only the reservation that, while eliminating clutter, it increases washing-up between sticky measurements, and that one of anything like this is too few.

All-in-One Plastic Slide Measure   1.5

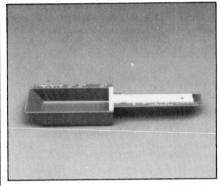

Plastic; 9¼″ long overall; section 2¾″ wide measures ¼ tsp. to ½ cup; section 1¼″ wide measures from ¼ tsp. to 3 tsp.
$1.25 ▲

Here is a second proof that, by rethinking traditional concepts, you can come up with really innovative solutions. This all-in-one measure eliminates so many implements that it makes us nervous—it makes us think that the time we might save by not having to take out and put away separate measures would be spent in washing this gadget over and over again as we dole out the ingredients for a particularly complicated cake. However that may be, it works on the same principle as the preceding plastic measure—by lengthening and shortening a space within a set area. This is a large wheelbarrow-shaped affair sans wheels and with one single long handle. The large scoop makes tablespoon and fractional cup measurements up to ½ cup; a hoelike slide lets you block the space to measure the amount you want. The troughlike handle is also a measure; it is adjusted by the same slide, whose larger end functions in the larger space. The handle section measures from ¼ teaspoon to 1 tablespoon. The whole business is a little over 9 inches long, is made of heavy plastic, and looks as though it would stay together fairly well. We don't think that it should be the only measuring cup in your kitchen —for one thing, its capacity is small— but it might very well be an auxiliary.

Plastic Cup for Weight and Volume   1.6

Plastic; 5¾″ high; 3¼″ base diam.; 4¼″ top diam.; measures up to ½ liter.
$1.98

Europeans measure dry ingredients by weight, not volume, and there is really no way to follow a recipe in *Larousse Gastronomique* if you don't have a set of kitchen scales. But if you don't—and you don't, right?—this inexpensive cup provides a not completely accurate but sufficiently valid way to approximate the correct measures. It is shaped like a funnel with a spout and has a round base for a solid footing. The body is marked in vertical bands, each of which is headed by the name—in German—of a common foodstuff: raisins, barley, flour, sugar, salt, cocoa, dried beans, and oats. Beneath that is a scale in milligrams. If you scoop oatmeal into this cup up to the 75 mg. level, then you will have oatmeal weighing approximately that much. Not ideal, but better than nothing and certainly adequate if you seldom use Continental recipes. The cup is of medium-weight transparent plastic, and it stands something under 6″ high. This is, you will notice, the first measure we have seen which has as a requirement that you be able to see through it so that you can check the level of the contents against the markings on the outside.

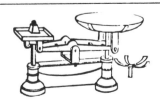

A "weighing machine," 1848.

Pyrex Measuring Cups 1.7

Pyrex glass; 5" diam., 5¼" deep, 1-qt./1-liter capacity. Also avail. 4" diam., 4¼" deep, 1-pint/½-liter capacity, or 3" diam., 3½" deep, 1-cup/¼-liter capacity.

$1.80 ▲ $1.40 ▲ $1.00 ▲

The ubiquitous Pyrex measuring pitcher for liquid measure, here available as a trio holding 4 cups, 2 cups, and 1 cup. We don't have to tell you about Pyrex, because we're sure that you own one or another of these—that you, too, grew up with them. But now they have a new attraction, a liter scale in addition to the cup scale for the moment when the whole world goes on the metric system. A minor change in a wonderful staple. These are easy to clean, a dream to see through, and they can hang on hooks on a pegboard or stand on a shelf in your cupboard. But don't forget that they are made of Corning's familiar ovenproof glass, just like the double boiler and the baking dish we show you, and that they can also be put into a bain marie, in a preheating oven, or, very carefully, over a gentle flame for melting butter or chocolate or for heating maple syrup. One tip: before you measure honey, molasses, or syrup in this cup, grease it lightly. In that way you will be able to get every last drop out, and cleaning the pitcher will not be the agony it might otherwise be. And don't forget that you can use it for measuring fats by the displacement method. Suppose you have a free-form lump of lovely farm-fresh butter, and you need half a cup of it. Just pour half a cup of cold water into your measure and then begin to drop chunks of butter into it until the water, with all the butter submerged, reaches the 1-cup level.

Small Plastic Measuring Cup 1.8

Plastic; 3" diam.; 2¾" deep; 1-cup capacity.
$.59

At first glance this doesn't compare with the Pyrex cup, being small and, unfortunately, made of plastic. But it is a plastic which will not deform on contact with boiling liquids and which is, therefore, dishwasher-proof. It is a neat little design, with the characteristic pouring spout which is nearly always found on cups for measuring liquids. And it is one of those wonderful things to have when one is introducing the children to the glories of the kitchen: an unbreakable utensil. Drop it and it bounces—what more can we say? We can say that it has a useful scale of liquid ounces on one side of the cup, and that a woman we know has one of these permanently in residence in each of her canisters of flour, sugar, and rice.

Liter Measure from Italy 1.9

Heavy-gauge aluminum; 4¼" diam; 4¼" deep; 1-liter capacity.
$7.50

We don't think that you should buy this for your kitchen, unless it be to hold the spoons that stand next to your stove or a bunch of daisies on the window sill. But we wanted to show you what a European liter measure is like. This, from Zucchi, is made in Italy, where it is used like a cup measure for liquid ingredients. It is of restaurant-quality heavy-gauge aluminum with a good handle and simple design—so simple, in fact, that it has no markings other than "Litro," indicating that it holds 1 liter when filled to the brim; no fractional measures are given and, in fact, they would be difficult to use in this measure. If you have that kind of a kitchen, you might stick a couple of pounds of different shapes of pasta into it for an amusing bouquet.

CALGIONETTI

This pastry has a provincial honesty that is a delight. It is a Christmas specialty from the Marches and was always my favorite. My mother made calgionetti only during the Christmas holidays and they were made two different ways. The first was with grape concentrate (set aside when we made wine in the fall), mixed with bits of chocolate and almonds. The other way was with chick peas (ceci beans) and honey.

FILLING
¾ cup shelled almonds
1½ cups canned or dried chick peas, soaked overnight and cooked until tender
2 tablespoons grated orange rind
¼ teaspoon cinnamon
4 tablespoons honey

DOUGH
3 cups flour
½ cup dry white wine
½ cup water
½ cup olive oil
Pinch of salt

Put almonds in boiling water. Boil for about 1 minute or less, drain and remove brown skins. Place in tray and put in 400° oven, mixing occasionally. Remove when brown, cool and finely chop. Set aside.

Drain chick peas and put through mill or sieve. Add almonds, orange rind, cinnamon, and honey. Mix well and set aside.

Make a well in the flour. Put other ingredients in well. With a fork gradually work in flour until mixture thickens. Then continue mixing with hands. Knead dough until well blended. Roll into a ball, then cut in half and make 2 balls. Flour a board, roll out one ball with rolling pin to a circle about ¹⁄₁₆ inch thick. About 2 inches from the top of the circle put 1 teaspoon of filling every 2 inches across the width. Roll 2-inch strip over top. Seal bottom edge. With sharp knife or pastry wheel, cut out individual calgionetti in half circles as you would ravioli. Seal edges with a fork and set aside. Repeat process until all of the circle is used. Then roll out other half of dough and repeat process.

In a skillet put about 1 inch of corn oil or peanut oil. When oil is very hot add 5 or 6 calgionetti, one at a time, and deep-fry until they are golden brown on both sides. Remove from oil, blot with paper towels and repeat process. Sprinkle sugar over calgionetti when finished. Yield: About 60 calgionetti.

(From ITALIAN FAMILY COOKING, by Edward Giobbi, illustrated by Cham, Lisa, and Gena Giobbi. Copyright © 1971 by Edward Giobbi. Reprinted by permission of Random House, Inc.)

Porcelain Measuring Pitcher   1.10

Porcelain; 4″ diam.; 5″ deep; capacity 1 Imperial pint.
$8.50

Here is another measuring device which we recommend that you use for other than measuring purposes. Not that it isn't clearly marked on the creamy porcelain interior into divisions indicating ¼, ½, ¾, and 1 pint; only unfortunately those are divisions of the Imperial pint, that strange English convention which confuses the American cook by being a quarter again as large as the American pint—20 ounces instead of 16. Which means that you can't use this lovely thing for measuring unless you have an English cookbook or want to do some

fancy figuring. Broad blue and white stripes encircle the outside, and there is a gently curved white handle. It is so terribly pretty, such a deft fusion of dairymaid simplicity and sophisticated design, that we urge you to buy it in spite of the uselessness of the measuring gauge. Your children will be thrilled to use it for pouring their own milk or cocoa; and you could mix pancake batter right in it and have it ready to pour onto the griddle.

POTATO AND CHERVIL SOUP

Using this recipe of Elizabeth David's would be an opportunity to use for its intended purpose the attractive English measuring pitcher (1.10) we show you, marked into divisions of the Imperial pint.

POTATO AND CHERVIL SOUP
[British measuring units]
½ lb. of potatoes, 1 oz. of butter, 1 pint of water, ¼ pint of milk, seasonings of salt and nutmeg, 2 oz. of double cream, a heaped tablespoon of fresh chervil cut with scissors.

Cut the peeled potatoes into small strips or dice. Melt the butter in a heavy soup pot. Put in the potatoes, let them cook extremely gently in the butter for about 10 minutes until they are beginning to soften. They must not brown. Sprinkle them with a little salt and a grating of nutmeg. Pour in the water. Cover the pot. Let the potatoes simmer for 20 to 25 minutes. Sieve them through the mouli, preferably twice. Return the purée to the rinsed-out pan. Add the milk, first brought to the boil in another pan. (This point is important.) Taste for seasoning. Before serving stir in the chervil and the cream. Quantities given make three good helpings.

For all its primitive simplicity this is a very excellent and light little summer soup. It should be on the thin side, but creamy and white. The flavour of the chervil with the potatoes is very subtle. For those who cannot get this useful and delicate herb, the same soup can be made using watercress or ordinary cress or chives. Be careful not to overdo the herbs, whichever you use. It is the few green flecks and the contrast of tastes which make the charm of the soup.

(From SUMMER COOKING, by Elizabeth David. Copyright © 1955, 1965, 1971 by Elizabeth David. Published by Penguin Books. Reprinted by permission of Elizabeth David.)

SCALES AND BALANCES

Measuring by weight is both more exact and more sensible than measuring by volume or number. "Take two eggs": a superficially precise instruction, but one which is dependent on the highly variable size of eggs. The canny consumer knows that nothing that cost 69¢ in one size and $1.09 in another can be truly interchangeable. As for cup measure, it can vary remarkably depending on the way in which the flour is placed in the cup: was it sifted until airy and light, or was it packed down in the canister and lifted into the cup in near-solid spoonfuls? But a given number of grams of flour or salt means only one thing.

In European recipes the ingredients are listed by weight in grams, if they are solids, or in liters, if they are liquids. Opened at random, a French cookbook in our office calls, in a recipe for chicken, for 100 grams of butter and 4 deciliters of Cognac. With one of the new dual-scale Pyrex measuring pitchers you'd have no trouble measuring the Cognac, but if you don't own a scale with metric markings, you are in difficulty with the butter. Of course there are conversion tables available in the better general cookbooks, and these give you rough cup equivalents so that you can cope with an occasional French recipe; they can tell you, for example, that 100 grams of flour will measure ⅔ of a U.S. cup. But if you think that you might be using Continental cookbooks, you'd be wise to invest in a good kitchen scale. You can use even the simplest kind for checking on the suspiciously tidy roast the

Continued from preceding page

butcher sent you, and at the other extreme you can always use one of the bigger ones for weighing the baby.

See-Saw Balance Scoop 1.11

Plastic; 14½″ overall; measuring cup 5″ diam., 4″ deep; capacity 17 oz. or 500 grams.

$12.98

The best kitchen scales are invariably made abroad, since this is not a common item in the American kitchen. In Germany, "Dr. Oetker" is the brand name of a line of more than 200 baking and kitchen utensils, as well as a number of German-language cookbooks. The Dr. Oetker balance shown here is an ingenious and convenient system for measuring small amounts of ingredients. It is actually a miniature plastic see-saw, with a measuring cup for ingredients at one end and a counterweight at the other end. The weights in ounces and grams are printed along the flat top surface of the beam. A fulcrum-rocker in the middle slides back and forth to balance the two ends, and indicates that a proper balance has been achieved by means of a small bubble like that on a carpenter's level. The cup is of clear plastic, with markings indicating British, American, and metric measurements; it holds 17 ounces or 500 grams. Its one drawback is that unless the ingredients distribute evenly in the cup, as flour does, the weight may be inaccurate. A wall bracket permits you to hang it all conveniently—and decoratively—out of the way for storage.

CRACKLING BISCUIT— TEPERTOS POGACSA

30 biscuits

Note on Cracklings: Pork cracklings can generally be purchased in a Hungarian, Czech, German or Austrian butcher shop. If they are not available to you, take a slab bacon and leave on the skin a layer of fat about ½ inch thick. Cut the slab into 2-inch pieces. Put in a heavy pan with about 3 tablespoons water and 2 tablespoons milk. This will make it taste almost nutty. Cook slowly until most of the fat is rendered.

With goose cracklings you use a slightly different method. When you cut off goose fat, make sure that you cut it with skin on one end and a little bit of the breast meat on the other. Make a few incisions on the inside, leaving the outside skin intact. Cut into about 2-inch squares. Put the pieces into a pot and barely cover with water. Start the cooking under a cover, over medium-high heat. When the water evaporates, remove the cover and increase the heat to render and brown the cracklings. Turn the pieces and move them around to make sure that they don't burn.

At the strategic moment, remove the pot from the heat and sprinkle it with a few drops of cold water. The best way is to dip your hands into cold water and just shake the water over the cracklings; make sure that your face is not directly above. Remove cracklings; if they still contain too much fat, gently press them with a spoon. (Save the precious fat, of course.)

When you cut pieces of pork or goose fat, try to cut them as evenly as possible so one piece will not burn before the other is done. When the color resembles the crust of a hard roll, the cracklings are generally done.

In peasant houses, where saving was vital, instead of washing out the pan in which fat was rendered, after removing the cracklings and the fat, the cook threw flour into the pan to absorb the fat remaining; the resulting mixture was then used at a later date as *roux*.

This crackling biscuit is another perfect accompaniment to a glass of beer. It can be made in any size. For a stag party double the size of the biscuits.

3 tablespoons milk
1 pound flour
1 envelope of yeast
1 whole egg
½ pound pork cracklings, ground or chopped
1 tablespoon rum
1 tablespoon salt
1 teaspoon pepper
¼ pound lard, melted
⅓ cup dry white wine
1 extra egg yolk

1. Heat milk till lukewarm. Make a starter dough with the milk, 1 tablespoon of the flour and the yeast. Let the starter rise for 10 minutes.
2. Mix remaining flour with 1 whole egg, the cracklings, rum, salt, pepper, melted lard and wine. Mix in the starter, and knead well.
3. Let the dough rise in a lukewarm place until it doubles in bulk, 30 to 45 minutes.
4. Roll out the dough on a floured board and fold it. Cover it with a clean cloth and let it rest for 10 minutes.
5. Repeat the same procedure twice or three times—rolling, folding, resting. Preheat oven to 400°F.
6. Finally roll the dough to 2-inch thickness. With a biscuit cutter 1½ inches in diameter, punch out biscuits.
7. With a sharp knife score the tops of the biscuits in a lattice pattern. Beat the egg yolk with 1 teaspoon water, and brush the glaze on the biscuit tops. Let them rest until this glaze dries, about 10 minutes.
8. Bake in the preheated oven until golden brown, about 25 minutes.

(From THE CUISINE OF HUNGARY, by George Lang. Copyright © 1971 by George Lang. Reprinted by permission of Atheneum.)

Compact French Plastic Scale 1.12

Plastic; 6¼″ X 4¼″; 4½″ high; weighs up to 9½ lbs. or 4000 grams. Also avail. with a weight capacity of 5 lbs. or 2000 grams.

$17.00 ▲

The German scale we showed you (1.11) works according to the principle of balance, like the one that blind Justice carries around with her. This marvelously attractive mechanism works, instead, by spring balance, a somewhat less accurate way of determining weight, but one

GERMAN KITCHEN

Continued from preceding page

which is adequate for kitchen use. In a spring scale, the dial registers according to the degree to which the spring is depressed by a weight: compare a doctor's scale—balance—with your bathroom scale—spring—and you will have an idea of the two principles as well as a comparison of the degrees of accuracy. (Why is it we always weigh *less* on the everyday bathroom scale?) This scale by Terraillon would never do in a jeweler's workshop, but it is a perfectly good choice for the sort of measurement required in the kitchen. This is a compact, rounded little rectangle in brightly colored plastic, with a magnified dial on the front showing measurements in pounds and grams. The measurements go up to 9½ pounds or 4 kilograms—4000 grams: as a matter of fact, that is the reason why it is called the *4000*. How would *you* like to be called by your weight? There are two plastic boxes, one fitting inside the other, that are to be inverted over the machine when not in use, covering it snugly. To weigh food, you set one of them tidily onto the ridges on the top of the scale and use a wheel on the side to adjust for the weight of the box. This is adequate as a machine, but superb as a design: compact, easy to clean and read (the figures are magnified by the lens over the weight indicator), and brilliantly colored, demonstrating that plastic can be gorgeous when it is treated with respect.

Danish Wall Scale 1.13

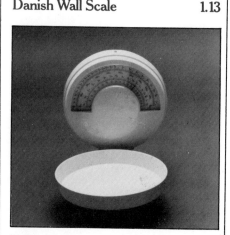

Plastic; 8" diam.; tray extends 10" from wall when open; weighs up to 6 lbs. 10 oz. or 3 kilograms.

$21.50

This scale is the one that all of our experts wanted, even those who confessed that they scarcely ever measured by weight. They wanted it because it is one of those perfect designs you meet only now and then—and which so often come to us from Denmark. Taking up no more space than a kitchen clock, it hangs on your wall, the face covered by a weighing tray. When you want to use it, you lower the tray until it is horizontal, and pile your beans or your flour into it. Then it is a simple matter to slide the tray out of its chrome loop handle and dump the contents into a bowl. The plastic case comes in avocado, blue, orange, red, or yellow, but we show it, and would buy it, only in white, looking as pure as a scale in a meat market or a laboratory. This works on a pendulum mechanism, with no springs to go out of kilter. It has two dials, one finer in gradation than the other. On the fine scale you can weigh, by quarter-ounce and ten-gram increments, up to a hair over 2 pounds 3 ounces or 1 kilogram (1000 grams); the indicator then goes onto the grosser scale, which weighs by ounces and by kilograms plus grams. There you can weigh up to 6 pounds 10 ounces or 3 kilograms. There are two indicators—the big hand and the little hand—which eliminate any confusion as to which of the two dials to look at.

WILD DUCK WITH QUINCES— VADKACSA BIRSALMAVAL

2 servings

1 young wild duck, 3 to 4 pounds, dressed
Salt
6 quinces
¾ cup melted butter
½ cup dry white wine

1. Preheat oven to 300 F. Wash the duck as little as possible. Just clean inside and outside with a moist cloth. Salt well inside and outside.
2. Peel quinces and cut into segments. Stuff them into the cavity of the duck.
3. Place duck in a roasting pan and pour melted butter over the bird. Roast in the preheated oven for about 10 minutes.
4. Pour the wine on top of the duck and put it back in the oven. Continue to roast the duck, basting all the time with the butter and wine in the pan, until it is almost done. This will be 1 hour, or less.
5. Increase oven heat to 500 F. and roast for 3 or 4 minutes longer, until skin is crisp.
6. Total roasting time for a young wild duck depends on how bloody you like it. In Hungary they prefer it well cooked.

Serve with a *risotto* made with the giblets of the bird, and with braised red cabbage.

NOTE: Only the breasts of wild duck are used, since the legs are tough. As a result the duck will make only 2 servings.

(From THE CUISINE OF HUNGARY, by George Lang. Copyright © 1971 by George Lang. Reprinted by permission of Atheneum.)

Selling underweight loaves of bread was a frequent crime during the Middle Ages. If his bread weighed less than it was supposed to, the baker was pulled through the town on a hurdle with the offending loaf hung around his neck.

French Beam Balance 1.14

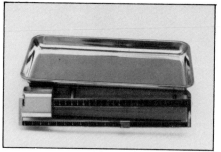

Chromed steel weighing pan with enameled steel base; 12" × 7"; 3" high; weighs up to 22 lbs.

$31.00 ▲

This beam balance from Terraillon is not nearly so attractive as their neat little plastic-housed spring scale, but it makes up for it by being far more accurate and having a much larger capacity. The manufacturer suggests that you can use this scale, with the addition of a separately sold folding hammock, for weighing the baby; and it is the same scale which they sell for weighing letters and packages in your office. It has a base of brilliantly colored enameled steel and a removable mirror-finished chrome tray. In front there is a double row of balances, each with its chrome slide. And it works in precisely the same way as the scale in your doctor's office: you move the upper slide to the correct number of pounds, up to 22, and then move the lower slide to the ounce indicator which causes the scale to balance. You can have this scale for weighing in either pounds or grams; the latter would be somewhat more useful for a kitchen, since kitchen scales are most often needed when you use a European cookbook. If, however, you buy the scale for weighing in pounds, you can always learn how to do those fearsome mathematical conversions (see the tables in a good general cookbook). Pile the tomatoes or butter directly onto the easily cleaned tray, or add a bowl, remembering to adjust the scale, by means of the white knob on the side, to take into account the weight of the bowl. This scale is useful principally because it has the ability to weigh such a large amount.

English Portion-Control Scale
1.15

Plastic; base 8¾″ diam., 3¾″ high; bowl 7¼″ inside diam., 5⅛″ deep; weighs up to 5 lbs. or 2200 grams; bowl capacity up to 4 U.S. pints, 4 Imperial pints, or 2½ liters.

$12.95

As far as we are concerned, this is plastic at its ugliest: flimsy, badly colored, easily stained. Our scale is yellow-orange and black, with markings of avocado green! But the whole scale is well made and extremely useful, being the first one that we can show you which has a system for adjusting for portion control. That means that you can place your butter in the large rigid, plastic weighing bowl and then move the circular weight gauge so that the pointer is once again at zero; then you can add the sugar without removing the first ingredient, and so on ad infinitum. In fact, you can undoubtedly mix certain kinds of cakes right in the bowl after adding, successively, eggs, flour, and flavorings. With the bowl removed, a weight-watcher can put his dinner plate on the scale, turn the indicator back again to zero, and then weigh his meat and his spinach without taking off anything but pounds. The scale shows both gram and pound weights; the easy-pouring bowl is marked in U.S. pints, plus liters and Imperial pints, so it is usable for measuring liquids as well as for weighing solids. It is hard to make a

judgement of this scale: the bowl is well made and marked, and the movable gauge is smooth and easy to use. But on the other hand, it is awkwardly large, it works on less-than-ideal spring balance, and it is really awful looking.

INSALATA DI MARE— HERB-FLAVORED SEAFOOD SALAD

This may well be the most popular cold seafood dish in Italy. Every region has its own version, each slightly differing in ingredients and seasonings. The one thing they all have in common, and the most notable characteristic of this dish, is the delectable juxtaposition of the varied textures of such crustaceans as shrimps, *scampi,* and *cannocchie* and such mollusks as clams, mussels, scallops, squid, and octopus. You can try making your own combinations, as long as they result in a variety of delicate tastes and interesting textures.

For 6 persons

½ pound medium shrimps, preferably the very tiny shrimps from Maine or the Pacific, if available
7 tablespoons vinegar
Salt
2 medium carrots, peeled and washed
2 stalks celery, washed
2 medium yellow onions, peeled
½ pound squid, cleaned
1 pound octopus tentacles, peeled like the squid
¼ pound sea scallops
1 dozen mussels, cleaned
1 dozen littleneck clams, the tiniest you can find, washed and scrubbed
6 black Greek olives, pitted and quartered
6 green olives, pitted and quartered
⅓ cup broiled sweet red pepper, cut into strips ½ inch wide
¼ cup lemon juice
½ cup olive oil
Freshly ground pepper, about 6 twists of the mill
1 good-sized clove garlic, lightly crushed with a knife handle and peeled
¼ teaspoon dried marjoram or ½ teaspoon fresh

1. Wash the shrimps in cold water, but don't shell them. Bring 2 quarts of water with 2 tablespoons of vinegar and 1 teaspoon of salt to a boil. Drop the shrimps into the boiling water and cook for 2 minutes after the water returns to a boil. (Very tiny shrimps may take 1½ minutes or less, depending on size.) Drain. When cool, peel and devein the shrimps

and cut into rounds ½ inch thick. If very, very tiny, leave whole. Set aside.
2. Using two separate pots, put 3 cups of water, 2 tablespoons of vinegar, 1 teaspoon of salt, 1 carrot, 1 celery stalk, and 1 onion in each pot. Bring to a boil. Add the squid and their tentacles to one pot and the octopus tentacles to the other, and cover. Cook at a slow, steady boil, testing the squid with a knife or sharp-pronged fork for tenderness after 20 minutes. Drain when tender, and when cool cut into strips ⅜ inch wide and 1½ inches long. Test the octopus tentacles for tenderness after 40 minutes. Drain when tender, and when cool cut into disks ⅜ inch thick. Set aside.
3. Rinse the scallops in cold water. Bring 2 cups of water, with 1 tablespoon of vinegar and ½ teaspoon of salt, to a boil. Add the scallops and cook for 2 minutes after the water returns to a boil. Drain, and when cool cut into ½-inch cubes. Set aside.
4. In separate covered pans, heat the mussels and clams over high heat until their shells open. Detach the mussels from their shells and set aside. Detach the clams from their shells and rinse them one by one in their juice to remove any possible sand.
5. Combine all the seafood in a mixing bowl. Add the quartered olives, the red pepper, the lemon juice, and the olive oil and mix thoroughly. Taste and correct for salt, and add pepper, the crushed garlic clove, and the marjoram. Toss and mix all the ingredients thoroughly. Allow to rest for at least 2 hours, and retrieve the garlic before serving.

NOTE
You can prepare this salad many hours ahead of time, if you like, but it is best if it is not refrigerated. If you absolutely must refrigerate it, cover it tightly with plastic wrap. Remove from the refrigerator well in advance of serving so that it has time to come to room temperature.

(*From THE CLASSIC ITALIAN COOKBOOK, by Marcella Hazan, illustrated by George Koizumi. Copyright © 1973 by Marcella Hazan. Reprinted by permission of Alfred A. Knopf.*)

Before scales were used in the determining of meat prices, the ancient Romans arrived at the cost by a most curious procedure: "The buyer shut one of his hands: the seller did the same: each of them suddenly opened the whole or a few of his fingers. If the fingers were even on each side, the seller had the price he pleased: if they were odd, the buyer gave his own price. This was called micare." Mication was suppressed in the year 360, with the following decree: "Reason and experience have proved to us, that it is of public utility to suppress the practice of mication for the sale of cattle, and that it is more advisable to sell by weight than to trust to a game with the fingers."

The Pantropheon, *by Alexis Soyer, 1853*

BEAN SOUP A LA JOKAI— JOKAI BABLEVES

8 servings

2 smoked pig's feet
½ pound smoked pork ribs
1 knob celery, peeled and diced
¼ pound fresh shell beans (see Note)
1 medium-sized onion, peeled and
    chopped
1 tablespoon lard
1 tablespoon chopped flat parsley
1 tablespoon flour
½ tablespoon paprika
1 garlic clove, mashed
½ pound smoked pork sausage
Salt
2 tablespoons sour cream

1. Cook smoked pig's feet and pork ribs in 2 quarts water till the meat comes off the bones. Bone them, and put meat pieces aside.
2. Add the diced knob celery and the beans to the meat broth, and cook till beans are done.
3. Meantime, fry onion in lard over low heat. When onion is wilted, add chopped parsley and flour and make a brown *roux* over the lowest heat possible. Stir often to prevent burning.
4. When the *roux* is light brown, mix in paprika and garlic; immediately add 1 cup of cold water. Whip till smooth, then pour into the cooked beans.
5. Add smoked sausage and ½ tablespoon salt. Simmer for 10 more minutes.
6. Cut smoked meats into small pieces, and add to the soup. Adjust salt. Add the sour cream.
7. Serve with dumplings.

NOTE: *The best time to make this soup is when fresh shell beans are available.*

However, the soup can be made with the usual dried beans, too. Almost any type can be used—cranberry or pinto beans, for instance. If you use dried beans, soak them overnight first.

Smoked pork rib and smoked pig's feet are generally sold in the United States in Southern-style butcher shops. Any parts of pork can be used.

(From THE CUISINE OF HUNGARY, by George Lang. Copyright © 1971 by George Lang. Reprinted by permission of Atheneum.)

Pelouze Portion-Control Scale   1.16

Enameled steel with plastic dial; 6½″ X 6½″, 8½″ high; aluminum "Adapto-Plate" 18″ X 14″; weighs up to 25 lbs.
$25.95 (Scale), $10.95 (Adapto-Plate)

None of the scales we have shown you are legal for commercial use; for that, they have to meet stringent specifications and receive a government seal. But this scale by Pelouze is of highly professional quality, will weigh items up to 25 pounds in weight, and possesses an unbreakable plastic dial which, like that on the British scale above, can be set back to zero after the addition of each ingredient in a series. Only there is no comparison at all: this one is not lovely, but it is honestly designed, shining-clean looking in enameled steel, patently well made, with a highly readable dial in black and brilliant blue. An additional feature is what the maker calls the Adapto-Plate, a 14″ × 18″ aluminum sheet which attaches securely to the platform of the scale and permits you to weigh large items, such as an 8-rib roast, or many items, such as the vegetables for a daube or the tiny cucumbers for a batch of home-pickled cornichons. The

plate distributes the weight for greater accuracy; anyone who has stood on a bathroom spring scale, putting his weight first on one foot and then on the other as the dial leaps up and down, knows that position on the scale platform can be crucial unless there is some sort of equalizer like this one. This is an admirable machine: moderately compact, easy to clean, accurate; on the platform you could weigh out 25 quarter-pound hamburgers without removing a single one, and be sure of reading the dial with ease.

Original Pocket Balance   1.17

Brass face with chromed-steel ring and hook; 10½″ overall; weighs up to 50 lbs.
$3.95

The style of this small brass-faced scale probably hasn't changed for a hundred years. Look at it and you will understand how a spring scale works: you can see, through the slot in the front, a thick spring which stretches as heavier and heavier weights are hung on the bottom hook. It is, of course, actually a meat scale, able to weigh up to 50 pounds; it therefore ignores the subtleties, moving in two-pound leaps between readings. Unless you are dealing with gargantuan hunks of meat and the like, you are likely to find it more ornamental than essential. Attach it by its chrome ring to the ceiling of your country kitchen, and suspend from it a string of red onions or a basket of autumn fruits.

THERMOMETERS

The mention of temperature in cooking always seems to bring to mind stoves and freezers; but just as much kitchen work in which temperature is important is done in the open, in what we call the ambient temperature. There you mix and beat and measure and blend and chop: all these in the natural atmosphere of your kitchen. Does it make a difference? Well, dough rises beautifully in a modern American house, heated to a voluptuous 72 F. in the winter; but years ago (and today in England) it was necessary to put bread dough into a warming oven so that the yeast could grow. Piemakers find that their pastry melts in a hot room, and the best restaurants provide chilled rooms for their pâtissiers—better by far than a cold marble slab sweating in a hot room. Mayonnaise is hard to make on a summer day, when the oil thins out and the dressing refuses to become thick. Yes, the context of our cooking does make a difference, but short of making the room comfortable for ourselves and avoiding certain tasks in an obviously unsuitable temperature, there is not much that we can do about it. You know what Mark Twain said about the weather.

On the other hand, there is a lot that we can do about temperatures in enclosed areas. We heat them and chill them, and then we want to know just how hot or cold they are. This temperature control is an important part of the technology of cooking, and it applies both to the environment of the food—the oven, the boiling water, the freezer—and to the food itself—the dough or the ice cream. You can always tell a professional cook by the little penlike instant thermometers (1.26) which he carries in his breast pocket, ready to be whipped out at an instant and stuck into a soup or a roast to get an instant reading on their temperature. Of course, there are still the subjective tests, like flicking drops of water onto a griddle to see if it is hot enough, or watching to see when the butter foam subsides in a frying pan to indicate the right moment for food to be added. But aren't we lucky that we no longer have to test our ovens by putting a piece of paper into them and then watching to see how long it takes for it to brown? Or that we now needn't drop sugar syrup into cold water and then judge the quality of the ball which forms in order to tell what stage the candy has reached? Far better to have at your disposal a good set of cooking thermometers.

OVEN THERMOMETERS

No matter how good your oven is, we are willing to bet that the temperature that you set it for is not the temperature that it actually reaches. When you consider how important oven temperature is to the success of your cooking, that fact is outrageous. You can turn the dial to 350 F. or 500 F.—or, even less precisely, to Moderate or Hot—but there is no way that you can be assured that your oven is actually reaching and holding the temperature you want unless you test the interior space. We suggest that you buy a very good oven thermometer and then put it

Memorable advertising copy from the **Washington Post,** *1936.*

FLORENTINES

½ cup sugar
⅓ cup heavy cream
⅓ cup honey
2 tablespoons butter
¼ cup candied orange peel, finely
    chopped or ground
1½ cups blanched, sliced almonds
3 tablespoons sifted flour
8 ounces semisweet chocolate
1 tablespoon vegetable shortening

Set oven at 400 degrees. Grease baking sheets very well.

Combine sugar, cream, honey, butter in a heavy saucepan. Stir over low heat until sugar is dissolved. Raise heat and boil without stirring until a ball forms when a bit of mixture is dropped into cold water, or until mixture registers 238 degrees on a candy thermometer. Cool slightly.

Stir in orange peel, nuts, and flour. Drop small rounds of batter on prepared cooky sheets, leaving at least 2 inches between cookies. Flatten each cooky with a fork dipped in milk.

Bake 8 to 10 minutes, or until cookies are golden brown. They will spread in baking. Therefore, immediately upon removing them from the oven, pull each one back into shape with a round, greased 3-inch cutter. Using the cutter will insure their final roundness.

When cookies are firm, remove them from cooky sheet and finish cooling on a rack.

Melt semisweet chocolate. Stir in shortening. Coat underside of each cooky thinly with melted chocolate. Place in refrigerator long enough to set chocolate.

Yield: approximately 16.

(From THE ART OF FINE BAKING, by Paula Peck, illustrated by Grambs Miller. Copyright © 1961 by Paula Peck. Reprinted by permission of Simon & Schuster.)

into your heated oven, moving it about so that you can identify the hot spots. Then you can adjust subsequent oven settings to the heat which you know that it actually achieves.

Not only are oven thermostats notoriously inaccurate, even when they are adjusted frequently, but the most widely sold oven thermometers are also virtually useless. The most common sort consists in its working parts of a spring made of two different metals which expand at variable rates with the application of heat. As the spring heats up, it moves an attached pointer around the dial to indicate the temperature. Unfortunately, the accuracy of these oven thermometers is short-lived, and a slight jar will destroy their accuracy forever. For that reason we show you only two oven thermometers; and both of them work on the principle of mercury rising in a glass tube when heated.

horizontal glass tube clamped into place on a piece of stainless steel bent into an acute angle to form a stand. It is cheaper than the preceding thermometer, and it obviously lacks the wonderful protection afforded by the folding box of that one; but for as long as it lasts it will do the job better than the dial type, which we don't recommend. Black lettering on the face of the steel indicates readings from 100 F. to 680 F. or, as a concession to directions in inaccurate cookbooks, Slow, Moderate, Hot, and Very Hot. A hook on the top permits you to hang it from an oven rack to test the heat in different areas of the oven compartment.

Mercury Oven Thermometer with Folding Case   1.18

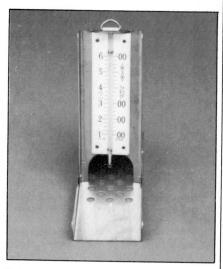

Stainless-steel case, thermometer with enameled-steel face; 5¼" × 2⅛" × ⅝" closed; 5" high when standing open; registers up to 600 F.

$15.00 ▲

This extraordinary piece of equipment is a mercury thermometer which is set securely against a white enamel background in a steel case. The case folds up into a tight box to protect the glass tube when it is put away. The box opens easily, forming a stand to place on the oven shelf. The base of the stand is perforated so that warm air can circulate up to the thermometer. The large, easily read markings go from 100 F. to 600 F. by 25-degree steps; and the tube of mercury is somewhat magnified, appearing as a silver ribbon against a clear yellow background. This is an excellent product, easily the best in its field.

From the famous diary kept by Samuel Pepys in the seventeenth century, we might assume that his wife had some difficulty getting dinner together and would have benefited from an oven thermometer. On one occasion she burned her hand preparing turkey leftovers, on another she baked pies and tarts in her oven "but did heat it too hot, and so did a little overbake her things, but knows how to do better another time."

Quoted in Kitchen and Table, *by Colin Clair, Abelard-Schuman, New York, 1964*

Taylor Mercury Oven Thermometer   1.19

Stainless steel; 4⅞" × 2¼"; registers up to 680 F.

$5.95

Taylor, one of the best domestic producers of cooking thermometers, makes this mercury thermometer, which is a

NUT MERINGUE LAYERS FILLED WITH CHOCOLATE BUTTER-CREAM—DACQUOISE AU CHOCOLAT

1 to 2 teaspoons sweet butter, softened
2 tablespoons flour

MERINGUE LAYERS
½ cup whole almonds
½ cup filberts
⅔ cup granulated sugar
1½ tablespoons cornstarch
6 egg whites

BUTTERCREAM FILLING
3 squares (ounces) semisweet chocolate
½ cup granulated sugar
¼ cup water
3 egg yolks
½ pound (2 sticks) sweet butter, cut in pieces

ASSEMBLY AND GARNISH
1 cup heavy cream
2 tablespoons dark rum
1 tablespoon confectioners' sugar

Preheat oven to 330 F. to 350 F. Butter and flour 2 cooky sheets. Mark a 9-inch circle on each sheet, using a layer-cake pan as a guide. (Alternatively, butter two 9 × 1½-inch layer cake pans. Cover the bottom of each with a round of waxed paper and spread lightly with butter. Flour both pans.)

MAKE MERINGUE LAYERS: Finely grate nuts at high speed in the blender. Combine with sugar and cornstarch. Beat egg whites until they hold a stiff peak.

With a rubber spatula, gently fold in the nut mixture. Spoon half of the meringue into a pastry bag fitted with a ½-inch plain tube.

Pipe the mixture onto one prepared cooky sheet, to completely fill the marked circle. Repeat with remaining meringue. Or spoon half of meringue into each prepared layer cake pan and smooth tops.

Place pans in oven and bake 35–40 minutes. Turn off oven but do not remove meringues. Leave in oven until cool, then remove pans from oven and place on cake racks to cool another hour at room temperature. Gently lift meringue layers off cooky sheets. (Or loosen edges of meringue layers in cake pans with a small knife. Invert on cake racks and lift off pans. Carefully peel off waxed paper.)

MAKE BUTTERCREAM: Melt chocolate in the top of a double boiler over hot (not boiling) water. Combine sugar and water in a saucepan. Bring to boil, stirring, over medium heat. Boil syrup until it reaches temperature of 230°–234° on a candy thermometer, or spins a thread when dropped from a fork. Place egg yolks in medium-size mixing bowl (or bowl of electric mixer). Beat at medium speed. As yolks are beating, slowly pour syrup into bowl. Continue beating for 6 to 8 minutes, or until eggs are thick as a light mayonnaise and very pale yellow. Beat in one stick of butter, bit by bit. Beat in the melted chocolate. Beat in the remaining butter, bit by bit. If the cream starts to break down, the butter is probably too cold. Place the bowl of buttercream in hot water for a few seconds and let it start to melt around the edges. Work again with the mixer or a hand whip. It should smooth out. Refrigerate.

ASSEMBLY AND GARNISH: Just before serving, whip cream until it holds a shape. Add rum: beat until stiff.

Place one meringue layer, flat side down, on serving plate.

Spread top with all but ½ cup of the buttercream. Then, using a pastry bag, pipe the whipped cream over the buttercream.

Place the second layer, flat side up, on top of the cream. Sprinkle confectioners' sugar over the top. Place remaining buttercream in pastry bag and decorate top of cake. Cut in small wedges.

The oven temperatures you would use, if you followed the directions in early cookbooks, were highly variable, depending on your degree of delicacy or hardiness: "For pies, cakes and white bread the heat of the oven should be such that you can hold your hand and arm [in it] while you count 40: for brown breads, meats, beans, Indian puddings and pumpkin pies, it should be hotter, so that you can only hold it in while you count 20."

The Kitchen in History, *by Molly Harrison, Scribners, New York, 1972*

FREEZER THERMOMETERS

Yes, you do need a freezer thermometer. Do you know why? Not because you will get food poisoning if you don't have one: few bacteria grow at all below 20 F., and almost none below 10 F. And not for the rare occasions when the power goes out for more than 36 hours: there's not much point in knowing just how high the temperature has risen when the ice cream is lying all over the floor of the freezer and the turkey doesn't resist the pressure of a probing finger. (In such cases your best bet is to leave the freezer closed as long as the power is off, keeping its contents as cold as possible—so don't even look inside until the motor is humming again.) No: you need a freezer thermometer because the quality of frozen food is affected enormously by the temperature at which it has been held.

Preserving techniques are only as good as the palatability of the end product, as anyone who has eaten a carbon-dioxide-stored apple, still delicious after many months, can testify. There isn't much point to having a freezer if it doesn't give you food that you will be happy to eat. And both vitamins and aesthetics are best preserved when the freezer temperature is kept around zero, or even below. Above 4 F. or so, enzyme action within the frozen food will alter its flavor, color, and texture. Commercial standards require that a freezer be kept within a range of no more than two degrees above or below zero; any higher than that, and the quality, although not the safety, of the food is threatened. A piece of meat or a container of peaches held for a year at zero will be of the same quality as food stored for 5 months at 5 F., for 1 month at 15 F., and for 1 *week* at 25 F. But notice that at each of these temperatures the food will be hard-frozen to the touch; but just being frozen isn't good enough. That's why your refrigerator ice-cube compartment isn't cold enough to ensure good frozen food, although it's fine for short-term storage in a pinch, no more than a day or two.

So get yourself a freezer thermometer and use it. Remember that the temperature will go up in the freezer when a lot of unfrozen food is first added; and that, in accordance with the rule that warm air rises, you will get a higher reading near the top than near the bottom of your freezer, and nearer the door of an upright freezer it will be warmer than at the back. Freezer burn, by the way, is another matter and rather a misnomer, being a result of dehydration of the food's surface because of poor wrapping rather than incorrect temperature.

"At Agua Amarga . . . the women, by turns sacrificing one of their goats, cut for each buyer, with an ordinary axe, one piece after another, starting at one end of the animal, and selling for so many pesetas a chunk the weight of a stone chosen by themselves as their own absolute measure. (And seeing these women how could I help thinking of Robert Fulliou and his measured objects which signify a revolt against the absolute and definitive weights and measures chosen for all times, like a god, a woman or a way of life?) The inch is death, the banner of the bourgeois, and the fact that each of these Spanish women can have her own rock worth such and such almost makes me forget the lack of skill with which they chop up those poor animals."

"A Gastronomic Itinerary," in The Mythological Travels, *by Daniel Spoerri. Translated by E. Williams. Something Else Press, 1970*

Taylor Refrigerator-Freezer Thermometer   1.20

Enameled-steel and stainless-steel case with glass face: 2½" X 2⅜"; registers from −35 F. to 75 F.

$3.50

At first glance only the chilly blue enamel case offers a clue that this is not your run-of-the-mill spring-operated oven thermometer. Upon closer inspection, you will see that the dial registers from −30° to 75°F. There are two shaded areas on the dial—one showing a range of −10° to 5° for the freezer and another covering 35° to 45° for refrigerated food. We recommend that you use it in the refrigerator rather than the freezer. You may prefer this alternative to the mercury-operated thermometer following (1.21) because you might just find the shaded area on this dial a trifle easier to read than the tiny strip of comparable shading on 1.21. If you are intelligent enough to select a refrigerator thermometer in the first place, you probably won't be too confused by the fact that the below-zero temperatures are not shown as minus on this trapezoidal dial. The thermometer will hang or stand and comes with a one-year warranty.

CECELIA'S SAUERBRATEN

(12 servings)

1 cup red wine vinegar
½ bottle red wine
12 peppercorns
1 teaspoon salt
1 bay leaf
6 cloves
2 cloves garlic, chopped
2 thin strips yellow rind of lemon
1 onion, halved
¼ teaspoon nutmeg
3 stalks celery, chopped
2 carrots, chopped
4 sprays parsley
6-pound rolled top round of beef
2 cups beef stock
3 tablespoons cornstarch

In earthenware or enamel container large enough to hold the roast, combine vinegar, red wine, peppercorns, salt, bay leaf, cloves, garlic, lemon rind, onion, nutmeg, celery, carrots, and parsley. Add beef, cover, and let marinate in refrigerator for at least 3 days, turning meat occasionally.

Remove meat from marinade; reserve marinade. Dry meat well with paper towels.

Bring marinade to a boil and simmer over low heat while meat is cooking.

Heat a heavy kettle or Dutch oven. Put meat in the pot, fat side down, and brown it well on all sides. This will take about 1 hour. When a rich brown all over, pour off excess fat from kettle.

Add half the beef stock to the meat. Cover tightly and cook over low heat for 3½ hours, basting occasionally with remaining cup of stock and with the hot marinade until all marinade has been added.

Remove meat to a hot platter.

Strain gravy, pressing vegetables through the sieve.

Remove fat from surface. Return gravy to heat and stir in cornstarch mixed with a little water.

Serve the sauce separately from the meat.

TO FREEZE REMAINING MEAT AND GRAVY: Slice remaining meat into serving pieces and arrange in a round shallow freezer container, or in a cake pan lined with foil. Cover with sauce and freeze. When frozen, wrap, label, and store.

TO DEFROST AND SERVE:
Remove from freezer 1 hour before heating. Empty into large heavy skillet. Cover and defrost over low heat for about 30 minutes, or until hot. Do not let sauce boil.

(From THE COMPLETE BOOK OF FREEZER COOKERY, by Ann Seranne. Copyright © 1953, 1966 by Ann Seranne. Reprinted by permission of Doubleday & Company.)

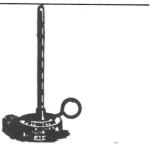

Turn-of-the-century thermometer, from The Encyclopedia of Practical Cookery.

Taylor Freezer Thermometer   1.21

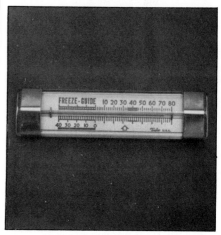

Plastic and stainless steel with enameled-steel face; 4¾" X 1⅛"; registers from −40 F. to 80 F.

$3.75 ▲

The alter ego of the compact Taylor oven thermometer we have shown you is this neat little freezer thermometer. (Notice, by the way, that while oven thermometers stand, freezer thermometers hang, on the theory that the proper condition of a freezer is chock-full.) This has a 4¾" plastic case bound with polished aluminum bands which curve into hanging hooks; a mercury thermometer registers temperatures from −40 F. to 80 F. and is easily seen from behind its magnifying lens. This is rustproof and carries a one-year warranty. A good buy.

Centigrade Freezer Thermometer   1.22

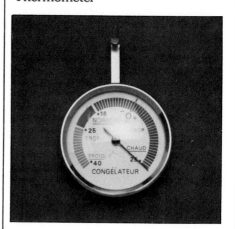

Aluminum and chrome case, glass face; 2" diam.; registers from −40 C. to 25 C.
$4.00

A range advertised shortly after the turn of the century included among its features an oven thermometer "in order to keep . . . strictly up to the minute."

Continued from preceding page

At first glance, it seems foolish to have a freezer thermometer which registers in Centigrade rather than in Fahrenheit; we were becoming reconciled to having to discard this shiny little dial, the best-looking of all the thermometers. And then we realized that the simplicity of the gauge, with the safe area clearly marked in green from −25 C. to −16 C. (roughly −13 F. to 3 F.) makes it perfectly adequate for its use. There are no subtleties to freezer temperature control, and if you see the hand going beyond the green Normal band, you can simply fiddle with your freezer's control knob until the indicator returns to the proper area. This dial is 2″ in diameter, encased in shiny chrome, with a plastic-covered circular key which shows clearly the areas which are *trop froid* (too cold), *normal*, and *trop chaud*. There is a lightweight aluminum hook so that you can hang it from a freezer rack or shelf.

Inside-Outside Freezer Thermometer

1.23

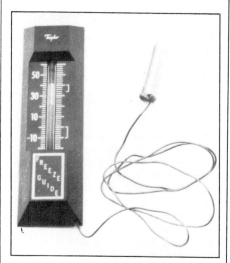

Plastic case with copper wire and stainless-steel sensor; case 5⅜″ × 1½″; wire 28″ long; registers from −20 F. to 60 F.
$5.95

If you live in an area where the power regularly goes out because of September hurricanes or generator failures—and if every time that happens you hold your breath for a day, afraid to open the freezer to see whether all is lost—then this is the thermometer for you to have. As a matter of fact, it is probably the thermometer for all of us to have, being

the only one we show you which can be read without opening the freezer door; and every time you open that door you are damaging the depth of your chill by a warm breath. The sensor, a bulletlike piece of stainless steel, lies on the freezer rack; from it extends a long copper wire, thin enough to go between the rubber gaskets of the door without admitting any air. The wire connects with a mercury thermometer which can be attached to the door on a rectangular plastic frame made, unfortunately, of the flimsiest-looking plastic we have seen. The gauge goes from −20 F. to 60 F. The area from −10 F. to 0 F. is marked as "Safe," which is perhaps an error in the direction of caution—but far better than a higher "Safe" area.

Oven temperatures were determined in various personalized ways before controlled heat became common. Della T. Lutes writes of a "brown paper oven." This referred to an oven that would turn a sheet of white writing paper a delicate brown.

Della T. Lutes, The Country Kitchen, *Little, Brown and Company, 1936*

APPLE APRICOT TART

(Makes one 8-inch tart)

Pastry for a lattice-topped pie
3 large cooking apples, peeled, cored, and thinly sliced
1 tablespoon lemon juice
¼ teaspoon nutmeg
½ cup broken walnuts, pecans, or pistachios
12 ounces apricot jam
1½ tablespoons butter

Line an 8-inch pie plate with pastry. Cover neatly with apple slices beginning in center and overlapping in circles to the edge. Sprinkle apples with lemon juice, nutmeg, and nuts. Spread with apricot jam and dot with butter.
Cover filling with a lattice topping.
Freeze, then wrap and return to freezer.

TO BAKE FRESH OR FROZEN:
Bake in a preheated 425° F. oven for 40 minutes if fresh; 45 to 50 if frozen.

(From THE COMPLETE BOOK OF FREEZER COOKERY, by Ann Seranne. Copyright © 1953, 1966 by Ann Seranne. Reprinted by permission of Doubleday & Company.)

FOOD THERMOMETERS

When we have tested and corrected the temperature of the room, the oven, and the freezer, then we still have to deal with what is, after all, the point of the whole thing, and test the internal temperature of the food. Thermometers which do this all work on the same principle, being inserted into a median level of the food and remaining there until the mercury settles at a reading. With solids, of course, we are careful not to permit the tip of the thermometer to touch a bone or a pocket of fat, either of which would give a distorted reading; we always pay due respect to the pointed probe, never forcing it into place. And we always warm the thermometer in a little hot water before we plunge it from a comfortable room temperature into a pot of seething fat or boiling sugar. These instruments are sensitive over a wide range of temperatures, according to their purpose: the dough thermometer we show you registers only up to 120 F., but a deep-frying thermometer (1.33) gives readings up to 460 F.

MEAT AND OTHER TESTING THERMOMETERS

Rare meat, like raw meat, is soft to the touch, while well-done meat is firm; between the two there is a range of resistance which is, apparently, easily read by those with tactile sensitivity—they simply give it a poke with their finger—or long experience. Or maybe you prefer, when judging the doneness of meat, to rely on the fact that a cut made into a rare roast will produce red juices, a medium roast will give pink juices, and a well-done roast will yield colorless juices. A good-enough gauge, but you don't want to risk losing juices from the meat with repeated cuts. No, it is better to time your roasts according to a chart in a cookbook: a given number of minutes per pound—use the minimum figure for the degree of doneness you want—in a preheated oven with a trusted temperature. And at the end—not the beginning—of that period, you stick a meat thermometer into the meat to check that the center has reached the proper temperature for rare, medium, or well done, as the case may be.

Professional chefs carry around with them little instantly registering thermometers which they stick here and there into various foods, checking on temperatures, and you should learn to use your regular meat thermometer in the same way. It is foolhardy to stick it into a cold rib roast, leaving it there for hours in the oven: for one thing, it will conduct heat rapidly to the center of the roast; for another, it will leave an open hole out of which the juices will bleed. Treat the thermometer with respect: warm it in water before you stick it into a hot roast near the end of the estimated roasting time; don't let it be knocked about in a drawer; and test it every now and then by putting the probe into boiling water and watching to see that it registers 212 F. (If it doesn't, remember what allowance to make for its error when next you use it.) When you test meat with it, take into account the fact that the internal temperature of a roast can rise 10 degrees while it sits out of the oven, firming up for the carver's knife. Take it out of the oven before it reaches the temperature you want and let it "coast" to doneness. And, when using recipes, regard the recommended readings with skepticism; the cookbook author's Rare may not be your Rare, nor that of our experts, who tend to come down on the side of lower "done" readings.

H-B Dough Thermometer   1.24

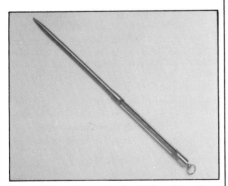

Glass; 10" long; immersion depth 5"; registers from 0 F. to 120 F. Stainless-steel case, 11" long.
$18.00 Thermometer, $18.00 Case

This is not so much a dough thermometer as one element in a System: the H-B Instrument Company's armored thermometer system. You buy a beautiful stainless-steel case shaped like an extremely elongated bullet, with one end pointed and the other closed by a screw cap with a loop attached. A long window for viewing the markings on the actual thermometer is placed a little less than halfway between the two. The point is that you can insert different H-B thermometers—long slender mercury tubes—into the case, which then acts as protection from the dangers of a kitchen drawer as well as from resistance in the food into which it is inserted. It also works as a transmitter of temperature changes. This thermometer, made of etched glass, is for testing the temperature of rising dough and, therefore, registers only from 0 F. to 120 F.; yeast doughs grow best when they are kept somewhere between 70 F. and 85 F. You should also buy the glass meat thermometer insert below, which registers from 100 F. to 220 F., and use it in the same case. This is not only a thrifty and effective system, the thermometer case is beautiful. It comes packed in the most unaffectedly Japanese-looking wooden tube we have ever seen from a Western manufacturer.

H-B Meat Thermometer   1.25

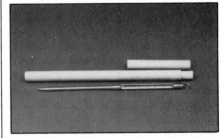

Glass; 10" long; immersion depth 5"; registers from 100 F. to 220 F. Stainless-steel case, 11" long.
$18.00 Thermometer, $18.00 Case

Stage Two of the armored thermometer system we describe above—for Stage One we refer you back to 1.24. That thermometer was for dough, while *this* one is for roasting meat, but they both fit into the same sleek elongated stainless-steel case, which protects them while in use from the slings and arrows of your kitchen. (You can, of course, buy a metal case for this one too, if you'd prefer not to switch the tubes back and forth.) Notice how cleverly the etched glass is shaped so that it forms its own magnifier for the mercury tube. Notice the bright yellow background laid behind the silvery mercury, the handy little loop on the end. If you want to look ahead to the third insert you can purchase, look at the deep-fat thermometer (1.31). This meat thermometer is a precision instrument of the highest quality. Of course, you will not leave it sticking into your turkey thigh for the whole four hours preceding Thanksgiving dinner; only the most nonreactive instrument would be able to deal with that span of unrelieved heat. Which is like saying that only a horse with a completely numb mouth could tolerate being used for hire in a stable: true enough, but who would want to ride him?

ROAST LAMB WITH GARLIC AND OLIVES

Serves 10-12

5½-6-pound leg of lamb
12 large cloves garlic (or more, if small), peeled
1 bottle dry white wine
2 cups pitted ripe olives
Salt and pepper
A few sprigs fresh rosemary

Have your butcher bone the lamb. Some butchers are dexterous: without cutting the leg apart, they can remove the bone and leave only a pocket. Have the lamb

Continued from preceding page

boned with a pocket, if possible; if not, tie it together in several places. (With the bones make stock.*)

In a shallow pan, put lamb on a rack over the lightly crushed garlic cloves, and pierce meat well all over with the tip of a sharp knife, or use an ice pick so that the lamb will absorb the lovely steam from the wine. Pour the white wine over, and put in a preheated 350 F. oven. Roast, basting with the pan juices every 10 minutes or so until a meat thermometer inserted in the lamb reads 135 F. (Do not cover the pan.)

Remove meat to a warm platter and keep warm. Strain stock and add to pan juices. By this time, the sauce should be slightly thickened by the garlic; if not, add a little *beurre manié*** or some other thickener such as a mixture of arrowroot or cornstarch with water, and finally, stir in the olives, either whole or sliced.

Arrange the meat on a serving dish, garnish it with rosemary sprigs and surround it with small new potatoes dressed with parsley and butter. Pass the sauce separately.

* *To make stock:* Put bones in a saucepan, cover with water, add a teaspoon of salt, and bring to a boil. Skim; then add half an onion stuck with 2 cloves; a small carrot, sliced; a few celery leaves; a sprig of parsley; and a few peppercorns. Cook covered until vegetables are completely soft, 35-40 minutes. Strain and reserve.

** *Beurre manié* is composed of slightly softened butter and flour in a one-to-one proportion, worked together to make a smooth paste.

(From THE GREAT COOKS COOKBOOK, by The Good Cooking School, Inc. Copyright © 1974 by The Good Cooking School, Inc. Reprinted by permission of Ferguson/Doubleday.)

Tiny Instant Thermometer 1.26

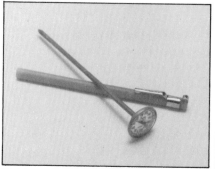

Stainless steel with glass face, nylon pocket sheath; dial 1″ diam.; 5″ stem; registers from 0 F. to 220 F.
$12.00 ▲

Unfortunately, the common method of using a meat thermometer is to stick it into a roast and then leave it in place until something registers Done—a method that can damage meat by conducting heat rapidly to its interior and by creating a large hole for juices to escape from. This tiny instrument, a Bi-Therm from Taylor, is used in precisely the opposite manner. It is, in a way, the emblem of a professional, who tends to have a row of these sticking out of his breast pocket just as your doctor will have his small instruments handy. The chef will pop one of these into whatever food he might want to check up on, whether it is a steak grilling on the fire, a sauce which must be kept at all costs below the boiling point, or a dish finishing in the microwave. It is tiny, but it's neither inexpensive nor a toy: the dial is only 1″ in diameter and is moisture resistant, with an unbreakable crystal. The stainless-steel stem, only 5″ long, is thin but extremely strong and fits into an unbreakable nylon pocket sheath. The sheath has a pocket clip that includes a loop near the end. Through this loop you can slip the thermometer, then use the sheath as a holder when testing, say, a boiling pot. The thermometer is made so that its scale can be manually adjusted should it become inaccurate in the course of time. It registers from 0 F. to 220 F. with a high degree of accuracy and could, therefore, be used to test the interior of your freezer or of frozen food as well as that of your pork roast. Just stick it into whatever it is that you want to test, placing it if necessary in the loop of the sheath, and it will give a quick and accurate reading. The perfect gift, we think.

Bi-Therm Fahrenheit/ Centigrade Testing Thermometer 1.27

Stainless steel with glass crystal; dial 2″ diam.; stem 5″ long; registers from −20 C. to 100 C. and 0 F. to 220 F.
$13.00

Not so cute, but twice as useful, especially if you use European cookbooks, is this larger Bi-Therm dial testing thermometer from Taylor. It shows temperatures both in Fahrenheit and in Centigrade readings, and could be used for freezer testing and jellymaking as well as for meats, liquids, and doughs. It reacts just as quickly as its little brother; has the same shatter-proof and moisture-resistant dial crystal and a similarly slender stem, with the Bi-Therm sensor in its tip. ("Bi-Therm," by the way, means that these thermometers register according to the expansion of two different metals exposed to heat.) We especially like the 2″ dial for the fact that it presents its information—Fahrenheit readings on the outer ring, Centigrade readings on the inner one—in phenomenally readable form. Although it is an instantly reactive thermometer, not intended to be left in the food, it looks a lot like the dial meat thermometers you are most familiar with; it is, however, both more accurate and informative than those, which are too often marked in descriptive terms—"Rare" beef at a too-high 140 F., for instance, or pork at 190 F., when the recommendation of experts is now that pork be cooked to 165 F. to 170 F. This instant thermometer is meant for general testing, so it is suitable for any kitchen use in foods within its temperature range—obviously you won't put it into boiling fat that may reach 390 F.

LAMB LOIN

Serves 4

Lamb loin is best known for those suc-culent small loin chops, so good simply broiled and served with salt and pepper as the sole embellishment. But the loin makes a splendid little roast too, with the bones removed and the tail wrapped around the eye of the meat and tied or skewered in place. It should weigh about 2-2½ pounds. Put it on a rack in a roast-ing dish and cook in a preheated 400 F. oven until the exterior is crisp and brown, the center quite rare—about 15-20 min-utes or until inserted thermometer reads 130 F. Beforehand, make stock with the bones, cooking it down until you have a cup [see preceding recipe]. Add a cup of white wine and cook at high heat to re-duce to 1 cup in all. Meanwhile, cook 2 finely chopped mushrooms and 2 peeled and minced garlic cloves in 2 tablespoons of butter until soft. Stir them into the re-duced stock and wine mixture. Season with salt, pepper, and a little tarragon, and serve over the meat.

(From THE GREAT COOKS COOK-BOOK, by The Good Cooking School, Inc. Copyright © 1974 by The Good Cooking School, Inc. Reprinted by per-mission of Ferguson/Doubleday.)

Thermoelectric Food Thermometer   1.28

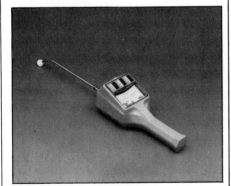

Plastic with stainless-steel tube; body 9½″ × 3½″ × 3¼″; tube 10½″ long; registers up to 280 F.
$124.50

The first thing that will surprise you about this thermometer designed for pro-fessional kitchens is that it looks like a casting rod: a design concept so aston-ishing that it tends to obscure the really basic factor, which is the way in which it probes the food and registers heat. It takes temperatures by means of a ther-mocouple: there is a needlelike probe containing the thermocouple, a joining of two wires of dissimilar but conductive metals in such a way that they form a circuit on which the action of heat gen-erates a small but measurable current of electricity. When the thermoelectric cur-rent is measured, the reading appears on the front of the device on a dial with markings graduated from −20 F. to 280 F. The thermometer was developed by the president of an electronics firm in partnership with a Vermont firm making fishing and hunting equipment; thus the innovative and highly accurate method of temperature registration in conjunc-tion with the outdoorsy look of the thing. In your hand you hold a heavy but well-balanced plastic grip, above which an en-larged section holds the recording dial and a list of the preferred "done" tem-perature readings for commonly eaten meat and game, plus potatoes, fish, and lobster. From the grip there extends a curving chrome rod 10½ inches long, capped at the end with a white plastic button. When you slide another button on the back of the hand-piece, you cause an extremely thin hollow needle to pro-trude from the white button. This is the probe containing the thermocouple which records the temperature on the dial. This thermometer, as bulky and peculiar-looking as it is, has a multitude of vir-tues. It is extremely accurate; the long curving rod and needle permit you to measure the temperature of a piece of meat cooking over charcoal without burning your fingers; the slender needle pierces the meat without permitting much juice to escape; and the slide that operates the needle has markings and a locking device that permits you to choose the length that will insure that the probe reaches precisely to the center of the food you're testing. It is sold to hunters as well as restaurants, but it would be equally useful in the home kitchen, stretching to record the temperature of a chicken roasting at the back of your oven or, at the other extreme, the tem-perature of food being refrigerated or frozen.

CANDY, JELLY, AND DEEP-FAT THERMOMETERS

Sugar changes its character when it is cooked, and the basic technique in candymaking, jellymaking, and in the production of certain frostings is to control the behavior of the crystals of sugar. We are told that you can do this without a good candy thermometer, by using instead one of the cold-water temperature tests, involving dropping small amounts of the candy solution into a glass of cold water. There are charts in your cookbooks which will tell you when the various temperatures have been reached, from the Soft Ball stage to the Hard Crack stage; but we think that this method is of only archaeological interest, now that there are good candy and jelly thermometers available. Because only when you can control the temperature of your solution absolutely can you make beautifully jelled glasses of raspberry-plum jam or crocks of ginger marmalade; only then can you pull taffy or pour successful lollipops with your children; only then can you contrive luscious pink frostings which stand an inch deep on the top of a birthday cake.

Highly specialized techniques are involved here, with their own separate ranks of equipment and cookbooks; these are kinds of cooking which are all but impossible to do when you don't have the proper equipment, and relatively simple when you do have it. Candy thermom-eters, like other thermometers, should be of the highest quality; should register, by preference, with mercury; should never never be plunged into boiling syrup without a preliminary warming; and should be de-signed to be tested by insertion into boiling water for a few minutes. If the test shows that the thermometer is off—that it registers 215 F., for example, instead of 212 F.—then change, not the thermometer, but the recipe, adding three degrees to every temperature given.

Continued from preceding page

We also show you some thermometers designed specifically for deep-frying; you can, of course, use these to check the temperature of your broth, jam, or candy solution as well.

Glass Candy Thermometer 1.29

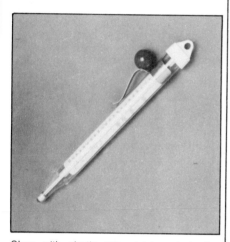

Glass with plastic cap, stainless-steel clip, wooden ball-shaped handle; 9″ long; ¾″ diam.; registers from 120 F. to 360 F.
$1.39

This gaily colored candy thermometer is an inexpensive version of the stainless-steel armored thermometer system we have shown you; only here the thermometer fits into an outer tube made of glass, not steel, and the casing is a permanent one. At one end of the tube the thermometer and casing become one; at the other is a flimsy plastic cap which, we are told, will pop off to warn you should the pressure inside become near-explosive from overheating. The thermometer is held in place within the tube by means of a round red disc, described as a Stabilizer. On the thermometer's scale are indicated temperatures from 120 F. to 360 F., with Soft Ball, Hard Ball, Soft Crack, and Hard Crack inserted at the proper points. The maker says this thermometer can be used for deep-frying, but note that it won't record as high as 375 F., the most commonly used frying temperature; and neither does its scale show the reading for the jellying point of preserves, although it's also called a jelly thermometer. A wide steel clip slides up and down to hook onto the sides of pots of varying sizes; and it has attached to it as a handle a red wooden ball which will be cool to the touch when you pick the thermometer up. It is a good little product, well made as far as it goes. The manufacturer warns you never to use it in the oven; we add our own warning never to touch a hot glass thermometer with a damp cloth or potholder, lest the steam created should crack the glass.

CANDIED FRUIT PEEL

½ pound lemon peel, or ½ pound orange peel, or ½ pound grapefruit peel, or a combination of the three, totaling ½ pound

First day: 2 cups sugar
    1 cup water   Cook to 220° F.
Second day: ¼ cup sugar
    ¼ cup Karo syrup   Cook to 222° F.
Third day: ¼ cup sugar
    ¼ cup Karo syrup   Cook to 226° F.
Fourth day: ¼ cup sugar
    ⅓ cup Karo syrup   Cook to 230° F.

Total ingredients for syrup:
    2¾ cups white sugar
    1 cup water
    ¾ cup + 2 tablespoons Karo syrup
    *China or stainless steel bowl

FIRST DAY: Peel lemons, oranges, or grapefruit carefully, using a short, pointed knife to cut about ¼ inch deep all around the fruit; cut the peel into 4-6 sections and take it off with your fingers. Cut the sections into strips ⅜-½ inch wide and 2-3 inches long, or into oblong shapes about ½ inch wide and 1 inch long. Wash and rinse the peels in cold water.

Put the pieces into a pot, and add enough water to cover, when they are pushed down into the pot, and put the pot on the stove at medium heat. When the water begins to boil, reduce the heat and let simmer for 25 minutes. Take the peels from the stove, strain off the hot water, and hold the strainer with the peels under cold running water for a minute. Put the peels back into the pot and fill it with cold water, and set aside.

Put the 2 cups of sugar and 1 cup of water into a pot and on the stove at medium heat. Wash the adhering sugar crystals down from the sides of the pot and the stirring paddle when the batch boils up for the first time. Put the thermometer in the pot and cook to 220° F. Strain all the water from the peels and add them to the cooked syrup in the pot. Put the pot back on the stove at medium heat and boil it up once. Then pour the batch into the china or stainless steel bowl. Completely cover the surface of the batch with a piece of wax paper, directly on top of the peels and syrup, in order to keep in the heat as long as possible. Set the bowl aside at room temperature for 24 hours.

SECOND DAY: Remove the wax paper from the bowl and pour the whole batch into a small pot. Put it on the stove at medium heat and boil up once, stirring carefully. Strain the syrup from the peels. Put the syrup back into the pot; wash and dry the bowl and put the drained peels back into it.

Add ¼ cup of sugar and ¼ cup of Karo syrup to the syrup in the pot, stir, and cook to 222° F. Pour the hot syrup over the peels in the bowl, cover the surface of the batch with wax paper, and set aside at room temperature until the next day.

THIRD DAY: Repeat the procedure as described for the second day, adding ¼ cup of sugar and ¼ cup of Karo syrup to the syrup and cooking it to 226° F.

FOURTH DAY: Repeat the procedure as described for the second day, adding ¼ cup of sugar and ⅓ cup of Karo syrup to the syrup and cooking it to 230° F. But then, put the peels back into the pot, boil it up once, and pour the batch into a 1-quart Mason jar or similar glass container with a wide opening. Cover the surface of the batch in the jar with another piece of wax paper, but do not close the jar itself until the next day, when the batch has cooled, to prevent condensation of moisture in the jar. The peels are now preserved, and can be kept this way in a cool place until needed.

To prepare the peels for chocolate dipping, pour the peels and the syrup back into a pot and on the stove at low heat and stir carefully, until the syrup boils up again. Drain the peels and place them on a screen or a wire rack, with the help of two forks, while the pieces are still hot, to permit all the syrup to drop off. Set aside overnight, or until cool and dry enough for dipping in chocolate.

The remaining syrup has an excellent, natural citrus fruit flavor and can be used, slightly thinned down with hot water, on pancakes and waffles.

(From THE ART OF MAKING GOOD CANDIES AT HOME, by Martin K. Herrmann, illustrated by John Herrmann. Copyright © 1966 by Martin K. Herrmann. Reprinted by permission of Doubleday & Company.)

Large Taylor Candy Thermometer 1.30

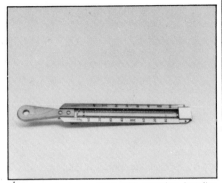

Stainless-steel mounting with wooden handle; 16" long; 2" wide; registers from 46 F. to 370 F.
$22.50 ▲

Everyone we talked to who makes candy recommended this thermometer; and every candy cookbook which named a specific brand named this one. It is extremely practical, easy to read, and accurate, with temperature markings from 46 F. to 370 F. The glass tube magnifies for ease of seeing the slim column of mercury inside that shows as a band of metallic gray against the white of the glass and the grey of the stainless-steel body. This frame has been bent into a flat trough to protect the thermometer tube, and the tip of the frame holds the glass half an inch above the floor of any pan, from a cauldron of boiling jam to a small copper pot in which you are making fondant. The large wooden paddle-shaped handle at the top allows you to move the thermometer even when one end is in boiling syrup, and a steel pan clip on the back has positions that are adjustable to the height of the sides of your pan. Our only concern is that, because of its protective construction, this superb thermometer might be somewhat difficult to clean; but a soak in warm water immediately after use should dissolve any sugar syrup left on the surface. We strongly recommend it.

ALMOND TOFFEE

1 cup toasted, chopped almonds
1½ cups white sugar
¼ cup water
⅓ cup Karo syrup
8 ounces margarine*
½ teaspoon salt
¼ teaspoon baking soda
1½ cups toasted, chopped almonds, additional
*Greased baking sheet

Warm the first cup of toasted almonds in the oven at 175° F. and keep them there until they are needed. Put the sugar, water, and Karo syrup into a pot and on the stove at medium heat and stir. When it boils up for the first time, wash the sugar crystals down from the sides of the pot and the stirring paddle. Keep boiling and stir in the margarine.* When the margarine is completely melted, take out the stirring paddle. Put in the thermometer and cook to 290° F., stirring carefully with the thermometer.

Then take the pot from the fire and stir in the salt, baking soda, and the one cup of warmed almonds with a dry stirring paddle.

Pour the batch onto the greased baking sheet, spreading it evenly and about ¼ inch thick. Move the sheet to a cooler spot on the table every few minutes to cool it evenly. Soon, when the batch feels plastic, like caramel, run a palette knife or spatula under the batch to release it from the tray, turn the batch over, and score it with the palette knife, making parallel lines about ½ inch apart. Then turn the baking sheet 90° and score the batch in parallel lines 1-1¼ inches apart. Cool the scored batch near an open window or in a cool room, but not in the refrigerator, or it will get sticky. Soon the pieces will be firm and will come off the sheet easily. Break the pieces apart at the score lines.

Spread the additional 1½ cups of cold almond pieces on a baking sheet with borders or in a wide, flat bowl. Dip the toffee centers in chocolate and roll them in the almonds right away, or else sprinkle the almonds on top. When the chocolate on the toffee centers has set for a few minutes, they can be taken out and set on a baking sheet covered with wax paper, for cooling and to make room for more centers on the almonds. When the pieces are completely cool, you may either wrap them individually in foil or leave them unwrapped. Store them in a cellophane bag or closed jar or tin, in a cool place.

*If you wish to use butter instead of margarine, be sure to add ¼ teaspoon of lecithin, necessary to bind the fat with the other ingredients. Margarine already contains lecithin.

(From THE ART OF MAKING GOOD CANDIES AT HOME, by Martin K. Herrmann, illustrated by John Herrmann. Copyright © 1966 by Martin K. Herrmann. Reprinted by permission of Doubleday & Company.)

H-B Candy or Deep-Frying Thermometer 1.31

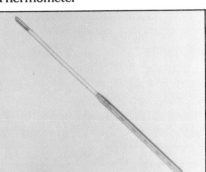

Glass; 10" long; registers from 200 F. to 450 F. Stainless-steel case, 11" long.
$18.00 Thermometer, **$18.00** Case

Part three of the H-B armored thermometer system, of which the other two parts are the dough thermometer and the meat thermometer we have shown you (1.24, 1.25). These have a long stainless-steel bullet-shaped case with a window through which you can see the markings etched into the interchangeable glass thermometers calibrated to the temperatures required in the different kinds of cooking. This third H-B instrument was originally sold as an asphalt thermometer, used to test boiling tar; but because it registers temperatures up to 450 F., we think it ideal for testing the contents of your candy kettle or your deep-fryer. It does have one drawback—the absence of a clip on the case to hold it to a pan to prevent its tip, which encloses the sensor, from resting against the pan bottom. You would have to devise your own Rube Goldberg way of suspending the thermometer—perhaps by a skewer run through the ring and laid across the pot—or else you'd have to stand there holding this dangling from the tines of a pot fork. If this doesn't discourage you and if you have bought the stainless-steel case and one or both of the other inserts, then by all means buy this wonderfully accurate and well-made third partner in the set.

In the newly settled city of New Orleans a French lady yearned for an almond confection of her youth that was named after the Count Plessis-Praslin. Her cook made a version of the sweet, using the wild pecans which grew nearby to create the Southern pecan praline.

25

DEEP-FAT FRYING THERMOMETERS

Most of the thermometers designated for either candymaking or deep-fat frying are interchangeable, as you have seen from our descriptions in the preceding section. Here we show you two deep-fat thermometers, each a version of one in the last section and each capable of registering to a higher temperature. Look at the section on deep-frying in Chapter 11 to understand their use; their care is that of any sensitive instrument. Warm them before using, don't touch their glass with a damp cloth or potholder when they are hot, and try not to let them knock around in a kitchen drawer. And be careful: hot fat and hot sugar are probably the most dangerous things in your kitchen.

Colorful Candy and Fat Thermometer   1.32

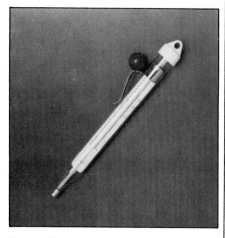

Glass with plastic cap, stainless-steel clip, wooden ball handle; 9" long; ¾" diam.; registers from 100 F. to 400 F.
$1.39

This is another version of the colorful little candy thermometer encased in a glass tube we showed you above. The manufacturer says that you can use it for making candy and jelly as well as for deep-frying, and sure enough there are markings along the scale for candymaking stages from Soft Ball to Hard Crack, and then others on up to Doughnuts, Fish, and Potatoes (400 F.). However, as on the companion instrument for candy, no reading is given for Jelly. Because the scale covers a wider range of temperatures, the markings are a little smaller and harder to read than on the candy thermometer, but not enough to disqualify the instrument. This tube, like its sibling, has, at one end, a pop-off plastic cap to warn of imminent explosion from overheating, and there is a sliding steel clip which holds a heat-resistant red wooden ball to use as a handle. Only 9" in length, it is pretty, inexpensive, and adequate for the purpose.

Taylor Deep-Frying Thermometer   1.33

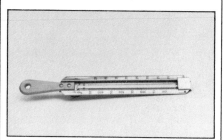

Stainless-steel mounting with wood handle; 16½" long; 2" wide; registers from 55 F. to 460 F.
$22.50 ▲

Another big beauty from Taylor. Like the one for candymaking we have already shown you, this involves a mercury thermometer in a flat trough in a stainless-steel casing. On the back there is an adjustable clip to hold the instrument to the side of the pan, while at the top there is a wooden paddle-shaped handle that permits you to touch the thermometer without burning yourself. It registers from 50 F. to 460 F. in 5-degree steps; the usual range of temperature for deep-frying foods is from about 360 F. to 390 F. Deep-frying is one process, by the way, in which you leave the thermometer in place. Clip it into place in the cool oil or the melting shortening, and watch the indicator climb to the desired temperature as the fat is heated, so that you can avoid overshooting the correct point and risking damage to your fat as well as the food you put into it. Then watch the temperature drop when you lower the food into it, to begin its slow rise all over again. An excellent product, the best of its kind.

CHERRIES IN RUM FRITTERS— CSERESZNYEK RUMOS PALACSINTABAN

25 to 30 pieces

2 eggs
½ cup flour
1 tablespoon powdered sugar
Pinch of salt
1 tablespoon rum
½ cup clarified butter
½ cup vegetable oil
1 pound firm Bing cherries with their stems
Additional powdered sugar
Vanilla sugar

1. Mix eggs, flour, 1 tablespoon powdered sugar, salt and rum till smooth. Let the batter rest for 1 hour.
2. Heat butter and oil in a frying pan. When frying temperature is reached, turn heat to low.
3. Dip cherries into the batter and stand them up in the butter and oil. Turn them carefully by their stems to make sure they will become crisp and golden brown on all sides. Blot them in powdered sugar on paper toweling.
4. Pile up the fritters in pyramid shape. Sprinkle with vanilla sugar.

(From THE CUISINE OF HUNGARY, by George Lang. Copyright © 1971 by George Lang. Reprinted by permission of Atheneum.)

Thermo Spoon   1.34

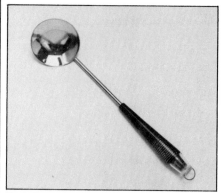

Hard chrome stem and bowl, melamine handle, plastic capped thermometer; 12¼" overall; bowl 3" diam.; measures from 50 F. to 450 F.
$7.99

Neither so accurate nor so professional as the thermometers we have been showing you, this combination spoon and thermometer is an amusing gadget nonetheless. Use it to stir jam, to retrieve doughnuts from their bath of boiling fat;

Using a section of broomstick as a wand, a lady practices the gentle art of making spun sugar to decorate a dessert. Using a candy thermometer to test the boiling syrup makes success more certain today.

Continued from preceding page

better still, use it to stir custards and milk-based soups and chowders, watching all the while to be sure that the temperature gauge does not reach the boiling point. A shallow bowl 3″ wide is welded to a hard chrome rod forming the handle, and the sensor element of the thermometer is at the point where they are joined. The upper end of the rod is encased in a melamine handle topped with a plastic-covered cylindrical scale. On the scale there are large numbers indicating temperatures from 50 F. to 450 F.; and at the very top is a metal loop for hanging. The spoon shape limits the use of this device as a thermometer, while the care essential for a thermometer limits its use as a spoon; it is a caprice, to be sure, but it is not without its uses.

WINE THERMOMETERS

Wine, like bread, is a miracle created daily by the action of yeast on natural substances. And yeast, as we know, is highly responsive to temperature changes, perishing silently when the heat rises and becoming sullenly paralyzed with too much cold. When wine is fermenting, the cellar is kept somewhere between 50 F. and 90 F., and skilled cellar-masters are able to control the rate and degree of fermentation by adjusting the temperature of the interior of the vats full of wine. Every vintner has in the cellar a thermometer with which the maître de chai tests the temperature of the wine.

But the wine in your cellar or closet or on your kitchen shelf is already fermented. And a wine thermometer in the home is not used like a dough thermometer, to help to control the creation of the product, but rather like a meat thermometer, to tell you when it is at a proper temperature to be served. Red wines are served at room temperature, most properly somewhere between 65 F. and 72 F. Except, of course, for the very light and dry red wines, which are sometimes served 10 degrees colder than this. And white wine, which we know is to be chilled, can be served iced, as Champagne is, or only slightly cooler than a red wine, like a very fine white Burgundy. We show you two wine thermometers which are inserted in the neck of the bottle in place of the cork to help you determine when the wine for dinner is at the perfect temperature.

mometer. Set into the bar is the scale of degrees and a set of markings indicating the proper temperatures at which to drink Cognac, vin rouge, vin de dessert, vin blanc, Champagne, and eau-de-vie: this last, at 5 C., nearly freezing. Around the stem below the wooden portion is a cork to hold the thermometer in position in the bottle. We question the use of a wine thermometer like this one—for one thing, would there be any change of taste from a metal rod left in place in the wine for any length of time?—but if you want to have one, then this is probably the best of the Centigrade group.

Swiss Vinometer   1.36

Plastic with aluminum sensor; 6½″ overall; cylinder 1¾″ diam., 1⅜″ high; registers from 30 F. to 90 F.
$15.00

If you prefer readings given in Fahrenheit rather than in Centigrade, here is a wine thermometer that will suit you. It is a black plastic cylinder bound in aluminum; the top of the cylinder holds a handsome temperature gauge, with a bright red pointer indicating temperatures from 30 F. to 90 F. Around the sides of the cylinder there are printed the recommended temperatures at which to serve various wines, with, unusually enough, Swiss wines (*Swiss* wines?) being included in the categories, Switzerland being the country of origin of the thermometer. The underside of the cylinder has attached to it a 5½″ aluminum rod to lower into your bottle. We have the same reservations about it that we had about the preceding Centigrade thermometer, but, like that device, this is a good one.

Thermovins from Germany   1.35

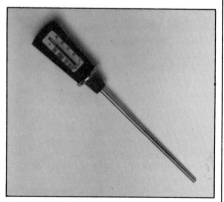

Tropical wood and cork with polished chrome sensor; 11½″ overall; registers from 5 C. to 25 C.
$18.75

When you have taken the wine from your cellar or temperature-controlled closet and brought it into the living quarters to allow it to reach room temperature, when you have perhaps set it in a cradle to settle the sediment and have also removed the cork to permit it to breathe, then why in the world would you want to plug it up again, even with such a relatively nonoffensive contraption as this? It would be simpler, surely, to lower the stem of the Taylor instant thermometer (1.26) into the neck of the bottle if you wanted to check the temperature of the wine. However, this is an item for the person whose pleasure in the wine he drinks is compounded by the assurance that he is doing precisely the right thing, and this is exactly the right device for temperature-taking. It consists of an attractive wooden bar into which has been set a long stemlike liquid ther-

DEVICES TO MEASURE TIME.

We have measured by cups and liters and tablespoons, by American and Imperial pints, by degrees of Centigrade and of Fahrenheit, and by ounces and kilograms; and we have seen that there is by no means a universality of agreement about the standards of measurement, and that a good set of conversion tables is an essential part of your batterie de cuisine. Until you come to time: and then there is an absolute agreement. For, once you are past the subjective school of thought, the school which tells you to cook "until done" or to beat "until light," then you deal always with the same measures: seconds, minutes, and hours. To be sure, once you are an experienced cook you can show less respect for the recommended cooking times—you'll know that you can speed up the roast if you also raise the temperature, and that, because ingredients vary, so does the time that they take to cook. But by and large you can rely on time directions. And the first and most important time measurer you will have is the clock on your kitchen wall. We are not taking into account the fact that you probably have a timer that came with your stove, since many of those are notoriously inaccurate, especially when measuring tiny bits of time—the three-minute egg, the mere seconds it takes for a meringue to brown. We show you a wall clock, an hourglass, a clockwork timer, and then one of those wonderful delayed-action timing devices that let you start the turkey cooking while you are away from home, or the coffee percolating while you are still asleep, or that will turn off an electric appliance after the period of time you decree.

There is much to be said for the hourglass, free as it is from any dependence on exterior sources of energy, using only a small portion of the world's infinite supply of gravity. Perhaps a large hourglass would not be useful in the kitchen, but we can think of any number of uses for this little one, which measures a rough three-minute chunk of time. Try it the next time that you cook a three-minute egg; or, after you get your next phone bill, use it ruthlessly for measuring out message units. This has a heavy little metal frame plated in chrome, with three supports standing around a glass hourglass. Inside the hourglass there is a pink granular substance which runs slowly through at—we must admit—a slightly variable pace. Still and all, it is inexpensive and sturdy and has a shape so classic and evocative that it would be worth having around to look at, even if it served no function.

Recipe indications have not always been given in minutes: "Then take the third or fourth part of warm white wine and mix all together. Then take the fairest wheaten flour that you can get and beat them together long enough to weary one person or two. . . ."

The Goodman of Paris (Le Ménager de Paris), c. 1393. Translated by Eileen Power. George Routledge & Sons, London, 1928

OEUFS A LA COQUE—BOILED EGGS

Although eggs are cooked in such a variety of exquisite ways by French cooks, the ordinary boiled egg is not their strong point. One would be lucky, I think, to get boiled eggs as good as those described by Henry James after a luncheon at Bourg-en-Bresse, which was composed entirely of boiled eggs and bread and butter. 'They were so good that I am ashamed to say how many of them I consumed.' *An oeuf à la coque* in fact usually means, in France, an egg plunged in boiling water, taken out again, and there you are. But Madame Saint-Ange, thorough in this matter as in all others, gives no less than five different methods of boiling an egg in her incomparable *Livre de cuisine*, starting off her chapter on eggs with the remark that 'a true boiled egg must have been laid the day it is to be eaten'. Not an easy rule to observe, but certainly few people will quarrel with the rule that an egg more than three days old had better be cooked some other way.

Sunbeam Wall Clock   1.37

Plastic; 9″ diam.; 2½″ wide.
$12.95

We hung this one on our office wall and have been going to meetings and taking coffee breaks by it for a few years now. It is simplicity itself: a round electric wall clock, 9″ in diameter, with a plastic frame in black, red, green, or gold. The white face has on it big black arabic numbers, pleasantly old-fashioned look-ing, and bold black hands with tuliped ends. There is also a gold sweep-second hand to help you count the fractions of minutes. A raised crystal protects the face and lets you see the time clearly from nearly any angle. It keeps good time, is relatively inexpensive, and will last as long as your electrical current.

Egg Timer   1.38

Cast-aluminum and chrome-plated frame, glass hourglass; 3⅛″ high; 1⅞″ diam.: 3-minute timer.
$2.29

Continued from preceding page

Here are the Saint-Ange methods, summarized:

(1) Allowing ¾ pint of water for 2 eggs, bring it to the boil in a fairly deep saucepan. Off the fire, lower the eggs into the water in a tablespoon. Cover the pan and cook 4 minutes without further boiling.

(2) Put the eggs into a saucepan; cover them plentifully with cold water. When the water reaches a full boil, the eggs are cooked. Remove them at once.

(3) Bring a saucepan of water to the boil; remove from the fire to put in the eggs. Cover the pan. Put back on the fire. From the moment the water comes to the boil again allow 3 minutes. If the eggs are very large leave them a further minute off the fire.

(4) Plunge the eggs into the pan of boiling water. Taking it immediately from the fire, keep it closely covered for 10 minutes.

(5) Plunge the eggs into boiling water. Cover; leave *one* minute over the fire. Remove from the fire and leave 5 minutes.

From all these alternatives everyone should surely be able to choose that which suits them best. Personally, I prefer systems No. 4 or 5, which produce boiled eggs with nice creamy whites. With the first method they are insufficiently cooked for my taste, and methods No. 2 and 3 are useful if you are in a hurry but do not produce such lovely whites.

(From FRENCH PROVINCIAL COOKING, by Elizabeth David. Copyright © 1960, 1962, 1967, 1969 by Elizabeth David. Published by Penguin Books. Reprinted by permission of Elizabeth David.)

Terraillon Timer 1.39

Plastic; 2⅝″ diam.; 1″ high; 1-hour timer.
$10.50 ▲

Speaking of design, isn't this wonderful? It is a little round plastic timer which runs on clockwork and which reminds us that Italy is second only to Scandinavia in the production of the very best modern design. Look at this beautiful thing. It is only 2⅝″ in diameter and stands 1″ high, a sandwich of two colored discs in red, white, yellow, brown, blue, or chrome on either side of a central ring of numbers from one to sixty. A cutout in the top helps you to locate the numbers with greater ease. Turn the top clockwise past the desired number and then back onto it, and then set the timer down on its three tiny rubber feet. When the time is up, a quiet and fuzzy-sounding bell will ring. This is the modern version of the hourglass, with the advantage of drawing your attention, through the bell, to the moment when the time is up, but it is equally marvelous to look at.

Time-All 1.40

Plastic; 4⅛″ × 3″; 3⅝″ high; 24-hour timer.
$10.00 ▲

We are showing this to you in a cooking catalog, but we would be lax if we didn't tell you that its greatest current use is helping to pretend that an empty house is, in fact, occupied. With it, you can arrange to have your lights go on at six every night and off again at 11:30, even though you are in Morocco; a burglar will either believe that you are a very orderly person or will suspect that you are using an automatic timer. But for remote-control cooking it is terrific, so long as you have electrical appliances to work with. Suppose the baby wakes every night at two. Just plug the electric bottle warmer—or the hot plate on which a saucepan full of water rests—into this timer set for 1:55, and he will have his meal in no time. Use it with your Farber rotisserie or your Hoover oven (see Chapter 8) to begin cooking a chicken or a stew while you are still out at work; or with your electric kettle or percolator to have tea or coffee ready the moment that you awaken. This is, compared with the preceding three timers, a homely thing, made of fake wood and black, orange, and cream plastic. First you set it for the times at which you want it to go on and off, find the current time, add that setting, and plug it into the wall. Then plug your appliance into the top of it and you're in business. It's no beauty, but it is useful.

"The merit of each dish lies two-thirds in its flavor and one-third in its texture. The latter is an inescapable quality of the food, whether good or bad. . . . The texture is always a perfectly definite quality, which is in a way harder to control than the flavour, because it cannot be corrected. You cannot unboil an egg. That is why the perfect soft-boiled egg is rarely to be had. A great deal of art and experience goes into its making."

Chinese Gastronomy, *by Hsiang Ju Lin and Tsuifeng Lin, Pyramid Publications, 1972*

SALOMETERS AND HYDROMETERS

When you taste freshly made lemonade to see if it is sweet enough, then you are testing the density of the sugar solution. And when you sip a spoonful of broth from a pot before you season it, you are testing the density of the salt solution. In both of these cases, your testing apparatus is the set of taste buds on your tongue, a sensitive enough instrument to inform you whether the relationship of seasoning and liquid is correct. There are, however, occasions when density is important not because of taste but because it will have some effect on the quality of the finished product. Jellies, for example, contain sugar for sweetness and for its preservative qualities, and also because sugar is essential to the formation of gel and the consequent firming of the jelly. A jam made with too little sugar will be soft, while one with a great oversupply of sugar will become either crystalline or syrupy. And sherbets and ices made with too much sugar will never freeze properly, no matter how heavenly they taste in liquid form.

Tasting a salt brine to gauge the density of the solution would not only be unpleasant, but insufficiently exact. Salting is one of the oldest forms of food preservation, working by impregnating the food with a heavy concentration of salt; the spoilage is retarded in direct proportion to the strength of the solution. Many foods which are salted go on then to be further preserved by smoking, canning, or freezing, and it is, therefore, essential to be able to judge the strength of the original solution in order to carry out the next step properly. Whether you are curing vegetables, such as cucumber pickles or sauerkraut, or meat or fish products, such as corned beef, bacon, or smoked fish, you will need to know the density of the brine. Old recipes, when recommending a very strong brine—10 per cent, we would say—described it as one "strong enough to float an egg." Luckily, we have instruments at hand which help us judge in a less subjective manner.

Salometer   1.41

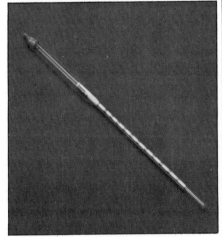

Glass; 11½" long; readings from 0 to 100.
$9.00

This salometer, or salt measurer, works on the same principle as the old cook's advice to make brine "strong enough to float an egg." No dials or mercury or thermocoupling here, rather a weighted glass tube which is read according to how far it sinks into a brine. Little salt, and the tube will sink way down, so that at water level you can read 10—a light solution. Much salt, and it will bob along the top like a swimmer in the Great Salt Lake, and at water level you will see a reading of 80 or 90. It is a simple method, complicated only by the problem of converting regular percentage points from your cookbook to the standard on the salometer. The thing to re-member is that the 100° mark on the salometer represents a saturated solution—one holding all the dissolved salt it will take—35 pounds of salt to 100 pounds (10 gallons) of water. A 10 per cent brine, therefore, would give a reading of 36° on the salometer, since it contains about one-third as much salt as a saturated solution. Otherwise this is the simplest possible contraption, an 11″ long weighted and sealed glass tube with a marked piece of paper rolled up inside it to give you the readings.

Baumé Hydrometers   1.42, 1.43

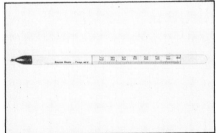

Glass; 11¼″ long; readings from 0 to 70.
$7.50

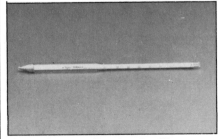

Glass; 12″ long; readings from 0 to 35.
$9.00

This is called a hydrometer, or water measurer, and thus it approaches the question of density from the other side: How much sugar is in your coffee (the salometer) vs. how much coffee is in your sugar (the hydrometer)? It works just as the salometer does, however, by registering the point to which a weighted glass tube sinks in a solution of salt, sugar, or anything else that dissolves. We show you two shapes, one a simple straight tube like a sealed test tube, and the other narrowing halfway up its length away from the nipplelike weight. They are both the same in their readings, however, registering according to a scale developed by Antoine Baumé, a French chemist, to measure the density of sugar syrups. One of these hydrometers indicates degrees from 0 to 75 and the other from 0 to 35, but either would be sufficient for use by the jellymaker or the home canner, or to test the amount of sugar you have added to your raspberry juice when making fresh-fruit sherbet in your new ice-cream freezer.

TO SOUSE OR PICKLE A TURKEY, IN IMITATION OF STURGEON

An old recipe showing the rather casual measuring methods used in pickling, this is credited to one Mary Kettilby, a contributor to *A Collection of Above Three Hundred Receipts, by Several Hands,* 1734.

Take a fine large Turkey, dress it very clean, dry, and bone it, then tie it up; put into the Pot you boil it in, one Quart of White-wine, one Quart of Water, and one Quart of good Vinegar, and a very large Handful of Salt; let it boil, and scum it well, and then put in the Turkey; when 'tis enough, take it out, and tie it tighter; let the Liquor boil a little longer; and if it wants more Vinegar or Salt, add it when 'tis cold; pour it upon the Turkey, 'twill keep some Months; you eat it with Oil and Vinegar, or Sugar and Vinegar; 'tis more delicate than Sturgeon, and makes a pretty Variety, if that is not to be had; cover it with Fennel, when it is brought to the Table.

(From THE CORNUCOPIA, by Judith Herman & Marguerite S. Herman. Copyright © 1973 by Judith Herman and Marguerite S. Herman. Reprinted by permission of Harper & Row.)

The preliminaries of preparing food for cooking have only begun when the shopping has been done; once it is purchased and carted home, the food must be washed and put away, although not necessarily in that order. Fruit washed too soon will rot quickly in the cupboard; on the other hand, things being what they are in modern agriculture, there is much to be said for the practice of rinsing off whatever pollutants industry has chosen to spray on your pears or your blueberries. In general, however, it is better to wait until you have portioned out the food for that particular evening's meal, and then to wash that small amount. Meanwhile, you'll keep the food cool (greens and vegetables), or at room temperature (fruits to be ripened).

A whole series of utensils have been developed which allow you to run water over food and out the other side; they are also, of course, used for dealing with cooked foods which have to be separated from the liquids in which they have been cooked. On a scale from solid to void, at one end there is the colander, a shaped bowl made of a sheet of metal perforated by holes, while at the other end is the strainer, a collection of air spaces surrounded by thin metal wires. In between there are variations, but all colanders and strainers are similar, each of them a variation on the idea of the net. We show you our choices among these, then proceed farther along to salad dryers, then to the things you need for scrubbing and other cleaning jobs in the kitchen.

METAL WITH HOLES: THE COLANDER

The single most useful tool for washing and draining food is the colander. You should buy the largest one that your sink will accommodate, because you can always drain a few boiled new potatoes or gently rinse a half-pint of raspberries in a basin-sized colander, but you will never be able to rinse three heads of lettuce or drain a couple of pounds of spinach in a tiny one. Here is a case in which Bigger is definitely Better And be sure that you get a colander that sits firmly on its base: some of them come in, like Carl Sandburg's fog, on little feet: poetic but unstable. Try to empty a couple of pounds of boiled pasta into one of these unsettled things, and the whole mass will undoubtedly tip out of it and disappear in slippery strands down the disposal.

John Evelyn's book Acetaria, A Discourse on Sallets, *gives directions for preparing greens that can scarcely be improved on. "Let the herby ingredients be exquisitely cull'd and cleans'd of all worm-eaten dry-spotted leaves. Then discreetly sprinkled with spring water, let remain for a while in a cullender, then swing gently in clean napkin."*

Restaurant-Size Aluminum Colander   1.44

Heavy-gauge aluminum with tinned loop handles; 15″ diam.; 6⅞″ high; 11-qt. capacity.

$33.00 ▲

Our first choice, if you have the room for it. This capacious aluminum colander, restaurant size, is basic equipment for a commune, a dorm, a parish house, or any family kitchen when you are cooking for a crowd; but it's just as good on a daily basis when you have to wash lettuce, drain fruit for canning, or manage the hot, hard-to-handle mass of freshly boiled spaghetti in gallons of water. This is a solidly constructed piece of equipment 15″ across and standing almost 7″ high, and it holds 11 quarts of food. Its steel-riveted handles are curved for shapely looks and satisfactory grip, and, best of all, the base is a heavy-gauge aluminum ring that will never tip over. Although the aluminum will theoretically become stained if you use the colander for draining certain foods that interact with that metal, the food stays in the colander for only moments at a time, lessening the risk of discoloration: and the light weight and sturdiness of aluminum thoroughly justify its use here. The holes look small because the colander is so large, but each of them is actually a decent ⅜″ in diameter. And if you have no proper storage space for this helpful giant, then by all means put it on a counter and fill it with all of the grapefruit you bring home from the supermarket.

Farberware Stainless-Steel Colander   1.45

Stainless steel with plastic handles; 9½″ diam.; 5⅞″ high; 5-qt. capacity.

$14.00 ▲

If you don't have room in your sink for the big aluminum colander above, you just buy this shiny, tubby-looking piece of equipment made by Farber. It is small, but it is nevertheless able, because of its high sides, to hold a full 5 quarts of food. The tall and narrow shape allows it to fit into a large, lidded stockpot and serve as a steamer. Although it stands on a triangular base of tippable little feet, it is actually quite stable as a result of its low center of gravity. And the heat-proof black plastic handles are a decided advantage when you are trying to lift it after pouring into it quarts of boiling water and scalding-hot green beans. All in all, it is quite pretty with its silvery finish and its carefully applied pattern of little holes; and the 9½″ diameter is manageable enough to allow you to find a place for it among your pots and pans.

WILTED SPINACH SALAD

Spinach is an increasingly popular salad green, either alone or mixed with other types. The leaves should be fresh, young, and thoroughly washed.

Serves 4-6

4 tablespoons olive oil
1 large or 2 small cloves garlic, crushed and chopped
2 tablespoons soy sauce
½ cup thinly sliced water chestnuts
Freshly ground pepper
2 tablespoons lemon juice
1 pound spinach, washed, dried, and crisped
Salt to taste
2 hard-boiled eggs, coarsely chopped

Cook olive oil and garlic over medium heat for 2 minutes. Add the soy sauce, water chestnuts, and pepper. Cook one minute, tossing the water chestnuts. Add the lemon juice and blend. Then add the spinach and toss as you would a salad until the spinach is just wilted. Taste for salt and correct the seasoning, if necessary. Transfer to a salad bowl and garnish with the chopped egg. Serve warm.

(From AMERICAN COOKERY, by James A. Beard, illustrated by Earl Thollander. Copyright © 1972 by James A. Beard. Reprinted by permission of Little, Brown and Company.)

Porcelain Colander or Strainer   1.47

Porcelain; 7¼″ diam.; 4″ deep. Also avail. with diam. of 4¼″ or 5½″.

$27.50

There are times when simply nothing else will do, when you have to rinse or drain foods that are so delicate that they should not be touched by metals at all. And so we show you this beautiful but fragile porcelain colander—or is it a strainer?—with a handle like that on a teacup, the sides delicately fluted and with rows of perforations along each ridge. You won't use this small beauty for draining spaghetti or for rinsing lettuce, but it would suffice for rinsing raspberries or for straining the bay leaf and thyme from the hot milk in which you have steeped them for a sauce. Its fluted shape suggests a mold. Use it over a bowl to drain the whey from a cheese dessert, or from whipped cream. It comes in two sizes, from 5½″ to 7¼″ in diameter, and it has a sturdy ring in its handle

so you can display it as it deserves. A luxury, but not a foolish one.

Spaghetti Strainer or Colander   1.48

Heavy-gauge aluminum with tinned cast-iron handle; bowl 10″ diam., 4¾″ deep, 5-qt. capacity. Also avail. with capacity of 2 or 3 qts.

$11.20

More often than not, when you use a colander you don't care about what happens to the water that drains through it —it is either the starchy liquid in which the spaghetti has been boiled or the cold fresh tap water which has been pouring through the fresh blueberries, and it disappears down the sink with no regrets. But, should you want to save the liquid after separating it from the solid food, then you could do it by means of this gargantuan version of the slotted spoon: half strainer, half colander. Of very heavy metal and flat-bottomed, it is called a spaghetti strainer, but if you look at it, you will see that there is a hook which will fit onto the rim of a large pot or bowl and so makes it easy to save the liquid that pours through the openings. We used ours for straining the bones and vegetables from a simmering beef stock, and it was strong enough to stand up to the heavy beef bones which fell into it, being made of an extremely heavy-gauge aluminum. The tinned iron of the handle makes it possible to hold onto it barehanded without being burnt, even when boiling-hot liquids make the body of the colander scalding hot; a difference in metals is one of the best ways to retard the passage of heat. This colander meets all the criteria for pots in commercial use, from the open edges, for ease of thorough cleaning, to the extra metal that reinforces the bottom

Continued from preceding page

and the corners. We have the 10-inch, 5-quart size, but there are two smaller versions, holding 2 or 3 quarts, which would be even more useful in the home kitchen.

Stainless-Steel Spaghetti Strainer or Colander   1.49

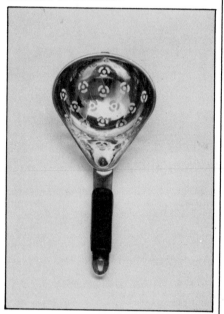

Stainless steel with plastic handle; 17″ long overall; bowl 8½″ × 6½″, 3″ deep.

$8.95

We think that it's enchanting, this pretty scoop shaped like a little lacrosse stick. And notwithstanding its nonculinary appearance, it is a very useful implement. A hook at one end catches onto the edge of a pot so that vegetables can be poured into it and the broth saved for soups; or you can grasp the plastic handle and use the scoop as a ladle, going down into a pot of bubbling water to scoop out pasta shells or bow ties. It was made in Italy of black plastic and stainless steel, with the bowl of the scoop welded to the metal portion of the handle, which extends for the entire length of the handle inside a sandwich of black plastic. A hook at one end allows you to display this strainer from a hook, as you will certainly want to do. The perforations in the bowl are in a pattern that looks like a William Morris stencil: terribly pretty, but not to be used with pastina or any other very tiny pasta shapes.

A nineteenth-century French lettuce-washing basket.

Wire Spaghetti Drainer   1.50

Tinned-steel wire with wood handle; 23″ long overall; bowl 12″ × 8½″, 4½″ deep.

$6.25

Same shape, different concept: or, is the glass half-full or half-empty? This tear-drop-shaped pasta drainer is not made of solid metal perforated by tiny holes in the fashion of a colander; instead, it is formed of miles of tinned-steel wire looped round and round on a frame. The frame itself is very large—23″ in length—and so heavy that it would take a hammer to bend it out of its irregular figure-eight shape. Thinner wire has been swirled around and around on the wider end to make the business end, while a dowel of bleached wood has been inserted into the narrow end to serve as a heatproof handle. This is the chef's version of the pasta strainer, useful for getting down into a commercial-sized cauldron of boiling water for lifting out and draining all kinds of foods—a super-size wire ladle in effect—but also dandy

for lifting doughnuts or zeppole out of their bath of boiling oil and for removing solid foods from soups-in-progress. Because there is no hook to attach this large ladle shape to a bowl's edge, you would have to possess strong arm muscles to hold it steady while quarts of boiling water are poured through it; its best use seems to us to be as a dip-and-lift draining tool.

Small Scoop-Strainer or Drainer   1.51

Stainless steel with plastic handle; 12″ long overall; bowl 5½″ diam., 2½″ deep.

$12.95

A tiny item that dwells in the area where the functions of colander, strainer, and slotted spoon overlap. It is a colander, but with no feet; a strainer, but it is not made of wire mesh; a spaghetti drainer, but a small one; a spoon in shape, but not in size. Still, it would be useful for many purposes in the kitchen, from removing tea leaves when you are making a really large quantity of iced tea, to scooping a single serving of fresh vegetables from their quarts of water where they are cooking à la Française. It is a bowl-shaped piece of stainless steel which has been perforated all over like a colander; it has a hook at one end, and a good heat-resistant plastic handle at the other. Because of its small size—it's only 12″ long overall—it might be your choice for a smallish all-purpose kitchen strainer. Because it is of perforated stainless steel it has no tinning to erode, no wires to be pushed out of shape, and its holes should never be seriously clogged with food.

Stainless-Steel Spaghetti Strainer or
Colander
Wire Spaghetti Drainer

Small Scoop-Strainer or Drainer
Bowl-shaped Wire Strainer
American Aluminum Strainer
Double-Mesh Strainer

WIRE STRAINERS

We have been talking about the spaghetti scoops a bit as though they are strainers, but in fact the invariable mark of a strainer is that it is made of wire mesh; and, in function, it is often a refining tool—see the sieves in Chapter 4 to which it is a sibling. In fact, a strainer is the modern industrial version of the fisherman's net or the layer of cheesecloth stretched over the top of a bowl. It is as useful in the kitchen as a paring knife or a wooden spoon, and with its extreme versatility it can do any of a number of jobs almost but not quite perfectly. Thus, it can take the place of a colander, or a sieve, or a tamis or drum sieve, or a slotted spoon or a skimmer; but it is not the best tool for any of these purposes.

When you buy a strainer, look for strength in the wire construction so that the mesh, no matter how fine it is, will not be damaged by a stirring spoon with which you urge the liquid or pulp through the mesh. Then look for large, firm ears to hook the sieve onto the edge of the pot or bowl that you are straining into; and, if you have a choice, buy a strainer with a wooden handle, so that you will not be burnt by the heat of the liquid you are pouring through the mesh. And since even good strainers are cheap, buy at least three: a tiny one for tea, a 6-inch strainer for journeyman jobs, and one enormous and tough semi-colander like 1.52.

This is the best of the American-made strainers because of the reinforcing bars which form crossed semicircles under the mesh bowl. It comes in different sizes and with different finenesses of aluminum mesh, so that you can have it with a basket which is either 5″, 6″, or 8″ in diameter, and with mesh which is either medium or coarse. The aluminum will not discolor or corrode as readily as tinned steel will and it is extremely easy to clean, but it is less sturdy than the tin-plated mesh. And so the manufacturer has provided the two supporting bands of heavier metal to bolster the mesh against the buffeting of ordinary kitchen use and abuse. There is a black plastic handle, and two sturdy ears permit you to prop the strainer on the edge of a bowl. Storage, by the way, may be a problem: a strainer looks like a hand-held utensil, but it is really as big as a saucepan. Hang this one out of the way on a pegboard—there is a hole in the handle. There it will not be knocked about as it would be in a drawer.

Bowl-shaped Wire Strainer 1.52

Tinned-steel frame and mesh, with wood handle; 18¼″ long overall; bowl 10″ diam., 4¼″ deep.

$3.95

Every strainer being made contains some accommodation for counteracting the fragility of the mesh. Here is a large, bowl-shaped strainer whose sturdy 10-inch frame has been hung with a medium tinned-steel mesh which is so strong that it is virtually rigid. This Italian import is designed for professional use, having an extra-large capacity and tinning of extremely high quality. But it is neither too good nor too expensive to use at home; so fine is it that we don't hesitate to recommend it for straining a sauce or for sifting flour. (And did you ever stop to think that a sifter is just another variation of the strainer?) This one has a flat wooden handle and two extremely strong ears for hooking it onto the rim of a bowl. A good choice for the sturdy-work-horse strainer category.

American Aluminum Strainer 1.53

Aluminum with plastic handle; 13″ long overall; bowl 6″ diam., 5″ deep. Also avail. with diam. of 8″.

$4.00 ▲ $4.50 ▲

Double-Mesh Strainer 1.54

Tinned-steel wire with wood handle; 18¼″ long overall; bowl 10″ diam., 4⅝″ deep.

$8.00

Fine mesh, although it does a more thorough job of sifting and straining than coarser mesh, is also less strong, more easily damaged by the pressure of a spoon or the edge of a pan against the netting. Here is an interesting solution to this problem, not unlike the chinois with crossbars which we show you in Chapter 4. Here a layer of the finest tinned-steel mesh has been reinforced by a second, coarser, layer which has been stretched as a support dome over

Continued from preceding page

the entire outside of the bowl. This strainer has its virtues, especially if you are using it for sifting flour, but it is also damnably difficult to clean, having just that many more spaces where food can become trapped. This is a huge piece of equipment, possessing an extremely rigid frame, measuring 10″ across the bowls and with a nice flat wooden handle adding another 8″ in length for a total of more than 18″ overall.

"The mother went then and dipped rice with a gourd from the basket where they kept it stored, and she leveled the gourd with her other hand so not a grain was spilled and she poured the rice into a basket made of finely split bamboo and went along the path to the pond's edge, and as she went she looked down the street . . . She stepped carefully down the bank and began to wash the rice, dipping the basket into the water and scrubbing the grain with her brown strong hands, dipping it again and again until the rice shone clean and white as wet pearls . . ."

Pearl S. Buck, The Mother, *The John Day Company, 1934*

Shallow Stainless-Steel Strainer   1.55

Stainless steel; 13½″ long; bowl 7½″ diam., 2½″ deep. Also avail. with diam. of 2¾″, 3½″, 4½″, 5½″, or 6½″.

$10.00 ▲

We have shown you strainers with mesh made of aluminum and tin-plated steel; here is the fairest of them all, with its wide bands of shining stainless steel and its flexible stainless-steel mesh. When you add the attractive triangular hook welded to the bowl and the flaring stainless-steel handle, you have a remarkably pretty utensil and one which is relatively sturdy. It comes in six sizes: 2¾″, 3½″, 4½″, 5½″, 6½″ and 7½″ across the bowl—but the capacity is not so great as that of the preceding strainers because of the extreme shallowness of the bowl. This is undoubtedly a way of dealing protectively with the fineness of the mesh so that the pressure will be equally distributed throughout. In addition, the flexibility of the mesh ensures that, like a tree branch which sways and therefore does not break, this strainer will crumple rather than become dented in the drawer. As we have said, this one is terribly pretty and has a reasonably strong frame; watch out, though, that you don't burn yourself on the metal handle when using it to drain very hot food. We see this strainer as one that you can use as an auxiliary food mill, pressing peas or tomatoes through the mesh with the back of your wooden spoon for babies, making puréed peaches and strawberries in season.

Stainless-Steel Strainer-Skimmer   1.56

Stainless steel; 15½″ long overall; bowl 4¾″ diam.

$9.00

With a skimmer such as those in the section on deep-frying in Chapter 11 you lift out the doughnuts bubbling on the surface of boiling fat, the dumplings floating on the top of the chicken stew;

and, if the mesh is fine enough, you can also do jobs that are really straining—as when you skim off the rather dry froth of protein which appears on the surface of liquid in which you are beginning the boiling of meat. Here is a good hybrid implement for all of those purposes, being more flat than domed, but with a slight lift to the edges so that it will hold the food on the mesh. Made in Italy and framed of stainless steel, it has a fine mesh netting, also of stainless steel, which sets it apart from the frying skimmers we've mentioned. The long, long handle is welded firmly to the rim. The bowl of the skimmer is just a little less than 5″ across, large enough to remove a fritter or a pikori from its bath of fat, small enough to maneuver at the top of a tall, narrow stockpot. For more skimmers, look at Chapter 11, and see the perforated and slotted spoons in Chapter 6.

Cylindrical Strainer of Stainless Steel   1.57

Stainless steel; 9″ long overall; bowl 3½″ diam., 1½″ deep. Also avail. with diam. of 2½″.

$10.00

Suppose you want to render chicken fat, and keep both the fat and the savory, browned onions which you fried in it for flavor; or suppose you want to try out cubes of pork fatback and remove the cracklings before you pour the fat into your terrine full of baked pâté as a sealing layer: you can prop this small stainless-steel strainer on the rim of a Mason jar for the chicken fat, or the edge of the terrine, and you let the clear, melted fat flow through the mesh. And you will have caught in your strainer the bits of delicious fried onions to mix later into cooked squash or mashed potatoes, or you will have saved the pork bits for later use in Crackling Biscuits (see George Lang's recipe). This is a good strainer that comes in two sizes, 2½″ in diameter—perhaps for tea—or 3½″ in diameter, to sit comfortably inside the top of a storage jar during use. It looks a little like a butter warmer, being different from the other strainers in that the sides are of solid metal, while the bottom is made of a very fine stainless-steel mesh. Good-looking and very sturdy.

Tiny Conical Strainer　　　　1.58

Tinned-steel wire with wood handle; 7⅛″ long overall; bowl 3″ diam., 2½″ deep.

$1.35

Now, the fact is that food is strained not only through mesh screens, but also through other foods. And so, if you pour very good goose fat from your roasting bird through this conical strainer, you would rapidly collect a mass of crackling fragments and impurities in the point of the cone, and that mass would serve to purify further the fat which filters through it. (This is the same principle which the cigarette manufacturers rely upon when they tell you that the smoke of their cigarettes is filtered through the tobacco itself.) But this implement, which has a family resemblance to the chinois (Chapter 4), is not at all hazardous to your health; it is a small tinned-steel strainer with a rather rigid cone-shaped bowl of fine mesh, the handle a continuation of the rim of the strainer into which there has been pressed a flat wooden bar to protect your fingers from the heat. This would be a reasonable choice for straining tea, and it is sure to come frequently to hand when you want to clarify a small amount of any other liquid.

DRYERS FOR SALAD GREENS

The problem is not in washing salad greens, but in drying them. A wet spinach leaf, a damp piece of Boston lettuce will turn limp in the bowl and dilute the dressing to boot, wasting the priceless olive oil and herbs you have put into it. And oil will never cling to wet greens, but will instead pool in the bottom of the bowl. But there are many methods of accomplishing the perfect drying of salad greens. One of our experts washes them in a sinkful of cold water and then wraps them in a Turkish towel and stores them in the refrigerator for an hour. Another cuts the core out of a head of lettuce, puts it in a colander, allows it to split apart with the pressure of water from the tap running into the hollow, and then dries it leaf by leaf with an overall patting with paper towels. And still another puts the half-dried greens into a plastic bag with paper towels which absorb the remaining moisture.

There are, in addition, a number of faster, because mechanical, methods of drying salad greens, all of them calling on the principle of centrifugal force. As a matter of fact, we heard of a woman in East Hampton who prepared a salad for a really big party by washing the greens in her bathtub and then drying them immediately in the clothes dryer with, we trust, the temperature control turned down to No Heat. If this seems excessive, then remember that you can use the same principle with a rather low expense of energy by using a French salad basket. (Look ahead to Chapter 11 for the section on deep-frying, in which we show a flexible mesh basket that can also be used as a colander when its handles are bent down to act as legs, and as a salad dryer when the handles are turned back to the top of the basket.)

With any salad basket you grasp the handles and make a great sweeping ring with your arm, your shoulder marking the central point of the circle and the bottom of the basket moving along the circumference. The greens are forced to the circumference and the water is pulled out past them. Neat people go out of doors to do this, but if you live in a high-rise apartment or if it is raining, then we should mention that we know plenty of people who dry their greens this way in the bathroom; there are fewer things to be damaged than there are in the kitchen, fewer fragile items to be ruined by the wildly swinging basket or the splattering about of the water; and there's always the shower curtain to act as a backsplash.

Lettuce, from Le Boire et le Manger, by Armand Dubarry, 1884.

"In the foregoing receipts you will perceive that I have used each salad herb separate, only mixing them with the condiments or with vegetable fruit. I have a strong objection to the almost diabolical mixture of four or five different sorts of salad in one bowl, and then chopping them as fine as possible; the freshness as well as the flavour of each is destroyed; they agree about as well together as would brandy and soda water mixed with gin and gingerbeer. . . ."

Soyer's Cookery Book, by Alexis Soyer, 1854

Decorative Salad Basket   1.59

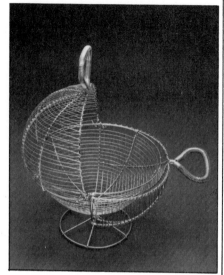

Tinned-steel wire; 8″ diam.; 12¾″ high.

$11.00 ▲

The ordinary French salad basket collapses for storage into a heap of limp mesh mounted on rings; the basket we show you now deals with the problem of storage by never needing to be put away. With its hinged sections raised and its handles held aloft, as they would be during use as a drainer for salad greens, it looks rather like a Victorian hat form with a bow on top, a wire sculpture in which a basket has been constructed around a globe of thin air to stand on a fragile wire pedestal. When it isn't in use, it can sit, the top sections of the globe folded down, in the middle of the kitchen table, holding fresh fruit; or on a counter, holding yellow and red onions; or even, if you have a cool pantry, on a shelf, holding a collection of white and brown eggs. The basket is constructed of an ingenious web of interlocking thin and thick tin-coated wires; and although the bowl itself is only 8″ in diameter, the pedestal and the wire-bound handles make it much larger than that overall. Next winter, take it to your hostess, filled with Christmas balls; next spring, it could be an equally welcome gift filled with tinfoil-covered eggs. Besides being one of the prettiest things in this book, this is extremely useful, even better than the collapsible basket because of its sturdy construction and the good quality of the tinning.

Mouli Metal Spin-Dryer   1.60

Tinned steel with plastic knob and stand; 9″ diam.; 4″ deep.

$8.50

This is as mechanized as we think a salad dryer ever needs to be. It has the traditional flexible mesh basket, here fitted with a removable central post, brace and suction cup to secure it to the bottom of your sink. A threaded plunger rod pushes in and out of the central post, so that it builds up momentum like a child's top and the basket spins round and round, hurling water against the sides of the sink. It is good not only for salad greens but for delicate berries which ought not to sit wet in a bowl; you can regulate the speed of the spinning according to the fragility of the basket's contents. Mouli makes this as well as the one that follows—and we are willing to bet that this sells nowhere near the number that that one does, in spite of its honest looks, absolutely satisfactory functioning, and lower price. See 11.96 for another use.

Mouli Plastic Spin-Dryer   1.61

Plastic; 10″ diam.; 6¼″ high.

$12.95

An intensely practical plastic salad spin-dryer from Mouli, also the maker of the metal job above. Far better looking than the model it replaces in the manufacturer's list—that one looked like a plastic Colosseum—it is of unbreakable polypropylene. It sits snugly in a kitchen sink or on the counter. The greens go into the slotted basket that in turn sits inside a solid white plastic bowl covered by a smoke-colored lid with the gears for the spinning mechanism inside. When you turn the knob on the top the slotted basket spins, the water is forced out to the sides, hits the inside of the plastic bowl, and drizzles down into its bottom —no splashing about with this one, if that feature is worth the difference in price between #1.60 (above) and this.

Danish Salad Dryer   1.62

Plastic; 8½″ diam.; 7½″ high.

$25.00

Infinitely prettier than most objects of plastic is this Scandinavian salad dryer: maybe other nations are just too ambivalent about plastics in the kitchen to use them effectively. This is a handsome container colored bright red, blue, orange, yellow, or avocado, with an interior slotted basket in white which is turned by a side crank and which has a cover of clear plastic. When the basket turns, the water on the greens is forced out to the side by our old friend centrifugal force, and it then drains down into the body of the machine. Because of the side crank, it must be used near the side of a counter, but since the water is contained, that makes no difference. This machine is used all over Europe not only as a salad dryer, but, with the addition of a sandpaper-finished inner disc and a collar, as a potato peeler: we didn't believe it either, but it works, although not spectacularly well. This dryer is more expensive than the Mouli and just as difficult to store, but it is so much prettier that we don't hesitate to recommend it.

FRENCH KITCHEN

Brushes And Other Cleaning Tools

In some supermarkets there are as many aisles for detergents as there are for foods, a good index of how concerned we are with cleanliness. Our bathrooms and entrance halls sparkle with wax, our clothes dissolve under the onslaught of constant washing, and our dishes are sterilized every time they are used. There is a nationwide mania for cleanliness, and one woman we know told us that on her first trip to France she was shocked to find that she felt so drip-dry. But with all of that, there are not so many ways of cleaning food. Water flushes away juices from meat and fruit, and they, therefore, are best rinsed off quickly in comfortably cool water; if food is exceptionally dirty, it can be scrubbed with water and a soft brush; but only in times of plague and pestilence would we think of touching it with soap—after all, cooking does as good a job of killing bacteria as soap would, and it is unwise to eat uncooked food where germs are rampant, anyway. And so we begin this section with three little German brushes for scrubbing potatoes and carrots and pots, and then go on to an array of utensils for washing down the rest of the kitchen.

The brushes are nearly all made of hardwood and natural bristles, and are well enough made to stand up to scalding-hot soapy water. And they are attractive to look at; they cry out for anthropomorphizing, turning under our gaze into rigid British Guardsmen and cuddly blonde animals. When you add to this the fact that they are inexpensive and sturdily made of natural materials, then you can see why they have been among the most admired items to go through our offices.

handle and out the other end, where the metal forms a hook. The brush itself is set at an obtuse angle from the handle, it is securely fastened together, and it all fits comfortably in the hand. The only question is which brush to buy: we suggest two, one of either natural or nylon bristle for root vegetables, and the one with extra brass bristles for cleaning pots and pans.

Visp	1.66

Fiber bristles, unfinished wood handle; 8¾" long.
$2.50

It is called a Visp, which is not a dialect joke, but the Swedish name for this endearing little scouring brush. Now, obviously we have left the realm of food and have moved on to describe the ways in which we clean our pots. And one of the most primitive ways is to use this fairy-tale creation, this miniature broom for elves. It has a rounded handle of natural wood and a brush of very coarse fibers which has been glued together and then bound round and round with metal wire. In *Cold Comfort Farm*, one of the classics of English parody, an Old Family Retainer is presented over and over again with a nice little plastic sponge for washing the dishes, but keeps going back to scraping and poking at them with a bent twig; the English relative, no doubt, of this Scandinavian folk device.

Three Brushes	1.63, 1.64, 1.65
from West Germany	

Nylon, fiber, or fiber with brass-wire bristles, all with wood handles; 9½" long overall; heads 2½" diam. .

$4.00 ▲

We don't want to seem unduly meticulous, but still and all, there are times when a simple rinse in cold water isn't enough to render food clean enough to cook, much less to eat au naturel. Potatoes come to us crusted with earth; fruit is covered with toxic sprays; and with the resurgence of home gardening, more and more Americans have come to realize that earth and ants are the natural companions of foods which come from the ground. And so we scrub the carrots and beets with a good bristle brush to dislodge the dirt. We have examined many brushes and were not surprised to discover that the best examples come from West Germany. We show you three: one with natural bristles, one with nylon bristles, and one, made for cleaning pots and pans, which has an outer ring of natural bristles and an inner cluster of brass needles. Each brush has its bristles set into an unpainted disc of wood the size of a large checker; a metal tong-like device clasps this disc and narrows to run all the way through a wooden

"Cleanliness was a fetish with my mother. There were few commercial cleaners on the market when I was a small child, but there was the brick board onto which dust from a fine brick was shaved with an old knife, and with this and a piece of soft cloth the steel knives and forks for the table, as well as the kitchen cutlery, were scoured. Wood ashes were used to clean the

spider when fish was fried—to remove the odor—and were generally employed for other purposes as well. Soft soap also had its part in keeping chopping bowls, cutting boards, and wooden-topped tables clean."

Della T. Lutes, The Country Kitchen, Little, Brown and Company, 1936

Huge Pot Brush   1.67

Light Tampico bristles, wood handle; 23" long.

$1.80

The Visp above and this brush may look alike in the photographs, but are they ever different in person: the most obvious difference is that the Visp is less than 9 inches long, while this brush for cleaning coffee urns and stockpots is 23 inches overall. The Visp has a bunch of brittle fiber bristles at one end, while this has a ravishing blonde bush of bristles made of Tampico, a stiff natural fiber that resembles jute. Still and all, the construction is not so dissimilar after all, each brush having a pole handle to which bristles have been attached in one way or another—nailed, in this case—and then finally bound round with metal wire. This is a marvelous tool for institutional use, but we are convinced that any household that possessed one would soon find any number of ways to use it. It's big enough to strike any little boy as a good battle tool, and cheap enough to strike his parents as a good investment. And anyone would admire it as a creaturelike object, reminding some of us of

Pogo's head, others of an endearing badger from a children's book.

Pot-scrubbing Brush   1.68

Palmyra fiber bristles, hardwood handle; 10½" long overall; head 6" wide.

$3.75

When you have a really big cleaning job to do—say, miles of butcher block counter or the roasting pan in which you have just baked a honey-glazed ham—then this is the brush to use. The bristles are made of palmyra, a natural fiber which you will recognize as being the kind used in the manufacture of doormats. And frankly, if palmyra can clean the mud out of your children's waffle-stompers when they reach the doormat, it should be able to take on pretty much any job in the kitchen. The shape of this brush makes it somewhat easier to grasp than that of the usual scrub brush, being like that of an ordinary man's hairbrush; bristles included, it measures 10½" in length, with the head of bristles 6" wide. It's inexpensive and useful, and you might as well hang it on the wall right over your griddle and count yourself a Time Study Expert.

After the kneading, the clean-up: A good brush does the best job on a pastry-coated board.

Bottle and Glass Brush   1.69

Stiff black bristles, hardwood handle; 15" long.

$3.50

When we began to look at brushes with a cleansed and speculating eye, we were astonished at their beauty and variety. Look at this, now: it resembles a topiary tree, part of the garden in *Alice in Wonderland*. It is actually a brush for hard-to-clean shapes like coffee pots and bottles and vases, and why is it that nobody ever talks about how disgustingly smelly a vase can become after five days of last Saturday night's centerpiece? With this brush you can clean out that vase as well as the wine decanters, flushing out the sediment at the bottom and leaving them sparkling for the next use. It has a 15-inch handle of hardwood to which are attached stiff black bristles. And although the overall tool is large, the bristle end would not be too wide to use for cleaning coffee cups or milk tumblers. This is one of the most useful brushes we show you.

As late as the end of the eighteenth century, sand was the principal material used to scrub kitchen utensils. It was sold by peddlers, like the one in this ditty:

*Who liveth so merry in all this land
As does the poor widow who selleth
　　the sand?
And ever she singeth as I can guess,
Will ye buy any sand, any sand,
　　mistress.*

The Kitchen in History, *by Molly Harrison, Scribners, New York, 1972*

Human dishwashers in the nineteenth century in France had a pretty grim time of it: closed in a tiny, windowless room that was designed to prevent the water from chilling too quickly, they could stay at their task only as long as they could survive in the airless steam bath. But the resourceful plongeur *had a sideline. He would collect the layer of fat which formed on the water, put it in kegs, and sell it for use in the manufacture of soap.*

Christian Guy, An Illustrated History of French Cuisine

Baby-Bottle Brush 1.70

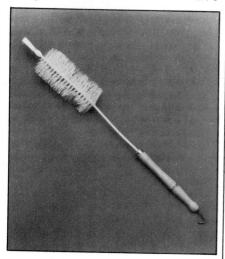

Nylon bristles, wood and plastic-coated wire handle; 17¼" long.

$.89

The advantage of this brush is not so much that it is narrower than the one before—although it is—but rather that it is flexible. It has a wooden handle and a set of white nylon bristles, and connecting the two there is a plastic-coated wire handle which bends easily when any pressure is exerted, so that you can reach into the corners and crevices of a thermos bottle or a wine decanter as well as baby's nursing bottle. In that last use it enters many of our lives at one time or another, being the most common brush for scraping and rinsing out the dreadful dried layers of formula or fruit juice which cling to their interiors. Its length — 17¼" — makes it actually 2" longer than the preceding brush, but the flexibility of the wire makes it usable in smaller spaces.

Narrow Steel-bristled Brush 1.71

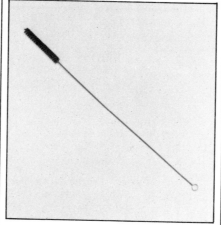

Stiff bristles with steel wire handle; 22" long.
$1.00

For the central post of your percolator; for the spout of your teapot; for behind wheels and into corners on every appliance in your kitchen. Use it on the cutter of your can opener; use it down the drain of your sink the next time it clogs up. It is a very narrow and very long metal brush for reaching far into tight places. It has a steel ring at one end for hanging, and it is extremely inexpensive. The bristles, by the way, are attached in a unique manner, being caught in the twists of the spiral-wound metal handle.

Twin Bar Brushes 1.72

Nylon bristles on hardwood posts with cast-aluminum base, rubber suction mat; base 6½" × 4⅜"; 8½" high.
$10.00

Here are the Tweedledee and Tweedledum of the brush world, Siamese twins in black nylon bristle which you attach by suction to the bottom of a sink full of hot and soapy water. When your party is in progress and the highball glasses are needing refills, then whoever is in the kitchen can take each dirty glass as it comes in, dip it into the suds, then press it down over one or the other of these bristly fellows, twisting it back and forth. Then a dip into another sink full of clear hot water, or a quick pass beneath the faucet, and the job of cleaning is done. This is not a tool for everyday use, but it is a useful accessory in a household where large parties are given, even one or two a year. We know three teen-age girls who do catering in the resort town where they live year-round, and we are considering giving these brushes—Guardsmen in their bearskin hats—to one of the girls for an eighteenth birthday present. It is made of two hardwood posts set into joined cast-aluminum pedestals which are in turn screwed onto a figure-8 rubber mat. Each post is thickly set with medium-soft black nylon bristles that are bound to it with brass wire. The brushes stand up 6¼" tall, and they will spend more time in the cabinet than in use, unless you run a household which has a bar with a double sink in it. But whenever they are on duty, you'll be glad to own these staunch helpers.

A coffee urn in the style of the last century came with its own long-handled cleaning brush.

Baby-Bottle Brush
Narrow Steel-bristled Brush
Twin Bar Brushes

Bronze and Stainless-Steel
Scrubbing Pads
Coiled-Plastic Scrubbing Pads
Stainless-Steel Scrubbing Cloth

Bronze and Stainless-Steel Scrubbing Pads

1.73, 1.74

Avail. in either bronze or stainless steel; 3" diam.; 1" thick.

$.98

If some of the brushes we have shown you look like lovable stuffed animals, then these metallic pads in bronze alloy resemble the backs of Harpo Marx's and Shirley Temple's heads. The same type of pad also comes in a continuous coil of fine-gauge stainless-steel wire, and we are absolutely devoted to both of these cleaners made by modern technology. In our opinion, the most overpriced, least practical item in your kitchen is the commercial steel-wool pad—with or without a pink or blue core of cleanser—turning rusty and claggy in your soap dish. Instead of boxes of steel-wood pads, buy two of these curly marvels. They come in various sizes and degrees of gentleness to the hand. They do not rust, do not throw off splinters, and do not die; if one should become clogged with food, then you can simply turn it inside out and use the clean part; a few pulls this way and that while you hold the pad under the faucet will leave it clean for next time. They are better than brushes for cleaning vegetables and scrubbing mussels or clams, since they are flexible, easy to use, and of course nontoxic. They are superb for cleaning barbecue grills and dirty pans, and strong and gentle enough to use on a waxy kitchen floor. Keep one, free of contact with soap, for foods, and another, used with soap or detergent, for other clean-

ing. They cost next to nothing, last forever, and do their job better than any other similar tool.

"When Gokul's wife came out she saw her bending accusingly over a pile of pots and pans which were stacked together in a corner of the verandah. She pointed to one of them with her finger. 'Just look at that one now. Haven't you got eyes in your head? It's got water stains on it. And what's more, it's one of these that Shorno has taken for the milk. To begin with, the bucket wasn't cleaned properly; and secondly it's been handled by a low-caste woman. Moreover, it's going to be taken into the kitchen. What's going to happen to the purity of our caste. My ancestors have preserved it for generations, and now it's ruined, I tell you; and all because of you.'"

Pather Panchali, *by B. Banerji, Indiana University Press, 1968*

Coiled-Plastic Scrubbing Pads

1.75

Plastic mesh; package of 3, each 3½" diam.; 1" thick.

$.69

Lesser versions of the pads of fine, coiled metal strips above are these similar productions in plastic mesh. The pads come three to a package, are quite inexpensive and colorful, but are truly useful only on pans with a little soft food adhering lightly, or pans with release "nonstick" finishes. Which is not saying much, since nonstick pans—not our favorites—should

never have food sticking to them anyway. This pad is so gentle as to be almost ineffective, and if you want that much delicacy—for example, if you are cleaning fine china—then you are better off using a natural sponge. So we are showing this set of three 3½" pads only for the benefit of those who are mad for release-finish cookware and want to use the Authorized Equipment.

For some, pot-scrubbing is not a serious concern.

Stainless-Steel Scrubbing Cloth

1.76

Stainless-steel mesh; 22" × 7¼".

$2.65

And now for something completely different: a gentle length of stainless-steel mesh, a piece of soft chain mail, in fact, for cleaning your pots and pans. We recommend it highly because it leaves no splinters, because it never rusts, it lasts forever, scrubs as well as a brush,

Continued from preceding page

and because it is marvelously easy to clean, rinsing out under the faucet more thoroughly than a sponge. It is a length of four-ply mesh 22″ long and 7¼″ wide, and it is wonderfully flexible: you can wad it into a ball, use it flat under the hand, or bend it into a thin strap like a shoeshine cloth. And every Halloween it can be sewn together temporarily to make the niftiest chain-mail vest any seven-year-old knight would ever want. It is made by Wearever to use with their own pans, and it is the best item of its kind.

Griddle Screen 1.77

Carborundum mesh; package of 8, each 5½″ X 4½″.
$2.00

When we tell you about griddles in Chapter 6, we will recommend that you clean them the way professional chefs do, by pouring water on while the griddle is still hot, and then scraping away with a spatula while the water boils the bits of food loose. But, should that not do the full job, then you ought to have a grill cleaner such as this one. It is a fine screen made of Carborundum, a mixture of silicon and carbon which acts as an abrasive. You hold a damp cloth in your hand and place the inflexible Carborundum pad flat on the griddle, with a little oil or fat beneath it. Then you scrub it back and forth, and the griddle will be cleaned by the water and the abrasive action, and there will be a slight film of oil left on the surface for protection. These come eight to a pack of 5½″ by 4½″ pads, and they are easily cleaned under running water after use.

Serious cooking utensils require serious cleaning equipment.

"Marvellous to the little girl was the celerity with which Miss Asphyxia washed and cleaned up the dinner dishes. How the dishes rattled, the knives and forks clinked, as she scraped and piled and washed and wiped and put everything in a trice back into such perfect place, that it looked as if nothing had ever been done on the premises!"

H. B. Stowe, Oldtown Folks, *1869*

French Pop-up Sponges 1.78

Cellulose; package of 3, each 4″ X 3″.
$1.50 for a pack of 3 ▲

The wonder of the ages is this French sponge which lies around dry, looking

like a piece of pale melba toast until it is held under water, when it blossoms into a real cellulose sponge more than half an inch thick—into something which rather resembles a slice of white bread, as a matter of fact. You may think that we are being insanely francophile, telling you to import your sponge from Europe, but this is in truth better than the synthetic sponges in the supermarket, as it has tiny holes which release the water very slowly. These are not expensive, and they last far longer than the domestic variety, and are softer and more pliable. So if you are going to use a sponge, why not use the best you can find?

Chamois-covered Sponge 1.79

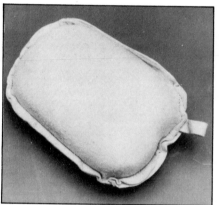

Chamois leather over sponge; 5½″ X 4″; 1¾″ thick.
$3.50

This is at the opposite end of the scale from the Griddle Screen, a cleaner meant for the times when you have to clean something very fine or very fragile, such as your fine silver or vermeil or some very old china. It is a French sponge covered in chamois leather, a luscious-feeling wad of buttery yellow softness which acts as a slipcover for a puffy French sponge. You could polish the furniture or bathe the baby with it, so smooth and resilient is it to the touch. A tab of chamois in one corner allows you to hang it up to dry, a procedure which will prolong the life of this opulent cleaning device indefinitely. It is not inexpensive, but then, how many will you ever need?

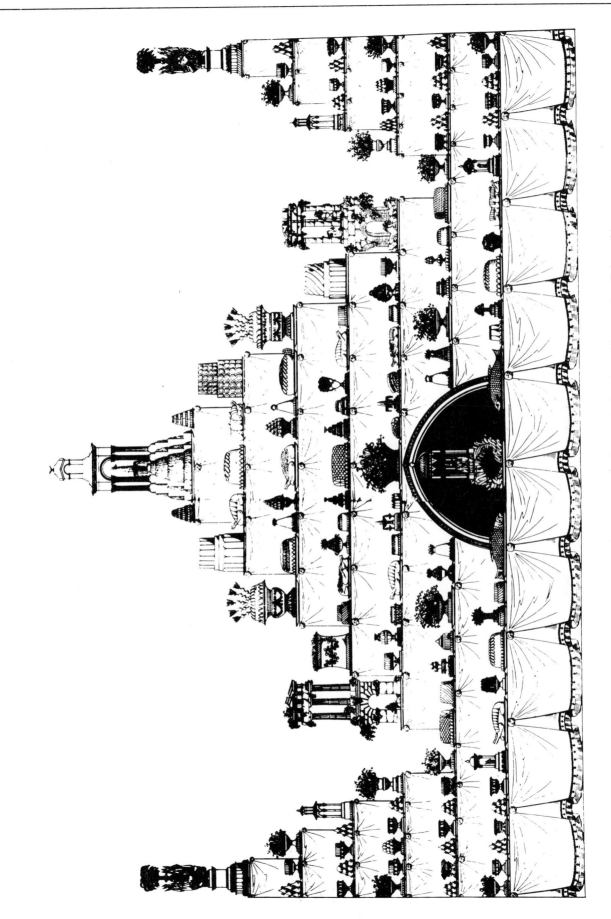

Imagine the clean-up . . . Carême's idea of a "grand buffet de cuisine modern," from his
Le Maître d'Hotel Français, 1842.

Knives, Sharpeners, and Cutting Boards

Since men became meat-eaters, implements for cutting food have been essential. Knives are the oldest known manmade objects, but even before our ancestors learned to make tools, they cut with sharp stones and shells.

In this chapter we describe a modern multitude of knives and related accessories: sharpeners, racks, cutting boards, and chopping blocks.

PEBBLE CHOPPERS AND HAND AXES

The first tools were small stones or pebbles sharpened by striking one stone with another to flake off fragments and form a crude cutting edge. They have been found alongside the bones of prehistoric men in the Olduvai Gorge in Tanzania and Koobi Fora in Kenya, and date back at least two and a half million years. These tools were used for butchering game by people who lacked fire or clothing.

Later in prehistory, man improved his methods of stone-tool manufacture, creating more efficient implements of finer workmanship and design. A new technique was in use by the period known as Acheulean, from about one million to 100,000 years ago. The "soft hammer" was a piece of bone or wood held so that it would impinge upon the face of the rock being worked at a sharp angle. The soft hammer, which used pressure rather than striking force, broke off thin, even flakes of stone, and resulted in a flat tool with carefully trimmed edges. The variety of tool types was growing. Hand axes, cleavers, scrapers, and chisels of this period have been found in Europe, East Africa, India, and China.

Physically modern men (*Homo sapiens*) worked stones with great precision and were able to fashion fine, thin, symmetrical stone flakes. They also produced edges that were notched or denticulated; these edges were the first ancestors of our familiar serrated knives. A great profusion of tools from this period has been found in France, Italy, and elsewhere in Europe, as well as in the Middle East, Central Asia, and in Africa.

We've come a long way from pebble choppers. Today's cutting utensils are available in a myriad of sizes and shapes intended for a myriad of specific functions. The Stone Age is long past, and modern knives do their work by means of a sharp-edged metal blade that is almost always made of iron or one of its alloys.

IRON AND STEELS

To understand knives, we must understand iron and its derivatives. Iron is the fourth most common chemical element, composing about 5 per cent of the earth's crust. Usually it is found as an ore—that is, in combination with other elements. One familiar ore is iron pyrites or "fool's gold," which so glistens that it has often tricked the gullible.

True metal-working, unlike the stone-working of antiquity, is less than 10,000 years old. Copper was probably the first metal to be separated from its ore, or smelted. Basic metal-working techniques were swiftly discovered, but at first metals were considered so rare and valuable that they were used only for ceremonial equipment, weapons, and

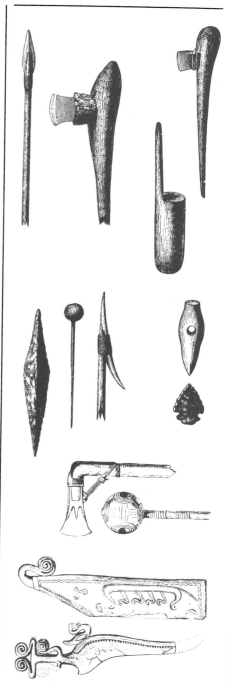

Cutting implements of the Neolithic, from Meyer's grosses Konversations Lexikon, 1902 (top); and of the Bronze Age, from A Popular History of the United States, from the First Discovery of the Western Hemisphere by the Northmen to the End of the Civil War, by William Cullen Bryant, c. 1878.

ornaments.

The great metallurgical breakthrough came with the invention of iron refining about 4000 years ago. Knives of bronze (an alloy of copper and tin) had been too expensive to be owned by ordinary people, who had been making do with stone. Iron was plentiful and inexpensive.

Refining separates iron from the other elements in the ore, resulting in crude or cast iron. When molten, it can be poured or cast into a form or mold; when it cools it remains in the shape of the mold. Iron in this form was used for almost all purposes for which a strong, malleable substance was required: knives and pots, swords and plowshares, horseshoes and weathervanes, and even, about a hundred years ago in American cities, buildings several stories high.

By the Middle Ages in Europe, people were carrying short swords or daggers about with them and bringing them to the table to use for spearing and cutting up cooked food. But in about the year 1600 table knives, probably invented by craftsmen seeking to expand sales by offering a new and useful product, came into fashion.

Iron is a fascinating substance with unique properties, both good and bad. On the plus side, it is abundant and strong, and it takes a sharp edge. But iron oxidizes when exposed to humid air; the red flaky stuff we know as rust is ferric oxide, iron combined with oxygen from air. Another disadvantage of iron is that it becomes very brittle when it is cooled rapidly during the refining process; and while it becomes less brittle when cooled more slowly, it also becomes less hard.

A rusty knife that isn't very sharp and that shatters when it encounters a tough job is not much use. To eliminate its worst qualities and bring out its best, iron must be made into steel—refined iron to which other elements are added. Steel is at least 85 per cent iron and up to 15 per cent other elements. High-carbon steel has about 12 per cent carbon and is the alloy most similar to cast iron. It can be formed in the same ways as cast iron, and it too will rust; it is harder than cast iron, but still quite brittle.

Low-carbon steel, which is harder but tough and resilient, was invented in the Near East more than 3000 years ago. Crude iron and grass were burned together in charcoal furnaces. When the grass had charred until it was almost pure carbon, it combined with the molten iron. The amounts of grass and crude iron were measured to control the proportions of each element in the resulting alloy. Nonindustrialized societies still make steel in this, or a similar, way.

Rust resistance finally came with the much more recent invention of such alloys as nickel steel and aluminum steel. Most rust-resistant of all is stainless steel, developed in England. Stainless steel's high chromium content—4 per cent or more—gives it great tensile strength and excellent resistance to abrasion and corrosion. Some stainless steels have other elements added.

Stainless can be shaped by *forging*, which involves beating and hammering the metal into shape while it is hot; by *rolling*, in which red-hot ingots of the metal are placed between shaped rollers to be pressed into the desired forms; and by *machine forming*, in which the desired

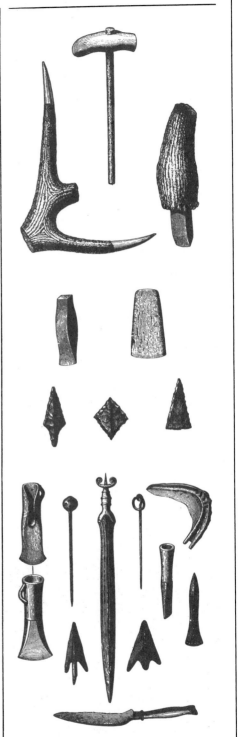

Implements of stone and bronze, some with attached handles of wood and staghorn, from Meyer's grosses Konversations Lexikon, *1902.*

Continued from preceding page

shape is stamped out of the sheet of metal. But it cannot be cast, since it tends to shrink away from the mold and settle back into its original mass.

STAINLESS VERSUS CARBON STEEL

Stainless steel is the only metal that can honestly be recommended for use in coastal areas or anywhere that pitting and rusting from humid or salty air is likely to occur. It is needed for the blades used for cutting high-acid foods such as tomatoes. Until recently, however, stainless steel was always a compromise steel, since it did not take a good edge and was hard to sharpen. Stainless steel is not the answer for knives; high-carbon stainless is.

On the other hand, some people insist on carbon steel. This prejudice used to be justified. Carbon-steel blades take a sharper edge than plain stainless and keep it longer—and that is what you want in a knife. Because stainless is a harder metal than carbon steel, knives made of stainless steel can be too hard to sharpen. Knives should be sharpened on a steel or stone every time they are used. With regular sharpening a good blade can be kept in good condition for many years. But unless the sharpener is harder than the blade it will not be able to abrade the metal, and most sharpening steels are not hard enough to sharpen most stainless blades. There are even some knives of stainless, especially those made in the Orient, which cannot be sharpened at all: they are made of an alloy that is harder than almost any sharpener. If you see the words "never needs sharpening" near a knife blade, stay away from it; what it really means is "you will never be able to get a sharp edge on this blade."

Today we have high-carbon stainless steel, sometimes called "no-stain." It can be given a sharper edge than the older stainless compositions, and it will never pit or rust. If you use the correct steels, it will sharpen wonderfully.

Decide on the metal you want for each of your knife blades individually, bearing in mind where and for what the implement will be used. While a matching set of knives may look great on a wall rack, the same metal and shape might not provide the qualities needed for such diverse kitchen chores as slicing rare roast beef, chopping spinach, or filleting fish.

STRENGTHENING BLADES

A knife is only as good as the metal in its blade. All steels are unstable: their physical properties change when they are heated. These properties are used to advantage to make blades as hard, tough, and strong as possible. Steel for blades is heat-treated by tempering and annealing. In *tempering* the molten metal is heated slowly up to a desired point and then cooled rapidly by immersion in a chemical bath. This hardens the steel but leaves it so brittle it will shatter. In subsequent *annealing* the steel is heated to a lower temperature and then air-cooled slowly;

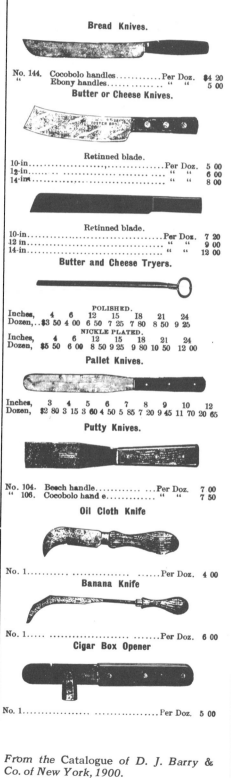

Bread Knives.

No. 144. Cocobolo handles............Per Doz. $4 20
  "   Ebony handles............ "   "   5 00

Butter or Cheese Knives.

Retinned blade.
10-in. ....Per Doz. 5 00
12-in. .... "   " 6 00
14-in. .... "   " 8 00

Retinned blade.
10-in. ....Per Doz. 7 20
12 in. .... "   " 9 00
14-in. .... "   " 12 00

Butter and Cheese Tryers.

POLISHED.
Inches,	4	6	12	15	18	21	24
Dozen,	$3 50	4 00	6 50	7 25	7 80	8 50	9 25

NICKLE PLATED.
Inches,	4	6	12	15	18	21	24
Dozen,	$5 50	6 00	8 50	9 25	9 80	10 50	12 00

Pallet Knives.

Inches,	3	4	5	6	7	8	9	10	12
Dozen,	$2 80	3 15	3 60	4 50	5 85	7 20	9 45	11 70	20 65

Putty Knives.

No. 104. Beech handle............Per Doz. 7 00
  " 106. Cocobolo hand e......... "   "   7 50

Oil Cloth Knife

No. 1................................Per Doz. 4 00

Banana Knife

No. 1................................Per Doz. 6 00

Cigar Box Opener

No. 1................................Per Doz. 5 00

From the Catalogue of D. J. Barry & Co. of New York, 1900.

this toughens it.

Heat-treating causes steel molecules to link up in loose chains going every which way. *Grinding* aligns the chains of molecules to give the blade strength. Grinding, the most important factor in knife manufacture, makes the difference between a good knife and a poor one. For a good blade this is not a machined operation; it can only be performed by a skilled craftsman who treats each blade as the unique piece of metal it is. As the craftsman passes a blade across the grinding wheel, the loose molecular chains are forced to line up in the desired direction. If you look at a good knife blade you should be able to see grinding marks all along the blade at right angles to the cutting edge.

A knife blade, especially along its cutting edge, is very thin, since thinness is what makes sharpness. Grinding makes this thin strip of metal strong where strength is required; otherwise the thin edge would curl and bend. The quality of a steel blade is directly related to the strength of its molecular chains after grinding.

A hollow-ground blade has been shaped by machine and has an abrupt concave profile near the cutting edge on one or both faces. The molecules have not been aligned for strength, and the rest of the blade is relatively thick. Hollow-ground edges cannot be sharpened, because the sharpener would be working against the thick part of the blade. However, this edge is used to advantage on serrated blades.

Dishwashing machines can ruin a good knife because of the effect of heat on the steel blade. The grinder's skilled craftsmanship has been completely wasted if molecular chains are constantly realigned by repeated alternation of heating and cooling.

WHAT IS A KNIFE?

There are three main parts to a knife: the blade, the handle, and the tang. Examine every knife for the quality and construction of each part before deciding which one to buy.

A *blade* should be judged by how well it will do the job and how easily it can be sharpened, since you will be sharpening it every time it is used. A too-hard blade cannot be sharpened; a too-soft blade will lose its edge so rapidly you will spend more time sharpening than using it. Hardness is measured precisely in degrees on the Rockwell scale. The most desirable hardness for a knife blade is between 55° and 58° Rockwell; knives of these hardnesses will take an edge readily and hold it for a reasonable length of time. Metal with a Rockwell number higher than 58° will hold an edge longer but will be too hard to sharpen; metal below 55° will be too soft. Good blades have been tempered, annealed, and hand ground.

Judge a *handle* by how it feels and by the quality of its finish. Beware of very elaborately shaped handles, ostensibly designed to fit every curve of your fist. They are less likely to fit your particular hand than a more basic shape.

Handles are made of wood, sometimes raw, sometimes stained and varnished; of wood impregnated with plastic for safety in dishwashers

Continued from preceding page

and for longer wear; of solid plastic; of very hard rubber; and sometimes of solid stainless steel.

Brazilian rosewood is preferred for handles because it does not have a straight grain. It is a hard wood whose grain goes in all directions, resisting cracking and splitting. Also, it is a tacky or sticky wood, which gives it a naturally nonslip surface that actually improves with use—an important consideration. The wood of a handle can shrink, so do not allow it to soak. Avoid slick, shiny plastic handles; they will attract grease like magnets and slip around in your hand. Today, professional butcher's knives, must, by law, have plastic handles for sanitary purposes. We think they are ugly and usually avoid them.

The differences in handle sizes are not important, although many people take notice of them. There is only slight variation in hand widths, and almost every hand will "fit" around all but the most exaggeratedly large or small handles.

The *tang* is the part of the blade extending into and attached to the inside of the handle. You usually can see it sandwiched between the two halves of the handle. A full tang is the same length, width, and shape as the handle; it is completely visible all around the edge of the handle. A rattail tang is, as the name implies, long and skinny; it extends the full length of the handle but is only partly as wide. A part or half tang is as wide as the handle but extends for only a part of its length.

Rivets, tubelike "snaps" that must be machine-attached, secure a tang to the handle. Their heads should be completely smooth and flush with the surface of the handle. Some (usually inexpensive) knives have half tangs held in place with gum or glue, which expands and loosens after much washing; these should be avoided. If there is a wooden handle and even a part tang, you should be able to see the tang and two or three rivets. The length of the tang gives a knife good balance and supports the blade.

The thickest part of the blade or tang shows you the quality and thickness of the blank of steel from which the knife was made. In a good knife, the thickness of the spine of the blade is continued in the tang.

A WORD OF CAUTION

Remember always that knives are dangerous tools. People are seldom hurt by things of which they stand in awe; more often they are hurt by those of which they feel sure.

Place a knife on a work counter so that the entire implement rests on the surface; it is too easy for someone passing by to brush a protruding handle off a table or counter and onto the floor.

Dry knife blades from the spine to the cutting edge, not from the handle to the tip. *Never* test the sharpness of a blade by running your finger along the edge! If necessary, brush your fingertip lightly *across* the blade.

Never work with a dull blade. People tend to fear sharp knives, but the truth is that a sharp knife is safer than a dull one.

MUTTON.

VEAL.

Always store knives in racks, whether wall-mounted, standing on a counter, or built into a cutting table. Never put a knife in a drawer where it might carelessly be picked up blade first, and where its edge may be nicked or dulled by contact with other knives or utensils.

WHAT'S IN A NAME?

The "three S's" of knives are Sheffield, Solingen, and Sabatier, but none of these names is a guarantee of anything. Both Sheffield in England and Solingen in West Germany are cities famous since the fourteenth century for their cutlery, produced originally by skilled guild craftsmen. Large numbers of metal-working factories are now located in both of these cities. In France, Sabatier was at one time the name of a specific factory, but the name has now been leased to at least twelve different manufacturers in that country and some in South America as well. Consequently, there is no quality control or common standard. However, knives labeled Sabatier have a recognizably French "look," because that is what people expect. Choose a knife for its individual qualifications for the job you want it to do and not by the name of the town or factory it comes from.

A "WARDROBE" OF KNIVES

There are three basic categories of knives according to function: chopping, butchering, and slicing and cutting. The smaller paring and utility knives overlap both the chopping and slicing categories. Some knives are multipurpose, designed to be used for both cutting and chopping.

Minimally, you could make do with one good chef's knife and one paring knife. A more complete "wardrobe" would consist of several parers in different lengths, at least one good chef's knife, one basic slicing knife, one rigid boning knife, and one serrated-blade knife about 8 inches long for slicing tomatoes and bread.

CARE OF KNIVES

Every knife blade should be sharpened after use. See the end of this chapter to choose your sharpeners.

All blades should be washed in hot soapy water as soon as possible after use. Rinse and then wipe them dry with a cloth. Coat carbon-steel blades with grease of some kind if they are not in constant use. It is best to avoid using a dishwasher even for knives claimed to be dishwasher-safe because it affects the tempering.

Never soak a knife; it is harmful to the handle and does no good for the blade either. Soaking should never be necessary anyway; there should never be caked-on food on a knife blade. If a wooden handle loses its sheen, restore it by wiping with a cloth dipped in salad or furniture oil; be sure to wipe the oil residue off before using the knife.

Do store knives in slotted or on magnetic racks, not in drawers.

Do not hold knives in a flame or dip them into a pot of hot food; don't use them to pry up jar lids; and don't use a lightweight tool for a heavy-duty task.

PRACTICAL CARVING

BY THOMAS J. MURREY, Author of 50 Soups, 50 Salads, Breakfast Dainties, Puddings, Entrees, Cookery for Invalids, Etc

A useful book on a tricky subject, published in 1887.

"The art of carving at the table consists, above all, of working easily, without abrupt movements, without impatience. Dissection at the table is not an easy operation for everyone, but those who by taste or obligation carry it out, should try to acquire a few ideas about the natural construction of complicated cuts that they might be called upon to carve. I mean by complicated cuts, those with bony and hinged frameworks, such as large poultry and feathered game; as for large joints and big game, a little instinct will suffice."

L'Ecole des Cuisinières by Urbain-Dubois.

Chef's or Cook's Knives

The terms "chef's knife" and "cook's knife" are used interchangeably, an indication of how basic this tool is to every kitchen, whether professional or home. It is used primarily for chopping, when the knife blade rapidly and repeatedly strikes the surface of a chopping board, cutting to smithereens any food in its path.

The professional way to chop is to rock the knife handle up and down with one hand while the fingers of the other hand rest lightly on the tip of the blade. This rock-chop method is suitable for most foods, whether they be firm vegetables for a mirepoix, delicate mushrooms for duxelles, or ripe tomatoes for a fresh pasta sauce. Sometimes a chopping technique with greater impact is required: hold the knife parallel to the work surface with its cutting edge raised slightly above the chopping surface; lower it firmly and raise it slightly several times in rapid succession. In either method, you need a handle shaped in such a way that your hand does not hit the cutting board, and the blade must be shaped so its entire edge does.

Since a chef's knife mainly chops, every part of it is designed to give the strong support necessary for the impact of blade on the chopping surface. It has a thickened section at the handle end of the blade, known as a bolster, to give your movements additional leverage and to keep your fingers from riding up on the blade. The *bolster* is a protective barrier between your hand and the cutting edge. Knives of German manufacture usually have particularly thick, sturdy bolsters. In most of these knives, the rear part of the handle curves downward to support and cushion the back of your hand against the force of impact when you bear down.

A *collar,* most frequently found in French knives, is an extension of the blade past the bolster and into the handle; the collar is the lower part of, and has the shape of, the handle.

The blade of a chef's knife is rigid, although there may be some flexibility at the very tip. It should taper evenly from bolster to tip and from spine to edge. A smooth, even curve on the broad blade surface is necessary for proper balance and will prevent food from clinging to it.

Most chef's knives have a full tang. (This is not true of most butcher's or slicing knives.) The impact of chopping vibrates all through the blade, and so the blade must be firmly anchored at the handle end. The weighty tang balances the long, heavy blade and increases the power of your movements. You should be able to balance a well-designed chef's knife by laying the part of the blade just below the bolster flat across your finger.

These blades range in length from about 7 to 13 inches; they vary considerably in weight as well. You'll probably want at least two in different sizes. The size should be proportionate to the task. Don't be afraid of handling really big, heavy knives. They require less energy; the weight does the job.

Henckels Chef's Knife with Plastic-impregnated Handle   2.1

No-stain high-carbon Friodur steel blade with black Durawood handle, nickel-silver rivets; 13" long overall; blade 8" long, 1⅞" wide. Also avail. with blade 6", 9", or 10" long.

$23.50 ▲ $18.50 ▲ $28.50 ▲

This chef's knife has a stainless-steel blade and a plastic-impregnated handle. It is said by its manufacturer to be dishwasher-safe, but we advise against putting any good knife in that hot environment. Normally, to get the virtues of stainless, we must sacrifice the virtues of carbon steel. This blade, made of a high-carbon stainless steel trade-named Friodur, will not stain, pit, or rust. It is finely machined, rigid enough to withstand any demands you are likely to make on it, and it retains a very satisfactory degree of sharpness because of its high carbon content. Wide at the bolster end, the blade tapers in a smooth curve to a point at the tip. It is best of its class, and expensive.

"FRENCH COOK'S KNIFE. *Made of best steel. It can easily be kept very sharp, and made of almost constant use in preparing dishes. It is especially useful for boning. It costs seventy-five cents, yet, with proper care, should last a lifetime. These knives are so light, sharp, and easily handled, that when once used, a person would consider it very awkward to cook without one."*

Practical Cooking and Dinner Giving, *by Mrs. Mary F. Henderson, Harper & Brothers, New York, 1891*

Henckels Chef's Knife with Plastic-
impregnated Handle

Carbon-Steel Chef's Knife from
France
Lighter French Stainless-Steel
Chef's Knife
Professional Stainless-Steel
Chef's Knife

A chef at work in medieval England.

Carbon-Steel Chef's Knife from France 2.2

Carbon-steel blade with rosewood handle, brass rivets; 17⅛″ long overall; blade 12″ long. Also avail. with blade 4″, 6″, 8″, or 10″ long.

$25.00

Absolutely the most elegant-looking chef's knife we've seen is made by Sabatier Jeune, one of the top manufacturers among the more than a dozen licensed to use the Sabatier name; a crown is incised over the letter K on the blade as a trademark. It has such typically French touches as a finely grained rosewood handle of a warm brown tone accented by three brass rivets. A smoothly gleaming collar of steel wraps around the base of the handle. The blade is made of the finest carbon steel; it is firm and heavy, culminating in a full tang. You won't want to spoil this knife by letting it become food- or water-spotted, so be sure to wipe it clean immediately after each use and never, never put it in the dishwasher. It is extremely satisfying to use, and in our opinion, it is the best carbon-steel chef's knife we know. If you plan to buy only one knife, this could be the one. If you want knives in every conceivable size, this is also the one, since it is available in five different lengths, from a 4″ size for paring to this one.

Lighter French Stainless-Steel Chef's Knife 2.3

Stainless-steel blade with black wooden handle; 11¾″ long overall; blade 8″ long, 1⅜″ wide. Also avail. with blade 10″ long.

$15.00

This nicely finished French knife resembles the classic chef's knives, but it is shorter and quite lightweight. The stainless-steel blade, available 8 or 10 inches long, is moderately flexible. It has a smoothly curved edge tapering to the point, and a pleasing satinlike finish. Although no tang is in sight, the knife is well balanced. The bolster is small but in good proportion to the size of the blade, and the circumference of the smooth black wooden handle is slightly greater than that of the collar. These features add up to a good tool for lighter cutting tasks. This is a moderately priced knife, a sound value for the money.

"One must never, in English and United States belief, give a knife as a gift; at least some small token payment must be made for it, otherwise the knife will cut the friendship. . . . In England, India, and elsewhere, knives crossed at table lead to a quarrel. Such crossed utensils may be uncrossed without bringing bad luck by uncrossing them withershins (right to left, against the sun's direction)."

Funk & Wagnalls Standard Dictionary of Folklore, Mythology, and Legend

Professional Stainless-Steel Chef's Knife 2.4

Stainless-steel blade with rosewood handle, nickel-silver rivets; 15¼″ long overall; blade 10″ long, 2⅛″ wide. Also avail. with blade 8″ or 12″ long.

$10.10

This knife, of stainless steel by Victorinox of Switzerland, has a very hard, elongated, almost triangular blade that is beautifully ground and very, very sharp. The handle of dark-brown rosewood, shaped moderately to fit the hand, is actually rather good-looking for a professional knife. There is neither a bolster nor much widening of the handle for support, but the handle end of the blade and the cutting edge are diagonally angled to protect the hand. The not-quite-full tang, secured by three nickel-silver rivets, results in a knife that is a bit blade-heavy. A large and heavy knife like this will do the cutting for you; you will feel confident about tackling anything with it at hand.

53

The Largest Chef's Knife 2.5 of Them All

Stainless-steel blade with rosewood handle, nickel-silver rivets; 19″ long overall; blade 13″ long, 3″ wide.

$34.00

Our feelings toward this enormous tool—one is almost tempted to call it a weapon—have alternated between awe and admiration. We have nicknamed it, affectionately and unanimously, "the monster." It is a professional knife, as can be seen from the canting of the blade and handle. Its owner, one of our editors, says, "It's the nearest knife to heaven I know." Then she warns, "Just because it's heavy, don't abuse it." If you are tempted by its heft to use it as a cleaver and whack a lobster in half with it, forbear! Treasure this knife and protect your investment in it, which will be sizable. Thorough washing and drying immediately after every use, plus regular sharpening, should keep "the monster" performing sublimely for a lifetime. The angling of the blade and handle, as well as the ample proportions of both, provide protection for your fingers in the absence of a bolster or collar. It is incredibly heavy. The weight is in the blade. This is an exceptionally good-looking piece of equipment. It is 19 inches in total length and has a stainless-steel blade that really gleams and a polished rosewood handle punctuated by three nickel-silver rivets. It has instructions incised on the blade: on the tip side of a dividing line it says: "for cutting / zum schneiden / pour couper / per tagliere"; and on the handle side of the line it says, "for chopping/zum spatten/ pour battre/per battere."

Paring and Utility Knives

Paring knives look very much like chef's knives, but they are on a smaller scale. Larger parers can be indistinguishable from smaller chef's knives; this intermediate size is sometimes referred to as a utility or kitchen knife. However, the curve of a paring-knife blade is usually not as pronounced as that of most chef's knives. This is because a parer is basically not an impact tool, although it can be used in the same way as a chef's knife—to chop small amounts of parsley, for example. Instead, a paring knife works more as an extension of your hand.

It is a great temptation to acquire a number of inexpensive paring knives, since they are sold in every dime store. But a cheap knife with a poor blade and an uncomfortable handle is of little use. It won't stay sharp, and it can't be sharpened. The thin, hard blade will chip; it is not flexible; it does not have a good pointy tip; and its handle is sure to split or pull away from the blade. A cheap paring knife is a poor investment—especially when even those on limited budgets can afford a good one.

To use a paring knife move your hand up on the handle so that your thumb is on the side of the blade nearest you and your index finger is curved against the opposite side of the blade; the heel of your hand rests on top of the handle. This grip allows your entire hand to swivel from the wrist and gives you control over the tip of the blade as well as the edge. You can move the knife toward you (to dig the tip into a potato and scoop out the eye) or away from you (so you can scrape a carrot). Foreshortening the blade in this way balances the knife for easy working. With your thumb on the blade you will feel the resistance of the blade scraping against the food and be much less likely to cut yourself. It is important to feel the food when you work in close with a small knife; this is what we mean when we say these knives act as extensions of your hand.

Henckels Paring Knife 2.6

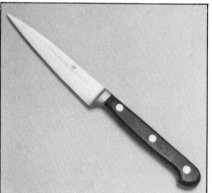

No-stain high-carbon Friodur blade with black Durawood handle, nickel-silver rivets; 8″ long overall; blade 4″ long. Also avail. with blade 3″ long.

$9.50 ▲

This German import in chef's knife form is a no-stain version of the paring knife from Henckels below (2.7). "If I had to go out in the world with one knife, this is the knife I'd choose," announced our expert. "It is short enough, sharp enough, strong enough, and long enough to do almost anything." The blade, of Henckels' forged high-carbon Friodur nonstaining steel, is rigid, curving to taper to a fine point. The handle is made of black plastic-impregnated Durawood, and is shaped like the handle of a chef's knife handle. There is a full, tightly riveted tang as well as a heavy bolster, making it possible to use this knife as an impact chopper as well as a parer. It is a first-rate knife and sells for a well-deserved first-rate price.

James Beard's knife cart

Knives, Sharpeners, and Cutting Boards

2

Henckels Carbon-Steel Paring Knife from Brazil 2.7

High-carbon-steel blade with brown wooden handle, brass rivets; 8⅛″ long overall; blade 4″ long.

$5.70

This knife is a very good-looking, and a less expensive alternative to 2.6. There are two points of view about paring knives. Either you feel: "I must get a very fine one because I'm going to be using it all the time." Or you feel: "I'll get a less expensive one so I won't mind when it needs to be replaced." These knives certainly do get banged around a great deal. This one, from the Henckels factory in Brazil, is about half the cost of the Friodur blade we have just shown you and has excellent qualities. No one could fault you for choosing it. The two knives are essentially the same in shape and size; but this one is of high-carbon steel, which of course requires more care than Friodur. It has a brown wooden handle with brass rivets to hold the full tang—a warmer, less "hostile" look than the black-with-silvery-rivets of the higher-priced Henckels. It met with an extremely enthusiastic response from the people here. It is really a very nice-looking tool, could be used as a steak knife, and is a good find.

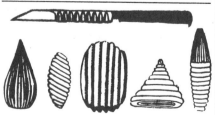

From French Domestic Cookery, *published in New York in 1885.*

"Then, with the servants bustling in all directions, a boiled calf was borne in on a silver dish weighing two hundred pounds, and actually wearing a helmet. Then came Ajax, and rushing at it like a madman slashed it to bits with his naked sword, and making passes now up and down, collected the pieces on his point and so distributed the flesh among the astonished guests."

The Satyricon *of Petronius Arbiter*

Superb Stainless-Steel Parer 2.8

Stainless-steel blade with rosewood handle, nickel-silver rivets; 8¼″ long overall; blade 3¾″ long.

$7.50

Alfred Zanger is a manufacturer who really cares about knives, and he makes them with the most sensational blades of any we have ever seen. They are crafted in Solingen, to his specifications, from a formulation of stainless steel that is extremely beautifully machined and finished with hand grinding by a master craftsman. This knife is a beautiful and keen-edged piece of steel, set in a one-piece rosewood handle. Zanger prefers a three-quarter tang because of the evenness of the matching grain in the single piece of wood. Unlike those of most of our paring knives, the handle is drawn down to cover the entire rear of the blade; this knife cannot be used for chopping. The blade is broader than most and hard to use for finicky jobs; but it is truly a pleasure to use. If you come to this tool, as some of us have, after years of using parers with inferior blades, you will instantly feel the difference. Your carrot sticks will be thinner

and more even, your raw mushroom slices will be works of design to grace any salad.

Petite Paring Knife from France 2.9

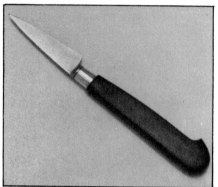

High-carbon-steel with Ebonite handle; 6⅝″ long overall; blade 2″ long.

$3.75 ▲

Some paring knives are specialized in form. This knife, from one of the Sabatier licensees, has a tiny 2-inch blade of high-carbon steel. It has a shiny collar, a straight black Ebonite (very hard rubber) handle, and no visible tang. Because of its small size and very sharp tip, the blade is a small triangle. Said to be one of Julia Child's favorite knives, it might well become a favorite of yours too, particularly if you like to serve food with decorative garnishes. The small blade gives you ultimate control of the tip, whose sharpness really serves a purpose. Use it to score or flute mushroom caps, nick the eyes out of potatoes, and shape tomato rosettes.

Tiny Dishwasher-Safe Parer 2.10

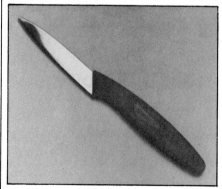

Stainless-steel blade with yellow Grilon plastic handle, 7″ long overall; blade 3″ long.

$4.00

Henckels Carbon-Steel Paring
Knife from Brazil
Superb Stainless-Steel Parer
Petite Paring Knife from France
Tiny Dishwasher-Safe Parer

All-Purpose Stainless-Steel Cleaver
Heavy Carbon-Steel Cleaver

Here is a small paring knife with a sharp short blade of stainless steel. The yellow plastic handle is particularly good in a short parer because it really goes inside the food. When you use this knife to scoop the seeds out of zucchini, sever the pit from a peach, or do any number of messy jobs, you will be glad you can toss it into the dishwasher.

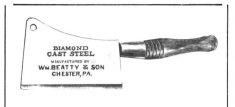

Cleavers

Cleave, *v.i.* To adhere closely, cling, remain faithful.
Cleave, *v.t.* To split or divide as by a cutting blow; to sever.

The most important thing about a cleaver is its weight. This is one of the rare instances in which a blade-heavy knife is desirable. You really swing down with it, and you let the weight do the splitting for you.

While the primary function of a cleaver is to go through bones, it also can be used for general chopping, as it is in Chinese cuisine. After chopping or slicing, simply slip the blade under the cut-up pieces, scoop them up, and carry them on the flat side to your pot or mixing bowl. The flat side of the cleaver can be used to smash garlic or pound meat for scaloppine or braciole.

We encourage you to select a larger, heavier cleaver than the one you think might be comfortable. You will get used to the heft and be glad. With a lightweight cleaver you will have to work too hard to cut through cartilage and bones.

All-Purpose Stainless-Steel Cleaver 2.11

No-stain high-carbon Friodur blade with black Durawood handle, nickel-steel rivets; 11" long overall; blade 6" long, 3" wide.

$23.50 ▲

This is a highly recommended general-purpose implement from Henckels of Solingen. It is a heavy object, and its thick rectangular blade is made of beautifully ground and polished Friodur no-stain high-carbon steel. The highly polished surface of the thick blade does not taper gradually on a plane to the keen cutting edge, but diminishes suddenly with an abrupt roll just above the edge. This is a professional-quality cleaver.

"Prince Huei's cook was cutting up a bullock. Every blow of his hand, every heave of his shoulders, every tread of his foot, every thrust of his knee, every whshh of rent flesh, every chhk of the chopper, was in perfect rhythm—like the dance of the Mulberry Grove, like the harmonious chords of Ching Shou.

"'Well done!' cried the Prince. 'Yours is skill indeed!'

"'Sire,' replied the cook, laying down his chopper . . . 'A good cook changes his chopper once a year—because he cuts. An ordinary cook once a month—because he hacks. But I have had this chopper for nineteen years, and although I have cut up many thousand bullocks, its edge is as if fresh from the whetstone.

For at the joints there are always interstices, and the edge of the chopper being without thickness, it remains only to insert that which is without thickness into such an interstice. Indeed there is plenty of room for the blade to move about. It is thus that I have kept my chopper for nineteen years as though fresh from the whetstone.

"'Nevertheless, when I come upon a knotty part which is difficult to tackle, I am all caution. Fixing my eye on it, I stay my hand, and gently apply my blade, until with a hwah the part yields like earth crumbling to the ground. Then I take out my chopper, stand up, and look around with an air of triumph. Then, wiping my chopper, I put it carefully away.'

"'Bravo!' cried the Prince. 'From the words of this cook I have learnt how to take care of my life.'"

Hsiang Ju Lin and Tsuifeng Lin, Chinese Gastronomy, *Pyramid Publications, 1972*

Heavy Carbon-Steel Cleaver 2.12

Carbon-steel blade with natural-wood handle, nickel-silver rivets; 11⅜" long overall; blade 6" long, 3¼" wide.

$20.00

Even heavier than 2.11, this cleaver is meant for some serious bone-cracking, although you can, of course, use it for lighter bones, such as those of duck or other fowl. The solid, hand-forged, steel blade has some curve to it, making this a versatile tool that can be used for chopping as well as cutting. Using it to mince carrots might be considered overkill, however, given the weight of this implement. The surface of the massive carbon-steel blade has been emery-rubbed to within an inch of the edge, where the polished cutting area takes over. The full

Continued from preceding page

tang is perfectly fitted into the smooth blond wood handle and secured with three heavy rivets. It is carbon steel, so be sure to keep it wiped clean at all times. There is a hole in the blade so it may be hung out of the way on a very, very secure and sturdy hook.

Butchering Knives

Butchering knives are designed for cutting rather than chopping. They are not impact knives and therefore they do not need a full tang, a bolster, or a collar. Almost all butcher knives have a handle whose end nearest the blade is enlarged to form a thick, protective shoulder. This acts as a support and cushion for your hand and gives you leverage for the large arm and hand motions required to cut up sections of meat.

In this section only knives for cutting up raw meats will be described, especially large slicing, scimitar-shaped and boning knives. For descriptions of knives for fish preparation, see Chapter 11.

Superb Stainless-Steel Butcher Knife 2.13

Stainless-steel blade with rosewood handle, nickel-silver rivets; 15¼″ long overall; blade 10″ long, 1¾″ wide. Also avail. with blade 8″ long.

$30.00

From the Zanger line comes this superior stainless-steel blade, beautifully hand-ground. If you are buying only one all-purpose kitchen knife, buy this one. In form it is a larger version of their parer (see 2.8). It has the three-quarter tang preferred by this manufacturer, tightly fitted to a slot in a one-piece Brazilian rosewood handle and fastened there by three nickel-silver rivets. Zanger calls this a chef's knife, and indeed the long rigid blade has the gradually tapered curve characteristic of that category. But the handle is that of a butcher's knife; it is drawn down so it

comes just beyond the cutting edge of the blade. There is no bolster, but the supportive handle has a sizable shoulder which makes it unnecessary. Zanger says this grip is better for slow chopping and for the vast majority of chopping jobs. This knife might take some getting used to. Partly because of the handle shape and partly because of its lighter weight (resulting from the lack of a full tang), it will feel different from other chef's knives. Nevertheless, it is highly recommended because of the exceptionally strong, sharp blade and because of its superb overall quality. We like it as a butcher's knife, but you can certainly use it for chopping as well.

Wüsthof Stainless-Steel Butcher Knife 2.14

High-carbon stainless-steel blade with black wood handle, nickel-silver rivets; 18″ long overall; blade 12″ long, 1¾″ wide. Also avail. with blade 10″ long.

$25.00

This is the quintessential butcher's knife. It is a professional tool with a highly finished, very long high-carbon stainless-steel blade, and a generous handle. It will section a quarter of beef, cut up a whole roast, or slice scaloppini. The blade has a gently curved upper edge. The cutting edge curves more sharply to a crescent shape near the tip, resulting in a blade wider at the end than the handle. The smoothly finished handle encloses a full tang. This knife is wonderful in the hand.

Scimitar Knives

In such knives as these, the upward curving of the blade tip is exaggerated until the whole thing resembles a scimitar; and with its length of blade of hand-forged carbon steel, it is a formidable weapon. You use a scimitar-shaped knife by inserting the point first into the side of the meat furthest from you and then rocking down and back on the handle in one strong, definitive motion to cut directly through—watch a good butcher to see one of these blades in action. These tools are ideal for slicing off whole cuts, primarily large steaks or individual portions from a whole fillet.

It is clear from an eighteenth-century recipe for pork that housewives needed to know how to wield knives wisely: "As it may sometimes be necessary for the cook's killing the pig herself, it may not be improper to inform her in that case how to proceed. Stick the pig just above the breast bone and let the knife touch its heart, otherwise it will be a long time dying."

Superb Stainless-Steel Butcher
Knife
Wüsthof Stainless-Steel Butcher
Knife

Henckels Scimitar Knife
Stainless-Steel Skinning Knife
Tanqueuer
A Superb Blooding Knife

Henckels Scimitar Knife 2.15

No-stain high-carbon Friodur steel blade with black plastic handle; 15¾" long overall; blade 10" long, 1⅜" wide.

$21.00

This scimitar-shaped tool by Henckels has a blade of that manufacturer's no-stain high-carbon Friodur steel and a strong black plastic handle. It is a super-sanitary knife that can go in the dishwasher (although we don't recommend frequent machine washing for any knife), and it complies with all sanitary codes. The blade is wide and stiff, with a wonderful curve. In general, a scimitar-shaped knife is more limited in usefulness than a straight butcher's knife, but if you like to deal with your own large cuts of meat—perhaps to divide them into portions for freezing—this one is worth considering.

Stainless-Steel Skinning Knife 2.16

Stainless-steel blade with yellow Grilon plastic handle; 11¾" long overall; blade 6½" long, 1½" wide. Also avail. with blade 5" long.

$10.00

At a quick glance this looks like a smaller scimitar knife, but there are significant differences that set it apart. The short, 6½-inch blade is more curved and set at a more deliberate angle. Look carefully and you'll see that the thinnest and finest part of the cutting edge is at the curve near the tip, and the thickest, sturdiest part of the blade spine is exactly opposite in the concave curve. This is a skinning knife. Most people don't need a skinning knife; but if you are going to skin something, you will need this knife or one very much like it. The extremely sharp edge is for pushing through the fine membranes between skin and flesh. You do this by sliding the blade between meat and skin, pushing away from you and at an upward angle toward the skin to separate it from the meat. The point is bent up to avoid puncturing either the meat or the skin.

Tanqueuer 2.17

Stainless-steel blade with brown wooden handle, nickel-silver rivets; 10½" long overall; blade 6⅜" long.

$13.50

What looks like a knife but isn't a knife? A tanqueuer, an impact instrument to hold meat to the cutting board. It has a very thick rigid "blade" with a very sharp tip and no cutting edge at all. There is absolutely *no* sharpness to the blade. A full tang extends to the widened blunt end of the handle. Use a tanqueuer by putting your hand over the top of the handle and driving it through the meat into the wooden block. When making steak tartare you would use a tanqueuer to stab through the filet mignon and pinion it to the board. Then you'd remove any fat or membrane covering the meat and use the edge of a silver spoon to scrape toward you across the grain. It can also be used to

hold an eel at the tail while you cut around the skin at the neck (with any good sharp-pointed boning or paring knife) and peel it back like a glove. A knife cannot be substituted for a tanqueuer: the tip would break off and the blade would be ruined; it might also fly out of the table as if shot from a bow, possibly causing serious damage. Remember that a knife blade is ground to align the molecules for strength *in one plane only;* the impact of stabbing demands strength in a completely different area. If you don't have a tanqueuer handy when you need one, substitute a hammer and a very long, strong nail.

A Superb Blooding Knife 2.18

Stainless steel blade with rosewood handle, 10½" long overall; blade 5¼" long, 1" wide. Also avail. with blade 6¾" long.

$8.60

This is called a blooding knife, but don't be put off by its official title. It is a tool of many uses, a superb all-purpose kitchen knife, and one of the most attractive-looking knives we know of. In France there are two kinds of butcher shops—one primarily for beef and one for horsemeat; this knife belongs in the latter. It is straight-bladed, with a very sharp point for letting the blood out of a vein. It is a perfect tool for close cutting of anything. The very rigid blade is stainless steel. The handle is shaped like a standard butcher-knife handle; it is a particularly good-looking soft, warm brown color, pleasantly finished and just plain good to hold. It would be a fabulous steak knife.

Boning Knives

In many cases your butcher will do any boning you require; but you might want to have the bones and trimmings to make broth. You must, if you are going to stuff something, know how the meat is organized; this is possible only when you bone it yourself and see it laid out flat before you. Sometimes you will change your mind about how you want to use a particular cut of meat after you've taken it home, and it's too late to ask the butcher for special favors. And sometimes, especially if there is a hunter in the family, there will be fresh meat and no one available to do the cutting up for you.

There is a rule of thumb for boning knives: the rigidity of the blade is directly proportionate to the size of the beast (or bone). For boning large roasts a strong, rigid blade is required. A flexible one striking against hard bone could pop back at you and even snap off, and a rigid blade used on delicate bones would mangle them totally. A flexible knife is used on delicate fowl such as small chickens, pigeon, squab, or quail. You could not feel their tiny chest bones if you worked with a stiff knife. A flexible one is more responsive, giving greater sensitivity to your hand.

American High-Carbon-Steel Boning Knife 2.19

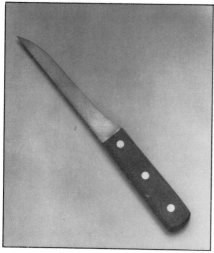

High-carbon-steel blade with beechwood handle; 10½″ long overall; blade 6″ long. Also avail. with blade 6½″ long.

$6.60

This stiff boning knife has the unmodulated handle typical of those made by American manufacturers. It is made of natural beechwood with a glazed finish, although it doesn't look or feel like what we usually mean by "glazed." The block-like form feels surprisingly secure in the hand, a perfect illustration that a shaped handle is not essential. However, the handle doesn't have the bulge of wood at the blade end that would protect your hand, so be careful! There is a firmly riveted full tang. The thin, rigid blade sharpens very well indeed.

Wüsthof High-Carbon Steel Boning Knife 2.20

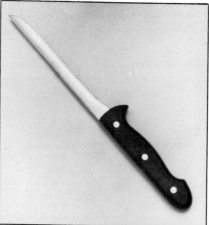

High-carbon-steel blade with black wooden handle; nickel-silver rivets; 11¼″ long overall; blade 6″ long. Also avail. with blade 5″ long.

$11.50 ▲

This boner can be distinguished from most others by its narrow blade. A butcher would employ it only for working around thinner bones, but in the average kitchen it could be very useful indeed. The blade is stiff, but you could certainly use it on all but the most delicate of bones. It is of high-carbon steel, hand-forged and beautifully ground. The one-piece handle is shaped for a comfortable safe grip.

Zanger Boning Knife 2.21

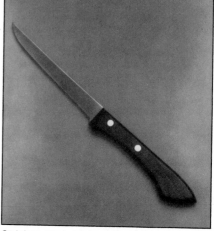

Stainless-steel blade with rosewood handle, nickel-silver rivets; 11″ long overall; blade 5½″ long.

$13.50

This knife, with a slightly flexible blade of gorgeous quality, is highly recommended. It is very narrow, long, and of the superb stainless steel found in every Zanger knife. The three-quarter tang preferred by this manufacturer is secured to a slot in the one-piece handle by two rivets of nickel-silver. The blade is fitted tightly to the Brazilian rosewood handle, with not a jot of a gap. This is a most acceptable knife, with a superior blade, at a moderate price—an extremely good value, especially if you want one multipurpose boning knife.

Cookbooks from the fifteenth through nineteenth centuries awarded a large chapter to the art of carving, a serious and respectable skill. This quotation from Modern Domestic Cookery (1853) is typical of the food books of the period: "Although carving with ease and elegance is a very necessary accomplishment, yet most people are lamentably deficient, not only in the art of dissecting winged game and poultry but also in the important point of knowing the parts most generally esteemed. Practice only can make a good carver; but the directions here given, with accompanying plates, will enable any one to disjoint a fowl and avoid the awkwardness of disfiguring a joint."

American High-Carbon-Steel
Boning Knife
Wüsthof High-Carbon-Steel Boning Knife
Zanger Boning Knife

Henckels Flexible Boner
A Versatile Stainless-Steel Slicer

Henckels Flexible Boner 2.22

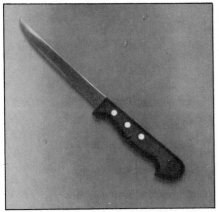

No-stain high-carbon Friodur steel blade with black plastic handle, 11″ long overall; blade 5½″ long.

$9.90

We particularly recommend this knife, which is manufactured by Henckels. It is almost exactly like 2.21, except that it has a narrower and much more flexible blade. The hygienic no-stain Friodur steel blade and black plastic handle denote this as a tool for professionals. A skilled butcher would use it to bone the most delicate fowl, and you can too.

"Boning is not a difficult operation. It only requires time, a thin, sharp knife, and a little care. Cut off the neck, and also the legs at the first joint. Cut the skin in a line down the middle of the back. Now, taking first one side and then the other of the cut in the fingers, carefully separate the flesh from the bones, sliding the knife close to the bone. When you come to the wings and legs, it is easier to break or unjoint the bones at the body-joint; cutting close by the bone, draw it, turning the flesh of the legs and wings inside out. When all the bones are out, the skin and flesh can be readjusted and stuffed into shape. As the leg and wing bones require considerable time to remove, they may be left in, and the body stuffed with lamb or veal force-meat."

Practical Cooking and Dinner Giving, by Mrs. Mary F. Henderson, Harper & Brothers, New York, 1891

Slicing Knives

When we talk about slicing knives we mean tools intended to cut through cooked meats of every kind. The blades of these knives vary in respect to four qualities: flexibility versus rigidity; width; pointed or rounded tip; and edge, either smooth or modulated by some hollow-ground shaping. The terms *slicing knife* and *carving knife* are usually interchangeable; to be technical about it, though, carving is a subsection of slicing.

Carving is the kind of cooked-meat cutting that is most frequently done at the table. Knives intended for this purpose tend to have thinner, more flexible blades. In a carving knife trueness of line, or absolute straightness, is of particular importance—more so than in the heavier, thicker-bladed chef's knives, for example. In a blade this thin, the stronger stainless steels are the best, since they are less likely to snap and are hard enough to hold an edge. If you have the proper sharpening equipment you will be able to keep a good stainless carving knife blade in tip-top form.

The heavier, harder-bladed slicers are designed to cut broader slices through hot, softer meats. If the surface of the meat is firm and relatively dry (as in a cold roast or a ham), the meat is less resistant, and the thinner, narrower blades are suitable. For chops and rare hot roast beef (which are soft and mushy) a heavier, more rigid blade is needed. While a full tang isn't a necessity for a slicer, you would certainly appreciate the extra muscle it gives when you deal with a heavy rib roast or a rack of lamb. For information on mechanical slicers, see Chapter 3.

A Versatile Stainless-Steel Slicer 2.23

Stainless-steel blade with rosewood handle, nickel-silver rivets; 15″ long overall; blade 9½″ long, 1⅛″ wide.

$22.50

This is an all-purpose slicer, with the superb stainless-steel blade and one-piece solid Brazilian rosewood handle for which Zanger is known. Within the realm of the slicing knife it is the least specialized; it is versatile enough to perform a variety of slicing and carving jobs. There is a sharp tip on the finely ground hard blade; the very comfortable and secure handle is neither too big nor too small and has a good shoulder to protect your hand. The blade is stiff enough to use for carving large slices of hot prime ribs of beef or any other heavy cuts of meat; yet it is slender enough to cut a fairly thin slice from a turkey breast or other firmer, dryer roasts. It is not ideal for extra-fine slicing—for prosciutto, for example—which requires a flat, broad blade without a point at the tip. We recommend this knife without reservation for roasts of almost any size.

Official carvers of the seventeenth century were not only responsible for the perfect slicing of meats. Their manuals also included directions for the decorative whittling of vegetables and the execution of whimsically peeled fruits.

Henckels Heavy-Duty Slicer 2.24

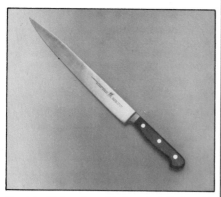

No-stain high-carbon Friodur steel blade with black Durawood handle, nickel-silver rivets; 15" long overall; blade 10" long, 1³⁄₁₆" wide. Also avail. with blade 8" long.

$22.00 ▲ $18.50 ▲

This stainless-steel slicer from Henckels of Solingen has a stiff blade and a full tang. The cutting edge is as fine as that of 2.23, but because of the really thick and long tang there is more weight at the handle end, and therefore the balance is much better. You don't feel the weight as much when you hold the knife in your hand, but you'll be glad to have it on your side when cutting through a rare rib roast or carving a selle d'agneau. This is the best slicer we have seen for cutting heavier meats.

YORK HAM

a pungent fruit conserve flavoured with spirits."

Buddenbrooks, by Thomas Mann, 1924

Round-tipped Stainless-Steel Slicer 2.26

Stainless-steel blade with rosewood handle, nickel-silver rivets; 15⅛" long overall; blade 10" long, 1" wide. Also avail. with blade 12" or 14" long.

$9.60

Ham Slicers

There is a whole confusing range of slicers known as "ham slicers." All this term really means is that these knives were designed to make a long, thin, even slice. In general, these are long, narrow blades. It is particularly important when choosing a slicing knife to ignore the manufacturer's terminology and follow your own preferences. Some like a thin blade with a little drag to it, and others find they get more "bite" out of a broader blade. Some like a sharp tip to use for going around the bone, and others prefer a round-tipped blade because they fear a pointed tip will make gashes in an even slice. Some like extreme flexibility, and others prefer firmness in a blade.

For those who feel more secure with a round-tipped blade, this one from Victorinox of Switzerland is the most versatile of the lot. As you can see from the photograph, the blade width diminishes very slightly and gradually, ending in a smooth rounded curve instead of a sharp point. The blade is of finely ground and very sharp stainless steel and is quite flexible. The grip-shaped handle is of rosewood. A full-length rattail tang, secured by three rivets, gives it good balance but too much weight. The 10-inch blade length is the most useful, but this knife comes with 12- and 14-inch blades as well.

Flexible-bladed Ham Slicer 2.25

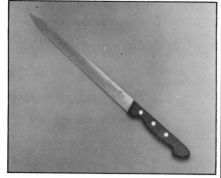

No-stain high-carbon Friodur steel blade with black wooden handle; nickel-silver rivets; 15¼" long overall; blade 10" long, ⅞" wide.

$16.00

The long, narrow, and flexible blade with a very pointy sharp tip is perfect for ham. The three-quarter tang is firmly secured; the handle is well shaped; and although the knife is fairly lightweight, it has good balance. It is a fine choice.

"The plates were changed again. An enormous brick-red boiled ham appeared, strewn with crumbs and served with a sour brown onion sauce, and so many vegetables that the company could have satisfied their appetites from that one vegetable-dish. Lebrecht Kröger undertook the carving, and skilfully cut the succulent slices, with his elbows slightly elevated and his two long forefingers laid out along the back of the knife and fork. With the ham went the Frau Consul's celebrated 'Russian jam,'

"A whole ham boiled, as its producer pridefully announced, in cider which was just at the sparkling point—together with a handful of raisins—until almost tender, and then skinned and baked long enough to set and brown the crust of brown sugar, mustard, and spices. The knife, cutting through the crunching crust, slipped into the rosy meat like the blade of a scythe before ripened grain, while one thin pink slice after another rolled down upon the cutting board."

The Country Kitchen, *by Della T. Lutes, Little, Brown and Company, 1936*

Henckels Heavy-Duty Slicer
Flexible-bladed Ham Slicer
Round-tipped Stainless-Steel Slicer

Slicer with Hollow- ground
Ovals on Edge
Narrow Slicer with Hollow-ground
Ovals on Edge

Slicer with Hollow-ground Ovals on Edge   2.27

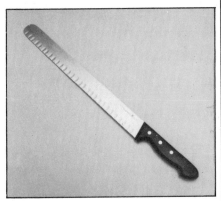

No-stain high-carbon Friodur steel blade with black wooden handle, nickel-silver rivets; 20" long overall; blade 14" long, 1½" wide. Also avail. with blade 12" long.

$26.00 ▲

This Friodur knife, which has a long, fairly wide blade for cutting thin slices of roasts, is distinguished by its cutting edge. It is punctuated by oval areas which have been made very sharp and thin by hollow grinding. These ovals are staggered in position, so they are not all on an even line, and they are ground into both sides of the blade. Their purpose is to break the friction of slicing at the edge. Note that this is not a serrated or scalloped edge, which would tear up the meat instead of slicing smoothly through it. The same style is also available with a 12-inch blade.

As Elizabethan ladies were responsible for carving the joints of meat at the table, they came up with a few dainty devices: "That she might be able to grasp a roast chicken without greasing her left hand, the gentle housewife was careful to trim its feet and the lower part of its legs with cut paper. To preserve the cleanness of her fingers, the same covering was put on those parts of joints which the carver usually touched with the left hand, whilst the right made play with the shining blade. The paper-frill which may still be seen round the bony point and small end of a leg of mutton, is a memorial of the fashion in which joints were dressed for the dainty hands of lady-carvers, in times prior to the introduction of the carving fork."

John Cordy Jeaffreson, A Book About the Table, *London, 1875*

Narrow Slicer with Hollow-ground Ovals on Edge   2.28

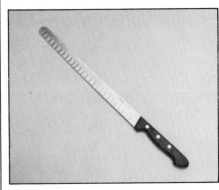

No-stain high-carbon Friodur steel blade with black wooden handle, nickel-silver rivets; 17¼" long overall; blade 12" long. Also avail. with blade 10" long.

$24.00

This Henckels Zwillingswerk slicer of Friodur steel has a thinner, more flexible blade than 2.27, but it has the same hollow-ground ovals along both sides of the blade. If you look carefully, you will note that the ovals are not all at the same level but at staggered heights. Use this knife to carve even slices of the more delicate cooked meats, such as turkey breast or veau poêlé.

"Knife falls, gentleman calls;
Fork falls, lady calls;
Spoon falls, baby calls."

Funk & Wagnalls Standard Dictionary of Folklore, Mythology, and Legend

HAM BAKED IN CIDER

A dish that used to be favored in New England, Pennsylvania, and sometimes in the West—in fact, wherever apples are a major crop and cider is made in the fall.

Serves 8-12

1 10-pound ham (not aged)
Cider
1 cup brown sugar
2 teaspoons mustard
Cloves
2 cups breadcrumbs

Soak the ham in cider overnight, skin side down. Remove the ham and place it on a rack in a roasting pan. Bake at 350 degrees, allowing 20 minutes per pound. Baste from time to time with the cider. Remove the ham from the oven, and strip off the skin. Spread with brown sugar, mustard and crumbs, and stud with cloves. Return to the oven to glaze for about a half hour at 350 degrees. Baste occasionally with the cider.

SAUCE
2 cups cider from the ham
¼ cup applejack (optional)
½ cup seedless raisins
¼ teaspoon nutmeg
¼ teaspoon cloves
1 tablespoon cornstarch mixed with 1 tablespoon cider

When the ham is done, prepare the sauce. Cook the cider, applejack, and raisins about 5 minutes and add the spices. Stir in the moistened cornstarch and continue stirring till it thickens slightly. Serve the sauce with the ham. Also serve fried apple rings and cornmeal mush cut in slices, floured, and fried until crisp in butter.

(From AMERICAN COOKERY, by James A. Beard, illustrated by Earl Thollander. Copyright © 1972 by James A. Beard. Reprinted by permission of Little, Brown and Company.)

Knives with Serrated Blades

You will notice that we have chosen no old-fashioned saw-toothed serrated-blade knives. They simply do not keep their sharpness. Even as bread knives, they are useful only for evenly textured loaves. They would tear a coarse-grained bread, resulting in a crumbly surface instead of a smooth slice. You must have a serrated knife for bread and tomatoes, and for whenever else you must get through a crust to a fragile interior without hacking into it. We do not recommend them for

Continued from preceding page

meat, as they do not produce an even slice. Your choice of a serrated knife is mostly a matter of individual preference. Some people like serrated blades for fruits and vegetables; others prefer a flat-ground but sharp edge for these things. For bread, tomatoes, and other citrus fruits where you don't want a mush, you need a little purchase on the blade. The various hollow-ground toothed edges will also give you this.

The steel along the edge of a serrated knife must be strong enough so that the teeth don't bend out of shape. The serrations on the blade edge are formed by two successive processes. First the scalloped or toothed profile is cut out from the metal blank. Then the metal along one or both sides of each cut-out is thinned sharply by hollow grinding. This method, in which the metal is virtually scooped out to form a shallow hollow, was developed about 60 years ago for use on straight razors of carbon steel; and it was a perfect device for putting a very thin, sharp edge on a thicker blade. Even straight edges that are hollow ground cannot really be resharpened beyond a certain point; and serrated edges cannot be resharpened at all. All the serrated-edge knives we show are stainless, because of their frequent use with acid fruits and vegetables.

French Stainless-Steel Bread Knife   2.30

Stainless-steel blade with brown wooden handle, brass collar, nickel-silver rivets; 12¼″ long overall; blade 7¾″ long, 1″ wide.

$10.00

If you are one of those people who is baking your own bread more often, you will sometimes want to display an entire loaf on a handsome bread board, bringing it to the table along with an equally handsome knife. This is that knife, with a beautiful shape, a beautiful and fine-quality mirror-finished blade, and a beautiful collar of brass gracing a handle of warm brown-toned, even-grained wood. Bread stays hotter and fresher when it is cut immediately before serving.

Bread was not simply for slicing and eating in the Middle Ages, but cut to form bowls and plates when it became stale. Among the needs for a fourteenth-century dinner for forty were: "Item, two knife-bearers, whereof one is to cut up bread and make trenchers and salt-cellars of bread and they shall carry the salt and the bread and the trenchers to the tables and shall make for the hall two or three receptacles, wherein to throw the large scraps, such as sops, cut or broken bread, trenchers, pieces of meat and other things."

The Goodman of Paris (Le Ménager de Paris), c. 1393. Translated by Eileen Power; George Routledge & Sons, London, 1928

White-handled Bread Knife from England   2.31

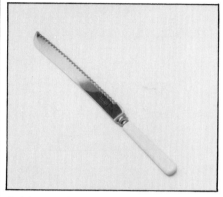

Stainless-steel blade with white plastic handle; 12⅝″ long overall; blade 8″ long.

$5.00 ▲

Another knife that can be brought to the table proudly is this very practical and attractive one. It comes from Sheffield, the traditional steelworkers' guild town in England, and the stainless-steel blade certainly witnesses the quality of the Sheffield products. The long, somewhat flexible, narrow serrated blade has a mirror finish and widens into a protective small bolster at the handle joint. What we like best about this knife is its handle, made of the same fine white plastic now used instead of ivory for piano keys.

Tea Bread Knife.

FRUIT, VEGETABLE, AND UTILITY KNIVES

Some of the most useful serrated knives are the little ones commonly used for fruits and vegetables. They are particularly good for tomatoes, where the resistant skin has to be pierced without crushing the tender fruit beneath. In the same way they are good for lemons, making neat slices without forcing out the juice. Once you have the knife, you will find many secondary applications, such as cutting baguettes or slicing sausage.

Within this area, too, come utility knives—often better known as bar

From The Wonderland of Work *by Clara L. Mateaux, 1883.*

Continued from preceding page

knives. They cut fruit, but they usually have a combination of blade surfaces for other functions as well.

French Tomato Knife 2.32

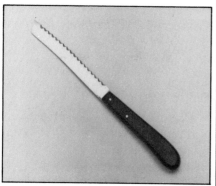

Stainless-steel blade with black wooden handle, nickel-silver rivets; 8¾" long overall; blade 4½" long.

$2.50 ▲

You will use this knife a lot. It makes it easier to peel small citrus fruits if you prefer not to use a peeler, to cut through rolls, to slice Polish or German sausage, or to slice skinny loaves of Italian bread —to do anything that requires you to get a grip on something small. Made of somewhat flexible, serrated stainless steel, this 4½-inch blade has a good point that can help in dealing with the heavy-textured outside layers of things. There is a hole in the end of the straight, black, wooden handle that facilitates hanging. Relatively inexpensive, it is a very good value.

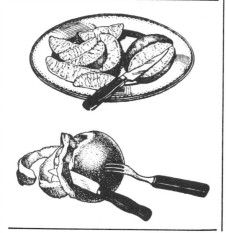

Utility Knife with Forked Tip 2.33

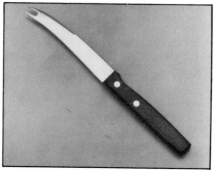

Stainless-steel blade with rosewood handle, nickel-silver rivets; 8½" long overall; blade 4⅜" long.

$4.50

Utility knives often have combination blades with two or more different edge treatments, and this one is a prime example. One edge of the blade is flat-ground for plain cutting and slicing; the other is serrated for tomatoes and citrus fruits; and the tip is bifurcated. It is the perfect bar knife with which to peel lemons, break the metal strips around some corks and caps, spear pickled onions or maraschino cherries, or cut orange slices. But it could be a very useful tool in the average kitchen, in a galley-type kitchen, a studio apartment, or on a cabin cruiser.

"Commodore Perry in his explorations among the Eskimos found them using bits of a three-ton meteorite which they called "the woman" and which they had reduced to about half of its original size. . . . The Spaniards found a few knives of iron among the Aztecs which were prized above gold and which they said came from heaven."

Funk & Wagnalls Standard Dictionary of Folklore, Mythology, and Legend

GRAPEFRUIT KNIVES

A special category of fruit knives is designed for grapefruit. There are two different ways to prepare a grapefruit for neat eating: the first one is to loosen each section from its pocket; the second, to completely remove the membrane surrounding each section. In the latter case the knife blade used must have a fairly good angle and be stiff enough to pull through the membrane.

Grapefruit Knife with "Ivory" Handle 2.34

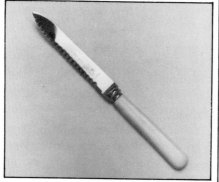

Stainless-steel blade with white plastic handle; 7¾" long overall; blade 4" long.

$6.00

This knife, by Taylor of Sheffield, England, is eminently suited for eliminating all segmenting membranes from grapefruit. However, it is fairly broad of blade and may require some getting used to if you customarily prepare grapefruit by loosening individual sections. It is an attractive knife, with a polished stainless-steel blade and the closest-thing-to-ivory white plastic handle. It is dishwasher-safe and has keen-edged serrated hollows along both edges of the blade.

"The Indonesians use a knife with a specially guarded blade for cutting rice; the hidden blade will not arouse the anger of the rice spirit."

Funk & Wagnalls Standard Dictionary of Folklore, Mythology, and Legend

American Stainless-Steel Grapefruit Knife   2.35

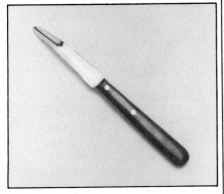

Stainless-steel blade with brown Pakkawood handle, nickel-silver rivets; 7¼" long overall; blade 3¼" long.

$4.75 ▲

After examining many, many grapefruit knives and trying them all, we decided that this simple inexpensive one from Case, an American manufacturer, did the best job of loosening sections. The width and curve of the blade are just right. Slip the shiny serrated blade between grapefruit sections or between the flesh and the shell. Simply wiggle the Pakkawood handle around gently and the job is done.

"See how a man becomes immortal by his good taste! Who would have remembered the Earl of Sandwich if he had not brought the sandwich into vogue in the last century? The gratitude of mankind has for ever, and all over the habitable globe, honored it with his name."

Kettner's Book of the Table, *1877*

FROZEN-FOOD KNIVES

Cutting through solidly frozen foods is another use of serrated knives, in a class by itself. If they are available to you, it is an enormous economy to purchase frozen vegetables in one large block and then cut off portions as needed. In certain parts of the country fish is available only in the form of large frozen blocks. If you freeze your own vegetables or fruits, it is often easier to do so in large solid blocks than in individual packages. And if you make several hearty loaves but want to use only part of one loaf at a time, you will surely need to saw through a hard-frozen crust. With a frozen-food knife, blade strength is essential. Characteristically these knives have heavy toothing on one blade edge: in most, this is combined with a finer-toothed opposite edge to make a multipurpose tool.

French Frozen-Food Knife   2.36

Stainless-steel blade with black plastic handle; brass rivets; 13" long overall; blade 8½" long.

$7.00

This French knife is the sturdiest of the frozen-food knives we have seen, and it has the biggest, strongest teeth. On one cutting edge there are two different sizes of large teeth. The opposite edge, with finer scallops, would be quite good as a bread knife. A double-riveted half tang adds to its overall strength. With a strong and heat-resistant black plastic handle and a polished stainless-steel blade, this is a sanitary, useful knife that can be put in the dishwasher.

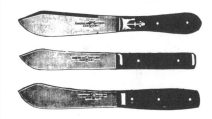

Knife Sharpeners and How to Use Them

How often have you read instructions in a recipe book or watched a demonstration on television or in a cooking class, and try as you might, not been able to achieve the same results? Nine times out of ten your inability to duplicate the result is not because of your inexperience, but because you either do not have the correct knife or because the one you do have is not sharp enough. You can read Julia Child or James Beard for instructions in technique every day for a month, but it will not do you the slightest bit of good unless your blades are always sharp.

Throughout this chapter we have mentioned the importance of regular sharpening. It is not so much cutting through food that dulls a blade but rather the repeated contact, usually with impact, of the cutting

67

Continued from preceding page

edge against the firm surface of the chopping block or board. It is always much easier to give knives a few strokes with a sharpener every time you put them away than to attempt to bring them back from the dead after you have been negligent. Knives can be brought back (particularly by the Zip-Zap, 2.37), but it is not a fun task. Steel tends to shrink back into itself, though, so if you are about to work with a knife that was sharpened the last time you put it away but hasn't been used in a while, it would be wise to retouch it.

In sharpening, it is most important not to disturb the finish painstakingly put on a blade by a master grinder. Work just on the very cutting edge of the blade, holding the sharpening steel or stone at 20° angle to the edge. There are some who prefer to work at a 10° angle. The idea is to affect the minimum amount of the blade.

SHARPENING STEELS

There are five factors to consider in a sharpening steel: hardness, fineness of grain, magnetism, shape, and protection.

The degree of *hardness* of the steel should be proportionate to the hardness of the blade (hardness is measured on the Rockwell scale —see the introduction to this chapter). The higher the Rockwell of the blade, the higher should be the Rockwell of the sharpener. Sharpening can take place only when a hard substance abrades or wears away a portion of a less-hard substance. A sharpener must be at least 8° Rockwell harder than the thing it is sharpening. Some knives have no malleability; they are of so hard an alloy of steel that no traditional sharpener can hone the edge.

A finishing steel has a *very fine grain;* the most useful steels for home use have *medium-rough grain.* A professional chef or a butcher is likely to work a knife on a rough steel first and then give it a few final swipes with a finer steel or a stone for a supersmooth finish.

Some steels are *magnetic,* so that the alignment of the molecules in a blade is reinforced, an especial advantage with carbon-steel blades. These steels will also collect the residue of sharpening.

The conventional *shape* for a sharpener is cylindrical, but many steels are oval or broadened out. A flat, broad shape gives more sharpening area. The shape of a sharpener is mostly a matter of what you prefer or are used to. However, if you already have or plan to purchase one of the knife racks with a round slot for a round sharpener, you will probably prefer to keep a round sharpener handy. Storage is not a major consideration, though. Most steels have rings at the end of the handle so they can be hung anywhere. They are certainly too weighty for a magnetic rack.

For your *protection,* a sharpener should have a guard or hilt at the base of the the handle, since when you are using a steel you will be bringing the sharp edge of the knife toward you.

The Zip-Zap 2.37

Ceramic sharpener with brown wooden handle; 5½″ long overall; sharpening surface 3½″ long.

$3.00 ▲

With great pleasure and enthusiasm we introduce you to the Zip-Zap, created by Alfred Zanger, whose superior steel we have discussed. This odd-looking little gadget is easily worth many times its weight in conventional sharpening steels. It is of a special ceramic which, if ceramics were measured on the Rockwell scale (which they are not), would be about 92°. Thus it is harder than any knife steel around. It looks almost like a midget sharpening steel. It is designed so that, held between the thumb and forefinger, it will automatically be at the correct angle—20°—for sharpening. The motion you use with this device is the same as in traditional sharpening, but you hold the knife stationary with your left hand and move the Zip-Zap across it diagonally. Remember that the shorter and lighter object should always move across the heavier one. If you are accustomed to using a large, heavy steel, you may find this a bit awkward the first time you try it, but you will soon discover that the little sharpener is quite long enough. It is so convenient that you can easily get into the habit of giving a knife a few strokes with it every time you pick the knife up or put it away. The shaft is round, so it can be stored in the circular slot in conventional knife racks. You will notice after using the Zip-Zap for a while that grayish steel filings may appear on the surface. Simply go over it with a soapy brush, rinse, and dry. The Zip-Zap is not unbreakable, but it is the most effective sharpener we know, and it is as inexpensive as it is handy.

Traditionally most sharpeners are of hard steel, but a new and novel form, made of very hard ceramic, has been devised (see 2.37). Also in the sharpening category are stones and whetstones for honing; these are naturally abrasive and are harder than some, but not all, blade steels. Not all of them will work equally well on all blades. Then there is the old razor strop (which we do not show), with smooth, heavy leather on one side and an abrasive of some sort on the other. It is still used by some barbers to hone long single-edged razors. These really give a smooth finishing touch.

Only a hand-operated sharpener should be used on good knives (or any knives, for that matter). We do not recommend any electric or mechanical sharpening devices. Blades vary in shape and thickness; you must get the feel of each individual blade as you sharpen it. You cannot assure yourself of precision sharpening with any of the electrical, ball-bearing, or other devices which sharpen between wheels or stones at a fixed distance and angle. These contraptions, ingenious though they may seem, are almost guaranteed to chip and dull any blade. They shorten the useful life of any tool by inevitably wearing away more than is needed and by distorting the edge.

This warning against electrical and mechanical sharpeners does not hold for the old, "knives to grind, scissors to mend" itinerants, familiar in many neighborhoods of large cities, with their bicycle-powered rotary sharpeners. They are probably the last of a dying breed of craftsmen who can be counted upon to do a commendable job.

For those knives whose manufacturers claim "never need sharpening; of the hardest stainless-steel alloy; has a permanently sharp edge," you can always draw the blade across the edge of a china dinner plate to reestablish the molecular alignment. This is because a fine ceramic has a higher Rockwell than even a hard stainless steel.

Multicut German Sharpening Steel   2.39

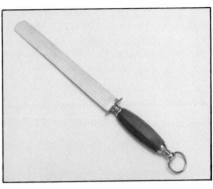

Multicut steel sharpening surface with ebonized wooden handle, nickel-plated fittings; 17¼″ long overall; steel sharpening surface 12″ long.

$50.00▲

This very flat oval steel is multicut, having vertical ridges of both fine and rougher grain running the entire length of its 12-inch magnetized shaft. It thus is a compromise between first and finishing steels; and it offers the equivalent of sharpening a blade on several steels at once, since a blade drawn diagonally across it makes contact with several grain levels in the process. There is a substantially sized handle of ebonized wood, necessary for you to get a firm grasp on this not-lightweight tool. Whether you feel at ease with this somewhat unusual but functional design is a matter of personal preference. Try it; perhaps you'll like it. We do.

FRIED ONIONS, TOMATOES,
AND CORN WITH OLIVES

Serves 4-6

3 large onions, peeled and thinly sliced
4 tablespoons butter
4 tablespoons bacon fat or oil
4 large tomatoes, peeled, seeded, and chopped
1½ teaspoons salt
1 teaspoon freshly ground pepper
1½ cups freshly cut corn or whole-kernel corn
1 cup pitted ripe olives

Sauté the onions in the butter and fat in a heavy skillet till just soft. Add the tomatoes and seasonings, cover and simmer 25 minutes over low heat till thoroughly blended. Add the corn and olives and heat through for 10 minutes. If using

Classic Round Sharpening Steel   2.38

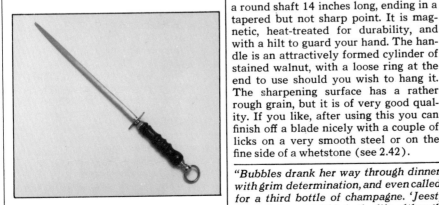

Hard chromed-steel sharpening surface with walnut-finished handle; 20¼″ long overall; steel sharpening surface 14″ long. Also avail. with sharpening surface 10″ or 12″ long.

$21.00

This is the sharpening steel used by James Beard and, no doubt, by many others who have fine knives to care for. It is a classic of hard chromed steel, with a round shaft 14 inches long, ending in a tapered but not sharp point. It is magnetic, heat-treated for durability, and with a hilt to guard your hand. The handle is an attractively formed cylinder of stained walnut, with a loose ring at the end to use should you wish to hang it. The sharpening surface has a rather rough grain, but it is of very good quality. If you like, after using this you can finish off a blade nicely with a couple of licks on a very smooth steel or on the fine side of a whetstone (see 2.42).

"Bubbles drank her way through dinner with grim determination, and even called for a third bottle of champagne. 'Jeest, honey,' she said, 'this is the life, although between you an' I, that steak cou'nt be cut with a battle ax.'"

Auntie Mame, *by Patrick Dennis*

Continued from preceding page

chili powder, add after the corn has cooked 5 minutes. Correct the seasoning and serve with hamburgers, barbecued pork, or barbecued spareribs.

(From AMERICAN COOKERY, by James A. Beard, illustrated by Earl Thollander. Copyright © 1972 by James A. Beard. Reprinted by permission of Little, Brown and Company.)

Standard Carborundum Stone 2.41

Carborundum stone; 6″ X 2″; 1″ thick.

$10.00

A standard carborundum stone is the least expensive of the traditional sharpeners (the Zip-Zap, 2.37, is less expensive, but it is a very new development in sharpeners indeed). Carborundum is the name of any of several abrasives, usually composed of silicon carbide. From the many sizes and varieties available we select this rectangular block 6 x 2 inches and an inch thick. It has one quite rough side, and another smooth side. For this reason it is known as a double-grit stone, and its shape is the one we prefer—it is never advisable to get a carborundum stone with a handle or with an eccentric shape. To use this stone, place it on a flat surface, support it with one hand, and draw the knife across it at the same 20° angle and with the same motions you would use with the largest steel. It is a little harder to use than a steel, because you have to steady it on a counter. Work across the coarser grit side first; then finish with the finer grit. A carborundum stone tends to wear out; when it does, replace it. You cannot sharpen a blade well on a stone with a pitted and uneven surface.

"Throughout Europe iron is one of the most potent charms against witchcraft. Sometimes it will even keep a witch out of the neighborhood, yet both witches and sorcerers use iron vessels and instruments in the preparation of their brews."

Funk & Wagnalls Standard Dictionary of Folklore, Mythology, and Legend

A Set of Whetstones 2.42

Whetstone; 2 pieces in wooden container; each stone 3⅞″ X 1⅞″, ¾″ thick.

$36.00

The ultimate finishing tool is this set of whetstones, two fine blocks of a fine silicon dioxide of a kind first quarried by prehistoric Indians to use as arrowheads. It is mined in the Ouachita Mountains of Arkansas, the only place it is found. This set consists of two rectangular blocks, one soft and the other hard. They come nestled inside their own box of varnished natural wood, with instructions for oiling and using them. The initial oiling, however, stimulates a natural luricant. Use this whetstone set after using any other sharpener—such as a steel—for the finest possible finish. If you get a burr at the tip of a blade, as sometimes happens, it can be removed by holding the blade lightly and working it in a rotary motion over the hard block and then the soft. This set is a luxury item. Since it must be kept in its box and stored in a drawer, it is a bit of a nuisance to have to take it out every time you want to use it. But it is a lovely thing to have and to use.

Pocket Steel 2.43

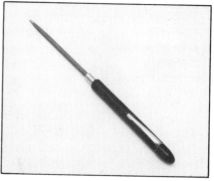

Magnetized steel sharpening surface with black plastic handle and sheath; 7″ long overall; sharpening steel surface 3″ long.

$4.00

Every professional chef carries a miniature but functional sharpening steel with him or her at all times when a knife may be used, and if you are well known as a skilled carver, you will probably want one too. This one is tucked into its own protective case, which has a clip for fastening it to a pocket or the inside of a purse; it is a magnetized, fine little bit—less than 3 inches—of steel. A brass cap at the end of the blade is threaded so it can be screwed in one direction into the case, which doubles as its handle, or screwed in the other direction to keep the blade securely in the case. When fully extended and ready for use, this tool is a great big 7 inches long! It is a nice present for the man or woman who likes to carve, or for yourself; it would also be a nice house-gift for the host or hostess whose knives last frustrated your best efforts.

"She begins meticulously cutting up the bird on her plate. Despite the smallness of the object, she takes apart the limbs, as if she were performing an anatomical demonstration, cuts up the body at the joints, detaches the flesh from the skeleton with the point of her knife while holding the pieces down with her fork, without forcing, without ever having to repeat the same gesture, without even seeming to be accomplishing a difficult or unaccustomed task. These birds, it is true, are served frequently."

Jealousy, *by Alain Robbe-Grillet, translated by R. Howard, Grove Press, 1959*

Pocket-Size Sharpening Steel   2.44

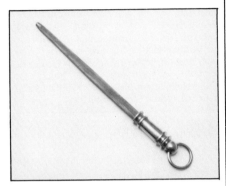

Magnetized steel with stainless-steel handle; 4⅜″ long overall.

$3.60

This tiny pocket steel is so pretty, with a large ring at the end so that it might hang on a chain from a pocket or around a neck, that we have dubbed it the lavallière of the future. It is particularly appropriate as a gift for the woman who has achieved equality in certain culinary matters by carving as well as any masculine expert. She can surely wear this badge of achievement with pride, and she'll use it frequently too. Only 4⅜ inches long, including the ring at the end, it is a little jewel of a sharpener.

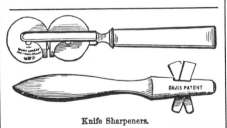

Knife Sharpeners.

Vatel, chef to Louis IV, explained the carver's role: "A carver should be well bred, inasmuch as he should maintain a first rank among the servants of his master. Pleasing, civil, amiable and well disposed . . . he should station himself by the side of his master, carving with knives suitable to the size of his meats. A carver should be very scrupulous in his deportment, his carriage should be grave and dignified, his appearance cheerful, his eyes serene, his head erect and well combed, abstaining as much as possible from sneezing, yawning, or twisting his mouth, speaking very little and directly. . . ."

Where Should You Keep Your Knives?

There are two basic solutions to the knife-storage problem: magnetic racks and slotted racks. Unless you have small children and feel more secure with knives kept out of their reach, never put knives in a drawer. First of all, this is dangerous to you—it is easy to get gashed while lifting out a knife. Drawer storage is not good for knives, either; blades are damaged if they get bumped and knocked around. So if you must keep knives in a drawer, try to protect the blades in some way, and keep the handles toward the front of the drawer for easy lifting. Still another disadvantage is that in a drawer the range of knives is hidden from your view. If your whole knife selection is out in the open where you can see them, you are more likely to pick up the best one for the job at hand.

On the whole, it is probably no less safe to keep knives in or on a proper rack. No one is likely to place a rack at toddler height, near a child's chair, or near a stepladder. If a good rack is suitably located, at adult height, it is much safer in almost any situation than any other means of storing knives.

Make sure all wall-hung racks are well secured. A magnetic rack is especially heavy to begin with, and when loaded with a full complement of knives, this is a weighty and dangerous item. Install a knife rack as you would a bookcase. Usually these racks come complete with screws and instructions, but if you have a problem wall, you will probably have to add some additional hardware: lead anchors for a masonry wall, toggle bolts for a hollow wall. In some cases all you need do is locate the wooden studs in your wall and attach the rack to them. In other cases you may have to install a wooden backboard on the wall with masonry nails and then secure the rack by screwing it to the backboard. When in doubt, consult your local hardware dealer or the man at the lumberyard.

The Magnabar XII   2.45

Cherrywood with two magnetic bars; 12″ × ⅞″; 1⅝″ high. Also avail. in 18″ length.

$7.00 ▲ $10.00 ▲

Some people believe that a magnetic rack may cause molecular distortion in the steel of a knife blade. We have not found any significant distortion and recommend a strong magnetic rack, such as the Magnabar XII, without reservations. A rack must, however, have a **strong** magnet, because you just don't want to have knives skidding around. We recommend only racks with a double row of magnets. This one, of cherrywood, has two thick bars. You can see for yourself, by looking at the end of the rack, that each of them is large; together they are formidable. This is one of the best, and best-looking, solutions to the problem of knife storage. Be sure, by the way, that there is absolutely no grease on your knife or it may not adhere to even such strong magnets as these.

Modular Slotted Wooden Rack   2.46

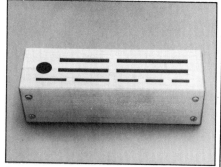

Bird's-eye maple rack; 9½" × 2½".

$12.50

This beautifully styled wooden rack has slots for a circular steel and for knives of a variety of sizes. Of a most attractive light-colored polished bird's-eye maple, it has well-arranged slots, placed in three rows for maximum storage on minimum wall space. It will hold four good-sized chef's knives or a small cleaver and five other knives too. One advantage of this rack over the magnetic ones is that it can be attached to a chopping block (the vibrations would shake the knives loose from a magnetic rack). If you do attach this or any other wooden rack to a chopping block, be sure to leave at least an inch of clearance between the top of the tallest knife handle and the top of the block. Never put a knife rack on the side where you're going to be working; always put it on the side away from the action. This rack comes with clear instructions for hanging.

One-Row Slotted Wooden Knife Rack   2.47

Walnut-stained knotty-pine rack; 12" × 1¾". Also avail. 18" long. Both sizes avail. in natural finish.

$6.00

If reaching behind a knife to get out another knife makes you nervous, you'd probably be more comfortable with one or more single-row slotted wooden racks like this one, of walnut-stained knotty pine. It has one round space and one long, straight slot. It is neither as attractive nor as commodious as the one just described, but neither is it as expensive; and it, too, will fit flush against a wall or on the side of a chopping block.

A fifteenth-century book includes this description among the duties of "A Pantler or Butler": "In the pantry you must always keep three sharp knives, one to chop the loaves, another to pare them, and a third sharp and keen, to smooth and square the trenchers with. Always cut your lord's bread, and see that it be new; and all other bread at the table one day old ere you cut it, all household bread three days old, and trencher bread [used as plates] four days old."

Chopping Blocks and Boards

We are not talking about cheese boards, rustic-styled serving planks, or meat-carving boards, but about chopping and cutting boards used primarily for food preparation.

The whole point of a chopping and cutting board is to receive the brunt of the action of a knife blade at work. A pastry board can be of pine, and lots of chopping bowls are of pine, but ideally a cutting board is made from a hard wood such as maple.

WHY WOOD?

Why are the best of these made of wood? Because wood is neither so rigid that it will ruin a knife blade nor so unyielding that it will give your wrist the cook's version of tennis elbow. It has some resilience; it does not add any flavor of its own to the food; it *works*.

A real chopping block, not a kitchen counter, is best made from laminated squares of the end grain of wood. Old-fashioned butchers' blocks were held together by tongue-and-groove arrangements. This is not so important today, because of the even stronger bond made by modern synthetic glues and other methods. The chopping blocks and boards made by J. & D. Brauner (see 2.48) are laminated electronically for a completely secure bond.

Buying old blocks is risky, but not for reasons of hygiene. Cleaned wood can be very clean indeed. But old blocks are sure to have uneven surfaces, and these can't be sanded until level again because the end-grain sections of which they are made are certain to be of unequal hardness.

There is no such thing as an optimum height for a chopping block or work counter. The important considerations are how tall you are and how your arms, and especially your shoulders, move. Chopping is a movement of the arm, primarily of the forearm. You should not have to use the relatively weak shoulder muscles, or even raise your shoulder, at all. Most chopping surfaces are too high for most people.

The best possible chopping surface is a freestanding block you can approach from any side. A well-designed kitchen has a more or less triangular layout, with stove, refrigerator, and sink at the angles. Ideally, a chopping block would be located smack in the middle of that triangle. But most kitchens are not ideally laid out, and they do not have enough space for a freestanding block. For those who do not have the luxury of ideal kitchens, we recommend chopping boards made of laminated lengthwise strips of wood. These are not as strong as end grain blocks, but they are stronger than simple flat pieces of wood, which tend to split along the grain lines. If you can find one, an end-grain board is a perfect answer.

Get the largest block or board you have room for and feel comfortable with. Round ones are not practical; food will inevitably slide off the edge at the least opportunity.

CLEANING CHOPPING SURFACES

The best way to clean wood is to scrape off all food residue with a knife blade or a scraper and then to sprinkle kosher or other coarse salt over the board. Then use half a lemon, from which you have already extracted the juice, to scrub and remove stains. Rinse off with cold water only. If a board is badly stained, it can be sponged with ordinary household bleach. Be sure to wash off all bleach with cold water; and be careful, because wood is porous and may absorb the bleach. Never use soap or detergent, which weaken wood fibers.

We are not showing any well-and-tree boards for meat carving, because they are hard to clean and can turn bad very quickly from the seepage of meat juices and accumulated gook. Those with set-in metal prongs are especially difficult to work on, since you cannot move the meat easily and the prongs will tear up the outer flesh. All in all, the simplest solutions are the best. And the simplest solution for carving a roast is to put the meat on a large china platter, let it rest for about 20 minutes so its juices are reabsorbed instead of flowing all over your platter, and then carve.

Butcher-Block Cutting Boards 2.49

Laminated edge-grained maple boards; 18" × 12", 1¾" thick. Also avail. 20" × 15", 24" × 18", 30" × 18", 36" × 18", or 24" × 24"; all 1¾" thick.

$10.90

These Butcher-Block cutting boards are made of laminated edge-grained maple —not end grain, good but not ideal. They are cured and electronically glued to form a single warp-resisting strong plank; they are sanded to a satin-smooth finish and hand-rubbed with protective oil. The natural medium-light appearance of these boards, with slight variations in color of adjoining strips, is very pleasant to look at. They are available in 1¾-inch thickness in a variety of sizes, from 18 x 12 inches up to 36 x 18 inches and 24 x 24 inches. Other sizes can also be specially ordered from the manufacturer. Countertops and cabinet tops, 1½ inches thick by 25 inches deep, are available in standard lengths or can be specially ordered too; a matching backsplash is available. You can place one board on your kitchen counter, cover a dishwasher with one, or top every surface in the kitchen. Whether you choose a little or a lot of the butcher-block look, it is most attractive, functional, and long-lasting.

Butcher Block 2.48

Laminated and dovetailed end-grain maple chopping block; 18" × 18" × 12" thick, 34" high overall. Also avail. 24" × 18" × 12", 24" × 24" × 12", 24" × 24" × 16", or 30" × 30" × 16"; overall height 34".

$133.00

This professional chopping block stands on four thick, sturdy legs. The 12-inch-thick top is of end-grain maple, electronically laminated for permanence. It comes in several sizes that are larger than the 18 x 18-inch top shown here, and the overall height is 34 inches, comfortable for most people. Casters are available for this block, but we don't advise that you buy them; even though you may think you will want to move this heavy thing around, consider the fact that is is not a piano. It is a work surface, and should be stationary. Moreover, its height without casters is preferable. This table also comes with a knife rack securely attached to the side. With space for a round steel, a good-sized cleaver, and several other large knives, it will keep your tools where you need and use them. When you order the rack with the chopping block, Brauner will attach it for you. If you have space for this butcher block, it is a handsome piece of kitchen furniture and the best possible chopping surface you can buy.

End-Grain Cutting Board 2.50

Pacific red alder cutting board; 16″ X 12″, 2″ thick. Also avail. 19″ X 14″ or 22″ X15″, 2″ thick.

$20.00

Slice the top two inches off the butcher block (2.48) and you have this end grain cutting board. There is one other difference, a strictly botanical one. This handsome board is constructed of laminated sections of Pacific red alder, while the Brauner boards and blocks are of maple. We have explained the superiority of the end grain as a cutting surface, and with this board you can have it without buying a piece of furniture. Both sides are usable and, but for the board's size and weight, it would be handsome for serving as well as chopping and cutting.

Hard-Rubber Chopping Board 2.51

Hard rubber board, 24″ X 18″, 1″ thick. Also avail. 18″ X 12″, 20″ X 15″ all three avail. either ¾″ or 1″ thick.

$36.05

The day of wood in the kitchen is unfortunately coming to an end in this country. Federally mandated sanitary codes for wholesale food processing now prohibit the use of wooden chopping boards and blocks. Wood, because it is porous, will accept grease, which is not easily removed, and there is a consequent tendency to breed bacteria. If you decide against wood for sanitary, or any other, reason, we do not recommend plastic. Plastics scratch and mar easily, and they crack and chip if you chop with real impact. Furthermore, plastic is brittle and will inflict terrible torture on your wrist and elbow; it has no resilience at all. The best of the nonwood chopping boards is this one, which is made of very hard rubber. However, when it arrives in your kitchen you will hate us for recommending it. Not so much because of its tan, bland appearance; you'll soon get used to its looks. But, when brand new, it smells like a pair of old galoshes. We warn you so you at least won't be surprised. Eventually the smell will die out in the open air, and the board's virtues will surely outweigh this defect. It is very heavy; its weight keeps it lying flat on your counter. It is virtually indestructible, but if you try hard you might be able to scratch it. It has excellent resilience and is waterproof, nonporous, and sanitary. It has a juice rim running completely around on all sides just inside the perimeter. You could have it built in as the topping for all your counters. All that, and it comes with the seal of the National Sanitation Foundation Testing Laboratory, too. Because it is waterproof it is the perfect counter surface to build into your outdoor barbecue area. This one is 24 x 18 inches and is 1 inch thick; it also comes in three smaller, but still generous, sizes and in thicknesses of ¾ inch as well as 1 inch.

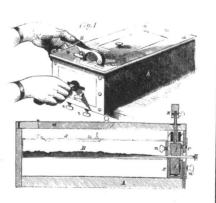

This ingenious contraption for cleaning knives was shown in the Scientific American *in 1860.*

Ceramic Cutting Board 2.52

Ceramic board with rubber feet; 20″ X 14¼″, white. Also avail. in white with Spice o' Life and Autumn Harvest designs in corner.

$14.95

The only hard-surfaced cutting board that we suggest you consider is this one made of Corning's famous space-age ceramic. You can chill it like a marble pastry board or put hot pots on it—it is impervious to temperature extremes. It will not scorch, crack, or chip. However, it is not scratchproof. We like the large 20 x 14¼ inch all-white one, but the board is also available in other sizes and with two colorful designs on a white background. It can be built into a countertop—consider setting one in at the bar, or beside your stove. Because it is nonporous and easily wiped clean, it will not hold food residues or odors. The top surface is smooth, but the underside has a pebbly texture. There are six removable rubber feet. We don't suggest that you even consider using this as a chopping board: it has no resilience at all, and if you chop on it, your wrist will remember the effort for many days.

One of the defenses of gourmandism put forth by Brillat-Savarin is as follows: "For even those who sleep apart (and there are many such) eat at the same table; they have a theme of conversation which never grows stale, for they talk not only of what they are eating, but of what they are about to eat, what they have met with on the tables of their acquaintances, fashionable dishes, new inventions, etc., and such table-talk is full of charm."

Illustrated in A Diderot Pictorial Encyclopedia of Trades and Industry, Manufacturing and the Technical Arts, edited by Charles C. Gillespie, New York, 1959.

Cutting Instruments Other Than Knives

With a knife and a couple of sticks—their famous cleavers and chopsticks—the Chinese have managed to create one of the world's great cuisines. And, as a matter of fact, a really skillful craftsman can still do most of the preliminary preparation of food with a good chef's knife; only, in the words of the old joke, thank God he doesn't have to. And he doesn't have to because the mechanically minded Western world has created a whole artillery of devices other than knives which are used to cut food apart in one manner or another.

There are tools for removing the thick skins of oranges, or the barest sliver of the zest of a lemon; for slicing a main-course serving of rare roast beef, or the most transparent shavings of baked ham; for chopping onions, or parsley, or potatoes; and, if not quite for removing the bones from a fowl, at least for doing the equivalent in the vegetable world by removing the core from an apple. And if you have a nifty little swiveling peeler which removes a thin layer of potato peel, why should you struggle to do the same job less efficiently with a paring knife?

THE RELATIVES OF THE KNIFE

Some of the cutters in this chapter show their familial relationship to knives very clearly—think of scissors and shears and the great two-handled blades for slicing cheese, the curved blades for chopping in a bowl. Others hide their kinship cleverly, like the mandoline or the stretched wire for slicing cheese. Sometimes the blades are hidden, appearing only as triangular bits of sharpened steel or knife-thin edges on a cutter; but if you look carefully enough, you will see a sharpened metal edge on every item in this chapter except the nutcrackers.

More often than not, these edges are on implements of stainless steel and so cannot be resharpened easily; but then, the blades themselves come in shapes that make them impossible to resharpen at home. But they are there, in the middle of a tool or in a row of disc-shaped cutters; and it is this edge that tells you that you are still dealing with knives of sorts and still performing the knifely functions of peeling, slicing, chopping, and otherwise dividing food into parts.

HANDLE WITH CARE

Oddly enough, there were more accidents, more cut fingers and Band-Aids when we were testing the items for this chapter than when we were examining hundreds of knives in order to evaluate them. For one thing, everyone knows that knives can cut; but why worry about a funny little machine that looks like a toy truck? There was unquestionably a totally unwarranted lack of respect in approaching these edges which are, in fact, often as sharp as those on the best knives. One German mincer earned a reputation as something of an item of slaughter as one person after another handled it carelessly and wound up with bleeding fingers. But there is also the very real consideration that these cutters are not grasped simply, as knives are, with one hand. A knife is held in one manner and then used with a limited range of movements, but the items in this chapter call into use a variety of hand positions and muscle movements. You use them by pressing down with two hands, or by

CUCUMBER AND MINT SALAD

Serves: 4 to 6
Preparation time: 10 minutes
Cooking time: none

Cucumbers have a natural affinity to dill, but why confine them to this combination? For a change of pace use mint!

INGREDIENTS
1 tablespoon lemon juice
½ cup heavy cream or crème fraîche
3 to 4 cucumbers
Salt
1 tablespoon finely minced mint
1 tablespoon finely chopped parsley
Freshly ground white pepper

PREPARATION
1. In a bowl, combine the lemon juice and cream and let the mixture stand for 2 to 3 hours.
2. Peel the cucumbers and cut them in half lengthwise. Remove the seeds with a spoon or melon-ball cutter. Cut the cucumbers into ¼-inch slices. Sprinkle with salt and let them stand in a colander for at least 30 minutes.
3. Drain the cucumbers and dry well with a paper towel. Combine with the cream. Sprinkle with the mint and parsley. Season with additional salt and pepper. Serve well chilled.

REMARKS
The salad can be made several hours ahead of time. If prepared the day before, the cucumbers will lose some of their crispness, but they will still be delicious. You can combine cucumbers and sliced radishes for a variation and use fresh dill instead of mint.

(From THE SEASONAL KITCHEN, by Perla Meyers. Copyright © 1973 by Perla Meyers. Reprinted by permission of Holt, Rinehart and Winston.)

rocking your wrist back and forth, or by squeezing your fingers together, or even by rubbing food back and forth across a blade.

THE SPECIALISTS

The other fact that distinguishes the non-knife cutters from the knives is that they are specialized—each one is a tool for a given task. A really good knife can be used for slicing eggs and peeling peaches and disjointing a chicken; a meat slicer is used for slicing meat and bread, and that's about it. That means that you should consider, before you buy anything in this chapter, whether the function is one that you perform frequently enough to justify the price of the tool and the storage space it will need.

PEELERS

Skillfully handled, a good paring knife is the best peeling tool in your kitchen. With it you can remove the skin from any fruit or vegetable, making a dazzling display as you carve off an apple skin in a single ribbon or pull long purple strips from the surface of an eggplant. The soldier doing KP, a comedy figure as traditional as any in the commedia dell'arte, was always shown with a paring knife in one hand and a potato in the other.

But other tools have been developed to help you do this job with greater ease. The simplest is the swivel-action peeler, which you surely already have in your gadget drawer or hanging from a hook on a pegboard—with it you can remove a paper-thin layer from a potato or a carrot, doing it with a natural shucking motion. Then there are other, more specialized, tools for removing the thick skins from citrus fruits. You will certainly want to have the peeler in your kitchen; and the others are interesting. If you think that you will find them useful, we can assure you that they work well.

ers is resharpen them. As a matter of fact, you have to be aware that they will become dull and should be thrown out after a year or so of use. Don't just fuss about the edges becoming dull; bear in mind what you paid for it in the first place, and get another one when you need it.

"To peel a boiled potato of good quality is a choice pleasure. Between the pad of the thumb and the point of the knife, held in the fingers of the same hand, one grasps—after incising it—that rough thin paper by one of its lips, and pulls it toward one to detach it from the appetizing flesh of the tuber.

"The easy operation, when performed without too many tries, leaves one with a feeling of inexpressible satisfaction.

"The slight rustle made by the detaching tissues is sweet to the ear, and the discovery of the edible pulp delightful.

"One feels—on observing the perfection of the bared fruit, the difference, the similarity, the surprise, and the ease of the operation—that one has accomplished something right and proper long foreseen and desired by nature, but which one has the merit of fulfilling nonetheless..."

Francis Ponge, The Voices of Things

French Swivel-Action Peeler   3.2

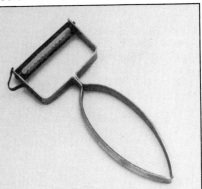

Stainless steel with high-carbon-steel blade; 4⅞" long; blade 2" wide.

$1.25

Europeans use a different type of swivel peeler. The blade is the same as that of the American model above, but it is attached at both ends to its stainless-steel handle, which swells into a comfortable hollow oval for your hand to grasp. It is used with a pulling motion rather than a shucking motion; grasping the handle in

Swivel-Action Peeler   3.1

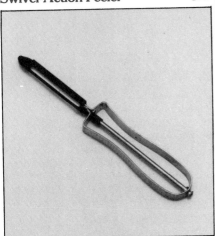

Carbon-steel blade with stainless-steel handle; 6¼" long.

$.49 ▲

This is the familiar swivel-action peeler: the best made, and still costing a great deal less than a dollar. Can you think of *anything* else about which those two remarks can be made? It is sometimes called a knee-action (or even nee-action) peeler, through a misunderstanding of the movements of that particular joint; the name indicates the fact that it rotates slightly as it moves, and thus can accommodate itself to the contours of various vegetables. The handle is of waffled chrome steel, and it is attached to the cutting blade by means of a steel axis. The blade itself is made from half a tube of carbon steel which has had a lengthwise slice cut out of it; and both edges of the slice have been sharpened so that, as it moves back and forth across a potato—or as it is wielded by a righty or a lefty—it cuts under the peel to remove a thin, neat layer. There are peelers like this available with stainless-steel blades, but they are not so sharp, and one thing you cannot do with these peel-

Continued from preceding page

your right palm, you hold a carrot in your left hand and pull the scraper down its length from the tip, aiming for your left hand. It does a good job, paring off a paper-thin sheet of peel: we tried it on the tough stalks of some elderly aspara-gus and on carrots, and both times it worked just fine. As a useful extra, it has a small, thin extra blade, curved in a half-circle, for removing the eyes of potatoes. It is inexpensive and easy to clean. But Americans who are not used to the direction of the movement might just get their knuckles scraped the first few times they try it.

CITRUS PEELERS AND ZESTERS
There is a whole armament of tools designed for coping with the peels of citrus fruits, and a whole branch of cookery for transforming them once they are removed. After all, you can choose whether to peel an apple or a potato—and we dare you to peel a plum—but nobody, *nobody* is going to bite into an unpeeled grapefruit. On the other hand, once citrus peel is removed there are lots of things you can do with it. Begin by freezing it for future use: it freezes beautifully. Then twist it into your martini; or grate it into your oatmeal cookies; or boil it in a sugar syrup to make one of those pretty bittersweet candies that are so inherently repulsive to any right-thinking child, so welcome to more sophisticated palates. In short, orange peel and lemon peel are of value only after they have been removed; and thus we show you a variety of tools designed to help you remove them.

Citrus Shell Cutter 3.3

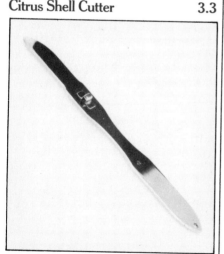

Stainless steel; 5¼″ long.

$3.00 ▲

This is one of the most frequently tested items in the catalog: nobody could believe that it worked the way that we said it did. And thus it kept going home with one or another expert or editor, weekend after weekend, and being brought back by passionate converts. It is a 5¼″ blade of stainless steel shaped rather like a ski with a tiny metal box on the underside. And it is excellent at its job, which is to remove the peel from citrus fruit in two perfectly intact halves. It does this by means of the tiny cutter on the back of the blade, scarcely visible in our picture, which peels away a narrow strip of skin to form an equator around the orange or grapefruit. Then the slightly curved edge of the tool is inserted between the peel and the fruit, gently teasing them apart; and before you know it, an intact half can be removed from the surface of the orange. What do you do with it? Well, you could fill half of a lemon with an ice or a sherbet, and serve it on a bed of lemon leaves from the florist. Or you could spoon balls of vanilla ice cream and orange sherbet into orange halves, forming your very own Creamsicles. This is a simple, well-made tool that performs one of life's less essential tasks, but performs it perfectly.

SALSA GREMOLADA— GREMOLADA SAUCE

½ cup finely chopped lemon peel
2 teaspoons finely chopped garlic
3 tablespoons finely chopped parsley, Italian if possible
2 tablespoons olive oil
Salt and freshly ground black pepper to taste

Mix together all ingredients and add to sauces or stews during the last 5 to 10 minutes of their cooking time. Yields about ¾ cup. Use with stews, especially osso buco.

(From ITALIAN FAMILY COOKING, by Edward Giobbi, illustrated by Cham, Lisa, and Gena Giobbi. Copyright © 1971 by Edward Giobbi. Reprinted by permission of Random House, Inc.)

Lemon Zester with Rosewood Handle 3.4

Stainless steel with rosewood handle, brass rivets; 6¼″ long.

$5.40

Some people like olives in their martinis; some people like onions; some don't even like martinis; but if you know someone who takes his martini with a twist of lemon peel, then this Swiss zester is an essential tool for you. You can use it for cutting strips of orange and grapefruit peel for candying as well, but in most households it would be primarily a bar tool. And it is a pretty one, with a handle of rosewood into which there has been sunk the tang of a stainless-steel blade, which is further secured by two rivets. The blade is an inflexible strip of metal with a hole cut into it, and the very end has been bent up into a peak. The near edge of the peak is sharpened so that it will cut a wide but shallow strip of peel—the zest—when it is pulled towards you over the surface of the fruit.

Citrus Shell Cutter
Lemon Zester with Rosewood Handle
Lemon Zester with Plastic Handle
Citrus-Peel Shredder
French Citrus-Peel Shredder
White Mountain Apple Parer and Corer

Citrus-Peel Shredder — 3.6

Stainless steel with rosewood handle, brass rivets; 6″ long.

$6.30

This is a tool that removes even less of the skin of the orange than a zester, making doubly sure that you won't pick up any of the bitter white pith beneath the colored surface. You can never use a grater on a lemon peel successfully; instead, the next time that you need really tiny shavings of peel to flavor the filling of your lemon-meringue pie or to mix with parsley and garlic for a gremolada (recipe), do it with this neat little tool. And remember that once you have denuded the orange or lemon, you should store it in a plastic bag in your refrigerator so that the juices won't dry out before they are squeezed out. This tool is the fraternal twin of the rosewood-handled Swiss zester; only this one has, cut into the end of the bent stainless-steel blade, a row of tiny circles and a pretty scalloped edge. You pull it toward you over the skin of the fruit and you get minute shreds of pure flavor and color. You may never have seen anything like this before, but it is, if anything, more useful to the cook than the more familiar tool which cuts larger strips of peel. It is 6″ long, sturdily made, and can be used, if you run that kind of household, for decorating pats of butter as well.

French Citrus-Peel Shredder — 3.7

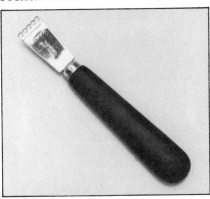

Stainless-steel blade with plastic handle, aluminum collar; 5⅞″ long.

$2.50 ▲

Again we show you a less expensive French version of the rosewood-handled tool (3.6), its handle made of smooth black plastic and its metal blade significantly thinner than that of the first. And again we tell you that, for the number of times you will use this tool, you could do very well by buying the less expensive version. The cutting edges of the tiny holes are just as sharp; the blade is fitted to the handle nearly as well; the whole thing goes safely into the dishwasher; it is, in short, a good and valid economy. As a matter of fact, it is considerably sturdier than the zester made by the same company. Made of rounded black plastic and stainless steel, it is 5⅞″ long.

White Mountain Apple Parer and Corer — 3.8

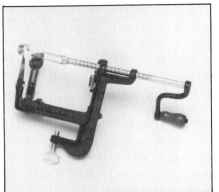

Painted cast-iron frame with stainless-steel shaft, slicer, and peeling blade, tinned cast-iron prong, wooden knob handle; 9¼″ × 6½″.

$14.95

Lemon Zester with Plastic Handle — 3.5

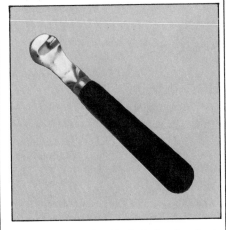

Stainless-steel blade with plastic handle, aluminum collar; 5½″ long.

$2.00 ▲

Another zester, this one French rather than Swiss, with a handle of black plastic rather than rosewood and with a correspondingly significant difference in price. This is far less expensive than the previous tool, and it works just as well; notice that the gesture will be different, involving a scraping motion, like the one you use with swivel-action peelers, rather than a pulling motion. There are other matters which account for the difference in price, notably the greater flexibility of the stainless-steel blade and the less secure and less hygienic manner in which it has been attached to the handle.

But it also happens that the feel of the handle in the palm is one of the most luscious we have experienced; and since this is a tool of infrequent use, it is one where economy might well be practiced.

The heavy cast-iron meat grinder which your grandmother used to screw onto the end of her kitchen table has a relation in this apple parer, corer, and slicer. It has been made for years by the Goodell Company and was recently taken over by another firm who are working to modernize and refine it without destroying its early American looks and practicality. And it is not the foolishly quaint thing you might at first suppose: in the fall, when there are barrels and bushels of apples for sale at farm stands, you could well use it to help you in making pies, applesauce, brown betty, and chutney—and how about a huge pot of apple butter from fruit puréed through your chinois or food mill (Chapter 4)? You mount this on the table, then pull the wooden handle and central shaft all the way back and impale an apple on the three-pronged fork. Now, when you turn the handle, the apple moves forward to come into contact with an upright holding a sharp blade. This, working on a spring, adapts itself to the contours of the apple, removing the peel as it goes. Finally, the apple is forced onto a sharp hook, which removes the core while cutting the rest of the fruit into slices. It is a machine which is nearly as seasonal as apples, since it works best on fresh hard fruit: and it has the heavy smoothness in the hand of good old-fashioned cast iron. Ours is painted green and has a red-painted wooden handle, a cheerful combination repeating the colors in the baskets of apples.

> I stretch my arms for apples
> anyway, feel how the ripe ones
> slide in my hands like cups
> that want to be perfect. Juices
> locked up in the skin.
>
> She used to slice them in quarters,
> cut through the core,
> open the inside out. Fingers
> steady on the knife, expert
> at stripping things.
>
> Sometimes she split them sideways
> into halves to let a star break
> from the center with tight seeds,
> because I wanted that,
> six petals in the flesh.
>
> ...

From "Apples," by Shirley Kaufman, in Poetry *magazine, 1970*

Corers, Ball Cutters, Citrus Slicers, and Pitters

From peeling to coring and pitting is a reasonable step, since both of these actions can be performed with a good knife. But in the array of non-knife cutters available to you there is a spectacular assortment of devices for removing one piece of a plant from another in any number of ways—the hull from the strawberry, the corn from the cob. They resemble one another not at all, but they all have a knife edge concealed somewhere in their varying shapes: sometimes you have to look hard to find the beveled and sharpened surface which, like the royal birthmark of the house of Graustark, will remind you of the ancestry of what looks to you like a pretty silly tool.

SILLY OR SUBLIME?
Because that is the other problem with these highly specialized gadgets. Either you can't live without them—you wonder what you ever did before you discovered your melon-ball cutter or your strawberry huller—or you find them totally laughable, like somebody else's passion for a popular singer you can't abide. You can decide for yourself how to react after seeing our miscellany of cutters for apples, for squash and corn on the cob, for strawberry hulls, for lemons. Then, later, we go on to offer information on devices for pitting fruits and olives.

Apple Corer 3.9

Stainless-steel blade with varnished light wood handle, nickel-steel collar; 7¾" long overall; blade 3⅞" long.

$2.50 ▲

It isn't so easy to use an ordinary apple corer, even though Americans have had generations of practice in using instruments for this purpose, including our wonderful machine (3.8). To begin with, you have to attack the core head-on and not at the slightest angle, or you will get a transverse section of core and leave a remnant in the fruit. And then you have to deal with the fact that cores, like apples, come in different sizes, and that you are just as likely as not to leave a whole mess of seeds and sharp bits embedded in the flesh of the apple. But there are times when an apple has to be cored—when you make baked apples, for example, and want to stuff the center with cinnamon candies—and then you ought to have the best apple corer you can get to help you. This one is from France, and is very well made of bleached and varnished wood and stainless steel. The blade is trough-shaped and has at the tip a thick ring of metal with a sharpened end; the two are attached by means of a metal collar. Put the apple down on a counter and attack it from above with the sharpened end of the ring: it should slip easily through to the other side. Then pull back with the core in the trough, and the job is done.

Apple Corer and Slicer   3.10

Cast aluminum with stainless-steel blades; 4″ diam.

$4.50

Now, if you should want to core and section your apple in one mighty motion, here is another one of those rigidly designed tools for non-standardized foodstuffs. It's a great idea, and this is an extremely popular tool; the trouble is that we can't figure out why. Apples come in different sizes, with cores of different sizes, and although in theory it would be lovely to be able to clomp down on top of one, simultaneously coring and slicing it, we just couldn't make that happen every time we tested this tool. Actually, it worked better on pears than on apples—they are softer and have narrower cores. If, however, you are determined to own one of these, then this is the one to buy, an extremely well-made device in polished cast aluminum with stainless-steel blades. It is made in one piece, with the blades firmly embedded; it is extremely strong, and has two good grip handles and highly sharpened blades. The frame is 4″ across, the space for the core is ¾″ across, and the blades will cut your apple or pear into 14 slices.

POTAGE AUX POMMES—APPLE SOUP WITH CAMEMBERT CHEESE BALLS

4 tablespoons salt butter
½ teaspoon finely chopped garlic
1 teaspoon tomato paste
3 tablespoons all-purpose flour
4 cups chicken stock
Salt
Freshly cracked white pepper
½ teaspoon chili pepper
¾ cup heavy cream
1 tablespoon chopped fresh chives
2 firm apples
Camembert cheese balls

Melt 2 tablespoons butter in a large heavy pan, add the chopped garlic, and cook 2 minutes. Off the heat, add the tomato paste and flour. Stir until smooth, then add the chicken stock. Return to low heat and stir until the mixture boils. Season with salt and pepper, add the chili pepper, cream and chives, mix well, and set aside. Skin, core, and cut the apples into bite-size pieces, and sauté in the rest of the butter until golden. Add them to the soup, reheat a little, and serve with a separate dish of frozen Camembert cheese balls [below, Camembert Glacé]. Net: 4 to 6 servings.

CAMEMBERT GLACE—ICED CAMEMBERT
8 ounces Camembert cheese
¼ cup dry white wine
¼ cup heavy cream
Salt
A few grains cayenne pepper
2 tablespoons dry white breadcrumbs
¾ cup freshly grated Parmesan cheese
A little paprika
A few sprigs fresh crisp watercress

Rub the cheese through a wire sieve or fine strainer, rind and all. In an electric mixer, beat the cheese until it is almost liquid with the wine, cream, salt, cayenne pepper, and breadcrumbs. Freeze. When it is solid, cut into bite-size pieces and roll them in the grated Parmesan cheese and paprika. Stick a toothpick into each piece. Serve on a small round platter garnished with the fresh watercress. Net: 12 to 16 pieces.

(From THE DIONE LUCAS BOOK OF FRENCH COOKING, by Dione Lucas and Marion Gorman, illustrated by Joseph S. Patti. Copyright © 1947 by Dione Lucas. Reprinted by permission of Little, Brown and Company.)

An antique apple parer, corer, and slicer.

Zucchini Corer   3.11

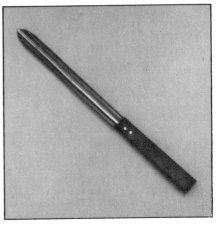

Stainless-steel blade with rosewood handle, brass rivets; 10⅜″ overall; blade 6¼″ × ⅝″.

$2.00 ▲

En garde! It's a zucchini corer, this long trough-shaped stainless-steel blade with one end held in a rosewood handle. And it's one of those tools we keep telling you about, which is either utterly useless or is the only thing that will do the job you need done. In Italy, they stuff zucchini with savory mixtures of chopped meat, parsley, and pignoli; and the Middle East has its own stuffings for this squash. In this country, we stuff cucumbers with softened mixtures of cheese and herbs, chill them thoroughly, and then slice them for lovely cool summer hors d'oeuvre. We remember an old lady who served us iced tea, cookies, and cucumber slices stuffed with Roquefort cheese in a shady corner of her front porch. This is a well-made utensil, more than 10″ in length, with a blade more than 6″ long; and it could also be used, so as not to make it too specialized, for coring apples and pears.

"Independently of its exquisite flavour, the melon passed, among the Greeks and Romans, as being very beneficial to the stomach and head. It is possible that they may have gone a little too far; but then man is so ready to give imaginary qualities to what he loves, that we cannot wonder at their praises of this delicious plant, which we generally eat in the most simple manner."

The Pantropheon, *by Alexis Soyer, 1853*

Double Melon-Ball Cutter 3.12

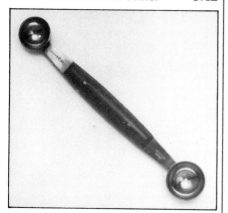

Stainless steel with wood handle, brass rivets; 6⅝″ long; cup diam. ⅞″.

$2.75 ▲

Still preparing fruits and vegetables, we move on to show you two tools that work as tiny scoops. They are melon-ball cutters, used in a time-consuming fashion to create those cornucopias of fruit which are displayed in scooped-out pineapples and watermelons. But you could also use them to carve small balls of potato and turnip which are then sautéed and served around your roast chicken or duckling; to scrape out the centers of cherry tomatoes and mushrooms, then to be filled with scoops of steak tartare or crabmeat. Or to make balls of softened nougat which are then rolled in powdered chocolate or crushed almonds. In short, unlike the zucchini corer, the melon ballers have uses beyond the obvious. We show you first a double-sided melon baller, useful because you can make two sizes of spheres. A heavy bar of stainless steel, 6⅝″ in overall length, is held in the center in a sandwich of wood; at each end of the wooden handle there is a rounded cup-like shape, its edges honed to a significant degree of sharpness, to do the actual cutting. You invert the cutter over the surface of the food, press it in a bit, then rotate the head to dig out a perfect globe.

Turnips and carrots "turned" into shapes for garnishing.

William Alcott grudgingly accepts melons in The Young Housekeeper, or Thoughts on Food, *1838: "The muskmelon and the watermelon . . . when perfectly ripe, and raised in a natural manner, without the use of strong fresh manures, and without any forcing or hotbed process, are by no means as injurious as writers have represented them to be. Indeed, I regard them both, in the absence of the summer fruits, which are preferable, as rather useful. An occasional meal of either is much better than no fruit at all."*

Gerhard Recknagel 3.13 Melon-Ball Cutter

Stainless steel with rosewood handle, brass rivets; 7″ long; cup diam. ¾″. Also avail. ½″, ⅝″, ⅞″, 1″, or 1⅛″.

$3.60

We asked one of our experts what he used to carve out the insides of cherry tomatoes, and he said that he used his children. But if the whole idea intrigues you, and you think that you might get into the food-decoration business in a big way, scooping globes of gelatin and chopped liver and carrots and bananas, then you will need more than one size of melon-ball cutter. This good-quality scoop from West Germany comes in a variety of sizes, producing balls from roughly ½″ to 1⅛″ in diameter; just choose the ones you want and get to work. It is a well-made tool of stainless steel, the tang held in a wooden handle and attached to it with brass rivets. There is in this, as in the preceding

melon baller, a hole cut into each hemisphere to help you release the ball shape once you have formed it.

Round French 3.14 Melon-Ball Cutter

Stainless steel with high-carbon-steel cup, rosewood handle; 6″ long; cup diam. ⅞″.

$5.00

From France: the first of three excellent little melon ballers. This is in the familiar shape and size, with a hemispheric high-carbon steel cutter soldered to a stainless-steel shaft. The shaft extends into a full tang which is sandwiched between two lengths of rosewood to form the handle. The whole thing is 6″ in length; the edges of the cup are beautifully sharpened, and the same manufacturer makes, as you will see, some interesting variations on the theme.

Oval French 3.15 Melon-Ball Cutter

Stainless steel with high-carbon steel cup, rosewood handle; 6″ long; cup 1¼″ × ¾″.

$7.00

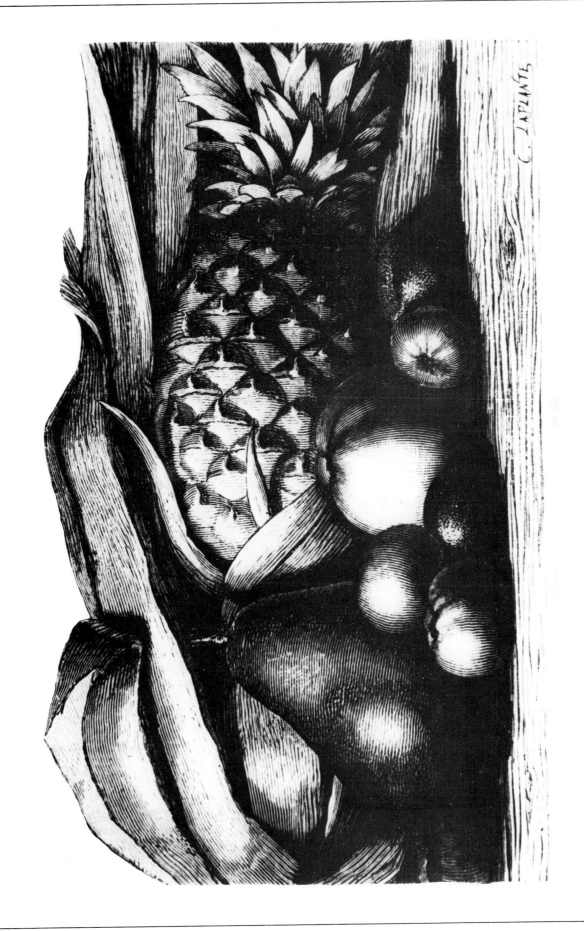

Entitled simply "Dessert," this still-life of fruits appeared in Le Livre de Cuisine by Jules Gouffé, published in Paris in 1874.

Continued from preceding page

As we discussed the preceding cutter, we promised you variations. Such as . . . an oval cutter, sharp enough to form those tiny olive-shaped balls of sautéed potato, carrot, and turnip which lie, fragrantly bathed in sauce, alongside a roasted chicken. Or to cut ovals of very firm lemon ice which you will then pile into the larger oval of an eviscerated lemon shell. Again, here we have an implement of superb quality in rosewood, stainless steel, and high-carbon steel, the shaft forming a full tang through the wooden handle and the edges of the cutter sharpened to a knife edge.

Fluted French Melon-Ball Cutter 3.16

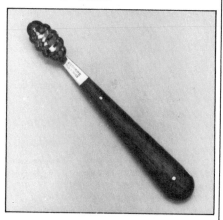

Stainless steel with nickeled-steel cup, rosewood handle, brass rivets; 6" long; cup ¾" × 1¼".

$8.00

This one will amaze them all: a melon-ball cutter made like a little scalloped pasta shell. With it you can make beehive-shaped pieces of sweet butter; astonish the family by carving gelatin into fluted shapes for garnishing; or simply do a rather pretentious fruit salad by cutting cantaloupe into this shape, apple into ovals (3.15), and watermelon into rounds (3.14). Then a few sprigs of mint, a general bath in a little syrup and light rum, and you will have turned a family dessert into a celebration. In spite of its frivolous uses, this is a good tool, strongly made in rosewood and stainless steel, with tiny brass rivets in the handle. We want to emphasize the absolute strength of all three of these well-made gadgets from France.

MELON IN STRAWBERRY SAUCE

Serves: 4 to 6
Preparation time: 25 minutes
Cooking time: 3 to 5 minutes

4 cups fresh strawberries
¾ cup sugar
½ cup currant jelly
2 tablespoons Grand Marnier
¼ cup kirsch
1 large ripe casaba or Spanish melon
Juice of 1 lemon

PREPARATION:

1. Wash and hull the strawberries. Reserve 1 cup of the most perfect berries. Place the remaining berries in the top part of the blender together with the sugar and blend at high speed for 3 minutes or until the sugar is completely dissolved. Pass the mixture through a fine sieve and reserve.
2. Combine the currant jelly with the liqueurs in a small saucepan and heat until the jelly is completely dissolved. Beat the mixture into the strawberry purée and reserve.
3. Cut the melon into small cubes or balls with a melon-ball cutter. Sprinkle with lemon juice and a little sugar and marinate for 30 minutes.
4. Add the strawberry purée, fold lightly and top with the whole strawberries. If you wish, sprinkle the whole strawberries with a little sugar and dribble a little Grand Marnier on them. Chill for 2 hours before serving.

REMARKS

A mixture of melons may be used, except watermelon, which does not lend itself well to fruit salads.

(From THE SEASONAL KITCHEN, by Perla Meyers. Copyright © 1973 by Perla Meyers. Reprinted by permission of Holt, Rinehart and Winston.)

Two vegetable or fruit cutters are explained in French Domestic Cookery, New York, 1855.

Tomato Spoon 3.17

Steel blade with stainless-steel collar, painted wood handle; 6" long; blade 1⅞" × ¾".

$1.75

A tomato spoon is the tool you use to remove the seeds and pulp from the inside of a tomato. Yes, we know—the experts all tell you to cut the fruit in half and then squeeze each half until the insides come out—but the problem is that they never *do* all come out. Which is no catastrophe unless you are a perfectionist, in which case you should buy a tomato spoon to insure that your tomato shells for shrimp salad are impeccable. Or suppose you are making tons of tomato sauce with the abundant harvest of those tomato plants you planted in a frenzy last spring. You can use the squeeze method; or you can wait until the sauce is done and then let the Mouli food mill or your chinois strain out the seeds. Only, if you had removed them before you began you would have achieved a much finer flavor. This is a nice tool, with a molded wooden handle attached to a sharpened, pointed spoon bowl: it looks as though someone had taken a teaspoon and decided to sharpen it into a weapon. It is a single-function object, not for everyone, but not useless, either.

STUFFED TOMATOES BERGERETTE

Serves: 6
Preparation time: 25 minutes
Cooking time: 20 minutes

A cold stuffed tomato is one of summer's most attractive appetizers. It is a marvelous way to use leftovers creatively and even with a simple filling such as this one you can create a refreshing and delicious hors d'oeuvre. You may vary the filling by adding to it finely minced poached salmon, a few poached mussels or even flaked tuna.

INGREDIENTS
6 medium-sized tomatoes
Salt
¾ cup vinaigrette dressing
½ cup Italian rice
⅓ cup heavy cream
1 teaspoon Dijon mustard
Freshly ground white pepper
2 tablespoons finely minced scallions
2 tablespoons finely minced parsley
2 tablespoons finely minced green
    pepper
2 tablespoons finely minced pimientos
4 anchovy filets

GARNISH:
6 whole cooked peeled shrimp or 6
    whole rolled anchovy filets
Black olives
Bed of watercress
Juice of ½ lemon
2 to 3 tablespoons olive oil

PREPARATION
1. Cut a slice off the top of the tomatoes. Gently loosen the flesh with a small knife and remove it. Discard the seeds but reserve the pulp. Sprinkle the tomato shells with salt and place them cut side down on a plate for 30 minutes.
2. After 30 minutes, sprinkle the tomato shells with ¼ cup of the vinaigrette and let them marinate while you prepare the rice.
3. In a saucepan, bring to a boil 1½ cups of water seasoned with ½ teaspoon salt. When the water comes to a boil, add the rice, reduce the heat and simmer, covered, until it is tender (about 20 minutes). Then remove the rice to a mixing bowl and cool completely.
4. Whip the cream. Add the Dijon mustard, salt and pepper and reserve.
5. When the rice is quite cold, add the minced vegetables and anchovies. Bind the rice salad with the whipped cream mixture and add the remaining vinaigrette. The tomato pulp, finely chopped, may be added to the rice too. Be sure not to include any of the seeds. Refrigerate the rice for 30 minutes to 1 hour.
6. Drain the tomato shells and fill them with the rice. Top each shell with 1 whole shrimp, anchovy filet or black olive. Put the tomatoes on a bed of watercress seasoned with lemon juice and olive oil. Serve chilled but not cold.

(From THE SEASONAL KITCHEN, by Perla Meyers. Copyright © 1973 by Perla Meyers. Reprinted by permission of Holt, Rinehart and Winston.)

Strawberry Huller 3.18

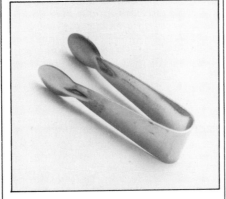

Stainless steel; 2½″ long.
$.75 ▲

For a few weeks every spring, those of us who like to use seasonal produce go out of our minds with strawberries. Strawberries and asparagus—not a day goes by when one or the other isn't served, and then suddenly it's all over. But while it lasts it is wonderful: strawberry shortcake, strawberries with orange peel, kirsch, and heavy cream, strawberries served plain with a mound of powdered sugar and a glop of crème fraîche on every plate. And for those few weeks this little tool is highly overworked—and is then put away to await another June. It is a strawberry huller; and it looks like a blunted tweezer, being a tiny metal pincers formed of one strip of stainless steel bent in half, the ends formed into concave circular shapes. It works better than a paring knife to remove the leaves, since it does not cut into the flesh of the fruit and let the juices out. It's a simple little thing, 2½″ long and quite inexpensive; but it is not always easy to find and it is extremely useful. You could use it for plucking poultry feathers as well, but ours more than pays its way every spring when it runs mad during the strawberry season.

"It is not elegant to gnaw Indian corn. The kernels should be scraped off into the plate, and then eaten with a fork. Ladies should be particularly careful how they manage so ticklish a dainty lest the exhibition rub off a little desirable romance."

Hints on Etiquette, by Charles Day, 1844

Corn Cutter 3.19

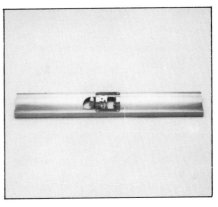

Stainless steel; 15″ × 2¼″.
$3.98

When corn is in season, you eat it every night, barely cooked in boiling water and then covered with melted butter, salt, and lots of black pepper. But when it's not in season, not so local, but still there in your supermarket, then what do you do with it? Or when three sets of guests arrive on Sunday, each with 12 ears of corn sparkling fresh from their local farm stands, then what do you do on Monday? You use one of the many recipes which are indigenous to this continent and which make use of corn cut off the cob. There is corn relish, sparkling in primary colors with red and green peppers; corn chowder, made of corn, heavy cream, and pepper; succotash, the old Indian dish of corn and beans; or corn pudding, with corn, bacon, and onions held in a custard. And in order to make any of these, you need a way to get the corn off the cob. Which means either a sharp knife or this corn cutter. You will use it all the time or never at all; take your choice, but we can assure you that it works, removing the kernels with never a bit of the cob. It is a trough of stainless steel 15″ in length which you lay across the top of a mixing bowl. Halfway along it are some complicated and vicious cutters and shredders. You scrape the ear of corn along the trough, and the cutters shred and scrape the kernels off easily with no mess. The parts are adjustable for different-sized kernels and to deliver whole grains or grains prepared for creaming.

Radish Cutter 3.20

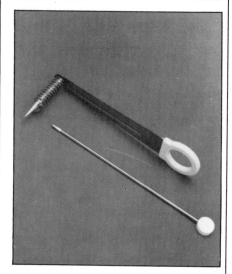

Stainless steel with plastic handles; cutter 4⅝" × 1⅝"; needle 5" long.

$5.00

This is a complicated mechanism that performs a useless function. It is pure fantasy, but it is workable fantasy: science fiction, we guess you could call it. It is a radish cutter, and once you have mastered it you wind up with a radish cut into a coiled-up spiral ribbon. Terrific, right? You can't live without it, right? But there are people, we assure you, who use them: witness the sales. And they are not really as silly as we are pretending: they are useful when you want to decorate cold platters and salads for the buffet table. This is how it works. There is a round plastic loop that serves as a handle for a blade that looks like a small, round-ended paper knife. A pointed screw is attached to the underside of the tip of the blade, and a spindle fits into the top of the screw, on the upper surface of the blade. You stick the point of the screw into one end of your radish, insert the spindle in its sockets, and begin to turn the blade round and round it, holding the spindle steady. The sharpened edge of the blade cuts a continuing section through the vegetable—you are actually unscrewing the radish! This is made of stainless steel and plastic and is small, inexpensive, and easy to clean. It was, for obvious reasons, one of the most *tested* items in the *Catalogue*; the problem seemed to lie in understanding the instructions, but, once that was accomplished, the testers all found it easy to use.

"In times of popular tumult [the radish] was often transformed into an ignominious projectile, with which the mob pursued persons whose political opinions rendered them obnoxious to the majority, as we might say in the present day."

The Pantropheon, *by Alexis Soyer, 1853*

Lemon Slicer 3.21

Plastic with chromed-steel supports, cast-aluminum collar, and stainless-steel blades; 4" diam.; 5⅝" high.

$30.00

This is an expensive, heavily engineered gadget in plastic and chromed steel which lets you slice a whole lemon into ten even wedges. It's not for everyone; its job could be performed just as well with a cutting board and a good knife; and for that matter, how often do you need to cut up a whole lemon at a time? But if you are looking for a present for a man with a bar which he loves, the sort of man who dares you to ask for a drink that he can't make, then this might be just the answer. It is well constructed and works excellently. You insert a lemon into a hollowed-out red plastic base which looks rather like an egg cup. There are two metal posts on which you insert a black plastic cylinder which holds ten triangular cutting blades. One good shove on the two handles and the lemon is—what?—decasected? What is the word which means bisected into *ten* pieces? This device is easy to clean, efficient, and well made. And the use, of course, is not limited to the saloon; you could just as well bring it out on the day when you serve shrimp cocktail or grilled fish. Whether you think it expensive depends on whether you would use it a lot or a little.

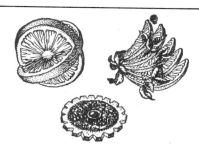

PITTERS

If knives are used to slice, to peel, to chop and to bone, then what is the equivalent of the last function in the vegetable world? Why, pitting, of course: removing the inedible from the heart of the edible. Pitting instruments are not in common use in this country except in those kitchens where a lot of preserving and jam-making is done. And quite often, it is true, removing the pits is a matter of aesthetics and ease of eating rather than of taste. When you add olives to a dish of Duck with Olives or to a Sauce Provençale, the pit will do no harm to the flavor, but *will* challenge the ingenuity of the diner; so the same dish might be prepared with pitted olives for company, unpitted for the family dinner table. Cherries, on the other hand, should be pitted before they are put into pies or made into homemade preserves; tiny beach plums are pitted before they are made into jam. And it is a rather simple thing to accomplish, so long as you have the proper tools.

Cherry or Olive Pitter   3.22

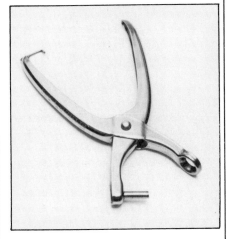

Nickeled steel; 7½″ long; pitting rod ⅞″.

$4.50

This is the simplest of the lot, a nickeled-steel cherry pitter which looks like the gadget you use to punch holes in notebook paper. It is made of two curved metal forms held together with a coil spring at the joining. When you squeeze the long ends, the action brings the shorter ends together, too. And in one of these is a ring to hold a single cherry, while in the other there is a short metal rod for poking out its pit. A little hook, like the one on the ends of the handles of your poultry shears, helps you to keep the instrument closed when it isn't in use. Perfectly adequate and sure to give a neat result, but limited by the fact that it takes one cherry, one olive at a time.

CHERRY FLAN TART

Serves: 6 to 8
Preparation time: 35 minutes
Cooking time: 45 minutes

INGREDIENTS
1 9-inch baked tart shell

THE CHERRIES:
3 cups pitted Bing cherries
Sprinkling of sugar
Juice of ½ lemon
⅓ cup sweet port wine

THE CUSTARD:
2 whole eggs
2 egg yolks
1 cup heavy cream
⅓ cup sugar
1 teaspoon vanilla
1 teaspoon lemon rind

THE MERINGUE:
3 egg whites
Pinch of salt
8 tablespoons sugar

1. Preheat the oven to 350°.
2. Pit the cherries and place them in a bowl. Sprinkle with sugar, lemon juice and wine and marinate for 30 minutes to 1 hour.
3. In another bowl combine the whole eggs with the yolks, cream, sugar, vanilla and lemon rind and whisk until the mixture is very well blended. Set it aside.
4. In a large bowl combine the egg whites with the salt and beat, adding the sugar a little at a time, until the meringue is stiff and glossy. Set it aside.
5. Drain the cherries thoroughly and place them in the baked tart shell. Top them with the egg and cream mixture.
6. Return the tart to the oven and bake until the custard is set (about 30 to 40 minutes).
7. Remove the tart again and spoon the meringue on it, covering it completely.
8. Turn the oven to 450°. Return the tart to the oven for 3 or 4 minutes or until the meringue is lightly browned. Remove the tart and let it cool.
9. Carefully unmold the tart and slide it onto a serving platter. Serve the same day at room temperature.

(From THE SEASONAL KITCHEN, by Perla Meyers. Copyright © 1973 by Perla Meyers. Reprinted by permission of Holt, Rinehart and Winston.)

Plum Pitter   3.23

Cast aluminum with stainless steel blades; 6½″ long.

$4.50

There are no plums, alas, in plum pudding, the name being the result of a confusion about what to call various dried fruits. But there are plums in fruit soup, that heady mixture of fruit, white wine, and cinnamon; in plum dumplings, made of blue plums pitted, stuffed with cubes of sugar, and then encased in pastry; and in any of the many plum tarts and plum cakes which flourish in Europe. And in order to make any of them you have to find a way to get the stones out of the plums. Try this simple device from West Germany, cast-aluminum pincers with tension supplied by a simple spring. One end has an open cup for holding a small plum; the other has crossed blades which push into the ring, pitting and quartering the fruit at the same time. It is sturdy, inexpensive, and very simple to operate and to clean. If you are fond of the small purple plums available late in the season which are more properly called fresh prunes, then this would be a handy tool for dealing with them.

Cherry and Plum Pitter   3.24

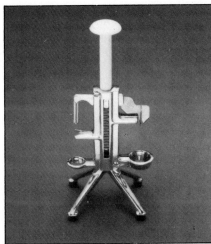

Cast aluminum with stainless-steel blades, plastic plunger; base 3⅝″ × 3⅛″; 9″ high.

$9.50 ▲

The photograph makes it look as though it were three feet tall, some mighty machine used in restaurant kitchens. But in fact it is a mere 9 inches high and as light as a mixing spoon or a whisk; it is mighty only in function. This little contraption pits pretty much anything: cherries and olives on one side, plums on the other. The individual machines work like the ones we have already shown you,

Continued from preceding page

with a rod on one side to push the stones out of olives, and a crossed blade on the other to pit and quarter small plums. The news about this machine is not only that it does both, but that it sits upright on its little rubber-covered feet, so that you can slam down hard on the white plastic plunger, using a much more effective form of leverage than is applied in working the other pitters. It is quicker, does more with less effort on your part and less strain on your hand, and we heartily recommend it.

"My sisters used to have cherry contests. They stuffed themselves with cherries all week long and counted up the pits on Saturday. It made them feel exuberant . . . I'd eat a few and I'd feel sick. But that never stopped me. I never missed a single contest. I despised cherry contests, but I couldn't stand being left out. Never. Every week I'd sneak off to the woods with bags full of cherries. I'd sit on a log and pit each cherry with a knife. Then I'd bury the fruit in a deep hole and fill it up with dirt. I cheated so hard to be in them, and I didn't even like them. I was so scared to be left out."

Mrs. Constable in In the Summer House, *a play by Jane Bowles, published 1948, 1954 by The Noonday Press*

Old cherry stoner.

Spatulas

Spatulas look like big blunt-edged knives, forming part of a visual equation which states that a spatula is to a chef's knife as a child's blunt scissors are to shears. Although they are only occasionally used for cutting—as in making three thin, thin layers from a single round of Génoise—their resemblance to knives is more easily recognized than that of some of the other, sharper items in this chapter. As a matter of fact, the very best spatulas are made by the companies which also manufacture knives, and a spatula from, say, Le Roi de la Coupe, will have the same marvelously regal look as knives from that same firm.

Spatulas have a million uses. Look at the rubber ones used in pastry making—see Chapter 10—and then look at the metal spatulas we use to turn pancakes or hamburgers on a griddle and which we show you in Chapter 6, or the wooden, spoon-like ones in Chapter 5. Before the advent of rubber scrapers, only metal spatulas were used for cleaning griddles and pastry boards. But they are also used for turning, for cutting and cutting in, for folding and spreading: in short, they are as close to being an assistant chef as anything that most home cooks are likely to have at their disposal.

Oddly enough for such important objects, you will discover that spatulas of the very best quality are rather hard to find, although flimsy ones abound in heaps on counters in the local five-and-ten. Most American spatulas are of rather shoddy quality, so that if you live someplace where you simply cannot find a European tool, then you might want to Make Do instead with an artist's palette knife: really too thin to be the object of choice, but pleasantly flexible and useful for spreading icing and sandwich fillings.

WHAT TO LOOK FOR
What makes a good spatula? In general, the same solidity of construction that makes for a good knife. But we deal also with a great variation in flexibility, which ranges all the way from a tough blade that bends scarcely at all as it lifts a sheet of pastry to the thin steel one that bends

MOUSSE AU CHOCOLAT VENITIEN —VENETIAN CHOCOLATE MOUSSE

Rich chocolate mousse encased and layered in delicate chocolate genoese cake. Chocolate heaven!

CHOCOLATE GENOESE CAKE
6 eggs
1 cup superfine granulated sugar
4 ounces dark sweet chocolate
4 tablespoons liquid coffee
1 cup sifted cake flour (without baking powder)
4 tablespoons cool melted sweet butter (and extra for the cake pan)
A little rum or liqueur

CHOCOLATE MOUSSE
6 ounces dark sweet chocolate
5 tablespoons frozen sweet butter
3 egg yolks
2 tablespoons rum or any desired liqueur or brandy
3 egg whites
1 cup heavy cream, whipped

DECORATION
2 cups shredded dark sweet chocolate
A little confectioners sugar

CHOCOLATE GENOESE CAKE. Preheat the oven to 350°. Brush a 9-inch springform cake pan with cool melted sweet butter. Cut wax paper to fit the bottom of the pan, put it in, butter the pan again, and dust it lightly with flour. Beat the eggs and sugar in the mixer until very light and fluffy. Break the chocolate into small pieces. Put it in a little pan with the coffee and melt it over very low heat. Cool it a little, and fold it into the egg yolk mixture. Fold in the flour a little at a time. Sprinkle the melted butter over the top and mix it into the batter. Pour the mixture into the pan and bake 50 minutes. When it is baked, slide a sharp knife around the edge to loosen the cake and unmold it at once, very carefully, onto a wire cake rack. Allow it to cool a little.

Clean the springform pan, brush it lightly with vegetable oil, and invert the pan on a paper towel to drain excess oil. Line it with slices of the cake, as follows.

Cut one complete round of cake for the bottom of the pan, and set it in. Cut fingers (strips) of the cake to fit around the edge of the pan, and line the whole pan in this manner (reserve about a third of the cake for the layers). Sprinkle the cake with a little rum or liqueur. Set the cake aside.

CHOCOLATE MOUSSE. Cut the chocolate into pieces and put them on a glass ovenproof dish over a pan of simmering water. Work the chocolate with a spatula until it is melted, then take it off the heat and work in the sweet butter (cut in pieces) and the egg yolks (one at a time) in the same manner, with the spatula. Flavor with the rum or liqueur, and add a little warm water if the mixture is too thick. Beat the egg whites to soft peaks. Add the chocolate mixture to them and fold it in well, then fold in the whipped cream.

Spread a layer of the mousse in the cake-lined springform mold, then a layer of cake slices. Sprinkle the cake with more rum or liqueur, and continue to layer with the chocolate mousse and cake slices until the pan is full. Cover the mold with wax paper and put it in the refrigerator for about 2 hours, or in the freezer, to set. To serve, carefully turn the mousse out onto a cold flat serving platter. Sprinkle the top with the shredded chocolate, also stick some around the sides. Dust the top with a little confectioners sugar.
Net: 6 servings.

(From THE DIONE LUCAS BOOK OF FRENCH COOKING, by Dione Lucas and Marion Gorman, illustrated by Joseph S. Patti. Copyright © 1947 by Dione Lucas. Reprinted by permission of Little, Brown and Company.)

like a sapling as it follows the contours of a layer cake to spread the icing.

There is variation in size, too, from the little sandwich spreaders to the great majestic rods with which you slice horizontally through a cake layer. And there is a variation in edge. All spatulas are thin, but some have edges which are all-but-knife edges; and many of those meant for the pastry cook have serrated edges to help them deal with freshly baked cakes. In general, the metal used in spatulas is thinner than in the knives which are produced by the same companies; and thus we recommend that you treat these utensils with special care. Treasure them, because a good one, like a good man, is hard to find.

French Spatula 3.25

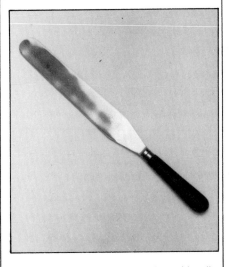

Stainless steel with black-painted wood handle, brass collar; 15½" overall; blade 10⅜" × 1⅝".
$10.00

This beautiful French spatula from Le Roi de la Coupe is one of our favorites, with a characteristic French look given by the brass cap joining the blade to the handle. Some of the more expensive of the Italian spatulas have full tangs running through the handles, which undoubtedly makes them strong, but unnecessarily strong, as it happens. This one has a moderately flexible blade with edges which are thin enough to cut through a Génoise layer or a pan of brownies but which are far from sharpened. The handle is made of wood, and the metal rod which runs through it is visible down at the very end. A lovely implement, which we dub *la reine de la coupe.*

Serrated Spatula 3.26

Stainless-steel blade with wood handle, brass rivets; 13½" overall; blade 9" × 1¼".
$8.00 ▲

The logo on the blade of this spatula shows the Alps, a bird, and William Tell's crossbow: how Swiss can you get? One edge of this blade is serrated sharply enough to let you use it as a lightweight bread knife or for cutting freshly baked cake layers; the other is blunt for spreading icings; and the two add up to a preferred baker's tool—or, for that matter, a tool for spreading butter on bread and then cutting the slices in half. There is no visible tang, but the blade is well secured by two brass rivets in the wooden handle. The stainless-steel blade is extremely flexible and strong, and the price is relatively low. A good buy.

Enormous Italian Spatula 3.27

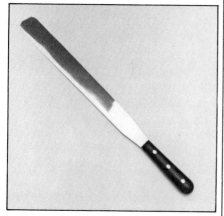

Stainless-steel blade with ebonized handle, brass rivets; 19¼" overall; blade 14" × 1½".
$17.50

A mammoth spatula which you will use for lifting a cake onto its serving plate, for removing a pizza from the oven, or for keeping a not-too-large fish intact while lifting it out of its poaching liquid. It is extraordinarily well-constructed, with a full tang which is thicker than the appropriately heavy-gauge blade. The metal blade is rigid from the handle halfway to the tip, and then becomes flexible. Although the blunted edges might make you think that this spatula was designed for use as a spreader, the weight and length of it—it is 19¼" from tip to tip—make it clear that it is a tool for lifting and moving—a fit companion and a good match for the enormous barbecue turner (6.115) in Chapter 6. By the way, we are only showing you spatulas with blades of stainless steel, since these implements do not have to take a great edge and the advantages of stainless are great in such tools.

A nineteenth-century spatula for lifting fish slices from their pan or their poaching broth.

Lighter Italian Spatula 3.28

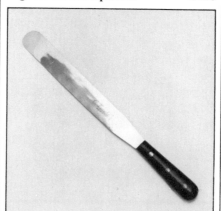

Stainless-steel blade with ebonized handle, brass rivets; 17" overall; blade 11¾" × 1½".
$12.00

A lighter, more flexible spatula from the maker of the preceding one. This is lighter but not flimsier, because it, too, has a full tang through the handle and three strong brass rivets. You will use it for mixing—it would fold and blend ingredients to perfection when used on a marble slab—and for most of the maneuvers you do with pastry. Once you get the knack of it, you will soon realize that a cold steel blade is always preferable to warm hands when you have to lift pastry into a pie plate or onto a cooky sheet. This is very well-constructed in stainless steel and ebonized wood; it has no sharp or pointed edges, and would be an excellent spreader—with it, you could frost whole acres of sheet cakes for the school bake sale with only a few generous swipes.

"He acted entirely for himself; in any circumstances he did what seemed pleasing to himself, what was most convenient, but at once the snobs would start copying him . . . If he was eating some special sweet and instead of taking his spoon used a knife, or a special implement of his own invention which he had had made for him by a silversmith, or with his fingers, it at once became wrong to eat it in any other way . . ."

Proust, *"Within a Budding Grove,"* from Remembrance of Things Past, *Random House edition, 1934*

Victorinox Flexible Spatula 3.29

Stainless steel with rosewood handle, nickel-silver rivets; 14⅞" overall; blade 10" × 1½". Also avail. with blade 8" or 12¼" long.
$9.35

You may have less trouble finding this spatula than many of the others we have shown; although it originates in Switzerland it is widely distributed in this country, and this size is especially popular here. It has an extremely flexible and lightweight blade which makes it useful for folding in egg whites if you, as the French do, have beaten them on a platter; it will do the job perfectly, preserving the air held in the whites while cutting neatly into the batter. Use it for spreading icings and sandwich fillings, too. We show you the largest size, nearly 15" in overall length, but you can also have it in smaller sizes. An adequate choice.

Small American Spatula 3.30

Stainless-steel blade with stained wood handle, brass rivets; 11½" overall; blade 7" × 1¼".
$1.50

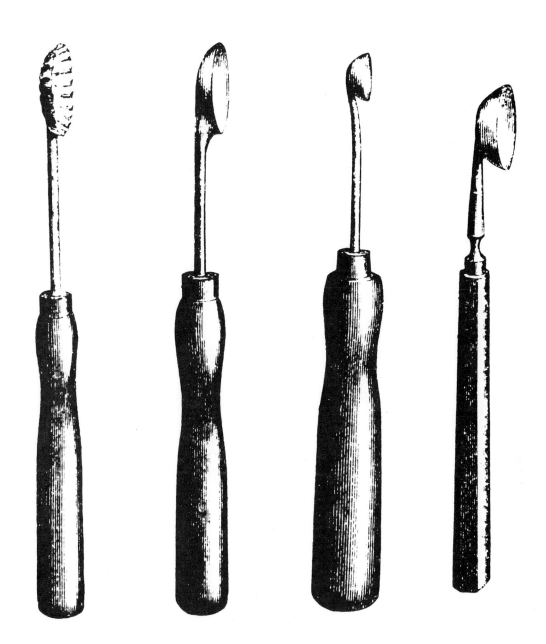

VEGETABLE SCOOPS

Cutting Instruments Other Than Knives

3

Continued from preceding page

Another easy one to find: inexpensive, domestically made, and useful for many small chores. The blade is fairly flexible, the reddish wooden handle is the only one of the lot which has a hole in the tip for hanging, and the whole thing is put together with a half-tang secured by two brass rivets. This is just under a foot in length; it is neither the most beautiful nor the sturdiest of the spatulas we show you, but it is perfectly adequate for many kitchen functions: for example, it will do all of those jobs you are now feeling a little uncomfortable about doing with a dinner knife.

Narrow Spatula for Lifting 3.31

Stainless-steel blade with rosewood handle, nickel-silver rivets; 14″ overall; blade 8″ × 1⅜″.
$12.00

We are so used to getting our cooking ideas from Europe that it comes as a pleasant shock to recognize an American influence on European cookware which is on a higher level than quick lunches. This slender-bladed spatula is actually a development of the broader American griddle spatulas, but it comes from Switzerland. The stainless-steel blade bends down sharply from the handle and then bends to become parallel again—technically, this is called an offset blade—and this shape makes it a logical support during lifting. We also see it as a useful mixing tool when you are working on a large and fairly flat surface—a pastry slab, for instance. The whole tool is about 14″ in length, of good quality, with a flexible blade. It has no tang, but rather has two heavy nickel-silver rivets.

BEURRE D'ANCHOIS–ANCHOVY BUTTER

8 tablespoons sweet butter
6 anchovy fillets
teaspoon lime juice
½ teaspoon freshly cracked white pepper
Beat the butter in an electric mixer until it is creamy. Mix in the anchovies, lime juice, and pepper. Roll up in wax paper and foil, freeze and use when needed. Net: 4 ounces (8 tablespoons).

(From THE DIONE LUCAS BOOK OF FRENCH COOKING, by Dione Lucas and Marion Gorman, illustrated by Joseph S. Patti. Copyright © 1947 by Dione Lucas. Reprinted by permission of Little, Brown and Company.)

Swedish Sandwich Spatula 3.32

Stainless-steel blade with rosewood handle, brass rivets; 8⅝″ overall; blade 4⅛″ × 1¼″.
$5.50

There is a special form of spatula which is used for making sandwiches; and what is more appropriate than that we show you first one from Sweden, where open-faced sandwiches are a tradition? This is short—8⅝″ in overall length—with a rounded blade that is serrated on one edge, smooth on the other. Think of it for spreading herb butters on thin white bread (does anyone remember watercress sandwiches?), or anchovy paste onto black bread, and then turning the blade over and cutting the bread into geometrical shapes with the serrated edge. Or, for that matter, you could use the serrated edge for creating decorative

patterns on the soft spread. This is a versatile tool; it can also be used for slicing tomatoes, or making paper-thin cuts of a cucumber. It is handsome and lightweight, with a flexible blade and a comfortable rosewood handle.

American Sandwich Spatula 3.33

Stainless steel with rosewood handle, brass rivets; 8¼″ overall; blade 3⅝″ × 1¼″.
$1.30

The American version of the sandwich spatula, slightly lesser in quality than the Swedish spreader but still very good. The stainless-steel blade is flexible, but not so flexible as the Scandinavian model; the handle is of rosewood, but not so well finished as the import. This spatula is slightly odd in that it has a handle shaped like that on a knife, a handle which imposes a given position on the user. Which is fine with a knife, but which makes no sense at all when you are dealing with a tool such as this one, which has two equally useful edges on the blade. But it would not really be uncomfortable to hold the handle backwards in order to spread peanut butter on your cracked-wheat bread, or cream cheese on your bagel. This is a tool which should be found in more kitchens than it is now; think of it the next time you are asked to bring the sandwiches to a picnic, or the next time you have to make twenty-four bologna sandwiches for a children's party.

Scissors and Shears

Scissors are marvelous kitchen tools, although we tend to think of them in the context of the rest of the house. But consider: with them you cut string for trussing poultry, and parchment and waxed paper for lining cake pans. With them you mince parsley, chives, and other herbs, you snip the ends off of green beans, you trim the lacy edges of poached eggs and the untidy protrusions of fish fillets and veal scallops. And all of these functions are performed by common shears, no different from the ones that you have in your desk drawer or your sewing box. The only requirement which sets them apart is that they be washable, without too many little spaces in which bits of food can hide and be spoiled.

If you loosen your preconceptions and think of scissors freshly for a moment, you will see that they are actually two knives, joined in the middle, with the meeting edges similar to the cutting edges of knife blades: a double lever, with the pin serving as fulcrum. Because of this fact, they are both singular and plural; "scissors are," but "a scissor is." Being two knives, they will rust and stain like knives if made of certain metals; they must be dried carefully, like knives; and they can be sharpened, like knives. But the thing that most sets them apart from knives is the muscular action which sets them in motion; and many people find that scissors are easier to control than a knife. Here in our office we have two warring factions whenever we have chives to cut: those who do it with a chef's knife and a wooden board, and those who do it with the biggest, sharpest pair of scissors in the supply closet.

All-Purpose Kitchen Shears 3.35

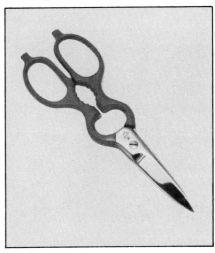

No-stain high-carbon Friodur steel; 8" long overall; blades 2⅝" long.

$19.50 ▲

This all-purpose pair of scissors is a version of the classic European kitchen shears. And when the makers say "all-purpose," they really mean it. Not content with producing a strong pair of shears with nonstaining, high-carbon steel blades of excellent quality, the manufacturers claim that various parts of the tool can be used as well for cracking nuts, for crushing sugar cubes, for removing bottle caps, for untwisting screws, hammering in nails, and prying off the lids of jars. We doubt it, frankly, although it's awfully nice of the company to try to supply us with such a versatile tool: but we're just as happy to accept it as a pair of well-made scissors for the kitchen. There is a serrated edge on one blade, making it easy to cut up pieces of chicken breast or fish. The steel handles have been coated in a bright orange plastic which will help you to locate it easily in a kitchen drawer and which provides some assistance to wet and slippery hands.

For the record, though, between the finger holes and the blade there are two oval openings, one with serrated edges, designed for the auxiliary uses we've mentioned: one is clearly meant for cap-prying, and the other should take charge of nutcracking jobs and unscrewing small bottle caps. The handles end in small flat tabs like the head of a screwdriver; using these as screwdrivers (or screw looseners) would undoubtedly mar the plastic finish.

Stainless-Steel Kitchen Shears 3.34

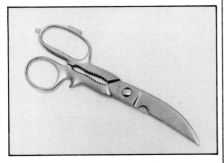

Stainless steel; 8½" long overall; blades 3¼" long.

$11.50

Not an inch of edge of these shears goes to waste. A pair of heavy-duty, high-quality, stainless-steel shears, fine for the job of cutting recipes and equipped to perform a multitude of other functions as well. In a pinch, you might have used regular scissors to tighten a screw or pry off a bottle top, which was sure to shorten the life span of your scissors. With these, your worries are over. They double as a bottle opener, poultry shears, screwdriver, and so forth, thanks to jutting nibs and serrated edges along the handles and blades. Nor do they sacrifice comfort. The handles have the delineated thumb and hand holds of regular sewing shears. A final bonus: the blades lift apart for cleaning when the shears are open to their fullest, an advantage they possess over the following example, 3.35.

93

Black-handled Shears   3.36

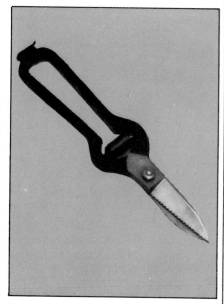

Carbon steel with plastic-coated handles; blue-steel spring; 8¾″ long overall; blades 2½″ long.

$21.50

This heavy, ugly little utensil is, as it clearly appears, extremely strong. It stands somewhere in between a pair of scissors—you *could* cut twine with it—and a pair of poultry shears; and we wouldn't doubt that you could do a little wire-snipping besides. The first thing you will notice that makes it different from the preceding scissors is the tension spring between the handles. Scissors work as primary levers—the blade goes down as the handle goes up. But a pair of shears like this has, in addition to lever action, a mighty spring which flares apart when the handles are unhooked and which takes a certain amount of effort to close. This means that your effort will be passed along in the form of cutting power in order to cleave whatever substance you're dealing with. The catch on the handle is there because this is beginning to be a dangerous instrument: notice the sharpness of the short, thick, sharp blades and the closeness of their fit. One blade is serrated, which is especially good when you are dealing with raw foods and with lobsters. And it has a lethal-looking spring; remember that the spring will have to be cleaned, and as it stands it creates a welcome environment for all of the chicken and meat juices that will surely flow into it.

Faceted Poultry Shears   3.37

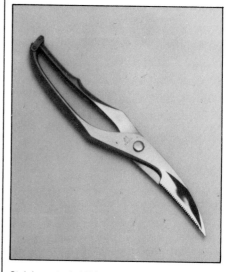

Stainless steel; 10¼″ long overall; blades 4″ long. Also avail. in chrome-plated steel.

$27.50

A beautiful pair of poultry shears, a 10¼″ length of faceted stainless steel. This is one of the most elegant pairs of shears we have to show you—a judgment due, in part, to the fact that all the workings are invisible, and in part to the handsome handles. The ugly spring which is such a dirt-catcher in the preceding pair is built into the joining of the blades here. And the catch that prevents that little bone-crusher from springing open in your drawer is here transformed into a flattened screw with an ornamented edge which you tighten to hold the blades together. This screw, unfortunately, has no stop to it, so it can be untwisted right out of its hole and lost; but this is probably not an implement that you will be using carelessly. Notice the slight curve of the blades (one of which is serrated), a shape preferred by some chefs when dealing with a chicken's bone structure. And notice that design is of some importance in poultry shears because of the fact that they will be brought to the table; these are far more than merely presentable.

CHICKEN AND APPLE CASSEROLE —CSIRKEBECSINALT ALMAVAL

4 servings

1 chicken, 3 pounds, cut into stewing pieces
2 carrots
2 parsnips
1 small onion

Salt
4 green or sour apples
1 tablespoon sugar
½ cup sour cream
2 tablespoons flour

1. Get a nice yellow-colored, plump chicken and not one that looks as if it died of starvation. Put chicken pieces in 2 quarts water in a large pot and bring to a boil. Skim.
2. Peel and trim vegetables and cut into chunks. Add to the chicken with 1 teaspoon salt. Cook very slowly till chicken is done.
3. Peel apples, core them, and cut into quarters. Put half of the chicken broth in a separate pot. In it cook the apple quarters with the sugar till they are almost soft.
4. Mix sour cream with flour and add to the apples. Stir and simmer for 2 more minutes.
5. Add chicken pieces and cook slowly for another 5 minutes. Adjust sugar and salt to taste according to the sourness of the apples.
6. Mix the cooked vegetables with the apple and chicken, or serve them separately.

(From THE CUISINE OF HUNGARY, by George Lang. Copyright © 1971 by George Lang. Reprinted by permission of Atheneum.)

Stainless-Steel Poultry Shears   3.38

Stainless steel; 10″ long overall; blades 4″ long.

$15.00

Another pair of shears clearly designed to come to the dinner table where, like a well-behaved child, it would offend no one. This pair has a concealed spring, cleaner but not so strong as the visible spring in our first heavy shears (3.36). But it also has a closing latch at the end of the handles which is far preferable to the closing screw of the preceding pair, 3.37. We find these awfully good looking, made entirely of stainless steel, polished on some surfaces, satin-finished on others. You will notice that most of the shears we have shown you have stainless-steel blades, since these are tools which will be involved constantly in the juices of foods, and since the uttermost sharpness of the blade is not essential. This is an elegantly curved tool, 10" long overall and with 4" blades; one of the gently curving blade edges has a generous rounded indentation for dealing with poultry bones.

Eagle Shears 3.39

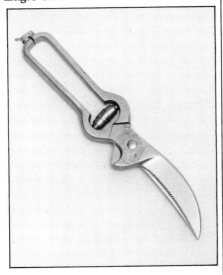

Chromed steel; 10¼" long overall; blades 4½" long.

$18.00

No, we don't expect you to barbecue an eagle for the Fourth of July, and then use these to cut it up for serving. As we are delighted when form and function marry, we don't deny this partnership an occasional whimsical turn. At the point where a heavy bolt joins the two blades of these chromed-steel shears, an eagle's head has been etched. This eagle really means business. When the slender, curving blades of the shears open, so does the eagle's beak, creating a small snipper suitable for those bits of bone or cartilage which the main blades can't handle with-

out mangling the bird. These shears are equipped with a strong tension spring and a secure catch at the base of the handles. The no-slip grips have a crosshatched pattern, vaguely resembling a bird's leg.

BRAISED GOOSE

In preparing goose, always consider the age of the bird. Young goose is tender and delicate, and excellent when roasted. On the other hand, an older goose—excellent in flavor—is rather tough, and should always be braised to tenderize it.

Serves 6-8

8-9 pound goose, cleaned and eviscerated
Salt and freshly ground black pepper
Goose neck, gizzard, liver, and heart, chopped
2 cloves garlic
½ teaspoon dried sage, crushed
Salt
2 cups dry white wine
5-6 cups beef stock or bouillon, as needed

Heat broiler. Wash goose and wipe dry, inside and out. Pull lower fat from inside goose. Rub cavity with salt and pepper. Place goose in heat-resistant glass baking dish and slide into hot broiler not too close to the flame. Broil approximately 15-20 minutes, turning frequently to brown on all sides. Remove from broiler; save the fat drippings.
Heat oven to 350 F. Put 2 tablespoons of the fat drippings into a roasting pan large enough to hold the goose. (The pan must have a cover). Add the gizzard, neck and heart, and sauté over moderate heat until lightly browned. Add garlic, sage, salt, and wine. Stirring, over low heat, bring just to the boiling point. Put goose into the mixture in roasting pan; immediately, add enough beef stock to cover goose ¼-way-up. Still over low heat, bring to a simmer. Cover and place in preheated 350 F. oven for 2-2½ hours. While it cooks, either rotate from time to time or turn over at least twice. Goose is done when leg moves easily at joint and juices run clear yellow. Strain pan juices, skim off fat, and serve juices as gravy.

(From THE GREAT COOKS COOK-BOOK, by The Good Cooking School. Copyright© 1974 by The Good Cooking School, Inc. Reprinted by permission of Ferguson/Doubleday.)

Curved Steel Shears 3.41

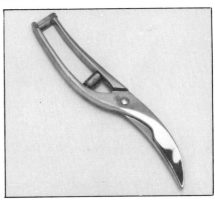

Chromed steel; 10" long overall; blades 4" long.
$22.50 ▲

The same company which made the beautiful stainless-steel shears we showed you above (3.38) also makes this variation with deeply curving blades. Now, the sense of the meeting among our experts was that straight blades are better, easier to control, more effectively sharpened than curved. But there are times when it is necessary for you to get down into something that you are carving, times when you are dealing with a big bird or a tricky anatomical problem, and when it would be useful to have a curved blade. This is a moderately curved pair of shears 10" long, with a visible spring for greater strength and a latch at the end of the handles to keep everything under control when you store the implement. Beautifully made in highly polished chromed steel, these shears should come elegantly to Thanksgiving dinner or to any other meal in which the carving is a part of the evening's entertainment.

COLVILLE APPLES

Highly Curved Steel Shears 3.42

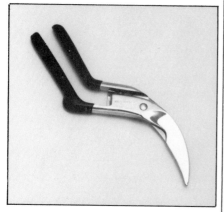

Chromed steel with black plastic-coated handles; 10¼" long overall; blades 3¾" long.

$20.00

Curved into an extreme arc, these are the shears which you would reach for to disjoint a large goose or a whole baby pig—a big job in which you want to get the blades down into the roast without your hand necessarily following. This is a marvelously constructed pair of shears with a hook latch on the joining and a visible spring, made of twisted wire, that is far easier to clean than the more common exposed springs of flattened, coiled steel. One blade has a serrated edge and a bone-breaking arc cut into it. The handles are of black plastic, the blades of German chromed steel; it is not awfully attractive, but it is most definitely a hard-working and serious piece of equipment.

Call it mincing knife or mezzaluna or hache-viande—the curved chopper has changed very little over the years. From French Domestic Cookery, *New York, 1855.*

Curved Chopping Devices

Because of the pre-eminence of France in the world of great cooking, we tend to think first of French recipes and French methods. And since the chef's knife is the ultimate French tool for chopping, we are sometimes so limited as to think that using it is the only way of cutting food into little pieces. (Oddly enough, it is also the essential cutting tool in that other great cuisine, the Chinese.) But in truth, the chef's knife is used in a variety of ways. When you hold down the tip with one hand and slap the back of the blade so that it bounces up and down over a bunch of parsley or a few flattened cloves of garlic, then it is being used with a rocking motion. And in many other parts of the world, that same rocking motion would be performed instead by a curved blade in a wooden bowl.

One of our experts remembered his grandmother chopping chicken livers and hard-boiled eggs in such a bowl; another recalled that his aunt used to chop garlic, lemon peel, and parsley together with a crescent-shaped blade in a little trough, and then have them ready to sprinkle over bubbling stews. These cutters to use in a bowl are either one-handed or two-handed, but they are at best crescent-shaped knives of the highest quality that are used by exerting pressure on both ends of the blade. You always use them on wood: a board if you must, but preferably in a trough or a bowl which matches the curve of the blade. And they are as valid a tool as a chef's knife; they are simply not the French way of doing things. And who are we, after all, to be chauvinistically French?

French Wooden Bowl and Chopper 3.43

Light, uncoated wood bowl and chopper handle, stainless-steel blade; bowl 5⅝" diam., 1¾" deep; chopper 6½" long overall; blade 4⅞" long, 2½" wide.

$15.00

Now that we have sworn that the French don't use these things, we will eat our words by showing you one from France. And it is true that this bowl would not be used there for chopping lots of onions or parsley or hard-cooked eggs. But for a tablespoon or two of parsley, for a few cloves of garlic, this bottom-heavy little bowl and its single-handled crescent knife would be just the thing. Did you know about chopping garlic on a half-teaspoonful of salt so that you don't lose any of the garlic juices? If you try it, just remember to subtract the salt from the total amount indicated in the recipe. This is a very appealing set, with the dark-brown, almost black ornamental bands burnt rather than painted onto the wooden bowl; with a light-colored natural wood finish on bowl and knife handle; and with a stainless-steel blade whose curve matches that of the bowl and which is meant to be used seriously, although perhaps not so seriously, as a great knife.

Highly Curved Steel Shears
French Wooden Bowl and Chopper
Mezzaluna I
Mezzaluna II
Birch Chopping Bowl
Carbon-Steel Double-Crescent Chopper

Mezzaluna I 3.44

Stainless-steel blade with dark wood handles, nickeled-steel collars; blade 10¾" along curve, 1⅞" wide.

$12.00 ▲

In Italy they call it a mezzaluna or half-moon, and it is a well-made, respectable, and expensive form of cutlery. This is no flimsy or occasional instrument, no gadget for erratic use, but rather a form of knife and conceivably the most reached-for item in the kitchen that possesses it. Look at the beautifully designed handles, made of smooth wood with flattened tops so that you are able to exert downward pressure comfortably with your palms. The knobs are attached to the long, curved stainless-steel blade with attachments surrounded by metal collars. Beautiful; easy to sharpen; and easier than a chef's knife to learn to use. We have to admit an affection for the romantic name; the only English name which really fits is *mincer*, which we feel does not express the heavy-duty, serious quality of this tool.

Mezzaluna II 3.45

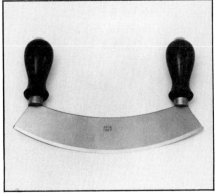

Stainless-steel blade with painted wood handles, nickeled-steel collars; blade 10⅜" along curve, 1⅞" wide.

$5.00

If Mezzaluna were the name of an automobile instead of a food chopper, the difference between this one and the one above would be very easy to illustrate. Both models have the same working part—a sharp, stainless-steel curved blade. The Mezzaluna I is the equivalent of the car with the mahogany dashboard and leather seats, while Mezzaluna II, with its simpler, less expensive painted wood handles, is the model with the vinyl upholstery. The handles for this model are knobs which you grasp as you would the gearshift of your Fiat—which means that there is not such a great ease of downward pressure. Nonetheless, it is a marvelous blade, able to cut through food with great dispatch, whether in a bowl or on a board. In any case, your *salsa di vongole* will be memorable.

Birch Chopping Bowl 3.46

Natural birch; 12½" diam.; 4" deep; 3-qt. capacity. Also avail. with capacity of 1 or 2 qts.

$9.99

To go with your mezzaluna you ought to have a wooden chopping bowl like this one. Made of good hard birch, it was carved from a single piece of wood and left untreated but smoothed to a silken finish. Although the interior will inevitably become scarred with the marks of your blade, it will also respond well to a good scrubbing with a rough sponge and soapy water. In it you chop hard-cooked eggs and mince turkey for cold salads, you prepare the livers for chopped chicken livers, and you shatter a cabbage into a million tiny pieces for coleslaw. We show you the 3-quart size, which is 12½" in diameter, but there are also two smaller sizes available. Resist the temptation to use this for a family-sized salad bowl, for you will never, never get the odor of garlic out of it once it is in.

Carbon-Steel Double-Crescent Chopper 3.47

Carbon-steel blades with natural wood handles, nickeled-steel collars; blades 14¾" along curve, 2⅛" wide.

$24.00

If we compared the Mezzaluna (3.44) to fancy automobiles, then this is the Land-Rover, the 4-wheel drive vehicle that is all work and no play. It is, first of all, uglier than the shining Italian examples. Its homeliness is relieved by the reassuring stamp "Peugeot" etched on the blades by means of business-like nuts and bolts. While perhaps the least esthetic mounting, it is the most practical. It permits you (carefully) to disassemble the razor-sharp carbon-steel blades in order to clean and dry them thoroughly, and to sharpen them. The generous (14¾") sweep of the double blades will cover a lot of territory in no time. Just be sure you have a bowl that is compatible with it.

A delightful approach to the first greens of spring, from The Scots Week-end *by Donald and Catherine Carswell, 1936: "The dumplings are made in the ordinary way with suet and flour seasoned with pepper and salt, but they are green with some of everything that grows in spring freshness, which you gather unobtrusively during the day. Pick the green buds of hawthorn, the succulent tips of nettles, grass and other green things, remembering that in this condition nothing is poisonous; include dandelion leaves, daisy stems, shoots of young corn and turnip-tops or anything that tastes sweet and harmless. Wash them and chop them fine. Work them into your dough until it is green through and through. For soup make small dumplings not more than an inch across; for stews and meats make them larger so that they can be cut up. They go with anything, are delicious and play the part of salad in wholesomeness."*

Other Mincing Devices

The pattern becomes clearer: we begin to understand that the essential thing in a cutter is the blade; all the rest is variation. The blade can be set at the end of a handle or between two knobs, it can be straight or curved or even round, or it can be part of such variously shaped devices as melon-ballers and swivel-bladed peelers. And its use varies according to the ways in which your hand can move. But always there is the sharpened edge. We now show you three utterly peculiar ways of applying a knife edge to food: two rolling mincers, which look like toy trucks and are pushed back and forth over your herbs like a child's toy over the rug; and one wonderful parsley chopper which ought to be brought to the table as frequently as your pepper mill, if you love the flavor of this delicate herb as much as we do.

French Rolling Mincer 3.48

Plastic with stainless-steel blades; 6" × 2¼"; 3⅝" high.

$7.50

It looks like nothing so much as a character in one of those Japanese sci-fi cartoons—it's not the hero, perhaps, but the puissant captain of a battalion of space creatures. What it is, is a clever French device for mincing: five good-sized wheellike steel blades rolling on a single axle, the whole thing enclosed in a plastic frame that covers the mechanism. A comfortable curved handle rises from the top of the machine, and a plastic shield with five slots in it covers the working parts and keeps food from getting into them to any serious degree. Lay your parsley or your onion slices on a board and then roll this little terror back and forth over the food until it is cut into sufficiently small pieces. The shield is removable—not too handily—so that you can turn the whole business upside down under a faucet for cleaning. It is strong and rather endearing to look at; and it can be used for cutting noodles and for tenderizing meat as well as for mincing.

Double Rolling Mincer 3.49

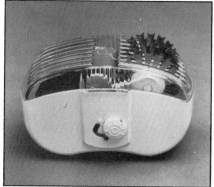

Plastic with stainless-steel blades; 5½" × 2¼"; 3¼" high; blades 2" diam.

$13.50

If the mincer above is a character in a sci-fi movie, then this is his Ultimate Weapon—people in our office kept cutting themselves on it. Which was completely unnecessary, by the way, had they only followed the simple instructions so haltingly written in that particular English which you know was looked up word for word in an office dictionary: "the casing made of chemical cleaners-resistant SUPER-plastics." It is a double terror, this one, with one set of five razor-edged wheels and another set of jagged-edged wheels. Each is held on an axle, and the two axles are attached to a see-sawlike device controlled by a button on the outside of the case. When the smooth wheels are up, then the jagged wheels are down, and vice-versa. And when the button is in the central position, then both sets of wheels are covered for safety. The main casing is of orange plastic which helps by shielding whatever knives are not in use. The mechanism comes apart for easy cleaning under the faucet, and it certainly works efficiently, cutting our trial cabbage and chives to a fine mince.

PUREE D'OSEILLE—SORREL SAUCE

[British measures]

Wash and chop very finely a small handful of sorrel leaves, not much more than ¼ lb. Melt it gently in ½ oz. of butter. Stir in, bit by bit, ¼ pint of cream previously boiled (this is important, for sorrel is very acid and there is a risk of the cream curdling when the two come into contact) and then thin it with a tablespoon or two of the stock from the dish the sauce is to accompany—usually veal or fish. A very excellent little sauce, which also makes, in larger quantities, a good accompaniment to poached eggs.

(From FRENCH PROVINCIAL COOKING, by Elizabeth David. Copyright © 1960, 1962, 1967, and 1969 by Elizabeth David. Published by Penguin Books. Reprinted by permission of Elizabeth David.)

Parsley Chopper 3.50

Aluminum with stainless-steel crank, plastic knob; 2¾" base diam.; 1¾" top diam.; 6⅜" high.

$13.50

Onions, the most minced of vegetables since time immemorial. These varieties were illustrated in an old British encyclopedia of cookery.

There is no agreement about the best way to chop parsley. We have told you about the interoffice strife here, involving the scissors crew versus the knife people; but there are other methods, too. We have just shown you the circular cutters which pass mercilessly back and forth over the parsley, chopping it into small pieces. Having tried them all, we feel that this device is probably the best solution: a cone-shaped parsley chopper made of satin-finished and black-surfaced aluminum. In the first place, it works, chopping up the herb handily in its rotating blades. In the second place, it fits over a jar when you want to mince a quantity of parsley for storage, but it is attractive enough to pass over a platter of meat right at the table. And finally, the whole thing is marvelously easy to take apart for cleaning and then to reassemble. Try putting both garlic and parsley in it before you turn the handle over a dish of stew. Pass it with cheese when you serve onion soup, with chives for the baked potatoes, with chocolate with ice cream, or with mint when you have a big fresh fruit salad.

"PARSLEY. *If there be nothing new under the sun, there are, at any rate, different uses found for the same thing; for this pretty aromatic herb was used in ancient times, as we learn from mythological narrative, to adorn the head of a hero, no less than Hercules: and now—was ever fall so great?—we moderns use it in connection with the head of —a calf. According to Homer's 'Iliad,' warriors fed their chariot steeds on parsley; and Pliny acquaints us with the fact that, as a symbol of mourning, it was admitted to furnish the funeral tables of the Romans.*"

Isabella Beeton, The Book of Household Management, *1861*

Mandolines

We've talked about knife edges which were straight and serrated, flat, crescent-shaped, round, and jagged. The one constant element is that they all move in one way or another over the food. But some clever person, dissatisfied even with such an abundance of uses, figured out that you could also move the food over the knife blade. This is, of course, the principle of the grater (Chapter 4); it is also the principle of the mandoline, a device widely used in Europe for cutting vegetables into consistently shaped strips. It is a narrow wooden board into which there have been fixed one or more cutters; depending on the size and shape of the cutters you can slice, julienne, or produce rippled cuts of cabbage, potatoes, carrots, beets, and any other firm food. The name, one assumes, derives from the musical instrument, and a distant derivation it must be—an honest eye sees that the musical instrument it really resembles is the washboard. We assume that some ancestor of the modern mandoline was made with steel wires instead of knife blades and that some poetic apprentice chef, astonished by the resemblance, dubbed it a mandoline. Lucky for the French tongue that he wasn't a ukelele player.

| **Swiss Mandoline** | 3.51 |

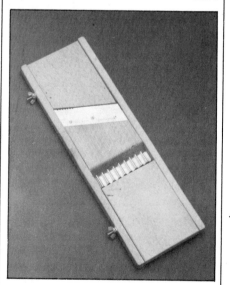

Light, uncoated wood frame with stainless-steel cutters; 14⅜" × 4½" overall; straight cutter 4" long; scalloped cutter 3⅝" long.
$15.95

This is the classic mandoline, a smoothly sanded, uncoated wooden board with two stainless-steel cutters set into it. The board is actually a frame holding three wooden inserts at minutely different levels; you can adjust the height of the inserts, and thus the thickness of the finished product, by tightening or loosening the screws on the side. With one surface up, you have a slanted steel cutting edge interrupted by a few notches at one end to catch your slippery potato and help to lead it into the blade. On the other surface are two bars that help to grab the food and guide it into the cutter, a rippled cutting blade or waffler. Remember that the virtue of this instrument is that it permits you to cut both consistently and rapidly, making paper-thin slices of cucumber or onion in minutes. It is, in a funny way, the ancestor of the super Cuisinart machine in Chapter 5.

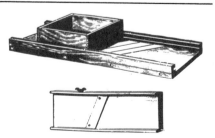

Slaw cutters and kraut cutters of an earlier day.

"I saw the magnificent entry of the French Ambassador Colbert, received in the Banqueting House. I had never seen a richer coach than that which he came in to Whitehall. Standing by his Majesty at dinner in the presence, there was of that rare fruit called the King-pine, growing in Barbadoes and the West Indies; the first of them I have ever seen. His Majesty having cut it up, was pleased to give me a piece off his own plate to taste of; but, in my opinion, it falls short of those ravishing varieties of deliciousness described in Captain Ligon's History, and others . . ."

The *Diary of John Evelyn, 1620–1706*

LES CRUDITES—RAW VEGETABLES

These are for the raw, crisp element of an hors-d'oeuvre. They consist of sliced very firm raw tomatoes, dressed with the minimum of oil, lemon and seasoning, sprinkled with finely chopped parsley. Cucumber sliced very thin and dressed in the same way. Radishes, washed, trimmed of excess greenery but left otherwise as God made them, rather than disguised as water lilies. Raw Florentine fennel, the outer leaves removed, the heart cut into quarters, and sprinkled with plenty of lemon juice to prevent it turning brown. Or alternatively cut into fine strips and dressed with oil, salt, lemon. Celery treated the same way. Very young raw broad beans piled on a dish in their pods, to be eaten *à la croque au sel*, i.e. simply with salt. Raw red or green peppers, cut into the thinnest of rounds, all seeds and core carefully removed, dressed with oil; prepared in advance and perhaps mixed with a few black olives.

Raw carrots (*carottes râpées*) very finely grated, the red part only, the yellow core being discarded; the resulting preparation, almost a purée, is mixed with a very small amount of finely chopped shallot, a little oil, lemon juice, salt, and a pinch of sugar if necessary, depending on the quality of the carrots.

Céleri-rave rémoulade, peeled and washed raw celeriac, shredded on the special crinkled blade of the *mandoline* into match-size strips, put straight into a bowl of acidulated water to preserve its colour; blanched a few seconds in boiling salted water, drained very dry, mixed

with a thick mayonnaise very highly seasoned with salt, mustard, and a good deal more vinegar than is ordinarily allowed.

One would not, of course, have all these things at the same time, the choice depending a good deal upon the time of year; only very small quantities of each should be served, so that nobody will be tempted to eat too much before the main course.

With a *plat de crudités* is usually served either a slice or two of *pâté de campagne*, salame sausage, or raw ham; in the south, olives and anchovies, or tunny fish in oil; in the north, pickled gherkins and sardines or fillets of mackerel in white wine; and if there is no other rich sauce, possibly an egg mayonnaise.

(From FRENCH PROVINCIAL COOKING, by Elizabeth David. Copyright © 1960, 1962, 1967, 1969 by Elizabeth David. Published by Penguin Books. Reprinted by permission of Elizabeth David.

German Cabbage Cutter　　　3.52

Light uncoated wood frame with high-carbon-steel blade; 20¾" × 7⅞" overall; food guide 7¾" × 6" × 2¼"; blade 7⅛" long.

$26.00

For those who take their coleslaw and sauerkraut seriously, we offer this monster mandoline, more properly called by the German equivalent of cabbage shredder. It is a simpler and more dramatic contraption than the mandoline above, with only one cutting blade, a length of sharpened carbon steel which lies diagonally across the wooden board. A big wooden box runs on tracks which are raised along either side of the board. You fit half of a cabbage into the box, lay your palm on top of it, and rub it

back and forth over the cutting edge. This is really big—nearly 2 feet long—and totally specialized—you would scarcely be able to shred a carrot or a few potatoes with it. And, like all graters and shredders, it will tend to cut your knuckles if you use it incautiously. But we do rather admire its drama and its unity of purpose.

Cutfix　　　3.53

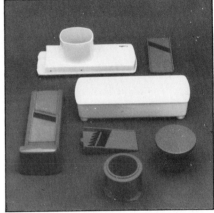

Plastic with stainless-steel blades; 9½" × 3¼"; 5⅞" high; cutting edges 2¼" long.

$16.00

We can give you a hundred reasons why we should have hated this, and yet we love it. It is a device developed in Germany for containing the works of a mandoline, for putting it at a distance from your knuckles so that you don't hurt yourself when you are slicing and julienning the food. And it's plastic; and it's small; and it's just the sort of bastardization of a grand old machine that we most detest. The trouble is that it works awfully well. Now picture this: a low plastic box on legs, about the size of an ice-cube tray, over which fits a cover with a chimney on top and a plunger to push things into the chimney. Between the cover and the box you insert a sliding frame into which you can fit various cutting edges; you slide the frame back and forth while you use the plunger to push a potato down through the chimney. With each slam of the frame, you get another cut off the potato. And it really works, making better French-fries than any other cutter we saw, keeping onion slices away from our sensitive noses, and letting us make potato or turnip or carrot cubes. So what if it *is* white and orange plastic; so what if the chimney is a little small, forcing you to cut your potatoes into slim shapes before you insert

Continued from preceding page

them. And so what if it isn't a Beautiful and Classic Device? It is efficient and easy to clean and to store. You could buy a mandoline, hang it on your pegboard for show, and keep this as your secret closet slicer.

Professional Steel Mandoline 3.54

Nickel-plated steel with high-carbon steel blades, varnished wood knob; 15½" × 4½"; 10¼" high with legs extended; cutting edges 4" long.

$66.50

A professional mandoline: no nonsense of pretty woods or flimsy plastic here, but rather heavy-gauge, nickel-plated steel with high-carbon steel blades. It is designed to be attached permanently to a table, although it can be used free-standing. Think of the classic mandoline such as 3.51, then make it of heavy non-staining metals, and then equip it with hinged V-shaped legs something like those on a deck chair. The legs prop the mandoline in position when you tilt it up on one end or the other to use the two blades, one rippled and one plain, or the julienne cutter, or the cutter that makes a wider strip suitable for French-fries. Levers control the thickness of all these cuts, making it possible to regulate the size of your pieces to a nicety. By making rippled cuts at right angles on the same piece of food you can make a waffled surface. To hold the food being cut there is a metal carriage on rails; the food is held down by a hinged lid with a knob, and this whole arrangement protects your fingers completely. There

might be a problem in cleaning it if you choose to screw it to your countertop, but a soapy sponge would undoubtedly remove the scent of onion before you slice apples. This is an expensive device, one that you'll find in the finest professional kitchens, and one well worth learning how to use—it's a bit complicated as well as costly. A first-rate slicer, it cuts with more versatility than even the magical Cuisinart machine. However, it will not grind, mix, grate, or purée—score one for the mechanized marvel.

GRATIN DAUPHINOIS— SCALLOPED POTATOES IN GARLIC AND CREAM

Serves 8

Gratin dauphinois, one of the simplest potato preparations, might very well be the most sublime manner of treating this lowly vegetable. A specialty of Grenoble, a town bordering the Alps, it is well known in the eastern part of France, particularly around the Rhone Valley, and is made in many restaurants with varying degrees of success. In Grenoble it is considered heretical to sprinkle the dish with cheese, but it is accepted in Lyon. The cheese is necessary if the dish is made mostly of milk, for it will help the gratin to achieve a beautiful golden color. However, many fine restaurants use a large amount of cream, or often only cream is used. In these cases, the potatoes will color beautifully without the help of the cheese. *It is essential that the potatoes, once sliced, are not soaked or rinsed in water as they would lose the starch needed for the dish to be smooth and creamy.*

Around the Grenoble area any left-over *gratin dauphinois* is eaten without reheating, accompanied by a green salad seasoned with oil, vinegar, and a generous amount of chopped garlic.

2 pounds boiling potatoes, peeled (about 5 to 6 cups)
2 cups milk
1½ cups heavy cream
1 large or 2 small cloves garlic, peeled, crushed, and minced to purée
¾ teaspoon salt
½ teaspoon freshly ground white pepper
1 tablespoon butter
½ cup grated Swiss cheese (about 2 ounces)

Wash the potatoes well and dry them thoroughly. Slice the potatoes ⅛ inch thick into a large saucepan. Add the milk, cream, garlic, salt, and pepper and bring the liquid to a boil over moderate heat, stirring with a wooden spatula to prevent scorching. Remove the pan from the heat. Pour the potato mixture into a well-buttered gratin dish or a shallow baking dish. Sprinkle the grated cheese over the mixture and bake on a baking sheet in a preheated 400° oven for about 1 hour. The potatoes are done when they are nicely browned and the tip of a knife pierces a potato easily.

Let the dish stand for 15 to 20 minutes before serving.

(From JACQUES PEPIN: A FRENCH CHEF COOKS AT HOME, by Jacques Pépin. Copyright © 1975 by Jacques Pépin. Reprinted by permission of Simon & Schuster.)

Slicing Machines and a French-Fry Cutter

Just another way of dealing with the circular blade, which we first discussed in considering the rolling mincers; but here the blade is single, enormous, and turned by a handle rather than by the resistance of a board. These are the machines that sit on the counter of your neighborhood deli, peeling off paper-thin slices of ham and roast beef for sandwiches. A man who works here confessed that he had always dreamed of having one, but that it had never occurred to him that they were available for home use. Yet in fact they are a standard item in home kitchens in Europe, where they are used for slicing bread and meat.

What you want is a slicer which is easy to clean, which has some means of adjusting the thickness of the slice, and which is designed to protect your fingers from the sharpness of the blade. If you decide to own one, then the next time you have a funny-shaped knob left over from the end of the ham you will be able to slice it neatly instead of giving up and chopping it up for hash or—shame—gnawing bits of it from the whole as you stand near the refrigerator. These slicing machines are especially good because they cut standard-sized slices rapidly and with a low expense of effort. When we were testing them, we found one of the temporary office workers listening intently. We learned that she is a member of a commune; frequently makes and serves dinner for 100; and had been so convinced by our comments that she planned to go out after work and buy a slicer for the commune. Nonelectrified, of course.

The slicer has a secure vacuum suction base and, in spite of the industrial look of it, folds up for storage to a width of only 3½ inches.

Bosch Electric Slicing Machine   3.57

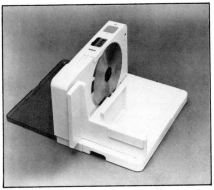

Plastic housing with stainless-steel blade; base 12⅜" X 9½" when open, 12⅜" X 3" when closed; 7½" high; blade 6⅝" diam.

$79.50

How careful are you? This Bosch slicer has numerous advantages over the preceding machine by Eva, save one. With the Eva, it is impossible to keep the blade spinning once you lift your finger from the control button, an absolute safety device on a potentially lethal machine. The same holds true of half the large orange button on the Bosch machine—the side of the button with the little depression. Press the other side of the button, however, and it stays down until pressed again for release. If you can remember what you are doing at all times, select this machine over the Eva. Its cover doubles as a tray to catch sliced food. The feeder tray comes off for cleaning (slide the black lever on the side); you can adjust the speed of the blade according to the hardness of the food; you are able to regulate the slice from tissue-thin to 1¼ inch thickness—quite a range. It comes with one of those double food pushers which interlock and fit into a ridge in the base. The whole affair folds to a slender four inches.

White Enamel Slicing Machine   3.55

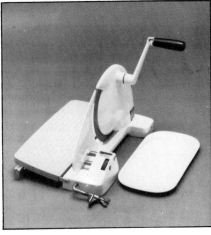

Enameled cast-aluminum body with plastic platform and handle, stainless-steel blade; 13" X 9½"; 8¼" high; blade 7¼" diam.

$57.50

This could well have come right from the neighborhood delicatessen, fresh from making roast-beef heroes and ham-and-provolone on rye. It is offered simply in white-enameled cast aluminum, with a grey plastic platform to catch the slices and a serrated wheel of stainless steel. It really looks just like a commercial slicer, although it is somewhat smaller, being only 8¼" high. You turn the handle with your right hand, causing the blade to rotate, and you push the meat towards the blade with your left hand, hoping that you don't cut your fingers. The thickness of the slices you get is determined by setting a calibrated dial, graded from 0 to 20 mm. A clamp and screw help to stabilize the machine by attaching it to the countertop, and the side platform folds up snugly for storage when the machine is not in use.

Eva Electric Slicing Machine   3.56

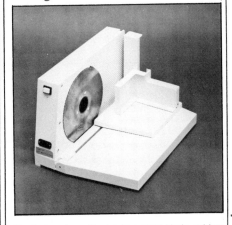

Plastic housing with stainless-steel blade, rubber suction base; base 14" X 10" when open, 14" X 3½" when closed; 8" high; blade 6⅝" diam.

$75.00

The advantage this slicer has over the preceding one is that it runs by electricity. This and the fact that the manufacturer has equipped it with a couple of safety devices. The machine is operated by a button on the side and the lethal blade will continue to rotate only so long as the button is depressed. Lift your finger and the machine stops: you can't leave this machine on and walk away. There is also a hand shield assembled from two pieces of squared-off ridged white plastic, for protection when slicing small pieces of food. Like the manual slicer, this one has a dial for adjusting the thickness of the slice from near transparent to ¾ inch, but it does not provide a tray for catching the slices as they emerge. The serrated blade twists off easily for washing. The rest of the machine cannot be immersed in water for washing, making cleaning the plethora of ridged and creviced surfaces somewhat tricky. Use a brush and running water.

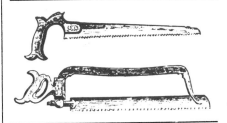

French-Fry Cutter 3.58

Tinned steel with stainless-steel blades, painted wood handles; 7¾″ × 3⅛″ overall; cutting grid 3⅛″ square.

$10.00

Our heretofore-mentioned commune member, planning dinners for her 100 really good friends, asked us about a French-fry cutter. This was a different matter from the meat slicer—we could show her three models of that device—but, unfortunately, there is no mechanical French-fry cutter which we feel offers substantial advantages over the chef's knife and board skillfully managed. The Cutfix (3.53), it is true, makes nicely shaped julienne strips, but it really wouldn't make a large amount quickly enough for her purposes; the professional mandoline (3.54) is effective, but it is expensive. The very best gadget we could find for cutting strips of potato was this simple device from Holland. It has been in the kitchen of one of our experts for 15 years, where it has apparently done yeoman service. But beware if offered a similar design: this is a tool of excellent quality, and the same design in a lesser-gauge steel might well cause you grief—so check on its construction. We have here a square frame of tinned steel from which handles bend upwards, bridged by cylindrical wooden knobs. In the square frame is a grid of stainless-steel knife blades. You cut one of the ends off your potato so you can stand it on end, and then grasp the handles of the cutter in both fists and slam it down hard, cutting through the vegetable. Even should the ends of the strips remain caught in the little squares, they would be pushed out by the pressure of the next potato.

Butter and Cheese Slicers, Scrapers, and Samplers

Butter presentations tend to be fanciful and slippery—those little curls floating in melting ice water in hotel dining rooms—or too simple to be considered food preparation at all. One woman we know unmolds a tub of whipped sweet butter onto a salad plate and serves it forth as a simulated country block of butter; and in Normandy, where the butter is the best in the world, it comes in lidded cylinders which fit upside down into stoneware crocks. But, given your ordinary American brick of butter, what are you doing with it? You could leave it alone—always a refreshing suggestion. Or you could cut it neatly into pats so that each of your guests can take a measured amount onto his plate. Or you could, Heaven help us, make curls, and then cope with the problem of keeping them firm. No real butter lover, however, would be contented with the paltry amount contained in the average butter curl. Nonetheless, we show you a choice of gadgets for preparing your butter for serving.

CHEESE CUTTERS

Cheese is fermented milk. Which is like saying that candy is cooked sugar, scarcely allowing for the great variation between a sourball and a Milky Way. And with cheese the spread is even wider, from the rich creamy curds of cottage cheese to the brittle tang of Parmesan, from the chalky bite of a fresh Chèvres to that high point of American culture, the individually wrapped slice of yellow processed cheese. We still recoil in horror from the memory of a piece of cheese we were served on an airplane which tasted of nothing—not soap, not butter, not chalk, but nothing, the absolute negation of taste—a crime when you consider the large number of wonderful cheeses that exist in the world.

Given the fact that cheeses vary, so does the equipment for dealing with them. You can make a pretty good guess about where a device comes from if you know the origin of the cheese it was meant for. A case in point: look at the beautiful long blades we show you first, for cutting slices and hunks out of large firm cheeses. They are made in Switzerland and Germany and are meant for Swiss and German cheeses such as Appenzeller and Münster. The little spade-shaped tool for gouging out chunks of hard cheese (3.65) is from Italy, as are the Parmesan and the Provolone on which it would be used. A parlor game, but fun to play. One more example: the gadget armed with a wire stretched taut to cut rubbery fresh cheese like Mozzarella; it comes, of course, from Italy.

"Nurse Andrews was simply fearful about butter . . . she had that maddening habit of asking for just an inch more bread to finish what she had on her plate, and then at the last mouthful . . . taking another helping. . . . 'When I was with Lady Tukes,' said Nurse Andrews, 'she had such a dainty little contrayvance for the buttah. It was a silvah Cupid balanced on the—on the bordah of a glass dish, holding a tahny fork. And when you wanted some buttah you simply pressed his foot and he bent down and speared you a piece. It was quite a gayme.'"

Katherine Mansfield

Butter Slicer 3.59

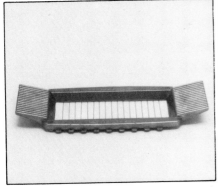

Cast aluminum with steel cutting wire; 7½″ × 3″.

$2.00 ▲

The simplest way of cutting pats of butter is with a knife; or you could use this inexpensive device, not unlike the apple corer and slicer (3.10) in concept, being a cast-aluminum frame which is pressed down over the food—in this case, a quarter-pound of butter—so that the set-in cutting edges can divide it neatly into 18 slices. The cutting edges here are wires rather than sharpened blades, reminding us of the fact that butter and cheese were once ordinarily cut with a taut wire. The slicer is a 7½″ light-weight frame of a pewter color, with a continuous wire looped back and forth across it at regular intervals. You could slice hard-cooked eggs with it, too, if you lack one of the special egg slicers such as those in Chapter 11. Remember that one of the cutters we have shown you in this chapter was called the mando-line? This little gadget shows the connection quite clearly.

Butter Curler 3.60

Stainless steel with rosewood handle, brass rivets; 7″ long; curling loop 1¼″ wide.

$2.50 ▲

If you should want to get pretentious with your butter, then you could carve it with one of the nifty sculptured melon-ball cutters we showed you earlier—how about 3.16? Or you could buy a real butter curler from Germany, like this one. It is a small tool with a rosewood handle and a curved stainless-steel blade. The blade is bent into something resembling Little Bo-Peep's crook and has a sharpened serrated edge. Not for chastising the sheep, but for scraping across the top of a hard slab of butter and pulling off a shell-like ribbed curl. Of course, then your troubles begin as you try to keep it from melting out of its lovely contours (a bowlful of finely pulverized ice is your best bet)—but this gadget will help you to make an attractive form to begin with. It is 7 inches long in its most useful size.

Double-handled Cheese Cutter 3.61

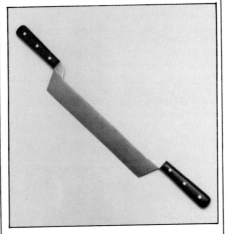

Stainless-steel blade with rosewood handles, nickel-silver rivets; 23″ overall; blade 11½″ × 1¾″.

$25.00

This cutter is shaped so that you lean your weight on it, pressing down hard to overcome the resistance of a large, firm cheese such as a Gruyère, a Sapsago, or a Cheddar. We are talking, of course, not of the tinfoil-wrapped tidbits you buy in your supermarket, but of great heavy wheels, cheeses which would defeat your dinner knife or paring knife entirely. And so you buy a tool which is as eminent as the cheese itself: expensive and well-made, with a full tang held within each of the rosewood handles by three nickel-silver rivets. The raised handles allow you to press down hard with no fear that your knuckles will be bruised on the table top. This is beautifully constructed and *huge:* just under two feet long, with five-inch handles. Made in Germany, it is in the same tradition as the superb German knives in Chapter 2.

Swiss Cheese Cutter 3.62

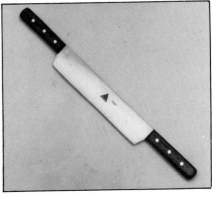

Stainless-steel blade with wood handles, nickel-silver rivets; 19″ overall; blade 9½″ × 2″.

$24.00

Don't be misled by the double handles; this cutter and the preceding one are both really knives, and they are fine knives. This one is from Switzerland where, according to our theory, it was made to cut wedges out of the great wheels of firm cheese—Emmenthaler, Appenzeller, and Gruyère, among others made in that country. It has a good stainless-steel blade and rosewood handles, and it is designed so that you can bear down on it with both hands, pressing down on a large wheel of cheese. It is not quite so beautiful as the German cutter, but neither is it so expensive; and it is wonderfully made, arrow-straight across the top and 19″ long, with the blades extending into rattails which are encased in the wooden handle on either end.

Pat of Butter.

Curled Butter.

105

Single-handled Cheese Cutter 3.63

Stainless-steel blade with rosewood handle, nickel-silver rivets; 13½″ overall; blade 8¼″ × 1½″.

$24.00

This is basically the same knife as the double-handled Swiss one, 3.62, coming from the same manufacturer and made with the same solid construction in stainless steel and wood. But it has only one handle and is, therefore, likely to be more useful than the previous two, since with it you can attack a cheese from one side alone. Use it as you would a dinner knife in cutting into a Brie, or as you would a paring knife in cutting a slice out of an Edam or a Gouda. In addition to being more versatile, it is sufficiently lower in price than the two-handled knife to make it worth considering. The handle is raised above the blade to help you make a straight, firm cut into a piece of cheese, or a cheesecake, or, for that matter, a chocolate cake or a cucumber. It is, in fact, closer to a knife than the others, and is well made, with a three-quarter tang and an 8¼-inch stainless-steel blade.

"It is well known that some persons like cheese in a state of decay, and even 'alive.' There is no accounting for tastes, and it may be hard to show why mould, which is vegetation, should not be eaten as well as salad, or maggots as well as eels. But, generally speaking, decomposing bodies are not wholesome eating, and the line must be drawn somewhere."

Isabella Beeton, Book of Household Management, *1861*

Cheese Chopper 3.64

Stainless steel with rosewood handle; 8⅜″ × 5⅞″ overall; blade 5⅞″ × 5⅛″.

$24.00

So far we have approached our cheese from two sides and from one side; now, with this tool we attack it directly from above with a guillotine-like knife. This is a large, rigid blade of stainless steel, nearly square in shape, with tangs that extend upward from either end of the blade to be incorporated into a wooden handle that arches over the blade. It is interesting because it is so much more blade than handle, but it is probably not the very best way to slice cheese, being difficult to use with the proper amount of force. As a matter of fact, it would work well on a board to chop parsley or onions; or perhaps you could use it to chop already sliced cheese into a fine mince for sprinkling on top of a gratin.

Cheese Scraper and Gouger 3.65

Stainless-steel blade with painted wood handle; 9¼″ long overall; blade 5⅛″ × 2¼″.

$10.00

Suppose it's a winter's evening and you take a half-wheel of Gruyère or Emmenthaler and prop it up on a platter so you can toast its cut surface in front of the fire in your fireplace. As the cheese melts, you scrape it off with—surprise—just such a handy little scraper as this, catching the buttery mass on a pewter-plate filled with boiled new potatoes and pickles. That is a raclette, and it is heaven. Or take this same little scraper and use it to approach the hardest cheese you can find, the sort of aged Parmesan which has defeated every middling-size knife with which you have foolishly tried to cut it. You just gouge out a chunk of cheese with this and stick it in your table grater, or nibble it with a perfectly ripened pear. This is a small tool from Italy, its stainless-steel blade caught in the chromed collar of a painted wooden handle. The blade is extraordinarily rigid and thick, sharpened only halfway up from the point, and it will not—*will not*—break. It is uncannily like a sculptor's tool, but it is in addition both useful and inexpensive.

Cheese Sampler 3.66

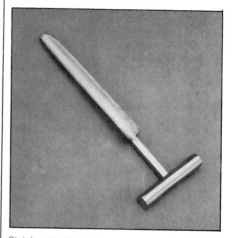

Stainless steel; 6¼″ long.

$7.00

Once cut, an unready Brie will not continue to ripen, but will show its chalky core forever and ever as it decays; but how are you to tell whether it is ripe or not if you can't cut it in the first place? You can pinch and sniff, of course; and we are sure that real cheese people have other tests known only to the cognoscenti. But one simple thing you can do is pierce it with this stainless-steel sampler, pull out a piece of cheese to

Antique cutting tools from the collection of James Beard

Continued from preceding page

check its condition, and then put it back again, leaving the cheese intact for all practical purposes. This is a professional's tool, made in Italy to stick into the heart of a Taleggio or a Bel Paese; it has a T-shaped handle which you grasp in your palm as you pull, and well-sharpened edges on the troughlike blade. In fact, it is not unlike the simplest form of corkscrew, and we admire it—unlike the guillotine-shaped chopper (3.64)—because it seems to have taken into account the proper use of specific muscles in performing a specific action.

"Cheese is to be chosen by its moist and smooth coat; if old cheese be rough-coated, rugged or dry at top, beware of little worms or mites: if it be overfull of holes, moist or spongy, it is subject to maggots. If any soft or perished place appear on the outside, try how deep it goes, for the greater part may be hid within."

Mrs. Hannah Glasse

SCALOPPINE DI VITELLO CON
PISELLI—VEAL SCALOPPINE WITH
PEAS

1 pound veal scaloppine, cut into 4-inch
    strips and as thin as possible
1 cup green peas
1 medium onion, finely chopped
4 tablespoons butter or half butter and
    half olive oil
1 cup chopped tomato
1 teaspoon dried basil or 1 tablespoon
    chopped fresh basil
Salt and freshly ground black pepper
Flour
½ cup imported Marsala
½ pound mozzarella cheese, sliced
    ½ inch thick
Grated Parmesan cheese

Cover peas with water and cook until they are almost tender. Drain and set aside.

In a separate pot, sauté onions in 2 tablespoons of the butter. When onion wilts, add tomato, basil and salt and pepper to taste. Cover, and simmer over low heat for 10 minutes. Then add peas and simmer for 5 minutes more. Set aside.

Dust the veal with flour. Heat remaining butter in a wide skillet. When the butter is hot, add veal and cook over high heat, turning constantly. As soon as veal colors, add wine and salt and pepper

to taste. Continue tossing veal.

When wine thickens, after several minutes, turn off heat. Place a slice of mozzarella on each piece of veal and broil under high heat. When edges of mozzarella begin to brown, pour peas and tomatoes over it, sprinkle with Parmesan cheese and return to broiler for 2 to 3 minutes. Serve immediately to 4.

(From ITALIAN FAMILY COOKING, by Edward Giobbi, illustrated by Cham, Lisa, and Gena Giobbi. Copyright © 1971 by Edward Giobbi. Reprinted by permission of Random House.)

Double-Wire Cheese Cutter   3.67

Walnut handle with stainless-steel rod, wire cutter; 9½″ overall; cutting wires 4¾″ long.

$16.00

What do you use when you want to cut slices out of a cheese which is too hard for a table knife but which crumbles pathetically under the onslaught of a heavy stainless-steel blade? You retreat to the oldest method of cutting cheese, and use a wire. Now, if you want to be really folksy you could draw a wire taut between your fingers and pass it through a wedge of cheese; but it is more sensible to use this double-wire cheese cutter. There is a steel rod extending about 5 inches from a walnut handle; at the end of the rod is a cap which holds the wires away from the rod and which controls the tension. With this implement you can cut thin slices of Mozzarella for your Eggplant Parmesan or your Scaloppine di Vitello con Piselli (recipe.)

Scandinavian Cheese Slicer   3.68
and Server

Stainless steel with stained wood handle; 8⅞″ long overall; head 3¼″ × 3″.

$4.50 ▲

Of all the cheese cutters we have discussed, this is the one that you are most likely to possess; every cheese shop sells them to hungry shoppers, seducing them on the way with tastes of their fine Fontina and Edam cheeses. Many manufacturers make these, and we are recommending a very nice-quality cutter from Sweden, suggesting that you use it to shave thin pieces of Havarti or Jarlsberg, which you will then lay on rye toast and cover with equally thin slices of radish and cucumber. Or use it at the table to cut and serve your cheeses, whether with water biscuits or slices of apple; it is quite presentable enough to appear at the festive board. If you can't get our brand, then look for a similar cutter with a good wooden handle and a stainless-steel blade with the sharpened slit set at a proper angle for cutting. This one is nearly 9 inches long, solidly made, and has a five-year guarantee from a respected manufacturer. It is a bargain when you consider the really insignificant price.

Carême illustrated this use of aspic cutouts in Le Pâtissier Royal.

Cutters for Truffles and Other Garnishes

Given the state of the economy, it seems sheer madness to offer you an Italian cutter for white truffles, then six different sets of tools for cutting black truffles into decorative shapes. Never cheap, both kinds of fungi have become astronomically expensive, so that *Larousse*'s warning that fresh truffles must be lightly cooked in butter seems like a cautionary note from a fairy tale, and the recipes for making fritters out of thick slices of this dark fungus, or for roasting whole truffles in the coals, read like alchemists' notes. You aren't going to use truffles for your main course, but they are still available in cans, and the thrifty cook knows that a truffle goes farthest when it is cut into tiny pieces and tucked into a pâté or used to decorate a chaud-froid or an aspic-glazed bird.

The sets we show you are both very expensive and very high in quality, with cutting edges as sharp as those on a set of knives. They are beautifully made so that they will not deform when they are impressed on a resistant slice of truffle, or anything else you might wield them on. Because, of course, their use is not restricted to cutting truffles. You can use them as well for cutting aspic into decorative shapes for ornamenting cold salads, or for forming tiny crescents out of puff pastry to decorate the surface of a pâté en croûte. You could decorate a rice salad with tiny spades and diamonds of pimiento and black olives; cut hearts and stars from skinned and seeded tomatoes to lay at the center of a canapé; or make leaf-shaped forms of candied angelica to tuck under a butter-cream posy on top of a decorated cake.

Italian Truffle Cutters 3.70

Tinned steel; set of 12, with container; each ⅝" to ⅞" diam., ¾" deep; container 2½" diam.
$9.25

The tiniest set of cutters we are going to show you: the box itself is no bigger than a slice out of the center of a good-sized truffle. And into it fit 12 tiny cutters, each one different, each one made from a single piece of tinned steel bent into shape, one raw edge folded over, the other knife-sharp. The shapes are heart, spade, club, triangle, crescent, teardrop, five- and six-pointed star, barquette, rosette, and curved square. These are tiny and well-made, and they fit snugly into their own 2½-inch tin box. They are, in addition, by far the least expensive set we are showing you, and far from the least in quality. The good construction and low price make this our pick of the lot.

Truffle Slicer 3.69

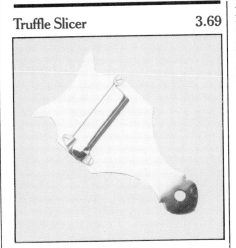

Stainless steel; 7¾" X 3¼", blade 2¼" long.
$6.00

Anyone can slice cheese, but it takes a person of substance to slice white truffles. This elegant utensil is, in truth, just another version of the cheese scraper we have just shown you, but it is more elegantly made, as befits an implement for slicing those expensive fungi. This is a paddle of stainless steel, 7¾ inches long, shaped rather like a small colonial horn-book; in the wide part of the paddle there is an opening with a covering blade of razor-sharp stainless steel. This blade is adjusted before use with a twist of a metal screw which raises and lowers it as though it were the awning of a house in the tropics; this action makes the slices you are cutting thinner or thicker. Use this pretty little thing to slice cheese, if you like, or dark chocolate; but remember that it was made in Italy for cutting thin slices of the wonderful, garlicky Piedmontese white truffles, and respect it accordingly.

Truffle Cutters in Plastic Box 3.71

Tinned steel with clear plastic container; set of 42, ranging from ¼" to 1½" diam.; each ¾" deep; container 3¼" X 2⅛".
$44.00

Forty-two cutters in a clear plastic box only 3¼ inches long: a feat achieved by tucking one form inside another so that you end up with only seven shapes, each one in six sizes graduated from small to infinitesimal. There are miniature circles, squares, triangles, barquettes, diamonds, teardrops, and parallelograms, each elegantly formed from a single piece of tin. This set was produced in Germany by a company that makes fine knives; it is of superb quality. But we ought to ask you to notice the price, and compare it with the price of the less ambitious Italian set just above.

"Pliny was very much inclined to range the truffles amidst astonishing prodigies. He fancied that he saw it at its birth increase without roots, without the slightest fibre, without the least capillary vessel likely to transmit to it nutritious juices; therefore he believed that, sown by thunder-bolts in the autumnal storms, this daughter of thunder grew like minerals by juxta-position."

The Pantropheon, *by Alexis Soyer, 1853*

Larger Truffle Cutters 3.72

Tinned steel with clear plastic container; set of 24, ranging from ⅜″ to 1½″ diam.; each ¾″ deep; container 4½″ diam.

$44.00

From the same company that distributes the preceding cutters comes this set of slightly larger ones suitable for cutting pastry and aspic shapes as well as truffles; as a matter of fact, these are getting rather large for the truffle category and would take altogether too much of that priceless black fungus for each shape. This is one of the most beautiful sets we have ever seen, with its elongated Gothic triangle, trefoil, and shield, its clearly molded pig, bird, rabbit, and fish, its elegantly formed heart and cloverleaf and stars and fleur-de-lys. It is also formidably expensive; but if you took one of the tin forms between your fingers and tried to press it out of shape you would understand the reason for the cost—no matter how hard you squeezed, you could scarcely affect it. Most of the shapes are formed without a single seam, just pressed with enormous precision from a cylinder of tin. There are 24 perfectly rigid shapes altogether, the largest being a four-leaf clover nearly large enough to be a cooky cutter.

Large Tin of Truffle Cutters 3.73

Tinned steel with tinned-steel container; set of 75, ranging from ¼″ to 1½″ diam.; each ¾″ deep; container 5⅞″ diam.

$115.00

The Rolls-Royce of the group: an enchanting round tin of 75 assorted cutters, including all of the shapes in the last two sets, which come from the same distributor, and adding some new ones. For example: a tiny man-in-the-moon, a tulip, a mother rabbit and a baby rabbit, and comma-shaped paisley-print forms. We brooded over these in the office, loving them because they are so beautifully made, but a little shy of them because of the monumental cost. But look: if you cut aspic or hard-boiled egg whites instead of truffles, that would be a tremendous saving right off, right? Pour a really stiff aspic into a flat jelly-roll pan; let it harden; and then have a marvelous time cutting out diamonds and Christmas trees and stars and the most glorious flower shapes available. Made of tin in Germany, and sold in a flat round tin just under 6″ in diameter, these are an enchanting gift for the person with an almost-perfect batterie de cuisine.

French Gelée Cutters 3.74

Tinned steel with clear plastic container; set of 12, ranging from 1″ to 1¼″ diam.; each 1⅛″ deep; container 5¼″ diam.

$25.00

A French set of rather large cutters in a plastic box; these are interestingly made in that the noncutting edge of each has been soldered to a flat base, with the joinings smoothed out and made nearly invisible. They are strong and easy to hold, each one about an inch across; they are made of tin and come in 12 useful shapes—heart, diamond, cross, spade, star, comma, clover, crescent, semicircle, teardrop, half-ring and Gothic square. Not so evocative of gasps of admiration as the German sets we have shown you, but of really good quality and really sturdy construction.

Some historians and etymologists believe that the word aspic *comes from the serpent, the asp, "whose icy coldness recalls that of the jelly," but Prosper Montagné, who compiled* Larousse Gastronomique, *considers it more reasonable to assume that the word came from the Greek* aspis, *meaning shield, the form in which the first aspic molds were made.*

Larger Truffle Cutters
Large Tin of Truffle Cutters
French Gelée Cutters
Alphabet Cutters
Chrome-plated Steel Nutcracker
Double Wooden Nutcracker

Alphabet Cutters	3.75

Tinned steel with tinned-steel container; set of 27, ranging from 1¼″ to 1½″ diam.; each ¾″ deep; container 6″ diam.

$59.50

Every letter of the alphabet fits into this tin box 6 inches in diameter: every one from A to Z, plus a funny squared-off funnel which is meant to produce a period when its base is applied to your raw material. The letters are clearly formed in block writing, each one about an inch high, and where the shape is a fragile one they have been reinforced by the application of a bar of tin across the noncutting edge. Most of them are made of two strips of tin, neatly welded together. A good set, and quite useful for someone who loves to decorate foods. We know lots of people who don't like layer cakes. If you have one in your family, why not surprise him on his next birthday by baking a cherry pie and spelling out your Best Wishes in pastry letters over the surface of the fruit?

Any modern cook with plenty of truffles and aspic could reproduce this nineteenth-century design by Carême.

Nutcrackers

We began the chapter with peeling, and we will end it in the same way. But now the peels are hard and woody rather than soft and slippery: in fact, they are the shells of nuts. Nuts taste better and are much cheaper when you buy them whole. When you use them immediately after they are shelled there is less chance for the oils to become rancid upon exposure to air; and by the way, we wonder how many people know that there is a season for nuts, just as there is for apples and grapes? They are at their best—because they are freshest—in autumn, and so there is good reason for the walnuts in your Thanksgiving cornucopia and the boxes of pecans given as gifts at Christmas time.

Chrome-plated Steel Nutcracker	3.76

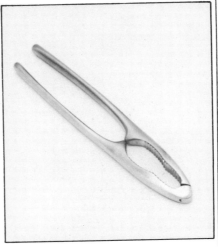

Chrome-plated steel; 7″ long.

$3.00

The simplest form of nutcracker, made of two lengths of chrome-plated steel, with a good stiff hinge at one end and the tips of the smooth handles some 7″ away. And somewhere in between those extremities the metal is molded and carved into ridges which grasp the nut as you press on the ends, exerting enough pressure to crack the shell. A classic design, neither markedly cheap nor especially expensive, and just as useful for cracking lobster and crab claws as it would be for filberts and pecans.

Wilfred Funk has traced the word walnut from the Anglo-Saxon wealhhnutu, wealh meaning foreign, hnutu meaning nut. Hence, the name of a nut that was foreign to the British Isles.

Double Wooden Nutcracker	3.77

Lacquered light wood; 2″ base diam., 4⅝″ high.

$3.95

We said that the steel nutcracker (3.76) was the simplest. Perhaps we should take that back. This is the inexorable nutcracker, employing the force of turning a screw in order to crack the shell of the nut placed in the round opening. Bits of shell are guaranteed not to fly about the room, nor will the nutmeat be pulverized. You are, indeed, likely to wind up with it still intact. The nutcracker is well-polished wood. Use by turning the screw up from the bottom into the desired opening, the large one for your Grade A walnuts, and the smaller one for fresh filberts. When not in use, it will stand on your tabletop or counter like a rustic toy. This sturdy, effective tool receives our enthusiastic recommendation.

English Nutcracker   3.78

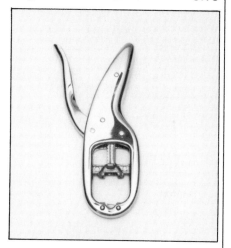

Chrome-plated steel; 7½″ × 2⅜″.

$12.00 ▲

What the world needs now is a really innovative nutcracker, like this chrome-plated crank-operated gadget from England. It looks and feels rather like a staple gun or a hole-puncher. One end has two hand grips which, when squeezed together, serve to crank up a rack and a lifting knob which fit into an oval opening. You squeeze the handles and with each squeeze you raise the rack another step until the nut which rests on it is cracked by the pressure you have created. The theory is that sudden pressure causes the nut to shatter, while gradual pressure merely breaks the shell. This gadget is not bad; it's inexpensive; and it really does do a good job, better than most, of cracking the shells without shattering the meat. Useful for crab and lobster claws also, of course, and valuable in that it comes with a three-year guarantee.

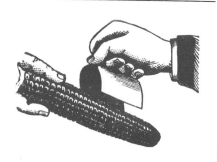

CORN GRATER

LONG, OR VEGETABLE, CUTTER BOX

Texas Native Inertia Nutcracker   3.79

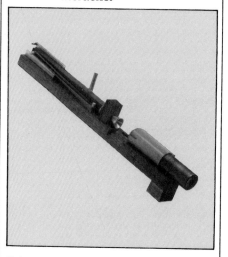

Oak with steel weight, aluminum guides; 17½″ long.

$12.98

Why do nutcrackers tend to be so nutty? This one is a dilly, the wacky contraption which we chose to end the chapter. Despite its looks it is neither a Rube Goldberg device nor a project made in Boy's Shop IV, but rather an effective method of cracking pecans; it was sent to us from North Carolina, where cracking nuts is a major industry. The maker tells us that this machine cracked the pecans that went to the moon on the Apollo flights, and that it is the official Show Nutcracker of the Texas Pecan Growers' Association; in short, it is the Real Thing, and not some baroque hoax. It is, as you see, a thick, 17½-inch bar of oak on which a short upright post has been strongly fastened. On one side of the post there is attached a heavy metal cup, backed by a metal disc on the other side of the post. On the other side of the post there is mounted on the base a simple battering-ram mechanism that works on rubber-band power, forcing its ram—another oaken rod—against the metal plate on the post with great force. Got that? There's even more. On the cup-bearing side of the post a removable cylinder of weighty steel lies on the base of the machine. Between the end of this cylinder and the cup place a pecan. You pull back on the catapult, using the little handle provided, and at the same time you lean on the cylinder so as to keep it in place and you let go; and miraculously, the shell of the pecan cracks and the meat remains intact. Billing itself as the Texas Native Inertia Nutcracker, not only does this machine work on all sorts of nuts, but it is remarkably inexpensive. One woman in our office ordered a dozen, planning to give them as thank-you gifts for the next few years.

"All the classical allusion which connect nuts and marriage have reference to the walnut. The nut was also supposed to be precious for its uses. Its oil was good for bald heads, for the painter's palette, for lamps, and for worms. . . . The walnut not only cured worms, it cured hydrophobia: and was . . . an antidote to poison."

Kettner's Book of the Table, *1877*

American Nutmeg Grater, 1896, from the collection of George Lang

Grinders, Crushers, Mashers, Refiners, and Extractors

The quality of the flavor and texture of your ingredients distinguishes cuisine from food, determines whether you dine or eat. The Chinese are eminently aware of the interdependent relationship of these two elements. But while they achieve wonders by cutting and stirring with mainly a cleaver and a wok, the modern kitchen can avail itself of tools of every description, hand or electrically operated, primitive or the most advanced, to refine texture and, in the process, enhance and intensify flavor. They will allow you to begin with raw materials, the basic ingredients, rather than settling for the preflavored and preprocessed foods that have flooded the market, are expensive, and do no credit to the cook. You can have custom spice blends rather than packaged combinations, freshly grated cheese rather than sawdust.

THE TEXTURE-CHANGING OPERATIONS

Changing the texture of food involves you in tenderizing, smoothing, reducing, concentrating, blending, expanding, and separating it, either in the raw or cooked state. Aside from knives (see Chapter 2) the tools for pounding, grinding, crushing, mashing, refining, extracting, and puréeing are mortars, pounders, sieves, food mills, graters, grinders, presses and other extractors, blenders. Sometimes these are used in combination—food may be put through a sieve, then processed in a blender to refine it further. The tools are occasionally interchangeable, too, depending upon the food: pepper may be ground in a mill or a mortar, but coffee needs a coffee grinder. It is up to the cook to decide upon his equipment in terms of his needs. A container that is too large or too small, a frame that is too light or too deep, a multipurpose appliance that carries out none of its functions well, a hand tool that requires more strength than a person has, will cause the cook to struggle in frustration. In some categories of tools there is a single, outstanding example, the *ne plus ultra,* while other groups offer a wider range. Be guided by our selections in the light of the results you wish to achieve.

Meat Pounders and a Tenderizer

A cut of meat must suit the recipe, its structure and the method a happy marriage. In most cases, the knife edge you use for slicing or boning is the only utensil you will need for altering the size and shape but not the integrity of the muscle; but in some situations, the very absence of grain is required, fibers that offer no resistance. Anyone who plans to prepare escalopes de veau (see "About Veal") may rely on a good butcher to pound the raw meat, as he has the proper tools. But, as with every other endeavor in this world, if you want to be certain of good results, do it yourself. First be sure that your precious veal has been sliced carefully on the bias (across the grain at a moderate angle), permanently Sanforizing it. Veal is too expensive to allow it to shrink or curl grotesquely in the pan, and careful slicing will prevent this. Then you pound it flat, uniformly, carefully, so every mouthful will be first-rate.

SCALOPPINE DI VITELLO AL LIMONE—SAUTEED VEAL SCALOPPINE WITH LEMON SAUCE

For 4 persons

2 tablespoons vegetable oil
¼ cup butter
1 pound veal *scaloppine,* thinly sliced and pounded flat
¾ cup all-purpose flour, spread on a dish or on waxed paper
Salt and freshly ground pepper to taste
2 tablespoons lemon juice
2 tablespoons finely chopped parsley
½ lemon, thinly sliced

1. Heat the oil and 2 tablespoons of the butter in a skillet, over medium-high heat. (It should be quite hot. Thinly sliced veal must cook quickly or it will become leathery.)

2. Dip both sides of the *scaloppine* in flour and shake off the excess. Slip the *scaloppine,* no more than will fit comfortably in the skillet at one time, into the pan. If the oil is hot enough the meat should sizzle.

3. Cook the *scaloppine* until they are lightly browned on one side, then turn and brown the other side. (If they are very thin they should be completely cooked in about 1 minute.) When done, transfer to a warm platter and season with salt and pepper.

4. Off the heat, add the lemon juice to the skillet, scraping loose the cooking residue. Swirl in the remaining 2 tablespoons of butter. Add the parsley, stirring it into the sauce.

5. Add the *scaloppine,* turning them in the sauce. Turn on the heat to medium very briefly, just long enough to warm up the sauce and *scaloppine* together—but do not overdo it, because the *scaloppine* are already cooked.

6. Transfer the *scaloppine* to a warm platter, pour the sauce over them, garnish with the lemon slices, and serve immediately.

(From THE CLASSIC ITALIAN COOKBOOK, by Marcella Hazan, illustrated by George Koizumi. Copyright © 1973 by Marcella Hazan. Reprinted by permission of Alfred A. Knopf.)

No French is needed in order to associate the term *batterie de cuisine* with meat pounders, although there was a time when the only blunt instrument found in American kitchens was the rolling pin with which Maggie chased Jiggs. And even that, compared to professional and European models, was a mere toy (see Chapter 10). All too frequently, pounding equipment is inadequate. Be prepared to apply force, otherwise don't attempt it. Meat pounders must be heavy, weighing at least 24 ounces. Select the one which you find comfortable to use. Some require a slapping arm motion; others have you punching down on the meat. Consider the size of the head. Is it large enough? Has it been beveled or tapered so sharp edges do not damage the meat? Is the handle long enough? Easy to hold? Balanced? Is the pounder a comfortable weight? To these specifications must also conform design and materials.

While pounding veal for scaloppine does tenderize it, that is not the main object—the cuts of meat we pound (rump or leg of veal or lamb, chicken breasts) will be of good quality to begin with. What is needed is to eliminate the grain without pulverizing the meat. We have also included one tool whose primary function is tenderizing, and we would recommend it only for that purpose.

Rectangular Carbon-Steel Pounder 4.1

Carbon steel; head 5¼″ × 4½″; 11″ long overall; 2 lbs. 6 oz.
$27.00

Unquestionably utilitarian and professional, this massive French pounder dispenses with special hand grips, mirror finishes, and other refinements. Yet, if your aesthetic sense covets function above all other attributes, it is indeed the most elegant instrument in the heavy arsenal. There is work to be done; this is the Trojan. A large (about 5-inch square) surface of heavy steel applied to morsels of boneless meat will reduce them to delicate, melting tenderness with a single blow. The thicker center area tapers to beveled edges which have been honed to blade sharpness. Turn it on its side, deliver another whack with this pounder-cum-cleaver, and your scaloppini is trimmed to size. It is an uncompromising design, to be treated with respect, and it is very heavy. The handle, on the same plane as the striking surface, must be held clear of the counter or fingers will be converted to scaloppine as well. And the proletarian carbon steel must be babied, carefully washed and dried after each use lest it become a rusting hulk. Only then do you hang it carefully out of the way on a very very sturdy hook.

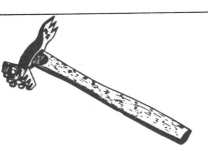

Meat tenderizer and ice pick.

Rectangular Stainless-Steel Pounder 4.2

Stainless steel; head 4¼″ × 4″; 11½″ long overall; 1¾ lbs.
$30.00

Put a heavy-duty French pounder like the preceding one in the hands of Italian designers and presto! it is transformed into an elegant, streamlined object. Although this pounder is by no means all shine and style, the renovation required some sacrifices. At 28 ounces, it has been trimmed of a third of its weight (an advantage for some users, who find lifting a very heavy instrument uncomfortable). The pounding surface, about 4 inches square, is some 20 per cent smaller. Still, it is an effective tool for flattening boneless veal, chicken, beef, or lamb to fragile morsels for a quick sautéing, a whiff of garlic, a splash of wine. The gracefully elongated handle, an improvement over the prototype, makes it easier to smash the meat and not the knuckles. Display this pounder on your wall, hanging it from the hole at the end. The polished stainless steel will never submit to rust, but avoid marring its gleaming finish with an abrasive cleaner—treat it as you would your finest polished pot.

Beaten biscuits are a venerable American institution. In the Virginian Cook Book *(1885) their preparation is nostalgically described: "Let one spend the night at some gentleman-farmer's home, and the first sound heard in the morning after the crowing of the cock, was the heavy, regular fall of the cook's axe as she beat and beat her biscuit dough." Recipe books of the time recommend a full half hour's beating with a mallet or wooden pestle.*

Round Professional Veal Pounder — 4.3

Nickel-steel plate on iron; head 4¼" diam.; 12¾" long overall; 2½ lbs.

$20.00 ▲

Perfection is approached in this stunning instrument. It combines prodigious weight with effective, considerate design and material. The area which must come in contact with your cutlet is circular, 4¼ inches in diameter, a trifle skimpy if traditional wiener schnitzel, as big as a dinner plate, is on the menu. The sleek handle is elevated from the plane of the striking surface, facilitating repeated, comfortable use with the fingers safely clear of contact with the board. Its shining nickel-steel surface is a joy both to use and behold. This Rolls Royce of meat pounders would be a justifiable expense for the kitchen where only the finest plume de veau is tolerated.

"When the chestnuts and corn are green and full grown, they half boil the former and take off the rind: and having sliced the milky, swelled, long rows of the latter, the women pound it with a large wooden mortar, which is wide at the mouth, and gradually narrows to the bottom: then they knead both together, wrap them up in green corn-blades of various sizes . . . and boil them well, as they do every kind of seethed food. This sort of bread is very tempting to the taste, and reckoned most delicious to their palates."

James Adair, The History of the American Indian, *1775*

About Veal and Other Meats That Are Pounded

The average American manages to consume less than two pounds of veal a year in between his 116.3 annual pounds of hamburger, roast beef, and steak. Since the days of the Chisholm Trail, the beef critter has been king in the United States. Raised to be red-blooded beef, cattle must fulfill this destiny and not be slaughtered as veal. Lack of demand has made veal a luxury here, despite the millions of calves of suitable breeds that are born each year.

Veal, when it is sold at all, is found in urban markets, often those catering to a population of Italian, French, or German extraction. In the lands from which these people have come, where limited grazing area makes it almost necessary to slaughter calves for meat, veal is a regular menu feature. The best veal is milk-fed, from very young animals that have not yet begun to graze. The flesh of such calves is pale, soft, and virtually free of fat. Less choice veal—that from older animals—is darker, with more fat. The most expensive cuts of veal come from the rump or the round, solid meat with little muscle separation, suitable for roasts and sautés. (Other cuts of veal may be braised or roasted.) With such solid cuts there is no waste; however, there can be shrinkage as the heat of cooking tightens the muscle. To assure perfect texture and lessen shrinkage, small slices—scallops—of veal are frequently pounded before cooking.

VEAL SCALLOPS
Meat for scallops must be carefully butchered. A pound or two of solid veal rump or round will contain only two or three muscle divisions to interrupt the grain. The meat is cut across the grain at a slight angle—somewhat on the bias, as it were—into slices half an inch thick. These slices are then divided where there are natural muscle separations and cut where there are none, so you end up with uniform pieces. These small portions, trimmed of any membrane or fat, are placed between sheets of waxed paper and pounded to quarter-inch thickness or less with a meat pounder or a mallet, and the flat of a cleaver or a knife. The resulting scallops—escalopes in France, scaloppine in Italy, schnitzel in Austria and Germany—are suitable for innumerable exquisite preparations, the most typical being a quick sauté and a finishing sauce. Veal cut into bite-size pieces is often described as piccati—on menus, you'll see Piccata of Veal listed.

OTHER MEATS FOR SCALLOPS
The same names—scallops, escalopes, scaloppine, and schnitzel—are applied to beef, lamb, or pork slices prepared in the same fashion. Scallops of veal are often stuffed and rolled—think of such dishes as paupiettes or oiseaux (French), involtini, rollatini, spiedini (Italian), rouladen (German). Rolled and stuffed pieces of pounded beef, pork, or lamb may also be prepared as braccioletti or ballotini (Italian). Large pieces of these meats, pounded, rolled, and stuffed to be sliced like a

roast, are called variously roulades, ballotines, and bracioles. Boned breasts of chicken are often pounded. So prepared they are called cotelettes, cutlets, escalopes, or suprêmes; and, finally, split jumbo shrimp may also be pounded before cooking. Small pieces of boneless meat prepared without pounding will be listed on menus as medaillons, noisettes, or grenadins.

This confusing welter of terms is frequently misused. The term cutlet (cotelette, costatelle, costalette) is often applied to any or all of these meats, whether cut into chops or not, boneless or not, pounded or not. There are also unique examples of dishes using pounded meats from various cuisines. Wiener rosbraten, an Austrian dish of round steak smothered in onions, begins with a pounded slice of beef; and the American culinary repertory has for generations included so-called Swiss steak, made with floured and browned beef that has been beaten drastically to break the fibers and tenderize it.

Stainless-Steel Pounder with Plastic Handle   4.4

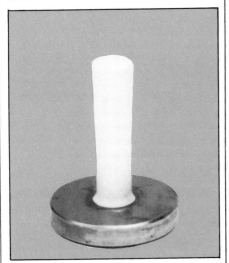

Stainless steel with plastic handle; head 3½" diam; handle 3¾" long; 1¾ lbs.

$20.00

A compact, innocent shape belies the knockout punch which this instrument can deliver. The weight—almost 2 pounds—of the thick, solid disc of stainless steel will subdue the most resistant fiber, transform your veal to a supple slice fit to meet the demands of your best recipe for escalopes de veau Vallée d'Auge. Several blows must be struck in order for the head, 3½ inches in diameter, to cover a respectable portion of meat, but the beveled edge will not cut through the meat as a sharp edge would do. In function, the white plastic handle does not hinder (the meats with which

it will come in contact have little fat to cause it to become slippery), although in form it disappoints—it is clearly a sheathing, seamed and styleless. Nevertheless, the implement is practical and a fine value.

Brass Pounder   4.5

Brass; 3½" diam; handle 4" long; 1¾ lbs.

$25.00

A sculpture stand should be provided for this exquisite brass meat pounder when it is not in use. Though it was made in France, one would have thought Brancusi had a hand in its design. It would be a unique addition to the kitchen where burnished brass is uncommon but where art is treasured. The 3½-inch disc and its sculptural, curving finger-grip handle are fashioned of a single piece of very heavy polished brass—a felicitous union

of utility and beauty. It asks to be held, fondled, loved. The warm, glowing sheen will deepen with memories of magnificent meals, but it will not tarnish.

Aluminum Meat Tenderizer   4.6

Cast aluminum; head 4¼" × 2⅜"; 9½ long overall.

$5.00

Now we cross the boundary between fine, boneless morsels, flattened as your recipe requires and guaranteed against shrinkage and toughness by correct cutting and pounding, to the nether world of compromises—meat that needs to be tenderized. Butchers roll mediocre boneless steaks through a machine which waffles their surfaces, half chewing them before they are cooked, so the diner's teeth are spared an inordinate effort. This gadget serves the same function, pounding or flattening while actually breaking the fibers to tenderize the meat. Made of cast aluminum, in construction it is sturdy enough and it is balanced and comfortable to use, but it lacks adequate weight and the surface of meat that would be covered by the head seems to be on the small side.

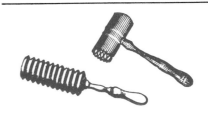

The Victorian cook often had to deal with very tough beefsteak. Here are two weapons for subduing its texture.

117

Several Mortars and a Grain Mill

Aside from the cutting edge, the mortar is the most primitive tool commonly in use to prepare food, whether in remote native villages or three-star kitchens. When humankind discovered that grain was easier to digest if ground rather than left as whole kernels—if it was pre-chewed, if you will—people began to pound it on a tree stump or a flat rock, and so the mortar was born. An object of some sort was used for pounding —the ancester of the pestle. If the average American household survives without the mortar and pestle it is because commercial food processing has made this tool almost superfluous. However, grinding spices and nuts yourself always assures fresher and better results. Use your mortar and pestle, secure in the knowledge that this is not some esoteric or pretentious piece of equipment but the most historic and utilitarian of utensils, almost as basic as the wheel.

MATERIALS AND SIZES

The best and most expensive mortars are marble—hard, clean, relatively nonporous—the garlic for pesto will not end up as a living memory in the spices you are later grinding for fruitcake. The inside of a marble mortar is fairly smooth, but it is left unpolished to permit the necessary friction. The most practical alternative to marble for a mortar and pestle is ceramic, although in *The Cuisines of Mexico* Diana Kennedy recommends native black basalt. Ceramic—usually porcelain—offers properties of marble, except perhaps for weight and permanence. Wood, another material commonly used for mortars, is not suited for grinding any ingredients liable to exude moisture, even when it is the most closely grained hardwood. Some of the essence may linger. Wooden mortars (and pestles, too) are fine for spices and seeds.

A medium-sized mortar is the best for most purposes, although a well-equipped kitchen will have several sizes. The mortar should never be filled more than halfway, or it will overflow during the grinding. Be sure your mortar is heavy enough to withstand vigorous pounding, and that the pestle fits both the mortar and your hand comfortably. It is preferable for the mortar and pestle to be of the same material to equalize pressure and assure even grinding—marble with marble, wood with wood.

LA BRANDADE DE MORUE— CREAM OF SALT COD

This is not really a dish to be made at home and, indeed, nowadays, the majority of housewives in the Languedoc and in Provence buy it ready made for Friday lunch at cooked food shops which specialize in it. There is one such shop in Nîmes, Raymond, 43 rue d'Avignon, from whence it is sent all over France. It is one of those dishes which you either like or detest. Personally, I find it delicious, although even then a little goes a long way.

Briefly, you must soak 2 lb. of salt cod in cold water for 12 hours at least. Drain and rinse it, put it into a pan of fresh cold water and bring it very gently to the boil, then remove it at once from the fire. Take out all the bones, flake the fish, add a crushed clove or two of garlic, and place over a low flame. In separate small saucepans have some olive oil and some milk. Keep all three saucepans over a flame so low that the contents never get more than tepid. Crushing the fish with a wooden spoon you add, gradually and alternately, a little milk and a little olive oil, until all is used up and the cod has attained the consistency of a thick cream. All this, however, is quicker said than done. It requires great patience and also considerable energy (the famous chef Durand of Nîmes, who has a recipe in his book, published in 1830, specifies that two people are needed to make the *brandade*, one to pour, the other to stir and rotate the pan), and if you own a pestle and mortar, it is better to crush the fish first in this. It can be done in an electric mixer, which I believe is nowadays used by the people who make the *brandade*, on a commercial scale. In south and south-western France, the *brandade* is usually to be found at the restaurants and in the cooked food shops on a Friday, but rarely on other days.

The *brandade* is served warm, surrounded by triangles of fried bread or pastry. . . .

NOTE: Salt cod should always be soaked and cooked in porcelain, glazed earthenware, or enamelled vessels. Metal tends to discolour it. And if your *brandade* has oiled or separated, the remedy is to mix in a small quantity of smooth potato purée.

(From FRENCH PROVINCIAL COOKING, by Elizabeth David. Copyright © 1960, 1962, 1967, 1969 by Elizabeth David. Published by Penguin Books. Reprinted by permission of Elizabeth David.)

Marble Mortar and Pestle   4.7

Marble; mortar 11″ diam. × 6¼″ high; bowl 5″ deep; body 1″ thick; pestle 10½″ long.
$200.00 to $300.00

The classic mortar we show you here belongs to James Beard. One like it can be crafted for you in France and shipped by boat, to be assigned a place d'honneur in your kitchen. Only a serious interest in fine cooking justifies the size and expense of this majestic object. It is very heavy and has a large capacity (it would be ideal for Elizabeth David's Brandade de Morue recipe), almost two quarts—yet it is effective for much smaller quantities, since its interior curves sharply like the pointed end of an egg. The marriage of mortar and pestle is perfect, and their unpolished rock-hard surface offers just enough resistance to permit efficient grinding. Four cloverleaf ears, provided for carrying, will probably be used only once, in assigning the mortar to its permanent working location. Although one ear has a trough for pouring, the weight of this massive mortar, again, makes it seem unlikely that it will be used for that purpose.

Porcelain Mortar and Pestle 4.8

Porcelain; mortar 5⅝" outside diam., 4¾" inside diam.; bowl 2⅝" deep. Also avail. with outside diam. of 4⅛", 6", or 6¾".

$27.00

Vitrified porcelain, hard and nonporous, is an acceptable stand-in for marble in this fine French mortar. It is generously rounded, with a well-formed pouring spout and a heavy, stable base. Although the mortar is highly glazed and the bottom of the pestle is not, the two finishes seem to correlate well to produce a good result. While its size is ample for making a cup or so of pesto (see recipe), it will also accommodate a few cardamom pods for a pinch of seasoning, or it will crush the juniper berries for a game marinade.

Set of Three Porcelain Mortars and Pestles 4.9

Porcelain; set of 3. Small mortar 2⅞" diam., 1½" deep, pestle 3⅝" long; medium mortar 4" diam., 1⅞" deep, pestle 4½" long; large mortar 5" diam., 2⅝" deep, pestle 6¼" long.

$9.00

A nest of three white porcelain mortars with matching pestles is a practical idea —the only disadvantage is that when they are not in use, the three pestles do not quite fit neatly into the top (and smallest) mortar. You *could* put the two smaller pestles away and use the large one for all three mortars, unless you see fit to reserve one set for a specific use, such as mashing garlic. The largest of the three mortars would be big enough to pulverize at least a cup of ingredients at a time, although it would be equally efficient for grinding a handful of dried thyme. White glaze gleams on the exteriors and inside rims of the mortars and the handles of the pestles, while the grinding interiors and the lower part of the pestles have been left unglazed to facilitate grinding. The pouring spouts, shaped like ashtray depressions, are silly.

MORTAR PESTO

NOTE: The quantity of basil in most recipes is given in terms of whole leaves. American basil, however, varies greatly in leaf sizes. There are small, medium, and very large leaves, and they all pack differently in the measuring cup. For the sake of accurate measurement, I suggest that you tear all but the tiniest leaves into two or more small pieces. Be gentle, so as not to crush the basil. This would discolor it and waste the first, fresh droplets of juice.

2 cups fresh basil leaves (see note above)

2 tablespoons pine nuts
2 cloves garlic, lightly crushed with a heavy knife handle and peeled
A pinch of coarse salt
½ cup freshly grated Parmesan cheese
2 tablespoons freshly grated Romano *pecorino* cheese
½ cup olive oil
3 tablespoons butter, softened to room temperature

1. Choose a large marble mortar with a hardwood pestle. Put the basil, pine nuts, garlic, and coarse salt in the mortar. Without pounding, but using a rotary movement and grinding the ingredients against the sides of the mortar, crush all the ingredients with the pestle.
2. When the ingredients in the mortar have been ground into a paste, add both grated cheeses, continuing to grind with the pestle until the mixture is evenly blended.
3. Put aside the pestle. Add the olive oil, a few drops at a time at first, beating it into the mixture with a wooden spoon. Then, when all the oil has been added, beat in the butter with the spoon.
4. As with blender *pesto,* add 1 or 2 tablespoons of hot water from the pasta pot before using.

(From THE CLASSIC ITALIAN COOKBOOK, by Marcella Hazan, illustrated by George Koizumi. Copyright © 1973 by Marcella Hazan. Reprinted by permission of Harper's Magazine Press in association with Harper & Row.)

Bernard Leach Mortar 4.10

Porcelain; mortar 5" diam., 3⅛" deep; pestle 3½" long.
$10.00

Continued from preceding page

This most elegant of the ceramic mortars could handle sizable quantities of seasonings, say a cup of pistou to dramatize a rich Provençal Soupe au Pistou (see recipe), delighting the palate as this mortar delights the eye. The elegant, hand-thrown sandy body of this porcelain mortar, glazed the palest celadon green, exhibits the distinctive Bernard Leach artistry. Beauty enhances rather than intrudes on the item's utility: the flat bottom is an exceptionally ample three inches in diameter, before the slope of the sides accelerates. The unusual, almost flat base of the pestle corresponds exactly in shape with the inside of the mortar, while its well-proportioned stubby handle fits the fist comfortably. The slightly rough, almost white glaze slipped over the interior of the mortar and the bottom of the pestle facilitates grinding without being rough enough to become clotted with food.

Ash Mortar and Pestle   4.11

Ash; mortar 4″ outside diam., 3″ high; 2″ inside diam., 1¾″ deep; pestle 4″ long.

$10.00

Both the mortar and the pestle in this set are carved from single pieces of ash, an exceptionally close-grained hardwood. Only a small bowl has been scooped out of the mortar, the chunky pestle fitting it exactly. This little set is a real charmer, ideal for grinding spices, and it's so irresistible that you may find yourself adding quatre épices to everything. The edge of the mortar curves inward to help prevent the contents from flying out of the bowl.

Ironwood Mortar and Pestle   4.12

Ironwood; mortar 4″ diam., 5″ high, 3″ deep; pestle 6½″ long.

$34.00

This mortar of ironwood—the rare lignum vitae—receives its high marks on performance, not looks. The wood is literally as hard as iron, hence impervious to the pungent oils of the items you are likely to pulverize. It is also a comfortable, deep shape, and the base can be held securely to the countertop with the flat of your hand. The pestle, of the same wood, is slender and comfortable to hold. As these mortars are one-of-a-kind, size (and price) may vary.

LA SOUPE AU PISTOU

[British measuring units]

A famous Niçois soup of which there are many versions, the essential ingredient being the basil with which the soup is flavoured, and which, pounded to a paste with olive oil, cheese and pine nuts makes the sauce called *pesto* so beloved of the Genoese. The Niçois have borrowed this sauce from their neighbours, adapted it to suit their own tastes, and called it, in the local dialect, *pistou*. It is the addition of this sauce to the soup which gives it its name and its individuality. Without it, the soup would simply be a variation of *minestrone*.

Here is the recipe given in *Mets de Provence* by Eugène Blancard (1926), a most interesting little collection of old Provençal recipes.

In a little olive oil, let a sliced onion take colour; add 2 skinned and chopped tomatoes. When they have melted pour in 1¾ pints of water. Season. When the water boils throw in ½ lb. of green French beans cut into inch lengths, 4 oz. of white haricot beans (these should be fresh, but in England dried ones must do, previously soaked, and cooked apart, but left slightly underdone), a medium-sized courgette unpeeled and cut in dice, 2 or 3 potatoes, peeled and diced. When available, add also a few chopped celery leaves, and a chopped leek or two. After 10 minutes add 2 oz. of large vermicelli in short lengths.

In the meantime prepare the following mixture: in a mortar pound 3 cloves of garlic with the leaves of about 10 sprigs of very fresh basil. When they are in a paste, start adding 2 or 3 tablespoons of olive oil, drop by drop. Add this mixture to the soup at the last minute, off the fire. Serve grated Parmesan or Gruyère with it. Enough for four.

(From FRENCH PROVINCIAL COOKING, by Elizabeth David. Copyright © 1960, 1962, 1967, 1969 by Elizabeth David. Published by Penguin Books. Reprinted by permission of Elizabeth David.)

Separate Wooden Pestle   4.13

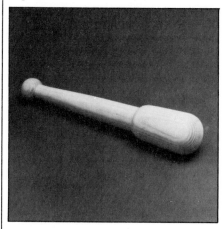

Unfinished light hardwood; 9″ long.

$2.50

A well-balanced, light, unfinished hardwood pestle from France will come in handy when you least expect it. Not only will this one, 9″ long, provide a spare for your mortar, but if you decide to crush the anchovies directly in the bottom of your salad bowl when you make a Caesar salad, you'll have the tool for the job. Inexpensive, useful.

A MILL FOR GRAIN

Grinding grain is as old as civilization itself. Until a few generations ago, two millstones, powered by man, beast, wind, or water, accomplished most of the task, pulverizing the grain, extracting nothing. Later mills, especially the great roller mills of the midwestern United States, which were introduced from Hungary during the 1870s, were infinitely more efficient, making available to the nation's bakers quantities of cheap wheat flour. Wheat, the more desirable ingredient, began to replace corn meal in most American bread, and a lighter, more refined loaf emerged from more ovens. Unfortunately, refinement got out of hand and the quality of flour and bread declined steadily. Both the bran and the germ were removed from the wheat being milled, bran because the demand was for white, fine-textured flour and the fiber interfered with milling, the germ because the oils became rancid in the heat of the mills and whole-grain flour did not keep well. What nutrients were not discarded with the bran and the germ were largely destroyed by the heat of the milling process. As time went on, various additional "improvements" were made, such as bleaching flour chemically—again, to the detriment of its nutritiousness.

The inevitable reaction set in during the 1960s, although the health-minded had long muttered about overrefined flour. A resurgent interest in natural foods and nutrition, provoked in part by the "flower culture" and the back-to-the-land movement, had people across the country buying yeast and making their own bread from the best flour they could find. Bleached white flour would never do. Specialized outlets carried stone-ground grains, of course, and even the commercial millers began selling whole-wheat and unbleached flours, but many serious home bakers have been turning to home grinding with more devotion than if they were spinning flax into gold.

There are several very sound reasons for grinding your own grain rather than buying flour. First, as Pillsbury discovered in the 1870s, the oils in the protein-rich germ of the wheat do indeed turn rancid, making stone-ground flours highly perishable—to keep well for more than a short time they need refrigeration. This is true of both store-bought and mail-order brands. Second, you do not have the flexibility of custom quantities or textures if you buy ready-ground flour. Finally, retail prices for stone-ground grains are astronomical, making home-baked whole-grain bread hardly more economical than store-bought, which is not as it should be at all. The ideal solution to these problems is to grind your own. Fine, you say, just as soon as I build my house by a running stream. But read on—we show you the Magic Mill.

"In the article of diet, they were necessarily temperate. The different dishes into which they had learned to manufacture the Indian corn and pumpkin, afforded a variety of the most nutritious food. Near by every house stood the samp mortar, a large log hollowed out at one end, with a pestle attached to the extremity of a long pole suspended over it. The other end of the pole was planted in the ground, and a crotch of some ten feet in height supported it midway. This instrument might be heard in operation every Saturday afternoon, preparing the samp and hominy for the coming week. Who that has read our countryman's poem upon samp, porridge and hominy, can but admire a dish that could have inspired the bard to sing its virtues in strains of such unbounded praise."

"Chronicles of East Hampton" [*New York*], *by David Lion Gardiner, 1940*

Magic Mill for Grain 4.14

Hardwood cabinet, stainless-steel hopper and drawer, 2 mill stones; 18¼" deep × 11¼" wide; 15¾" high; hopper capacity 8 cups with lid closed, 12 or more cups with lid open; flour drawer capacity, 6½ qts.

$300.00 ▲

If you're fully convinced that you love to bake bread and that you'd like to find an old mill to restore in order to have your own stone-ground flour, the Magic Mill is a more convenient alternative. Buying it is a three-figure investment, however—but still less than the cost of that picturesque ruin—and it should only be considered for the household where bread baking is frequent enough to be a way of life. Of the increasing number of home grain mills on the market we consider this one the best, from the standpoint of ease and flexibility of operation and reliability. Although it is powered by a ¾-horsepower electric motor, it can easily be converted to other power sources. An optional attachment will allow it to be run by a gasoline motor, a bicycle, or water power (if you build that house by the stream after all). The entire unit, which measures 11¼" by 15¾" and is 18¼" high, is housed in a

Continued from preceding page

furniture-finished hardwood cabinet which can be recessed in a cupboard in such a way that only the front and the top of the hopper are exposed. The stainless-steel grain hopper, enclosed in wood, holds 2 quarts of grain at a time (3 quarts if the lid is left open), enough to produce 2 pounds of flour. The capacious flour drawer is also lined with stainless steel, meeting sanitary codes for commercial use. The motor drives the two grindstones, which are easily adjustable for textures from crunchy cracked wheat to the finest pastry flour. A rather sophisticated version of the old mortar and pestle, the Magic Mill will grind away at the rate of a pound a minute. The hinged lid allows for simple cleaning and the machine is covered by a two-year guarantee on motor, stones, flour drawer, and cabinet.

Cream of barley soup was prescribed to soothe upset stomachs in the nineteenth century. A chinois was used to strain it.

The Family of Sieves

Changes in the texture of food may be produced through the use of heat or cold, as we do constantly when cooling, chilling, or freezing, or by mechanical means—by pounding, grating, grinding, sieving, and mashing. We have seen what pounding can do; here we consider sieving. By our definition involving texture change, sieves, not strainers (although the terms are often used interchangeably) belong in the category of utensils we are examining. A strainer separates liquids from solids, while sieves are meant to refine texture. In a sieve, as the food passes through the holes in a wire screen, or perforated metal, or a mesh made of such another material as horsehair or nylon, it is broken into particles whose size is determined, of course, by the size of the holes.

A sieve made in a classic drum shape of wood or, more recently, of metal, is also called a *tamis*—think of the "tammy cloth" called for in old cookbooks. Most of the drum sieves allow the mesh to be replaced.

Wooden sieves are used primarily in connection with baking. Small sieves and coronets work their final magic, drifting clouds of confectioners' sugar onto feathery pastries or pastel-tinted Turkish delight. (Sifters also perform this function in baking—they are discussed in Chapter 10.)

DRUM SIEVES AND THE CHINESE CAP

Metal sieves, stronger and more sanitary than wooden ones, are replacing the wooden tamis for refining moist ingredients into purées. These, called metal drum sieves, are a modern improvement over the wooden classic.

The sieve called a chinois is, in essence, a stable jelly bag; originally it was held by two people, or hooked over a couple of chairs. Named fancifully because their shape resembles a pointed coolie hat, metal chinois are made of perforated sheet metal or wire mesh, attached to a circular frame that is equipped with a handle and, in the best examples, a bracket for resting the sieve on the rim of kettle or bowl.

When foods are puréed in a metal sieve or chinois, a wooden pestle-like implement is the most efficient tool for hastening the progress of the ingredients through the mesh. For use with a drum sieve, the wooden tool is called a champignon, a clearly descriptive name. With the chinois we use a pointed pusher or pestle which is tailored to fit closely

POTAGE CREME DE POTIRON AUX CREVETTES—CREAM OF PUMPKIN AND SHRIMP SOUP

Peel a 2-lb. slice of pumpkin, throw away the seeds and the cottony centre, cut the flesh into small pieces, salt and pepper them, and put them into a thick saucepan with a stick of celery cut in pieces. Cover them with 1½ pints of milk previously boiled, and 1 pint of mild stock or water, and simmer until the pumpkin is quite soft, about 30 minutes. Sieve the mixture; return the purée to a clean pan. Mash or pound in a mortar 4 oz. of peeled prawns or shrimps (buttered shrimps will do), adding a few drops of lemon juice. Dilute with a little of the pumpkin purée, add this mixture to the soup, simmer gently for 10 minutes or so, sieve again if the soup is not quite smooth, taste for seasoning and, when reheating, thin with a little more hot milk or stock if necessary. Immediately before serving stir in a good lump of butter. Ample for six.

(From FRENCH PROVINCIAL COOKING, by Elizabeth David. Copyright © 1960, 1962, 1967, 1969 by Elizabeth David. Published by Penguin Books. Reprinted by permission of Elizabeth David.)

Urbain-Dubois, in his Ecole des Cuisinières, *illustrated four methods of straining: A nap-*
kin is tied to the legs of a bottomless stool and consommé is strained into a pot; two pairs of hands
squeeze a fine sauce through woolen cloth; a felt bag, suspended like the napkin,
clarifies aspic; and a tamis is propped on two wooden spoons in order to filter fruit juices.

down to its very depths. It is important that your sieves and chinois have the proper mesh to refine food to the degree required and to prevent seeds, stems, skins, and the like from passing through. The sizes of the sieves must also be proportionate to the kettles, bowls, platters, and baking pans over which they are to be used. To be sure you'll have the proper utensil at hand, you'll need sieves with several sizes and types of mesh.

THE FOOD MILL

Clearly related to the sieve by its product—food refined to a greater or lesser degree—is the food mill. Think of it as a mechanized sieve—it stands in the same relation to the tamis as to the flour sifters in Chapter 10. The tamis or the drum sieve will do the same job as either the mill or the sifter, but the mechanically advanced utensils will do them better.

Aluminum Drum Sieve 4.15

Aluminum with tinned-steel mesh; 16″ diam.; 3½″ deep.
$44.00

This generous-sized professional-weight aluminum drum sieve means business. Gallons of tomatoes for sauce, a year's supply of glace de viande, or enough beurre d'écrevisses for a banquet can pass through the tinned-steel mesh stretched across its 16-inch diameter. Its wide, flat sieving area allows the food to be spread so that you are pushing the food through the sieve with a broad, flat motion which is not tiring. It is strong enough to withstand the pressure of heavy puréeing and, although initially expensive, it is destined for a long and productive life. The wire mesh fits into the round frame much like the fabric in an embroidery hoop—it is clamped into place with a metal band and held by a sturdy bolt, making the most vulnerable part easily replaceable. If the size of this sieve makes it impractical for your kitchen, select a chinois instead.

Zucchi Wood and Metal Sieves 4.16

Wood frame with stainless-steel mesh; 12″ diam.; 4½″ high. Also avail. 7½″ diam., 3″ high, or 15″ diam., 5½″ high. Also avail. with horsehair mesh.
$18.00

From Italy we have a wardrobe of drum sieves in sizes and meshes to suit every purpose, ranging from a 15-inch behemoth with a coarse metal mesh to a 7-inch baby strung with gossamer scrim. They are all constructed with double unfinished wooden frames, the mesh tightly stretched between them. They are quite sturdy for the most part, certainly adequately strong for sifting dry ingredients; the 7-inch sieve fitted with brass mesh might be used for finishing chestnut purée or a crème pâtissière—but remember that very fine mesh must be used advisedly with moist ingredients, since the wire may prove difficult to clean.

Wood-framed Horsehair Sieve 4.17

Wood with horsehair mesh; 10¾″ diam.; 4⅜″ high.
$7.95

Nostalgia and history insist that this prototype sieve be included—it is the ancestor of almost all the sieves we show you. Horsehair was once the most common material for the mesh of sieves, which were long made almost entirely with wooden frames. The only model available on the contemporary market had to be imported from Colombia. An unfinished wooden frame holds a circle of horsehair woven in a tight random herringbone pattern. It would be a lovely addition to the kitchen with an inventory of hand-hewn or rustic implements on display. The horsehair mesh is quite fine and will not corrode, but, unlike nylon, it is virtually impossible to replace.

Wood-framed Sieve with Nylon Mesh 4.18

Wood frame with fine nylon mesh; 12″ diam.; 4½″ high.
$15.00

Aluminum Drum Sieve
Zucchi Wood and Metal Sieves
Wood-framed Horsehair Sieve
Wood-framed Sieve with Nylon Mesh

Wood-framed Coronet Sieve
Mouli Food Mill

Made in the same fashion as the metal-mesh Italian sieves by Zucchi we have shown you, the wooden frame of this 12-inch one is fitted with a nylon mesh as fine as bridal veiling. The nylon is, of course, utterly clean and noncorroding, a modern replacement for horsehair. While flavors will not linger in its threads, it may be difficult to render them spotless; however, you can use this sieve with impunity for atomizing dry ingredients, or heedless of any harmless staining, for a special purée.

BEIGNETS DE CREME

4 cups milk
½ pound almond macaroons
6 egg yolks
Grated rind of 1 lemon
1 tablespoon orange-flower water
6-8 cups peanut oil for deep frying
1 cup confectioners' sugar

Boil the milk until it is reduced to half its volume, about 2 cups.

Crush the macaroons very finely and blend them with the egg yolks, grated lemon rind and orange-flower water into a smooth paste. Gradually stir in enough of the hot milk to make a mixture that will just hold its shape, and blend thoroughly.

Drop by the teaspoon into the oil heated to 375 F. on a frying thermometer. Fry until puffy and golden, drain on kitchen toweling, sprinkle with confectioners' sugar, and serve very hot.

(From LA CUISINE, by Raymond Oliver, translated by Nika Standen Hazelton with Jack Van Bibber. Copyright © 1969 by Tudor Publishing Company. Reprinted by permission of Tudor Publishing Company.)

Among the many specific utensils mentioned in The Pantropheon *(1853) of Alexis Soyer are sieves of several kinds. In this excerpt from a description of an ancient Roman kitchen the* archimagirus, *or chief cook, looks at the work of a second cook and remarks: "Never will this* despicitius *bread obtain the necessary lightness by baking: the flour should have been passed through a Spanish sieve of linen thread; use the Gallic sieve of horsehair for the* artocreas *(meat pie) and one of papyrus, or Egyptian rush, for the coarser kinds of flour."*

Wood-framed Coronet Sieve   4.20

Unfinished light wood with stainless steel, or nylon mesh; 11½" × 7¼"; 3¼" high.
$10.50

This sieve is a unique specialty item that is not for every kitchen. The design is efficient and aesthetically pleasing: the sieve consists of a band of wood curved around in a teardrop shape and stapled. A second, identically shaped piece fits inside it, holding a wire sifting screen in place. The end where the wood is joined forms a convenient flat handle, making these coronet sieves easy to use with one hand to dust your marble slab with flour as you knead your bread dough. Unusual enough to justify including your sieve in a display of your most interesting kitchen objects.

Mouli Food Mill   4.21

Tinned steel with plastic knob handle; 9" top diam., 5" bottom diam.; 3⅝" deep at sides; 3 sieving discs, each 5¼" diam.; 2-qt. capacity. Also avail. with capacity of 1 or 3 qts.
$13.00 ▲

In a category dominated by simple shape clearly expressing function, the Mouli food mill is a baroque interruption, all jutting angles, twisted wires, scalloped edges, and curved plates stamped with holes, messages, and designs. Yet it is a highly utilitarian example of simple mechanics harnessed for efficiency by makers without stylists on the payroll. The advantages with which the Mouli is endowed make it superior to all other types of hand-cranked food mills. Like a sieve or chinois, it will separate as it purées, leaving seeds and skins of tomatoes behind, sorting out the peels and cores of your cooked apples as the sauce drops into the bowl beneath. Our staff jester, watching this being tested, murmured, "The quality of the sauce is not strained, it droppeth as the gentle rain of heaven upon the plate beneath". What our jester meant is that food is refined to the degree you control by the openings in the disc you select, but it isn't liquefied to death as in an inexorable blender. The mill, of course, also eliminates hand mashing. You simply turn the crank, topped by a plastic knob, which causes the flat, curving blade to rotate over the perforated disc placed in the open bottom of the mill. This forces the food through the holes. While you crank you grip the handle for stability. There are three interchangeable discs—a fine one for baby food or other smooth purées; a medium one which permits some texture to pass through, giving character to applesauce and such potages as the one in the next recipe; finally, a coarse disc for jobs like ricing potatoes or preparing tomatoes for cooking into a sauce. Any jammed particles of food are freed by simply reversing the direction of your cranking. The discs are easy to remove by releasing a simple tension spring. Made of acid-resistant tinned steel, the whole works can go into the dishwasher or can be easily cleaned by hand when disassembled. The 2-quart capacity is adequate for most purposes; you can also choose a 1-quart or 3-quart size. The adjustable padded retractable legs on the mill will fit a container up to 11 inches in diameter. While the coarse disc may be used for chopping nuts, we do not recommend it for chopping or grating such hard raw ingredients as vegetables.

Aluminum Chinois 4.22

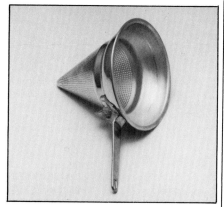

Aluminum with cast-aluminum handle; 7⅞″ diam.; 8¾″ deep.
$12.00

This aluminum chinois is the most à la mode of our Chinese caps. Light in weight yet extremely sturdy, it is molded, cone and all, of a single sheet of metal; and, but for the handle, there's not a welded seam in sight. Nor are there any narrow rims or crevices to harbor particles of prior purées. The medium perforations in the sieve would be perfect for purée Bretonne, the soul of earthy white beans, but not for making seedless raspberry jam—also, you must remember that aluminum is not suitable for prolonged use with highly acid foods. With its handle and a convenient bracket to balance it over a bowl, it is not dependent on a container with a specific diameter, although, because of its shape, it must be used with a kettle or bowl at least 6 inches deep. To its durability and stability, add the advantage of economy—the price is a gentle one. When not in use it can be hung out of the way from the hole in its handle, the best means of storing awkwardly shaped utensils.

POTAGE CREME DE TOMATES ET DE POMMES DE TERRE—CREAM OF TOMATO AND POTATO SOUP

[British measures]

The white part of 2 leeks, ½ lb. tomatoes, ¾ lb. of potatoes, 1½ oz. butter, a little cream, chervil or parsley.

Melt the butter in a heavy saucepan; before it has bubbled put in the finely sliced leeks; let them just soften in the butter. Half the success of the soup depends upon this first operation. If the butter burns instead of just melting or the leeks brown the flavour will be spoilt.

Add the roughly chopped tomatoes; again let them cook until they start to give out their juice. Add the peeled and diced potato, a seasoning of salt, and two lumps of sugar. Cover with 1¼ pints of water. After the soup comes to the boil let it simmer steadily but not too fast for 25 minutes. Put it through the food mill, twice if necessary. Return the purée to the rinsed-out saucepan. When it is hot, add about 4 oz. of cream. In warm weather it is advisable to bring this to the boil first, as if it is not quite fresh it is liable to curdle when it makes contact with the acid of the tomatoes. Immediately before serving stir in a little chervil or very finely chopped parsley. Enough for four good helpings.

For all its simplicity and cheapness this is a lovely soup, in which you taste butter, cream and each vegetable, and personally I think it would be a mistake to add anything to it in the way of individual fantasies. It should not, however, be thicker than thin cream, and if it has come out too solid the addition of a little milk or water will do no harm.

(From FRENCH PROVINCIAL COOKING, by Elizabeth David. Copyright © 1960, 1962, 1967, 1969 by Elizabeth David. Published by Penguin Books. Reprinted by permission of Elizabeth David.)

Stainless-Steel Chinois 4.23

Stainless steel; 8″ diam.; 8¼″ deep.
$45.00

This Italian-made chinois, neat headgear for the Tin Woodman, is made of perforated stainless steel. Although the mesh is quite fine, the sieve is very sturdy and has an advantage in the nature of its material: stainless steel will survive infinite batches of acid fruit purées, its finish unblemished. Because it is made of six different parts, neatly welded together, this sieve does have vulnerability of another kind: seams will eventually give in to pressure, and they also tend to trap particles of food—this chinois will require meticulous care. The hook at the base of the handle allows it to be cantilevered at the side of a bowl of any diameter; the hole at the end enables you to hang it for storage.

Stainless-Steel Chinois 4.24

Stainless-steel frame with tinned-steel mesh; 9″ diam.; 10″ deep.
$33.00

In this large-capacity stainless-steel and tinned-steel chinois, you can purée the spinach for pounds and pounds of lasagne verde or, if you are a cook who makes frequent large quantities of jams and fruit butters, you can keep your preserving kettle well filled. Its weight is proportionate to its size. Of very heavy-gauge metal and noncorroding, it is reinforced with five rods welded to the sides and joined at a metal cap over the tip of the cone. The cone is finely perforated, but the sieve is not finished as smoothly as the smaller, more elegant Italian chinois above. Utility rather than appearance is the primary consideration here. All the parts are welded together, creating those unavoidable crevices which are a nuisance to clean. Its size requires that it be used over a container at least 10 inches deep; the diameter of the receptacle is not restricted, however, since it may be hooked over the rim. Its open handle can be looped over a large hook for storage.

A nineteenth-century riddle:

> *A riddle, a riddle,*
> *As I suppose:*
> *A hundred eyes,*
> *And never a nose.*

Answer: A sieve.

The Cornucopia, *by Judith Herman and Marguerite S. Herman, Harper & Row, New York, 1973*

Fine-meshed Tinned-Steel Chinois   4.25

Tinned-steel frame with tinned-wire mesh; 8″ diam.; 9½″ deep.

$21.00

Like a piece of silk, the supple mesh of this Swiss-made chinois is tightly woven of the thinnest tinned-steel wires to prevent the merest atom of impurity from intruding upon the glorious bouillon you strain through it. (Your grandmother probably used a linen napkin.) This chinois has a handle, but a hook or bracket for balancing it on the side of a kettle would have been a thoughtful addition. The mesh cone is fitted into the tinned-steel frame and is protected by an outside skeleton of four rods welded to the frame. Because of this construc-

tion, you will have to be meticulous in cleaning, lest traces of food remain under the rods. The handle has a hole for hanging your sieve out of the way when it is not being put to its very specific use.

BOUILLON POUR LES SAUCES— STOCK FOR SAUCES

[British measuring units]
The *bouillon* from the *pot-au-feu* is often used in household cookery as a basis for sauces, but when you have no such meat stock available and when it is necessary to make a foundation for a sauce independently of the ingredients of the dish which it is to accompany, the following method will produce a well-flavoured clear stock without any great expense of either time or materials. It is a method simplified to the greatest possible degree for household cookery.

The ingredients are: ½ lb. each of lean stewing veal, preferably from the shin, and good quality minced beef; 2 scraped carrots, 2 halved tomatoes, 2 medium-sized onions, washed but not peeled, 2 sprigs of parsley with the stalks; no salt or pepper until a later stage.

Put all the ingredients in a small pot or saucepan which will go in the oven; cover with just over a pint of water. Cover the pot and cook in a low oven for 1½ hours. Strain through an ordinary sieve. Leave in a bowl until the fat has set. Remove the fat. Heat up the stock, strain through a muslin to get rid of any sediment. There should now be about ¾ pint of clear straw-coloured *bouillon* ready to make any sauce requiring stock.

As it has been cooked without salt, it can also be reduced to a thick syrup-like consistency, a sort of improvised meat glaze or *glace de viande,* in the following manner: put a large soup ladle of the *bouillon* into a 6-inch frying-pan or sauté pan. Let it bubble fairly gently for about 10 minutes, during which time you remove the little flecks of scum which come to the surface with a metal spoon dipped frequently in hot water. When the liquid starts to stick to the spoon and is reduced to about 2 tablespoons, it is done. The flavour is now three times as strong as it was to start with but, of course, had there been salt in it, it would have been uneatable. Pour it into a little jar, keep it covered, and when it is to be used heat it up in the jar standing in a pan of water. Although this has not the deep colour of professional meat glaze, it has the right amount of body to

strengthen a sauce, plus a freshness and clarity of flavour unusual in the lengthily cooked, more elaborate confection of the chefs.

For large households the stock can be made in double quantities, and for the reduction to glaze, use a larger, 10-inch pan.

(From FRENCH PROVINCIAL COOK-ING, by Elizabeth David. Copyright © 1960, 1962, 1967, 1969 by Elizabeth David. Published by Penguin Books. Reprinted by permission of Elizabeth David.)

Chinois with Stand   4.26

Tin-plated steel with hard-maple pestle; 8½″ high overall; chinois 7″ diam., 7¼″ deep; pestle 10⅛″ long.
$4.98

Take a perforated steel chinois and set it into a stand—there you have a convenient arrangement for use with almost any size bowl or container, no balancing acts required. The American manufacturer of this chinois has thought of everything; for cleaning, the cone snaps out of the stand, an essential arrangement since both stand and sieve are a labyrinth of crevices. A hard-maple pestle, tailored to the deep cone, is efficient. The metal of this chinois was formerly coated with somewhat-less-than-durable enamel in nice enough colors, but the makers have, we think wisely, changed to a tinned finish over steel, which should prove more durable and make this sieve eligible for heavier duty than its predecessor. The perforations produce purées of medium texture. All in all, we can recommend this one as an inexpensive, convenient chinois.

Large Wooden Pestle for a Chinois   4.27

Unfinished light hardwood; 11¼" long.

$4.40

A graceful, pointed hardwood pestle, looking somewhat like a yarn spindle, this pusher fits ideally into a chinois—with a simple, rotating motion it rubs the food through the perforations. Its weight and balance are excellent, and it has been polished to a satin sheen. If you own a chinois which did not come equipped with its own pestle, the small investment involved in buying this tool is essential. If you lack a chinois, this pestle is made to match 4.22.

Wooden Champignon   4.28

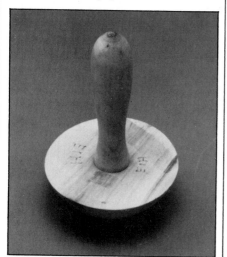

Unfinished light hardwood; head 5" diam.; 7" long overall.

$7.00

Why are some pestles called champignons? The answer is here—this looks so much like a mushroom you would expect it to smell of the damp earth. It is Italian, made of smooth, unfinished hardwood, and it is of a good size and shape for rubbing purées through any of the drum sieves we recommend for moist mixtures. It is easy to manipulate and control, and it has terrific visual appeal.

Large Wooden Champignon   4.29

Unfinished light hardwood; head 4½" diam.; 10¼" long overall.

$6.00

A more refined version of the preceding champignon—the wood is smoother, the head is flatter and wider, and the whole seems to be better constructed. However, the longer, more slender handle might be less comfortable for someone with a large hand. Just as you do not buy a chair without sitting in it, never select a hand-held kitchen tool without first grasping it as you would when using it—this touch-and-hold test will let you decide whether the utensil is for you.

SALSA AL MARSALA—MARSALA SAUCE

½ cup dry Marsala, imported if possible
1 clove garlic, chopped
Salt and freshly ground black pepper
3 cups veal stock
1 tablespoon butter

Put wine in a skillet or pot with garlic and pepper to taste. Turn up heat and cook, uncovered, until reduced to ⅔ of its volume. Add veal stock and continue to reduce for 1 minute. Add salt to taste and put liquid through strainer. Remove from heat, add butter and blend well. Serve hot on veal or chicken. Yields about 2 cups.

(From ITALIAN FAMILY COOKING, by Edward Giobbi, illustrated by Cham, Lisa, and Gena Giobbi. Copyright © 1971 by Edward Giobbi. Reprinted by permission of Random House.)

One of the simplest strained sauces is the raspberry purée for the well-known Pêche Melba. Escoffier recorded the invention of the celebrated dessert as follows: "Madame Nellie Melba, the grande cantrice . . . sang at Covent Garden in 1894. She stayed at the Savoy Hotel . . . at which time I was directing the kitchens of that important establishment. One evening when Lohingrin (sic) was to be performed, Madame Melba gave me two seats . . . As you know, in that opera a swan appears. The following evening Madame Melba gave a petit souper . . . and to show her that I had profited from the seats . . . I sculpted in a block of ice a superb swan, and between the two wings I buried a silver bowl. I covered the bottom . . . with ice cream and on this bed . . . I placed peaches . . . soaked for several minutes in a syrup of vanilla . . . A purée of fresh raspberries covered the peaches completely."

Apricot-Wood Champignon   4.30

Apricot wood; head 2⅜" diam.; 10½" long.

$3.00

Large Wooden Pestle for a Chinois
Wooden Champignon
Large Wooden Champignon
Apricot-Wood Champignon
Hardwood Champignon
Potato Ricer

The distinction between kitchenware and objects of folk art is a tenuous one. Take the case of this apricot-wood champignon from Damascus. Certainly less efficient than the Italian models with their larger heads, it is nevertheless undeniably beautiful, with its graceful silhouette terminating in a series of carved knobs. Reserve it for making hummus bi tahini, and between Middle Eastern feasts display it with your Colombian horsehair sieve.

Hardwood Champignon 4.31

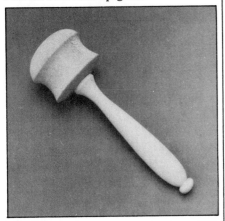

Unfinished light hardwood; head 3″ diam., 2½″ thick; 9½″ long overall.

$2.50

This is a nicely turned champignon of smoothly sanded, unfinished hardwood. The handle is very comfortable to grasp, longer than that of our classic mushroom, thicker than that of our slender example (4.29). The head is somewhat smaller, however—it is only 3 inches in diameter —making your sieving a little more work.

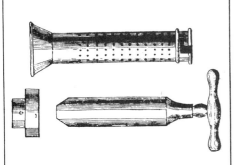

A purée presser, nineteenth century.

Presses

In order to refine certain foods, a viselike press is more efficient than a sieve or a mortar. While it is not necessary to use a press for making mashed potatoes, many people prefer to, particularly if they have no need for a food mill or a chinois in their kitchens; for them we have included one effectively designed potato ricer. On the other hand, it would be impractical to submit a clove or two of garlic to a chinois. Assuming you do not prefer to smash the garlic with the flat of a knife blade and then chop it up, as James Beard does, summon the garlic press.

A good garlic press will accommodate a healthy, robust clove of garlic, even a large one. It must be made with precision, so coarse bits of garlic do not squish out in every direction. The mesh must not be too fine to successfully press unpeeled garlic (a major advantage in using a press), or to clean with ease. Look for these features when you buy a garlic press; in most they are notably absent. We have found that the item sold as an onion press is more functional than most garlic presses.

What of some writers' objection to pressed garlic as being stronger, altogether more overpowering, than minced or sliced garlic amounting to the same original quantity? Here we have a failure of perception of surface as a function of quantity: when finely reduced, as the output of a garlic press is bound to be, a lot of garlic surface is exposed, and therefore a little garlic goes a long way. If you use a press, simply reduce the total quantity in a recipe calling for chopped or sliced garlic and all is well. In other words, the garlic press can't make garlic ''stronger,'' it simply makes every atom of flavor more available.

Potato Ricer 4.32

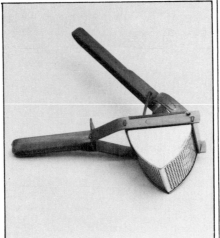

Enameled-steel frame with tinned-steel pusher and bin; 9½″ long overall; bin 3¼″ × 3″, 2¾″ deep.

$5.50

There is something incredibly soul-satisfying about warm, soft food—a security blanket of freshly mashed potatoes, drenched with butter and served piping hot, nourishes puerile fantasies. Must you use a special implement to gratify this need? Your sieve, chinois, food mill, or the multiplex Cuisinarts Food Processor (Chapter 5) are effective in producing this comforting food; but, while hand-held potato mashers and potato ricers are sold in every housewares store, most of them are inadequate. The only potato ricer we have found to be satisfactory is a Swedish import. It consists of two light-green enameled-steel handles attached to a flat pusher that operates on potatoes placed in a triangular, pierced bin of tinned steel. It is operated with a squeezing motion, and the bin will hold a fairly large potato comfortably. The ricer presses out the light, riced potatoes downward, into the bowl or pot where they belong. Not a pretty gadget, but very sturdy. Use it to rice potatoes for a French purée seasoned with a bit of meat stock and beaten to chiffon texture,

Continued from preceding page

or go the American route and beat in butter, salt, pepper, and heated cream for a sinfully rich and deliciously comforting dish to accompany your fried chicken.

"About 1773 [the potato] was beginning to be cultivated in [Scottish] gardens, but still with a hesitation about moral character, for no reader of Shakespere requires to be told that some of the more uncontrollable passions of human nature were supposed to be favoured by its use."

Traditions of Edinburgh, *by Robert Chambers, 1825*

Large Aluminum Onion or Garlic Press   4.33

Cast aluminum; 7¼" long; head 1¾" wide.
$10.00

Actually an onion press, this German cast-aluminum press is excellent for garlic as well. Its curved, triangular container will hold several cloves of garlic for a profoundly redolent ratatouille or an aioli for a crowd. The garlic cloves will not have to be peeled, and the holes of the press are large enough to permit easy cleaning. The top pressing section fits the container snugly, so there is little chance of the garlic escaping out the top as you squeeze the handles together. Use this for onions, too—try adding onion essence to the gravy of your slow-simmered pot roast just before you thicken and serve it.

An old Gaelic rhyme:

> *Garlic with May butter*
> *Cureth all disease:*
> *Drink of goat's white milk*
> *Take along with these.*

Aluminum Garlic Press   4.34

Cast aluminum; 6¾" long; 1" wide.
$4.50 ▲

What this aluminum garlic press lacks in capacity it makes up for in design—it is considerably smaller than the preceding one. A sleek, handsome instrument, polished to a chromelike finish, it departs from the traditional shape. The close-fitting hinged presser section comes down over the garlic, forcing it through the flat, perforated face of the utensil. The unit is easy to clean, but it will only accommodate a single clove of garlic at a time.

PISSALADIERE

This is one form of the Provençal version of pizza. It calls for tomatoes, puréed onions, anchovies, and ripe olives and is baked using a brioche dough or a plain white bread dough. I prefer the brioche . . . flattening the dough out into a wide pan and spreading the filling over it. It makes an attractive, delicious hors d'oeuvre or luncheon dish. I used to buy it in a bakery in St. Rémy in Provence, where I lived several summers, and found it much to my liking, as I am sure you will.

8 to 12 servings
1 recipe brioche dough [for 2 8" × 4" loaves]
6 large ripe tomatoes or 1 one-pound can Italian plum tomatoes plus 2 tablespoons tomato paste
Olive oil
1 or 2 cloves garlic, peeled and crushed

3 medium Spanish onions
3 tablespoons butter
Freshly grated Parmesan cheese
½ teaspoon rosemary, crushed in a mortar
Anchovy fillets
Ripe olives, preferably the soft Italian or Greek type

Prepare the brioche dough. While the dough is rising, prepare the filling:

Peel, seed, and cut the tomatoes in very small pieces (or, if using canned tomatoes, drain, seed, and chop). Heat 2 tablespoons olive oil in a skillet, add the tomatoes and garlic, and let them reduce to a paste over medium heat, stirring occasionally. Peel and chop the onions and steam them in the butter over low heat, covered, until they form a rather thick purée.

After the first rising, roll the dough out to about ⅜ inch in thickness and line two 9-inch-square cake tins or one 12-inch tart pan. Brush with softened butter and put in a warm place to rise slightly.

Sprinkle the brioche shell with the grated Parmesan. Spread the onions over it, and sprinkle with the rosemary. Cover with the tomato purée. Arrange the anchovies in a lattice pattern on the tomatoes, and place an olive in the center of each opening. Brush the olives with a little olive oil. Bake in a preheated oven at 375°, until the crust is golden and cooked through, about 25 to 30 minutes. Brush the top with more olive oil before serving hot as an hors d'oeuvre or a main luncheon dish.

(From BEARD ON BREAD, by James A. Beard, illustrated by Karl Stuecklen. Copyright © 1973 by James A. Beard. Reprinted by permission of Alfred A. Knopf, Inc.)

Gravy Strainer

Graters

Eventually, a blunt instrument will not suffice when you are dealing with certain foods. Some of them are too firm to be pushed through a sieve, not brittle enough to be ground in a mortar, not small enough to be forced through a press. The only way to refine their texture is to use a cutting edge. With the proper sharp knife (see Chapter 2) you can mince garlic, chop nuts, julienne carrots, or shred cabbage, but obviously five, ten, fifty, or a hundred knives working at once would complete the task faster and more uniformly. A grater, essentially a surface covered with small cutting edges, is precisely that proliferant knife.

Some hand graters are multipurpose units capable of producing a variety of textures, and so are suitable for use with scores of foods. Others are distinctly single-minded. The grater operated by rubbing food (and, when you get down to the nitty-gritty, your knuckles) over a sharply perforated surface is the simplest kind, and remember—if it doesn't work on your fingers, it will not work on your food. Good rotary graters, mechanical but not electric, are faster, more efficient, and more expensive than hand graters and they operate in the reverse fashion: the cutting surface is rubbed against the food, which is held in place by the pressure of a plate.

GRATING SURFACES

Graters are equipped with two types of surfaces. One is made up of punctures, the torn edges of the holes protruding to create the rasplike surface that is characteristic of hand, not rotary, graters. (Exception: the electric meat grinder-graters we show you.) This is the kind of grater that crumbles and abrades the food and is murder to clean. The other type has holes or slits with a raised cutting edge on one side. This type will shred food into so many strings, the fineness or thickness of which is determined by the size and placement of the openings. Food processed by a shredding surface will retain more of its integrity and lose less moisture than if it is grated over ragged punctures. Some such graters have slits that will slice, but none of the slicers on a hand grater, rotary or otherwise, has the talent of a mandoline, which we show you in Chapter 3. A rotary slicer is reasonably efficient if uniform pressure is applied to the food.

A fine shredder and a medium grater may be used interchangeably on such foods as hard cheese, potatoes, orange peel. Many electric appliances will also grate and shred, providing the optimum answer to many culinary prayers (see our selection of grinders, farther along in this chapter). Nevertheless, hand graters have their moments of glory in the most mechanized kitchen, for a pinch of nutmeg, a touch of lemon zest. Select one or several—look for graters that are comfortable to use, sturdy, and made of noncorrosive metal. If, with all that, they are easy to clean, you are home free.

LEMON BREAD

This is a tart, deliciously refreshing bread with a character all its own. I had a feeling that lemon flavor in a baking powder bread might work out very well, so I experimented and came up with this. I am delighted with it, and find that it keeps extremely well.

1 small loaf

1 stick (½ cup) butter
½ cup granulated sugar
Rind of one lemon, finely chopped or coarsely grated
2 eggs
½ cup lemon juice
2 cups all-purpose flour
3 teaspoons double-acting baking powder
1 teaspoon salt

Cream the butter and sugar together, then add the lemon rind and the eggs, one at a time, beating well after each is added. Stir in the lemon juice, then sift in the dry ingredients gradually. Beat well after each addition until you have a light, workable batter. Pour into a buttered and floured 8½ × 4½ × 2½-inch bread pan and bake at 350° for 50 to 60 minutes. Turn out on a rack to cool. Do not slice until the next day. Serve with butter and preserves as a tea bread.

(From BEARD ON BREAD, by James A. Beard, illustrated by Karl Stuecklen. Copyright © 1973 by James A. Beard. Reprinted by permission of Alfred A. Knopf, Inc.)

"Horse-radish was another harbinger of spring, the first green thing to shove its rapier blades above the chilly earth. A few weeks later the lacquered emerald leaves would find their peppery way to the simple planning of our menus as 'greens'... In the first pale days of early spring, however, its part was merely to lend zest as a relish to the diet. Washed, scraped, and grated—with salt, vinegar, and sugar added, and conserved in a glass jar—it was ready to be used on baked beans, salt pork, or corned beef."

The Country Kitchen, *by Della T. Lutes. Little, Brown and Company, 1936*

Fisko Flat Stainless-Steel Graters   4.35

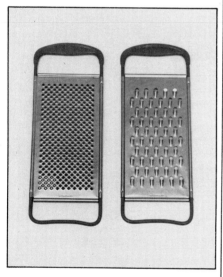

Stainless steel with plastic-covered grip and foot; 2 pieces, each 10¾″ X 4″ overall; grating surface 7½″ X 4″.

$4.00

These flat grater-shredders by Fisko are simple functional tools—the wooden Indonesian coconut grater in twentieth-century terms. Each consists of a separate plate with rolled edges. Wire slipped into the edges along each side forms a curved handle and base which for comfort and non-skid considerations have been coated in plastic. We would have preferred not to have to think about matching these to our kitchen, especially since yellow, orange, red, and avocado seem to be the predominate colors. That off our minds, we now deal with the practical. There are actually five different grater plates available, but we recommend these two: a coarse shredder for carrots or potatoes for your Rosti; and a punctured grating surface, fine for a bit of onion to sharpen a salad dressing. The advantage to a flat grater is that you may lie it flat over a small bowl, or stand it up inside it. These are reasonably well made, and the stainless steel will not be affected by acid foods.

AVOCADO SOUFFLE WITH LEMON SAUCE

Serves 6

BECHAMEL
4 tablespoons butter, approximately
4 tablespoons flour, approximately
1 cup milk
1 teaspoon salt
Freshly ground white pepper
Good pinch freshly grated nutmeg

SOUFFLE
4 whole eggs, separated
2 very ripe medium avocados or 1 large (1½ cups, puréed)
2 extra egg whites
Pinch of salt
Pinch cream of tartar

Butter heavily a 2-quart glass soufflé dish, then coat with flour, dumping out any excess. Refrigerate. Place a baking sheet in the oven and turn oven heat to 375 F.

Melt 4 tablespoons butter in a heavy saucepan (not aluminum). Stir in the flour until smooth to make a *roux*. Cook slowly, stirring constantly with a wooden spatula, until the mixture froths—about 3 minutes. Take care not to allow it to brown. Beat in milk. Continue cooking slowly, beating constantly with a wire whip, until the Béchamel comes to a boil and thickens noticeably. Remove from the heat and beat in the seasonings. Cool slightly. Add the 4 yolks, one at a time, to the cooled Béchamel, beating hard after each addition. Set aside. *The soufflé can be made in advance to this point* —in which case, seal with plastic wrap to prevent a skin forming.

Peel the avocados; discard the pits and scoop the flesh out with a spoon. Push through a fine sieve, or purée in a food mill. *Measure exactly 1½ cups.* Combine with the Béchamel and egg-yolk base.

Add to the 6 egg whites a pinch of salt and the cream of tartar. Beat in an electric mixer or with an electric beater until the whites hold firm shiny peaks when the beater is held straight up. Using a wire whip, beat about a third of the whites into the avocado mixture. Pour the whole mixture over the remaining whites, and fold in with a rubber spatula.

Taste for seasonings. It may need both salt and pepper. Pour into the prepared soufflé mold, place on the baking sheet and bake for 35 minutes, or longer if you like a dry soufflé. Serve immediately on a tray with a folded napkin under it.

LEMON SAUCE
1 package (8-ounce size) cream cheese, softened
3-4 tablespoons finely chopped parsley
3-4 tablespoons finely chopped chives
Juice 2 lemons (about), strained
Salt
Freshly ground white pepper

Place the cheese, herbs and half the lemon juice in the container of the electric blender and blend at high speed to a smooth purée. Add salt and pepper to taste. Taste here, too, for lemon and add more if you like. Serve in a suitable sauceboat at room temperature. Makes about 1½ cups.

(From THE GREAT COOKS COOKBOOK, by The Good Cooking School, Inc. Copyright © 1975 by The Good Cooking School, Inc. Reprinted by permission of Ferguson/Doubleday.)

Stainless-Steel Heavy-Duty Grater and Shredder   4.36

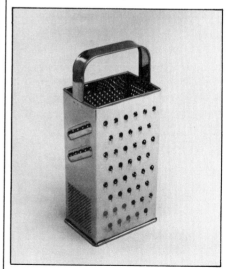

Stainless steel; 7½″ X 4″ X 3″; 10″ high with handle.

$6.75

The potato, root and branch: The vegetable most often mashed, puréed, fluffed, or riced in the centuries since its introduction into Europe.

Continued from preceding page

Take the old-fashioned metal box grater, add a little modern know-how, and you have a classic with clout. First of all, this version is made from heavy-duty stainless steel, to withstand the abuse of pounds of carrots for a rich carrot torte or the acid in the fruit you are grating for orange bread. The welded handle is extremely easy to grip, and all the edges have been rolled around wire frames for strength and comfort. Five different surfaces are offered for every job—they range from the finest grating perforations, perhaps for a pinch of nutmeg to top a custard, to slits for slices of apples for tarte aux pommes. Use the small shredding holes to produce a fine zest of lemon (see recipe for Lemon Bread), the large shredder for a raw-vegetable salad. The medium grating grid is perfect for dry bread crumbs. An extremely well-constructed kitchen tool, versatile and well-nigh indispensable for those who prefer not to overmechanize their kitchens.

Stainless-Steel Grater and Shredder 4.37

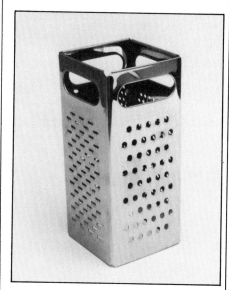

Stainless steel; 4″ square; 9″ high.
$11.20

Unlike the sturdy stainless-steel box grater above, this one shows how modern design got a bit carried away. It's made of stainless steel and is box-shaped, but the box has gone square in its horizontal dimensions and each side ends in a cut-out hand grip, allowing for one-piece construction. The result is handsome but rather bulky and awkward to grasp comfortably. The rolled edges are not finished as tightly as we could wish, with the result that the grater is somewhat unpleasant to hold. It has coarse, medium, and fine shredding grids (the fine one also has a scalloped slit), as well as a commodious slicing side. Its size makes it easy to clean. However, the individual flat shredders we have shown you plus a mandoline (see Chapter 3) would be preferable manual equipment; or you might buy the stainless-steel classic grater-shredder just preceding.

French Nutmeg Grater 4.38

Tin; 4½″ × 1¾″; 1″ deep.
$1.50

There was a time, in the not too distant past, when the only way you could buy nutmeg was whole (and, long ago, according to legend your nutmeg might turn out to be wooden). You grated it yourself—the real one, not the fake—using a special nutmeg grater so the pungent spice would not show up later in your bread crumbs. In earlier centuries nutmeg was used to season foods to a far greater degree than it is today—a pity, as this is a subtle spice, with many uses in vegetable and meat dishes as well as in sweets. If the modern palate has less taste for nutmeg, that is all the more reason to grate your own rather than to rely on a ground product which may have been sitting on the shelf for months on end, a faded remnant. Your apple pie will never be the same, and don't forget a little nutmeg in your next spinach soufflé or blanquette de veau. Both these nutmeg graters function in an identical fashion. A fine, curved rasping surface is surmounted by a hinged storage compartment into which to tuck a nutmeg, and there is a hole for hanging the whole contraption. A charming reminder of times gone by, and an indispensable tool for the cook with a fine palate for seasonings.

Large English Nutmeg Grater 4.39

Tin; 6½″ × 2½″; 1⅛″ deep.
$2.55

This large nutmeg grater from England costs about the same as the French one above and is perhaps a better choice. Not only is it more attractive, but in it several nutmegs can be stored, instead of one. Fine graters such as these are never easy to clean; your best method is to give it a rap against a towel-covered hand, or the counter, to dislodge tired bits clinging to the surface; rinse it under hot water once in a while, making sure that it is well dried afterward—try putting it in a warm oven for a short time.

"Along with a number of other spices nutmeg was used—piteously—as a fumigant against the plague. At the same time it was immensely popular in the kitchen. During the seventeenth, eighteenth and nineteenth centuries English sweet dishes and cakes appear to have been crammed with nutmeg, mace, cinnamon and cloves. For nutmegs, English silversmiths devised marvels of pocket graters, little boxes hinged and folded, with sharp grating surfaces and a compartment for the nut. No fastidious traveller need ever have been without a nutmeg to grate upon his food, his punch, his mulled wine, his hot ale, or comforting posset."

Elizabeth David, Spices, Salts and Aromatics in the English Kitchen, Penguin Books, 1973

DRIED FRUIT CAKE

½ cup dried prunes, apples, peaches, apricots, or a mixture
½ cup water
²/₃ cup butter
1 cup sugar
1 egg
2 cups sifted all-purpose flour
1 teaspoon baking soda
½ teaspoon salt
½ teaspoon each of cinnamon and nutmeg
½ teaspoon grated orange rind
¾ cup wine or juice from soaking dried fruit
½ cup toasted chopped walnuts, pecans, almonds, filberts, or hickory nuts

Obviously this, a museum piece, was the kind of fruit cake that used to be depended on during the winter and was often the holiday treat of the pioneer. Sometimes several types of fruit were combined for this cake, and old recipes generally called for four times this amount. We have livened the recipe with orange.

Combine the fruit and water in a small saucepan. Bring to boil, cover, and remove from heat. Let stand until cool. The fruit needs only to be softened. When cool, cut the fruit in pieces about the size of a seedless raisin. Pit the prunes. Cream the butter well and cream in the sugar until light. Beat in the egg and stir in fruit. Add the sifted dry ingredients alternately with the juice or wine and grated orange rind. Do not overstir. Add the nuts at the last. Turn into a greased and floured loaf pan or pans, and spread the dough up the sides of the pan a bit to produce a more

uniform top. Bake in a preheated 350-degree oven about 55 minutes. Test the center with a fingertip; when the cake springs back from light pressure and has shrunk from the sides of the pan, it is done. Let it stand in the pan on a rack about 10 minutes, then loosen from the pan and turn out on the rack to cool. This cake was generally not frosted but was stored in a crock or tightly covered tin until next day before being sliced.

(From AMERICAN COOKERY, by James A. Beard, illustrated by Earl Thollander. Copyright ©1972 by James A. Beard. Reprinted by permission of Little, Brown and Company.)

Two-Piece Round Cheese Grater with Bowl   4.41

Stainless steel; 7¾″ diam.; 2½″ deep; 6-cup capacity.
$6.50

Here is a large-capacity, round, Italian cheese grater fitted with its own bowl in a sleek, simple design. The roomy bowl will hold 6 cups of grated cheese without overflowing, and you can clearly see the amount of cheese you have through the air holes which encircle the grater. The stainless-steel bowl and grater come apart for easy cleaning. Although the bowl itself can be used on the table, assuming that a simple round of metal coordinates with the crockery, we do not recommend this unit as is for storing grated cheese. It lacks a cover—its only lapse—so the cheese may dry out or waft its fragrance over the pots de crème if it is stored in your refrigerator. Because most American kitchens are too warm to leave grated cheese unrefrigerated, perhaps the solution would be to cover the top closely with foil or plastic wrap and refrigerate the whole thing.

CROUTES AU PARMESAN—PARMESAN WAFERS

USE:
1 C. flour
1½ C. grated Parmesan cheese
7 T. butter
3 T. water
salt, cayenne

Prepare puff pastry, making eight turns using the flour, butter, water, salt, and a few grains of cayenne. Each time you give the dough a turn, sprinkle it with the finely grated Parmesan. Let it rest for fifteen minutes. Roll it out to a quarter-inch thick, cut it into diamond shapes, brush with egg, and bake in a hot oven.

Serve on a napkin.

Gruyère wafers may be prepared the same way.

(From ENCYCLOPEDIA OF PRACTICAL GASTRONOMY, by Ali-Bab, translated by Elizabeth Benson. Copyright © 1974 by McGraw-Hill, Inc. Reprinted by permission of McGraw-Hill Book Company.)

Plastic Cheese Grater   4.42

Plastic with stainless-steel grater; 3″ diam.; 3¾″ high; saucer 5″ diam.
$3.25 ▲

If the generous-sized round metal grater above can be faulted for lack of a cover, this nifty Italian plastic grater cannot be faulted. It is basically a clever design, a

Continued from preceding page

three-piece plastic unit looking like a little fire hydrant and available in several attractive colors. The bottom part is a double-walled cylinder fitted with a small metal grater across the top. The domed, fluted cover extends to fit down between the walls of the bottom cylinders, and it has a series of metal spikes inside it to hold the cheese against the grater. It is operated simply by placing the cheese on the grater, inserting the lid, pressing down on it, and twisting it back and forth. The cover is easy to grip, so grating is easy. The little custom-fitted saucer, upon which it sits, prevents crumbs of cheese from littering either the table or the refrigerator. It is ideal for storing a small piece of hard Parmesan, ready to go on the table to be dusted over plates of linguine. It has not been designed for easy cleaning; using a small, stiff-bristled brush, but no water, would be your best bet.

Rotary Grater with Three Cylinders 4.43

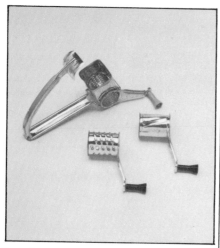

Tinned steel; plastic handles on grating cylinders; 7½" × 2", 3" high; 3 cylinders, each 1¾" diam., 2⅛" wide.

$4.50 ▲

This grater is Mouli at its best—it has become a homely kitchen classic and deservedly so, because the design is extraordinarily efficient and uncomplicated. You hold this grater by a pair of tinned-steel handles, the lower one of which terminates in a hinged hopper, the receptacle for the cheese, beneath which there is a cradle to hold the sepa-

rate grating cylinder, which is turned by its own small handle during use. The upper handle is fitted with a plate for pressing down on the food in the hopper in order to hold it against the rotating grating surface. Since the Mouli grater has this holding plate, you can use it to grind nuts—for instance, pistachios for sprinkling on servings of mousse au chocolat. It comes with a fine shredding cylinder, a coarse shredder, and a slicing cylinder. Although it is often packaged with only the fine shredder, it pays to buy it with all three. Although the food receptacle is small, with continual refilling your kitchen could eventually be knee-deep in grated Gruyère with little effort. The cylinder can be switched for left-handed as well as right-handed use—good news for southpaws. The grater is very easy to clean—just swish the parts through hot suds, rinse, and dry.

For reasons obvious to those possessing taste buds, cheese should be freshly grated for use in any recipe. A hazard other than staleness occasionally encountered by purchasers of pre-grated cheese is adulteration. Reay Tannahill writes in her book Food in History *of a case which occurred in 1969: An Italian manufacturer was found to have added an odd secret ingredient to his grated Parmesan cheese—umbrella handles.*

PAIN DE FRUITS (FRUIT BREAD)

Interesting in flavor and nicely textured, this French fruit bread is excellent for toast. It bakes to a delicious-looking rich brown and is a very attractive gift bread.

1 loaf

4 eggs
½ cup granulated sugar
1½ cups all-purpose flour
1½ teaspoons double-acting baking powder
½ teaspoon ground cinnamon
1 teaspoon salt
6 tablespoons butter, melted and quickly removed from heat
3 ounces filberts, ground
4 ounces almonds, ground
4 ounces dried figs, cut into small pieces
2 ounces candied citron, diced
½ cup golden seedless raisins, presoaked in warm water for 1 hour

Line a 9 × 5 × 3-inch bread pan with buttered waxed paper. Beat the eggs

and sugar until they form a ribbon. Sift together the flour, baking powder, cinnamon, and salt and add, along with the melted butter, to the eggs and sugar. Then add the nuts, figs, citron, and raisins and blend thoroughly. Pour into the prepared pan and bake in a preheated 350° oven for 50 to 60 minutes. Cool slightly in the pan, then remove the loaf to a rack to finish cooling.

(From BEARD ON BREAD, by James A. Beard, illustrated by Karl Stuecklen. Copyright © 1973 by James A. Beard. Reprinted by permission of Alfred A. Knopf, Inc.)

Quick Mill for Cheese 4.44

Nickel-plated housing, chrome-plated grating parts, stainless-steel retaining pan; 20¼" × 10½"; 17⅛" high.

$550.00

For high-speed grating of a lot of cheese, such as a caterer or a restaurant or a very large, very hungry family might require, there is no substitute for this Italian electric cheese grater. It will pulverize approximately 75 pounds of hard cheese in an hour, but it does have a limitation—it will accommodate only hard cheeses such as Romano or Parmesan, and it reduces them to a granulated texture. It won't make fine shreds of Swiss cheese for your gratin, but it will give you fresh cheese for the bowls on the tables, however large your restaurant. This sort of electric efficiency is available at a price, not for every budget; but the Quick Mill is well made, with all working parts of noncorroding metals, and is substantial in size, taking up more than 14 inches of space in one direction, more than 12 inches in the other.

Zyliss Mechanical Grater   4.45

Cast aluminum with rubber suction base, stainless-steel grating cylinders; 4½″ base diam.; 9⅛″ tall; 3 grating cylinders, each 3¼″ diam., 3⅛″ deep.
$50.00

For versatility and good looks in the category of mechanical but nonelectric appliances, this hand-cranked grater is the best for the price. The futuristic body and handle are of gleaming cast aluminum, not a seam in sight—obviously a product of the same design school that produced items like the gleaming meat pounders and espresso machines we have shown you. The strong suction base will cling fiercely to a smooth surface; you would have to lift the table before it is likely to let go without the intervention of the release lever. All the parts are rustproof. The hinged cover permits you to exert steady pressure on the food being processed without risking skinned knuckles. Three drums, each stemmed to screw into the machine's handle, are of stainless steel, with cutting edges that will stay sharp; these permit fine and coarse

grating and shredding and slicing as well. The perforations on the fine drum look like scalloped slits; with this one you produce carottes râpées for a refreshing hors d'oeuvre, or ground nuts in which to roll your rum balls. The coarse shredder will cope with fairly soft cheeses, and you can also use it for vegetables, cooked or raw, for salads. Making thin onion rings, or thin potato rounds for Pommes Anna, or thinly sliced cucumber, is the province of the slicing drum. A superfine drum for grating hard cheese or bread crumbs and a special drum for making juliennes—think of Céleri-rave Rémoulade—are optional extras. Before you opt for this grater, remember that starting in the same price range you can buy an electrically powered machine which will perform the same functions and more. It is important to evaluate your equipment and your needs before investing in an expensive nonelectric appliance, although this, using no current and powered only by the cook's arm, is perhaps more versatile than most, if more strenuous to use.

Mouli Salad Maker   4.46

Plastic frame with plastic handle, rubber feet; 12½″ long × 9¼″ wide overall; 4″ high excluding crank; hopper 5″ diam., 1¾″ deep; 5 steel grating discs, each 4⅝″ diam.
$6.98

One buys Mouli mechanical gadgets for their utility, never for their beauty. In the case of this salad maker that utility is somewhat limited, but we have included it as a reasonably efficient alternative to the Zyliss mechanical grater above at a mere fraction of the price. The hand crank turns the various shredding and slicing discs, while a hinged plate holds the food in the kidney-shaped hopper firmly against the cutting surface. The drawback is precisely the odd contour and limited size of the food receptacle, which, further, must be positioned over a countertop or platter—its legs do not allow sufficient clearance to use a bowl underneath. However, the rubber feet, set on hinged legs for convenient storage, hold it to a surface with relative stability. The frame is of plastic and is of course rust-free; the entire contraption dismantles for easy cleaning. Five interchangeable discs are provided. Three are grater-shredders—fine, medium, and coarse—two are slicers, thick and thin. From cabbage to chocolate, bread crumbs to betteraves, the Mouli is an inexpensive improvement over flat graters.

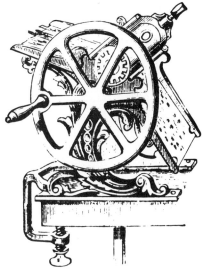

An English vegetable cutter of the last century, recommended as a rapid means of preparing ingredients for soup.

Meat Grinders

The quality of their beefsteaks separates the wealthy from the wanting, but ground meat is the great equalizer. For making dishes from polpette to pâté, in huts or hotels the world over, meat is ground, to be

Continued from preceding page

seasoned, shaped, cooked, and served in a thousand ways. In grinding the fat and muscle—often of tough meats—are cut and torn, the grain and fiber obliterated as they are forced inexorably through the blades. Finally, the particles emerge, compliant, ready to be lightened with mellifluous cream or kindled with violent spices to tempt the palate. Culinary sleight of hand extends ground meat, even doubles it—economy for epicures. A good meat grinder will pay for itself by allowing you to use cheaper cuts, to combine small amounts of different ingredients, or to use your leftovers inconspicuously.

GRINDERS AND ALTERNATIVES

Whether hand or electrically powered, a meat grinder operates with a rotary action. A large screw drives the pieces of meat toward the knife blades—which usually look like the propeller of a steamer or some such—forcing them through openings which determine their ultimate texture. Instead of a meat grinder you *could* select a food processor or other multipurpose electric appliance that has attachments for shredding, slicing, grating, or juicing (see Chapters 3 and 5); with some of these you can prepare the beef for the filling and the lettuce and cheese to garnish your tostadas all on one machine. If your needs run primarily to hamburger rather than homemade sausage—for which your own grinder is essential—a cooperative butcher is another alternative. Any but the simplest hand grinder will be expensive, so examine your options carefully.

Moulinex Meat Grinder 4.47

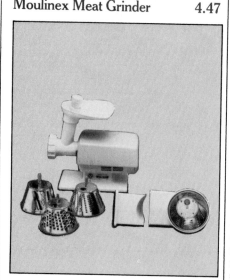

Plastic housing with boilproof nylon hoppers, tinned-steel salad-making cones, tempered-steel grinding discs; 6½" × 4¼"; 6" high; 4 cones, each 4" diam., 2⅜" deep.
$39.95

The clean lines of this plastic grinder conceal a multiplicity of talents, not the least of which is an electric can opener which positively will *not* sharpen (or ruin) your knives or do anything else but open cans. If you own a blender as well, this grinder equips you for mechanizing most food-processing jobs. Even with the powerful fan-cooled 150-watt motor, the whole machine weighs only seven pounds, so it is easily carried with one hand. It is compact—6½ by 4¼ inches, and 6 inches high—dimensions that permit handy countertop storage in the tightest kitchen. Using the parts is not a formidable undertaking; it is meant for daily service; but be sure to unplug the machine before removing or inserting parts. The Moulinex comes equipped with a salad maker and a grater, four interchangeable tinned-steel cones providing textures from slices to shreds. The machine will also grate over a punctured surface like that of a hand grater, an unusual feature. These various drums surpass other sets of cones in their capacity to finely grate soft cheese as well as in yielding professionally powdered hard cheese. The citrus juicer does not depend on hand pressure to activate the reamer, making fresh juice effortlessly. Two tempered-steel grinding discs, designed to stay sharp, are provided with the meat grinder. A sausage stuffer almost completes the picture. There is also a hamburger press—a less useful item which does not improve your hamburger, making it too firm and dense. The salad hopper and pusher block, the tray, funnel, spiral screw, and hand ring of the meat grinder are of dishwasher-safe and virtually indestructible nylon. Add to this highly competent combination a surprisingly low price.

POLPETTE ALLA PIZZAIOLA— BEEF PATTIES WITH ANCHOVIES AND MOZZARELLA

Although it is very far from being a national dish, Italians do eat "hamburger." This is particularly true of some areas of the south where the beef is rather tough and it is chopped to make it tender. The following version of "hamburger," in its frank, zesty taste, in the simplicity of its approach, and in its decorative appearance, is undeniably Italian.

For 6 persons
1 3-by-3-inch piece white bread, crust removed
3 tablespoons milk
1½ pounds lean beef, preferably chuck, ground
1 egg
Salt
¾ cup fine, dry unflavored bread crumbs, spread on a dinner plate or on waxed paper
¼ cup vegetable oil
6 canned Italian tomatoes, opened flat, without seeds and juice
1 teaspoon orégano
6 slices mozzarella, 4 inches square, ¼ inch thick
12 flat anchovy fillets

1. Preheat the oven to 400°.
2. In a saucer or small bowl, soak the bread in the milk and mash it to a cream with a fork. Put the meat in a bowl, add the bread and milk mush, the egg, and 1 teaspoon salt, and knead with your hands until all the ingredients are well mixed.
3. Divide the meat mixture into 6 patties 1½ inches high and turn them over in the bread crumbs.
4. Over medium heat, heat the oil in a skillet until the meat sizzles when it is slipped in. Add the meat patties and cook 4 minutes on each side, handling them delicately when you turn them over so they don't break up. When done,

transfer to a butter-smeared baking dish.
5. Cover each patty with a flattened tomato, reserving a small strip of each tomato, no larger than ½ inch, to be used for garnish. Season lightly with salt and a pinch of orégano. Over each tomato place a slice of mozzarella, and over the mozzarella place two anchovy fillets in the form of a cross. Where the anchovies meet place the reserved strip of tomato. Put the dish in the uppermost level of the oven and bake for 15 minutes, or until the mozzarella melts.

NOTE

These patties can be prepared several hours ahead of time before they are put in the oven.

(From the CLASSIC ITALIAN COOK-BOOK, by Marcella Hazan, illustrated by George Koizumi. Copyright © 1973 by Marcella Hazan. Reprinted by permission of Alfred A. Knopf.)

The Tritacarne Three   4.48

Housing, hoppers, food pushers, and some working parts of plastic; stainless-steel shredding/grating cylinders, tempered-steel meat grinding blades and cylinders, and tinned-steel tomato-pulping cone. Base 9¼″ × 4″, 6¾″ high; base with tomato pulper 18½″ long, with meat grinder 11⅜″ long, and with grater 10⅛″ long.
$80.00

The Bialetti Tritacarne Three will process every ingredient you need for a full-dress spaghetti dinner except the pasta. Unfortunately, there is an incredible welter of parts which comes packed in a box big enough for an electric train under the Christmas tree, and it takes a bit of time to get acquainted with all of them. The parts are all meant to be attached to a fairly compact

white plastic pedestal unit which houses the 115-watt fan-cooled motor. First, to prepare the beef and pork for the polpette: The meat grinder is equipped with coarse and fine cutting heads, plates, and a sharp knife blade, all of tempered steel. The rotary grinder screw is plastic. Move on to the salsa di pomodoro: the tomato press forces the pulp through a mesh of fine holes while the seeds and skin, detained in the machine, are not crushed into the purée to mar its flavor, as they would be in a regular food mill. A commodious plastic hopper and funnel are provided for such puréeing jobs. (The instructions caution that the tomatoes must not be boiling-hot when they are puréed. On the other hand, the conical sieve you use heats up from the friction when in use, making this attachment all right for tomatoes, but inadvisable to use with raw fruit.) Ready to grate the cheese? Fitting into another plastic attachment with a food hopper and pusher plate are the slicer/shredder/grater/ drums of stainless steel and aluminum. Like the Moulinex we have shown you above, the grating drum is covered with fiercely-looking perforations which will pulverize hard cheese with authority. Needless to say, you'll unplug the machine to change or remove the attachments. Suction feet secure the machine to the countertop during use. The plastic parts are designed to withstand the rigors of dishwasher cleaning.

Spong Meat Grinder   4.49

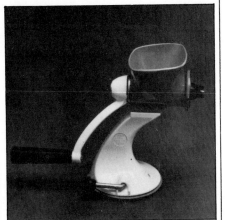

Enameled die-cast steel base with hard nylon hopper, tinned cast-iron worm, and tempered-steel grinding discs; 4″ base diam.; 7¼″ high.
$20.00 ▲

In a kitchen which places only moderate demands on a food grinder and which does not have an electric appliance with an attachment for grinding meat, there is a place for this small hand grinder by Spong. It is light, sleek, and compact. The hard-nylon food hopper has a small capacity, but the tinned cast-iron rotary screw will force strips of meat through any of four tempered steel grinding discs at the rate of a pound a minute. The stationary cutter, bladelike in shape, is fixed into place, and you place the coarse, medium, or fine disc over it according to the grind you need. A satisfactory solution to the problem of grinding with armpower instead of electricity.

Kichka's recipe for steak tartare:

"On a plate, a quarter to a half pound of ground filet of beef, preferably, and an egg yolk.

"At your disposal on the table: oil, vinegar, mustard, Worcestershire sauce, ketchup, chopped onions, chopped parsley, capers, salt, pepper and if you have any, cognac.

"Begin by preparing it with everything in the desired proportion, tasting the mixture as you go along, never finding it just right, and continue until there is nothing left on the plate."

"A Gastronomic Itinerary," in Daniel Spoerri, The Mythological Travels

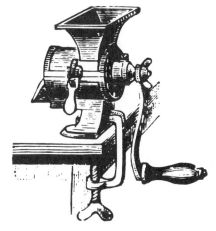

Nineteenth-century English food grinder.

Hand-operated Meat Grinder 4.50 with Attachments

Cast-iron base with double-dipped zinc coating; zinc-plated steel attachments; cutting plates and cutting edges of worm self-sharpening hard steel; worm extensions with juice-extractor and nut-grater attachments chromed steel; 7" wide, 12" high overall; height from counter top 7".

$21.95 meat grinder only

This very heavy-duty hand grinder from Czechoslovakia, as essential to the kitchen as Pilsener glasses are to the table, will crank out pounds of pork for klobasy, or bread crumbs in which to roll tender topfenknödel. It means business, making no compromises with modern concepts of style. Although yours may come packed with directions in original, untranslated Czech, it will not flinch at grinding corned beef for old-fashioned red-flannel hash. The cast-iron body and handle, as well as some of the attachments, are zinc-plated to resist rust and corrosion. The massive rotary worm has self-sharpening steel cutting edges, a feature found on few other grinders,

that permits it to handle large pieces of meat. The worm fits through the base of the grinder: the handle is secured by a bolt at one end of the worm, and at the other end the four-sided steel knife blade is fitted, sharpened edges facing out. Then a steel cutting disc, coarse or fine as you choose, fits over the end of the blade and is held in place by a zinc-plated screw-on ring. If you remove the cutting blades and disc, such optional attachments as a nut grater, a cooky press, or a fruit press can be substituted, ready to prepare nuts or fruit for your Linzer torte or other baking. The fruit press, which yields only pulp—no seeds or skin—has a finer mesh than either the electric or manual tomato presses we have shown you, making it more effective for berries—conceivably you could even purée huckleberries. Be sure the base clamp, with its plastic insulator, is tightly secured before using the machine—one would not want to see all ten pounds of it go crashing to the floor. The parts should be washed and dried carefully after use; take care not to drop the considerable weight of the grinder in your sink, either.

WONDERFUL MINCEMEAT

2 pounds lean uncooked beef
2 pounds uncooked tongue
1 pound beef suet
4 cups seedless raisins
4 cups seeded raisins
2 cups currants
1 cup diced citron
1 cup diced orange peel
½ cup diced lemon peel
1 cup chopped figs
2½ cups sugar
2 teaspoons salt
2 teaspoons nutmeg
2 teaspoons cinnamon
2 teaspoons allspice
1 teaspoon cloves
5 cups cognac (approximately)
4 cups sherry (approximately)

Cook beef and tongue in water to cover until tender. Grind through the coarse blade of meat grinder, adding uncooked suet.

Add all remaining ingredients except cognac and sherry. Add enough cognac to make a thick, soupy mixture. Place in a clean crock. Cover and let stand at least 1 month. Refrigeration is unnecessary. Check after 1 week. If mixture has absorbed most of liquid and seems dry, add enough sherry to moisten it again. Continue to check every 2 to 3 weeks, adding cognac and sherry alternately as mincemeat absorbs mixture. It will keep indefinitely.

Add 1 cup chopped tart apples to each 1¼ cups mincemeat before using. Drain mincemeat before mixing with apples.

(From THE ART OF FINE BAKING, by Paula Peck. Copyright © 1961 by Paula Peck. Reprinted by permission of Simon & Schuster.)

Peppermills and Salt Grinders

Oriental spice routes have been paved with peppercorns since the most ancient era—man's culinary history has been seasoned with more *Piper nigrum* than any other spice, and to this day pepper is the most widely used seasoning in the world. Unless it has been freshly ground, however, pepper might as well not season at all. Whether in the kitchen to enliven the Southern fried chicken, or at the table, dusted over a crisp salad, pepper should be dispensed at the source, directly from the peppermill, the encapsulated and mechanized little grinder, the successor to the mortar and pestle.

A good peppermill will hold at least two tablespoons of peppercorns so you can avoid continual refilling. And when it comes time to replenish the supply, it should be possible to fill the mill without an advanced degree in engineering. Filling the peppermill and adjusting the grind (an adjustable grinding mechanism is another important feature) should be independent operations. With the plethora of peppermills on the market, it is not difficult to find one which is efficient and also satisfies your taste in objects. The examples we show you have excellent mechanisms, and have both the grinder and the case made by the same manufacturer.

SALT GRINDERS

While it is essential to grind pepper—unless you're using the peppercorns whole in the stockpot—the same is not true of salt, a stable chemical in pure form. Ordinary table salt contains chemical additives, however, that adversely affect the flavor of food. French or English sea salt or kosher salt (neither of which actually needs to be ground finer, except possibly for some very coarse kinds of sea salt) are good alternatives. For table use, some people find a salt mill filled with coarse rock salt or sea salt more convenient than the historic expedient, an open salt dish. Those who use sea salt at the table are firmly convinced that their favorite salt tastes better than the packaged grocery-store kinds with additives. Buy one of the salt mills we show, and decide for yourself.

Perfex Peppermill   4.51

Cast aluminum with tempered-steel mechanism; 2¼" base diam.; 4¼" high. Also avail. 3½" high.

$16.50 ▲

To have coined the name Perfex for this French peppermill was not arrogance—it is accurate and descriptive: one could want nothing better in a functional piece of equipment. No frills—a simply designed cylindrical cast-aluminum mill is fitted with a small practical pull-out chute for inserting the peppercorns. There is a crank handle on top and an adjustable tension nut on the bottom. Loosen the tension nut to the end of the shaft for very coarsely crushed pepper suitable for a steak au poivre, or set it for a fine grind by tightening it, and go on with your pfeffernusse. If your hands

are covered with dough as you grind, the satin finish of the mill is easily wiped clean. The Perfex comes in two sizes; it makes more sense to own the larger one.

POULET LYONNAISE—CHICKEN LYONNAISE

Serves 6 to 8

Whenever the adjective *lyonnaise* is used in a French recipe it implies that onions are part of the recipe.

2 3½-pound chickens
3 teaspoons salt
1½ teaspoons freshly ground black pepper
4 tablespoons butter, softened
1 tablespoon vegetable oil
3 cups sliced onions
2 cloves garlic, peeled, crushed, and chopped
1 cup breadcrumbs (fresh if possible)
½ cup water

Trim the chicken wings by removing the tips at the last joint. Split the chickens through the back and flatten them until they lie even on the table. Sprinkle on each side with 2 teaspoons of salt and 1 teaspoon of pepper. Rub 2 tablespoons of the butter on the skin of the chicken and place them on a tray, skin side up, in a 425° oven for 25 minutes. Turn the chicken over and cook an additional 15 minutes on the other side. Meanwhile, melt the remaining butter and the oil in a saucepan and add the onions, 1 teaspoon of salt, and ½ teaspoon of pepper. Cook on medium heat on top of the stove for 12 minutes, turning the onions once in a while. Add the garlic and cook another 2 minutes. The onions should be cooked

through and light brown in color. Arrange the onion mixture on top of the chicken (*i.e.*, the onions go on the skin of the chicken). Top with breadcrumbs and moisten the topping with the fat accumulated in the pan. *Tip the pan to one side and use a spoon or a baster to pick up the juices and coat the bread mixture with it.* Place the chicken back in the oven for 25 minutes, or until nicely browned. Place the chicken on a serving dish and add the water to the cooking pan. Melt all the solidified juices and bring to a boil. You may serve the chicken cut into quarters with the sauce poured on top.

A nice Beaujolais like Morgan, Chiroubles or Moulin-à-vent would be excellent with this dish.

(From JACQUES PEPIN: A FRENCH CHEF COOKS AT HOME, by Jacques Pépin. Copyright © 1975 by Jacques Pépin. Reprinted by permission of Simon & Schuster.)

Pepper is the fruit of an East Indian plant. The berries are bright red when they are growing, black when dried. When the outer layer of dried black pepper has been removed the remaining part of the fruit is used as white pepper —actually beige in color—which is somewhat milder in flavor than the black.

Peugeot Wooden Peppermill   4.52

Natural or walnut-stained beechwood with stainless-steel mechanism; 2" base diam.; 3¾" high. Also avail. 8⅝" high.

$10.00 ▲

The Peugeot peppermill mechanism sets a standard of excellence and has a well-deserved reputation for durability. It may be found in peppermills of every imaginable shape and size, as well as this one of classic silhouette, as familiar as the Coke bottle. In use, the walnut body is held in one hand, while the top section is turned with the other. Peppercorns inside the hollow core feed into the metal mill at the bottom from which the pepper drifts, freshly ground, onto soup or salad. The knurled nut at the top is turned to adjust the grind—the tighter it is screwed the finer the grind—or unscrewed completely to let you remove the cover and refill the peppermill. While replenishing this mill is more complicated than in the Perfex, it is trouble-free because of the precision construction of the mechanism. The mill we show you is unfinished walnut and is available either light or dark, in the familiar squat shape we show you or elongated to be 8⅝" high. Two Peugeot peppermills, one in a dark-stained wood and one light, would be useful to have for black and white peppercorns. Matching salt shakers are also available.

Stainless-Steel Peppermill 4.53

Stainless steel with wooden knob handle; 2½" base diam.; 3" high.

$21.00

W. M. Fraser makes a good peppermill mechanism, here housed in a commodi-

ous case of heavy-duty solid stainless steel, an improvement over some stainless-steel mills consisting of a metal sheath over a wood body. The steel cylinder is interrupted in midsection, suggesting a sturdy hour-glass shape, an attractive modern design, easy to grasp. A crank handle at the top is attached to the grinding shaft. Unlike the Perfex and Peugeot mechanisms, the Fraser shaft is not wrapped with a tension spring which is loosened or tightened with a nut for adjusting the grind. Instead, this peppermill has a small tension screw at the bottom, establishing a more limited range of adjustment. A black plastic cap on the bottom of the mill unscrews, revealing an opening for refilling in the base of the mechanism. Be careful not to adjust the tension unless the bottom cap is in place or the entire mechanism will loosen, postponing the sauce poivrade while you struggle to realign the parts.

Wooden Peppermill 4.54

Unstained varnished walnut with steel mechanism; 3½" square; 2⅞" high.

$12.50

The old-fashioned wooden coffee mill, miniaturized for pepper. The small wooden box, dovetailed and varnished, has on its top a greenish metal crank, a chute for filling the mill with peppercorns, and a clip that fits into any of four notches for adjusting the grind. The mechanism is of stainless steel. Made in France by Grulet, it is strictly a kitchen item—one does not dust pepper directly from this mill to season food at the table—one spoons the pepper from the wooden drawer near the bottom.

"In those days there were none of the thousand ameliorations of the labors of housekeeping which have since arisen—no ground and prepared spices and sweet herbs; everything came into our hands in the rough and in bulk, and the reducing of it into a state for use seemed one of the appropriate labors of childhood. Even the very salt that we used in cooking was rock salt, which we were required to wash and dry and pound and sift, before it became fit for use.

"At other times of the year we sometimes murmured at these labors, but those that were supposed to usher in the great Thanksgiving festival were always entered into with enthusiasm. There were signs of richness all around us—stoning of raisins, cutting of citron, slicing of candied orange peel . . ."

H. B. Stowe, Oldtown Folks, 1869

Salt and Pepper Mill Set 4.55

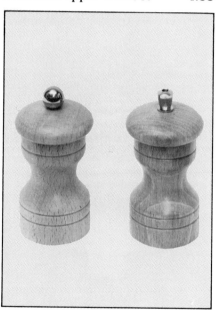

Unfinished light wood with hardened-steel mechanism in pepper mill, stainless-steel mechanism in salt mill; 1⅞" base diam.; 3¾" high.

$11.00

Again French, again efficient classics. The blond pepper mill in a classic shape has a good French mechanism. Not quite the premier quality of Peugeot perhaps, but close. You can't really adjust the grind on the pepper mill, but that is generally the sacrifice you make when you select a salt and pepper set. (You could buy a salt

The Old Way

Continued from preceding page

shaker to match your Peugeot pepper mill, but then you could not use Kosher or sea salt.) The salt mill operates just like the pepper mill, but here the mechanism is of non-corrosive stainless steel. It also looks just like the pepper mill—the slightly different screw buttons at the top are the only way to tell them apart. The small (less than 4″) size is sufficient for a pepper mill, but the salt mill will probably need refilling every other day.

Pocket Peppermill 4.56

Brass with stainless-steel mechanism, leather carrying case; 1″ diam.; 2″ high.

$12.95

Culinary demands certainly exist away from home. In a fine restaurant, the peppermill will be proffered. In others, often where the plat du jour is most in need of support, a peppermill is unavailable, only preground grains sitting in a shaker offered as the pallid substitute. This pocket peppermill, an innocent conceit, can provide small pleasures by making indifferent food bearable. The elegant fluted 2-inch brass cylinder containing a stainless-steel mechanism is made in Italy and is housed in its own red leather case. Shades of the epicures of an earlier century, who carried their own nutmegs and a special silver grater.

My mill grinds pepper and spice;
Your mill grinds rats and mice.

The Oxford Nursery Book, *edited by* Iona and Peter Opie. Oxford University Press, 1955

Wooden Salt Mill from France 4.57

Beechwood with boxwood key and grinding ball; 1⅛″ base diam.; 3¾″ high.

$7.50

As simple as the salt it dispenses, this smoothly sanded, unfinished wood salt mill from France is naively attractive. It stands on a flat base. To use it, turn it upside down, turn the wooden key-shaped handle, and the grinder—a sharply ridged hardwood ball—moves against the salt grains to grind them and release them through a small opening. The smooth bottom part, bulb-shaped, unscrews from the turned wood upper section for refilling with coarse sea or kosher salt.

Glass Salt Mill 4.58

Glass with cork stopper, plastic handle and grinding ball; 2⅝″ diam.; 3″ high.

$14.00

Variation on a theme. This Scandinavian salt mill is a squat, heavy glass cylinder. The key-shaped handle and the grinding ball are of hard white plastic. It is stoppered with a rustic cork which, like the translucent salt grains, is revealed through the glass. The design is more assertive than that of the French wooden mill, the glass more fragile and more decorative. In either case, salt is dispensed at the table without spoons, dishes, and other accessories. The companion peppermill, while beautiful looking, is difficult to fill and impossible to adjust.

Coffee Mills

There is no question that once a roasted coffee bean has been ground, its quality begins at once to go into a serious decline. The best cup is brewed from freshly ground coffee, and having a home coffee mill makes that possible every day, or several times a day. The beans are ground only as they are needed, so you can guard the flavor and fragrance of your supply of beans (ideally in the freezer) until the last possible moment. Infinite possibilities of custom blending are limited only by the availability of beans.

It is not necessary that your coffee mill have a large capacity—a six-cup pot of strong American coffee will take less than a cup of ground coffee. What a coffee mill must have, however, is an easily adjustable grind system, so that the requirements of a Turkish jezve, if you have

Pocket Peppermill
Wooden Salt Mill from France
Glass Salt Mill

Cast-Iron Clamp-on Coffee Mill
Wooden Coffee Mill
Braun Electric Coffee Mill
All-Purpose Quick Mill

brought one of these slightly conical brass pots back from your travels, can be met as readily as those of an ordinary percolator.

Cast-Iron Clamp-on Coffee Mill   4.59

Enameled cast iron; 5″ wide; 8″ from wall brackets to tip of crank; 11″ high. Also avail. 13″ or 15″ high.

$18.50 ▲

Our respect for the historic development of food-processing equipment prompts us to insist that this shiny black cast-iron English replica of an old mill be included. It would be a charming accessory in the country kitchen, serving more than a strictly decorative function. It works, down to the end of its bright red crank handle (fashioned, unfortunately, of plastic). The grind is adjustable, within narrow tolerances, by setting a lever in the back. The coffee mill can be clamped on one end of your old pine farmhouse table, or mounted on the authentic barn siding of your kitchen walls—there are strong brackets with holes provided for convenient fastening. The container for the ground coffee is removable, and the whole thing has touches of gilded trim suitable for The Age of Innocence.

"Frederick the Great used to make his own coffee, with much to-do and fuss. For water he used champagne. Then, to make the flavour stronger, he stirred in powdered mustard. . . . Now to me, it seems improbable that Frederick truly liked this brew. I suspect him of bravado, or perhaps he was taste-blind."

M. F. K. Fisher, Serve It Forth

Wooden Coffee Mill   4.60

Dark-stained wood with steel mechanism, copper-washed steel lid and crank; 4⅞″ square; 4⅜″ high; drawer capacity 4 oz.

$16.50

The time-honored classic wooden coffee mill is still being made in France, just as it was at the turn of the century. You might discover an old one in an antique shop or at a yard sale—if so, it might be finished more beautifully than this dark-stained wood and imitation-copper example. The stolid cube shape of the base is fitted with a drawer which collects the ground coffee, up to a total of 4 ounces. The crank handle extends from the copper-finished top, which slides back for filling the mill. By simply setting a clip into any of the five notches under the handle you can adjust the grind.

Braun Electric Coffee Mill   4.61

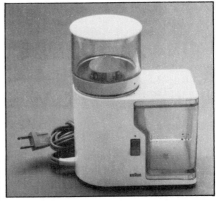

Plastic; 5⅝″ × 3⅛″; 7½″ high; container capacity 1½ cups.

$45.00 ▲

Unless your taste runs to the old-fangled, select this paragon of electric coffee mills. Neat and compact, typical of its maker (Braun) in design, it is made of easy-to-clean white plastic. The hopper for the beans and the container for ground coffee are of blue-tinted clear plastic, the better to see quantities. By rotating the bean hopper, the grind can be set for any of nine textures, from coarse to powder. The motor produces a quiet hum, likely to be drowned out by the water boiling, and the mill has a good capacity, 1½ cups.

All-Purpose Quick Mill   4.62

Plastic with stainless-steel blade and hopper; 3⅝″ × 3″; 6½″ high.

$14.95

Continued from preceding page

In attempting to provide a small appliance for every milling purpose, Salton has solved no problems—the Quick Mill looks better than it works. A slick beige-plastic elliptical cylinder has a clear brown plastic top. By depressing a white button on its side, the mill is activated, its blender-type blades madly whirling inside; take your finger off the button and the blades stop. As in a blender, texture is determined by the length of time the grinding action is allowed to continue. The Quick Mill does an un-even job on coffee beans; such variables as quantity affect the timing and make your chosen grind impossible to achieve with accuracy unless your taste runs to Turkish, in which case you can run the mill until your beans are pulverized to a powder. The container is too small to make this a practical machine to use for grain or bread crumbs, and a mortar would be preferable for grinding spices. Similar multipurpose milling machines now coming on the market are no more effective in performing their various functions than this one; we include it as a typical example of the genre.

Juice Extractors

Moses smote the rock at Meribah with his rod and water issued forth—seemingly an unlikely event, but to some no more unlikely than extracting juice from a carrot. Moses had his rod, and extracting juice from various foods also takes special equipment. Greater pressure than the hand alone can exert, reduction into finer particles than the knife can achieve, will induce the release of every drop of vital juice, whether from fruits, vegetables, or meats, to flavor and to fortify. Electrically and hand-operated equipment has been devised to force foods to yield drops or buckets of juices as they are needed. Clever miniatures or bulky behemoths, juice extractors and juicers come fitted with pressers, reamers, whirling blades, and straining meshes, a multiplicity of parts that require careful, often tedious cleaning.

These machines are highly effective within their fairly narrow limitations: a citrus juicer, for example, will not make a dent on a carrot; the meat press would destroy your tomato. Rather than a special machine for preparing juice, you could consider a juicing attachment for multipurpose electric appliances if freshly squeezed orange juice is not your family's required eye-opener every morning, or carrot juice its passion.

FRUIT JUICES

Most fruit juices, including cranberry, cherry, grape, raspberry and strawberry, apple, and citrus and tomato juice, make excellent frozen products and retain their fresh flavor from one season to another. They make refreshing drinks thawed and served cold, or they can be made into fruit juices, ice creams, and sherbets, or boiled up with sugar and made into clear and sparkling jelly.

ORANGE AND GRAPEFRUIT need only be squeezed to extract the juice. The juice is then packed into liquid-tight containers and frozen. Select fully ripe fruit and chill thoroughly in refrigerator. Cut fruit in half, ream out juice, and strain through a stainless-steel or plastic strainer or cheesecloth. Pour juice into containers, leaving 1 inch head space, and freeze immediately.

APPLES as well as citrus fruits need no heat treatment. Extract the juice from sound winter apples, pour into moisture-vaporproof, liquid-tight containers, allowing 1 inch head space, and freeze at once. The secret of really fresh-flavored golden apple juice is in the speed with which it is handled and put in the freezer. Fermentation starts almost immediately, and if the juice is allowed to remain at room temperature for even an hour, it begins to darken and develops a "cider" flavor.

CHERRIES, GRAPES, AND BERRIES must be heated to extract the juice. Select fully ripe, flavorful fruit. Wash, sort, and drain fruit and put it in a stainless-steel or aluminum preserving kettle. Crush fruit with a potato masher and heat very gradually to between 160° and 170° F., stirring occasionally, to soften the fruit and release the juices. Strain juice through a muslin jelly bag and cool by floating the saucepan containing it in ice water. Sweeten juice with from ½ to 1 cup sugar per gallon, or sweeten to taste. Pour the juice into moisture-vaporproof, liquid-tight containers, leaving 1 inch head space for expansion during freezing, and freeze immediately.

APRICOTS, PEACHES, AND RHUBARB must also be heated to extract the juice and since these are drier fruits than cherries or berries, a little water should be added. Wash, sort, and drain the fruit. Put it in a stainless-steel or aluminum kettle and add about ½ cup water for each pound of fruit.

Bring the fruit to a simmer, mashing occasionally with a potato masher, and simmer very gently for 10 minutes. Strain juice while hot through a jelly bag and cool by floating the saucepan containing it in ice water. Sweeten the juice to taste, pour into moisture-vaporproof, liquid-tight containers, leaving 1 inch head space for expansion, and freeze immediately.

TOMATOES should be fully ripe and sound. Wash, core, and quarter, discarding any green portions. Heat tomatoes slowly in a stainless-steel or aluminum kettle until juice begins to boil and press juice and pulp through a fine sieve. Cool juice over ice water and add 2 tablespoons salt to each gallon of juice, or salt to taste. Other seasonings such as pepper and celery salt, or herbs such as fresh marjoram, garlic, or thyme, may also be added to taste. Pour the seasoned juice into moisture-vaporproof, liquid-tight containers and freeze immediately.

(From THE COMPLETE BOOK OF FREEZER COOKERY, by Ann Seranne. Copyright © 1953, 1966 by Ann Seranne. Reprinted by permission of Doubleday & Company.)

An old juice extractor.

Tomato Juicer and Pulper 4.63

Cast-aluminum base with chromed cast-iron shaft and crank, stainless-steel perforated spout, aluminum chute, and plated, acid-resistant metal hopper; 16″ × 16″ × 7¾″ overall. Countertop height 12¼″; hopper 7¾″ diam., 5¾″ deep.

$21.95

Cognoscenti insist on fine tomato sauce, the pulp and juice used without a hint of seed or skin to mar texture or add bitterness. These high expectations require a high degree of specialization. In a tamis or a chinois or a food mill the tomato is effectively peeled, but manually forcing it through the mesh may cause bitter essences of crushed seeds to invade the purée. Electric juice extractors are too selective, permitting juice only and very little rich pulp to emerge. Europeans with understanding and appreciation of the particular properties of foods have tailored this machine to the tomato or other fruits or vegetables with small, undesirable seeds. It looks like a giant clamp-on meat grinder, of which it is a variation. The Czechoslovakian meat grinder (4.50) has a fruit-press attachment very similar to this, and the Bialetti Tritacarne Three (4.48) provides an electric puréeing attachment which is smaller and which tends to heat up from friction. Your entire tomato harvest can be fed through the commodious chromed-metal hopper of this machine. The crank handle turns the heavy spiral shaft, forcing the fruit toward the conical appendage that strains the pulp into the chute underneath. We know a family that rigged theirs to a small motor. Waste material, seeds and skin, exit from the opening at the end—a container of some sort should be used to catch this residue, and you may have some trouble finding the right bowl to fit under the chute to collect the purée. Tension springs, wing nuts, and a series of gaskets insulate and tighten the connections between various screw-on parts. The machine disassembles easily for cleaning, but putting it back together is another matter entirely. Clamp the machine tightly to the countertop, set the spiral screw in place with the rod and tension spring inside it and with the cone, chute, and alternating gaskets over it. Attach the two hinged screws by exerting considerable pressure on the entire assemblage—by the third try you should make it. Tighten the wing nuts and, finally, add the handle. Never remove the cork at the end of the cone. While raw tomatoes may be juiced in this machine, more flavor is obtained from cooked fruit. Be sure to carefully wash and dry all the parts. A brush would be useful for scrubbing the cone.

Electric Vegetable and Fruit-Juice Extractor 4.64

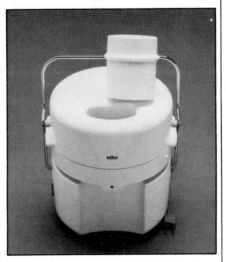

Plastic housing and sieve with stainless-steel strainer basket and pulverizing disc, chromed-steel handle; 8″ diam.; 10½″ high overall, 9½″ high excluding feeder.

$60.00 ▲

Heating destroys vitamins, so in order to extract without heat the juice from many hard raw fruits and vegetables to make various healthy potions, a special machine is required. There are many of these machines on the market. Some, sold at health-food stores, are outrageously expensive. Larger models of juice machines, while useful when it comes to feeding a commune, are unnecessary in the average household. Because these machines will only extract the juice of vegetables and fruits and will do nothing else, you should select other equipment if you intend to juice only citrus fruits, which must be peeled before they are juiced in these machines, an impractical limitation. Braun makes this good-looking white plastic cylinder, compact to store and, with its handle, convenient to carry. Its electric motor spins a roughly perforated stainless-steel disc inside to pulverize the food. Extracted juice and fibrous residue are flung, by means of centrifugal force, to the perimeters of the inner basket. The juice is forced through the strainer at its circumference and exits through the built-in spout at its base. An extra-fine white plastic straining mesh may be inserted in the machine, but it does not appreciably affect the thickness of the juice. To operate the machine, the top section is fitted into place, with the handle swiveled upward to clamp it. Food is inserted through an opening at the top by means of a pusher. A simple on-off switch activates the motor. The entire machine disassembles into a stunning array of parts, white, yellow, gleaming stainless steel, which must be carefully cleaned so as not to acquire the tie-dyed look that might be imparted by beet, carrot, and spinach juice over the surfaces.

Oster Electric Juicer-Extractor 4.65

Plastic housing with stainless-steel grid and strainer; 10¾″ × 6½″; 10″ high; juice container has 1-qt. capacity.

$80.00 ▲

Continued from preceding page

Like the Braun juice extractor above, Oster's version, a cubist interpretation in a gold plastic box, will pulverize your fruits and vegetables, releasing their vitamin-rich juices for homemade V-8 and beyond. The Oster machine has some convenient features: there is an internal compartment for storing the cord, and an elongated toothbrush-like gadget has been included for cleaning the stainless-steel grid and strainer. The built-in clear gold plastic juice container holds up to 4 cups of juice, allowing for almost continual operation; it slides in and out on tracks, but placing it properly can be tricky. There is a two-speed centrifuge motor, but the difference in texture between the high- and low-speed products is insignificant. Two handles on the sides unlock the top. The large container can then be lifted off, along with the strainer and grid, everything coming apart for the inevitable, thorough, tedious cleaning job. While some obscure cookbook written in the natural-food subculture may outline a use for the fibrous debris left inside these machines once the juice has been forced out, we are unaware of any potential use for them—these desiccated remains are to be discarded, or fed to the compost heap.

SAUCE BIGARADE—ORANGE SAUCE

[British measures]

This is to serve with wild or domestic duck. *Bigarade* is the French name for bitter oranges.

Two Seville oranges, a teacupful of veal or game stock, 1 oz. of butter, 1 tablespoon of flour, 4 lumps of sugar, salt and pepper.

Pare the rind of the oranges very thinly, cut into fine shreds, plunge them into boiling water, and boil 5 minutes. Strain. Prepare a brown *roux* by melting the butter in a small saucepan, stirring in the flour and continuing to stir over a gentle flame until the mixture is quite smooth and turns *café au lait* colour; now add half the warmed stock, stir again, then add the other half. Cook very gently another 5 minutes. Add the seasonings, the strained juice of one of the oranges and the peel. A few drops of Madeira or port added at the last moment are an improvement and the juices which have come from the bird while roasting should also be added.

Those who prefer a milder sauce can omit the orange juice and make up the quantity with a little extra stock. In any case, this is not a sauce to be served if you are drinking a fine wine with your duck; it would overwhelm it. If it is to go with a domestic duck, the stock can be made from the giblets.

(From FRENCH COUNTRY COOKING, by Elizabeth David. Copyright © 1960, 1962, 1967, 1969 by Elizabeth David. Published by Penguin Books. Reprinted by permission of Elizabeth David.)

Presse Viande   4.66

Cast iron; 5½" × 4½"; 3" high.
$25.00

You may have thought that this concept went out with the mustard plaster, but the idea of feeding the juice extracted from meat to an invalid has merit. Consider, first of all, that when a frozen piece of meat thaws, the juices released naturally can contain up to 20 per cent of the protein—just imagine the food value of juices forced from fresh meat that has been compressed until all that is left is connective tissue. Health-giving, fortifying, restorative protein, iron, vitamins, minerals without affronting the digestive system. If raw meat juice is not your cup of tea, it can be added to broths, doubly enriching them. This meat press, a heavy iron vise on four legs, has two ridged plates on the inside. The meat is placed on the base, the lid is brought down and the large bolt swiveled upward into its socket. By tightening the wing nut on the bolt the

juice is tortured out of the meat. This device should be set on a dish or a bowl during use so none of the precious effusion is wasted.

Sunkist Citrus Juicer   4.67

Chromed-steel housing with stainless-steel reamer and strainer, plastic splash guard and funnel; 8" base diam.; 16¼" high.
$315.00

Once again, freshly squeezed orange juice is a luxury. Before World War I, an orange was a traditional find in the toe of a child's Christmas stocking because oranges, particularly in winter, were scarce and expensive. In those days, fresh orange juice was a rare treat. Today, orange juice—*not* freshly squeezed—inundates the nation: concentrates, powders, and chilled containers are stacked in the supermarkets. But that quart of orange juice costing less than fifty cents is not fresh orange juice; not even the "fresh" juice, not reconstituted, in containers is as fresh as the juice that brims to the surface of a cut orange, ready to be squeezed into a glass. That juice is expensive and can be tedious to make. But to know it is to love it, particularly if an indelible memory of the flavor of pristine juice exists in your consciousness, still not rinsed away by a lifetime of juice from the store. You must then make room in your kitchen for the most masterful juicer of them all. It is bulky and ugly, and it must be left out on the countertop because it is too heavy to move about.

If you are ready for the aesthetic sacrifice, your life will be blest with fresh orange juice for the foreseeable future. The massive chromed body of this machine houses the motor and is surmounted by a vaguely spherical white plastic collar and funnel. The collar cradles the stainless-steel reamer and strainer. The collar, funnel, strainer, and reamer lift off easily for cleaning. When replacing the strainer, secure it in place with the small lever at the central shaft. The motor is powerful and a grounded cord (three-prong) is provided, so be sure that your outlets will accept it. The machine is activated by an on-off switch and does not require hand pressure on the fruit to extract the juice. And you can be sure that every last drop of precious juice will be removed from the fruit, directly into the glass to brighten your morning and refresh your day. Sunkist makes it and they ought to know.

Large Hand-operated Citrus Juicer   4.68

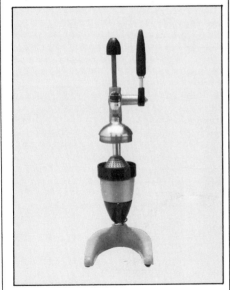

Enameled cast-iron and stainless-steel body; stainless-steel reamer; chrome pusher; plastic funnel, juice container, and handle; base 8½″ × 7″; 9½″ tall.

$90.00

Sitting next to the malted-milk machine at the soda fountain you will see one of these gangling devices. We have included it, not with a nod to nostalgia, but as the most efficient nonelectric orange-juice squeezer we found. It operates on leverage, not electricity. You twirl the handle

to lower the steel cap over the orange half sitting on the stainless-steel reamer. Give the handle a little extra push and the juice flows from the bottom of the reamer section into the glass or pitcher you have set below. A black plastic swivel cup will snap in place over this bottom opening to catch any drops of juice which have been loitering on their way down. The parts that touch the fruit—the black plastic and stainless-steel cup, strainer, and reamer—lift off for washing, and the upper cap that presses on the fruit unscrews. This bird-like gadget is 19½ inches tall, so be sure you have a clear space to keep it ready for action.

Electric Citrus Juicer   4.69

Plastic; 6¼″ diam.; 7⅛″ high; juice container holds 3 cups.

$40.00

Assuming that Sunkist's oranges but not their juicing machine are for you but that you *do* want electrically squeezed orange juice, you have dozens of options, from sleek little electrics to attachments for such multipurpose units as meat grinders and electric mixers. It is impractical to depend on one of the multipurpose-machine attachments for daily use—ideally, the orange juicer should be left out, conveniently placed, for the children to use instead of reaching for a soft drink; and you do not want to have their thirst interfere with your making of pâté or Génoise. This inexpensive electric machine is simple to assemble, efficient to use, and easy to clean. Its territorial demands are insignificant—it occupies a mere seven-inch space, and it is not at all an eyesore. The small motor forms the base. You can

keep it plugged in: when you want fresh juice, set the plastic juice container (cum-pouring-spout-and-handle) over it. Add the plastic strainer and then the deeply scored reamer, and you're ready to go. You place the orange half on the reamer, which rotates automatically under pressure. What makes this machine preferable to many others is that the reamer does not take a tremendous amount of pressure to function. A child can use it, and that is exactly what you want. The juice container holds three cups, enough to serve several people, and the juice need never drip over the motor or mess up the countertop. There is also a neat cover provided which will keep the dust out between juicings. The machine may be ordered in white, black, or transparent blue.

Stoneware Citrus Reamers   4.70

Stoneware; orange juicer 6½″ diam.; 2¾″ high; 1-cup capacity; lemon juicer 5⅛″ diam.; 2¼″ high; ⅔-cup capacity.

$11.00, $9.00

These two handmade stoneware citrus squeezers, the large one for oranges and the small one for lemons and limes, are an inspired creation almost too beautiful to use. It is hard to believe they are meant to serve the same function as our antediluvian hand-cranked monster (4.68). The noted potter Cynthia Bringle has turned and shaped stoneware for these and glazed it a shimmering gray or luminous brown enlivened with random spatters. The visual pleasure is intensified by the utterly functional design. The sharply ridged reamers, a contrast to the generous bowls, score the flesh of the fruit effectively, inducing it to release every drop of juice. Their stunning spiral fluting, repeating the lines in the turned bowls, improves their efficiency, making them among the best hand reamers we've seen. The handles are meant for hanging, not for grasping. This near-perfection lacks only a strainer—small price to pay for such beauty.

An anxious Samuel Pepys noted in his diary for 1825 his first experience with orange juice: "Here, which I never did before, I drank a glass, of a pint I think, of the juice of oranges, of whose peel they make comfits: and here they drink the juice as wine, with sugar, which is a very fine drink, but, it being new, I was doubtful whether it might not do me hurt."

Quoted in Kitchen and Table, *by Colin Clair, Abelard-Schuman, New York, 1964*

Plastic Citrus Reamer 4.71

Plastic; 5½" diam.; 3¾" high; ⅔-cup capacity.
$1.50

Even if black coffee is all you need in the morning and there is no permanent juice station in your kitchen except the refrigerator, you still cannot cook without a citrus juicer. Fresh orange juice for your Sauce Bigarade over duckling (see recipe). Lemon juice to add to your macedoine, assuring untarnished pieces of apple and pear. If you want the bare minimum in a citrus squeezer, this small plastic juicer does double duty. The orange or yellow plastic bowl is fitted with a small reamer and pouring spout and is ideal for lemon juice—it will hold six ounces of juice comfortably. Fit the large reamer and strainer made of clear plastic over it and you are all set for oranges. (You must press down and rotate the citrus half on this type of implement.) Clearly, it is both more difficult to use and less efficient than the electric machines, and less beautiful than the Bringle stoneware reamers above, but for small jobs it will suffice.

Porcelain Lemon Squeezer 4.72

Porcelain; 3¼" diam.; 2" high; 1-oz. capacity.
$3.95

Another white porcelain kitchen classic from Pillivuyt. This lemon squeezer is faithful to the prototype: there is a small reamer with its own spouted saucer and handle, and that's all—it's lemon-sized, one-piece. It is lovely to look at, a nuisance to use. An ashtray? A spoon rest, perhaps? As a lemon squeezer, its sun has set. The reamer is indeed effective enough, but the saucer for the juice is too shallow, barely adequate for the 1 to 1½ tablespoons of juice in the average lemon half. And you must either seed your lemon before squeezing it or be obliged to pick out the pits from the saucer, chasing them all around, or pour the

juice through a strainer. This last choice, if the juice is destined for a measuring spoon, requires three hands. The squeezer cannot be hung up out of the way, and it could most certainly be broken. Not your first choice, unless you plan a total Pillivuyt kitchen.

Plastic Lemon Squeezer 4.73

Plastic; 2⅞" diam.; 4⅜" high; 2-oz. capacity.
$9.00

If you liked the Italian plastic cheese grater we showed you (4.42), you will love this gadget. For one thing, it is neater to use than most squeezers. A central core of white plastic, narrowly fluted for easy grasping, has a small reamer-strainer fitting snugly inside. The bottom, a yellow or white plastic juice container with a pouring spout, screws on. The top, scored for grasping, is screwed down over the lemon half, forcing out the juice. Give another twist, a little more juice. The whole thing comes apart for cleaning, and the German manufacturers recommend it for table use. There is certainly merit in that, unless you feel your shrimp cocktails would seem naked without the inevitable garniture of lemon wedge. Certainly a handy item to have at the bar.

A lemon squeezer.

CHICKEN WITH LEMONS AND OLIVES EMSHMEL (DJEJ EMSHMEL)

I first ate this dish in a home in the city of Meknes, sometimes called the City of Olives. *Djej emshmel* (pronounced *meshmel* or *emsharmel*) is a classic Moroccan dish—chicken served in an intricately spiced, creamy, lemony, and sublime sauce with a scattering of pale-hued olives.

Serves 8

INGREDIENTS
2 to 3 chickens, whole or quartered, with their livers
6 cloves garlic, peeled
Salt
1 teaspoon ground ginger
1 teaspoon sweet paprika
¼ teaspoon ground cumin
¼ teaspoon ground black pepper
¼ cup salad oil
2½ cups grated onion, drained
¼ teaspoon pulverized saffron (mixed with turmeric, if desired)
½ cup mixed, chopped fresh herbs (green coriander and parsley)
1½ cups ripe "green-brown" olives, such as Royal-Victorias (quartered and salted in a jar for 1 month)
2 preserved lemons
2 to 3 fresh lemons

EQUIPMENT
Large bowl
Paring knife
6-quart casserole with cover
Strainer, if necessary
Small mixing bowl

Working time: 30 minutes
Cooking time: 1 hour (approximately)

1. The day before, using 4 cloves of the garlic and 2 tablespoons salt prepare the chickens [see BASIC METHOD FOR PREPARING POULTRY, below], then marinate both chickens and livers in 1 teaspoon salt, the remaining 2 cloves of garlic, sliced thin, the spices, and the oil. Refrigerate, covered.
2. The next day, place the chickens, livers, and marinade in the casserole. Add ½ cup of the grated onion, the saffron, herbs, and 2 cups water. Bring to a boil, cover, and simmer 30 minutes, turning the chickens often in the sauce.
3. While the chickens are cooking, rinse and pit the olives. (If they seem a little bitter, cover with cold water, bring to a boil, and drain.) Set aside.
4. Remove the chicken livers from the casserole and mash them fine. Return to the casserole with the remaining grated, drained onions. (This will give a good deal of heftiness to the sauce.) Add

water, if necessary. Continue cooking 20 minutes, partially covered.
5. Rinse the preserved lemons (discarding the pulp, if desired) and quarter. Add the olives and preserved lemon quarters to the sauce when the chickens are very tender and the flesh falls easily from the bone. Continue cooking 5 to 10 minutes, uncovered.
6. Transfer the chickens to a serving dish and spoon the olives and lemons around them. Cover and keep warm. By boiling rapidly, uncovered, reduce the sauce to 1½ cups. Add the juice of 2 fresh lemons to the sauce in the pan. Add more salt (and more lemon juice, if desired) to taste. Pour the sauce over chickens and serve at once.

BASIC METHOD FOR PREPARING POULTRY

For most of the recipes . . . prepare poultry as indicated below—the timings in the recipes include these steps:
1. Wash the chickens or other poultry in salted water and drain. Pound 4 cloves garlic and 2 tablespoons salt into a paste. Rub the paste into the cavity and flesh of the poultry, at the same time pulling out excess fat from under the skin and from the neck and rump ends. Pull out the thin translucent membrane from under the skin of the breast. Rinse the poultry well under running water until it no longer smells of garlic. (The garlic is used to rid the poultry of any bitterness that might spoil a sauce; it also acts to bring out its flavor, much like MSG.) Drain the poultry well.
2. If you suspect that your poultry is tasteless on account of "scientific breeding," use a method invented by Janet Jaidi to improve its taste: Rub it with the spices to be used in the recipe, a little butter or oil, and marinate it overnight. (If you do this, remember that you may have to readjust the spicing of your sauce at the end.)
3. If you are using whole poultry, it must be trussed. Trussing poultry is easy; clip off the wing tips and discard; slip the ends of the legs into a horizontal incision made just above the rump (turkeys often come this way), or slip the legs into incisions made on the lower sides of the breast.

(From COUSCOUS AND OTHER GOOD FOOD FROM MOROCCO, by Paula Wolfert, with Introduction by Gael Greene. Copyright © 1973 by Paula Wolfert. Reprinted by permission of Harper & Row.)

Tiny Juice Extractor 4.74

Cast aluminum; 1" diam.; 3" long.
$1.50 ▲

Regardless of what array of food processors, mixers, blenders, juicers, graters, grinders, sophisticated utensils, and professional pans you have in your kitchen, you need one of these. This little gadget is dynamite. A few drops of lemon juice, neatly. Not tablespoonfuls or fractional cups for sherbet or avgolemono, but just a few drops to finish a blanquette de veau, to freshen a ratatouille. How is it accomplished easily, without seeds in your juice and without destroying an entire lemon? Insert the sharp end of this cast-aluminum tube into your lemon (or lime, or orange) and squeeze, measuring the drops. Forcible entry with feeling. Enough juice? Replace the lemon, still containing the extractor, in the refrigerator to use as you need it. It makes sense to own at least two juice extractors, one for a lemon and one for a lime: you can then banish those plastic imitation lemons filled with reconstituted juice forever from your culinary life. You will wonder how you ever lived without this clever citrus squeezer. And for little more than a dollar. When was the last time that happened?

A Special Lemon Squeezer 4.75

Cast aluminum; 3" diam.; 9" long.
$5.00

Until now, we have been concerned with the fresh juice of lemons and oranges. The fragrant oils which imbue their skin barely mingle with the clear taste of the juice. In certain dishes, however—Italian piccata of veal, Greek avgolemono—the oils, in moderation, enhance and intensify the flavor. So you want them, but not at the price of shreds of zest in your food. This rustproof and acidproof aluminum lemon squeezer, in which the lemon half is pressed point down, allowing the juice to run over the skin and pick up the oily essences, has been tailored to this requirement. The hinged top and bottom are clamped together in the hand and the juice is poured from the spout with the squeezer still closed. While you obtain the oils, you miss plenty of juice, since this squeezer does a less than efficient job in reaming the fruit. It is large enough to accommodate an orange.

BLENDER MAYONNAISE

Makes about 1¼ cups

2 egg yolks
½ teaspoon dry mustard
½ teaspoon salt
2 tablespoons vinegar or lemon juice
1 cup vegetable oil or half vegetable and half olive oil

Place the yolks, mustard, salt, vinegar and ¼ cup of the oil in the container of the electric blender. Cover and turn the motor to high. Remove cover at once, and add remaining oil in a slow, steady stream. When all the oil has been added, turn off the motor.

TO SALVAGE CURDLED MAYONNAISE:
Place 1 tablespoon of the curdled mayonnaise in a warm, dry bowl with 1 teaspoon prepared French or domestic mustard. Beat with a wire whip until creamy. Add remaining mayonnaise, tablespoon by tablespoon, beating vigorously after each addition until creamy.

(From THE GREAT COOKS COOKBOOK, by The Good Cooking School, Inc. Copyright © 1974 by The Good Cooking School, Inc. Reprinted by permission of Ferguson/Doubleday.)

The good-humored ecclesiastic Sydney Smith, who flourished in the first half of the nineteenth century, had his own method of obtaining bread crumbs: "It is great proof of shyness to crumble your bread at dinner. I do it when I sit by the Bishop of London, and with both hands when I sit by the archbishop."

Bon-Mots of Sydney Smith and R. Brinsley Sheridan, *Walter Jerrold, ed., J. M. Dent & Company, London, 1893*

Electric Blenders

Once there was a tribe of blender-worshipers. They displayed their vertical idols in their kitchens, and daily they consulted volumes instructing them in the practice of their faith. They filled the little glass towers with sacrificial offerings and wept with joy at the blessings the blender gods bestowed upon them. Delicate purées. Gossamer mousses. Mountains of bread crumbs in a twinkling. Oh, there were doubters who belittled their devotion, trying to expose these godlings as charlatans. "Show us almonds less pulverized, Hollandaise more buttery, purées with texture!" demanded the doubters. But the believers did not need these proofs. They sat reverently at the feet of the high priestess, Ann Seranne. The blender reigned, unchallenged, for decades. Then, one day, a new god rose to confront the blender, and the former skeptics bowed in turn. The almighty Food Processor, the rotund, gleaming Cuisinart. The blender believers warned that the quenelles would never be as velvety, the milkshakes as thick. But the Cuisinartists sang anthems as their onions were neatly chopped, their dough was smoothly kneaded, their meat ground fine. Fortunately, good food encourages a spirit of toleration, and many kitchens could afford to enshrine both deities in the culinary pantheon.

Although militant blenderites may still insist "there is not much a blender cannot do, and what it does do, it does to perfection," as Ms. Seranne has declared, we regard the blender as a limited-use machine. Its capacity (except for the one-gallon behemoth we show you) is small, even smaller than the rated capacity of the jar, which can never be filled more than about half or two-thirds full. Even with all the new gadgetry with which it has recently become encumbered—20 speeds, flashing lights, timers, heaters and such—the makers have not removed these limitations. The early blender, equipped with a simple on-off switch, four madly whirling blades in the base of its jar, and a secure lid, could liquefy food and purée it to the finest possible degree. It was the drink-mixing wizard. Carefully monitored, it could grind bread into crumbs and nuts into powder, if you were willing to ignore the small mass that congealed at the bottom of the jar. It opened culinary vistas, Hollandaise in households which knew only ketchup, mousse au chocolat instead of My-T-Fine packaged pudding. There were several worthwhile refinements on the prototype in the early days. Blenders were given two speeds, high and low (all you ever need); jars that opened from the bottom to facilitate removal of thick mixtures; lids with openings for slowly adding ingredients during mixing without spraying the entire kitchen. But subsequent developments have served to complicate matters without improving them much. The old-fashioned on-off two-speed blender is unavailable except as a bar blender, which we have included for its efficient simplicity. A large-capacity commercial blender would be useful in many kitchens, and we also show you two of the latest multispeed models. They are typical of what is readily available.

[beaten] for a long time: and afterward take unpeeled almonds, and let them be brayed with the shell in what is abovesaid and with them bray bread crumbs browned on the grill."

The Goodman of Paris (Le Ménager de Paris), c. 1393. Translated by Eileen Power, George Routledge & Sons, London, 1928

Single-Speed Blender 4.76

Enameled base with chrome top, heat-resistant glass container, stainless-steel blades; 7" base diam.; 14" high overall; 1-qt. capacity.

$50.00

This blender from Waring may look like an anachronism and it is, with its simple, sturdy base and its simple on-off switch, particularly today when blenders tend to look more complicated to drive than an airplane. Nevertheless it is not only all that you need, but it is the best you can get. The manufacturer intends it for heavy and continual use in bars, so its motor is of better quality than those of most household blenders.

And, with its lack of an elaborate switch system it has the minimum number of components to get out of order. We say it is all you need because it does all the things a blender does best—it makes drinks and fine purées, it grinds nuts and spices, it makes bread crumbs, and it grates firm cheese. If you decide, as we advise, to buy the simplest blenders you can find, be careful: all bar blenders, though powerful, are not necessarily as effective as this one. Many have their blades set too high for good use with foods. For instance, in several other bar blenders you would have to make an enormous amount of mayonnaise in order to have enough egg yolks in the container to touch the blades at the beginning of the operation. The disadvantage of this blender is that the container does not detach from the blades, which is a problem during emptying and cleaning but which makes for great safety of operation. We favor the glass jar, which lets you see what you are doing, although there is also available an all-but-indestructible stainless-steel container. This blender is our choice for utility and long-term economy, although its initial cost is higher than that of some more elaborate but less desirable machines.

Old recipes such as this make one most grateful for the modern electric blender:

"Take cooked crayfish and remove the flesh from the tails: and the rest, to wit tails and carcase, must be brayed

Large Commercial Blender 4.77

Base die-cast zinc with baked-enamel finish; container and blending assembly stainless steel; 23" high overall; base 9" square; 1-gal. capacity.

$443.00

There are families and situations where a large-capacity blender jar would be put to frequent use, short of circumstances in which the total Ann Seranne fan might prepare everything but the roast in a blender. This professional-quality blender is very expensive, but it would be a worthwhile addition to the kitchen which prepares fine purées and liquid mixtures in quantity—the kitchen of a home caterer, for example, or a person who produces dozens of richly smooth cream-cheese pies to supply a local shop. The stainless-steel container has a one-gallon capacity and the lid clamps closed. The controls on the enameled-metal base offer three simple choices: high, medium, and low. The motor is a powerful, dependable one, capable of sustaining frequent heavy use. Waring, the manufacturer, also makes two-speed commercial blenders in 1- and 2-quart sizes; the 1-quart size is more than twice the price of a comparable bar blender, but we recommend it as the better choice.

Waring Fourteen-Speed Blender and Accessories

4.78, 4.79

Chrome-plated steel base with heat-resistant glass jar, plastic lid; 9¾" × 8⅛"; 14¾" high; 5-cup capacity.

$52.95

Shatterproof Lexan plastic with plastic lid; 3" diam.; 4¼" high; 8-oz. capacity.

$1.50

Often the availability of a piece of kitchen equipment determines what your final selection will be. Waring's Futura blender is their most up-to-date model generally available for home use. While we do not feel the latest blender is necessarily the best, this one can be used for all blender jobs if you understand its limitations. Plan to use just the high and low speeds, ignoring the gradations in between. Do not expect it to produce shredded carrots, minced onions, or even nuts chopped uniformly and coarsely. It will not happen. Velvet purées, yes—cold watercress soup to set a summer table—quenelles that literally drift into your sensibilities—frothy milkshakes for the youngsters, or tangy sours for adults will pour from this neat, ele-

gant machine, The calibrated glass container, with a capacity of 5 cups, is fitted with a handle and a pouring spout, and the lid has a measured opening covered by a cap that is a small measuring cup. The jar base containing the blades is removable for cleaning. The base of the machine is chrome and steel and has a timer, a plethora of control buttons, and a handy compartment for storing the cord. Small half-pint blend-and-store jars, useful for processing baby foods or a little bit of dip, are also available; these fit on to the same base that holds the large blender jar.

CREAM OF VEGETABLE SOUP

Here's a marvelous cream soup that can be made from practically any vegetable—freshly cooked, canned, or leftover from dinner the previous day. It has infinite variations, but the basic recipe demonstrates the technique of making a purée, the basis of all creamed soups. The vegetable may be carrots, spinach, broccoli, cauliflower, peas, string beans, squash, beets, lima beans, or any combination.

To make a purée, always begin with enough liquid to cover the blades, or about ½ cup. The liquid may be chicken or beef stock, milk, tomato juice, fruit juice, wine, or even water.

Serves 4

1 thin slice onion
1½ cups chicken, beef, or vegetable broth
½ cup cooked potatoes, mashed or diced
1 cup cooked vegetable
½ teaspoon salt or celery salt
Dash of pepper
1 cup milk or cream or ½ cup of each
1 tablespoon butter

1. Put the onion slice and ½ cup broth into container. Cover and blend on high speed for 10 seconds to liquefy the onion so that it will cook quickly.
2. Add potatoes, cover, and blend on high speed for 10 seconds.
3. Add remaining broth, the vegetable, salt, and pepper. Cover, rest hand lightly on cover, and blend on high speed for 5 seconds.
4. With blades spinning, remove cover or inner cap and gradually pour in the milk or cream.
5. Pour soup into a saucepan, add butter, and bring to a simmer over moderate heat, stirring constantly.

(From GOOD FOOD WITH A BLENDER, by Ann Seranne. Copyright 1974 by Ann Seranne. Reprinted by permission of William Morrow Co., Inc.)

Oster Dual-Range Pulsematic Blender

4.81

Chromed-plastic base with glass jar, plastic trim and lid; 8" × 5½"; 15" high overall; 5-cup capacity. Three plastic Mini-Blend" containers, each 1-cup capacity.

$58.95

If you believe the writers of promotional copy, Waring does not make blenders, they make "blendors," and Oster makes "Osterizers." All the same, you can be sure that Oster has a model competitive with the Waring fourteen-speed Futura we have just shown you. Here it is, called the "Dual-Range Pulsematic." The whirling blades mix drinks and purée beautifully, and also liquefy to perfection. It offers to do your grating, chopping, shredding, grinding, and such, but the results are not matched by its enthusiasm. The glass container nominally holds 5 cups, although its useful capacity is less. The two-ounce glass cap covering the opening in the lid can be removed for adding ingredients to the blender jar without redecorating the entire kitchen in Hollandaise Gold. It also comes with three 8 oz. containers. The base is plastic with metal trim, and there is the usual array of buttons. In addition to hitting "high" or "low," the buttons that select your overall category of speed, you must then select the exact speed within the category to activate the motor, a nuisance to say the least. The "off" button releases the sub-speed, not the high or low selection. Depending on the category, some buttons release instantly when you lift your finger. We recommend, as always, that you consult your instruction booklet in order to pilot this machine. While we regard blenders as a less than ultimate piece of equipment, try yours for various food refining and mixing jobs to see what its capabilities are in your kitchen.

The New Way

Multipurpose Machines, Beaters, and Bowls

The plot thickens. For that matter, as we mix and beat, so do your eggs, your roux, your choux, your stews. In the last chapter, we were concerned with refining food materials by means of graters and grinders. Now we mix and beat ingredients together, transforming tastes and textures, stirring, tossing, whisking, folding. We use complex machines, wire contraptions, simple wooden spoons. We mix in bowls and basins, small and large, of copper, plastic, glass, wood, ceramic, and steel. Omelets and quenelles, salads and Génoises, pâtés à choux and pâtés en terrine—you can't cook a thing in French or any other language without getting involved to some extent with these utensils.

Multipurpose Appliances

Some machines make close passes at being the ultimate kitchen accessory. Depending on your needs, you may find one to be the ideal solution for almost all of your beating, mixing, and blending needs. But some flaws do exist in the multipurpose machines, and certain operations are performed inadequately. We have discussed two multipurpose machines in Chapter 4, but those machines will not mix or beat. If you can put up with certain shortcomings or adapt your culinary life style to them, you may find they work for you. On the other hand, you may prefer to acquire the several specialized machines which will perform each function to the ultimate degree of perfection: a blender for fine purées, the KitchenAid K-5A for Génoise, and so forth. You would eventually own a whole pantheon of cooking equipment, with thousands of noninterchangeable shredding discs, plastic bowls, reamers, beaters, nuts, and bolts. You would have a somewhat redundant assortment to boot.

The American "appliance centers" made by Norelco and Ronson are major attempts to produce the ultimate kitchen machine. These are compact installations: their motor housings, set directly into the kitchen countertop, are able to operate a number of attachments. The possible problems are several, not the least of them being difficulty in getting repairs on the motors—which are basically blender motors, not up to heavy batters or bread dough. Although they make for an uncluttered countertop, we are not recommending them.

CONTINENTAL MODELS
Several European manufacturers produce free-standing machines which are essentially appliance centers. The motor base has two couplings, one for a mixer as well as attachments such as vertical cutters, citrus juicers, meat grinders, and peelers, to name a few. There is another coupling for high-speed centrifugal attachments: blender, juice extractor, coffee mill. The units are compact and good-looking on your counter. Somewhere underneath, however, you will have to file away a million parts. Although these imported machines are expensive when bought here, we do not recommend purchasing them in Europe since

HAM MOUSSE

2 cups Sauce Velouté*
3 envelopes unflavored gelatine
2 cups diced, leftover ham**
1/8 teaspoon cream of tartar
Salt
Freshly ground white pepper
3 egg whites
1 cup heavy cream

Line the bottom of a 6-cup mold with kitchen parchment and brush the sides only with vegetable oil. Turn upside down to drain on paper towels. Set aside.

TO MAKE THE MOUSSE: Sprinkle the gelatine over the hot Sauce Velouté. Place back over a low heat for 2 minutes, stirring constantly, to dissolve the gelatine. Take off the heat and add the ham.

Purée half the ham and half the sauce in the electric blender at high speed or in the electric food processor. Then purée the remainder. Return to the saucepan and keep warm over low heat.

Sprinkle the cream of tartar and a good pinch of salt over the egg whites and beat with a rotary or electric beater (or in the electric mixer) until the whites hold firm, shiny peaks when the beater is held straight up. Pour the ham mixture over the whites and fold in with a rubber spatula. Refrigerate, giving mixture an occasional stir, until almost cool and beginning to set.

Fold the whipped cream into the cooled ham mixture, then spoon into the prepared mold. Refrigerate until firm. It will take at least 3 hours.

To serve, unmold on a chilled serving platter and garnish with leaves of Bibb lettuce or bouquets of watercress. Serve with toast points to about 10.

*Make the Sauce Velouté in these proportions: 3 tablespoons butter or margarine, 3 tablespoons flour, 2 cups chicken broth, salt and freshly ground pepper to taste.

**The same amount of cooked chicken can be used in place of the ham.

(From WASTE NOT, WANT NOT: A COOKBOOK OF DELICIOUS FOOD FROM LEFTOVERS, by Helen McCully. Copyright © 1975 by Helen McCully. Reprinted by permission of Random House.)

"Sargent's Gem Food Chopper," 1902.

they may not have been fully adapted to use with American electric current.

Of course you may already own, say, a blender, in good condition and dependable for cold soups and so on. And you may own some other mixing equipment as well. Selections should then be tailored to fill the gaps that exist. Armed with a decent blender, you would find the K-5A extremely useful. Or if you add a Cuisinart Food Processor, you could scale the highest culinary peaks without even owning every K-5A attachment. Or you might manage very well with a Sunbeam Mixmaster, assuming most of your cooking is for a nuclear family or an occasional small dinner party rather than a commune, and that extraneous functions such as peeling potatoes mechanically do not loom large in your life.

If baking is but a sometime thing for you, you might find the Cuisinart Food Processor alone to be more liberating than a self-cleaning oven. This machine is designed to process food dropped down a vertical chimney to encounter one of four whirling flat blades or shredding or slicing discs (as opposed to a rotary process, in which the food is held against a rotating cylindrical cutter). The blade selection determines the finished product—grated, ground, sliced, shredded, puréed, kneaded, mixed. The big multipurpose European machines are also vertical cutters, but they lack the compactness—which means ready availability—of the Cuisinart. Consult the table in this section for assistance in selecting a multipurpose appliance.

Cuisinart Food Processor   5.1

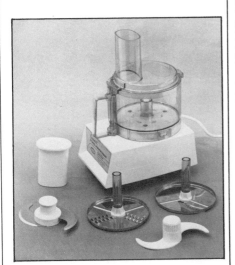

Painted cast-aluminum housing with shatter-resistant Lexan bowl, cover, and pusher; stainless-steel cutting blades and discs, plastic blades and spatula; base 9″ X 6½″, 5″ high; bowl 6½″ diam., 3¾″ deep; 7-cup capacity.

$225.00 ▲

To many people in this day and age, when kitchen staffs are nonexistent (except in restaurants, many of which have been using machines like this for a number of years—see the Robot Coupe, 5.2), the Cuisinart Food Processor is becoming indispensable. This French import has been playing to rave reviews from the day it first arrived on these shores. People everywhere are gladly parting with over two hundred dollars in order to be able to chop, slice, shred, grind, and knead to perfection in seconds, effortlessly. Processed food, the worst thing that can be said about the American supermarket, will become the best thing that can be said about its kitchens, so long as it means food prepared in this machine. Fresh nut butters, minced herbs, graham cracker crumbs or mayonnaise, the cabbage for slaw, dough for bread, forcemeat for terrines, or minced spinach for timbales are at your fingertips. The time-consuming chores that determine whether the family will have plain veal shanks or jarret de veau Provençale (with chopped carrots, onions, leeks, celery, tomatoes, and garlic) for dinner are all but eliminated by this compact phenomenon.

It consists of an enameled metal base about 5″ high, with a motor shaft protruding from the top; a 3¾″ deep work bowl with handle that fits over the motor shaft; a cover that locks over the top of the bowl, with an oval chimney through which food is added, and a pusher which fits into the feed tube. A double-bladed multipurpose knife, a slicing disc, a shredding disc, a plastic mixing blade, and a plastic spatula are the only parts with which you need bother, making storage of accessories an uncommonly easy matter for such a versatile machine. The motor base can sit neatly on the countertop, occupying an area about 6 by 9 inches, with the blades you are not using tucked into the drawer. One of the reasons that cooks begin to rely on the machine from the minute they own it is that setting it up is no hassle. Drop in the appropriate blade and it's ready to go. (Most of the time you will leave the double knife blade in the machine.) There isn't even an on-off switch—you start the proceedings by turning the cover slightly to lock it into place. Then, to maintain your love affair with the machine, everything but the base can go into the dishwasher. The motor, which operates without gears, has a circuit breaker so it will positively not burn out; if it should heat up from overlong use, the cutoff functions until the motor has cooled. If you observe the minimum precaution of always using the food pusher, the whirling blades pose no danger. It is truly amazing, but—there's always a "but"—it has its limitations. It will not whip egg whites well, for instance, so you will still need an electric beater or wire whisk. While it does knead bread dough and other heavy mixtures, its container is not large enough to produce more than a couple of loaves at a time; it will hold up to 7 cups, but the bowl of a mixer or beater should never be filled to capacity. (Be sure to read the instruction booklet carefully before using the machine.) Even in the quiet of your rural kitchen, the Cuisinart Food Processor intrudes with but the merest hum, a kitchen helper which neither talks back nor rattles on.

This dough mixer appeared in a manufacturer's catalogue in 1900.

Robot Coupe 5.2

Plastic housing and accessories, with stainless-steel cutting blades and discs, aluminum strainer; base 9″ × 7¾″, 7¾″ high; bowl 7⅜″ diam., 3¾″ deep; 2½-qt. capacity.

$399.00

If the limited size of the Cuisinart Food Processor's work bowl is too much of a drawback for you, consider the professional model, the Robot Coupe, definitely the Papa Bear of this family, available in sizes holding from 2½ to 48 quarts. Although it cannot cook the porridge, every task it is assigned will come out just right. Beautifully cut vegetables, julienne crudités, French-fries, of course—these have long been the province of the European kitchen, and the machines to make them easily possible have been European inventions. For years, the restaurants of France have been relying on the Robot Coupe for slicing, shredding, chopping, cutting, grating, grinding, mixing, and kneading. The Cuisinart machine (5.1) is the stripped-down home model. The Robot Coupe is a more versatile machine, with a substantial inventory of assorted parts and accessories. Like that of the Cuisinart, the heavy-duty motor set into the blocky white base is equipped with a circuit breaker for trouble-free operation, and it, too, cannot be activated unless the cover is locked in place atop the food container. The basic food cutter setup—a curved blade which fits down on the spindle in the container, a cover, and a food pusher—is the prototype for that of the Cuisinart machine. Other functions—slicing, shredding, mixing, kneading, juicing—require blades, funnels, pushers, covers, and plates that are tailored to the operation. There is very little that it cannot do well, quickly, and in quantity. But unless very large capacity interests you, we recommend the Cuisinart over the Robot Coupe for its simplicity and efficient operation.

"North: 'May I ask, with all due solemnity, What are rumbledethumps?'

"Shepherd: 'Something like Mr. Hazlitt's character of Shakespere. Take a peck of purtatoes, and put them into a boyne [large pot]—at them with a beetle [crusher]—a dab of butter—the beetle again—another dab—then cabbage—purtato—beetle and dab—saut [salt] meanwhile—and a shake o' common black pepper—feenally, cabbage and purtato throughither—pree [taste], and you'll fin' them decent rumbledethumps.'"

Christopher North, Noctes Ambrosianae *(1825–1835)*

Bosch Magic Mixer 5.3

Plastic housing with plastic and stainless-steel attachments; base 15″ × 10¼″, 8¾″ high; liquidizer 4¾″ diam., 8½″ high; 1½-qt. capacity; mixing bowl 9¾″ diam., 5½″ deep; 5-qt. capacity.

$250.00 ▲

Of all the machines we have investigated, this one comes closest to performing every kitchen function except for the actual cooking. First the good news. This utensil consists of a compact, well-designed stand with two attachment-coupling centers, one for a mixing/beating/vertical-cutting assembly, the other for high-speed centrifugal blade action for blending and liquefying. The mixing and beating mechanism is unique. The beaters, activated from below, are attached to the bottom of the mixing bowl. A double whisk and a beating/stirring/kneading blade are both provided. Adding ingredients while the machine is in motion is very simple, since access to the bowl is virtually unobstructed by motor heads

and the like. A handy splash guard prevents a kitchen full of batter. Remove the beaters or whisks and atop the mixing bowl you can assemble a vertical cutter, juicer, potato peeler, sieve, or small-capacity ice-cream maker. Turn the machine on its side and attach a meat grinder with the dazzling capability of not only making mince of your meat but also pressing out noodles or spaghetti, shaping cookies or biscuits, filling sausages, pressing seedless fruit purées, and grating cheese or chocolate. The blender is equipped with a 6-cup plastic jar, a set of sharp blades, and a simple on/off switch. A coffee mill and a centrifugal juice extractor use the same connection. Virtually all the parts, except for items such as meat-grinder blades and worms, are safe in the dishwasher. The heavy-duty motor is not likely to fail you. Now for the bad news. The 5-quart mixing bowl is made of plastic. (A stainless-steel 6-quart bowl is an optional extra.) The blender jar is also of somewhat insubstantial plastic. While there is a small beater and bowl which operate on a circumferential basis, the bowl is plastic, and this attachment is another optional extra. None of these parts will whip your meringues with the élan of the Kitchen-Aid K-5A, nor can you easily heat or chill the plastic bowls. And, of course, you have to store all the parts. The entire affair is a serious, but wise, investment. Be sure to read all operating instructions before using this machine.

Braun Kitchen Machine 5.4

Plastic housing with plastic, steel, stainless-steel, and cast-aluminum fittings and attachments, glass blender jar; base 13¼″ × 6¼″, 8½″ high; blender 4¼″ diam., 8¾″ deep; marked capacity 32 oz.; large bowl 9⅛″ diam., 6⅜″ deep, 4½-qt. capacity; small bowl 1½-qt. capacity.

$200.00 ▲

Guide to Multipurpose Electric Appliances in Chapters 4 and 5

	Bosch	Braun	K-5A	Sunbeam	Robot Coupe	Cuisinarts	Blenders	Moulinex	Bialetti Tritacarne
Beating/Mixing:									
Light	X*	X*	X*	X*	X*	X*	X		
Heavy	X*	X	X*	X*	X	X			
Hot/Cold Collar			X*						
Whipping	X*	X*	X*	X					
Kneader	X*	X	X*	X	X*	X*			
Blending	X*	X*			X*	X*	X*		
Liquefying	X*	X*					X*		
Fine Puréeing	X*	X*			X*	X*	X*		
Slicing/Shredding:									
Rotary			X*					X	X
Vertical	X*	X	X		X*	X*			
Grating	X	X*	X		X*	X*	X	X	X
Meat Grinder	X*	X*	X*	X*	X*	X*		X	X
Citrus Juicer	X*	X*	X	X*	X*			X	
Non-citrus Juicer	X*				X*				
Fruit/Tomato Press	X*								X
Cooky Press	X								
Noodle Maker	X								
Sausage Stuffer	X*		X*					X	X
Coffee-Grain Mill	X	X							
Ice Crusher	X		X		X*	X	X*		
Ice-Cream Maker	X		X*						
Potato Peeler	X*								
Strainer/Sieve	X*		X*						
Can Opener	X		X					X	
Heavy-Duty Motor	X*		X*		X*	X			
Stainless-Steel Bowls	Xc		X*	X*					
Large-Capacity Bowl/ Container	X*		X*		X*		Xb		
Compact Storage of Parts				X		X	X		

X —Machine has this feature
* —Recommended for this purpose
a —Available on the Waring Futura
b —Available on commercial models
c —Optional

Continued from preceding page

Like the Mercedes-Benz, Braun appliances bespeak quiet elegance. If only they operated as well. The mechanisms barely hum, and their serene, uncluttered lines are exquisite to behold. But their motors have been known to falter or fail at moments of greatest stress. This Braun multipurpose kitchen appliance is absolutely the best-looking one we show. It is also the least expensive of the mixer-blender-cutter combinations, at less than the price of the Bosch Magic Mixer—but it has about half as many attachments. It comes with a whisk, spatula, dough hook, blender, and vertical cutter. The meat grinder, citrus juicer, and combination coffee grinder and cheese-nut grater are optional extras which increase the price of the unit. Don't buy it without including at least the meat grinder in your purchase (unless you already own a good electric one). The Braun machine consists of a simple L-shaped white plastic base. The motor operates on three speeds. The 4½-quart mixing bowl (interchangeable with a 1½-quart bowl, an advantage, but both of plastic, a disadvantage) sits on the flat part of the base. The mixer head is coupled onto the high section of the base and extends over the bowl, to be fitted with whisk, spatula, or dough hook. You remove the mixer head to attach a blender or a small vertical cutter equipped with four different blades, or any of the optional attachments. The meat grinder is of fairly standard design, with a well-made sharpened cast-aluminum worm. It has only one tempered-steel cutting disc, however—a medium one. The grinder feeds its output nicely into the mixing bowl, which also serves to accumulate juice from the juicer or nuts or cheese from the grater. The simplicity with which all this sets up and operates, without having attachments running off in all sorts of cockeyed directions, is a pleasure.

If your kitchen does not demand a wide range of exotic attachments or a great deal of heavy mixing and beating, the performance of this machine will not disappoint you.

KitchenAid K-5A   5.5
Electric Mixer

Baked enamel on steel with stainless-steel trim, mixing bowl, and whip, enameled cast-aluminum flat beater and dough hook; 13 separate attachments avail.; 13½″ × 10⅜″, 16½″ high; bowl 8″ diam., 7″ deep; 5-qt. capacity. Copper beating bowl avail.

$240.00 ▲ Basic mixer only

The Hobart KitchenAid K-5A is generally conceded to be the best American-made machine for beating, mixing, whipping, and kneading. Any kitchen that regularly turns out brioches for breakfast, spinach soufflés for supper, or dacquoises for dessert is inadequately equipped without one. It will beat and whip faster and more thoroughly, incorporate more air to create a greater volume, than any other machine. The large flat beater or generous wire whisk rotates in one direction while revolving around the stationary bowl in the other, beating from the edges toward the center. The relatively narrow 5-quart stainless-steel bowl is the key to the K-5A's efficient operation with both large and small quantities, and it is also the key to its one drawback. Between the large head of the machine, close over the bowl, and the beater, which occupies much of the diameter of the bowl, for the cook to attempt to get an ingredient in edgewise while the machine is in operation amounts to an intrusion. Even the pouring chute for ingredients, which can be cantilevered off the side of the bowl, doesn't help much. The contents of a large sifter will still dust the top of the beater, the sides of the machine, and half of the kitchen counter as well. But even though this machine is not perfect, the meringue you pipe out onto your baking sheet for that dacquoise will be.

Balance the inconvenience of having to stop the operation from time to time to add sifted flour or cocoa against the extraordinary advantage of having a hot or cold jacket, an extra bowl which fits around the mixing bowl, to hold warm water for assuring proper volume for your petits-fours batter, or to hold ice for your bavarois aux fraises. The sturdy enameled cast-aluminum paddle beater will cream butter even before it comes to room temperature, an advantage for the cook who does not always plan ahead. The dough hook kneads efficiently, with no effort on your part. An additional treasure is the unlined copper bowl which can be ordered from the Bridge Kitchenware Corporation to complete the partnership with the wire whisk, assuring beaten whites of Alpine splendor. The two arms that hold the mixing bowl in locked embrace can be raised or lowered to assure proper alignment of beater and bowl. While the demands of the bakery are the forte of the K-5A, the powerful ten-speed motor performs a host of other functions as well. The various attachments which couple onto the front of the motor without disturbing the mixing area are optional. Meat grinder, sausage stuffer, can opener, silver buffer, colander and sieve, citrus juicer, vegetable cutter (rotary or vertical), splash guard, grain mill, and ice-cream maker are offered. Order them only if they are suited to your particular needs. For example, if you own a Cuisinart Food Processor (5.1), skip the vegetable cutters and slicers for your K-5A. Of particular note is the ice-cream maker, of fairly typical design, which makes a generous four quarts and will not burn out. The meat grinder is well designed and easy to use, with sharp cutting edges not only on the blades but also on the worm (see the meat grinders in Chapter 4). The attachments are remarkable for the virtual absence of plastic parts. Solid steel to last a lifetime is what we're talking about. Even a purist like Julia Child has confessed that she cannot live without her K-5A.

Sunbeam Mixmaster 5.6

Chrome-plated steel with plastic bowl tray, handle, and dial, stainless-steel beaters and bowls; 11½" × 7", 12¾" high; small bowl 6" diam., 4" deep, 1½-qt. capacity; big bowl 9" diam., 4⅜" deep, 4-qt. capacity.

$100.00 ▲

American electric mixers are on the whole not really serious. The Hobart KitchenAid K-5A, originally a professional machine, stands out as the shining exception. While the Sunbeam Mixmaster is not fit to wipe the K-5A's beater blades, it is a satisfactory machine. If you require a simple standing electric mixer/beater and you have no intention of parting with hundreds of dollars so you can save money on cake, select this one. The sleek, chrome-plated machine comes equipped with two stainless-steel bowls. The advantages of stainless steel are legion (it is noncorroding, a good conductor of heat and cold, unbreakable, dishwasher safe); there is also the advantage of having two bowls (do your batter in the big bowl, and then whip the two egg whites you need for the cake in the small one without having to wash in between). In what is basically a simple hand eggbeater gone electric, the beaters rotate as the bowl turns, providing thorough mixing, beating, and whipping through a range of twelve speeds. The beaters are billed as "extra large," rather an exaggeration: their size is adequate. A tight lever on the side of the base adjusts the turntable to the bowl, setting the beater off center for the large bowl to cover the area. The motor housing and beaters can be removed from the stand and used as a portable. A dough hook is provided for breads. A meat grinder and juicer are optional extras. The Mixmaster—a name which has approached generic usage—has a good motor. All told, if we were the Westminister Kennel Club, we would call it "best of its class."

Farberware Hand Mixer 5.7

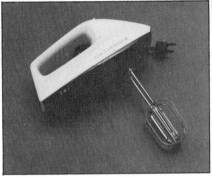

Plastic with chromed steel beaters; body 8½" × 3", 4½" high; beaters 6½" long.

$11.99

The cook whose baking amounts to an occasional quiche Lorraine can manage with a portable electric beater rather than the K-5A. Actually, the difference between a hand beater and a portable electric beater is not considerable. The electric version is more powerful and requires the use of only one hand, but with either you are committed to standing there and holding the thing. This Farberware model is not heavy, and it's fairly easy to grasp—without its beaters, it could be mistaken for an electric iron. The controls and beater release are all within range of the hand that is holding the appliance, freeing the other hand to turn the bowl, add or sift in ingredients, or scrape the sides of the bowl while you beat. You can carry it over to the stove to beat while food heats. And, of course, you can beat whatever you like in any bowl you wish. It is a good idea to own at least one extra set of beaters with these machines, so that washing the beaters between steps of a recipe is unnecessary. The heavy-duty motor has three speeds. The cord is detachable and a hole in the bottom of this little machine allows it to be hung out of the way. Match it to your kitchen decor: it comes in white, avocado, or a yellow called "golden harvest."

OLD-FASHIONED SPONGE CAKE

6 eggs
Pinch of salt
1 cup granulated sugar
1 tablespoon lemon juice
1 teaspoon grated lemon rind
1 teaspoon vanilla
1 cup sifted flour

Set oven at 350 degrees. Grease and dust with flour the bottom of a high, 9-inch tube pan or two 9-inch layer-cake tins. Do not grease sides of pan. Cake will cling to sides as it rises.

Separate eggs. Beat egg whites with salt until they form soft peaks. Beat in sugar gradually, a tablespoon at a time. Continue beating until egg whites are very stiff, about 5 minutes in all.

Stir egg yolks with a fork to break them up. Add lemon rind, juice, and vanilla. Fold ¼ of the stiffly beaten egg whites thoroughly into egg yolks. Pour egg-yolk mixture over remaining stiffly beaten whites. Sprinkle flour on top. Fold all gently together, using hand or mixer turned to lowest speed. Fold only until no separate pieces of egg white show, with batter still very fluffy and light. *Do not overmix.*

Pour batter into prepared pan, spreading it with a spatula. Hit the pan sharply on table twice to remove air pockets.

Bake cake 35-40 minutes in preheated oven.

Cake is done when top is golden brown and springy to the touch. Remove cake from oven and cool in pan. It is not necessary to turn it upside down while cooling. When completely cool, loosen sides of cake with a knife and remove it from pan.

(From THE ART OF FINE BAKING, by Paula Peck. Copyright © 1961 by Paula Peck. Reprinted by permission of Simon & Schuster.)

Whisks

Like the shaman and the alchemist, the cook is dependent on the basic elements of fire, water, and air to work his magic. Of the three, air is the challenge. It is an ingredient never mentioned in recipes, although the finished creation may contain more air than anything else. Air may be incorporated by both chemistry and physics—the heat of the oven causes expansion of air or gas within the batter or dough; in mixtures leavened by yeast or baking powder, the gases formed by the leavening

Continued from preceding page

are further expanded by the heat. Or the deft cook can capture some of the surrounding atmosphere, entrap it among other ingredients, and thus use air to lighten and leaven. The method is whipping, the tool the whisk.

The whisk, made of many wires, multiplies a single stroke to many, and within minutes, billows of egg white or cream fill the bowl. The wire whisk is a concise and graceful design: a number of wires, curved around and the ends gathered together and clustered in the hand, it is the modern tool that has replaced the little bundle of twigs once used as a beater. The length, thickness, and material of the wires determine the flexibility and function of the whisk. The lightest balloon whisk is a tracery of tenuous strands for ethereal egg whites. Much stiffer unyielding whisks, large or small, are for blending and beating sturdier sauces.

While the electric machines we show you have limitless ability to substitute for a battery of whisks—and you might even use a manual eggbeater for most purposes—one whisk does not a kitchen make. Collect all sizes and stand them in a jar on the countertop as an artist would his paintbrushes, selecting the proper one for the particular medium in which you are working.

Ekco Eggbeater 5.9

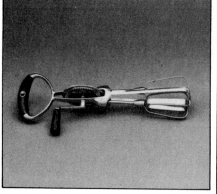

Chromed frame with stainless-steel beaters, nylon gears, plastic handle and knob; 12" long.

$7.95

As we said at the end of the section on multipurpose appliances (5.1 through 5.8), the small portable electric mixers are little more than glorified eggbeaters, and only a moderate improvement over the typical hardware-store Ekco model shown here. This chrome-and-stainless-steel mechanical eggbeater, equipped with smoothly meshing nylon gears, operates easily enough to allow you to tackle almost any whipping and beating job with reasonable efficiency, from egg whites to pancake batter. The range of speeds is, of course, infinite, limited only by your own arm capacity. On the other hand, this isn't a good utensil with which to tackle heavy mixtures such as pound-cake batters; hence the rationale for owning an electric beater, either a portable one or, better still, a standing mixer.

CRAB TURNOVER

THE FILLING
3 tablespoons unsalted butter
3 tablespoons flour
1 cup milk
1 pound crabmeat, with all cartilage picked out
¼ teaspoon cayenne pepper
1 teaspoon salt
2 tablespoons chopped chives
2 tablespoons chopped fresh parsley
THE PASTRY
8 sheets filo pastry (see note)
¼ pound unsalted butter, melted

To make the filling: In a heavy, 1-quart saucepan, melt the butter over medium heat. Add the flour and mix well. Stirring with a wire whisk, pour in the milk and cook over high heat until mixture comes to a boil and thickens. Reduce heat to low and let simmer for 2 or 3 minutes. Remove from heat, and stir in the crabmeat, pepper, salt, chives, and parsley. Taste for seasoning and cool to room temperature.

To make the turnovers: Preheat the oven to 400 F. Spread one sheet of 12 x 16-inch filo flat, and brush the entire surface with about 1 tablespoon of the melted butter. Fold the pastry over once from a

12-inch side and once from a 16-inch side. The pastry now has four layers and measures 6 x 8 inches. Brush 2 inches of the edge of one 8-inch side with butter and fold over to make a 6-inch square. Spread ⅛ of the crabmeat filling onto the center of the square.

Brush the edges of the square with additional melted butter. Fold the squares in half, diagonally, to form a triangular turnover. Press the edges down to seal. In the same fashion, make 7 more turnovers. Place them on a lightly buttered cookie sheet and bake in the middle of the oven for 15 to 25 minutes or until the pastry is crisp and lightly browned.

(From THE GREAT COOKS COOKBOOK, by The Good Cooking School. Copyright © 1974 by The Good Cooking School, Inc. Reprinted by permission of Ferguson/Doubleday.)

Flat German Whisk 5.11

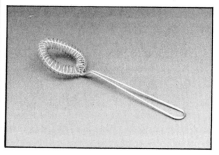

Tinned steel; 11½" long overall; head 3" diam.

$1.50

This tin-plated German contribution, a little less than a foot long, has a spiral of springy wire looping around an oval bowl. At first glance, it looks more like a spoon than a whisk. Picture gently lifting a whole boiled egg with it. Actually, its destiny is the raw white rather than the whole egg. *Joy of Cooking* describes in detail how to use a flat whisk such as this one for beating egg whites on a platter. Some recipes even specify using flat whisks ("Mildred Knopf's Orange Puff Cake" in Maida Heatter's *Book of Great Desserts*). It is perfect for melding a roux or mixing cream and egg yolks in a shallow pan or sauteuse. It is ideally suited for attacking lumps along the edges of the pan that elude a conventionally shaped whisk or spoon.

An eighteenth-century recipe begins: "Take the Yolks of twenty-four Eggs, beat them for an Hour."

Ekco Eggbeater
Flat German Whisk
Heavy-Wire Stainless-Steel Whisk

Thin-Wire Stainless-Steel Whisk
Heavy Tinned-Steel Wire Whisk
Heavy Stainless-Steel Whisk

Heavy-Wire Stainless-Steel Whisk 5.12

Stainless-steel wires with tinned-steel handle; 12″ long. Also avail. 10″, 14″, 16″, 18″, 22″, or 24″. Avail. with tinned wires.

$6.25   10″ $6.50▲   14″ $8.00▲

Thin-Wire Stainless-Steel Whisk 5.13

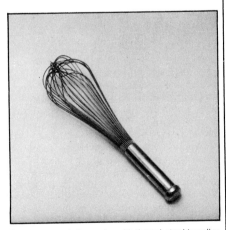

Stainless-steel piano wire with tinned-steel handle; 16″ long. Also avail. 10″, 12″, 14″, or 18″ long.

$7.00

Here are two no-nonsense whisks of stainless-steel with tinned handles, a 12-inch model with strong, thick wires and a 16-inch one with thinner wires. Thanks to their sealed, all-metal construction, these tools can be scalded at the highest possible heat to utterly sanitize them. They are made for professional use but they deserve wider exposure. On both, the innermost wire is looped around all the other wires, holding them together and making them sturdier than some more flexible models. Use the heavy wire whisk (also available with tinned wires), a satisfyingly rigid implement, for a thick béchamel, the foundation for your croquettes, or instead of a wooden spoon for the pâte à chou you're using as a base for your quenelles. The whisk with thinner wires has 50 per cent more of them than the other. Lighter and more flexible, it would work better in a lighter sauce, and it is the ideal tool for egg whites, provided you use a capacious bowl.

"The weenie eggbeater with the long handle created a version of mayonnaise that is rapid and economical. Dry mustard-salt-pepper or paprika in quantity in a bowl with one entire egg. Beat with the Sam gadget eggbeater for three minutes—while you do something else with the left hand—then gradually add oil in the usual way—and when it is stiff, lemon juice in small quantities. When a third of a cup of oil had been added stir in a dessert spoon of boiling water. Add a few tablespoons more oil. Eh voilà. As it will be more than you need for one time it can be put in the ice chest for the next day but no longer because of the white of the egg. Cannot be made without the use of a Sammie gadget eggbeater . . ."

Letter to Sam Steward, October 24, 1952, from Staying on Alone—Letters of Alice B. Toklas, *Vintage Books, 1975*

ZABAGLIONE WITH FRESH STRAWBERRIES—EGG AND WINE CUSTARD

If strawberries are not available, substitute sliced fresh, frozen, or canned peaches, pitted fresh or canned apricot halves, or sliced bananas. Be sure to drain frozen or canned fruit very well.

1 pint fresh strawberries, washed and stemmed
8 egg yolks
½ cup sugar
⅔ cup Marsala or sweet Sherry wine

Divide strawberries among six stemmed wine glasses.

Put egg yolks, sugar, and wine into a round-bottomed copper pot or glass double boiler top of at least 2-quart capacity, as egg yolks almost triple in volume. Sprinkle with a little cold water.

Place the copper or glass pot over a pan of simmering water and beat mixture rapidly with a wire whisk until it becomes a thick, creamy custard.

Immediately pour over the strawberries in the wine glasses, dividing evenly, and serve at once. Serves 6.

Heavy Tinned-Steel Wire Whisk 5.14

Tinned-steel wires with tinned-steel handle; 16″ long. Also avail. 18″ long.

$7.50

This 16-inch tinned-steel whisk from Metropolitan Wire is large and heavy, with sixteen sturdy wires rigidly braced together. The handle is stainless steel and the joints are sealed to permit thorough cleaning. The shape of the whisk is quite bulbous, but this is not a resilient balloon whisk to mate with an unlined copper bowl for beating egg whites. Quarts of heavy batter requiring mixing without the incorporation of much air are its forte—a gross of fudgy brownies for the next bake sale, and the chocolate frosting as well; a gallon of boiled dressing for the Fourth of July picnic. If you volunteer your services for such tasks, you will appreciate this whisk.

Heavy Stainless-Steel Whisk 5.15

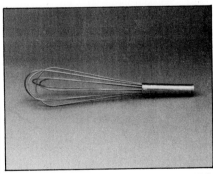

Stainless steel; 15¾″ long. Also avail. 13¾″, 17¾″, or 23½″ long.

$12.00

This whisk feels more like a bludgeon than a whip, so heavy is it. Nevertheless, it is extremely well balanced, and from

Continued from preceding page

the standpoint of construction, it is a thing of beauty, the most elegantly finished whisk of all. Of solid stainless steel, twelve heavy wires set into the handle through a perfectly fitted stainless-steel cap, a matching cap topping the steel handle. Billed as a confectioner's whisk, it will delight either the professional or the serious amateur. Despite its rigid wires, the utensil is still quite flexible, since the wires are not braced.

Large Wooden-handled Stainless-Steel Whisk   5.16

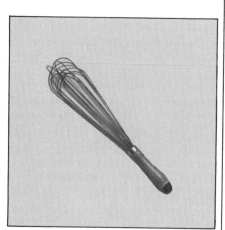

Stainless-steel wires with varnished wood handle; 16″ long.

$10.00

This large whisk is a near-balloon in shape and is extremely comfortable to hold. The contoured wooden handle is smoothly varnished. The sturdy wires are gathered into a riveted stainless-steel cap on the handle. They are not braced at the top, so a flexible cluster of rounded wires, 3 inches deep, will beat and aerate your eggs and quickly lighten your purées. It is not the ideal instrument for whipping egg whites into high peaks for mousse au chocolat: a trifle too heavy, a shade too narrow. But oh, you will love using it for crème pâtissière.

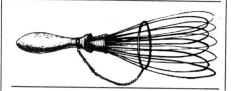

Wooden-handled Tinned-Steel 5.17 Whisk

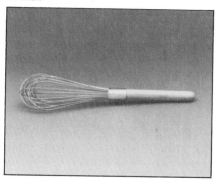

Tinned-steel wire and cap, uncoated light wood handle; 14″ long. Also avail. 10″ or 12″ long.

$5.00 ▲ $3.75 ▲ $4.25 ▲

If your kitchen has need for but one whisk, this might be the one to select. A dozen flexible medium-weight tinned-steel wires interlace and curve back to be fastened into the smooth unfinished wood handle, held tightly in place by a generous tin cap. It is well constructed. While it will produce drifting clouds of egg whites in your bowl, it has enough heft and rigidity to handle a medium-dense batter, a mayonnaise, a crème anglaise. The bottom of the metal cap is open, exposing the unfinished wooden handle. The space thus created between the wires, cap, and handle, is the second most difficult to clean of any in this entire catalogue. The prize for the most difficult crevice of all goes to the next example (see 5.18), in which a smooth cap is replaced by wrapped wires. While these dubious distinctions may not deter the prospective owner of these otherwise admirable whisks, they bear consideration.

Wooden-handled Balloon   5.18 Whisk

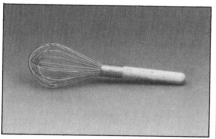

Tinned-steel wires and collar with coated light wood handle; 14″ long. Also avail. 10″, 12″, 16″, or 18″ long.

$4.00

Not that owning a whisk is all that essential—you could survive very nicely with a common eggbeater (see 5.9) and increase your egg whites five, maybe six times in volume rather than the ultimate seven. However, for poetic mouthfuls of spuma di cioccolata to enrapture your dinner guests, a proper light balloon whisk to fit your unlined copper bowl is de rigueur. This French example is the best in our collection for the purpose. The 14-inch size is shown, but larger sizes may be obtained. The light, unfinished wooden handle is fitted with flexible tin wires and held by a wire wrapping. This arrangement is neither the most sanitary nor the easiest to clean, but if you reserve this whisk for egg whites only, you will minimize the problem.

SPUMA DI CIOCCOLATA— COLD CHOCOLATE FOAM

For 6 persons

6 ounces semisweet chocolate drops
2 teaspoons granulated sugar
4 eggs, separated
¼ cup strong espresso coffee
2 tablespoons rum
⅔ cup very cold heavy whipping cream

1. In a 250° oven, melt the chocolate in a small saucepan.
2. Add 2 teaspoons of sugar to the egg yolks and beat with a whisk or the electric mixer until they become pale yellow. By hand mix in the melted chocolate, the coffee, and the rum.
3. Whip the cream in a cold bowl until it is stiff, then fold it into the chocolate-and-egg-yolk mixture.
4. Whip the egg whites until they form stiff peaks, then fold into the mixture. When all the ingredients have been gently but well combined by hand, spoon the mixture into glass or crystal goblets, custard cups, or any other suitable and attractive serving container. Refrigerate overnight. (This dessert can be prepared even 3 or 4 days ahead of time, but after 24 hours it tends to wrinkle and lose some of its creaminess.)

NOTE
Don't exceed the recommended amounts of rum and coffee, or you may find a liquid deposit at the bottom of the dessert.

(From THE CLASSIC ITALIAN COOKBOOK, by Marcella Hazan, illustrated by George Koizumi. Copyright © 1973 by Marcella Hazan. Reprinted by permission of Alfred A Knopf.)

Small Wooden-handled Stainless-Steel Whisk 5.19

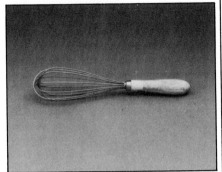

Stainless-steel wires and cap with beechwood handle; 11¼″ long. Also avail. 9½″, 10½″, or 14″ long.
$3.50

This is an elegant little whisk. The gracefully pear-shaped wire cage is gathered into a gently curving unfinished wooden handle. It will leap into your hand for a thousand different purposes. Mixing vinaigrette moments before the salad is served, stirring the batter for crêpes, adding honey to fresh applesauce to just take an edge off the tartness, or cream to your broccoli purée to enrich it; lightly beating eggs for omelets, eggs and cream for quiche, or eggs and lemon for broth, smoothing sour cream before adding it to beef Stroganoff, stirring melted chocolate into pots de crème, or lightly blending flour into eggs and sugar for ladyfingers. The list is long for so small a whisk. It is light but quite rigid, constructed of 18-8 stainless steel, suitable for mixing, lifting, stirring, and combining ingredients with each other rather than with air.

Thomas Jefferson, that man of many talents, was dedicated to fine food. Wherever he traveled he kept a record of what he had most enjoyed, making notes so that his cook at home could reproduce the delicacies he favored. This recipe for meringues, an odd mixture of languages, is typical: "12 blanc d'oeuf, les fouettes bien fermes, 12 cuillières de sucre en poudre, put them by little and little into the whites of eggs, fouetter le tout ensemble, dresser les sur un papier avec un cuiller de bouche, metter les dans un four bien doux, that is to say an oven after the bread is drawn out. You may leave them there as long as you please."

Thomas Jefferson's Cook Book *by Marie Kimball. Garrett and Massie, 1949*

Small Tinned-Steel Rigid Whisk 5.20

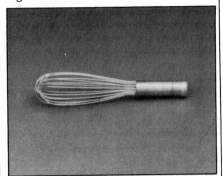

Tinned-steel wire; 8″ long. Also avail. 12″ long.
$4.50

Here is the mini-whisk, no job too small. Beat the sour cream while it is still in the container. Stir the chocolate syrup with the milk right in the glass. Combine a little lemon juice and prepared mustard in the bottom of the bowl to start a marinade. This little item is small and quite rigid, made of tinned steel. The closely spaced wires have been deprived of much of their flexibility and shortened to inhibit aeration. The tin handle is hollow, a framework into which the wires are set, wrapped in place by wire. It is a useful kitchen item.

Early whisks were made from bundles of twigs fastened together. The wood used might impart a fragrance to the batter, as in this eighteenth-century Shaker recipe quoted in the American Heritage Cookbook: *"Cut a handful of peach twigs which are filled with sap at this season of the year [February]. Clip the ends and bruise them and beat the cake batter with them. This will impart a delicate peach flavor to the cake."*

Spoons and Spatulas

Inevitably, foods must be combined. They may be stirred together lightly, beaten together vigorously, folded in delicately. You might use your hand for mixing if you lack an implement—people do. Over an open campfire you would pick up a stick. In the kitchen, you turn to wooden spoons and spatulas, as cooks always have. Wood is traditional, of course, but more important, it is practical. Wood is a poor heat conductor, so the cook may stir for hours with no danger of fried fingers. Also, a wooden spoon or spatula reacts hardly at all to sudden temperature changes; you can use it at high heat, then moments later in a chilled mixture with no ill effects.

Unlike implements of metal, those of wood are highly unlikely to discolor food or affect flavors. Remember the childhood game "Rock, Scissors, Paper"? Paper covers rock, rock crushes scissors, scissors cut paper. Wood wasn't in the game at all because it doesn't crush and it doesn't cut. It will never accidentally scratch a pan the way metal might. At the same time, it is resilient enough to cushion the impact on a bowl of heavy beating done in it. It is only fair to add that wood is porous and liable to absorb the flavors or odors of foods, hence the wisdom of owning several wooden utensils. We do not recommend tasting

Continued from preceding page

from wooden utensils for this reason: the wood distorts the flavor of the sample. Use a tablespoon or a porcelain spoon instead, allowing a few moments for the food to cool so you do not burn your mouth and curtail your tasting career for a time.

GOOD WOOD

Precisely because of the problem of porosity, hardwoods should always be used in cooking. Unfortunately, the manufacturers of soft pine-wood utensils don't see it that way. Avoid buying cheap pine spoons and spatulas. They splinter easily and will not last as long as better implements. The very closely grained woods, beautifully patterned olive or golden boxwood, go into the making of spoons and spatulas for delicate sauces, chocolate, and custard. Beech, cherry, and maple are normally fashioned into more workaday tools—spoons to stir a stew, for example. Delicately finished or lacquered spoons should never be used with high temperatures.

SPOONS VS. SPATULAS

On the question of spoons vs. spatulas, it is a matter of personal preference. Their uses are roughly the same: stirring, beating, and mixing ingredients; creaming them or rubbing them through sieves; lightly tossing or folding; and, of course, serving. Spoons have bowls, and spatulas end in flat or slightly curved paddles. Spatulas can be scraped clean against the sides of a pan or bowl, and bits of unmixed food will not collect in them; but spoons generally lift, move, or dish ingredients more efficiently, especially when there are numerous pieces to deal with.

Whether you're considering spoons or spatulas, the available sizes, shapes, and contours are dizzying. Serious cooks treasure their collections of time-worn favorites and their interesting acquisitions as well. James Beard stores his wooden implements in a decorative ceramic pot near the stove. You might insert a screw eye into the handle of any tool that is not equipped with a hole and hang it up for both decoration and convenience.

Treat wooden utensils with loving care. Do not leave them near an exposed source of heat, lest they scorch. Never soak them in water or put them in the dishwasher; they will soften and crack. Rinse and dry them thoroughly after use. With reasonable care, you will always be able to depend on them for soup or sauce, and through thick and thin.

"The English language is very deficient in terms descriptive of culinary processes. The Scots retain the word 'to skink' in defining the process of continually lifting high a sauce or gruel by spoonfuls, and rapidly letting it fall back into the pan. The French language, which is peculiarly rich in culinary terms, calls what is signified above by stirring, to vanner a sauce or soup; and to see a French cook thus engaged at the stove with the velouté or sauce à la Lucullus, an Englishman might well suppose that life and death were depending on a process for which his language has no name."
From The Annals of the Cleikum Club, *incorporated in Meg Dods's* The Cook and Housewife's Manual, *1826*

Beechwood Mixing Spoon 5.21

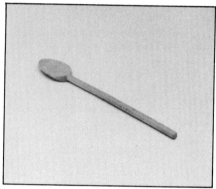

Polished beechwood; 14″ long. Also avail. 8″, 10″, 12″, or 16″ long.

$.89

The beau idéal of spoon. Smoothly finished, with an oval carved bowl and cylindrical handle—who could ask for anything more? Yet this French spoon delivers in excess of expectations. The moderately shallow bowl has a flat bottom so it will stay put if you set it down with food in it; and it is sturdy enough for heavy beating. The grain is centered in the bowl, creating a lovely pattern of whorls like a thumbprint. The handle is scored near the end: tie a cord around to hang it within reach. We'd consider having this one in all five sizes, from 8 to 16 inches.

Thin-handled Wooden Spoon 5.22

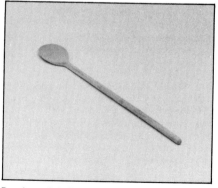

Beechwood; 14″ long. Also avail. 8″, 10″, 12″, or 16″ long.

$.69

Beechwood Mixing Spoon
Thin-handled Wooden Spoon

Beechwood Stew Spoon
Boxwood Chocolate Spoon
Cherrywood Chocolate Spoon
Curved Olivewood Spatula

The same company, Artsam, that imports 5.21 offers this 14-inch beechwood spoon with a longer handle and a smaller, rounder, flatter bowl. It is quite light and the bowl is shallow, making it useful for testing the consistency of a sauce or lightly stirring a creamed soup in a fairly deep pot, but not for going at a thick batter. It is utterly utilitarian and simple.

Beechwood Stew Spoon   5.23

Beechwood; 12″ long. Also avail. 10″, 13¾″, or 15¾″ long.

$1.19

No frills, just a homely, rough-textured tool that's all business. This simple beechwood stew spoon has a generous oval bowl with a 10-inch flattened handle, widely squared off at the end and tapering toward the neck. It is such a nice implement you will pick it up for more than shuffling things around in your stews. Creaming butter, for example, tossing salad, stirring batter.

Boxwood Chocolate Spoon   5.24

Varnished boxwood; 11″ long. Also avail. 8″, 8¾″, 10″, or 13″ long.

$3.88

Long wooden chocolate spoons, the aristocrats of wooden utensils, were designed for stirring bubbly hot chocolate in tall porcelain pots. Boxwood, the material of this spoon, will not conduct heat or lend any flavor of its own to the brew. This 11-inch-long chocolate spoon is delicately carved from golden fine-grained boxwood and varnished to protect it from discoloration by the chocolate, one of the most invasive of substances. The bowl is small, thick, and quite shallow, almost paddlelike. The handle is a gracefully tapering cylinder terminating in a decorative knob at the end. Fine varnished wood like this should not be subjected to high heat, but then, neither should chocolate.

Cherrywood Chocolate Spoon   5.25

Varnished cherrywood; 9¾″ long.

$2.69

From cordial cherry candies to Schwarzwalder torte, the combination of cherries and chocolate is classic. Thus, the appeal of a cherrywood chocolate spoon is more than purely visual. The fine wood, kind to the porcelain of the tall chocolate pot, is varnished so the chocolate will not stain it. The delicate, egg-shaped bowl is gently scooped and polished to accentuate its lovely graining. The slender, cylindrical 7½-inch handle tapers ever so slightly, terminating in a decorative spool turning at the end, a lovely detail.

A spoon that has not withstood the test of time is described by Mrs. Beeton, who gave the following account of a medieval kitchen: "In the larger establishments of the middle ages, cooks with the authority of feudal chiefs, gave their orders from a high chair in which they ensconced themselves, and commanded a view of all that was going on throughout their several domains. Each held a long wooden spoon, with which he tasted, without leaving his seat, the various comestibles that were cooking on the stoves, and which he frequently used as a rod of punishment on the backs of those whose idleness and gluttony too largely predominated over their diligence and temperance."

Curved Olivewood Spatula   5.26

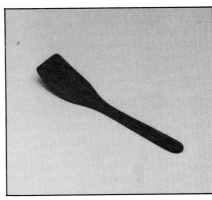

Olivewood; 12″ long; 2½″ wide. Also avail. in beechwood.

$3.50 ▲

We breach the frontier between spoon and spatula with a most elegant example. The rich brown whorled grain of olivewood and its ultrasmooth texture when polished make it one of the most attractive materials for cookware; its hardness and lack of porosity enhance its advantages. This is a spatula, flat and without the receptacle of a spoon, but the gentle curve with which it has been shaped would make a pair of these useful as servers. The spatula is 12 inches long, the curved paddle portion 5 by 2½ inches. It is finely finished and the tip is tapered to a delicate edge to facilitate getting under or around food. For stirring or creaming, it is lovely to handle. The slight curve makes it perfect for folding egg whites into soufflé, turning potato pancakes, or scraping the tasty bits from the bottom of a chicken fryer as you make cream gravy. The right-left slant to the paddle makes it a tool for right-handed people. A hole at the end of the handle has been provided for hanging.

A nineteenth-century French chocolate beater, illustrated in L'Ecole des Cuisinières *by Urbain-Dubois.*

Beechwood Spatula Set   5.27

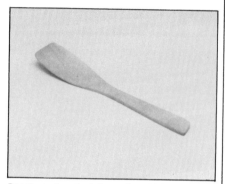

Beechwood; set of 2, each 11½" long, 2⅜" wide.

$1.50

Another compromise between spatula and spoon, this set is a pedestrian version of the olivewood beauty above (5.26). Each spatula of the pair has gently curved paddles to allow smooth scraping of the sides of the mixing bowl or saucepan, as well as a slightly rounded back surface for creaming. The paddle tips are squared off with rounded corners. They slant slightly downward from left to right, making them awkward for a left-handed person to use. The pale beechwood of these utensils has little grain. The finishing is somewhat negligent, the edges splintery. Don't expect these to last a lifetime, but they will be useful while they last.

Boxwood Spatula or Spatula Set   5.28

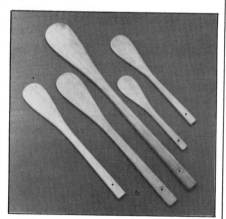

Boxwood; 8" long, 1½" wide. Also avail. individually 10", 12", or 14" long, or in sets of 4, including the 8", 10", 12", and 14" sizes.

$1.50

These Berard Frères beauties are the great classic spatulas, the very best you can buy. They're of smooth, golden-grained boxwood, with paddles that are flat but distinctly spoon-shaped, tapering to thin, rounded edges. The wood is highly resistant to penetration by moisture or grease. We recommend the extra-long (18-inch) model for extra-big jobs like making pan gravy; it's extremely well balanced despite its length, with most of the weight centered in the 2¼-inch paddle. The medium-sized (12-inch) spatula would be fine for stirring anything that can be made in a saucepan or double boiler, from cream sauce to custards; its paddle is 1¾ inches across at the widest. These are available singly, or you might prefer to order a set of four in graduated 8-, 10-, 12-, and 14-inch lengths. Like all the spatulas we show, these have small holes in the handles for hanging.

In the kitchen, everything has its lore and mystery, even stirring: "A survival of an old Druidical belief, mentioned by Sir James Frazer in The Golden Bough, *and still prevalent in some parts of the Highlands, is that in kneading bannocks, stirring porridge or kail, sending a glass round the company, etc., the movement must be 'deiseal,' sunwise—i.e. the right-hand turn. This is the lucky way. Widdershins—i.e. the left-hand turn—is unlucky."*

The Scots Kitchen, *by F. Marian McNeill*

Beechwood Spatula or Spatula Set   5.29

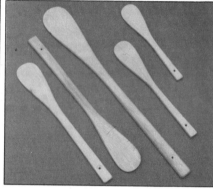

Beechwood; 18" long; 2¼" wide. Also avail. individually 8", 10", 12", 14", or 16" long, or in sets of 4, including the 8", 10", 12", and 14" sizes.

$1.80

Beechwood doesn't have quite the deliciously smooth feel of boxwood, and its beige color isn't as rich-looking, but when beechwoodware comes from Berard Frères, as these spatulas do, it's as good as beech can be. These spatulas are available in the same sizes as 5.28, or they, too, can be bought as a set. They are a wee bit thicker than their boxwood counterparts, except at the very tip, and very nicely finished, with no splinters. If you don't need something as fine as boxwood, buy these.

Bowls

Bowls are for mixing, for serving and, when made of ceramic or oven-proof glass, even for cooking.

An unlined copper bowl is the utensil of choice for whipping egg whites, the cachet of the professionally equipped kitchen. Metal bowls range from that ultraspecific copper bowl to the stainless-steel bowl at the opposite end of the spectrum, the ubiquitous workhorse of the kitchen. Metal is unbreakable. It is light. A metal bowl will respond more rapidly than any other material to heating and chilling. The K-5A mixing machine (see 5.5) is conveniently equipped with a jacket—a second bowl to hold hot water or ice to heat or chill the food you are processing in its stainless-steel bowl. Lacking this extraordinary piece of equipment, use bowls within bowls. For example, to speed-set a bavarois au citron, simply heap the mixture into a large metal bowl—which will assure the greatest amount of surface for contact with the

Beechwood Spatula Set
Boxwood Spatula or Spatula Set
Beechwood Spatula or Spatula Set

Copper Egg-White Beating Bowl
Stainless-Steel Mixing Bowl
White Ceramic Pudding and
Mixing Bowl

cold—and place it in another large container (a still larger bowl, preferably not metal, or your kitchen sink) filled with ice. As it cools, gently fold the mixture in from the sides to the center, avoiding crystalline edges. Conversely, while preparing lemon chiffon pie filling or Génoise, you can heat while you beat.

Always match the bowl size to the beating or mixing implement, or vice versa. A whisk should fit precisely into the bottom of the beating bowl, the better to deal effectively with the food being operated on. Small whisk in a big bowl means more energy expended, less material incorporated—total inefficiency. And big beater in a too-small bowl means, simply, a mess all over the place.

It's a good idea to accumulate bowls in different materials and sizes. Bowls are one thing that you can never have too many of, and best of all, they are multipurpose. A sizable wardrobe of them adds versatility to your kitchen.

depths and have rings for gripping or for hanging fixed just below the rims. And in recommending metal bowls, we emphasize the importance of using wooden spoons and spatulas with them for greater resiliency and less racket.

"If a recipe calls for more than 1 egg white or yolk, it is a wise precaution to use 3 bowls.

Crack each egg in turn over the small bowl and deposit its white therein; then put the yolk into the middle-sized bowl, or throw it away if the egg should happen to be bad, in which case the white also should be thrown out, and the whites and yolks already separated will not be spoiled by the bad egg. If the whites are to be beaten, it is of the utmost importance that not the smallest speck of the yolk get into them. If there is even the least amount, they cannot be beaten."

The Emily Post Cookbook, *1951*

Copper Egg-White Beating Bowl   5.30

Hammered copper with brass ring; 12½″ diam.; 6″ deep; 7-qt. capacity. Also avail. with diam. of 9½″, 10¾″, or 14″.

$60.00 ▲

If you can hang only one bowl on your wall, let it be this one, a commodious (7-quart) beauty from France. Make no mistake about it, this will spend most of its time hanging out of the way; it is definitely not an everyday item. But then, neither is soufflé de saumon fumé. The chances are that you will fall in love with it for its appearance: its copper body gleams with a high polish on the outside and is hammered on the inside, the hammering providing texture as well as added strength. The shape of the bowl keeps the whipping action going continuously as you incorporate air into egg whites with one of the many-wired balloon whisks we show you, achieving volume that cannot be achieved by any other beating method. It is the copper itself that assures this marvel, reacting

chemically with the egg whites. After use, simply rinse and dry your copper bowl (be very careful to keep it free from any speck of fat or oil, which would affect the egg whites unfavorably). To neutralize the surface of the bowl before every use, toss in a handful of salt, slosh some vinegar around with the salt, rinse, and wipe dry. That is how the French chefs who care about their egg whites care for their copper beating bowls.

Stainless-Steel Mixing Bowl   5.31

Stainless steel; set of 3; 1-, 2-, and 3-qt. capacity.

$10.00 ▲

This set of three stainless-steel bowls, in 1-, 2-, and 3-quart sizes, is our choice for continual kitchen use. Unlike ceramic, these metal bowls have little personality—so little, in fact, that stainless steel will keep to itself and not influence your food's color or flavor. These are not perfect hemispheres but are of useful

White Ceramic Pudding and Mixing Bowl   5.32

Ceramic; 8½″ diam.; 5″ deep; 3-qt. capacity. Also avail. with capacity of 1, 1¼, or 3¾ qts.

$8.50   2¾ qt. **$4.00**▲   5½ qt. **$7.00**▲

Examine any English or American cookbook written before 1920 and you will discover vast chapters of recipes for pudding. Dessert puddings, main-course puddings, snack puddings. In those days, ovens were unreliable, convenience foods unheard of. Where today's cook bakes, our forebears would pud. Sweet or savory mixtures, heaped into basins, were steamed to custard or cakelike consistency. Leftovers from meats to vegetables to breads became puddings. It was not uncommon for a meal to comprise three courses, each featuring pudding. These white-glazed ceramic bowls

Continued from preceding page

are pudding basins. Deep. Ovenproof. Their characteristic inch-deep rim, permitting the pudding mixture to be covered with cloth that is tied in place under the lip, has now become a decorative feature. They have a solid, comfortable simplicity, but enough of the right kind of style to take them to the table. The glaze is nonporous, so we recommend them for salad, unless you prefer Proustian memories of prior garlic in your greens, in which case use a wooden bowl by all means. We show the 3-quart pudding bowl here, as the most versatile for all purposes. You will come to depend on the other sizes as well, the smaller ones for mixing or serving sauce, the larger to marinate shrimp to serve sixty.

Blue- and- White Striped Ceramic Bowl   5.33

Ceramic; 6½″ diam.; 3¾″ deep; 1¼ -qt. capacity. Also avail. with capacity of ¾ qt.

$4.00

If you find a white ceramic pudding basin unexciting, this traditional Cornish type with blue stripes may brighten your culinary life. The glazed ceramic pudding basin shown is small, with a capacity of 1¼ quarts. Deep in proportion to its diameter, it sits solidly on its flat bottom. Functionally, this English ware is the same as that of 5.32. Visually, it makes an aesthetic statement that agrees with modern or traditional, Anglo-Saxon or Continental environments. The authentic charm of the bands of blue can follow from kitchen to table, not only in these bowls of various sizes but in mugs, pitchers, dishes, and other items of tableware in the same pattern. Spoon berries into one to chill, crème fraîche or Devon-

shire cream in another, and then serve from them. Or array a dozen of the smaller size on your table for hors d'oeuvre variés, family style.

Glazed Ceramic Gripstand Bowl   5.34

Ceramic; 10″ diam.; 4½″ deep; 3¾-qt. capacity.

$5.50	2½ qt. $5.00▲	6½ qt. $11.00▲
	4½ qt. $7.00▲	12½ qt. $27.50▲

This bowl has old-timey good looks, in a warm buff glaze, the color of rich batter and boxwood spoons, with a geometric design in relief on the outside, ivory within. As solidly British as well-worn tweeds, it is just as sensible and comfortable, with its patented gripstand. Normally, we prevent a bowl from traveling across the countertop while we mix by wadding a dish towel underneath, or by setting it on a rubber mat or some such. This bowl has a flattened area on one outside surface; this allows it to rest steadily for beating at an angle. It also has two small lip handles, good to focus pouring or for butter-fingers to cling to. The glazed ceramic will emerge from the oven undamaged if you wish to bake in it. The mouth is quite wide in relation to the height of the bowl, making it good for breadmaking, beating, creaming. We show the 10-inch, 3¾-quart size, but they range both upward and down. We think their practicality and nostalgic appeal make them eminently collectible.

GATEAU BASQUE—BASQUE CAKE

Serves 6-8

ALMOND PASTRY
6 tablespoons butter
2 tablespoons shortening
1½ cups all-purpose flour
Pinch of salt
3 tablespoons ground, blanched almonds
¼ cup sugar
1 egg yolk
½ teaspoon almond extract
2–3 tablespoons ice water

FILLING
¾ cup plum jam, preferably damson

GLAZE
1 egg white, lightly beaten
Granulated sugar for dusting

In a bowl, rub butter and shortening into flour and salt. Add ground almonds and sugar.

Mix egg yolk with almond extract and water and add to flour mixture. Work lightly with a spoon to a smooth dough and chill, covered, for about 1 hour.

Preheat oven to 400 F. Roll out two-thirds of the dough on a floured surface and line an 8-inch flan ring or 7½-inch oven-proof glass pie plate. Fill with jam. Roll out the remaining dough to a 9-inch circle and cover the cake. Seal the edges and mark the top in cartwheel fashion with the point of a knife, cutting through to the layer of jam.

Bake for 15 minutes or until the top is golden brown.

Just before the end of cooking, brush the top of the GATEAU with the beaten egg white, sprinkle with granulated sugar and return to the oven for about 2 minutes. (Sugar must be dusted onto egg white quickly so that the heat of the pastry has a chance to make a meringue-like topping of frost.)

Serve hot or cold.

(From THE GREAT COOKS COOKBOOK, by The Good Cooking School, Inc. Copyright © 1974 by The Good Cooking School, Inc. Reprinted by permission of Ferguson/Doubleday.)

Leach Stoneware Bowl   5.35

Stoneware; 9⅛″ diam.; 4¾″ deep; 1½-qt. capacity. Also avail. with capacity of ¾ pt. or 1 qt.

$11.00

Bernard Leach, whose work we discuss in Chapter 7 as well, is one of our greatest contemporary potters. These handsome stoneware bowls are made at Cornwall St. Ives by his students to his specifications, and thus are fairly uniform. Typical of Leach pots, they are unglazed on the outside, of a roughly sandy texture and rich reddish color, and are beautifully glazed within, in a variety of harmonizing, randomly mottled colors ranging from oatmeal to pale celadon. These smallish, well-proportioned round bowls, holding from 12 to 48 ounces, have a straightforward, handcrafted appeal. The stoneware is so highly vitrified that the bowls can actually be used on top of the stove as well as in the oven. While they make wonderful small casseroles, you would also be doing them justice if you served hard sauce for holiday puddings in them or set them out filled with freshly shelled nuts, plump raisins, and slivers of crystallized ginger to nibble on at the end of Thanksgiving dinner.

Ron Garfinkel Salt-Glazed Bowl   5.36

Salt-glazed stoneware; 14″ diam.; 6¾″ deep; 10-qt. capacity.

$30.00

The bowls just described (see 5.35) are small, exquisitely crafted kitchen utensils. By comparison, this salt-glazed bowl by Ron Garfinkel is on a monumental scale. It makes its statement as effectively when empty as it does containing the dough for five loaves of whole-wheat bread or with a peck of crisp autumn apples from the orchard piled in it. The design reflects the dynamism of the salt-glazing process. At the moment when the heat of the kiln is at its most intense, the potter throws in handfuls of rock salt. The fire dictates how the white-hot stoneware objects become fused with sodium molecules from the salt to form rock-hard sodium silicate, a glasslike, semigloss sheen, slightly pitting the sur-

face, which becomes a rich blend of speckled browns, blues, or greens. We cannot imagine any dining room, no matter how formal, which would not be glorified by an object like this. It is a work of art, instantly recognizable to collectors, a special experience to the owner, and a compliment to the recipient.

MOROCCAN BREAD—KISRA OR KHBOZ

INGREDIENTS
1 package active dry yeast
1 teaspoon granulated sugar
3½ cups unbleached flour
1 cup whole-wheat flour
2 teaspoons salt
½ cup lukewarm milk
1 teaspoon sesame seeds
1 tablespoon aniseed
Cornmeal

EQUIPMENT
Small and large mixing bowls
Electric mixer with dough hook (optional)
2 baking sheets
Towels

Working time: 35 minutes
Rising time: 1½ to 2 hours
Baking time: 40 to 50 minutes
Makes: 2 six-inch round loaves

1. Soften the yeast in ¼ cup sugared lukewarm water. Let stand 2 minutes, then stir and set in a warm place until the yeast is bubbly and doubles in volume. Meanwhile, mix the flours with the salt in a large mixing bowl.
2. Stir the bubbling yeast into the flour, then add the milk and enough lukewarm water to form a stiff dough. (Since flours differ in their ability to absorb moisture, no precise amount can be given.) Turn the dough out onto a lightly floured board and knead hard with closed fists, adding water if necessary. To knead, push the dough outward. (It will take anywhere from 10 to 15 minutes to knead this dough thoroughly and achieve a smooth, elastic consistency. If using an electric beater with a dough hook, knead 7 to 8 minutes at slow speed.) During the final part of the kneading, add the spices. After the dough has been thoroughly kneaded, form into two balls and let stand 5 minutes on the board.
3. Lightly grease a mixing bowl. Transfer the first ball of dough to the greased bowl and form into a cone shape by grasping the dough with one hand and rotating it against the sides of the bowl, held by the other hand. Turn out onto a baking sheet that has been sprinkled with cornmeal. Flatten the cone with the

palm of the hand to form a flattened disc about 5 inches in diameter with a slightly raised center. Repeat with the second ball of dough. Cover loosely with a damp towel and let rise about 2 hours in a warm place. (To see if the bread has fully risen, poke your finger gently into the dough—the bread is ready for baking if the dough does not spring back.)
4. Preheat the oven to 400°.
5. Using a fork, prick the bread around the sides three or four times and place on the center shelf of the oven. Bake 12 minutes, then lower the heat to 300° and bake 30 to 40 minutes more. When done, the bread will sound hollow when tapped on the bottom. Remove and let cool. Cut in wedges just before serving.

VARIATION—KHBOZ MIKLA
A flattened circle of the dough is cooked, over an open fire, on a dry earthen griddle called a *mikla* until browned on both sides. To my mind this is absolutely delicious with fresh butter and crystalized honey.

(From COUSCOUS AND OTHER GOOD FOOD FROM MOROCCO, by Paula Wolfert, with introduction by Gael Greene. Copyright © 1973 by Paula Wolfert. Reprinted by permission of Harper & Row.)

Three-Piece Pyrex Bowl Set   5.37

Pyrex glass; set of 3; 7″, 8¼″, and 10″ diam.; 1-, 1½-, and 2-qt. capacity.

$6.00 ▲

Pyrex is a term as generic as the Jell-O chilling in it. A Pyrex bowl can be used in the oven, in the freezer, and also on the table, assuming it contains a gelatine dessert for a party of toddlers. These are utilitarian and practical equipment. The nicely rounded bowls have flat bottoms (stamped with their capacity—1, 1½, or 2 quarts) and a broad top rim, handy for securing a wrapping of plastic or foil. Glass bowls can have no secrets. If all

Continued from preceding page

the fruits in your gelatin hit bottom and stay there, you'll know about it. (But then, you might also notice it in time to correct it before the jelling is complete and your family is served less than perfection.) The round shape simplifies unmolding. Glass, even glass treated to be as sturdy as Pyrex, must be handled with care. Keep it away from direct heat, and don't let it go directly from hot to cold or vice versa. As a precaution, allow its contents to cool before putting the dish into the refrigerator. You can always tell whether your Pyrex bowls are perfectly clean, in sink or dishwasher, but avoid abrasive cleaners which will scratch them. Observe these caveats and the bowls will provide long and efficient service.

"Elvira watched her sister mix the bread. Jane did not lose a grain of flour in the process; her knotty fingers were deft and delicate from faithful practice. She left the mixing-bowl polished quite clean when she finally deposited the dough in the pans."

"A Pot of Gold," in A New England Nun and Other Stories, by Mary Wilkes Freeman, 1891

Ten-Piece Duralex Mixing Bowl Set 5.38

Heat-resistant Duralex glass; set of 10; 2¼" to 10¼" diam. range; 1½-oz. to 3½-qt. capacity.

$15.00 ▲

As usual in matters culinary, here the French tend to go us one better. These tempered glass Duralax (French equivalent of Pyrex) bowls are lighter-looking and have a more graceful, open silhouette than their American counterparts. They have been designed with two sets of outer ridges, one across the mid-

dle and one near the bottom. In addition to providing relief from all that plain glass, the ridges serve as a good grip for your hands. The range of sizes of these bowls lends itself to a vast number of functions, from that of saltcellar to salad bowl. The middle and larger sizes will be your mixing bowls and ovenware, and the smaller ones come in handy for storing leftovers in the refrigerator. Of course, to obtain four of a single size to use for individual fruit service, you are faced with the impractical circumstance of acquiring several complete sets, forty bowls! The careful treatment recommended for Pyrex (see 5.37) applies to these as well.

Danish Melamine Bowl 5.39

Melamine with rubber grip ring; 8½" diam.; 5" high; 3-qt. capacity. Also avail. with capacity of 1½, 2, or 4 qts.

$6.50 ▲ $7.50 ▲ $9.00 ▲ $10.50 ▲

Plastics are among the miracles of our time. Every day new uses are being found for these synthetically produced materials, which sometimes seem to be taking over the world. In recent years the Scandinavians and Italians have been producing high-grade plastics which are not only practical but aesthetically competitive with other substances. Plastic is, by nature, light, flexible, and utterly nonporous. It can add a shock of bright color, insulate against heat or cold, cushion the stroke of a rigid whisk, or resist penetration by acid substances. While it is non-biodegradable, its form is not permanent. The heat of oven or stovetop will mold it to a sad distortion. It is susceptible to scratching and cannot be cleaned with abrasives. This melamine bowl from Denmark is the very best one can expect from a plastic bowl. It is bright, heavy, heat-resistant, and safe in the dishwasher. Sizes from 1½

quarts to 4 quarts are available; we show the 3-quart size. It has a pouring spout on one side and a grip lip on the other. Its outstanding feature is a built-in non-skid device, a rubber ring on the bottom (removable for thorough cleaning of the bowl). Its deeply rounded shape is good for mixing—you can plunge right in with both hands. Its lighthearted cheerfulness—in red, orange, purple, avocado, or sunflower—will accent an informal table, whether you fill it with the contrast of deep green spinach, or the compliment of stewed peaches.

Stoneware Batter Bowl by Cynthia Bringle 5.40

Stoneware; 5⅞" diam.; 4¼" deep; 1½-qt. capacity. Also avail. with capacities up to 2 qts.

$12.00

If the modern breakfast table is set at all, it is with cream and sugar, possibly irritation. In an earlier era, a pitcher of maple syrup or molasses and one of fresh milk sat on every farmhouse table. The batter for the griddle cakes was poured onto the wood stove's cast-iron griddle from a squat, spouted batter bowl. Cynthia Bringle, one of the finest contemporary American potters, has translated the rural tradition into beautifully handcrafted personal terms. This handsomely turned, solidly proportioned stoneware bowl has been supplied with a generous spout. The grooved handle affords a good grip. Except on the very bottom of its flat base, the bowl has been glazed a gleaming deep greige, spattered with warm brown, and fired with a stunning free-form design of white, bright blue, and metallic brown. The bowl will comfortably hold one quart. It would be a joy to use in the kitchen for preparing or serving breakfast, for mixing and pouring out pancake or muffin or popover batter, or even the batter for

Ten-Piece Duralex Mixing
Bowl Set
Danish Melamine Bowl
Stoneware Batter Bowl
by Cynthia Bringle

Stoneware Batter Bowl
by Licht-Tomono
Arabia Enamel Bowl
Handmade Walnut Bowl
Large Teakwood Bowl

crêpes. When not in use, it should be on display, filled with a big bunch of cornflowers in season.

Stoneware Batter Bowl by Licht-Tomono 5.41

Stoneware; 6½" diam.; 3¾" deep; 1-qt. capacity. Also avail. with capacity of 3 or 8 qts.

$12.00

This hand-thrown batter bowl of stoneware is in the same great tradition of the artisan potters as the preceding bowl, but it is more openly bowl-like, simpler in shape, and somewhat heavier. The handle and the spout are both smaller than those of the Bringle bowl, making this one somewhat less comfortable to hold and to pour from. Its surface is marked with the broad, shallow horizontal stripings left by the potter's fingers, and its satiny warm-gray glaze is overlaid here and there by random brown speckles and areas of a deeper tone. The base is unglazed, and the piece is signed by the potter, the noted Doris Licht-Tomono. A beautiful piece, useful and satisfying to look at as well.

Arabia Enamel Bowl 5.42

Enameled steel; 8¼" diam.; 5½" deep; 3-qt. capacity.

$12.50

Stun them at a large dessert buffet by heaping mousse au chocolat in a pristine white service bowl (perhaps the matching bowl, in white) and pairing it with this gleaming deep, deep brown Arabia bowl brimming with whipped cream. Or imagine its depths filled with freshly churned fudge-ripple ice cream, creamy vanilla ribboned with dark fudge sauce. The appearance of this bowl, one of the most fundamentally pleasing ones we've seen, will complement less naive delights: saffron rice; pale endive salad with dark watercress highlights; richly somber molé poblano. If you prefer another color, choose it in white or yellow instead of brown. The 3-quart bowl is made of special enamel over steel, and it can even be used directly over flame if you are careful to observe the precautions of not letting it boil dry and not adding liquid while it is hot. For our money, the durability and all-around usefulness of this bowl is simply A-plus. Its shape is so remarkably appealing that we have yet to show it to anyone who hasn't immediately wanted to hold it, stroke its surface, and turn it this way and that to admire it as it deserves.

Handmade Walnut Bowl 5.43

Black walnut; 13¼" diam.; 4¼" deep.

$70.00

We do not recommend using wooden bowls for salad: they become rancid. But if you must have one, here is our first choice: a magnificent smoothie from California, handcrafted by Bob Stockdale, a master. It is carved of black walnut and treated with a tasteless oil, which prevents your dressing from being absorbed into the finish and allows you to clean it with never more than a light washing. The finish is beautiful, absolutely silky, enhancing the extraordinary grain which flows over its curving surfaces. This one is generously large: from its smallish flat base the sides slope very gently upward to the full circumference and then turn sharply vertical to form

almost straight sides. Use it for a quantity of absolutely first-rate salad greens, or a centerpiece of freshly roasted nuts and autumn fruits. And if you haven't got enough of the perfect edibles to fill it, leave it beautifully empty.

Large Teakwood Bowl 5.44

Teak; 15" diam.; 7¼" deep. Also avail. with diam. of 10", 12", or 20".

$49.95

There are times when one needs a truly gigantic container. Salad for the big buffet you give to reciprocate every invitation you have ever received. A place to pile the doughnuts for the hundreds of small witches, goblins, and ghosts who mob your house on Halloween. This Brobdingnagian bowl is mighty impressive and, for the money, excellent value. It is made of solid teak of excellent quality, hand carved, seasoned with a "secret" treatment, and hand rubbed until it attains the dark lustre of antique teak. The narrowed hemisphere of its silhouette is simple and uncluttered. If you plan to use it for salad, be sure your servers are at least 14 inches long, lest they vanish from sight in the greenery, forcing your guests to rummage in the damp underbrush to retrieve them. And need we remind you to care for it as for all wooden utensils?

Stovetop Cooking Utensils

The Very Short History of Stovetop Cookery

Throughout most of prehistory and history, the basic food of the vast majority of mankind has been boiled whole grain—whether called grits, mush, foufou, polenta, couscous, or porridge. Cooking, or the use of heat to break down tough fibers, is more necessary for vegetable foods such as roots and grains than for meats. This is not cooking for palatability; foods to tempt the taste buds are a quite recent luxury. Even the toughest raw meat can be chewed and digested without cooking, but some foods *must* be cooked to be safely eaten. Manioc root, a staple in the diet of various Pacific Islands people, is literally inedible when raw, being toxic as well as tough; and acorns, a basic food of the Indians of California, are neither wholesome nor palatable unless they are leached and cooked.

Among the most basic of human inventions, the development of stovetop cookery is a relative newcomer, more recent by millennia than simpler methods of cooking such as barbecuing or even oven roasting Well, not *stove*top really; what we're actually talking about is cooking-in-a-container-on-top-of-a-heat-source. And you will see what a tricky business it was for our prehistoric forebears if you consider that above-fire cooking required a container that was waterproof, fireproof, transmitted heat, and did not interact chemically with the food.

There were several primitive solutions to the container problem. Most universal was the earthenware pot. It was fireproof, safe, and did not change the taste of food—but it was not waterproof. On the contrary, it was porous. But after being coated inside and/or out with some sort of plant gum it became waterproof enough to contain thick porridges or stews. Glazed pottery, the ancient ancestor of our enameled pots, came much, much later, and with it came, in some places, another problem: slow poisoning over a period of time, due to lead being used in the glaze. This problem still exists in many parts of the world where coarse pottery is used.

Earthenware did not (and does not) transmit heat very efficiently. Over the fire, it required long cooking, with much stirring to prevent scorch and to distribute the heat. In just this manner did Jacob cook up the mess of pottage that proved the undoing of his brother Esau.

How to get the heat from the fire to the food inside the pot was another problem. The contents of a pot placed on the ground next to the fire would become heated, but slowly. Another simple solution was to place the pot directly in the fireplace; some ancient vessels with conical pointy bottoms have been excavated in various parts of the world; these could be pushed directly into the hot coals or ashes.

In some places the heating process was accelerated by dropping hot rocks (real ones, not stolen gems) into the stew. Among the Indian natives of California, even into the twentieth century, food was cooked in tightly woven basketry pots lined with pitch to make them watertight. Water and the food to be cooked—usually stone-ground acorn meal—were placed in the pot, and stones heated in the fire were added to keep the mush simmering.

Cooking equipment of the prehistoric Lake Dwellers, from Meyer's grosses Konversations Lexikon, *1902.*

Various methods were devised to keep a pot above the heat source. A stack of rocks surrounding the fire provided a simple stand. Neolithic hearths of 30,000 and more years ago have been identified, not only by charred remains but by the circle of stones surrounding them. At one ancient site, Molodova in the western Ukraine, 15 small stone-ringed hearths and more than a hundred bones and tusks remain as evidence of early man. Another method of supporting a pot was to construct a sort of tripod or lean-to of poles, set in the ground surrounding the hearth. The poles crossed each other near the top, providing a rung from which pots could be suspended by means of animal sinew or braided reed ropes. And in some cases the stand was incorporated into the clay pot itself, which was made with three or four thick legs of clay attached beneath the base as a sort of built-in tripod.

Even after the developments that ushered in the successive metal ages of bronze and iron (see the discussion of metals in Chapter 2), it took a long time for these valuable materials to be used for such mundane purposes as cookery. At last someone, somewhere (or more likely several persons in several places) decided to mimic the form of the earthenware pot in cast bronze and iron.

It was a natural choice. Metal pots were virtually indestructible, could be made in a variety of sizes and shapes, could be used indefinitely in the cooking fire, and would transmit heat rapidly and efficiently. The proliferation of sizes and shapes began almost instantaneously, based on the abundant models provided by clay pots. And voilà! *Homo sapiens* was on the way to dining, instead of simply eating food. But the origin of cookery vessels as pottery has remained with us in the etymological sense, and we speak of all such containers generically as "pots."

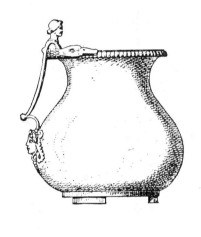

Before serious cookery could get under way, however, ritual had literally to be served. In China during the Shang dynasty, in the thirteenth century B.C., bronze vessels fashioned over pottery molds were used to prepare food offerings. Early writings describe these cooked offerings as being made of bones with the marrow in them and some meat on them, and refer to the contents being ladled out and ceremonially eaten. The soup consumed at the ritual banquet was offered in a round three-legged vessel, a *ting* or tripod-cauldron, sometimes covered with a mat of woven rushes and sometimes topped with a bowl-cover that could be used for serving the contents.

Metal pots were still too valuable in their early history for daily use by most people, and the earthenware pot, by then usually glazed, continued to serve for most purposes. It was inexpensive enough to be replaced easily when it broke, which it often did. Utility-grade earthenware such as primitive folk made was and is quite fragile, being fired in kilns which can never get hot enough to produce such resistant ceramics as stoneware. (If you search out street markets as you travel, you may be able to find such wares still being made and used today; people on our staff have collected delightful examples from Barbados, Mexico—especially Oaxaca—Guatemala, Peru, and Portugal, as well as in Pueblo Indian communities in the southwestern United States.)

Bronze pots from Pompeii, illustrated in La Vie Privée des Anciens *by René Joseph Ménard, 1880-1883.*

In the meantime, however, the ancient Romans came up with a way to improve on the open fireplace. By enclosing a hearth in clay, tile, or brick, a stove was created. It provided a more concentrated source of heat and, more importantly, a safer and warmer source. Because stoves could be safely used in the home and they conserved scarce fuel, the stove idea spread rapidly throughout Europe. Cast-iron plates were first used to surround clay-tile stoves in the late fifteenth century, a progressive development that likewise spread slowly but surely. Colonists brought iron stoves with them to America, and some were manufactured here by the earliest iron foundries. But these were warming, not cooking, devices, and most families didn't own one.

In a colonial home the hearth was in the common room and, because of the comfortable warmth and light it provided, it became the center of activity for the household. The fireplace was topped with a long, broad mantel, often made from a solid tree trunk; it was a shelf for storage of utensils, and from it hung hooks for kitchen tools and pots. A wooden bar suspended above the fire held pots during cooking. Later an iron crane that was fastened to a side wall of the fireplace was used. The free end could be swung out into the room so that the housewife could load its pothooks, and then swing it back into position over the fire.

Many years passed before stoves became generally available, and even then they were regarded as accessories to the fireplace. The one stood alongside the other, and the stovepipe was usually vented into the fireplace chimney. The stove was used for warming and, at last, for baking; the fireplace remained the place for all cooking done in a pot or skillet until coal-burning ranges became available around the middle of the nineteenth century. Real stovetop cooking is, then, practically brand-new. In all likelihood, your great-great-grandmothers were the first in their families to enjoy or be amazed at its possibilities.

However, pots for over-the-fire use in the fireplace existed long before. The batterie de cuisine in an early American household was often as basic as "1 frying pan, 2 skillets, 3 bake pains (*sic*), iron pothooks, warming pan and trivet" (*Treasury of American Design,* Abrams, 1973). The cooking vessels were almost always of iron and might include long-handled skillets as well as pots and tea kettles, sometimes standing on three or four legs (the built-in tripod again) so they could be placed directly on the hearth close to the fire. They had to be tended carefully and their position changed frequently so that all sides of the pot had a chance to come into contact with the heat. There would also be lids for the pots and kettles, and instead of handles as we know them, there was a large loop or semicircle of wire attached to the top at opposite sides of the rim. The pot could be suspended by this bail handle.

Blacksmiths could not keep up with the demand for their wares (which included tools for agriculture and warfare as well as the kitchen), and all of their output was strictly utilitarian in appearance: there was no time for such adornments as curves or scrolls. The first working forge in America dates back to 1644, when the Saugus Ironworks in Massachusetts began operations. The ironworks has been restored under the sponsorship of the iron and steel industry, and among the

After an engraving of the Nef des fous, 1497, as illustrated in the Dictionnaire de l'Ameublement et de la Decoration depuis le xiii° Siècle jusqu'à nos Jours, *by Henry Harvard, 1887-1890.*

exhibits is the first object produced: appropriately, a cast-iron cooking pot.

Brass and copper utensils were mostly imported, and were within the reach of only the wealthy. However, there was a copper foundry in Lynn, Massachusetts, as early as 1664; and kettles were hand-crafted of brass and copper in Philadelphia fifty years before the Revolution. The first sheet-rolling mill for brass was established in Waterbury, Connecticut, in 1802, and the city remains a center of brass manufacture to this day. A year earlier, Paul Revere had put up the first copper rolling mill near Canton, Massachusetts. But in early America a kitchen replete with an assortment of polished brassware was a rarity and sure proof of affluence (just look at the kitchen of the Governor's Palace the next time you visit Colonial Williamsburg).

But while American pots were almost exclusively of iron through the colonial years, elsewhere copper and brass utensils were just as frequently found. In Europe, very good pots of these metals were in everyday use in middle-class as well as upper-class kitchens. And throughout the Mediterranean region and into Asia, thinner hammered copper and brass pots could be found before or over every fire.

Whether a household used copper or iron kettles, long cooking over the fire and frequent stirring were necessary. And a good thing too—meat and poultry were both tough and scarce, and the long cooking was needed to tenderize and also to distribute the flavor throughout the essentially vegetable stews and grain mushes that were the everyday food of the average family.

HOW HEAT COOKS
In cookery, heat changes foods in various ways. We are concerned with how a particular pot makes heat available to its contents, and with how those contents make use of the heat.

Conduction of heat occurs when heat passes through a solid substance, so we say that materials which transmit heat easily are "good conductors." Most metals are good conductors, because heat spreads or diffuses (as the layman perceives the process) throughout the metal. Glass is less satisfactory because, although it transmits heat directly, the heat does not spread or diffuse. A glass pot, therefore, will carry heat from the burner to the contents only through its bottom, which is of course the surface receiving the heat. But heat received through the bottom of a copper saucepan will spread rapidly through the walls of the pot until the food is surrounded by it. Poor conduction on the one hand, good conduction on the other.

Some metals, however, are not good conductors. Stainless steel is little better than glass. Primarily, it allows the heat to pass straight through but does not spread it around; in fact, glass responds instantly to heat and will actually transmit it directly even faster than stainless.

Convection is the way that heat spreads through liquids or gases. In fluids, a rise in temperature generally results in a decrease in weight or density. When you cook boeuf bourguignonne, for example, the portion of the cooking liquid nearest the source of heat is the first to reach a

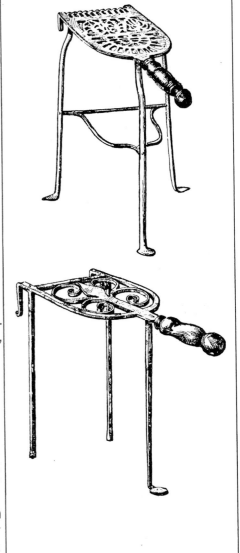

Eighteenth-century trivets.

higher temperature and become lighter. Then the cooler and heavier portion of liquid above it sinks to displace the already heated portion, which, because it is warm, tends to rise on its own. This starts a current moving so that there is a continual flow of warmed liquid upward and cooler liquid downward throughout the pot. Heat is transferred from one point in the stew to another by this convection current, and eventually all of the beef gets cooked. When you cook clams or vegetables in or over a very small amount of liquid, that liquid vaporizes—it becomes steam, a near-gas. The steam circulates in convection currents throughout the closed kettle, thus cooking the food without the necessity for immersing it completely in a liquid.

(A third method of heat transfer, called *radiation,* is what goes on in an oven or over coals or under a broiler: the radiant heat within an oven is transferred directly to foods, as in roasting, or through conduction and/or convection, depending on the type of food and its container.)

All stovetop cookery involves both conduction and convection, and requires some liquid in the pot. In choosing pots we are concerned with the ability to conduct heat from an external source (the range) to the food inside. Different foods have different heat requirements, and therefore pots of different materials must be considered for different purposes. When it comes to choosing pots for their ability to spread heat evenly, there is nothing to beat copper. A fine sauce in the making requires surrounding gentle, even heat, and only copper, with its superb heat-diffusion capability, fits the bill.

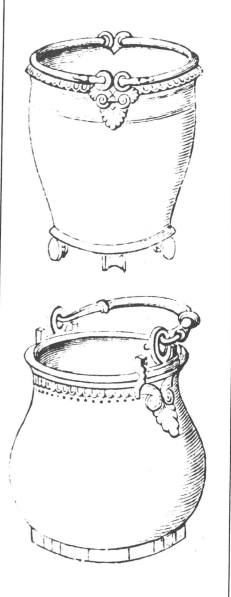

In fine cooking it is also important for a pot to lose heat as quickly as it accepts and diffuses it. Copper wins in this category too; it radiates the heat off, being extremely sensitive to temperature changes. Aluminum, on the other hand, holds the heat and therefore is not recommended for saucemaking, where it is important to be able to remove heat at the precise moment when the proper consistency has been achieved. But aluminum, because it does hold heat and has excellent diffusion properties as well, is excellent in pots for casseroles and stews, and for griddles too.

Heat transfer is the significant factor in the type of handles used on cookware. Heat slows down when it goes from one material to another, and for this reason handles are usually made of a metal that is different from the basic pot metal—the immediacy of heat transfer is reduced. Handles can be welded on, and in some inexpensive kinds of cookware they are. But this kind of joint is likely to weaken and loosen with overheating. More usually, metal handles are secured by thick bolts, which can be retightened if necessary, and which by introducing still another metal slow heat transfer a bit more. Brass handles are customarily found on copper pots not only for heat-reducing reasons and because of their decorative appearance, but also because they are lighter in weight than the copper. On a very heavy copper pot, however, iron would be the metal of choice for the handle. It is lighter than both copper and brass and it will transmit less heat than either, being completely different in composition from the copper (brass, of course, is a copper alloy).

THE MAKING OF A POT

Today most of our cooking vessels are of metal. Pottery in various forms is still used, of course (we show you many casseroles and other pots of stoneware, porcelain, and other types of earthenware), and stone is still used for griddles such as the one in this chapter. But for almost everybody, everywhere, when we talk of something to cook food in nowadays we are understood to be speaking of metal containers.

There are two basic methods for shaping metal utensils. In *casting,* the molten metal (usually iron or aluminum) is poured into a mold. If there is to be a handle, the shank to which it will be attached is cast in one piece with the pot. After the metal cools and sets, the shaped utensil is removed from the mold. If there are surface irregularities they must be removed by grinding. Then the whole utensil is polished. An additional finish (cladding or enameling, perhaps; see below) may be put on at this point. The mold can be reused.

Cast-metal utensils are often somewhat porous and the metal may contain impurities arising in the casting; there is also a tendency for the surface to pit. Elimination of such problems is a major reason for covering a cast utensil with a different finish or, at the very least, for sealing its surface somewhat by giving it a high polish. Unprotected by any applied finish, cast iron must be seasoned before use. You can easily do this yourself (see "The Care and Cleaning of Cooking Vessels" below).

The manufacture of *drawn* utensils is more complicated, and involves a series of from two to ten or more stamping (shaping) operations, during which the metal is stretched and formed. In stamping, the rough shape of the object is cut out of the metal sheet or blank by a huge machine that acts like a monster cooky cutter. A brittle metal cannot be stamped or drawn as, instead of bending and stretching, it would break. Such metals must first be heat-treated to improve their tensile strength and flexibility. Another problem that drawing overcomes is that, as they cool, cast metals tend to shrink back or return to their original shape. In drawn containers the position of the molecules is maintained, thereby holding the shape to prevent this shrinkage and eliminating flaws due to trapped air bubbles or to stress or tension in the metal.

If you have ever tried to smooth out a crumpled piece of aluminum foil that has been used to cover a jar tightly, you will have a small idea of what is involved in the drawing process. You may rub and smooth it repeatedly, but some of the creases and bulges remain where the foil was stretched out of shape.

In addition to being formed by casting and drawing, metal utensils may be shaped by *forging,* or hammering the metal when it is red-hot, as with iron, or simply by cold beating and hammering. This ancient technique is widely used even today in North Africa and the Indian subcontinent, where copper and brass are available and human labor is much less costly than technological improvements.

One way to join metal to metal is by welding. Two pieces of iron can be hammer-welded together: they are brought to bright-red heat, then cleaned and covered with a flux to keep them clean. Then they are

Heating bronze: A Frenchman's drawing of men of the Bronze Age at work (detail). From Cyclopedia of the Universal History: Being an Account of the Principal Events in the Career of the Human Race, from the Beginnings of Civilization to the Present Time, *Cincinnati, c. 1885.*

placed one on top of the other on an anvil and hammered together. Iron must first be heated to be joined in this way, but softer metals with lower melting points, such as lead, silver, gold, and platinum, can be cold-hammered. (Try it yourself with two pieces of solid-core solder.) Nowadays, welding is usually done by electricity. You can see electrical spot-welding on some utensil handles and other kitchen items. In this process the two pieces of metal are held together and electric current is passed through them, heating the metals instantaneously on one small spot and thereby joining them.

A similar process bonds or fuses sheets of two different metals together, with electricity and under pressure. This is the way some multi-layered pot bottoms are constructed (see "Sandwiches and Other Combinations" below).

All metals expand or contract, or become distorted to some degree, with changes in temperature. Aluminum is the least likely of metals to become distorted by heat. Many pot manufacturers allow for this probable expansion and contraction by building a concave area into the bottom of their pots; the idea is that, while heated, the bottom will become flat. But some pots with aluminum as one of two or more layers in their "sandwich" bottoms are completely flat (witness Cuisinarts and Paderno). Single-metal steel or aluminum pot bottoms that are flat are very likely to become permanently misshapen—the metal will find its own room for expansion by humping up in the center, and you will find that your cooking oil or other liquid stands in a ring around the sides of the pot, while the food sits high and dry in a hot spot in the center.

THE STUFF OF WHICH POTS AND PANS ARE MADE
Even in this best of all possible worlds, there is no such thing as the perfect metal for pots. Each possibility has its plusses and its minuses. To understand pots and choose them wisely according to our unique individual requirements, we must first understand the metals and other materials of which they are made.

IRON AND STEELS. Until this century, the most common metal for pots and pans in the Western Hemisphere was iron. This is one of the most plentiful elements on earth. Almost always iron is found in ores in which it is combined with other elements, never by itself. About 4000 years ago people learned how to refine iron from its ore, using very high heat to melt it out. Molten iron can be poured—cast into a mold—and this was how, for centuries, pots were usually made—and in many cases still are.

Cast iron is heavy; it absorbs heat slowly and evenly, retains it, and is a good conductor as well—excellent qualities all for a cooking vessel to possess. But there is a negative side too. Cast iron is rather brittle. It rusts, stains, and becomes pitted on exposure to air, dampness, and some foods, and it tends to become distorted when heat is applied. Iron is malleable and can also be formed in sheets by rolling. Drawn utensils made of *sheet iron* are thin and absorb heat unevenly. They are particularly likely to become warped if subjected to high heat or sudden extremes of temperature. Iron is talented stuff, but it comes with severe problems.

Steel is iron from which a number of problems have been removed by the addition of carbon and, usually, other elements. High-carbon steel (just iron and carbon) is harder and stronger than iron, but it is still brittle and subject to corrosion. For cooking utensils, stainless steel is the most important alloy.

Stainless steel, a wonderful metal, was discovered in 1913 in Sheffield, the English town whose steelworking tradition dates back to the Middle Ages. A metallurgist named Harry Brearley was experimenting with various steels for use in gun barrels. He had discarded a number of unsuitable ones, and after some months he noticed that one of the pieces in the discard pile was still bright and shiny. It turned out to be a steel in which he had put 14 per cent chromium. Brearley patented the combination, and also several others containing additional elements such as nickel. A modern example of turning swords into plowshares!

Stainless steel is "stainless" because a very thin, usually invisible oxide forms on the surface. This film protects the metal underneath, since it does not combine with any other element or compound. Stainless steel does not interact with any food acids or alkalies, and is therefore completely nontoxic. Because of its high chromium content, stainless not only keeps bright and shiny, but also has great tensile strength and is not easily dented. Sounds perfect, doesn't it? But wait! This otherwise ideal alloy is a very poor conductor of heat. (What to do? Not to worry! See below, "Sandwiches and Other Combinations.")

COPPER AND BRASSES. Copper, like iron, was one of the first metals known to man, and was probably the first to be smelted, or removed from its ore by heat. But despite its long history, it remained a somewhat expensive metal until American mines began producing in quantity in the mid-nineteenth century. Until then, the major source of copper in this country was junked metal; recycling of all materials was a way of life for our forefathers, and we would do well to study their habits of thrift.

Copper is an extremely good conductor, of electricity as well as heat. It is softer than iron, and can be beaten and hammered to shape. But it is quite hard enough, and can be formed by casting or drawing as well. However, it distorts significantly when heated. And the big problem with copper is that it interacts with everything it touches. It reacts with the moisture in the air, resulting in a greenish surface film —verdigris—that protects the metal underneath but is devastating in a pot because it is ultimately poisonous. Copper is also corroded by salt water, and therefore by salted foods, in contact with which it forms a chloride. As a result of these chemical reactions, food cooked in copper vessels, even when there is no noticeable corrosion, may take on a metallic taste. All copper vessels must be kept scrupulously clean, and require constant polishing if they are to be completely safe to use.

Despite its shortcomings, and due primarily to its exceptional ability to conduct heat (and not a little to its warm, glowing appearance), cop-

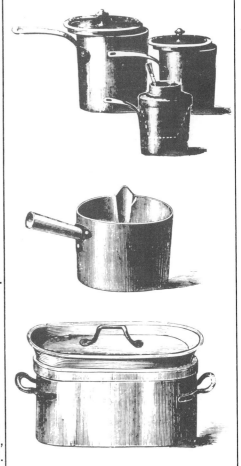

Copper pots, illustrated in L'Ecole des Cuisinières *by Urbain-Dubois.*

per is the preferred metal for pots used by chefs. No other metal will surround the food with heat so effectively, and none other will as responsively lose heat when the fire is doused. You, too, would enjoy cooking with a kitchenful of gleaming copper stockpots, saucepans, and skillets. But there is that tendency to corrode; therefore, your pots should have a lining of tin or silver or stainless steel to protect you and your loved ones from slow poisoning and to guard your food from taste changes. In the copper pots we show you, all surfaces that come in contact with food are lined.

The negative aspects of copper are mitigated to some extent in its alloys. It has a natural ability to combine with other metals, and there are literally hundreds of copper alloys. Best known, and most used in cookery in the past, are the brasses, in which 55 to 90 per cent copper is combined with 10 to 45 per cent zinc, along with smaller amounts of various other elements. The properties and uses of the different brasses vary according to the proportions of each combination. Brass can be shaped by being beaten or hammered, rolled into thin sheets, machined, and cast. Aluminum brass, with 3 per cent or less of aluminum, has the greatest resistance to corrosion. Also resistant are the tin brasses, in which tin substitutes for part of the zinc, sometimes along with other elements. The so-called nickel silvers are silvery-white brasses in which nickel is substituted for part of the zinc. However, brass is more brittle and more expensive than copper, and while you may occasionally come across a brass pot, for the most part it has gone out of use.

THE COATING METALS. Tin is very soft; it is not strong enough to be used by itself for pots. But tin is completely unaffected by moisture, completely nontoxic, and it does not corrode or rust or pit. It is very malleable and can be rolled, pressed, or hammered into extremely thin sheets or foil. Tin is therefore used as a coating to protect other metals—in the culinary department, especially for pots of copper and the steel for tin cans. A tin coating results from dipping a sheet of the base metal into molten tin, a layer of which remains on the sheet surface. A similar coating can be applied by an electrolytic method, which requires less tin. Tin can also be sprayed onto the base; the iron or steel thus coated is tin plate, used in tin cans. A layer of tin only about 1/10,000 of an inch thick is necessary to prevent corrosion of the underlying metal. Because tin is pliable, it can be applied to sheet metal before a utensil is formed by stamping and drawing.

Tin becomes darkened by food acids; but this surface tarnish is a protective coating and should not be removed. Tarnished or darkened tin absorbs heat effectively, and the darkening is therefore advantageous; never scour a tin-plated utensil merely for the sake of making it bright. Besides, because tin is so soft, scraping and scouring tend to scratch the surface and may expose the steel or iron underneath, encouraging rust.

Tin melts at a relatively low temperature, and an empty tinned vessel should never be left over heat, lest the lining bubble up and separate from the core. There are a number of very attractive French pots

Nineteenth-century French copper charlotte molds, tin lined. French tin milk pan, shaped to prevent boiling over.

of carbon steel completely dipped in tin, inside and out. However, the exterior surface that must be exposed to heat in these pots is just too fragile to be practical. Such a pot will, however, do for a fish poacher, in which you cook at low to moderate heat with a substantial quantity of liquid.

We caution you to cook in real pots only, and never to mistake a tinned mold for a vessel to use over direct heat. If you were to do so, the tin solder would melt and the mold would come apart. If a recipe directs you to caramelize sugar in a mold, don't—unless you know your mold is heatproof, in which case it certainly is not tin-lined.

Like tin, *silver* is soft, nontoxic and noncorroding. It does not interact with or contaminate food. It is applied by electroplating over other metals, usually copper. It forms a tarnish which is easily removed by polishing. Because it is one of the more expensive metals, however, it is very seldom used for cooking utensils, even though it perfectly well could be. We show some that are silver-lined, but these are more for presentation purposes than for heavy cookery.

ALUMINUM. This element, which has revolutionized the manufacture of cooking utensils and made possible such miracles as airplanes of enormous size, was not isolated until the nineteenth century, although compounds had been known and used much earlier. It is the most abundant metal in the earth's crust, but it is never found free in nature—only in combination in various ores, of which bauxite is the best known and most important. Bauxite is very stable, and great ingenuity was required to free the aluminum in it in commercial quantities. Minute amounts were isolated in 1825. But chemical procedures produced very little metal, and at midcentury aluminum was so rare that honored guests at the court of Napoleon III dined with aluminum flatware, while ordinary guests used ordinary gold and silver. More than sixty years passed before a young American, Charles Martin Hall, decided to try an electrical process, since chemical methods had failed. The big problem was to remove pure aluminum from its oxide, which had the extremely high melting point of 3632 F. After much trial and error, working in a woodshed behind his family home in Oberlin, Ohio, with equipment that, for the most part, he himself had devised, he was at last successful. Using the current from homemade batteries and carbon-lined containers, and employing cryolite (sodium aluminum fluoride) as a flux, or a substance to aid flowing or melting, he was able to reduce the melting temperature to a manageable 1832 F.

Aluminum is very light in weight, fairly strong and tough. It is an excellent conductor of heat. It is one of the metals least likely to distort from a rise in temperature. It is chemically active, but it forms a self-protective coating of oxide that prevents deeper corrosion. Aluminum becomes even harder and stronger when it is alloyed with such substances as magnesium, manganese, nickel, chromium, zinc, iron, copper, and silicon. Those pots trade-named Magnalite are of an alloy containing about 5 per cent magnesium. As with copper, there are hundreds of alloy combinations. Your aluminum pot is very likely to be composed of one of them rather than being made of the pure element.

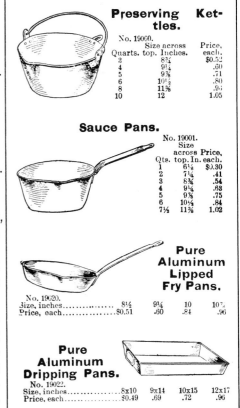

PURE ALUMINUM WARE.
Beautiful as Silver—Pure as Gold.

Preserving Kettles.

No. 19060.

Quarts.	Size across top. Inches.	Price, each.
3	8¾	$0.52
4	9¼	.60
5	9⅞	.71
6	10½	.80
8	11⅜	.96
10	12	1.05

Sauce Pans.

No. 19001.

Qts.	Size across top. In.	Price, each.
1	6⅛	$0.30
2	7¼	.41
3	8¾	.54
4	9¼	.63
5	9⅞	.75
6	10½	.84
7½	11⅜	1.02

Pure Aluminum Lipped Fry Pans.

No. 19020.

Size, inches	8½	9¼	10	10⅞
Price, each	$0.51	.60	.84	.96

Pure Aluminum Dripping Pans.

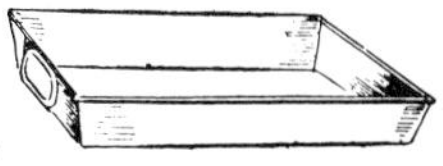

No. 19022.

Size, inches	8x10	9x14	10x15	12x17
Price, each	$0.49	.69	.72	.96

From the 1897 Sears Roebuck Catalogue; *New York: Chelsea House Publishers, 1968.*

Since aluminum is tough, lightweight, and an excellent conductor, why then are not all pots made of it? The reason is twofold: First, copper is a still better conductor, and second, aluminum causes some foods to discolor. If spinach or a wine sauce were to be cooked for more than a short time in an aluminum pot, the interaction of the food, if the acid concentration were high enough, and the pot would turn the food a dark color and give it a nasty taste.

Pure aluminum itself becomes stained and darkened by the alkalies found in some foods and in hard, or alkaline, water.

Aluminum can be cleaned with an acid substance that counteracts the alkali (see "The Care and Cleaning of Cooking Vessels" below).

In manufacturing utensils, aluminum may be cast or stamped and drawn. Because of its conductive qualities, it is frequently allied with other metals for pot bottoms, as in Cuisinart and Farberware examples; see below, "Sandwiches and Other Combinations," for how it is done.

Since it is an excellent conductor of electricity, aluminum can be given a special *anodyzed* finish. After shaping, the utensil becomes the conductor in an electrically charged chemical bath and thus gets coated with an oxide, sometimes with color added. Utensils of anodyzed aluminum should not be placed directly over high heat or put in the dishwasher; the finish is only superficial, and much too fragile for practicality.

We have paid particular attention to finish in the pots we recommend. Especially in aluminum cookware, it makes all the difference. If you are deciding between cast aluminum and drawn aluminum, you should know that they will cook equally well. Drawn-aluminum pots are probably less expensive. But the finish may be the deciding factor. A cast-aluminum pot, if it has a shiny, polished finish, is to be preferred. The polish gives added strength, protects the surface, and improves the looks.

SANDWICHES AND OTHER COMBINATIONS

With this array of metals from which manufacturers can choose, it is no wonder that you have such a wide selection of pots. By combining metals in various ways the negative properties of some of them can be overcome and the positive qualities enhanced. It was early discovered, for example, that when copper or brass was coated with tin, its excellent heat conduction was maintained and oxidation problems eliminated. Of course, the soft tin would eventually be worn through, exposing the base metal—but it was a simple enough matter to have the pot retinned. Today, too, it is often well worth the expense of tinning a worn old copper pot—and you just might come across one at a garage sale or flea market. In fact, the popularity of these antique and near-antique items is growing and there is more than one shop where you can buy "copper-by-the-pound." As long as it isn't too beat up, bumped and banged out of shape, or hopelessly scratched, it's probably worth considering.

Since copper has always been valued it was often repaired in earlier days. When buying old utensils, look carefully at every centimeter of the surface. Make sure that all joinings, whether of patches or attached

Pure Aluminum Bellied Sauce Pans.
No. 19002. Size, 6¾ inches by 4¾ inches
Price, each..**96c**

Pure Aluminum Milk or Rice Boilers.
No. 19003, Size of inside pot, 3 quarts. Price, each.....**$1.70**

Pure Aluminum Coffee Pots.
No. 19012.
Size, pints, 4 5 6 8
Price, each, $1.50 1.60 1.75 2.05

Pure Aluminum Tea Pots.
No. 19013.
Size, pints, 4 5 6
Price, each, $1.69 1.75 1.94
Special Notice. We will furnish an improved pattern of above aluminum tea and coffee pots which are tapering, and have a bead around the bottom adding much to their appearance and are very much handsomer than cut.

Pure Aluminum Tea Steepers.
No. 19016. Size, 4½x4 inches. Price, each..**40c.**

Pure Aluminum Tea Kettles.
No. 19017. Pit bottom.
No. 19018. Flat bottom.
Size, No. 8. Price, each..................**$2.80**

"Pure Aluminum Ware" was shown in the 1897 Sears Roebuck Catalogue; New York: Chelsea House Publishers, 1968.

elements such as handles, are still completely solid. With copper there is a direct correlation between weight and quality; a thin, light pot is the more likely to be banged up and bruised and also less reliable as a sturdy saucemaker. Be sure, also, that the tinning is intact on the old pot you are considering, and be prepared to go to the additional expense of retinning before you can make use of your find. Or you might want to look into the possibility of having an old copper pot lined with silver. We looked into it, and found that nowadays it is not significantly more expensive than tinning. A really unusual find might well deserve the more elegant treatment. For tinning specialists, look in the Yellow Pages, or consider the International Retinning & Repairing Company, Inc., located at 525-531 West 26th Street, New York, N.Y. 10001; they say people mail them pans from as far away as Alaska for retinning. Their fee is based on a formula which involves the diameter of the pan, the depth, and some multiplication.

The qualities of stainless steel as an inert surface in contact with food were too good to be ignored—and its good appearance was also a plus factor. But its lack of conductivity had to be compensated for. The solution was to make a "sandwich" bottom, with cast iron or aluminum for the filling. You see a shiny stainless pot, your food comes in contact with harmless stainless—but the more conductive metal core, out of sight (or sometimes in a plate on the base) delivers heat efficiently. Technically known as *cladding,* the process involves the joining by electrolysis of one layer of metal to another under pressure, creating a strong permanent bond. For example, the stainless-steel Farberware pots have been given better heat conductivity by electroplating their bottoms with thick aluminum: they are thus described as aluminum-clad stainless. Cuisinart pots have bottoms with an actual sandwich in which the filling is an aluminum core. The two outer layers of stainless steel not only look handsome but give the pot additional stability, while the aluminum core prevents distortion from rapid heat changes and transmits heat superbly.

We recommend only pots of this construction that have substantial layers of metal in the sandwich. Beware of those with thin cladding—some of them have such a thin layer of the more conductive metal that it hardly makes a difference, except in the appearance. We admit, though, that there are drawbacks even to the thick sandwich bottom. For one thing, these pots are bottom-heavy (thin-clad pots are not, and that is one way to judge them—simply lift them). Then, because the conductive metal is only on the bottom or, at most, extends a bit up the side, heat does not diffuse well into the pot walls. Also, because of the thickness of the bottom, heat is not lost rapidly enough by these pans for use in situations where great sensitivity is required. And lastly, the heat transfer is not, despite the addition of a conductive layer, perfect. (If you look back to our discussion of handles above, you'll understand why; with every addition of a different material there is some heat loss.) So we must say that, while we heartily recommend them, clad-bottom pots are not the best, the ideal solution for all cooking purposes. The fact is, there is no ideal pot.

Stovetop cooking utensils as illustrated in L'Ecole de Cuisinières, Modern Domestic Cookery, *and* The Practical Housekeeper.

But still another possibility is to coat a highly conductive metal core with a nonmetallic surface that does not interact with food and protects the metal underneath. A porcelain enamel coating over a cast-iron base provides us with some of our most handsome and useful cooking vessels (by Copco, Lauffer, and Le Creuset, among others). These pots are resistant to acids, won't rust (unless chipped), and are easy to clean. There are minor problems: sometimes the porcelain, which is actually a form of glass, chips or cracks under extremes of temperature or rapid temperature change, or if it receives rough handling. It may develop hot spots unless the pan contains sufficient liquid, and food might therefore tend to stick and perhaps scorch. And this finish does interfere with heat conduction (the addition-of-a-different-substance problem again), and it makes sautéing all but impossible. If you try to brown chicken parts for paella in a large porcelain-coated skillet, the bird will be cooked through before it develops a healthy tan. Also on the minus side, some enamels can be scratched or otherwise marked up by metal pot forks and spoons. But if you exercise minimal care and recognize the minor limitations of this material, you will find these among the most useful utensils in your kitchen, and all of them are beautiful enough to be brought to the table for serving.

The technique by which the glaze is fused to the metal core dates back to the third or the second century B.C. At first, though, enameling was used only for such decorative purposes as the crafting of jewelry or elaborate priestly and royal decorations. To make a pot, the metal base, often of iron, is formed into the desired shape and the handles and spouts are welded on. The first coat of enamel, usually a dark-blue glaze of cobalt and nickel oxides, is applied as a liquid by dipping or spraying. At temperatures of 1400 F. to 1800 F. in an enameling furnace, the glaze melts and fuses into the pores of the cast-metal base. Additional layers, colored and made opaque by metallic oxides, are applied and the furnace treatment is repeated. The quality of enamelware depends on the ingredients of the glaze and the number of coats applied. Note that porcelain enamel should not be confused with synthetic or baked enamel, which is fused onto metal at low heat and is used for appliance exteriors.

Release (nonstick) surfaces, most of them of nylon plastic, are another nonmetallic finish found on modern cookware. We do not find them particularly satisfactory, for several reasons. As with the porcelain enamels, they don't do a good job of sautéing. The surface is quite fragile, and even the more resistant compositions tend to get scratched up. Furthermore, with age they lose their release capacity. Although they are recommended for special-diet cookery where no fat should be added, in reality they do not work well unless a coating, albeit a light one, of oil is present.

THE CARE AND CLEANING OF COOKING VESSELS

In our day and age cleaning problems are usually solved by resort to commercial cleansers. It is important to use one which will interact chemically only with the surface of a pot, and not deeply or permanently alter the metal. Choose the right cleanser for the job.

Enameled ware, illustrated in American Kitchen Collectibles *by Mary Lou Matthews, 1973.*

Nonchemical cleaning can be accomplished by the abrasive qualities of the cleaning instrument or agent. In general, however, it is best to avoid strong abrasives of any kind. Wherever possible, cleaning by gentle polishing is to be preferred. Even crusted-on food is best attacked gently. You can dig in with Brillo pads, but it's far better to let the crust soften by soaking overnight in baking soda and water. You will save time and energy and preserve your pot surfaces as well.

Here, metal by metal, is a brief rundown of procedures and materials:

With *iron,* the big upkeep problem is rusting and staining. The best measures are preventive. New iron pots should be seasoned before use. Wipe the entire interior with a paper towel dipped in edible vegetable oil, making sure that the surface is filmed. Then pour a little oil into the pot and set it over moderate heat for at least 15 minutes. Don't use furniture oils, which may be toxic, or olive oil, which will leave its essence in the porous metal surface. Cool the pan and wipe it clean with paper towels. Once you have seasoned a pot or pan, if you can avoid washing it, do so. In the olden days there would have been a supply of sand at hand to use to scour. Now, use coarse dry salt instead as an abrasive; scour the pot or pan gently and wipe it out with a paper towel. If wash you must, do so immediately after use in hot soapy water, and dry immediately and thoroughly so that not a jot of dampness remains to encourage rust: turning the pot upside down over a low-burning stove flame will dry it very satisfactorily.

If you and your pots live in a humid seaside climate, you must take special preventive measures. It *is* true that the old chowder pot was iron, but it was used daily and did not stand idly around waiting to be attacked by damp salt air. Unless your iron pots are similarly well occupied and out of mischief, they should be completely filmed with a protective layer of grease and further covered with plastic wrap. Otherwise they will become hopelessly pitted in no time.

Once rust gets a foothold on iron, however, that is a whole other kettle of fish. Good rust removers are available, and you are more likely to find them at the hardware store or marine suppliers than in your local supermarket. For surface rust, a maritime product such as Naval Jelly can't be topped; but leave it on only as long as necessary and not a minute longer, be sure to rinse it off very well indeed, and do not let it get on any enameled or polished surfaces (read the label!). If you have a cast-iron pot that is really pitted, nothing will help; it is too far gone for cooking. (You can paint it with rust-preventive outdoor enamel and use it as a planter.)

Cleaning *stainless steel* pots can be a tricky business. There is no way for you to be sure of the actual proportion of metals in a given stainless utensil. Therefore, always follow the manufacturer's advice; only he knows what went into his pots, and surely he wants you to keep them in good condition. There are various commercial cleaning products that are quite good; use them as recommended by the manufacturer. Occasionally, some stainless steels develop a blue-gray or brownish tinge from surface oxidation if they have been overheated—at temperatures of 450 F. or higher, stainless steel will inevitably discolor, and if it is

subjected to extreme or repeated overheating, the discoloration may go completely through the metal. Stainless steel should never be used in those ceramic broilers that heat up to as high a temperature as 800 F.; the stability of the metal can be crucially affected by such high heat. Surface discoloration can sometimes be removed with special stainless-steel cleaner, or try any mild detergent mixed with vinegar. And unless you don't care a feather or a fig, never use steel wool on the mirror-finished or satin-finished exterior of a gleaming stainless pot.

For *copper* you can use a chemically formulated copper polish. However, these are usually strong enough to completely strip the metal of its patina and change its color. Some people like even old copper to look newly minted, but we prefer the warm, mellow gleam that comes with age. It's better to use coarse (kosher) salt and either lemon juice or vinegar for cleaning copper; this gives the same chemical reaction as commercial cleanser, but in a weaker form. Whatever cleans copper will do the same for *brass*.

There is no way to clean *tin,* short of such severe scouring that you literally remove the metal. Tin will darken but this is not a problem, since the dark surface increases absorption of heat and therefore enhances the cooking quality of the tinned vessel. To repeat: *never* scour tin. Mild detergent and warm water should do the trick. If necessary, soak it overnight.

For *silvered* presentation pans, snail dishes, and the like, simply use silver polish just as you do on your flatware, then rinse and wipe dry.

Aluminum becomes darkened by the alkalies found in some foods and by hard water. It should not be washed with strong alkaline soaps. Use special aluminum cleaner or, better still, cook an acid food such as rhubarb or tomatoes in it, or boil lemon or vinegar water. Another good cleaner is a solution of cream of tartar (tartaric acid) and water, boiled in the pan. Use coarse salt if an abrasive is needed, and rinse immediately and thoroughly. Pitting may occur when salty water or moist foods, especially if salty, are allowed to stand in an aluminum pot.

Porcelain enamel finishes should be washed in warm water with a mild soap or detergent. Use baking soda for scouring; harsh powders will destroy the glaze. Soften cooked-on gook by overnight soaking in warm water to which a little baking soda or mild detergent has been added. Use ordinary household bleach if necessary to remove stains; be sure to rinse very thoroughly after using bleach.

Finally, a few don'ts: Never use commercial steel-wool pads on anything. Use only the products we recommend (see Chapter 1), such as those pads made of curly ribbons of bronze. Copper scratches easily, as does mirror-finished stainless steel, so don't use anything that might mark these metals.

Never let an empty pot stand over high heat. And naturally you will try not to burn anything—but who hasn't been called to the phone and forgotten that the fire was on under the rice or the lentil soup? When such disasters occur, empty and cool the pot, and try soaking it with a detergent or soap solution. Then, proceeding from gentle to more drastic measures if necessary, loosen the burned material with a straight-

Complete Kitchen Furniture Assortment.

From the 1897 Sears Roebuck Catalogue; New York: Chelsea House Publishers, 1968.

edged wooden spatula or, if your pot can take such treatment, scrub off the scorch with the bronze scrubber we've mentioned. Persistence pays off, so soak and scrub repeatedly until you succeed in exorcising the burned deposit.

CHARACTERISTICS AND CARE OF POT MATERIALS

POT MATERIAL	EFFICIENCY OF HEAT TRANSFER	METHODS OF FORMING	SURFACE CHANGES AND FOOD INTERACTION	CLEANING METHODS
Iron	Absorbs heat evenly; excellent conductor.	Cast, forged, or stamped or drawn.	Rusts, stains, and pits.	Cast iron must be seasoned before use. Wipe with coarse salt after use or wash and dry thoroughly. Use commercial rust remover if necessary.
Stainless steel	Poor conductor	Drawn	No food interaction. Sometimes turns bluish or brownish from overheating.	Use special commercial preparations.
Copper	Excellent conductor	Cast, forged, or stamped or drawn.	Corrodes easily; forms poisonous surface coating. Interacts with salted foods.	Use salt and vinegar or lemon juice, or use commercial polish.
Brass	Good conductor	Cast, forged, or stamped or drawn.	Less easily corroded than copper, but tends to discolor.	Use salt and vinegar or lemon juice; or use commercial polish.
Tin	Used as lining only; too soft to be used alone.	Applied by dipping base metal or by electroplating.	No food interaction. Completely nontoxic, but tends to darken with age.	Gentle detergent; do not scour.
Silver	Good conductor, but usually used as lining.	Usually applied by electroplating.	No food interaction. Completely nontoxic; tends to darken with age and in air.	Remove tarnish with commercial silver polish; handle gently to avoid scratching.
Aluminum	Excellent conductor	Cast, or stamped or drawn.	Interacts with acid foods to darken them and change taste; discolors from alkalies.	Lemon or vinegar, or use commercial cleanser.
Porcelain enamel (nonmetal, glass-based finish).	Poor conductor; used as applied finish only.	Fused or kiln-fired onto cast-metal core.	No food interaction, but can chip or crack with temperature changes and can be scratched.	Baking soda or mild detergent solution; use household bleach to remove stains, and rinse well.

Over-the-fire cookery takes a novel turn in this engraving by Israel von Meckenern (1450-1503) (N.Y. Public Library Picture Collection).

Stovetop Cooking Utensils

The first time we had a kitchen of our own to fit out, we headed right for the local hardware store and bought a bunch of pots—a small one for boiling eggs and a large one for heating up cans of soup, a couple of frying pans, and one big soup pot for boiling spaghetti. And only then did we go off to the gadget rack and get ourselves a wooden spoon and a can opener. Our tastes and our skills may have become more sophisticated since then, but the first thing we think of when we hear of a batterie de cuisine is still a set of pots: the basic implements of top-of-the-stove cooking.

We need hardly mention that that first set is by now greatly reduced in size. One saucepan, battered out of shape, is being used as a makeshift bain-marie for warming up jars of baby food, while one frying pan, scorched, serves only to heat up leftovers for the (admittedly coddled) dog. One pretty and shiny pot melted when it was left, empty, over a flame, and one charming little sauté pan, lined with some kind of nonstick coating, was scraped down to the metal, releasing when in use green material that we suspected of being poisonous in action as well as in appearance. In short, our first brave little collection, bought because it was cheap and attractive, has long since been replaced by a somewhat more expensive—and far more sensible—group of pots, chosen with our own cooking habits in mind.

THE POT IS BORN

These pots we use today are the descendants of those that originated when some early man, sitting by a fire, laid strips of meat on a hot rock or perhaps on the searing-hot blade of a simple iron tool. An enormous step forward was made when he learned to add sides to his griddle, either by shaping the metal, by selecting a rock with a hollow core, or by forming a simple bowl of clay. At last burning had become cooking, and composed dishes of the simplest sort replaced what had been, until then, a perpetual barbecue. As the sides of the pots grew higher the cook could create soups and stews, and eventually the artisans made pots just for specific dishes until we wound up with the whole range of stovetop cooking utensils we show you here.

WINNING METALS

These utensils go all the way from the griddle, perfectly flat, to the tall-sided stockpot; they include utensils like the soapstone griddle, on which the food is cooked bare; those utensils for cooking with fat, like the frying pan and the sauté pan; and the wide range of pans for cooking with water, like the soup pot, the saucepan, the steamer, and the double boiler. All are utensils which sit right on top of the flame or electric heat, with bottoms through which the heat must be transmitted both to the sides and to the food. That means that these pots are almost all made of metal. Look at our discussion of the properties of different materials (Chapter 6) and you will understand why we offer you frying pans of low-grade steel, but stockpots of aluminum and saucepans of copper; and why we think that you can't do better than to have a double boiler made completely of glass.

DO YOU LIKE SETS?

Every few months, in those advertising handouts which arrive with regularity from every department store at which we have been weak enough to open a charge account, we see advertised sets of excellent cookware at considerable savings in price. And every few months we nearly succumb, until we reflect that the very material and design which might make for the perfect casserole in a set are precisely the wrong material and design for the frying pan in the same set. And, further, the sizes of pots offered are all wrong for real families. A very eminent authority hinted to us that these problems are intentional—that some stores put together sets with peculiar sizes of pots just so that you will be forced to come back later and buy what you really need—that these are "starter sets" in a very real sense. You are, in short, better off choosing each pan individually, buying each one in the material most suited to its function and in the size most suited to your kitchen.

Nonetheless, we are snobs enough to admit that we would not sneer if someone offered us a set of tin-lined copper pots, and we also realize that many people admire the look of a row of beautiful matching pots and pans. There must, after all, be a reason for the fact that the starter set is an ever-popular gift for someone who is setting up a household. We will give you, therefore, a list of manufacturers from whose products you may select a set of matching pots to fit your own needs.

What will you choose? We asked four authorities, and we were prepared to get widely varying answers. Instead, our experts more or less agreed on the rock-bottom basics for cooking; disagreement among them was mainly about quantity, about how many saucepans and so on you need. And all of our experts, we are proud to say, hastened to add that the pots of the brands we list below are the ones that they themselves would choose. You will, of course, have to decide for yourself on the sizes best suited to your own kitchen.

They suggested that most of us need two saucepans, holding perhaps 1 and 2½ quarts; a large and a small frying pan or sauté pan—an 8" size for scrambled eggs and the like and a 12" pan for other frying. Then a 5-quart metal or enameled casserole would complete the basic set. It can also serve as a minimal stockpot for those who don't anticipate extensive soup and sauce making. But remember that the sizes are up to you: if twelve of

FORM AND FUNCTION

Think about shape and its relationship to function: the way, for example, in which a low, wide pan encourages evaporation, as in the reduction of the sauce of a classical sauté, while a stockpot reduces evaporation while blending the flavors of many ingredients into a broth. Think of why a frypan—used for quick, searing cooking with dry heat—is most efficient when it has scarcely any sides at all. Since pots use heat most efficiently when they fit directly over a burner, then why are restaurant presentation pans nearly always oval? The answer, of course, is that these are not *cooking* pans: they serve to warm food just before it is served, and they appear at tableside—so appearance is more important than shape or material in these pans.

Consider the virtues of different styles of handles: most rangetop pans are, after all, pots which you will be manipulating all of the time, putting them on and off the flame, tilting them, tossing the food in them—and the handles had better be friendly to your palm. Wood and plastic feel lovely in the hand and remain comfortably cool to the touch, but either can be damaged if the pot should be left askew over the flame or if it is put, for a moment, under the broiler. And metal handles, which are not harmed by fire, can feel like a handful of nuts and bolts in your hand, and scalding-hot nuts and bolts at that.

THE COVER STORY

Finally, look at the lids farther along: lids, which turn pots into ovens. We once had a professor of architecture who advised us to walk along the streets of the city looking *up,* toward the rooftops. And pow! It was a revelation, an entirely new world-view that we suddenly perceived. The same thing happened when we first began to look closely at different types of lids. These—simple discs of metal, in their basic form—serve not only to keep the bubbling contents of a pan from splashing all over the cook; they also control both the speed of evaporation of the contents and the level of heat within the pot. Among pot covers there is a remarkable degree of variation in the type of seal, in the fit, and in the way in which design has been adapted to function. Consider the edges of an earthenware casserole, left unglazed so that the lid will not slide around on it; consider the absolute seal of the Cuisinart saucepan lids (6.95); and look at the minute bumps designed to catch evaporating steam on the underside of a lid like 6.98.

SUITING THE POT TO THE COOK

Once you have thought of metals, of shape, of handles, and of lids, then think most seriously about your own needs. What kind of cooking do you do? Are you the sort of person who is chagrined if forced to use canned chicken broth, and always, therefore, has hundreds of cubes of frozen homemade stock in the freezer? (One of our editors taught us to freeze stock in refrigerator trays and store the cubes in plastic bags.) If you recognize yourself here, then you should have a stockpot of really high quality. If, on the other hand, you use a large pot once a year when you invite the gang from the office over for spaghetti, then don't put

you sit down to supper every night, a 1-quart saucepan would do nothing for you.

Here are our choices of the best manufacturers' brands of matching pots and pans from this and other chapters—particularly matching casseroles:

COMMERCIAL ALUMINUM. *A professional-quality brand of heavy-gauge aluminum with handles made of tinned iron in order to retard the passage of heat. See 6.10, 6.34, 6.44, 6.45, 6.71, 6.79, 6.92, 6.93, 8.47.*

COMMERCIAL ALUMINUM WITH CALPHALON. *The same excellent professional cookware with tinned iron handles as the Commercial Aluminum brand above, this has, in addition, the advantage of a really exceptional release (nonstick) finish which is integral with the metal. See 6.11, 6.33, 6.46.*

COPCO. *Danish cookware of brilliantly colored enamel over cast iron, made in striking modern shapes. Many of the pots have turned teakwood handles and flat-ground bottoms; all have interiors of white or black. See 6.4, 6.9, 6.25, 6.56, 6.85, 7.14, 8.15.*

CUISINART. *Stainless-steel pots with a triple-layered bottom of steel, aluminum, and steel again which prevents warping and encourages heat conductivity. A wide range of design; pressed-wood handles. See 6.13, 6.30, 6.31, 6.54, 6.73, 6.95, 6.96, 7.2, 8.13, 8.14.*

Continued from preceding page

DANSK CAST ALUMINUM. *Really beautiful modern design in handsome, lightweight, molded aluminum. See 6.14, 6.48.*

FARBERWARE. *A good weight of stainless steel with heavy aluminum bottoms; the workhorse of American cookware. See 6.22, 6.63, 6.64, 6.72, 6.101, 6.102, 7.9, 8.42.*

LAMALLE. *This is the name of a firm of distributors of French tin-lined heavy copper cookware. The pots are expensive, but they are in classic designs and of the highest quality. See 6.19, 6.36, 6.86, 6.87, 6.88, 7.10, 7.21, 8.9.*

LAUFFER. *An English line of black-enameled cast-iron ware made in modern designs. These pans have speckled gray interiors and a raised ring on the bottom prevents the enamel from burning off on an electric element. See 7.8, 7.18.*

LEGION. *Separately made stainless-steel and copper pots are bonded permanently together to form Legion's incredibly heavy professional Bi-Metal cookware. Available in very large sizes. See 6.29, 6.40, 6.50, 6.77, 6.94, 7.7.*

LE CREUSET. *Enamel over cast iron in traditional designs, warm colors. The interiors are white or lightly tinted. See 6.24, 6.55, 7.20, 7.42.*

LEYSE. *An American brand of professional-quality aluminum cookware, available in many of the shapes used in the French cuisine. See 6.80, 7.1.*

MAGNALITE. *Universally available; these pots are cast from an alloy of aluminum and magnesium which is thick, lightweight, relatively stainproof, and moderately priced. See 6.23, 6.47, 7.17, 8.35, 8.36, 8.46.*

PADERNO. *High-quality heavy Italian stainless-steel pots with a thick layer of aluminum on the bottom. Hard to find, but excellent. See 6.12, 6.32, 6.51, 6.76, 6.100, 7.4, 7.13, 7.24, 8.43.*

PORCELAINE DE PARIS. *Fine porcelain in beautiful patterns; available, as you would expect, in oven dishes, but also in saucepans and frying pans. See 6.58, 6.97, 7.47, 7.52, 7.67, 7.68, 8.19, 10.16, 11.71.*

PYREX WARE. *Heat-resistant clear glass made by Corning for top-of-the-stove or oven use See 6.66, 7.64, 9.13, 9.34, 10.5.*

WEAREVER. *Aluminum cookware, available both in a heavy professional weight and in a lighter gauge for home use. See 6.82, 6.91, 8.39, 8.40, 8.41.*

your money here—an inexpensive, lightweight pot will cook your occasional pasta to perfection. Perhaps you do most of your cooking for one or two people. Then by all means buy small frypans and saucepans which are just right for half-broilers, the two pork chops, the half-cup of rice that you will cook in them. Do you give lots of parties? Do you like to serve from your cooking pots? Do you cook with long-simmered sauces? Think of such questions before you decide: as always, our recommendation is to spend the most money on the pots that you will be using the most. And if for any reason you must buy a really inadequate pot for a given purpose, then do it, but consider the pot disposable, to be replaced when you can find the right replacement and can afford to buy it.

ABOUT ELECTRIC POTS

One further word—a postscript—about electric pots, skillets, and so on. We use them, but we use them sparingly. The kinds that use high heat drain too much electricity for our energy-sensitive consciences, and all such appliances take up counter space which might be better employed for kneading bread or chopping onions; and they are nearly always more difficult to clean than a simple top-of-the-stove utensil. Notice, please, that we have no section in this book for small appliances—instead, when an appliance proves itself to be better than the combination of utensil-plus-fire (the toaster versus the toasting fork is the clearest example), then we put it into the chapter which deals with its type of cooking. Thus, in this chapter you will find an electric griddle, a waffle iron, and a grill; in another section you will find, near the casseroles, a slow cooker (7.49), which is thrifty in its use of current; and elsewhere, near the roasting pans, there will be several electric ovens. It's a safe rule of thumb that, given the choice, you are almost always better off using a really good pot and your stove rather than an electrical appliance designed for a special and often limited use.

In the Beginning: Griddles

Living in an intimate relationship with the fire surface, a griddle—one of the earliest cooking utensils—transfers heat immediately from the flames to the food. There is no amenity of liquid and, often, no sizzling fat to serve as intermediary: here the key word is *fast*. A griddle can be a flat rock seasoned with salt and laid on the hot coals of a campfire, or the top of a cast-iron stove made portable—an iron frying pan without its sides. On a griddle we cook pancakes, or scones, or crumpets in encircling rings; we grill thin pieces of bacon or meat or fish; we fry eggs. The cooking method is as simple as the utensil; and the only demand made of the utensil is that it reach and maintain a high heat in order to "seize" and cook simple foods quickly. Your griddle may be built into the top of your stove, or it may be a portable one.

Soapstone Griddle 6.1

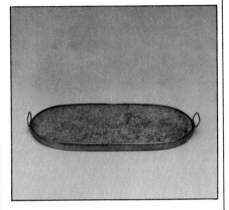

Soapstone with copper frame; 18¼″ × 9¼″; ⅞″ thick. Also avail. 16″ × 8″ or 24″ × 12″ in oval shape, and in diam. of 10″, 12″, 14″, or 16″ in round shape.

$40.00 ▲

In some Japanese restaurants you can order Steak Cooked on a Hot Rock. No esoteric Oriental practice this, but rather a harkening back to one of the earliest ways to cook. Stone, when heated, provides a searing heat for fast cooking, and in early New England every kitchen had a soapstone griddle. Laid on a wood- or coal-burning range, the soapstone absorbed the heat quickly, and then, because it is nature's own nonstick material, it readily gave up the flapjacks or eggs or ham slices when they were done. This contemporary version was made in Vermont from locally mined stone, cut out in a generous oval or circle, and then bound in copper to prevent chipping of the edge and for the glory of it all. Copper loops at either end will help you to lift it on and off your stovetop, but be careful where you set it down after use, because this griddle really retains heat: it would be wise to let it cool off on the range. And it is heavy, especially in the largest size, which is two feet long. Before using it you must season the soapstone by scouring with a thin layer of salt and a cloth until the surface is as smooth as glass; after that, you need never grease it. This griddle is particularly good for those lucky few who have wood-burning stoves.

"Gargote *(low-class eating house)* is used *to describe a place where the food is terrible. The word* gargoter *means to boil noisily.*

"*The Zuñi Indians cook maize cakes, which form their staple diet, on stone slabs which have been heated gradually while oil and resin are rubbed into them. During this essential operation, 'no word must be spoken above a whisper, the stone would crack.'*"

Claude Levi-Strauss, The Raw and the Cooked, *Harper & Row, New York*

Farberware Griddle 6.2

Heavy cast aluminum with plastic trim; 21¼″ × 12″ overall; 3″ high; cooking surface 18″ × 12″; sliding tray 13″ × 9″.

$35.00 ▲

We don't show many electrical pots and similar appliances because some of them use a great deal of energy and they create storage problems. Far better for you to get a large stove with extra burners to begin with, and then to put your money into good pots. But this electric griddle from Farber is awfully good, too good to be ignored simply because it works on an independent heat source. Do not confuse it with an electric frying pan, although some of the functions of the two may overlap: this has a nearly flush surface and is to be used with a minimum of fat. The surface is of well-ground heavy cast aluminum. The griddle can be heated to 425 F. and will then hold that temperature, or any intermediate temperature to which you set it. On its ample surface—8 by 12 inches—you can cook half a pound of bacon, or 8 hamburgers, or 6 pancakes easily. The shallow drawer below the cooking surface will keep the first batch of pancakes warm while you finish cooking the rest; or, if you are cooking bacon or hamburger, a drain in the griddle channels the surplus fat into this drawer, which of course is removable for cleaning. There are two large plastic handles which extend downward into legs for the appliance, and a plug-in temperature control. To clean the griddle in the manner of a professional chef, unplug it when you are finished cooking, pour water onto the hot surface immediately and, while it is bubbling away, scrape it with a metal pancake turner (6.113), or try Griddle Screen (Chapter 1). Imagine this appliance in the kitchen of a ski house, cooking breakfast for a mob before a day on the slopes; or imagine the bliss of making flapjacks for your family right at the table, rather than all alone in the kitchen, and you will see its virtues.

BASIC GRIDDLECAKES

2 cups sifted all-purpose flour
1 tablespoon sugar
4 teaspoons baking powder
1 teaspoon salt
2 eggs, lightly beaten
1½ cups milk
¼ cup melted butter or oil

Combine all the dry ingredients and sift into a mixing bowl. Combine the eggs, milk, and butter and stir into the dry ingredients until the large lumps disappear. It is wise to remember that as this batter stands, it thickens. If this should happen while you are baking the cakes, add a little more milk, stirring it in with a wooden spoon or spatula. To bake, pour the batter on a hot, lightly greased griddle. The cakes should be about 4 to 6 inches in diameter. They are ready to turn when bubbles form and break and the edges seem cooked. Turn, and brown lightly on the reverse side. These are best served with melted butter and hot syrup or honey.

(From AMERICAN COOKERY, by James A. Beard, illustrated by Earl Thollander. Copyright © 1972 by James A. Beard. Reprinted by permission of Little, Brown and Company.)

Cooking utensils found at Pompeii.

Stovetop Cooking Utensils

A STOVETOP GLOSSARY

BAIN-MARIE. *This is a device for keeping food warm by setting it, in its container, in a bath—in French, a bain—of simmering water. It is typically a large shallow pan to contain the hot water plus one or more cylindrical containers for food. It differs from a double boiler in that the hot water—the heat—surrounds the food rather than merely sitting under it.*

BRAZIER. *A short-handled metal pot with a good bottom, used both on top of the stove and in the oven; a braising pan.*

CASSEROLE. *In the United States, a short-handled or handleless covered pot for use in the oven or on the top of the stove. In France, oddly enough, casserole means a saucepan.*

CHICKEN FRYER. *A high-sided frypan with a domed lid, an American utensil used for browning and then slow-cooking foods: it is somewhat like a long-handled round brazier.*

DOUBLE BOILER. *A saucepan which fits closely into another saucepan. The lower section holds a shallow pool of boiling or simmering water whose steam serves to transmit a gentle heat to the food suspended over it in the upper section.*

ELECTRIC FRYPAN. *Just what it says: a frypan which gets its heat from built-in electrical elements rather than from contact with a stove burner or element.*

FAIT-TOUT. *Literally, "does-everything." A multipurpose pan, like 6.36 and like the casseroles given this name in Chapter 7. In both contexts, a term of endearment.*

FRYPAN OR FRYING PAN. *A shallow, flat-bottomed metal pan with a long handle that is used for cooking with fat over a flame. American frypans typically have sides which are not perpendicular to the bottom but which flare out from it. In French, such a pan is a poêle à frire.*

GRIDDLE. *A thick, flat pan of metal or stone, having the faculty of absorbing and retaining heat and commonly used for cooking flapjacks, bacon, scones, and other "griddle breads." In France, griddles are used for grilling large pieces of meat.*

GRILL. *In the United States, a wire rack which is fitted over a shallow pan for oven broiling, or which is used over the coals for charcoal broiling. In France, a grill commonly is in the form of a griddle with raised ridges on its surface (6.4). Larousse Gastronomique says that the metal grill was one of the earliest cooking utensils, second only to the spit.*

MARMITE. *A tall, narrow or bulging-sided stockpot of copper, enameled iron, earthenware, or porcelain, named for the dish cooked in it, petite marmite. The cylindrical shape encourages the blending of flavors while it discourages evaporation.*

POELE A FRIRE. *In the United States, what we call a frypan.*

PRESENTATION PAN. *A long-handled pan used on top of the stove or with a rechaud and then brought to the table for service; sometimes used for last-minute flambéing. Presentation pans are often oval, with a handle attached to one narrow end. They may be made of heat-resistant glass or of beautiful metals such as copper and silver, and are designed more for appearance than for their cooking quality.*

PRESSURE COOKER. *A heavy saucepan with a mechanically tightened seal which cooks the food inside by means of compressed steam. Just as in a steam engine, the water boiled in such a sealed pot causes pressure to build up inside, in this case both raising the boiling point and forcing the steam into the food, thus shortening cooking times.*

SAUCEPAN. *In France, these are called casseroles. In any home, good saucepans are the workhorses of the kitchen: heavy, with straight high sides and long handles, made of metal, enameled metal, or heat-resistant glass and meant to be used on the top of the stove.*

SAUTE PAN. *The French pan—like a frying pan but with straight sides, solid construction, a long handle. It is designed for easy manipulation over a burner. Most properly made of materials that are highly responsive to heat.*

SAUTEUSE. *A heavy, long-handled metal pan with low sides rising perpendicularly from the bottom; a sauté pan, used for cooking with fat over the fire.*

SAUTOIR. *Similar to a sauteuse, but with higher, outward-sloping sides, like a very deep American frying pan or skillet.*

SKILLET. *Another name for a frypan or a sauté pan.*

SPIDER. *Old name for a black-iron frypan.*

STEAMER. *A perforated trivet, or a basket-like device, or a perforated double-boiler insert, placed in or over a pot of boiling water so that the contents of the steamer can be cooked by the rising steam. See Chapter 11 for steaming devices.*

STOCKPOT. *A large metal or enameled-metal pot used for making soups and stocks. This is one of the few pieces of top-of-the-stove cookware which has two short handles rather than a long one, because of its great weight when filled with liquid and the fact that you don't have to move it about while you are cooking. A marmite (see above) is a special version.*

TRIVET. *A plate with legs, often ornamental, which is used underneath a hot dish on the table. When made of metal, trivets are also used underneath cooking pots on the range; in this second use, they work to slow the cooking by distancing the bottom of the pot from the flame. "Trivet" is also a name for a steaming rack (above).*

WAFFLE IRON. *A utensil made for cooking waffles; nearly always electrically heated, and nearly always having patterned plates which can be reversed to form a smooth-surfaced grill. The iron heats the waffle batter (or grilled sandwiches, if the plain surfaces are used) from both sides, pressing the waffle surfaces into typical designs.*
(See p. 252 for ovenware)

SEB Minute Grill 6.3

Chromed steel with enameled-steel top, plastic trim; cast-aluminum grids with nonstick cooking surfaces; 10½" × 8¼"; 3¾" high.
$45.00 ▲

Americans have long loved to eat broiled meat; that is, meat cooked below a very hot heat source. Only recently has broiling in this way spread to France, where the usual method of grilling is to cook the meat on a ridged iron plate heated on the top of the stove. This appliance from France recreates that method for the electrical age, but it cooks both sides of the meat at once, sealing in the juices instantaneously and permitting a radically shortened cooking time. Imagine a waffle iron or sandwich grill with removable grids that are neither waffled nor flat, but ridged instead; that will give you an idea of the appearance of this grill. It is well made and extremely handsome in stainless steel, black plastic, and red enamel. The expansible hinge between the two grilling surfaces controls the space between them, permitting you to cook a two-inch sirloin as well as a filet of flounder. There are, to be sure, some disadvantages: there was considerable spattering of grease when it was tested, and the spout for surplus fat has nothing to drain into—the user must supply a receptacle. And like most electrical appliances with a heating cord that can't be removed, it is difficult to clean. Although we don't usually like release surfaces, the nonstick coating on the grids seems to be a good one, and the fact that no scraping or poking should occur during use means that the surface is unlikely to be damaged. This is the only appliance we know which produces good grilled meat without the use of a high-heat broiling element. There is a recipe booklet translated from the French; and although the cooking times seemed very short, they proved reliable when they were tested.

Scones, still popular throughout Scotland, England, and Ireland, are a form of muffin, rather like a baking-powder biscuit, that is still often baked on a griddle—a "girdle" to some Scots—rather than in the oven. Old books suggest that they should be consumed by those who desire more beautiful skins and sweeter tempers.

GIRDLE SCONES

Sift 2 cups flour, 1 teaspoon cream of tartar, ½ teaspoon salt, 1 teaspoon soda and 1 teaspoon sugar together. Take a cupful and mix it with enough buttermilk or sour cream to make a soft dough. Pat it with the hand on a floured board. Form it into a circle ½ inch thick. Cut it in triangles or squares with a knife and bake them on a floured griddle (girdle) over a medium heat, turning them to brown both sides. They may be split and eaten hot, or, if cooled, split and toasted. (Note: Many people serve them cold but we always felt that heated scones make a much more appealing dish with jam.)

(From DELIGHTS AND PREJUDICES, by James Beard, illustrated by Earl Thollander. Copyright © 1964 by James Beard. Reprinted by permission of Atheneum.)

Copco Grill Pan   6.4

Enameled cast iron; 11″ diam.; 1⅝″ deep. Also avail. 9″ diam.

$31.00 ▲

The French, as we say above, like to cook on a ridged griddle. Here is that griddle grown into a near-frypan of cast iron covered in porcelain enamel, available in five clear colors including yellow, red, blue, or brown, plus plain white (all with a black interior). It is handsome, heavy, and expensive, and comes in both 9″ and 11″ sizes. The pan is designed with an integral handle that has a slight concavity for a better grip, and it also has a smaller handle on the opposite side to help you lift it easily even when it holds a heavy steak. There is a flat-ground bottom, so the pan will sit firmly on your stovetop; it can also be used, preheated, under your broiler. This is something of a hybrid between a grill and a frypan, and it would prove most useful to those on a low-fat diet, since the ridges on the bottom keep the meat from sitting in its own melted fat. There is a pouring lip which encourages you to remove the fat as it collects.

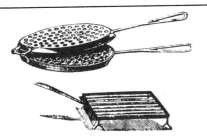

Old American grip broiler (above) and gridiron.

Waffle Iron   6.5

Chromed steel with plastic trim, Teflon-coated, cast-aluminum grids 10⅜″ square; longest dimension 13½″; 5″ high.

$37.00 ▲

This Farberware appliance is both grill and waffle iron, and it makes the best grilled-cheese sandwiches you can imagine: crunchy brown, soaked in butter, with bits of bubbling American cheese oozing out the sides. And if these were delicious, then the ones made with the wafflemaking side of the plates were ambrosial, every bit of creamy cheese sealed into a crisp waffle. The waffle side makes a delicious croque monsieur, too—ham and Gruyère toasted to perfection. The grill is quite handsome, heavy and solid-looking in chromed steel with black plastic trim. There is a thermostat for temperature control and the cast-aluminum grids have a release coating of Teflon on both their patterned and plain sides. We don't usually like release coatings for utensils, but for waffle irons, which need never be touched by a stirring spoon or a probing fork, it will not matter should the surface become slightly scratched. Just forget that it is coated, and remember to brush oil over the grids or the grill surfaces every time they are used. This appliance makes four good-sized waffles, or four pieces of French toast made in the waffle iron, or four grilled sandwiches. The cooking surfaces are 10⅜″ square and the appliance has legs that raise it an inch above the kitchen counter. A short and commendably realistic recipe booklet comes with it—by "realistic" we mean that it does not recommend that you try to make fried chicken or other such unlikely dishes on the grill.

Frying Pans

Griddles are flat, with at most a very low rim, and are meant to hold nothing but the simplest food. Cooking foods quickly, little gravy is produced. On a griddle none is saved, nor is there any way of adding fat or liquid to moisten the proceedings. If the griddle sides were raised slightly, you could cook as you do on a griddle (except for oddly sized food), or you could add fat or liquid to the solids in the pan. You would still have a simple utensil, but your cooking would be less simple to the extent that butter and onions or a little wine or stock would change it. With these more sophisticated materials, you would want to be able to turn the heat down once the food was seared so that it could be cooked through.

We are talking now about frying pans, the pans you reach for when you want to cook liver and onions, or hashed-brown potatoes, or pork chops. Although we say that you "fry" in these pans, sometimes you also sauté: which means a rapid cooking in a small amount of fat and, often, the addition of other ingredients to the pan—cooking such as you do in the French sauté pans—specialists. The frying you do in frying pans is entirely different from deep-frying, which we discuss in Chapter 11 and which involves immersing the food in a deep bath of hot fat. The pans we show you now are made of metals which heat quickly and transmit the heat evenly. They are, in a way, bent griddles; but, of course, with history they have evolved—often to be some of our most useful and sometimes most elegant pans.

The dour author of The Young Housekeeper, or Thoughts on Food *(1838) gives the following description of what some consider to be a pretty cheery food: "Pancakes, sometimes called slap-jacks or flap-jacks, were formerly much used throughout the eastern and middle United States. They were in special demand during the winter; and are in many places, very fashionable still. They are a very inferior kind of food, but are most wholesome when eaten alone and nearly cold, or with a very little milk; whereas, they are commonly used hot, and with molasses, or, what is a thousand times worse, covered with melted butter."*

Lightweight Steel Skillet 6.7

Low-grade steel; 12″ diam.; 2″ deep.
$6.00

A simple frypan of low-grade steel, lightweight and with a long handle, this is a version of the all-purpose pan you will find in restaurant kitchens. It has none of the graces—no brilliant colors or easy-to-grip handle—it is a simple utensil for cooking quickly and efficiently. This version from Italy will heat and cool off rapidly, will brown a veal scallop in no time, and will respond at once when you turn down the heat below it. Because of these qualities, it wouldn't be a bad choice for Chinese stir-frying, if you lack a wok. Notice that the handle is spot-welded to the pan, as is typical of professional cooking pans; but this handle, with its unmodulated edges, might sit painfully in a small palm until the user learned to adjust his grip, grasp the handle close to the pan and take advantage of the shallow trough for a thumb rest.

Cast-Iron Skillet 6.6

Cast iron; 10½″ diam.; 2¼″ deep. Also avail. 6½″, 8″, 9″, 11¾″ diam.
$7.50 ▲

The granddaddy of them all, a cast-iron skillet. In New England these are called spiders, so named because they used to be made, like tripods, with three legs to hold them out of the fire, and thus they resembled spiders—or octopi—or milking stools. These pans are absolutely functional, heating uniformly with no hot spots and holding their heat well. They are inexpensive and become more and more attractive as they darken with age. Yes, they *can* rust, but it is easy enough to prevent that if you remember to dry them out over a stove burner after washing them; yes, they are heavy; and yes, they are slightly porous and so will absorb some flavors and thus be ruled out for making really delicate sauces. Nonetheless, they are classics, the absolute favorite of at least one of our experts for all journeyman kitchen chores. Remember, this is not a pan for subtle cooking; it doesn't cool quickly enough for fragile procedures and, with time, the seasoned surface could emit a slight taste—harmless, but not a friend of delicate flavor. This skillet comes in six sizes, from 6½″ to 13⅜″ in diameter; but the largest size might be really too heavy for many people to lift. We'd recommend the 10½″ or 11¾″ skillet for the greatest all-around usefulness. The manufacturer makes a domed glass lid (6.98) to fit this pan.

Our sample rusted easily, even though it was kept generously greased; it was obviously designed for a kitchen in which it would be in constant use, where it would wear out rather than rust out. It is worth considering for the home kitchen because of its sensitivity to heat and its low price.

STUFFED PORK CHOPS

Use either rib or loin chops and have them cut thick. Ask the butcher to cut a pocket in each—or do it yourself, following the directions below.

6 rib or loin pork chops, 1–1½ inches thick
¼ cup butter
1 medium onion, finely chopped
1 rib celery, finely chopped
1 garlic clove, finely minced
¼ cup finely chopped mushrooms
1 teaspoon thyme or rosemary
1¼ cups dry bread crumbs
¼ cup chopped parsley
1 teaspoon salt
½ teaspoon freshly ground pepper, or to taste
3 tablespoons vegetable oil
Boiling water
1 cup brown sauce or gravy (Alternate: 3 tablespoons flour and 1 cup beef broth or bouillon)

With a sharp knife, cut a pocket in the fat-edged side of each pork chop about 2½ inches long and deep into the meat, until the point of the knife touches the bone.

Prepare the stuffing: Melt the butter in a medium skillet. Add the onion, celery, garlic, mushrooms and thyme or rosemary. Cook until the vegetables are softened, about 5 minutes. Stir in the bread crumbs, parsley, salt and pepper. Blend thoroughly. The mixture should be fairly dry.

Using a teaspoon, fill the pocket in each chop with the prepared stuffing, dividing the mixture evenly. As each chop is stuffed, press the cut edges together to enclose the stuffing, securing the pocket with small skewers or round wooden toothpicks.

Use a heavy skillet with a tight-fitting lid, large enough to hold all the chops. Heat the oil. Add the stuffed chops and brown well on one side.

Using a two-pronged fork and wide metal spatula, carefully turn the chops, taking care that the puffed-up stuffing is not disturbed. Brown the second side. Add just enough boiling water to cover the bottom of the pan. Cover the skillet.

Lower heat and simmer 25 minutes. Carefully turn the chops, replace lid and simmer 10 to 20 minutes longer, depending on the thickness of the chops. Chops should be tender but not dry. When they are done, transfer to a hot platter and keep warm.

With a large spoon, skim off fat from pan juices. Add brown sauce or gravy to the pan and heat, stirring occasionally, just to a boil. (Alternate: stir flour into pan juices, blend well and cook for several minutes. Then add broth or bouillon and stir over medium high heat until the mixture thickens.) Taste to check seasoning; correct if necessary, then spoon over chops.

Italian Iron Frypan 6.8

Heavy-gauge iron; 13½″ diam.; 2¼″ deep.
$14.50

This solid, attractive, but simple pan does the same journeyman jobs, the same quick frying as the flimsier steel pan above. But it is larger, measuring 13½″ across the top, and has a 14″ handle, spot-welded to the pan in six places. It's also very heavy, solid, and well constructed. Although the manufacturer supplies oil which the pan's purchaser is advised to use in order to keep it rust-free, nonetheless the metal seems less likely to rust than does the steel of the thinner pan. For either of these pans—or any skillet of iron or low-grade steel—don't forget the trick of drying it thoroughly over a stove burner turned low after washing and rinsing the pan well.

Copco Skillet 6.9

Enameled cast iron; 12″ diam.; 1¾″ deep. Also avail. 10″ diam.
$36.00 ▲ $31.00 ▲

For those who feel that the ideal cooking material is enamel over cast iron, this is the best-of-class frying pan. We have, however, our reservations: this material will never, never brown food as well as bare metal does; and there is always the danger that the enamel will chip or crack if it is carelessly treated. But it is beautiful, as different from the workaday Italian iron frypan above as you can imagine. It is wide and shallow, enameled in brilliant blue, yellow, brown, red, or white, all with a shining white interior. The handle is a deftly turned rod of teak with a cast-aluminum perforated tip, fitting sensuously into the palm; and to help you manage the really considerable weight of either the 10″ or 12″ size, there is also a secondary loop handle on the opposite side of the pan. A handsome

Continued from preceding page

and well-fitting cover (6.85, available separately) has a flat disc knob in its center. The base of the pan is ground flat to sit well on a burner, and it has been left without an enamel coating to help the distribution of heat and to prevent chipping and burning. So: beautiful in color and shape and pleasant to the hand, this skillet nevertheless has nothing like the sensitivity to temperature changes of the less costly frypans. Rather, think of it as a kind of brazier: use it, for example, for some chops which you will brown delicately, coat with sauce, and then cover for a long simmer on the stovetop.

Aluminum Frying Pan   6.10
Frying Pan with Calphalon   6.11

Heavy-gauge aluminum with tinned-steel handle; 7″ diam.; 1½″ deep. Also avail. 8″, 10″, 12″, or 14″ diam.

$7.50

Heavy-gauge aluminum with Calphalon finish, tinned-steel handle; 7″ diam.; 1½″ deep. Also avail. 8″, 10″, 12″, or 14″ diam.

$11.85

Two frying pans from Commercial Aluminum, identical in size and shape but with a difference in finish, a difference which miraculously eliminates the chemical problems of cooking with aluminum, at the same time providing an easily cleaned release (nonstick) surface. (Where are the trumpets?) It is a satiny charcoal finish called Calphalon and it is exclusive with this manufacturer. It cannot be easily harmed because it is integral with the metal. Before use, season the pan by first oiling it well, then heating it gently. Cool the pan before washing it. The shape of both pans is simple, with a flat bottom and sides which arch generously upwards, and the metal is thick. The heavy-gauge tinned-steel handle is held quite securely in place by three strong rivets: compare its gentle edges with those on the handles of the professional Italian frypan (6.8) and see how much more comfortable they are to hold. Both these pans have heavy-gauge bottoms and they come in a range of sizes from 7″ to 14″ in diameter. Nothing fancy, nothing pretentious here: these are simple, well-made, and serviceable pans at a good price. The Calphalon makes an important difference: we'd cast our vote for the pan with that finish.

ONIONS BRAISED WITH MADEIRA

2 tablespoons olive oil
2 tablespoons butter
4 large onions, peeled and sliced 1 inch thick
1 teaspoon salt
½ teaspoon freshly ground pepper
¼ cup beef broth
¼ cup Madeira

Melt oil and butter in a heavy pan. Add onions and sear over high heat 2 minutes. Season with salt and pepper; add broth; cover and simmer for 10 minutes, or just until tender. Add Madeira and let the sauce cook down slightly.

(From THE GREAT COOKS COOKBOOK, by The Good Cooking School. Copyright © 1974 by The Good Cooking School, Inc. Reprinted by permission of Ferguson/Doubleday.)

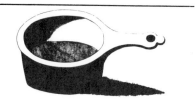

Ancient bronze pan, from Alexis Soyer's The Pantropheon.

Italian Frying Pan   6.12

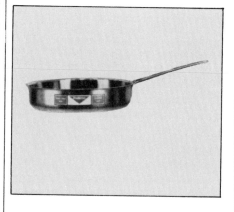

Heavy-gauge stainless steel with aluminum sandwich; 11″ diam. Also avail. 12½″ or 14″ diam.

$55.00

If we say Pyrex or Magnalite, you know immediately what we mean; but unfortunately, when we say Paderno, no picture is likely to come to your mind. And a shame it is, because this is a superb line of Italian cookware which is virtually impossible to find in this country. Paderno makes pans which are so strong, so well constructed, and so functionally designed that they put to shame the obvious allures and trickery of the pots on the shelves of our department stores. This 11″ frying pan, now: it is of brushed stainless steel with a good, well-set handle. The pan is perfect for sautéing because its bottom is a metal sandwich more than a quarter of an inch thick, with aluminum next to the burner—a superb conductor of heat, it is bonded to the sides and totally warp-proof. The sides rise straight up, reminding us that this is probably an adaptation of the Italian braziers or low casseroles (7.4). It has our complete admiration: if you can find it, it is indeed a find and well worth the money.

A fanciful figure in which a brassware seller is costumed to represent a large part of a good cook's batterie de cuisine.

Cuisinart Frying Pan   6.13

Stainless steel with aluminum sandwich; compressed-wood handle; 11″ diam.; 1¾″ deep. Also avail. 6¾″, 8″, 9½″, or 10¼″ diam.

$41.00 ▲

In the price range we have moved into now, the pans are all beautiful and well-designed as well as expensive. Take, for example, this stainless-steel skillet from France by Cuisinarts, which comes in a range of sizes from 6¾″ to 11″ in diameter. Its design is reminiscent of the American frypan (or the French poêle à frire), with sides curving widely up from the base. This pan was made with a very French attention to detail: the heat-conducting bottom is of heavy aluminum sandwiched between two layers of stainless steel: this bottom is perfectly flat and dull in finish, and it provides the unique heat diffusion of aluminum without its problem of affecting the taste and color of certain foods. The handle frees you from potholders, being made of two bars of compressed wood riveted to a stainless-steel rod. The wood has been treated to withstand oven heats up to 375 F. (But watch out for the brass rivets in the handle—they can get hot enough to burn!) There is a mirror finish of so high a quality that we were able to fry an egg in this pan without using butter. A wonderfully versatile pan—you must consider it not only for pork chops or fried potatoes, but also for a large omelet or oversized crêpes. If you require a lid, see our 6.95.

GRENADINS AU VERMOUTH—VEAL GRENADINS WITH VERMOUTH

The grenadin is really a cut of veal rather than a particular portion. The meat comes from the topside of the young calf and is cut into small, round, thick collops that resemble beef tournedos. French butchers automatically encircle the grenadin with a strip of pork fat (which is immediately removed for this recipe). If you cannot get the real grenadin, then slices of boned and rolled veal rump can be substituted.

The delicacy of the veal is not overwhelmed by the vermouth. This is a dish of great subtlety that is merely coated with a discreet amount of sauce, not bathed in it. Whether you are lucky enough to get the plump grenadins or have to use another cut, this is a presentation of distinction.

6 servings
6 veal grenadins or rump steaks at least
   ¾-inch thick
¼ cup flour
3 tablespoons polyunsaturated
   margarine
½ teaspoon grated lemon rind
½ cup dry white vermouth
3 tomatoes
12 small white onions
herb bouquet (4 parsley sprigs tied
   around 1 bay leaf)
¼ teaspoon thyme
½ teaspoon basil
salt and pepper
1 tablespoon flour mixed with 2
   tablespoons cold water
1 tablespoon polyunsaturated margarine
1 teaspoon cognac

Remove any fat from around the veal and lightly flour the meat. Heat the margarine in a heavy skillet and brown the veal on both sides over medium heat. While the veal is browning, grate the lemon rind into the vermouth and pour over the veal. Cover the pan at once and remove from the fire. Shake the pan to loosen the juices that have fried to the bottom. Let the covered pan stand for 5 minutes off the fire to infuse the meat with the vermouth.

Meanwhile, cut the unpeeled tomatoes in quarters, lengthwise, and squeeze out the seeds and pulp. Peel the onions and prepare the herb bouquet.

Return the skillet to the fire and add the tomatoes, onions, herb bouquet, thyme, basil, salt and pepper. Cover and simmer over very slow heat for 30 to 40 minutes, or until the onions are soft when pierced with a sharp knife. Baste several times during the cooking.

Discard the herb bouquet and arrange the veal and vegetables on a serving platter; keep them warm while finishing the sauce. Turn up the heat under the skillet and add the flour-and-water mixture, a little at a time, to thicken the liquid slightly. The sauce should be the consistency of heavy cream. Add the margarine and cognac, give one good boil (about a minute), then spoon the sauce over the veal and vegetables.

(From HAUTE CUISINE FOR YOUR HEART'S DELIGHT, by Carol Cutler. Copyright © 1973 by Carol Cutler. Reprinted by permission of Clarkson N. Potter, Inc.)

Dansk Aluminum Frying Pan   6.14

Cast aluminum with plastic handle; 7½″ diam.; 1½″ deep. Also avail. 9″ or 11″ diam.

$19.95

The top-of-the-line frying pans, the absolutely first-rate ones we have been talking about, have all been made of stainless steel, aluminum having, as we know, certain problematic qualities when brought into contact with acid foods. But here is a marvelous pan from Dansk—"the people who brought you teak"—which is made of one piece of cast aluminum. The black plastic handle, able to withstand oven heat to 475 F., is not screwed on, but is securely heat-welded to the pan, never to loosen and come off. The balance between handle and pan is such that we found this among the easiest of all the frying pans to lift. The design is simple and beautiful; in the 7½″ size we can imagine it coming to the breakfast table holding two perfectly fried eggs; in the 9″ or 11″ size, think of a big dessert pancake sprinkled generously with powdered sugar and served with a bowl of gently butter-fried apple slices.

Glass Frying Pan 6.15

Heat-resistant glass with asbestos stovetop pad; 9″ diam.; 2½″ deep; 2-qt. capacity.
$32.50

Speaking of coming to the table, just imagine yourself carrying in this seemingly fragile Swedish glass skillet full of fluffy scrambled eggs and chicken livers. Or picture hovering over it while you fry eggs, watching the burners (or the asbestos pad, if you use it) disappear as the eggs become opaque. This is scarcely your run-of-the-mill frying pan, but rather essentially an amusing presentation piece that is nevertheless perfectly usable; like glass pots and baking pans to be used in the oven, it can withstand cooking heat. This is an attractive if slightly frivolous product, made of clear hand-blown glass with a short, broad handle. The sides are molded with wavy indentations around the base, making it look rather like a soufflé dish. It holds 2 quarts and is ovenproof; when it is put over direct heat you are advised to use the asbestos pad which is provided. A showpiece and rather a nice one; treat it gently, never heating it empty and never putting anything cold into it when it's hot, and it can perfectly well survive to become an heirloom.

Silver-lined Frying Pan 6.16

Copper with silver lining and stainless-steel handle; 10⅜″ diam.; 1½″ deep.
$100.00

The absolute ultimate: it is perfectly accurate so to describe this presentation pan (or frying pan) in three metals, copper, stainless steel, and—yes—silver. As a matter of fact, silver is not so frivolous a metal for lining a copper pan as you might think, as it is actually longer-lasting, less fragile, and able to withstand higher temperatures than tin—in short, it is as functional for cooking as less costly metals. But we are recommending this not primarily as a cooking pan, even though it has its virtues; the pot is lined with silver because it can be polished to perfection to become the *ne plus ultra* in presentation pans. Use it with tremendous éclat for flambéing food at the table, or for making an omelet with truffles over a chafing-dish burner. Now, the drawbacks: the pan is enormously heavy, and the long, elegantly forked handle is one of the most uncomfortable to hold that we have encountered. And the cost is something that we don't like to think about. But does anyone expect a dancer to cook? A singer to wash floors? The role here is pure drama, pure display, and this is a pan of star quality.

Presentation Pans and Other Ovals

Pans are supposedly designed to fit both the stove burner and the food —clearly an impossibility, as most foods aren't round—and so most pans are made in the shape of the round burner, that being at least predictable. But what foolishness: even a shell steak fits better in an oval pan than a round one, and what, after all, is the real shape of two fried eggs? Yet we go on trying to manage our chickens, our fish, our broccoli and asparagus by squashing them into too-small round pots, or else we have to deal with empty areas in pots that are too large for their contents. Oval pans make sense for cooking, but they have another virtue: they are useful for serving, their shape making them suitable for offering food between two guests at a table. And in this latter incarnation they are called flambé or presentation pans.

Meant to be used half as frypan and half as serving platter, presentation pans are vessels in which the food is cooked quickly or, more often, is finished by being heated or by having a sauce completed. They are then brought to the table—if, indeed, the finishing isn't carried out at tableside. This means that they must, like our incredible glass skillet (6.15), be at least as attractive as they are sturdy. And that is why we can recommend some copper presentation pans which are not of the highest quality: if they are to be subjected only briefly to the heat, then they need not be as sturdy as a stewpot or a brazier. You have a choice in this section among a widely varied group of oval pans: some are of as good quality as anything we show, while others are your ordinary copper-clad Lily of the Field. Don't overlook the last pan in this section, 6.20—scarcely beautiful, it nevertheless has the virtues of a useful shape and good materials.

Nineteenth-century French frying and sauté pans.

STEAK AU POIVRE— PEPPER STEAK

Serves 4

4 shell steaks, boned and well trimmed, about 8 ounces each
1 teaspoon salt
3 tablespoons crushed black peppercorns
4 tablespoons (½ stick) sweet butter
3 shallots, peeled and minced (1½ tablespoons)
2 tablespoons good cognac
¼ cup red wine
1½ cups brown beef gravy

Sprinkle both sides of the steaks with salt, then coat both sides with the peppercorns. This is done by spreading the crushed pepper on the table and pressing the steak on the pepper. Heat 2 tablespoons of the butter in a large, heavy skillet. When the butter is a rich hazelnut color, sauté the steaks 3 to 4 minutes on each side till medium-rare. Lift the steaks from the pan to a warm platter and keep warm in a 180° oven. Add the shallots to the pan and sauté for 1 minute. Add the cognac and ignite. When the flames die out, add the wine and bring to a boil. Reduce to about half, add the beef gravy and bring to a boil again. Boil for a few minutes to reduce the sauce and bring it to the right consistency. Add the remaining butter, strain, and taste for seasoning, as it may need salt. Pour the sauce over the steaks.

Sometimes the shallots and wine are omitted and the steak is made just with cognac and brown gravy.

Or the steaks can be deglazed with cognac and 3 to 4 tablespoons of heavy cream can be added to the brown gravy before it is reduced.

(From JACQUES PEPIN: A FRENCH CHEF COOKS AT HOME, by Jacques Pépin. Copyright © 1975 by Jacques Pépin. Reprinted by permission of Simon & Schuster.)

A sautoir, from L'Ecole des Cuisinières *of Urbain-Dubois.*

Copper Pan from Portugal 6.17

Medium-gauge copper with stainless-steel lining, brass handle; 5½″ diam., 1¼″ deep. Also avail. 6½″, 7⅛″, or 9½″ diam.
$15.00

Also made of three metals and also attractive, this engaging little pan from Portugal is of medium-gauge copper lined with stainless steel. It has a brass handle, attached to the pan with three copper-headed rivets, and comes in four sizes, from 5½″ in diameter—of limited use except for sautéing a garniture, such as a few mushrooms—to a respectable 9½″. Far from costly, it is of reasonable quality and has shining good looks; altogether, a good finishing and presentation pan.

Copper Presentation Pan 6.18

Medium-gauge copper with tin lining, brass handle; 10″ × 7″; 1½″ deep. Also avail. 12″ × 9″.
$27.00

In an oval pan you can sauté a trout, or half a chicken, or a steak, with the least risk of burning your butter on an un-

covered expanse of unnecessary pan bottom: if you want to improve an idle half hour, make a list of foods which are oval and another of foods which are round, and you'll be surprised at the results. Here is a pretty oval pan, more suited to quick sautéing or to finishing than to long cooking. It is of medium-gauge copper with a highly polished tin lining and a brass handle which is held to one end of the oval by rivets. The pan measures 10″ in length and is also available in a 12″ size.

THE GARLIC MEAT LADY

We're cooking dinner tonight.
I'm making a kind of Stonehenge
*   stroganoff.*
Marcia is helping me. You already
*   know the legend*
*   of her beauty.*
I've asked her to rub garlic
*   on the meat. She takes*
*   each piece of meat like a*
*   lover and rubs it gently with*
*   garlic.*
I've never seen anything like this
*   before. Every orifice*
*   of the meat is explored, caressed*
*   relentlessly with garlic.*
There is a passion here that would
*   drive a deaf saint to learn*
*   the violin and play Beethoven at*
*   Stonehenge.*

Richard Brautigan, The Pill versus the Springhill Mine Disaster, *Delacorte Press, New York, 1968*

Lamalle Oval Pan 6.19

Medium-gauge copper with tin lining, brass handle; 11⅞″ × 7⅞″; 1⅝″ deep. Also avail. 10⅜″ × 7″, 13⅜″ × 9″, or 15⅞″ × 10⅛″.
$45.80

If you want a copper pan which can be used for more than presentation, this is the one to buy. In it you could do a duck or a steak au poivre from the beginning, instead of using the pan only for the final flaming with brandy at the table. This Lamalle pan is a sturdy product, as befits their motto, "Heavy tinned copper our specialty." (How nineteenth century! How bourgeois! What a far cry from a contemporary advertising slogan!) The pan is shallow, nearly a foot long, with sloping sides; the whole is of highly polished copper lined with tin. A bronze handle, secured by two rivets to one end of the oval, slants upward, ending in a pointed arch. You can't do better than this pan for both versatility and looks.

Lamalle Oval Iron Frypan　　6.20

Heavy black iron; 14″ × 10″; 1¾″ deep.
$30.00

A good illustration of the importance of materials: here is a pan that is more or less identical to the preceding one—it's the same shape and roughly the same size and is from the same source—but there is all the difference in the world between the two. That one is shining copper, tin, and brass, while this one is dull black iron. That one was elegant, while this one is rough-hewn, heavy; with its hammered edge it could have come to you right from the blacksmith's anvil. With this iron pan we have moved once again away from presentation and back to pure function, to pans for quick grilling, for good responsiveness to heat change. As for hygiene, it's more or less the same; copper needs polishing, while iron needs careful drying and greasing. If you don't intend to use it for table service, this pan, at half the price of its Lamalle copper sibling, is a good choice. It is 14″ long and a good 10″ wide; the long iron handle is no beauty, but it feels good in the hand.

BRAISED ENDIVE

8 to 10 medium sized Belgian endives
2 tablespoons butter
1 teaspoon salt
½ tablespoon sugar
Juice of ½ lemon, strained
⅓ cup water
Minced parsley

Trim the base of the endives and remove any bruised leaves. Wash carefully under cold running water. Drain.

Arrange the endives in an enameled, ovenproof casserole. Dot with the butter, sprinkle with salt and sugar, then pour over the lemon juice and water. Cover with a piece of waxed paper, then place a saucer or plate on top to keep it in place. Add the cover and bring to a boil. Reduce heat and braise on top of the stove or in a preheated 325 degree oven for 35-40 minutes, or until tender when pierced with a paring knife.

At this point, the endives can be placed in a tureen with their juices and refrigerated, covered, for 1 to 2 weeks. Or, they can also be served just as they are, hot from the broth. To serve, drain the endives, flatten with a large knife, then cut the large ones in half lengthwise.

Heat butter in a large skillet and sauté the endives for 5 to 6 minutes until golden. Garnish with minced parsley. You may also pour 1 or 2 tablespoons of brown gravy on top at the last moment, 2 to 3 tablespoons of melted butter, and top with chopped parsley.

(From JACQUES PEPIN: A FRENCH CHEF COOKS AT HOME, by Jacques Pépin. Copyright © 1975 by Jacques Pépin. Reprinted by permission of Simon & Schuster.)

Chicken Fryers

We began this chapter with the griddle: perfectly flat, perfectly simple, perfectly able to transfer heat from flame to food. But as the cooking became more complicated and the sides of the pan became higher, we saw that the skillet was to evolve in two directions. The first was towards quick frying, the food finished perhaps by a rapid deglazing of the pan to make a little sauce, or perhaps by flambéing; for such cooking we recommended lightweight pans which heat and cool off quickly. The second line of development was towards pans for prolonged cooking, either of foods that take considerable time to cook or of dishes for which the cook wants to make a sauce whose flavors should combine slowly. In America such a pan has been called a chicken fryer; in France, it is a sauteuse—a sauté pan.

There are, to be sure, minor differences in design between the two. All of the chicken fryers we show you have a kind of straight and stubby handle which lies parallel to the stovetop and which is short enough to fit tidily into the oven, unlike the longer handle which rises diagonally from the side of a sauteuse. And the chicken fryer has a pouring lip for removing some of the fat from the pan; some have two lips in order to accommodate both left- and right-handers. But the real difference is the material of which they are made. Chicken fryers are always made of cast iron or heavy aluminum or enameled ware—materials which hold and distribute heat well, some of which (like iron and aluminum) might do harm to a delicate sauce but all of which are perfectly suited for long cooking in fat.

The sauteuse, as we will see, is made of materials which are hospitable to saucemaking. Now, of course you can make dishes other than fried chicken in your American pan; but if you should decide to add mushrooms and peppers and tomatoes in order to prepare a chicken cacciatore, you should be aware that the aluminum and tomatoes will not react well together. So for more versatility, consider one of the pans we show you in stainless steel or porcelainized cast iron.

Farberware Frying Pan 6.22

Stainless steel with aluminum-clad bottom, heat-resistant phenolic-resin handles; 12″ diam.; 2½″ deep. Also avail. 7″, 7½″, 8½″, or 10½″ diam.
$24.00 ▲ $20.00 ▲ $16.00 ▲

Always a good value: when you balance quality and availability against cost, Farberware often turns out to be the best cookware for the price. In spite of our caveat about the handle—why can't they design one whose darling little screw doesn't repeatedly come loose?—you can't go wrong with this standard American product in stainless steel, with a well-fitting, slightly domed lid and an aluminum-clad bottom. (This bottom conducts heat better than the copper bottoms of stainless-steel pans in the same price range; the copper on these turns out to be a mere glaze, rather than a useful layer, of metal.) The steel here is of heavy gauge, and the black plastic handle, unwittingly removable though it may be, fits your hand like a dream. In the 12″ size, the pan has a second handle to help you when lifting; smaller sizes, without the auxiliary handle, are available down to 7″ in diameter. What really interests us here is the shape: the pan is really a little deeper, a little less flared, than an ordinary frypan; one glance shows that it can handle more than a veal cutlet or a couple of fried eggs. It is, in short, on its way to being that most American of cooking pots, the chicken fryer. If you want to use this pan for covered cooking, see the separate Farberware lids (6.101 and 6.102).

SAUTE OF CHICKEN TROPEZIENNE

Serves 6
Preparation time: 35 minutes
Cooking time: 2 hours 45 minutes

A tender chicken, sautéed with fresh herbs and finished with a lovely creamy sauce, can bring the essence of southern France to your table. You may want to change your selection of herbs, but remember that no dish should ever be completely taken over by herbs. The chicken, not the herbs, should dominate.

INGREDIENTS
2 egg yolks
½ cup heavy cream
2 2- to 2½-pound chickens, cut into serving pieces (use the wings and giblets for stock)
2 carrots
1 leek
1 bouquet garni, including 1 large celery stalk with leaves
Salt
5 peppercorns
Basil leaves
1 large sprig fresh tarragon
1 large sprig fresh rosemary
Freshly ground white pepper
4 tablespoons sweet butter
1 tablespoon oil
¾ cup dry white wine
4 whole garlic cloves, peeled
2 tablespoons finely chopped fresh herbs (parsley, chives and chervil)

PREPARATION
1. In a small bowl combine the egg yolks and cream. Blend the mixture and reserve.
2. In a saucepan, combine giblets and wings with the carrot, leek and bouquet garni. Cover with 4 cups of cold water, season with salt and the peppercorns. Bring the mixture to a boil, reduce the heat and simmer, partially covered, for 1 hour to 1 hour and 30 minutes. Strain the stock, reduce it to 1 cup and reserve.
3. Dry the chicken pieces well on paper towels and place basil leaf, 2 tarragon leaves and 2 rosemary leaves under the skin of each piece. Season with salt and pepper.
4. In a large chicken fryer, heat the butter and oil. Sauté the chicken pieces a few at a time until evenly browned. Remove them to a side dish; continue sautéeing.
5. Add the wine to the pan, bring it to a boil and scrape the bottom of the pan well.
6. Return the chicken pieces to the pan. Add the stock and garlic cloves. Reduce the heat and simmer the chicken covered for 45 to 50 minutes, or until tender.
7. With a slotted spoon remove the chicken pieces to a serving platter. Raise the heat and reduce the pan juices by ⅓.
8. Take the frying pan off the heat and beat in the cream and egg yolk mixture. Return the pan to very low heat and whisk it constantly until it thickens. Do not let it come to a boil.
9. Taste the sauce and correct the seasoning. Spoon it over the chicken and sprinkle with the fresh herbs. Serve with tiny buttered potato balls, simply cooked young green beans, followed by salad and a bowl of fresh fruit.

REMARKS
The chicken can be kept warm in its sauce in a 200° oven for 20 minutes.

(From THE SEASONAL KITCHEN, by Perla Meyers. Copyright © 1973 by Perla Meyers. Reprinted by permission of Holt, Rinehart and Winston.)

Magnalite Chicken Fryer 6.23

Cast magnesium and aluminum alloy, phenolic-resin handle; 12″ diam.; 3″ deep. Also avail. 10½″ diam.
$31.00 ▲ $28.00 ▲

The trouble with Magnalite ware is that we've grown accustomed to its face—we have seen it around for so long and, though virtuous, it was no beauty to begin with. Homely and familiar, it has really exceptional cooking qualities that tend to be undervalued when it is compared with some of the more dazzling products on the market. But the Magnalite alloy of aluminum and magnesium has all of the advantages of aluminum, which is second only to copper in heat conductivity, and few of its drawbacks. The alloy is hard enough to be buffed and polished until there are virtually no surface pores, and thus the metal's vulnerability to pitting and tarnishing is reduced. (Nevertheless, it's wise never to let salty or acid foods stand unnecessarily long in this ware.) This chicken fryer is heavy, but nowhere near so heavy as it looks; imagine the burden of lifting a pan of this size—12″ across—made of thick stainless steel or copper.

The high polish of the exterior is not continued onto the bottom of the pan, which is dull and absolutely flat for maximum heat absorption; there is a rounded lid which fits extremely well, covering the two pouring lips of the pan and permitting you to cook with surrounding moist heat when you wish to. But despite its shiny looks this pot is not beautiful. For the money, however, and considering its weight and its well-fitting lid, it is a really good choice.

Le Creuset Chicken Fryer   6.24

Enameled cast iron; 10¼″ diam.; 3¼″ deep; 5-qt. capacity. Also avail. 8½″ diam.

$37.00 ▲

A remarkably handsome pot of enameled cast iron, the outside a brilliant blue, flame, yellow, or brown and the inside a matte black. By making it black inside and brightly colored outside, the manufacturer reached a splendid resolution of the problem of the materials: enameled ironware does not brown food well in any but its dull black finish, and non-enameled cast iron works none too well with the ingredients in many sauces. But a pot in dull black overall can be dreary in the kitchen, while these colors are radiantly beautiful. This pot has the typical short handle of the chicken fryer, with a stubby subsidiary grip on the opposite side to help you lift the pot; and very necessary that is, because it is *heavy*. Two pouring lips are covered tightly during cooking by corresponding curves on the edge of the lid. This pan is 3¼″ deep, substantial, nearly a saucepan in shape. A good product, but watch out for the weight. And be warned that enameled ware can crack and chip if treated casually; avoid sudden temperature changes, and never set this pan over the heat while it is empty.

Copco Chicken Fryer   6.25

Enameled cast iron; 12″ diam.; 2½″ deep.

$56.00 ▲

The Le Creuset chicken fryer (6.24) with its enameled outside and matte black interior was a superb reconciliation of the beauty of bright enamel with the cooking quality of iron. Put white enamel on the inside, as Copco has done, and you no longer have an effective chicken fryer, but something more like a shallow casserole. Use it when you want a simmering sauce to reduce as it cooks. It comes in many colors of enamel—blue, yellow, brown, red, and white. This is a 12″ skillet, quite deep and with slightly sloping sides. The cover fits closely. The base of each piece has been ground flat and left unglazed. This means that the pan will sit solidly on an electric burner and that there is no enameled surface on the outside of the bottom to be shattered by the expansion the pan undergoes when it is heated. A treat to look at.

BRODETTO ALLA SAN BENEDETTO—FISH STEW SAN BENEDETTO STYLE

½ pound squid, cleaned at fish market
2 medium whiting, with heads on [other white-meat fish in season may be substituted for whiting or bass]
1 pound striped bass
12 mussels
½ pound raw shrimp
6 clams
1 medium onion, plus 2 tablespoons, chopped
½ cup, plus 2 tablespoons, olive oil
4 tablespoons chopped parsley, Italian if possible
½ green pepper, pickled in vinegar if possible
¼ cup wine vinegar
¾ cup chopped tomato
Salt and hot pepper
¼ cup dry white wine

Wash squid and all fish. Cut whiting and bass into 3-inch pieces, squid into ½-inch pieces. Scrub the mussels well under running water. Shell and de-vein shrimp. Sauté squid and all but 2 tablespoons of the onion in 2 tablespoons of the olive oil in a small skillet for 5 minutes. When onion looks wilted, set the mixture aside. Do not overcook.

Meanwhile, place remaining olive oil and onion, 3 tablespoons of the parsley, and green pepper in a large skillet. Cook over high flame for several minutes, and add vinegar. Cook for several minutes and add tomato, salt and hot pepper to taste and continue cooking, uncovered, for 5 minutes. Add bass and cook for 5 more minutes. Add whiting and cook for several minutes. Add clams and cook for several minutes. Add mussels and cook until they begin to open, then add the shrimp. As soon as shrimp change color, add wine. Cover and simmer for about 5 minutes, add remaining parsley and simmer a few minutes more. Serve hot over toasted French or Italian bread to 6.

(From ITALIAN FAMILY COOKING, by Edward Giobbi, illustrated by Cham, Lisa, and Gena Giobbi. Copyright © 1971 by Edward Giobbi. Reprinted by permission of Random House, Inc.)

Sunbeam Electric Frypan   6.26

Aluminum with plastic trim; 11½″ square; 6⅝″ high overall; base 1⅞″ deep, lid 3″ high, legs 1⅝″ long.

$28.95

A few years ago electric frypans were the rage; one bride we know got six for wedding presents. And then the furor died down, and they were no longer This Year's Appliance—this past year another

Continued from preceding page

girl we know received four yogurt makers. Electric frypans have their flaws: their responsiveness to heat—the rate at which they heat up and then cool down at the cook's demand—is seriously limited; and it is difficult to shake them during use in the manner which is usual with frypans. But they continue to be made; one of our editors swears by hers, saying that she loves it because it frees one burner in her small apartment kitchen and because, once set, she can trust it to maintain a steady heat while she attends to the rest of the meal. Of the electric frypans we saw, we liked this one from Sunbeam the best. First plus was that it came with a simple chrome finish: no sickly shades of gold or avocado. Second plus: the heat control detaches from the pan when the cord is unplugged from it, and the pan itself is thus immersible for washing. This is a square shallow pan with a very high domed lid, tall legs which remove it a good distance from the kitchen counter, and strongly anchored plastic handles. The heat goes from a Warm setting, below 250 F., up to 420 F. There is a simple adjustable vent on the lid for use when you want steam to evaporate. A recipe book included with the pan goes a bit wild, giving instructions for baking pound cake in your frypan; but for scrambled eggs, fried chicken or fried eggs or pork chops, stir-fried vegetables, even for cooking asparagus lying flat or for baking pancakes, this is a reasonable appliance to purchase, of special interest if you have limited stovetop space.

An American dual-purpose stove of the nineteenth century.

The Pans for Sautéing

The French verb *sauter,* meaning to jump or to leap—grasshoppers are *sauterelles*—applies to cookery in its transitive form: to cause to jump, or to toss—a nice image for the action in a frying pan when the cook is moving it rapidly back and forth over high heat. In sautéing, food is cooked in a small amount of fat while it is kept in motion either by being tossed, stirred, or shaken as the pan is drawn back and forth vigorously across the burner. The sauté pan—in French, a *sauteuse* or a *sautoir*—has evolved a wide and flat shape to provide a bottom that will give ample room for the food and also move easily over the burner. The intense heat of sautéing requires that the pan be of heavy-gauge and highly conductive metal that will transmit heat evenly and steadily without any spot burning. When the sides of such a pan grow higher, we call it a saucepan instead of a sauté pan.

WHAT TO LOOK FOR

The best metals for sauté pans are also the best for saucemaking—copper lined with tin—although there are good sauté pans made of stainless steel or aluminum. If you are going to spend the money on copper, here is the place to do it. What you don't want is a stainless-steel pan which has a thin wash of copper on the bottom, causing trouble for the pot-washer without a compensatory increase in heat sensitivity; in the bottom of a stainless-steel pan only a thick layer of copper, or a "sandwich" of aluminum or mild steel, will improve the pan's cooking quality.

Because you will be moving the pot over the heat constantly, a good handle is essential. It will be long, slanting upwards from the edge of the pan, and it should be both easy in the hand and cool to the touch: a brass handle is both handsome and expensive, but iron is cooler and cheaper. Either is adequate; the essential factor is to have the handle made separately, then joined to the pot, and it should be made of a different metal in order to limit the passage of heat from one to the other.

A lid is a useful thing to have, also, because sautéing is often only the first step in a recipe, to be followed by a period of covered cooking. You will find that lids to fit many of the pans we recommend can be purchased separately from the manufacturer of the pot; most of them will fit equally well on either a saucepan or a sauté pan of the same line. Think of the sauté pan as a French frying pan, a transition between a skillet and a saucepan.

Alexis Soyer, the great French chef who was virtually adopted in England (as were his confrères Carême, Escoffier, Ude, and Francatelli), made clear the distinction between frying and sautéing: "You will perceive . . . that the word fried is often wrongly used in cookery instead of the word sauté. . . . Sauté means anything cooked in a very small quantity of butter, oil, lard, or fat, on one side of the article at a time, whilst the other requires about a hundred times more of the above-named materials to cook properly."

Copper Sauteuse from Kitchen Glamor 6.27

Heavy-gauge copper with tin lining, brass handle; 9⅝″ diam.; 2¼″ deep; 3¾-qt. capacity. Also avail. 8″ or 11″ diam.

$32.95

Fait-tout means "does-everything," and there is no French kitchen where you will not find some version of the pans given this name: in fact, the batterie de cuisine is likely to include three or four in different sizes and shapes. This faittout—a sauteuse—is in the heaviest weight of copper available in pots sold in the United States. It is the classic of its type: the heavy tin-lined copper absorbs, conducts, and reflects heat well and also loses it quickly, displaying a sensitivity which is essential in a sauté pan but which would be pointless in, say, a stockpot. The tin lining prevents the food from interacting with the copper but does not interfere with the conductivity of the metal; and the cast-iron handle remains relatively cool in the hand—the difference in the metals forms a mechanical barrier to the passage of heat. We show this sturdy pot in the 9⅝-inch size; it's also available with a diameter of either 8 or 11 inches. Copper lids with brass loop handles are also available separately (see 6.86).

SALSA MARINARA—MARINARA SAUCE

This recipe was given to me by a Florentine while we were living in Florence. It is the best marinara sauce I have ever tasted.

¼ cup olive oil
2 cups coarsely chopped onion
½ cup sliced carrot
2 cloves garlic, finely minced
4 cups canned Italian plum tomatoes
Salt and freshly ground black pepper
4 tablespoons butter
1 teaspoon dried oregano
1 tablespoon chopped fresh basil or
  1 teaspoon dried basil

Heat the oil in a large open skillet and add the onion, carrot and garlic. Cook, stirring, until the vegetables are golden brown. Pour the tomatoes through a sieve, pushing the pulp through with a wooden spoon. Discard the seeds. Add the puréed tomatoes to the vegetables and add salt and pepper to taste. Partially cover and simmer 15 minutes. Put the sauce through a sieve and push the solids through with the wooden spoon. Return to the skillet and add the remaining ingredients. Partially cover and simmer 30 minutes longer. Yield: 3 to 4 cups.

VARIATIONS
With mushrooms: Quarter ¾ pound of fresh mushrooms and cook them in 2 tablespoons olive oil, plus 2 tablespoons butter, until golden brown. Add the mushrooms to the sauce for the last ½ hour of cooking.

With meatballs: Combine ½ pound twice-ground pork or veal with 1 egg, lightly beaten, ¼ cup chopped parsley, ½ cup bread crumbs, grated rind of ½ lemon, 2 tablespoons grated fresh Parmesan cheese, ¼ teaspoon grated nutmeg, and salt to taste. Add ½ garlic clove, finely minced, if desired. Shape the mixture into 12 small balls and dust them lightly with flour. Brown on all sides in 2 tablespoons oil, plus 2 tablespoons butter. Add the meatballs to the sauce for the last ½ hour of cooking.

With sausages: Broil 2 sweet or hot Italian sausages, turning occasionally, until done. Cut the sausages into ½-inch-thick slices. Add to the sauce for the last ½ hour of cooking.

(From ITALIAN FAMILY COOKING, by Edward Giobbi, illustrated by Cham, Lisa, and Gena Giobbi. Copyright © 1971 by Edward Giobbi. Reprinted by permission of Random House, Inc.)

Hammered Copper Sauteuse 6.28

Heavy-gauge hammered copper with tin lining, cast-iron handle; 8″ diam.; 2½″ deep; 2-qt. capacity. Also avail. 8¾″ diam., capacity 2½ qts., and 9½″ diam., capacity 3 qts.

$45.00 ▲

This sauteuse is rather like the preceding one—it is of equally heavy-gauge copper and it, too, has a tin lining and an iron handle, but it has, in addition, been hammered all over, producing a leaflike surface pattern on the polished metal. Now, this is not simply an aesthetic variation, but a method by which the metal has been tempered for added strength—think of Siegfried remaking his sword. If you have a gas stove, then the added strength is all to the good; it is, however, less desirable on an electric range or over a heat-sensor element, where a perfectly flat bottom is desirable. A good pan: costly, heavy, beautiful, and made to last forever. In the 8″ size it holds 2 quarts, and it also comes in 8¾- and 9½-inch sizes. A long-handled lid to fit this pot can be purchased separately (6.103).

Legion Copper and Stainless-Steel Sauteuse 6.29

Heavy-gauge copper exterior with heavy-gauge stainless-steel interior and handle; 12¼" diam., 3½" deep; 6½-qt. capacity. Also avail. 6¼", 7¼", 8¼", 9", 10¼", 14¼", 16¼", 18", 20", or 22" diam.
$110.00

Now, suppose that instead of lining your copper sauteuse with tin, you bonded it to a completely separate pan made of stainless steel. The reactivity to heat would still be good, though not so good as that of a copper-and-tin pan, and you would gain a great deal in durability. More and more restaurant chefs like this Bi-Metal cookware made of two layers of metal joined together; it never burns or discolors inside, nor does it have to go back to the manufacturer to be retinned. Instead, it will last for the rest of your life, the low-gloss finish of the copper becoming softly lustrous as it patinates. It comes in sizes from 6¼" to 22" in diameter and is phenomenally heavy; taking pity on the chef, the manufacturer has provided him with a good secondary grip, a loop handle of stainless steel, on the larger sizes. The primary handle is of stainless steel and is relatively comfortable in the hand. Strong and all but indestructible, this is the pan to buy if you have need for a really heavyweight sauteuse. For matching lids, see 6.94.

Cuisinart Sauté Pan 6.30
Cuisinart Sauté Pan with Grip 6.31

Stainless steel with aluminum sandwich, compressed-wood handle; 8¾ diam.; 3" deep, 2¾-qt. capacity. Also avail. 7" diam., 1½-qt. capacity, and 10¼" diam., 4½-qt. capacity.

$33.00 ▲

Stainless steel with aluminum sandwich, compressed-wood handles; 11" diam.; 3⅜" deep; 5½-qt. capacity. Also avail. 8" diam., 2-qt. capacity, and 9½" diam., 3½ qt. capacity.

$53.00

More decorative and less commercial versions of the sauté pan are these in stainless steel by Cuisinarts. Leaving out heat sensitivity—in which nothing can rival heavy copper—these heavy-gauge pans have all of the virtues of copper and none of its limitations. The stainless-steel interior will never need retinning, while the quarter-inch-thick aluminum sandwich on the bottom eliminates the spotty heating typical of steel. Let us enthuse: Cuisinart pans have superb lids and bottoms. Unlike most other pans, which are made with slightly concave bottom surfaces to allow for expansion when the metal is heated, these have bottoms made absolutely flat to hug an electrical element or the flat sur-

face of a ceramic range as well as a gas burner. Some pans with a double-layered bottom will arch when heated, because one metal expands more rapidly than the other; but in the three-layered Cuisinart bottoms—steel, then aluminum, then steel again—the steel acts like a vise on the aluminum, preventing it from bending one degree away from perfection. These pans have superb covers, so well-fitting that they are difficult to lift once sealed in place by heated vapor in the pot; these are sold separately (see 6.95). Watch out for the handles: although the pressed wood will stay cool, the brass rivets which attach it most decidedly will not. These pans are expensive, but not so expensive as copper ones of equal quality. They come in six sizes, three of which—and not the three largest—are provided with a secondary handle for easy lifting. Handsome to begin with, they will be easy to keep so, and will come beautifully to the table.

Paderno Stainless-Steel Sauteuse 6.32

Stainless steel with aluminum sandwich; 8" diam.; 3" deep; 2½-qt. capacity. Also avail. 9½", 11", or 12½" diam.
$50.00

Because sauté pans are so versatile, coming to hand equally appropriately for poaching an egg or frying a chicken, we have chosen only the finest to offer you: this is not the place to scrimp on quality. On the same level of excellence as the Cuisinart pan but of a more commercial design, its handsome shining surface not so easily ruined by scratches, is this superb stainless-steel sauté pan from Italy. The manufacturer calls it a casseruola bassa, the name also given to some braziers (Chapter 7), and it is precisely that: a brazier with one long handle to use on top of the stove. It is deeper than the Cuisinart pan; it is not so eligible to travel on its looks from stove to dining room; and the bottom is not so fine. But it is impeccably made of heavy stainless steel with an aluminum sandwich on the bottom for better heat conductivity, and the austerely functional design has won the affection of all our experts. It would be perfect for a stovetop stew or for osso buco or other braised dishes. The manufacturer also makes matching lids—see 6.100. Unfortunately—and we have had to say this about several very fine Italian pots—it is difficult to find in this country. If you do find one, don't pass it by, since it is better than any American-made stainless-steel sauteuse we have seen.

ALUMINUM SAUTE PANS

We now show you three aluminum sauté pans, each quite different from the others. If you choose to have a range of sauteuses in different materials rather than a set, you would do well to buy the smaller sizes in copper or stainless steel and the larger ones in aluminum. Aluminum transmits heat well, and it is not only lighter but less expensive than the other metals (although, with the price of aluminum escalating daily, we may not be able to say that much longer). When using aluminum there is always, you will remember, the problem of the metal interacting with certain foods and thus affecting both their taste and color. But look at 6.33, a sauteuse which is protected by an inert nonstick finish called Calphalon, for what may be the ideal solution to the problem of which really large pan to buy. Because of their size and their plain appearance, these aluminum pans are definitely a commercial solution, but they are of good quality and they have the virtue of being both less heavy and less expensive than either copper or stainless steel.

Calphalon-finished Sauteuse   6.33

Heavy-gauge aluminum, Calphalon finish, tinned-steel handle; 12″ diam.; 2⅝″ deep; 5-qt. capacity. Also avail. 6″, 8″, 9¾″, 14″, or 16″ diam.

$51.95

This professional-quality aluminum sauteuse made by Commercial Alumi-

num is not light, but neither is it heavy for its size—it has a generous 5-quart capacity in the 12″ diameter. The point here, however, is not the weight of the pan but the finish, a handsome charcoal satin which is actually a trademarked release and protective finish named by the manufacturers Calphalon. The Calphalon finish is produced on fully crafted pots by an electrochemical process, and it protects the metal of the pan from the pitting caused by certain foods and, in turn, protects vulnerable foods from the discoloration or flavor damage that occurs when they are cooked in aluminum. Because it is integral with the metal, the finish cannot be damaged by poking or stirring. You are advised to oil the pan well and heat it gently in order to season the finish before you use the pan for the first time; then you will have a pan with a release agent which for once we heartily recommend because it eliminates the usual drawbacks connected with cooking in aluminum. This pan is shallow, with the correct straight sides, and is made of heavy-gauge aluminum; its tinned-steel handle is riveted securely to its side. The size range of the six pans of this design is from 6 to 16 inches. You can, if you like, buy a lid for the pan you choose—see 6.92 and 6.93.

SHRIMP-AND-HAM JAMBALAYA

To serve 6 to 8

2 cups water
2 teaspoons salt
1 cup short-grain white rice
2 pounds uncooked medium-sized shrimp (about 20 to 24 to the pound)
6 tablespoons butter
1½ cups finely chopped onions
2 tablespoons finely chopped garlic
A 1-pound can tomatoes, drained and finely chopped, with all their liquid
3 tablespoons canned tomato paste
½ cup finely chopped celery
¼ cup finely chopped green pepper
1 tablespoon finely chopped fresh parsley, preferably the flat-leaf Italian variety
3 whole cloves, pulverized with a mortar and pestle or finely crushed with a kitchen mallet or the flat of a heavy cleaver
½ teaspoon crumbled dried thyme
½ teaspoon ground hot red pepper (cayenne)
¼ teaspoon freshly ground black pepper
1 pound cooked lean smoked ham, trimmed of excess fat and cut into ½-inch cubes

Bring the water and 1 teaspoon of the salt to a boil in a small saucepan set over high heat. Add the rice, stir once or twice, and immediately cover the pan. Reduce the heat to low and simmer for about 20 minutes, or until the rice is tender and the grains have absorbed all of the liquid in the pan. Fluff the rice with a fork, cover, and set it aside.

Meanwhile, shell the shrimp. Devein them by making a shallow incision down their backs with a small sharp knife and lifting out the black or white intestinal vein with the point of the knife. Wash the shrimp briefly in a colander set under cold running water. Drop the shrimp into enough boiling salted water to cover them completely and cook briskly, uncovered, for 4 to 5 minutes, or until they are pink and firm. With a slotted spoon, transfer the shrimp to a bowl and set aside.

In a heavy 5- to 6-quart casserole, melt the butter over moderate heat. When the foam begins to subside, add the onions and garlic and, stirring frequently, cook for about 5 minutes, or until they are soft and translucent but not brown. Add the tomatoes, the tomato liquid and the tomato paste, and stir over moderate heat for 5 minutes. Then add the celery, green pepper, parsley, cloves, thyme, red pepper, black pepper and the remaining teaspoon of salt. Stir-

Continued from preceding page

ring frequently, cook uncovered over moderate heat until the vegetables are tender and the mixture is thick enough to hold its shape lightly in the spoon.

Add the ham and, stirring frequently, cook for 5 minutes. Then stir in the shrimp and, when they are heated through, add the reserved rice. Stir over moderate heat until the mixture is hot and the rice has absorbed any liquid in the pan.

Taste for seasoning and serve the shrimp-and-ham jambalaya at once, directly from the casserole or mounded in a heated bowl.

(From AMERICAN COOKING: CREOLE AND ACADIAN (Foods of the World Series), by Peter S. Feibleman and the Editors of Time-Life Books. Copyright © 1971 by Time, Inc. Reprinted by permission of Time-Life Books.)

Commercial Aluminum Sauteuse 6.34

Heavy-gauge aluminum, tinned-steel handle; 9¾" diam.; 2½" deep; 3-qt. capacity. Also avail. 6", 8", 12", 14", or 16" diam.
$34.35

Similar to the preceding sauté pan, this one, by the same manufacturer, lacks the Calphalon protective coating. Here is a heavy-duty sauteuse, strong in construction, dark grey in color, made without seams, of extra-thick aluminum and with corners rounded for easy cleaning. The bottom is made heavier than the sides for better heat conductivity and to prevent sticking and burning. This is a solid pan whose cooking qualities are nearly as good as those of copper, but whose price is considerably less. The comfortable tinned-steel handle is attached with rivets, and in spite of the relatively light weight of these pans there is a secondary handle on the largest size. You can order lids separately—see 6.92 and 6.93. A good choice if the drawbacks of uncoated aluminum pose no problems for you.

French Hammered Aluminum 6.35 Sauteuse

Heavy-gauge hammered aluminum with black-coated cast-aluminum handle; 10½" diam.; 3" deep. Also avail. 8" or 9½" diam.
$27.00

Not every French cook has a batterie de cuisine composed entirely of shining copper pans: in a nation which admires thrift there is recognition of the virtues of aluminum. Here is a hammered aluminum pan of French manufacture, the metal heavy in itself and then made even stronger by being hammered all over in a leaflike design. There is a black-coated cast-aluminum handle which should stay cool in the hand while you move the sauteuse back and forth over the burner. This pan is somewhat deeper than the equivalent American sauté pan—it's fully 3" deep—and it is available in three sizes ranging from 8" to 10½" in diameter.

SUPREMES DE VOLAILLE, SAUCE SUPREME—CHICKEN BREASTS WITH SAUCE SUPREME

---

3 whole chicken breasts—skinned, boned and split in half
½ lemon
Salt
White pepper
Unsalted butter (for the waxed paper)
6 tablespoons unsalted butter
Hot cooked rice
Sauce Suprême (follows 6.37)

Preheat oven to 400 F.

Flatten each half chicken breast by pounding lightly with the side of a chef's knife. Squeeze a few drops of lemon juice over each piece and sprinkle with salt and pepper.

Cut a round of waxed paper to fit the inside of a 12-inch ovenproof skillet. Butter one side of waxed paper.

Heat 6 tablespoons of butter in the ovenproof skillet until the foam subsides. Add the chicken. Spoon butter over.

Lay the waxed paper, buttered side down, over the chicken. Cover the skillet and put it in the oven for about 8 minutes. The chicken is done when the flesh is white and resilient.

Serve on a bed of hot cooked rice. Spoon a little Sauce Suprême over each breast and pass the rest in a sauceboat.

Hammered Copper Fait-Tout 6.36

Heavy-gauge hammered copper with tin lining, cast-iron handle; 8¾" top diam.; 7" bottom diam.; 3¼" deep; 2-qt. capacity. Also avail. 5", 5¾", or 6½" top diam.
$60.00 ▲

Let's be honest: if you had a limited amount of money to spend on kitchenware, you would probably go out and buy an inexpensive saucepan and skillet and teapot and blow the rest on two perfect roses. But in fact you would do better to sink it all into this one superb pan. Imported from France, where it is known as a sauteuse evasée—literally, a flaring sauté pan—it is in reality a true fait-tout or "does everything" pot, able to perform any number of cooking tasks really well. The sloping sides resemble at the same time a low Windsor saucepan (6.50), a skillet and the classic French sauté pan

Yankee inventiveness and thrift: Without any waste of fuel, cooking, baking, roasting, and water heating went on simultaneously in some ranges of the last century.

Continued from preceding page

termed sautoir. We admire it because it is of the heaviest-gauge copper lined with tin, and we also admire the hammered pattern on the outside, which adds both beauty and strength. (The bottom, however, remains unhammered, making it equally useful on either electric or gas burners.) The curved iron handle will remain cool long after the pan has become fiery hot. In this pan you could sauté several suprêmes de volaille and then add liquid to complete the cooking; in the smaller sizes you could make a sauce, since the pan functions perfectly to expose a wide area of liquid surface for sauce reduction. And, because of the sloping sides, the bottom is easy to reach for stirring. All in all, a pan endlessly useful for dealing with a range of quantities in the food you cook: the pan will brown a single slim veal cutlet, or a quart of sauce will find ample space to reduce. And, to add to its versatility, you can buy a lid separately—see 6.86, 6.87, and 6.88. It is the pot we chose to complete this section, because in it you can perform skillfully both the functions of the sauteuse and the saucepan.

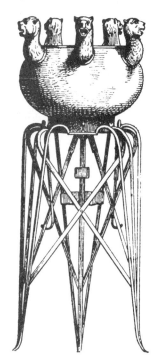

An ancestral pot—an Etruscan tripod vessel.

Saucepans

The saucepan is the workhorse of the kitchen—in it we make not only a perfect Hollandaise, but cook frozen spinach; not only do we use a saucepan to prepare a few tablespoonfuls of roux, but we reach for the same kind, if not the same size, of pan to cook three pounds of linguine. And although saucepans are not, strictly speaking, presentation pans, in this era of the hostess-cook one of our editors often serves soup to her guests from a copper saucepan. It is obvious, then, that we need saucepans in a variety of sizes and materials. The batterie de cuisine should contain at least three or four, so that the right size of pan can be used for a given quantity of food; but in addition there should be saucepans of different materials: a copper pan is worth every penny of its hefty cost to the saucemaker, but a lighter and cheaper pot will do to hard-cook eggs, heat up a can of soup, or boil pasta.

A BUYING STRATEGY

We recommend that you economize by buying the smallest and largest of your saucepans in stainless steel or aluminum, so that you don't waste money on pans for simple tasks that involve boiling for the most part; then spend as much as necessary for one or two copper pans of impeccable quality in the medium sizes. Enameled iron, so useful for skillets and casseroles, is an uncommon material for saucepans because it is so heavy, making it unsuitable for a pot which, like the sauteuse, needs to be manipulated constantly: tilted, shaken, moved on and off the flame. For the same reason, pay attention to the handle, both the way it feels in your palm when it is cool and the possibility that it will burn you when it is hot.

FACTS, THEN FANTASY

Once you have thought about the practical whys and wherefores of choosing saucepans, consider your aesthetic and sensual response to these pans. We offer such a range of choices that you should be able to choose a pan which fits your own fantasy of its purpose. Look at an Arabia pot, sparkling white in enameled steel (6.57), transmitting the message "hygiene," and you will certainly want to use it for porridge and light egg custards. Then look at the big charcoal-satin Calphalon aluminum pan from Commercial Aluminum (6.46), of restaurant quality and restaurant size, and see how suitable it seems for your next batch of spaghetti sauce. This is the fantasy connected with cooking: we can only supply you with the facts and leave the poetry up to you.

COPPER: OLD CAN BE GOOD

There is nothing so gratifying in a kitchen as the warm bellies of copper pots hanging on the wall, reflecting both the sunlight and the flames of your stove. These pans, if originally well made, will last forever: they need not be bought new to give you good value, and their beauty only increases with age. They are among the most collectible items of kitchenware, turning up with diminishing frequency in antique and junk shops. And what you look for in an old pan is more or less the same as in a new: thick metal, good construction, riveted handles. The state of the tinning inside the pot is unimportant—although the cost of retinning is not inconsequential, the service is available. (In Chapter 6 is a discussion of retinning.) Watch out, though, for the quality of tinning in new pans: ask questions about both the thickness of the lining and whether it was applied by dipping or plating or—less desirably—by painting on. (We can assure you that all the manufacturers we recommend do a good tinning job on their pots.)

When you buy an old pot, look carefully at the bottom. If there has been a repair, you will see a saw-toothed circle inside the circumference of the pan, and you should, accordingly, pay less for it. Handles come either in brass or iron, and the story that there are no really old brass handles is apocryphal: both materials will show up on antique pans. Just remember that old iron, like new iron, is both cheaper and cooler than brass.

Copper, like gold, is sold by weight, and at today's price it should be counted among the precious metals. Ultimately, however, you buy copper pans neither because they are precious or beautiful nor to complete a collection, but because only with copper can you be sure that the time and money you spend on making a really great sauce will not be wasted.

In the Middle Ages the office of master saucemaker was one of great importance. He was a chief functionary in great houses, with many servants at his command. Similarly, the sauce chef in a restaurant is considered to rank at the head of the kitchen staff.

Kitchen Glamor Copper Saucepan 6.37

Heavy-gauge copper with tin lining, cast-iron handle; 8" diam.; 4⅜" deep; 3-qt. capacity; 5 lbs. Also avail. with capacity of ¾, 1, 2, 4, or 7 qts.

$37.29

Heavy, gleaming, solidly made, this hand-finished, extra-heavy copper saucepan is of heirloom quality no less than your silver teapot, and you'll use it a lot more often. On the inside you can see the tinner's tool marks, and the well-shaped cast-iron handle is firmly attached to the pan with three copper

rivets. The pan we show you is 8″ in diameter, holds 3 quarts, and weighs a substantial 5 pounds. There are smaller sizes, down to a 3-cup miniature for melting butter, and larger sizes up to an awe-inspiring 7-quart pot weighing 6 pounds—you would think twice before taking *that* one off the shelf. For lids to fit these pots, see 6.89. Note that this ware is not only heavy but expensive; consider, however, that the copper of which it is made is by now nearly a precious metal; that it is all but indestructible; and that these pots are among the very best of their kind.

Snails eager for saucing. From the Almanach des Gourmands, 1904.

B.I.A. Copper Saucepan 6.38

Heavy-gauge hammered copper with tin lining, cast-iron handle; 7" diam.; 4" deep; 2½-qt. capacity. Also avail. with capacity of ¾, 1¼, 1¾, 3½, or 4½ qts.

$95.00

Improving on the already perfect is a logical impossibility, but it seems to happen all the time in the kitchen. Suppose you take a tinned copper pan like the preceding one—heavy, well-made, with a good cast-iron handle—and then you see to it that it is hammered all over the outside. And *voilà:* you increase the strength

Continued from preceding page

of the metal without increasing the weight, not to mention adding an attractive leaflike pattern on the surface of the pan. What you lose in adding the hammered finish is the wonderful, perfectly flat bottom of these classic pans, so that they sit less closely on electric elements and ceramic ranges than an unhammered pot would. (Some manufacturers make a pan which is beaten only on the bottom, but we feel that the gain in strength is too slight to justify the sacrifice of a flat bottom surface.) This pan comes in six sizes, ranging in capacity from 1½ pints to 4½ quarts; the weight of each, like the quality, is substantial. And yes, you can buy a lid for your pan: see 6.103.

ALTERNATIVES TO TIN LININGS FOR COPPER

There are copper pans which have linings of metals other than tin; but before we show them to you, it occurs to us that we might discuss why copper pans must have a lining in the first place. After all, aluminum, steel, and even rust-prone cast iron can be used uncoated. But copper, it seems, reacts with certain substances in common foods to produce verdigris, a poisonous greenish substance; and although perhaps only relatively few have been killed by this poison, it can make you very, very sick; and so copper cookware is always lined with a harmless metal. Tin is the lining of choice, but it is not the only solution. Here are the alternatives: First, steel, which is expensive; then stainless steel, which diminishes the conductivity of the copper; then aluminum, which has its own (nonpoisonous) ways of reacting with certain foods. Then why use these metals? Because the cost of retinning is not small, and the process must be repeated, at some inconvenience, every few years. For our money, no other lining is as good as tin—except possibly for the silver lining of such pots as 6.39—but you should know that not everyone agreed with us on this point.

Silver-lined Copper Saucepan   6.39

Heavy-gauge copper with silver lining, stainless-steel handle; 7¾" diam.; 3¾" deep; 2½-qt. capacity.
$100.00 pan only

Once again, the silver lining (see 6.16) which, we insist, is not less practical than tin, being less fragile, longer lasting, and able to withstand higher temperatures than the more plebeian metal. But we don't pretend that anyone would pay the price of silver if it were not that it makes a simply smashing surface and if this copper and silver pan designed by Georg Jensen were not, in fact, handsome enough to serve as a presentation pan. We have criticisms—the stainless-steel handle is impossible to hold without developing blisters, the overhang of the separately available lid (see 6.90) permits vapor to run down the outside of the pan, and the pot would be an unforgivably expensive utensil for cooking your beans and rice. But expressing our reservations is a little like wondering whether Robert Redford is good to his mother: beauty is beauty and should be enjoyed for its own sake. This stunning pan has a pronged stainless-steel handle, holds 2½ quarts, and is meant to be brought to the table.

Bi-Metal Saucepan   6.40

Heavy-gauge copper, with heavy-gauge stainless-steel interior and handle; 7½" diam.; 4" deep; 2½-qt. capacity. Also avail. with capacity of 1½, 4, 5, 7, 12, 21, 34, 49½, or 61½ qts.
$57.00

There used to be a vogue in this country for stainless-steel pans which had a coating of copper washed onto the bottom; a nice idea, but not functional in the quality which was produced. Here is what the makers of those pots should have been aiming for: a complete stainless-steel inner pan bonded to a complete copper outer pan, and fitted with a stainless-steel handle. The copper provides excellent heat diffusion and the stainless steel makes for ease of cleaning and prevents interaction between the food and the copper. Obviously good, say, for making sauces which are bound with eggs. Now, stainless steel is the least sensitive of the metals used to line copper pans, and the finished product is certainly enormously heavy, but this Bi-Metal cookware is used with no problems by restaurant chefs, who like its strength, stability, and good proportions. Separate stainless-steel lids are available—see 6.94. These pans come in 9 sizes holding from 1½ quarts to 61½ quarts—the last is not your run-of-the-mill solution to poaching an egg.

The gluttonous Emperor Heliogabalus offered huge rewards to cooks who invented new sauces. But there was a catch—if the sauce did not please him, he kept them in confinement until they had produced one that did.

ALUMINUM SAUCEPANS

Aluminum conducts heat nearly as well as copper; aluminum is light and was, until recently, quite inexpensive. It has, as we know, certain drawbacks: it can be corroded by both acids and bases in certain foods, which cause its surface to pit, and interaction between the metal and foods cooked in it can cause "off" flavors and discoloration. There have been more or less successful attempts to solve this problem by means of special finishes—see, for instance, 6.46—but the problems of using pure aluminum and aluminum alloys are not insurmountable, and in most kitchens aluminum does the journeyman jobs. Which *doesn't* mean that you should run out to your five-and-ten-cent store and buy a range of pans; as a matter of fact, the chances are that the manufacturer of those very same dime-store pans makes a much better line of products which can be bought in housewares departments. There is a disconcertingly wide range of quality in aluminum pans: generally speaking, the gauge or thickness determines the quality, and gauge is represented by numbers in an inverse series—thus, 8-gauge aluminum is thicker than 20-gauge. In the pans we show you you will see a range of design—at one extreme is a pot which, save for the color of the metal, could be of the finest copper, and at the other are utensils of the dullest commercial appearance. All of them, however, are of good quality.

Hammered Aluminum Saucepan 6.42

Heavy-gauge hammered aluminum with black-coated cast-aluminum handle; 7¼" diam.; 4" deep; 2½-qt. capacity. Also avail. with capacity of ¾, 1, 1½, 3, 4, or 5 qts.
$32.50

Quick: Look at the picture and say what the saucepan is made of. Wrong. It's not copper, but heavy-gauge aluminum, hammered and highly polished on the outside. This is easily the best and most attractive of the aluminum saucepans. Imported from France by Lamalle, it is made by the same manufacturer who produced the hammered aluminum sauteuse (6.35). Thick enough to cook well, light enough for the cook's comfort, it's not for making egg or wine sauces (again, an aluminum handicap), but it's ready to do everything else in your kitchen. Notice the wonderful black-coated cast-aluminum handle, securely riveted on; we wish you could feel its combination of light weight and unbendable strength.

Banded Aluminum Saucepan 6.41

Heavy-gauge aluminum with cast-aluminum handles; 8" diam.; 5¼" deep; 4-qt. capacity. Also avail. with capacity of 1½, 2, or 5 qts.
$33.00

We have selected several heavy-gauge aluminum saucepans. Basically, they all involve simple, straight-sided shapes, proportionately wider or narrower, with long, securely-riveted cast-aluminum handles. Styling plays a part only in this example and the next (6.42). Here the Norwegians have strapped inch-wide bands of aluminum to the top and bottom perimeters of the saucepan, giving the no-nonsense of professional aluminum cookware definite éclat. The bands have been emery-rubbed to contrast with the satin finish of the rest of the pan. In this line, the saucepans are slightly wider than they are high, a median between the narrow 6.44 and shallow 6.45, and good for general cooking. The heavy, flat bottoms are extra thick and, in conjunction with the even heat distribution characteristic of aluminum, are an especial deterrent to scorching problems. Well-fitting lids are included with each pan. There are 4 sizes available, ranging from 1½ to 5 quarts in capacity.

Saucepan of a Roman type, found in Scotland.

Grimod de la Reynière, the pseudonymous French editor of the nineteenth-century Almanach des Gourmands, *who also wrote books of advice for hosts, is emhatic on the subject of sauces: "Without sauces a dinner were as bare as a house that has been levied on by the officers of the sheriff."*

Nest of Aluminum Saucepans 6.43

Medium-gauge aluminum with cast-aluminum handles; set of four with diams. of 4¾″, 5½″, 6¼″, and 8″; capacities of ¾, 1¼, 1¾, and 3½ qts.

$15.00

A different quality entirely, but not to be discounted, is this set of medium-gauge polished aluminum saucepans from France. They are better than most American pans of equivalent weight and are very attractive, relatively inexpensive, firmly made in rather thin metal, and have cast-aluminum handles. And although they won't give food the protection needed during long cooking, still and all there are nice touches in the pouring spout, in the doubly thick bottom, and in the riveted handle. Let's face it—we don't spend every minute in the kitchen making fine sauces. Sometimes we boil an egg or heat milk for baby bottles, or we rapidly warm up the remains of last night's soup. For all such tasks, and for cooking frozen vegetables, this nest of four pans, from 4¾″ to 8″ in diameter and holding from 3 cups to 3½ quarts, will be eminently useful.

QUENELLES MOUSSELINE DE BROCHET—POACHED PIKE MOUSSE DUMPLINGS

To serve 8 to 10

9 tablespoons unsalted butter, softened, plus 2 tablespoons unsalted butter, cut into ½-inch bits
½ cup cold water
Salt
½ cup all-purpose flour
1 pound skinned pike fillets, cut into 2-inch pieces
1 whole egg
2 egg whites
¾ cup heavy cream, chilled
¼ teaspoon ground nutmeg, preferably freshly grated
⅛ teaspoon freshly ground white pepper
Sauce Nantua [following 6.53]

With a pastry brush, spread 1 tablespoon of the softened butter over the bottom and sides of a flat-bottomed dish about 4 inches in diameter.

In a heavy 1-quart saucepan, bring the water, 2 tablespoons of butter bits and a pinch of salt to a boil over high heat, stirring occasionally. As soon as the butter has melted, remove the pan from the heat and pour in the flour. Beat vigorously with a wooden spoon for a few seconds until the mixture (known as a *panade*) is smooth. Then return to moderate heat, and still beating vigorously, cook until the *panade* is thick enough to pull away from the bottom and sides of the pan into a solid mass. Spoon the *panade* into the buttered dish, spreading it evenly. Cover with a piece of buttered wax paper and refrigerate until thoroughly chilled.

Meanwhile, purée the fish in the jar of an electric blender, 5 or 6 pieces at a time, or put it through the finest blade of a food grinder. As it is puréed, transfer the fish to a bowl. When all the fillets have been blended or ground, add 6 tablespoons of softened butter, a few tablespoonfuls at a time, beating vigorously with a wooden spoon. Refrigerate for at least 30 minutes.

Then transfer the *panade* to a deep chilled bowl and, one at a time, beat in the whole egg and the egg whites. When all of the eggs have been absorbed, beat in the puréed fish a little at a time. Then force the mixture through the finest disc of a food mill into a clean bowl set in a pot of crushed ice or ice and water. Beating constantly, add the cream a tablespoon at a time. Beat in the nutmeg, pepper and 1½ teaspoons salt. Cover with foil or plastic wrap and chill for at least 30 minutes.

Spread the remaining 2 tablespoons of butter evenly over the bottom and sides of a heavy 12-inch sauté pan. Bring two 1½- to 2-quart saucepans half filled with water to a boil over high heat.

To shape each *quenelle*, fill a soupspoon generously with the fish mixture. Dip another soupspoon into one pan of boiling water and invert it over the first spoon to mold the fish mixture into an oval shape. Then use the second spoon to push the *quenelle* gently into the buttered skillet.

When all the *quenelles* have been shaped, pour the second pan of boiling water down the sides of the skillet and add 1 teaspoon of salt. Cover the pan at once and poach over low heat for 10 minutes, or until the *quenelles* feel firm when pressed lightly with a finger. With a slotted spoon, carefully transfer the *quenelles* to a heated platter. Pour the

sauce Nantua over them and serve.

NOTE: If you wish to prepare the *quenelles* in advance, you may transfer them to ice water as soon as they are poached. Let them cool completely and then transfer them to a dampened towel spread out on a jelly-roll pan. Cover with plastic wrap or foil and refrigerate until ready to serve. To reheat them, bring 1 quart of water to a simmer in a 2-quart saucepan, drop in the *quenelles* and simmer for 3 or 4 minutes.

(From CLASSIC FRENCH COOKING (Foods of the World Series), by Craig Claiborne, Pierre Franey, and the Editors of Time-Life Books. Copyright © 1970 by Time, Inc. Reprinted by permission of Time-Life Books.)

Tall Aluminum Saucepan 6.44

Heavy-gauge aluminum with tinned-steel handle; 8½″ diam.; 6½″ deep; 6½-qt. capacity. Also avail. with capacity of 1½, 2½, 4½, or 8½ qts.

$35.65

Now shift your point of view. We are talking no longer of pans for fine sauces, or of lightweight pans in which we boil a little water to dissolve gelatin, but rather of restaurant ware: pots in which you can cook large quantities of food for a long time. This pan, made by Commercial Aluminum, is of heavy-duty professional quality and is not particularly beautiful, but if you are accustomed to giving large parties, it is what you need. It is of the best quality you can get in aluminum: food cooked in this pan will never scorch, the pot will never burn out, and it can sit on a burner for hours, cooking efficiently with the heat barely turned on. The junction of sides and bottom is rounded for easy cleaning, and the bottom is of thicker metal than the sides. The pan is straight-sided and very deep, with a tinned-steel handle attached by three heavy rivets; there is a flat lid (6.93), available separately, which sits firmly on the edge. It comes in five sizes, holding from 1½ to 8½ quarts. You will love this excellent pot for its soul, not its beauty.

Large Shallow Aluminum Saucepan   6.45

Heavy-gauge aluminum with tinned-steel handle; 12" diam.; 4½" deep; 8½-qt. capacity. Also avail. with capacity of 2½, 5, or 15 qts.

$37.50

Remember the brazier? This is the same pan in another shape—a brazier with one long handle, designed for the American trade. Like the brazier, it is meant for browning meat and then reducing the liquid in which it cooks. And also like the brazier, it is strictly utilitarian, designed not at all for beauty. Wide and heavy, it has rather low sides, a bottom even thicker than the quarter-inch metal of the rest of the pan, and a tinned-steel handle secured to the pot by three rivets. Commercial Aluminum, the manufacturer, also makes a range of lids in sizes to fit these pots (see 6.93). This is basically restaurant ware and *large:* a pan to use when you are cooking curried chicken or jambalaya for a crowd, and are intending to transfer the finished dish to beautiful earthenware bowls for serving.

Aluminum Saucepan with Calphalon Finish   6.46

Heavy-gauge aluminum with Calphalon finish, tinned-steel handle; 7" diam.; 3⅞" deep; 2½-qt. capacity. Also avail. with capacity of 1½, 4½, 6½, or 8½ qts.

$20.80

Yet another variation on the theme of restaurant ware, this time a heavy-duty professional-quality saucepan with straight sides and a tinned-steel handle. But this one has a bonus, the finish called Calphalon that we have already described (6.33). This gives the pan a satiny dark-gray, virtually stick-free surface which can't be damaged by stirring or scraping because it is integral with the metal. (You'll remember we advise seasoning these pans before their first use—oil your pan and heat it gently, then let it cool, wash and dry it, and your pan is ready.) Good enough, and the finish is a pleasant surprise for whoever is washing the pots, but in addition—and more important—Calphalon eliminates the problem of interaction between aluminum and food; if the food can't damage the aluminum, then the aluminum can't damage the food. So good is it that we hope the manufacturer distributes its Calphalon-finished pans more widely. You can, by the way, choose this pan in any of five useful sizes holding from 1½ to 8½ quarts, and the manufacturer offers lids to fit (6.93).

SUGO DI CARNE—MEAT SAUCE

Almost any bony pork parts, such as spareribs and neck bones, may be used with or instead of pig's feet and pork chops. Sweet Italian sausages may also be substituted.

4 cups fresh or canned ripe tomatoes
½ cup olive oil or 1 cup cubed salt pork
1 pig's foot or 1 large pork chop
1 shin of veal or shank of veal, if available
¾ pound chicken wings, necks or backs
1 beef soupbone
¾ pound chuck, preferably with bone
1 onion stuck with 4 cloves
2 whole garlic cloves
1 teaspoon whole crushed peppercorns or freshly ground pepper to taste
½ cup dry white wine
1 tablespoon dried fresh basil or 6 fresh basil leaves
1 can (6-ounce) tomato paste
Salt to taste
2 tablespoons butter

Heat the oil or render the salt pork in a large deep skillet [6.46] or in a kettle and add the pig's foot, veal, chicken, beef bone and chuck. Cook, stirring with a wooden spoon, until meat starts to brown. Add the onion and garlic and continue cooking until meat is *thoroughly* browned. Add the peppercorns, wine and basil, and continue cooking until the wine evaporates. Set the kettle aside.

If fresh tomatoes are used, core and peel them. Work fresh or canned tomatoes through a sieve or strainer to remove the seeds, which give a sauce a bitter taste. Bring the tomatoes gradually to a boil. Add the tomato paste and salt. Stir to blend and add to the meat and bones. Add the butter and partially cover. Simmer gently for 2 hours, stirring all around the bottom frequently, taking care that the sauce does not scorch or burn. (If it is not stirred, it will burn.) Yield: Enough for 2 pounds of pasta.

(From ITALIAN FAMILY COOKING, by Edward Giobbi, illustrated by Cham, Lisa, and Gena Giobbi. Copyright © 1971 by Edward Giobbi. Reprinted by permission of Random House, Inc.)

Magnalite Saucepan 6.47

Cast magnesium-aluminum alloy with phenolic-resin handle; 8½″ diam.; 4½″ deep; 4-qt. capacity. Also avail. with capacity of 1½, 2, or 3 qts.

**$26.00   1 qt. $19.50▲   2 qt. $22.00▲
3 qt. $24.50▲**

The Magnalite saucepan is the most successful of the American aluminum pots. Some of our experts hate the way it looks, while others rather like its honest, shiny-faced plainness. It is made of an alloy of magnesium and aluminum and is polished to a high-gloss surface which is somewhat less vulnerable than plain aluminum to the insults of acid foods. Further, the material, though thick, weighs less than aluminum of the same gauge. A good tight seal exists between the cover and the pan, reminding us that these pots were designed in the 1930s when there was a vogue—Depression-created—for waterless cooking. In this method, as the food is heated the liquid in it evaporates, forming a vapor seal and bonding the lid even more firmly to the pan: after long slow cooking, it sometimes requires a bit of a tug to get the cover off. Advocates of waterless cooking claim that fewer vitamins are lost to the cooking liquid and, therefore, fewer nutrients are poured down the sink. In four sizes, holding from 1½ to 4 quarts, this saucepan needn't be limited to any one kind of cooking: it is as versatile as an aluminum pot can be.

The Prince de Soubise, like so many nobles of the eighteenth-century French court, was an accomplished amateur cook. The delicate soubise sauce of puréed onions and Béchamel sauce (which in its turn was named after another noble) is one of the many preparations which bear the names of aristocratic French families or individuals: Richelieu, Condé, Orléans, d'Uxelles.

Cast-Aluminum Pan from Dansk 6.48

Cast aluminum with heat-resistant plastic handle; 7½″ diam.; 4¾″ deep; 3-qt. capacity. Also avail. with capacity of 1¼ or 2 qts.

$29.95

Back from the world of the leviathans and the plain-Janes, back to good looks: this pan, looking a little like an Art Deco object and a little like a pressure cooker, is nonetheless beautiful. We love good design, and we would like you to admire with us this superb 3-quart cast-aluminum saucepan from Dansk. It is well-balanced, handsome, with a good heat-resistant plastic handle heat-welded to the pan and a metal knob attached to the lid by a gasket that prevents the heat from passing between pan and cover. There is not a positive seal between the lid and the pot because of the two pouring lips, one of which is spanned by a tooth-like strainer on the cover: a good device for draining off liquids. A unique pot, very beautifully designed.

RISOTTO PIEMONTAISE

Serves 6

1 cup rice (any unconverted rice, or rice that is not par-boiled)
2 tablespoons sweet butter
1 medium onion, peeled and sliced very thin (1 cup)
1 teaspoon real saffron pistils
2 cups chicken broth
½ cup dry white wine
½ teaspoon freshly ground white pepper
Salt, depending on the saltiness of the chicken broth

Melt the butter in a heavy pot with a cover, and add the onion. Cook on low heat for 3 to 4 minutes, stirring with a wooden spoon. Do not allow the onion to take on any color. Add the rice and mix well so that all the grains are coated with the butter. Add the saffron, broth, wine, pepper, and salt and bring to a boil, stirring to avoid scorching. Reduce heat to a very low temperature, cover the pot, and let cook for 25 minutes.

²/₃ cup good grated Swiss cheese
2 tablespoons grated Parmesan cheese
1 tablespoon sweet butter

Five minutes before serving, add the above ingredients to the rice and mix in with a fork. The rice mixture will become quite sticky and mushy, similar to potatoes, but quite delicious.

(From JACQUES PEPIN: A FRENCH CHEF COOKS AT HOME, by Jacques Pépin. Copyright © 1975 by Jacques Pépin. Reprinted by permission of Simon & Schuster.)

STAINLESS-STEEL SAUCEPANS

Stainless steel is steel to which has been added nickel, chrome, or other elements, producing an alloy with an attractive and impervious surface that will take and hold a high polish, that will not rust or corrode, and that discolors only when sorely abused. So far as use is concerned, it is the negative image of aluminum, having virtues where aluminum has flaws, and flaws where aluminum has virtues. Stainless steel has a wonderful surface which never interacts with food—you can make a Hollandaise or a sauce espagnole in it without a qualm. On the other hand, it has abominably poor heat conduction, allowing food to scorch and stick when another pan would hold an even heat. That is why we seldom see stainless steel used alone in cooking pots—why a number of different methods of lessening its liabilities by combining it with other metals have evolved.

SOLUTIONS TO THE STEEL PROBLEM

There are in existence, but terribly difficult to find, pans with a substantial copper layer covering the bottom and extending part way up the sides. Wonderful, but we might as well be talking about unhomogenized milk and Good Clean Fun: they're hard to find. The second solution to the heat-diffusion problem is to make the entire pan of a conductive metal—aluminum or mild steel—pressed between two thin layers of stainless steel: this is not a bad solution. But the most common way of making an acceptable stainless-steel saucepan is to add either a thick layer or a sandwich of heavy-gauge aluminum to the bottom of the pan. This goes far toward eliminating the problem of hot spots and resultant burning; in a saucepan—which, by definition, is meant to hold sauces—you can also rely on the liquid to finish the diffusion of the heat that is begun by the conductive aluminum. And although stainless steel retains heat quite well and will not cool off as soon as the flame goes off, this is no drawback unless you are making a sauce that involves eggs.

Windsor Saucepan 6.50

Stainless steel with mild-steel core; 8″ diam.; 4″ deep; 2½-qt. capacity. Also avail. 5-qt. capacity.
$19.00

This is by no means a beautiful pot; the finish is dull, the design undistinguished. Why, then, is it so expensive? If you could feel the weight and try it out on your stove you would understand that it is an elegant solution to the problem of using stainless steel in pots. The entire body has been built of a combination of materials which the manufacturer calls **Tri-Ply**: layers of stainless steel on either side of a layer of mild steel. Now, mild steel, used by itself, is a difficult material, liable to rust and absorb flavors; but it has the quality, which stainless steel does not possess, of distributing heat evenly and quickly. Like a perfect marriage, then, each partner provides what the other lacks. The shape of this pan, by the way, is called Windsor; such pans are also made of other materials. It is a pan rarely used outside restaurant kitchens, but it has many admirers nonetheless. Note that its flaring shape allows a stirring spoon or whisk to get down to the bottom of the pot with a minimum of difficulty. For a lid to fit this intriguing pan, see 6.94.

Paderno Saucepan 6.51

Stainless steel with aluminum sandwich; 9½″ diam.; 6″ deep; 7-qt. capacity. Also avail. with capacity of 2¼, 4¼, or 11½ qts.
$80.00

Every time we come to a **Paderno** pot we could weep: they're smashingly designed, the very best professional line in stainless steel that we have seen, and they are all but impossible to find in this country. This saucepan is constructed of extra-heavy stainless steel with a heavy aluminum sandwich bottom. The beauty of this saucepan comes entirely from its quality, which makes it far better than the many popular pans in this metal which are all over the place. If you can find a Paderno pot—or a whole range of them—buy it—or them. (And look at the same time for lids to fit—see 6.100.) We can imagine nothing more satisfying to own. Here, a simple saucepan 9½″ in diameter, with sides of gleaming brushed stainless steel and with a narrow, highly polished ridge around the top edge. Simple, and simply stunning.

Finnish Stainless-Steel Saucepan 6.52

Stainless steel with aluminum-clad bottom; 7¼″ diam.; 4¾″ deep; 3-qt. capacity. Also avail. with capacity of 1½ or 2 qts.
$21.95

Saucepan for the 21st century? Will we still be cooking our own food by then? This unorthodox design from Sarpaneva exposes mirror surfaces of stainless steel...verticals, horizontals and perfect circles...gleaming geometry. In this case, stainless does not mean smudgeless. This piece of cookware must be babied, as you would fine silver. Every fingermark shows, and any abrasive cleaners or cloths will irrevocably mar the finish. We were pleased with its top-of-the-stove performance. The heavy aluminum-clad bottom gets the heat going evenly. The lid fits well. You must use a mitt of some kind with the handle, for both comfort and protection. Use the enormous cut-outs to hang the saucepan and lid out of the way.

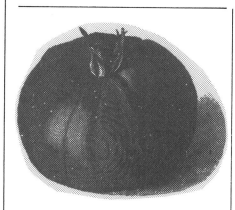

Farberware Saucepan 6.53

Stainless steel with aluminum-clad bottom, phenolic-resin handle and knob; 6¾″ diam.; 2¾″ deep; 1½-qt. capacity. Also avail. with capacity of 1, 2, 2½, 3, or 4 qts.

$13.99

We said it before and we'll say it again—for the price, Farberware is the best quality stainless steel with aluminum bottoms. Here we show you the smallish 1½-quart, all-purpose saucepan, which you can use for everything, from warming up last night's vegetables, to reducing the vinegar and herbs for your dollop of béarnaise to go on tonight's steak. The pan comes in other sizes too, one smaller, and several larger. If it had cleaner lines, we might recommend a "set." Anytime you buy a Farberware pan, equip yourself with a Phillips screwdriver, the kind that matches the four-notched screw head in the handle of the Farberware pan. We ruined a couple of paring-knife tips before we got smart and bought a screwdriver to tighten the forever-loosening handles on our Farberware pans. The saucepans come with matching flattened onion-dome Farberware lids.

SAUCE NANTUA

8 tablespoons (1 stick) unsalted butter
2 teaspoons chopped onion
3 tablespoons flour
1½ cups milk
⅓ cup clam juice
¼ cup heavy cream
⅛ teaspoon ground nutmeg
⅛ teaspoon white pepper
⅛ teaspoon thyme
3 ounces raw shrimp, with shells
2 teaspoons tomato paste
Salt, to taste

Melt 3 tablespoons of the butter in a heavy saucepan over low heat; add onions and cook for 2 minutes. Remove pan from heat and gradually stir in the flour. Return the pan to low heat and, constantly stirring, cook for about 2 minutes longer.

Combine milk, clam juice and cream; gradually add to butter and flour mixture, beating with a wire whisk until the ingredients are thoroughly blended. Add the nutmeg, white pepper and thyme. Increase the heat and, still stirring, cook until the sauce comes to a boil and thickens. Reduce heat to low, simmer for about 10 minutes. Set this white sauce to one side.

Wash shrimp. Chop the unshelled shrimp coarsely and sauté in 5 tablespoons butter until just pink and opaque. Place shrimp and butter in container of electric blender; blend on high speed for 30 seconds.

Force this shrimp-butter purée through a fine sieve with the back of a wooden spoon. Chill.

Before serving, bring the white sauce to a simmer; remove the pan from the heat and whisk in the shrimp butter, a few tablespoons at a time. Add the tomato paste and taste to see if any salt is needed.

A Victorian gravy pot, designed to extract meat essences.

Cuisinart Saucepan 6.54

Stainless steel with stainless-steel and aluminum sandwich, metal and compressed-wood handle; 7″ diam.; 3½″ deep; 2-qt. capacity. Also avail. with capacity of ⅔, 1, 1½, or 3 qts.

$28.00 ▲

This is the year that everyone wants the products of Cuisinarts; that firm's output has become what the fashion industry calls a "Ford," the dress that everyone is buying. And with good reason: witness this sleek stainless-steel saucepan with a rim that makes for easy pouring and a thick sandwich of aluminum and stainless steel on the bottom which is so finely made that it stays flat at any temperature: the perfect solution for cooking on electric stoves. (If you want to understand the construction of the Cuisinart pot bottom, look at our discussion in Chapter 6.) The metal handle of this pan is sandwiched between two layers of compressed wood and the whole thing is held together by three rivets; remember to watch out for the heat of those rivets if you should try to lift the pot without using a potholder. The same wood is used for a simple knob to top the lid, which is available separately (6.95); both handle and knob can withstand oven temperatures up to 375 F. There is a mirror finish on the entire outside, and the pot, although heavy, is so exceptionally well-balanced that it feels lighter than its weight. It comes in five sizes, with capacities ranging from ⅔ of a quart to 3 quarts.

The first version of the ubiquitous tomato sauce was not enthusiastically received when a chef at the Spanish court served it to an Englishman in the late sixteenth century: "In Spaine and these hot Regions, they use to eat the Apples of Love prepared and boiled with pepper, salt, and oyle; but they yeeld very little nourishment to the body."

The many-talented nineteenth-century chef Alexis Soyer published several books, among them a personal view of the cookery of the ancient world, The Pantropheon, *issued in 1853. From it comes this illustration of a "stockpot with ladle and cullender."*

ENAMELED-IRON SAUCEPANS

As a material for cookware, enamel cannot be compared with other materials, being in fact a mediation between metal and food. The enamel prevents the cast-iron core of the pan from rusting, or an aluminum core, when it is present, from turning a tomato sauce or other acid food muddy. In cooking quality it is not so good as a cast-iron pan; but as its main limitations are its inability to sauté and its lack of rapid cooking, neither of these is a major drawback in saucemaking.

Enamel pots are either warmly colored, hearty, and evocative of the metal on which the finish rests, or else they are terribly pure, Alp-like, with no visual reference to their dark cores, and plainly ready to make a porridge or to coddle eggs for an invalid. It is true that enamel makes a surface of special cleanliness: its lack of porosity creates the perfect environment for cooking eggs and delicate sauces. Clorox—well washed out afterwards, of course—cleans any blemishes on the perfectly white escutcheon. Remember that James Beard recommends that you keep a pan which is consecrated solely to boiling eggs, and that only plain porcelain and glass are as good as enamelware for the purpose of cooking foods which are easily damaged.

If you want to understand enamel, look at the discussion of earthenware in Chapter 7, and then consider enamel as a thin, thin layer of vitrified pottery material laid over the surface of metal. Sprayed on, the raw enamel coat covers the surface of the pan, sinking into the pores of the cast metal. Then a high-heat firing vitrifies the coating, making a fusion so complete that the finished pot becomes highly chip-resistant: one manufacturer claims that it would be easier to chip a bathtub than one of his pans, but, then, you are less likely to drop a bathtub on the floor. "Vitrified," of course, means turned to glass, and that is precisely what this enamel is: a sturdy glass finish that is almost inseparable from a heavy pot. You use such pots without fear of their rusting, or absorbing flavors during long slow cooking, or transmitting the ghostly essence of garlic from one dish to another and more delicate food you may cook at another time.

Le Creuset Saucepan (Mijotin) 6.55

Enameled cast iron; 7¼" diam.; 3" deep; 1¾-qt. capacity.
$24.00 ▲

Here we have enamelware expressing its basic metal—heavy cast iron. A tubby little saucepan with a short handle and a black knob on its lid, this has a brilliant blue, flame, yellow, or spice-brown glaze on the exterior. The black interior looks like raw cast iron but is in fact enameled just as much as the outside; because the interior is less highly fired, however, it lacks a high glaze and thus is a more efficient vehicle for sautéing foods or for browning meat to begin a stew. The pot, holding 1¾ quarts, has two pouring lips, one on either side; there are corresponding curves in the cover, so a good seal is created. The short handle and lack of extraneous materials make this a good pot for starting food on the range top and then stashing away in the oven.

Ancient bronze pot, from Alexis Soyer's Pantropheon.

CLASSIC HOLLANDAISE

Makes 2 cups

4 egg yolks
2 tablespoons water
3 sticks (1½ cups) sweet butter, melted and hot
Salt
Freshly ground white pepper
Cayenne
1 tablespoon lemon juice, strained

Combine the yolks and water in the top of a double boiler (not aluminum). Beat for 1 minute with a whip; place over simmering water, or on a "flame-tamer" [6.61] over medium heat. Using a wire whip, beat vigorously for 8 to 10 minutes or until the mixture is thick and creamy. Take care not to curdle the eggs. When perfectly combined, you can see the bottom of the pan between strokes and the mixture will never be so hot you can't dip your finger into it.

Remove from the heat and place the pan on a damp cloth to keep it from turning as you beat. Add the hot butter in dribbles—beating constantly. When all the butter has been added, season with salt, pepper and cayenne to taste. Finally, stir in the lemon juice. Keep warm in a pan of tepid water, not hot or your sauce will separate. Hollandaise is always served lukewarm or tepid.

(From THE GREAT COOKS COOKBOOK, by The Good Cooking School. Copyright © 1974 by The Good Cooking School, Inc. Reprinted by permission of Ferguson/Doubleday.)

Copco Saucepan   6.56

Enameled cast iron with wood handle; 8″ diam.; 3½″ deep; 2-qt. capacity. Also avail. with capacity of 1 or 3 qts.

$33.00 ▲ $28.00 ▲ $38.00 ▲

Curiouser and curiouser: the burnt orange enameled exterior of this pan makes you expect rabbit stew or onion soup within, but when the lid is lifted what you see is a clean white enamel which would not be amiss for making a fine Hollandaise. The pot has a well-turned wooden handle with a metal tip, and there is a flat-ground bottom to assist in heat diffusion. And the manufacturer, recognizing the heaviness of his product, has added a secondary handle to help you lift it, even though this pan comes in only 1-, 2-, and 3-quart sizes. It is available in several colors: yellow, blue, brown, red, and white, all with the characteristic white interior.

White Arabia Saucepan   6.57

Enameled steel with wood handle; 6¼″ diam.; 4¼″ high; 1½-qt. capacity.
$28.50

When we were children, some of us were lucky enough to have grandmothers who cooked delicious things in white enamel pots, and perhaps that is why this little white enamel saucepan seems to promise treats both mild and nourishing: custards or bits of chicken gently stewed, all made to tempt the appetite of a child or an invalid. Here we have creamy white enamel laid over light steel in a small round pot with straight sides and with a wooden cylinder for a handle. There is a well-fitting lid which has six tiny holes, provided either for ventilation or for straining off liquids; the bottom has been enameled black for heat conduction. Holding 1½ quarts, the pan is 6¼″ across, and comes in brown and yellow as well as white. This is a pan in which the enamel makes the point: it would be perfect for cooking anything which needs gentle handling, such as sauces bound with egg, or puddings which begin with scalding milk.

Porcelaine de Paris Saucepans   6.58

Porcelain and chromed steel; 4½″ diam.; 2½″ deep; 1-pint capacity. Also avail. with capacity of ¾, 1, 1½, or 2¼ qts.
$38.00

Perhaps we'll be able to convince you that you can really set this fragile porcelain saucepan over a direct flame; on the other hand, maybe you believe that such a deed would be an altogether outrageous desecration of a ravishingly beautiful piece of china. But look at it this way: the manufacturer has made saucepans out of the stuff, saucepans with real handles and lids and pouring spouts, and he made them so expensively that they were surely meant for more than display. And it is really not such a long step from saucepans of porcelain enamel—like the preceding Arabia pot

—to saucepans of porcelain, and, as you have already seen, to stovetop pans of glass. The fact is that these pans are made of so beautiful a china, of such a high quality, that they would enhance the quality of anything you cook which requires gentle and respectful care of the ingredients. But of course they require certain care themselves; just remember to keep the flame low and to be sure that they are never set down empty over the fire. Each pan is encircled with a strip of metal which then extends in a long narrow loop that holds the porcelain handle. There is a lid to match each of the five sizes of saucepans, which hold from 1 pint to 2¼ quarts; the lids are available separately (6.97) and the pots and lids can be bought as a set, complete with wrought-iron racks for both. We show them to you in the Vieux Chine pattern: we don't expect to have to work at convincing you that these pots are very beautiful.

If you have run out of ideas for sauces, you might try this recipe of F. Scott Fitzgerald's for Turkey with Whiskey Sauce: "This recipe is for a party of four. Obtain a gallon of whiskey, and allow it to age for several hours. Then serve, allowing one quart for each guest. The next day the turkey should be added, little by little, constantly stirring and basting."

Fitzgerald, The Crack-Up [including The Note-Books], New Directions, New York, 1956

Gense Glass Saucepan   6.59

Heat-resistant glass; 5½″ diam.; 4¼″ deep; 1¼-qt. capacity.
$29.50

Continued from preceding page

This is the pan in which you can make the Hollandaise and then bring it to the table. (Gasps of admiration; cries of disbelief.) Made of hand-blown glass, it can be used on both electric and gas ranges with an asbestos pad, or it can be set in a pot of water to make an improvised bain-marie. It is, moreover, guaranteed to be ovenproof. Measuring 5½″ in diameter and 4¼″ in depth, it has a wide, flat handle, and there is a pouring spout exactly 90 degrees away from the handle. Notwithstanding its delicate appearance and beauty, it is stronger than ordinary glass and will take kindly to dishwashers. A limited-use pot, and a handsome one.

"But still now it is 1939 and war-time, well it was just beginning and everything was agitating and one day we were with our friends the Daniel-Rops they are our neighbors in the country and he was expecting a call to go to Paris and the telephone rang. He went quickly to answer it, he was away some time and we were all anxious. He came back. We said what is it. He said the quenelles the Mère Mollard was making for us have gone soft. Quenelles, well quenelles are the special dish of this country made of flour and eggs and shredded fish or chicken and pounded by the hour and then rolled and then hardened in the cold air and then cooked in a sauce and they are good.

"We all laughed we regretted the quenelles, but it was French of her with a son at the front to be worried about her quenelles."

Gertrude Stein, Paris France, *Liveright paperbound edition, 1970*

Double Boilers and Bains-Marie

In both the double boiler and the bain-marie, water is used to mediate mechanically between the container of food and the heat. We have seen, in looking at other pots, that there are other means by which this mediation can be accomplished: the aluminum sandwiches in the bottom of stainless-steel pots are one example, and the Flame-Tamer (6.61) is another. But water works equally well in diffusing heat, making it easier to control. That is why you melt chocolate in a double boiler: you want the heating process to be gentle (hence you use barely simmering water), and you want to be able to stop the heating process before the chocolate has scorched—and you can lift the top of the boiler away from the water at the exact instant the melting is complete.

DEFINITIONS

What is the difference between a double boiler and a bain-marie? Well, they look different, a double boiler being two ordinary pots, one made to rest snugly inside the other, while the bain-marie is most typically a shallow bath of water in which the contents of one or several tall cylindrical pots may be kept warm. But the real distinction is in function. In the double boiler, water is placed in the bottom pot and the insert is then set over it and you actually cook the contents—the scrambled eggs or custard—over the gentle heat provided by simmering or boiling water. The pans of the bain-marie, on the other hand, are filled with already completed sauces or other food and then set into a large tub filled with hot or actually simmering water. All is then kept warm in the gentle bath, an ancestor of the electrical Hotray. You can improvise a bain-marie out of a roaster and a number of small pans—just look out for sloshing. One of our experts uses a copper bain-marie of restaurant quality on her buffet table, filling each saucepan with a different type of curry and placing a huge bowl of cinnamon-flavored rice to the side.

MOVING TOWARD THE STEAMER

Then we have the double boiler or stockpot with an accessory steamer section (or a basket, for the stockpot). One double boiler (6.64) is usable in four ways—the steamer can be used separately over the base or sandwiched between the two solid pans, and the two solid pans can be used one above the other or separately. With this utensil we move in the direction of the full-fledged steamers presented in Chapter 11.

"So long ago as the time when emperors ruled in Rome, and the yellow Tiber passed through a populous and wealthy city, this utensil was extensively employed, and it is frequently mentioned by that profound culinary chemist of the ancients, Apicius. It is an open kind of vessel . . . filled with boiling or nearly boiling water; and into this water should be put all stewpans containing those in- gredients which it is desired to keep hot . . . and if the hour of dinner is uncertain in any establishment by reason of the nature of the master's business, nothing is so certain a means of preserving the flavour of all dishes as the employment of the bain marie."

Isabella Beeton, The Book of Household Management, *1861*

Metal Trivet   6.60

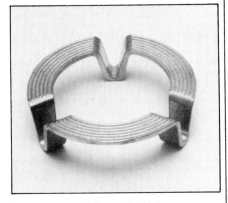

Cast aluminum; 5″ diam.; 1½″ high.
$3.00 ▲

We begin this section with neither a bain-marie nor a double boiler, but rather with a device that helps us to replace either at need: a cast-aluminum tripod stand which turns any saucepan-and-skillet combination into a bain-marie. You set the trivet in a large pan filled with water, hot or simmering, depending on what you want to keep warm, and then you place a smaller pan on the trivet, so that the water rises around its bottom and sides. The top surface of this round 5″ trivet is ridged to keep pots from slipping off; it costs next to nothing; and it is reasonably well-made out of a single piece of aluminum. All you need is a skillet, a saucepan, and this. Ingenious.

Flame-Tamer   6.61

Siliconized steel for gas ranges, chromed steel for electric ranges; 8″ diam.; ⅞″ thick.
$5.50 ▲

Using the same principle of heat regulation as Thermopane windows and thermal underwear, this Flame-Tamer from Tricolator works by maintaining a layer of air between stove burner and pot. It consists of a thick 8″ disc of steel, its top grooved to let pots sit securely—it's not unlike a silver Frisbee—and is rigidly constructed to contain a ¾″ layer of space. But the air in this space is far from the nothing we usually consider it: it is the element that modifies the potency of the fire so that you can keep coffee hot over it, can put fragile glass or earthenware casseroles on top of it, and can eliminate totally the burning and scorching of those foods for which you generally use a double boiler. Just as a double boiler intrudes a hot but not scorching liquid between the fire and your Hollandaise, the Flame-Tamer intrudes a moderating layer of air. This gadget comes in two models, one for gas ranges, one for electricity; it is sturdily made, quite heavy, and well worth having.

Gentle Cooker from France   6.62

Enameled-steel ring with chromed-steel rack, wood handle; 7½″ diam.; 2⅛″ high in lowered position; 3″ high in raised position.
$10.00

There are two sides to the story of heat regulation. You want to be able to turn a gas flame up high without having to worry about scorching your food or breaking a fragile pot, but you also want to be able to turn it down low, holding a tender simmer without having the flame go out. This contraption from France—a CuiDoux, meaning gentle cooker—performs both functions well, permitting you to raise the bottom of a porcelain or earthenware casserole well away from the danger of direct contact with the fire and also leaving plenty of

room for air to circulate beneath the pot, feeding necessary oxygen to the gas burner. In this way it is unlike the asbestos pads and the flat Flame-Tamer, which work by insulation rather than by distancing. It is a ring of heavy enameled steel pierced by three slanted openings; into each opening fits one leg of a chromed-steel, star-shaped stand. When a wooden handle is pushed to the left, those legs go high, lifting the stand a full 3″ off the stove; when it is pushed to the right, they slide down so that the stand is barely more than 2″ off the stove. A screw at the joining of handle and stand permits you to halt this elevation and make the stand secure at any height. This device is extremely well made and sensibly designed; it is not cheap, but it will protect your pots better than the familiar flat asbestos pads.

Farberware Double Boiler   6.63

Stainless steel with aluminum-clad bottom, phenolic-resin handles; base 6½″ diam., 4⅜″ deep; insert 6½″ diam., 4⅛″ deep; full height 6¼″; base capacity 2½ qts., insert capacity 2 qts.
$24.99

We can't help but feel that, with a good double boiler, you are actually getting two—or three—pots for the price of one. In this Farberware package you have the base, which is a good stainless-steel saucepan, available alone (6.53), plus a secondary pan of adequate quality (all that it lacks is an aluminum-clad bottom), which make a double boiler when they are used together. The quality is excellent, the capacity good—the bottom saucepan holds 2½ quarts and the insert, 2 quarts—and there is a nicely fitting lid. There is also a minor annoyance in the ridge which encircles the top pot in order

Continued from preceding page

to hold it snugly within the base; unfortunately, it also encircles the interior, lying in wait to trap bits of food, which are difficult to remove without using a small, hard-bristled brush. And we have to warn you about the Farberware handle, likely to loosen and really the only drawback in this really excellent product. Compare the price of this with that of similar European pans, and you may find yourself buying American.

TEJFELES TORMAMARTAS— HORSERADISH SOUR-CREAM SAUCE

About 2½ cups sauce

¼ pound grated horseradish
3 tablespoons butter
2 tablespoons flour
½ cup meat broth
½ cup milk
1 teaspoon sugar
1 teaspoon salt
1 to 2 tablespoons white vinegar
  or lemon juice
Pinch of pepper
½ cup sour cream

1. Pour ½ cup boiling water over grated horseradish. Let it stand for a couple of minutes, then drain.
2. Make a *roux* with the butter and flour. Stir, then dilute with the broth and milk. Add sugar and salt. Bring the mixture to a simmer, then let it cook over very low heat for about 5 minutes.
3. Add grated horseradish together with vinegar and pepper and cook for another 10 to 15 minutes.
4. Adjust salt and sweet and sour to your taste, with more accent on the sour.
5. Just before serving, whip in the sour cream.

(From THE CUISINE OF HUNGARY, by George Lang. Copyright © 1971 by George Lang. Reprinted by permission of Atheneum.)

Bain-marie, from L'Ecole des Cuisinières of Urbain-Dubois.

Farberware Double Boiler with Steamer   6.64

Stainless steel with aluminum-clad bottom, phenolic-resin handles; each piece 7½″ diam.; base 4¼″ deep; inserts 3⅜″ deep; full height 5⅞″; base capacity 3 qts., insert capacity 2 qts.

$33.00 ▲

Before we leave Farberware, we ought to mention another of their double-boiler combinations. For this, instead of the 2-quart saucepan, you buy the 3-quart size; then you can also choose two inserts to fit it, a short-handled upper bowl and a steamer of identical shape. In this way you wind up with a saucepan, or a double boiler, or a steamer, or all three at once: let's say you might be cooking rice in the bottom, steaming green beans in the middle, and reheating creamed chicken in the top. A triple threat.

White Enamel Double Boiler   6.65

Enameled steel with plastic knob on lid; both base and inset 6″ diam., 3″ high; overall height 5″; each piece 1½-qt. capacity.

$5.00

As ordinary as a double boiler can be, this porcelain enamel-and-steel set made by General Housewares Corporation is simple, old-fashioned, and inexpensive.

Neither steel nor enamel could be called a superior heat conductor but, since you have the water to act as insulation in any double boiler, neither the material nor the light weight of this utensil is particularly important. This boiler is ideal for heating baby food because the white enamel lets you know that the pan is thoroughly clean; it is the pan you will take down for melting chocolate, scrambling eggs, or making cocoa. The sides of the inset pan meet the bottom in a commendably gradual curve that is ideal for whisking sauces; the lid fits either pan, and the handles of both have holes for hanging. The protruding ridge on the inset pan can pose a cleaning problem, but it is a feature to be found—and tolerated—in most double boilers. Small— only 6″ in diameter—this pan is inexpensive, with a great deal of homely charm.

The ancient Greeks had double-bottomed amphorae—earthenware pots—which allowed water to be placed in the bottom part, creating a double-boiler effect when the pot was used for cooking.

Pyrex Double Boiler   6.66

Pyrex glass and stainless steel; both base and insert 6″ diam., 5¼″ deep; full height 6¾″; insert 1¼-qt. capacity, base 1½-qt. capacity.

$15.50 ▲

At last: a pan for which glass is not an interesting variation but the very best material imaginable. Clear glass is the best answer to the ever-present problem of cooking over water, the problem of knowing how the water is behaving— whether it is at too high a boil or sitting there, dead, far below a simmer, and whether it needs replenishing. Make your Hollandaise or Béarnaise in a Pyrex glass double boiler and you will not only have a wonderful nonporous surface for your pan, but you will be able to control the simmer of the water in the bottom pot and keep an eagle eye out for the slightest sign of curdling of the sauce in the insert pan. This pan comes with a nasty hairpin-shaped thing which is supposed to enable us to use it over electric stoves. We regularly use Pyrex right on the burners, but, if this makes you uncomfortable, buy an asbestos pad. Metal rings around the tops of both the base and the insert secure the comfortable glass handles. There is a nice lid with a glass knob; the insert has a 1¼-quart capacity, the base, 1½ quarts. A good product, low in cost. The handle and ring will fit a replacement pan, so don't discard them if you suffer breakage.

Copper and Ceramic Double Boiler 6.67

Copper with tin lining, brass handles, and ceramic insert; base 6¼″ diam., 3¾″ deep; insert 5¾″ diam., 4½″ deep; full height 6″; base capacity 2¼ qts., insert capacity 1¾ qts. Also avail. 1-qt. capacity.

$58.00

We gave high points to the Pyrex double boiler above; nonetheless we have to show you the classic French answer to the problem of how to cook over boiling water. In this combination there is a tinned copper bottom pan with a good brass handle and a secondary loop handle opposite it. Like almost every other traditionally designed example of this genre (and unlike, say, the Farberware boilers), the bottom pan is practically useless by itself because of the way in which the sides slant inwards: but this is a structural necessity because of the need to stabilize the weight of the extremely thick white porcelain upper pan. A flat copper lid sits loosely over the edge of the porcelain pot. We have never seen this set in anything but copper and porcelain, despite the fact that the bottom pot is never used for cooking and so could easily—and less expensively —be made of heavy-gauge aluminum. The porcelain insert is nonporous and thick enough to maintain a steady low temperature. Replacements are available if it should be broken, and it is a simple matter to release and remove the metal band which encircles it and anchors the handle, and then to put it back into place around the new bowl. This double boiler can be purchased with an insert of either 1- or 1¾-quart capacity: it weighs, we must warn you, 6 pounds in the smaller size, 10 pounds in the larger. This utensil will cost you approximately five times as much as the Pyrex double boiler but, apart from the beauty of the metal and a greater durability in the lower pan, it has no great advantage that we can see.

Aluminum Double Bain-Marie Pan 6.68

Aluminum with cast-aluminum handles, plastic knob on lid; base 5″ diam., 6″ deep; insert 5″ top diam., 4¼″ bottom diam., 7″ deep; full height 8¼″; each piece 1¾-qt. capacity.

$20.00

A compromise between a double boiler and a bain-marie, this has the cylindrical shape of a bain-marie insert but it comes in two parts, one fitting inside the other like stacked water tumblers. The upper pan rests in an inch of water in the lower pan, while the water rises in the quarter-inch of leeway between the sides. The problem here: there is not room for enough water so that you can feel comfortable that what's there will not cook out; furthermore, the extremely tight fit of insert and outer pan, while useful for conducting heat through the aluminum walls, creates a vapor seal that is difficult to break. Finally, aluminum is scarcely the metal of choice for the kind of delicate sauces that a double boiler is meant for making and a bain-marie is designed to keep warm. However, this pot (the top holds 1¾ quarts) wins points for its neat shape: the inevitable trench around the circumference should be easier to clean than some that tend to catch bits of food. As a half-step between types of utensils, it is interesting but not totally successful.

SAUCE BEARNAISE

½ cup wine or tarragon vinegar
1½ tablespoons chopped shallots
½ teaspoon freshly ground pepper
4 egg yolks, slightly beaten
1½ cups hot clarified sweet butter, about ¾ pound
Salt
1 teaspoon chopped fresh tarragon
1 teaspoon chopped parsley
½ teaspoon chopped fresh chervil (if available)

Combine the vinegar, shallots and pepper in a saucepan (not aluminum), and reduce over high heat until you have about ¼ cup left. This takes about 5 minutes. Cool slightly. Then gradually and briskly whip in the egg yolks with a wire whip. Place over very low heat and cook, whipping constantly, for 6 to 8 minutes. You should have a creamy sauce with the consistency of a soft whipped cream.

Take off the heat and add the hot butter, drop by drop, whipping steadily. Stir in the salt, strain the sauce, and add the chopped herbs.

Like Hollandaise, sauce Béarnaise is served lukewarm. It, too, is kept warm over tepid water. Makes about 2 cups. Delicious with filet mignon, fried or boiled fish.

NOTE: If you are apprehensive about cooking the sauce over direct heat, as instructed, pour reduced liquid into the top of a double boiler. When it has cooled, stir in the beaten egg yolks, place over simmering water, and cook to a creamy consistency, whipping constantly. This takes somewhat longer but it's undoubtedly safer.

(From THE OTHER HALF OF THE EGG, by Helen McCully, Jacques Pépin, and William North Jayme. Copyright © 1967 by M. Barrows & Company, Inc. Reprinted by permission of William Morrow & Company, Inc.)

Hammered Aluminum Bain-Marie Pan   6.69

Hammered aluminum with black-coated, cast-aluminum handle; 4¾″ diam.; 5½″ deep; 1½-qt. capacity.
$12.00

This is a true bain-marie pan, not a hybrid with the top of a double boiler. It is a pan meant not for cooking, but to set in a large container of gently simmering water, keeping delicate sauces warm until they are needed. It is a deep, narrow (4¾″), straight-sided saucepan of hammered aluminum with a truncated black-coated cast-aluminum handle perfectly suited to its use, since this is a pan meant to be moved only in and out of the water bath. The shape is logical, also: the pot is made high-sided so that the water in the bath cannot spill into it. Good-quality metal, a flat lid of a lighter gauge, and a capacity of 1½ quarts make this pan precisely suited to its function. If you are planning to keep foods warm in this manner, you should probably have more than one of these.

This curious account of the origin of the bain-marie is given by Alexis Soyer in The Modern Housewife, *published around 1850: "Bain-marie, or as it is called in the English kitchen, Beaumére Pan, is a pan which contains water kept at a boiling state, in which are placed the other saucepans, &c., so that the contents should not be acted upon too strongly by the fire. This term is old, having its origin with the alchymists, who, finding that sea water boiled at a high temperature, and did not evaporate so quickly, used a pan containing sea-water (maris, in French, of the sea); hence the term Bain Marie, or Seawater Bath."*

Copper Buffet Bain-Marie   6.70

Copper and brass; each insert 2-qt. capacity.
$210.00

Although you can improvise a buffet bain-marie with a Hotray, a baking dish, and some pots, here you have the real thing to covet—superb, efficient, and outrageously expensive. It is enormous, gleaming with copper and brass, suitable for setting on a mahogany sideboard to serve breakfast before the hunt, or for presenting a variety of soups for a late supper. A generous oval basin of copper is supported on four legs over a butane burner. The bottom of this pan is covered by a plaque with either two or three spaces, into each of which an insert pan fits; the plaque covers the simmering water so that it cannot splash out. Each pan has a capacity of 2 quarts and is fitted with a lid. This magnificent utensil is total luxury, not of this century, and when you come right down to it, it's not altogether unlike a steam table: but it is wonderful nonetheless. For the hostess who, until now, has not possessed the Mostest.

Enormous Double Boiler   6.71

Heavy-duty aluminum with tinned-steel handles; base 9¾″ diam.; 7½″ deep; inserts 9¾″ top diam.; 7½″ deep; each piece 9-qt. capacity. Also avail. with capacity of 11, 15, 17½, 25, or 36 qts.
$85.35

As different from the bain-marie above as night from day, this is an enormous double boiler of professional quality: we show you the size with a 9-quart capacity, but it comes large enough to hold 36 quarts! This pot represents a transition between single-purpose double boilers and the stockpots in the next section: each of the two main parts of this utensil *is* actually a stockpot. In addition to the insert there is a steamer, and all three parts have flat bottoms and are made of heavy-gauge aluminum with extra thickness in the bottoms. The tinned handles are square and riveted on, standing well away from the sides, so you won't burn your knuckles when using them. In short, this is a double boiler and steamer set of superb quality. Can you use it? That depends on your style of life; we'd guess that you would use it far more often than the glamorous bain-marie just above. Think of making and keeping hot enough soup or porridge for a houseful of ski weekenders; think of preparing rice for a big buffet, or steaming potatoes for an enormous salad; or remember the Chinese attitude toward saving fuel and stack the three parts—broth on the bottom, another food in the perforated insert, and then vegetables in the top, topped off with a lid. Granted, if you live alone or your family is small you can live without it; but these are good pots, and the purchase of an extra cover will give you two large stockpots.

Stockpots

Double boilers cook by transmitting heat through the water in the base and so creating steam, which rises to cook the contents of the upper pan. In stockpots, on the other hand, heat is also transmitted through water, but the food is actually in the liquid, so that it can impart its own savor to the broth. Stockpots, however large, are tall and narrow, and for good reason. The narrowness of the pot permits the existence of only a small area of surface from which evaporation can take place, and so conserves the liquid; and the pot's relative height forces the liquid to bubble up through layers of goodies—flavors which start at the bottom build up through layers of broth, meat, bones, and vegetables, blending and enriching each other.

You can buy a stockpot in any size beginning with about 4 quarts, and only you can make a judgment about what size to buy on the basis of how you live. Our advice is to decide on the largest capacity you will need, and then double it: there is no point in buying a pot holding less than 10 quarts, and you may want an even larger size. Remember that you need a 20-quart pot to end up with a tiny container of glace de viande after five days of simmering and reducing meat stock; and even this large pot is none too large if you're serious about making fine chicken or meat stocks, which require a lot of space for the bones, meat, and vegetables.

WHAT WEIGHT OF METAL?

Because of the modifying action of the water on the heat, you need not buy a stockpot in the same high quality as your saucepans; a medium-heavy gauge of metal is quite adequate, since the enormous quantities of water in the pot will act to diffuse the heat. Aluminum is fine because it is light, but the bottom must be of good quality—and thicker than the sides—because it must support heavy bones that must not be allowed to stick or scorch. Hours of work can go to waste if bones, onions, and the like at the bottom of a stockpot should burn: one taste of scorch and the broth is ruined.

APPLESAUCE

Our most common apple dish is applesauce, which has done duty as a dessert for generations and has also been used as an accompaniment to meats and poultry—notably pork, duck, and goose. In the days when people had apple trees in their backyards, the first fallen fruit was gathered, split, cored, and cooked with a little sugar. Then it was forced through a sieve and seasoned to taste. This made the initial applesauce of the season, much prized for its fresh flavor. However, sauce made from maturer apples is what most of us know.

6 to 8 cooking apples, 4 to 8 ounces each
½ to ¾ cup water
Sugar to taste

Peel, core, and cut the apples into sixths. Place in a heavy saucepan and add a small amount of water—just enough to create the steam necessary to soften the apples. Cover, and cook over medium heat till the apples are done. Then stir with a wooden spoon or spatula and add sugar to taste, along with whatever spice you like, such as nutmeg, cinnamon, mace, or ginger. Apples vary so much in sugar content that it is folly to sweeten them before they are cooked.

(From AMERICAN COOKERY, by James A. Beard, illustrated by Earl Thollander. Copyright © 1972 by James A. Beard. Reprinted by permission of Little, Brown and Company.)

Farberware Stewpot   6.72

Stainless steel with aluminum-clad bottom, phenolic-resin handle on lid; 12½" diam.; 8½" deep; 16-qt. capacity. Also avail. with capacity of 4, 6, 8, or 12 qts.
$20.00 $26.00 $29.00 $45.00 ▲

Farberware is the maker of this perfectly good stainless-steel pot with an aluminum-clad bottom. It has a well-fitting lid, a satinlike finish, two handles, and the typical Farberware knob on the lid. Furthermore, you can have it in any of 5 sizes, from 4 to 16 quarts in capacity. A nice pot, but not quite the stockpot shape; we, carping, consider it a brazier or a stewpot, but Farber, its maker, calls it a saucepot. It would be lovely for making a lot of applesauce or stuffed cabbage, or for cooking pasta. (Rule of thumb: never buy a large pot like this if you can't fit a stick of spaghetti into it unbroken. Have you ever stood there, *melting* your spaghetti into the water?) But, lacking the tall cylindrical shape of the stockpot, this pot wouldn't be our first choice for making a consommé.

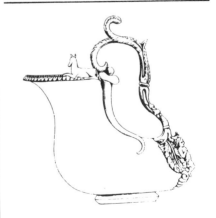

Ancient bronze stockpot shown by Alexis Soyer in The Pantropheon.

Large Cuisinart Pot 6.73

Stainless steel with aluminum sandwich, compressed-wood handles; 11″ diam.; 8¼″ deep; 8½-qt. capacity. Also avail. with capacity of 1½, 3, or 5 qts.

$70.00 ▲

Again, this time from Cuisinarts, a beautiful pan which is of high quality but which is less than perfect as a stockpot, both because it is not quite the right shape and because it holds only 8½ quarts in its largest size. It is made with the finesse characteristic of Cuisinart cookware: of stainless steel and drumlike in shape, it has a highly polished mirror finish, compressed-wood handles, and an aluminum and stainless-steel bottom fully ⅜″ thick. The lid creates a firm seal with the edges of the pot, and the whole affair is handsome enough to come to the table. If you bought it, you could use it to cook vegetables in the French manner, by throwing handfuls into lots of boiling water; or it would be fine for poaching whole pears in wine or spiced syrup for a winter dessert. And of course, it could be used to make a soup, even though it is undesirably low and wide for making the classic meat stocks.

Ornamented bronze stockpot of the classical age.

Some authentic soups have their limitations. The bacon broth of Lübeck was described by Thomas Mann in Buddenbrooks: "A bouillon made of sour cabbage, in which was served the entire meal—ham, potatoes, beetroot, cauliflower, peas, beans, pears, sour plums, and goodness knows what, juice and all —a dish which nobody except those born to it could possibly eat."

FOND DE GIBIER—GAME STOCK

1¼ pounds venison trimmings, cubed
¼ pound hare trimmings, cubed
½ mature wild rabbit, dressed and cut into serving pieces
1 partridge, plucked, cleaned, and cut into serving pieces
1 mature pheasant, plucked, cleaned, and cut into serving pieces
1 carrot, peeled and sliced in rounds
1 onion, peeled and chopped
¼ teaspoon sage
3 juniper berries
1 bay leaf
2 parsley stems
1 teaspoon fresh or ¼ teaspoon dried thyme
1 cup dry white wine

1. Preheat oven to 400 degrees.
2. Brown the meats, carrot, and onion in a roasting pan in the oven. As each item finishes browning, transfer it to a stock pot.
3. Add sage, juniper berries, bay leaf, parsley stems, and thyme to the stock pot.
4. Pour off excess fat from the browning pan and deglaze it rapidly with the white wine: Pour the wine into the pan, bring to a boil over medium heat, and scrape loose as much of the meat drippings as you can from the bottom of the pan, incorporating them into the wine. Pour all liquid into the stock pot. Add 1 cup of water. Then reduce liquid to a glaze (until it has evaporated and started to caramelize). Immediately add enough cold water to cover the ingredients. Bring to a boil, skim thoroughly, reduce heat and simmer, uncovered, for 3 hours. Add water, if necessary, to keep up the level.
5. Remove large solid ingredients. Strain the stock through a chinois. Let cool without completely covering.
6. Refrigerate. When the stock has solidified, remove the layer of fat that has formed at the top. Then heat the stock gently to liquefy it. Pour it into small containers and freeze.

(From THE SAUCIER'S APPRENTICE, by Raymond Sokolov. Copyright 1976 by Raymond Sokolov. Reprinted by permission of Alfred A. Knopf, Inc.)

Vollrath Stockpot 6.75

Stainless steel with aluminum-clad bottom; 10½″ diam.; 8¾″ deep; 12½-qt. capacity. Also avail. with capacity of 8, 16, or 20 qts.

$45.00

Enfin a real stockpot, this one a businesslike affair that gives good value for the money. Notice the rim: it is not rolled over a wire, as are the edges of some saucepans, because this is no longer a permitted design in commercial kitchens —it was felt that this provided refuges for food which were impossible to clean to the level required by the law. This is your clue that here we have a professional pan. The curved lip on the pot coincides with the raised lip on the cover, which can be purchased separately. We question the value of the flat, rodlike handle used for lifting the cover; when the stock reaches boiling, the cover, and the rod, will be boiling hot as well. There are two good handles that curve well away from the sides of the pot to protect the chef's knuckles. The whole thing is properly high and narrow in shape, and comes in sizes holding from 8 to 20 quarts.

Jonathan Swift, in a parody of books of the "good advice to housewives" genre, showed his opinion of the Frenchification of English cuisine: "If a lump of soot falls into the soup, and you cannot conveniently get it out, scum it well, and it will give the soup a high French taste."

Directions to Servants, *1731*

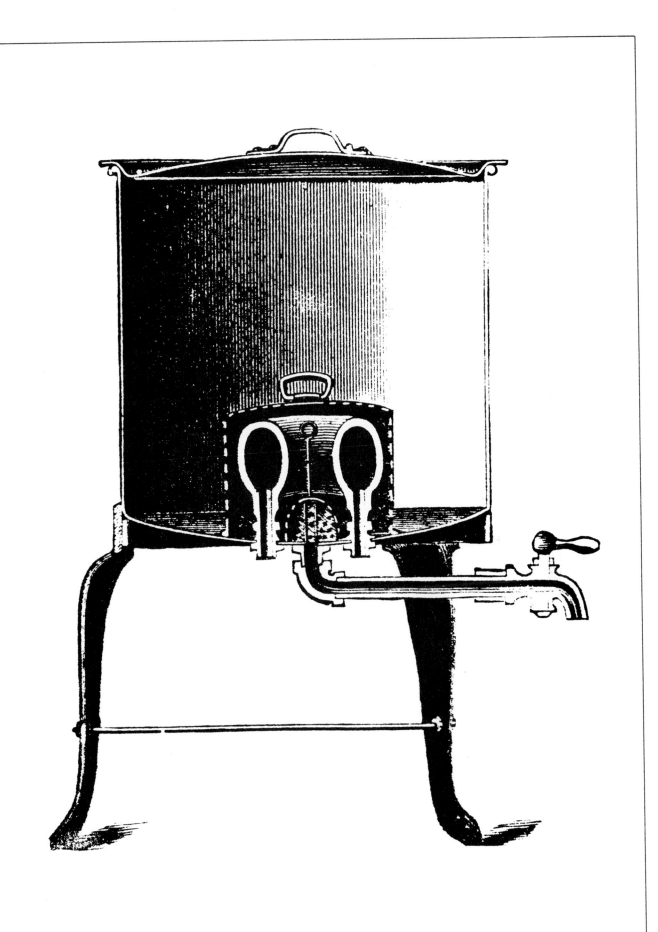

With intricate plumbing, steam-heated stock boilers advertised by a Philadelphia manu-facturer in 1900 were prepared to deliver from 20 to 100 gallons of bouillon per batch.

Paderno Stockpot 6.76

Stainless steel with aluminum sandwich; 15¾"
diam.; 15¾" deep; 53-qt. capacity. Also avail.
with capacity of 10½, 17½, 25½, 38, or 74 qts.
$300.00

Here is a mighty pro of a pot, 15¾" high
and 15¾" wide, holding 53 quarts, massive enough to stock a freezer. The construction is more than heavy: the double
bottom, containing an aluminum sandwich more than ¼" thick, keeps the heat
under control. The exterior is brushed
stainless steel with a highly polished rim.
Welded loop handles are something you
can really take hold of. Although this pot
is heavier than one of this size in aluminum, it has none of the drawbacks of
aluminum—nothing but stainless steel
will touch your food. It is a major investment, meant, in this size, for
quantity-minded cooks with good muscles. You will find it in Italian restaurants, providing a pot in which to cook
the best bollito misto. There are five
other sizes, too—the smallest in the series holds 10½ quarts, the largest, 74
quarts. For lids, see 6.100. As always
with Paderno pots, we urge you: if you
can find it, buy it. It is superb.

*With tripod legs shrunk to mere feet, a
stockpot shown in* The Pantropheon of
Alexis Soyer.

Copper and Stainless-Steel 6.77
Stockpot

Heavy-gauge copper exterior with heavy-gauge
stainless-steel interior and handles; 12" diam.;
12" deep; 22-qt. capacity. Also avail. with capacity of 13, 35, 52, 75, or 118 qts.
$290.00

Heavier and heavier: this stainless-steel
and copper Bi-Metal stockpot holding 22
quarts is expensive and nearly impossible to lift, but it is the ultimate in quality, with the best heat distribution we
know. It is gargantuan in the largest
sizes—imagine a pot that holds 118
quarts! And don't even try to imagine
the cost, which is in line with the price of
the metals and the quality of the manufacture. You can have it with lid (see
6.94) as well as a faucet and a grate, all
at extra cost, if you feel up to it; and you
can choose it in any of six sizes, beginning with a pot of 13-quart capacity. The
outside is of sumptuous brushed copper,
with stainless-steel handles set part way
down; the stainless-steel inside is a full
pot joined permanently to the copper
outer pot—it is not a mere thin lining. A
lifetime investment, but perhaps over-
whelming for a noncommercial kitchen.

*Stocks and sauces have always been con-
sidered the soul of French cuisine. In the
introduction to his 1739 book,* Les Dons
de Comus, *Marin writes: "With proper
pots and pans, fresh food purchased each
morning, and a good bouillon, even third-
class persons can dine with grace."*

ALUMINUM STOCKPOTS
Once again a word about metals. We aren't showing any all-copper,
tin-lined stockpots; they are available, but we don't recommend them
unless you can find a wonderful buy in an old one. We happen to feel
that money spent for a new copper stockpot is a silly expense, producing no compensatory benefits; if you care to go to the expense of copper, then buy the Bi-Metal pot, 6.77. It will not be so responsive to heat
as copper lined with tin or silver, but neither will you have to spend
your good money to have it relined; and besides, great sensitivity to heat
is not needed in this form of cookware. And you simply have to be concerned about weight: remember, not only the metal but the contents
have weight, and anyone who has tried to lift a fish tank or a pail full
of water knows that water weighs a lot. The obvious solution to the
problem of metal for a stockpot is aluminum. It makes the whole concept manageable, and even the propensity of this metal to discolor is
not a major drawback in a stockpot. Therefore, we show you our
experts' choices among large pots of this material.

A HANDLING HINT
A final word: all of these stockpots, even those of aluminum, are heavy.
Instead of tipping them to get at the contents, try using a small saucepan as a large ladle, steadier than an actual ladle and with a larger
capacity than most ladles (but see 6.120). A 1- or 1½-quart pan is fine
for this purpose.

Hammered Aluminum Stockpot

6.78

Hammered aluminum with cast-aluminum handles; 12″ diam.; 11½″ deep; 22-qt. capacity. Lid 12½″ diam., 2″ deep.

$85.00

We turn now to aluminum with a sense of relief, since the large stockpots of other metals were becoming altogether too difficult to move. (In restaurant kitchens such pots rest on swivel bases, and besides, there are all those apprentices running around eager to be of help; the home cook has no such assistance, either mechanical or manual.) Here, from Lamalle, is an impressive heavy-gauge aluminum pot with a water-ripple surface created by hammering the outside. It is about as deep as it is broad, about 12″ each way, and it has a cover 2″ deep which can double as a flat pan for browning soup bones in the oven before adding them to the stock ingredients. The cast-aluminum handles of the pot and lid meet, so you can easily pick up both at the same time. This is of the finest quality and, therefore, it is expensive. The size is ideal for the home kitchen—holding 22 quarts, the pot is large enough to make a substantial amount of stock but not too massive to be stored; and aluminum makes its weight manageable.

For centuries fishermen in Brittany were accustomed to contributing their daily catch to "faire la chaudière"—prepare the cauldron—which meant making a hearty fish stew, often over a beach fire. When they crossed the Atlantic and arrived in Newfoundland long ago they brought with them both the chaudière and their method of making fish soup, which became known in America as chowder.

BOILED BEEF—POT AU FEU

3 to 4 pounds brisket of beef
2 to 3 pounds shin of beef
1 onion stuck with 2 cloves
1 garlic clove
3 leeks
1 carrot
1½ teaspoons rosemary
Cold water
1 tablespoon salt
6 medium onions
6 additional small carrots
6 turnips
6 to 8 pieces marrow bone
1 tablespoon freshly ground pepper
Croutons of crusty French bread
Grated cheese
Boiled potatoes
Boiled cabbage
Coarse salt
Sour gherkins
Mustard

Put the brisket and the shin of beef into a large kettle with the stuck onion, garlic, leeks, carrot, and rosemary. Add cold water to cover and bring to a boil. Boil rapidly 5 minutes, removing any scum that forms on the surface. Add salt, cover, and simmer 2 hours. Then add the onions, carrots, turnips, and marrow bones. Simmer another hour or until the meat and vegetables are tender. Meanwhile cook the potatoes and cabbage, each separately. Finally add pepper to the pot au feu, and correct the seasoning.

Serve the broth in bowls with croutons and cheese. Follow with the beef, marrow bones, and vegetables. Pass the coarse salt, gherkins, and mustard.

Stockpot by Commercial Aluminum

6.79

Heavy-duty aluminum with tinned-steel handles; 9¼″ diam.; 8¼″ deep; 11-qt. capacity. Also avail. with capacity of 16, 18, 20, 25, 30, 32, 36, 40, 50, 60, 80, or 100 qts.

$59.60

Somewhat heavier and nowhere near so beautiful as the preceding pot by Lamalle, this professional-quality stockpot was made to stand up to the stresses of a restaurant kitchen, so you can be sure it would not buckle under the stress of a rhythm section composed of kids with wooden spoons. The bottom is made extra-thick to prevent scorching; the corners, also reinforced, are nicely rounded so that they may be easily cleaned. While this pot is heavy, it is not so heavy as one of stainless steel. We are showing you the smallest pot in this line, which holds 11 quarts; it can be purchased in a ladder of 13 sizes reaching 100 quarts. Lids are available seperately —see 6.92. We ought to mention that this same manufacturer makes a lighter-weight stockpot, as well as one in this heavy weight that is equipped with a faucet and strainer in its larger sizes. Straight sides and good handles of tinned steel make this one an intelligent choice.

Steamer-Boiler with Basket Insert

6.80

Heavy-gauge aluminum with tinned handles, steel-mesh basket insert; 13″ diam.; 14″ deep; 32-qt. capacity; insert 12½″ diam., 11½″ high. Also avail. with capacity of 60 qts.

$65.00 ▲

A super value: Here is a large professional Leyse stockpot of heavy-gauge aluminum with a cover; with it comes a three-legged steel steamer or strainer basket that sits inside. Put your lobsters —or your brisket—or your fowl and vegetables into the basket, plunge it into the liquid in the pot, and cook. When your food is done or your broth ready, lift the solids out in the basket. Think of the convenience of using this pot for cooking corn on the cob for a large crowd. There is also a metal stand (6.81, be-

Continued from preceding page

low) which you can buy separately—it helps to solve the problem of storing such a large vessel. (One of our experts suggested that you set the pot on its stand in your front hall and plant a tree in it.) More realistically, it could sit comfortably in a corner of your kitchen or pantry in this black trivet. On summer evenings, go out and dig a hole in the ground (or in the sand, if you are fortunate enough to be at the shore), plant a bonfire in it, add the trivet, and set your clambake ingredients to steaming in the pot. This pot is very big—you can choose a capacity of 32 or 60 quarts —and remarkably inexpensive. We repeat: a super value.

Stand for Leyse Stockpot 6.81

Black-painted steel; triangular, each side 13½″ long; 16″ high.

$11.95

Here is the stand for the Leyse stockpot. It is of steel, painted black, welded together into a triangle which is set on legs. The high legs extend up the sides of the pot for steadiness, while the short legs sit on the floor. A nice adjunct to a good pot; use it as a base for storage or, as we suggest, to steady the pot during outdoor cooking over a firepit.

Wearever Stockpot with Spigot 6.82

Heavy-gauge aluminum with nickel-plated steel spigot; 12″ diam.; 13″ deep; 25-qt. capacity. Also avail. with capacity of 32, 40, 60, or 80 qts.

$170.00

Don't be misled by the spigot—this pot is not the world's largest dispenser for iced tea. Rather, this is a common type of professional stockpot in Europe. The rationale? Remember that fat rises. You may be making a huge pot of stock from which you will eventually skim off the fat and strain the vegetables, but in the *meantime* you want to drain off a cup or so of stock. And when it comes to draining all of it, you will want to bless the spigot. A filled 25-quart pot is impossible to lift and tedious to ladle. As for many of the stockpots in this section, a cover is available (6.91), but it is not included in the price of the pot. This is a big, substantial, heavy-gauge aluminum pot with a doubly thick rim and bottom and with superb heat distribution. It is rather expensive, and can withstand the roughest handling. We show you the 25-quart size, but you can have it in a larger size holding 32, 40, 60, or even 80 quarts.

Cooks in old English kitchens boiled down their rich stocks to make a "veal glew," which they formed into little cakes and dried in the sun. In America, the New Englanders made a similar extract which they called "soup in the

Red Enamel Marmite 6.83

Enameled steel; 9″ diam.; 9″ deep; 8-qt. capacity.

$29.95

We have been rather cavalier about metals for stockmaking, implying that you can't really damage a stock by making it in a pan of the wrong metal. Which is usually true: except that there are those times when a stock *must* be clear, perfect, and light in color. You may want to make an aspic to coat a fish, or may plan to cover a chicken suprême with a clear glaze, or to make oeufs en gelée. For such uses you need perfectly limpid stock, and you are best advised to make it in a stockpot with a porcelain finish. Here is an enameled marmite of mild steel, made by Cousances. The interior is a fine bird's-egg speckle of ultramarine and mauve, while the exterior enamel is a vivid cadmium red. Here is solid value in a stockpot of medium (8-quart) capacity. It is neither too ponderous to lift nor too high-priced, nor will it hog storage space. It has a double-thick bottom, a matching snug-fitting cover, and two solidly welded handles. It is infinitely prettier than the standard stockpots we have shown you, and for that reason it has our hearts; but it is also a good value.

pocket." Both preparations are ancestors of our bouillon cubes and also are close kin to the French glace de viande, or meat extract, made by reducing stock to a thick paste that will keep indefinitely for use in enriching sauces.

Pressure Cookers

When you need stock in a hurry, your choice may very well be between opening a can and pressure-cooking last night's chicken bones with some vegetables. We would unhesitatingly choose the homemade version for thrift, for taste, and for good use of time. But just as we think you can taste the difference between homemade and canned stock, so we think you can taste the difference between pressure-cooked stock and the product of more traditional methods. The process of making a good stock is not just a softening of the ingredients, but a blending of the flavors; to our mind, this just doesn't happen satisfactorily in a pressure cooker, because it cooks food fast—albeit with moisture—and at a high temperature.

Honest to our fingertips, we admit that we may be influenced by the fact that we are—collectively—scared silly of pressure cookers, and never mind telling us again about the safety valves that remove the risk of using them. Nonetheless, many swear by them, and for all of those people in a hurry, especially people of great courage, we have chosen what we feel is the safest as well as the most attractive pressure cooker made.

SEB Pressure Cooker   6.84

Heavy aluminum with plastic handles; 9½" diam.; 6⅝" deep; 6-qt. capacity. Also avail. with capacity of 4, 8, or 22 qts., and also avail. in stainless steel.
$27.95

Since the beginning of the energy crisis there has been a renaissance of interest in pressure cookers, those wonderful pots that permit you to cook almost anything in roughly half the time you ordinarily take, sometimes even less. The saving of fuel is impressive, although our experts are in agreement that pressure-cooked food is in general inferior to the same food prepared by traditional methods. Here is the SEB pressure cooker from France, a round aluminum pot with a flat bottom and plastic handles; the lid, which has a rubber gasket, is fastened tightly in place during use by a plastic screw handle. SEB makes some twenty models of pressure cookers, both round and oval, and they claim to be the world leaders in their field. The instructions with their cookers emphasize their safety devices. To wit: on the lid there is the familiar rotating valve, which controls pressure during cooking; then there is a safety valve that releases the pressure should it reach the danger level, a much higher point than the level controlled by the primary valve; and then, finally, there is a safety clamp across the lid, held in place by two latches, which acts as an additional safety device: if both of the valves should be obstructed, this bar springs up between its latches, allowing the lid to lift slightly and the high-pressure steam to dissipate harmlessly. A wire-basket insert and a hard-cover book, with excellent photographs, come with the pot; there are also 200 recipes and a list of parts. This is a well-made cooker, far handsomer than the one your grandmother had, and it is available in sizes holding from 4 to 22 quarts. You will want one of the larger sizes if you plan to use the pot for processing home-canned foods.

Digesters, shown in Modern Domestic Cookery, *1853.*

CONIGLIO ALLA MARCHIGIANA— RABBIT MARCHIGIANA

A 3-pound rabbit
1 cup dry white wine
½ cup olive oil
4 cloves garlic, finely chopped
1 tablespoon rosemary
Salt and freshly ground black pepper

Cut rabbit into serving pieces as you would chicken. Place rabbit pieces in one layer in a skillet. Do not add oil but cook the pieces, turning occasionally, until the external moisture on them evaporates. Begin with a low heat and increase heat as liquid is drawn out. Do not brown.

Add remaining ingredients, cover, and simmer over medium heat until rabbit is tender, about 45 minutes to 1 hour. Add a little more wine if the pan becomes too dry. Serves 4.

(From ITALIAN FAMILY COOKING, by Edward Giobbi, illustrated by Cham, Lisa, and Gena Giobbi. Copyright © 1971 by Edward Giobbi. Reprinted by permission of Random House, Inc.)

The thrifty nineteenth century discovered that steam, intensely contained to build up pressure, "digested" food; therefore containers with the food sealed inside were placed in rather dangerous, magical steam-containing shells called "conjurers," to create the necessary pressure for the procedure. Meat glazes and sauce bases were created in this way. In Modern Domestic Cookery, *by a Lady, 1853, they were described: "Various steam-kettles, known to cooks as 'conjurers,' ought to be kept in every kitchen and used at intervals when the fire is not otherwise engaged. Into one of these a digester should be placed, containing a quantity of water just sufficient to cover the ingredients to be acted upon; into it are to be put all the scraps of meat which are usually thrown away, together with the bones of all the meat daily dressed and consumed . . . whether left upon a dish or a plate. Fastidious ladies will probably be shocked at the idea of again bringing such matters to table, but they should recollect that the bones are only scraped with a knife."*

Separate Lids

A lid can be anything from the top crust of a pie to a heavy iron dome for a pot; from a sheet of waxed paper to the depressed top of a doufeu, which is designed to be filled with burning coals. The variables are weight, shape, and quality of seal, and there are any number of possible combinations of these factors to fit any number of cooking needs. There is no single solution to covering a pot: rather, the lid must suit the type of cooking you are doing. The Cuisinart lid 6.95, for example, slightly domed and forming a positive seal with the edge of the pan, prevents the evaporating steam from escaping and makes it roll back into the pan as it condenses—good for stews and soups. But if you are, instead of making soup, reducing a tomato sauce for pasta, watching it bubbling energetically on a back burner, you may want to cover the pan so that you don't get spatters all over the stove: for this, a flat, lightweight lid, placed slightly askew so that the steam can escape, is the proper covering.

HEAT CONTROL UNDER COVERS

Most importantly, a lid helps you to regulate the heat in the pot. Any lid at all—even pie crust—will raise the heat of the food beneath it to some extent, although a glass lid allows heat to radiate off somewhat. A heavy-gauge lid of a diffusing metal creates, with the pot, a tight little oven which closely surrounds the food and holds its temperature at a high point. This permits the cook to lower the flame radically, even to shut it off entirely if the intent is simply to keep finished food warm—a real fuel-saver. A covered pot should be checked after it has been over the heat for fifteen minutes or so—the chances are that the heat can be reduced greatly at that point.

CHOOSING LIDS

Most manufacturers of pans make what they call "universal lids," designed to fit any of their pots of a given diameter. Thus, the Wearever 10″ lid will fit both a skillet and a large saucepan; and, for even more versatility, see the Cuisinart universal cover, 6.96. We are showing you lids from a number of companies which sell them separately from their pans: remember that, with few exceptions, you need not match a lid to a pan from the same manufacturer—there are enough sizes here to cover all the pots that need a lid.

POLLO CON CAVOLFIORE—
CHICKEN WITH CAULIFLOWER

A 3-pound fryer, cut in pieces
3 tablespoons olive oil
3 cloves garlic, unpeeled
Salt and freshly ground black pepper
1 head of cauliflower, broken into
   flowerets (or you can use 1 pound of
   Brussels sprouts)

¼ cup wine vinegar
1 tablespoon chopped rosemary
1 tablespoon chopped parsley, Italian
   if possible
½ cup chopped tomato
½ can (pitted) black olives, drained

Sauté chicken in olive oil with garlic and salt and pepper to taste over moderate heat in wide uncovered skillet. Turn

---

pieces occasionally. While chicken is cooking, blanch cauliflower in boiling water. Drain and set aside, but keep warm. When chicken is brown, add vinegar, rosemary and parsley. Cover, lower heat and simmer for 3 minutes. Take off cover, turn up heat and boil until the vinegar has evaporated. Add tomatoes, and when they begin to boil, add black olives and cauliflower. Cover, and simmer 15 to 20 minutes. Discard garlic. Serves 6.

(From ITALIAN FAMILY COOKING, by Edward Giobbi, illustrated by Cham, Lisa, and Gena Giobbi. Copyright © 1971 by Edward Giobbi. Reprinted by permission of Random House, Inc.)

Copco Lid   6.85

Enameled steel; 12″ diam. Also avail. 10″ diam.
$18.00 ▲ $16.00 ▲

The lid for the Copco skillet, very special, very much made to go with that pan in either its 10″ or 12″ size. It comes in blue, brown, red, yellow, or white porcelain enamel to match the colors of the pans; is extremely heavy; has an edge which forms an excellent vapor seal; and has a nice flat knob which is comfortable to grip and lift. Rather flat in shape, it somewhat resembles a beret.

Copper pot with lids; nineteenth-century French.

Lamalle Copper Lids   6.86, 6.87, 6.88

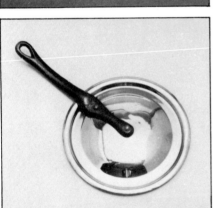

Copper with tin lining and either brass or cast-iron handles; 8¾″ diam. Also avail. 4⅞″, 5⅝″, 6½″, 7¼″, or 8″ diam.
$22.80 each

Once you have invested in expensive copperware, you may as well improve your investment by acquiring the proper lids to make your pans both more beau-

tiful and more useful. Lamalle has these lids to fit its round pots in sizes which go in many steps from 4⅞″ to 8¾″. They are of heavy-gauge copper, are lined with tin, and they come with a choice of three handles: a flat, non-protruding loop secured by a rivet at either end, a long black cast-iron handle, and a long brass handle. Each lid has a raised rim which rests flat on the edge of the pot; the long handle is secured by rivets, both in the center and at the point at which it bends to conform to the raised rim.

Kitchen Glamor Copper Lid   6.89

Copper with tin lining, cast-iron handle; 8″ diam. Also avail. 5″, 5¾″, 6½″, 7½″, 8¾″, or 10″ diam.
$10.00

A perfectly simple disc of copper: there is no rim and only a slight swelling into a low dome. This lid is made in sizes to fit copper pots from 5″ to 10″ in diameter, but the lack of a rim means that any lid of this design will fit any pot smaller than itself in circumference. There is a long, black cast-iron handle, riveted in two places and with a hole in the end for hanging the lid over your stove. Expensive, as you would expect, but well made and with a beautiful simplicity of design.

Jensen Copper and Silver Lid   6.90

Copper with silver lining, stainless-steel handle; 8″ diam.
$35.00

One way to increase the versatility of a pan is by providing it with a lid. This lid, bearing the mark of Georg Jensen, matches the sumptuous silver-lined pan, 6.39, already versatile enough to serve both for cooking and for presentation at table. Like the pot, the lid has an elegant stainless-steel handle. Highly polished and extremely expensive, the lid is 8″ in diameter and is of copper lined with silver.

Wearever Aluminum Lid   6.91

Aluminum; 11⅞″ diam. Also avail. 6⅞″, 7⅞″, 8⅞″, 9⅞″, 10⅞″, 12⅞″, 13⅞″, 15⅞″, 17⅞″, or 19⅞″.
$6.00

We respect this ugly duckling, this simplest possible aluminum lid from Wearever. Using a design which is flat-edged,

Continued from preceding page

with a slightly recessed inner surface, it lies absolutely flat on almost any pot edge you can imagine. It will not form a positive seal, nor will it provide maximum condensation of vapors building up inside the pan; but it is nearly universal in usefulness, made of a good conductive material, and comes in a good range of sizes, growing in one-inch steps from just under 7″ to just under 20″.

Lid from Commercial Aluminum   6.92

Heavy-duty aluminum with tinned-steel handle; 12″ diam. Also avail. 8½″, 9¾″, 10¾″, 11″, 12¾″, 14″, 15¾″, 16″, 17¾″, 18″, 20″, or 23¾″.

$6.75

This excellent universal lid is from Commercial Aluminum—the manufacturers clearly believe in it, because they show it with all of their pots. It is of a relatively heavy-gauge aluminum and has a tinned-steel ribbon handle attached by strong rivets. The wide flat edge lies commendably flat on the pan, while the slightly domed shape of the center section is designed to collect rising vapors and return them to the food in the form of moisture. The lid can be purchased in any of thirteen sizes, ranging from 8½″ to 23¾″ in diameter.

French lidded pot, nineteenth century.

Lighter Lid from Commercial Aluminum   6.93

Aluminum with tinned-steel handle; 7″ diam. Also avail. 6″, 7¾″, 8″, 8¾″, 9⅛″, 9⅞″, 10⅝″, 11⅜″, 11⅞″, or 14″.

$4.40

The universal lid from Commercial Aluminum we have just shown you has a lightweight version, too, which is made of thinner material, which costs less than the other, and which fits on their smaller pots. In design it is virtually indistinguishable, however, having the same wide, flat edge, the same low-domed central area, and the same tinned-steel ribbon handle strongly attached by rivets. The sizes are made to fit the smallest Commercial Aluminum saucepans and skillets as well as certain of the larger ones; fit should be your only consideration here, since this lightweight lid performs its functions perfectly adequately on the pots it is designed for.

Legion Stainless-Steel Lid   6.94

Stainless steel; 12½″ diam. Also avail. 6¼″, 7¼″, 8¼″, 9″, 10¼″, 14¼″, 16¼″, 18″, 20″, or 22″.

$18.00

A beautiful lid from Legion to go with their Bi-Metal pans. Like the pans, it is well-made and handsome; the lid, however, is of one metal, heavy stainless steel, stamped in one piece. The edges are rolled back and pressed to form a narrow raised rim; inside this rim the lid fits snugly down within the pot, then rises very slightly into the flattest of domes. There is a handle made of an arched strip neatly welded to the top of the lid. Remember the enormous size of Legion's pots? These lids are available in eleven sizes to match, from 6½″ to 22″ in diameter.

Cuisinart Stainless-Steel Lid   6.95

Stainless steel with compressed-wood handle; 11″ diam. Also avail. 4¾″, 5½″, 6¼″, 7″, 8″, 8¾″, 9½″, or 10¼″.

$15.00 ▲

This Cuisinart lid is slightly dome-shaped and is topped by a Danish-modernistic wooden knob. The curved edge of the cover clasps, with a perfect fit, the curved edge of the pan, forming a fabulous seal. The outlook for continued good fit is excellent, since the lid is of durable heavy-gauge stainless steel. Available in 9 sizes, from 4¾″ to 11″ in diameter.

Until Catherine de' Medici arrived in France in 1533 as the bride of the future King Henry II, ladies of the court had eaten their meals in the privacy of their chambers, claiming that the movements of the jaw in eating deformed the shape of their faces and made them unattractive. Catherine changed both French dining habits and the quality of the food for the better, introducing into her future realm the varied and delicate cookery of Florence as well as the table manners and customs of her urbane homeland.

Lid from Commercial Aluminum
Lighter Lid from Commercial Aluminum
Legion Stainless-Steel Lid
Cuisinart Stainless-Steel Lid

Cuisinart Universal Cover
Porcelaine de Paris Lid
Domed Glass Lid
Paderno Stainless-Steel Lid

Cuisinart Universal Cover   6.96

Stainless steel with compressed-wood handle; 6¼″ outside diam. Also avail. 8″ or 8¾″ outside diam.
$9.00

The beauty of the preceding Cuisinart cover was its precise fit to the pot, achieved by making it in many sizes; but this lid, their Universal Cover, is just the opposite. In a clever design concept it has been made in three different diameters, each of which will fit three sizes of pans. On the lid there is a wide border consisting of three concentric rings pressed into the steel, each stepping downwards, rather like seats in a stadium, toward the low-domed center of the lid. The ridges formed on the underside by these rings match three pot sizes; the smallest pot one of these lids will fit is 4¾″ in diameter; the largest, 8¾″. This is made in the usual Cuisinart heavy stainless steel, with a heat-resistant compressed-wood knob and a perforated tab on the edge that makes it possible to hang the lid from a hook.

Porcelaine de Paris Lid   6.97

Porcelain; 4½″ diam. Also avail. 5¼″, 6″, 7″, or 7¾″.   **$14.00**

To cover your Porcelaine de Paris saucepans: an array of beautiful porcelain lids in the appropriate sizes and patterns. The lid to a Fruits Sauvages saucepan, say or one in the Vieux Chine pattern (6.58) will have the same design on it as the pan it covers; a flat knob in the center allows you to lift it on and off. You can, by the way, purchase a rack to hold the lids as well as one for the pots: a good idea, since they are both easy to break and wonderful to display.

Domed Glass Lid   6.98

Heat-resistant glass; 10½″ diam. Also avail. 8″, 9″, or 11¾″ diam.
$6.25 ▲

Isn't this terrific? It's a heavy domed lid of heat-resistant glass, with ridges on the inside that are like those on a doufeu lid; and it's made to sit on a cast-iron pan for a truly exciting visual combination. General Housewares' glassware for cooking is comparable to Corning's, ovenworthy and able to resist heat but not sudden great changes in temperature; however, the manufacturers say that 90 percent of the time it could go from the freezer to a preheated oven without breaking—a claim that we'd rather not test, cowards that we are. The great merits of this lid are the good visibility it affords and the way it collects vapors for self-basting the food. In four sizes, from 8″ to 11¾″ in diameter.

HARE OR RABBIT WITH 40 CLOVES OF GARLIC

5-5½ pound hare or rabbit, skinned and eviscerated, sectioned into 8 serving pieces
¾ cup peanut oil
2 tablespoons butter
2 medium onions, sliced
6 stalks celery, cut in julienne
2 large carrots, peeled and cut in julienne
1 fennel, cut into 8 slices
6 to 8 sprigs of parsley
½ cup Madeira or dry white wine
40 cloves garlic, peeled
2 teaspoons salt
1 teaspoon dried tarragon
1 bay leaf
Pepper, freshly ground, to taste
Dough

Wash and dry rabbit well. Place peanut oil in shallow dish or a plate, and turn hare or rabbit in it until well coated on all sides. Set aside.

In a heavy casserole which has a lid, put the butter, onions, celery, carrots, fennel, parsley, Madeira or white wine, and 10 cloves of the garlic. Place pieces of rabbit or hare in a layer over the vegetables; sprinkle with some of the salt and tarragon, and 10 more cloves of the garlic. Layer again with rabbit; season with more salt and tarragon, some of the pepper, and 10 more cloves of garlic. Repeat process with remaining rabbit and seasonings, ending with rabbit, salt, pepper, tarragon, and garlic. Place the bay leaf on top.

Heat oven to 375 F. Cover tightly, and seal together the edges of casserole and lid with a paste made of flour and enough cold water added to make it soft and pliable. Bake for 1½ hours without removing lid throughout cooking time.

(From THE GREAT COOKS COOK-BOOK, by The Good Cooking School. Copyright © 1974 by The Good Cooking School, Inc. Reprinted by permission of Ferguson/Doubleday.)

Paderno Stainless-Steel Lid   6.100

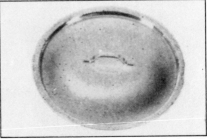

Stainless steel; 11″ diam. Also avail. 6¼″, 8″, 9½″, 12½″, 14¼″, 15¾″, or 17¾″.   **$15.00**

Continued from preceding page

Here is Paderno's lid, to go with all of those Paderno pans which we have told you are so difficult to find but so super. Made of extra-heavy stainless steel, it is a simple round shape with a flat raised ridge around the circumference and a loop handle in the center. If you are lucky enough to find a Paderno pot, then by all means buy the lid to match it; there are eight sizes, from 6¼″ to 17¾″ in diameter.

Farberware High-domed Lid	6.101
Farberware Low-domed Lid	6.102

Stainless steel with phenolic-resin handle; 12″ diam. Also avail. 10½″ diam.

Stainless steel with phenolic-resin handle; 12″ diam. Also avail. 7″, 8½″, or 10½″.
$13.00 ▲ $8.00 ▲ $9.00 ▲

Most Farberware pots come with matching lids, but there are some, such as the frying pans, which don't, and for these, lids of two designs are available. You can get a simple low-domed lid to fit four sizes of pans from 7″ to 12″ in diameter, or you can buy a high-domed lid either 10½″ or 12″ in diameter—this one will turn your large frying pan into a chicken fryer. All are well made, with the typical Farber phenolic-resin knob in the center; they fit only the pans of this manufacturer, but they fit well. It is also rather consoling to know that extra lids are available if you should lose one in moving or through infant vandalism.

Hammered Copper Lid	6.103

Heavy-gauge hammered copper with tin lining, cast-iron handle; 7″ diam. Also avail. 4¾″, 5½″, 6¼″, 8″, 8¾″, or 9½″.
$20.00

Beautiful but redundantly finished is this copper lid from France: we say "redundantly" because the hammering, which is done to make metal stronger, serves no useful purpose on a lid. But the lids are available, looking like wonderful golden Inca suns, lined in tin and with long black handles. They are available in seven sizes from 4¾″ to 9½″ in diameter, and we like to imagine a range of these hanging in order against a kitchen wall.

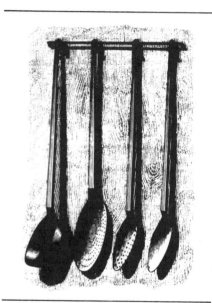

Stovetop Cooking Implements

In France, where the intellectuals were the ones to discover Jerry Lewis, there is currently a vogue for the cheapest American cooking spoons and spatulas, the sort that gather dust on counters in the back of Woolworth's and, probably, the sort that still linger in your kitchen drawer. You can't quite exactly remember buying them, but they are there, and the chances are that you use them constantly. Food cooked on top of the stove requires a lot of manipulating—stirring, flipping, mixing, tasting—either to blend it, or keep it from burning, or to satisfy the cook's curiosity and need for fussing. The novice spends altogether too much time nervously poking and prodding his food as it cooks, but even the master chef sometimes has to stick a spoon in there and test or blend the ingredients. Does it matter what he uses? The Chinese, who have never developed a fork, who save their little spoons for soup-eating, manage the whole business of cooking with a good assortment of knives, a broad spatula curved to fit a wok, a wire skimmer, and cooking chopsticks. But in the West, where technology has reached a high level, we eat with a knife, a fork, and a spoon, and our cooking implements tend to be variations on these, only a little skewed.

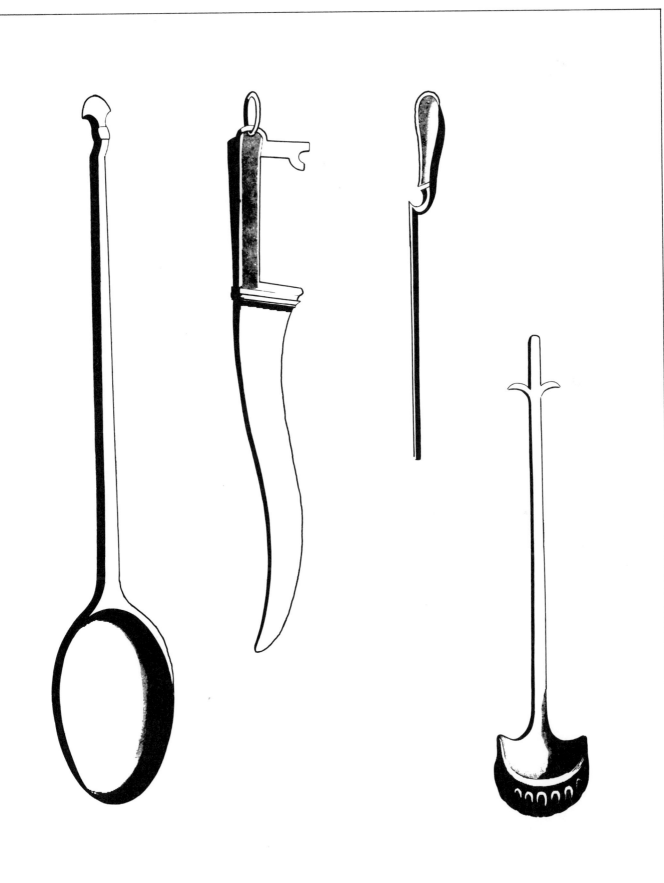

From left to right, a Roman silver spoon for eggs and fish; a brass knife, probably for sacrifices, from Herculaneum; a simpulum, or spoon for salt or eggs; a long-handled wine ladle. From Alexis Soyer's The Pantropheon.

Continued from preceding page

We cook not with a knife but a spatula: flat, generous in size, used for turning and lifting pancakes, hamburgers, bacon. Cooking spoons, yes, but also a wooden spoon, a skimmer, a ladle. And we use a fork for actual cooking only in its strongest, simplest form: two-tined, heavy, long of handle, able to spear a piece of meat cleanly and lift it when necessary. Go ahead and use whatever versions of these utensils you have; we will show you what we consider a good selection, in case you should want to upgrade your collection. Remember that this is an area in which, for a modest expenditure of money, you can buy really superior cooking tools. And look at Chapter 5, where we show implements used for mixing or beating.

KITCHEN TOOL SETS

We show you first a set of tools for the kitchen, near-perfect and fairly affordable. (We are not recommending an endearingly lovely set we have seen, made with decorated porcelain handles by Porcelaine de Paris—but we do show you one porcelain spoon for tasting.) And then we will go on to recommend other implements which you can buy separately. Because we discuss wooden spoons in Chapter 5, where we have put the tools for mixing and beating, you will notice that here all the tools are made of non-rusting metals, that they are all strong, all easy to clean, and nearly all have a whole or hook at the end of the handle so that they can hang on the wall over your stove—a proper stirring spoon, like *le mot juste*, should come to hand as soon as you think of using it. We'd like you to make a special note of the appearance of these implements, because they were formed with nothing but perfect function in mind, and they are all extremely handsome. It is hard to imagine any designer improving on the appearance of, say, the skimmer in the Lauffer stainless-steel set (6.104), or of the Hoan ladle (6.122).

Stainless-Steel Implement Set   6.104

Stainless steel; 7 pieces ranging in length from 9″ to 14″; wall rack 15½″ long.
$49.00 ▲

These are the tools you are going to need the most, chosen for you in satin-finished stainless steel by the H. E. Lauffer Company. For lifting flat things, there is a broad spatula or pancake turner, for lifting bulky things, there is a fork. For lifting and tasting, a spoon; for lifting and straining, a skimmer; and for lifting liquids, two soup ladles and a crêpe ladle. This is a beautiful set, equipped with a 15½″ wall rack so that the implements can be kept right at hand. The strong handles are firmly welded on and they will not bend or snap back under the weight of their burdens. So lovely are these pieces that any one of them could go easily to the table. The crêpe ladle, for example: although its traditional function is to measure out precisely the correct amount of batter for one crêpe, it could serve beautifully as a gravy ladle. And look at the skimmer, a European version of the American slotted spoon, with a design which is reminiscent of a Chinese basket skimmer. Use it to lift a whole fish out of its poaching liquid. Far from inexpensive, this set is beautiful and beautifully made.

White Porcelain Tasting Spoon   6.105

Porcelain; 9″ long. Also avail. 6″ or 7½″ long.
$6.00 ▲

The Chinese, who don't use spoons in cooking, do use them for tasting, and those spoons are made of porcelain, just like the little ones you are given when you eat your Hot Crab and Melon Soup. Not only is the use of porcelain absolutely the best way to ensure that the food you are tasting will neither be tainted by flavors from other foods nor by the metal of the spoon, but such a spoon is also the finest utensil available for stirring a custard or a delicately flavored sauce. Compare this spoon with the wooden ones we show that are also used for mixing, and you will realize the immaculate qualities of its material. And here it is, made in France, a spoon of the purest white porcelain. It comes in three sizes, of which we'd choose the longest—9″—as the most suitable for reaching down into a pot. There is a hole for hanging at one end of the handle. It is really very expensive as well as eminently breakable, and one of our staff was seized with a nearly irresistible urge to whack it down *hard*. Nonetheless, what a superb gift for a friend who cooks and who has, until now, had everything!

SPOONS FOR STOVETOP USE

Cooking spoons are not only for transporting and stirring, but for tasting. One of our editors swoons even today, thirty years later, when she recalls being given a mixing spoon coated with chocolate pudding to lick. And spoons for cooking are lovely and large; they have long handles and copious bowls. They are soup spoons grown gargantuan, except that they are made of cast aluminum or stainless steel rather than sterling silver. We show you wooden spoons in the chapter on mixing and beating (Chapter 5), but those, useful and beautiful as they are, are not so well suited as these for use in top-of-the-stove cooking. For one thing, a wooden spoon carelessly left sitting in a saucepan might burn; for another, the wood is permeable to flavors, and thus is more likely than metal to retain the flavor from one dish to pollute the palate which tastes the next, so that there may be a hangover of tomato and oregano in your crème anglaise. Here we show you spoons both plain and perforated or slotted, as well as a skimmer and tongs for lifting pieces of solid food out of sauces and for removing poached eggs from their poaching liquid and bones from a simmering broth.

Stainless-Steel Spoon 6.106

Stainless steel; 11¾″ long. Also avail. 13¼″ or 15½″ long.
$3.00

It looks like a teaspoon for giants, this spoon from Vollrath that has been pressed out of a single piece of stainless steel. The handle is molded and pierced for hanging, the bowl is slightly pointed, and the spoon is available in three lengths from a comfortable 11¾″ to a substantial 15½″. This is a professional utensil whose handle was designed to fit the large hand of a chef, and it may take some getting used to when it is used in the home kitchen.

SPEZZATO DI VITELLO CON CARCIOFI—VEAL STEW AND ARTICHOKES

4 tablespoons olive oil, or half oil and half butter
1 pound veal shoulder, cut into 1-inch cubes
4 fresh artichokes about the size of lemons [available in Italian markets], cut in quarters (one box frozen artichoke hearts or one can artichoke hearts, drained, may be substituted)
3 garlic cloves
1 cup chopped onion
Salt and freshly ground black pepper
½ cup dry white wine
1 tablespoon rosemary
2 bay leaves
2 tablespoons chopped parsley, Italian if possible
1 cup roughly chopped tomato

Preheat oven to 400°. Heat oil in a skillet and add veal. Cook over high heat, stirring constantly. Remove tough outer leaves and tips of artichokes. Add artichokes, garlic, onions and salt and pepper to taste. When onion wilts, add wine and herbs. Cover and lower heat. Cook gently for about 5 minutes. Add tomato and cook 3 to 5 minutes more.

Put skillet in oven, cover and bake 15 to 20 minutes or until artichokes are tender. Discard garlic. Serves 6.

(From ITALIAN FAMILY COOKING, by Edward Giobbi, illustrated by Cham, Lisa, and Gena Giobbi. Copyright © 1971 by Edward Giobbi. Reprinted by permission of Random House, Inc.)

Aluminum Spoon 6.107

Cast aluminum; 13″ long.
$2.50

This spoon from West Germany is lustrous, airy-light, and smoothly cast in aluminum. It is, in addition, rather beautiful, precisely like a dinner soup spoon in its proportions, but mammoth, like a child's nightmare of a medicine spoon—it is 13″ long. Yet as light as it is, you could lift a whole chicken or a pot roast of beef on it with no fear of it snapping or bending. It is, moreover, downright inexpensive—we try not to say "cheap"—and one of our editors brooded for an afternoon over the fact that she doesn't own one, since it is so beautiful, so strong, and so low in price.

TOMATO COMPOTE

2 pint baskets cherry tomatoes
Their weight in sugar
Approximately ½ cup water
Juice of ½ lemon
Heavy cream, whipped cream or sour
    cream

Scald the tomatoes for 1 minute and peel carefully, being certain you do not break the flesh. Combine weighed sugar with the water; bring to a boil; reduce heat to medium and cook for 10 minutes. Add the tomatoes and cook very slowly, skimming off any scum that rises to the top, until the tomatoes are thoroughly tender but not mushy. Stir in lemon juice; remove to a serving dish and cool. Serve with heavy cream, whipped cream or sour cream.

(From THE GREAT COOKS COOK-BOOK, by The Good Cooking School. Copyright © 1974 by The Good Cooking School, Inc. Reprinted by permission of Ferguson/Doubleday.)

Perforated Stainless-Steel Spoon   6.109

Stainless steel; 11¾" long. Also avail. 13¼" or 15½" long.
$3.00

The fraternal twin of the Vollrath stainless-steel spoon we discussed above (6.106), this one has a perforated bowl that makes it perfect for lifting eggs out of their poaching liquid, broccoli out of boiling water, or a herb bouquet out of a sauce. The spoon is available in three lengths, from 11¾" to 15½"; its handle has a hole near the end for hanging. It does present the same problem as the other Vollrath spoon, however: the large handle may prove uncomfortable to anyone with a small hand.

Slotted Stainless-Steel Spoon   6.110

Stainless steel; 11¾" long. Also avail. 13¼" long. Also avail. 13¼" or 15½" long.
$3.00

Another variation on the theme of the slotted spoon, a category which will ultimately lead us to skimmers. This is the Vollrath stainless-steel spoon once again in its three sizes, 11¾", 13¼", and 15½". Our sample has a self-handle; The same spoon is available with a plastic handle in the 13¼" length; it is probably to be preferred in that form. The bowl has several slots instead of a scattering of circular perforations. What's the difference? Well, this spoon allows liquid to drain out more quickly than the perforated spoon does, but the difference is rather small; you pay your money and you take your choice. Like all of this manufacturer's spoons it is of high quality, designed for professional use. There is a hole in the handle for convenient hanging.

RISOTTO CON SUGO—RISOTTO WITH SAUCE

3 tablespoons butter
1 cup rice, imported Arborio if possible
1 quart chicken stock
Salt and freshly ground black pepper
3 tablespoons meat sauce [after 6.46] or
    marinara sauce [after 6.27]
Grated Parmesan cheese

Heat butter in a deep pot. Add rice and cook, stirring constantly until rice takes on color. Add 1 cup broth, salt and pep-per to taste and cook, uncovered, over moderate heat, stirring constantly. Add more stock as it is needed. When rice begins to soften, about 15 minutes later, add meat or marinara sauce, continuing to stir constantly. Rice should be tender, but firm to the bite, al dente. Sauce should be thick. Serve hot with grated cheese to 3 to 4.

NOTE: Green peas, freshly cooked, are excellent in this dish. Add them during last 5 minutes of cooking.

(From ITALIAN FAMILY COOKING, by Edward Giobbi, illustrated by Cham, Lisa, and Gena Giobbi. Copyright © 1971 by Edward Giobbi. Reprinted by permission of Random House, Inc.)

Stainless-Steel Skimmer   6.111

Stainless steel; 14¼" long overall; 4¼" diam.
$6.00

Having promised an eventual discussion of skimmers in our earlier discussion of slotted spoons, here we are, right on target. This all-purpose, flat, perforated skimmer, a disc of stainless steel with a sunburst of holes in its surface, is almost flat enough to resemble a very sturdy strainer. Use it to pick the meat out of a simmering stock. It will be up to the task no matter how heavy the portion. You can rely on it for removing fruits from their poaching bath or wine. The stainless steel will not discolor. It is long enough to plumb the depths of most pots. The simple, straight handle is comfortable to hold, and its sharp curve adds to the ease of handling, as well as giving you the means to hang it on a rack.

Perforated Stainless-Steel Spoon
Slotted Stainless-Steel Spoon
Stainless-Steel Skimmer

Stainless-Steel Tongs
Flexible Pancake Turner
Perforated Pancake Turner

Stainless-Steel Tongs   6.112

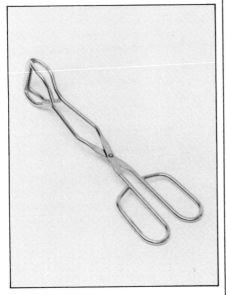

Stainless steel; 8½″ long.
$5.50

In the finest French restaurants, the waiter deftly transfers your slices of tournedos from the presentation pan to the plate using two spoons, one on top of the other, and held between thumb, forefinger, and middle finger. While you might amuse yourself and acquire that kind of dazzling technique, it is hardly necessary in the kitchen. A pair of strong, serviceable tongs, the edges blunted so as not to tear the food, are extremely useful for turning meat in the pan. Most of the tongs we have seen are inexpensive, chromed steel. You can buy them in any hardware store, and they are serviceable. However, for durability and good looks, as well as the kind of finish we would rather put to our tournedos, we show you these, of stainless steel, 8½ inches long.

COOKING SPATULAS AND A POT FORK

In our discussion of baking we went into a paean about various scrapers and spatulas, rhapsodizing about them as the cook's third hand, the most useful tools in the kitchen. Well, these are something else. Although they are called spatulas, they are also, and more properly, called turners: they are the extensions of your right hand with which you can reach down to a griddle or a hot frying pan to flip over a hamburger or a rasher of bacon or a pancake. Where the baking spatulas all had handles in the same plane as the blade, these have their handles set at an angle that permits the utensil to go down into a pan. They have wooden handles so that your hand will not be threatened by heat transmitted from the hot griddle to the blade, and they are big: why not have a turner with which you can turn over three hamburgers or a half-pound of bacon at one swipe? Notice that, like spoons, both solid and perforated turners are available; and whereas the perforated ones can be used for any task, you would not want to use a solid turner to deal with lifting or turning foods cooking in much fat — fried potatoes, for instance.

Flexible Pancake Turner   6.113

Stainless steel with rosewood handle, brass rivets; 14″ long overall; blade 7¾″ × 3″.
$8.75 ▲

Since Julia Child first showed us how she keeps her tools handy for use, everyone with a pretense to cooking well has next to the stove a crock full of implements for mixing, turning, and lifting. And this is the turner which should be in every such crock, kept close at hand for the moment when the bubbles explode through the griddlecake and the edges just begin to look dry. A simple, blunted blade of stainless steel, rounded at the tip, the turner bends upward at an angle as it narrows; the thin extension of the blade is encased between two strips of rosewood and the whole handle is riveted together with brass. Some 14″ in length, the turner blade is made of Jap-anese steel, but the implement was put together in this country. We especially like its generous size, its flexible but strong metal, and its good feel in the hand.

Perforated Pancake Turner   6.114

Stainless steel with rosewood handle, brass rivets; 14″ long overall; blade 7¾″ × 3″.
$5.25

Another spatula from the manufacturer who made the preceding turner, this one is neatly perforated by sixteen circular holes. Because of those holes, fat can drain off when you pick up frying onions or potatoes. There is something pleasant about the looks of the tidy rows of perforations; but beyond that, the tool is made of the same flexible Japanese steel, is of the same generous size, and has the same pleasantly smooth rosewood-clad handle as its sibling.

245

Extra-long Turner 6.115

Stainless steel with rosewood handle, brass rivets; 19½" long overall; blade 7¾" × 3".
$11.00

This is the turner that cooks use in hash houses; with it, they can reach back to the farthest corners of their smoking griddles, flipping pancakes and hamburgers and eggs. There was some discussion among our experts over whether it is in fact a useful tool for the home cook—it is, after all, a formidable 19½" in length. But the ayes won, that party maintaining that bigger is better, that the turner could be stored in the convenient range-side crock of implements, and that the extra-long handle is ideal for use in summer barbecuing. The nays, on the other hand, pointed out that, for all of the increase in handle length, you get a blade of the same size as that of the preceding two turners.

Turner with Beveled Edges 6.116

Stainless steel with rosewood handle, brass rivets; 11" long overall; blade 5" × 2⅞".
$2.75

The three working edges of this attractive and sturdy stainless-steel turner are beveled so that it may be slipped under the thinnest of crêpes, or be used to remove still-soft cookies from a baking sheet, or be used to scrape up all of the burnt onions on the bottom of the frying pan. A useful version of the spatula, with a stubby blade 5" long and the usual pleasantly shaped rosewood handle, which is held in place with two brass rivets. This turner has a blade which was made in Japan; unlike the other blades we have shown, however, this one is not flexible and therefore might well serve also to help you to lift heavy pieces of meat or baked goods.

Utensils have a mediatory function: the head scratcher, the drinking tube, and the fork are intermediaries between the subject and his body.

Claude Lévi-Strauss, The Raw and the Cooked

Cast-Aluminum Turner 6.117

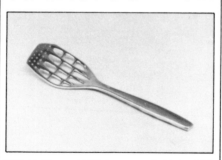

Cast aluminum; 11½" long overall; blade 4½" × 3".
$2.50

If you were to believe the manufacturer, this tool is the real do-everything in the way of implements; they show it slicing bananas, turning fried potatoes and meat patties, lifting fish into breadcrumbs, and beating eggs. Without losing our heads, we *will* say that it is a nice, modestly priced perforated *and* slotted turner made of aluminum, and that it has dinosaur-backbone ridges along the underside of the handle that allow you to rest it on the side of the pan without having it slide into the fat. What the makers *don't* tell you is how to pick up the handle without burning yourself once it has been resting on a hot pan for a while. One of our experts has this at home and adores it, finding it useful for a multi-

tude of jobs; most of us thought it goofy-looking but no less valuable than the more expensive turners, except for the fact that it does not have a wood-clad handle. It is sturdily made of lightweight, rigid cast aluminum and is nearly a foot long. The end of the blade is slanted, beveled, and also perforated for about ¾" before the large slots of the blade begin. The edge, by the way, is not really sharp enough to use as a cutter of anything *but* bananas.

Narrow Perforated Turner 6.118

Stainless steel with rosewood handle, brass rivets; 11" long overall; blade 5⅛" × 2⅛".
$5.00

Once again we find ourselves questioning the claims of a manufacturer: this well-made flexible turner from Sweden comes with the assurance that it can be used on pans which have a release (nonstick) surface—it is claimed that the leading edge is especially polished so as not to damage such coatings. We don't believe it, on the basis of our experience with the fragility of most release coatings. But the point is that this is a good turner anyway, made of a highly flexible stainless steel with one end of the blade totally encased in a riveted-on rosewood handle, leaving no spaces for dirt to invade. It is 11" long, quite narrow, and the blade is perforated by long slits. The handle has been especially treated so as not to be harmed either by the hot edges of a pan or by the hot water of a dishwasher. The turner is also available with a handle of nontreated beechwood.

"Item, *wot you well that pea or bean pottages or others burn easily, if the burning brands touch the bottom of the pot when it is on the fire. Item, before your pottage burns and in order that it burn not, stir it often in the bottom of the pot, and turn your spoon in the bottom so that the pottage may not take hold there.*"

Pot Fork 6.119

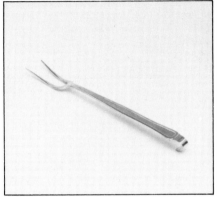

Cast aluminum; 12½″ long.
$2.50 ▲

A fork used in cooking needs to be long, strong, lightweight, and easy to clean: that is all there is to it. Which means that you should get rid of that little stainless-steel four-pronged fork from the five-and-dime and buy instead something resembling this rigid cast-aluminum fork. It has two sharp, widely spaced prongs which curve slightly away from one another, the better to penetrate and hold securely a heavy piece of meat. It is cast in one piece, so that there is no niche or space between fork and handle in which dirt can hide; and it has a hook at the end for hanging and, just possibly, keeping the fork from sliding into a high-sided pot. It is part of a set made in Germany, but it is available separately. We like it because it is strong, lightweight, very inexpensive, and long enough—12½″—to keep the cook's knuckles away from hot food.

LADLES

Of all the implements which stand like a bouquet in a crock next to your stove, the ladle is the most likely to be brought to the table. There it will be used to serve not only soup, but stews and even dishes of rice and other grains. Isn't it lucky that kitchen ladles are so beautiful? You can manage with an inexpensive ladle from the five-and-ten so long as the wooden handle (it is sure to have one) is well attached and not covered with a high-gloss paint which will be sure to peel off and flake into your soup. Check the manner in which the handle is attached to the bowl: there should be no gaping spaces in which food can collect. And notice the angle at which they are joined: are you going to want to plumb deep into a stockpot, or will you, instead, be skimming liquid out of a relatively shallow pan? Think of size: a really small ladle, like those in most utensil sets, is useful for serving small bowls of soup and for adding liquids and melted butter to foods during cooking; the large one in the same sets is needed to help you deal with the contents of an unmanageably large pot. In other words, there is no reason why you shouldn't find an adequate ladle—like a million-dollar baby—in a five-and-ten-cent store. But if you are willing to spend more money for what will be, after all, a once-in-a-lifetime expense, then you can choose from among the ladles we show you here.

PETITS CHOUX BRAISES— SMALL BRAISED CABBAGES

Serves 6

1 large green cabbage
10 slices of bacon (½ pound), coarsely chopped
1 medium-size well-ripened tomato, cubed (1 cup)
2 medium onions, peeled and thinly sliced (1¾ cups)
5 cloves garlic, peeled, crushed and coarsely chopped (1 good tablespoon)
5 carrots, peeled and thinly sliced (1½ cups)
¼ teaspoon freshly ground black pepper
½ teaspoon dried thyme
2 bay leaves, broken into pieces
1 teaspoon salt
2 cups chicken stock
1 tablespoon good wine vinegar
2 tablespoons water
1 tablespoon arrowroot or cornstarch

Clean cabbage and remove any bruised leaves. Cut out the central core to separate the leaves. Try not to damage the large leaves; you will need them later to use as wrappers for the inside of the cabbage. Drop all the leaves into a large pot of salted boiling water. Push the leaves into the water and bring to a boil again. It will take at least 5 minutes for it to start boiling once more; when it does, cover, and continue to boil for 12 minutes more. Place the whole pot of cabbage under cold running water until the leaves are thoroughly cold. Drain in a colander. Select 10 of the largest leaves and set aside to use as wrappers. You will make about 10 little cabbages of these leaves. Cut away the triangular rib sections, which are tough.

Have a 6-ounce round ladle handy. Place a large leaf in the cup of the ladle so that it hangs over the sides. Fill the center of it with more cabbage, pushing to make it compact. Fold the overhanging leaf onto the center, and unmold. You will have a nice round little cabbage. Press it gently to draw out some of the excess water. Repeat until you have used all of the cabbage to make about 10 miniature cabbages.

Heat oven to 400 F. Put the chopped bacon in a large, flat, ovenproof glass baking dish. Top with the tomato, half of the onion, the garlic, half of the carrots, and the pepper; arrange the little cabbages on it. Sprinkle over them the remaining carrots, onion, thyme, bay leaves, and salt; pour the chicken stock over. Bring to a boil on top of the stove. Cover tightly with a large piece of aluminum foil, place on a cookie sheet in oven for 1 hour. Reduce oven to 350 F. and cook 1 hour longer.

Remove from the oven. Take off the aluminum foil; place little cabbages on a platter, and garnish by sprinkling all of the cooked vegetables on top of them.

You should have about 1½ cups of juice left in the gratin dish; mix the vinegar and water with the arrowroot until smooth and add it to the juices. Stirring constantly, bring to a boil. Let boil for a few seconds, then pour over the cabbages. Serve hot as a whole meal with a salad. (Very good reheated.)

(From THE GREAT COOKS COOKBOOK, by The Good Cooking School. Copyright © 1974 by The Good Cooking School, Inc. Reprinted by permission of Ferguson/Doubleday.)

Stainless-Steel Ladle 6.120

Stainless steel; handle 12⅝" long; 4-oz. capacity. Also avail. with capacity of ½, 2, or 8 oz.

$5.25

Isn't this pretty? Its beauty is all the more remarkable because it seems to have been accomplished without effort, without deliberate thought being given to design: the good looks of this stainless-steel ladle come from its functional form. It is made of heavy, rigid stainless steel, the handle curved at one end to form a hook for hanging and the other end neatly welded to the bowl. The bowl itself forms a perfect hemisphere and is joined to the handle in a nearly perpendicular manner, enabling you to go very deep into a pot. We show you the 4-ounce size, a good one for general kitchen use, but you can have it with a bowl holding anywhere from half an ounce to 8 ounces. It is also available with a plastic handle in a medium-large size.

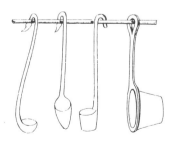

Ladles found in the ruins of Pompeii. From The Pantropheon *of Alexis Soyer.*

Large Stainless-Steel Ladle 6.121

Stainless steel; 22" long overall; bowl 5½" diam., 1¾" deep; 1-pint capacity.

$15.00

This is what a ladle looks like when it holds a full pint. It is simply very, very big: the bowl is larger than half of a large melon, the handle, of necessity, a good-sized bar of heavy-gauge stainless steel. The whole thing weighs a pound when it is empty. And that means that, the weight of liquid being what it is, this ladle could be a problem to lift when it is full of chicken soup. When we were testing this one, we found ourselves worrying about this ladle; would handling it be like trying to lift a pail of water at the end of a rod? In professional kitchens, the size we show here is undoubtedly useful, and even in the home kitchen it offers a most practical method for emptying a stockpot too large to be lifted—an operation like bailing water out of a rowboat with a bucket, or emptying a fish tank with an empty ice-cream container.

"And note as soon as thou shalt perceive that thy pottage burneth, move it not, but straightway take it off the fire and put it in another pot."

The Goodman of Paris (Le Ménager de Paris), *c. 1393. Translated by Eileen Power. George Routledge & Sons, London, 1928*

"Hot soup at table is very vulgar: it either leads to an unseemly mode of taking it, or keeps people waiting too long whilst it cools. Soup should be brought to table only moderately warm."

Hints on Etiquette, *by Charles Day, 1844*

Copper Ladle 6.122

Copper bowl with tin lining, brass handle; 14¼" long overall; bowl 4" diam., 1½" deep.

$16.00

All the qualities which make copper perfect for pots and pans make it all wrong for utensils. It is highly conductive of heat; it is heavy; it needs to be lined with tin or another innocuous metal lest it come in dangerous contact with the food. For those reasons it is highly impractical to use for cooking implements. But it is also utterly beautiful: and for that reason it's an alluring thought to have a copper ladle to bring to the table with your copper pot in order to apportion your onion soup or your ziti with seafood. Just a sex object after all, loved for its looks. This ladle is a hemisphere of shining copper lined with tin (and a lot of good that's going to do, since the whole bowl gets dipped into the food), with a brass handle attached to the bowl by two copper rivets. That this is meant for gracious serving rather than serious kitchen transportation of food is shown by the fact that the bowl is set nearly in line with the handle—it is thus shaped to be used in small, rather shallow serving pots or dishes. How to prevent the potential problems arising from copper in direct contact with food? Just remember that this ladle is for serving, and don't let it stand around for hours in food. And, of course, you will want to keep the metal brilliantly clean.

Partisans of the new, "cool" cookstoves of the last century contrasted the comfort of using such ranges, above, with the discomfort of "the old-fashioned wood cook stove and steamy kitchen," below.

Oven: Casseroles and Pots

7

A radical change in the source of the heat: In this chapter we move away from pots which sit over a gas flame or electric burner and in which energy is conducted from the pot's bottom throughout the sides of the pan. The movement here is towards the casserole in its many incarnations: short-handled or handleless pots, usually covered, in which the quality of the bottom is indistinguishable from that of the sides, or for that matter, of the lid, because these pots are meant to go into an oven or to reproduce, on top of the stove, the all-enveloping oven heat. In the oven, the heat penetrates the pot from all directions and is absorbed through the bottom, the sides, and the top. An intermediary form is the brazier, half-frypan and half-casserole, which has a sturdy bottom for sitting over a burner and short handles for fitting into an oven. The bottoms are reinforced, either with an extra plate or by being drawn more thickly—they are usually one and a half times as thick as the sides.

In looking at casseroles you will notice first the absence of the long handle: this makes them not only thrifty of space, but tells us that the cook need not be actively involved with manipulating these pots. Instead, they are designed for slow cooking done in an oven. They are pots of earthenware or porcelain, enameled steel, copper or other thick metal, pots of good quality, able to diffuse and hold the heat well. And, because there are nearly always covers, you will know that these are pots from which the evaporating steam cannot escape and in which the cooking is therefore done with moist heat. The humidity may come from the foods themselves—for example, the juices released from a mirepoix stewing in butter—or it may be added by the chef—a splash of red wine. When we come to the terrine we will see that the moisture can also consist of fragrant steam released by the cooking meat and forced back into it by the sides of the pot. When we examine the flat baking and roasting dishes in this chapter, we see utensils in which the liquid evaporates as the food cooks. In any of these ways, moisture serves to blend flavors and to soften textures and to create sauces.

Braziers—A Transitional Form

Small world: an American cook is more likely to have a wok in her batterie de cuisine than a brazier. For some reason, this common European cooking pot, half sauté pan and half casserole, has never become a familiar item in the American kitchen. What is a brazier? The name—whose kinship to the equivalent term "braising pan" is evident—comes from a French word meaning live coals or embers; thus, it is a pan—in French, a braisière—meant to be used over direct heat. Once the food is seared in hot fat over the fire, however, it's bathed in a liquid of some sort, covered, and set on the back of the stove or placed in the oven for prolonged cooking.

Most commonly, braziers look like rather high-sided sauté pans with two short grips in place of the sauté pan's long handle. The shape—wider and shallower than that of a saucepan—is particularly suited for making composed dishes in which you want the sauce to reduce: a

Leyse Handleless Sauteuse 7.1

Aluminum with tinned-steel handles; 12″ diam.; 2½″ deep; 5-qt. capacity. $16.20

If this pan had a long handle it would be a covered skillet; if it had higher sides, it would be a casserole. Having neither, it is instead a covered sauteuse, which can be used over a direct flame and then placed in the oven for long cooking. It is a type of pan less familiar to American cooks than it should be, and it is a suitable transition to the more spacious and, therefore, more useful Italian pots which follow but which may be very difficult to find. This American pan is readily available and has its uses in the American kitchen: consider, for example, a less than tender fowl, first sautéed in butter, then, with sherry and tomatoes added, covered and tucked away in an oven set low for gentle cooking. This 12″ pot is of fairly heavy-gauge aluminum and is made with straight sides, a well-fitting flat lid, and two tinned-steel handles. Consider it before you look at—or for—the Italian braziers that follow the next casserole.

Cuisinart Casserole 7.2

Stainless steel with aluminum core, compressed-wood handles; 9½″ diam.; 3″ deep; 3½-qt. capacity. Also avail. with capacity of 2 or 5½ qts.
Max. Temp. 375 F. $43.00 $50.00 ▲
Higher-sided than the sauteuse (7.1) and obviously so attractive that it can

chicken sauté, for example, or a vegetable braised in beef stock. Compare the shape of the brazier with that of a tall, narrow stockpot, which offers a smaller surface to evaporation, and you will understand the difference. And then there is the matter of weight: it is difficult to lift a heavy pan by a single long handle—there are in existence, as a matter of fact, enormous sauté pans which have opposite the long handle a short grip for the cook's assistance. In braziers, which are made of heavy-duty metals and are meant to hold considerable amounts of food, the problem of weight is solved by providing two short handles, thus fitting the pots equally well for use in the oven and on a crowded range top. In fact, many restaurant chefs in this country use braziers rather than sauté pans for browning or sautéing foods for this very reason; and in Italy you will seldom see a frying pan.

A CHOICE OF BRAZIERS

We offer you five braziers, a handleless sauteuse (7.1) that might be called a modified chicken fryer; another, an elegant French beauty; and three superb Italian casseruoli bassi, or low casseroles. The three casseroles are of stainless steel and are nearly identical in shape; we show them all because this common Italian pot is not readily available in this country, and you should count yourself lucky if you can find any one of them. If you are accustomed to browning meat in an iron frypan and then transferring it to an earthenware casserole for further cooking, a simple adjustment of technique, a less daring attitude toward spattering fat, will enable you to use these pots for browning on top of the stove before they are set over a back burner or tucked away in the oven for slow, gentle cooking.

Casseruola Bassa I　　　　7.3

Stainless steel with aluminum bottom; 12″ diam.; 4″ high; 6½-qt. capacity.
$50.00

This is a cooking pot of impeccable quality, of a design seldom seen in this country outside professional kitchens. Imagine osso buco browned with its vegetables in this stainless-steel brazier, then simmered on the back of the stove while the sauce reduces to a thick glaze. This is a roomy pan with aluminum inlaid in the bottom for improved heat distribution. The inside has a brushed finish, the outside is highly polished. The joinings are solidly done, the pot quite strong; it makes us wonder why we don't see more Italian pans in this country. This casseruola bassa holds 6½ quarts and measures 12 inches across the bottom; the sides are only 4″ high.

go from stove to table, this excellent casserole from France looks less foreign to the American cook, but it is in fact the same sort of pot. It is a more elegant version, with better heat conduction, and it is made of stainless steel rather than aluminum. This extends its usefulness to fish, egg sauces, and other discolorables. Cuisinart pots rate high marks for their excellent quality and attractive design. This casserole has a mirrorlike stainless-steel finish and satiny compressed wood handles, while its special thermal bottom, in which a core of aluminum is welded to the steel body, is designed to conduct heat even better than copper. The stainless-steel cover has a knob of the same compressed wood as the handles; care must be taken that the oven temperature does not exceed 375 F. lest damage be done to the handles and knob. In both family (2-quart and 3½-quart) and party (5½-quart) sizes, this pot will repay you for its steep price by its durability and good looks.

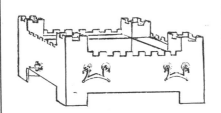

Another kind of brazier, a Roman model described in The Pantropheon. The hollow walls contained water and the charcoal went in the center; over the fire the cooking pot hung from a tripod.

Braising was formerly accomplished in a pan that held coals on the cover, to heat its contents from both sides—see our examples of the doufeu, 7.15 and 7.19. This way of cooking is described in this passage from The Modern Housewife by Alexis Soyer, published around 1850: "Braising . . . like the sauté, belongs entirely to the French school from which it takes its name, braise being the remains of the wood burnt in the oven, or live charcoal: this plan of cookery requires the action of the fire under and over the braising pan, which is air-tight, in order that the aromatic flavour arising from its contents may be imbibed by the meat or poultry, and give it that succulence so esteemed by epicures. The braise is put on the cover, which in some cases is made deep on purpose to hold it."

Casseruola Bassa II   7.4

Stainless-steel with aluminum sandwich bottom; 9½" diam.; 3½" deep; 4½-qt. capacity. Also avail. with capacity of 7, 10½, 15, 20½, or 28 qts.

$75.00

Another beauty from Italy, this one, in our first-choice size, smaller than the preceding low casserole but of equally high quality. The bottom measures 9½" across, while the pot is only 3½" deep; the whole is of good stainless steel of a very heavy weight, with handles welded on and an aluminum plate on the bottom for an even distribution of heat. The unusual dimensions of the stainless-steel handles, the body's satin finish, and the rim's thickened, mirror-finished band qualify this casserole to appear at table. There is a matching lid which must be ordered separately; in design it resembles the Cuisinart Universal Cover (6.96), and it, too, is of stainless steel.

Casseruola Bassa III   7.5

Heavy-gauge stainless steel; 7½" diam.; 5" deep; 4-qt. capacity.

$65.00

Smaller still across the bottom and with even higher sides (5") than its sister pots, this Italian brazier begins to resemble a saucepan divested of its long handle. But notice the set of the handles of all three pans: all imply that you will be lifting a rather heavy weight from above, a whole chicken or a pot roast. Then try to imagine lifting such a weight in a long-handled pan and you will appreciate the logic of the design. This is another amazingly well-made pot from Italy in stainless steel of a heavy gauge. The handles are welded solidly to the sides, and the bottom is of double thickness for even distribution of heat.

AN OVEN GLOSSARY

Pots are called by many names, often depending on the country or region in which they are made or used. Often the pot and the characteristic dish cooked in it developed together and they share a name: thus, terrine, marmite. To some extent the terms which designate the covered pots we use in oven cooking are interchangeable; and when they are not, it is because a certain pot has a very specific purpose—every bean pot is a casserole, but not every casserole is a bean pot. If we err in applying names to pots, it will be in the direction of generality: vagueness is not a stance to be admired, but it's preferable, we think, to making definitive but misleading pronouncements. And the fact is that most of these definitions overlap and become blurred; one man's daubière is another man's Dutch oven.

Every country has its own earthenware pots; some of those that don't appear here can be found in other chapters.

BEAN POT. *A tall covered casserole with a lid often bulbous in shape and usually made of glazed earthenware. The shape helps to encourage the mingling of flavors of the various layers of ingredients within.*

BRAZIER. *A twin-handled metal pot, with or without a lid, and usually having a reinforced bottom so that it can be used for top-of-the-stove cooking; a braising pan.*

CASSEROLE. *A covered pot of earthenware or metal, having two short handles or no handle at all, and meant for use both on a stove burner and in the oven. In French, casserole means simply "saucepan"; but in English it has come to mean only the pot without a long handle.*

CASSERUOLA BASSA. *In Italy, a fairly low casserole. More specifically, what we call a brazier.*

CASSOLE. *An earthenware casserole resembling a clay flower pot, used in the south of France for making a cassoulet.*

COCOTTE. *The same as a casserole. Larousse Gastronomique tells us that the terms en casserole and en cocotte are synonymous. Small individual ramekins are also called cocottes.*

DAUBIERE. *A pot in which we prepare daube or stew; usually of earthenware. Daube comes from Old French and it is not clear whether the root was in the idea of clay—as in an adobe wall—or the covering of seasonings with which the meat was customarily daubed (another extension of the word).*

DIABLE. *A round, single-handled pot with a cover that is a mirror image of the bottom. Of unglazed earthenware, it is used to roast potatoes and chestnuts without any liquid.*

DOUFEU. *A covered casserole distinguished by a depression in the lid into which it was once the custom to shovel hot coals. It is now recommended that the cook pour water into the depression to encourage condensation within the pot.*

DUTCH OVEN. *Historically, a covered stewing or baking pot which hung on a hook over the open fire or was set among the coals. In the Midwest today, Dutch oven is the term used for an oval, domed roaster; in the East it is used for a heavy, round, short-handled (or top-handled) pot intended for top-of-the-stove cooking. The term is also abused by stove manufacturers, who sometimes miscall their slow-cooking wells "Dutch ovens."*

FAIT-TOUT. *Literally, "does-everything." A round or oval enameled cast-iron covered casserole; not unlike a brazier.*

KETTLE. *A large metal pot with a lid and a wire loop handle, usually made of iron; can be a name for a Dutch oven.*

MARMITE. *A pot for cooking petite marmite; actually a bulging-sided stockpot, most often made of porcelain but also of earthenware or metal. The shape helps to reduce evaporation of the broth.*

POELON. *A small, uncovered earthenware or metal casserole with a short, fat handle and a pouring lip.*

SLOW COOKER. *A covered electrical pot made to resemble a casserole; it may be of metal and plastic or metal and ceramic and it will hold a steady temperature as low as 200 F. for long, gentle cooking.*

STEWPOT. *The Anglicized version of the daubière.*

TERRINE. *From the French* terre, *or "earth," and, therefore, an earthenware casserole. Oval or rectangular, usually with a cover, and used for cooking the ground-meat mixtures which are called* pâtés *when they are unmolded for service and* terrines *when they are served from the baking dish.*

TIAN. *The name of a pot and the food cooked in it—a mixture of vegetables typical of Provence. There are other casseroles strongly identified with one*

region of France—a toupin, *a* caquelon, *for example.*

TRIPIERE. *A covered earthenware casserole used for cooking tripes à la mode. The tripière has one of two highly distinctive but totally different shapes, being either nearly totally flat, like a flying saucer, or else tall and long-necked.*

TUREEN. *This doesn't fit here, being a porcelain or pottery covered dish from which soup is served at table. We included it to help you distinguish it from a terrine.*
(See p. 194 for Stovetop Utensils)

Round Casseroles

If a brazier is a convenient way to add humidity and slow cooking to the virtues of a frying pan, the next step is the cozying of meats and vegetables to blended warmth in casseroles.

On long winter afternoons when the fireplace or the stove is lit against the damp and the chill, when dinner takes its place not as an interruption of outdoor play but rather as the chief occupation of the end of the day, and when the seasonal foods tend to be those which need long and gentle cooking, what is more appropriate than to take advantage of these facts and make your supper in a casserole? Tucked away in the oven to cook slowly all afternoon, it will fill the warm kitchen with good smells. Let summer people and Californians eat their freshly picked vegetables raw, their slices of meat barely charred over a quick fire; in the winter when hearths are warm we want food long-cooked in simmering broths. To cook the food we crave come winter, onions and turnips and carrots are turned as they heat in butter, then are bathed in the remains of last night's wine to serve as a bed for an inexpensive roast, all under a lid which catches the condensing steam and sends it back to baste the meat.

MATERIALS FOR OVENWARE

For this we need pots which will take heat from a surrounding source and transmit it evenly through a liquid; the liquid will amplify the heat, as earthenware does, so that a stove turned way down (or even a corner of the fireplace distant from the flames) will provide enough energy to keep the contents bubbling. Earthenware (see "Pottery Pots" for our crafted casseroles), then, and heavy porcelain and glass, enameled iron and the metals which are not so responsive to temperature changes—all these are good for our ovenware. We don't require long handles, because these are dishes which, once put in the oven, will scarcely be touched until they are taken out again, and long handles are wasteful of both oven space and of effort when you lift a laden pot.

DEFINITION BY FUNCTION

A picture emerges, then, of what we call casseroles: fairly low and wide, made of earthenware or a conductive metal, handleless or having short

Heavy Iron Kettle 7.6

Cast iron with heat-resistant glass lid; 10" diam.; 3¼" deep; 5-qt. capacity.
$16.25

The primeval pot; the Ur-pot; that from which the others all come and towards which they all aim is the prototype for this one. You should be thrilled to discover that these pots are still being made, scaled-down versions of kettles which once hung from enormous hooks in kitchen fireplaces or stood on their metal legs over the glowing coals. Of course, they are extraordinarily heavy, and all but impossible to move with one hand; of course, the handle will burn the cook's hands with the slightest unwary touch; and, of course, they will rust if given any but the most attentive care. What matter? Here you have a folk classic, the ultimate gift for friends with a country house, and a pot not to be discounted for use in the fireplace during power failures. If you are willing to maintain it, to dry and oil it carefully after every use, you will find this a pot that heats and maintains its heat better than one of enameled iron or steel. In other words, it is not a cute tourist item; it is a real kettle for cooking real food the old-fashioned way. This one, by General Housewares, is superior to Oriental imports, but its cover, alas, is glass.

A man went to a great fair and bought a glorious three-legged iron pot. It would hang in the fireplace and be used for stews. On the way home the pot grew heavier and heavier. The man set it down and said to the pot, "I have carried you this far. You have three legs and I have two. Now it is your turn to carry me." He stood there waiting but the pot refused to walk. The man waited for a while and then angrily continued home, leaving the pot to come home by itself.
Paraphrased from The Stone Soup: The Magic of Familiar Things, *by Maria Leach, 1954*

handles, and usually fitted with a snug cover. Keep your eye on these covers: they make all the difference, providing a means for condensation of moisture (and thus providing self-basting), and they also reflect heat down onto your ragout or bird, making the pot into a sort of oven which cooks by enveloping the food in moist heat. (Some recipes even specify that you seal the edges of the casserole lid with pastry to enclose the food more completely.) With this next group of casseroles, we have moved completely away from the sauté pan and into the area of pans designed entirely for cooking with moisture. What you call these pots is another problem. We include a glossary (after 7.5) of the more-or-less interchangeable terms for the group to which this kind of pot belongs, with their more-or-less interchangeable definitions. Only be aware that categories and definitions overlap; that one man's Dutch oven is another man's casseruola bassa; and that most of the pots in this group can be called casseroles with no apologies.

Copper and Stainless-Steel Casserole 7.7

Heavy-gauge copper with heavy-gauge stainless-steel interior and handles; 10¼″ diam.; 5½″ deep; 7-qt. capacity. Also avail. with capacity of 10½, 15, 27, 38, 49½, 50, 61½, or 74½ qts.
$92.40

This Bi-Metal casserole is made of the best metals for cooking that you can buy; once that is said, we must add that it is astonishingly expensive and terribly heavy. But if you have the money and the space and the strength, then look into this line, of which we show several: each consists of a copper utensil lined with a stainless-steel utensil. That's right—one metal is not painted on the other, not washed on, not applied to the bottom, but both are used to make two pots of superior quality bonded permanently together to create a superb and all-but-immortal instrument for cooking. It is the very best restaurant-quality equipment around, and although the stainless half of the sandwich does limit the sensitivity of the copper somewhat,

it makes up for it by its contribution in strength and invulnerability. There is a whole line of pots like the one we show you, ranging in size all the way up to a little beauty holding 74½ quarts; we suggest either the 7- or 10-quart size. The smaller one is 10¼″ in diameter; the larger, 12¼″. There are stainless-steel covers to fit all sizes (6.94).

Black Lauffer Casserole 7.8

Porcelainized cast iron; 9″ diam.; 4¼″ deep; 4-qt. capacity. Also avail. with capacity of 2, 3, or 5 qts.
$38.00

Again we are dealing with a whole line of fine cooking ware, but unlike the Bi-Metal pots, most of which are made huge for use in professional kitchens, these Lauffer pans from England are designed specifically for the home kitchen. You will be hearing about them in their many shapes because of the good design and excellent quality of the product. Here is a large round casserole with a lid shaped like a ramekin, made of heavy cast iron and lined with a speckled white porcelain finish. There is an interesting ten-

sion between the design, which is elegant and modern, and the material, which reminds one of the past. These pots go comfortably from the freezer to the oven and are resistant to the food acids which do so much damage in aluminum and unlined iron pans. They range in capacity from 2 to 5 quarts; the 4-quart size seems to us most useful. Extremely handsome, almost intrusively interesting in design: a good gift. Remember that these pots, due to the design of the bottom (an all-around ridge lifts the pot up slightly) and the fact that the bottoms are enameled, are better for use over gas than electricity.

". . . [But] for supper Grandma made hasty pudding. She stood by the stove, sifting the yellow corn meal from her fingers into a kettle of boiling, salted water. She stirred the water all the time with a big wooden spoon, and sifted in the meal until the kettle was full of a thick, yellow, bubbling mass. Then she set it on the back of the stove where it would cook slowly. . . . At supper time Pa and Grandpa came in from the woods . . . Pa and Grandpa had brought the syrup from the big kettle in the woods . . . Grandma made room for a huge brass kettle on the stove. Pa and Grandpa poured the syrup into the brass kettle, and it was so large that it held all the syrup from the four big buckets . . . everybody ate the hot hasty pudding with maple syrup for supper."

Laura Ingalls Wilder, The Little House in the Big Woods, *Harper & Row, New York, 1932*

QUEUE DE BOEUF AUX OLIVES NOIRES—STEWED OXTAIL WITH BLACK OLIVES

For 2 oxtails the other ingredients are olive oil, brandy, white wine, stock or water, a big *bouquet* of bay leaves, thyme, parsley, orange peel and crushed garlic cloves, about ½ lb. of stoned black olives.

Have the oxtails cut into the usual pieces by the butcher. Put them to steep in cold water for a couple of hours so that the blood soaks out. Take them out and drain them. Heat 2 or 3 tablespoons of olive oil in a big heavy stew-pan or *daubière*. Put in the pieces of oxtail and let them sizzle gently a few minutes. Pour over 4 to 6 tablespoons of warmed brandy and set light to it. When the flames have died down, add a large glass, about 6 to 8 ounces, of white wine. Let it bubble fiercely a minute or so. Add just enough stock or water to come level with the pieces of oxtail. Bury the *bouquet* in the centre. Cover the pan. Transfer to a very slow oven, Gas No. 1, 290°F. Cook for about 3 hours.

Pour off all the liquid and leave until next day. Remove the fat. Heat the remaining stock; pour it back over the oxtail. Add the stoned olives. Cook for another hour or so on top of the stove, until the oxtail is bubbling hot and the meat coming away from the bones. Serve with a dish of plain boiled rice.

This dish can, of course, be cooked all in one operation but, for those who don't like very fat rich food, the system of getting rid of most of the fat from the sauce makes a better dish. The flaming with brandy also does much to strengthen the flavour of the sauce, but it can be left out if it seems a rather extravagant ingredient in a dish which should really be a cheap one.

These quantities should make plenty for six people, but the dish is one which can very well be made with one oxtail only.

(From FRENCH PROVINCIAL COOKING, by Elizabeth David. Copyright © 1960 by Elizabeth David.)

Round Farberware Casserole   7.9

Stainless steel with aluminum bottom, stainless-steel handles; 12″ diam.; 4″ deep; 6-qt. capacity. Lid has heat-resistant, phenolic-resin handle.

Max. Temp. 425 F. $37.99

This is really a round casserole, though Farberware, its manufacturer, calls it a "roaster." In the familiar line of American cookware made of stainless steel

with a thick layer of aluminum bonded to the bottom, they are a consistently good buy. The stainless steel is easy to clean, while the aluminum provides good heat diffusion: this is a pan in which you will be able to first sear and then stew your beef. The domed, tight-fitting lid, with a phenolic-resin knob, permits the cook to use this 6-quart pot as a capacious casserole as well as a brazier; but because the heat resistance of the knob extends only to 425 F., take care not to overheat the oven in which this pot is used. It is of good quality, neither the best nor the worst of its category, and is one of the few American pans with the shape of a brazier.

French Copper Casserole   7.10

Heavy-gauge copper with tin lining, brass handles; 8″ diam.; 4″ deep; 3½-qt. capacity. Also avail. with capacity of ¾, 1¾, 5, or 6¾ qts.

Max. Temp. 425 F. $67.50

This tin-lined copper casserole with brass handles, imported by Lamalle, could do nearly any job in your kitchen. Copper is marvelous for sautéing—and thus the pan could serve as a small brazier; copper provides superb conductivity without forming any hot spots—and thus the pan might well be a saucepan; and the pot itself has short handles and a tightly sealed, domed lid, as befits a casserole. All in all, a casserole that embodies the concept of the fait-tout, the French pot that does everything. This is the very best quality imaginable in this material; the pot is not at all cheap, but owning it is a goal to which we might well all aspire. We show you the 3½-quart size, 4″ deep and 8″ in diameter, a size in which you could make anything from a generous amount of Hollandaise sauce to a pot of the hottest chili in town.

"Cooking was done largely in the open, with venison and turkeys and geese turning on the spits, lobsters and oysters roasting in the coals, and clam chowder and venison stew simmering in iron kettles over the fire. One can imagine the weariness of the women during those festival days. . . . Fortunately they were spared the task of dishwashing, since there were no utensils except knives to cut up the meat and a few wooden spoons . . ."

Commentary on the first Thanksgiving from We Gather Together: The Story of Thanksgiving, *Ralph and Adelin Linton, Abelard-Schuman, London and New York, 1949*

Portuguese Copper Casserole   7.11

Medium-gauge copper with tin lining, brass handles; 4¾″ diam.; 2½″ deep; 1-pint capacity.

Max. Temp. 425 F. $30.00

If you put this small Portuguese copper pot on a shelf next to the Lamalle casserole (7.10) in its smaller size, you would always reach for the latter; but if you saw it all by itself you would be happy to have it. Although it is not a sable like the Lamalle, it is not a plain cloth coat either. It is formed of medium-gauge copper, polished to a high shine, with a good tin lining and polished brass handles. The sides are straight and the lid close-fitting; it is 4¾″ in diameter and holds 1 pint. Altogether, a reasonable version of a classic concept.

A hare and two rabbits ready to cook, 1824.

Large French Aluminum Casserole   7.12

Heavy-gauge aluminum; 10⅛" diam.; 5⅜" deep; 8-qt. capacity.

$37.50

When is a brazier a casserole? When the sides are high enough for a large mix of ingredients and a top goes on to retain juice and steam. We are on record already: we don't *prefer* aluminum for cooking mixed dishes, because you have to be concerned about discoloration of certain ingredients, like white wine, for instance. But who could help loving this big beautiful aluminum pot? It is of heavy-gauge metal, hammered for extra strength, with an attractive leaf-like pattern all over the outside. It also is a boon for people who don't want to lift a pot this size in steel or iron or copper. The bottom is large and the sides medium high, so that any stew cooked in it will reduce properly without boiling away entirely. Unfortunately, the lid provided is lightweight and not especially vapor-tight, but the pot itself is a beauty. This heavyweight from France, with a capacity of 8 quarts, is one of those delightful pots that just feel good when you handle them.

The culinary equipment of the ancient Greeks was rudimentary, but the basic pieces were well-wrought and quickly perfected: among the fundamentals were marmites, cauldrons, casseroles, and spits. Most cooking vessels had covers, which permitted the slow stewing of meats with little added liquid. The Greek pots were generally made of bronze, iron, or earthenware, but elegantly decorated gold and silver versions have also been unearthed.

Italian Aluminum Casserole   7.13

Unpolished, unalloyed aluminum with cast-aluminum handles; 11" diam.; 5½" deep; 9-qt. capacity. Also avail. with capacity of 13½, 19, 26, or 38 qts.

$50.00

Yet another beautiful big pot, this one of unpolished, unalloyed aluminum with a dull, satiny finish and thick, shiny cast-aluminum handles. Similar in shape to an Italian brazier we described earlier (7.4), it is from Italy, holds 9 quarts, and has easily gripped handles and a comfortable heft in the hand. Straight-sided, heavy, solid: only you can decide whether the drawbacks of aluminum (see Chapter 6) are made up for by the quality of this pot.

Copco Casserole   7.14

Porcelainized cast iron; 8¼" diam.; 4" deep; 2½-qt. capacity; lid 8" diam., 1¼" deep. Also avail. with capacity of 1½, 5, or 7 qts.

$37.00 $25.00 $49.00 $59.00 ▲

Among Denmark's finest exports is Copco ware (see also 8.15 and 6.9, for example), the durable enameled cast-iron pots which ornament many American kitchens. This casserole comes in a range of sizes with capacities of 1½ to 7 quarts and in a range of clear colors: blue, yellow, red, brown, and white. One glance; you know it's European. The gently sloped, well-balanced shape communicates the clean design produced on that continent, and the bright colors (even the white) are far from the omnipresent dead-avocado of recent American ware. As both the pot and the lid have handles of the same enameled iron as the bodies, this casserole can be used safely in an extremely hot oven. We like the Copco pans because there is no enamel on the special flat-ground bottoms, which sit as well on an electric stovetop as over gas, with no risk of burning off the enamel and with the perfect contact between pot and burner essential to electric cooking. One flaw: porcelain-interiored pans simply do not sauté well; food cooked in them will never be "seized" as well as it would be in a metal pan. For ideal results in a pot with a light, bright, shiny enameled interior, sauté the meat in a heavy iron frying pan, then cook it gently in the enameled pot until done.

The raw material: A fine pullet shown in an old cookook.

Large French Aluminum Casserole
Italian Aluminum Casserole
Copco Casserole
Round Doufeu

Finnish Casserole with Metal Handles
Round Magnalite Casserole

Every cooking utensil in the camp was needed to produce the black duck dinner served by Paul Bunyan for his loggers: "The black ducks, of course, received first attention. And great as the plates were, by the time one was heaped with a brown fried drumstick, a ladle of duck dumplings, several large fragments of duck fricassee, a slab of duck baked gumbo style, a rich portion of stewed duck, and a mound of crisp brown dressing, all immersed in golden duck gravy, a formidable space was covered. Yet there was still room for cabbage, mashed potatoes, potato cakes, stewed tomatoes, corn on the cob, baked beans, peas, applesauce, lettuce, cornbread, hot biscuits and condiments. And then there was dessert to ponder upon . . ."

James Stevens, Paul Bunyan, *Alfred A. Knopf, New York, 1948*

Round Doufeu 7.15

Enameled cast iron; 9½" diam.; 4¼" deep; 4-qt. capacity. Also avail. with 6-qt. capacity.
$45.00 ▲ $50.00 ▲

A doufeu is, literally, a "gentle fire," from the French words *doux* and *feu*. The pan so named has a deeply recessed cover which was originally filled with hot coals so that the meat within was cooked, without benefit of oven, between two fires. Today we have ovens and stoves with even heat, so we use the recessed space for cool water. This encourages condensation within; the steam formed in cooking will gather on the bumps on the inside of the lid and drip back to baste the meat. Here, an enameled cast-iron round doufeu from France. It comes in both 4- and 6-quart sizes and in a variety of colors. Choose from flame, yellow, green, or brown. The point is that, even if you don't intend to do the business with the water, the pot itself is a handsome, good-quality cooking utensil.

Finnish Casserole with Metal Handles 7.16

Stainless steel with aluminum bottom and stainless-steel handles; 7" diam.; 6½" high; 3-qt. capacity. Also avail. with capacity of 1½", 2, 4, or 5 qts.
$28.50

A perfectly beautiful pot. This manufacturer's most attractive top-of-the-stove design has a sleek, uncluttered shape with handles made of nicely turned loops of stainless steel. Today's cook, servantless, needs pans like these which can go elegantly to the table and eliminate one level of dishwashing. The casserole is of stainless steel with an aluminum bottom, all gentle curves and smooth finish, and is available in sizes holding from 1½ to 5 quarts. The lid serves both to establish the tightest seal in town and as a beautiful gratin pan. But be careful about using the cover as a pan over a burner—remember that it has no mediating layer of aluminum or copper, and the thin stainless steel, used alone, can produce scorching and uneven cooking. Such a very beautiful product, this, that it seems ungallant to mention that we might have preferred a metal of a somewhat heavier weight.

ESTOFAT DE BOEUF ALBIGEOIS — BEEF STEW WITH RED WINE AND BRANDY

A fine large piece of topside or top rump of beef is required for this dish, and it is not worth attempting with less than 4 to 5 lb. The other ingredients are a little pork or goose dripping or oil, carrots, onions, garlic, half a bottle of red wine, brandy if possible, a big faggot of aromatic herbs including bay leaves, thyme, and parsley, about 1 lb. of streaky salt pork, and 2 pigs' trotters.

Have your beef rolled and tied in a good shape; melt the dripping in a heavy pot which has a well fitting lid; put in the meat, surround it with 2 large sliced onions, 4 or 5 carrots, a couple of cloves of garlic. Start off over a gentle flame for 15 minutes, and when the fat is running and the onions beginning to colour, pour in 4 oz. (8 tablespoons) of brandy; let it bubble; add the wine; put in the salt pork, the trotters (split) and the *bouquet*, and a very little salt. Cover the pot, transfer to the lowest possible oven, and there leave it for about 7 or 8 hours.

The result of this lengthy, almost imperceptible cooking is a beautifully tender piece of meat and a rich, aromatic, but rather fat sauce; to counteract this, serve with it plenty of plain boiled or purée potatoes or rice if you prefer. The dish is also delicious cold, and resembles a *boeuf mode*, except that the meat is not larded, and the jellied sauce is thicker and darker. The vegetables must be strained off, and the fat removed when the sauce has set. The trotters, from which the bones will have almost fallen out, can be coated with melted butter and breadcrumbs, gently grilled and, with a *sauce tartare*, make a little hot hors-d'oeuvre.

(From FRENCH PROVINCIAL COOKING, by Elizabeth David. Copyright © 1960 by Elizabeth David.)

Round Magnalite Casserole 7.17

Cast magnesium-aluminum alloy with phenolic-resin handle; 10" diam.; 5¼" deep; 6-qt. capacity; 6 lbs. Also avail. with capacity of 5 or 7½ qts.
Max. Temp. 400 F. $28.25

We cannot imagine a greater contrast to the Sarpaneva designs from Finland than this homely but worthy American casserole. It's a pot you can find easily and, once found, can afford: nothing to sneer

257

Continued from preceding page

at. Magnalite pots—versatile utensils that are worthy to be put into the fait-tout class—come in several sizes. One holding 6 quarts weighs only 6 pounds, its solid body of a magnesium and aluminum alloy making it appear much heavier. It would be hard to find a better utensil for quick and even heating and browning as well as for the long, slow braising of large pieces of meat. We show you the oval version of this pot in another chapter as a roaster (8.46), but the distinction is merely a matter of semantics: "roast" indicates a *thing* as well as a *process,* and roasts tend to be long rather than round. But you could do a chicken paprikash as well as a cut of beef in that one, a fat little rolled roast in this; as a matter of fact, a meat rack is included for the moderate price.

Oval Casseroles

They've all been round, the casseroles we have discussed so far: round to sit neatly on a burner without wasting one bit of heat, round to rest in the center of your oven, equidistant from all four walls. And after all, you can make lentil soup or a risotto in a pot of any imaginable shape. But sometimes the pot must suit the contents, and when the pot is to hold a whole chicken or a boned leg of lamb or a filet of beef, we prefer to use a large oval casserole. (Smaller casseroles of this shape are terrines.)

BEAUTY FOR THE BEEF?

An interesting philosophical point: just how important is beauty in a pot which will never be brought to the table? Large cuts of meat are removed from the casserole, sliced on a board, and then presented on a platter, rather than in the pot in which they were cooked: when you are balancing comparative cooking qualities and durability against cost, how much will you pay for beauty? A point to be considered when making a choice among the pots we show you in this section.

Lauffer Oval Casserole   7.18

Porcelainized cast iron; 9″ × 6″; 3½″ deep; 2¾-qt. capacity. Also avail. with 4-qt. capacity.
$28.00

An oval casserole made by H. E. Lauffer in England of enameled cast iron with a matte black exterior, all lined with a speckled white porcelain glaze. Two sizes—2¾ quarts and 4 quarts—to accommodate two sizes of poultry, or to make terrines for large or small dinner parties. These are heavy pots with close-fitting lids and the ability to withstand great extremes in temperature. Excellent quality; miles ahead of the Magnalite oval roaster (8.46) in looks; moderately ahead in price.

LA POULE FARCIE EN DAUBE A LA BERRICHONNE—BONED STUFFED CHICKEN IN JELLY

Around Easter time and the early summer, when the old hens no longer useful for laying are killed off, different versions of this dish are made in many of the country districts of central France. It is a method of turning an old boiling fowl into a civilized and savoury dish. Apart from a large boiling hen, the ingredients [British measures] are ½ lb. each of minced pork and veal, and all the seasonings one would ordinarily use for a pâté, i.e. a little white wine and cognac, garlic, parsley, pepper, salt, an egg, perhaps pistachio nuts, a calf's foot and, if possible, a pint or so of veal stock, plus carrots and onions.

The poulterer or butcher must be persuaded to bone the bird for you; there are still many competent ones who will do this, and you never know till you ask.

Mix the pork and veal together, add the liver of the bird first stiffened in butter, then cut into little dice. Season with about 2 teaspoons of salt, pepper, a chopped clove of garlic, a tablespoon of chopped parsley, and about a dozen halved pistachio nuts if you have them. Add a coffee-cupful (after-dinner size) of white wine, a tablespoon of brandy, and 1 whole beaten egg. Stuff the chicken with this mixture, reshape it as much as possible in its original form, tie round with string, and secure the openings with little wooden skewers. Place on a bed of sliced onion and carrot in a deep oval pot which will go in the oven; put the calf's foot, divided into four, all round. Pour over the stock, fill up with water just to cover, add a *bouquet* of bay leaf, thyme, and parsley, and cover with two layers of foil or greaseproof paper and the lid. Cook in a very slow oven, Gas No. 2, 310° F., for 3 hours or a little over.

Remove the bird carefully; it is now advisable to continue cooking the liquid with the calf's foot for another hour at least in order that the jelly which it ultimately produces shall be really firm. Strain it into a bowl; leave to set. Remove the fat. Just melt the jelly; remove the strings from the bird and, in order to facilitate serving, carve into slices obliquely downwards as if you were cutting a sausage. If the leg bones have been left in, as they usually are, they will be soft enough to be carved right through with a good knife. Reshape the bird, put it in a deep serving dish, pour over the jelly and leave to set again.

Serve with a green salad or a potato salad; if you want to give a rather copious meal, it can serve as a first course in the same way as a pâté; otherwise as a main course.

(From FRENCH PROVINCIAL COOKING, by Elizabeth David. Copyright © 1960 by Elizabeth David.)

In nineteenth-century France the word casserole still denoted a baked, molded crust of rice filled with a fricassee of white meat or a game purée. Here is an elaborate casserole from the collection of James Beard.

Oval Doufeu 7.19

Enameled cast iron; 12″ × 9½″; 4″ deep; 6-qt. capacity. Also avail. with 4½-qt. capacity.
$50.00 ▲

Not unlike the Lauffer casserole in appearance is this oval doufeu from France, of cast iron with a matte-enamel finish inside and out. If you have had enough of our passion for black pots, you may prefer one of the other colors: flame, brown, yellow, green, or blue. The top of this pot has the unique doufeu depression, into which the cook pours cold water to encourage condensation and self-basting on the inside. This is a more primitive-appearing pan than the one by Lauffer, probably because it is like the original casserole of this type, which had a depression in the lid to be filled with hot coals to simulate a small oven. Heavy, costly, formidable: the pot we show you is a foot long and can hold 6 quarts.

Le Creuset Oval Casserole 7.20

Enameled cast iron; 9½″ × 7½″; 3¾″ deep; 3½-qt. capacity. Also avail. with capacity of 2, 5¼, or 7¼ qts.
$34.95

This oval casserole illustrates the latest improvement in design from Le Creuset: a bottom which has been glazed lightly and then fired only once, so that it retains the appearance of untreated iron, resists chipping, and heats up rapidly. This bottom sits securely on a burner, far more securely than possible for bottoms treated with the typical porcelain enameling. A nice pot on all counts: oval, 9½″ long, available in any of an assortment of soft colors (plus one loud chartreuse) on the outside; all the pots have a soft beige interior. Identify it by the peculiar T-shaped handles, odd to look at but nice to use, and also by the smoothly domed lid with a flat knob as a handle.

CANARD AUX NAVETS

At the bottom of a fireproof casserole, of a size to hold the duck comfortably, arrange 3 or 4 slices of bacon, 2 onions cut in rounds, 2 or 3 carrots also in rounds, a bayleaf and a small stick of celery.

Place the trussed and seasoned duck on this bed and braise it gently for 10-15 minutes, then pour a glass of white wine over it and let it reduce, add 2 glasses of brown stock and continue cooking very gently with the lid on. A medium-sized duck will take about 1¼ hours. When the duck is cooked take it out and keep it hot. Put the contents of the pan through a sieve, making a fairly thick brown sauce; skim off the fat as much as possible.

Return the sauce and the duck to the pan, and place all round it 2 or 3 dozen baby turnips [cooked as for glazed turnips] which you have prepared while the duck is braising.

Let the whole dish get very hot and serve it in the casserole.

(From FRENCH COUNTRY COOK-ING, by Elizabeth David. Copyright © 1951 by Elizabeth David.)

Ancient classical influences are seen in the design of this seventeenth-century bell-metal marmite.

Oval Copper Casserole 7.21

Heavy-gauge copper with tin lining, brass handles; 9½″ × 6½″; 4″ deep; 3-qt. capacity. Also avail. with capacity of 1 qt. 5 oz. and 2, 4, or 7 qts.
Max. Temp. 425 F. $86.00

From *la bête* to *la belle:* from the Beast to Beauty. This and the oval doufeu (7.19) are both French, and both are in the grand tradition, but there the resemblance ends. Here is an oval casserole of highly polished copper with brass handles riveted securely on either end. It is tin-lined, as we would expect, and it has its own handsome, brass-handled cover; it is of a good weight, holds 3 quarts, and will last for generations with nothing more than an occasional retinning. Superb in function and in appearance; make it a gift to yourself for mastering your most-admired recipe.

Oval Doufeu
Le Creuset Oval Casserole
Oval Copper Casserole

Shallow Nambé Casserole
Deep Nambé Casserole
Paderno Stainless-Steel Casserole

DISCOVERING NAMBE

One of our editors learned about Nambé while in the south of France at the home of an expatriate American friend. Oh, didn't she know this marvelous American cookware? It was light in weight, nonporous, with fabulous heat retention and the ability to go from the freezer to the oven with ease. And it was, as she could readily see, terrific to look at: pots of a shiny, smooth aluminum alloy had won prizes for good design awarded by the Museum of Modern Art. Further investigation exposed further facts: Nambé is not only the name of the alloy but of the factory (just like Magnalite). It is a small, relatively new plant outside Santa Fe, New Mexico, where a slowly growing group of craftsmen dedicate themselves to the production of hand-finished metalware. There they use the technique of sand casting, in which a wax model is imbedded in sand, the wax is melted away, and the molten metal is poured into the resulting space. And then the hardened metal is hand-finished and polished by craftsmen, placing the operation at the level of industrialization, say, of the Bennington Potters, and at least fifty wonderful years backwards in the Industrial Revolution.

but these are unimportant. We are more interested in the size and the shape. You are less likely to use this 2-quart casserole as a braising pan and more likely to assemble in it a casserole of rice and beans or a small stew of chicken and hot peppers. (Our mouths get ready for Mexican food when we see it because it is made in Santa Fe and because it has visual qualities which remind us of American Indian jewelry.) You can use this pot over the flame, or in the oven, or even in your deep-freeze to prepare a frozen dessert, and its lid can be used separately as a baking dish. Should this ware become discolored, there is a special Nambé polish which will take care of that.

Paderno Stainless-Steel Casserole 7.24

Heavy stainless steel with aluminum sandwich bottom; 10¼" long. Also avail. 11¾" long.
$60.00

An oval casserole, measuring 10¼" along its longest axis, with nothing whatsoever to be said in favor of the design except that it is perfectly suited to the function. This Italian pot by Paderno is of extra-heavy construction in brushed stainless steel and it has a double aluminum sandwich for a bottom. It has straight sides, a well-fitting lid set into a flared lip, and no handle because the lip makes it unnecessary—in short, it is another of those pots from Italy which make us wish that there were more of them readily available to the American cook.

Shallow Nambé Casserole 7.22

Sand-cast aluminum alloy; 10¾" × 8½"; 3⅛" deep; 3-qt. capacity; lid 10⅛" × 8⅞", 1⅛" deep. Also avail. with 4-qt. capacity.
$65.00

This pot haunted us with its resemblance to something we knew well but couldn't quite remember: and then we realized that it looks, in fact, like a beautiful sister of the Magnalite roaster (8.46), the Mary to its Martha. Similar in shape, similar in the smooth, sensual look of cast metal, this sand-cast aluminum alloy pot from Nambé is different in that it is ravishingly beautiful. It is formed in a gently curved rectangle, with squarish self-handles on both the lid and the base: a raised ridge inside the lid fits snugly into a lip on the bottom. (That lid, by the way, can also be used as a

gratin pan or a flat roaster.) Our sample casserole holds 3 quarts, but there is another size with a capacity of 4 quarts. Each pot has slight, distinctive irregularities because, as befits the work of individual craftsmen, it is hand-finished. And, as befits the work of individual craftsmen, it is quite expensive.

Deep Nambé Casserole 7.23

Sand-cast aluminum alloy; 8¼" × 6⅛"; 3½" deep; 2-qt. capacity; lid 8⅛" × 6⅛", 1" deep.
$58.00

Taller, flatter in shape, but with the same luscious curves and shiny surface, this casserole much resembles the lower Nambé aluminum-alloy pot above. There are actually minor differences between the two, mostly involving the way in which the lid and the pot fit together,

Pottery Pots

To those brought up on aluminum and stainless steel let us introduce pottery, the oldest and one of the finest forms of cookware. Civilization began not with the wheel, but with the potter's wheel. There is no non-nomadic culture which does not make some sort of clay ware—once a people goes beyond simple chipped stone tools to form objects, they reach out to work with clay. Thus, when we move to the consideration of earthenware pots, we find ourselves talking about some of the earliest manmade objects: utensils whose origins go back to prehistory. Archeologists, in fact, date civilizations by the shards they find in a given layer of excavation.

Pottery is a general term used for utensils or objects made of molded wet clay which are fired at high heat to fix their shape. In aristocratic form it is porcelain, also called china; translucent, white, nonabsorptive, and vitrified. In its bourgeois or peasant form it is earthenware: opaque, clay-colored, absorptive if not glazed, and most often not vitrified. Now, some people say that earthenware and stoneware are two names for the same thing, while others distinguish between stoneware, which is vitrified, and earthenware, which is partially vitrified. A matter of nomenclature: they resemble one another far more than either resembles porcelain.

This matter of vitrification, now: unfired clay can be freely mixed with water, in which it partially dissolves. Once it has been heated in a kiln to around 1100 F., however, it is fixed in shape and its material is no longer dissolvable. If clay is heated to even higher temperatures it becomes even harder until, at around 2000 F., it becomes vitreous—meaning that its components fuse together in a glasslike mass. (Whether the *surface* appears glasslike depends upon whether it is glazed, and with what substance.) So, because pottery can be fired at different temperatures, you can have earthenware objects which are hard but not vitrified, or vitrified but not glazed or shiny.

COOKING IN EARTHENWARE

Earthenware is wonderful for very slow cooking because, although it does not heat up quickly, once it is hot it will retain its temperature for a very long time; thus it is the very opposite of copper, which is so effective for frying pans because it heats and cools off quickly. No, earthenware makes the SuperPot for the energy crisis, as it will keep its contents simmering for ages in an oven which is scarcely turned on. Best are those pots which are glazed only on the inside, while the outer surface is left bare for the greatest absorption of heat. Glazes were developed to seal the surface of the clay, which is both porous and absorptive if left baked but pristine (as in the upper part of the Schlemmertopf, [7.38], and similar clay cookers). The user sometimes "seals" such surfaces, as by soaking a porous pot in water before each use; and you will see one casserole (7.27) which is supposed to be sealed before its first use with the oil left after a thorough rubbing with garlic!

Leach Casserole with Handle   7.25

Stoneware; 6″ diam.; 3⅛″ deep; 1-qt. capacity. Also avail. with 1-pint capacity. $12.50

These 1-pint and 1-quart casseroles, made in the workshop of Bernard Leach, the British potter, are as functional as they are aesthetically satisfying. The stoneware from which they are made permits a minimal amount of fuel to bring the contents to a gentle simmer and then to retain the heat, keeping everything bubbling away without further ado. There is a close-fitting lid with a chunky knob, and the stout handle is hollow so as to remain cool. A rough beige exterior, left unglazed for the greatest absorption of heat, complements a choice of interior glazes: celadon green, a mottled gray-brown, or a glossy black tenmoku, all vitrified and thus as strong as glass. As responsible citizens, we are supposed to tell you that these pots should never be used over a direct flame; but one of our editors has had a Leach pot for ten years and says that she has used it over a burner with no damage done, always being careful to heat it slowly and to have the pot at least one-third full while it is heating.

Eventually, the necessity for sealing surfaces was transformed into an art form: the study of Japanese glazes is the work of a lifetime, and almost every society makes its own distinctive glazed pottery.

LOOK-ALIKES: A WARNING

One warning: You really ought not to buy the cheap clay pots which are sold in the markets of the cities where your cruise ship puts in. Although they may look like some of the primitive-appearing casseroles which we will show you—such as those from Vallauris in the south of France—the glaze of inexpensive tourist ware may have a high lead content, causing it to make actually poisonous any food put within it. If you have such a suspect pot, use it as a flower pot, not for food.

Leach Casserole with Strapwork Handle 7.26

Stoneware; 11¼″ diam.; 4¾″ deep; 4-qt. capacity. Also avail. with 1- or 2-qt. capacity.
$30.00

Another design from Bernard Leach: this, a stoneware casserole in three sizes, each with a handsome strapwork handle on the lid; choose a 1-, 2-, or 4-quart pot. It has the same unglazed exterior and beautiful internal glazes as the other Leach pots. This British potter went to Japan in the years before World War I, and learned there to make the classic Japanese glazes. He returned to Cornwall to make the most beautiful stoneware of his period and, incidentally, to produce serviceable hand-thrown pots of highly vitrified stoneware from his native soil. Young potters from all over the world come to him to learn to make these simple standard shapes in cookware. When you buy a Leach pot, you are buying the work of a very fine atelier, designed and supervised by a master potter.

THE TWO POTS

One fine day the Iron Pot
Asked the Pot of Earthenware
To come out and take the air;
But he thought he'd better not,

"I'm so brittle, I shall be
Safer on the hearth," said he;
"For the slightest jostle means
I am smashed to smithereens.
As for you, of course, your skin
Is as thick as mine is thin:
You've no reason to stay in."
"Nay," said t'other, "I can screen you.
If by chance we meet
Some hard object in the street,
I will interpose between you,
And preserve you free from harm."
Thus he brought the waverer around.
Well in step and arm-in-arm
The unequal couple strode
Clippety-cloppety down the road,
Bumping together every time
They crossed a roughness in the ground.
Earthenware came to grief: in a few yards
Nothing was left of him but shards;
And he had no one but himself to blame.

Live with your peers, not higher seek
to climb
Else your sad fate may be the same.

La Fontaine, Fables

Clay Marmite 7.27

Earthenware; 9″ diam.; 4½″ deep; 5½-qt. capacity. Also avail. with capacity of 3 or 4 qts.
$45.00

How can you help but love a pot when you are advised to rub it all over with garlic before you use it? Not a matter of taste, but of good sense: the oil of the garlic, once heated, forms a glaze over the soft earthenware exterior. This is a primitive-looking clay pot from Vallauris in the south of France, where Pablo Picasso also obtained clay for ceramics; it is of far better quality than the inexpensive pottery it resembles. In three sizes holding 3 to 5½ quarts, it has a loose-fitting top and an interior that are both glazed in shiny brown. Wonderful for oven-to-table service of peasant cuisine: a cabbage soup or a risotto baked with seafood. If you use it on top of the stove, remember—heat it gently (or use a mat or a trivet between it and the flame) and be sure there is some non-cold liquid inside the pot.

Japanese Casserole 7.28

Stoneware; 8″ diam.; 3″ high; 2-qt. capacity.
$18.00

Oriental pottery is at once delicate and sturdy, as shown by this ovenproof stoneware casserole with a durable hand-thrown look and a dainty pussy-willow design. The colors on this pot are subtle and earthy, a rich brown and smoky blue; there are hand-painted white pussy willows and a smooth off-white interior. The lid, when reversed, makes a useful footed serving plate. This is not an expensive casserole, and it will serve two quarts of soup or a family-sized casserole meal agreeably.

Karnes Casseroles 7.29, 7.30

Stoneware; 8½″ diam.; 5″ deep; 3½-qt. capacity.
$42.00

Stoneware; 9″ diam.; 6½″ deep; 5½-qt. capacity. Also avail. with capacity of 7 qts.
$55.00

To own a casserole made by Karen Karnes is to own a work of art: unlike the products of the Leach atelier, which are made by students according to the master's designs, each Karnes pot has been hand-thrown by the artist herself —the evenly ridged interior was made that way by the potter's hands as she molded it on the wheel. Here are two beautifully functional casseroles, both with short handles but subtly different from each other in contour. (There is also a third, larger pot, holding 7 quarts.) The rough exterior glaze comes in rich and earthy, slightly mottled shades of brown. The tight-fitting lid is furnished with Karnes's characteristic ribbonlike handle. This pot is incredibly tactile: you want to reach out and touch its bulging sides.

Karnes Bean Pot 7.31

Stoneware; 8″ diam.; 7″ deep; 4½-qt. capacity. Also avail. with capacity of about 5 to 6 qts. or 6 to 8 qts.
$36.00

Another pot from the doyenne of American potters, Karen Karnes. Here she turns her hand—and wheel—to a bean pot: huge, tall-sided, roughly glazed, with a beautifully fitting lid. Karnes fits her lids better than any potter we know: notice that the touching edges of both lid and pot are left unglazed to prevent chipping and to hold, if necessary, a strip of sealing dough. A museum-quality piece. Earthenware pots take space to store, since you dare not fill them with other, smaller utensils, which might do damage. But a Karnes pot should be on proud display on your bookcase or sideboard when not in use. And lest we forget to mention it—this pot is fantastic to cook in, doing wonders with anything which benefits from very long, very slow cooking. Imagine a chicken fricassee for six close friends, made in the 4½-quart pot; or cassoulet for a crowd in the largest size, which will hold at least 6 quarts.

A timeless pot—nineteenth-century French earthenware.

The celebrated beans of Boston were a useful Sabbath preparation for the Puritans, as they could be made ready for baking in their pot before the fire ceased being stoked at sundown Saturday and left to cook slowly overnight in the remaining heat. When the brick oven came into use in the nineteenth century, the beans were accompanied by other traditional East Coast dishes that benefited from slow, long cooking—such dishes as slumps and pandowdies, forms of fruit cobbler, which, with the beans, made a hearty Sunday meal.

Leach Bean Pot 7.32

Stoneware; 7″ diam.; 4⅞″ deep; 2½-qt. capacity. Also avail. with 1½-qt. capacity.
$15.00

Another bean pot, this beauty made by the students of Bernard Leach, perhaps the best—and certainly the best-known—potter in the world today. It is made of stoneware—clay that has been fired to such a heat that it has the strength of glass. The outside has a reddish-brown pebbly texture, the interior has a sensuous celadon-green crackle glaze inspired by ancient Chinese pots. It is also available in a black-to-rust tenmoku or a mottled gray-brown glaze. Sensibly designed with two handles (or lugs, as the British call them), it has a solid flat bottom and a closely fitting lid. It comes in 1½- and 2½-quart sizes, but we recommend the larger pot, since slow-cooked dishes cook better when made in relatively larger quantities. By all means serve from this pot; that is half the pleasure of owning it.

THE
KITCHEN COMPANION,
AND
HOUSE-KEEPER'S
OWN BOOK,
CONTAINING ALL THE MODERN, AND MOST APPROVED METHODS IN
COOKERY, PASTRY, & CONFECTIONARY,
WITH AN EXCELLENT COLLECTION OF
VALUABLE RECIPES,
TO WHICH IS ADDED, THE
WHOLE ART OF CARVING, ILLUSTRATED.

Title page of a cookbook published in Philadelphia in 1844.

THE WORK OF OTHER POTTERS

Before we leave Leach and Karnes, before we immerse ourselves totally once again in the products of the commercial world, we should mention that there are other fine potters whose works can be seen elsewhere in the book—people such as Ron Garfinkel, Cynthia Bringle and Doris Licht-Tomono, all of whom (as well as Leach and Karnes) could be contacted about making casseroles. All are serious potters who, out of affection for the medium, have addressed themselves to making cooking pots as well as decorative pieces. It is an unequaled opportunity for you to do what the Renaissance princes did: to commission a work of art. Still pottery but not entirely handmade are the next, still handsome and serviceable, pots. They are also easier to come by than the one-of-a-kind, artisan-made vessels.

Bennington Oval Casserole 7.33

Stoneware; 11″ × 8⅝″; 4½″ deep; 4-qt. capacity. Also avail. with capacity of 2 or 6 qts.
$14.00

The Bennington Potters stand halfway between the artisan-potters and the good commercial factories. They hand-throw many of their products, they use quality glazes, and they produce beautiful designs which are, nonetheless, clearly "modern" rather than a product of the artisan aesthetic—no craftsman's fingerprints are left on a Bennington pot. Here is a beautiful oval casserole with either a creamy-white or a tawny glaze produced by firing a wash of clay and water at 2350 F.: this is the ancient technique of making slipware, which has the very modern advantage of being dishwasher- and oven-proof. The lid fits snugly and has interior ribs to promote self-basting and to enable it to serve, after it has cooled, as a trivet when the casserole is brought to the table. Very simple, very beautiful; in 2-, 4-, and 6-quart sizes.

". . . he felt his belly crave for its food. He hoped there would be stew for dinner, turnips and carrots and bruised potatoes and fat mutton pieces to be ladled out in thick peppered flour fattened sauce. Stuff it into you, his belly counselled him."

James Joyce, Portrait of the Artist as a Young Man

Dansk Casserole 7.34

Stoneware; 7″ diam.; 5½″ deep; 3-qt. capacity.
$34.95

Dansk makes everything for the table, from carving sets to casseroles, and among its products is a handsome table service in the Generation Frost Whisper pattern which includes this marvelously designed casserole. But you can also buy the pot by itself, and you very well may once you see it: a handsome tall, off-white casserole, bordered in brown or blue and irregularly speckled in brown. It is noticeably more "commercial" in appearance than the hand-thrown earthenware pots we have shown you, with its tall, straight sides, a lip for catching spills, and a flat, fairly well-fitting lid. Holding 3 quarts, it also makes a good-looking soup tureen.

Stangl Double Dish 7.35

Earthenware; 9¼″ × 6¾″; 2″ deep; 1¼-qt. capacity. Lid 9¼″ × 6¾″, 1¾″ deep.
$25.00

From the old New Jersey firm of Stangl comes this native product, not quite a terrine, but a useful oval pottery casserole nonetheless. Stangl has long made a good product, well-made, handsome, and by no means inexpensive. They call this double dish a "medium cooker"; the top and bottom are nearly identical and could be used separately as twin vegetable dishes or together for braising a chicken with a minimum of liquid. It has an attractive finish, with white flecks shooting through a bright blue, green, or yellow glaze. The dish matches dinnerware made by the same manufacturer.

Covered Porcelain Pot 7.36

Porcelain; 6½″ diam.; 3½″ deep; 1-qt. capacity. Also avail. with capacity of 1½ cups and 2 or 3½ qts.
$24.00

Bennington Oval Casserole
Dansk Casserole
Stangl Double Dish
Covered Porcelain Pot

Glass Casserole
Schlemmertopf

Continued from preceding page

A neat, fat little covered pot of good-quality porcelain from France. The pattern we show is of thistles in olive green and brilliant blue on a creamy background, but the pot is also available in several other flower patterns as well as in plain white. (And by the way, as is often true of expensive porcelain, you can get the same shape, the same good glaze, in an undecorated, cheaper version.) This porcelain is extremely dense, is nonporous and light in weight, and it would go from oven to table elegantly. A good lid with an unglazed lip seals the casserole well; when it is lifted, steam smelling wonderfully of onions and red wine will escape to pique the appetite. We show it in the 1-quart size; it comes also as an individual soup bowl and in larger sizes.

for use in a microware oven (or a conventional oven) and it is far sturdier than it looks. Take off the lid and use the dish for a soufflé: what an elegant table presentation that will be!

THE CLAY COOKER

Here is a pot designed for a method of cooking that grew from the practices of peoples so simple that they could not form and fire a cooking vessel. For even before there were clay pots there was simple clay, and primitive people, intent on dinner, took wet mud, presumably with a high clay content, daubed it all over their chicken or fish, and then put it among the embers to cook. (A method not, by the way, unlike that of the Sunday barbecue chef or the Eagle Scout who wraps his potatoes in aluminum foil and then buries them deep among the charcoal briquettes.) The wet clay and the moisture in the food, all firmly sealed in by the hardening mud, kept the food from drying out; when it was all done, the cook or the diners simply took a hammer or a boulder, cracked the clay shell open, and peeled it off. Underneath was tender, gently steamed food inside a probably inedible skin. You can try this method yourself by spreading any firing clay—not plasticene!—over next Sunday's roasting chicken before you put it into the oven. And there are actually firms, intent on capitalizing on this earliest form of cooking, which offer to sell you kits with the proper kind of clay for daubing over your food; but the real modern evolution of this method is exemplified by the pot we show you here, the Schlemmertopf.

Glass Casserole 7.37

Ovenproof glass with cork trivet; 7½″ diam.; 2½″ deep; 1¼-qt. capacity. Also avail. 7½″ diam., 3⅞″ deep, 2½-qt. capacity.
$10.00

Look back at the heavy round doufeu (7.15), and if you have an eye for structure you will see that it was the inspiration for this elegant and airy glass casserole, straight-sided with a deep depression in its tight-fitting lid. The lid itself is high with rounded sides, and this construction forces the steam to circulate and baste the contents of the pot. Endives, mushrooms, pearl onions, fruits—anything which calls for gentle oven braising with a minimum of liquid and perhaps a little butter can be brought to perfection in this unusual dish. It comes from Corning in two sizes —1¼ and 1½ quarts—and each has its own cork trivet. Unlike some Corning glassware, this utensil cannot be used in the freezer, nor on top of the range, nor under the broiler. It is, however, ideal

Schlemmertopf 7.38

Earthenware; bottom 13″ × 9¼″; 3¼″ deep; 3-qt. capacity; lid 13¾″ × 9½″, 2¾″ deep. Also avail. with 2-qt. capacity.
$18.00

What is it? It's a rough, baked clay pot, more or less oval in shape, with a top and bottom of the same size. The outside is roughly decorated with scratched designs—what potters call sgraffiti—and the entire pot, with the exception of the in-

terior of the bottom section, is left unglazed. (This inside glazing, by the way, is a late development, meant to add to the ease of cleaning; ordinarily Schlemmertöpfe and similar clay cookers are left totally unglazed.) The point of the whole thing is that it is a means of simulating the primitive method of cooking in rough wet clay; so, before it is used, the pot is soaked in cold water until, like a clay flower pot, it becomes wet through. Then food is put inside, the cover is put on, and it all goes into a cold oven. You turn the heat up high, and some time later your dinner is cooked. The advantage seems to be that you can produce tenderly braised meat or poultry or whatever without using any fats, with little additional liquid, and without letting any of the nutrients in the food escape—in this, the pot is not totally unlike a pressure cooker or the waterless cookers of the 1930s. We show you a Schlemmertopf large enough to hold a family-sized roasting chicken or a five-pound rolled roast; the pot comes with a lengthy recipe booklet which tells you how to make stews and vegetable mélanges as well as roasts of meat and poultry.

Terrines

Consider the kinship of the words *earthenware* and *terrine:* Anglo-French cousins born of the synonymous English word *earth* and the French *terre*. A terrine is, therefore, by definition an earthenware pot: usually oval, lidded, and more often than not having an opening cut into the top to function like the slashes made in a pie crust to vent the steam and so prevent the contents from exploding. *Terrine* is also, like *marmite,* one of those words which serve for both pot and contents. A terrine is a dish of ground and chopped meat; actually, it is a pâté served from this specific dish, not unmolded. Like the words, the pots come from both sides of the English Channel, and you will notice an extraordinary number of English products in this section. (You will also see porcelain terrines and Le Creuset's porcelainized metal terrine, all, in their materials, exceptions to the rule.) Not only steak and kidney pie, but also the Four and Twenty Blackbirds must have been baked in just such a dish as some of those we show you.

White Terrine from France 7.39

Porcelain; 8½" X 6½"; 3½" deep; 2-qt. capacity. Also avail. with capacity of 1,1¼, 1½, or 1¾ qts.

$17.00 ▲

To the etymological purist, a terrine should be made only of earthenware; nonetheless, this is a classic terrine from France. It is a simple oval in white porcelain made in 1, 1¼, 1½, 1¾, and 2-quart sizes. There is a bottom unglazed on the outside, a lid which fits neatly onto the rim around the edge, and a depression on the top across which lies a bar-like handle. Very simple, very neat. The smallest size will hold a pâté, while one of the larger sizes might well be used for two little game hens, or a dish of pasta baked in sauce.

Mock Pâté en Croûte 7.40

Porcelain; 9" X 4½": 3" deep; 1-qt. capacity. Also avail. with capacity of 1 pint or 1½ qts.
$48.00

A wonderful terrine from France in the form of a pâté en croûte: the outside has been sculpted to imitate pastry, and the handle is made in imitation of the head of whatever game you have used to make the terrine. We show you the duck's head, but you can also have a rabbit, a pheasant, a partridge, or a snipe. The interior is a fine creamy white porcelain, while the outside is glazed to resemble baked pastry—it is rough in finish and the color of perfectly done toast. There are three sizes, holding 1, 2, or 3 pints. Fill it with a pâté mixture of duck livers, ham, and Madeira and set it to bake in your oven; the hole in the lid allows steam to escape, thus serving the same function as the funnel with which you pierce the top crust of a real pâté en croûte. And, of course, you will serve the terrine from this dish when it has cooled and mellowed.

Brown English Terrine 7.41

Earthenware; 7" X 4⅞"; 2¾" deep; 1-qt. capacity.
$20.00 ▲

A neatly made little terrine from England in highly glazed brown and tan, with a suggestion of a floral design under the glaze of the lid. In the British Isles they make pork pies and veal and ham pies of cubed meat in aspic, which are turned out and served free-standing in their thick pastry shells. But you could just as well bake a French pâté mixture in this tidy little covered dish only 7" long with a capacity of 1 quart. Each slice would be roughly 5 by 3 inches: one slice for a first course with tiny sour pickles and mustard, two slices for Sunday supper with brown bread and butter. The terrine has suggestions of handles barely raised from the surface of the sides of the pot, and a faint legend, like a child's drawing, on the bottom, which says, "Made for T. G. Green England." A pot that looks as though it belongs in *The Wind in the Willows,* or in an English workman's kitchen: honest, simple, and rudely attractive.

Pâtés and terrines.

*Here we show another delightful item, a
terrine from James Beard's collection.*

TERRINE DE CAMPAGNE – PORK AND LIVER PATE

This is the sort of pâté you get in French restaurants under the alternative names of *pâté maison* or *terrine du chef*.

The ingredients [British measures] are 1 lb. each of fat pork (belly) and lean veal, ½ lb. of pig's liver, an after-dinner coffee-cup of dry white wine, 2 tablespoons of brandy, a clove of garlic, half a dozen each of black peppercorns and juniper berries, ¼ teaspoon of ground mace, 4 oz. of fat bacon or, better still, if your butcher will provide it, either flare fat, or back fat, which is the pork fat often used for wrapping round birds for roasting.

An obliging butcher will usually mince for you the pork, veal and liver, provided he is given due notice. It saves a great deal of time, and I always believe in making my dealers work for me if they will.

To the minced meats, all thoroughly blended, add 2 oz. of the fat bacon or pork fat cut in thin, irregular little dice, the seasonings chopped and blended (half a dessertspoon of salt will be sufficient), and the wine and brandy. Mix very thoroughly and, if there is time, leave to stand for an hour or two before cooking, so that the flavours penetrate the meat. Turn into one large 2-pint capacity terrine, or into 2 or 3 smaller ones, about 2 to 2½ inches deep. Cut the remaining fat or bacon into thin strips and arrange it across the top of the pâté. Place the terrines in a baking tin filled with water and cook, uncovered, in a slow oven, Gas No. 2, 310 deg. F. for 1¼ to 1½ hours. The pâtés are cooked when they begin to come away from the sides of the dish.

Take them from the oven, being careful not to spill any of the fat, and leave them to cool. They will cut better if, when the fat has all but set, they are weighted. To do this, cover with grease-proof paper and a board or plate which fits inside the terrine and put a weight on top. However, if this proves impractical, it is not of very great importance. If the terrines are to be kept longer than a week, cover them completely, once they are cold, with just melted pure pork lard.

When cooking the pâtés remember that it is the *depth* of the terrine rather than its surface area which determines the cooking time. The seasonings of garlic and juniper berries are optional.

Serve these pâtés as a first course, with toast or French bread. Some peo-ple like butter as well, although they are quite rich enough without.

Lastly, the proportions of meat, liver and seasonings making up the pâtés can be altered to suit individual tastes, but always with due regard to the finished texture of the product. A good pâté is moist and fat without being greasy, and it should be faintly pink inside, not grey or brown. A dry pâté is either the result of overcooking, or of too small a proportion of fat meat having been used. And ideally all the meat for pâtés should be cut up by hand rather than put through the mincing machine, which squeezes and dries the meat. But this is a counsel of perfection which few people nowadays would care to follow.

Alternative proportions for those who like more liver and less meat
1 lb. 2 oz. pig's liver, 1¼ lb. belly of pork, ½ lb. lean veal, a coffee-cup of dry white wine, 2 tablespoons brandy, 2 cloves garlic, 6 to 8 juniper berries (optional), 1 dessertspoon salt, 4 black peppercorns, mace, 4 oz. of back pork fat or 4 rashers of fat bacon.

The procedure is exactly as in the first recipe.

(From FRENCH PROVINCIAL COOKING, by Elizabeth David. Copyright © 1960 by Elizabeth David.)

The directions for the preparation of food have improved considerably since the time of Richard II of England, when cooks were given a recipe for rabbit which held little more than: "Take rabbits and smite them to pieces: seethe them in grease. . . ." Or for chicken: "Take chickens and ram them together, serve them broken. . . ."

Le Creuset Enameled Terrine   7.42

Enameled cast iron; 11″ × 4¼″; 3¼″ deep; 1-qt. capacity. Also avail. with 1½-qt. capacity.
$25.00 ▲

A long and narrow cast-iron terrine which holds, like the English terrine from T. G. Green (7.41), only 1 quart. The fact that the shape is so attenuated means that each slice will be quite small, 3 inches square, in fact: small enough to fit on a large wheat cracker, small enough to justify serving three slices on a bed of lettuce for a first course. This terrine is well made by Le Creuset of enameled cast iron with integral handles, a domed lid, and a steam vent. We fell in love with the butter-yellow enamel, but it also comes in red, brown, or blue; each color has the same creamy-beige interior.

Large Rectangular Terrine   7.43

Porcelain; 8″ × 5½″; 3½″ deep; 2½-qt. capacity. Also avail. with capacity of ¾, 1, 1½, 1¾, or 3 qts.
$45.00

We show you this rectangular terrine for pâté mixtures in its 2½-quart size: large enough for a party, but not the largest size which is available. Made by Pillivuyt, it can be purchased in seven sizes, one as small as a pint and a half, and one as large as 3 quarts; the larger sizes will produce pâtés which can be cut into slabs substantial enough to serve as the main course at an evening meal. This is a creamy-white terrine made of good-quality porcelain, with the bottom and the lid edges left unglazed. A strapwork handle is set into an indentation in the domed lid, which is perforated by the usual steam hole.

Round Mock Pâté en Croûte   7.44

Porcelain; 5½″ diam.; 2½″ deep; 3-cup capacity.
$11.00 ▲

In contrast to the elegant austerity of 7.43 is this warm little porcelain game terrine, also from Pillivuyt. It's been molded and glazed on the outside to resemble the pastry crust in which pâtés are often baked (see pp. 462 and 463 for real pâté en croûte molds), with fluted sides and swirled cover in a mottled brown that is surprisingly realistic. The inside has a simple non-porous white glaze; the lid fits snugly in the fluted rim of the dish. Most of this manufacturer's items come in a vast range of sizes, but we're glad this terrine is available only in this 3-cup size, just over 5″ in diameter. It wouldn't be near so charming in a 1½- or 2-quart size. With the charm comes practicality, for this is the perfect size for a pound of chicken liver pâté or other meat spread.

English Stoneware Terrine   7.45

Stoneware; 8½″ X 5¾″; 2¾″ deep; 1-qt. capacity.
$7.50

Somewhat cruder, heavy, attractive, this terrine is made to sit decoratively on the shelf of a country kitchen when it isn't in use. The exterior is glazed a dark brown, the inside is a creamy beige. The edges of the lid and the surface it rests on are left unglazed to prevent chipping. Stoneware terrines like this make us think of recipes which call for game, for roughly cut pieces of pork and for country brandies. This comes in a handy 1-quart size. It's rustic, inexpensive and altogether different in style from the elegant French porcelain terrines. Think of steak and kidney pie—think of tankards of dark ale.

White Terrine with Blue Flowers   7.46

Porcelain; 8″ X 5½″; 3¼″ deep; 1¾-qt. capacity.
$24.00

The contrast could not be greater between this dish and 7.45: this one conjures up not steak and kidney pie but pâtés of the whitest veal, the most finely puréed goose livers. This beautiful porcelain casserole is oval, white, and decorated with rather full-blown blue peonies—it is more delicate in appearance than to the touch. It will hold 1¾ quarts nicely; the domed lid invites you to cook a roasting chicken within the pot. This will bake well and then come to the table, where it will harmonize with your finest Canton ware or Royal Copenhagen dinner plates.

ESTOUFFADE DE CERF AU VIN ROUGE — VENISON STEWED IN RED WINE

Buy about 2 lb. of shoulder or flank of venison in one piece. Tie it in a sausage shape and put it to marinate, in a glazed earthenware or china bowl, with 4 tablespoons each of port and wine vinegar, and 1 tablespoon of olive oil. Leave for 24 hours, then take out the meat, wipe it dry, roll it in flour, and put it in a small oval earthenware dish in which it will just about fit. On top put a layer of sliced onions and then cover completely with thin slices of fat bacon. Pour over the marinade, add a seasoning of salt and pepper, cover with greaseproof paper and the lid of the dish and cook in a very slow oven, Gas No. 2, 310°F., for 4 to 4½ hours.

Serve in a very hot dish with very hot plates, for nothing gets colder or congeals more rapidly than venison. Redcurrant or rowan jelly, or any sweet-sour pickled fruit goes well with venison.

(From FRENCH PROVINCIAL COOKING, by Elizabeth David. Copyright © 1960 by Elizabeth David.)

Decorated Porcelain Terrine   7.47

Porcelain; 7″ X 5″; 2½″ deep; 1½-pint capacity. Also avail. with capacity of 1¾ or 2½ qts.
$36.00

271

Continued from preceding page

Baking dishes of porcelain possess their own air of incongruity; how is it possible that a casserole or terrine so elegant, so beautifully decorated, so light in the hand, can also hold a boiling stock, a baking pâté, a heavy fowl? How can it be not only as strong as a pot made of earthenware, but actually stronger? The senses cannot be trusted: you must take our word when we say that this ravishing casserole from Porcelaine de Paris, fragile in appearance with its brown and gold flowers scattered over the exterior, is as suited to the oven as your heaviest aluminum pot. It comes in three sizes, from 7 inches to nearly 10 inches in length: all are oval and straight-sided, and each has a lightly domed lid which fits nicely into the rim around the top. As a matter of fact, this is one of the best-fitting lids we have come across; a real triumph in porcelain.

Timbale Milanaise 7.48

Porcelain; 4¼″ diam.; 2⅜″ deep; 1-pint capacity. Also avail. with capacity of ¾, 1, or 1½ qts.
$23.00

A timbale, among other things, is a high-sided pot which is lined with pastry; "milanaise" means, in addition to its other culinary implications, a mixture of macaroni and grated cheese with truffles, mushrooms, ham, and tongue, held in a tomato sauce. This nice little porcelain pot has the pretend-crust finish which takes care of the pastry, its sides a dull tan and brown, its lid swirled, presumably, by the pâtissière's knife. But whether you will fill it with macaroni is another matter. We see it stuffed with a pâté of goose livers and set on a cocktail table; or even filled with sweet butter and served at a festive breakfast. This pot is tiny, holding just half a quart, but it. comes in other sizes, all the way up to a pot with a 1½-quart capacity: a size which you might just want to try filling with a "milanaise."

THE SLOW COOKER

It happens not only to us mortals but also to the experts, the nightmarish equipment breakdown on the eve of a dinner party. The difference is that the experts are better able to cope, less likely to throw up their (sticky-fingered) hands and send out for Chinese food. One of our editors tells us that on the morning of a day when she had invited ten for dinner—including a Hungarian physician of discriminating palate—she discovered that her stove had died during the night. After an hour or so of weeping and moaning, she remembered that her electric Hotray could be set at 250 F. So she put together a hasty matelote d'anguilles, set it on the tray in an earthenware pot at ten in the morning, and served it forth, fully cooked, at nine that night. She hasn't yet told us what she did about the coffee—perhaps she sent out for that. This is not an introduction to a blurb on Hotrays, but rather to the principle of cooking embodied in the electric slow cooker: the principle of cooking at a very low heat for a very long time, as ancient as embers and as modern as a thermostat. Also see Chapter 8, Electric Roaster.

Orange Plastic Slow Cooker 7.49

Plastic exterior with stoneware insert; 11″ diam.; 9″ high; 5-qt.capacity.
$34.00 ▲

A modern outgrowth of the idea of cooking slowly in earthenware, this cooker is worth serious consideration. Even in this time of high electricity costs you can keep a slow-cooking pot at a constant temperature of 200 F. or 300 F. for a few pennies a day if the appliance uses only 70 watts at its low setting; the cost is equivalent to that of one not-very-bright light bulb burning. This pot should be of special interest to people who are out of the house all day; to people who are tired of being in debt to the electric company; to people who want to cook tough cuts of meat by a method which produces a flavorful and nutritionally sound

result. This, the Crock-Pot made by Rival, is the best electrical slow cooker we have seen: a fat little tub on legs which comes in one size, with a total capacity of five quarts. We like it because of the thick earthenware cooking insert and the insulating outer wall which carries the heating element all the way up the sides; this all-around heat is essential in a unit which heats and cooks so slowly. The stoneware is mustard-colored and the plastic shell comes in a flamboyant orange, green, or yellow. It is terrible looking, having a flimsy-looking Lexan plastic lid and a truly dreadful polyethylene outer wall. Yet incredibly enough, it was not only the best, but the best-looking slow cooker we examined. There is a removable heat control that allows you to clean the pot conveniently and a good cookbook comes along to teach you this method of cooking.

Carême's version of a timbale de macaroni à la Milanaise.

Special-Purpose Pots

If you look at cookware long enough you begin to believe that there is some sort of Platonic Ideal for pots, so suited are some utensils for cooking a specific food. Thus, bean pots, tripières, onion-soup pots: if you want, you can serve spaghetti or hot-fudge sundaes in any of them, but each takes its name from the specific food which it was designed to cook the best. We start here with bean pots, go on through various specialty casseroles which have evolved for cooking and serving soupy foods and grains, and then wind up with a cluster of small containers in earthenware, outbursts of creativity by individual potters, which are included in part because they were too fine to leave out.

English Bean Pot 7.50

Stoneware; 6½" top diam.; 6" deep; 2-qt. capacity. Also avail. with capacity of 1 cup and 1, 1½, or 3 qts.

$9.95

As brown as the beans bubbling within, this glazed bean pot from England is actually called a Dutch Pot. Perhaps it straddles the line between Dutch oven and bean pot. Its shape is somewhat more squat than the more traditional example from France which follows. It can be used to bake a stew as well as to cook slowly a rich, nourishing kidney-bean-and-barley mixture to warm the family on a winter evening. The pot is very nicely shaped, with a pair of handles protruding from its sides, a knobbed lid, and decorative bands of beading under the glaze across its circumference—a minor touch, but one which makes this pot distinctive. Do not restrict it to beans. Use it for any savory combination of meats and vegetables that must bake gently. And rather than ferreting it away when not in use, fill it with dried fruits or nuts in their shells to set out for autumn nibbling, a quantity of pickles at a big party, or even cookies, easily reached through the generous mouth of the pot.

French Bean Pot 7.51

Earthenware; 5" diam.; 4½" deep; 1¾-qt. capacity.

$9.95

The shape is fat, round, and homey. You could hug it. The traditional bean-pot shape—also that of the marmite—is taller than it is wide and narrows to the top so the toothsome contents bake to tenderness without losing much of the savory sauce through evaporation. The glazed earthenware in molasses brown, with just a band of buff near the top (and inside), is a perfect material for the sort of slow cooking required by a pot of beans. Inexpensive and multipurpose, it is a convenient size for a one-pot meal for two—lamb or sausage baked with white beans and garlic—or for Boston baked beans for a family of four.

LA POTEE

This is the traditional daily food of the peasants of eastern France, particularly in the Haute Marne. It is a simple rustic dish, made from freshly gathered vegetables and home-cured bacon.

It is cooked in a marmite, or heavy iron saucepan; you need a selection of vegetables in about equal proportions, say 12 small potatoes, 12 small carrots, 6 small turnips, and 6 small onions, 2 lb. of French beans or broad beans, 2 lbs. of green peas, the heart of a young cabbage cut in strips, and a piece of home-cured bacon, say about 1 lb. for six people.

Put the root vegetables and bacon on first, covered with water, and let them simmer slowly. Thirty minutes before serving add the green vegetables. The cabbage is put in, cut in strips, during the last 5 minutes.

The soup is served in a large deep dish or tureen, the vegetables almost, but not quite, crumbling, and the rose-pink bacon cut into convenient pieces.

(From FRENCH COUNTRY COOKING, by Elizabeth David. Copyright © 1951 by Elizabeth David.)

Porcelain Marmite 7.52

Porcelain; 5¼" diam.; 5½" high; 1½-qt. capacity. Also avail. with 3-qt. capacity.

$45.00

The simplest foods cooked to absolute perfection are the essence of fine cooking. A case in point is the marmite: a superb broth in which you have simmered some beef and chicken. In another pan you prepare vegetables just to the point of crispness, after which they are added to the stock and barely heated through. Then the presentation: cups of broth first, and then the meat, sliced, the perfectly cooked vegetables surrounding it. For cooking this dish (another of those named for the cooking pot) it is customary to use a marmite, a pot with sides which slope inward to increase condensation and to prevent the stock from reducing, the top fitting tightly for the same reason. We show a beautiful example from Porcelaine de Paris, decorated with vegetables as a hint of what

Continued from preceding page

is cooking inside. It comes in two sizes, holding 1½ and 3 quarts respectively, and is useful also as a tureen for any kind of soup. Porcelain is the purist's choice when making a marmite, because, being nonporous, it will never transmit the ghost of flavors from other dishes. It works, with the usual precaution—slow heating with liquid inside—on top of the stove or in the oven. It also works, ideally, for serving with the proper respect deserved by this dish, elevated from simple origin to elegance by attention to detail.

Stoneware Marmite or Tureen 7.53

Stoneware; 9″ diam.; 7¼″ high; 4-qt. capacity. Ladle 12″ long, ½-cup capacity.
$65.00

The same shape as the porcelain marmite (7.52) but of a different material, this beautiful stoneware pot is by a master potter, Cynthia Bringle. Over and over we have seen a model from the haute cuisine and then the simpler variations on the same shape. This pot is of excellent-quality stoneware with a good ring, it is beautifully glazed in greige, rust, and dark brown, and it has a rustic handle which looks like twisted rope. The pot itself holds 4 quarts, and the matching ladle holds ½ cup. Not marmite only but lentil soup, minestrone, anything warm and filling and nourishing can be cooked and served in this pot. It costs a great deal but it is one of a kind, a work of art. Many people would save it for serving—hence we call it "tureen"—but it will be perfectly happy in your oven.

Individual Marmite 7.54

Porcelain; 2¾″ diam.; 2⅝″ deep; 1-cup capacity.
$5.30

First catch your hare: That is, first make your soup in an immaculate porcelain marmite, carefully skimming off the fat and adding the vegetables at just the proper moment to ensure crispness. Then, before you present the meat on a platter, serve the broth in these individual marmite pots, covered to hold the heat, the sides sloping inward in imitation of the very functional shape of the larger pot. These porcelain marmite pots are white, with tiny handles which protect the diner's fingers and a creamy glaze which will not clash with the rest of the dinnerware on the table. They are not at all expensive, especially when you consider that they could also be used for individual pots of baked beans, or for individual deep main-course meat or game pies, or even for a baked dessert.

Earthenware Daubière 7.55

Earthenware; 8¾″ diam.; 9″ deep; 6-qt. capacity.
$42.50

A daube, the food cooked in the pot called a daubière, is another of the dishes taking its name from the utensil in which it is cooked. Thus *daube* has come to be the name of a stew, a staple of French country cooking. Thrifty peasants have long made daubes of meat so tough that it requires long marinating before it is cooked, and the peculiar shape of this pot, with its bulbous bottom and narrow neck, permits the smallest amount of marinade to tenderize the largest amount of meat. This French pot has a country look, made as it is of rough natural-colored earthenware which is glazed only on the inside and on the ill-fitting green cover. It comes in a six-quart size and must be seasoned before it is used, the recommended method being a good rubbing inside and out with garlic and then a long, slow baking in the oven. The clay and the pot are from Vallauris, a mecca for French potters and ceramists, including the late Pablo Picasso.

Another ageless earthenware casserole of the last century. From L'Ecole des Cuisinières of Urbain-Dubois.

LES DAUBES

"O, scent of the daubes of my childhood!

"During the holidays, at Gemeaux, in the month of August, when we arrived in my grandmother's dark kitchen on Sunday after Vespers, it was lit by a ray of sunshine in which the dust and the flies were dancing, and there was a sound like a little bubbling spring. It was a daube, which since midday had been murmuring gently on the stove, giving out sweet smells which brought tears to your eyes. Thyme, rosemary, bay leaves, spices, the wine of the marinade, and the fumet of the meat were becoming transformed under the magic wand which is the fire, into a delicious whole, which was served about seven o'clock in the evening, so well cooked and so tender that it was carved with a spoon."—Pierre Huguenin: *Les Meilleures Recettes de ma Pauvre Mère*, 1936

(From FRENCH PROVINCIAL COOKING, by Elizabeth David. Copyright © 1960 by Elizabeth David.)

LA DAUBE DE BOEUF PROVEN-CALE—PROVENCAL MEAT AND WINE STEW

There must be scores of different recipes for daubes in Provence alone, as well as all those which have been borrowed from Provence by other regions, for a daube of beef is essentially a country housewife's dish. In some daubes the meat is cut up, in others it is cooked in the piece; what goes in apart from the meat is largely a matter of what is available, and the way it is served is again a question of local taste.

This is an easy recipe, but it has all the rich savour of these slowly cooked wine-flavoured stews. The pot to cook it in may be earthenware, cast iron, or a copper or aluminum oven pot . . . wide rather than deep.

The ingredients are 2 lb. of top rump of beef, about 6 oz. of unsmoked streaky bacon or salt pork, about 3 oz. of fresh pork rinds, 2 onions, 2 carrots, 2 tomatoes, 2 cloves of garlic, a *bouquet* of thyme, bay leaf, parsley, and a little strip of orange peel, 2 tablespoons of olive oil, a glass (4 fl. oz.) of red wine, seasoning.

Have the meat cut into squares about the size of half a postcard and about 1/3 inch thick. Buy the bacon or salt pork in the piece and cut it into small cubes.

Scrape and slice the carrots on the cross; peel and slice the onions. Cut the rinds, which should have scarcely any fat adhering to them and are there to give body as well as savour to the stew, into little squares. Skin and slice the tomatoes.

In the bottom of the pot put the olive oil, then the bacon, then the vegetables, and half the pork rinds. Arrange the meat carefully on top, the slices overlapping each other. Bury the garlic cloves, flattened with a knife, and the *bouquet*, in the centre. Cover with the rest of the pork rinds. With the pan uncovered, start the cooking on a moderate heat on top of the stove.

After about 10 minutes, put the wine into another saucepan; bring it to a fast boil; set light to it; rotate the pan so that the flames spread. When they have died down pour the wine bubbling over the meat. Cover the pot with greaseproof paper or foil, and a well fitting lid. Transfer to a very slow oven, Gas. No. 1, 290°F., and leave for 2½ hours.

To serve, arrange the meat with the bacon and the little pieces of rind on a hot dish; pour off some of the fat from the sauce, extract the *bouquet*, and pour the sauce round the meat. If you can, keep the dish hot over a spirit lamp after it is brought to table. At the serving stage, a *persillade* of finely chopped garlic and parsley, with perhaps an anchovy and a few capers, can be sprinkled over the top. Or stoned black olives can be added to the stew half an hour before the end of the cooking time.

Although in Italy pasta is never served with a meat dish, in Provence it quite often is. The cooked and drained noodles, or whatever pasta you have chosen, are mixed with some of the gravy from the stew, and in this case the fat is not removed from the gravy, because it lubricates the pasta. Sometimes this *macaronade*, as it is called, is served first, to be followed by the meat.

Nowadays, since rice has been successfully cultivated in the reclaimed areas of the Camargue, it is also quite usual to find a dish of rice, often flavoured with saffron, served with a meat stew.

This daube is a useful dish for those who have to get a dinner ready when they get home from the office. It can be cooked for 1½ hours the previous evening and finished on the night itself. Provided they have not been overcooked to start with, these beef and wine stews are all the better for a second or even third heating up. The amounts I have given are the smallest quantities in which it is worth cooking such a stew, and will serve four or five people, but of course they can be doubled or even trebled for a large party; if the meat is piled up in layers in a deep pan it will naturally need longer cooking than if it is spread out in a shallow one.

(From FRENCH PROVINCIAL COOKING, by Elizabeth David. Copyright © 1960 by Elizabeth David.)

BOILING-POT

Dansk Buffet Casserole   7.56

Stoneware; 9½" diam.; 2½" deep; 2-qt. capacity. $34.95

Another casserole whose shape is suited to its function, in this case not only cooking but serving. Dansk calls it a buffet casserole because, being wider and shallower than most other 2-quart casseroles, it allows easy access to the contents. The large surface assists in the evaporation of liquids and makes this pot especially useful for making dishes which involve grains, such as jambalaya or bulghur mixtures. A nice-looking pot in Dansk's Generation Frost Whisper design, glazed in a speckled white and edged in a deep rich brown or blue. Although there is a cover, we would not recommend this casserole for cooking any dish in which you did not want the liquid to reduce considerably.

"'It's a stew of tripe,' said the landlord, smacking his lips, 'and cowheel,' smacking them again, 'and bacon,' smacking them once more, 'and steak,' smacking them for the fourth time, 'and peas, cauliflowers, new potatoes, and sparrowgrass, all working up together in one delicious gravy.' Having come to the climax, he smacked his lips a great many times, and taking a long hearty sniff of the fragrance that was hovering about, put on the cover again with the air of one whose toils on earth were over.

"'At what time will it be ready?' asked Mr. Codlin faintly. 'It'll be done to a turn,' said the landlord, looking up at the clock, 'at twenty-two minutes before eleven.'

"'Then,' said Mr. Codlin, 'fetch me a pint of warm ale, and don't let nobody bring into the room even so much as a biscuit till the time arrives.'"

Dickens, The Old Curiosity Shop

Individual Covered Casserole 7.57

Porcelain; 4½″ diam.; 2″ deep; 1½-cup capacity.
$20.50

A girl we know, who was lucky enough to receive a covered Royal Limoges porcelain dish as a wedding present, asked us if it was all right to put really hot food in it. She was astonished to hear that the dish was meant not only for serving but for cooking; that it was, indeed, the very finest of ovenware. Her confusion was understandable, since these small covered casseroles with their delicate tapestrylike design of multicolored flowers seem altogether too beautiful and fragile to be as useful as they are. Here, for example, is a miniature covered pot which is meant for serving soup but which could, as well, serve a portion of stew. In either case it could go into the oven and then directly to the table. This dish has a capacity of about 1½ cups and is only 4½ inches across the top.

Shallow Royal Limoges Casserole with Lid 7.58

Porcelain; 6¾″ diam.; 1¾″ deep; 3-cup capacity.
$32.00

In the same pattern as 7.57 is this shallow round casserole, only 1¾ inches

deep, to be covered with its own pretty lid. Two eggs could be broken into one of these dishes, which has been first heavily buttered, and then slipped into the oven to bake gently. Or a sauced combination of fruits de mer could be spooned in, sprinkled with cheese, and once again popped into the oven to melt the cheese and combine the flavors. In either case, the lid will insure that the contents come piping hot to the table; and what a pretty sight the shirred eggs would be on a breakfast tray!

Oval Royal Limoges Casserole 7.59

Porcelain; 12¾″ X 7¼″; 2½″ deep; 2-qt. capacity.
$84.50

This casserole in porcelain, the third we show you by Royal Limoges, is considerably larger than the first two and is designed less for individual serving than for cooking for two or four diners, depending on what you put in it. For example, a chicken or a game hen could braise in this long oval dish; or a dish of potatoes au gratin could cook slowly in the oven while you sauté your fish on top of the stove. There are several matching pieces in this ware (see 7.57 and 7.58, for instance), so that a complete oven-to-table service may be purchased; we think it prettier, however, to have only a few pieces in this pattern, which will go well with nearly any dinnerware. This small, charming pot holds 2 quarts and has an extraordinarily well-fitting domed lid which rests in a groove around the inside edge.

"...I should like to set one or two simple and almost mystical phrases I heard from the lips of Mme. Yvon, a thoroughbred cordon bleu. One day at her house, after I had eaten a boeuf à l'ancienne which completely gratified at least three senses out of the five—for apart from its dark, velvety savor and its half-melting consistency, it shone with an amber-colored, caramel-like sauce, ringed at its circumference with a light shimmer of fat the color of fine gold—I cried:

"'Madame Yvon, it's a masterpiece! What do you put in it?'

"'Beef,' Mme. Yvon replied.

"'Heavens, I can tell that . . . But all the same, there must be a mystery, some sort of magic in the way the ingredients are combined . . . With a marvel like this, it should surely be possible to give it a name?'

"'Of course,' Mme. Yvon replied. 'It's a beef casserole.'

"All it would take to preserve, to rescue, and to justify France's pride in her gastronomy would be a few more Mme. Yvons. But she is a rare species in an age that is bent on making silk without silk, gold without gold, pearls without oysters, and Venus without flesh . . ."

Colette, "Prisons et Paradis," in Earthly Paradise, *Robert Phelps, ed., Farrar, Straus & Giroux, New York, 1966*

Covered Onion Soup Pot 7.60

Earthenware; 4½″ diam.; 3¾″ high; 2-cup capacity.
$3.50

This little covered casserole is the traditional French-style onion soup dish. It comes from Japan in the familiar tan and dark-brown earthenware and has a dark-brown lid. The pot is ovenproof but somewhat more fragile than hardier stoneware vessels; nonetheless, a set of

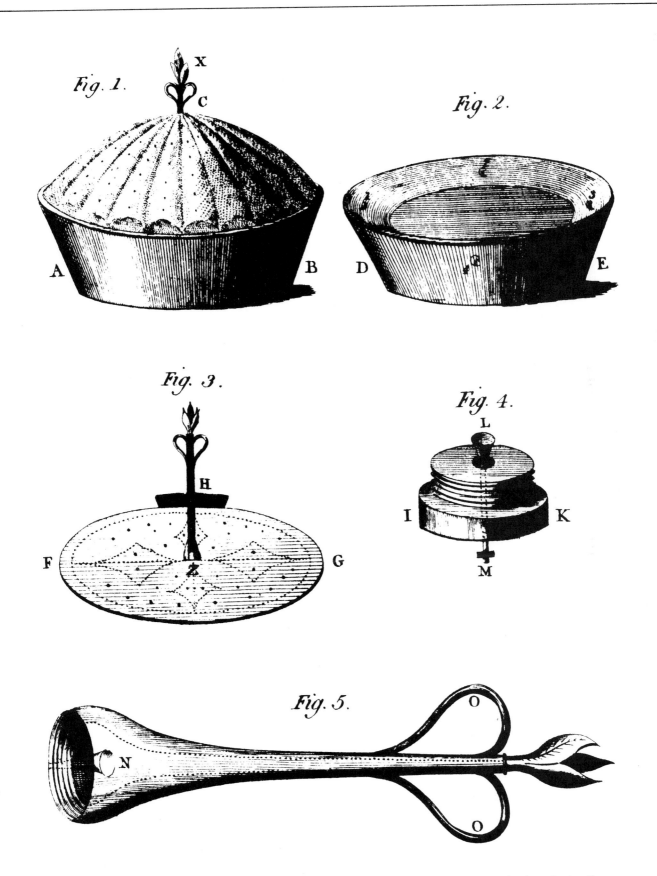

Fig. 1.

Fig. 2.

Fig. 3.

Fig. 4.

Fig. 5.

A late-eighteenth-century dish for a potato pasty. All the bits and pieces were put together in order to allow mashed potatoes, heaped on the central disc (Figure 3), to be permeated by the vapors of meat simmering in the pan below and at the same time to brown on top.

Continued from preceding page

these will serve well enough to hold the bubbling soup and then be passed under a broiler to transform the bread and cheese topping into a delicious chewy amalgam. There are rounded sides on the pot—memories of the marmite—and it has self-handles and a well-fitting lid. An attractive and practical way of serving any soup.

Ron Garfinkel Crock 7.61

Salt-glazed stoneware; 4¼″ diam.; 3¾″ high; 2-cup capacity.

$5.00

Totally idiosyncratic: a small, high-sided crock by the talented potter Ron Garfinkel, colored in brown, green, blue, or bone and stippled with a white salt glaze. The glaze is made by throwing rock salt into the kiln at the moment when the heat is at its maximum intensity; the result is of an elegance quite unrelated to the rather unpredictable method. This crock holds just 2 cups, and we'll let you imagine what you will serve in it, keeping in mind that earthenware retains cold as well as heat. Eggplant caviar? Chicken-liver mousse? Potted shrimp for the cocktail table? Once you have seen it you will have to find a use for it, because it is smashingly beautiful.

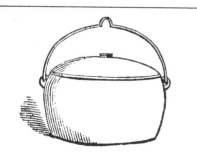

RILLETTES DE PORC—POTTED PORK

As an alternative to a home-made pâté, *rillettes*, which might be described as a kind of potted pork, are quite easy to make at home, and as they keep well, can be made in a fair quantity and stored.

Get the butcher to remove the rind and the bones of approximately 2 lb. of belly or neck of pork and 1 lb. of back pork fat. Rub the meat well with salt and leave it to stand for 4 to 6 hours in summer, overnight in winter. Cut it in thick strips along the grooves from where the bones were taken out, then again into little strips rather shorter than a match and about twice as thick. Put all these into an earthenware or other oven dish, with the pork fat also cut into small pieces; bury a crushed clove of garlic and a bouquet of herbs in the centre, season with a little pepper, add a soup ladle of water, put on the lid of the pan, and cook in a very low oven, Gas No. 1, 290° F., for about 4 hours.

By this time the meat should be very soft and swimming in its own limpid fat. Taste to see if more salt or pepper are needed. *Rillettes* are insipid if not properly seasoned.

Turn the contents of the pan into a wire sieve standing over a big bowl, so that the fat drips through. When well drained, partly pound and then with two forks pull the *rillettes* until they are in fine shreds rather than a paste. Pile lightly into a glazed earthenware or china jar or two or three little ones. Pour the fat over the top of the *rillettes,* leaving behind any sediment and juices, and completely filling the jars. Cover with foil. *Rillettes* should be of a soft texture, so if they have to be stored in a refrigerator, the jars should be removed several hours before serving time.

As I have described in the introductory chapter dealing with the food of the Loire valley, *rillettes* and another version of the same dish, called *rillons,* in which the pieces of pork are much larger, are to be bought in every *charcuterie* and are served in every restaurant. Nowadays the final shredding of *rillettes* is often done by machine, but the good *charcutiers* will tell you that this is not satisfactory, for it reduces them to too purée-like a consistency.

(From FRENCH PROVINCIAL COOKING, by Elizabeth David. Copyright © 1960 by Elizabeth David.)

Tiny Leach Pot 7.62

Stoneware; 3⅜″ diam.; 2⅛″ deep; 6-oz. capacity.
$2.50

A tiny Bernard Leach stoneware pot, roughly finished on the outside and with a black and rust tenmoku glaze within. It is about half the size of the Garfinkel crock (7.61) and is far less elegant in feeling, but it can be used to serve demi-portions of any of the cocktail accompaniments which we recommended you present in the other. We tested it in the oven with eggs shirred in cream: not only were they delicious, but once they were eaten, Leach's handsome swirl design was exposed at the bottom. (Memories of childhood bribery: eat your cereal so that you can see Mickey Mouse on the bottom of the dish.) We ought to mention again the really good prices of pottery from the Leach atelier, which make it possible for everyone to own the work of a really great artist.

The ancient Greeks frequently used earthenware pots, which they discarded when they became too encrusted with foodstuffs. A new pot was used when a recipe called for particularly delicate flavors, as does the following: "Having pounded a quantity of the most fragrant roses in a mortar . . . put in the brains of birds and pigs boiled . . . and the yolks of eggs and with them oil, and pickle-juice, and pepper and wine. And having pounded all these things carefully together . . . put them into a new dish, applying a gentle and steady fire to them."

Baking Dishes

Not all oven dishes are high-sided and covered; there is also a group of fairly shallow pans which were designed to be put on the middle rack of an oven where the heat can penetrate their walls from all directions. Europeans tend to call them roasters, identifying them with the shallow pans for cooking meat which we discuss in the next chapter (Chapter 8). Of course, they could be used for this purpose. But because they are made of earthenware, porcelain, or oven glass, all of which permit a gentle absorption of heat from all sides, they are particularly good for making dishes cooked with liquids which benefit from a slow gentle cooking. The shape, too, relatively shallow and straight-sided, makes them appropriate for fish, for eggs, and for anything cooked with evaporating moisture, such as the great variety of ethnic dishes which are made with grains. Look into all of the chapters dealing with those foods before you decide on one of these shallow pans.

What do you cook in these baking dishes? First of all, of course, anything flat . . . fish, beef roulades, braised vegetables lightly covered with oiled or waxed paper. Then, anything which need not be covered with liquid but which would benefit from the gentle steam produced by a mirepoix, a shallow layer of diced vegetables simmering in wine. And, of course, anything which you wish to solidify: custard, corn bread, lasagna, rice mixtures, anything which has to be of an even, shallow density throughout so as to set properly or cook evenly.

These dishes are undoubtedly the descendants of the shallow pans which were once placed beneath turning roasts: whole baby lambs or loins of beef or rows of pigeons turning on a spit over an open fire. As the spit was turned, fat melted by the heat rolled back onto the turning meat or fell into a pan placed underneath to catch the drippings. And one day, we assume, some domestic genius put a handful of leeks or potatoes into this pan to cook, and noticed that their flavor was immeasurably improved. Yorkshire pudding, that simple combination of flour, salt, milk, and eggs, was originally cooked under a turning roast in just this manner, the simple batter gaining its flavor from the melting fat. In old New England, where the fireplace was needed for heating as well as for cooking, a hole—an oven—was built into its wall, and then a shallow pan would be placed in it where that night's dinner could cook slowly all afternoon. All of the glass, porcelain, and earthenware dishes which we show you are appropriate for just that sort of slow and gentle cooking.

Légumier

Karnes Baking Dish　　　　7.63

Stoneware; 15¾″ diam.; 3¼″ high; 5½-qt. capacity.
$36.00

We begin with the star, **Karen Karnes's** outrageously large, outrageously beautiful baking dish, its sides curving gently to hold enough to feed a troop of Boy Scouts or the entire Académie Française. The glaze has the rich brown perfection of a superb sauce; there are coiling finger-formed ridges on both the inner and outer surfaces, and two sturdy handles are placed under the rim. It is most assuredly not for everyone: this dish is hard to store and really uncomfortably large, since it will hold 5½ quarts. But consider a huge paella or risotto for a party, a lentil and smoked-meat casserole, a choucroute garnie, its ingredients cooked separately and then the whole baked together briefly at the end. Too shallow for a tossed salad, it would, however, serve well for a composed salad or a graphic arrangement of crudities. Don't even think about storage; instead, between its trips to the oven fill it with fruit or pine cones or Christmas balls and count yourself lucky to have it.

JAMBON A LA CREME AU GRATIN

[British measuring units] Make a cream sauce with 1½ oz. of butter, 2 tablespoons of flour and, when these have amalgamated, 4 tablespoons of warmed white wine. Then add ½ pint of warmed milk. Season with a little salt and a generous amount of freshly milled pepper. Simmer this sauce, very gently, stirring frequently, for 15 minutes. Now transfer the saucepan in which it is cooking into another large and shallow one containing hot water (or, of course, a proper *bain-marie* if you happen to possess such a thing) and add 4 or 5 tablespoons of fresh thick cream. Stir again. Lastly, add 2 tablespoons of grated Gruyère or Parmesan cheese. The cheese must not dominate the sauce but is there to give it pungency, as a condiment. Add more salt if necessary, always taking into consideration the saltiness of the ham. Of this you need ½ lb., cooked and cut in thin even slices. Into a shallow *gratin* dish, pour a little of the cream sauce. On top put the ham, in one layer, with the slices overlapping each other. Cover completely with the rest of the sauce. Add some minuscule little knobs of butter. Place in a hot oven, near the top, for 5 to 10 minutes. Finish under a hot grill for a minute or two and serve immediately, when the surface is blistering and bubbling.

(From FRENCH PROVINCIAL COOKING, by Elizabeth David. Copyright © 1960 by Elizabeth David.)

Rectangular Pyrex Baking Dishes   7.64

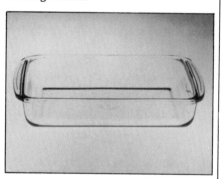

Pyrex glass; 10″ × 6″, 1¾″ deep; capacity 1½ qts. Also avail. 11¾″ × 7½″, 1¾″ deep, capacity 2 qts., and 13½″ × 8¾″, 1¾″ deep, capacity 3 qts.
$2.10 ▲ $2.70 ▲ $3.10 ▲

If your ambition is to own the Karnes baking dish, then these are probably the baking dishes that you already have; and as far as function is concerned, you should not feel at all cheated. They are practical, easy to clean, inexpensive and, being transparent, they allow you to oversee the contents closely. Because they are glass, oven temperatures should be lowered to 25 F. below the heat recommended for metal pans; and thus, they are thrifty not only in the original purchase but in the future fuel bill. Not only that, but these simple rectangular dishes come in a variety of sizes, having a capacity of 1½, 2, and 3 quarts; since the price is so reasonable, you could easily have at least two. Good for lasagna, for brownies, for gratinéed vegetables; not beautiful, but full of homely good qualities.

Porcelain Baking Dish with Blue Flowers   7.65

Porcelain; 13½″ × 8¼″; 1¾″ deep; 2¾-qt. capacity.
$23.00

Because we urge you to think of the decorative as well as the functional, because we think it is sometimes more practical to have a dish which can be used for both baking and serving without any apologies, we show you this classic French version of the rectangular baking pan. From Pillivuyt, it is similar in shape to the oblong Pyrex pan (7.64), but it is made of a highly glazed white porcelain which has been decorated on the outside with a blue flower design. And, strange to say, porcelain has all of the wonderful qualities of glass, save only the low cost: it is easy to clean and retentive of heat, permitting you to lower the oven temperature for a given dish by 25 F. The pan comes in only one size, 13½ inches in length, and it is of a simple shape and a pleasant design, with an unglazed bottom (for better heat absorption) and narrow handles flaring from the sides. You can have it in a multi-colored floral design or in a plain white glaze as well as in our version, decorated with slightly Victorian-looking blue roses.

GRATIN DAUPHINOIS

[British measuring units]

Dauphine and *dauphinois*, similar though they sound, are two very different preparations of potatoes, both most excellent in their ways. *Pommes dauphine* make an ideal accompaniment to steaks and small roasts, for those who are not daunted by last-minute deep frying. *Gratin dauphinois* is a rich and filling regional dish from the Dauphiné. Some recipes, Escoffier's and Austin de Croze's among them, include cheese and eggs, making it very similar to a *gratin savoyard*: but other regional authorities declare that the authentic *gratin dauphinois* is made only with potatoes and thick fresh cream. I give the second version which is, I think, the better one; it is also the easier. And if it seems to the thrifty-minded outrageously extravagant to use half a pint of cream to one pound of potatoes, I can only say that to me it seems a more satisfactory way of enjoying cream than pouring it over tinned peaches or chocolate mousse.

Peel 1 lb. of yellow potatoes, and slice them in even rounds no thicker than a penny; this operation is very easy with the aid of the mandoline. Rinse them thoroughly in cold water—this is most important—then shake them dry in a cloth. Put them in layers in a shallow *earthenware* dish which has been rubbed with garlic and well buttered. Season with pepper and salt. Pour ½ pint of thick cream over them; strew with little pieces of butter; cook them for 1½ hours on a low oven. Gas No. 2, 310° F. During the last 10 minutes turn the oven up fairly high to get a fine golden crust on the potatoes. Serve in the dish in which they have cooked. It is not easy to say how many people this quantity will serve: two, or three, or four, according to their capacity, and what there is to follow.

Much depends also upon the quality of the potatoes used. Firm waxy varieties such as the *kipfler* and the fir-apple pink which appear occasionally on the London market make a gratin lighter and also more authentic than that made with routine commercial King Edwards or Majestics which are in every respect second best.

Two more points concerning the proportions of a *gratin dauphinois*: as the quantity of potatoes is increased the proportion of cream may be slightly diminished. Thus, for 3 lb. of potatoes, 1¼ pints of cream will be amply sufficient; and the choice of cooking dish (for the appropriate shape, see the *tian*) is also important, for the potatoes and cream should, always, fill the dish to within approximately three quarters of an inch of the top.

The best way, in my view, of appreciating the charm of a *gratin dauphinois* is to present the dish entirely on its own, as a first course to precede grilled or plain roast meat or poultry, or a cold joint to be eaten with a simple green salad.

(From FRENCH PROVINCIAL COOKING, by Elizabeth David. Copyright © 1960 by Elizabeth David.)

Stangl Baking Dish   7.66

Earthenware; 9″ X 6½″; 1½″ deep; 1¼-qt. capacity. Also avail. 12″ X 9½″, 1½″ deep.

$15.00

An American beauty, similar in shape to both of the preceding dishes. This speckled blue earthenware dish from the Stangl pottery firm was originally produced for Tiffany & Company. In spite of Tiffany's Fifth Avenue address, however, the dish has a simple old-fashioned look and would go well in an Early American kitchen. Again, this dish is a rectangle with rounded corners, but the handles are small and have a thumbprint impressed on the top. There are two lengths—9 and 12 inches—in yellow, green, or blue (our preference). A white fleck runs through the glaze of the yellow, green, and blue dishes. On all the dishes the glaze is continued over the bottom. Simple, heavy, and quite costly, but handsome.

Rectangular Porcelaine de   7.67 Paris Baking Dish

Porcelain; 9½″ X 6½″; 1½″ deep; 3-cup capacity. Also avail. 10¾″, 12″, or 13¼″ long.

$34.00

Elsewhere you can read our rhapsody on Porcelaine de Paris, that holdover from a time when beautiful designs were handpainted on china rather than slipped on with decals. Here we will limit ourselves to a description of the practical beauties of these porcelain pans, called roasting dishes by the manufacturer. They are large and meant to hold main courses; actually, a roast could be done in one of these rectangular dishes and then brought to the table for the host to present to the guests before carving. The porcelain is of the highest quality. The bottom of the dish is unglazed on the outside, and a pattern of Persian flowers is painted onto the interior in the most vibrant colors. There are four lengths, 9½″, 10¾″, 12″, and 13¼″, and the dishes are rather wide in proportion to their length. A raised rim encircles each dish, widening into small handles at either end.

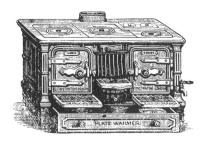

CONSTANTINE'S TREASURE RANGE (No. 84) WITH ROASTER AND OVEN

Oval Porcelaine de   7.68 Paris Baking Dish

Porcelain; 11″ X 6½″; 1½″ deep. Also avail. 11¾″, 13″, 13¾″, or 15″ long.

$41.00

Ignore our photograph: baking dishes like these simply must be seen to be believed. Imagine them standing on edge, leaning against the back of a Breton dresser; visualize them coming to the table with your most modern dinnerware or your finest antiques. These are oval porcelain dishes with shallow flutings around the sides, rather like quiche pans pulled out of shape. Were that all it would be enough, but these lovely baking dishes are painted with a breathtaking series of vegetables, a different one for each size: leek, eggplant, carrots, tomatoes—all of a dewy freshness. The porcelain sounds with a bell-like ring when it is touched, the light shines through the translucent china as though it were skim milk. (For more on Porcelaine de Paris, look in Chapter 11). Each dish is unglazed on the outside of the bottom to prevent chipping. They range from 11″ to 15″ in length, and you would do well to buy two in different sizes in order to get two different designs. They are worth every penny they cost.

Unless we are to believe Charles Lamb and accept his theory that the first cooking pot was the burning house, then we must agree that the earliest form of cookware was the spit. On some simple stick, a piece of freshly caught meat was offered to the fire; seared, roasted, the scent of raw meat transformed into the scent of prehistoric grande cuisine.

Until now we have been discussing pots in which food is cooked in some sort of liquid: a chicken braised in the evaporating juices of a bed of wine-drenched vegetables, or a tall casserole of lentils, tomatoes, and bits of leftover ham. This kind of cooking demands that the pans have good covers, for one thing, to hold the juices in; and they must be made of materials which lend themselves to the slow diffusion of heat. Think of a Karnes earthenware pot (Chapter 7) as the perfect example of this sort of dish. Then remember that food can also be cooked perfectly dry, as it was in the culinary beginning, with neither pot nor liquid to stand between it and the flames. This food need not, of course, be freshly slaughtered rabbit over a fire started by lightning. It can be done in an oven, with the heat rebounding onto the food from all sides: a beautiful sirloin of beef standing proudly in a low roasting pan, the oven door left slightly ajar to allow the evaporating juices to steam off because roasting, after all, is not steaming. In this chapter we'll tell you about the dishes and devices designed to present their contents directly to a flame in any number of ways.

SOURCES OF HEAT

Direct heat can be applied to food from above, from the side, and from below; and of these, the best way is from the side.

The most primitive method of roasting or broiling is that by which the flame sits immediately beneath the charring food: a whole ox turning, skewers of marinated lamb on a rack, or a few hot dogs pierced by twigs and hand-held over a campfire. This is related to the form of cooking which, domesticated, we use in home barbecues and hibachis and in such useful compromise solutions as the Farber broiler-rotisserie, 8.7. Unfortunately, in many such arrangements there is the problem of managing the flames which result from the melting fat catching fire; and it is by necessity a simple form of cooking, since all of the lovely essences that emerge from the meat are lost during the roasting.

When the fire is above the food, you have a quieter and quicker method, with a receptacle below the meat to catch melted fats and juices for use in later saucing or embellishments. The most familiar application of this method is the broiling done in your home oven; another is the use of the broiler heat to brown the top of a gratin—a task for which chefs sometimes use a salamander, a specially shaped piece of steel (8.20) which is heated in the stove like an old-fashioned pressing iron and then held over the food to melt and brown the top. Then there is the food-above-the-fire arrangement, the one best known to us all. For we are a nation of barbecuers: if the national bird were not the eagle, it would be the barbecued chicken. Whether the barbecue habit comes from some collective unconscious memory of meals along the

"Steak is part of the same sanguine mythology as wine. It is the heart of meat, it is meat in its pure state; and whoever partakes of it assimilates a bull-like strength . . . Like wine, steak is in France a basic element, nationalized even more than socialized. It figures in all the surroundings of alimentary life: flat, edged with yellow, like the sole of a shoe, in cheap restaurants; thick and juicy in the bistros which specialize in it; cubic, with the core all moist throughout beneath a light charred crust, in haute cuisine. It is a part of all the rhythms, that of the comfortable bourgeois meal and that of the bachelor's bohemian snack. It is a food at once expeditious and dense, it effects the best possible ratio between economy and efficacy, between mythology and its multifarious ways of being consumed. . . . Steak is here adorned with a supplementary virtue of elegance, for among the apparent complexity of exotic cooking, it is a food which unites, one feels, succulence and simplicity . . ."

"Steak and Chips," essay in the collection Mythologies, by Roland Barthes, Hill and Wang, New York, 1973

ROASTED LAMB (MECHOUI)

I am not going to suggest you spit-roast a whole lamb; I realize that for most readers that is out of the question. Instead I recommend that you make *mechoui* with a ten-pound forequarter. Though it may taste a little better if you can dig a pit, fill it with charcoal, and set up a roasting spit in your back yard, I guarantee that with this adaptation you will obtain good results in the oven of your home, be it country house or city apartment.

Actually, the same problem confronts the Moroccan city dweller. She knows that the best place to eat *mechoui* is in the *bled,* because if she cooks it in the city, where most people do not have a full-sized stove, she will have to send her meat to a community oven, and there the workers will be extremely casual about basting the lamb. The best Berber *mechoui,* you see, is swabbed down every ten minutes with butter and spices.

Fortunately, most Americans have large stoves in which a forequarter can easily be roasted, and are therefore in a better position to cook *mechoui* than the average person in Rabat or Casablanca. Buying a whole forequarter in America can, however, be an amusing experience.

The paste used to flavor the meat in this recipe is in the style of Rabat.

INGREDIENTS

1 forequarter lamb (10 pounds)
1½ tablespoons ground coriander seed
4 to 5 cloves garlic, peeled and mashed
2 teaspoons ground cumin
1 teaspoon sweet paprika
6 tablespoons sweet butter, softened
Salt to taste

EQUIPMENT

Sharp paring knife
Roasting pan large enough to hold the lamb
Large spoon or bulb baster

Working time: 10 minutes
Roasting time: 3 hours
Serves: 8 (as part of a Moroccan dinner)

1. Carefully remove extraneous fat from the lamb, then make deep incisions under the foreleg bone along the breastplate. Blend all the other ingredients into a paste and rub into the meat. Let stand 10 minutes.

2. Preheat the oven to 475°.

3. Place the lamb, fatty side up, in a large roasting pan. Place on the middle shelf of the oven and roast 15 minutes. Reduce the heat to 350° and continue to roast for about 3 hours, or until the meat can easily be removed from the bones with your fingers. Baste every 15 minutes with the juices in the pan. Serve at once, while still burning hot. Eat with your fingers and have a bowl of ground cumin and salt ready for those who like to dip their meat.

NOTE: The secret of a good *mechoui* is to obtain a crisp, beautifully browned crust while the meat inside is sweet, juicy, and meltingly tender. The lamb should not be pink, as the French like it, or tough and dried out, as it is so often served in the United States.

(From COUSCOUS AND OTHER GOOD FOOD FROM MOROCCO, by Paula Wolfert, introduction by Gael Greene. Copyright © 1973 by Paula Wolfert. Reprinted by permission of Harper & Row.)

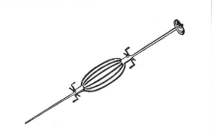

A cradle spit, ancestor of the tambour (8.2).

Chisholm Trail or whether it is a simple matter of not wanting to wash out the oven broiling rack, every weekend hordes of American families manage to cook their suppers out of doors: on patios, on beaches, at roadside picnic stops, and even on high-rise apartment terraces where the smoke of burning fat can rise and mingle graciously with hundreds of car exhausts. Isn't it peculiar, then, that we have never had available to us the best equipment for the best way of cooking with direct heat, which is most emphatically not any of the three ways we have described?

THE SIDE APPROACH

In the great outdoor restaurants of France there are huge vertical broilers—walls, really—with great spits standing before them on which roasts, even sides, of beef are slowly turned. In the Near East, a roast of lamb is turned on a vertical spit before the fire, and slices are carved off as they are cooked. These arrangements are similar to that in an old-fashioned colonial cooking fireplace, where a revolving spit was placed before the fire, while a pan underneath it caught the drippings. In this manner, the meat was constantly basted by its own melting fat as it turned, but it was never polluted by the smoke of fat falling into a fire. And there, in the dripping pan, there might be potatoes roasting in a constant shower of melting goose fat, or a huge puff of Yorkshire pudding being flavored by the browning beef with which it was to be served. This is the best method of open-fire cooking, a method which has for some reason not been available in this country, unless you improvised a dripping pan and used a banked fire toward the back of an outdoor barbecue with electrical rotisserie equipment—possible, but clumsy.

THE ULTIMATE EQUIPMENT

It seems too good to be true, but we have found a company in France which makes grills which allow the cook to roast and broil in the only truly correct way, with a lateral heat source. And these appliances are beginning to be imported into this country. They are made by Cocambroche, a name familiar in France as the manufacturers of outdoor cooking equipment. In a variety of models, using as heat source either your fireplace, a bed of charcoal, or your stove oven with the door standing open, you erect a spit alongside the heat source. This spit turns slowly by means of an electrical turner or one which rotates on a loosening spring, and the fat from the turning food falls into a dripping pan: often the tilted dripping pan which the French call a *lechefrite*. This general method is expressed in several ways: there is a simple erection of spit, turner, and dripping pan which sits on your open oven door (8.1); another assemblage, a mammoth affair of wrought iron that encompasses andirons, spits, and electrically powered turners, transforms your fireplace into a machine for roasting a flock of chickens (8.4); or you can choose an outdoor barbecue capable of cooking two steaks, two chickens, a leg of lamb, and a grillful of sardines at once. And while you are cooking all this, you would still have a big spit left over: spanning the two fireboxes and above the grills, this spit is literally large enough to roast a whole lamb. Clearly a contraption to delight the acquisitive outdoor partygiver, whether in Dubuque or Rouen.

Continued from preceding page

We don't want to make too many jokes; we are absolutely mad for these affairs and would like to see them replace every tinny backyard grill in the country. We'll show you enough of them to let you know that they are available in every size and degree of complication, whatever your requirements. Once you have tasted steak cooked *alongside* the fire, with no coating of nasty burnt charcoal smoke, you will never again want to return to the old method.

The Cocambroche Four Rotisserie   8.1

Enameled-steel base with nickel-steel supports and spit; base 13¾" × 9"; spit 15" long; supports 7" high.
$90.00

Here is the side-fired grill in its simplest form, light enough to sit on your open oven door and use the heat supplied by your local power and light company, or to place on the hearth of your fireplace in front of a good blaze of hardwood. Though perhaps not the ideal solution to the problem of roasting on a spit, it does use a lateral source of heat and it is infinitely better than built-in oven rotisseries, especially those that cannot be used with the oven door open and which thus force the food to be partly steamed. The Cocambroche Four has as its base a simple enameled-steel pan measuring about 14" by 9"; the pan has a slanted bottom to catch the drippings and allow you to spoon them back over the meat. To this pan you attach two upright supports; across the supports you lay either a spit or a tambour or wire cage 8.2, depending on what you plan to cook. At one end of the spit or the tambour frame goes a clockwork mechanism which will turn the spit, or the basket, for about an hour; you can set a little control to govern the speed of turn-ing, and if you need more time, you simply rewind the mechanism. The spit is equipped with two forklike prongs to bite into a roast or a bird and be tightened there by screws; the prongs simplify the problem of balancing the meat on the spit. The tambour is adjustable, so that it will hold snugly something as thick as a fine fish or as thin as a small steak; and for another kind of cooking, openings in its end plates accommodate six skewers for your shish kebab or shashlik. That's it. The meat turns and cooks, while the fat drips off into the pan. And it all comes apart for easy cleaning.

Cocambroche Tambour   8.2

Nickel steel; 12¾" × 6¾"
$37.00

Chickens are all very well for roasting with lateral heat, but what do you do about steak? Or hamburgers? Or meat which has a bone so placed that you cannot pierce the roast with a spit? This basketlike accessory, called by the makers a tambour, is, so far as we are concerned, half the value of the Cocambroche grills: an adjustable cage made of wire in which you can place and hold snugly anything from a single fish to the two halves of a broiler. The cage is then fitted to the spit-turning mechanism of your grill, which will rotate it before the fire. This tambour has end pieces with tiny holes around the circumference into which you can put skewers of meat.

SPITTED BARBECUED SPARERIBS

2 sides spareribs
Salt and freshly ground pepper

MARINADE OR BRUSHING LIQUID
½ cup honey
½ cup soy sauce
2 garlic cloves, crushed and chopped
3 tablespoons catsup
½ cup water or white wine

Salt and pepper the spareribs and weave them on the spit. Mix the ingredients for the marinade. Start the ribs revolving and roast slowly, brushing them frequently with the marinade. After 1 to 1½ hours they will be beautifully glazed and will have absorbed the delicious flavors of the marinade. Cut the ribs in sections. Serve as an hors d'oeuvre or as a main course with fried rice and a tomato salad.

(From AMERICAN COOKERY, by James A. Beard, illustrated by Earl Thollander. Copyright © 1972 by James A. Beard. Reprinted by permission of Little, Brown and Company.)

Cocambroche Living   8.3

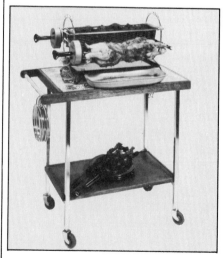

Wrought iron with steel supports, brass trim; grilling surface 17½" × 8"; 2 spits 17½" long.
$285.00

One step above the Cocambroche Four in capacity and sophistication is the Cocambroche Living, a small, portable appliance on which you can cook enough grilled meat for a large party. At the

The Cocambroche Four Rotisserie
Cocambroche Tambour
Cocambroche Living
Cocambroche Gargantua
Cocambroche Residence

center is a deep mesh box for charcoal, roughly triangular in cross-section, which allows the heat to radiate up onto a flat horizontal grill measuring 17½″ by 8″ and, at the same time, to radiate laterally towards the wonderful turning spits, one along each side of the firebox. The spits are turned by clockwork—no electricity is needed. The design of this cooker greatly reduces the amount of charcoal that you will need. The grill is extremely compact and could be used in a fireplace, next to a window, on a balcony, or on a table out of doors. On it you can make grilled shrimp for a first course on the flat grill, while your main course turns in a leisurely fashion on either side. Four chickens or two legs of lamb will fit on the spits, and, to add to the versatility of this device, long skewers are provided for broiling small pieces of meat and vegetables. We can't imagine anyone who wouldn't want to own this.

Cocambroche Gargantua 8.4

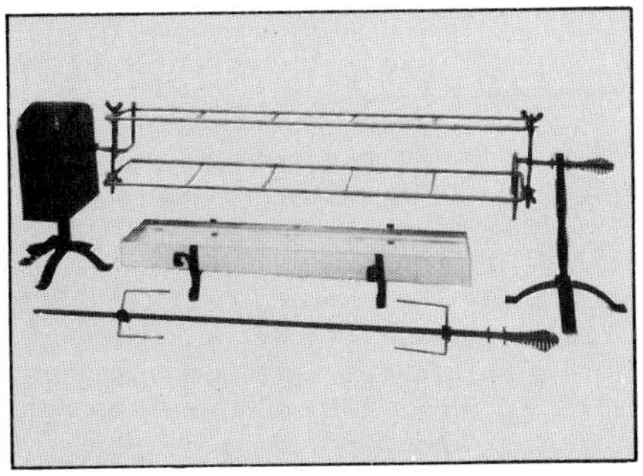

Wrought-iron supports, steel drip pan; avail. with spit 31½″ long, drip pan 23½″ long, or spit 39″ long, drip pan 31½″ long.
$400.00

The manufacturer calls it Gargantua, and what else? Here your heat source is neither Con Edison nor a box of charcoal, but rather your fireplace or a mammoth bonfire; you are provided with two cast-iron uprights, an enormous lechefrite for catching the drippings, and an electrically powered turner for the spit. And this apparatus *is* decidedly gargantuan, not only in size but in feeling; think of a large party in the country with three or four large roasting chickens caught in the heavy prongs of the spit, with vegetables browning in a bath of drippings in the lechefrite. There are other fireplace models available, some with full andirons, and all the others with clockwork mechanisms for turning the spit. Notice how cleverly we have managed to provide you with the very model of direct-heat cooking: the true descendant of our primitive ancestors' sapling spits, holding the hunters' catch up to the heat of the communal fire.

SKEWERED AND GRILLED LAMB (QUODBAN)

One of the most famous dishes of the Middle East and the Arab world is skewered lamb or beef, known variously as *shish kebab, shaslick,* brochettes, and so on. In some parts of Morocco these are eaten with a good sprinkling of hot spices, followed by a soothing glass of highly sweetened mint tea. On the road between Meknes and Rabat there is a small town called Khemisett, which specializes in serving spicy *quodban* to travelers. Here, the vendors of the many competing stalls grill the meat on skewers, then remove it and place the pieces within pieces of barley bread encrusted with salt crystals.

INGREDIENTS
1½ pounds boned leg of lamb, cut into ¾-inch cubes
1 cup beef or mutton fat, cut into ¼-inch cubes
1 onion, grated
¼ cup finely chopped parsley
Salt to taste
½ teaspoon freshly ground black pepper

EQUIPMENT
Shallow dish
Broiler or outdoor grill
12 skewers

Working time: 10 minutes
Marinating time: 2 hours
Grilling time: 5 to 8 minutes
Serves: 6

1. Place the lamb in the shallow dish with the chunks of fat and all the other ingredients. Toss well and let stand for 2 hours.

2. Heat up the grill.

3. Thread the meat alternately with the fat chunks, pressing the pieces together. (There should be 6 to 8 small pieces of meat and 4 pieces of fat on each skewer.) Broil the meat a few inches from the heat, then turn when well browned and grill the other side. (Moroccans usually grill the meat until well done.)

4. To serve, each guest slides the pieces of meat, one by one, into a wedge of Moroccan bread, and then sprinkles on some cayenne, cumin, and salt, which are served in separate bowls, to taste.

NOTE: For a spicier *kebab,* add a scant teaspoon paprika and cumin. Also, 1½ pounds beef fillet can be substituted for the lamb.

(From COUSCOUS AND OTHER GOOD FOOD FROM MOROCCO, by Paula Wolfert, with introduction by Gael Greene. Copyright © 1973 by Paula Wolfert. Reprinted by permission of Harper & Row.)

Cocambroche Residence 8.5

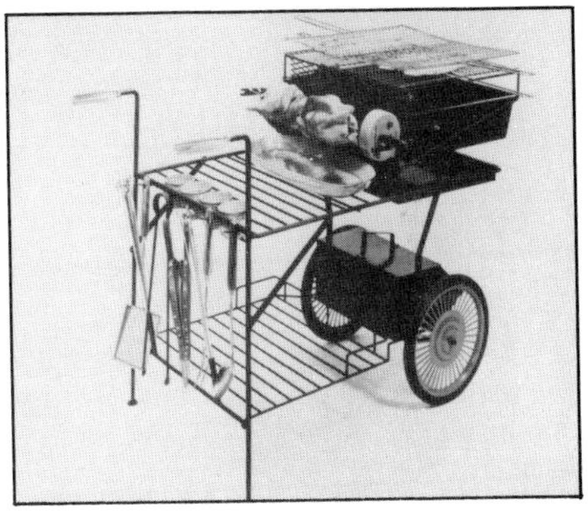

Wrought iron and enameled iron with steel accessories; 31½″ × 19½″ overall; grilling surface 17¾″ × 8¼″.
$420.00

This begins to look more like what we recognize as a barbecue grill. Here is a cooker built in two levels on a portable metal cart. At one end are the cart handles, at the other end are the wheels. On the lower level are a box for storing charcoal and a shelf made of iron bars. On the upper level is a rack near the handles for cooking accessories, then a shelf like the lower one, then the actual cooking area. This turns out to be an ash pan on the bottom and a raised firebox above. Over the firebox is space to lay a portable grill or skewers, and in front of the fire, which is contained in the metal mesh of the firebox, is a spit that turns by clockwork over a dripping pan. There is an awful lot of cart for the small cooking area, it is true. But in the sense that a tank is a way of making a big gun portable, so this is a way of making a small grill portable. You could lay a wooden board across the front part of the cart for carving, and you could put a covered bowl of salad on the bottom shelf, away from the heat. There is another model that is similar but slightly larger: called the Grande Famille, it is for those who have a *famille* large enough to be called *grande.*

Cocambroche Touraine 8.6

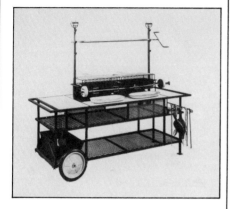

Wrought iron with steel accessories, ceramic inserts, wood chopping board; 70″ long, 27½″ wide overall; full height 60″; 2 grills, each 17¾″ × 8¼″.

$1,500.00

Moving upward by mechanical progression, this is the ultimate cooker from Cocambroche, and we would assume that on it you could cook enough to feed the entire French army, or half of a boys' camp. It is so complete as to be almost embarrassing, and it is divine. To wit: a huge wheeled cart, with a top level which is paved with tiles and equipped with a carving board and into which is set the cooking mechanism. Below this, a second level of metal mesh —here you warm food, hang accessories, and catch in a pan the ashes from the charcoal fire above. On the lowest level, also of metal mesh, you store plates, food, and charcoal (a metal box is provided). The actual cooking area holds two stoves. One is a V-shaped firebox like that of 8.3 , radiating heat upward and to two sides so that you may broil over it while you cook on a spit to the side. But there is in addition a flat bed of coals, also blessed with a mechanically turned spit to the side. Plus drip pans, in which you can cook vegetables, and a mammoth spit over the whole affair. What do you have? Well, enough equipment to cook for a mammoth party. You can roast hot dogs for the children on a grill or in the portable long-handled hinged grill provided, while at the same time you also lay over the other fire skewers of marinated shrimp for hors d'oeuvre. Then on one of the spits you can roast something special for the adults, something that the children would consider yukky—like a small suckling pig—or something that is simply too ex-

pensive to serve the little dears—like a couple of whole fillets of beef. You could, of course, also do a bird on the second main-level spit and cook a whole lamb on the large top-level spit that spans both fireboxes, but let's assume that you have enough to eat for this meal. There is another, slightly smaller and wheelless model called the Manoir, with which you have the choice of using an electric spit turner. The final word in grills; a ravishing addition to your entertaining equipment.

Farber Broiler-Rotisserie 8.7

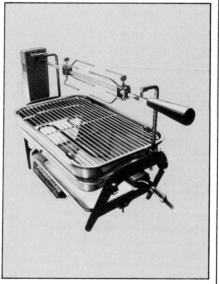

Stainless-steel body with aluminum drip tray, plastic legs; 15″ × 10″ broiling surface; stainless-steel and black plastic rotisserie accessories.

$50.00 ▲

The American cousin of the wonderful French Cocambroche cookers, using electricity rather than charcoal as its heat source. This, called the Open Hearth, allows you to broil your hamburgers or steak or to turn spitted meat—even a large roast or a good-sized turkey—in surrounding heated air. It is from our old friend Farber and, save for the fact that the heat comes from below rather than the side, it is as good as the French product and is, further, adaptable to apartment kitchens, where charcoal cooking is scarcely feasible. The Open Hearth is perfectly suitable for use indoors—its maker says flatly that it's smokeless and spatter-free—and we have found that to be true, due to ingenious design that

prevents the meat fat from being heated by the cooking element to the point where smoke might be produced. You buy a stainless-steel broiler unit that sits in a frame supported by black plastic legs. This holds the broiling element, which is heated via a removable plug and cord set. Over the broiling element goes a grill and under it a drip pan, which is almost completely sheltered from the heat. This is the basic grill. You will also get, if you are wise, the rotisserie mechanism—a support, with adjustable spit positions, for the spit and motor; a sturdy spit with two strong four-pronged forks to hold the meat; and an electrically powered heavy-duty motor. You can also buy a set of five long skewers and a rack for broiling foods en brochette. The Open Hearth comes in two sizes, a smallish 12″ by 8½″ for people with small kitchens or small families, and a commodious and more useful 15″ by 10″ size. All parts but the self-cleaning heating element and the rotisserie motor can be immersed in soapy water for easy cleaning. If you have no earthly way of finding in your house accommodations for one of the Cocambroche grills, this is your next best choice for grilling and spit roasting.

In Tudor England, cooks in great houses spit-roasted their meat, often using trained dogs, encouraged by live coals thrown at their feet, to turn the spits. There are even records of geese being trained as turnspits. Upon seeing a goose turning a turkey on a spit, one observer remarked: "Alas! We are all turnspits in this world: and when we roast a friend let us be aware that many stand ready to return the compliment."

SKEWERED AND GRILLED LIVER, BERBER STYLE (KOUAH)

INGREDIENTS
1 pound lamb's liver, in one piece
¼ pound mutton fat
Salt
½ teaspoon cumin
1½ teaspoons paprika
Pinches of cayenne to taste

EQUIPMENT
Griddle or wire rack for charcoal grilling or a seasoned skillet
Broiler or outdoor grill
12 skewers

Working time: 10 minutes
Grilling time: 5 to 7 minutes
Serves: 4 to 6 (as part of a Moroccan dinner)

1. Firm the lamb's liver by lightly searing on both sides on a hot griddle or in a well-seasoned skillet. Cut into smallish chunks. Cut the fat into smaller chunks.

2. Mix the liver and fat with salt and the spices and thread on skewers, beginning and ending with pieces of liver. Grill quickly on both sides and serve very hot, with Moroccan bread. In Tangier thinned Harissa Sauce [a very hot pepper sauce] is often served with *kouah*.

(From COUSCOUS AND OTHER GOOD FOOD FROM MOROCCO, by Paula Wolfert, with introduction by Gael Greene. Copyright © 1973 by Paula Wolfert. Reprinted by permission of Harper & Row.)

A roast-cook spitting birds. From an old Hungarian cookbook.

Gratin Pans

Remember that in discussing broiling and roasting we are talking not only about pots but principles, and that two contraptions which look very different can, in fact, use the same cooking methods. And if grills are devices for exposing food to direct open heat, then so are the gratin pans we show you next. The food which rests in them is meant to be offered directly to the flames of an overhead broiler. These pans are shallow, to begin with. And although they may resemble the low earthenware casseroles we showed you in the last chapter, there is a subtle difference in function, for these are basically presentation pans. Food for gratins is cooked elsewhere, turned into the au gratin pan, often with a sauce and a sprinkle of crumbs or another topping, and then set briefly under the intense heat of a broiler, or placed on the upper shelf of a very hot oven until the topping browns and the food is hot throughout. Afterwards, it is seldom removed from its dish, but is rather brought directly to the table.

WINNING LOOKS

This means that gratin dishes are beautiful but not necessarily serious, that they can be made of a lightweight copper or aluminum or a fragile porcelain, because they do little actual cooking; and although they are related to the pans which we show you elsewhere for cooking eggs and fish (Chapter 11), those pans must have better cooking qualities. Far better, for gratin pans, to have a beautiful exterior, a wide area of exposure to the browning fire, and adequate handles for carrying the finished dish to the table.

The word gratin *refers to the thin crust that is formed over a sauced dish when it is browned in the oven or broiler. The term* au gratin *first appeared in eighteenth-century French cookbooks, where it applied to foods that were sauced and cooked in the same dish until the sauce "caught" at the bottom and sides of the dish. Today we use* gratin *and* au gratin *to refer to a shallow, crumb-topped preparation of food, usually in a sauce, and also the dish or pan containing the food.*

Aluminum Gratin Set   8.8

Aluminum with cast-aluminum handles; 5 pieces, in lengths of 8″, 9½″, 11″, 12¾″, and 14½″; capacities of ¾, 1, 2, 3, and 4 qts.

$37.50

Good design in a less-than-perfect material. Here are five aluminum gratin pans from France, each oval, with a flat bottom, straight sides, and two heavy cast-aluminum handles secured with rivets. A versatile group which will not endure much rough handling, but which is nonetheless adequate to most jobs of gratinéeing, during which the pan is never expected to stay long in the oven. You mix your beautifully braised spinach with a Mornay sauce, turn it into one of these pans, top it with a mixture of crumbs and cheese, perhaps, and pass it briefly under the broiler; no thickened bottoms are needed here for top-of-the-stove cooking. The largest size (4 quarts) will hold a whole array of poached and sauced fish fillets, while the smallest (1½ pints) can handle a breast of chicken covered with Béchamel.

Oval Copper Gratin Pan   8.9

Copper with tin lining, brass handles; 10½″ × 7″; 1½″ deep; 1½-qt. capacity. Also avail. 12″, 14″, or 16″ long.

Max. Temp. 425 F. $42.00

Continued from preceding page

A beautiful tin-lined copper dish, much better than the pans in the aluminum nest. But do you need it? Technically no, for all the reasons we cited above. But it is beautiful, and it will inevitably be used as a presentation dish. And it is made of wonderfully conductive copper, so we must admit that some cooking will go on in your pan even in the five minutes it sits under the broiler. And finally, if you can afford it, why not have the best: beautiful, well-made, with brass handles, the whole thriftily formed of lightweight copper in the classic oval shape and lined with tin. Suppose you sauté some veal cutlets covered with a mixture of seasoned bread crumbs and Parmesan cheese. Then cover them lightly with a good tomato sauce and slices of mozzarella and let it all finish cooking in this ravishing pan, while the cheese melts and the flavors become blended. Choose from four sizes, from 10½″ to 16″ long.

"Au Gratin is something toasted or baked so as to produce a surface that is grated. A sole or cauliflower au gratin is a sole or cauliflower strewed with breadcrumbs or raspings, and baked in the oven to a golden tint. In strict reason, the phrase ought to apply equally to a sole fried with breadcrumbs. But language is not obedient to reason, and custom has ordained that what is called a Gratin shall be baked."

Kettner's Book of the Table, *1877*

Round Copper Gratin Pan   8.10

Heavy-gauge copper with tin lining, brass handles; 8″ diam.; 1¾″ deep; 1-qt. capacity. Also avail. 6¼″ or 9½″ diam.
Max. Temp. 425 F. $30.00

A round copper pan, in a shape most familiar for egg cookery. This is a tin-lined copper dish of heavy gauge with prominent uplifted brass handles. It comes in an assortment of sizes, 6¼″, 8″, and 9½″ in diameter, that will serve a variety of purposes. In the smallest, of course, you can bake two eggs in crème fraîche or butter; consider a resuscitating of leftovers in the medium-sized pan: vegetables and chicken chopped small, bound with a sauce, topped with buttered breadcrumbs, and then slid under the broiler to brown. For two diners, it will be quite enough when the meal is amplified by a salad, some fruit and cheese. This pan is of nice quality, and rather deeper than usual for the type.

FILETS DE SOLES BONNE FEMME —POACHED FILLETS OF SOLE WITH MUSHROOMS AND HOLLANDAISE SAUCE

4 large fillets of sole or flounder
A little lemon juice
Salt
Freshly cracked white pepper
4 large firm white mushrooms
7 tablespoons salt butter
½ cup dry white wine
¼ cup water
2 egg yolks
A few grains cayenne pepper
2 tablespoons tarragon vinegar
2 tablespoons heavy cream
6 tablespoons frozen sweet butter, cut in pieces
Optional: Thinly sliced black truffles
5 tablespoons all-purpose flour
⅔ cup light cream
Duchess potatoes
4 firm white mushroom caps, fluted if desired, sautéed in a little butter

Preheat the oven to 350°. Wash the fillets in lemon juice and water. Dry well. Season the skin side with a little salt and pepper. Fold over lengthwise. Arrange them on a buttered baking dish. Slice the mushrooms and sauté in 2 tablespoons salt butter, 1 teaspoon lemon juice, salt, and pepper. Cook briskly 2 minutes. Add the wine and water, bring to a boil, simmer a minute or two, and spoon over the fish. Cover the fillets with buttered wax paper and poach 15 minutes in the oven. While they are cooking, prepare the sauce.

HOLLANDAISE SAUCE. Put the egg yolks in a small bowl, add salt, the cayenne pepper and vinegar, and mix well with a little whisk. Add the heavy cream. Stand the bowl in a shallow pan of hot water over low heat. Beat with the whisk until it is as thick as you want. (You must achieve the desired thickness before adding butter.) Then add the frozen sweet butter bit by bit, and 2 drops lemon juice. When the Hollandaise sauce is finished, cover the bowl with plastic wrap and stand it in a bowl of lukewarm water (not hot) and it can hold all day. (Thinly sliced truffles may be put in the Hollandaise sauce.)

When the fillets are cooked, set aside to keep warm. Strain the stock the fish was poached in and reserve the sliced mushrooms.

FISH VELOUTE SAUCE. Melt 3 tablespoons salt butter in a tin-lined copper pan. Remove the pan from the heat and stir in the flour, then stir in ¾ cup strained fish stock. Stir over low heat until the sauce thickens. Add the light cream and bring to a boil. Add another 2 tablespoons salt butter, bit by bit.

The proper way to serve this dish is as follows. Encircle an oval platter with piped scallops of Duchess potatoes, dot with butter, and brown under the broiler (use a pastry bag and star tube to pipe the potatoes). Arrange the cooked fillets in the center and spoon the sliced mushrooms neatly on the fillets. Spoon the fish velouté sauce over the fillets but not over the potatoes. Then spoon a wide ribbon (4 to 5 inches) of Hollandaise sauce down the center of the dish over the velouté. Brown quickly under the broiler (not too long or the Hollandaise sauce will separate). Put one fluted sautéed mushroom on top of each fillet. Serve at once. Net: 4 servings.
(From THE DIONE LUCAS BOOK OF FRENCH COOKING, by Dione Lucas and Marion Gorman, illustrated by Joseph S. Patti. Copyright © 1947 by Dione Lucas. Reprinted by permission of Little, Brown and Company.)

THE
ROYAL COOKERY BOOK

(LE LIVRE DE CUISINE)

BY

JULES GOUFFÉ

CHEF DE CUISINE OF THE PARIS JOCKEY CLUB

TRANSLATED FROM THE FRENCH AND ADAPTED FOR ENGLISH USE

BY

ALPHONSE GOUFFÉ

HEAD PASTRY-COOK TO HER MAJESTY THE QUEEN

COMPRISING

DOMESTIC AND HIGH-CLASS COOKERY

ILLUSTRATED WITH ONE HUNDRED AND SIXTY-ONE WOODCUTS FROM
DRAWINGS FROM NATURE BY E. RONJAT

NEW EDITION

LONDON
SAMPSON LOW, SON, AND MARSTON
CROWN BUILDINGS, 188 FLEET STREET

1869

Copper and Stainless-Steel Oval Gratin Pan 8.11

Copper with stainless-steel lining, brass handles; 15¾" × 8⅝"; 1½" deep; 2¼-qt. capacity. Also avail. 9", 10⅝", 12⅝", or 14⅛" long.
$59.00

This beautiful gratin pan from Spring Brothers, made in Switzerland, is lighter in weight than the stainless-steel and copper Bi-Metal pans we showed you in other chapters. The medium-gauge copper is substantially lined with brushed stainless steel, meaning that there will be no problem of tin wearing thin or melting in high oven heat: and thus there is no need to panic should the recipe direct you to bring the food to a boil on the top of the stove, or to finish it in a very hot oven. There is a flat rim around the circumference, the square brass handles are both modern in design and easy in the hand, and they are firmly soldered to either end of the oval pan. There are a number of sizes available, from 9" to 15¾" in length; and the pan may also be obtained in all stainless steel. Trim, modern, expensive.

GRATIN OF LEEKS AURORA

Serves: 6
Preparation time: 30 minutes
Cooking time: 25 to 30 minutes

INGREDIENTS
12 leeks of even size, about ¾ to 1 inch thick
Salt
5 tablespoons sweet butter
1 cup finely cubed cooked ham
3 tablespoons flour
2 teaspoons tomato paste
2 cups chicken stock
Freshly ground white pepper
2 egg yolks
2 tablespoons crème fraîche
½ cup grated Gruyere cheese

PREPARATION
1. Cut off some of the green, leaving the leeks about 4 to 5 inches long. Wash them thoroughly under cold running water, then soak them in cold water for 1 hour to remove all possible sand.

2. Place the leeks in a casserole and cover with salted water. Bring the water to a boil, reduce the heat and cook the leeks, partially covered, for 15 to 20 minutes or until tender. Test them several times as some stalks may be done before others.

3. Drain the leeks on paper towels and then place in one layer in a well-buttered baking dish.

4. In a small skillet heat 2 tablespoons of butter, add the ham and sauté it for 3 minutes until coated with butter and heated through. Reserve.

5. In a heavy saucepan melt the remaining butter. Add the flour and cook for 3 minutes without browning. Add the tomato paste and blend it with the flour.

6. Add the chicken stock all at once and stir until the sauce has thickened and is very smooth.

7. Season the sauce with salt and pepper and remove it from the heat.

8. In a small bowl, beat the egg yolks and crème fraîche until well blended.

9. Add the cubed ham and the egg yolk mixture to the sauce.

10. Place the sauce over a very low flame to reheat, but do not let it come to a boil. Pour the sauce over the leeks, sprinkle with the grated cheese and run under the broiler until the cheese is melted and lightly browned.

REMARKS
For a variation, wrap each cooked leek in a thin slice of ham and then coat with the sauce.

(From THE SEASONAL KITCHEN, by Perla Meyers. Copyright © 1973 by Perla Meyers. Reprinted by permission of Holt, Rinehart and Winston.)

The huguenote, a French earthenware roasting pan for large birds or cuts of meat, came into use as the spit declined.

"What is a cooker without a loving cook? . . . Even our severely utilitarian and almost foolproof ovens of today, with their marvelous ingenuities for saving time and temper, ask for that appreciative sense of creation. . . . After all, apart from that great comforter, the bed, the stove is the most important object in the home. It certainly has a personality of its own, and often approximates human behavior. If treated with contempt, or if looked on as an energy thief, it can retaliate with a bad dish.

"Man always felt the need of a cooking stove, and his affinity with it is not likely to leave him. From its beginning as a heap of hot stones in which baked a clay-encrusted bird, or perhaps, a piece of a captured tribal enemy, it has been essential to our well-being and wish for variety."

"The Stove," by Rhys Davies, in These Simple Things *(Essays from* House and Garden*), Simon & Schuster, 1965*

Rectangular Nambé Gratin Pan 8.12

Sand-cast aluminum alloy; 11" × 7¾"; 1½" deep; 1¼-qt. capacity.
$42.50

If you are interested in beautiful cookware, then you should look into products made of the Nambé aluminum alloy, a unique metal resembling highly polished pewter which is made in a small factory in New Mexico. Pewter, while beautiful, melts when exposed to temperatures that are fairly low, too low for cooking; but the Nambé alloy goes from freezer to a preheated oven with ease. The pot is cast, like a statue, in a sand mold and then finished by individual craftsmen, so that each piece is a work of art. Now, cast metals, being lighter, are also somewhat more porous than others, and thus they are more sus-

Copper and Stainless-Steel
Oval Gratin Pan
Rectangular Nambé Gratin Pan

Cuisinart Round Gratin Pan
Handle for Cuisinart Gratin Pans
Copco Oval Gratin Pan

ceptible to staining; that is why we haven't recommended more cast-aluminum pots despite their frequent good looks. High polishing, which seals the surface, helps; also Nambé products come with their own cleaner. This particular pan is extremely handsome and quite deep, making a good vegetable casserole. It is shaped in a rectangle with rounded corners, and its flat, pierced handles resemble those of a silver porringer in design. We tested it with a dish of broccoli and cheese and found it both attractive and serviceable. As befits the works of individual craftsmen, these pans are not cheap, but neither are they as expensive as French copper gratin dishes. And there is a great beauty in their gentle curves and high polish.

Cuisinart Round Gratin Pan   8.13

Stainless steel with aluminum sandwich; avail. in 6¼"diam. Also 8", 9½", 10¼", or 11"; all 1½" deep.
$28.00 ▲

A marvelous contemporary adaptation of the gratin pan by Cuisinarts: a round dish, in a whole range of sizes, of mirror-finished stainless steel. From 6" to 11" in diameter and quite deep (1½"), they can be used, especially in the larger sizes, as small roasting pans; also, being full pots with sandwich bottoms of aluminum and stainless steel, they can be used on the stovetop as well. Two thin loop handles on each pot are designed to accommodate a removable black plastic and stainless-steel handle, available separately (8.14). This detachable handle is not absolutely stable, but is remarkably so; it snaps into place without a clip or other mechanical device, which adds points in its favor, since such devices are all too likely to become en-

crusted with food and stuck. We don't recommend this as a sauté pan, but it would not be impossible to use it as one; notice that the round shape creates a better balance with the handle than an oval shape would. The pan is quite expensive, as are all Cuisinart products, but its marvelous versatility of use—stovetop to oven to table without compromising at any point—could make it a thrifty choice in the end.

Handle for Cuisinart Gratin Pans   8.14

Plastic and stainless steel; 8½" long.
$4.50 ▲

The Cuisinart handle for the firm's gratin pans (above), in black plastic and stainless steel. The handle fits neatly in the hand, while the steel prongs at the end fit snugly over the loop handle of the gratin pan and are braced under its rim. Open the oven door, snap this into place, and remove the hot gratin from the oven. Place the dish on an asbestos pad or a trivet, push down with your thumb, and off comes the handle. Perfectly useful: 8½" long.

Copco Oval Gratin Pan   8.15

Enameled cast iron; 12" × 7¾"; 1¾" deep.
$26.00 ▲

A gratin dish shaped like a small boat, a barque 12" long with sides which swing upward to form handles. The inside is a creamy white enamel, while the outside

is available in a number of colors: bright yellow, red, brown, blue, or white. We like it for fish because of the porcelain-enameled interior, which is able to withstand the onslaughts of wine-based sauces and which gives gentle care to fragile foods. The pan's cast-iron core is left bare on the base, thus eliminating the problem of the chipping and burning of an enamel bottom over a burner. Not the traditional design, but very good-looking, sturdy, and useful, and moderate in price as well.

GRATIN DE COURGE BRESSANE— PUMPKIN AU GRATIN

Serves 6

It is unusual in the United States to utilize pumpkin in ways other than in pumpkin pie. In the part of France from which I come, Bourg-en-Bresse, pumpkin is never served sweet as dessert but cooked, *au gratin*, and served as a vegetable.

1 small to medium-size pumpkin; peeled, seeded, and cut into 3" chunks (approximately 3 pounds raw pulp)
2 teaspoons salt
1 teaspoon sweet butter, softened
3 large eggs
1 cup heavy cream
½ teaspoon freshly ground white pepper

Place the pumpkin chunks in a large saucepan with 1 teaspoon of the salt. Cover with cold water and bring to a boil. Cover, and simmer slowly for 20-25 minutes, until the pumpkin is tender when pierced with a fork or tip of a knife. Drain thoroughly in a colander. Put through a food mill to give it the consistency of a nice purée.

Heat oven to 450 F. Butter a shallow gratin dish, approximately 1½ inches deep and large enough to hold 6 cupfuls. With a fork, beat the eggs until well combined and mix with the cream until blended. Combine the pumpkin purée, egg mixture, remaining salt and the pepper, and pour into the gratin dish. Place dish on a cookie sheet (to catch any spills, and to conduct and distribute the heat more evenly), and transfer to oven. Cook for about 1 hour, until golden brown. Remove from oven; let rest 10 minutes before serving. This is very good with broiled steak, lamb chops or chicken.

(From THE GREAT COOKS COOK-BOOK, by The Good Cooking School, Inc. Copyright © 1974 by The Good Cooking School, Inc. Reprinted by permission of Ferguson/Doubleday.)

Pillivuyt Oval Porcelain Gratin Dish   8.16

Porcelain; 12″ × 7″; 1⅝″ deep. Also avail. 10″ or 14″ long.

$12.50 ▲ $10.00 ▲ $16.00 ▲

More comme il faut than the Copco boat, perhaps—an oval porcelain gratin dish from the fine old French firm of Pillivuyt. It is exceedingly simple but exceedingly well-made in a plain oven-proof white porcelain; you can have it 10″, 12″, or 14″ long. There is a flat-ground base and low, slanting sides with integral handles gently ridged to resemble shells. Which makes us wonder: is this motif the final refinement of the scallop shell as a cooking dish? Far from expensive, and quite useful.

POIRES BRAISEES AU CARAMEL— PEARS BRAISED IN CARAMEL

6 medium-sized pears, not too ripe (Anjou, Bosc, or Comice)
3 to 4 tablespoons sugar
⅓ stick sweet butter
1½ cups heavy cream
1 tablespoon confectioners' sugar
¼ teaspoon vanilla extract

Peel and split the pears lengthwise. Remove the seeds and core. Place the pear halves, flat side down, in a gratin dish. You need a large dish in order not to have the pieces overlap. Sprinkle the sugar on top, add the butter broken into bits, and place in a 425 degree oven for 35 minutes. By this time the sugar should have caramelized and the pears should be tender when pierced with the point of a knife. If the pears are still hard, cook another 5 or 10 minutes. Add 1 cup of the cream and place back in the oven. Cook for approximately 10 to 15 minutes, basting every 5 minutes. The sauce should have reduced, be thick, and of a nice ivory color. The caramel cooking with the cream will form a rich and delicious sauce. If it reduces too much and you see that the sauce is breaking down, add 3 or 4 tablespoons of water.

(From JACQUES PEPIN: A FRENCH CHEF COOKS AT HOME, by Jacques Pépin. Copyright © 1975 by Jacques Pépin. Reprinted by permission of Simon & Schuster.)

Oval Limoges Baking Dish   8.18

Porcelain; 13½″ × 8½″; 1½″ deep.
$34.00

Porcelain makes the most beautiful of all the gratin dishes, such as this shallow oval Royal Limoges example similar to those which we show you elsewhere for oven cooking (7.58). It is huge — 13½″ long—and shallow, useful for baked dishes which must be gratinéed at the end, such as a crusty crème brulée or Julia Child's spinach gratinée. (Is there a family alive that would eat *this much spinach?*) It is extremely beautiful, made of the pure white porcelain for which Royal Limoges is noted, over which there has been laid a pattern of pink, yellow, blue, and green flowers from an eighteenth-century print.

CREME BRULEE—BURNT CUSTARD

The original recipe came from Kings College, Cambridge, England, two hundred years ago. It was then served in shallow crystal dishes and a gold hammer was passed around to crack the clear caramel. This dish was served in Great Hall on special occasions. You should start it a day in advance of serving.

2 cups thick cream
½ inch vanilla bean
4 egg yolks
1 cup granulated sugar

Put the cream in a pan with the piece of vanilla bean, slowly bring it just to a boil, and remove it from the heat. Beat the egg yolks in a bowl with 4 tablespoons sugar until very creamy and light. Very carefully and slowly pour the warm cream over the egg yolks, stirring all the while. Transfer the egg and cream mixture to a heavy pan, and stir it over low heat until it coats the back of a metal spoon. Pour it into a shallow glass heatproof serving dish and chill it overnight in the refrigerator. Next day cover the top completely with granulated sugar, so that none of the cream shows through. Place the dish on a bowl of crushed ice and set it under a hot broiler to caramelize the sugar. When it has caramelized, return the custard to the refrigerator for at least 3 minutes before serving it. Net: 4 to 6 servings.

(From THE DIONE LUCAS BOOK OF FRENCH COOKING, by Dione Lucas and Marion Gorman, illustrated by Joseph S. Patti. Copyright © 1947 by Dione Lucas. Reprinted by permission of Little, Brown and Company.)

Porcelaine de Paris Gratin Dishes   8.19

Porcelain; 6½″ diam.; 1″ deep. Also avail. 5″ or 7¼″ diam.
$23.00 for set of two

More and more beautiful: here is a set of round gratin pans from Porcelaine de Paris, available in diameters of 5″, 6½″, and 7¼″. The dish has two small handles, showing it shares a common ancestor with the Pillivuyt dish (8.16); these handles are slightly ridged on top. Now, these are usually considered dishes for eggs, but we make the point here, as well as with the Pillivuyt example, that they are also useful for gratins. A creamy glaze covers the dish everywhere except on its base, and the Pavot pattern of floral tracery is applied over it. Think of this lovely dish to hold caramelized broiled pear slices for a winter dessert.

Salamander   8.20

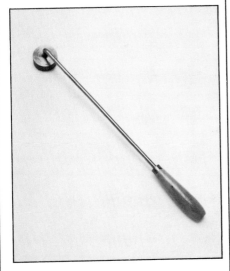

Steel with wood handle, brass collar; full length 18½"; head 2" diam.

$8.00 ▲

It looks like an instrument of torture or of far-out self-defense—take *that,* you swine—but it is, instead, a time-honored device for browning the top of otherwise finished foods. Suppose that your oven is fully occupied, roasting a pork loin and six baked potatoes; and that you have a dish of Tomatoes Provençale which is heated to a turn but which needs a quick pass beneath the broiler—which is inside your oven—to brown the cheese and crumbs on top. Just put the metal end of the salamander into your stovetop burner for a few minutes until it becomes red-hot, then pass it over the top of the tomatoes; you will see them turn crusty-brown before your eyes. Our salamander comes from France. It has a comfortable bleached-wood handle held by a brass collar to one end of a heavy steel rod which bends down at the other end to hold a thick hockey puck 2" in diameter made of the same steel. Professional ranges often have special ovens for top browning which are called salamanders; if you aren't fortunate enough to have one of those, then you can achieve a similar result, a similar perfectly controlled crust on your Crème Brûlée (preceding page) with this, the portable, and original, salamander.

GRATIN DE COURGETTES ET DE TOMATES—BAKED COURGETTES AND TOMATOES

For this recipe the courgettes are peeled and butter only is used in the dish, which is an unusually delicate one. Its disadvantages are the time it takes to prepare and the fact that, if it is served as a first course, two people can quite easily consume the whole lot. But it also makes a very good accompaniment to lamb, in which case it should be enough for four people.

3 oz. butter, 2 lb. courgettes, 1 lb. tomatoes, parsley, 1 small clove of garlic; salt and pepper. Breadcrumbs.

Pare the courgettes very thinly, leaving just a few strips of the green skin; slice them into even rounds about ¼ inch thick. This can be done on the *mandoline*. Put the courgettes in a colander, salt them lightly and leave them to drain. Skin the tomatoes; chop them roughly. Chop about 2 tablespoons of parsley with the garlic.

Shake the courgettes as dry as possible in a thick tea cloth. Heat 1 oz. of the butter in a frying-pan and put in half the courgettes (unless you have a very large frying-pan they won't all go in at once). Do not let the butter burn or even turn brown. Let the courgettes cook gently until they are soft and transparent-looking; transfer them to a gratin dish and cook the rest in the same way in another ounce of butter. Having transferred these also to the gratin dish, melt another half-ounce of butter in the pan and in this cook the tomatoes and the parsley and garlic mixture with a seasoning of salt and pepper until the tomatoes have lost the greater part, but not all, of their moisture; they should be in a thickish purée but not too dry. Amalgamate this mixture with the courgettes. It should completely fill the dish. Smooth down the top; strew with a light layer of pale golden breadcrumbs. Divide the remaining half-ounce of butter into little pieces and put them on the top. Put the dish on the top shelf of a hot oven, Gas No. 7, 425° F., for 25 to 30 minutes, and serve sizzling hot when the top surface is deep golden and bubbling.

Simple though this dish appears it is not easy to get it quite right at the first attempt; it is mainly a question of getting the tomatoes to the right consistency so that the finished dish is neither too liquid nor too dry, and this provides a useful demonstration of the treatment of tomatoes to go into any *gratin* or other oven dish. If they are put in raw they will give out so much moisture in the cooking that the result will be a thin and watery dish with a sadly amateurish air about it, whereas the preliminary cooking gets rid of excess moisture and also concentrates the flavour.

(From FRENCH PROVINCIAL COOKING, by Elizabeth David. Copyright © 1960 by Elizabeth David.)

Tools for Preparing Roasts

In gratin pans we put food which has been cut up—shredded, chopped, minced, ground, carved—food on which we have spent most of our energies and creativity before it goes into the pan. Roasting pans, on the other hand, hold whole pieces of meat, large, solid, and sometimes uninteresting. And although the preparation of such meat is inevitably less complicated than that which is done for the ingredients of gratins, still, some preparation often needs to be carried out—either by adding fat to lean meat, flavor to dull meat, or a better shape to the whole.

And this can mean anything from a gentle massage with herb butter to the creation of a complicated pattern of larding with strips of marinated fat. Larding means threading fat through a roast, while barding involves wrapping the roast in a sheet of fat; with it you can emulate your butcher by tying it into place with twine. Both processes are done to cheap cuts as well as to the more expensive cuts which are naturally lean, such as roasts of veal; and larding, especially, adds tenderness and flavor to the roast both from the fat's own succulence and also from the lardoons' being soaked in a marinade. The introduction of flavoring

Continued from preceding page

or tenderizing elements other than fat can involve anything from tucking slivers of garlic into slits cut in a leg of lamb to inserting truffles beneath the skin of a roasting chicken, or injecting a marinade into a roast with an ingenious needle-equipped bulb baster (8.31); from stuffing a turkey with corn bread and sausage to threading ham strips through sweetbreads to be braised. We begin here with the simplest of tools for preparing a roast: the lacers and skewers with which we lace up the cavity of a fowl or pin together the flaps of a piece of boned meat.

LACERS AND SKEWERS

Your grandmother, confronted by the indelicate end of a chicken, probably finished stuffing it and then sewed it up with heavy twine and a darning needle. A perfectly good technique, by the way, and one which you could use today with one of our butcher's needles (8.25); just be careful not to use nylon thread, which might melt, or waxed cotton, which might add an unpleasant taste to your bird—heavy white thread of the kind used for sewing on buttons is fine. On the whole we prefer to use turkey lacers, tiny skewers which are pinned through the skin of the fowl, and around which we then lace twine as though we were hooking up a child's stylish hiking boots. These lacers are always made with their blunt ends turned into rings so that the cook, confronted with scalding-hot needles in her freshly roasted chicken, can simply stick the tine of a fork through the ring and pull the lacer out. We show you a heavy set and a light set, the first sturdier and the second also useful in another way, for holding veal birds or braccioli in shape. We then go on to sets of skewers which come in different weights and sizes and which serve a number of purposes.

Stainless-Steel Turkey Lacers   8.21

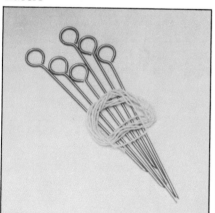

Stainless steel; set of 6 with lacing cord; each 4½" long.
$.79

The cost is minimal, you can buy them anywhere, they are altogether as common as can be, but like many common things—like onions or like chocolate-chip cookies—they are invaluable all the same. Here are stainless-steel skewers with pointed tips and ring-shaped ends. They come six to a card, and the manufacturer has thoughtfully supplied you with a bit of string just in case you have no kite-flyers or package-tiers or needle-pointers in your house. Each needle is 4½" long: a good size for lacing a turkey or for skewering, let's say, tiny marinated mushrooms for hors d'oeuvre.

THE VERSATILE TURKEY

TURKEY
1 14-18-pound fresh or frozen, thawed turkey
1 small onion
Celery leaves
Margarine, if not a self-basting turkey

Rinse turkey and wipe inside dry with paper toweling. Sprinkle interior with salt and pepper and place an onion and some celery leaves within. Rub skin with margarine if it's not a self-basting turkey. Roast, breast side up, at 325 F. in a shallow, open pan. Cover drumstick ends with foil and lay a loose sheet of foil over the bird for the last ½ hour in the oven.

Time for a 14-pounder, stuffed, is about 2½ hours; unstuffed, 2 hours. But follow the packer's guide, if directions are given. Time is variable. The bird I cooked took 2½ hours. I stuffed it, I must admit, this time. It's prettier! Test for doneness by pressing thigh, which should be soft or, better, check by thermometer inserted in the thickest part of the inside thigh muscle. Be careful not to touch the bone. Temperature should be 185 F. [or 175 F. to 185 F. if you prefer].

STUFFING STOCK
Turkey neck and giblets
Salt to taste
3 or 4 peppercorns
Tops of 1 bunch green onions (see Stuffing)
Sprigs of parsley
Celery tops

While turkey roasts, simmer neck and giblets in water to cover with salt, a few peppercorns, the tails of the onions, a few sprigs of parsley and some celery tops. You'll use the stock to moisten the stuffing, and in the gravy. (Leftover gravy goes into turkey bone soup.)

Take the turkey liver from the stock as soon as it is tender. It cooks quickly. Cover with a little stock, and refrigerate for later uses.

STUFFING
1 pan baked cornbread [8" pan]
3 cups coarse crumbs of French bread
2 cups chopped celery
2 tablespoons minced parsley
1 teaspoon poultry seasoning or ½ teaspoon crumbled sage and ½ teaspoon poultry seasoning
1 bunch green onions with parts of tops, chopped
¼-½ pound cooked old-fashioned pork sausage, optional for added flavor
1 stick or ½ cup margarine, melted
Salt and pepper to taste

Combine stuffing ingredients, moisten with stuffing stock and place in buttered casserole to bake along with the turkey for the last 45 minutes. If you do stuff the turkey, your procedure obviously starts with preparing the stuffing or, first of all, cooking the giblets.

GRAVY

Some giblets (see recipe)
Mushrooms

Take giblets from the stock, cut finely. Sauté mushrooms, sliced or chopped, to have them ready. Sometimes I strain the giblet stock and thicken it with a cornstarch paste, adding chopped giblets and mushrooms, so that the gravy base is ready when the turkey comes out of the oven. Then it is a matter of adding spoonfuls of drippings from the bird, tasting and adjusting seasonings. A great time saver.

NOTE: Don't forget to allow 15 to 20 minutes after roasting for the turkey to "set" for the carver's knife. It will be much easier to slice if kept warm on its platter for that much time.

(From PENNY-WISE, PARTY-PERFECT DINNERS, by The Good Cooking School, Inc. Copyright © 1975 by The Good Cooking School, Inc. Reprinted by permission of Ferguson/Doubleday.)

Fine Turkey Lacers 8.22

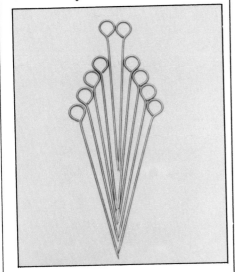

Stainless steel; set of 10, each 3⅞″ long.
$1.10

Same thing as the preceding lacers, only smaller, finer, lighter. Which is not altogether a drawback: we think you could use these successfully not only for poultry but to hold together small shaped pieces of meat, such as cotelettes à la Kiev, beef or veal birds, even stuffed cabbage if you don't trust your wrapping job. They will leave the smallest possible holes and can be removed once the meat or cabbage rolls have melded delectably in the cooking. These come ten to a card—no twine included—and are slightly under 4″ long. In stainless steel from West Germany.

BARBECUED SHRIMP

Shrimp have always been plentiful along our coasts, and in many varieties. These include the tiny Pacific shrimp, which are pink and tender and may be eaten by the handful; the sweet tiny shrimp from Maine; the very large, rather gray-green Gulf shrimp; and the Florida shrimp, which are of medium size and quite pink. Shrimp also come to our markets from Spain, Panama, Guatemala, and India, some weighing two and three to a pound and others over a hundred to a pound.

2 pounds shrimp (about 15 to the pound)
1 cup olive oil
1 teaspoon salt
2 cloves garlic, chopped
¼ cup chili sauce
3 tablespoons Worcestershire sauce
½ teaspoon Tabasco
1 teaspoon salt
1 teaspoon basil

Shell and devein the shrimp, leaving the tail shells on. Arrange in a shallow oblong dish approximately 6 x 9 inches. Mix the seasonings well and pour over the shrimp. Toss thoroughly and allow to stand several hours, turning occasionally. To broil over charcoal, string the shrimp on metal or bamboo skewers and invite each person to grill his own over medium coals, or place all the shrimp in a wire grill and broil them over the coals. To broil in a gas or electric broiler, arrange the shrimp on a flat pan and run under broiler about 4 inches from the heat unit for about 3 to 5 minutes or until the shrimp have turned color and the flesh is tender.

(From AMERICAN COOKERY, by James A. Beard, illustrated by Earl Thollander. Copyright © 1972 by James A. Beard. Reprinted by permission of Little, Brown and Company.)

Flat Skewers from Italy 8.24

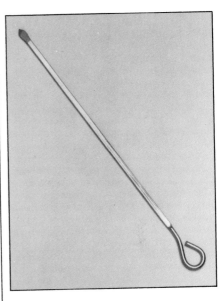

Stainless steel; set of 6, each 6″ long. Also avail. 7¾″, 9¾″, 10¾″, or 11¾″ long.
$1.50

A terribly good value is an assortment of stainless-steel skewers from Italy. We have these in five sets, in sizes from 6″ to 11¾″ long, one size per set. One end of each skewer is twisted into a ring, the other is pointed; but the thing to notice here is that the body of the skewer is flat, and thus will neither turn in the roast chicken, loosening the lacing twine, nor will it release its hold on pieces of skewered food as they lie over the fire. The stainless steel means these skewers can go over, or under, the hottest grill or broiler. Each size is a useful one—think of small skewers of chicken livers or shrimp for pacifying guests waiting for the grilled steak, or why not plan a main course of shashlik, broiled on the longest ones?

Mrs. Stephen J. Field, the author of Statesmen's Dishes and How to Cook Them *(1890), recommends this manner of making a bird eligible for roasting: "The turkey should be cooped up and fed some time before Christmas. Three days before it is slaughtered, it should have an English walnut forced down its throat three times a day, and a glass of sherry once a day. The meat will be deliciously tender, and have a fine nutty flavor."*

VERDURA MISTA IN GRATTICOLA —CHARCOAL-BROILED VEGETABLES

Americans have practically reinvented cooking over charcoal, but the uses to which all the marvelously practical barbecue equipment is put are incredibly few. Whenever our family goes barbecuing on a public campsite or picnic area, our grill topped with tomatoes, eggplant, peppers, onions, mushrooms, and zucchini is soon the object of ill-concealed wonderment as the only bright island in the midst of a brown atoll of hot dogs, hamburgers, and steaks.

Barbecuing vegetables is one of the most effective ways of concentrating their flavor. Charcoal-broiled peppers are all that peppers should be, and never are when done any other way. Zucchini turns out fresher-tasting than the most skillfully fried zucchini and is just as crisp and juicy. Even indifferent tomatoes are returned by the fire to their ancestral tomato taste and become nearly as full flavored as the vine-ripened tomatoes of San Marzano.

Doing vegetables need not interfere with the unquestioned pleasure of charcoal-broiled steak. Cook the vegetables in the first flush of the fire. When they are done, the fire is ready for broiling steak or whatever else you are having. With a full load of vegetables, calculate about 25 to 40 percent more coal than you would use ordinarily for steaks or hamburgers alone.

For 4 persons

1 large flat Spanish onion
2 sweet green or red peppers
2 large, firm, ripe tomatoes
1 medium eggplant
Salt
2 medium fresh, young, firm, glossy zucchini
¼ pound very fresh and crisp mushrooms
Olive oil
Crushed peppercorns
1 teaspoon chopped parsley (optional)
⅛ teaspoon chopped garlic (optional)
½ teaspoon fine, dry unflavored bread crumbs (optional)

1. Remove the outer, crackly skin of the onion, but do not cut off the point or the root. Divide it in half horizontally.
2. Wash the peppers in cold water and leave whole.
3. Wash the tomatoes in cold water and divide in two horizontally.

4. Wash the eggplant in cold water, then cut in half lengthwise. Without piercing the skin, make shallow cross-hatched cuts, spaced about 1 inch apart, in the eggplant flesh. Sprinkle liberally with salt and stand the halves on end in a colander for at least 15 minutes to let the bitter juices drain away.
5. Wash the zucchini thoroughly in cold water. Cut off the ends; then cut the zucchini into lengthwise slices about ⅜ inch thick.
6. Wipe the mushrooms clean with a damp cloth. Unless they are very small, detach the caps from the stems. You are now ready to light the fire.
7. When the highest flames have died down, place the onion on the grill, cut side down. Place the peppers on the grill as well, laying them on one side. After 4 or 5 minutes check the peppers. The skin toward the fire should be charred. When it is, turn another side of the peppers toward the fire, at the same time drawing them closer together to make room for the tomatoes and eggplant (see Step 10 below). Continue turning the peppers, eventually standing them on end, until all the skin is charred. Remove them from the grill and peel them while they are as hot as you can handle. Cut them into 2-inch strips, discard the seeds, put the cut-up peppers in a bowl, and add at least 3 tablespoons of olive oil plus large pinches of salt and cracked peppercorns. Toss and set aside.
8. While the peppers are still cooking, check the onion. When the side facing the fire is charred, turn it over with a spatula, taking care not to separate the rings. Season each onion half with 1 tablespoon of olive oil and ½ teaspoon of salt. Move to the edge of the grill, making sure there is some burning charcoal underneath.
9. When the onion is done, in about 15 to 20 minutes, it should be well charred on both sides. Scrape away part of the blackened surface and cut each half in 4 parts. Add it to the bowl of peppers, tossing it with another pinch of salt and cracked pepper. (The onion will be quite crunchy, which makes a nice contrast with the peppers, but it will also be very sweet, with no trace of sharpness.)
10. When you first turn the peppers (see Step 7 above), make room for the tomatoes and eggplant. Place the tomatoes, cut side down, on the grill. Check them after a few minutes, and if the flesh is partly charred, turn them. Season each half with ½ teaspoon of olive oil, a small pinch of salt, and the op-

tional parsley, garlic, and bread crumbs and cook until they have shrunk by half and the skin is blackened.
11. Shake off any liquid from the eggplant. Pour 1 tablespoon of olive oil over each half and place it on the grill with the cut side facing the fire. Allow it to reach a deep brown color, but don't let it char, which would make it bitter. Turn the eggplant over and season each half with another tablespoon of olive oil. From time to time as it cooks, pour ½ teaspoon of oil in between the cuts. The eggplant is done when it is creamy tender. Do not cook it beyond this point or it will become bitter.
12. When the eggplant is nearly done, put the zucchini slices on the grill. As soon as they have browned on one side turn them over and cook until done, 5 to 8 minutes. Remove to a shallow bowl and season with a large pinch of salt, pepper, and about ½ tablespoon of oil.
13. When you turn the zucchini over, put the mushrooms on the grill. These cook very quickly, about 1 minute to a side, including the stems. Add them to the bowl of zucchini and season the same way.

NOTE

It is unfortunate that the length of this recipe makes it appear so forbidding. It is actually about as simple to execute as grilled hamburgers and hot dogs. The whole secret lies in mastering the sequence in which the vegetables are put on the grill. Aside from that, there is very little to do except watch them. The fire does nearly all the work. The entire process should take about 35 minutes.

From THE CLASSIC ITALIAN COOK-BOOK, by Marcella Hazan, illustrated by George Koizumi. Copyright © 1973 by Marcella Hazan. Reprinted by permission of Alfred A. Knopf.

Split lamb kidneys held in shape for broiling by a skewer woven through the halves. From L'Ecole des Cuisinières of Urbain-Dubois.

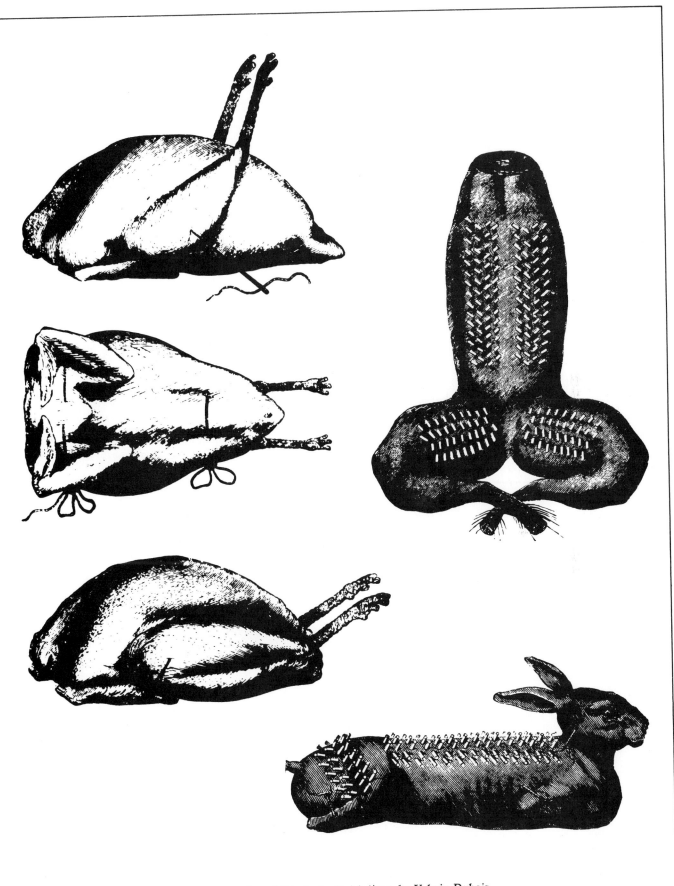

Illustrations from L'Ecole des Cuisinières, by Urbain-Dubois,
show the larding of a hare and how to truss a chicken with needle and thread,
basic skills for the nineteenth-century cook.

Roasting and Broiling Pans, Appliances, and Tools

BUTCHER'S NEEDLES

In moving from large-eyed lacers and skewers, which could never be drawn all the way through a piece of meat, to relatively small-eyed butcher's needles, we stop considering ways to pin together flaps or openings of meat or fowl and look toward stitching: the best and most secure way to fasten the skin of a bird for a galantine, or to pass twine through a roast in the process of tying it into a compact and attractive shape. Then we show you another kind of needle—those we use for larding lean meat with succulent strips of fat.

Set of Butcher's Needles   8.25

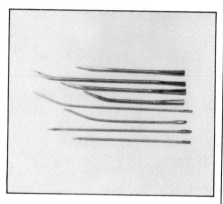

Stainless steel with plastic container. Set of 8: 4 larding needles ranging in length from 6″ to 9″; 4 sewing needles; 2 curved, 2 straight, ranging in length from 6¼″ to 9¼″.
$7.20

We once saw an upholsterer sewing up a sofa with a bent needle, the curve doing the work of overcasting for him: just the case with two needles of this set of eight from Germany. There are two needles in each of four lengths, and while one of each pair has an eye for holding twine, the other widens toward a hollow end that is split into four prongs meant to close over the end of a strip of larding fat. Excellent-quality stainless steel, in sizes from 6″ to 9″, all collected in a decent plastic tube with a heavy plastic cap on either end. We are talking, you will notice, about two processes. First of all, with the use of the eyed needles, whether curved or straight, you have the best way to hold meat together, a more efficient method than skewering for closing flaps in rolled roasts or in veal birds, and also the classic way, using a long straight needle, of trussing poultry. Why the curve, you ask, in two of the eyed needles? Two reasons: the curve makes it feasible to

stitch shallowly without struggling to make a curve with a straight needle, and it helps you to find your way around the bones in the meat. From stitchery with thread or twine we move, still within this set, to larding with these perfectly adequate lardoirs or larding needles, which hold the fat to be inserted through your beef or venison.

Butcher's Needle   8.26

Stainless steel with wood handle; 15½″ overall; needle 12″ long.
$6.50

This is a butcher's needle, a professional's tool for tying up a roast by stitching through it instead of looping string around it. Use it at home on the meat you buy from the supermarket to create neatly organized roasts on the European model. For example, buy a rib roast, cut away the bones for the stockpot, and form the eye into a neatly tied package wrapped in the flap of rib fat. You work the needle by shoving it through the meat close to one end, then threading butcher's twine through the eye (about 5 feet of twine for our rib roast). Leave about 12 inches or so free on the far side and draw the twine back through the meat, freeing from the meat the loose end of twine nearest to you. Move an inch or so along the roast and stitch through again, this time looping the far-side free end through the twine on the needle. Again withdraw the needle and the sewing length of twine, still threaded through the eye, then repeat the stitching and looping until the whole thing is firmly tied. Tie off the loose ends together. There is a stainless-steel blade with a spear-shaped, eyed point and a bleached and varnished wooden handle; the whole thing is 15½″ long. For the kitchen of the thrifty self-sufficient cook.

"Obtain a gross of small white boxes such as are used for bride's cake. Cut the turkey into small squares, roast, stuff, kill, boil, bake and allow to skewer. Now we are ready to begin. Fill each box with a quantity of soup stock and pile in a handy place. As the liquid elapses, the prepared turkey is added until the guests arrive. The boxes delicately tied with white ribbons are then placed in the handbags of the ladies, or in the men's side pockets."

F. Scott Fitzgerald, The Crack-up (including The Note-Books), New Directions, New York, 1956

LARDING NEEDLES

We are a nation tediously obsessed with low-fat cooking, to whom the French practice of larding lean meats seems all but suicidal. But the fact remains that some cuts, such as veal roasts, venison, or bottom round of beef, are greatly improved by being threaded through with seasoned fat. This bastes the meat from the inside as it cooks, adding both flavor and tenderness and producing a lower final fat content, for all that, than that of a prime rib roast, heavily marbled with its own built-in larding. Larding is done with strips—*lardons* or lardoons—of blanched salt pork, fresh pork fatback, or suet. In France and elsewhere in Europe the method is to lay a strip of fat in the trough of a *lardoir,* or larding needle, and then push it all the way through the meat, usually parallel to the grain. You do this at regular intervals throughout the roast, paying attention to the design which will be created when the meat is carved against the grain and, of course, across the lardoons. There are wonderful pictures in old books showing the designs which noted chefs once created with their larding needles.

If you would like to try larding—and remember that lean cuts and less heavily marbled grades of meat are less expensive than fatty ones —we can show you a variety of tools, beginning, of course, with the delicately pronged larding needles in the butcher's set above (8.25). But there are other, equally efficient utensils—read on.

Large Hinged Lardoir 8.29

Stainless steel with wood handle; 20½″ overall; needle 17⅞″ long.

$21.60

Another hinged lardoir, this one much more complicated, much larger than the others. But it is also the first we have seen, please note, that is big enough: big enough to shove all the way through a reasonably large roast. Julia Child recommends that larding be done *with* the grain of the meat; it will be easier to push the needle through in that direction, and the carver, cutting against the grain, will expose designs in the slice. This stainless-steel larding needle is nearly 18″ long, more than 20″ long with its handle. At one end is a removable bleached-wood handle and, at the other, a torpedo-shaped hinged affair, toothed within, that holds the leading end of the lardoon. Now: you catch the fat in the hinge and lay it along the trough of the needle; then you shove the loaded lardoir through the meat. When it is in place, you remove the wooden handle, release the fat from the hinge, move the handle to the other end to cover the hinged point (are you still with us?), then you triumphantly pull the blade the rest of the way through the meat. Leaving, we assure you, the lardoon in place.

For those weary of the same old roasts, there is this suggestion in an old manuscript which might revive jaded palates: "Take a capon and a little pig and smite them in the waist. Sew the hind part of one on the fore quarters of the other, and stuff, and roast, and serve them forth."

German Lardoir 8.27

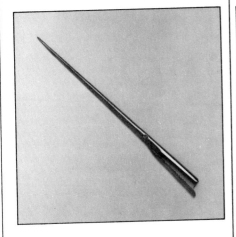

Stainless steel; 7¾″ long.
$1.65

We have two rather small larding needles, this one from Germany and the next one from Italy. Only it happens that the Italian needle is made in Germany too—God Bless the Common Market— if not at the same factory, then at least from the same model. First, the German: from Gerhard Recknagel—wonderful name—a hollow needle 7¾″ long made of stainless steel with a point at one end. The needle widens gradually and ends in an interesting device: the hollow tube is hinged to split into two for the remainder of its length. One half of the split section of tube has a single pointed tooth, while the other has a line of shallow dinosaur-like teeth along the sides. When a strip of larding fat is placed in the split tube and the hinge is closed, the fat is held firmly in place, and the needle is ready to be pushed through the meat, point first, with the lardoon drawn through after it.

Italian Lardoir 8.28

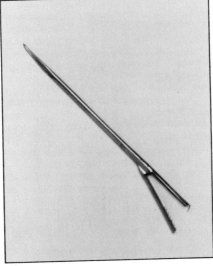

Stainless steel; 7½″ long.
$1.50

Now, this is nearly the same as the German larding needle above—7½″ long and hollow, it has a similar pointed tip and hinged end with toothlike edges. The clasp snaps open for the insertion of the lardoon and then is snapped closed. We like it better than the other one only because the tip is formed into a sharp, three-sided point that looks better than the German needle and will also go through the meat more easily. This needle is from Italy and is pleasantly inexpensive, considering its good construction and the medium-gauge stainless steel from which it is made. A hint: if you chill the fat strips in a cold marinade, or simply in the refrigerator, they will be far easier to work with and will be less likely to be torn by the teeth of the clasp.

ROAST VENISON

Serves 6-8

MEAT
6-7 pound rump of venison
½ pound pork fat, cut in strips about ⅓ x 6 inches long (lardons)
½ pound salt pork, thinly sliced

MARINADE FOR THE PORK FAT—LARDONS
½ teaspoon salt
½ teaspoon pepper
1 clove garlic, crushed
1 tablespoon parsley
2 tablespoons rum

MARINADE FOR THE VENISON
2 cups beef bouillon or stock
2 cups red wine
⅓ cup vegetable oil
1 large onion, peeled and sliced
1 carrot, peeled and sliced
2 ribs celery, including green tops, sliced
2 cloves garlic, peeled and crushed
1 teaspoon salt
10 peppercorns, crushed
Salt and pepper

SAUCE
1 cup beef stock
⅛ teaspoon dried thyme
1½ tablespoons flour
1 cup heavy cream

Prepare the marinade for the larding fat by combining all ingredients in a small bowl. Toss the strips (lardons) in the marinade and leave for an hour—or for as long as 4 hours, if it is convenient. Remove the lardons from the marinade and chill in refrigerator for 20 minutes to facilitate the larding.

To lard the roast: Place a chilled lardon in the groove of a larding needle and insert the tip of the needle into the meat. Moving the needle with a rolling motion of your wrist, gradually penetrate the meat. Place your thumb on lardon and hold it there as you withdraw needle, leaving lardon in its place. Repeat this procedure with the remaining lardons, studding the rump at 1-inch intervals. (The more larding the better the taste, and the more attractive the roast.)

Prepare the marinade for the venison, combining all the ingredients in a large glass bowl, just large enough to hold the meat and marinade. Place the larded venison in the marinade. Cover with plastic wrap and marinate in refrigerator for at least 48 hours—even another 24 hours, if possible — turning the meat about in the marinade at least several times each day.

Preheat oven to 400 F. Drain the meat and dry it thoroughly. Drain the marin-ated vegetables and make a bed of them in the bottom of a glass-ceramic roasting pan just large enough to hold the meat. Salt and pepper the roast; place on the vegetables; then, cover with the strips of sliced salt pork, securing them with toothpicks if they won't stay in place. Roast the meat for 20 minutes; reduce heat to 325 F., and continue roasting for about 50 minutes more, or until thermometer placed in center of meat reads 140 F., or until roast is browned on the outside and pink when cut. After the first 15 minutes of roasting, baste with the fat accumulated in pan. Continue to baste (about every 15 minutes) until roast is done. Remove the roast; let it rest on its serving platter for about 10 minutes while you prepare the sauce.

Pour off all but 2 tablespoons of the fat from the roasting pan. Add the beef stock and the thyme and stir to combine the brown bits that cling to the pan and the vegetables. Cook for 2 or 3 minutes, or until the stock boils. Strain the sauce, pressing the vegetables against the strainer to get all the juices before discarding them. Pour sauce back into pan.

Quickly combine the flour and cream; mix thoroughly and stir into strained sauce. Return to stove and, over moderate heat, whisk without interruption until the sauce thickens. Pour into heated sauce-boat. Serve the venison immediately, spooning some sauce over each serving; accompany with red currant jelly.

(From THE GREAT COOKS COOK-BOOK, by The Good Cooking School, Inc. Copyright © 1974 by The Good Cooking School, Inc. Reprinted by permission of Ferguson/Doubleday.)

A meticulously larded tongue shows what a culinary work of the last century considered an elementary method of preparing food for cooking.

Simple Lardoir
8.30

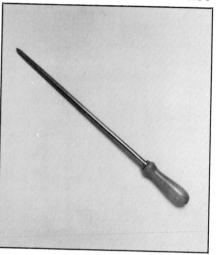

Stainless steel with hardwood handle, brass collar; 20½" overall; needle 15⅝" long. $21.50

Larding needles are uncommon in this country, and this one is found only in butcher shops. And, as with almost everything else, the simplest turns out to be the best: this minimally elaborate lardoir turns out to be, as mathematicians say, the most "elegant" solution to the problem. Here we have in effect half of a tube cut in two lengthwise: the section is formed into a fine point at one end and attached to a wooden handle at the other. You lay the lardoon in the deep trough and push the needle through the meat. When the tip comes out the other end, you grasp the end of the fat in your fingers and hold it in place while you pull back on the handle. *Voilà* . . . you wind up with the needle in your hand, the fat in the meat. This one is 20½" in length altogether, with a stainless-steel blade and a varnished handle of bleached wood, the two joined rather sloppily with a brass collar.

In seventeenth-century England a mechanical spit, set in motion by a clockwork device, was invented. A more elaborate version of this was used in one noble kitchen: "The musical turnspit, that, whilst causing joints to gyrate before . . . the fire, played four-and-twenty tunes. . . . The spits of this machine turned a hundred and thirty roasts at the same time; and the chef was informed, by the progress of the melodies, when the moment had arrived for removing each piece of meat."

Bulb Basters

Bulb basters look like large eyedroppers. The jazziest is the one that comes with a needle you screw into its tip in order to inject a marinade into the meat. But the common baster is an inexpensive and useful item in your kitchen. A spoon will do the same jobs, but it will not do them so well: you will burn your fingers reaching under the rack of the roasting pan, and you are sure to lose the juices if you try to spoon them up from around a large roast in a small pan. Better to buy a baster and use it to wash melted fat and liquids from the pan over the meat, keeping it moist, adding flavor, and creating a glaze.

It is important to have a rubber bulb on your baster which is firm enough so that it won't collapse and stick together with the suction—avoid flimsy ones, and shun plastic bulbs which are difficult to use and also tend to split. It's important that there be an opening at the lower end large enough so that your baster doesn't become clogged with every lovely bit of browned onion slurped up with the gravy.

You have a choice of three materials for the tubular shaft. Metal is both strong and easy to keep clean, but you can't see through it to judge how much liquid you are taking up. Glass does not have that limitation and is equally easy to clean, but it can shatter in a moment's exuberant gesture. And nylon, which is both strong and semitransparent, will melt at moderately high pan temperatures and also tends to collect memories of every fluid which goes through the baster.

According to the manufacturers, you can use basters for the tricky job of skimming fat from soups and gravies. Well, maybe: we think they work less well than a spoon, pulling up altogether too much at a time and being altogether too difficult to control. You may have better luck than we have had in using a baster for skimming, but we do recommend that you buy a baster and use it for its original purpose.

purée, a purée of bulbous chervil, a purée of chestnuts, or a lentil purée.

One may also substitute, for the madeira, port, or sherry, some white wine—chablis for instance—but one would have to use more of it.

(From ENCYCLOPEDIA OF PRACTICAL GASTRONOMY, by Ali-Bab, translated by Elizabeth Benson. Copyright © 1974 by McGraw-Hill, Inc. Reprinted by permission of McGraw-Hill, Inc.

Bulb Baster with Injecting Needle 8.31

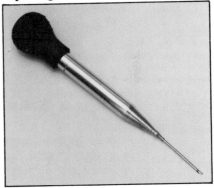

Stainless steel with rubber suction bulb; 12¾" long with injector. Aluminum cleaning brush with nylon bristles; 8½" long.

$2.50 ▲

A baster like the biggest hypodermic syringe in the world: almost 11" long, it has a stainless-steel tube and the regulation firm rubber suction bulb, and it can be used as it is, like any other baster. But it has, in addition, a thin stainless-steel needle that screws into place at the tip of the stainless-steel tube and permits you to inject a marinade or other liquid seasoning right into the middle of your roast. Melted fat injected into a less-than-well-marbled roast will work as well as larding, and an injection of wine and herbs will add flavor to the meat. A marinade like this helps to make your roast tender, as the wine or other acid softens the fibers. (On the other hand, because of the steam from the added liquids, an injected marinade tends to turn a roast into a pot roast.) You can choose your injection fluid to impart an interesting gamy flavor, like that of venison, to whatever cut you start with. This is fun, but scarcely a necessity. Worth buying as a basic baster, with the thought that you can always use the injecting needle when you're in a mood to experiment.

GIGOT D'AGNEAU ROTI—ROAST LEG OF LAMB

FOR THREE PEOPLE, USE:
½ lb. veal knuckle
4 oz. raw, smoked ham
3 oz. lean bacon
2 oz. mushrooms
1 small carrot
3 T. madeira, port, or sherry wine
3 T. butter
1 small onion
1 stalk celery
salt, paprika, pepper
1 tiny leg of lamb weighing about 2 lbs.
½ foot calf's foot
bouquet garni
quatre épices

Cut the smoked ham into strips to lard the lamb with. Save the trimmings. Trim the leg of lamb and either bone it or not. Lard it with the ham strips.

In a little butter, cook the onion, carrot, celery, bacon, the cut-up veal knuckle and the half a calf's foot, *bouquet garni*, ham trimmings, salt, and sufficient water. Cook these all together for three hours. Reduce the cooking liquid so as to have about three-quarters to one cup left. Skim off the fat and strain. Taste and add salt if necessary.

Spread the rest of the butter on the leg of lamb and place the meat on a rack in a roasting pan. Add the above cooking juices, the madeira, port, or sherry, season with paprika, pepper, and a little of the *quatre épices* to taste. Roast it in the oven, basting frequently, for about forty-five minutes. Or, if you prefer, roast it on a spit.

Arrange the lamb on a platter, skim the fat off the cooking juices, and reduce them. Coat the meat with this sauce.

Serve, sending along, at the same time in a vegetable dish, either a mushroom

Roasting and Broiling Pans, Appliances, and Tools

8

Aluminum Bulb Baster 8.32

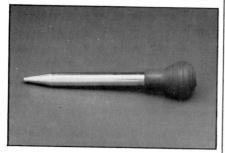

Aluminum with rubber bulb; 10″ long.
$.99

All things considered, the best basters are made of metal. They are better than glass, which breaks, and better than nylon, which discolors; and their only flaw is the fact that they are opaque —at times you may want to use a baster to add liquid to a dish, and therefore may want to have a clear view of the amount. We show you one baster made in Japan of polished aluminum and rubber. Although we prefer the stainless steel baster (8.31) that will neither discolor your sauce nor be discolored by it, this aluminum baster is satisfactory.

Glass Bulb Baster 8.33

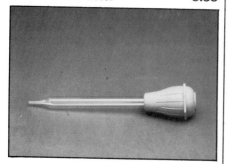

Heat-resistant glass with rubber bulb; 10½″ long.
$1.09

Pretty, isn't it? A glass baster, identical in shape to the aluminum one, but with the visual excitement of glass. It is, we are assured, heat-resistant; safe in the dishwasher; easy to clean. And it has the great advantage of transparency, so that you can see precisely the amount of pan juices you have sucked up into it. But you *know* it is going to break, right? Someone will put a pot down on

it, or you will wave it too close to the edge of a counter and—bam—it will be shattered. But it's cheap enough so that it will be no great loss of money, and in fact, if the looks, the visibility, and the hygiene mean enough to you, you might as well go ahead and enjoy it for as long as it lasts.

Nylon Bulb Baster 8.34

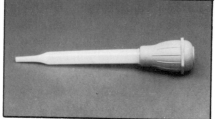

Nylon with rubber bulb; 11″ long.
$.89

Of the three materials used in the basters we show you, this is the least successful compromise, but it isn't terrible. There is a strong rubber bulb, easily removed for cleaning, and an unbreakable see-through nylon tube marked to indicate measurements from ¼ ounce to 1

ounce, which is near-capacity. You can't leave a baster of nylon in the oven or it will melt; but why would you *want* to leave it there? No, the only problem is the eternal problem with synthetics: the material discolors, it retains odors and flavors, and it sometimes passes them on. Now this probably won't make one bit of difference when you are basting your ham—the flavor of the pineapple juice probably won't get transferred to next Sunday's turkey; but we warn you anyway. The overall length of this baster is 11″, and the price is reasonable.

The spit-turners of the old English kitchen were among its lowliest drudges. They were often beggars or vagabonds who sought this transient employment in the great houses. In the sixteenth-century comedy Gammer Gurton's Needle, the drifter proclaims:

> *Many a mile have I walked, diverse and sundry waies,*
> *And many a good man's house have been at in my days,*
> *Many a gossip's cup in my time have I tasted,*
> *And many a broche-spit have I both turned and basted.*

Roasting Pans

The turkey is trussed, the roast is larded, the leg of lamb boned and then pinned or stitched together, the ham is ready to glaze with port wine and currant jelly: in short, it is time to cook the piece of meat you have just prepared so lovingly for the oven or the broiler. Which means, by and large, that the cook can retire from active participation for a while, returning only occasionally to check on the proceedings, perhaps to look at the meat thermometer or to baste the roast at intervals if basting is called for. Immediately beneath the broiler heat, a steak turns brown and crusty; we hope that you are lucky enough to have a really high-quality broiler supplied with your oven. If not, separate pans are very difficult to find, and you would not be wrong to use a flat roaster with a grill to support your broiling meat, rather than the pathetic enameled thing of thin metal which too often Comes With.

Roasting, as we have noted, is for most of us necessarily done in an oven, and so involves a less direct confrontation between the heat and the food than broiling; but, so long as there is space for air to circulate around the food, it doesn't matter that a pan stands between the fire and the bird or the beef—you will have a beautifully browned roast. The dry heat of the oven—try leaving the door slightly ajar to allow steam to escape—should bounce from wall to wall and back onto the food. It's not really that simple, of course—things seldom are—because there are disagreements about oven temperatures, the use of meat thermometers, and about the virtues of deep and shallow roasters.

THE HIGH WAY, AND THE LOW

The high *covered* roaster cooks with steam, making your meat more or less into a pot roast whether you want one or not, and is the subject of much controversy. James Beard, for instance, likes to roast in a heavy low pan with a V-shaped rack—see our 8.44—which holds the meat out of the fat and permits the circulation of hot air all around it. Others claim that nothing in the world can equal the moisture and tenderness of a really large turkey roasted in a high-sided pan and, further, that with a really good pan you can cut the cooking time virtually in half, because the hot walls of the pan magnify the oven heat. We'll show you both sorts of roasters and let you take your choice.

SIZE, MATERIAL, AND WEIGHT

Roasters are a sort of utensil in which the size and weight of the pan are more important than material. Except for a few expensive stainless-steel roasters, most are made of aluminum, an aluminum alloy, or enameled steel; after all, there is little contact between the pan and acid ingredients except perhaps briefly during gravy-making, so there can be little objection to aluminum here. It is true that a low stainless-steel roaster can also be used to make lasagna or moussaka, but we are not convinced that the price and weight are justified by such an occasional use: better buy a separate pan for the lasagna.

The weight or gauge of the material, however, is another matter: these pans are meant to carry heavy roasts. What else do you cook that can weigh 18 or 20 pounds? And so they need to be sturdy enough to bear the weight without adding unreasonably to the total number of pounds you must lift. Size, too, is another matter. Roasting pans are different from sauté pans, which need be only slightly larger than the food that is cooked in them. Instead, roasters take their size from the oven rather than the food; buy a pan as big as your oven will permit, always allowing for the circulation of air between the edges of the roaster and the walls of the oven—at least 2 inches of leeway should be left on all sides.

HANDLES

The final consideration is the handle. We discarded many attractive and sturdy pans which did not have handles that were either integral or rigid. Integral, that is, like those of the Magnalite roaster (8.36); or with positive stops like those of the Wearever pans and others with loop handles—these open out when the pan is lifted, to a point at which they either (for certain models) lock into place or encounter a sturdy stop that prevents their rising further as you hold them. We feel very strongly about this, since hot fat, like hot steam, is a real danger in the kitchen. You will be balancing an oddly shaped piece of meat, held insecurely on a rack over a pan full of hot fat; if the handles of the pan

"Dining at a friend's, Sydney Smith happened to meet Mr. B. . . . The conversation at the table took a liberal turn. Sydney Smith . . . happened to say that though he was not generally considered an illiberal man, yet he must confess he had a little weakness, one secret wish—he would like to roast a Quaker.

" 'Good Heavens, Mr. Smith!' said Mr. B. full of horror, 'roast a Quaker? But do you consider, Mr. Smith, the torture?'

" 'Yes, sir,' replied Sydney. 'I have considered everything. It may be wrong, as you say: the Quaker would undoubtedly suffer acutely, but everyone has his tastes,—mine would be to roast a Quaker. One would satisfy me, only one. It is one of those peculiarities I have striven against in vain, and I hope you will pardon my weakness.' "

Bon-Mots of Sydney Smith and R. Brinsley Sheridan, Walter Jerrold, ed., J. M. Dent and Company, London 1893

MARINATED PORK LOIN ROAST WITH PRUNES

This Scandinavian specialty is not only a delight to eat, it has great eye appeal as well, for each slice has a center bull's-eye of dark, delicious prunes. It must be started 2 days before your dinner. While easiest to prepare and slice boned, this dish may be made with the meat on the bone.

Serves 8-10

1 12-ounce box pitted prunes
Cognac
5-6-pound pork-loin roast, center or rib end (boned: loin in one piece, and bones in one piece. Reserve bones)
3 tablespoons butter
2 tablespoons oil
1 clove garlic, crushed
1 teaspoon dried thyme
Salt and pepper

MARINADE MIXTURE
2 large onions, peeled and sliced
2 carrots, peeled and sliced
2 stalks celery, sliced
4 bay leaves
6-8 peppercorns
Dry red wine (enough to cover meat)

Put prunes into a jar, cover with Cognac, and let stand for 24 hours.

Have your butcher bone the loin so that the meat is in one piece and the bones in one piece (the bones to be used as a rack on which to roast the loin). With a long, sharp-pointed knife make an incision in thickest part of meat and

Continued from preceding page

extending its entire length. If necessary, enlarge opening a bit to hold soaked prunes and stuff them in with a long-handled spoon or other long, blunt instrument. Roll meat and tie in several places with white cotton string. Put meat into 4-quart mixing bowl with marinade mixture and refrigerate for 24 hours.

Preheat oven to 450 F. Remove meat from marinade, drain and dry it; strain marinade to use as basting liquid. Heat butter and oil in a skillet and brown roast on all sides. Put reserved bones in roasting pan; place meat on them as if they were a rack; baste well with strained marinade, and roast for 15 minutes. Reduce heat to 350 F. and, basting from time to time with the strained marinade, roast until done—about 1 hour or until a thermometer inserted in meat reads 160 F.

Remove meat to a warm platter and keep warm while you make gravy with the pan juices, first skimmed, then seasoned with a little pounded garlic and finely minced fresh thyme (or crumbled, if dried). Cook it on top of the range over high heat, scraping up and stirring in the brown bits adhering to the pan. If it seems too thick, add more marinade. Serve roast sliced thin, garnished with sautéed apple slices, and with a little gravy poured over, the rest in a separate dish.

NOTE: This recipe may be prepared as above, using a pork loin that has not been boned. Stuff roast, but do not tie with string. Marinate as above, but roast 1½ hours or until thermometer inserted in meat reads 160 F.

(From THE GREAT COOKS COOKBOOK, by The Good Cooking School, Inc. Copyright © 1974 by The Good Cooking School, Inc. Reprinted by permission of Ferguson/Doubleday.)

The sixteenth-century turnspit was human, not mechanical.

are not firm, the fat can pour back over your wrists or even spill onto your body, causing serious burns. A calamity which you can help to prevent by having the proper utensils.

LOW ALUMINUM ROASTERS

We show you these pans first because, as we have noted, aluminum or an alloy, such as Magnalite, is a most logical material for large utensils designed to hold heavy pieces of meat in a hot oven. Finally, in this group we show you the Dansk pan (8.38), which really doesn't belong here, as it's made of enameled steel—but at least it's in good company.

Magnalite Roasting Pan   8.35

Cast magnesium-aluminum alloy; 13⅜" X 12⅞"; 1½" deep.
$23.00

Magnalite, the country cousin in the family of American cookware, turns out to make the perfect roasting pan. Like all Magnalite pots, this roaster is cast of an alloy of aluminum and magnesium, and thus is light in weight but wonderfully strong. The design is simple, unpretentious, effective: a gently curved rectangle of well-polished metal, with integral handles which are easily gripped, designed not to slip out of greasy fingers. The pan weighs 5 pounds and is 13⅜" long, almost 13" wide, and deep. One of our editors, scorning the flimsy broiler pan which came in her apartment oven, uses this roasting pan and a special technique instead. She lays the steak in this pan, preheats the broiler to the highest possible temperature, and broils the meat quickly very close to the burner, turning it once. She leaves the oven door ajar, so that her thermostatically controlled electrical broiler will receive a constant leak of cold air and will, therefore, never turn off. And when she is all finished, she lifts out the steak,

pours off surplus fat, adds a bit of red wine to the brown bits in the pan, and stirs the mixture over a stove burner to make a simple deglazing sauce.

Deeper Magnalite Roasting Pan   8.36

Cast magnesium-aluminum alloy; 15⅜" X 9⅝"; 2" deep.
$18.00

The difference here is in the proportions: both this Magnalite pan and the preceding one are cast of the same sturdy aluminum and magnesium alloy. It is, therefore, light in weight for its size and strength, weighing about 4 pounds. This pan is 15⅜" long, 9⅝" wide, and 2" deep. Whether you buy this one or the other pan can only be determined by the size of your oven: roast meats are, after all, roughly the same size. (You don't believe us, right? But think: the difference between a neat little French roast and a turkey for Thanksgiving dinner is not so great as that between corn on the cob for the two of you and corn for a clambake.) And, since roasts don't have to be matched to the size of your pan, you might as well buy the largest pan which will fit, with room for air circulation—two inches all around—in your oven.

BILL of FARE

Barr's Dining Rooms.

ROASTS.

Roast Beef, with Vegetables,	50
Roast Pork, " "	50
Roast Lamb, " "	50
Roast Veal, " "	50
Roast Chicken, " "	60
Roast Turkey, " "	60

COLD MEATS.

Roast Beef,	35
Roast Veal,	35
Roast Lamb,	35
Roast Pork,	35
Boiled Ham,	35
Boiled Tongue,	40
Corned Beef,	35
Roast Chicken,	40
Roast Turkey,	40

Guests will confer a favor by reporting any errors in Checks, however slight,
or inattention of waiters.

The role of the roast in the Gay Nineties.

French Aluminum Roaster 8.37

Heavy-gauge aluminum with cast-aluminum handles; 14" × 10"; 2½" deep. Also avail. 18" × 14", 3¼" deep.
$32.50

The shape is familiar: this roaster is the aluminum version of the rectangular earthenware baking pans we discussed in an earlier chapter. It is very much a European product in feeling and in size: the French and Italians don't eat as much meat as we, and they would put a nicely tied, fat little roast into a small pan like this. There are two upstanding, gently curved handles of cast aluminum. And although there is not one mite of unnecessary detail, it is the best-looking, most honest roaster we have seen. The impression is that function has been evolved gradually to its ultimate form in this pan. It is made of heavy-gauge aluminum, is only 14" × 10", and although the depth—2½"—may be too great for American purists of the shallow-pan school, it does help to cut down on spatter, a boon to those who do not have self-cleaning ovens.

This clockwork-operated spring jack operated in its cabinet ("roaster"), set before the fire.

In Mary Ronald's Century Cook Book *(1895) it is made clear that the old practice of spit roasting in the fireplace had by then given way to our modern method of bake-roasting: "To roast beef on a spit before a fire is unquestionably the best method of cooking it; but as few kitchens are equipped for roasting meats, baking them in the oven is generally practiced, and has come to be called roasting."*

Dansk Roasting Pan 8.38

Enameled steel; 12¾" × 10"; 2¼" deep. Also avail. 10¾" × 8".
$35.00 ▲ $26.00 ▲

The line of pans from Dansk to which this roaster belongs has always been rather problematic: madly attractive, but still and all, they can't be used on an electric stove, and the shiny enameled steel tends to reflect heat rather than absorbing it. But it is perfectly fine for oven roasting. The pan we show you has nice, thin, rigidly attached handles and would really star when doubling as a pan for baking moussaka or lasagna for a crowd. It's gilding the lily, rather, to use it for a roast chicken, because it is unlikely that anyone would then get to see the snowy-white interior of this handsome, brilliantly colored pan (ours is red)—unfortunately, there is little chance that one would use even this roaster as a presentation pan, since even these most shallow sides render it too deep for carving; also, the carving knife could easily harm the porcelain. This pan is small—12¾" × 10"—of moderate depth (2¼"), and it's handsome and easy to clean. If red isn't your favorite color, you may choose yellow, green, orange, or brown. Not a bad choice for a double-purpose roasting-baking pan, and especially good in a small oven.

Wearever Aluminum Roaster 8.39

Aluminum; 18½" × 12½"; 2" deep.
$16.00 ▲

Sometimes a specific pan produces such a string of successes that it becomes cherished out of all proportion to its apparent qualities. This medium-weight sheet-aluminum pan from Wearever is the dearest possession of one of our editors, in whose batterie de cuisine it keeps company with such sophisticates' delights as any number of copper saucepans and a brand-new Cuisinarts food processor. But she loves this roaster; swears that it is the most versatile pan in her kitchen. She uses it to make brownies, bar cookies, bread; once she made baked noodles for a party in it. And oh, yes: she roasts meat in it. It is on her recommendation that we show it to you. It is spacious, shallow, with a beaded rim and loop handles that are equipped with stops that prevent them from rising above the horizontal when they are lifted by the cook. There is a heavy, nonbuckling bottom on which you can fit two roasts at a time. And it is—not the least important point—a very good buy for the money. Measuring 18½" × 12½" and 2" deep, it is no beauty, but then, who can explain love?

CAPPONE FARCITO—STUFFED CAPON

1 medium-sized surgical capon*
2 cloves garlic
Olive oil
1 tablespoon fresh rosemary
Salt and freshly ground black pepper
1 cup dry white wine
4 strips salt pork

STUFFING
Capon gizzard, diced
2 small onions, chopped
1 tablespoon butter
1 cup grated Parmesan or
  pecorino cheese
½ cup chopped parsley
1 capon liver (raw), diced
2 tablespoons raisins
2 tablespoons chopped walnuts
2 cups bread crumbs
1 tablespoon chopped fresh basil or 1
  teaspoon dried basil
1 teaspoon thyme
2 eggs, lightly beaten

Preheat oven to 400°.

To make stuffing, sauté gizzard and onions in butter until onions wilt, adding more butter, if necessary. Cut gizzard in cubes—discard tough parts. Mix together all remaining stuffing ingredients. Stuff bird. Cut garlic in slivers and slip under skin of capon (remember to discard when chicken is roasted).

Truss the bird, then rub with a little olive oil, rosemary, salt and pepper to taste. Place strips of salt pork over bird. Roast capon on rack in shallow baking pan. When capon is brown, add wine by pouring over bird and allowing to collect in pan. Cover pan and lower heat to 350°. Baste often, and roast for about 1½ hours, or until tender. Serves 6 to 8.

*NOTE: A surgical capon is a rooster that has been castrated surgically. Other capons are the result of hormone injections. I personally frown upon the use of hormones in food, and though surgical capons are more expensive, they are worth it.

(From ITALIAN FAMILY COOKING, by Edward Giobbi, illustrated by Cham, Lisa, and Gena Giobbi. Copyright © 1971 by Edward Giobbi. Reprinted by permission of Random House.)

Professional-Weight Wearever Roaster   8.40

Heavy-gauge aluminum with nickel-plated steel loop handles attached by cast-aluminum plates; 19¾″ × 10⅞″; 3½″ deep.
$22.10

A Wearever pan of a different quality. This one is bigger, deeper, of a heavier gauge of metal, with the open-rolled rim which signals that it was designed for professional use: only rims such as these can be cleaned well enough to meet government standards of hygiene. The rolled edge makes it easy to pour off fats before you make your gravy by adding a hot liquid and then scraping like crazy at the browned bits at the bottom of the pan. Because the sides are higher—it is 3½″ deep—this is not at all as versatile as the pan above, but it is altogether more formidable and, because of its dimensions—19¾″ × 10⅞″—it is better suited to a long, thin roast such as a filet of beef or a boned loin of pork. The nickel-steel loop handles are fastened to the pan by cast-aluminum plates with stops that prevent the handles from being lifted above the horizontal and making your grip less secure. Another good buy, by the way, as most Wearever pans are.

Enormous Wearever Roaster   8.41

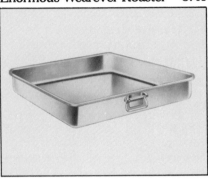

Heavy-gauge aluminum with nickel-plated steel handles attached by cast-aluminum plates; 21¾″ × 19¾″; 3½″ deep.
$33.00

A final aluminum baking-roasting pan from Wearever, this one designed for the people who are lucky enough to have Garlands or other professional ranges with oversized ovens. The only way to use these great cooking spaces correctly and efficiently is with such huge pans. You could use this one for large fish—it looks a bit like a turbotière—or for doing two smaller striped bass at once, or for roasting a whole baby lamb, or a suckling pig, or several pheasants. If any of this seems ridiculous, then it isn't the pan for you, but if you read it with a gasp of recognition—At last!—then perhaps you should look into it. As we said, it is big—21¾″ × 19¾″, 3½″ deep—it has an open-rolled edge for hygiene, and two nickel-steel loop handles, fastened to the pan's body by cast-aluminum plates which have the same positive stops as do those of 8.40; and it is relatively inexpensive. It is altogether professional in design and in weight—the aluminum is very thick indeed.

STAINLESS-STEEL ROASTERS AND A ROASTING RACK

Our reservations about stainless-steel roasters still hold: they are altogether too heavy and too expensive when compared with aluminum. We set aside one, made by the manufacturers of This Year's Favorite Cookware, because the price seemed altogether prohibitive, the weight totally inappropriate. But if you have a yen for the shine and the impervious surface of good-quality stainless steel—if you do a lot of roasting of meat bathed in an acid marinade, basting your chicken with wine and your ham with fruit juice—and if you should want to take advantage of an unadvertised bonus—stainless-steel roasters can be cleaned in your self-cleaning oven—then we offer you a choice of two. One is American, and the other, Italian; both are relatively reasonable

Continued from preceding page
in price and in weight.

Whatever kind of roaster you use—and especially if you want to improvise a roaster, using any flat pan of suitable size and weight—see our chromed-steel rack, 8.44, designed to lift your meat into the ideal conditions of oven heat surrounding it on all sides.

Farberware Roasting Pan with Rack 8.42

Stainless steel with chromed-steel rack; pan 17″ × 11″, 2½″ deep; rack 12″× 8″, ⅝″ high.
$19.99

An American roasting pan by Farber, a perfectly acceptable roaster in stainless steel. It has integral handles, open-rolled edges, rounded corners, and a slightly raised central area which allows the fat to run off and to pool around the outer edges of the pan. (And which, by the way, limits its usefulness for secondary purposes such as baking.) A sturdy rack sits on the bottom. The weight of the pan is moderate, but its bottom is sufficiently thick so that juices will not burn when the roaster is placed over a burner for deglazing. An altogether reasonable product; we think that you might do well to buy it.

Long-legged dripping pan and ladle.

Paderno Stainless-Steel Roaster 8.43

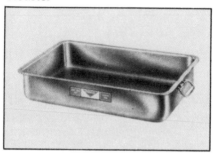

Stainless steel; 11⅞″ X 8⅝″; 2⅜″ deep. Also avail. 13¾″, 17¾″, 19¾″, or 23¾″ long.
$25.00

If you want the equivalent in stainless steel of the best-quality aluminum roasters, then you must look to Europe: specifically, to this pan from Paderno. Notice that it is available in very small sizes, because the Italians, like the French, being less carnivorous than we, are given to roasting compact, well-tied little pieces of meat. But notice also that it is, nonetheless, a pan of professional weight in a domestic size. There are open-rolled edges—made that way for ease of cleaning—loop handles, and a range of lengths from 11⅞″ to 23¾″. The only problem—always the difficulty with Paderno—is that it is very hard to find in this country. If you have a friend who is going abroad this summer, tell him to forget the leather pocketbooks and the reproductions of the *David* and to bring you, instead, a Paderno pot.

Roasts are a favorite English and American food for celebrations. Although food was scarce during the Revolution, one colonial family listed the following compromise Thanksgiving meal: Haunch of Venison, Roast Chine of Pork, Roast Turkey, Roast Goose, Pigeon Pasties, Creamed Onions, Cauliflower, Squash, Potatoes, Celery, 3 Pies and 2 Puddings. Lean fare.

PRIME (STANDING) RIB ROAST

The first three ribs are considered the best, although in my opinion a larger roast is preferable—the first five ribs, well trimmed, so that carving will be easy. This means a "7-inch cut," with the short rib section cut off and the chine bone, back cord, and feather bone removed. It is wise to have the roast barded with an extra piece of suet.

(1) *Low-heat method.* This requires a well-insulated, well-regulated oven. It is much in favor and works successfully with beef that is well fatted. Place the roast on a rack in a shallow pan and rub it with freshly ground pepper and, if you choose, with a little rosemary or thyme or garlic. However, fine beef should be roasted as simply as possible—peppered before roasting, salted later—with additional flavorings reserved for the sauce. Preheat the oven to 180 or 200 degrees, and place the roast in the oven bone side down. Allow it to roast without basting approximately 23 to 24 minutes per pound, until it achieves an internal temperature of 120 to 125 degrees for rare meat; or, for medium, approximately 28 minutes per pound until it achieves an internal temperature of 140 degrees. Salt the roast, remove it from the oven, and allow it to settle about 10 minutes before carving.

(2) *Medium-heat method.* This is more or less the standard method. Preheat the oven to 300 or 325 degrees. Prepare the roast as above. Roast, allowing 15 to 17 minutes per pound for rare (meat thermometer, 120 to 125 degrees) or 17 to 20 minutes per pound for medium rare (meat thermometer, 140 degrees). Allow the roast to stand 10 minutes before carving.

(3) *Searing method.* Preheat the oven to 425 to 450 degrees. Prepare the meat as above. Roast 30 minutes. Reduce the heat to 325 degrees and continue to roast, allowing about 12 minutes per pound for rare (meat thermometer, 120 to 125 degrees) or 14 to 15 minutes per pound for medium (meat thermometer, 140 degrees). Allow it to stand 10 minutes before carving.

(4) *Western method.* This is much used by Western housewives who lead active lives and entertain a great deal. The roast is started before midday for serving at dinner in the evening. For a 7:30 dinner, set the oven at 375 degrees at 11 A.M. (for an 8:30 dinner, advance it an hour to noon, and so on). Put the roast on a rack and place in the oven. Roast 1 hour. At the end of that time, turn off the heat, but do not open the

door of the oven. Leave the roast in the oven until evening. Approximately 1 hour before you are ready to serve, turn on the oven to 375 degrees and roast the meat another 45 minutes to an hour. Remove to a hot platter and let it stand 15 minutes before carving. Roasts of varying weight, up to 11 or 12 pounds, will cook in the same time by this method—the outside nicely browned and the inside rare. For roasts of more than 12 pounds, the final roasting should be started an extra hour in advance.

(From AMERICAN COOKERY, by James A. Beard, illustrated by Earl Thollander. Copyright © 1972 by James A. Beard. Reprinted by permission of Little, Brown and Company.)

V-Shaped Roasting Rack 8.44

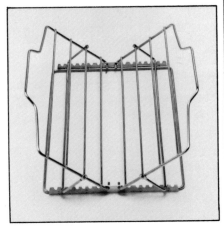

Chromed steel; base 12″ × 11″; adjustable racks, 12½″ × 5¾″ each side.
$4.50 ▲

True roasting involves not only a source of radiant heat, but also full air circulation around the meat. You can get this on a turning spit and in a toaster, but you can also contrive it in your oven if you use this V-shaped rack. It sits over a shallow roaster to hold your meat away from the bottom of the pan. And although most shallow roasters have, if they have any rack at all, a flat grill which sits in the bottom and lifts the food a mere useless half-inch above the pan, we suggest that you put that rack away (you can always use it for cooling cookies) and buy this one instead. With it you can turn anything—even a heat-proof glass or porcelain serving dish—into a roasting pan. A flat rectangular frame of rolled steel, chrome-plated,

lies in the pan, its upper edges serrated like teeth. Points on the ends of the two meat-holding sections of the rack fit into holes near the center of the end-pieces of the rectangle, and then the grills tilt out, to be held in place at the angle you choose by movable legs which slip into a set of the teeth. It all works rather like a reclining deck chair, only *double;* and the fact that the rack is adjustable means that you can put into it the skinniest eye-round roast or the fattest turkey. This rack is strong enough to hold a good-sized roast. One of our experts brought in to show us the rack that his mother had given him, second-hand, twenty years ago. That one, aged and discolored as it was, was strong enough to hold a buffalo. Awe-inspiring, but unnecessary: this rack will hold any roast you are likely to put into your oven—a turkey of 20 pounds, a 15-pound rolled rib roast.

This type of Dutch oven was for fireplace roasting. Steaks were broiled in the hanging gridiron.

DEEP ROASTERS

A culinary controversy as violent and as unimportant as that over Lobster à l'Armoricaine versus Lobster à l'Américaine exists over the merits of shallow versus deep roasters. The fact is that many people believe that the term "roaster" should not be used for a flat pan that holds a roast high, allowing the air to circulate around it, but that a roaster is, rather, a deep-sided pan, in effect a kettle. This party of deep-roasters maintains that the function of a roaster is not to reproduce the relationship between the side of beef and the open fire, but rather to create a second, smaller oven inside the stove oven. For, when it is surrounded by great heat, a high-sided pan does, indeed, become a small oven, bouncing the heat from wall to wall and greatly magnifying it in the process. (Which means, among other things, that you really have to watch your cooking time—the recommended cooking times may be all wrong for deep roasters.) In a really good high roaster you can cook a beautifully browned turkey in little more than half the time roasting would take in a flat roaster. Just use a meat thermometer the first few times you try the deep-roaster method. Our experts say that it's fine to use the cover for most of the roasting time of poultry, but don't put the cover of the pan over beef and other meats unless you want to retain the vapor and end up with pot roast. By no means should you discard the lid, however, if you never use it for roasting: with its help you can use your roaster as an improvised poaching kettle for a leg of lamb or for a salmon too stout for your fish poacher. Set it over two burners if it's long enough, or if your burners are close enough together.

Roast rack of lamb is today an extravagant meat course, fit for the purses of shipping barons and the like. Not so in 1836, when Lydia Maria Child, in The American Frugal Housewife, *had this to say about the cut: "That part of mutton called the rack ... is cheap food. It is not more than four or five cents a pound."*

Deep Oval Enamel Roaster 8.45

Enameled steel; 14" × 10"; 6½" deep. Also avail. in 5 other sizes, ranging from 11" × 7", 4½" deep, to 16" × 11¾", 7¾" deep.
$6.50

Like the inside of your oven, this roaster is made of porcelain over steel. And although porcelain-enameled steel can dent and chip if carelessly handled, it is also impervious to acid foods, it comes in an old-fashioned black and white glaze, and it is phenomenally inexpensive. Here is the classic oval high roaster, supplied with a domed cover. It can be used for a bird, a rolled roast, or secondarily, for boiling an awful lot of spinach, or for stovetop poaching when you need a longish pot that won't be harmed by your wine-based court bouillon. There are handles on either end and one at the center of the domed lid. The price makes it right, and our only reservation is that the steel beneath the porcelain is thin and might, therefore, heat in such a way as to cause a large piece of meat to stick to the bottom. The gravy well on the bottom is good in concept, but unfortunately, the reality doesn't match up, since the hollow just isn't deep enough to keep the meat from sinking into the fat; you could always use a low rack in this roaster when the roast has no supportive framework of bones such as that in a loin of pork. Available in six sizes.

DANISH ROAST GOOSE

Serves 6-8

1 goose liver, chopped
2 tablespoons Cognac
6-8 pound goose (ready to cook)
½ lemon
Salt and freshly ground black pepper
1 teaspoon ground sage
½ pound prunes
¼ cup (4 tablespoons) butter
½ cup chopped onions
3 cups tart apples peeled, cored and sliced
4 cups cooked chestnuts, chopped
½ cup coarsely chopped dried apricots
1 tablespoon chopped parsley
6-8 slices bacon

Place chopped liver in a small bowl and add the Cognac. Marinate 15 minutes, or until ready to use. Rub goose inside and out with the cut side of ½ lemon. Sprinkle inside and out with salt and pepper, but only inside with the sage. Set aside.

Plump prunes in a bowl of hot water 15-30 minutes, drain, remove pits, chop prunes coarsely, measure out ¾ cup and set aside.

In a skillet over medium heat, heat butter, add onions and sauté until they are limp. Add goose liver and Cognac, cook 1 minute or less, stirring. Remove skillet from heat and add apples, chestnuts, apricots, prunes and parsley. Mix together well. Taste and correct seasoning with salt and pepper. Stuff goose with mixture. Close the cavity, and truss.

Heat oven to 325 F. Put bacon in a saucepan and cook over low heat until it releases all of its fat. Discard bacon; soak cheesecloth in the bacon fat. Wrap fat-soaked cheesecloth entirely around the goose; place goose on a rack set in a roasting pan. Roast in preheated oven (basting frequently with any remaining bacon fat and the pan drippings) for 2½-3 hours, or until goose is tender and the joints move easily.

(From THE GREAT COOKS COOKBOOK, by The Good Cooking School, Inc. Copyright © 1974 by The Good Cooking School, Inc. Reprinted by permission of Ferguson/Doubleday.)

Deep Oval Magnalite Roaster 8.46

Cast magnesium-aluminum alloy with aluminum rack; 20" × 12"; 5½" deep.
$54.50   13" $31.50▲   15" $36.50▲
           18" $57.00▲

Still in the oval form is this Magnalite roaster, which comes with a rack to keep your meat from sticking to the bottom of the pan—rather a remote possibility, in view of the thickness and good conductivity of the Magnalite alloy. We are showing you the 20" size, large enough to hold a 25-pound turkey, but there are smaller sizes suitable for roasting neat little chickens or small shoulders of lamb: small enough, in fact, to use as stovetop braziers. A ten-year guarantee comes with this pot, reflecting the manufacturer's confidence in its quality. Start a turkey with the rather deep domed cover in place in a very hot oven; twenty minutes before it's done, remove the cover and allow it to brown. When a skewer in the thigh produces juice which runs yellowish or clear, not pink—and when the meat thermometer reads 175 F.—then you will have a beautifully done, superbly moist bird. (However, some of our experts prefer a slightly higher reading, to 185 F.) And two days later, when the meat is all but gone, you can use the same pot to boil the skeleton and scraps with vegetables to make a turkey soup.

Deep Aluminum Double Roaster 8.47

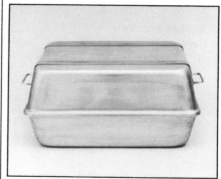

Heavy aluminum with steel strapwork; 20" × 16"; base 5" deep; lid 4⅝" deep.
$54.35

Metal strapwork, like that on a steamer trunk but considerably thicker, adds to the strength of this medium-gauge roaster by Commercial Aluminum. It is mammoth in size, suitable for holding a leviathan of a turkey or a whole haunch of venison; yet such a roast would be so heavy that, unsupported, it could cause the bottom of the pan to buckle. The strapwork, running the long way under the bottom, helps to distribute the stresses throughout the pan. Notice that this is a double roaster, the base and the top being virtually a pair of mirror twins, either of which could be used alone. There is a set of loop handles on each part, held to the pan and cover by strongly riveted plates. The handles hang against the ends of the pan when not in use and are prevented from rising beyond the safe horizontal position by the construction of their base plates. Check the size of your oven before you spend the substantial amount of money involved: the roaster is a bulky 20″ × 16″ in size. The lid, you will notice, is a mere fraction of an inch shallower than the 5″-deep base. A formidable pair, for a single formidable roast or a brace of fine birds.

Rectangular Aluminum Deep Roaster   8.48

Heavy aluminum with nickel-steel handles; base 14½″ × 9¾″, 6″ deep; lid 15¾″ × 10¾″, 1¼″ deep.
$57.00

The Italians often make ordinary pots in slightly extraordinary shapes. They call this one a brazier because it can be used on the stovetop, and we call it a roaster; but under either name the shape is utterly idiosyncratic. It is a big rectangular box—to one of our experts, it looks like the tin box in which he keeps crackers dry at his beach house—only this box is of very heavy-gauge seamless aluminum and is close to 15″ long and 10″ wide and 6″ deep without its cover, which adds another 1¼″ to the depth. Heavy steel loop handles actually lock horizontally into place when they are lifted; they are fixed to the pan by riveted plaques, and the shallow lid fits quite loosely over the top. The lid has its own fixed handles, so that it could be used separately as a low roasting pan. The whole thing is very big, relatively inexpensive, and funny-looking enough to be very appealing.

Electric Roasters: Second Ovens

Now, suppose you live in a rent-controlled apartment which features a smashing view, a really terrific address, and absolutely no kitchen worthy of the name: what do you do? Or suppose you are living in an impossible place for one year while you are trying to finish your thesis, and the kitchen has a stove which keeps trying to explode. Or suppose you are renting a beach house with incredibly poor equipment, and your husband has offered to entertain the whole gang from the Tennis Club at least once a week. Move? Impossible. Cry? Waste of time. No, you get yourself a good hot plate (Chapter 11) and an electric roaster, and you will soon be in business. Which is our roundabout way of saying that, although these appliances are never one's first choice for cooking supper, neither are they to be discounted; that when there is not a good stove oven available, they can do the job very well. And the prices are low enough so that you can buy, say, the Electric "Pot Luck" roaster (8.49) to get yourself out of a tight spot (the stove did explode), and then put it away to use as a secondary oven when you are having lots of company, or when you want to plug it into an outdoor outlet to make stew for twelve and keep it hot at an elegant déjeuner sur l'herbe.

Hoover "Pot Luck" Roaster   8.49

Baked-enamel exterior with porcelain-enamel interior, glass lid, plastic handles; chromed-steel roasting rack; 16⅛″ × 11½″; 9⅞″ high; 6-qt. capacity.
$50.00

This independent oven is made by Hoover, the same fine old firm that produces the vacuum cleaners. In construction it comes close to the slow-heat casseroles (7.49), and it can, like the slow cooker, hold a temperature of 200 F. But the heat can be raised to 500 F. as well, and you can use it for roasting meat. Don't try to sauté in it, however, because the enamel insert will never develop the proper kind of heat to "seize" the food. A roomy oval electrical pot holds 6 quarts and takes up only 14½″ of

your counter space. There is a dishwasher-safe glass lid, a porcelain-enameled cooking well removable for dishwasher cleaning, and a roasting rack made of chromed steel. A good buy for the money; although flour baking does better in a convection oven (8.55), our editors agree unanimously that this makes a better auxiliary "oven" for a summer house than the microwave ovens. So what if the exterior is orange or avocado, and covered with inane drawings. When you're in a fix, you can't be fussy.

PEKING DUCK

INGREDIENTS
1 Long Island duckling, 4 to 6 pounds
2 cups dry sherry
4 tablespoons Hoisin sauce
2 tablespoons sugar
10 to 12 scallions

PREPARATION
Wash and clean the duck. Hang by the neck for at least 8 hours, preferably overnight, in a cool, airy place.

Place the duck in a rectangular pan just large enough for the bird to lie flat. Pour the 2 cups of sherry over it. Marinate for 1 hour. Turn the duck over and marinate for another hour.

Hang the duck again until there is no dripping.

Wash and clean the scallions. Cut off ½″ above the roots and also discard

Continued from preceding page

green tops. The remaining pieces of scallion will be about 4" in length. Cross-slit both ends about an inch. Soak in ice water for 1 hour. Ends will open up like a flower. Arrange on 2 small plates.

Mix 2 tablespoons sugar with 4 tablespoons Hoisin sauce. Set out on two small plates.

COOKING PROCEDURES

Roast duck for 30 minutes in oven at 375 degrees, 1 hour at 250 degrees, and again for 30 minutes at 400 degrees.

To serve: Slice off skin and cut into pieces 1" × 2". Cut meat into pieces of similar size. Arrange skin and meat on a platter.

To eat: Spread a piece of doily (recipe below) on your plate. Place a piece of meat and a piece of skin in the center. Add 1 scallion and ¼ teaspoon sauce. Roll up the doily and turn over one end. Use fingers to hold roll and eat while still warm.

TIPS

There are many ways to prepare Peking Duck, but I believe that the above recipe is the simplest. In China, Peking Duck is usually prepared in restaurants and has to be ordered at least a day in advance. Shantung restaurants are famous for this method of preparing duck.

The ducks used for this dish in China are fed for many days on special feed so that they will grow fat and tender. But the Long Island ducklings in this country serve the purpose very well.

DOILIES FOR PEKING DUCK

INGREDIENTS

2 cups flour
1 cup boiling water
2 tablespoons sesame-seed oil

PREPARATION

Sift flour and measure 2 cups.

Gradually add boiling water and work with a wooden spoon into a warm dough. Knead gently for 10 minutes and let stand for 10 minutes.

Make into a long roll about 2" in diameter. Cut into ½" pieces and flatten them to ¼" thickness.

Brush a little sesame-seed oil over 1 piece of flattened dough and lay another piece over it. Roll out slowly, from the center out, until the piece is 4" to 5" in diameter. Proceed until all dough is rolled out this way.

Heat ungreased griddle over low flame and heat the dough. When it bubbles slightly, turn over and heat the other side.

While still warm, pull apart and fold at the center with the greased side inside. Repeat until all circles of dough are used up.

COOKING PROCEDURES

Steam for 10 minutes over boiling water before using to wrap duck as described above. Serve hot.

TIPS

These doilies can be made the day before and reheated in a double boiler. The first steaming, however, should be done in a steamer, so that enough vapor will be absorbed to make the doilies soft and easy to use. If no steamer is available use a deep saucepan and set a rack over a deep inverted bowl in this saucepan. Place a piece of cheesecloth over the rack and arrange the doilies on this. Steam, covered, for 10 minutes. Doilies prepared in this way can be frozen, kept for several weeks and resteamed without thawing when you are ready to use them.

(From THE PLEASURES OF CHINESE COOKING, by Grace Zia Chu, illustrated by Grambs Miller. Copyright © 1962 by Grace Zia Chu. Reprinted by permission of Cornerstone Library in association with Simon & Schuster.)

In a letter to his daughter, the Reverend Sydney Smith, the amiable and renowned nineteenth-century wit and epicure, writes of his friend who "came over a day from whence I know not, but I thought not from good pastures; at least, he had not his usual soup-and-pattie look. There was a forced smile upon his countenance, which seemed to indicate plain roast and boiled; and a sort of apple-pudding depression, as if he had been staying with a clergyman."

Wit and Wisdom of Sydney Smith, being Selections from His Writings and Passages of His Table Talk, *Evert A. Duyckink, ed., New York, 1856*

Microwave Ovens

Culinary history has been punctuated by revolution. The discovery that heat could effect palatable changes in staple foodstuffs sent human beings into the kitchen for good. Not only could they take it, they have been fascinated by it, spending millenia in attempts to perfect the art. Since the mid-19th century, advancing technology has changed the kitchen. The gas range, electric refrigeration, pressure canning were novelties of 100 years ago. The latest innovation is cooking without heat. It involves electronics, radar, molecular energy. In other words, post-World War II space-age discoveries have been harnessed for home use. The microwave may indeed be the wave of the future. It offers some incredible advantages, and we are impressed. They are becoming increasingly popular, but until the problems have been ironed out—and they are considerable—we are not ready to suggest all-microwave cooking.

As we have distinguished one method of cooking from another and so helped you decide between one piece of equipment and another, we have always had to deal with three variables: temperature, moisture, and time. Think of it as arithmetic: Higher temperature + less moisture + less time = broiled fish fillets; lower temperature + more moisture + more time = onion soup. But there is a method of cooking in which one of these variables has been eliminated, a fact that has created confusion among the method's users and lots of work for home economists. It is, of course, microwave cooking, performed entirely by "heat" generated within the food itself.

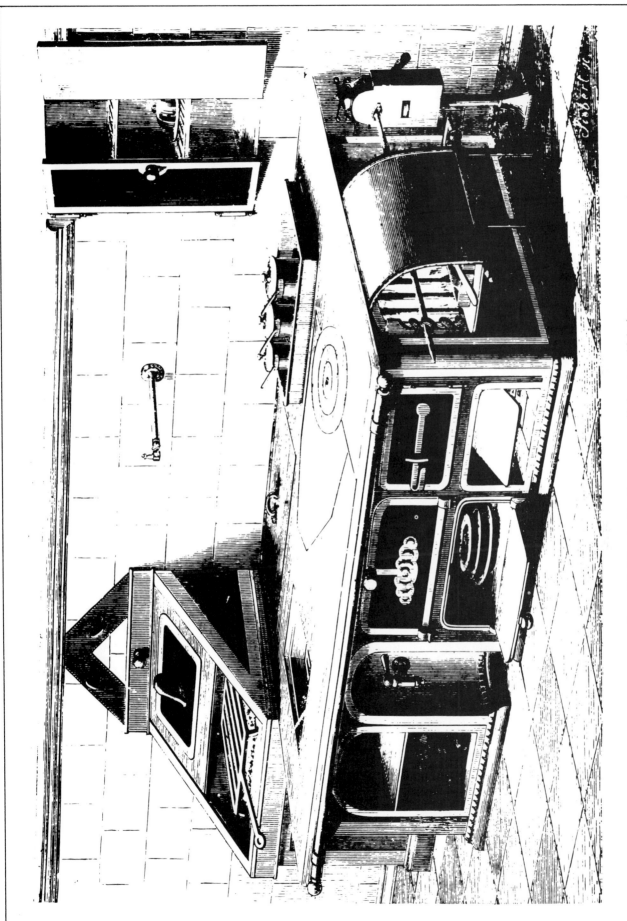

Everything the nineteenth-century cook's heart could desire for the cuisine bourgeoise: a cooktop, horizontal grill, warming oven, hot-water reservoir with faucet, bain-marie, and a vertical wall of heat for roasting meats on a spit turned by clockwork.

Continued from preceding page

HOW MICROWAVES WORK

To understand how microwaves work, the model to keep in mind is your two palms rubbing together, producing friction and heat. In microwave ovens, electrical energy is converted into electromagnetic energy through the mediation of a magnetron tube. The microwaves then fall on the food, causing the molecules of liquid in it to vibrate at a great rate (here the molecules correspond to your palms); and the resulting friction produces heat, which is then conducted through the food. And thus your supper is cooked not by a great cloud of heated air, but actually by itself, by its molecules; there is no loss of heat to the surroundings, not even to the dish on which the food rests, and the entire procedure is much faster than in the heat-cooking methods. You end up with hot food and a cold oven.

LEARNING MICROWAVE COOKING

Well, even the oven manufacturers admit that there are problems involved, adjustments which the new microwaver will have to make. Cooking pots, for example: whereas food absorbs the microwaves, and glass, paper, and most plastics transfer them, metal, unfortunately, reflects them away, slowing down the cooking. So inimical is metal to microwave cooking, in fact, that you are advised to wrap the narrow wings and legs of your turkey in aluminum foil in order to slow down the cooking while the waves have time to penetrate the mass of the breast. All of which means that you must use no metal at all, except for shallow aluminum-foil trays and the small skewers buried in your shish kebab. Even certain plastics have certain components that interfere with the cooking.

The other factor you have to learn to deal with is mass. Two potatoes take twice as long to bake, and four take four times as long, as one. Bulky and dense things take longer to cook than thin or loose-textured foods of the same weight. With the factor of temperature eliminated, you have to become adept at manipulating time and mass. (We begin to sound like Einstein.) One of the manuals we received with our test ovens told us solemnly that the bagel was the ideal shape for microwave baking, having more surface in relation to bulk than any other food. And there seems to be a special flair which good microwavers develop for arranging things cleverly within the oven cavity in order to get the best results.

The point is that this microwave technique can obviously be learned —after all, if we could learn to make puff pastry, why not this? But is it worth it? Certainly these ovens are widely used commercially, but unfortunately, in our opinion they never cook ideally, are never the mode of choice no matter how much you play with them. The oven tends to dehydrate food, leaving its four-minute miracle-baked potatoes finished but dried out. It doesn't brown food, no matter what the manufacturers say and despite the best efforts of one, Thermadore, to

---

Although kitchen ranges were invented in the late eighteenth century, many Americans still used a portable reflecting oven for roasting well into the nineteenth century. This device, designed something like a lean-to, was made of metal and sat with its open side facing the fire and its curved back toward the room. Meats were spitted, placed in the reflecting oven, and the spit was turned by hand. The effect of the heat reflected by the oven walls was like that in a rotisserie—meat became crustily browned and a pan set below the roast, safely away from the hot coals, could catch the drippings for use as basting liquid and ultimately in gravy.

COUNTRY-STYLE CHICKEN

1 frying chicken, cut up
Flour
Pepper
¼ cup butter or margarine
Salt

Coat chicken with flour; sprinkle with pepper. Melt butter in 7½″ × 12″ baking dish by microwave for 2 minutes. Roll chicken in melted butter. Place, skin side up, in baking dish. Cover and cook 4 minutes by microwave. Turn dish; cook 4 minutes. Uncover; rearrange and turn chicken in dish. Cook, uncovered, another 4 minutes. Remove from oven. Raise shelf; preheat infrared browning unit for 1 minute. Brown chicken for 3 minutes. Sprinkle with salt. Makes 4 to 5 servings.

(From RICHARD DEACON'S MICROWAVE OVEN COOKBOOK, by Richard Deacon. Copyright © 1974. Reprinted by permission.)

A portable oven for the nineteenth-century French kitchen.

provide a good infrared browning element (which of course uses a conventional form of heat), and despite the provision by others of so-called browning skillets, which are made of materials that permit them to become hot in the microwave oven and thus brown, after a fashion, the food put into them. And in recipes where you should be able to balance the cooking time of different elements—such as eggs coddled in cream—you may well find that nothing cooks at the same rate as anything else: and instead of eggs gently cooked in and subtly permeated with the cream and seasonings, you find yourself contemplating three masses of food—cream, egg white, and yolks—that are scarcely on speaking terms with one another. The newer models have several speeds to slow down the microwaves so your ingredients can have time to mingle—faster than, but closer to, a conventional process.

BALANCING THE REASONS
And yet—if you want to buy time with money; if you have a country house with a freezer full of meat and do half of your weekend cooking with frozen foods; if you work; if you have limited time but plenty of counter space—if any of these applies to you, then you might want to buy a microwave oven. Just don't expect to use it for grilling meat, or, as the manuals tell you is possible, for scrambling eggs. It is an auxiliary to your oven and your stove, not a substitute for either.

As we said, we don't love any of the microwave ovens, and so we are showing you a cluster and letting you choose among them. (But we confess to a sneaking fondness for the MicroMite in spite of its lack of beauty, simply because it is small: since the thing you are trying to save is time, you are best served by cooking small, separate bits of food.) But aren't the others marvelous to look at? We really thought they should be turned into TV sets. One final word: we have discovered that Hollandaise sauce, chilled to the point of solidity, can be liquefied without separating by placing it in the Litton oven set at Defrost for precisely 2 minutes. Now, that is a super accomplishment. Whether it's worth the $450 or so is another matter.

Thermatronic Oven 8.51

Vinyl top, stainless-steel sides and interior, black glass door and control panel, glass shelf; 23⅝″ × 14½″; 12⅝″ high; oven interior dimensions 16″ × 12½″, 7″ high. 83 lbs. **$575.00**

with turning electrical energy into electromagnetic power for microwave cooking; but if you have a 240-volt line, both can be done at the same time. This is a handsome unit, with no trumpery ornamentation: mainly shining stainless steel and black glass. It won a prize at the Museum of Contemporary Crafts. The latch works securely and the controls are relatively simple. We don't recommend the sequential unit that works on 120 volts; for even passable browning you need the simultaneous (240-volt) version of this oven. The oven also has a control for keeping food at serving temperature.

Amana Radarange Oven 8.52

Steel exterior with glass door, stainless-steel front panel and interior, glass shelf; 22¾″ × 17¼″, 15″ high; oven interior dimensions 14⅝″ × 13⅜″, 9⅛″ high. 91 lbs.
$475.00

The Amana oven has the inestimable virtue of possessing simple controls, a boon to anyone who has ever had to pay for a service call, and of offering a five-year guarantee. Two dials on the front panels control timing—one is for periods of up to 5 minutes, the other for up to 30 minutes; there is a switch to press for automatic defrosting of frozen foods; and that is absolutely all. The door closes with a nice comfortable *thunk*, like that on a big American car, and it is then automatically locked, which forestalls all of those nervous thoughts we all have about the microwaves somehow escaping. In short, it is strong, simple, and comes with a good guarantee. Amana provides what they call a browning skillet, a ceramic frypan with a bottom made of material which is able to transform the microwaves into heat. The claim is that this pan, properly preheated, will sear the surface of your meat and provide the browning which

Food done by microwaves cooks itself, as we told you. Which is of interest mainly in that your roast is never subjected to the searing heat which produces a nicely browned surface. No charcoal broiling, no thickened crust, no burnt bits of fat in these ovens—they've taken away all the fun, and it is just as though the meat consisted entirely of its own interior, no surface at all. Now, all of the manufacturers have had to deal with this fact, and they have provided different solutions. Thermadore's idea was the addition of a heating element that sears the meat by using the heat of infrared rays, just as though it were in an ordinary infrared broiler. Unfortunately, a 120-volt electrical line does not supply enough power to permit you to do this at the same time as the oven is involved

Roasting and Broiling Pans, Appliances, and Tools

Continued from preceding page
is usually missing from microwave cooking. There is also an extensive cookbook which seems remarkably sensible, remarkably free of the hyperbole usually provided by the industrial home economist.

HAM STEAK

½ cup brown sugar
1 tablespoon cornstarch
½ teaspoon ginger
1 (12-ounce) can apricot nectar
1 tablespoon lemon juice
1 (1½ to 2-pound) fully cooked ham steak

In 4-cup measure, combine brown sugar with cornstarch. Stir in ginger, apricot nectar and lemon juice. Cook by microwave 4 minutes or until translucent, stirring several times. Set aside. Place ham steak in 7½ × 12 inch shallow baking dish. Cover with plastic wrap or waxed paper. Cook 5 minutes. Turn ham; pour off juices and brush with apricot sauce. Cook another 2 minutes. Makes 4 to 6 servings. Serve with extra sauce.

(From RICHARD DEACON'S MICROWAVE OVEN COOKBOOK, by Richard Deacon. Copyright © 1974. Reprinted by permission.)

Litton Microwave Oven   8.53

Rosewood-grained vinyl on steel exterior with chrome and plastic trim, glass door; interior acrylic paint on steel; glass shelf; 24⅛" × 16⅞", 15" high; oven interior dimensions 16⅛" × 14⅛", 9" high.
$499.00

Litton has been in the microwave oven field longest of all and was the pioneer of some of the improvements made since the earliest days. The oven we show you here is the prettiest of the lot, a modern design in fake rosewood, black plastic, and chrome, with a white acrylic-painted interior that looks as though it had been designed for Star Trek. The door catch is excellent, working with the sort of pedal which used to be found on kitchen garbage cans, and providing an automatic lock. There are controls which permit you to Cook, Defrost, and Vari-Cook, an activity which includes a flexible range of cooking speeds, indicated on the dial by Warm, Reheat, Roast, and so forth; be warned, however, that these terms do not indicate the same processes as they do in ordinary cooking; rather, they are combinations of cooking time and resting time. There is an easy-to-read timer on the front—the whole thing looks remarkably like the prettiest television set you've ever seen—and you can also buy a complete line of glass cookware, as well as what the manufacturer calls the Micro-Browner Steak Grill, to replace Litton's browning skillet.

MEDITERRANEAN SEAFOOD STEW

George Lang, of the George Lang Corporation, which developed this recipe especially for the MicroMite oven, tells us that it works perfectly in that small version of the microwave cooker: because of its size, the MicroMite takes longer to cook a given amount of food than would one of the larger ovens. Designed to serve two, it illustrates one of the best ways to use these appliances—to cook stews and similar dishes in small quantities.

FOR 2 SERVINGS:
2 lobster tails in shells
½ lb. shrimps, shelled
½ lb. scallops
2 tbsp. olive oil
½ cup canned whole plum tomatoes
¼ cup dry white wine
2 tsp. salt
¼ tsp. ground bay leaf
¼ cup chopped parsley

With your kitchen scissors cut through the flat side of the shells on lobster tails. Cut through the meat to the bottom, leaving the rounded shell joined.

Combine all ingredients in a 1½-quart casserole. Cook in the MicroMite for 15 minutes. Remove lobster tails and place one of them, shell side down, in each of two deep soup plates. Spoon rest of stew over lobster tails.

Serve with boiled potatoes or rice. It's great with plenty of garlic toast wedges served in the rich sauce.

MicroMite Oven   8.54

Woodgrained vinyl exterior with plastic front panel, door, and shelf, stainless-steel and aluminum interior; 17½" × 12½", 12⅜" high; oven interior dimensions 10¼" × 10¾", 6⅛" high. 39 lbs.
$229.95

We liked this little oven, despite its being covered almost entirely in a fake wood which would fool no one and which makes it look as though it were designed to be built into your den, right next to the woofers and tweeters. Its door catch is perfectly workable, but never feels properly closed, since the locking operation is performed by turning the handle in an arc of only about seven degrees; it's functional but not satisfying. The designer has also seen fit to mar the front surface by putting on it a permanent chart of cooking times. All this said, we have to explain that we include it here because it is small. And unlike regular ranges, which get more wonderful as they get bigger, microwave ovens might just as well be small because they work best on small bits of food. It takes longer to cook two pieces of bacon than it does one, longer to do a 5-pound roast than a 3-pound roast; so the diminutive size of this oven makes it not only less intrusive in your kitchen space, but it's also perfectly adjusted to the small foods you will want to cook in it.

Legend has it that Edward III of England induced Flemish weavers to migrate to England and teach their trade, vital to British woolgrowers, by offering them roasted beef and mutton as a change from their accustomed diet of herring.

Convection Ovens

If you have been thinking of buying a microwave oven and are now deflated and cast down by our criticisms, consider instead the convection oven, the appliance that does what the microwave manufacturers have *said* their ovens can do. It cooks more quickly than an ordinary oven—although not so quickly as the microwave—and it does so while turning out a product which is browned and appetizing. It works on any outlet in your house, as it draws only 110 volts; it cleans itself; and it has been proved by years of use in commercial bakeries. This is the convection oven, a means of cooking in which the hot air is kept circulating constantly around the food. There are only two that we know of which are an appropriate size for the domestic kitchen: one is German, with no parts or repairs available in this country. And the other is from Farber.

Farber Turbo-Oven   8.55

Stainless-steel exterior with glass door; enameled-steel interior with catalytic coating, chromed shelves, slotted 2-piece broiling pan; 20″ × 13″, 14½″ high; oven interior dimensions 18″ × 12″, 9¼″ high.
$130.00 ▲

This is the Farber Turbo-Oven, a version of the convection oven, a cooking concept which is new to the home cook but which has long been in use in professional bakeries and pizzerias as well as in aircraft. In these ovens, heated air, kept at a uniform temperature, is kept continuously circulating around the food, touching all surfaces. Frozen food put in this oven defrosts in no time, being constantly stripped of layers of ice all around. Cooking, whether broiling or baking or roasting, is all done by the same operation: the heat comes from the bottom of the unit, and food can be placed on the slotted pan that comes with it, or set directly on the oven rack. If you use conventional cooking pans, thus preventing the hot air from reaching some of the food surfaces, the saving in time is reduced: the food will take only slightly less time than in a conventional gas or electric oven. A filter within the unit traps fat and bits of food and works with the air circulation for continuous cleaning of the walls, which have

a catalytic coating, while the oven is in use. At its messiest, such as when you have just broiled a very well-marbled steak, all that you have to do is remove the door, run it through your dishwasher, and wipe down the inside of the oven with a sponge moistened with detergent solution. The rest of the time it, like a kitten, takes care of its own hygiene. As for cooking times, they are variable. A large roast of meat or a turkey, set on the rack with no pan beneath it, will cook in half the ordinary amount of time, and will do it at a temperature of only 300 F. The unit is not large—as a matter of fact, it's no bigger than a breadbox—and Farber recommends that you keep it on a counter. If you want to have it built in, leave a 4″ allowance of space at the top, sides and back, since it requires surrounding air space. Our recommendation: don't buy a microwave oven—buy this one instead. It isn't the same: as a matter of fact, it is better.

Toasters

The chapter began with outdoor grills, and we were happy to tell you about a line of cookers, including some for indoor use, that allow you to apply direct heat to food from the side. But if you think for a moment, you will realize that we all cook something by lateral heat every day—every morning. Of course; we mean toast. Toastmaking is in a way the paradigm for this chapter: a means of cooking wherein heat is applied to food which is contained neither in a liquid nor in an enclosed space. Once, before any of us were born, toast was made by holding days-old bread up to the fire on the end of a toasting fork. Some of us can remember another early toaster (versions of this one can still be found):

Continued from preceding page

it sat over the burner of a gas range like a four-sided teepee, exposing one side of the bread at a time to a central core of heat radiated by its screenlike sides. Then there were early electric toasters which used the same idea, with electric elements running up the center and places on either side of the core for bread to lean against a grill. When the first side was finished we had to reach near the heat, in great danger of burning our fingertips, in order to turn the bread over and toast the other side.

Toasters have changed a lot since then, adding complications. They now expose both sides of the bread to the heat at once; there are timers which regulate degrees of darkness and which lift the bread up to us automatically from the toaster's slots when it is done. But they all still employ the same principle, the principle with which we began the chapter: the direct application of heat to food in an open environment. We will show you first a toaster oven, standing halfway between the independent oven and the true toaster, and then, with two true toasters, the circle will have become complete.

The world is divided between those who like their toast warm, soaked with melted butter and strawberry jam, and those who, like the English, cool and crisp it by standing it in racks so that it can be spread with sweet butter and topped with bitter-orange marmalade. However you like it, this is how you can make it: in a GE toaster which lets you make four slices at a time, while setting the controls for two different degrees of darkness. So much for quarreling children at the breakfast table! This toaster has a relatively pleasant design in chrome-plated steel and fake wood, and although GE makes another model— their 127—which is admirably designed in pristine chrome plate and black plastic, it unfortunately does not have a dual control. Our toaster has easily reached crumb trays underneath for simplicity of cleaning, and of course, the toast pops up as soon as it has reached the shade— or shades—of brown you have decreed.

GE Toast-R-Oven 8.56

Chromed steel with plastic trim and glass window; 15⅝″ × 10″; 7½″ high. Rack 10¾″ × 7½″.
$50.00 ▲

It looks like a small portable oven, but those who own it say that GE's model T95 is really the world's best toaster. Sure, you can bake potatoes or stuffed tomatoes or frozen dinners in it, at temperature settings ranging from Warm to 500 F, but that, it seems to us, is just a bonus—after all, you have a stove for all that. This appliance excels at toasting, and what makes it better than the ordinary is that you are not limited as to the thickness of the bread. It can do bagels, croissants, corn muffins, Danish pastry; and one man we know cuts French bread into inch-thick slices, butters it lightly with garlic butter, and

then permits it to dry out completely in his Toast-R-Oven, making a kind of garlic zwieback.

What this does best is toasting and top browning, and it does it with enough versatility so that it is significantly more useful than the ordinary appliance. In it you do four not-too-large slices of bread at once; you can brown the top of food only by using the oven tray, which blocks the radiant heat of the lower element; you can set your controls for any degree of darkness you prefer; and the toaster shuts off automatically.

GE Toaster 8.57

Nickel-chrome plated shell with woodgrained plastic and black plastic trim; 11½″ × 9½″; 6½″ high.
$39.98

Toastmaster Toaster 8.58

Chrome-plated steel with plastic trim; 8¾″ × 8⅛″; 7½″ high.
$30.00 ▲

Just as nice as the GE above: a four-slice toaster from Toastmaster which, like the GE, permits you to toast to two different degrees of darkness simultaneously. This one has perhaps a more honest finish of brushed chrome on steel, a surface which is easily wiped clean with a damp sponge. There are two easily reached crumb trays; the bread pops up nicely when the toast is done; it comes with a good guarantee. You choose the one you prefer, GE or Toastmaster.

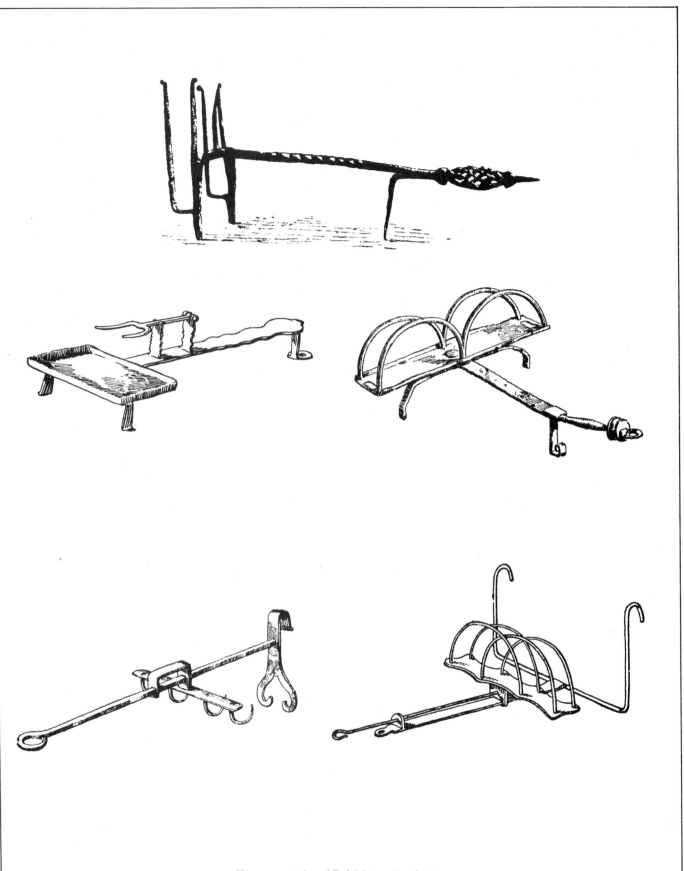

Three centuries of British toasting forks.
Top, iron fork, sixteenth century; center,
two down-hearth toasters of seventeenth- and eighteenth-century types;
below, two eighteenth-century fire-bar toasters.

Baking Pans for Batters

Baking is cooking in an oven by means of dry heat all around the pan. Baking of the kind we're discussing here involves the use of flour, or any of the products which, once ground, can be used as flour, such as nuts or potatoes or corn. Baking is a distinct area of cookery, more precise and scientific than any other, with recipes which must be followed as carefully as chemical formulas until one has achieved absolute mastery and can dare to vary the ingredients or the temperature or the pan size. In short, there is a scientific cast to the whole discipline —or perhaps it is better described as alchemy—this magic by which, with the simple application of heat, a sloshing pan of sweet batter is transformed into a layer cake and a small lump of resilient dough becomes a Parker House roll. Pans for batters and bread doughs will be considered here; we'll deal with equipment for preparing, baking, and decorating pastries in the next chapter.

THE BAKERS' REASONS

More people than ever are baking these days—a man in a commune making whole-wheat bread; a child laboriously pressing a walnut into the precise center of each of a panful of drop cookies; a woman reading three times over the complicated directions for making a Gâteau St. Honoré. And there are good reasons: the things that you make yourself are likely to be cheaper and purer and of higher quality than those you buy commercially. Consider the fact that baked goods, because they tend to deteriorate so rapidly, are more likely, when commercially made, to have preservatives added than nearly any other product. Consider the control you have over products which are made at home: you can add whole grains or powdered milk for a nutritional boost, or eliminate wheat flours, or salt, or anything else to which a member of your family may be sensitive. And finally, consider the price: home-baked goods simply cost less. Not only do they invariably cost less than the pastries you buy at the fancy bakery downtown, but less, probably, than the scarcely adequate bread and cookies, cellophane-wrapped and stuffed with BHT or other preservatives, lying on your supermarket shelves. The economy achieved by baking is a good argument, if one is still needed, for the ultimate economy of buying the very best equipment you can lay your hands on.

BAKEWARE STANDARDS

Our standards for this equipment are similar to those for other cookware; for discussions of metals and construction you might refer to Chapter 6, and then note carefully the different requirements for baking pans and pans for stovetop use. Pans used in the oven are subject to a different form of heat from that produced by a stovetop burner. The heat source is not direct; a pan for oven use, therefore, can be tinned or enameled on all surfaces, since we need not be concerned that the tin will melt or the enamel crack when it is subjected

Le blé (wheat), grain heads intertwined with morning glories. From Paul Bory's Nos Aliments, *published in 1887 in Tours.*

Heavy Aluminum Baking Sheet— Mirror Surface   9.1

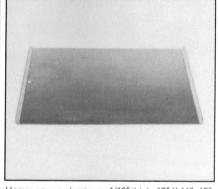

Heavy-gauge aluminum, 1/16" thick; 17" X 14"; 45°-angle rim ½" wide at each end.

$7.75

Unless you live in a big city and have access to a supplier of professional-quality cookware, this is probably the best baking sheet you are going to find. It has a mirrorlike finish that scarcely needs to be greased and that lends itself especially well to candymaking. While the two short sides have rims, the other two are rimless, so that cookies or flan shells can slide right off when they are done. The underside of this aluminum pan has a dull finish which absorbs the heat. An unusually sturdy 1/16" thick, the sheet is nonetheless a mere 2 pounds in weight, considerably lighter than a pan of the same size made of steel. Strong, lightweight, and well designed, this is, if not the Rolls Royce, at least the Buick of baking sheets.

to direct heat. Oven heat is general and even: the pan simply transfers the heat to the batter from all sides, rather than diffusing or transmitting it through the pan's bottom, set over a single intense heat source. It is for this reason that glass is a better material for a baking dish than a saucepan.

In baking pans we generally prefer weightiness and solidity of construction; but there are whisper-light pastries such as langues de chat which are best baked on a lightweight pan which heats and cools off rapidly enough not to overcook the tender cakes. Bakeware ought not to encourage foods to stick; anyone who has worked carefully over a cake batter, only to have the cake fall apart in its mad resistance to being taken out of the pan, will appreciate a surface which gracefully loosens its hold when required. Nonstick (release) surfaces are more acceptable in bakeware than in cookware. The ones developed for commercial bakeries are quite acceptable. Those found in your local stores are less so. Please notice that this is a reluctant endorsement, and that a well-greased, smooth surface is our first choice. Even with the most immaculate care, release surfaces will eventually become scratched or burned. Some pans are ruined forever, but some can be resurfaced.

USING BAKING PANS

A few words of caution. When we mention the capacity of a baking pan, such as "½ cup" or "1 qt.," this means the amount of batter that it will hold if filled to the brim. Of course, this would leave no room for rising, which is what you hope your batter will do; to allow room for rising, you must use only two-thirds as much batter as the pan will hold. Never put one baking pan immediately above another in the oven, or uneven and reflected heat will result in burned goodies. And remember that you must allow your pans to touch neither one another nor the sides of the oven; but allow the heat to flow throughout the entire oven cavity, leaving at least an inch—ideally more—between pans or between a pan and any side of the oven. This can be a problem if you have a small apartment stove, or any of certain types of old-fashioned ranges.

SHAPES

One last philosophical point. Think, if you will, of the unique shapes which so many cakes or breads have: consider brioches, madeleines, popovers. In baking, it seems, the pan and the product have evolved together, so that the pan is virtually an integral part of the recipe, as important as the eggs or the chocolate or the flour. A pot roast can be cooked in any of a number of large casseroles or pots and still be a pot roast. But brownies cooked in brioche tins? Lemon pies in loaf pans? Ridiculous—and thus is illustrated the enormous importance of the proper pan in the discipline of baking.

ALMOND ROUNDS

Typical of light, elegant cookies that require the best baking sheets are these of John Clancy's.

2 cups all-purpose flour
1¼ cups granulated sugar
¼ tsp. salt
1 cup (2 sticks) unsalted butter, plus 1 tbsp. softened butter
1 egg, separated
1 tsp. vanilla
1 cup finely chopped almonds
½ tsp. cinnamon

Combine flour, 1 cup of the sugar (reserve ¼ cup), and salt in a large mixing bowl. Add butter, egg yolk, and vanilla. Work the ingredients with your fingers until mixture is smooth and can be gathered into a ball. Shape dough into a cylinder about 2½" in diameter, wrap in plastic wrap, and refrigerate for 1 hour, or until very cold. Mix remaining sugar, chopped almonds, and cinnamon and set aside.

Preheat oven to 350 F. Butter two large baking sheets with the tablespoon of softened butter. Beat egg white with fork in small bowl until foamy.

With a sharp knife cut dough into rounds ¼" thick and place them on buttered cooky sheets about 1" apart. Brush cookies with the beaten egg white and sprinkle with almond mixture.

Bake cookies about 8 minutes, or until lightly browned. Cool cookies on wire cake racks. (10.81).

Makes 3 dozen cookies.

Heavy French Baking Sheet   9.2

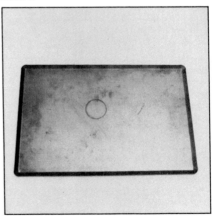

Heavy-gauge dark steel, 1/16" thick; 16" X 12"; 30°-angle sloping edge ½" wide. Also avail. 20" X 14".
$10.00

Continued from preceding page

Use two hands when you pick up this heavy-duty, no-nonsense French baking sheet: it weighs more than 4¼ lbs. The gray mild steel is about 1/16″ thick, so that one need never worry about it warping. It must, however, be treated with the same respect paid to cast iron: the surface should be seasoned and greased in much the same way as iron skillets (see Chapter 6); it should never be scoured and it must be well dried and greased after each use to prevent rust. Because it is thick it retains heat well, and thus it is particularly suited for such large baked goods as free-standing breads, tarts baked in flan rings, and those pâtés which are baked in bottomless molds. Like mother's linen tablecloth, this is a classic to be treated with respect.

PISTACHIO BREAD

This is a rather sweet bread—actually, more like a coffee cake, of the type once called a "race track"—flavored with delicious, beautifully green pistachio nuts. It is rolled, formed into a very large ring, and sliced before baking. It looks and tastes extraordinarily good, and is certainly one of the best breads of this kind I have ever had. It provides about 12 servings. [1 ring loaf]

1 package active dry yeast
Granulated sugar
¼ cup warm water (100° to 115°, approximately)
1 cup warm milk
½ stick (¼ cup) softened butter
2 teaspoons salt
3 to 4 cups all-purpose flour
¼ cup melted butter
1 cup shelled, salted pistachio nuts, coarsely chopped

Combine the yeast, 1 tablespoon sugar, and water in a large mixing bowl, and allow to proof. Then add the milk, the softened butter, the salt, and ½ cup sugar to the yeast mixture. Add the flour, cup by cup, beating well after each addition. (This dough is easy to handle but will be a little sticky at this stage.) Turn out on a lightly floured board and knead for a good 10 minutes, or until smooth and elastic. Form into a ball, place in a buttered bowl, and turn to coat the surface with butter. Cover with plastic wrap and set in a warm, draft-free spot to double in bulk.

Punch the dough down and turn out on a floured board. Let rest for a few minutes, then roll into a rectangle about 18 × 12 inches. Brush the surface with melted butter and sprinkle with ⅓ cup additional sugar and the coarsely chopped pistachio nuts. Beginning with

the long edge of the rectangle, roll up the dough like a jelly roll, pressing each seam as you do so. Join the ends of the roll and pinch together to form a ring. Place the ring carefully on a buttered baking sheet. Slice two-thirds of the way down into the ring, at ¾-inch intervals. Twist each slice to the right so that the interior of the slice is now facing upwards. Let the ring rise in a warm, draft-free place until almost doubled in size. Brush the entire surface with beaten egg, then bake in a preheated 375° oven for 30 to 35 minutes until nicely browned. Cool on a rack before serving. *(From BEARD ON BREAD, by James A. Beard, illustrated by Karl Stuecklen. Copyright © 1973 by James A. Beard. Reprinted by permission of Alfred A. Knopf, Inc.)*

Baking Sheets

You may call them cooky sheets, but we prefer to say baking sheets in order to emphasize the fact that they have many and varied uses. Sheets serve for any baked product that does not take its outlines from a pan: certain formed rolls, croissants, flat breads like pita, and all other free-standing breads. Cream puffs and meringue shells are spooned or piped directly onto a sheet for baking, bottomless flan rings rest on them, and individual tart (or tartlet) pans are balanced on them for support.

SUPPORTING OPERATIONS

If you find yourself with an assortment of battered and inadequate cake pans, you will find that a superb baking sheet placed under the old things will immediately raise them to a higher level of performance, just in the way that a good baking sheet, placed beneath a soufflé dish, serves to boost the conduction and retention of heat. In the case of the soufflé the sheet will also catch any spills that might occur before they are baked forever, seemingly, onto the bottom of your oven.

CHOOSING PANS

You will want to buy baking sheets in pairs so that you can prepare a second batch of cookies for the oven while the first panful bakes. Of course, you will never use two sheets at a time, one above the other, because the cookies on the bottom sheet will be likely to burn in the heat reflected from the one above. The largest sheet that your oven will accommodate is the most efficient; measure the oven before you buy and remember to allow leeway of at least an inch on every side to permit the even flow of heat.

Heavy American Baking Sheet—The Best

9.3

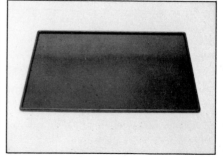

Heavy-gauge dark steel with silicone resin glaze; 16″ X 14″; rim ⅜″ wide.
$15.00

This sheet proves that even a classic can be improved upon. It is very similar to the French model (9.2). It is made of 22-gauge dark mild steel, but the manufacturer has solved the maintenance problem by applying a silicone glaze to both sides to eliminate rusting and prevent sticking; thus, the sheet is beautifully heavy and strong, retains heat well, but needs no special care except for very occasional commercial stripping and reglazing. All sides are rolled and beaded over a 5/16" welded rod; there are no sharp or unfinished edges anywhere. This is a beauty. It is an almost square 16" x 14" in size, and substantial in weight. Highly recommended: this Lockwood pan was the one our experts loved.

Lightweight but Good —Black-finished Sheets 9.4

Black-finished steel, 1/64" thick; 17" X 14"; rim ¼" wide. Also avail. 15½" X 12".
$2.39

It is a wonder that more manufacturers don't provide us with alternative sizes of pans. If you have a modern all-in-one range with a small oven, or an old-fashioned double-oven stove, this sheet in its mini-size may be the solution for you. It is thinner and lighter than the sheets we have been describing. Our experts were pleasantly amazed to find it didn't buckle and that it has a good surface and is, in addition, considerably less expensive than the heavier pans. The dull black finish, part of the metal and not a release (nonstick) coating, absorbs the heat and allows the cook to reduce oven temperatures and to cut baking time. In addition, no greasing is ever necessary. The manufacturer calls this surface Black Magic, and for the economy-minded buyer, the initial low price and the subsequent saving on fuel are indeed bewitching.

The ancient Saxons celebrated the rites of spring with the sacrifice of a sacred ox, or boun, which they dedicated to their goddess of light. This tradition was improved upon by symbolizing the sacrifice with a bun, marked to represent the horns of the boun; the form of the cake eventually became stylized as the hot cross bun. The early Christians adopted the design, along with the timing of the spring festival, in a new holiday, Easter.

Professional Perforated Bun Pan 9.5

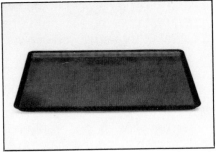

Heavy-gauge steel, dark tin coating; 24¾" X 17¾"; 1⅛" deep.
Max. Temp. 425 F. $15.00

If the current interest in convection ovens persists (Chapter 8), this may well be the prototype baking pan of the future. In cookery by convection, hot air is forced to flow all around the food, which is thus mainly cooked by the heat in the air surrounding it rather than by heat absorbed by the pan. And here is a pan, its entire surface perforated by tiny square holes, about seven to the square inch, permitting direct access of the heat to all surfaces of the dough. Professional bakers use it to bake formed doughs, such as those for buns and rolls: cooky or cake batters would drip through.

The pan itself is worthy of comment: it is made of tin-coated perforated sheet steel, with a heat-absorbing dark surface of tin oxide which the manufacturer calls Kolor Krust. Although the perforations help to reduce its heft, it still weighs a formidable 4¼ pounds. The construction is strong, and a 1⅛" rim all around prevents the contents from rolling off when finished. The baked product doesn't have to be transferred to a rack for cooling: the perforated tin serves as a rack if it is elevated from the surface upon which it rests. Between baking batches of sweet rolls, you could use it as a marvelously strong and attractive assembly tray for ingredients.

Jelly-Roll Pans

In a pinch, you could use a jelly-roll pan for baking cookies; our standards for both are pretty much the same, with emphasis placed on a sturdy, nonbuckling construction and a predarkened (or self-darkening) heat-absorbing surface. A nonstick (release) surface is not so important as it is in baking sheets, since, when you bake jelly rolls, you will always line the pan with waxed paper. On the other hand, anyone who tried to bake a Génoise or a sponge for petits fours on a baking sheet would wind up with batter all over the oven—which illustrates the rather obvious fact that the jelly-roll pan differs from the baking sheet in that it has sides an inch or so high. Only a soufflé-like batter with an integrity of form produced by beaten egg whites, such as Dione Lucas' Roulage Léontine in *The Cordon Bleu Cook Book,* p. 286, should be done on a cooky sheet, which will give a thinner, easier to roll, edge. For other recipes don't bother with second best when we have such attractive choices among the proper equipment. Unless you plan to make lots of petits fours, or unless you are accustomed to the assembly-pan technique of gathering cooking ingredients and want to reserve a pan for this purpose, you will need only one jelly-roll pan, so you might as well make it a good one.

Heavy Jelly-Roll Pan　　9.6

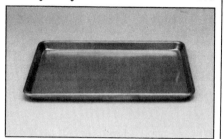

Heavy-gauge aluminum; 17⅞″ X 12⅞″; 1″ deep.
$8.00

The best of the standard pans is this approximately 18″ x 13″ heavy-gauge aluminum pan with a matte finish. It weighs about two pounds, heavy enough to feel solid in the hand. The edges are rolled over a rod, making for rigid construction, and the corners are rounded for easy cleaning and reinforced for strength. Altogether a satisfactory pan, and one which is used by many commercial bakers.

Predarkened
Jelly-Roll Pan　　9.7

Heavy-gauge steel, dark tin coating; 18″ X 12″, ⅞″ deep. Also avail. with standard tin finish.
Max. Temp. 425 F.　$5.50

If you can get it, this pan is slightly to be preferred over the preceding one. The weight and construction of both are about equal, but this one has the additional virtue of a predarkened tin-oxide surface laid over the sheet-steel base. The manufacturer calls this finish Kolor Krust; the dull, dark surface produces a uniform golden-brown color from the very first baking. As with all new tin-surfaced pans, this one should be greased heavily the first few times it is used. It also would make an excellent assembly tray for ingredients because of its exceptionally sturdy construction.

Loaf Pans

Either you bake bread or you don't—it's hard to imagine someone who is a little bit of a bread baker. If you don't, then one glass loaf pan will take care of your needs when you make the occasional pound cake or meat loaf or pâté. But if you do make bread—and these days, more and more people do—then you can scarcely have enough pans to hold the variety of loaves you will produce. There are small pans for fruit breads and larger ones for your daily bread. You ought to get at least two pans of each size, since most recipes are for more than one loaf. The magic of bread dough is that it can take on so many forms; the same mass of living dough can be made into a free-standing loaf on your baking sheet, or a proper sandwich bread in your covered bread pan, or a dozen rolls in your muffin pan. Once you learn the special feel of a dough fit for rising, you can vary the shape as you will.

FREEZING BREAD

Many of the best cooks take advantage of the fact that bread dough, either unbaked or preferably half-baked, freezes well, and arrest it in its course in order to have an ever-ready supply of bread for baking. They either wrap and freeze the dough before its last rising, or bake the loaves for half the time specified by the recipe. Once the shape of the half-baked loaves is set, they freeze the bread in its pans, and, once it is frozen, take it from the pans, wrap it in aluminum foil, and return it to the freezer. Then, when they want freshly baked bread, they defrost it and finish the baking on a baking sheet or directly on the oven rack.

BREAD BONUSES

We all know that it's marvelous to have homemade bread in the house. The bonuses are many—not least the sensual feel of the living dough itself and the smell of yeast dough baking. People who are interested in pure foods bake their own bread because it is nearly impossible to find commercially made bread which has not had preservatives added to it.

A final word of encouragement: don't be afraid. Women have baked bread for their families for centuries, and they weren't all fabulous cooks. A dough retarded by a slight chill will eventually rise, given enough time, some tender loving care, and a little improvement in its environment.

RAISIN AND NUT BREAD

This can be baked in two loaves with a mixture of raisins and nuts in both or with raisins in one loaf and nuts in the other. It is a good, all-purpose bread, which is enhanced by the extra sweetness of the honey and raisins. It toasts well; it is delicious cut thin, buttered well, and served with tea or coffee; it makes interesting sweet sandwiches when filled with chopped nuts and fruits, chopped figs, or even chopped olives and nuts; and it is also very good with marmalades of various kinds.

[2 loaves]

1 package active dry yeast
2 tablespoons honey
½ cup warm water (100° to 115°, approximately)
½ stick (¼ cup) butter, cut in small pieces
1¾ cups warm milk
5 to 6½ cups all-purpose flour
1½ to 2 teaspoons salt
½ cup raisins, or to taste (see note below)
½ cup chopped walnuts, pecans or unsalted peanuts; coarsely chopped filberts; or almonds, or to taste
Melted butter (optional)

Dissolve the yeast in the water with honey and allow to proof. Warm the butter in the milk, and add to the yeast mixture. Stir in the flour, mixed with the salt, 1 cup at a time, beating well with a wooden spoon after each addition. When the dough becomes rather stiff and difficult to stir, turn out on a floured board. Knead, adding small quantities of flour, until the dough is soft, velvety, and elastic. (It should spring back when pressed with the fingers and blister easily.) Shape the dough into a ball, place in a buttered bowl, and roll around to coat with butter on all sides. Cover tightly and let rise in a warm, draft-free place until doubled in bulk.

Punch the dough down. Turn out on a floured board and let rest for 5 minutes, then knead in the raisins and chopped nuts.

(If you are making one raisin loaf and one nut loaf, divide the dough into two equal pieces, and knead in the extra ingredients separately.) When the nuts and raisins are thoroughly amalgamated in the dough, cut it in half and shape into two loaves. Place in two well-buttered 9 x 5 x 3-inch bread pans, and allow to rise until doubled in bulk, or until the dough comes up above the tops of the pans.

Bake in a preheated 400° oven 25 to 35 minutes, or until the loaves sound hollow when tapped on the bottom with the knuckles. Remove from the tins and allow to bake on the rack in the oven for several minutes more to add color and texture to the crust. (For a tenter crust brush the loaves with melted butter just as you bring them out of the oven.) Allow them to cool on racks before slicing.

NOTES

1. It is better if the raisins have soaked in a little warm water or some Cognac for an hour or so. I sometimes add a tiny bit of cinnamon or nutmeg, too, because I like these flavors with the raisins.

2. These loaves freeze well, and will keep in plastic bags in the refrigerator for several days.

(From BEARD ON BREAD, by James A. Beard, illustrated by Karl Stuecklen. Copyright © 1973 by James A. Beard. Reprinted by permission of Alfred A. Knopf, Inc.)

Black Steel Loaf Pan 9.8

Black baker's steel; 10″ X 5″; 3½″ deep; 2¼-qt. capacity. Also avail. 12″ or 14″ long.

$6.50 ▲ $11.00 ▲

Current talk among bread-makers is that black steel pans have some special magic, producing a crust of unparalleled crispness, a crumb baked evenly all the way through. This is not a myth; here is the pan to try it with: a very heavy, sturdy, rectangular loaf pan hand made in black baker's steel. It was stamped out of a single sheet of metal, with the sides then folded up and welded together at the seams, the raw top edge rolled over a frame made of a heavy bent wire. Do not be surprised when you find that this pan is coarsely finished; function, not beauty, is the standard. A good quality pan: you can also have it in the 12″ and 14″ lengths.

Wearever Seamless Aluminum Pan 9.9

Heavy-gauge aluminum, 1/16″ thick; 8½″ X 4¼″; 3⅛″ deep; 1½-qt. capacity.

$12.45

If you know the Wearever brand only through the lightweight cookware sold in ordinary hardware and five-and-ten stores, you should be introduced to this manufacturer's professional line. This heavy aluminum loaf pan is of the type preferred by professional bakers and test kitchens. A single aluminum sheet fully 1/16″ thick is molded without seams to form a high-sided rectangular pan, 8½″ x 4¼″ and 3⅛″ deep, with rounded corners which are exceptionally easy to clean. The finish on the pan is dull and smooth, similar to that on many refrigerator ice-cube trays; the manufacturer calls it Aluminite, and it contributes to the ease of cleaning. This sturdy pan is as suitable for meat loaves and nut cakes as for bread baking. Heavy and needing little care, it's well worth its rather steep price.

Loaf Pan with Folded Ends 9.10

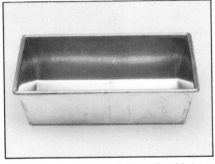

Heavy-gauge tinned steel; 8″ X 4″; 2½″ deep; 1-qt. capacity.

Max. Temp. 425 F. $5.50

Less expensive and just as good as the Wearever pan is this professional-quality pan of heavy-gauge steel coated with satin-finished tin from Lockwood. Its only disadvantage is that every ten years or so it might require retinning. The sheet metal is stamped out and then folded into a rectangular pan with seams in all four corners and tucks on the outside of the small ends; it looks like a neatly wrapped package. The rim is rolled over a heavy support rod, which keeps the pan rigid. Rather small in size, three of these pans are needed to hold the dough made by a standard two-loaf bread recipe: consider the advantages of having two loaves keeping fresh in the freezer while you eat the first. Don't forget to check your bread at an earlier stage of baking than usual. A smaller pan will allow you to reduce the baking time by as much as one-quarter.

Mini-Loaf Pan   9.11

Heavy-gauge tinned steel; top 5⅝" X 3⅛"; bottom
5" X 2½"; 2¼" deep; 2-cup capacity.

Max. Temp. 425 F.   **$4.25**

Also from Lockwood comes this mini-sized pan, not at all the frivolous product it might seem at first. Small loaves of bread stay fresher; freeze and defrost well; have more crust; can be varied, when a large recipe is used, by the addition of fruit, nuts, or wheat germ to portions of the dough; and they make marvelous gifts. Remember, too, heavy moist breads such as date-nut bake more evenly in small pans. Consider also a tiny meat or fish loaf for a family of two, and you will see the usefulness of this pan, a mere two cups in capacity. It is built rigidly for commercial bakery use, stamped out of a heavy-gauge steel sheet, heavily coated with tin, and then pressed into a seamless shape which cleans easily. The edge is rolled neatly around a steel rod. Try, if you can, to put toy cookware out of your mind and you will appreciate the many uses to which this tiny pan can be put.

Stoneware Loaf Pan   9.12

Stoneware; 10" X 4½"; 2¼" deep; 1¼-qt. capacity.

$6.50

With cookware, most of the time, we discover beauty in function. What a treat, then, to come upon this elegant and colorful stoneware loaf pan! It is hand-shaped at the Bennington Potters of Vermont, long a center of American pottery making. The matte-finished exterior comes in a choice of Williamsburg blue, yellow, or honey, while the inside has a white eggshell glaze. Smooth and heavy in the hand (it weighs more than two pounds), the high-fired vitreous stoneware absorbs and retains heat well. Like glass, it requires the lowering of baking temperatures by 25 F. in most recipes in order to avoid overdarkened crusts. It's too handsome to use for bread baking only and to leave in the kitchen; we think of it for the baking of meat, fish, and vegetable loaves which can then be brought proudly to the table.

Pyrex Loaf Pans   9.13

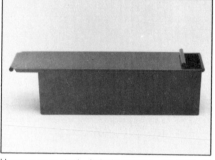

Pyrex glass; 8½" X 4½"; 2½" deep; 1½-qt. capacity.
Also avail. 9" X 5", 3" deep, 2-qt. capacity.

$1.70 ▲   **$2.10** ▲

The other side of the story; or, beauty is as beauty does. Since it was first patented by its developers at the Corning Glass Works in 1919, Pyrex Ware has proved so consistently useful and economical that it has acquired a homely attractiveness of its own. The glass conducts heat efficiently, and, colorless and transparent, it permits the cook to watch his dough achieve the crustiness characteristic of loaves baked in glass. All size information is stamped into the glass, so that whenever necessary you can easily check on the dimensions and capacity. Add to this the simple shape, the ease of cleaning, and the relatively low cost and wide availability of the product, and it is no wonder that Pyrex loaf pans in both sizes have been consistently popular for more than fifty years.

Breads are not good only for the stomach, as one can see from this prescription that Queen Elizabeth wrote out for Lord North's ear troubles: "Bake a little loaf of bean flour, and being hot rive it in halves, and into each half pour three or four spoonfuls of bitter almonds; then clap both halves to your ears at going to bed . . . and keep your head warm."

Pullman Loaf Pan   9.14

Heavy-gauge steel, dark tin coating; 13" X 4"; 4" deep; 2-lb.-loaf capacity.

Max. Temp. 425 F.   **$16.00**

Considering the quality of the bread available to us in supermarkets, it is no wonder that, when Americans bake their own bread, they tend to exalt crust over crumb (the technical term for the inside of the loaf). But for canapés, for toast, even for peanut-butter sandwiches, nothing is better than pain de mie, a long rectangular loaf of firm, close-grained, nearly crustless white bread. This can best be produced in a Pullman loaf pan, which has right-angled corners and a removable flat sliding lid. The cover keeps the air from touching the dough and forming a tough crust on any surface; it also forces the rising dough to swell uniformly into a flat top instead of making a bulging one. Our Pullman pan, made for use in commercial bakeries, is of heavy-gauge sheet steel with a dark preoxidized surface. The silicone glaze simplifies removal of the bread, and the construction is solid throughout, with riveted corners and a rim beaded around a wire rod. It is somewhat longer than the loaf pans we have been discussing—it will bake a two-pound loaf of sandwich bread. It's also useful for the production of pâtés and terrines, even icebox cakes, for large parties—anything in fact, which should be served in neat square slices. You probably don't have one; you probably should.

In the nineteenth century, all the fancies of architects were worked out with equal ornateness in pastry.
This illustration is from the Grand Livre des Pâtisseurs et des Confiseurs *of Urbain-Dubois.*

PULLMAN LOAF WHITE BREAD

(Elizabeth Susan Colchie)

This is a very firm, fine-grained loaf which is ideal for slicing, as it can be cut paper-thin without crumbling or becoming ragged or misshapen. It therefore makes a tidy sandwich or canapé as well as uniformly colored melba toast.

6 cups all-purpose flour
½ cup (1 stick) unsalted butter, cut into small bits
½ cup warm water (about 110 F.)
2 envelopes dry yeast
2 tsp. honey
1½ cups milk
3½ tsp. salt

In a large bowl combine the flour and butter, pinching them together with the fingertips to form tiny flakes. In a 2-cup measure stir together the water, honey, and yeast. Let the mixture stand for 5 minutes, or until it has doubled in volume. Meanwhile, warm the milk and salt to lukewarm, stirring to dissolve the salt. With a heavy spoon gradually stir the yeast mixture and the milk into the flour to make a rough dough. Knead the dough in the bowl for a moment to pick up all the flour.

Turn dough onto a floured board and knead it for 10 minutes. Butter a very large bowl (at least 4-quart capacity), form the dough into a ball, and turn it in the bowl to coat it with the butter. Cover the bowl with plastic wrap and place it in a draft-free place to rise for 2 hours, or until it has tripled in bulk. Punch it down, knead it for a moment on the floured board, and re-form it into a ball. Replace it in the bowl and cover it with the plastic. Let it rise again for 1½ hours, or until it has not quite tripled in bulk.

Again punch dough down and knead it for a moment on a floured surface. Slap and punch it to make a rectangle slightly longer than the Pullman pan (9.14). Beginning with a long side, tightly roll up the dough and pinch the open edge closed to secure the roll. Turn the ends under and place the dough, seam side down, in the ungreased pan, letting the ends of the dough touch both ends of the pan. Cover lightly with a towel and let dough rise in a draft-free place for about 1 hour, or until the pan is no more than three-quarters filled.

Fit on the cover and place the bread in a preheated 425 F. oven. Turn the heat down to 400 F. and bake the bread for 45 minutes. Remove it from the pan and bake it directly on the oven rack for 20 minutes. Let it cool completely on a rack, covered with a towel.

Crinkle-edged Tin Loaf Pan 9.15

Tin-plated steel; 11¾" × 5¼"; 2⅞" deep; 1½-qt. capacity.
Max. Temp. 425 F. $1.50

If you use your Pullman pan every week—and you very well might—you will scarcely use this unusually shaped French pan twice a year: but when you do reach for it, it will be the ideal solution to your problems. Think of nut breads; banana bread; steamed puddings; cold molds; or think of an elongated brioche. Halfway between a loaf pan and brioche tin, this pan has straight sides which flare out at both ends in deep folds resembling inverted drapery. In spite of the frivolous shape, the construction is quite serious; the pan is made of seamless sheet steel, lightly waffled over the entire surface for strength and coated with tin. Some care must be taken not to damage the thinnish tinning in cleaning and storing. The pan is generous in size, nearly a foot long and with a 1½-quart capacity. Not a necessity, but an amusing and inexpensive luxury.

Frame with Mini-Loaf Pans 9.16

Heavy-gauge tinned steel, 19½" × 9⅞" overall; each form 3⅞" × 2½", 1⅜" deep; capacity 6 fl. oz. per cup.
Max. Temp. 425 F. $24.00 ▲

This handsome pan is really a flat rectangular frame carrying twelve miniature bread pans, each holding a mere six fluid ounces. Is it also a tin for odd-shaped muffins? A tray for tiny meat loaves or meat pies? A means of baking a dozen small nut cakes for Christmas presents? It could be any or all of these. The frame is nearly 20 inches long overall, too big for some home ovens. It is of heavy, tin-coated sheet steel, with cups and frame securely interlocked at the top of the cups. There is a concealed support rod around the frame that makes for solid construction. This is not the sort of pan every kitchen must have; but if you do want one, this is the best.

White breads have been a status symbol for centuries. Early Greeks and Romans displayed loaves of fine wheat flour at feasts as a sign of their wealth, while peasants ate heavy, dark breads made of dense flour from whatever materials they had on hand: oats, peas, rye, barley, corn, millet, and even acorns. Juvenal, the first-century Roman satirist, summarized the status situation in his description of a dinner where the indigent guest is given "bread almost too hard to break . . . But for my Lord there is your soft snow-white bread . . . But hands off, remember: Respect the sacred bread-pan! And if you presume a tiny bit, there is someone standing over you to make you drop the bread. 'You saucy guest, kindly satisfy your wants from your usual tray and recognize the color of your bread.'"

The Danes use a rich variety of breads to make their smörrebröd (open sandwiches). In addition, they use bread dough to make crust for main-course tarts.

Baking Pans in Frames

As with the mini-loaf bread pans (above), other small pans may be grouped in small sets in a rigid frame. You will see the utility of this if you have ever tried to make popovers in custard cups or brioches in the traditional individual tin molds and, finding them hard to grasp with a potholder, burned your fingers and spilled the batter.

The problem can be solved in a makeshift way by setting the individual pans on a good baking sheet; even then, however, they tend to slide around if your hand is not precisely steady. Some culinary genius, some unknown Edison, some man whose wife had blistered her fingertips one time too many, eventually molded cups out of a cast-iron sheet or set individual molds securely into a sturdy metal frame.

The first pans we will deal with are mostly of cast iron; they include two pans for quick corn breads and one for that sublime twin of the Yorkshire pudding, the popover. Farther along, we will examine the full range of framed molds for baking quick breads: "quick" because they get their leavening power from other sources than from slow-acting yeast.

Here we have a modification of yet another traditional device for baking corn bread. Early Americans baked the bread in hot ashes, on stones, on boards, on the flat blades of hoes, or in three-legged "spiders" and other types of skillets; then they broke or cut the flat bread into individual portions. It must have been someone who loved the crusty surfaces of the corn-bread slices who invented this skillet with partitions, so that the unique corn-bread crust is on all sides of each slice. This skillet is made by Griswold, the oldest continuously existing brand name in American cookware. When the firm was founded in 1865, customers seasoned their own skillets by greasing and baking them in a slow oven; today Griswold does this at the factory, so that the pan comes ready to use and will maintain its seasoning, which prevents rust, with proper care. Like all cast-iron pans, it should be greased and preheated before it is filled. Unusually attractive to look at, the 9-inch skillet weighs a hefty 4½ pounds and has a hole in the handle for hanging.

Cast-Iron "Ear of Corn" Pan   9.17

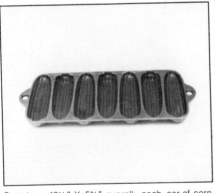

Cast iron; 13¼" X 5¾" overall; each ear-of-corn form 5½" X 1½", ¾" deep.
$6.00

Here is a set of joined miniature pans, shaped to make the traditional "ears of corn" baked in cast iron to come out crusty on the bottom and golden brown on the top. The thick cast iron holds the heat and prevents the crust from burning before the interior is cooked, while the individual size assures more crust—and crunch—per portion than is offered by corn bread baked in a conventional pan or skillet. You may have seen pans like these hanging in kitchens and antique shops; like Early American examples, this pan has seven ear-of-corn molds lined up in a heavy cast-iron rectangle with handles on both ends. It is preseasoned and ready for immediate baking after you grease and preheat it. If you aren't used to cast iron, the 4¼-pound weight may surprise you, but this pan is as much a classic as any quiche pan or soufflé dish.

Alexandre Dumas père, in his Grande Dictionnaire de Cuisine, *displays a Frenchman's low regard for an American favorite when he describes corn meal as a "kind of grain, formerly called Turkish wheat . . . from it there is made bread, which is digested with difficulty, which weighs on the stomach, and which is agreeable only to those persons with strong and robust constitutions."*

Skillet for Corn Bread   9.18

Cast iron; 9" diam.; 1" deep.
$5.50

Cast-Iron Popover Pan   9.19

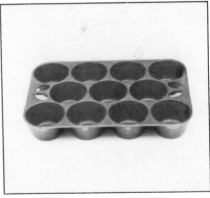

Cast iron; 11¼" X 7¾" overall; each cup 2½" diam. at top, 1½" at bottom, 1⅜" deep.
$7.25

Popovers, like corn bread, are traditionally baked in a cast-iron pan. The only leavening agent in these feather-light, hollow, crusty quick breads is very hot steam; tradition says that only a heavy iron pan which is sizzling hot when the batter is poured in will retain enough heat to create sufficient steam within the batter. Old standards change, and many cooks swear that ceramic custard cups or even aluminum cupcake tins will do just as well; Dolores Casella, in her book *A World of Breads*, maintains that popover pans need not in fact be preheated and the popovers can be

329

Continued from preceding page

started in a cold oven set at 425 F. Be that as it may, this heavy cast-iron, eleven-cup pan from Griswold remains a classic. Like all Griswold cast-iron products, it has been preseasoned at the factory and is ready for baking after the cups have been greased and heated.

To help you cope with the impressive 5¼ pounds the pan weighs, there are finger holes added on either end. Peek into your glass-windowed oven while the batter rises rapidly to a chef's cap, and you are likely to agree that this is still the best way to bake popovers.

The Non-Bread Pans

When is a bread not a bread? When it is richer than the bread we eat every day. When it is meant to be served alone with coffee or tea rather than throughout a meal. When it is of a distinctive shape as is, for example, kugelhopf, baked in the form often called a "Turk's head."

KUGELHOPF

This Middle European confection is a sweet yeast bread containing raisins and almonds. You can choose your own tale about the origin of this fluted cake, and, for that matter, your favorite spelling of its name—choices include kugelhopf, gougelhop, gugelhupf, gugelhopf. One favorite legend says that the shape was invented to commemorate the defeat of the Turkish armies which besieged Vienna in 1683. A cake shaped like the Sultan's turban was bound to be a success in the pastry shops of the day, along with the novelty of coffee. The beans were another trophy of the victory; coffee houses opened. Another story has it that the word *gugel* means monk's cowl and *hupf* means yeast; it is possible, therefore, that a molded round yeast bread, fluted in imitation of a monk's cowl, was an old Viennese favorite renamed in honor of the occasion.

The kugelhopf pan itself comes in a variety of swirled designs; it usually has a tube which conducts heat to the center of the dough and which also helps the yeast batter rise well by giving it something to cling to.

BRIOCHE

Brioche dough is golden and rich and eggy; it can be wrapped around a filet for Beef Wellington, or baked in a crown or a wreath or a cylinder or any other of the eight different shapes shown in *Larousse Gastronomique;* but traditionally it is baked in a round, flared, fluted mold and has a round knob of dough inserted into its top before the dough rises; this shape is the classic brioche à tête. For breakfast in Paris you are served a petite brioche à tête, which is a small version of the traditional cake. The large brioches with topknots, or grosses brioches à tête, can be baked in the tinned and ceramic pans shown here; miniature brioche tins are farther along in the chapter.

The traditional shape has certain advantages: the scalloped flutings indent the dough and provide a greater heat-conducting surface area than a smooth-walled pan would offer, and the flared sides permit the rising brioche to spread out generously.

Le maïs (corn) in all its stages.

Large Tinned-Steel Brioche Pan 9.20

Tinned-steel; 8″ top diam.; 3⅜″ bottom diam.; 3¼″ deep; 1¼-qt. capacity.
Max. Temp. 425 F. $1.50

First, the classic. This large tinned-steel brioche pan is properly fluted, generously flared, and is what French bakers have traditionally used to bake their rich, tender, cakelike breads. Aside from the standard shape and material, there are no amenities provided. The edges have simply been cut off—smoothly but sharply. No ornament interferes with the work of producing the perfect golden crust and feathery moist interior of your brioche. That it is a brioche tin will not prevent you from placing a ladyfinger in each flute, then filling the center with wonderful Bavarian cream which will quickly chill in the metal mold. Think of a splendid cold watercress mousse molded in this tin and served with a real brioche for a summer luncheon with a difference.

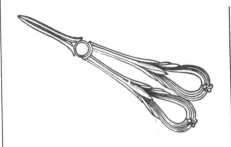

Small Tinned Turk's Head Pan 9.22

Heavy-gauge tinned steel; 6½" diam.; 3" deep; 5-cup capacity. Also avail. with tube.
Max. Temp. 425 F. $4.00

Another tubeless kugelhopf pan, this one is only about six inches across the top, so that you can bake a rich coffee bread in it without the help of a tube to conduct heat to the center. Of heavy-duty tinned sheet steel with a wire-reinforced rim, it is of professional quality. It can take frequent use without showing signs of wear, so you'll want to use it for baking other cakes as well as kugelhopf. Of excellent quality, it's a convenient size for a small family.

As Larousse Gastronomique *tells us,* "Faire une brioche" *is a colloquial expression translated as* "to make a blunder or a foolish mistake." *The provenance of the phrase is charming: musicians of the Paris Opéra were fined for wrong notes during a performance, the money being kept for the purchase of* brioches *for a subsequent informal party. At this gathering the wrongdoers suffered the indignity of wearing badges in their buttonholes in the form of brioches.*

Tube Pans

When you get right down to it, the kugelhopf and bundt pans are nothing but tube pans with a bit of fantasy added; the function of the central tube is the same for both the elegant versions and their simpler, unfluted sister, the tube pan. In all three the tube conducts heat into the center of a mass of batter which might otherwise remain somewhat uncooked. For this reason, the tube pan is especially suited for baking such heavy batters as those of nut cakes and pound cakes.

In addition, the sides of the tube give batters mainly leavened by air, such as those of angel, sponge, and chiffon cakes, a surface to cling to as they climb. The tube is seldom greased when baking these cakes, since greasing would give their fragile batters a less solid support to grasp. Other virtues of these pans: once unmolded from the tube pan, cakes of tender crumb can be cut more neatly when you don't have to worry about the fragile central point, and the cavity can be filled with a sweet filling, such as a pastry cream or a custard, for an elegant dessert.

California Brioche Pan 9.21

Ceramic; top diam. 8"; bottom diam. 3¾"; 2¾" deep; 5-cup capacity.
$6.50

This ceramic brioche pan is in the best European style; made in America, it is pleasingly less expensive than the imports. It does an excellent job in the oven if you remember to lower the heat by 25 F., as for glass and stoneware. A bright white, it is easily soaked clean in ordinary dishwashing solution. Treat it respectfully: if you avoid sudden temperature changes and remember that the material is not strong enough to withstand rough handling it will serve you well for making decorative cold molds, or even as a fruit or flower bowl, between bakings.

German Tinned Kugelhopf Mold 9.23

Heavy-gauge tinned steel; 8½" diam.; 3½" deep; 2¼-qt. capacity. Also avail. 6½" or 9½" diam.
Max. Temp. 425 F. $5.50 ▲

This pan, made in West Germany of heavy-gauge tin-coated steel, is the traditional mold for making kugelhopf. It is a pleasure to lift it and feel the weight, and the construction is excellent—the seamed, conical central tube is attached so well that it is hard to tell that it is a separate piece of metal. The tube extends half an inch above the pan's rim, providing a stand for the pan when it is turned upside down to unmold the cake. Well constructed, of classic design and made of heavy-gauge metal, this mold is nonetheless considerably less expensive than the Teflon-lined American versions of this pan. First class.

KUGELHOPF

1 envelope dry yeast
¼ cup water
1 cup plus 2 tbsp. granulated sugar
6 cups all-purpose flour
1 tsp. salt
1 tsp. vanilla
1 cup raisins
¾ cup slivered almonds
Grated rind of 1 lemon
2 eggs, beaten
½ cup melted butter
2 cups warm milk
4 tbsp. butter, for pan
Powdered or confectioners' sugar

Dissolve yeast in water and add 2 tbsp. sugar. Put mixture in a warm place for half an hour.

Sift flour into a warm bowl. Add 1 cup sugar, salt, vanilla, raisins, almonds, and the lemon rind and toss these ingredients to combine them. Make a well in the center of the flour, pour in the yeast mixture, and stir. Incorporate as much flour into the liquid as possible. Stir the beaten eggs and the melted butter into the dough, continuing to incorporate the flour, and gradually work in as much warm milk as you need to form a smooth dough.

NOTE: Depending on the moisture content of your flour, you may need much less milk. Use common sense. You are about to knead this dough, so do not add so much milk that it is sticky.

Knead the dough for 2 to 3 minutes. Knead dough gently—that is, do not pummel it as you would a nonsweet dough. The point is to distribute the yeast and start it working.

Dust the dough with flour. Place it in a large bowl. Cover it with a warm towel and let it rise in a warm place for 2 hours, or until it doubles in bulk. Turn the dough out on a floured board, punch it down, and shape it quickly into a ring. Put the ring in a well-buttered tube pan. (If using pan 9.23, have the pan warmed slightly to facilitate buttering. It usually requires about 4 tbsp. butter.) However, when doubling this recipe for pan 9.24, use 6 tbsp. Cover the pan and let the dough rise for 1 hour.

Bake the kugelhopf in a preheated 350 F. oven for about 1 hour. Test with cake tester (10.95). If the top browns too quickly, cover it with buttered paper. Unmold onto a rack (10.78) and cool.

Dust the cake with powdered or confectioners' sugar and let it stand overnight before slicing.

Handmade Stoneware Kugelhopf Mold 9.24

Stoneware; 12″ diam.; 6½″ high; 6-qt. capacity.
$24.00

This one is stunning. If you can forget expense and the fact that it is so big that you will use it only for large parties, then buy it because it is beautiful. Doris Licht-Tomono, an established potter, saw an early Pennsylvania Dutch mold and was inspired to produce this six-quart stoneware Turk's head. The unusual shape is similar to that of a mold illustrated in *Larousse Gastronomique*. A shiny glaze is applied to the surface, which is finished in pale earth colors. This mold has the excellent baking qualities and durability of ceramics produced by an expert in her profession; Licht-Tomono uses reduction stoneware firing, an extremely high-temperature kiln process, to produce an exceptionally durable stoneware. Enjoy the unusual shape, the caprice of the potter's adding a handle, the glaze, the sheer size of the thing. Then be appreciative of the fact that it works beautifully. See the recipe on this page.

Glass Kugelhopf Mold 9.25

Ovenproof glass; 9½″ diam.; 3½″ deep; 2-qt. capacity. Also avail. 7½″ diam., 1½-qt. capacity.
$18.00

Glass cookware tended until recently to be thick and heavy and all too obviously sturdy; here is a Jena glass kugelhopf mold from Germany which is surprisingly light in the hand and elegant to the eye, yet still perfectly suitable for use in the oven. It is made of thin glass and has gracefully swirled fluting and a smooth central tube. When the mold is inverted for cooling, it rests on the tube, which is about half an inch higher than the edges of the mold. The transparent glass makes us imagine jellies shimmering through, but these molds are perfectly oven-worthy as well as being suitable for cold molds.

Teflon-lined Bundt Pan 9.26
Teflon-lined Mini-Bundt Pan 9.27

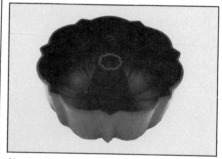

Aluminum with Teflon lining; 10″ diam.; 3½″ deep; 3-qt. capacity. Also avail. 9″ diam., 3″ deep, 9-cup capacity.

$8.00 ▲

A bundt is a German coffee cake of a denser texture and different form than a kugelhopf, although they are related confections. These bundt pans are made by the same manufacturer, with the traditional central tube. They are attractive and well made; the larger has been stamped out of a single piece of aluminum and is seamless. The thickness of the aluminum combined with the strength provided by fluting, makes the larger pan rigid, while the smaller pan is made of cast aluminum of exceptional strength, and is also available in formed aluminum like the larger pan. Both pans are lined with nonstick Teflon. There is a baked-on enamel exterior in a choice of colors; avocado, gold, tangerine, or white. The smaller, cast-aluminum pan comes without the enamel finish, too. (Remember that if a light color is chosen, baking time will have to be extended by about 5 minutes.) You could plan to use these pans as molds for cold foods since the space provided in the center of the tubed molds can be filled with fruit, a sauce, or other goodies.

COCONUT-ALMOND CAKE WITH CHERRIES

(Elizabeth Susan Colchie)

1 cup sweetened coconut, packed
    (3½ oz.)
½ cup blanched almonds,
    coarsely chopped
2½ cups all-purpose flour
¾ cup glacéed cherries (3½oz.)
1 cup (2 sticks) unsalted butter, softened
1¾ cups granulated sugar
5 eggs
1 teaspoon vanilla
1 teaspoon almond extract
1 tablespoon double-acting baking
    powder
¼ teaspoon salt
½ cup milk

Preheat oven to 350 F. Spread coconut and almonds on a baking sheet and toast them for 15 minutes, tossing several times, until coconut is lightly browned. Let cool and combine in bowl with ½ cup of the flour. In two batches grind the mixture in an electric blender until it is fine.

Heavily butter a bundt pan holding about 9 cups (9.27) and chill it for 15 minutes. Rinse the cherries in boiling water, dry them and slice them. Press them into the curves of the buttered mold and return pan to the refrigerator.

In the bowl of an electric mixer cream butter until light. Gradually add sugar, beating until light and fluffy. Add eggs, one at a time, beating well on high speed after each addition. Beat for 5 minutes. Add vanilla and almond flavorings.

Sift together the remaining 2 cups of flour, the baking powder, and salt into another bowl. Stir the dry ingredients into the creamed mixture, alternating with the milk. Fold in the coconut-almond mixture and spoon batter into the mold.

Bake in the center of the preheated 350° F. oven for 1 hour and 15 minutes. Invert mold on cake rack and cool for 15 minutes. Remove mold and cool cake completely.

Wrap cake tightly in plastic and let rest for at least 1 day at room temperature before serving.

The making of a cake was a long and arduous task before the development of modern culinary equipment and techniques. Sugar had to be pounded, flour dried and sifted, sheets of paper tied around hoops to make pans, and eggs and sugar hand beaten for 20 to 30 minutes to produce the proper consistency.

Professional Tube Pan   9.28

Heavy-gauge steel, dark tin coating; 8″ diam.; 3¼″ deep; 2¼-qt. capacity. Also avail. 10″ diam., 4-qt. capacity.

Max. Temp. 425 F. $11.00 ▲

Of impeccable quality, this professional baker's pan from Lockwood is made of tinned heavy sheet steel which diffuses oven heat rapidly through the batter. The tin has been predarkened to provide even browning from the first use, and a silicone release agent has been added to the surface. Since the bottom is not removable, you may, when the batter has no fat, want to use a paper liner. The central tube of this sturdily made pan does not extend higher than the walls, as some tubes do; for cooling after baking, the pan should be inverted over a funnel or bottle or on a rack, to provide air space beneath the cake. This is a deep pan, with a nine-cup capacity. Our experts agreed that this was the best product available in its class.

Le riz (rice).

SALLY LUNN

This is an old, old recipe for Sally Lunn. I like to bake it in a large tube pan and invert it. It makes a beautiful standing loaf that, when fresh, should be torn apart with forks rather than cut, to retain its lightness. Or, after cooling, it can be sliced and toasted. If you have some left, I recommend that you freeze it and use it sliced and toasted.

[1 ring loaf]

1 package actively dry yeast
⅓ cup sugar
½ cup warm water (100° to 115°,
    approximately)
½ cup lukewarm milk
1 stick butter, melted in the milk
1 teaspoon salt
3 eggs
3½ to 4 cups all-purpose flour

Combine the yeast, sugar, and warm water in a mixing bowl, and allow to proof. Add the milk, butter, and salt, and stir well to combine. Add the eggs and incorporate them well with a wooden spoon. Then add the flour in small amounts, and beat well with a wooden spoon after each addition. Make a stiff but workable batter, using up to four cups of flour if necessary. Cover the bowl, and let the batter rise slowly in a rather cool spot until doubled in bulk. Beat it down with a wooden spoon for about 1 minute. Scrape into a well-buttered 9- or 10-inch tube pan, and again let the batter rise—this time to the very top of the pan.

Bake in a preheated 375° oven 45 to 50 minutes or until the bread is dark and golden on top and sounds hollow when rapped with your knuckles. Turn out on a rack to cool, or serve warm, if you prefer, with a sweet butter.

(From BEARD ON BREAD, by James A. Beard, illustrated by Karl Stuecklen. Copyright © 1973 by James A. Beard. Reprinted by permission of Alfred A. Knopf, Inc.)

Ceramic Mold for Savarins 9.29

Ceramic; 8¼″ overall diam.; tube 4¼″ wide, 2½″ high; 5-cup capacity.
$6.50

This ovenproof ceramic savarin mold is as handsome as the large ceramic brioche mold also shown in this chapter (9.21); and no wonder, since they both come from the same manufacturer in California. Of easy-to-clean white ceramic, fluted like the brioche pan, it would make a natural companion for it. A savarin pan has a larger central tube than other tube pans—here it is a generous four inches across, making the pan resemble a ring mold to a degree. Although savarin dough resembles that of baba more closely than brioche dough, brioche and savarin doughs are similar enough so that one could be substituted for the other in using this pan. Think of baking one large batch of dough in two pans and then serving the brioche with butter and jam for breakfast and the savarin—kirsch-soaked, glazed, and decorated, with its center filled with whipped cream—for dessert at dinner.

Three-in-One Springform 9.30

Tinned steel; 10″ diam.; 2½″ deep; 3-qt. capacity. Also avail. 9″ diam.
Max. Temp. 425 F. $5.00 ▲

A springform pan is *not quite* a number of things: it's not quite a kugelhopf mold, not quite a tube pan, not quite a layer-cake pan. What it *is* is a superb solution to the problem of removing delicate cakes like torten and cheesecake from the pan without breaking them. The rim is separate from the bottom, which fits neatly into a groove running around the base of the rim. The sides spring free automatically when a clamp is released, and the cake can be removed without having to invert it. This four-piece springform set is made in West Germany of superior-quality tinned steel. The flat bottom is waffled with tiny circular depressions which add strength to the disc (the cakes made in a springform pan tend to be heavy). Of the other two interchangeable bottoms, one has a central tube and the other a mold-like ring of twirled fluting, making the pan in effect a semi-kugelhopf mold.

The *Génoise* cake, which the French borrowed permanently from the Italians, is based on eggs, which are heated during beating to increase their ultimate volume. Eggs did not figure as a raising agent in cakes until the seventeenth century. Earlier baked sweets were fairly dense affairs. Legends suggest that honey-sweetened discs of cake (introduced by the Romans) were broken over the heads of brides in Old English marriage ceremonies. Friends gathered the fragments as good-luck tidbits. Modern wedding cakes most often have their foundation in the Génoise, which is firm enough to support the wildest confectionary fancy, but delicate enough to stand eloquently alone when occasion requires.

ORANGE GENOISE CAKE
(Elizabeth Susan Colchie)

½ cup (1 stick) unsalted butter
1 tsp. vanilla
1 tbsp. grated orange rind
6 eggs
1 cup granulated sugar
1 cup all-purpose flour

Butter and lightly flour the bottom of a pan, keeping the sides clean. (Greasing and flouring won't be needed if you use the pan we suggest.)

Melt the butter over low heat, set aside, and let it stand for a few minutes. Skim off and discard the foam on top. Slowly pour the clear yellow liquid —the clarified butter—into a cup, discarding the sediment remaining in the pan. Stir in the vanilla and orange rind.

Blend together in a very large bowl the eggs and ½ cup of the sugar. Place the bowl over a saucepan of barely simmering water and heat the mixture until it is very warm, stirring frequently and thoroughly.

Meanwhile, sift the flour and salt together and return them to the sifter.

Preheat oven to 350 F.

With an electric beater beat the eggs, now off the heat, for 5 minutes at high speed. Gradually add the remaining ½ cup of sugar, continuing to beat the mixture at high speed for about 10 minutes, until it resembles a soft, glossy meringue.

Sift in about a quarter of the sifted flour and salt and delicately fold it into the eggs with a rubber spatula. Fold in about a third of the clarified butter, then alternate additions of flour and butter, working quickly and lightly.

Turn the batter gently into the pan. Bake the cake in the preheated 350 F.

Layer-Cake Pans

Bread becomes cake at a point somewhere near, but not precisely at, the point where yeast is eliminated. That said, we must admit that the distinction is blurred, and that such quick breads as popovers and corn bread contain no yeast, whereas kugelhopf and savarin obviously do. Still, the pans we have been discussing are nearly all for use with yeast-assisted doughs which have unique qualities—that is, for bread doughs. Now we must consider pans in which the batter rises through somewhat less potent agencies—air trapped in beaten eggs, or gas formed by baking powder or by baking soda plus acid—

the familiar round or square cake pans which produce baked batter suitable for stacking in layers.

QUALITY COUNTS

Since it cannot be said too often, let it be said again: cheap baking pans are no bargain. The best-quality and most practical layer-cake pans are to be found not in retail stores but in establishments that supply professional bakeries. These pans, which are manufactured to meet the demanding requirements of professionals, are offered to domestic consumers in this catalog. Metal cake pans of professional quality cost more than the five-and-ten kind, but they do a better job of baking, and they last, and last, and last—unlike the flimsy pans most often found in retail shops.

PAN SIZES

Recipes for cakes specify the proper pan size; the batter should fill the pan at least half but no more than two-thirds full. You can use round and square layer pans interchangeably if you remember that a square pan holds approximately the same amount of batter as a round pan whose diameter is one inch larger than the side measurement of the square pan; an 8-inch square pan holds roughly the same amount of batter as a 9-inch round pan, and so on. Check dimensions by measuring across the top, from inside to outside rim. Although square layers can be stacked, they are most often chosen for single layers when a wedge would be too fragile a shape to serve well; for example, the denseness of nut-studded brownies and the looseness of brown Betty make them more practical to serve in squares, not wedges.

Buy layer-cake pans in pairs or in threes. Buy extra-deep pans (9.32) in pairs if you want to split the cakes to make four or six layers.

oven for 55 minutes, or until the center is slightly springy to the touch.

Invert the cake on a rack and let it rest in the pan for 1½ hours. Run a thin metal spatula around the sides of the pan and unmold cake onto the rack. Let it stand for several hours before slicing it horizontally into two or three layers and filling and frosting it.

Alternatively, cool the cake, wrap it tightly in plastic, and refrigerate it for several days, or freeze it for as long as several months, before use.

Professional Layer Cake Pan   9.31

Heavy-gauge tinned steel; 9″ diam.; 1½″ deep; 6-cup capacity. Also avail. 6″, 7″, 8″, or 10″ diam., 1½″ deep, and 8″ or 9″ diam., 2″ deep.

Max. Temp. 425 F. $3.50 ▲

Here are two sizes of professional-quality cake pans from Lockwood: two well-made pans of seamless, tin-plated steel, noticeably heavier in the hand than any similar pans that are available. Both should be in the kitchen of any serious home baker; in fact, we recommend that you buy two or three each. Each pan is 9 inches in diameter; one is 1½ inches deep and the other, 2 inches deep. Buy both, and by all means do not ignore Lockwood's 3-inch-deep pan below, until now generally not available to the home baker.

Lockwood's Deep Layer Pan   9.32

Heavy-gauge tinned-steel; 8″ top diam.; 7¼″ bottom diam.; 3¼″ deep; 10-cup capacity.

Max. Temp. 425 F. $11.00 ▲

Our experts were delighted to discover that this third Lockwood layer-cake pan is now available to the home baker. It is 8 inches across and fully 3¼ inches deep, the prototype of the kind of heavy, deep cake pan heretofore unavailable to the amateur cook, who tended to use a tube pan when a tall cake was wanted. The pros know, however, that this pan, large as it is, works, because nonyeast cakes rise better in one deep pan than they do in two or three shallow ones. Served whole, the finished product is an impressive sight. Or the cake can be split with a spatula into two or more layers and filled with butter cream: and *voilà*, you have a tall layer cake with two rather than four—or six—possibly tough crusts. In addition, the uneven balancing of slightly mounded layers on one another is eliminated forever. Even if your cut is slanted, the finished product, reassembled with care, will be as shapely as the original cake. This method works better

Continued from preceding page

with the French recipe for the Génoise (see recipe, above), a close-grained, egg-raised cake, than for American layer-cake recipes, which produce cakes too moist or crumbly to be sliced horizontally with success. You don't need to grease this pan, or any other, when you use them for Génoise or other rich doughs that climb to rise.

Brownies are almost a staple in our chocolate-consuming country. Chocolate, their main ingredient, did not exist in the solid form in which we know it until the nineteenth century. Earlier recipes for confections now flavored principally by chocolate were immensely varied and usually contained great quantities of spices. An eighteenth-century Spanish preparation suggests the following: "Take 700 cacao nuts; of the finest white sugar half a pound; of cinnamon 2 ounces; of Mexican pepper 14 grains; of cloves half an ounce; of vanillotes, half a scruple, or in their stead 2 ounces of aniseseeds; and of annotto the bulk of a nut; to these some add a little orange flower water and a grain of musk."

Square Layer-Cake Pan 9.33

Heavy-gauge tinned steel; 8" square; 1½" deep; 6-cup capacity.
Max. Temp. 425 F. $6.00 ▲

Buy a square layer-cake pan to match your round ones of the same depth, and you can take your choice of round or square cake without having to adjust the recipe. Remember that an 8-inch square pan holds the same amount of batter as a 9-inch round pan, and so forth—very simple. Of course, you won't choose square pans when you want to stack and ice the layers; corners are

famously unreceptive to frosting, and the child who gets a center piece will feel forever cheated of his just portion of icing. Rather, use these pans for single layers of gingerbread, or for brownies, or for cakes, frosted only on the top, to carry in the pan to picnics. This tinned pan of heavy steel is of the same professional quality as the round Lockwood pans (9.30): same material, same weight, same impeccable construction. The corners are rounded for easy cleaning.

Square Pyrex Baking Pan 9.34

Pyrex glass; 8" square; 2" deep; 2-qt. capacity.
$2.10 ▲

Ovenproof glass baking pans offer a versatility that tinned layer-cake pans do not. This 8-inch square Pyrex glass dish, 2 inches deep, will not only bake a panful of brownies, but it can also be used for baking single-layer cakes and a wide variety of meat and vegetable dishes. Acid foods will not affect the glass as they would the tin coating of a metal pan; nor can the glass surface be scratched as easily as a thin layer of tin. For these reasons the glass pan is commendable. Remember that it must be treated with respect for all its relative toughness: care must be taken not to drop it, place it over direct heat, subject it to sudden extreme temperature changes, or scour it with abrasives that will scratch its surface. Because it transmits heat more quickly than tinned ware and because it holds heat longer after being removed from the oven, it should be used at baking temperatures about 25 F. lower than temperatures given for baking in metalware.

BANANA PECAN CAKE WITH CARAMEL FROSTING

(Elizabeth Susan Colchie)

CAKE:

1 cup pecan meats
2 medium bananas
1 tablespoon lemon juice
1½ cups all-purpose flour
1 teaspoon baking soda
1 teaspoon double-acting baking powder
⅛ teaspoon salt
½ cup (1 stick) unsalted butter, softened
½ cup granulated sugar
½ cup dark-brown sugar, packed
2 eggs
1 teaspoon vanilla
¾ cup buttermilk

FROSTING:

1 cup light-brown sugar, packed
6 tablespoons (¾ stick) unsalted butter, cut into bits
¾ cup heavy cream
½ teaspoon vanilla

Make the cake: Preheat the oven to 350 F., then toast the pecans on a baking sheet for 15 minutes stirring occasionally. Chop nuts coarsely. Thoroughly mash bananas with lemon juice (you should have ¾ cup). Sift flour, baking soda, baking powder, and salt into a bowl. In another bowl, cream the butter with an electric mixer until light. Gradually, add granulated and dark-brown sugars and beat until light and fluffy. Add eggs, one at a time, beating well. Add bananas and vanilla. Add flour to creamed mixture alternately with buttermilk. Fold in nuts and turn into a buttered 8"-square baking pan about 1½" deep (9.33).

Bake in the center of preheated 350 F. oven for 55 minutes, or until a cake tester (10.95) or skewer inserted in the center of cake comes out clean. Cool for 15 minutes in pan. Unmold onto wire rack and cool completely.

Make frosting: In a small saucepan combine light-brown sugar, butter, and cream. Stir over moderate heat to dissolve sugar. Raise heat to moderately high and boil mixture without stirring until it reaches the soft-ball stage (238 F.). Pour into bowl and stir in vanilla. Place bowl in a larger bowl of cold water and beat until frosting thickens to spreading consistency. Spread frosting on the cooled cake and let it cool thoroughly. If you wish, this cake keeps several days wrapped in plastic to keep. Wrap and seal well and freeze.

Large Shallow Aluminum Pan	**9.35**

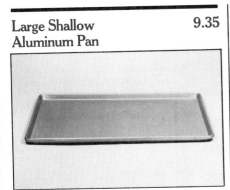

Heavy-gauge aluminum; 17⅞″ × 12⅞″; 1″ deep; approx. 2 lbs.
$8.00

A reprise here: look again at our 9.6, the heavy aluminum jelly-roll pan 1 inch deep. It is, after all, a cake pan of professional quality, and it needn't be limited to producing jelly rolls. The finished cake can be divided, for example, into three sections and stacked with a filling between them; or it can be cut into squares and diamonds for iced petits fours, particularly if it is a Génoise (see recipe).

Professional Mary Ann Pan	**9.36**

Heavy-gauge tinned steel; 7″ diam.; 1¾″ deep at sides, 1″ deep at center.
Max. Temp. 425 F. $4.00

Specialty Pans

Things somehow seem to taste different when they look different: if you don't believe it, try to get a four-year-old to eat a candied cherry which has been dyed green. And can anyone claim that the first bite of the ear of a chocolate Easter rabbit is not a different matter from the first bite of a Hershey bar? The pans which follow are generally meant to be filled with the same batters as flat layer-cake pans; but they mold the batter into such shapes as hearts, rabbits, or eggs, any of which is bound to influence our reaction to the finished product. In these highly specialized pans, standards are the same, but not so readily met, as for other bakeware: the pan should be thick, weighty, easy to clean, and effective in the diffusion of heat. Because of the multitude of corners and ridges in these specialty pans, great care must be taken to grease and flour them properly; release (non-stick) linings help to a point, but are not the panacea they at one time promised to be. Nothing can take the place of a good metal pan, well greased.

Here is an excellent-quality tinned steel Mary Ann pan made by Lockwood for commercial bakeries. The shallow depression in the top of the finished cake is formed by a raised circular platform in the bottom of the round pan: miraculously made without seams, the pan is easy to clean and has great strength. Only 7 inches in diameter, this pan will make a cake for six; the portions will be small but nonetheless satisfying because of the richness and sweetness of the topping. This heavy-gauge pan has all the good qualities which we have come to expect from Lockwood products.

Fluted German Obsttortenform	**9.37**

Tinned steel; 9½″ diam.; 1¼″ deep; 3-cup capacity. Also avail. 9″ or 11″ diam.
Max. Temp. 425 F. $2.25

MARY ANN PAN OR OBSTTORTENFORM

Think of the rather flat butter cakes you have seen in German bakeries: richly golden of crumb, with a shallow, level depression holding something like a wealth of apricot-glazed peach slices. At the other extreme there are the cellophane-packaged cakes which appear in supermarkets at strawberry time, with wide depressions meant to be filled at home with strawberries and whipped cream. The pan for making these distinctively shaped cakes is called a Mary Ann pan when it doesn't have fluted edges and an obsttortenform when it does.

Continued from preceding page

The Germans call this pan an *obsttortenform,* meaning fruit tart mold. It is not intended for the kind of fruit tart with fluted sides that is made with pie pastry; rather, it uses the attractive tart-pan fluting to ornament the sides of a single-layer cake with a circular depression for the fruit in its top. The pan is stamped out of a single sheet of metal, so it is seamless; the bottom has diamond-patterned waffling which adds strength to the thin metal—the whole pan is a generous size—enough to make a cake to be topped with strawberries for eight.

Obsttortenform with Bundt Fluting   9.38

Enameled heavy aluminum with Teflon lining; 10¼″ diam.; 1½″ deep; 1-qt. capacity. $4.49

The sides of this adaptation of the traditional German obsttortenform have bundt-type (or rather wide) fluting in place of the narrower ridges encircling the classic pan. This American version of heavy aluminum with a baked-on enamel outer finish comes in white, yellow, orange, or avocado. The white Teflon lining makes for easy release of the finished cake. The same size, if not so elegant, as the classic pan above, it is an interesting variation in design, easy to use and to clean.

The cake made in the "saddle of venison" mold made its debut when venison was a commonly served meat. The almonds stuck into the cake are meant to imitate lardoons, or the small strips of pork fat which were inserted into actual saddles of venison with a larding needle before roasting.

"Saddle of Venison" Rehrücken Mold   9.39

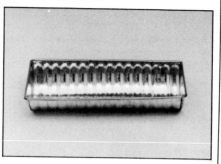

Tinned-steel; 10½″ X 4½″; 2½″ deep; 1-qt. capacity.
Max. Temp. 425 F. $4.25

The German word *Rehrücken* is literally "roe's (deer's) back," and, by extension, "saddle of venison." In delicious fact it is chocolate log cake with crosswise ribbing made by the mold, richly iced and studded with almonds, an Austrian delicacy of long standing. After feasting on a genuine saddle of venison, visibly and generously larded with strips of fat to add succulence to the meat, a successful hunter could enjoy the joke of a look-alike dessert; for the unsuccessful hunter, the *Rehrücken* could conceivably offer consolation. A flat one-inch "backbone" runs the length of the pan to balance it, and the sixteen "ribs" make it easy to divide the cake into uniform slices. The classic cake, made with ground almonds instead of flour, is so rich that the portions should be small. Use the pan for other cakes, too, or for bread.

This is Flaubert's description of the wedding cake that marked the transformation of Emma Rouault into Madame Bovary: "The base was formed of a cube of blue pasteboard representing a temple with a portico, colonnades, and statuettes of white plaster, with, between them, little alcoves studded with stars of gold paper. Above this was a castle made of Savoy cake, surrounded by tiny battlements of angelica, almonds, dried raisins, and oranges cut into quarters. Finally, at the very top, which depicted a green meadow complete with rocks, lakes composed of jam, and little boats made out of nutshells, was a small Cupid balancing himself on a chocolate swing, the two uprights of which were topped with natural rosebuds by way of finials."

LAZY DAISY CAKE

This cake has many names, but for the past forty years has generally been called by the "lazy" name. It does not have as fine texture as some other cakes, but is meant to be served warm with a fruit sauce or topped with a boiled frosting. This was one of those cakes to be made when you suddenly discovered there was no dessert or unexpected guests arrived just before meal time.

2 eggs
1 cup sugar
1 teaspoon vanilla
1 cup sifted all-purpose flour
¼ teaspoon salt
1 teaspoon baking powder
½ cup milk
1 tablespoon butter

Beat the eggs until light and beat in the sugar gradually until the mixture is light and thick. Beat in the vanilla. Sift the flour with the salt and baking powder. In the meantime heat the milk just to scalding (when a slight scum begins to form) with the butter. Add the dry ingredients to the beaten eggs alternately with the hot milk. Stir just to mix. Turn into a greased 9-inch square baking pan and bake in a pre-heated 350-degree oven about 30 minutes or until the cake springs back when pressed lightly in the center. Serve iced or plain while still warm, or with fruit, chocolate or caramel sauce, or ice cream. The cake may also be eaten cold with whipped cream, icing, or fruit.

(From AMERICAN COOKERY, by James A. Beard, illustrated by Earl Thollander. Copyright © 1972 by James A. Beard. Reprinted by permission of Little, Brown and Company.)

Victorian valentine.

This most elegant of decorated cakes could conceivably be made with the various sizes of pans and the decorating equipment we show you. Today, however, simpler decorations would be more feasible and more to our taste. This imposing structure, as much a monument to the confectioner's art as to true love, was made for the wedding of the Princess Royal of Britain to Prince Frederick William of Prussia.

Rabbit, Lamb, and 9.41, 9.42, 9.43 Santa Claus Molds

Cast aluminum, 1/16″ thick; 10″ tall; 10″ long; 3½-cup capacity.

$9.95

Cast aluminum, 1/16″ thick; 7″ tall; 11″ long; 3-cup capacity.

$9.95

Cast aluminum, 1/16″ thick; 10″ tall; 8″ wide; 1-qt. capacity.

$9.95

These molds for a rabbit, a lamb, and a Santa Claus are not—definitely not—the lightweight molds which you may have seen in your five-and-dime store, molds whose lack of quality is an absolute guarantee of failure of your efforts to use them. Put aside any prejudices: these are substantial cake molds worthy of investing in for festive occasions. They are heavier than you would expect, made of aluminum 1/16″ thick; each is cast in two pieces. To use the molds, you grease and flour both halves generously, and then pour in a Lady Baltimore cake batter (or other batter for a firm-grained, high-rising cake) up to the rim of the bottom half (expansion takes place into the top half). Stir the batter gently with a spoon to remove any air bubbles, and then put on the top of the mold. A steam hole permits steam to escape during baking. When the finished cake has cooled for about 15 minutes in the pan, you turn it over and remove the solid section first. Your creativity, of course, is further expressed in the decoration. General directions for the use of the molds are included by the manufacturer; for additional instruction see *The Joy of Cooking*. Each mold holds from three to four cups of batter.

We assume nowadays that cupcakes were so named because they are baked in individual cup shapes, but that is not the case. Cupcakes were originally baked in a full-sized pan, and the cake got its name because the ingredients were measured by the cupful. A typical cupcake recipe comes from the 1901 Picayune Creole Cook Book, and is a variant of the classic "one-two-three-four" cake, as is the recipe for what the 1896 Fannie Farmer described as "cup-cake" baked in "individual tins." It calls for 1 cup butter, 2 cups sugar, 3 cups flour, and 4 eggs. It was baked in a round pan. Today any batter baked in cupcake molds can honorably carry the title of cupcake.

CUPCAKES

½ cup (1 stick) unsalted butter
1 cup granulated sugar
2 tsp. vanilla
2 eggs
2 cups all-purpose flour
¼ tsp. salt
3 tsp. baking powder
½ cup milk

Preheat oven to 375 F.

In a large mixing bowl, cream the butter and sugar together with a large wooden spoon or an electric beater. When the mixture is light and fluffy, beat in the vanilla and then the eggs, one at a time.

Sift the flour, salt, and baking powder together. Add the dry ingredients alternately with the milk to the creamed mixture. Beat until smooth.

Pour batter into cupcake tins lined with paper cups and bake in the preheated oven for 12 to 15 minutes, or until a cake tester or a toothpick emerges dry from the center of a cake.

Remove the cupcakes to a wire rack to cool.

Breton Cake Mold Set 9.45

Six heavy-gauge tinned-steel molds; diam. from 3½″ to 7½″; depth from 2¼″ to 2¾″; 1½- to 9-cup capacity.

Max. Temp. 425 F. $95.00

An elegantly pleated headdress from Brittany inspired this French mold, a set of six fluted pans of graduated sizes ranging from 1½ to 9 cups in capacity. All but the smallest have flat bottoms, and the individual cakes, once baked, are intended to be stacked into a grand construction for a wedding cake. These French pans are of heavy-tinned steel each seamed up one side, and will produce a perfectly stunning cake for any ceremonial occasion.

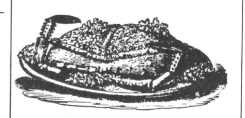

Muffin Tins and Other Miniatures

Until around 1850, breadstuffs were leavened either with yeast, a time-consuming process, or by air trapped in well-beaten eggs, or with saleratus (baking soda) or pearl ash (potassium carbonate). Cream of tartar was next often to be used with the baking soda. Then a Boston firm introduced the first version of baking powder—foolproof, as the other leaveners were not, and quick, unlike yeast. And quick is the operative word where muffins are concerned. The batter is mixed lightly and quickly for maximum tenderness and baked in small cups in a fraction of the time required for batter in large pans. Muffins are served at once, hot from the oven. And, of course, they are so tempting that they are consumed quickly.

CHOOSING A PAN

The special talent of the muffin pan is to produce individual portions without the problem of coping with numerous individual pans. Choose sturdy pans; the frame should be well-constructed with beaded, rounded corners, and the cups should be seamless. If you plan to bake muffins in large quantities, use two pans that can sit side by side on one oven shelf with ample air space around them, not touching one another or the walls of the oven. The pans should not be so large that you are tempted to put them one above the other on different shelves, an arrangement which invites burning or, at the least, uneven baking. We have an assortment of pans with cups of different sizes and shapes, as well as unique pans, like those for madeleines and miniature Mary Anns.

Some are more profoundly moved by muffins than others: "Mr. ———, who loved buttered muffins, but durst not eat them because they disagreed with his stomach, resolved to shoot himself; and then he eat three buttered muffins for breakfast, before shooting himself, knowing that he should not be troubled with indigestion."
Topham Beauclerk (1739-1780)

These, of course, were what we call "English muffins," and were not baked in but on tins. However, a contemporary New Englander might feel the same way about blueberry or cranberry muffins.

A beautifully decorated baba.

Lockwood 12-Cup Muffin Tin   9.46

Heavy-gauge tinned steel; 13⅞″ X 10⅝″ overall; each cup 2¾″ diam., 1⅜″ deep; capacity 3½ fl. oz. per cup. Also avail. with 24-cup frame.

Max. Temp. 425 F. $12.50 ▲

This is one baking pan you can't do without. A dozen regular-sized round muffins, cupcakes, rolls, or babas can be baked in this sturdy professional-quality muffin tin. Each cup holds 3½ ounces, is seamless, and is bonded securely to the frame in an interlocking construction which is rather beautiful to see. The pan is of tin-coated steel, with the outer edge of the frame rolled neatly over a concealed rod; the whole affair measures 13⅞″ by 10⅝″ and weighs a solid 1½ pounds. If you can buy only one muffin pan, buy this one.

Lockwood 24-Cup Muffin Tin   9.47

Heavy-gauge tinned steel; 17¼″ X 11¾″ overall; each cup 2-1/16″ diam., 1⅛″ deep; capacity 1¾ fl. oz. per cup.

Max. Temp. 425 F. $16.50 ▲

Baking Pans for Batters

Continued from preceding page
Of the same construction as 9.46, this pan has twice the capacity in terms of numbers of cups, but it turns out smaller muffins—the cups hold just half as much batter. The frame is far less than twice the size, measuring only 17¼″ by 11¾″ and so would allow much better use of your oven space than two of the twelve-cup pans. A good buy, but measure your oven before acquiring it.

Jumbo Muffin Pan 9.48

Heavy-gauge tinned steel; 17¼″ X 13⅛″ overall; each cup 3½″ diam., 1¼″ deep; capacity 6 fl. oz. per cup.

Max. Temp. 425 F. $21.00

In this one, both the frame and the individual cups are large: for hearty eaters who prefer jumbo-sized muffins, it turns out a dozen cakes, each fully 3½″ in diameter. A heavy pan, weighing more than 4 pounds, it is so large that you should measure your oven to see if it will accommodate the 17¼″ by 13⅛″ frame before you buy. (And don't forget to allow for air space around the pan!)

Pan for Square Cupcakes 9.49

Heavy-gauge tinned steel; 13¾″ X 10½″ overall; each cup 2¾″ square, 1¼″ deep; capacity 4 fl. oz. per cup.

Max. Temp. 425 F. $20.00

A good professional's pan, this one holds a dozen cupcake forms roughly in the shape of cubes. Each cake, measuring 2¾″ by 2¾″ and 1¼″ high, is a perfect individual portion, rather like an oversized petit four. At children's parties, think of the delighted faces if you served each child his own cake, with his own rosebud and his own candle. Or imagine serving these cakes, decorated like children's blocks, at a baby shower. The pan, measuring 13¾″ by 10½″, is as beautifully made of tin-coated heavy steel as the rest of the Lockwood series.

Pan for 12 Miniature Muffins 9.50

Tinned steel; 9¼″ X 7″ overall; each cup 1⅝″ diam., ⅝″ deep; capacity ¾ fl. oz. per cup.

Max. Temp. 425 F. $2.40

As good as the preceding pans, even though they are lighter because the cakes are so small, this tin from a different manufacturer makes twelve muffins which would be too small to satisfy most appetites. It is most useful for baking miniature tea cakes, cupcakes or plum puddings for parties. Each form holds only about three-quarters of a fluid ounce. Use it to make ladylike nibbles for teatime or a small indulgence for dieters, and what a marvelous gift it would be for a child who is interested in baking.

Fruitcakes have so long been associated with British baking that they have almost become a synonym for it. The remote ancestor of these cakes was a Roman confection made of barley mash, dried fruits, nuts, honeyed wine, and pomegranate seeds which was called satura. From the name of this delicacy is thought to have evolved the word satire, describing a heady literary mixture of sweet and sour elements.

Tin for Mary Ann Miniatures 9.51

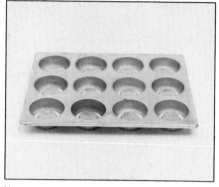

Heavy-gauge tinned steel; 16¾″ X 12⅝″ overall; each cup 3⅜″ diam., 1½″ deep at sides; capacity 5 fl. oz. per cup.

Max. Temp. 425 F. $20.00

A final offering from Lockwood in muffin and cupcake pans: a Mary Ann tin for twelve miniatures, each with the distinctive shallow depression on top for fillings. Top them with raspberry-glazed apricots? Four grapes and a cherry apiece? Or a mound of berry-filled whipped cream, making nontraditional strawberry shortcake? They would be nice, too, for gingerbread, served warm with a topping of spiced whipped cream.

A Breton cake (Gâteau Breton), with layers in place and decorated.

Jumbo Muffin Pan
Pan for Square Cupcakes
Pan for 12 Miniature Muffins
Tin for Mary Ann Miniatures

Pan for Miniature Bundt Cakes
Langues de Chat Pan
French Ladyfinger Pan
French Madeleine Tin

Pan for Miniature Bundt Cakes   9.52

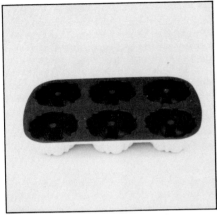

Enameled cast aluminum with Teflon lining; 14″ X 9″ overall; each cup 4″ diam., 2″ deep; capacity 8 fl. oz. per cup.
$8.95

We have here a frame with six miniaturized bundt tube pans, made of one solid piece of cast aluminum, a full 2 pounds in weight, with a baked-on enamel coating in green, yellow, or orange and a Teflon nonstick lining for easy unmolding. It is heavily made and easy to clean, and could be used for almost any cake batter. A final drizzle of thin icing is sufficient for the unmolded cakes: think of spice cakes with a lemon glaze. Each of the forms holds a full eight ounces and will serve two people plentifully, with the probable exception of adolescent boys.

Langues de Chat Pan   9.53

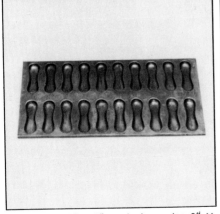

Black steel; 13″ X 7″; each depression 3″ X ¾″.
$21.00

One shape, two batters: a spongelike dough makes ladyfingers or biscuits a cuiller, while a dryer batter becomes the cooky which the French call langues de chat, the Italians, lingue di gatto. Whether lady's fingers or cat's tongues, this strong rectangular sheet with indentations for the cakes makes fully 20 of them, each one only 3 inches long; that is, rather too small to use for lining a mold, but precisely the right size to serve at an elegant tea. The pan is 13″ x 7″, made of darkened steel with edges folded down at right angles to the sheet to form a rim for it to rest and cool on.

French Ladyfinger Pan   9.54

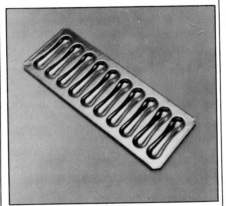

Tinned steel; 12½″ X 4⅞″ overall; each ladyfinger form 3½″ long.
Max. Temp. 425 F. $6.98

We looked all over for a pan which made shapely ladyfingers or cat's tongue biscuits of a size suitable for lining a dessert mold as well as for nibbling with tea or wine. What we finally found was this simplest possible pan from France. Measuring 12½″ x 4⅞″, it is stamped out of a single sheet of lightweight metal, and holds 10 shallow depressions, each 3½″ long, into which ladyfinger batter is to be spooned or piped from a pastry tube. The edges of the rectangle are folded over once, and the corners have simply been snipped off. This pan breaks all the rules we have set for good bakeware up to now, but it is nonetheless designed to make ladyfingers in the proper way. The relatively thin but sufficiently strong metal will heat up and cool off quickly, providing the rapid cooking essential for these ephemeral cakes.

While the barbaric early Europeans were barely subsisting on raw foods, *the miraculous Egyptians were producing elegant meals with the help of complicated utensils, making yeast-raised bread, and creating the first ovens. An inscription of the Twentieth Dynasty lists thirty breads and cakes in common use.*

French Madeleine Tin   9.55

Tinned steel; 14⅛″ X 7⅜″ overall; each form 1¾″ wide X 2¾″ long, ½″ deep; capacity ¾ fl. oz. per form.
Max. Temp. 425 F. $5.50 ▲

The Gingerbread Boy aside, the cooky with the greatest literary clout is undoubtedly Proust's famous madeleine. One wonders about the extraordinary number of cakes in forms inspired by the madeleine's scallops; perhaps, Darwin-like, we must conclude that they all come from a common ancestor, a small sweet cake cooked in actual scallop shells. This French pan for baking madeleines is really quite beautiful. Unlike American muffin pans, in which the cups are made separately and then joined to the frame, this pan is stamped out of a single sheet of metal. The edges are not beaded around a rod, but simply folded to the underside. Simply made as it is, the pan is utilitarian, with all the rigidity and ease of handling that it needs; like the ladyfinger mold (above), it is made of lightweight metal in order to heat and cool off quickly. The individual forms—there are 12 of them—hold only ¾ fluid ounce each; you will probably want two of the pans. And don't ignore the decorative possibilities of the molds—hang them, when not in use, as bas reliefs on your kitchen wall, one facing in and one facing out.

MADELEINES

2 tbsp. butter, softened, to grease molds.
2 eggs
¼ cup granulated sugar
½ tsp. vanilla
½ cup all-purpose flour, sifted
¼ cup unsalted butter, melted and cooled to room temperature

Preheat oven to 375 F. Grease madeleine molds with the 2 tablespoons of softened butter.

Place the eggs, sugar, and vanilla in the large bowl of an electric mixer. Beat until a thick ribbon drops from the beater when it is lifted from the bowl. The mixture should triple in bulk.

With a rubber spatula fold in the flour, a tablespoon or two at a time. Fold in the melted butter in the same fashion.

Place the mixture in a pastry bag fitted with a large plain tube. Fill the buttered madeleine pans two-thirds full and bake the cakes in the preheated oven for 8 to 10 minutes, or until delicately browned.

Remove madeleines from the molds to a wire rack to cool.

Yield: about 12.

Tin for Scallop-shaped Cupcakes   9.56

Tinned steel; 12″ X 9″ overall; each form 2⅜″ diam., ¾″ deep; capacity 1 fl. oz. per form.
Max. Temp. 425 F. $4.00

The French madeleine is shaped something like a scallop shell, but not quite; rather, it is modeled on some sort of imaginary elongated mollusk. This teacake tin from England also has scallop-shaped forms, but realistic ones. As with American pans, the molds were made separately and joined securely to the frame. Each form holds one fluid ounce. A well-made pan, it comes with 12 forms to a frame.

Tiny Scalloped Cake Forms from England   9.57

Tinned steel; 5¾″ X 4″ overall; each cup 1½″ diam., ⅝″ deep; capacity ½ fl. oz. per cup.
Max. Temp. 425 F. $2.00

Another set of miniatures based on a large original, this is a frame holding tiny scalloped forms which resemble shallow tubeless bundt pans. When the children help out in the kitchen, extra batter from a large cake can be poured into these miniature tins, each holding a mere ½ fluid ounce. This is not a toy, however, but a strong, well-made pan of English tin-coated sheet steel. A thrifty but elegant way to use up extra cake batter.

Individual Brioche Molds   9.58

Tinned steel; each tin 3¼″ diam. at top, 1½″ diam. at bottom; 1¼″ deep, capacity 5 fl. oz.
Max. Temp. 425 F. $.75

So strong is the power of design that not only is brioche a specific yeast-leavened bread enriched with eggs and butter; it is just as much a shape—a flared and fluted shape with a squat topknot. The two sides of classic brioche tins from France on this page fulfill all our needs for baking petites brioches à tête. One is 2¾″ in diameter and the other is 3½″; they are of light-weight tinned steel and are inexpensive. Remember that recipes for petite brioches à tête are for batches of from one to three dozen, so that you should have at least a dozen pans. Try these pans, too, for individual jellies or fish molds. The thinness of the tin coating makes it necessary to keep the pans well oiled between bakings.

Six Individual Brioche Tins   9.59

Tinned steel; 2¾″ diam. at top, ½″ diam. at bottom; 1⅛″ deep; capacity 2 fl. oz. Also avail. 3½″ diam.
Max. Temp. 425 F. $1.95 per set

Here is a set of six tinned French molds for individual petites brioches à tête. They are similar in size to the classic large brioche molds but are slightly different in design: in this set, each channel of the fluting is rounded at the bottom of the mold, as in some jelly molds or the Breton cake mold (9.45). Each tin is 3¼″ across the top and is stamped from a single piece of tinned sheet steel with a grained, silvery appearance. The set comes in a resealable plastic bag which can be used for storage. These are heavier gauge than the preceding brioche tins. If you choose these tins you should have at least two sets.

Brioche, according to Alexandre Dumas père, the great romancier-gastronome, was originally prepared with Brie as an ingredient, hence its name. Some etymologists maintain that the old words bris *(break) and* hocher *(stir) combined to form the noun, but the connections are rather vague.*

Tin for Scallop-shaped Cupcakes
Tiny Scalloped Cake Forms from England
Individual Brioche Molds
Six Individual Brioche Tins

Miniature Mold with Spiral Fluting
Stainless Steel Baba Molds from Italy
Individual Savarin Mold

Miniature Mold with Spiral Fluting — 9.60

Tinned steel; 2¾″ diam.; 1¼″ deep; 1½ fl. oz. capacity.
Max. Temp. 425 F. $2.00 Set of 6

This German tin mold only 2¾″ in diameter somewhat resembles large kugelhopf and brioche molds, but it lacks the central tube of the first, and the fluting has a strong spiral swirl from the center which makes it different from the usual brioche pan. It is of tin-coated sheet steel and (a warning) tends to be sharp on the edges. You will probably use it for small cupcakes and brioches.

Stainless-Steel Baba Molds from Italy — 9.61

Stainless steel; 2″ diam. at top, 1⅛″ diam. at bottom; 2″ deep; 3 fl. oz. capacity.
$3.00

Here is a small stainless-steel baba mold imported from Italy for making babas au rhum. The seamless mold resembles nothing so much as a large whiskey shot glass — only two inches

tall, it is perfectly plain, with slightly flaring walls. When making babas, the mold should be filled only halfway and the dough allowed to rise to the top before baking; while it is in the oven, the dough will rise still more to make the puffed cap which is characteristic of the baba. This is a mold you could also use for making timbales, small tarts filled with savory meat or vegetable mixtures. A dozen of these small pans would be a good number to have.

King Stanislaus I Leszczynski of Poland, exiled in France in the early eighteenth century, is generally credited with the creation of the first baba au rhum, which he first named Ali Baba after the hero of his favorite book, A Thousand and One Nights. His invention was actually an embellishment of the kugelhopf (recipe), a sweet yeast cake with raisins and almonds, which he soaked in rum and flamed. It became the specialty of a fashionable Parisian bakery, had a great success, and was soon dubbed simply "baba." In a somewhat similar evolution a cake born from the same dough was bathed in a kirsch syrup, christened "the brillat-savarin" in honor of the great gastronome, and soon found its name shortened to the familiar "savarin."

Individual Savarin Mold — 9.62

Tinned steel; 3⅛″ diam.; ¾″ deep; 2 fl. oz. capacity.
Max. Temp. 425 F. $.75

Savarin dough is rich with eggs and butter; it is baked in either a savarin pan or a baba mold, and then drenched in a syrup—often orange and rum—and given an apricot glaze. The manufacturer calls this shallow ring mold an individual savarin pan, but it

will scarcely allow for the rising necessary for true savarins. You could bake pound-cake batter in it and proceed with the drenching and glazing as for savarins, or make wonderfully creamy individual caramel custards. Whatever the use it is put to, this sturdy little mold is formidable: made of tinned metal, it has a beaded rim, an absolutely firm shape, and a small (two ounce) capacity.

Carême, the nineteenth-century culinary genius, explained the origin of the French name for small cakes, petits fours, in this way: cookies and little cakes were originally baked in a slow oven, a petit four, after the large cakes were done and the oven temperature had lowered. The thinnest and most delicate of petits fours—cornets, cigarettes, tuiles, langues de chat, and vanilla and lemon wafers—can all be baked on the heavy professional-quality sheets we recommend without the usual hazard of uneven browning.

"You wouldn't believe what a fine job it is to bake rolls, and especially to bake bread. My poor old dad had a bakery, so I know all about it. You see, in making bread, you've got two or three important secrets which are practically holy. The first secret is how to make the yeast; you have to leave it in the trough and then there's a sort of mysterious change takes place under the lid; you have to wait until the flour and the water turn into live yeast. Then the dough is made and mixed with what they call a mash-ladle; and thats a job that looks like a religious dance or something of that sort. Then they cover it with a cloth and let the dough rise; thats another mysterious change, when the dough grandly rises and bulges and you mustn't lift the cloth to peep underneath—I tell you, its as fine and strange as the process of birth. I've always had the feeling that there was something of a woman about that trough. And the third secret is the actual baking, the thing that happens to the soft and pale dough in the oven. Ye gods, when you take out the loaf, all golden and russet, and it smells more delicious than a baby, its such a marvel—why I think when these changes are going on, they ought to ring a bell in the bakeries, the same as they do in church at the elevation of the host."

"The Needle," from Tales from Two Pockets, *by Karel Capek.*

345

There is a mystique to making pastry: we are told that any literate person who owns a cookbook can learn to make a cake, but if we want to make pastry, then we had better watch someone who has already been initiated and copy what he does. In this pastry making resembles bread baking, where we are also advised to make ourselves apprentices before striking out on our own—perhaps it all has to do with touch, with the fact that our hands get directly involved in the manufacture of both kinds of dough. Pastry needs a "light touch": an expression that really means "do it quickly or you will melt the fat" and end up with tough pastry. Therefore, most of the directions for baking superior pastries have to do with keeping the dough cool yet workable.

This chapter will deal first with the various baking pans that impose a shape on pastries, from deep-dish pies to tiny barquettes; and later it will discuss the variety of utensils we use for preparing, shaping, finishing, and decorating pastries.

Baking Pans for Pastries

Pastry doughs are partly or entirely shaped before they are baked, they rest lightly within or upon their pans as they become firm during baking, and they are either freed to stand on their own, often as containers for fillings, or are brought to the table in the dishes in which they were baked. Doughs are handled in other ways, too: puff paste is rolled into sheets, baked in strips, and then cut into rectangles and filled with crème pâtissière to become napoleons; or it is cut into triangles, rolled up, and baked to appear as the lightest of croissants.

CHOOSING PANS

As for materials, completely precooked shells to be filled later with materials that require no further baking—such as fresh fruit tarts or lemon chiffon pies—are best baked in metal. Tart and pie shells partially baked and then filled to complete baking of the crust and the filling do better in ceramic, which retains heat well without burning the crust or its contents.

We prefer aluminum or earthenware to tinned steel for holding those pies that must be baked at first in an exceedingly hot oven—often as hot as 450 F.—so as to set the crust before the filling has time to make the unbaked crust forever soggy. You will recall, however, that tin melts at around 449 F., so, for obvious reasons, tin-plated pans are not suitable for baking pies.

In general, pie plates are serviceable rather than attractive, which is unfortunate, since pies always come to the table in their pans. (However, see our handsome 10.3 and 10.4.) Frontiersmen are said to have carried meat pies in their pockets; it is possible that crusts, like men, were tougher in those days.

Professional-Quality Pie Pan 10.1

Aluminum; 9″ diam.; 1¼″ deep. Also avail. 9″ diam., 1″ deep and 10″ diam., 1¼″ deep.
$3.35

A solidly made, high-quality pie pan, manufactured for use in commercial bakeries and, until recently, not available to the home baker. This pan has the familiar slope-sided shape for American pies and comes in both 9″ and 10″ sizes. It is seamless, pressed from a single sheet of standard-gauge aluminum, with a dull satin finish the manufacturer calls Aluminite. The finish is stain-resistant and retains heat more efficiently than do the shinier aluminum surfaces.

Pie Pan with Juice-Saver Rim 10.2

Stainless steel; inside diam. 9″; outside diam. 10¾″; 1¼″ deep; 1⅜″ high.
$4.00

Spilled sugary juices of pies that have bubbled over will bake onto the bottom of your oven in a hideous scorched wad, seemingly welded forever to the oven surface, so that the next time you bake potatoes you will get the ghostly odor of burnt apples. The juice-saver rim of this

THE PROBLEM OF SERVING

Like a turtle, a double-crust pie carries its house on its back, the sweet or savory filling resting snugly within its own edible shell—the crust itself is half pan, half food. But in thinking of pies, we find ourselves also considering open-faced American pies, not to mention tarts, flans, quiches, and tartlets. There is a problem of serving many of these—what do you do with your beautiful pastry once it is baked? In America, the pie is baked in a slope-sided pan which is necessarily used, sometimes apologetically, for serving—if the pie were lifted from its container, its sides would collapse. Europeans make tarts to be served both in the pan and free-standing. Quiches and other tarts are often brought to the table in their pans, which have, amazingly, been made as attractive as possible. Flans—the same as tarts except for the manner of their baking—are formed and baked in ugly steel rings placed on a baking sheet, whereas tarts are often baked in utilitarian loose-bottomed metal pans that are little better looking than the rings. But, once cooled, flans and tarts are placed for service, standing on their own, on elegant china serving plates. And the tiny tartlets are always removed from their pans: their appeal lies as much in the pastry as in the filling, and they are meant to be admired as a whole.

AMERICAN PIE PANS

Pies are American—"as American as apple pie," remember?—forever linked with those holidays which are especially patriotic. Mince and pumpkin for Thanksgiving; cherry for the Fourth of July and for Washington's Birthday. Pies go back to our earliest history—there is even the apocryphal story of the Massachusetts woman who was burnt as a witch because her accusers would not believe that she could get a filling between two crusts without resorting to the black arts. The tale is not true, of course, and absurd to anyone who knows that the early settlers had known and enjoyed a multitude of pies in England. But it's true that there is something especially American about a pie, and also about the familiar slope-sided pie pan, different from British or French pans. Ours commonly come in 8", 9", and 10" sizes, standardized not for the sake of the pastry—the same amount of dough can be rolled to fit a pan of any of these sizes—but so that the recipes for fillings will make the right amount. We suggest that you buy two pans of whatever size you think you will find the most useful, so that you can offer two different pies at a meal. (Pie pans are measured from the inside of the top of the rim to the opposite side.) Then get a deep-dish pan, too, although you can substitute a cake pan, round or square, or a casserole for this one. "Deep" can be defined as up to 3 inches—the deepest pies are those with a biscuit crust. A deep-dish pie usually has a top crust only.

Besides the most usual American pies with two crusts, there are also those made with a single bottom crust and no topping—consider custard pies, including pumpkin—or with a topping of lattice or streusel or meringue; and those with a single top crust over a deep fruit or meat filling.

pan solves that problem. To a standard-shaped pan is affixed a wide rim which dips into a shallow trough and then flares upward. If an overflow of juice burns in the trough, it is a cinch to remove because the pan is made of stainless steel, one of the easiest of metals to clean: a rinsing in hot running water and a swipe with a sponge usually does the trick. This pan is heavy and strong and the design concept is practical—it's nice to think of someone taking thought for the poor pot-washer, not to mention the oven-cleaner.

Bennington Pie Plate 10.3

Stoneware; inside diam. 9¾"; outside diam. 10¾"; 1⅝" deep; 5-cup capacity.
$6.00

We usually count ourselves lucky if a pie pan is not downright ugly, and hope that our guests will notice the elegant lattice crust and not the old thing in which the pie comes to the table. But here is a pie plate from Vermont's Bennington Potters which is beautiful: all elegant gentle curves and a variety of superb glazes: one is white freckled with brown inside and out, similar to another in tawny beige; two are available in blue or brown on the outside and white on the inside. This plate's beauty lies in its simplicity of design and color, but also in its practicality; the dish is easy to clean, unaffected by the foods we put in it, and amazingly resistant to chipping. The sides rise half an inch higher than those of the average pie pan, inviting you to bake deep-dish pies in it. This pie plate is beautiful enough to justify its cost—if you don't want to take our word for it, please note that examples of this pottery's work have been praised by the Museum of Modern Art.

TARTE A L'OIGNON—ONION TART

Carol Cutler, author of *Haute Cuisine for Your Heart's Delight,* has devised a crust with lowered cholesterol content as well as a spicy filling. You may use either pie crust recipe.

LOW-CHOLESTEROL ROLLED PIECRUST

This piecrust needs no chilling, so it can be stirred together and be ready at a moment's notice.

2 cups flour
1½ teaspoons salt
¼ cup cold skimmed milk
½ cup polyunsaturated oil

Sift the flour and salt into a mixing bowl. Pour the milk and oil into a cup, but do not stir. Add the liquid all at once to the flour and stir lightly with a fork. Form the dough into a ball, divide in half, and flatten each portion slightly.

Dampen the working surface and place on it a 12-inch square of waxed paper. (The water keeps the paper from slipping.) Put one portion of the pastry on the waxed paper and cover with another 12-inch square of waxed paper. Roll the pastry. When the dough reaches the edges of the paper, it is the right thickness for the piecrust.

Peel off the top sheet of paper, fit the dough, paper side up, into the pie plate. Peel off the other sheet of paper. Fill the pie and repeat with the other portion of dough, fitting it over the filling. Trim and flute the edges.

LOW-CHOLESTEROL STIR-AND-BAKE PIECRUST

This pastry will not have the smooth texture or yellowish color that most do. In fact, it will appear slightly lumpy and somewhat gray. Never mind, it all bakes out beautifully.

2 cups flour
1 teaspoon salt
1½ teaspoons sugar
½ cup polyunsaturated oil
¼ cup water

Place a sifter in a pie pan and sift the dry ingredients directly into the pan.

Mix the oil and water in a small bowl and slowly pour over the dry ingredients, stirring with a fork as you do. When all the flour has been dampened, beat it a few seconds with the fork.

Press the pastry to line the bottom and sides of the pan. Chill for at least 30 min-

utes, then push the firm dough further up the sides and make a fluted top by pinching the dough between thumbs and index fingers. The crust can be chilled again, or baked immediately.

ONION TART FILLING

Calories per serving 320

I have never liked the classic French version of Onion Tart. It comes out as just a variation on a *quiche,* that rich concoction of eggs, cream, and cheese, and the onions are almost incidental to the custard. In Alsace, however, where much of the cooking has Germanic overtones, the onion tart is another matter. There the onion dominates and only enough custard is used to hold the whole thing together.

In this recipe, the cholesterol-rich custard is replaced by a thick purée of cream of mushroom soup, skimmed-milk cottage cheese, and egg whites. This basic binder can be used for other vegetable tarts, too. It's fun to experiment with leeks, mushrooms, broccoli, asparagus, or cauliflower.

Don't be afraid of the quantity of onions. The long slow cooking reduces the onions' bulk to one quarter and also turns the strong flavor into a sweet one. The tart looks its best when fresh out of the oven and nicely puffed up, but it can be reheated with no loss of flavor.

This is an excellent main course at lunch. In smaller portions (8 to 10 servings) it also makes an unusual first course for dinner. For 8 servings:

1½ pounds onions, thinly sliced
¼ cup polyunsaturated oil
1 garlic clove, crushed
1 bay leaf
2 tablespoons flour
1 teaspoon meat extract (BV)
1 teaspoon salt
½ teaspoon pepper
2 tablespoons polyunsaturated oil
2 egg whites
1 cup condensed cream of mushroom soup, undiluted
½ cup dry skimmed-milk cottage cheese
¼ teaspoon freshly grated nutmeg
1 9-inch unbaked pie shell [above]
2 tablespoons grated low-fat cheese, or Parmesan

Slice the onions thin. Slowly heat the ¼ cup of oil in a heavy pot. Add the onions and mix thoroughly until the onions are well coated with the oil. Cover and simmer over very low heat for about 15 minutes, stirring often. Add the crushed garlic and bay leaf. Continue cooking for another 30 minutes, still

covered and still stirring often. Remove the bay leaf, sprinkle on the flour, and mix well. Add meat extract, salt and pepper; mix thoroughly. Cover and simmer for another 5 minutes. Cool slightly.

Meanwhile, put into the blender the 2 tablespoons oil, egg whites, mushroom soup, cottage cheese, and nutmeg; blend until you have a smooth purée. Spoon ½ of the purée into the cooked onions and mix thoroughly. Repeat with the other ½ of the purée. Taste for salt, pepper, and nutmeg; correct if necessary. Spread the mixture evenly into the pie shell and sprinkle on the grated cheese. Place in 375° oven for 35 to 45 minutes, or until nicely browned on top and slightly puffed. Serve hot, but not superhot.

Blue Pottery Pie Plate   10.4

Stoneware; 10½" diam.; 1¼" deep; 1¾-qt. capacity.
$15.00

It conjures up notions of Tom Sawyer, or a Norman Rockwell painting, or a book by Louisa May Alcott: it looks like a pie dish to set on a windowsill in some mythical American town, holding a fruit pie to cool while it taunts small boys with its aroma. This deep pie dish is made of a highly glazed stoneware; we have it in a rich bright blue shot through with white, but it is also available in white-speckled yellow or green, all of them quite attractive. It is a product of the Stangl Pottery Works, a fine Pennsylvania craft shop since 1805. There is a faintly raised band around the outside of the rim. This is not a plate for deep-dish pies, but rather a fairly deep pie dish: it is 1¼" deep and measures 10½" across the top. It is not inexpensive, but baking a blueberry pie in it would create a rhapsodic harmony, while a cherry pie would be a near-patriotic composition in fruit for red, pastry for white, and this plate for blue. It is fabulous for those pies whose shells are partially prebaked and then rebaked with the filling—it keeps the crust from burning—and for pies that enter the oven with both crust and filling uncooked.

From Kate Greenaway's Apple Pie, *1886.*

Pyrex Pie Plates 10.5

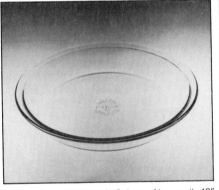

Pyrex glass; 9″ diam.; 1¼″ deep. Also avail. 12″ diam. **$1.20** ▲

No matter how often we bake in **Pyrex Ware**, it always seems a miracle; when milk tumblers and ashtrays shatter so easily, how is it possible that this glass bakeware survives high oven heats? But, as increasing generations of cooks can testify, it works, and well: it is easy to clean, relatively durable and far from costly. And it offers an additional advantage when baking delicate crusts—you can see through the glass how they are browning. There are two sizes of pie plates—9″ and also 12″—to take care of all your needs. Neither of the two drawbacks usually associated with ovenproof glass—its inability to withstand direct flame or the loose fit of its covers—applies to pie pans. The first Pyrex pans, as it happens, were pie plates, and the name Pyrex itself is a commer-

cial pun, combining the sound of *pyr* (from the Greek for *fire*) with that of *pie,* and adding the Latin *rex,* meaning "king," for good measure. Pyrex pans, in their practicality and variety of sizes, remain a good buy. Remember that glass allows food to cook more quickly than metal does—when using a Pyrex pie plate either lower the oven heat by 25 F. or shorten the baking time by 10 minutes.

Corning Pyroceram Pie Plate 10.6

Pyroceram; 9″ diam.; 1¼″ deep.

$3.95

Pyrex glass is sturdy and inexpensive—all the things we have said it is—but it cannot withstand great and sudden changes in temperature, the bakeware cannot be placed on direct heat or under the broiler, and it may shatter if it comes in contact with liquid while it is hot. Unfortunately, it isn't beautiful either.

So the Corning Glass Works developed a second line of cookware which, amazingly enough, has none of these faults. You really *can* take a Pyroceram pan directly from the freezer and put it into a hot oven; this is not an unimportant matter when you are dealing with pastry, which is often improved by being frozen. You really can put this ware under a broiler for top browning—consider a crème brulée, which you can serve forth in this pan without apology. The oven temperature should be 25 F. lower than for a metal pan—as with Pyrex. The ware is an attractive opaque white on which the manufacturer, on the principle of gilding the lily, has seen fit to place an inane floral design, mercifully small. No matter; this pan is durable, practical, and unbelievably easy to clean. It is considerably more expensive than its simpler Pyrex sister, but it is worth the price. For those who are forward-looking: take note that it can be used in microwave ovens (see Chapter 8).

"Sarah Penn's face as she rolled her pies had that expression of meek vigor which might have characterized one of the New Testament saints. She was making mince pies. Her husband, Adoniram Penn, liked them better than any other kind. She baked twice a week. Nobility of character manifests itself at loopholes when it is not provided with large doors. Sarah Penn's showed itself today in flaky dishes of pastry."
Mary Wilkins Freeman (1852-1930), "The Revolt of Mother," in A New England Nun and Other Stories, *1891.*

FLAN RINGS

Form follows function: the flan ring is the simplest and the least beautiful of all the devices in which we bake pastry, but luckily, no one but the cook need ever see it. To use this simple ring of steel—a cartwheel rim? An embroidery frame?—you set it on a baking sheet. Rolled-out dough is fitted into the ring, and then it is baked, either "blind," or empty (see recipe) or with a filling. The pastry shrinks somewhat during baking, so that, once cooled, it is easy to slide the shell off the sheet and remove the metal hoop. Because the walls of the baked pastry will have no support once the rim is removed, flans are usually filled with a shallow layer of fruit. However, various nonsweet tarts are also made in France—an unusual example is pissaladière, a pastry shell spread with an onion purée, crosshatched with anchovy fillets, and dotted with black olives—a Gallic pizza. Oh, yes; just to confuse the unwary, a flan can also be a sweet custard served for dessert in Spanish-speaking lands and in many Spanish restaurants in other countries. Needless to say, it is not cooked in a metal hoop.

Tinned French Flan Ring   10.7

Tinned steel; 7" diam.; ⅝" deep. Also avail. 3½", 4", 6", 8", 8¾", or 10¼" diam.

Max. Temp. 425 F. $2.25 ▲

This French, beautifully made, classic flan ring comes in seven sizes, ranging from 3½" to 10¼". The sides are less than an inch high. Each tinned-steel ring is straight-sided, securely spot-welded at the joining, and smoothly rolled at both top and bottom edges to protect the user's fingers and add strength. We suggest that you buy two rings of the same size—say, 8¾"—so that you can offer two kinds of tarts at your next party.

Deep Steel Flan Ring   10.8

Black steel; 8" diam.; 1½" deep. Also avail. 9½" diam., 1½" deep.
$1.85

Where less is more: from Vulcan's forge (well, actually from Germany) comes this simple strip of black steel that has been curved into a circular shape, with the ends welded together. That's all. It comes in two sizes, either 8" or 9½" in diameter, and it is unusually deep—1½"

—permitting a sumptuous layering of fillings: think of a liqueur-scented pastry cream, topped with fresh or poached fruit and a limpid glaze of jelly. Set it on a good baking pan, press your pastry gently into it (see recipe), and bake it, filled or not—and when you serve your creation proudly forth, no one would know that it had been baked in this ring. Heavy, inexpensive, serviceable, but far from beautiful, it is more solid than the tinned French model.

Fluted Flan Ring   10.9

Tinned steel; 8" diam.; 1¼" deep. Also avail 6", 7", 9½", or 10¼" diam.

Max. Temp. 425 F. $2.50

Another way to bake a fluted pastry shell or a flan with fluted sides: the most familiar method, of course, is to use a loose-bottomed tart pan or, for quiches, a porcelain mold. But here is a tinned-steel flan ring, to be used on a baking sheet: the inner ring is fluted, while the outer ring is flat, with nicely rolled edges. The two are welded together, forming a fairly rigid construction. You can have it in any size from 6" to 10¼". Inexpensive and well made, it is a rather unusual piece of equipment. Set it on a baking sheet, then line it in precisely the same way as Jacques Pépin directs for a fluted, loose-bottomed tart pan (recipe). When the pastry is done, the dough will have shrunken away from the sides and will be easily removable from the confines of the ring.

An English deep-dish pie of beefsteak, potatoes, and puff pastry.

Square Flan Form   10.10

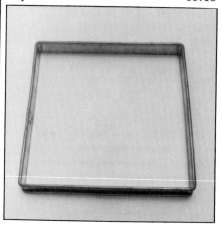

Tinned steel; 6½" square; ¾" deep.
Max. Temp. 425 F. $1.75

The size of this square flan form invites you to do a luncheon quiche of smoked salmon in a custard made with crème fraîche. Once it is baked, cut it into quarters for two modest portions, plus leftovers for second helpings. Or make a lobster quiche to serve four diners an elegantly small and rich first course. The form—and there is a terrible temptation to call it a "ring"—measures only 6½" along each side and is less than 1" deep. It is formed of tinned steel, and the ends of the strip are welded together; both the top and bottom edges have been rolled over wire, and the construction is extremely sturdy. The form is quite inexpensive and a special size and shape, suitable for people who live alone and for ménages à deux.

The so-called "cooked dishes" of Renaissance England (as opposed to the roasts—the "joints"—and other noncomposed preparations) were usually made of chopped meats in highly spiced sauces enclosed in a crust. The meat was chopped so that the often somewhat toothless Elizabethans could down the filling without much effort, and spiced to disguise the taste of the meat, which at times ran from high to putrid, depending on how soon after the slaughtering of the meat the dish had been prepared. The crust of an open pie was called a trap in the old English kitchen, and a closed pastry was invitingly called a coffin.

A flan ring, pastry crimper (pince-pâte), and jagger (roulette), nineteenth-century French.

Rectangular Flan Form 10.11

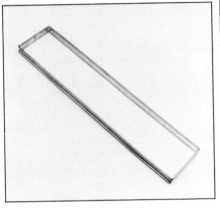

Tinned steel; 22″ × 4½″; 1″ deep.
Max. Temp. 425 F. $7.50 ▲

French pastry chefs construct long strips of flan in rectangular frames like these to make fruit tarts; with thin peach or pear slices laid crosswise, it is easy to divide the strips into servings. In bakeries, fruit strips are sold by length: "I'll have about six inches of the peach tart." At home using this frame, you will bake them in lengths of 22″. Because the frame is only 4½″ wide, you can fit three of them onto a baking sheet, thus using your oven most efficiently. Pastry, of course, freezes well, and an unbaked case, frozen in one of these frames set on a foil-covered pan, then wrapped closely in the foil, would be an invaluable resource to have in your freezer, ready to become a fruit flan on half an hour's notice. You may not feel that you need a circular flan ring if you are used to baking American two-crust pies, or if you use a loose-bottomed tart pan for open pastries, but you should think carefully about buying a few of these rectangular bands. They are of professional-quality tinned sheet steel, with top and bottom edges rolled over concealed wires, and the shape has too many advantages to be ignored.

PATE BRISEE

Jacques Pépin tells us all about this basic pastry:

This is one of the most useful pastry doughs. Easily and rapidly made, it is the base of countless open or latticed tarts, as well as pies, quiches, pâtés en croute, and other pastries. The dough is always better if it is made at least a few hours in advance and kept either in the refrigerator or the freezer—if you freeze it, allow it to defrost thoroughly in the refrigerator. However, you may, if you wish, use it right away. It will not be elastic and it will roll out perfectly if you follow the recipe.

Notice that the fat and the flour are worked together and the water is added at the end and incorporated rapidly. This is the reason why the dough is usable right away. If liquid is worked and kneaded with flour for a period of time, dough becomes rubbery and must rest before being used. [For a machine to protect you from this vicissitude, see the Cuisinart food processor, Chapter 5.]

1¼ cups pastry flour or all-purpose flour
6 tbsp. (¾ stick) unsalted butter, cut into bits
2 tbsp. lard or vegetable shortening
⅛ tsp. salt
¼ tsp. sugar
3 tbsp. cold water

Place all the ingredients except the water in a large bowl. Using both hands, toss the ingredients; then, using the fingers, start "mashing" and flaking the mixture until it has a uniform color and is a bit lumpy. Add the water and mix rapidly with your fingers, just enough to make it possible to gather the ingredients into a solid, smooth mass. Wrap in plastic wrap and refrigerate or freeze, or use immediately.

Yield: Enough dough for a 9-inch crust.

TO LINE A FLAN RING OR TART PAN

On a lightly floured pastry board (flour the rolling pin also), roll out the pâté brisée (above) about ⅛ inch thick and at least 2″ larger all around than the flan ring or loose-bottomed tart pan.

Place the ring or tart pan on a baking sheet, both ungreased. Roll up the pastry on the rolling pin, holding it in place with your thumbs, then place it over the ring or pan and unroll. Ease the pastry gently into place, taking care not to break it or to stretch it while pressing it against the sides and bottom.

When using a flan ring [10.7] make a fold of extra pastry about ½″ wide around the sides between the shell and the ring—this is to thicken the edge. Then with a sharp knife cut off the surplus dough, following the contour of the ring all around. Shape the top of the extra pastry around the rim into a smooth, rounded edge. Decorate the edge by pressing notches into it with the dull edge of a table knife, the tines of a fork, or a special crimper [10.96].

When using a loose-bottomed tart pan with fluted sides [10.9], after easing the pastry into place over the bottom, press it well into the flutings with the side of your finger. Roll across the top of the pan with the rolling pin to cut off surplus dough and, if necessary, press the flutings into place again with your finger.

TO BAKE A PATE BRISEE SHELL

It is often most satisfactory to bake tart shells partially before filling them. Even if the filling is to be cooked in the shell, preliminary baking keeps the crust from becoming soggy. If preliminary baking causes your shell to overcook when you bake it again with the filling, use a better-quality baking sheet under it [see 9.1], or use two sheets beneath it when the filled shell is replaced in the oven.

To proceed: Preheat your oven to 425 F.

After lining your flan ring or loose-bottomed tart pan, prick pastry with a fork every inch or so. Cut a piece of parchment paper [10.99], or use an appropriately sized parchment cake-pan liner [10.100], to cover the inner surface of the dough, sides as well as bottom, and fill the liner with rice or beans (which you will save for later use for this purpose only). Bake shell for 6 minutes, then remove pan liner and beans and bake about 4 minutes longer, or until shell is just lightly colored, if the eventual filling is to be baked in the shell. Bake the shell about 9 minutes longer, until golden brown, if it is never to return to the oven.

LOOSE-BOTTOMED TART PANS

Midway between the flan ring—whose "bottom" is provided by the baking sheet upon which the rings must rest during use—and the solid ceramic quiche pans are the loose-bottomed tart pans. Turning out tarts with fluted sides rather like those made by a quiche pan, they resemble the flan ring in that the tarts they make are served proudly on their own, not in the pan. Jacques Pépin's pâte brisée (see recipe) is eminently suitable for use with these pans.

Tinned Loose-bottomed Tart Pans 10.12

Tinned steel; set of 3; 8", 9½", and 11¼" diam.; 1" deep.

Max. Temp. 425 F. $2.00 $2.50 $3.00 ▲

Here is the set to buy if you are a novice at baking tarts and hesitate to try flan rings. Like the graduated sets of saucepans offered in department stores, it is a starter set, with pans of three sizes—8", 9½", and 11¼". The pans are easy to use—see recipe—and will give you invaluable experience in baking these delectable pastries. (To further encourage you, Paula Peck, in *The Art of Fine Baking* [p. 229], says that tart pastry is easier to work with than pie crust for the inexperienced baker, as it suffers less if it should be overhandled.) This beautiful set from France is a compromise between the bottomless flan ring and the one-piece quiche mold, since each pan has a removable bottom. We recommend nevertheless that you use these pans on a baking sheet, because the large surface of a heavy baking sheet holds and transmits heat to the bottom crust. The pans are of medium-gauge tinned steel, and their fluted sides will not bend or dent easily. To remove a tart or shell from one of these pans, slip your hand underneath—when the tart has cooled slightly—and push up on the bottom, allowing the outside ring to fall off onto your arm. Or you can set the pan on a tall can or other object smaller in diameter than itself, and allow the ring to drop down, free of the sides of the tart or shell. Slide the tart or shell gently onto a serving dish, either still on the loose bottom disc of the pan or not, as you choose. This kind of pan is particularly good for fragile prebaked pastry shells.

QUICHE PANS

Quiche pans, unlike flan rings and utilitarian loose-bottomed tart pans, are beautiful. From the beginning they were designed as dishes for both baking and serving, and as they have never lost that dual purpose, an unattractive quiche pan is difficult to find. With variations in size and fluting, the basic pattern remains constant: the dish is always opaque, nearly always white, and it has straight sides 1" to 2" high. Because the quiche remains within the supporting walls of the pan, it can be filled with heavy or quite liquid mixtures which might burst the sides of a less well supported shell. What we consider classic quiche pans are always made of ceramic ware, often of porcelain, so they conduct and retain heat well and will never scorch a bottom crust during long baking. Nevertheless, the quality must be good—the ware must be highly vitrified, and not too thick—so that the pan will heat quickly enough to allow the heat to "seize" the crust.

The term tart was originally derived from the manner of fashioning the pastry. Tart (in Italian, torta) comes from the past participle of the Latin verb torquere, to twist or torture. A tart was by definition a pastry whose dough had been twisted or tortured (as the procedure is called in some old texts). Consequently, an uncovered pastry of any kind was simply an open pie, not a tart, unless the crust was "tortured."

Black Steel Loose-bottomed Tart Pan 10.13

Black steel; 10" diam.; 15/16" deep. Also avail. 8", 9½", or 11" diam.

$2.75

Black steel has become a fabled medium for baking pastries, with the reputation of producing the best possible crusts in spite of any ineptitude on the part of the cook. The black finish gives an even color to your crust; the steel cooks it uniformly. For that reason we offer this black steel tart pan. If you use it for quiches, you could consider it the only exception to our description of quiche pans as beautiful; but then, if handsome is as handsome does, it begins to look pretty terrific, since it lives up to its advance notices. This pan from France is 10" in diameter and has the traditional fluted sides and a removable bottom. Once the pastry has been freed of the fluted rim after baking, no one will know that your creation emerged from anything as plain-Jane as this pan. Worth considering by the serious baker.

Californian Ceramic Quiche Mold 10.14

Ceramic; 9″ diam.; 1½″ deep; 6-cup capacity.
$6.00

After reviewing the functional severities of flan rings, what a treat it is to handle ceramic quiche pans! This one is a companion for two other molds, equally beautiful, all made by the same California manufacturer: the molds for large brioches (9.21) and for savarins (9.29). The flutings of this mold's sides are wider and a bit more baroque than we might expect: elegant, but possibly making it slightly difficult to remove slices of quiche from the pan. In all other respects, the mold is standard: the vertical sides are 1½″ high, and the mold has a highly glazed white finish which is as appropriate to table service as it is simple to clean. The pan measures 9″ across the top and has a 6-cup capacity. The only restraint to our enthusiasm is that the other quiche pans we recommend are lovelier yet. This is less expensive, however.

Directions for the manufacture of a fine English apple tart: "Take green quodlings [cooking apples] and quodle [coddle] them. Peel them and put them again into the same water, cover close and let them simper [simmer] on embers till they be very green, then take them up and let them drain, pick out their noses, and leave on the stalks, then put them in a pye, and put to them fine sugar, whole cinnamon, slic't ginger, and little musk and rosewater, close them up with a tight cover, and as soon as it boils up in the oven, draw it and ice it with rosewater, butter and sugar. Or you may preserve them and bake them in a dish, with paste, tart, or patty pan."

Surprise pies were a favorite in Tudor and Stuart England. They contained all manner of creatures which, when released from their pastry or mock-pastry cases, leaped or flew out, presumably to the delight of the unsuspecting diners. Live frogs and sparrows were favorites (blackbirds, too, as in the rhyme), but small dogs, squirrels, hares, foxes, and even the resident dwarf of Charles I have been recorded as the "filling" of these pastries. Today's bachelor party has history if not charm.

SING A SONG OF SIXPENCE

*Sing a song of sixpence,
   A pocket full of rye;
Four and twenty blackbirds,
   Baked in a pie.*

*When the pie was opened,
   The birds began to sing;
Was not that a dainty dish,
   To set before the king?*

Fluted French Quiche Mold 10.15

Porcelain; 10″ diam.; 1½″ deep; 5-cup capacity.
Also avail. 7½″, 11½″ diam.
$18.00 ▲ $20.00 ▲

The classic French quiche pan: made of fine, highly glazed white porcelain, it has fluted vertical sides and is available in 7½″, 10″, and 11½″ diameters. It is a handsome thing; it is also, we ought to mention, considerably more expensive than the similar American mold (10.14). It is also of a thinner, finer porcelain. This one has those French touches, reflecting immaculate attention to detail, that have made French cooking so fine. The bottom of this mold, for example, is left unglazed in order to increase heat absorption and thus insure that even a heavy filling will be cooked through. A classic; highly recommended.

From Kate Greenaway's Apple Pie, *1886.*

French Ceramic Fruit Tart Pan 10.16

Porcelain; 9″ diam.; 1⅜″ deep. Also avail. 8¼″, 9¾″, 10″, or 11¾″ diam.
$44.00

Pure luxury: but is sable any warmer than squirrel? This exquisitely decorated fruit tart mold from France doesn't function any better than plain white porcelain, but oh, what a lovely thing it is to behold! The sides ripple in shallow fluting around a dish glazed in milky white on which lie *les fruits sauvages*—wild strawberries, raspberries, and currants set against sprays of green foliage, incredibly à propos for a berry tart. It is made of the finest-quality porcelain in a country which is famous for such ware. Of course the bottom is unglazed for greater conduction of heat, of course the pan is easy to clean; and of course it comes in a selection of five sizes, from 8¼″ to 11¾″ in diameter. A beautiful pan of great quality.

TARTLET PANS

Pans for individual tarts or tartelettes, in their infinite variety of shapes and sizes, are as useful as they are decorative. Use them to bake tartlet shells of sweetened pastry dough for cases to be filled with fruit, cream, or custard, or use unsweetened dough to be filled with savory hors d'oeuvre mixtures.

Fitting the pastry into the molds is a chore that can be made quick and easy. Cut a cardboard pattern from a piece of pastry that you have painstakingly fitted over the back of one pan and trimmed to size; thereafter you can use the pattern to cut out pastry rapidly and accurately. After lining the pans, prick the dough thoroughly, and cut a piece of parchment or brown paper to cover the dough; fill the shells with beans or rice to prevent them from puffing as they bake, or cover the backs of pans with the dough and then cover the dough with a second tin of the same size to achieve the same effect. Whether you bake them upside down or right side up, place on baking sheets, an essential step in dealing with a large number of such small items. You can bake miniature tea cakes or petits fours in these pans instead of cutting the cake shapes out of large sheets of Génoise. The tiniest tartlet pans are used not only for hors d'oeuvre, but for elegant sweet bites to be nibbled after the dessert proper: a miniature orange cake glazed with chocolate, or a morsel of pastry holding one glazed strawberry.

HOW MANY TO BUY

We offer here a good assortment of pan shapes, but we could go on indefinitely. Remember that it is better to have twelve of one sort than two each of six kinds; in fact, you should buy no fewer than four of each shape, and if you buy either of the two sets of tartlet pans in frames, (10.26 or 10.27), you'll have at least six of a kind. The shells turned out by these small tins are so decorative in themselves that hors d'oeuvre and sweet tarts will need a minimum of garnishing for elegant service.

OTHER USES FOR TARTLET TINS

In Scandinavia, individual tart shells are lined with pastry, and then filled with almond paste to make Sandbakkelse.

Barquette Tin from France   10.17

Tinned steel; 3⅞" long; 1⅝" wide; ½" deep; 1 fl. oz. capacity. Also avail. 3¼" or 3¾" long.
Max. Temp. 425 F.   **$.40**

Little pastry boats laden with foie gras glazed with aspic are in the grand tradition of French hors d'oeuvre. Or, for dessert, raspberries and other small fresh fruits are at their most decorative placed in these elegant shells and topped with a little whipped cream or a coating of glaze. The flat-bottomed tins used, pointed at both ends, are called barquettes because of their resemblance to a bark, a kind of sailing ship. This pan, which comes in three sizes, is made in France of thin sheet steel coated with tin, stamped into a sturdy seamless mold. The middle size, perhaps the most useful, is 3⅞" in length and holds a single fluid ounce. Resist the temptation to think of these individual molds as toys: they are not for mud pies but are sturdy pans, altogether serious in purpose.

Fluted French Barquette Tin   10.18

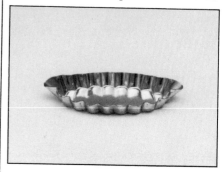

Tinned steel; 4" long; 2" wide; ½" deep; 1 fl. oz. capacity. Also avail. 3¼" or 4¾" long.
Max. Temp. 425 F.   **$.40**

This tinned-steel mold is an elaboration on the prototype barquette: it has fluted rather than plain sides. It comes in three lengths: 3¼", 4", and 4¾". It is made of unusually lightweight tin, but the gauge is quite adequate for the quick baking required by the tiny pastries you will cook in it. You ought to buy six or more and then handle and store them with care to prevent denting.

Fluted Italian Barquette Tin   10.19

Tinned steel; 3¼" long; 1⅜" wide; ⅜" deep.
Max. Temp. 425 F.   **$.40**

Another and rather smaller barquette mold, fluted rather than plain and Italian rather than French. This fleet of little boats comes in a set of twelve, each one stamped from a solid piece of tinned steel. The quality is exceptional; each barquette is absolutely solid and impossible to dent, in spite of its miniature size. These barquettes are 3¼" long and less than half an inch deep.

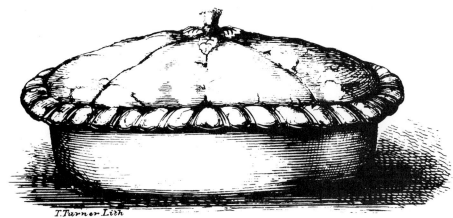

T. Turner Lith

PORTRAIT OF AN APPLE PIE

AS IT OUGHT TO BE

TAKEN FROM STILL LIFE.

STRIKING LIKENESS OF AN APPLE TART IN A PIE

AS THEY OFTEN ARE

TAKEN FROM REAL LIFE.

Made with the same materials, at the same cost, baked at the same baker's, at the same time, in the same oven, but executed by two different feminine artistes. We regret that neither portrait is signed.

Having seen both Pies made at two different houses, but by the same receipt, I sent my servant to watch the process of the baking of them; after waiting till they were done, she informed me, that about one o'clock a very cleanly dressed little girl presented herself at the baker's, with a ticket bearing the name of "Mrs. Armstrong," No. 1 Pie was then delivered to her.

"A few minutes after," says she, "a tall untidy looking girl, with a black face and still blacker hands, with her hair floating à la tempesta, called for Mrs. Jenkin's Apple Tart; No. 2 was handed to her, she exclaiming very loudly as she took it up, 'O Lor! aint it nice and smoking hot."
"In the crowd," says my Mary, "I lost sight of both tarts."

The Modern Housewife by Alexis Soyer, London, 1853.

Fluted Round Tartlet Pan   10.20

Tinned steel; 4″ diam.; 1″ deep; 4 fl. oz. capacity.
Max. Temp. 425 F.   **$.60**

No matter what their shape, all tiny tarts are properly called tarts or tarte-lettes, but the pastries turned out by this miniature pan have a special right to the name. It is a four-inch circle with fluted sides, stamped without seams from thin sheet steel and coated with shiny tin. Any filling recipe for a full-grown tart can be divided to fill these babies: you might create a family of tiny quiches, or tartlets filled with creamed shellfish or chicken—excellent for a first course—or a selection of miniature glazed fruit pies. When raspberries are most expensive, bake two tartlets and treat yourself and one lucky friend in-stead of bankrupting yourself to make one nine-inch tart.

Fluted Oval Tartlet Tin   10.21

Tinned steel; 3¼″ long; 2¼″ wide; ¾″ deep.
Max. Temp. 425 F.   **$.45**

Light as a feather, this fluted oval pan from France has shallow flutings radiat-ing from a flat oval bottom. Quite tiny—only 3¼″ long—it is pressed from a single sheet of tinned steel. The thin-ness of the metal permits fast baking but requires that you be careful not to dent or damage the molds. All such fragile ware should be washed by hand and kept oiled between uses to prevent rust.

Diamond-shaped Tartlet Tin   10.22

Tinned steel; 3¾″ long; 2½″ wide; ¾″ deep.
Max. Temp. 425 F.   **$.45**

Still another shape: this is a fluted dia-mond, pressed out of lightweight tinned steel and less than 4″ long. Buy at least four, keep them oiled between uses, and protect them from being crushed against one another or other equipment in a drawer, or you will wind up with dam-aged points and crumpled edges. If the Queen of Hearts had been a queen of diamonds, these would have been her knave's delight.

A tartlet, as the name indicates in both English and French (tartelette), is a small tart. It was known in the sixteenth century as a flannet, the diminutive of flan, a pastry preparation which derived its name from the metallurgical term flan, a metal disc. A medium-sized deco-rated open tart was called a tartelette by Richard II's cooks, who also made tiny tarts, of the same shape, which were served "swimming in pottage."

Tartlet Tins with Loose Bottoms   10.23

Tinned steel; 4″ diam.; 1⅛″ deep. Also avail. 4½″ diam., ¾″ deep.
Max. Temp. 425 F.   **$.85**

If these were full sized we would de-scribe them as sturdy tinned-steel, loose-bottomed tart pans of professional qual-ity and leave it at that; as miniatures, they are astonishingly well made. Avail-able in diameters of 4″ and 4½″, with snugly fitting removable bottoms, these small tins would be perfect for baking pastry crusts to be filled with curried seafood for a first course, or to be heaped with berries and whipped cream for dessert after a salad luncheon. These are unusual pans and hard to find.

Set of Tartlet Molds   10.24

Tinned steel; 6 different shapes, averaging about 1½″ in diam.; ⅜″ to ½″ deep.
Max. Temp. 425 F.   **$3.00**

In spite of our prohibition against think-ing of them as toys, tartlet molds are enchanting things in themselves; it is difficult to choose among their many shapes and sizes. So why not let some-one else select for you, and buy this set of eighteen tiny molds? They average 1½″ across and, on the average, hold only one-half of a fluid ounce. The pans are pressed out of tinned steel, and the set includes three each of six shapes: miniature kugelhopf molds, quiche pans, fluted diamonds, circles, fluted ovals, and fluted ovals with diagonally ridged bottoms. The quality is perhaps not so high as that of the individually chosen larger molds, but this set would be an excellent choice for anyone just begin-ning to make tiny hors d'oeuvre or sweet pastries.

Fluted Round Tartlet Pan
Fluted Oval Tartlet Tin
Diamond-shaped Tartlet Tin
Tartlet Tins with Loose Bottoms
Set of Tartlet Molds

Petit Four Pastry Set
Tin with Round Tartlet Forms
Tin with Oval Tartlet Forms

Petit Four Pastry Set   10.25

Tinned steel; 10 different shapes, 1″ to 2″ across;
⅜″ to ⅝″ deep.
Max. Temp. 425 F.   **$10.00**

These miniature tart-pastry molds are housed in a colorful tin box on which the luscious results, glazed and decorated, are depicted, ready to join a classic selection of petits fours, which often includes tiny tarts as well as iced cakes. The set consists of five each of ten differently shaped molds—oval, square, round, diamond-shaped, and so on. Each tin-plated mold makes a crust that will hold only a teaspoonful or so of filling, just enough for one sugary bite. And although they look as if they belong in a doll's kitchen, the molds are surprisingly sturdy. Think of them for making pastry shells to fill with cheese or a spiced fish concoction for a cocktail party; or place a single perfect strawberry, glazed, in each for a little girl's delight.

Pompeiian pastry molds.

Tin with Oval Tartlet Forms   10.27

Tinned steel; 14½″ X 5″ overall; 6 forms, each
4″ X 1⅝″, ½″ deep, 1 fl. oz. capacity.
Max. Temp. 425 F.   **$4.00**

TARTLET PANS IN FRAMES

Like muffin tins, tartlet pans in frames have the great merit of simplifying the handling of several small pastries at a time: when you use these, there's no need to juggle separate molds. Your oven needn't be overlarge to accommodate two pans of either design on a single shelf, with ample space left around and between them for the circulation of heat. These pans would probably benefit from the support of a baking sheet; but they are quite capable of standing on their own, whether you are baking blind (empty) shells or filled tartlets.

Tin with Round Tartlet Forms   10.26

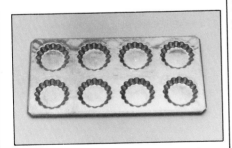

Tinned steel; 14¼″ X 7¼″ overall; 8 forms,
each 2¾″ diam., ½″ deep; 1 fl. oz. capacity.
Max. Temp. 425 F.   **$7.95**
A sturdy pan of heavy tinned steel with eight shallow circular impressions with sloping, fluted sides makes a whole set of tartlets: imagine these lined with a short dough and then filled with almond paste. Each tartlet mold measures 2¾″ in diameter and is only ½″ deep. There are no seams, since the pan is stamped out of a single sheet of metal. It is about

14″ long, with edges that have been merely bent under and corners that are simply cut off on the diagonal. Though there are no niceties of finish here, the pan is precisely good enough for its function—there is no waste of energy on fine finishing, but every detail is adequate to the job.

Pastry mold discovered at Pompeii.

Another tinned-steel pan from France, this one having depressions for the making of six long ovals with pointed ends. Each tartlet will be 4″ long and only ½″ deep; the entire pan is slightly over 14″ in length. Made of sturdy tinned steel, the pan has its edges folded back and the corners simply snipped off on the diagonal; but despite its simplicity, you can make in it the most elegant of pastries. To fill tins such as this, lay a sheet of pastry loosely over the entire pan and ease it slightly into the molds; allow it to rest for about five minutes while the dough sinks further into the depressions, then adjust the pastry to the molds with your fingers, if the fit is too loose. Run a rolling pin over the top of the pan to cut away the excess dough, which can then be peeled off easily—et voilà! Your tartlet shells are ready to prick and bake in the same fashion as pastries made in individual molds.

SPECIAL FORMS FOR PASTRIES

Not exactly pans, more nearly molds and all on the order of cones, the three special forms we show you next are sure to tempt the baker who would like to produce professional-looking filled pastries. The possibilities of the small molds for cornucopia shapes are infinite; and the croquembouche is not only delightful to eat—it's a spectacular construction worthy of the place of honor on a holiday buffet, where it can be admired as it deserves before being served.

CORNUCOPIA MOLDS

Here are the molds for shaping those Continental pastry cones which are variously known as cornucopias, cornets, cream horns, or lady locks. "Lady locks" because the long strip of pastry curling downward from the tip reminds one of a corkscrew curl; in Germany they are sometimes called *Schillerlocken* (Schiller's locks) in honor of the style in which the German romantic poet wore his hair. Whatever you call them, they are made by rolling inch-wide strips of pastry dough around the greased conical molds, and then glazing them and rolling them in sugar. When the horns have been baked, lying on their sides on a good baking sheet, the molds slip out easily and you can pipe whipped cream, custard, or pastry cream into the pastries. These molds are also used to make ham cornucopias filled with vegetable salad. Grease the *inside* of the mold; line it with a thin, twirled slice of ham and fill with a salad made of finely cubed cooked vegetables, mixed with homemade mayonnaise; then slip the filled shape out of the mold.

A simple dowel (above) was at first used to support a spiral-wound strip of puff pastry to make a cornucopia; metal molds have replaced dowels.

Narrow Cones for Lady Locks   10.29

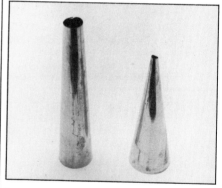

Tinned steel; avail. 5½" long, 1⅛" diam. or 4⅜" long, 1⅜" diam.

Max. Temp. 425 F.   **$.35**

The shape of this pastry mold resembles that of a megaphone more than a horn of plenty. It has many advantages over the French model (10.28): it has a smaller capacity and will, therefore, gobble up less of your whipped cream or pastry cream; it has double seams for extra strength; and it is—not the least of its virtues—considerably less expensive than the imported form—a point worth considering when you're buying an item you may not use often. The horn comes in two sizes, either 4⅜" or 5½" long, both narrow.

French Cornucopia Forms   10.28

Tinned steel; set of 4; each 4" long, 2½" diam.
Max. Temp. 425 F.   **$2.50 for four**

The open end cut at a slant gives this French mold a true cornucopia shape. It is of exceptional capacity, being a full 2¼" in diameter at the open end. Molded of tin-coated sheet steel and sturdily joined along the seam, it is well made but somewhat formidable in price when you consider that you should buy a dozen. A luxury, but a classic.

"Your old brick oven would have been ashamed of himself all his days, and blushed redder than his own fires, if a God-fearing house-matron, away at the temple of the lord, should come home and find her piecrust either burned or underdone by her oven or under zeal; so the old fellow generally managed to bring things out exactly right."
H. B. Stowe, Oldtown Folks, 1869

CROQUEMBOUCHE

A croquembouche is most usually a mountain of small cream puffs, each little boulder filled with vanilla or chocolate cream and the whole construction held together with a delectable caramel glaze. A formidable mouthful, seemingly even more formidable to produce, it is a large and festive pastry that can be accomplished by any cook who has the required mold, plus skill in making tiny cream puffs, plus patience.

Croquembouche Mold 10.30

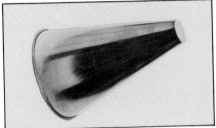

Tinned steel; 13″ tall; 8⅞″ bottom diam., 2″ top diam.
$11.00

If, on some snowy day with nothing else in sight, you should decide to construct a croquembouche, you must have this form, a large tinned-steel cone with a flattened top. You grease the outside generously and then build your pastry mountain around it, painting the little filled cream puffs with caramel glaze as you go. Once all is cool and set, you slip out the form and admire the architecture. We show you the 13″ size, large enough to shape a spectacular dessert for a party. The mold is expensive but absolutely essential for making this classic pastry.

Equipment for Preparing, Shaping, and Decorating Pastries

If we were following a recipe we would say that, now that we have selected and prepared a pan, we should begin to gather the specialized tools we will use for preparing the dough. First, though, take a look at Chapters 1 and 5 for a survey of the general preparatory tools you will need. And now that we have, in a manner of speaking, chosen a pan, preheated the oven, and weighed and measured our ingredients, we can begin to work with the dough itself and then, later, be ready to decorate pastries after they pop from the oven.

FLOUR SIFTERS

Sifting flour seems like such a boring waste of time when you consider the beautifully milled white flours we have to work with today; and the flour companies themselves seduce us into laziness by telling us that their products are presifted. Nonetheless, the best bakers still sift their flour, then sift their dry ingredients together in preparation for baking anything but bread. In this way they assure themselves that the flour has been aerated to produce a standard measure and that the dry ingredients have been sufficiently blended. Professionals use a single-action sifter, with only one layer of metal mesh, although sifter manufacturers have added more screens, with more complicated agitators. While this elaborate type of sifter may add slightly more air, it also requires more time to sift a given amount of flour and is harder to clean. Remember that moisture plus flour will create instant glue on any screen, and take care that your sifter is never washed, but rather shaken out thoroughly and then stored in a plastic bag after you use it.

Stainless-Steel Sifter 10.31

Stainless steel; 4¾″ diam.; 5¼″ high; 5-cup capacity.
$4.50

Neat, concise in shape, this carefree, stainless-steel sifter holds a full five cups. It is old-fashioned, well-made, easy to hold and use, and has the added virtue of an interior marked with measurements in both cups and fractions of a pound. An agitator shaped like a clover leaf moves horizontally over the mesh when the trigger on the handle is squeezed; all is sturdy, efficient, durable.

Lightweight Aluminum Sifter 10.32

Aluminum; top diam. 5½″; base diam. 4½″; 4″ deep; 5-cup capacity.
$2.98

An aluminum body makes this sifter somewhat lighter than others of the same capacity, a virtue for the cook whose arm gets tired when sifting large quantities of flour. Aluminum neither rusts nor chips; the ample body holds five cups and narrows to a base that is only 4½″ in diameter, enabling the sifter to rest conveniently on a large measuring pitcher. There is a single screen of exceptionally fine mesh and a spring-action handle coated in dark enamel. Lightweight and somewhat less sturdy than the English model (10.31), this sifter is nevertheless perfectly adequate for its purpose.

Triple-Screen Sifter 10.33

Tinned steel; 5″ diam.; 5¼″ high; 5-cup capacity.
$4.49

This sifter has three mesh screens and three flour agitators in pairs, one above another, so that the flour is actually sifted three times for, hypothetically, one expenditure of energy. The trouble is that you scarcely ever need triple sifting, and this sifter is both slower in action and more laborious to operate than a single-screen type. Still, it has homely virtues to recommend it: a good tin-plated steel surface, a steel-spring action, a well-made handle, sturdy coarse netting, and an ample (5-cup) capacity. The upper edge is slanted so that you can scoop flour into it, presumably from a barrel: evidence of its kinship to professional equipment.

Small German Shaking Sifter 10.34

Tinned steel; 3⅞″ diam.; 3″ high; 2-cup capacity.
$1.29

From the most complicated to the least: this 2-cup tinned-steel German sifter works by being shaken back and forth. The handle extends within the body, becoming a flat, forklike agitator that lies over the mesh. As you shake the sifter from side to side the movement causes the agitator to scrape over the screen and urge the flour through. It's comforting to realize that there is practically nothing that can break down here, although in using the sifter you may spread flour a little more widely than you intend. Good for dredging foods or for flouring a board; also good if you have limited storage space in your kitchen.

In the early 1800s it became common practice to bleach flour by chemical means. The Shakers spoke against it (much as do nutritionists today) when they wrote in a version of their Manifesto that "what had been the staff of life for countless ages had become a weak crutch" with the use of this process. Something of a full circle may be developing: in recent years, several major milling companies have added unbleached flour to their supermarket product lines.

PASTRY BLENDERS

The flour has been sifted and measured, and perhaps sifted again with other dry ingredients; now you must somehow cut in the fat. "Cutting in" is just that: two knives, with blades parallel and crossed in scissors fashion, pass each other closely over and over again in the bowl until the mixture looks like coarse meal, with each tiny piece of butter or lard coated with flour but retaining its individuality. Or—and we can't sell you the equipment for this method—do it with your fingers; the old cooks called it "rubbing in" the fat, and the trick, as always with pastry, is to do it quickly, flaking fat and flour together very briskly with the fingertips so that the heat of your hand doesn't melt the butter. Or try your food processor (Chapter 5). If you must buy a special utensil for this step, there are pastry blenders around, some of them (unlike 10.35) unsatisfactory and rickety, and a special and amusing blending fork which James Beard recommends as the preferred method for this step of pastry making—see 10.36

Pastry Blender 10.35

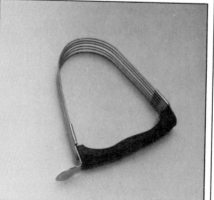

Stainless steel with plastic handle; 4¼″ wide; 5¼″ deep.
$1.75 ▲

If you really want a pastry blender, this one, made in Hong Kong, is of as good quality as any we have seen. Its oval shape, formed by six rolled steel wires, will get to the bottom of the deepest mixing bowl. An added feature is the metal thumb rest attached to the sturdy plastic handle to facilitate the mixing process. The utensil isn't very expensive, so if you want to try a blender, you might well buy this one—the construction is far sturdier than that of most others.

Blending Fork 10.36

Cast aluminum; 8½″ long; 1½″ wide; each tine 2⅜″ long.
$1.50 ▲

Mixing pastry dough requires not only dexterity but, at times, a strong arm. This blending fork will make the task easier because of its unique construction. While it resembles an ordinary but large fork from the front, turn it over and notice that each tine has a knifelike back, which makes the job of incorporating fat into flour go quickly. It can also be used for other kitchen jobs, such as mashing vegetables or fruits or blending any number of mixtures. This unusual tool isn't always easy to find, though it's eagerly sought for because of the recommendation of James Beard, among others.

"The making of pies [at Thanksgiving time] assumed vast proportions that waged on the sublime. Pies were made by forties and fifties and hundreds and made of everything on the earth and under the earth. The pie is an English institution, which, when planted on American soil, forthwith ran rampant and burst forth into an untold variety of genera and species . . . a thousand strictly American seedlings from that main stock . . . Pumpkin pies, cranberry pies, huckleberry pies, cherry pies, green currant pies, peach, pear and plum pies, custard pies, apple pies, Marlborough-pudding pies—pies with top crusts and pies without—pies adorned with all sorts of fanciful flutings and architectural strips laid across and around, and otherwise varied, attested to the boundless fertility of the feminine mind, when once let loose in a given direction."
H. B. Stowe, Oldtown Folks, *1869*

SCRAPERS AND RUBBER SPATULAS

A scraper is not just the thing your mother used in order to get nearly all of the frosting out of the bowl before she presented the denuded bowl to you; in its many guises it is also, for the professional cook, a second hand, steadier and stronger than his own. With the sturdy blade of a pastry scraper he reassembles dough on the surface of the board on which it is being kneaded, spreads jam on a cake layer, lifts the edge of a delicate strudel dough, and cleans his pastry board when mixing is finished. Other scrapers are used for other tasks, from the heaviest cleaning chores to scraping bowls and plates or getting the last of the purée out of the blender's damnably complicated bottom; obviously you will want to have a variety of sizes and shapes in your kitchen

Consider size and weight in choosing: since scraping is hard work these utensils should feel rather heavy for their size, but never unwieldy.

As for materials, hard rubber has many fine qualities. It is stiff enough to maintain a hard edge for tough jobs, but has flexibility and will not abrade the surface of equipment. We prefer wooden handles to plastic, which melts if forgotten for a moment too long on a hot surface; wooden-handled scrapers are increasingly hard to find (but see 10.39); but let it be said, in favor of plastic or nylon, that those materials have more flexibility than wood, often an advantage, and they are more perfectly sanitary. For cleaning large metal pans covered with cooked or burnt-on food, or for working with pastry and other doughs, a stainless-steel blade is useful, but should be used with care to avoid scratching. Shapes range from a plain square, edged on one side with wood, to elegant elongated wands with both rounded and angular edges on their flexible blades. They are all inexpensive; you will use them constantly, so buy several kinds and sizes.

Rubber Dough Scraper 10.37

Rubber; 4¾″ × 3¾″.
$1.30

It looks like a shovel without a handle, this dough scraper of hard rubber with gently rounded corners and no angles to poke or tear the dough. The extra leverage you get by grasping the blade directly enables you to get a good feel for the properties of the dough, making it ideal for the sensitive handling of delicate mixtures. It can lift sticky brioche dough during kneading where your hand would fail. A nice touch: it is heavy on the top where it is grasped by the hand, lighter on its tapered edges.

From Every Day Cookery, *by Juliet Corson, 1884.*

361

Metal and Wood Dough Scraper 10.38

Stainless steel with rosewood handle; 6" X 4⅞".
$5.75 ▲

With its hardwood handle and stainless-steel blade, this scraper is especially made for use on smooth, hard surfaces, such as those used for mixing some doughs and for rolling pastry. During the kneading of soft doughs it reassembles the mass after it has been spread by the heel of the hand, and it cleans the board when kneading is finished. The blade is secured firmly into the handle by two brass rivets; together, blade and handle form a rectangle, roughly 6" X 5", that is well balanced and easy to use. The blade, cut from a thin sheet of stainless steel, is so straight of edge that it will not damage the pastry-handling surface. As with any implement made even partly of wood, it should never be soaked in water; merely wash it quickly by hand and dry it at once.

Wooden-handled French Spatula 10.39

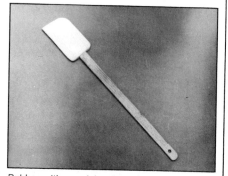

Rubber with wood handle; 13¼" long overall; blade 3⅜" X 2".
$1.10

An ample French spatula or scraper, this one is similar in many respects to the American one (10.41). However, the handle is of wood rather than plastic, a good point for those who fear that a plastic or nylon handle, left leaning in a hot saucepan, may melt. Here is a serviceable rubber scraper with a narrow hardwood handle, the entire utensil more than 13" long, with a hole in the handle so that it may be hung conveniently.

Narrow Rubber Scraper 10.40

Rubber with plastic handle; 10" long overall; blade 3" X 1¼".
$.50

This rubber scraper has a blade thin enough to fit into the narrowest spaces in your kitchen: between the blades of your electric blender jar, between the beaters and the walls of an electric mixer bowl, and even into the unforgivably narrow opening of a Dijon mustard jar. The blade is 3" long and a bare 1¼" wide and is made of good-quality white rubber. The hard plastic handle adds another 7" to the overall length and is meant to withstand the high temperatures in a dishwasher without melting into spiral spaghetti.

Large Rubber Scraper 10.41

Rubber with nylon handle; 13⅝" long overall; blade 4½" X 2⅞".
$1.00

This one has the largest blade of all the scrapers we show you. Made of durable rubber, the blade has both an angular and a rounded corner, making it suitable for entering all sorts of nooks and crannies, and especially for scraping batters or other foods from one container to another. Needless to say, it's also fine as a plate or bowl scraper. The strong nylon handle is firmly set into the blade and will not bend out of shape in dishwasher-hot water. Almost 14" in length, this scraper lets you get into deep utensils without getting your knuckles involved in the job.

A pastry chef's creations, 1824.

Small Rubber Plate Scraper 10.42

Rubber; 5⅝" long overall; blade 2½" X 2".
$.70

Designed for cleaning dinnerware, this hard rubber scraper is extremely sturdy despite its small size. Formed from a single piece of rubber, with no seams for moisture to creep into, its handle and blade are reinforced with rubber ridges. The handle fits comfortably into the palm of the hand, making it an easy implement to wield. The blade's gently curved edges handily dislodge food from the curves and flutings of plates.

From The Country Kitchen, *1850, reprinted in 1965 by* The Americana Review.

BOARDS AND OTHER PASTRY-MAKING SURFACES

As pastry bakers are constantly telling us, it takes a special touch to roll the dough. But, as in other endeavors, it helps to have the best equipment; maybe an Olympic skier could go downhill at top speed in old-fashioned boots, but we mortals need the help of the latest in buckled plastic. And maybe a Paula Peck can roll out dough with a wine bottle on an enameled kitchen table; for those less skilled, a better surface and a good rolling pin are almost essential.

SOME CHOICES

What is a good surface? The answer is a matter of opinion. Mrs. Peck, in *The Art of Fine Baking* (p. 23), recommends rolling dough between sheets of waxed paper, a method that, in the experience of many, results merely in sticky waxed paper. All that most home bakers really need is a well-floured, smooth wooden or Formica table or counter top without cracks, big enough to accommodate a large sheet of dough. The trouble with counter tops and kitchen tables, however, is that they often have traces of moisture left over from the last scrubbing or the last glass of spilled milk, and dampness is death to a well-rolled pastry. To play safe, then, you can buy a wooden pastry board, and keep it always dry and ready for use. Marble, of course, is the *ne plus ultra* of rolling surfaces because it remains always cool and will therefore not cause the fat in your dough to melt; further, it is a superb surface for mixing and kneading certain doughs. And one of our experts swears by his canvas pastry cloth (10.45) for rolling doughs: never washed in ten years, it has been shaken and aired after each use. You will have to choose the surface which suits you best, perhaps beginning with the old standby, the pastry board.

Marble Pastry Slab   10.44

Marble; 24″ X 18″; ¾″ thick.
$67.20

This is the pastry-making surface than which there is no better. If you want to spend the money and if you have the counter space to keep it always out—this is no portable object—you can't do any better than to buy this marble slab for working and rolling pastry. This one is 24″ x 18″ and ¾″ thick; large, heavy, with edges nicely beveled to prevent chipping. Marble never absorbs fat or moisture and remains always cool and dry. In fact, it makes the perfect pastry slab, if you take care that acid substances aren't allowed to attack the surface; wipe it clean with a well-dampened cloth after use, and dry it well. Your cooking habits and interests will determine whether this slab is a necessity or only a beautiful luxury.

There are available to professionals marble slabs with cooling elements set underneath, so that they can be used by pastry chefs working in hot kitchens. Our French pastry expert, Outhier of L'Oasis at La Napoule, and our American consultant, John Clancy, author of *The John Clancy Baking Book,* tell us that this type of slab is a far from ideal solution, even if you feel you can afford it. The refrigerating element causes the marble to sweat, which adds unwelcome moisture. If your kitchen is too hot, use an air conditioner, or direct the air flow of a fan over a block of ice, or put off making puff paste until a cooler day.

Wooden Pastry Board   10.43

Hardwood; 23⅞″ X 17¾″; ¾″ thick.
$16.99

Unlike marble, a wooden board can be put away easily when not in use—no small virtue in a cramped kitchen. And wood is a good surface: this board is large (about 24″ X 18″), made of good hardwood and sanded smooth. There is plenty of room to spread flour all over it and knead your dough or roll your pastry without getting the mess all over the counter. When you are done, scrape the board well (10.38) and allow it to dry in the air; you won't need to use water on it at all unless some especially moist or sticky mixture clings closely to the grain. In that case, use a nylon pot scrubber and as little water as possible; work fast, and dry the board well before airing it.

Canvas Pastry Cloth in Frame   10.45

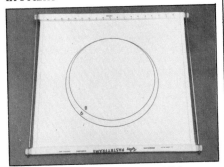

Canvas with wood and steel frame; 19½" square.
$5.50 ▲

Although this is the simplest and least expensive aid to rolling pastry, there are many who swear by its homely virtues. To make it, a canvas square has been weighted on two sides with removable wood and metal rods that form a frame. This keeps the cloth from slipping about during most operations, but if you have to exert exceptional pressure—as in kneading a heavy bread dough—you use the clamps provided to attach the cloth to a table or counter top. When it is heavily floured (which means working flour into the weave of the cloth as well as providing a surface film), this is a good surface for kneading dough and rolling pastry, and for the occasional baker it has the added merit of rolling up tightly for compact storage. Unfortunately, canvas is likely to absorb fats and moisture if not used carefully; shake and air the cloth after use, and if it should require renovation, lay it flat, scrub it with soapy water and a brush, rinse it repeatedly, and lay it flat to dry.

Chocolate Roll Board   10.46

Hardwood; 17¾" × 5"; ¾" thick. Also avail. 24" long.
$4.95

Rolled cakes—some of them actually soufflés—tend to be fragile affairs, awkwardly shaped and easily broken in the handling. For such cakes here is a wooden board which can go from working counter to freezer to refrigerator to dinner table under your chocolate roll, or jelly roll, or Bûche de Noël, providing support all the way. At Christmas time, place holly along the sides; on Washington's Birthday, lay sprigs of cherries on your cherry-tree log. This is a thick hardwood paddle with a smooth finish, nearly 18" long, made attractive by its simplicity. There is a hole for hanging drilled into the handle, suggesting that the board would make a good addition to a wall display of handsome and useful kitchen objects.

ROLLING PINS

Once the dough is sitting there in a pale chilled lump on your carefully selected rolling surface, somehow you have to turn it into a beautiful thin disc of unbaked pastry. The problem is to do this without either stretching it, or tearing it, or turning it into something resembling cardboard through overhandling. A skilled pastry chef could make do with the simplest rolling implement at hand—even a section of an old broomstick or an empty wine bottle. It's far better for most of us, though, to possess equipment that will work for and with us. We require certain things from a good rolling pin: a smooth finish in hardwood, which will prevent sticking and resist the absorption of fats and moisture; substantial weight so that the utensil, and not you, provides the flattening force; perfect balance, so that you do not have to work against your implement in order to roll a sheet of even thickness. Forget the widely advertised rolling pins which have hollow centers into which you insert ice cubes; unfortunately, they tend to sweat from condensation and deposit moisture all over your pastry. And forget the elegance of porcelain pins: they look cool and attractive, to be sure, but are far too fragile for use.

BASIC SHAPES

Your choice of basic rolling pins lies among the types advocated by two schools. The familiar American rolling pin has two handles with a heavy wooden cylinder that turns independently between them on ball bearings. This pin has a smooth action which makes it easy to produce dough of an even thickness. Typical French pins are longer, have no handles, and are straight (10.48) or tapered (10.49) hardwood cylinders. French chefs claim that it is essential to learn to get the feel of the dough into your palms through the use of such simple rolling pins. Both the French and American types are recommended; the choice is yours. All wooden rolling pins should be wiped clean with a damp cloth after each use and then dried immediately.

American Ball-Bearing Rolling Pin   10.47

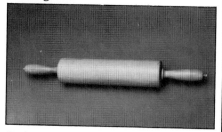

Hardwood with steel center rod and ball bearings; 25″ long overall; roller length 15″, diam. 3½″; 4½ lbs.

$12.50 ▲

Here is the ultimate in American-made rolling pins, heretofore unavailable except to professional cooks. It is made with a steel rod threaded through its heavy hardwood rolling cylinder and anchored with retaining nuts to polished and lacquered handles. The special ball bearings will never need lubrication, insuring smooth action for the life of the implement. While this rolling pin is available with cylinders in six lengths ranging from 10½″ to 18″, we recommend the 15″ Baker's Special as the most versatile for most pastry makers. This pin is a heavy implement and its weight does most of the work; with no pushing needed, there is much less chance of tearing the dough. This one is John Clancy's great favorite.

Straight French Rolling Pin   10.48

Wood; 17¾″ long; 2″ diam.

$4.00 ▲

To those pastry cooks who feel that ball bearings belong only in roller skates, this classic French rolling pin is the perfect utensil. Heavy but beautifully balanced and smoothly finished, it is the favorite of the renowned French chef Jacques Pépin; his reason for preferring it is that it affords the best feel of the dough when rolled gently beneath the palms. This is a knack to be learned, but once accomplished, permits the greatest variation of touch in rolling to accommodate differences in the textures

of various doughs. This rolling pin is a generous 17¾″ long and thus is ideal for rolling out large sheets of pastry.

Tapered Beechwood Rolling Pin   10.49

Beechwood; 20½″ long; diam. 1½″ at center, ⅞″ at ends.

$3.50 ▲

A SPECIAL PIN

Veritably a *rouleau magique,* or magic rolling pin, is 10.50, the Tutové pin—large, heavy, formidably ribbed, and designed to make perfect puff paste. This is one utensil many professionals swear by, and so will you if you treat yourself to the luxury of owning it.

Tutové Rolling Pin for Puff Pastry   10.50

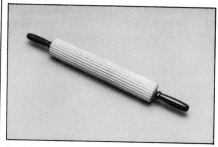

Hardwood with plastic handles; 25″ long overall; cylinder length 15½″, diam. 2½″; 3 lbs.

$45.00

In the loose amalgam which is pastry dough, the fat must always, by one means or another, retain its separate identity—it must not, in other words, soak into the flour. When a flour-and-water dough is stacked in hundreds of layers separated by layers of butter—that is, when it is being transformed into puff pastry—the segregation is even more essential. And although any good-quality plain rolling pin can be used to make puff pastry, the ultimate instrument for this purpose is this French grooved rolling pin with the trade name Tutové: the manufacturer proudly calls it a "magic rolling pin." The magic lies in the ⅛″ grooves which run lengthwise on the

Here is a French-style pin, made in the United States of native beech. It is carved from a single piece of wood to taper from the center to the somewhat thinner ends. Because its tapered shape cuts across the grain of the wood, this style of rolling pin will always have a slightly rougher surface than a strictly cylindrical shape. Nevertheless, this classic pin, slimmer than the straight French type and more than 20″ long, is well finished, with nice weight and balance. When using a tapered rolling pin, care must be taken to make the dough of even thickness without troughs and ridges. The best use of a tapered pin is to obtain a circle, or when purposely stretching the dough, as for croissants.

wooden roller; the rounded ribs separating the grooves distribute the butter evenly between the layers as the dough is rolled and as the layers become thinner and thinner and multiply in number with subsequent folding and rollings. The bite of the grooved pin is also effective in softening the dough when the pin is used to beat it after it has been chilled between workings. Made of hardwood, with black plastic handles, this is an expensive piece of equipment, but worth the price if you intend to make puff pastry: bouchées, puff-paste croissants, vol-au-vents, napoleons, crust for beef Wellington, or any number of other delights.

Vol-au-vent, a baked shell made of puff pastry.

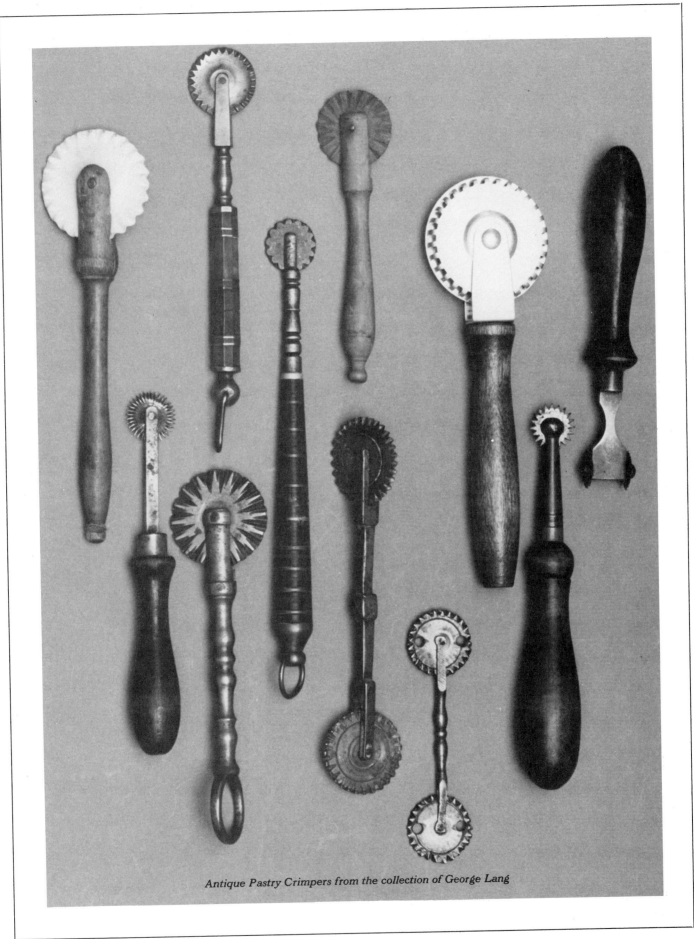

Antique Pastry Crimpers from the collection of George Lang

DREDGERS

Dredgers are halfway between canisters and salt shakers; they should neither be tucked away in a cupboard nor reserved for use on the dining-room table; they belong rather on a shelf at the cook's right hand. With dredgers, powdered sugar can be sprinkled on a cake or pastry, cinnamon sugar on plain cookies, or flour onto sticky fingers or a pastry board. Dredgers are rather marvelous looking, and one man we know has one on his breakfast tray full of cinnamon sugar to shake over his oatmeal. We give you an assortment, all well made, and leave it to you to choose the style that you prefer. Dredgers for flour have the larger holes, sugar dredgers the smaller.

English Flour Dredger — 10.51

Tinned steel; 2¾" top diam.; 4" base diam.; 5¼" high; 1½-cup capacity.
$3.00

This tinned flour dredger is new on the market, but it looks as if it might have been around when Queen Victoria was on the throne—surely Mrs. Beeton, the author of the famous Victorian book of household management, must have had one just like it. It is of heavyweight tinned ware, with a domed cap and large holes punched out to form a six-pointed star. The cap fits snugly without threading; when it comes off, this dredger looks rather like an ale tankard. It holds 1½ cups.

Elegant eighteenth-century English cinnamon casters or muffineers reflected the Georgian taste for spices. These perforated silver shakers held the sweet spice which each person sprinkled to taste over his muffins. In the United States, muffineer came to mean a taller shaker used to sprinkle a mixture of sugar and cinnamon.

Pair of English Dredgers — 10.52

Aluminum; 4¼" tall; base diam. 3⅜"; 1½-cup capacity each.
$3.60

More dredgers from **England**, but these are simpler, a pair in satin-finished aluminum. They have slightly domed caps with holes punched in a snowflake pattern, the flour dredger's holes larger than the sugar dredger's. They are lightweight, easy to keep clean by wiping with a damp cloth, and hold 1½ cups each. The caps lock on with a twist and come off easily for refilling.

French Sugar Dredger — 10.53

Tinned steel; 2⅞" diam.; 4¾" high; 1¼-cup capacity.
$6.00

Sometimes a strong, simple piece of equipment comes along that looks too good to have been made today; but this sugar dredger from France is absolutely contemporary. It is of far heavier-gauge metal than other tin-plated utensils of this nature. It won't dent, nor will the threads twist out of shape. It is simple, heavy, and handsome, and it holds 1¼ cups of sugar.

American All-Purpose Dredger — 10.54

Aluminum; 3¾" tall; 2¾" diam.; 1½-cup capacity.
$2.50 ▲

An American cousin of the imported special-purpose dredgers, this one is highly versatile. The holes in the lid of this shaker are sized to permit it to be used for salt, pepper, flour, or sugar. It is perfectly plain, of dull grayish aluminum; rather lightweight, but perfectly adequate for kitchen use.

Tools of a past age: A sugar dredger, pineapple stand, palette knife (spatula), and molds for sugar flowers.

English Flour Dredger
Pair of English Dredgers
French Sugar Dredger
American All-Purpose Dredger

Goose-Feather Pastry Brush
Flat Natural-Bristle Pastry Brush
Round Natural-Bristle Pastry Brush

PASTRY BRUSHES

If you are ingenious you can manage to get along without a single pastry brush in your kitchen by using paper towels, bulb basters, scrapers, or even the back of a spoon. But once you have a bunch of pastry brushes you will wonder how you got along without them—how did you lay an egg glaze on a pie crust or a loaf of challah? How spread a thinned coat of apricot jam on a delicate cake layer? How baste your turkey without splashing, or spread a herbal mustard coating neatly on Julia Child's Gigot à la Moutarde (*Mastering the Art of French Cooking* [vol. 1], p. 335). How did you grease your waffle iron, the pancake griddle, the bowl for raising yeast dough? Start with two, a goose-feather brush for applying fine glazes and a sturdy hog-bristle brush for applying fats, and you will never be without pastry brushes again.

Goose-Feather Pastry Brush 10.55

Goose feathers; average 7″ long.

$.69

Farm wives through the centuries have made pastry brushes from goose feathers; today, James Beard recommends that you use such a brush when you want to apply a light coating, since with them you can pick up the smallest possible amount of liquid. With this European brush made from pure white feathers, you can glaze a cooky or a pie crust with the lightest of coatings. A romantic-looking implement for all of its practical purpose, it consists of eight feathers, their quills intricately braided and lashed together.

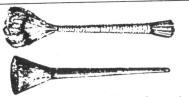

Nineteenth-century French pastry brushes, almost indistinguishable from those in use today.

Flat Natural-Bristle Pastry Brush 10.56

Natural hog bristles with wood handle, stainless-steel ferrule; 8″ long overall; bristles 1¾″ long, 1″ wide.

$1.50 ▲

What keeps this from being a paint brush, which it much resembles? The fact that it's made of pure sterilized natural white hog bristles, neither bleached nor dyed. (Only hog and nylon bristles are considered by experts to be satisfactory for kitchen use.) The ferrule or metal band that binds the bristles into the wooden handle is of stainless steel, grasping them so firmly that you will not find an unexpected brush hair in your currant-jelly glaze. This is a small brush, 8″ long overall and only 1″ wide, with a blunt-cut edge. Buy one, and we'll bet that you'll wish you had more.

Round Natural-Bristle Pastry Brush 10.57

Natural black hog bristles with wood handle, stainless-steel ferrule; 11″ long overall; bristles 2″ long, 1½″ diam. Also avail. with white bristles.

$5.60

As pastry brushes go, this is the granddaddy of them all. A king-sized 11″ long, it has white or black natural hog bristles set in epoxy, with a lacquered wooden handle and a stainless-steel ferrule. This brush is useful for buttering large sheets of pastry or baking pans, and is also marvelous for basting. The epoxy setting of the bristles guarantees that they won't shed all over your pie crust.

ALL KINDS OF CUTTERS

Cutters for pastry, whether knives, wheels, or shapes, must be very sharp and require little pressure to use, so that the dough will neither be torn, stretched, nor, in the case of puff paste, be sealed down so that air cannot get between the layers to permit rising.

PASTRY WHEELS

Of all cutting tools, pastry wheels come closest to knives: they are knives made mobile. You may have used one for cutting lattice strips for pies or for dividing pizza into slices, but they have other uses. In Italy they are called ravioli cutters, suggesting their uses in making pasta, and they can be used to cut neatly around a cardboard pattern to form tart shells or special shapes of cookies. They are, in short, the least specialized tools available for scoring or cutting dough, and therefore the most useful. A good pastry wheel has it all over a knife in that it presses evenly into the dough as it moves forward, never pulling or distorting by uneven pressure as a knife is likely to do.

Straight-edged Pastry Wheel · 10.58

Stainless steel, with wood handle; 7¼" long overall; wheel diam. 2½". Also avail. 8¾" long, wheel diam. 4".

$2.80

A knife made round: that is the definition of this beautifully simple cutting tool. A stainless-steel wheel is attached on an axle to a comfortable wooden handle; winglike finger guards keep the cook's fingers from getting involved with the cutting edge. The wheel is beveled on only one side to create a sharp cutting edge; the nonbeveled edge will run closely alongside a straight-edge or ruler (10.93). Good for both marking and cutting pastry, this tool comes with either a 2½" or 4" wheel.

Pastry Jagger · 10.59

Brass with nickeled steel frame and wood handle; 6¼" long overall; wheel diam. 1½".

$1.75 ▲

Less simple than the plain wheel cutter, this jagged-edged pastry wheel has sound historical credentials: our experts tell us that it was already being called a jagger in eighteenth-century English and American cookbooks. Its sharp wheel leaves an edge on pastry similar to that made by pinking shears on cloth, and thus makes an attractive finish on lattice strips or ravioli. This is a top-quality jagger with a well-shaped wooden handle, a nickeled-steel frame, and a strong brass wheel set so snugly into the shaft that it can't wobble.

Mardi Gras, or Fat Tuesday, or Shrove Tuesday, the day preceding the fast of Lent, has long been an occasion for gastronomic indulgence. In parts of colonial America doughnuts (a version of the olykoeks brought by the Dutch settlers) were tossed into the air for children to catch and consume. A fifteenth-century German treatise on the art of cake making includes a recipe for jelly doughnuts (eventually called Bismarcks, after the Prussian statesman) to celebrate the same holiday, Fastnacht. To this day Pennsylvania Dutch cooks treasure their family recipes for fastnachts, yeast-raised doughnuts made in honor of the day.

Double Pastry Wheel from Italy · 10.60

Chromed and stainless steel with wood handle; 6½" long overall; diam. of wheels 1½".

$2.25

Two for one: from Italy comes this professional-quality tool, with two cutting wheels, one plain and one a jagger, mounted on a sturdy wooden handle. The wheel is kept away from the cook's fingers by a metal hand guard. Simply flip the handle over to change from the plain wheel to the fluted: they curve gracefully away from one another rather like those swan-necked Siamese-twin containers for oil and vinegar. Although small—only 6½" in length—this implement is extremely well made.

There is much speculation about the origin of the doughnut. Excavations in the southwestern United States have revealed petrified cakes with holes in them which might give to a tribe of prehistoric Indians the honor of having created the ancestor of this pastry.

Old implements from France: combination pastry cutter, crimper, and wheel, top, and double wheel, below.

POPPY SEED STRAWS · PAULA PECK

Paula Peck, renowned for her baking skill, published this recipe in *The Art of Fine Baking*, from which we take it by permission. You might wish to use small cutters to vary the shape of your pastries, or consider cutting the bars with a pastry jagger (10.59).

SHORT HORS D'OEUVRE PASTRY

2⅔ cups sifted flour
1 cup butter, slightly softened
½ teaspoon sugar
2 teaspoons salt
4 hard-cooked egg yolks, mashed
4 raw egg yolks or 2 whole eggs

Place flour in a bowl. Make a well in the center. Add all ingredients. With finger tips, make a paste of center ingredients, gradually incorporating the flour to form a smooth, firm ball. Squeeze dough between fingers or with heel of hand, so that flour can be completely incorporated. If dough is very soft, wrap in wax paper. Chill two or three hours, or until firm enough to roll between sheets of wax paper or hand-mold into shapes.

POPPY SEED STRAWS

Short hors d'oeuvre pastry [above]
½ cup poppy seeds

Add poppy seeds to pastry as it is being mixed. Chill pastry. Roll it out ⅓ inch thick. Cut into small bars, ½ x 2. Place on ungreased baking sheet and bake in 350 degree oven until light brown, about 10 minutes.

Yield: approximately 4 dozen.

(From THE ART OF FINE BAKING, by Paula Peck. Copyright © 1961 by Paula Peck. Reprinted by permission of Simon & Schuster.)

Straight-edged Pastry Wheel
Pastry Jagger
Double Pastry Wheel from Italy

Dough Cutter for Circles
Six-sided Cooky Cutter
Cutters in Sets of Three
Assorted Cutters

COOKY CUTTERS

Cooky dough can be pressed from a pastry bag or a cooky press, sliced from a chilled cylinder, pushed off a teaspoon with your forefinger, or rolled out and then cut into shapes with a pastry wheel and a cardboard guide. But for rolled-out cookies how much simpler it is to use a cutter, especially made to cut dough neatly into fanciful shapes. And did you ever wonder why we cut cookies into these shapes, into little stars and Christmas trees and rabbits? It all began in pre-Christian times when the winter solstice was observed with animal sacrifices. Not everyone, alas, could afford to offer an animal; and thus the poor and the little children were allowed to give instead a symbol in the form of a sweet cake molded to look like an animal. From there, it was an easy step to the whole wonderful tradition of Christmas cookies and to special-occasion cookies in general.

Dough Cutter for Circles   10.61

Tinned steel with wood handle; 7½" long; cuts 1¾" rounds. Also avail. for 3" rounds, either plain or with hole in center, or for 3½" rounds, either plain or with either a small or a large hole in center.
$13.80

The wheel-toy to end them all: you could buy this tool if you never baked a thing, just for the fun of figuring out how it works. Curved oval cutters rotate on a tinned-steel frame which is attached to a wooden handle. Somehow, when this whole baroque affair is rolled over a sheet of dough, it turns out shapes that are beautifully round, wasting scarcely a scrap of dough. Big, heavy, funny-looking: a super addition to your kitchen and an intellectual puzzle to boot. The utensil is available with plain round cutters in three sizes, as well as a 3" cutter and two 3½" cutters, with holes of different sizes, suitable for making doughnuts or the tops of peek-a-boo sandwich cookies. And don't overlook the possibility of using this cutter for pasta shapes, too.

Pastry cutter, 1824.

Six-sided Cooky Cutter   10.62

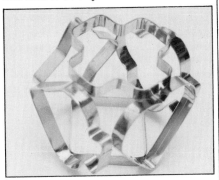

Chrome plate; 6 sides, each approx. 2¾" square.
$3.00 ▲

What a good idea! Here is a basically box-shaped metal frame with a cooky cutter of a different shape forming each of its six sides. As it is one unit, the cook need not search through kitchen impedimenta to assemble the various cutters needed. It is easier to handle than most cooky cutters because of its bulk, and it's also considerably stronger because of its shape. The cutters themselves are in the most usual shapes: heart, diamond, spade, club, cross and star.

Cutters in Sets of Three   10.63

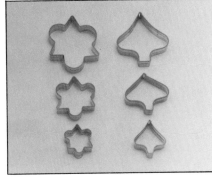

Tinned steel; 6 shapes, each in sets of 3; sizes range from 1½" to 3½" diam. per set.
$.69 per set

Each of these tinned cooky-cutter shapes comes in a set of three of varying sizes. Take your pick of three sizes of stars spades, rectangles, flowers, hearts, or Gothic trefoils. They are well made in Germany; the top edges are rolled, the bottom edges sharp, and each cutter is strengthened by having a narrow ridge folded into the metal around the entire circumference—a nice example of the manner in which a basically weak material can be made stronger by manipulating its structure.

Assorted Cutters   10.64

Tinned steel; 12 assorted shapes; 2" to 4" diam.
$.59 each

Cooky cutters come in an endless variety of shapes. These handmade tinned ones can turn out a whole barnyard population of cooky animals for a child's party, or a cluster of shamrocks for St. Patrick's Day. All of the cutters are sharp enough to make clean-edged cookies. Made in West Germany, they may be purchased in sets of twelve assorted shapes.

Gingerbread Cutter   10.65

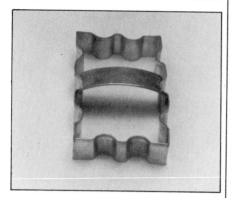

Tinned steel; 3⅝" long; 2¼" wide; ¾" deep.
$.69

This is the *other* shape into which gingerbread is cut: not a funny little man, but a rectangle with half-circles bitten out of its long sides. The traditional shape will evoke memories of the old-fashioned breadlike kind of gingerbread, its spicy dough dotted with raisins and glazed with slick, sugary icing. A generous 3⅝" long by 2¼" wide, the cutter is sufficiently deep for a heavy dough, and a curved handle with rolled edges makes it easy to use.

Bow-Tie Cutter   10.66

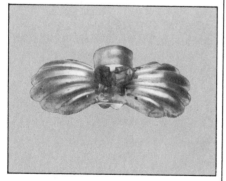

Tinned steel; 3¼" long; 1¼" wide.
$.59

This attractive cooky cutter resembles two tiny madeleines attached back to back. As it is 3¼" long, it makes a rather large cooky reminiscent of a bow tie with scalloped edges. The cutter is quite deep, which makes it usable for heavy doughs, such as that of lebkuchen. Made in West Germany, it has a sturdy rolled handle.

CREAM CHEESE PASTRY FOR HORS D'OEUVRE

Also from Paula Peck's *The Art of Fine Baking* and also for cutting with the smaller shapes (10.63 and 10.64) into crusty bites for drink delights.

This is a quick and easy recipe that can be made in the mixer. It makes a rich, crisp pastry which can be used in many ways and can serve as a substitute for short hors d'oeuvre pastry.

The easiest way to roll cream cheese pastry is between sheets of wax paper. Remember that in rolling any pastry between sheets of paper, and especially cream cheese pastry, it is necessary to loosen the upper and lower papers several times to prevent the pastry from sticking and to allow it to spread freely.

Cream cheese pastry can be frozen, unbaked, for 3 months or more. Shape it before freezing.

1 cup butter
1 cup cream cheese
¼ cup heavy cream
2½ cups flour
1 teaspoon salt

Cream butter and cream cheese together. Beat in cream. Gradually add flour and salt. Wrap dough in wax paper and chill several hours, or until needed.

Bake in a 350 degree oven.

(From THE ART OF FINE BAKING, by Paula Peck. Copyright © 1961 by Paula Peck. Reprinted by permission of Simon & Schuster.)

Santa Claus Cutter   10.67

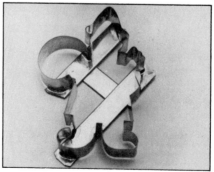

Tinned steel; 5½" tall; 3¾" wide; 1" deep.
$12.75

For making the ultimate gingerbread or sugar-cooky Santa Claus, this is the cutter to have. It turns out a large 5½" figure, suitable both for decoration and consumption. The cutter itself is hand-made, heavily tin plated, and has a con-venient grip shaped rather like the letter H. Although it is expensive, this is an heirloom-quality utensil sure to be passed on to succeeding generations of cooky bakers. When you have finished making the Christmas cookies, try hanging the cutter on the tree with a bright red ribbon.

Flower-shaped Cutters   10.68

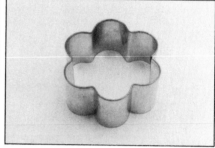

Tinned steel; set of 6, from 1⅜" to 3¼" diam.; 1⅜" deep.
$7.50

Six sizes of the same flower-shaped design are nested together in this set of pastry or cooky cutters from Italy. Each is formed of a single strip of tinned steel, bent into a six-petaled flower; the cutting edge is good and sharp and the top edge is rolled. These cutters are unusually deep—nearly 1½"—and could also be used as miniature flan rings.

Star-shaped Cutters from Italy   10.69

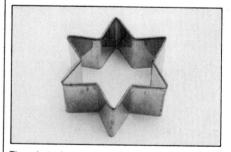

Tinned steel; set of 6, from 1½" to 3⅝" diam.; 1⅜" deep.
$7.50

Much like the flower-shaped cutters, this set of six cooky cutters, each in the shape of a six-pointed star, nests together neatly, offering the cook a variety of sizes with a consistency of shape. Like the flower cutters, they are also from Italy and are of good quality, made of tin-plated steel, with a rolled top edge and a really sharp cutting edge. And like the flower cutters, they are unusually deep.

Gingerbread Cutter
Bow-Tie Cutter
Santa Claus Cutter
Flower-shaped Cutters
Star-shaped Cutters from Italy

Biscuit Cutter with Arched Handle
Doughnut Cutter with Arched Handle
Oval Cutter for Puff Paste

BISCUIT AND DOUGHNUT CUTTERS

Why do you need a special biscuit or doughnut cutter? Why can't you make do with a kitchen glass for cutting biscuits, two sizes of kitchen glasses for doughnuts? Simply because tumblers do not have sharp cutting edges; if you press down on dough with one it will not cut cleanly but will compress the dough, often distorting the shape and always making it difficult to remove the uncooked dough from the cutter and then from the board to the baking sheet. Any cook who makes biscuits or doughnuts even occasionally will want the right cutters for the job. As a dividend, both cutters can be used for cookies too—use the doughnut cutter for the tops of sandwich cookies, so that the filling will gleam through the center opening.

Biscuit Cutter with Arched Handle 10.70

Tinned steel; 2″ diam.; 1½″ deep. Also avail. 2⅜″ diam.
$.50

Sometimes a functional design simply cannot be improved upon; a biscuit cutter like this one must have been used in colonial America. It is a strip of metal joined into a circle, with the overlapping ends welded securely together. The top edge is rolled, and an arched handle is securely attached to the cutter. Designed for making biscuits, the cutter is available in two sizes, both 1½″ deep, and can also, of course, be used to cut out cookies.

Doughnut Cutter with Arched Handle 10.71

Tinned steel; 3¼″ diam.; 1¼″ deep; center hole diam. ⅞″.
$.80

An elaboration of the biscuit cutter, with two circular cutters mounted in such a way as to produce the hole in the doughnut. This cutter and the preceding one are of the same good quality: bands of tinned steel have been joined by spot welding, and the cutter has an arched handle and a metal band across the top to hold the rings together and to increase the solidity of the whole construction. This cutter makes nice fat doughnuts with more cake than hole: remember to fry the cut-out "holes" for special treats.

Oval Cutter for Puff Paste 10.72

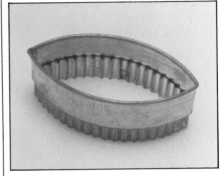

Heavy-gauge tinned steel; 4¼″ long; 2¼″ wide; 1½″ deep.
$2.95

Puff-pastry dough is especially sensitive to poor cutting; a blunt-edged cutter will seal the flaky leaves together, preventing the whole lovely buttery creation from rising. This cutter from France is of a kind traditionally used with puff pastry; it is of heavy tinned steel, with a fluted cutting edge welded neatly to a plain oval holding band. It's rather expensive, but then, so are the ingredients for making puff pastry; it would be an altogether false economy to scrimp on the cutting tool.

Vol-au-vents are lovely shells of puff paste, made in many sizes. To make individual ones to serve as a first course, filling them with the likes of sweetbreads in creamy sauce, you can cut out your ovals of puff paste with this cutter. Then, with a small sharp knife, make an incision ¾″ deep in each oval, parallel to the edge all around and about 1″ from it. When the paste is baked and puffed you can lift out this central portion, leaving a well for the filling and creating a lid.

Scalloped pastry cutters from a century-old French book are virtually identical with present-day sets.

SPECIAL-PURPOSE CUTTERS

Few pastries have been honored by having utensils designed solely for their making, and among those few is puff paste—witness the miraculous Tutové rolling pin (10.50), and now the array of cutters we show you. There are the fluted cutters, especially well made and sharp, for creating ovals, rounds, or crescents—classic shapes for this pastry—and a square cutter for making pastry cases, 10.74. Then, for the dedicated making of puff paste, see the ultimate machine for shaping vol-au-vents, 10.75, and the two rolling triangle-cutters for making croissants.

373

Oval and Round Puff-Paste Cutters 10.73

Heavy-gauge tinned steel; box of 7 ovals, from 3⅛″ long and 1″ wide to 4⅞″ long and 2⅞″ wide. Box of 7 rounds, from 1⅞″ to 4¼″ diam.
$15.00

Two sets of seven cutters each, in graduated sizes: one set is of ovals, the other of rounds, and all the cutters fluted on their lower edges. Because of the fluting they are not often used to cut ordinary cooky dough, which might shatter, but rather to cut puff pastry for garnishes and vol-au-vents. You can make crescents of puff paste to use for garnishing by using one edge each of a round and an oval cutter: Cut the pastry into rounds, then use the end of an oval cutter to remove a "bite" from each to create crescent shapes. For variety in your decorations, bake the cut-out fluted bits, too—their pointed oval shape is leaf-like. These cutters are of heavy-gauge tinned steel, rolled on the top edge and with well-sharpened blades. Expensive, but worth it.

Square Vol-au-Vent Cutter 10.74

Stainless steel; 4¼″ square; 1″ deep.
$17.00

For making vol-au-vents, these cutters turn out rectangular cases rather than the round ones made by the remarkable machine (10.75). Somehow we see them as destined to be filled with strawberries in whipped cream. Imagine a shiny square doughnut cutter 4¼″ on each side, with its inner cutter ⅝″ inside the outer one and with a reasonably sturdy handle spanning the entire construction. The inner cutter doesn't cut entirely through the dough at two of its corners, and thus the center square is anchored only lightly at those corners to the outer border of pastry. After cutting the pastry, you form the case by a procedure much easier to do than to describe: Beginning at an outer corner where the inner square is unanchored, you lift the border of dough and fold it diagonally, placing its point precisely over the opposite corner of the inner square. Then you lift the outer corner opposite to your beginning point and fold it in turn to lie over *its* opposite corner of the center square. The remaining two corners are twisted into points by these manoeuvres—they look somewhat like arrowheads. The case, when it has been baked, will be approximately square, with twisted knobs at two corners—decorative and effective. The top of the central square can be pried out to form a lid. The extra-sharp blades of this cutter pass cleanly through puff pastry without sealing the edges together, which would prevent it from rising.

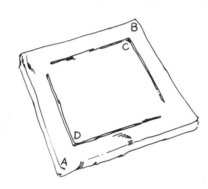

Cut out form of dough after use of 10.74. Moisten the outer rim.

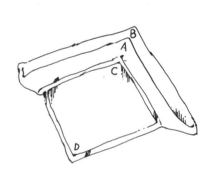

Lift corner A and place on point C, pressing firmly. Then lift point B and place on point D, pressing along edge firmly.

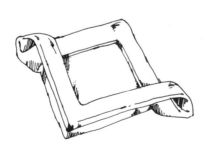

Form with both ends crossed over and ready to be placed on baking sheet to go in oven. Bake according to your recipe.

Completed, baked shell. With tip of sharp paring knife, make incision around center diamond and lift up top layers gently to form cap and shell.

Vol-au-Vent Machine   10.75

Cast aluminum and nylon with stainless-steel cutter; 6″ X 3½″ overall; 5½″ high; diam. of cutter 3¼″.

$57.00

For making individual vol-au-vents, airy cups of puff pastry to serve as edible containers for morsels of chicken or mushrooms or seafood bathed in a sauce, here is an ingenious device indeed. These pastry cases are usually cut from puff paste in two pieces, a circle for the base and a doughnut shape equal in diameter for the sides. The two are pasted together with egg wash and then rise in baking to become a high-sided cup. (Or you can cut out a circle or oval and then make a

case from it as directed previously.) But here is a third and highly professional method for making vol-au-vents with a machine which is very expensive and very formidable. There is a complicated cast-aluminum handle which includes an adjustable pressure gauge. The handle is attached to a stainless-steel blade which cuts out a scalloped circle a bit over 3″ in diameter while at the same time a nylon plunger creates a central well in the pastry. During baking this depression will never rise to the height of the sides, and thus the case is created. The machine comes with variously sized stainless-steel half-cubes on which you can prop a cake rack over the baking pastry at whatever level is desired to prevent it from rising irregularly.

Rolling Italian Croissant Cutter   10.76

Stainless steel with hardwood handles; 17″ long overall; cutting cylinder 5¹⁵⁄₁₆″ long, 2¾″ diam.

$48.00

Another marvelous cutter from Italy, in its way as fascinating as the device whose oval cutters miraculously make circles (10.61). This machine is easier to comprehend, but equally appealing. Wooden rolling-pin handles hold a stainless-steel frame with blades which, passed over a sheet of dough, produce a continual stream of triangular shapes. In Italy it is called a tagliatrianguli, or triangle cutter: we call it a croissant cutter, although it can also be used to cut dough for Danish pastry or apple turnovers. One complete revolution of the roller produces triangles that are roughly 4″ in the base and 6″ tall. Not a bit of dough is wasted or needs to be reworked by the cook.

Rolling French Croissant Cutter   10.77

Nickel steel with wood handles; 14″ long overall; cutting cylinder 5″ long, 3¾″ diam.

$35.00 ▲

This croissant cutter is smaller than the preceding one, is French in origin, and is made of nickel steel rather than stainless; otherwise it is similar, working on much the same principle as 10.76. It is also considerably more expensive than the Italian model. Both are mechanized circular cutters, a type of utensil virtually unknown in this country. They are exceedingly thrifty of dough, no small matter when you consider the cost of butter and the hours spent in folding, rolling, and chilling the dough for puff pastry.

COOLING RACKS

A woman we know used to remove her lemon cookies from their baking sheet onto freshly laundered tea towels; but alas for fond memories, it seems that she was all wrong. In theory it would work after a fashion, this genteel method of absorbing the moisture evaporating from cakes as they cool, but it's much simpler and more effective to place them on a wire cooling rack where air can reach beneath and all around them. Newly made cakes of all kinds are fragile and must, therefore, be allowed to cool slightly on or in the pan so that they will firm up enough to be removed safely. (There are a few exceptional cakes that are cooled completely in the pan—we're not talking about those, of course.) Then the cakes should be placed on wire racks which permit the air to circulate all around them and carry off the moisture they give off in the form of water vapor. If the vapor is prevented from escaping—for example, if a hot cake is put directly on a plate—then moisture will be trapped under the layer and the cake will be soggy. Cooling racks are important: choose big ones—10.80 if you have room to store it—and buy enough of them so that you will be able to cool everything that you take from your oven, even many dozens of cookies turned out in quick succession.

Circular Wire Rack from Germany 10.78

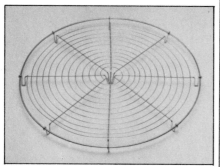

Tinned steel wire; 15" diam.; ⅞" high.
$6.00

It looks like a spider's web, but don't be deceived: this large circular cake rack from Germany is strong enough to hold your most substantial cakes. There are eight legs around the circumference and another in the middle to hold the cake about an inch above the surface of your counter. The legs are formed of the same sturdy tinned-steel wire that is woven into the circular mesh. Although the rack is a generous 15" in diameter and will hold a lot of cookies, you will nonetheless need a pair of them in order to cool two cake layers, even small ones.

Circular Wire Rack from France 10.79

Tinned wire; 11¹/₁₆" diam.; ¾" high.
$4.50

A single continuous coil of good-quality tinned wire, supported by a grid of crossed straight wires, winds around to form this French cooling rack; because of this construction the rack is exceptionally strong, even though the center is unsupported. Three triangular legs raise the whole affair ¾" off the table, so that air can circulate underneath. You will need at least two of these racks, which are just over 11" in diameter.

Heavy-Duty Wire Cake Rack 10.80

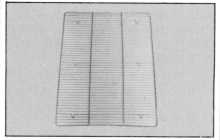

Nickel-plated steel; 24½" X 16½"; 1" high. Also avail. 16½" X 13", ⅞" high. **$10.00 $7.00 ▲**

The bakers on our staff are mad for these racks—a mania not easily explained by their simple appearance. But—breathed one editor, who makes dozens of cookies every weekend—they are so *big*. And—mused another, who turns out four loaves of bread once a week—they are so *strong*. And that's about it, and that seems to be enough: these are big, heavy, strong racks impeccably constructed of nickel-plated steel. We show you two sizes, one extremely large (24½" x 16⅜") and one medium-to-large (16½" x 13"): the larger has six, the smaller has four small rigid feet to lift them off the surface of the counter and permit air to circulate underneath. The frame, of four stout lengthwise rods, is crossed at half-inch intervals by rods of somewhat lighter gauge to form the cooling grid, and all the points of juncture are welded together. You can store these racks with your trays or baking sheets—to make the wherewithal to fill them, use the baking sheets, (9.2 or 9.3), and look at the recipe for Karen Zehring's lovely cookies.

Rectangular Wire Cake Rack 10.81

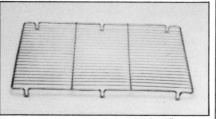

Heavy-gauge tinned steel wire;18½"X13"; 1⅛"high.
$10.00

What this rack has to offer is size, and a very useful one it is, midway between the two sizes of the preceding rack. The 18½" x 13" rectangle will accommodate two cake layers or a whole recipe's worth

of cookies. If you buy two of these, you'll be prepared for anything. Besides its size, the rack has the virtue of solidity, being made of heavy-gauge tinned-steel wire, with three U-shaped feet along each long edge lifting the surface more than an inch above the counter top. The only drawback we can imagine is that you might have trouble finding room to store it—we'd be inclined to put it with the baking sheets.

WALNUT COOKIES •
 KAREN ZEHRING

1¾ cups all-purpose flour,approximately
1 cup very fresh unsalted butter
½ cup confectioners' sugar
⅔ cup ground walnuts
¼ teaspoon salt
Pecan Cream Filling (below)
Vanilla-flavored confectioners' sugar for sprinkling

Preheat oven to 375 F.

Mix flour and butter with a pastry blender (10.35 or 10.36) until the mixture forms crumbs. Add sugar, walnuts, and salt and knead well (you may have to add a little more flour so the dough will not feel sticky). If possible, put the dough, wrapped in plastic, into the refrigerator for 45 minutes before rolling it.

Cut the dough into halves. Roll out each half ¼ inch thick between sheets of waxed paper. Cut dough with a small, scalloped cutter such as 10.73.

Place rounds at least an inch apart on a baking sheet and bake in the preheated oven for 12 minutes, or until cookies are only lightly browned around the edges.

Remove from oven and cool.

Fill pairs of cookies, bottoms together, with Pecan Cream Filling (below), making sandwiches of them. Sprinkle with vanilla-flavored confectioners' sugar.

PECAN CREAM FILLING
¼ cup milk
¼ cup sugar
1-inch piece of vanilla bean
¾ cup ground pecans
3 tbsp. lemon juice
⅓ cup unsalted butter

Bring milk, sugar, and vanilla bean just to a boil, then reduce heat. Stir in the ground pecans and lemon juice. Simmer the filling, stirring frequently, until thickened. Let the filling cool. Discard vanilla bean.

After filling has cooled completely, whip the butter in a separate bowl or in an electric mixer until it is very light and foamy. Then whip in the pecan mixture and fill the cookies. Yield: About 2 dozen.

Circular Wire Rack from Germany
Circular Wire Rack from France
Heavy-Duty Wire Cake Rack
Rectangular Wire Cake Rack

Revolving Decorating Stand
English Decorating Syringe

PASTRY BAGS AND DECORATING EQUIPMENT

Most baked goods require some sort of flourish at the finish, if only a powdering with confectioners' sugar or a drizzle of thin icing. Others of course, are glazed and frosted and adorned with icing rosebuds, and violets, crushed almonds, and the like. At any rate, your cake, having cooled on a wire rack, is in the perfect location for having its icing and any decorations applied. (Although there are those, to be sure, who prefer to apply finishing touches with the cake on a turntable, such as 10.82, believing its easy rotation to be a steadier movement than the human hand with an icing spatula can provide.) Before you begin to ice your cake, brush off all loose crumbs with a pastry brush (10.55) and look once again at the section on spatulas above.

A CHOICE OF METHODS

Once the coat of icing has been laid on, you have your choice of three basic methods for applying piped decorations: icing syringe, pastry bag, or a cone made of parchment paper. The syringe is easiest to control but least sensitive, rather like a student's violin when compared with a Stradivarius. A professional chef uses a pastry bag; and the real virtuoso can take a triangle of parchment paper, twist it into a cone, snip off the end in one of several frightfully clever shapes, and produce miracles of sculpture in butter cream.

All three decorating devices have other uses, too—with them you can pipe shapes for meringues or éclairs or cream puffs, or press cookies onto a baking sheet.

ICING SYRINGES

Perhaps most familiar to the home cook are the icing syringes: rigid metal tubes with insertable tips and a plunger to force out the icing. For the inexperienced cake decorator these are the easiest to control, and they can be bought in sets. As finesse is acquired, greater subtlety of control can be achieved with pastry bags and their tubes or nozzles.

Monumentally constructed stands were required to support chefs' towering pastry creations for great occasions of the Victorian era.

English Decorating Syringe 10.83

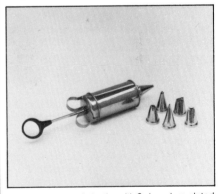

Stainless steel and plastic, with 6 chromium-plated tips; 7⅛" long overall; 1¾" diam.; tips 1⅜" long, ⅞" diam.; 3½ fl. oz. capacity.

$6.00

It looks like the child of the Tin Woodsman, this stainless-steel decorating syringe from England. Six interchangeable chromium-plated tips fit snugly onto a cylindrical body; at the other end are two rings to pull on with your fingers while you press the black plastic plunger with your thumb. In our tests, opening and closing the body of the syringe wasn't always easy; aside from that, this is a workmanlike piece of equipment, lightweight and comfortable in the hand, with a 6" tube and a capacity of 3½ ounces of icing.

Revolving Decorating Stand 10.82

Cast-iron stand, aluminum alloy turntable; 12" diam.; 4¾" high; 200-lb. capacity.

$26.00 ▲

Working like a potter's wheel, this neat cake-decorating turntable from Ateco adds the steadiness of machined bearings to a less-than-steady human hand. Put your cake on the thick aluminum top, which is 12" in diameter, and then revolve it with one hand while you apply frosting with the other. The precision machining permits the turntable to rotate smoothly and steadily above the heavy cast-iron stand. You can press ground almonds into the sides of the cake or scallop butter-cream shells around the edge as you make the wheel rotate slowly. The turntable is not beautiful, and although it may resemble a cake stand, it is decidedly not that, but rather a heavy, well-made piece of equipment for professional use that will serve superbly for years in the home kitchen. It is easy to take apart and clean; and it is inexpensive when you consider its probable longevity.

Aluminum Decorating Syringe   10.84

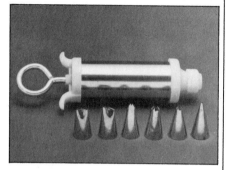

Aluminum and plastic, with 6 nickel-silver tips; 7" long overall; barrel 4¼" long, 1¾" diam.; 3½ fl. oz. capacity.
$6.50 ▲

When you buy this well-made American decorating syringe with six different nickel-silver tips you have the option of also buying a boxed set of 52 other tips (10.89) to augment the basic six. The barrel of the syringe is of a gold-tinted aluminum, and the ends of the cylinder are made of rigid white plastic. It is amazingly easy to disassemble the syringe for effortless filling and cleaning, a fact which makes us prefer it to the English model. In addition, the plastic trigger-like finger grips are much sturdier than those on the English syringe. A top choice.

THE SWEETEST CALLIGRAPHY OF THEM ALL: The Use of Writing in Pastry Decoration
by George Lang

Writing can be both functional and decorative. In pâtissèrie and confectionery, writing is used to give information and also purely for the sake of ornamentation. Sugar penmanship has just one advantage over conventional calligraphy: its three-dimensional quality can be much more dramatic. Unfortunately, most other aspects are disadvantageous, especially the fact that soon after it's made, it disappears.

The history of pastry calligraphy began rather recently. Carême, who flourished in the first third of the nineteenth century, is considered the greatest chef in culinary history, his most notable achievement being the introduction of architecture into the pastry art. For instance, his Le Pâtissier Pittoresque shows dozens of elaborate productions made out of pastry and sugar, ranging from an Egyptian cascade to a Chinese fort. Curiously enough, neither he nor his immediate successors used calligraphy in these extraordinary exhibition pieces. Francatelli, the disciple of Carême, headed Queen Victoria's kitchens and used calligraphic elements, not actually calligraphy, in his extraordinary creations.

The nearest to a definite date we can discern for the first writing on cakes is probably 1832. The great Viennese sugar baker, Franz Sacher, created his famous torte for the honor and pleasure of Prince von Metternich, to whom he was chef. On top of the smooth chocolate glaze, the name of its creator—"Sacher" —was written with delicate hand. From then on, the pastry chefs of the Danubian valley, especially in Austria and Hungary, invented cakes for celebrities and for important occasions, often with the appropriate name as part of the ornamentation. Later on, most probably in the beginning of the twentieth century, they also used writing to identify the particular kind of cake. Cakes marked "Marron" or "Noisettine" became standard presentations.

The next step came in the 1920s, when personalization became the order of the day. Even though everyone at a wedding knew the name of the bride and groom, suddenly lovely plaques with names on them appeared as part of the cake. The same thing happened with pastries for anniversaries, birthdays, and holidays. Like a child discovering the limitless possibilities of a particularly good toy, chefs went farther—they began to decorate cakes to look like a telegram, for example, or, on an anniversary cake, they might copy the original wedding certificate. At an exhibition in Cologne, I have even seen a faithful replica of a page from the Gutenberg Bible.

A cake calligrapher usually has to make his own pen and ink. For a "pen" one usually prepares a paper tube in the shape of a cone with an opening at the tip, generally formed of a triangular piece of parchment. (It is also possible to use a pastry or icing bag with metal tubes or nozzles which will make different designs, depending on the shape of the opening; and another device is a metal decorating syringe with interchangeable tips.) The "ink" for calligraphy is the so-called royal icing or an almost black royal chocolate icing. There are also various kinds of creams used and even, horribile dictu, something called chocolate plastic. Royal icing is made essentially with egg whites and powdered sugar whipped together with a pinch of cream of tartar. What makes royal icing indispensable to ornamental decoration and calligraphy is the fact that after the soft pastelike material is applied it hardens to the consistency of plaster.

Although sugar was known in Europe at least as early as the end of the fifteenth century, it was long the most expensive and rarest of all foodstuffs. As a matter of fact, it was only sold in pharmacies as a medicine. As a sweetener of foods and beverages, it was only used from the beginning of the eighteenth century. After Benjamin Delessert began to produce sugar commercially from sugar beets in the early nineteenth century, cakes and tortes became part of the baker's everyday repertoire. Royal icing, too, dates from this period.

Gingerbread, most probably an ancient invention by a Greek baker from Rhodes, was often gilded and embellished from the Middle Ages onward. It was eventually made in many forms, some highly decorated, and even appeared as "books" with an alphabet written on them so children could learn their letters the easy way. Now this might be an idea to solve the "Why Johnny can't read" problem . . . any child who had to "read" his cake before eating it would have sweet incentive indeed.

Decorating Pen   10.85

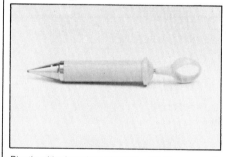

Plastic with chromium-plated tip; 7¼" long overall; ⅞" diam.; 1 fl. oz. capacity.
$1.25

"The moving finger writes". . . and in this case it writes in sugar. With it the kids can sign their own names to Grandma's birthday cake, or you can inscribe individual messages on cupcakes or cookies. Technically, we suppose that this is another decorating syringe, but we like to think of it as a sort of pen, the body a cylinder for holding icing and the point a detachable tip with a small round opening. It is thoroughly professional, easy to clean, and amazingly easy to use, made in England of plastic and metal.

The use of the pastry bag, illustrated in the Livre de Pâtisserie, *1873, by Jules Gouffé.*

PASTRY BAGS

Pastry bags used to be made of canvas, a fact which meant that they could be kept neither clean nor pliable; no matter how thoroughly you washed them, some of the former contents seemed to remain imbedded in the fabric. Today your choice is between a bag of nylon or of a fabric fused with plastic: the first is somewhat more supple and easier to control, the second, infinitely easier to clean. If we tell you that the first pastry bag we show you is the French and the second one is American, you will assume that here we have the old-fashioned conflict between beauty and hygiene, but not so: which one you choose is simply a matter of taste and of which feels better in the hand. The sizes of either bag you decide to buy will depend on the way you plan to use them—for making delicate ornaments on pastry, you will want a smaller size than for piping chou paste to form cream puffs, or for making scalloped borders on a grand scale.

French Nylon Pastry Bag   10.86

Nylon; 8″ long. Also avail. 9¾″, 11¾″, 13¾″, 15¾″, 17¾″, 19¾″, or 23¾″ long. $2.98

This French nylon pastry bag has many good qualities. It is more flexible than the ordinary canvas or plastic-coated fabric kinds and, because nylon dries so quickly, it is the easiest kind to wash and store. The flexibility helps you to control your results—only a slight increase in hand pressure produces a variation in the size or shape of what emerges from the nozzle. The bag comes in five lengths ranging from 8″ to 17″, and each size can be used with all standard pastry-bag nozzles.

CREAM PUFFS

Helen McCully tells us what pâte à chou is: a cream puff pastry that has innumerable uses. The dough can be made into cream puffs or éclairs, baked, filled with French pastry cream (vanilla, coffee, or chocolate), then frosted; or filled with mixtures such as lobster, crabmeat, or chicken to make hors d'oeuvre. The basic dough has many applications in cookery. Gnocchi à la viennoise, for example; in preparing potatoes à la dauphine, Duchess potatoes mixed with chou paste, shaped into balls, and deep fried.

PATE A CHOU

1 cup water
½ cup (1 stick) sweet butter
Pinch salt
1 cup sifted all-purpose flour
4 whole eggs

Crème pâtissière (see below)
Combine the water, butter, and salt in a heavy saucepan. Bring to a boil, take off the heat, and stir in the flour all at once. Place back over very low heat and beat vigorously with a wooden spatula until the dough leaves the sides of the pan and forms a ball. Take off the heat and beat in the eggs one at a time, beating briskly after each addition until the dough is smooth. Makes 16 to 18 puffs or éclairs.

To make cream puffs: Squeeze rounds, about 1 tablespoon in each, out of a pastry bag fitted with a medium-sized plain tube onto a greased baking sheet, leaving about 2 inches between puffs to allow for spreading.

To fill cream puffs: Fill a pastry bag, fitted with a small plain tube, with crème pâtissière. Make a small opening in the bottom of each puff with a paring knife. Insert the tube into the opening and fill the puff.

CREME PATISSIERE

2 cups milk
4 egg yolks
¼ cup sugar
1 teaspoon vanilla
¼ cup cornstarch

Bring the milk to a boil over moderate heat in a heavy saucepan. Set aside.

Combine the yolks, sugar, and vanilla in a bowl and beat with a rotary or electric beater until the mixture makes "ribbons" and turns a pale yellow—3 to 4 minutes. Add the cornstarch and beat until smooth. Add the hot milk slowly, whipping constantly. Pour the mixture back into the saucepan, place over moderate heat, and bring to a boil, stirring constantly with a wooden spatula. Cook very slowly, stirring constantly, until the crème thickens almost to a paste. Place a piece of plastic wrap flat on the surface so a skin won't form, and refrigerate. Makes about 3 cups.

NOTE: Crème pâtissière is a basic cream that can be used to fill cream puffs, éclairs, cakes, or as a base for sweet soufflés. If you wish to flavor it with liqueur such as cognac or kirsch, or other flavors such as coffee or almond (if you use almond do not use vanilla in the basic recipe), add the flavoring when the crème is cold.

Plastic-lined Pastry Bag   10.87

Plastic-lined fabric; 10″ long; 6¾″ top diam. Also avail. 7″, 8″, 12″, 14″, 16″, 18″, 21″, or 24″ long.
$.85

The fabric of this American-made professional-quality pastry bag is fused with plastic on its inner surface, while the outside has been left with a muslin-like texture for ease in gripping and manipulation. A little stiffer than the French nylon bag, it is supposed to become more supple with use; it's certainly worth giving a try when you consider its many excellent qualities. Try the 7″ size for piping rosettes on a cake and the 24″ size for such jobs as bordering a planked steak with duchesse potatoes.

French Nylon Pastry Bag
Plastic-lined Pastry Bag
Set of Tubes for Pastry Bags
Set of Decorating Tubes

Bismarck Pastry Tube
Tubes for Flowers and Leaves

Set of Tubes for Pastry Bags — 10.88

Tinned steel; 12 assorted pastry tubes averaging 2¼″ long; tubes from 1″ to 1⅜″ wide at large end.
$4.60

If you buy a pastry bag you will also need to acquire a basic set of tips, because the bag is only that—a container for the icing or other food you will force through it into decorative shapes made by metal tubes or nozzles. This set of assorted useful shapes can be used directly in the bag without a coupling: simply drop the tube in through the bag's wide end, and the narrowness of the opening at the other end will prevent it from falling through. The tubes have openings of various sizes and shapes—some round, some jagged, some slit-like (for ribbon shapes), some like stars; they are made of sturdy tinned steel for the use of professional bakers.

Set of Decorating Tubes — 10.89

Nickel silver; 48 tubes approx. 1¼″ long, ¾″ diam.; 4 tubes approx. 1⅝″ long, 1″ diam.; Deldrin coupling; 2 flower nails 2½″ long.
$24.15

This is the set of tubes that can be bought to supplement the basic six that come with the American decorating syringe (10.84). But better and better: they can also be used with any fabric pastry bag. A Deldrin coupling included in the set consists of two threaded pieces. One is attached to the tube you choose and dropped with it into the bag, to protrude from the narrow end; the other threaded piece is screwed over it, with the fabric of the bag caught in between. It all works very easily, and the set offers a fantastic range of decorative possibilities. All this and a see-through plastic storage case, too, not to mention two flower nails on which you can construct many-petaled blossoms for later transfer to cakes or confections.

The predecessors of Carême's elaborate sugar structures were the medieval "sotelties" (subtleties), which were molded of sugar and almond paste. They were presented at the end of each course at great feasts, and showed in great detail religious or pastoral scenes, military dramas, fully armed and peopled ships, and animals of all kinds.

Bismarck Pastry Tube — 10.90

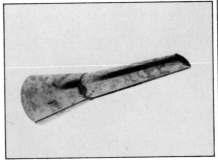

Nickel silver; 2⅝″ long; ⅝″ diam. at large end; 3/16″ diam. at small end.
$.95

Very, very special. "Bismarck" is the name long ago given to jelly doughnuts in honor of the Prussian statesman, and this is a special tube to be used for filling Bismarcks, and for nothing else that we know of. It is meant to be used with a pastry bag, but it is not included in any of the standard pastry-tube sets. With its slanted opening, it is designed to make the narrowest possible hole in the surface of the doughnut. The yeast-raised cakes are fried and allowed to cool, then a pastry bag is fitted with this tube and filled with thinned jam or jelly, which is then injected into the centers of the doughnuts. If you plan to make these jelly doughnuts, beloved of children, these tubes are worth getting. Following standard filled-doughnut instructions—to cut a hole in the cake and fill through it—will result in an unholy mess and leaking jelly coming from a too-large gash.

Tubes for Flowers and Leaves — 10.91

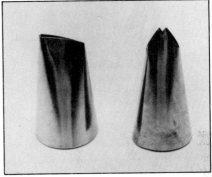

Nickel silver. Leaf tube 1⅞″ long; diam. at large end 1″; opening ¼″ wide. Petal tube 1¾″ long; diam. at large end 1″; opening ⅝″ wide.
$.55 each

Plant a garden on your next cake with these two tips and a pastry bag full of icing. One tube makes petals and one makes leaves, and with a little practice you will be able to combine them to create any flower in the garden. They are of nickel silver and fit all standard pastry bags; they're worth having because of the usefulness of this particular form of decoration. For example, you could do a different flower on each cup-cake or large cooky for a child's birthday party, or pipe a single perfect blossom on each of a trayful of iced petits fours.

Unchanged through the years, the pastry bag and plain tip for piping ladyfinger batter; these were shown in a nineteenth-century manual.

Cake-decorating Stencil 10.92

Aluminum; 5½" square. Avail. in 16 designs.
$2.55

If using this stencil was merely the easiest way to decorate a cake, we should not be as enthusiastic about it as we are—as it happens, it is also one of the most effective methods. Frost your cake lightly, let the icing set, and then place one of these lightweight steel stencils over the top: choose the carnation, say, or Charlie Chaplin. Now sprinkle powdered sugar or colored sprinkles or chocolate shot over the whole thing; lift it off carefully; and you have a beautifully finished design. If you are using a white frosting, you could set a part of it aside, tint it with food coloring, and then brush it gently over the stencil. On a dark chocolate icing, you could try painting a swan with a thick apricot glaze. These stencils will create a lovely powdered-sugar pattern on an unfrosted cake as well. The sixteen designs—which include flowers, various birds, butterflies, and even the man in the moon—are handsome, the price is good, and the construction perfectly adequate: a real treat.

ALMOND MERINGUES

(Elizabeth Susan Colchie)

⅔ cup finely ground, lightly toasted almonds
½ cup plus 2 tablespoons superfine granulated sugar
2 teaspoons cornstarch
3 eggs, separated
Large pinch (⅛ teaspoon) cream of tartar
Pinch of salt
¼ teaspoon vanilla
⅛ teaspoon almond extract

Butter and flour a large baking sheet (9.3) or cover it with baking parchment (10.99). Preheat the oven to 225 F.

Combine the almonds in a bowl with ½ cup of the sugar and the cornstarch. Rub the mixture carefully through your fingers to combine it well and remove any lumps.

Beat the egg whites in a bowl with the cream of tartar and salt until they form soft peaks. Gradually beat in the remaining 2 tablespoons of sugar until stiff peaks are formed. Add the vanilla and almond flavorings and beat for a minute more.

Delicately fold the nut and sugar mixture into the meringue, one-fourth at a time.

Fit a pastry bag (10.86 or 10.87) with a plain tube with a ¼" opening and gently fill the bag with the meringue. Pipe the meringue onto the baking sheet in 2" rounds.

Bake in the preheated oven for 1 hour, then turn off the heat and let the meringues remain in the oven for at least 3 hours. Cool them completely on a wire rack.

Store meringues in a tightly closed container.

Makes about 2 dozen.

Metal Ruler 10.93

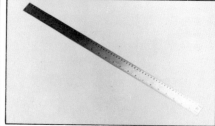

Aluminum; 24½" long; 1⅜" wide.
$1.65

Here is a washable metal ruler, an indispensable tool for every serious pastry cook. When making croissants, for example, each rectangle of dough, before being cut into triangles, must be no wider than 5" and no longer than 12" to produce a perfect result. Often dough must be measured and cut to fit a pan, or it must be cut into strips for various purposes. Use this ruler as insurance of fit and of straight edges, knowing that the metal will wash off cleanly and will leave no odds and ends of shellac on the dough. Marked for measurements up to 24", this ruler also measures in millimeters up to 61. There is a hole in the end so that you can hang it above your baking counter. The only problem will be to keep it from being stolen.

Rolling Pastry Piercer 10.94

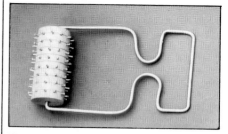

Wood with steel pins and handle; 9½" long overall; roller 4½" wide, 1¾" diam.
$9.00

Every pastry cook, gadget-minded or not, will want this professional dough piercer from Italy. It rolls smoothly over the dough, leaving punctures indistinguishable from the old-fashioned fork-made kind. While not precisely a kitchen necessity, it will be useful for cooks whose stock in trade runs to pie and tart shells or to masterpieces using large sheets of dough. It need not sit in the drawer between bouts of pastry making, however; it can also be used as a meat tenderizer.

MINOR INDISPENSABLES FOR BAKING

Like twine, like tweezers, like scissors, there are some things you never think you will need in the kitchen until you reach for them and they aren't there. You will need a kitchen-worthy (meaning washable) ruler for measuring rolled-out dough and checking the size of pans and for making a straight edge when trimming shapes or cutting strips. Less essential, but worth having if you make lots of pastry, is a tool for piercing dough. It looks like the inside of a music box, but is used to make hundreds of perforations in large sheets of dough or unbaked pie or tart crusts.

Cake-decorating Stencil
Metal Ruler
Rolling Pastry Piercer

Cake Tester
Pastry Crimper
Pie Bird

THE "GADGETS" THAT AREN'T

They are only called gadgets, disparagingly, when you don't need them; when you do, they become your right hand, your miraculous assistants, the very tools you can't do without. Here is a cluster of items—non-gadgets, to our mind—which are worth considering. Cake testers, pastry crimpers (you'll want one of these unless you possess an heirloom in brass or ivory), a pie bird to keep your pie crust in its place while letting steam escape—all such could no doubt be dispensed with, as can a reed banneton for shaping loaves (10.98) —but they will all make your baking a little easier and more efficient. And one more item, one we think indispensable—parchment paper, in any or all of its forms, for lining cake pans of any size or shape.

Cake Tester — 10.95

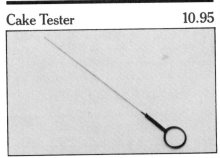

Wire with plastic-coated handle; 6¾" long.
$.30

When a cake is finished, a broom straw inserted into it will come out clean. Well and good, but what with plastic replacing straw in most brooms, it may not be so easy to find a traditional tester in your kitchen. Toothpicks don't work too well, being too short for comfort, and actually, many good cooks have always preferred to use a thin knife. But if you want to buy a special tool for testing cakes, one which will be always at hand and will scarcely create a dent in your budget, think of this sharp-pointed wire tester, with a plastic-coated loop for a handle, convenient for hanging.

Pastry Crimper — 10.96

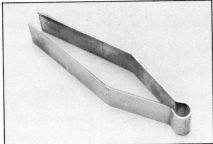

Stainless steel; 4" long.
$1.50

All filled pastries—pies included—require a tight seal between the top and bottom layers of crust. You can pinch them with your fingers, you can press them with the tines of a fork, or you can do the job effortlessly with this pastry crimper. It is well made from stainless steel and has serrated gripping edges. And lest you think you are spending your money for something you will scarcely ever use, the manufacturer advises us that it can also be used as a strawberry huller. A tip: always hull the strawberries at the last possible moment—and after they have been washed—to lessen the loss of juice.

Pie Bird — 10.97

Ceramic; 4" tall.
$2.25

"Four and twenty blackbirds baked in a pie"—in England they use one of these birds (not two dozen) very often in pies. This hungry little ceramic bird functions as a sort of funnel when it is placed in the center of the filling of a two-crust pie. It then helps support the top crust and allows steam to escape through its open beak, so that the crust will neither burst nor become soggy. With this little fellow around, you won't have to cut the usual slashes or other vents in the top of your pie. We grant that you'll make no incredible saving of effort or energy, but the pie bird is rather fun to use: imagine the children's faces when you cut the first piece of pie!

A raised pie, a British specialty.

PAIN DE CAMPAGNE— COUNTRY LOAF

Here is the recipe for the pain de campagne to fill the banneton (10.98). It is adapted from the recipe of Charles Williams of Williams-Sonoma, the source of the banneton.

1 envelope granulated dry yeast
Pinch of sugar
¼ cup warm water (110 F.)
2 tsp. salt
1¼ cups warm water (110 F.)
3 cups unbleached white flour
1 cup unbleached whole-wheat flour
Additional flour for kneading

Dissolve yeast and sugar in the ¼ cup of warm water and let proof (rise until foamy) about 10 minutes.

In a mixing bowl, dissolve salt in the warm water and add yeast mixture. Beat in the flour; then, knead the dough in the bowl until it becomes elastic and leaves the sides of the bowl and your hands clean. (If the dough is too soft, add a little more white flour.)

Form dough into a ball, flour it, and place it in a clean bowl in a warm place. Cover dough with a towel and let rise until doubled in bulk, about 1 hour.

Turn out onto a floured kneading surface and knead for 5 minutes. Form into a ball and place in a well-floured 8" round banneton. Let rise until it has doubled in bulk.

Preheat oven to 450 F. Turn dough carefully, upside down, onto a greased and floured baking sheet and bake for 15 minutes, then turn oven down to 400 F. and bake for 30 minutes more, or until loaf sounds hollow when rapped with the knuckles. Cool loaf on a wire rack.

Banneton for Raising Bread   10.98

Reed; 8″ diam.; 2½″ deep; holds 1½-lb. loaf.
$10.00

This is a banneton, a small basket made of reeds which is used for raising bread dough. Let your dough rise until doubled; then flour the basket heavily and set the shaped round loaf in it to rise again. When the dough has again doubled you turn it out upside down onto a baking sheet. Although the bread rises further in the oven, the impression of the reed pattern remains, giving the loaf a sweetly rustic appearance. And although the banneton, 8″ in diameter, could be used to make a 1½-pound loaf with any kind of bread dough, the recipe for pain de campagne—a true country loaf—on preceding page is just right: dense, smooth, and tasting pleasantly of the whole grain.

Roll of Parchment Paper   10.99

Parchment paper; 16½″ long; 15″ wide; 20 sq. ft. total.
$.98

Although we'll admit that you don't really need a pie bird, this item—parchment paper—is emphatically a necessity. The roll of specially treated parchment paper is packed in a dispenser box with a serrated metal cutting edge. You pull out and tear off a length, set your pan on the paper and draw its outline, and cut out the shape you have made. Then line your cake pan with the paper, pour in the batter, and waste not an instant worrying about the cake sticking to the bottom of the pan. It will lift right out, and it is a simple matter to peel the paper off the cake. You will find this paper invaluable for lining the bottoms of tube pans and for lining any old pans that have lost their finish; if using parchment paper eliminates the one time in twenty that you lose pieces of your cake to the adhesive qualities of a pan, then it is well worth it. The manufacturer recommends this paper for lining casseroles and baking sheets as well.

A cookbook published in 1788 in Edinburgh gives the following recipe for an old version of our hard sauce, deliciously christened Fairy Butter: "Take the yolks of three hard eggs, four ounces of loaf sugar, six ounces of fresh butter, as new from the churn as you can, and two spoonfuls of orange flower or rose water: beat them all very well until they are like a paste: then put it into a squirt, and squirt it on . . . in little heaps." This "squirt" is nothing but an eighteenth-century pastry bag.

Parchment Cake-Pan Liners   10.100

Parchment-paper pan liners; avail. 8″ or 9″ diam., 1½″ deep, 8 per box.
$.55

These fitted liners are less universally useful than the plain sheets of parchment paper. Looking like giant shallow cupcake-pan liners, with their flat bottoms and fluted sides, they are made to fit into 8″ and 9″ round cake pans. Instead of greasing and flouring the pan, you simply set a liner into it, pour in the batter, and bake. When the cake has cooled, the liner will peel right off. The plain roll of paper is preferable for its versatility, among other reasons, but these liners are rather pretty, will save time, and are perfectly serviceable. Try them, too, for holding the rice or beans with which you fill a pastry crust being baked without a filling.

Cupcake-Pan Liners   10.101

Paper, or paper with foil. Two sizes: 2⅛″ diam., 15/16″ deep, 1½ fl. oz. capacity, 110 per box; or 2½″ diam., 1¼″ deep, 2½ fl. oz. capacity, 48 per box (paper and foil) or 88 per box (plain).
$.39–$.49

Cupcake liners are peeled off the cakes at the last possible moment; there is even a special kid-technique of scraping every crumb off the paper with one's bottom teeth comparable to the kid-technique of scraping the cream off the separated wafers of a sandwich cooky. Here is a line of cupcake liners to fit two sizes of pan: the larger will hold 2½ ounces of batter, the smaller only 1½ ounces. The dazzler here is that, in addition to the bland pastels indigenous to this form of paper, the liners also come with a really stunning aluminum-foil finish on the outside of the paper. Paint the inside of the foil liners with a melted bitter chocolate and put them into your freezer to fill later with a champagne ice. Or use them to hold a classic frozen dessert, Biscuit Tortoni. Fabulous pans such as those we have shown you from Lockwood (9.46, 9.47) will only have their cooking action impeded by using these liners. A little added insulation may help your old cupcake pans, however. The cups with aluminum on the outside are somewhat stiffened and could stand alone on a baking sheet for baking at low heat, or could be filled with individual servings of mousse.

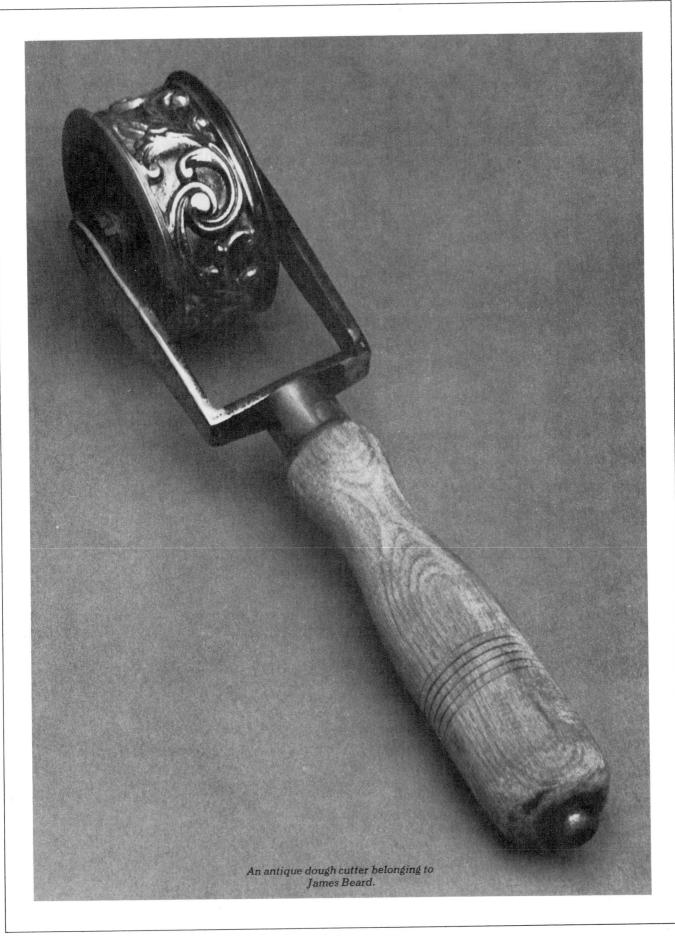

*An antique dough cutter belonging to
James Beard.*

The planet Earth is 70 per cent water. From Bangkok to Bangor its surface is studded with seas, lakes, ponds, rivers, sounds, and bays, all providing homes for a variety of edible beings. Swimming, crawling, or just burrowing peacefully into the bottom, these cold-blooded creatures provide the air breathers of the planet with an opportunity for sport, a source of protein, and very good eating.

As the varieties of fish, mollusks, and crustaceans that inhabit the waters are nearly limitless, so are the methods of preparing them. Raw, baked, steamed, poached, or broiled, seafood is superbly good, and good for you. Weight-conscious people know the value of seafood's low calorie count, and, while shellfish are high in cholesterol, swimmers with scales and fins have so little that they have become a staple of the healthful diet needed by people with heart trouble.

Those who live in the uttermost deserts must settle for frozen fish and shellfish, but the proximity of water to many areas of the nation and fast shipping under refrigeration make a plenitude of fresh fish available to most of us the year round. And that is the essential word in most seafood cookery—fresh. In some cultures, fish is fermented to make a sauce or a special dish with a taste that doesn't appeal to all palates—nuoc mam, such a sauce, is a staple of the Vietnamese diet. However, most of us prefer—however much we like anchovy paste or smoked salmon—to eat our fish fresh, to lift our catch wriggling on the end of a line from the water, or to rake our clams from their sandy bed. For market-goers, we give some guidelines to choosing fresh fish and shellfish further along.

Fish-eaters almost invariably become fish cooks, as do fishermen. For all of them we show here our choices of tools and utensils for doing everything from cleaning the smallest trout to poaching the largest striped bass, tools to pry a clam from its armored home and to probe the crimson carcass of a steamy lobster. We hope they will unlock for you many of the mysteries of these denizens of the deep.

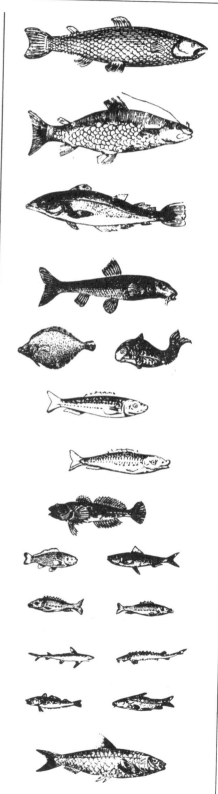

CHOOSING FISH

Anyone who has eaten a fish just plucked from its watery home knows the Lucullan delight of that experience. Whether you have caught it yourself or have purchased it from a market which specializes in really fresh fish, your entire attitude toward fish-eating is likely to be changed with the first bite, and changed for the better. The leaky supermarket packages containing the sodden remains of day-before-yesterday's catch have as much in common with a whole fresh fish as do frozen fish sticks.

The simplest way to be certain that your fish is truly fresh is to purchase it whole. A fish doesn't have to be flip-flopping to be called fresh, but it *must* be firm-fleshed (give it a poke), with red gills. Look at the gills for yourself and reject any fish that doesn't measure up. And don't ever buy a fish whose eyes look as if it's been to an all-night party: eyes should be shiny and full, not dull and sunken. And be sure it doesn't smell fishy: fresh fish smell like sea water, nothing more, and a fishy odor means "don't buy."

WHY PREPARE YOUR OWN?

To own a whole fresh fish is to love it. Think of the myriad ways it can be cooked—baked, charcoal grilled, steamed, poached. But before you reach for the recipe book you must prepare it for the pot, and that is a much less formidable undertaking than you might think. There are many advantages in knowing how to do the scaling, boning, or cutting up yourself instead of trusting the job to the fishmonger. It's cheaper, for one thing: think of the cost of precut fillets compared to that of a whole fish, and remember that what remains of the fish after the filleting operation—the head, skeleton, and meaty scraps—can be simmered to make a court bouillon, essential to most fish sauces, or even a fish soup or chowder—any of these is a bonus whose makings would otherwise be left to the fishmonger's garbage pail.

Then, too, remember that the delicate flesh of fish is protected by the skin from drying out, much as a shell preserves an egg or the rind protects an orange—the skin is Nature's own plastic wrap. If you buy your fillets or steaks precut, you will leave a lot of the vital fluids of the flesh on the market chopping block and on the butcher paper in which your fish is wrapped. So see our tools for cleaning, scaling, skinning, filleting, boning, and slicing fish and resolve to try them on a fine, fresh fish the next chance you get.

SHELLFISH

It is an absolute article of faith among seafood lovers that any shellfish—be it mollusk or crustacean—is certain to be more delicious, more succulent, more ocean-fresh, if you catch your own, or, failing that, if you buy the creatures alive and, figuratively at least, kicking. If circumstances are such that chilled, cooked crabmeat is the only kind available, most of us will use it cheerfully, or when pressed, we'll buy frozen shrimp or bay scallops, as those delicacies aren't available fresh off the boat in any but a few localities. But we prefer our crabs and lobsters, our clams and our oysters to be alive, and we keep them alive until they are prepared for cooking. So, unless your fishmonger is willing to come into your kitchen to open your clams or boil and crack your crabs—ours isn't—the job belongs to you. As these creatures are rather recalcitrant about yielding their delectable interiors to the consumer, special tools have been developed to make the task, if not easy, at least possible.

So the proper equipment, such as that we show you in this section, isn't just convenient to have, it is vital. You can make shift to cut a fish into steaks with any large, heavy, sharp knife, but you can't open clams or oysters with a paring knife without risking both your fingers and the blade of your unsuitable but innocent tool. Once you have mastered the art of piercing a lobster's armor or evicting oysters from their shells and have savored the plump morsels within, you will find the pleasure eminently worth the trouble.

How to Dress a Fish

There are many ways to skin a fish, or to fillet it, or to slice it into steaks, or to prepare it for cooking whole. Methods vary with the kind and size of fish you are preparing. Why not, you ask, have the fishmonger make your fish completely ready to cook? In many circumstances, that is a good idea. In others, it is either impossible (suppose it's a fish *you* caught) or impractical, as when the fish must be bought a day or so ahead and you fear it will dry out if it is prepared at the time you buy it. Fortunately, making a fish ready for cooking does not require surgical skill. The right tools—the ones we show you in this section—are imperative, however.

Now you see your catch, fresh and fine, staring at you from your chopping block. Line up your fish scaler, heavy shears, flexible boning knife or all-purpose fish knife, a filleting knife if you will need it, and your large, heavy knife. Roll up your sleeves and proceed.

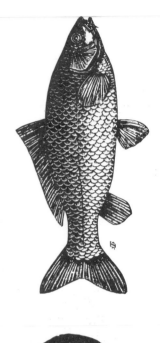

EVISCERATING

Here's how to draw a fish, if this hasn't been done at the market or by the angler who made the catch (it should be done as soon as possible after the fish is landed and before it is iced, if possible).

With a sharp knife—your boning knife, all-purpose fish knife, or filleting knife—begin at the fish's vent, the only opening on its belly. Insert the tip of the knife, with its sharp edge toward the head, and slit the skin from underneath as far as the collarbone near the base of the gills. Empty out the viscera, using your fingers to detach any clinging bits. Inside the fish, run the tip of your knife along each side of the backbone to pierce the membrane there and free any trapped blood. Rinse out the fish under cold running water.

SCALING

Almost any fish will require scaling once you get it home, even though the fishman may have made passes over it at his shop. To remove the remaining scales that are sure to be there, use one of the fish scalers we recommend, or a fish knife with a serrated edge. Holding the fish firmly by the tail, stroke the scaler toward the head—that is, against the direction in which the scales grow. Take extra care around the head and fins. Rinse the fish thoroughly under cold running water. Some anglers prefer to scale fish before drawing them when it's feasible—the round body is easier to work on than an eviscerated one.

EVISCERATING THROUGH THE GILLS

You may want to keep small fish intact–perhaps you plan to prepare small trout *au bleu* and you prefer not to slit them. (You must prepare them for this dish as soon as possible after they are caught if you want to achieve the intense blue color. And you don't want to slit them, because the slit edges will curl up and overcook in the boiling acidulated water.) Use a flexible, thin-bladed knife and a pair of scissors. Spread the fish's gill plates with your fingers, then reach inside to separate the gills from the top of the head—use scissors if necessary. Then pull on the gills, drawing out the viscera with them. Reach into the cavity of the fish to be sure you have removed all organs, then run the tip of the thin knife inside along either side of the backbone to puncture the blood sacs. Rinse the inside of the fish with cold water, and rinse the outside quickly and lightly. Don't scrape trout to be prepared *au bleu*—the less the skin is handled, the better for the looks of this dish.

FILLETING SMALL FISH
Sometimes you may want boneless fillets of small fish for use in quenelles or a mousse, or for frying quickly in butter. Rinse the whole fish (you don't need to draw it, nor need you scale it if the fillets are to be skinned). Lay it on its side on a board. With your very sharp small knife cut down along the midline running down the side from gill to tail. With the filleting knife, its blade held almost flat and parallel to the midline, cut along the fish's bones from the midline to the spine. Repeat from the midline to the belly, then turn the fish over and remove the second pair of fillets in the same way.

SKINNING FISH FILLETS
To skin fillets, large or small, lay the fillet with the skin side down. Cut into it crosswise, just down to the skin, at a point slightly above the tail end and grasp the tag end of the flesh firmly in one hand. With your knife blade pressing against the skin at a flat angle, work forward until the flesh and skin have been separated.

COPING WITH LARGE FISH
Almost invariably the large fish—bluefish, bass, salmon, and so on—whatever their source, will need careful attention in the kitchen. Scale them again (if the skin is dry, rinse them first), and use a short, blunt knife to scrape out any remains of the viscera in the cavity. Unless you're planning to poach or grill your fish whole, use your large, heavy knife to cut off the head behind the gills, slanting the cut on a diagonal in order to remove the bony structure and fins with the head. If the head is left on, be sure that all traces of the gills have been removed. To remove the dorsal (back) fin and its underlying bone structure from a fish to be used as steaks, cut down alongside the fin for its full length on either side, then pull out the strip you have released, yanking from the tail end toward the head. The fish is now ready to be filleted, or cut crosswise into steaks, or to be split for broiling.

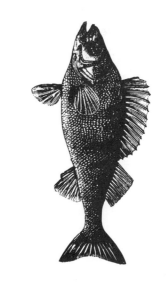

CUTTING STEAKS
Use your large, heavy knife and, if the fish is sizable, a wooden mallet such as the one we show you. Begin at the head end and slice into uniform steaks. To use the mallet, cut down until the knife blade rests against the bone, then strike the knife a sharp blow to drive it through the backbone and the lower half of the fish.

SPLITTING A FISH
As an alternative to filleting a fish to be broiled, splitting is preferred by some because the bones help keep the flesh moist. Hold the fish on its back, cavity upward. With your large, heavy knife cut carefully down along one side of the backbone for the entire length of the fish; stop

cutting before you pierce the skin. You can now lay the fish flat, butterfly-fashion, for broiling with the bone in.

FILLETING LARGE FISH OTHER THAN FLATFISH

For this, lay out your filleting knife and heavy shears. First remove the dorsal fin—when you're going to fillet a fish, it's satisfactory to simply cut the fin off with the shears so you won't jab yourself on the spines. Cut the belly of the fish fully open from vent to tail. On the outside of the fish, cut deeply along the backbone from head to tail, and cut down crosswise on each side just below the collarbone. Lay fish flat, skin side up, and use your filleting knife, the blade held almost flat and pressing against the bones, to cut the fillet free, beginning at the crosswise cut at the head end and ending above the tail. Repeat on the other side of the fish. You now have two large fillets with the skin attached. If you want to skin them, do the job as described above for small fillets.

FILLETING FLATFISH

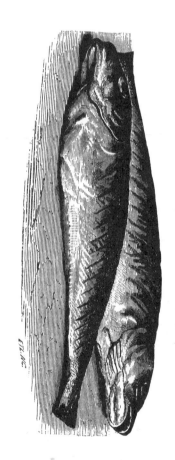

These pose unique problems. Undeniably funny-looking, flatfish have both eyes on one side of the head, and the skin of the underside is different in color and texture from the top side—typically a flatfish is lighter below, darker above, for camouflage while the fish is loafing on the silt of the sea bottom. You'll notice that these fish have spines that virtually encircle their bodies. You'll need heavy scissors, a heavy knife, and a filleting knife, preferably one designed for sole.

With your shears, first cut off the spiny ridge, and its roots, around the perimeter of the body. Remove the entrails, reserving the pink roe, if any, for your sauce. Remove the head with a semicircular cut, using your heavy knife. Then skin the fish: Use your fillet of sole knife and cut through the skin just above the tail. Work your knife under the skin and, keeping its edge pressed against the skin, which is held taut by your other hand, cut and pull the skin free, working toward the head. Alternatively, hold the tail with one hand and grasp the skin with the other; pull it sharply toward the head to strip it off. You'll see two fillets separated down the middle by the fish's backbone. First cut along either side of the backbone, then, with the knife held parallel to the spine, remove one fillet, pressing the blade against the bone and cutting toward the outside of the fish. Repeat for the second fillet, then turn the fish over and fillet the second side.

A BONUS

If you have a non-oily, mild-flavored fish—any kind you'd use for soup or chowder—use the head (minus all traces of gills), plus bones and trimmings, to make fish stock. (You mustn't use such fatty fish as salmon or bluefish, which would turn the stock dark and oily.) Don't need it at the moment? Freeze it for a later soup or sauce or for use as a superb poaching liquid for your next whole fish.

Fish Scalers and Fish Knives

Fish knives come in all sizes and shapes, from light, thin ones to heavy, solid ones, short and long, weak and strong, serrated blades and smooth.

Each is designed for a specific task in the process of getting your catch from the seaside or market to the table. Obviously, the serious fish cook will need an assortment of blades to deal with many different kinds of fish flesh.

Scaling is necessary, whether your fish is purchased or freshly caught. It can be made easier with the proper tool. Scalers are basically simple, inexpensive implements, but a well-designed one will make the difference between an arduous, messy job and a simple operation.

Sturdy fish shears are another required item for the fish cook. They have multiple uses, from opening the body of the fish to cutting out the gills, removing or trimming the tail, and cutting away the bony edges of flatfish.

To fillet or bone a fish, a very flexible blade is needed in order to follow the intricate bone structure common to our finny friends. These knives have a sharp point to pierce the skin without tearing, and they are light and easy to maneuver, with narrow blades and sturdy handles.

You will also find a large, heavy knife indispensable for cutting steaks from large fish such as striped bass, bluefish, and salmon. If your knife has a serrated blade it can also double as a fish scaler. This kind of implement must be strong enough to cut through the heavy skeletons of these big fish; see our wooden mallet, 11.11, for a means of adding power to the knife.

The common denominator of these implements is ease of cleaning. Fish is perishable and easily contaminated, so the tools used in scaling, boning, slicing, and so on must be absolutely sanitary. Stainless steel is the best material for blades, not only because it can be thoroughly scrubbed, but also because it will not discolor when it comes in contact with fish flesh. Waterproof handles, of rosewood, Pakkawood, or boilable plastic, are most practical for fish knives, both because they can be used with wet hands and also because they will survive the steamy water necessary for rendering them immaculate.

We list here a good selection of fish knives and scalers, but if you need an even larger variety, we refer you to the array of knives in Chapter 2.

steel—the material here—is ideal in fish tools because of its super-hygienic surface.

Aluminum Fish Scaler 11.2

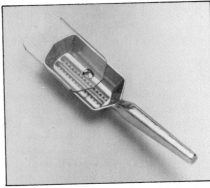

Cast aluminum with stainless-steel blade, plastic lid; 8¼" long overall; 2¼" wide.
$5.00

This tool was created to minimize the problem of fish scales flying up as you work. The very sharp stainless-steel blade, with square-toothed serrations along each side, is riveted lengthwise over the open bottom of a trough-shaped aluminum body about 1" deep and 4" long. Atop this body is a snap-on plastic cover, and a 4" metal handle, integral with the body, emerges from one end. What happens to the fish scales? They are neatly trapped within the trough, from which they are more easily cleaned than from your face and hair. Your fish will not be scaled as quickly as it would be if you used the preceding scaler, and it may be harder to work around the head and tail with this one, but it does make an essentially messy job neater. Surprisingly light yet sturdy, the implement is easy to use, easy to clean.

Stainless-Steel Fish Scaler 11.1

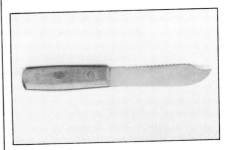

Stainless steel; 9¼" long.
$2.75 ▲

You will probably spy the twin of this fish scaler sitting on your fishmonger's chopping block. It won't win any design awards, but it will certainly make scaling your fish a simpler process (see our instructions under "How to Dress a Fish"). Made from a solid piece of stainless steel, it is 9¼" long. One end has deeply serrated edges, while the other is rolled into an easily grasped handle. The business end is curved upward so that you will not break the skin of the fish. The rakish angle also enables you to exert pressure easily on the fish's body to make quick work of the job. As the entire underside of this tool is open, there are no crevices to harbor residue, making the cleaning after use as simple as the scaling. And, as we have said, stainless

All-Purpose Fish Knife 11.3

Carbon-steel blade with beechwood handle, brass rivets; 9" long overall; blade 4⅞" long.
$2.50 ▲

Continued from preceding page

If you feel that one fish knife is all you need on your knife board, this would be a good choice. It is a rough-looking instrument with a 4⅛″ sanded but unvarnished beechwood handle that is fastened to the knife's full tang by two brass compression rivets. The blade, 4⅞″ long, can be used for a variety of purposes: the scimitar tip will gaff a small fish or, once it has been landed, slit its skin before it is eviscerated. The serrated back edge is designed for scaling, and the cutting edge will slice small steaks, split fish for broiling, or do other general chores. The blade isn't hollow ground, an advantage, as that means that the knife can be sharpened at home. That scimitar tip, by the way, with its sharp point, will open mollusks of all kinds. Don't be surprised if this knife is appropriated by the angler in the family when a fishing trip is planned—it would be at home in any tackle box.

Small All-Purpose Fish Knife　11.4

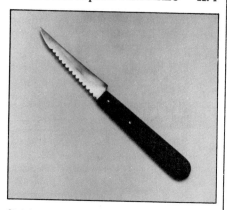

Stainless-steel blade with wood handle, brass rivets; 6¾″ long overall; blade 3″ long.
$1.50

This fish knife can perform all the functions of the preceding one, but it is about half the size. Its narrow 3-inch stainless-steel blade is serrated on the very blunt back edge, meant for scaling, and is sharp on the other, for slicing and cutting. It has a very sharp point—in fact, the tip is slightly bent downward—useful for digging out viscera, puncturing blood sacs, and piercing the skin when dressing fish. It is finished with a half rattail set into a straight wooden handle and secured with two brass rivets. While we do not recommend it in place of the larger all-purpose knife described above, we think you will find it invaluable for use on smaller fish such as trout or snapper blues.

PIKE COOKED IN HORSERADISH CREAM—CSUKA TEJFELES TORMAVAL

About 8 servings

1 carrot, peeled and sliced thin
1 knob celery, peeled and sliced thin
1 parsnip, peeled and sliced thin
1 medium-sized onion, sliced
1 tablespoon salt
6 peppercorns
Bouquet of parsley and celery greens
1 pike, 4 or 5 pounds, cleaned and gutted
1 tablespoon flour
¾ cup sour cream
4 tablespoons sweet butter
1 medium-sized horseradish, peeled and freshly grated (about 1 cup)

1. In a fish poacher cook all vegetables, salt, peppercorns and the herb bouquet in 1 quart water for 1 hour.
2. Place fish in slowly simmering vegetable broth and cook it very slowly for about 20 minutes, or until it is barely done. Flesh of fish must remain quite firm.
3. Remove fish and keep it warm. Strain broth and reduce it by half.
4. Mix flour with sour cream and butter. Add grated horseradish, then whip it into the boiling reduced liquid. Lower the heat and simmer for 2 minutes. Pour the sauce over fish, and serve.

NOTE: *This is an eighteenth-century recipe, with very few changes.*

(From THE CUISINE OF HUNGARY, by George Lang. Copyright © 1971 by George Lang. Reprinted by permission of Atheneum.)

Heavy Fish Knife　11.5

Stainless-steel with black plastic handle; 17½″ long overall; blade 11¾″ long.
$25.00

This massive knife weighs in at a hefty 12 ounces and bears a blade just a quar-ter of an inch under a foot. It is an elegant as well as an efficient tool, meant to make short work of the larger denizens of the deep. The satiny and very sharp stainless-steel blade is serrated, so it can be used for scaling as well as slicing. The extreme thickness of the back of the blade allows you to strike it sharply with a wooden mallet to cleave steaks from the boniest or biggest of fishes. Although it is meant for home use, the extremely fine manufacture of this knife gives it a professional quality. The black plastic handle is shaped for an easy grip and, although it has no bolster, the deep curve from handle to blade will protect your hand. The full tang is secured by three sturdy rivets. The entire implement is dishwasher-safe, but since the serrated edge requires expensive professional sharpening, we recommend hand washing. You will be inspired to take special care of this treasure, as it will give you a lifetime of service.

She is the one you call sister.
Her simplest act has glamor,
as when she scales a fish the knife
flashes in her long fingers
no motion wasted or when
rapidly talking of love
she steel-wool burnishes
the battered kettle

Adrienne Rich, first stanza of "The Mirror in Which Two Are Seen as One," in New York Review of Books, *1971*

Fish Shears　11.6

Drop-forged steel with black-painted handles; 10″ long. Also avail. 12″ long.
$20.00

Serious scissors are a sine qua non of fish cookery. How else to cut through the belly of the fish, snip around the gills, trim fins, and excise the spiny perimeters of flatfishes, or even make neat work of removing heads and tails? These heavy professional shears are made in Ger-

55.—In purchasing Fish it should be remembered that it is always most wholesome when in full season, and the following list will be found useful in ascertaining when it is best and cheapest.

NAME OF FISH.	IN SEASON.	BEST & CHEAPEST.	AVERAGE PRICE.
BARBEL	October to April	January to February	6d. to 8d. per lb.
BLOATERS	September to April	September to Feb.	1s. ,, 2s. doz.
BREAM	All the Year round	Autumn	8d. ,, 1s. per lb.
BRILL	All the Year round	August to April	1s. ,, 6s. each.
CARP	November to March	January to February	2d. ,, 6d. per lb.
COCKLES	All the Year round	Summer	2d. ,, 4d. per qt.
COD	November to March	February to March	4d. ,, 1s. per lb.
CHUB	June to December	Summer	4d. ,, 6d. per lb.
CRABS	April to October	Summer	6d. ,, 4s. each.
CRAYFISH	All the Year round	Summer	1s. ,, 3s. doz.
DACE	June to December	July to September	4d. ,, 6d. per lb.
DORY	All the Year round	Winter	1s. ,, 6s. each.
EELS	June to March	September to Nov.	8d. ,, 1s. per lb.
FLOUNDERS	All the Year round	August to November	2d. ,, 6d. each.
GUDGEON	June to December	July to September	6d. — per lb.
HADDOCKS	August to February	Winter	4d. ,, 1s. each.
HALIBUT	All the Year round	November to June	4d. ,, 1s. per lb.
HERRINGS	May to January	June to September	1s. ,, 2s. doz.
LAMPREYS	All the Year round	June to September	6d. ,, 1s. per lb.
LING	All the Year round	November to March	4d. ,, 6d. per lb.
LOBSTERS	All the Year round	Summer	6d. ,, 4s. each.
MACKEREL	Nearly all the Year	April to July	4d. ,, 1s. each.
MULLET (red)	All the Year round	April to October	4d. ,, 2s. each.
MULLET (grey)	All the Year round	Winter	4d. ,, 2s. each.
MUSSELS	January to April	January to April	2d. ,, 3d. per qt.
OYSTERS	September to April	Winter	1s. ,, 3s. doz.
PERCH	May to February	July to October	6d. ,, 1s. per lb.
PIKE	September to Feb.	October to January	3d. ,, 6d. per lb.
PLAICE	All the Year round	May to November	6d. ,, 1s. 6d. lb.
PRAWNS	All the Year round	May to December	6d. ,, 1s. 6d. doz.
SALMON	February to Sept.	Spring and Summer	8d. ,, 4s. per lb.
SHAD	February to Sept.	May to August	6d. ,, 9d. per lb.
SHRIMPS	All the Year round	April to November	3d. ,, 6d. per pint
SKATE	September to April	October to March	4d. ,, 1s. per lb.
SCALLOPS	January to June	March to May	6d. ,, 1s. doz.
SMELTS	October to May	Winter	6d. ,, 2s. doz.
SOLES	All the Year round	April to July	1s. ,, 2s. per lb.
SPRATS	November to March	Nov. and December	1d. ,, 3d. per lb.
STURGEON	April to September	Summer	6d. ,, 1s. per lb.
TENCH	November to March	Dec. to February	6d. ,, 9d. per lb.
THORNBACK	All the Year round	Summer	3d. ,, 6d. per lb.
TROUT	Feb. to September	April to July	1s. ,, 2s. per lb.
TURBOT	All the Year round	Spring and Summer	2s. 6d. to 15s. each.
WHITEBAIT	January to September	February to May	1s. 6d. ,, 2s. 6d. qt
WHITING	All the Year round	Spring and Summer	3d. to 1s. each.

Mrs. Beeton, in her famous Book of Household Management, conscientiously provided market information as well as recipes for her nineteenth-century readers.

Continued from preceding page

many of drop-forged steel. The massive blades are secured with a nut and bolt and have extremely sharp cutting edges. These shears are a precision instrument —the blades fit together perfectly with no separation. The lower ring of the handle has a flat edge which rests firmly on the cutting board, enabling the user to bring the blades together in a perfectly straight line. An added advantage is that at a weighty 12 ounces these scissors are unlikely to be borrowed by small fry for those blade-dulling paper projects.

Stainless-Steel Fillet of Sole Knife   11.7

Stainless-steel blade with plastic handle; 10¼" long overall; blade 6" long.
$9.00

Flatfish are delectable, among the finest fish we have, but many people avoid eating them for fear of swallowing one of the many small bones characteristic of these creatures—sole, flounder, fluke, and their kin. With the proper knife, and the proper technique in wielding it (see our directions for filleting in "How to Dress a Fish"), such fish can be rendered virtually boneless. This knife has the thin, sharp blade required to remove the flesh in fillets from the delicate underlying bones. Although it has no apparent tang, there is a piece of metal visible at the end of the black, dishwasher-proof handle. The 6-inch stainless-steel blade is fairly rigid at the base, but becomes more flexible as it tapers to the sharp point necessary for cutting through the skin of the fish. Because of this pliancy the blade has the responsiveness required for ease in feeling your way along the skeleton in order to remove all the flesh of a fillet in one neat piece.

BROCHET FARCI, BRAISE AU CIDRE—STUFFED PIKE, BRAISED IN CIDER

For four people, use:

1⅓ C. good cider
1 C. fish stock
1 lb. 7 oz. salmon
¼ lb. mushrooms
1 large carrot
5 T. butter
1 small onion
4 tsp. port wine
1 T. flour
few sprigs parsley
pinch thyme
2 eggs
1 pike, weighing about 2 lbs.
curry
dry, sifted breadcrumbs
fines herbes
salt and pepper

Make a good forcemeat with the fresh boneless and skinless salmon, the peeled mushrooms, *fines herbes,* some dry, sifted breadcrumbs, the port wine, some curry powder to taste, and salt and pepper. Bind the mixture with one egg and one egg yolk.

Scale, gut and trim the pike. Stuff it with the above mixture.

In 4 teaspoons of butter cook the minced carrots and onion, without letting them brown. Add the cider and the fish stock along with the washed mushroom peelings, the salmon trimmings, the aromatics and the parsley. Cook these for a half hour. Strain, cool, and skim the fat off the liquid.

Arrange the pike on the buttered rack of a fish pan or in any type of ovenproof and fireproof pan with a rack in it. Pour the cooled liquid over it and start the cooking on top of the stove over a hot flame. Then put the pan in the oven to braise for another twenty minutes, basting frequently.

When the fish is cooked, remove it, strain the cooking liquid and reduce it over a high flame.

Blend the flour into 4 teaspoons of butter and cook them together without browning. Blend in some of the reduced cooking liquid, reduce it a little further, and, last of all, enrich the sauce with the rest of the butter.

Arrange the pike on a hot serving platter, coat it with a little of the sauce, garnish the platter with *barquettes* filled with creamed asparagus, some croquettes made with crayfish tails, and fried carp milts.

Serve, passing the sauce separately in a sauceboat.

One may prepare other fish in this same way: whiting, for instance, stuffed with mushrooms, carp milts, shrimp tails and *Panada à la Frangipane.* The sauce would be enriched with a shrimp butter made with the trimmings and finished off the cream.

Carp may also be prepared in this same way.

(From ENCYCLOPEDIA OF PRACTI-CAL GASTRONOMY, by Ali-Bab, translated by Elizabeth Benson. Copyright © 1974 by McGraw-Hill, Inc. Reprinted by permission of McGraw-Hill Book Company.)

A curious discovery was made on Midsummer Eve, 1626, inside a cod which had been caught and sent for sale in Cambridge market. The fishmonger, when opening the fish, found a small book inside, wrapped in canvas. The book was cleaned, re-bound and sent to the Cambridge University Library. The volume was reprinted under the title: Vox Piscis or the Book Fish contayning Three Treatises which were found in the belly of A Codfish in Cambridge Market on Mid-summer Eve last, Anno Domini 1626.

Cambridgeshire Customs and Folklore, *by Enid Porter. Routledge and Kegan Paul, London, 1969*

High-Carbon Fillet of Sole Knife   11.8

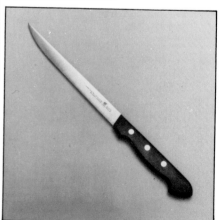

No-stain high-carbon Friodur steel blade with black wood handle; 12⅛" long overall; blade 7" long.
$11.00

More flexible and with a longer blade than the filleting knife for sole above, this implement will therefore be useful for the larger flatfish as well, such as halibut and turbot. The 7-inch blade is made of no-stain high-carbon Friodur steel, Henckel's brand of stainless steel, and it is attached to a formed grip of black wood with three rivets. The knife has a three-quarter tang, making it a sturdy tool. The extremely sharp tip will cut easily into the skin of fish without tearing. This is an expensive knife, but worth its price.

FILETS DE SOLE EN TURBAN—ROLLED FILLETS OF SOLE

Good fresh fillet of sole does not need much done to it. For a dish of perfect simplicity, it can be sautéed in polyunsaturated margarine, then lightly sprinkled with salt, pepper, and lemon juice. When a more impressive presentation is required, the fillets can be rolled around a light stuffing and poached in wine. They arrive at the table looking like a sheik's turban.

6 servings

2 tablespoons polyunsaturated
　　margarine
1 tablespoon minced shallots
¼ pound mushrooms, thinly sliced
salt and pepper
3 tablespoons polyunsaturated
　　margarine
1 teaspoon parsley
½ teaspoon tarragon
6 fillets of sole
½ lemon
salt and pepper
¼ cup vermouth
¼ cup dry white wine

Melt 2 tablespoons of margarine in a small skillet, add the shallots, and simmer

gently for about a minute. Add the sliced mushrooms, mixing them well with the shallots. Sprinkle with a little salt and pepper, cover the skillet, and simmer gently for about 3 minutes.

In a small bowl, cream together the 3 tablespoons of margarine, the parsley, and tarragon.

Rinse the sole fillets and dry on paper towels. Rub each fillet on both sides with the lemon half. Lay them on the counter skin side up (this is the darker side). Sprinkle each fillet lightly with salt and pepper. Spread some of the herb-flavored margarine over the entire length of each fillet, then spread the mushrooms. Do not extend the mushrooms to the very ends. Roll the fillet and secure the closing with a toothpick.

Select a heavy nonaluminum pan that will hold the 6 rolled fillets snugly. Stand the "turbans" in the pan and pour the wines over them. Put a piece of aluminum foil directly over the fillets, tucking it down inside the pan, then place a lid on the pan. The turbans can be prepared ahead and kept in the refrigerator for a few hours; the liquid should not be added, however, until just before cooking.

About 20 minutes before serving, place the pan of "turbans" on a very low fire and heat the wines gently. As they warm up they will begin poaching the fillets. Check from time to time to make certain that the wines are not boiling, for that toughens the fish. The wine should be kept just below a simmer. The fillets will be poached in about 10 minutes, depending on the size and thickness of the fish. Fifteen minutes should be the maximum. They are done when the flesh is white and flakes if pierced with a toothpick.

Carefully remove the "turbans" to a serving platter, take out the toothpicks, and spoon some sauce over each one. Serve at once.

(From HAUTE CUISINE FOR YOUR HEART'S DELIGHT, by Carol Cutler. Copyright © 1973 by Carol Cutler. Reprinted by permission of Clarkson N. Potter, Inc.)

Wilfred Funk, in Word Origins and Their Romantic Stories, *informs us that the Latin* filium, *meaning thread, preceded the French* filet, *little thread. In English the word* filet *was first applied to pieces of meat that were tied with string. Today, in English, it may be spelled with one l or two—either way, it means any one of many boneless cuts of meat or fish.*

Rowoco Filleting Knife　　11.9

High-carbon steel blade with brown wood handle, brass rivets; 10⅜" long overall; blade 6¼" long.
$8.00 ▲

From France, where the gastronomic term *filet* was coined, comes an extremely sharp, flexible knife which will be useful for boning jobs as well as for filleting small fish. The blade, which is only ⅜" wide at the base, tapers for 6¼" to a razor-sharp point. This knife is made of high-carbon steel, with a partial tang enclosed in a handsome wooden handle that is secured with three brass rivets. It has neither bolster nor crown and is not of as fine a quality as the Henckel knife, but for the money it is a more than adequate utensil.

The nineteenth-century chef spared no effort in building seafood structures as elaborate as anything he might create in pastry.

Smoked Salmon Knife   11.10

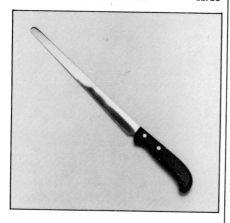

Stainless-steel blade with rosewood handle; 15"
long overall; blade 10" long.
$11.25

Sweden means smörgåsbord, that fabulous buffet which is a first course for aficionados but a full meal for most of us. Smoked salmon, which we usually think of as a Scottish or Nova Scotian product, is often included in the fish offerings, for the Swedes make a fine variety. Instead of the customary olive oil and capers, they serve it with feathery snippets of dill, pungent, freshly grated horseradish, and mounds of whipped cream. In order to carve this heavy fish into the traditional paper-thin slices, the Swedes have manufactured a knife which not only does the job efficiently, but is also beautiful to look at. The gleaming stainless-steel blade is attached by two brass rivets to a curved, dishwasher-proof rosewood handle. The lack of a full tang is unimportant in this instance, since you will use the knife only for delicate chores. As the blade is long and narrow with a rounded tip, it resembles a ham slicer, but it is much more flexible. This allows the carver to produce perfect slices of delectable pink meat.

ESCALOPES DE TURBOT PANEES—BREADED TURBOT FILETS

Clean and gut a turbot, remove the backbone, and slice off the filets. Season them with salt, pepper, and lemon juice, then roll them in flour, dip them in beaten egg, and, last, coat them with fine, dry, sifted breadcrumbs.

Arrange the filets, thus coated, in a low porcelain ovenproof baking and serving casserole which has been buttered. Cook for about ten minutes, basting it with the pan juices.

Serve in the same dish.

At the same time, send along a sauceboat with some Italian seafood sauce, *sauce italienne maigre,* which is prepared as follows:

Melt some butter in a saucepan and cook some chopped shallots and mushrooms in it. Allow the mushroom water to evaporate, then add some chopped parsley, some peeled, seeded, and chopped tomatoes, or some tomato purée, and season with salt, pepper, and flavor with fish fumet. Let this cook down so as to have a fairly thick sauce. Strain it and add some chopped *fines herbes.*

(From ENCYCLOPEDIA OF PRACTICAL GASTRONOMY, by Ali-Bab, translated by Elizabeth Benson. Copyright © 1974 by McGraw-Hill, Inc. Reprinted by permission of McGraw-Hill Book Company.)

Wooden Mallet   11.11

Hickory; 12" overall; head 6" × 3"; 1 lb. 5 oz.
$4.95

A large wooden mallet will perform a variety of services that are especially valuable to the fish cook. Some of our experts have been known when desperate to use a shoe in conjunction with a heavy knife in order to cleave a large fish into steaks, but you will find a mallet like this more serviceable for that purpose. Wood, because of its resiliency, won't injure the knife, nor will it demolish the fish if your swing should miss. And to render your already thin slices of smoked salmon nearly translucent, you can use this mallet: place the slices, one at a time, between pieces of waxed paper and pound them lightly. The same procedure will flatten fillets of sole, turbot, or flounder. The mallet is made with slightly beveled edges that won't tear the most delicate fish flesh; the smoothly sanded wooden cylinder is 3 inches in diameter, and fitted securely into it is a thick wooden handle 9 inches long. You will undoubtedly find a host of other uses for this tool in your kitchen—it can substitute for a meat pounder when you're preparing scaloppine or beef birds; with it you can thwack a split chicken into a flatter shape before broiling it; and a blow or two will force a stubborn cork back into a partly used bottle of wine.

Another elaborate construction of the last century, featuring slices of salmon garnished with eggs; everything was, no doubt, glazed with aspic.

Those tough odorous strips of dried fish known as stockfish were a staple in the Middle Ages, as they are today in many European countries. Thomas Coghan had this to say in his Haven of Health (1589): "Concerning which fish I will say no more than Erasmus hath written in his Colloquio—'There is a kind of fish which is called in England Stockfish: it nourisheth no more than a stock.'"

This was elaborated upon by Mouffet in Healths Improvement (1655): "Stockfish, whilst it is unbeaten, is called Buckhorne, because it is so tough: when it is beaten upon the stock it is termed Stockfish . . . howsoever it be sold . . . and made both toothsomer and delectable by good and chargeable cookery; yet a stone will be a stone, and an ape an ape, howsoever the one be set up for a Saint and the other apparelled like a Judge."

Kitchen and Table, by Colin Clair, Abelard-Schuman, New York, 1964

Fish and Seafood Poachers and Dishes

Water is the natural habitat of the fish. What better way to cook it, then, than in a liquid environment? Seaside dwellers can use actual sea water; landlocked citizens, a fragrant bath of wine and water, redolent with herbs and spices.

Fish flesh is delicate and should never be overcooked, as it will toughen and dry out. It is far easier to keep an eye on the cooking process if the fish is simmering on top of the stove than it is with any other method. The Canadian Fish Council suggests this rule of thumb: Measure the fish from side to side through the thickest part of the body and simmer it ten minutes for each inch. The end result should flake easily when pierced with a fork and yet be juicy and succulent. The cooking liquid may be turned into a delicious sauce by boiling it over high heat until it is reduced by half and then stirring in a beurre manié for thickening.

Now that we've talked you into poaching your fish, what are you going to do it in? A fish for four people measures about 16 inches from stem to stern. Even your most capacious saucepot isn't that ample. And, because of its fragile nature, fish will require cautious handling after cooking in order to bring it to the table intact. Fish poachers are specially designed to poach, to steam, and to produce a perfect whole fish at the table.

Poachers come in a range of sizes for everything from a miniature mackerel to a king-sized salmon. A 16-inch poacher is adequate for a small family, but in a larger pot you can cook either a fish of ample proportions or two smaller ones laid head to tail. All poachers have a common feature—a rack that protects your fish from the direct heat source beneath and enables you to lift the whole fish from the pot intact.

We do not recommend aluminum as a material in which to poach fish because it can discolor the liquid, giving a grayish cast to the sauce, if wine or other acid is an ingredient. A tin-lined copper fish poacher is a beautiful object, costly to purchase, but the sumptuous materials add nothing to the actual cooking quality, since the poaching liquid performs the same excellent job of heat diffusion as does copper. Stainless steel is excellent—also expensive. The most utilitarian poacher is one made of tinned steel. This is a satisfactory material because poaching is always done below the simmer, the liquid barely shimmering, so that you do not use the extremely high temperatures which damage the tin surface.

POACHING POINTERS

Wrap your fish in a double thickness of cheesecloth before placing it in the pot to insure its pristine appearance after cooking, especially if you want to eat it cold—cheesecloth acts as a gentle mold for a cooling fish. Be sure to remove it after cooling and before refrigerating the fish, however, as the natural gelatin will glue the fabric to the fish skin. To

POACHED RAINBOW TROUT AU BLEU

Even if you cannot move directly from stream to pot, you must try for trout no more than a few hours out of the water for this recipe to work. [We recommend that you clean the trout through the gills —see "How to Dress a Fish."]

Serve 1 trout per person

COURT BOUILLON
3 quarts water
1 onion, cut in half
1 bay leaf
1 tablespoon salt
1 cup white vinegar
6 peppercorns
THE FISH
1 live trout, about 1 pound
Melted butter
Lemon wedges
Chopped parsley
SAUCE HOLLANDAISE (¾ CUP)
2 egg yolks
2 teaspoons water
½ cup melted butter
Dash of cayenne
Pinch of salt
Lemon juice or white wine vinegar

In a large pot, bring the water, onion, bay leaf, salt, vinegar and peppercorns to a boil. Give the trout a blow on the back of the neck. Wash trout, cut it open and clean thoroughly, but leave head and tail on. Plunge trout into the boiling court bouillon and poach for about 4 minutes.

Put fish on a hot plate, and serve immediately with melted butter, Sauce Hollandaise or Sauce Mousseline, lemon wedges and chopped parsley.

SAUCE HOLLANDAISE: In the top of a double boiler, over simmering water, combine the egg yolks and water. Whisk until the eggs are well mixed and slightly thickened. Continue to whisk, making sure the water does not boil underneath, and gradually add the butter, a dribble at a time. If the sauce becomes too thick, dilute with a little warm water. If it curdles, add a little boiling water, and mix it briskly. When it turns thick and creamy, add cayenne, salt and lemon juice or vinegar to taste.

SAUCE MOUSSELINE: If you wish a very delicate sauce, combine the Hollandaise with an equal amount of whipped cream after you remove from over the hot water. This sauce must be served immediately.

(From THE GREAT COOKS COOK-BOOK, by The Good Cooking School. Copyright © 1974 by The Good Cooking School, Inc. Reprinted by permission of Ferguson/Doubleday.)

Continued from preceding page

insure a moist and delicious fish, turn the heat off under your poacher 10 minutes before it is done, and allow it to cool to room temperature in the liquid. Garnished and sauced, a whole cold fish makes a sumptuous summer buffet dish or the most elegant substitute for sandwiches at a picnic.

Most fish poachers will accommodate two mayonnaise-jar lids beneath the rack, raising it enough to suspend your fish above the liquid for steaming. Let your imagination be your guide when seasoning the poaching or steaming broth. About the only mistake you can make when using this method of fish cooking is overdoing it: season with a discreet hand, as you can always add a larger amount of thyme or bay another time. And, speaking of overdoing: If your kitchen begins to smell fishy, remove your dinner from the heat immediately—it is being overcooked. And take the fish from the liquid at once, as it will continue to cook in the hot broth if you leave it there.

FISH DISHES

The oval is the classic shape for the pots and dishes used in fish cookery for obvious reasons—there are few if any round or rectangular fish. The baking dishes for fillets of sole we show you in this section are closely related to the gratin pans in Chapter 8. However, all of these dishes for fish are oval. They are also relatively deep because you will be using liquids—wine, broth, even cream—when you cook certain fish by oven poaching, and you'll want space for your sauce and garnish on finished dishes.

These are handsome dishes, superbly useful both for cooking and presenting your fish handsomely, whether laid flat and blanketed with a creamy sauce or rolled in neat turbans. Earthenware dishes are especially suited to fish cookery because they provide gentle, yet diffuse heat which is retained after they are removed from the oven. Always leave fillets slightly underdone when cooking them in earthenware, as they will continue cooking on the way to the table.

Bail-handled Fish Poacher 11.12

Tinned steel; 16″ × 5½″; 4″ deep; tinned steel rack. Also avail. 20″ × 6″, 24″ × 7″, 28″ × 7″, or 36″ × 8″.
$62.00

In its smallest size, this is a good fish poacher for a small family or a couple. It measures 16″ overall, and its rack will hold a 14″ fish. Four larger models are available, ranging up to 36″ in length. Made of tinned steel with rolled edges, this poacher has a bail handle similar to that on a bucket—a holdover from the day when the fish cooker was suspended over an open fire. As part of a seaside clambake, you might want to use this pot to cook this way, adding a little romance to your poaching. The handle swings, of course, so be cautious when lifting—the contents are hot and heavy and you don't want a spill. The inside rack, also of tinned steel, is equipped with two curved handles through which you may slip a pair of wooden spoon handles to lift it, bearing your fish, from

the cooker. There is enough space above the tops of these handles and below the lid to allow you to slide a couple of metal jar lids beneath the rack when you want to steam a fish instead of poaching it. The lid, like that on all tinned-steel pots, has a tendency to warp. If this should be a problem, simply weight it down with a couple of cans of food when in use.

Double-handled Fish Poacher 11.13

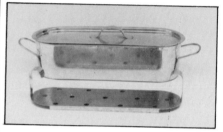

Tinned steel; 16″ × 6″; 4¼″ deep; tinned-steel rack. Also avail. in lengths of 20″, 24″, 28″ or 36″.
$45.00 ▲

This poacher is identical in shape to the preceding one, but instead of the wire bail handle it has handles welded to the outside of the pot for a more secure grip. It comes in a range of sizes from 16″ to a full 36″, this last large enough to poach something just slightly smaller than Moby Dick. It is made of tinned steel and has a tinned-steel rack identical to that of the preceding model. Gently priced, it is a good value.

Stainless-Steel Fish Poacher 11.14

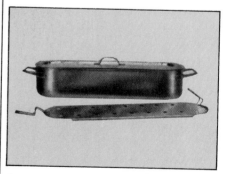

Stainless steel; 15¾″ × 4¾″; 3½″ deep.
$75.00   16″x5½″x4″ $34.00▲
         17″¾x5¾″x4¼″ $40.00▲

Stainless steel is more expensive and also more durable than tinned steel. If you are planning to own your fish poacher for a lifetime and don't wish to bother with retinning from time to time, this is probably the model for you. We show you one 15¾" long, but it's also available in 19¾" and 27½" lengths. The rack, also of stainless steel, has adjustable handles which fold down and which may also be clipped over the edges of the poacher to suspend it above the bottom of the pan, nice when you want to keep your fish warm above the steaming liquid while whipping up the sauce. The loop handles are sturdily welded to the outside of the pot, and another handle is attached to the heavy, warp-proof, tightly fitting lid.

HADOCK POCHE, AUX POMMES DE TERRE SAUTEES, SAUCE AUX OEUFS DURS

This recipe for poached haddock with sautéed potatoes and hard-boiled-egg sauce will serve six to eight.

2 lbs. potatoes
1½ lbs. haddock filets
2 C. milk
14 T. butter
7 T. cream
4 T. flour
2 hard-boiled eggs
1 small carrot
1 small turnip
1 small onion
bouquet garni
chopped parsley
lemon juice
nutmeg
salt and pepper

Boil the potatoes in salted water, peel, slice, then sauté them in 7 tablespoons of butter. Season them with salt.

Poach the haddock filets in a small amount of salted water or milk (the milk used here would be over and above the 2 cups listed above). Finish cooking the fish over a very low flame in a covered pan. Cooking time should be about fifteen minutes in all.

At the same time prepare the sauce.

In 3 tablespoons of butter cook the chopped carrot, turnip, and onion until they are lightly browned. Add the flour and stir around a few minutes without browning. Add the boiled milk, season with the *bouquet garni*, salt, pepper, and nutmeg. Let this all simmer until the sauce is thickened. This should take about one hour. Strain the sauce and whisk in the rest of the butter and the cream. Heat it up. At the last minute put in some chopped parsley and the hard-boiled eggs, either coarsely chopped or pushed through a coarse sieve.

Arrange the haddock filets on a platter, surround with the sautéed potatoes,

and serve. Pass the sauce at the same time.

(From ENCYCLOPEDIA OF PRACTICAL GASTRONOMY, by Ali-Bab, translated by Elizabeth Benson. Copyright © 1974 by McGraw-Hill, Inc. Reprinted by permission of McGraw-Hill Book Company.)

"... *Brillat-Savarin, the greatest of all Epicurean writers, wrote that the perfect lunch consists of a turbot poché au gratin, a glass of sherry, and a slice of bread and butter. When we degust such a lunch, this is what happens to us: The turbot, that most exquisite of all flatfish, having the consistency and basic flavour of the Rye Bay sole, has above that flavour something equivalent to the bouquet of wine—a faint suggestion of the flavour and perfume of the cucumber. As soon as the first forkful of the turbot spreads its influence on our tongues and palates, we are in a fresh wind on a sparkling sea off Dungeness, the long spit of shingle that has at its end the lighthouse that is the perpetual rival of Gris-Nez on the cliffs of France.*"

"Dinner with Turbot," by Ford Maddox Ford, from Vogue's First Reader, *Condé Nast, 1942*

Oval Fish Poacher or Casserole   11.15

Stainless steel; 14⅛" × 7⅞" inside dimensions; 3⅞" high, with lid. Also avail. 10⅝" × 5⅞" or 15¾" × 8⅝".
$110.00

A handsome modern fish poacher or casserole of the finest-quality brushed stainless steel, with a slotted rack equipped with multi-purpose handles. Fold them down and place the rack in the pot for cooking; extend them and hook them

over the liplike handles of the pot for serving, or for keeping your fish warm under the high, flat-domed lid. This casserole makes an excellent steamer because of its vapor-tight lid. You can also remove the rack and cook your fish on a bed of vegetables for a sublime difference in flavor. The pan's oval interior is the basic shape for sole, but in the size shown, 14⅛" long, it will hold anything from a pair of sea trout to a whole flounder or a school of sauced fillets of sole. This casserole is so attractive you will take it right from the stove to the table, and you'll also want to keep it in mind for use as a gratin dish.

Turbot Poacher   11.16

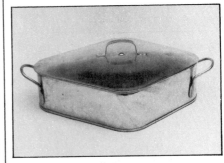

Tinned steel; 18" × 15¼"; 4⅜" deep.
$100.00

A turbot kettle or turbotière—lovely extravagance—is made solely for cooking turbot, but if you are in the sublime position of having this most elegant of fish to cook, you will need and want this poacher. Its diamond shape is designed to hold an entire turbot, a virtually scale-free flatfish related to the American halibut which swims only in European waters. Confronted with an imported specimen, take off the head or leave it intact as you prefer, snip off the spiny outer perimeter with your stout shears (11.6), and poach the fish exactly as you would a more ordinary breed. Except for its shape, this poacher performs in the same manner as the ones we describe above. It is of tinned steel, with a rack of the same material, and has a strong loop handle at either end and a flat handle atop the exceptionally well-fitting lid.

Seafood Cooker   11.17

Sand-cast aluminum with walnut knobs; 10½" diam.; 7¾" deep; 11-qt. capacity.
$65.00

A capacious clam pot of serious construction is hard to come by, but we have found one. Made of very heavy sand-cast aluminum with a highly polished exterior ornamented by a textured band and with a brushed interior, it will hold 11 quarts of liquid or a correspondingly large mess of clams or mussels. The lid fits very tightly, so you may steam your bivalves in this cooker in the smallest possible amount of liquid. No chance of these handles separating from the pot as you lift it off the fire with a steaming supply of shellfish—they are cast in one piece with the pot. The only detachable piece is the handsome walnut knob screwed onto the lid. The stable bottom is very thick, so the danger of scorching the contents is minimal: but you don't want to use this pot on a burner with a heat sensor, as the indented center in the bottom would prevent the pot from making contact with the thermostat. Many pots are good for fish cookery, but this is a star.

"Once when Picasso was coming to lunch I decorated a fish in a way that I thought would amuse him. I chose a fine striped bass and cooked it according to a theory of my grandmother, who had no experience in cooking and who rarely saw her kitchen but who had endless theories about cooking, as well as about many other things. She contended that a fish, having lived its life in water, once caught should have no further contact with the element in which it had been born and raised. She recommended that it be roasted or poached in wine or butter, or cream. So I made a court bouillon of dry white wine with whole peppers, salt, a laurel leaf, a sprig of thyme, a blade of mace, an onion with a clove stuck in it, a carrot, a leek, and a bouquet of fines herbes. This was gently boiled for half an hour and then put aside to cool, until it was put in the fish kettle and the fish was then placed on the rack, the kettle, covered, placed on the fire and slowly brought to boil, and poached for twenty minutes (for a fish weighing four pounds). Taken from the fire it was left to cool in the court bouillon. It was then carefully drained, dried, and placed on the fish platter. A short time before serving I covered the fish with an ordinary mayonnaise, and, with a pastry bag, decorated it with a red mayonnaise, not made with catsup, horror of horrors, but with concentrated tomato juice. Then I made a design with sieved hard-boiled eggs, the whites and the yolks apart, with truffles and with finely chopped fines herbes. I was proud of my chef-d'oeuvre when it was served and Picasso exclaimed at its beauty. 'But', said he, 'should it not rather have been made in honour of Matisse than of me?'"

"Food, Artists and the Baroness," by Alice B. Toklas, in Vogue, March 1950. Reprinted by permission.

Fillet of Sole Dish   11.18

Stoneware; 12¾" × 8⅝"; 1¾" deep; 1¾-qt. capacity.
$8.50

Four people can enjoy a meal served from this rustic-looking stoneware sole dish. Slicked with a delicate beige glaze, it is nonetheless solid and sturdy. The base is left in its natural state, both to absorb oven heat better and to sit steadily on the oven rack or the table trivet. The glaze on the rest of the dish makes for ease in cleaning and is completely impervious to fish flavors. Deep enough to hold a generous amount of liquid for oven poaching, this baking dish can also be placed briefly under the broiler to brown the top of your finished dish.

STEAMED CLAMS

You will need 20 or so clams per person—more or less according to the diners' appetites and the quantity of other food you are serving.

Scrub the clams thoroughly with a brush and rinse several times. Be sure they are tightly closed. Place them in a large kettle with a half inch of salted water at the bottom, and cover the kettle tightly. Steam just until the shells open, which will take about 6 to 10 minutes. Serve immediately, and do not use any clams that do not open. Taste the broth for seasoning, and serve in cups to accompany the clams. Provide plenty of melted butter in bowls for dipping the clams as they are removed from the shells.

(From AMERICAN COOKERY, by James A. Beard, illustrated by Earl Thollander. Copyright © 1972 by James A. Beard. Reprinted by permission of Little, Brown and Company.)

Deep Oval Baking Dish   11.19

Porcelain; 15¾" × 10¼"; 2¼" deep. Also avail. 13" × 8" or 14⅓" × 9".
$35.00

Filets de Soles Véronique (see the recipe), with its creamy sauce studded with green grapes, looks as beautiful as it tastes when you bring it to table in this heavy white porcelain baking dish. Formed in the classic oval, it has a chaste rope border and a faintly swirled pattern on the outside, but it is perfectly smooth within. The unglazed base will absorb and distribute the oven heat, and it is engraved with a series of squiggles so that it will remain planted firmly on whatever smooth surface you place it. For all its elegant appearance, it is a sturdy dish, safe both in the oven and the dishwasher. Although it's good in its smaller sizes, we recommend this, the largest size, for parties; almost 16 inches long and more than 10 inches wide, it's destined to hold many of your most festive foods.

FILETS DE SOLES VERONIQUE— POACHED FILLETS OF SOLE WITH FRESH WHITE GRAPES

4 fillets of sole or flounder
A little lemon juice
2 tablespoons salt butter
2 firm white mushrooms, sliced
Salt
Fresh cracked white pepper
½ cup dry white wine
¼ cup dry sherry
¼ cup water

SAUCE

4 tablespoons salt butter
4 tablespoons all-purpose flour
Salt
A few grains cayenne pepper
Strained fish stock (from the sole)
⅔ cup light cream
2 egg yolks
1 tablespoon Cognac or good brandy
1 tablespoon tarragon vinegar
2 tablespoons heavy cream
6 tablespoons frozen sweet butter

GARNISH

1 tablespoon salt butter
¾ cup skinned and seeded fresh white grapes
1 teaspoon chopped fresh parsley
1 teaspoon Cognac or good brandy
Salt
Freshly cracked white pepper

Preheat the oven to 350°. Wash the fillets in water and a little lemon juice. Dry well and fold them lengthwise with the bone side (white) out. Put them on a buttered baking dish. Make a court bouillon as follows. Melt the butter in a sauté pan and add the mushrooms. Cook over brisk heat with ½ teaspoon lemon juice, salt, and a little pepper. Add the wine, sherry, and water. Bring slowly to a boil. Spoon this court bouillon over the fillets. Cover with buttered wax paper and poach 15 minutes in the oven. Remove from the oven and arrange the fish on a warm serving platter. Strain the stock and reserve it.

SAUCE. Melt the salt butter in a saucepan. Off the heat, stir in the flour. Season with salt and the cayenne pepper. Add the strained stock from the fish. Stir over low heat until the sauce comes to a boil. Add the light cream and simmer gently 10 minutes. Put the egg yolks in a medium-size bowl. With a wire whisk

mix in the brandy, vinegar, salt, and a little cayenne pepper. Mix in the heavy cream. Stand the bowl in a shallow pan of hot water over low heat. Beat until the yolk mixture is as thick as you want it. Cut the frozen sweet butter into little pieces and beat it into the yolk mixture piece by piece. Mix this egg sauce (which is a Hollandaise) into the white wine sauce and set aside.

GARNISH. In another little pan melt the butter. Add the grapes, parsley, and brandy. Season with salt and a little white pepper. Heat gently over low heat.

To serve, scatter the grapes over the fillets. Spoon the sauce evenly over the dish. Brown quickly under a hot broiler.
NET: 4 servings.

(From THE DIONE LUCAS BOOK OF FRENCH COOKING, by Dione Lucas and Marion Gorman, illustrated by Joseph S. Patti. Copyright © 1947 by Dione Lucas. Reprinted by permission of Little, Brown and Company.)

BROTH BASIN

Stainless-Steel Sole Dish   11.20

Stainless steel; 14⅛" × 7⅞"; 3¾" high, with lid. Also avail. 9" × 5⅛", 10⅝" × 5⅞", 12⅝" × 7½", or 15¾" × 8⅝".
$66.00

Stainless steel is a supremely utilitarian material, but this fillet of sole dish is made from a sumptuous variety. Originally made for use in fine hotels and restaurants and shaped from the finest-quality stainless steel, it is very heavy, with a dull, expensive gleam. One advantage of this dish is the vapor-tight lid, which obviates the necessity for covering your fillets with buttered waxed paper as they oven-poach. When not in use as a fish cooker, it will double as a vegetable server, an out-of-the-ordinary casserole, or a gratin pan. A sensuously beautiful dish, modern and sleek.

In medieval Europe monks were allowed to eat fish at any time, but meat only on specified days. For this reason, frogs, being water creatures, were classified as fish, while the unborn young of rabbits, a favorite delicacy, were, like eggs, considered not to be meat.

Fish Grills

Tired of hamburger, had it with steak for outdoor meals? Add novelty to your next barbecue by grilling a fish. It's not only fun to do, but the result is surprising and tasty. The surprise comes at the contrast in each mouthful—crisp, crunchy skin covering moist, tender flesh. The fortunate few whose kitchens are equipped with open charcoal or ceramic broilers can enjoy this pleasure all year round. For others, the backyard barbecue or picnic fire at lake or seaside must suffice.

The elongated shape and curved, closely set wires of the specialized fish grills (see also the Cocambroche tambour, 8.2) are designed to cradle the entire body of the fish without breaking it. Because a cooked whole fish, or even fish steaks or thick fillets, are fragile, they can't easily be grilled unsupported. An ordinary hinged hamburger grill, with its two flat sides held together by slides on their long

Continued from preceding page

handles, can be used for grilling steaks, medium-to-thick fillets, and such small fish as trout and tinker mackerel, but there is the danger both of the fish slipping through the open side while flipping the grill over and of crushing delicate flesh with the pressure exerted by the flat grills. A better solution is the tambour we mention above, if you have the Cocambroche rotisserie equipment, or one of our fish-shaped wire grilling baskets.

USING A FISH GRILL

Before lighting your fire indoors or out begin by marinating the fish in oil, lemon juice, and seasonings for several hours; or be a purist and join the anti-marinating school—simply rub the fish with salt, pepper, and herbs and brush it lightly with oil at cooking time. Sometimes, for a change, omit the oil and try tying several pieces of bacon around your fish to baste it and to give it a smoky flavor; or baste your fish with melted butter. A small or medium-sized fish can be grilled with the head and tail intact and will be moister and better this way. Larger beasties may have to be decapitated to fit into your fish grill or hinged broiler. And always slash the body of the fish diagonally and shallowly on both sides, two or three slashes per side, to prevent it from curling up during cooking. To add flavor, place a few slices of onion, a smattering of celery, a piece of orange or lemon, or herbs and other favorite seasonings in the cavity of a whole fish. Then lightly grease the wires of the grill and place the fish within it. The fire should be gray with no red coals to flame up and burn the delicate skin. Settle the legs of the grill in the coals and broil the fish for about 5 to 10 minutes a side, depending on its size, brushing on a little more oil or melted butter once or twice. When the first side is done, flip the entire grill to cook the other side. If, despite the oiling, a bit of skin adheres to the grill after you have turned it over, flick it down and back into its proper place with the sharp point of a small knife.

FINE FLAVORINGS

There are other ways to flavor fish during grilling: if you cover the fire with dried stalks of herbs or with clippings of fresh herbs—think of rosemary for bluefish—the fish will be enveloped in and seasoned by their fragrant smoke. The famous loup de mer au fenouil of southern France is flavored by dried fennel branches added to the fire as well as by feathery fennel leaves placed within the body of the fish before grilling. As a final fillip, just before removing a fish seasoned in this way with fennel, you might want to pour a bit of warmed pastis—that strong anise-flavored aperitif beverage—over the fish and the coals. The resultant flames will produce a fish with a very crisp skin strongly perfumed with the herbs and the pastis.

Fish grills are of simple but sturdy manufacture and, consequently, inexpensive. They come in a range of sizes for every fish from bigger to smaller. We think that of the many utensils available for fish cookery, few will give you more pleasure for the money.

MUSTARD SAUCE

2 egg yolks
½ teaspoon dry mustard
1 teaspoon Dijon mustard
A few grains cayenne pepper
⅛ teaspoon each of mace and nutmeg
¼ teaspoon very finely chopped garlic
1 tablespoon tarragon vinegar
½ teaspoon salt
2 teaspoons Cognac or good brandy
1 cup vegetable oil
3 tablespoons sour cream
¾ cup whipped cream (about ½ cup heavy cream)

In a mixer bowl put the egg yolks, mustards, cayenne pepper, mace, nutmeg, garlic, vinegar, salt, and brandy. Beat thoroughly. Add the vegetable oil drop by drop, beating all the time. Remove from the mixer, fold in the sour cream and whipped cream, cover the bowl with plastic, and set it in the refrigerator to chill.

(From THE DIONE LUCAS BOOK OF FRENCH COOKING, by Dione Lucas and Marion Gorman, illustrated by Joseph S. Patti. Copyright © 1947 by Dione Lucas. Reprinted by permission of Little, Brown and Company.)

"The most common, because the cheapest, way of cooking fish is to grill it over food embers—or more correctly—palm branches. This is done by inserting it in a split palm stalk which is then laid across the fire. When done, they are stuck up in the rafters of the house to be kept till wanted. Fish may also be salted slightly or rubbed in tumeric before grilling. Dried fish is fried in coconut oil. Fresh fish is also cooked this way."

Housekeeping Among Malay Peasants, *by Rosemary Firth. Percy Lund, Humphries and Company, Ltd., London, 1943*

Fish Grill   11.21

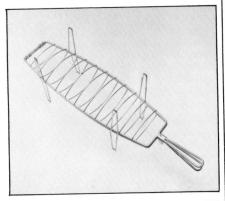

Tinned steel; 25½″ long overall; grill alone 20″ × 6″; legs 4½″ long.

$17.50 ▲

This is a classic fish-shaped grill made of tinned steel. It is a good standard size, holding any fish up to about 20″ long. The 4½″ legs are looped so that you can slip the handles of two wooden spoons through them to remove the grill and its contents painlessly from the coals. The legs and the handles are sturdily welded to the body, and the handles can be snapped together with a clip—if this loosens after repeated use, simply tighten it with a pair of pliers. The front end of the grill is blunt, so it will fit a fish whose head you've removed so the whole critter will fit within the basket. As the legs are narrow at the bottom, this grill will be easy to settle into the coals of your fire.

Fish Grill with Folding Legs   11.22

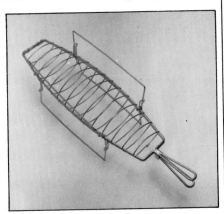

Tinned steel; 30″ long overall; grill alone 24″ × 7″; folding legs 4¼″ long. Also avail. 12″, 16″, or 20″ long.

$20.00

The difference between this fish grill and the one above is that this one has hinged legs—actually, two folding rectangular wire supports per side—that are collapsible, a boon for those with limited storage space or for fishermen who anticipate grilling their catch over a campfire. The grill comes in four sizes, from 12″ to 30″. Dedicated anglers might wish to buy a small, a medium, and a large size and be prepared for whatever swims in the waters they are fishing. The only disadvantage of the hinged legs here is that they may be more difficult to settle in the coals than the looped ones of the classic grill. In every other respect, however, the two grills are similar. Made of tinned steel wire welded to form a fish-shaped basket, this grill, like the other, has a blunt end to accommodate either whole or decapitated fish, and the fairly long handles are secured by a metal clip that keeps the whole apparatus closed while you flip it over.

Individual Fish Grill   11.23

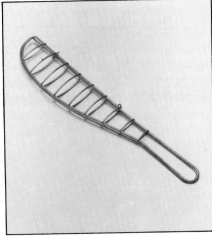

Tinned steel; 18″ × 3″.
$7.50

Recalcitrant children who claim to hate fish might change their minds if allowed to cook their own over the backyard barbecue in this grill. Just be sure to have plenty of potholder mitts on hand to protect small hands from hot handles. This mini-grill for trout or other small fish measures only 18″ in length, handle and all, so a fish of modest size (under 12″) is all it can handle. Made of tinned steel, it operates on the same principle as a hinged hamburger grill, but the sides are made convex to accommodate the plump, delicate body of a fish without crushing it. A separate ring-shaped fastening holds the handles together, keeping the grill closed while you turn the fish. A set of six or so would make the perfect present for that trout fisherman you know.

Sardine Grill   11.24

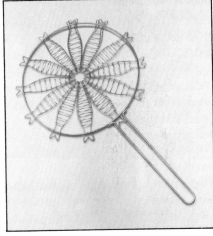

Tinned steel; 14¼″ diam.; 12 individual grills, each 7½″ × 1¾″.
$32.50

Even if you plan never to cook a sardine or a smelt, this grill will be a great addition to your kitchen decor. Hung silhouetted on the wall, it is a sculpture, sure to evoke comments and compliments. The two round frames, meeting face to face, form 12 small fish-shaped baskets with their noses meeting in the center. The 7½″ baskets and the very long handles are welded to the frame. Not just a conversation piece, this sardine grill will cook a dozen tiny fish to succulent crunchiness. Dip each delectable body in a mild mustard sauce or a piquant mixture of sour cream and dill for a great gustatory experience.

From La Grande Cuisine Illustrée, *1902.*

Tools for Opening Shellfish

Some of the most delectable sea creatures are the laziest—no rapid swimming through the deep for them. Clams burrow cozily into the mud or sand, mussels secrete themselves among the seaweed which clings to submerged rocks, oysters attach themselves for life to any suitable support they find, and the crustaceans—crabs and lobsters—amble along the ocean floor in a rather leisurely way. The scallops are more energetic than most; they swim by opening and closing their shells, thereby developing a hefty cylindrical muscle which is very good to eat.

Most shellfish fall into one of two categories, bivalves and crustaceans. Bivalves—clams, mussels, oysters, scallops, for instance—are a class of mollusks whose distinguishing feature is the presence of two shells hinged together and held shut by a strong muscle. Crustaceans wear their skeletons on the outside and have lots of sweet meat within—witness lobsters and crabs of all sizes. Since bivalves are either sedentary or not too swift, and crustaceans can't swim particularly fast, Mother Nature has provided them with heavy armor to protect them from their predators, one of whom is you. Man, the toolmaker, has developed an ingenious collection of implements to pierce, hack, and pry apart these outer coverings in order to devour the delicious interiors. We show you an array of these, beginning with knives and other devices for opening bivalves.

Oysters, clams, scallops, and mussels are plentiful in shallow coastal waters throughout the world. There are hundreds of kinds of each, and shellfish fanciers will travel miles to enjoy a variety native to a particular region. Oysters, clams, and scallops may be eaten raw as well as stewed, baked, broiled, creamed, or scalloped. Mussels are never eaten raw, but once cooked they lend themselves to numberless methods of final preparation.

SHUCKING THE BIVALVES: HARD-SHELLED CLAMS AND OYSTERS
All the edible bivalves have a common characteristic: healthy ones (and they *must* be healthy as well as alive if they're to be safe to eat) clamp their shells shut with the determination of a toddler with a penny in his mouth. Unlike the tot, they can't be talked into opening up. Seagulls deal with the problem in a practical fashion. They just pick the mollusk up and drop it from a great height on a rock or a seaside road until the shell shatters. Efficient, but messy. Of course, you can always plunge your prey into steam or boiling water—all sound bivalves will open after a short period in the pot. (Throw out the ones which remain clamped shut after they've had plenty of time to give up.) But who wants to eat a steamed cherrystone or bluepoint, which should be served raw and thoroughly chilled? Of course, if you are preparing Oysters Rockefeller or Clams Casino—two dishes in which the bivalve is arranged in its shell with a delectable stuffing and then baked—you may take the easy way out. Just slide the clams or oysters into the

FRESH OYSTERS AMBASSADEUR

Serves 2 at lunch or 3 for appetizers
12 large oysters on the half shell
3 shallots, finely chopped
½ cup finely chopped parsley
1 teaspoon chopped fresh chervil, or a pinch dried
Dash Tabasco sauce
1 teaspoon Worcestershire sauce
5 ounces (⅔ cup) butter
6 ounces lump crabmeat, picked over

BECHAMEL *
2 tablespoons butter
2 tablespoons flour
2 cups milk
¾ cup grated Gruyère cheese (about 3 ounces)
Fresh lemon

Preheat oven to 450 F. Arrange oysters on the half shell in a baking dish. Mix the shallots, parsley, chervil, Tabasco sauce, Worcestershire sauce and butter, and top each oyster with a teaspoonful of the mixture. Arrange some fresh crabmeat over each oyster.

To make the Béchamel: Melt butter over moderate heat; whisk in flour; allow to cook for 2 minutes. Whisking constantly, gradually add milk. When all the milk has been added, allow to cook for approximately 5 minutes longer, or until thickened. Cover each oyster with this sauce Béchamel. Sprinkle the grated cheese over the oysters and bake for about 8-10 minutes, or until golden brown. Squeeze fresh lemon juice over the baked oysters, and serve hot.

*You can use Fish Velouté instead if you like a fishier taste.

(From THE GREAT COOKS COOKBOOK, by The Good Cooking School. Copyright © 1974 by The Good Cooking School, Inc. Reprinted by permission of Ferguson/Doubleday.)

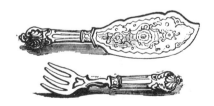

Fish Knife and Fork.

oven, preheated to 350 F., for a minute or two; the shells will open themselves with a minimum of injurious heating.

If they are to be eaten raw (or for that matter, if you plan to cook them), oysters and clams are more easily shucked if they are placed on a cookie sheet in a single layer and let rest for an hour or so in the freezer, or for a longer time in the refrigerator. This makes them sleepy and careless. Once it has been lulled, take the chilled bivalve and hold it firmly with the hinge in your palm. Wear rubber gloves to protect your hands, especially when dealing with oysters. For clams, force your clam knife between the halves of the shell near the hinge and twist with a scraping movement, to cut the muscle loose from the upper shell This will cause the shell to open a bit and make it easy to run the curved edge of the knife between the second muscle and the upper shell, then between the body of the clam and the lower shell. Done after a bit of practice, this leaves you with the clam quite intact and resting in its delicious juice in the lower shell.

Oyster-opening technique is similar. Hold the oyster with its deep shell down and with the hinge away from you. Force the oyster knife under the flat upper shell, twist the knife, then run it, held flat, along the upper shell until it cuts one or both of the muscles. Finish by cutting the remaining connections as you do for clams.

MUSSELS AND STEAMERS

Mussels and soft-shelled clams—"steamers"—must be soaked in cold water for several hours before cooking to force them to disgorge the sand from their interiors. Some people add a half-cup of flour or corn meal to the soaking water—they swear this results in fatter shellfish. Before the soaking process, mussels must be thoroughly scrubbed and "de-bearded," a process rendered much easier by the use of a stiff brush such as those we show you. (That beard, by the way, is actually closer to being the bivalve's hands—it is the fibrous growth that makes it possible for mussels to hold fast to rocks underwater.) Steamers will be more attractive and sand-free if they, too, are scrubbed with a brush and rinsed vigorously.

stainless-steel and the handle is black plastic, the entire implement may be put in the dishwasher after use. This is the Rolls Royce of oyster knives, but what you spend on the purchase you are likely to save on frayed tempers and fingers.

Oyster Knife with Wooden Handle   11.26

Stainless-steel blade and guard, light wood handle; 6″ long overall; blade 1⅞″ long; guard 2″ × 1¾″.
$2.50

This oyster knife, also with a blade shaped like a lopsided arrowhead, is similar in design to the one above, but it is less sturdy and, consequently, less expensive. The stainless-steel blade is attached with a tinned collar to a round wooden handle. A tinned bolster similar to that on a fencing foil protects the knife hand from contact with the oyster shell and also prevents the blade from piercing your oyster-holding hand. The handle, unlike that of the other knife, has no thumb rest, although the bolster is cut away at the top in such a fashion that you can rest your thumb against it for better leverage. The curved edge of the blade runs to the right rather than the left on this knife; it will be more efficient for southpaws than the preceding knife would be.

Oyster Knife with Plastic Handle   11.25

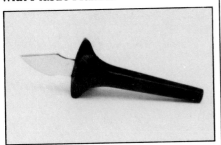

Stainless steel with plastic handle; 6½″ long; blade 1⅞″ long.
$2.75

Not a thing of beauty, this oyster knife makes up in efficiency for its lack of glamor. The short, sturdy blade looks lethal and it is—to an oyster. It has a broad and razor-sharp tip shaped much like an arrowhead that is straight on the right side as you hold the knife and curved on the left side. Obviously made for right-handers, it makes short work of separating the meat from the shell. A scalloped indentation in the tapered handle gives you a thumb rest for the firm grip necessary to force the shell apart, and a heavy bolster or guard at the blade end of the handle prevents the point of the blade from gouging the hand holding the oyster as well as protecting your knife-wielding fingers from the sharp edges of the shell. As the blade is of

Carbon-Steel Oyster Knife   11.27

High-carbon steel blade with nickel-steel collar, unfinished wood handle; 7″ long; blade 4″ long.
$4.50

Continued from preceding page

There are nearly as many varieties of oyster openers as there are of oysters, and each seaport has its particular favorite. This one is beloved among the fishermen of Boston. The 4″ blade is attached with a metal ferrule to a short bulb-shaped handle of unvarnished wood. The tip of the rigid, high-carbon steel blade is very sharp for making its way between the shells, but the edges are dull. Brute force to some degree is needed in attacking the oyster shell (although skill counts), and, since there is no guard to protect your fingers, a great deal of care is required when using this knife if you want to save both your hand and the oyster meat from injury. For professionals and those who look on oyster shucking as a blood sport, this is a very satisfactory tool.

Lady Mary Wortley Montagu, the eighteenth-century English poet and letter writer who traveled all over Europe, observed of the Viennese: "The plenty and excellence of all sorts of provisions are greater here than in any place I was ever in, and it is not very expensive to keep a splendid table. . . . They (lack) nothing but shellfish, and are so fond of oysters, they have them sent from Venice, and eat them very greedily, stink or no stink."

OYSTER STEW

If there is a traditional Christmas Eve dish in the United States, it is oyster stew.

5 tablespoons butter
1 cup milk
2 cups cream
1½ pints oysters and liquor
Salt and freshly ground pepper
Cayenne
Chopped parsley or paprika

This may be made with cream only or with milk. Heat soup bowls. Add a good pat of butter to each bowl. Keep piping hot. Drain the oysters, then heat the milk, cream, and oyster liquor to the boiling point. Add the oysters and bring again to the boiling point. Season to taste with salt, ·pepper, and cayenne. Ladle into the hot bowls and add a sprinkling of chopped parsley or of paprika.

Sautéed Oyster Stew. Combine the oysters and butter in a skillet and cook until the edges curl. Add the hot cream and milk, and bring to the boiling point. Season, ladle into hot bowls, and serve with crisp biscuits or buttered toast.

(From AMERICAN COOKERY, by James A. Beard, illustrated by Earl Thollander. Copyright © 1972 by James A. Beard. Reprinted by permission of Little, Brown and Company.)

Clam Knife from Japan   11.28

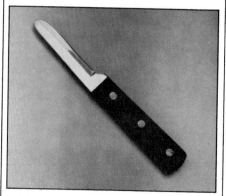

Stainless-steel blade with hardwood handle, brass rivets; 6¾″ long overall; blade 3¾″ long.
$1.50

The clam is a somewhat more tractable creature than the oyster, with a more clearly revealed opening between its shells. Hence, clam knives have blunt rather than sharp blades as well as rounded tips, which minimize the danger of cutting into the meat. This sturdy knife comes from Japan, where clams are plentiful. The tempered stainless-steel blade is heavier along the back than on the cutting edge, which is only moderately sharp, and is attached by three brass rivets to a flat, unvarnished hardwood handle. The full tang gives the whole implement the heft necessary to pry a clam shell open.

Unbreakable Clam Knife   11.29

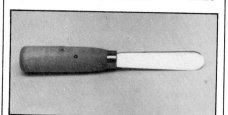

Stainless-steel blade with unfinished beechwood handle, nickel-steel collar; 7¼″ long overall; blade 3¼″ long.
$1.85

This clam knife comes with a guarantee against breaking and, as you might expect, it is a more massive tool than the one above. The stainless-steel blade is rounded on both sides, with no sharp edges. It is attached with a metal ferrule and a pin to a round handle of unvarnished beechwood. For working long hours with wet hands, this would be a comfortable instrument to use, and it's well worth considering even if your clam-opening is limited to an occasional first course for two, on the half-shell with lemon.

Clam Opener   11.30

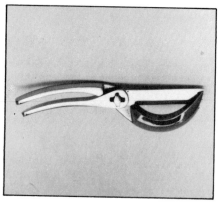

Nickel steel with stainless-steel blade; 7¾″ long.
$8.50

Our experts prefer that you learn to open your clams by the old-fashioned method we have described, so that none of the delectable juice is lost. But if despite your best efforts you cannot master the technique, this gimmick will do the trick. When you use this tool, the clam is opened in a vertical position instead of a horizontal one, so you would be wise to perform the entire operation over a bowl so the fluid is retrieved, to be used with the opened clams. You place the clam between the jaws of the implement, with its thin edge toward the hinge. By squeezing the scissorlike handles together, you cause the cutting edge of the blade to pass between the halves of the shell. But—and here's the catch—the blade also cuts through the body of the clam—a decided disadvantage if you want to serve your clams attractively on the half-shell, but no problem if the mollusks are to be chopped before use. The blade has a forked tip to lift the meat from the open shell. The apparatus is of nickel-steel with a stainless-steel blade. It's very sturdy, and it disassembles for easy cleaning.

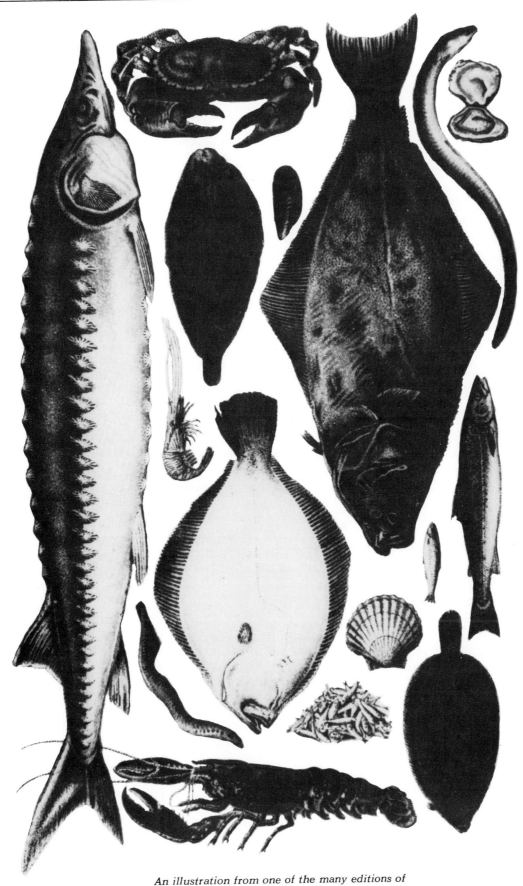

An illustration from one of the many editions of
Mrs. Beeton's Book of Household Management,
a nineteenth-century standby.

CLAMS ORLEANS

Serves: 6
Preparation time: 15 minutes
Cooking time: 20 to 25 minutes

Here is a clever way to prepare clams and the recipe is equally good made with fresh oysters. When clams are used, I prefer Little Necks or "steamers," which do not get chewy; but whichever clams you choose, the dish will still be delicious.

INGREDIENTS
30 clams (Little Necks)
½ cup white wine
1 bouquet garni
4 tablespoons olive oil
1½ cups homemade white bread crumbs
½ cup finely chopped parsley
1 tablespoon finely minced chives
Salt and freshly ground black pepper
2 small tomatoes, peeled, seeded, chopped and well drained
½ to 1 cup heavy cream
2 to 4 tablespoons sweet butter

PREPARATION
1. Preheat oven to 350°.
2. Wash the clams thoroughly in cold water to remove all sand.
3. In a large saucepan combine the wine, bouquet garni and clams and cook them covered, over medium heat, until they are all open.
4. Discard any clams that have not opened and reserve the others.
5. In a skillet heat the olive oil; add the bread crumbs, parsley and chives. Cook the mixture for 1 or 2 minutes or until the crumbs are just coated with oil. Season with salt and pepper.
6. Add the tomatoes and cook the mixture for 2 or 3 minutes.
7. Remove the clams from their shells, being careful not to break them. Discard the shells and strain the clam juice through a double layer of cheesecloth.
8. Flavor the heavy cream with 2 or 3 teaspoons of the clam broth. Do not use too much of the broth for it may be quite salty.
9. Place a layer of the bread-crumb mixture in individual baking dishes or scallop shells. Place 5 clams in each dish. Top with another layer of bread crumbs and dot each one with ½ tablespoon butter. Pour a little of the clam broth and cream mixture into each dish.
10. Bake the clams for 10 minutes and serve immediately.

REMARKS
The tomatoes must be well squeezed or else the bread-crumb mixture will become too soggy.

If you like the combination of bacon and clams, you may add ½ cup of finely minced crisp bacon to the bread-crumb mixture. The baking dishes should be ¾ filled with the cream mixture, so you may need a little more than the ½ cup, according to the size of the baking dish.

(From THE SEASONAL KITCHEN, by Perla Meyers. Copyright © 1973 by Perla Meyers. Reprinted by permission of Holt, Rinehart and Winston.)

"Number 32: Paring Knife with a black wooden handle and a very rusty blade, point broken off, bought for 3 francs and 40 centimes only a week ago along with two snail tongs at the cutlery shop at the foot of the Rue Mouffetard. I made this purchase because I liked the contrast between the long handle and the short blade, but without noticing that it wasn't stainless steel. The point was broken off the same day trying to open clams, the most hermetically sealed of all shellfish. The only way Kichka found to open them was to wait until they opened up slightly to breathe, then insert the blade rapidly, which took her the whole day. (If anyone knows a more efficient method, please write me.)"
An Anecdoted Topography of Chance, by Daniel Spoerri, Something Else Press, 1966

Oyster and Clam Knife 11.31

Stainless-steel blade with stained wood handle; 5¼" long overall; blade 2¼" long.

$2.00 ▲

If you wish to invest in only one tool for opening bivalves, this might be the very thing. Billed as a clam knife, it has the sharp, pointed blade of the oyster opener, and like that knife it has one straight edge and one curved edge, the latter for detaching the muscles from the shell. In addition, the blade is notched at the base of the curved edge for ease in twisting and then holding the shell open. The full tang is enclosed in a stubby, attractively stained wooden handle that is gently curved to fit the user's hand. The whole implement is only 5¼" long, just the right size for carrying on clamming expeditions by those who prefer to consume their catch on the beach.

STEAMED CLAMS A LA PROVENCALE

Serves: 4
Preparation time: 20 minutes
Cooking time: 20 minutes

Here is a simple yet delicious way to prepare either clams or mussels. Serve right out of the casserole in which they have steamed. An earthenware casserole is particularly attractive. The clams can also be steamed in the oven.

INGREDIENTS
4 quarts small clams or mussels
½ cup olive oil
2 hot chili peppers, dry
3 large garlic cloves, finely minced
2 tablespoons finely minced shallots
2 tablespoons finely minced fresh oregano, or 1 teaspoon dried
1 cup finely minced parsley
Freshly ground black pepper

PREPARATION
1. Put the clams or mussels in a colander and rinse them well under cold running water. Scrub them with a stiff brush to remove all sand that may cling to the shell, then soak them for 30 minutes in ice water.
2. Combine the olive oil and chili peppers in a large kettle or earthenware casserole.
3. Add the garlic and shallots. Cook until they are soft but not browned.
4. Add the clams, oregano and ¾ cup of minced parsley. Shake the kettle to coat the clams well with the oil and herbs.
5. Cover the kettle and cook the clams over low heat for 10 to 12 minutes or until they have all opened. Discard any that have not opened. Sprinkle with salt and pepper.
6. Sprinkle with the remaining parsley and serve right from the pot with crusty bread.

(From THE SEASONAL KITCHEN, by Perla Meyers. Copyright © 1973 by Perla Meyers. Reprinted by permission of Holt, Rinehart and Winston.)

Bay-Scallop Knife 11.32

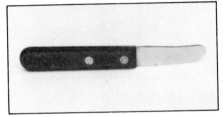

Stainless-steel blade, Pakkawood handle, brass rivets; 6¼″ long overall; blade 2¼″ long.

$2.20

Scallops are usually sold shucked because, once taken from the water, they promptly gape and dry out, expiring very quickly unless kept in cool sea water. If you can somehow acquire scallops in their natural state—one of our editors reports having scooped up bushels last fall in an idyllic Long Island bay—you may discover a delightful surprise in certain seasons. Adorning the familiar edible adductor muscle, the part you buy at the market, is a lump of pink roe, which will tint the sauce for your Coquilles St. Jacques a delicate shade and give it a wonderful flavor. This sturdy opener for scallops resembles a shorter, heavier clam knife. It is designed to deal with the delicate bay scallop, which is about 3″ in diameter, much smaller than the deep-sea scallop. The 2¼″ stainless-steel blade is set into a water-resistant Pakkawood handle with rounded edges and is secured with two brass rivets. The slight upward curve at the tip of the blade facilitates both opening the shell—an easier task than with clams or oysters—and cutting the plump muscle free from its moorings. And, as a bonus, the knife is guaranteed against breaking.

Sea-Scallop Knife 11.33

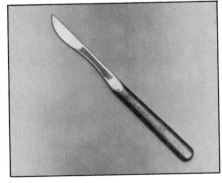

Stainless steel; 8″ long overall; blade 4″ long.
$3.30

This is a knife your grandchildren will inherit, so indestructible is it. The blade and the handle are made from one piece of stainless steel. The handle has a dull finish for a more secure grip, while the blade is mirror-bright. The shape of the blade is ingenious: from a sharp point it widens into a curve mimicking the curve inside a scallop shell, then indents again in a shallow arc until it again widens to become the handle. In addition, the blade thickens toward the handle to permit you to rest your thumb or forefinger there (depending on your personal technique) while you dislodge the large edible muscle. For the money, this is a very useful, durable tool, worth buying if you know of a source of fresh-caught sea scallops.

The imperial Romans preferred their fish ghoulishly fresh, as can be seen in this quotation from Seneca: "A mullet is not considered to be fresh unless it has expired in the hands of the guest. They are exposed in a glass bowl where can be observed the various nuances of colour through which they successively pass in their slow and painful agony. At other times they are doomed to perish in brine where they are pickled alive. What can be more lovely, they say, than an expiring mullet!"

Kitchen and Table, *by Colin Clair, Abe-lard-Schuman, New York, 1964*

SEA SCALLOPS A LA CREOLE

Serves: 6 to 8
Preparation time: 15 minutes
Cooking time: 35 minutes

Even though sea scallops have a less delicate flavor than bay scallops, they are excellent when prepared with a strong marinade such as the one given here. This dish is at its best if it is prepared the day before it is to be served. In the summer, the addition of 1 or 2 tablespoons of finely chopped fresh herbs will give it a whole new zest.

INGREDIENTS
1 cup dry white wine
1 cup water
1 large bouquet garni
2 celery stalks
6 peppercorns
1 onion stuck with a clove
1 teaspoon salt
2 pounds fresh sea scallops
6 tablespoons olive oil
1 teaspoon dry mustard
1 teaspoon Dijon mustard
1 small red onion, thinly sliced

THE MARINADE:
Juice of 2 lemons
1 tablespoon wine vinegar
1 bay leaf
½ cup sliced olives (preferably Greek olives)
1 whole unpeeled lemon, thinly sliced
3 tablespoons finely chopped pimientos
2 tablespoons finely chopped parsley
1 garlic clove, finely minced
Salt and freshly ground black pepper
Pinch of cayenne

PREPARATION
1. In a large enamel saucepan, combine the wine, water, bouquet garni, celery stalks, peppercorns, onion and salt. Bring the mixture to a boil, then simmer partially covered for 30 minutes.
2. Add the scallops and cook for 5 minutes over low heat. Drain and cool.
3. In a serving bowl combine the lemon juice, vinegar and oil. Add the dry mustard and Dijon mustard and whisk the dressing until it is very smooth.
4. Add the scallops, sliced onion, bay leaf, olives, lemon slices, pimientos, parsley, garlic, salt, black pepper and cayenne. Carefully blend the scallops in the dressing and chill until serving time.
5. Serve with crusty bread and a bowl of sweet butter.

REMARKS
For a variation you may add ¼ pound of sliced fresh raw mushrooms to the dressing. Instead of 2 pounds of scallops, you may use 1 pound of scallops and 1 pound of cooked shrimp.

(From THE SEASONAL KITCHEN, by Perla Meyers. Copyright © 1973 by Perla Meyers. Reprinted by permission of Holt, Rinehart and Winston.)

Tools for Preparing and Serving Crustaceans

The first man to eat a lobster or a crab must have been an intrepid soul. Who could have imagined that such ugly beasts would be so good to eat? After that gastronomic explorer managed to fish one of these crustaceans out of the water, probably suffering pinched fingers in the process, he had to figure out how to get to the meat under those bony carapaces. He probably bashed them with a rock, producing a result the right consistency for mousse. The tools we show will enable you to do a better job than early man, and to extract the flesh from a crustacean of any size or kind with maximum ease.

The diversity which exists in the worlds of the finny fishes and the bivalves extends to crustaceans. Many people have been startled to discover their Caribbean lobster—or perhaps one from the Mediterranean or the Pacific Coast—served without claws. No, it wasn't an accident in the kitchen: nature has not seen fit to supply these southerners, actually related to crawfish, with the appendages some consider the most delectable part of the northern, or true, lobster. So, to eat a spiny lobster, as these pinchless crustaceans are called, you won't need our claw crackers at all.

Crabs come in all sizes from the majestic Alaskan king crab, which averages five feet across, to the dime-sized or smaller oyster crab. Floridians are fond of the stone crab with its black-tipped claws, while West Coast epicures prize the meaty Dungeness, found from northern California to Puget Sound and beyond. In the waters of the East Coast roams one crustacean that is considered two, the blue crab. During its growing season the blue crab molts—sheds its shell—and becomes temporarily the delicacy known as the soft-shelled crab. While it's in this state the entire body, after cleaning, can be deep-fried, sautéed, or broiled and consumed down to the last morsel. When the blue crab is encased in its newly re-grown hard shell, the meat must be artfully picked from its shell and all its claws after the creature has been steamed or boiled. Tidewater types treasure the female of this species for its tasty eggs; she-crab soup is a regional specialty. Because of advanced freezing techniques, the meat of all the commercially caught crabs is available year-round and country-wide.

Shrimp, too, come in a wide range of sizes. On Fisherman's Wharf in San Francisco, the fishmongers sell paper cups filled with the tiniest cooked and chilled bay shrimp, each one the size of your pinky nail, to be devoured on the spot. The warm waters of the Gulf of Mexico yield gigantic gray monsters, a dozen to the pound, and other waters of the world supply pink, brown, or bright scarlet shrimp ranging from tiny to enormous. No matter what the size, provided they are not overcooked, shrimp are one of the most delectable crustaceans we know. Most shrimp come to market without their heads (they keep fresher that way). If you have a choice, buy raw, chilled shrimp in the shell in preference to frozen shrimp.

HOW TO COOK A LOBSTER

Like all seafood, lobsters, crabs, and shrimp are amenable to a range of cooking methods and presentations, but it is helpful to know the basic modes of preparation.

HOW TO COOK A LOBSTER

Lobster is most often served boiled (or steamed) or broiled. Each method has it devotees, few of whom know that lobster can also be eaten "raw": Kill and clean the lobster, slice in small pieces, and marinate in a bath of lime juice, onion, and green pepper with a heavy sprinkling of freshly grated black pepper. This will "cook" the meat—actually tenderizing and flavoring it—for the tangy dish known as seviche.

The most humane way of boiling a lobster is a subject of argument wherever fish cooks gather. Some people insist that the beast be placed in cold, salted fresh water and brought slowly to the simmer so it will expire peacefully some time before the water boils. Others prefer plunging the living lobster head first into the boiling pot to bring it to a quick end. Whichever method you choose, be sure the lobster shows ample signs of life before cooking. A freshly caught lobster is black or dark green and fights back—it will wave its claws pugnaciously when lifted by the back, which is the safe way to hold it. (Don't be fooled by the wooden pegs inserted in the claws, or the rubber bands wrapped around them—these are mainly to keep the lobsters in the tank from injuring each other. But even a pegged lobster can sometimes inflict a painful nip on the finger of the unwary handler, so approach your catch from the rear.) Once cooked, the lobster is a brilliant crimson with a tightly curled tail. It will take anywhere from 5 minutes up to 40 or so in boiling salted water (or sea water, if you're at the shore) to produce this result, depending on the size of the creature. Do not overcook—time the beast carefully and remove it from the pot when it's done—it will continue to cook if left in the water. If you need roe (coral) for a sauce, or if you just wish to enjoy its excellent flavor, choose a lobster with two soft, short swimmerets rather than long, rigid ones on the underbelly. That's a female—a "hen"—and it should have coral if the season is right.

Broiling requires that the lobster be killed before cooking. To do this, place the lobster on its back on a cutting board. Insert a heavy sharp knife at the juncture between body and tail; this is easier than cutting between head and body, as you are often advised to do. This cut severs the spinal cord and kills it. Now slit the underside of the body from head to tail (use scissors) and remove, if it is visible, the black vein down the center of the tail and take out the stomach sac just behind the eyes. Crack the claws. Brush the shells with oil, lay the split lobster on a broiler rack, shell side up, and broil for 12 to 15 minutes. Don't, we beg you, broil the flesh side unless you want the meat to dry out. When the lobster is done, turn it over, anoint the flesh side with melted butter, and serve.

HOW TO EAT A LOBSTER

Half the fun of eating a lobster is prying out the meat, each creamy morsel to be dipped in golden melted butter spiked with lemon. You also

Continued from preceding page

need to remove the meat if you're making such a dish as Homard à l'Américain or a lobster salad. A couple of tools are essential to crack the large hard claws and to pull out the delicate flesh within them and within the many small legs. A nutcracker will serve the first purpose adequately if not elegantly, but see our lobster pincers and see also the marvelous heavy shears we show in Chapter 3. A long, narrow pick (11.36) is vital to the job, too. If you plan to serve lobster as a grand-occasion food, you will probably want table-worthy tools such as these, which have been designed for the job.

Now the flame-red body of the lobster is before you. Go to work. First the easy part. Slit the tail down the center of the underside and remove the black vein. (It's sometimes invisible—don't worry if you can't find it.) Remove the tail meat in one big piece and cut it into bite-size morsels. If the lobster is for your own delectation, dip each piece into your lemon butter and consume it as you go. Yummy! But adventure awaits. Next, twist the big claws from the body. Each of these comes in reticulated sections joined by a tough, fibrous skin. Crack the largest part of the claws with lobster pincers or a nutcracker. Sometimes the whole piece of claw meat will come out of the shell with the tiny "thumb" section intact. If it doesn't, pry out this small piece with the pick. Now twist apart the joints of the rest of the claw and extract the meat. The shell texture becomes softer as it meets the body—the last section is flat and requires a little work to get the flesh out intact. The small legs, too, will require skillful maneuvering with the pick.

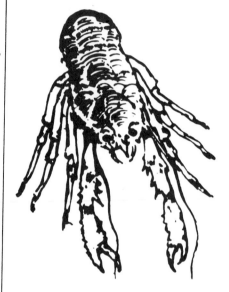

Now for the body. Along the juncture of the legs with the body there is a bony series of compartments, each translucent division holding a lump of meat. Pick these out carefully—these bits are among the most tender. If you have been lucky or smart enough to land a lady lobster, you will discover in the body cavity one or more large lumps of bright coral or roe. This is delicious—the very essence of lobster. The coral can be used to flavor a sauce, to make a flavored butter to spread on crackers for hors d'oeuvre, or you can just, sybaritically, dip it into butter and eat it on the spot. Larger lobsters contain meat in the back fins at the tip of the tail which can be picked out once the fins have been detached from the body.

HOW TO COOK AND CLEAN CRABS

Hard-shelled crabs are usually cooked before cleaning; their wildly waving claws, which can reach backward, make it impossible to scrub them while alive. Plunge the live, well-rinsed crabs into a pot of highly seasoned boiling water—use a long pair of tongs. The addition of a small amount of vinegar and a healthy sprinkling of cayenne pepper will give your crabs a wonderful flavor, or use the commercially prepared spice mixture called crab boil. Once cooked, crack the carapace with the heavy end of a crab knife (11.34). Pull off the top shell and scrape out the spongy, inedible gill material. Take out the spongy stomach, which lies in the middle of the body. Some of the sweetest meat lies in the back fins—the sides of the shell—which will be accessible

to your pick once you have cleared away the inner skeleton. In good-sized crabs, the small legs will yield meat, too. Crack them if necessary, or just probe them with your lobster pick or a nutpick.

Soft-shelled crabs must be cleaned before frying. First, wash them (they can't pinch). Plunge the point of a large sharp knife between the eyes to kill the crab, then lift the top shell at each side and clean out the gills and the other inedible matter. Flip the crab over and remove the apron—the pointed flap of shell. Cut off the front of the crab, just behind the eyes. Rinse again, drain, pat dry, and the crabs are ready to cook.

HOW TO PREPARE SHRIMP

Many people buy their shrimp cooked and cleaned in order to avoid the lengthy shelling and deveining process necessary when preparing fresh, or green, shrimp. Then they are disappointed to find that those fat pink crustaceans which looked so appetizing on their bed of ice at the market have all the taste of a schoolboy's eraser. This is because few fishmongers season the poaching broth, and virtually all of them overcook shrimp.

A short cooking period produces moist, tender shrimp. To boil, preferably in the shell, add plenty of salt plus onion, celery, and herbs to a large pot of water and set over a high flame. Once it is bubbling, add the shrimp. As the water comes to a full hard boil again, you will notice that your gray shrimp have turned a lovely shade of pink. Remove the pot from the heat immediately and drain the shrimp under cold, running water. They are now ready for shelling. Adventurous hosts can devise a new party game and let each guest shell his own. If you plan to sauce the shrimp or make a salad, cleaning is a do-it-yourself activity.

Shrimp may be shelled raw to stir-fry or broil them. Whether they are raw or cooked, the cleaning process is identical; use one of the tools we describe (11.38, 11.39), or lacking one of these invaluable devices, do it thus: If the shrimp have their heads, break them off. Hold the body under running water and peel off the shell, beginning with the top and working toward the tail fins. Then with a small sharp knife make an incision along the back curve and lift out the black or gray intestinal vein which runs along under the curved back. (Sometimes this vein can't be located—no cause to worry, as removing it is mainly a cosmetic operation.) Rinse the shrimp if necessary, and they're ready to use. Remember when you purchase uncleaned shrimp to allow for shell weight—1½ pounds of green shrimp will yield approximately 1 pound, cooked and cleaned.

Shrimp shells are a tasty by-product of cooking these crustaceans yourself. Washed, then pounded in a mortar or whirled in a blender with a little of the shrimp cooking liquid, they can be strained through a very fine sieve into melted butter, then chilled to create a delicious shellfish-flavored butter. Add a dollop of this essence to ordinary Béchamel sauce for a delicious topping for any fish, or use the butter on canapés. Strain and freeze the liquid in which you boiled your shrimp for later use for poaching fish.

Crab Knife   11.34

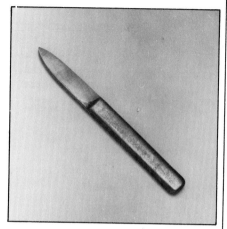

Stainless steel; 6″ long overall; blade 2½″ long.
$3.20

A solid piece of forged and hardened stainless steel, this knife has two business ends. A sharp thwack with the heavy handle will crack open the body and claws of the toughest crab, and you can neatly excise the meat from the cracked shells with the short, pointed blade. Use the same sharp point to kill soft-shelled crabs before cleaning and cooking them, if you're lucky enough to find these succulent morsels in your fish market. Only 6″ long, this knife packs a lot of power in a little body.

Fish Scaler.

GRANCHI—SOFT-SHELL CRABS

5 soft-shell crabs (live)
2 tablespoons olive oil
2 tablespoons butter
2 tablespoons chopped fresh basil or 1 tablespoon dried basil
2 tablespoons chopped parsley
1 teaspoon chopped garlic
Salt and freshly ground black pepper
¼ cup dry white wine

To clean live soft-shell crabs, lift end flaps and remove gills. Snip off front of crab where eyes protrude. Turn crab over, remove flap and wash. Crab is now ready to cook.

Heat oil and butter in a large skillet. Add cleaned crabs and cook, uncovered, over high heat for 3 to 5 minutes. Turn crabs over and cook several minutes more. Add basil, parsley, garlic, salt and pepper to taste. As soon as the garlic discolors (do not burn), add wine. Lower heat and simmer for several minutes. Serve hot to 5 as a first course.

(From ITALIAN FAMILY COOKING, by Edward Giobbi, illustrated by Cham, Lisa and Gena Giobbi. Copyright © 1971 by Edward Giobbi. Reprinted by permission of Random House, Inc.)

"Every year before the crab season starts, I begin to save money. People say crabs are my life, and my hoarded money is the ransom. From the first day of the season until the last, I do not miss a single day. People know I have a weakness for crabs and invite me. I call September and October the crab autumn. It is easily used up, and expensive to keep up. I tell the servants to scour the bottle and brew wine, both raw and clear, so that I can get tipsy, and I call those wines the crab wine and the crab brew, and the bottles crab bottles. I used to have a maid servant whom I called the crab maid, but she is now dead. Her sole job was to attend to the crab feast."

Li Liweng, quoted in Chinese Gastronomy, *by Hsiang Ju Lin and Tsuifeng Lin. Pyramid Publications, 1972*

Lobster Pincers   11.35

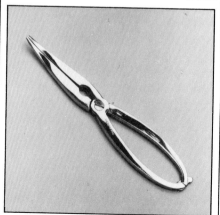

Stainless steel; 7⅜″ long.
$22.50

This tool is a piece of sculpture: the fact that it works supremely well is miraculous. Made in France of mirror-bright stainless steel, these pincers are designed both to crack the rigid shell of the lobster and to extract the meat from the larger sections with the long, slightly upcurved tips. The inside edges of these tongs are scored to provide a good grip on the smooth shell. And the small hole in the pincers near their base will close around a small leg to enable the diner to grip it while picking out the meat within. The pincers are operated on a spring mechanism which is totally enclosed—no chance that lobster juices, or the butter in the sauce, will invade the works. A small hooklike latch at the base of the comfortable handles keeps the pincers safely closed when not in use. In conjunction with the pick below, these pincers make an expensive and luxurious individual service for the consumption of the most elegant crustacean we have.

Lobster Pick   11.36

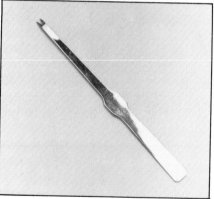

Stainless steel; 8″ long.
$3.00

This simple, beautiful pick is meant to be used with the elegant lobster pincers we show you above. It is a heavy piece of highly polished stainless steel with a wide flat handle tapering to a pair of tiny, sharp, curved tines. Intended for lobster, this pick can double for crabs, or even for periwinkles or snails. Although a nutcracker or, in a pinch, a pair of pliers, will suffice for cracking a lobster's shell, we know of no substitute for a pick in getting the last luscious morsels from the shell. This one makes the hardware-store variety look pretty primitive; a set of them, paired with the companion pincers, would be an ideal house gift for a seaside-dwelling friend, sure to elicit an invitation to return.

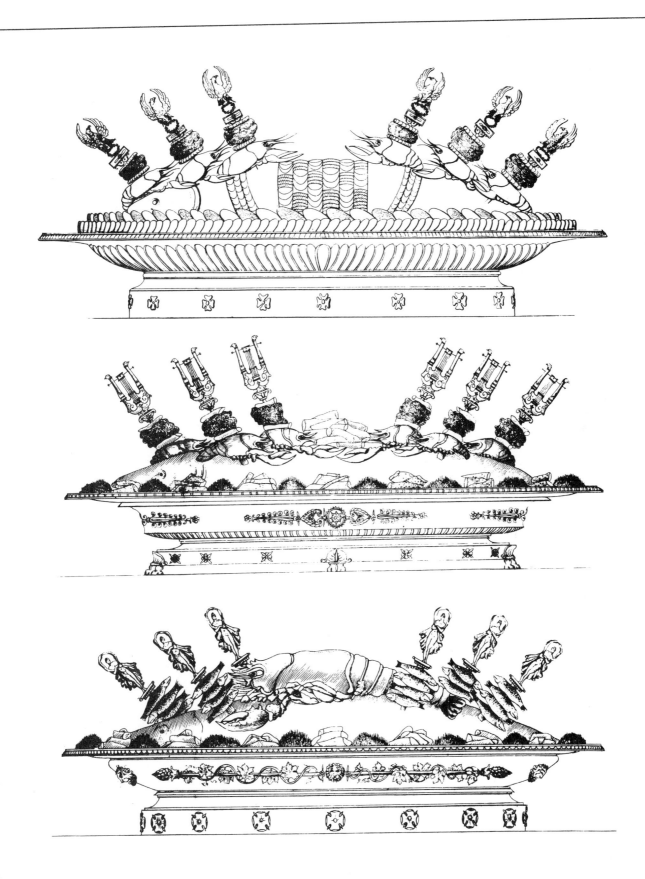

*Some of Carême's fantasies: Seafood presented
with garnishes indicating their appropriateness for
military, musical, or terpsichorean occasions.*

HOMARD NORMANDE—LOBSTER NORMANDY STYLE

Serves 6

Like all people living close to the sea, the *Normands* are very fond of shellfish, fish, and any other ocean-going delicacies. Although lobsters are very expensive in France, they are featured quite often in Normandy restaurants. As in the majority of the dishes made in that part of the country, cream, butter, and wine are used generously.

4 fresh, live lobsters, about 1½ pounds each
½ cup (1 stick) sweet butter
2 teaspoons salt
1 teaspoon freshly ground white pepper
6 shallots or ½ cup finely chopped scallions
½ cup calvados
3 cups heavy cream
3 tablespoons all-purpose flour
juice of ½ lemon
dash cayenne pepper
2 tablespoons fresh parsley, finely chopped

Split the lobsters lengthwise with a big knife and break the shells off the claws with a hammer or a cleaver. Pour the liquid and the tomalley [liver] into a small bowl. Discard the stomach. Melt half the butter in a large, heavy saucepan. When the butter turns to a hazelnut color, add the lobsters and sprinkle with salt and pepper. Cook on high heat for 8 to 10 minutes, turning the lobsters as you go along. They should turn an even red all over. Remove the lobsters from the saucepan. Arrange in a large roasting pan and place in a preheated 200 F. oven to keep them warm and to finish the cooking. Add the chopped shallots to the saucepan and sizzle 1 minute without burning. Add the calvados, ignite, and when the flame dies out, add the cream. Work together the remaining butter and the flour. When the sauce starts boiling, add the flour mixture bit by bit, stirring vigorously with a wire whisk to dissolve any lumps. Slowly bring to a boil. Then mix in the tomalley and lemon juice. Taste for seasoning and add salt and cayenne pepper if necessary. You may let the sauce reduce a bit if you like it thicker. Stir in the parsley. Pour the sauce over the lobsters and serve piping hot.

(From JACQUES PEPIN: A FRENCH CHEF COOKS AT HOME, by Jacques Pépin. Copyright © 1975 by Jacques Pépin. Reprinted by permission of Simon & Schuster.)

A domestic manual of times gone by advises the housewife to instruct her footman in the proper manner of breaking a lobster's claws: "He is not to crack it between the hinges of a dining room door, but take it into the kitchen."

Lobster Shears 11.37

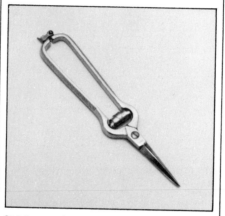

Stainless-steel blades with chromed-steel handles, nickel-steel spring; 7½" long.
$5.50 ▲

During their molting season lobsters have a very soft shell which will bend beneath your lobster pincers rather than crack. At such times these lobster shears will be especially useful for cutting away the shell. They can also be used instead of pincers on small-to-medium lobsters at any time; stout as they are, though, they won't cut the shell of that 10-pound monster you bought for salad. These shears are a kitchen tool—not in the same class with the opulent lobster pincers meant to appear at table—but they're sufficiently sharp and pointed to cut easily through the tough membrane on the underside of the tail, and as we say they'll cleave actual shell so long as it's not too thick. Made of heavy drop-forged stainless steel, they are powered by a strong exposed spring, which needs care in cleaning lest it harbor the ghost of lobsters past. The long, curved handles are scored for a secure grip, and there is a pin at the base of the handles to keep them safely closed when not in use.

"In general, the Bretons practice only one method of preparing their lobsters, true or spiny—boiling them in seawater, which is fine if what you want to taste is lobster. In lobster à l'américaine, on the other hand, the sauce, which cannot be produced without the lobster, is the justification of the indignity inflicted on him. If the strength of this dish, then,

lies in the sauce (as I deem indisputable), its weakness, from a non-French point of view, lies in the necessity of mopping up the sauce with at least three linear meters of bread. Bread is a good medium for carrying gravy as far as the face, but it is a diluent, not an added magnificence; it stands to the sauce of lobster à l'américaine in the same relationship as soda to Scotch.

"But a good pilaf—each grain of rice developed separately in broth to the size of a pistachio kernel—is a fine thing in its own right. Heaped on the plate and receiving the sauce à l'américaine as the waitress serves the lobster, the grains drink it up as avidly as nymphs quenching their thirst. The grains do not lose form or identity, although they take on a bit of rondeur. Mere rice cooked any old way won't do the trick; it turns to wallpaperer's paste. The French in general are almost as bad with rice as the Chinese, who are the very worst. The Armenians, Greeks, and Turks are the best with it. The conjunction of my Greek cook's langouste and his pilaf was a cultural milestone, like the wedding of the oyster and the lemon."

"Dietetics," by A. J. Liebling, in The Most of A. J. Liebling, *Simon & Schuster, New York, 1963*

Shrimpmaster 11.38

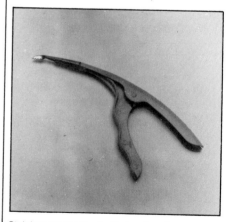

Stainless steel with plastic handle; 9" long.
$3.30

What will they think of next? The Shrimpmaster, that's what, and they've already thought of it. It is designed to make short work of the time-consuming task of shelling and deveining shrimp—it will perform both operations in one easy motion. You slip the tip of this implement between the shell and the flesh, beginning where the head used to be and following the curve of the top of the shrimp; while the tool lifts the shell free, it's also slitting the flesh to release the vein. Then you exert pressure on the plastic handles as you would on a pair of scissors and the vein and the shell are removed from the shrimp in one easy motion. You can, if you like, perform this operation under cold running water to keep both shrimp and utensil free of bits of shell and vein; you'll end up with beautifully cleaned crustaceans, whether raw or precooked. The ingenious business end of the Shrimpmaster is of stainless steel, fitted to yellow plastic handles joined by a spring. The bottom handle is shaped for an easy grip. It is not an elegant tool, but it does a yeoman job.

"We ate in pavilions on the sand. Pastries made of cooked and shredded fish and red and green peppers and small nuts like grains of rice. Pastries delicate and flaky and the fish of a richness that was incredible. Prawns fresh from the sea sprinkled with lime juice. They were pink and sweet and there were four bites to a prawn. Of those we ate many. Then we ate paella with fresh sea food, clams in their shells, mussels, crayfish, and small eels. Then we ate even smaller eels alone cooked in oil and as tiny as bean sprouts and curled in all directions and so tender they disappeared in the mouth without chewing."

Ernest Hemingway, For Whom the Bell Tolls

Shrimp-Ease   11.39

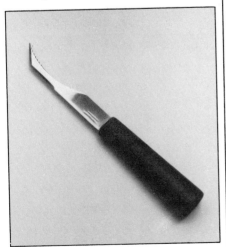

Stainless steel with stained walnut handle; 7¾" long overall; blade 3⅞" long.

$2.75

Heavier in the hand and lacking the scissorlike mechanism of the Shrimpmaster, this shrimp deveiner is nevertheless both simple and efficient. Attached to a satiny round wooden handle is a stainless-steel blade of intricate design. This blade is a mosaic of cutting surfaces which, in combination, make slicing through the shell and removing the black vein a one-step operation. A curved, serrated tip tapers in a gentle arc shaped to the body of a shrimp. The saw-like ridge removes the intestinal vein while the razor-sharp upper edge slices through the shell. This knife-like upper surface will also whack off the heads of the shrimp, if they have come to you that way—highly unusual, but possible. All in all, a handy tool to own when a large shrimp-cleaning chore looms.

SCAMPI CON ASPARAGI—SHRIMP WITH ASPARAGUS

1 pound raw shrimp
1 pound fresh asparagus
3 tablespoons olive oil
3 tablespoons butter
1 cup chopped celery
1 half-ripe tomato, diced
½ cup chopped parsley, Italian if possible
1 teaspoon fresh chopped mint or ½ teaspoon dried mint
Juice of ½ lemon
Salt and freshly ground black pepper

Shell and de-vein shrimp. Cut asparagus into 1-inch pieces, splitting the thick stalks and discarding all tough ends. Heat oil and butter in a wide skillet. Add asparagus, celery, tomato and parsley. Cook over high flame until celery is tender, mixing often. Add shrimp, mint, lemon juice, salt and pepper to taste. Toss, and cook shrimp about 5 minutes —do not overcook. Excellent with rice. Serve hot to 6.

(From ITALIAN FAMILY COOKING, by Edward Giobbi, illustrated by Cham, Lisa, and Gena Giobbi. Copyright © 1971 by Edward Giobbi. Reprinted by permission of Random House, Inc.)

Scallop Shells and Dishes

The scallop is the classic shell shape found in art—think of Botticelli's *Venus*—and in architecture through many centuries. It is the easily identifiable trade symbol of a major oil company on the one hand, and on the other the traditional emblem of St. Jacques, after whom the French have named both the bivalves—coquilles St. Jacques—and a number of the dishes made from them.

Like the snail's, the shell of the scallop is not just a home for the creature, but also an attractive serving container. "Give me my scallop-shell of quiet," said Sir Walter Raleigh, but you will probably want to fill yours with something more substantial—say Coquilles St.-Jacques à la Lyonnaise (see the recipe). We show here both the genuine article and a copy-cat version of the shell.

COQUILLES SAINT-JACQUES A LA LYONNAISE

Serves: 4 to 6
Preparation time: 40 minutes
Cooking time: 1 hour

Without doubt fresh Long Island bay scallops deserve the most elaborate preparation. Here is a lovely winter dish,

Continued from preceding page

elegant and subtle in taste. Follow it with a simple roast veal and a light dessert. You can serve this also as a main course, accompanied by buttered rice and followed by an endive salad.

INGREDIENTS

1 cup dry white wine
1 cup water
1 large bouquet garni
1 onion, stuck with a clove
1 teaspoon salt
6 crushed peppercorns
1½ pounds bay scallops

THE SAUCE:

2 egg yolks
¾ cup heavy cream
2 teaspoons Dijon mustard
½ teaspoon dry mustard
3 tablespoons sweet butter
3 tablespoons flour
Dash of lemon juice
2 tablespoons cold sweet butter

THE VEGETABLES:

2 tablespoons sweet butter
2 small carrots, cut into 1½-inch-long matchsticks
2 leeks, white part only, cut into 1½-inch-long matchsticks
2 small tender celery stalks, cut into 1½-inch-long matchsticks
4 large mushrooms, stems removed (reserve for stock), cut into matchsticks
½ cup dry white wine
Salt and freshly ground white pepper

PREPARATION

1. For the sauce, combine in a small mixing bowl the yolks, cream and both mustards. Whisk the mixture until well blended and then reserve.

2. Melt 2 tablespoons of butter in a heavy skillet. Add the carrots, leeks and celery. Cover the pan and simmer the vegetables until they are tender but not falling apart.

3. Add the mushrooms and ½ cup of white wine. Let the mixture come to a boil and cook, uncovered, over high heat until the wine has completely evaporated. Season lightly with salt and pepper and reserve.

4. While the vegetables are cooking, combine in a 3-quart enamel saucepan 1 cup of wine, water, bouquet garni, onion, 1 teaspoon of salt and the peppercorns. Bring the mixture to a boil, reduce the heat and simmer, covered, for 30 minutes.

5. Add the scallops, cover the saucepan and simmer for 5 minutes. Remove the

scallops with a slotted spoon and keep them warm.

6. Strain the broth into another saucepan and reduce to 1 cup.

7. Melt 3 tablespoons of butter in a heavy saucepan. Add the flour and cook for 3 minutes without browning, stirring constantly. Add the hot scallop broth all at once and whisk constantly until the sauce is smooth and thick. Correct the seasoning and add the lemon juice. Cook the sauce over very low heat for 20 minutes.

8. Add the cream and egg yolk mixture. Heat the sauce but do not let it come to a boil or it will curdle.

(From THE SEASONAL KITCHEN, by Perla Meyers. Copyright © 1973 by Perla Meyers. Reprinted by permission of Holt, Rinehart and Winston.)

Natural Scallop Shells   11.40

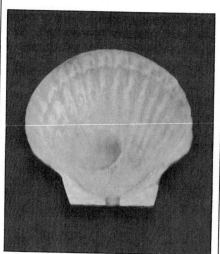

Natural shell; set of 4, each about 5″ diam.
$2.00

Scallops are such widely distributed bivalves that beaches around the world are strewn with their shells in many sizes and colors. Lucky beachcombers can gather their own, but for those who seem to discover only broken pieces, these natural shells from Japan can be purchased for a small price in sets of four. Once the outer covering of the giant sea scallops, they are, consequently, pearly within with a creamy white exterior striated with beige. They are shallow, so their cooked and sauced contents will turn the desired crispy brown under the broiler. The bottoms are naturally curved and so not very stable—a layer

of rock salt in a jelly-roll pan will hold them upright for baking, or you may want to fill several escargot plates (11.48) with the salt, center a shell in the middle of each, and take them from oven to table after baking your Coquilles St.-Jacques. While any ordinary au gratin dish can of course be used for your scallops, however you prepare them, how much more elegant and authentic such dishes would look in these shells. And don't overlook using them for other hot seafood too—deviled crab would be smashing, lobster Newburg most attractive—and there's no reason why they can't hold a first course of chilled poached mussels and sauce Rémoulade.

Porcelain Scallop Shell   11.41

Porcelain; 5¼″ × 4¾″. Also avail. 4″ × 3⅝″ or 4″ × 4″.
$5.00

A porcelain replica of the scallop shell, this French import will do both the baking and the serving of your gratinéed seafood in style. Unlike the natural shells, which tend to rock a bit on a flat surface, this doesn't—it has three projections on the bottom which seat it firmly on a baking sheet or serving plate. These dishes are so pretty you might even want to use them as ashtrays or for mints or nuts. The fluted interiors are deeper than natural shells, and they do not require the same care in handling and cleaning; just deposit them in the dishwasher after use. Although they look like a million, they cost a pittance.

Snail-Serving Equipment

To a gardener, snails are pests who fatten themselves on the choicest greenery; to the dedicated eater they are a delicacy known as escargots which he orders in the finest French restaurants. The pest and the gastronomic delight belong to the same family—they are gastropod mollusks—and both are edible, but there is a difference. The snails served in American restaurants and found in cans on the shelves of fine food shops are a special breed harvested from the moist vineyards and stone walls of Burgundy. They are large, lazy creatures who spend their lives gorging on grapevines and other goodies and growing fatter and more succulent within their biscuit-brown shells. Bathed in butter, garlic, and herbs, they make a delicious first course or, for real devotees, an entire meal.

Fresh snails are generally unavailable in markets in this country, more's the pity. Except for sea snails such as periwinkles and the tiny black delight of the Chinese, of course, if you have a vineyard or damp orchard you can collect your own. The canned ones that are sauced, heated, and served in restaurants are to be found in food shops, often paired with a separate package of shells. These shells may be washed and saved for re-use; thus you can pay less the second time around by buying only the tin. Always choose the largest size of canned snails. Drain them and simmer them in a little white wine to which you have added salt, chopped shallots, and butter—this will remove the "tinned" taste. Then proceed with your Escargots en Coquilles (recipe).

HOW TO PREPARE SNAILS

If, perchance, you do happen to harvest or purchase a mess of big, fat snails, here's how to prepare them. First, let the snails fast for at least a week or, say some experts, for a month, so that they will rid themselves of anything harmful they might have eaten. To do this, put them in a box with some small holes for ventilation, or in a closely woven basket; cover them closely (and weight down the cover, or else the future dinner will stroll away), and place the box in a cool place. On the day you plan to cook them, cut off the calcified protective flap, the "door" to each shell, and wash the snails well in several changes of cold water. Soak them for an hour in a water bath containing salt (quite a lot), vinegar, and a pinch of flour. Drain and rinse them. Bring a large pot of water to the boil and blanch the snails for 5 minutes. Drain them, rinse them under cold water, and remove them from their shells, cutting off the black intestinal portion from the end of each one; rinse them again. They are now ready to be simmered very gently for about three hours in a mixture of half salted water and half beef bouillon which has been spiked with carrots, onions, and a bouquet garni. While the snails are simmering, boil the shells, after scrubbing them, for 30 minutes in a solution of baking soda. Once the snails are cooked they may be drained, cooled, and refrigerated, or you can cool them, then stuff them immediately into their shells with a glob of the seasoned snail butter you have prepared and then heat them in the oven.

Snails to be cooked receive a characteristically straightforward treatment in a quaint old recipe: "Snails that be called escargots, must be caught in the morning. Take those snails that be young and small and have black shells, off vines and elder bushes, then wash them in water until they put forth no more slime. . . . Then it behoves you to draw the aforesaid snails out of their shells . . . and then you should remove their tail which is black (for that is their turd): and then wash them."

The Goodman of Paris (Le Ménager de Paris), c. 1393. Translated by Eileen Power. George Routledge & Sons, London, 1928

ESCARGOTS EN COQUILLES— SNAILS IN THEIR SHELLS

The snail is a gastropod mollusk of the Helicidae family. The choicest species are those large, fat, white snails known as *Helix pomatia.*

Certain people refuse to think of snails as edible because they are often hard and indigestible and they get a feeling similar to that produced by chewing on a piece of rubber. Others declare that the seasoning alone makes them passable. In reality, however, the snail is delicate, which is precisely why it is important to prepare it with care; otherwise it loses its taste very easily. Properly cooked and aromatized with well-chosen condiments in proper quantities, the snail is savory, tender, and digestible. One of my friends who has a delicate stomach, having prepared snails precisely according to the method outlined below, and, having found them delicious, let himself go so far as to eat 4 dozen of them and was surprised to find that he had no ill effects from his imprudence.

FOR SIX PEOPLE, USE:

½ lb. salted butter
½ c. dry white wine
10 T. coarse salt
4 T. chopped parsley
3 tsp. table salt
1 medium clove garlic
freshly ground black pepper to taste
72 big fat Burgundy snails (if possible) (preferably vine snails)
well-seasoned court bouillon prepared with water, salt, pepper, carrots, parsnips, garlic, thyme, bay leaf, and parsley

Realize, first of all, that it is important to prepare the snails the day before one is going to eat them. They then have a

Continued from preceding page

chance to absorb the seasonings and have a much better flavor than when prepared the same day.

If you are preparing them in winter the snails will have fasted and will be covered with a film. Remove this film and soak the snails in coarse salt for one hour, then wash them five or six times in cold water, changing the water each time. If you are preparing them in another season, start off by letting them fast for two days and then proceed as above.

Cook the court bouillon for thirty minutes. Put in the snails and cook them for one hour. Let them cool in the liquid. Remove them from the court bouillon, take the bodies out of the shells, wash the bodies and the shells in hot, salted water, and dry them. If necessary, remove any black portion (which is the intestine), which in summer tends to have an earthy taste.

Mash together the butter, parsley, table salt, garlic, and freshly ground pepper. Mix these well so as to get an absolutely smooth paste.

Put the mollusks back in their shells and pack in the seasoned butter.

At serving time, place the snails, opening up, in an oven-proof dish in which you have placed a little water to avoid having the shells or the dish burn. Sprinkle each snail with a little dry white wine, with a dropper, and heat this over a slow fire until the butter begins to boil in the shells. At this point the garlic is cooked and everything is ready.

Serve at once with special forks and special tongs *ad hoc,* so that your guests will not soil or burn their fingers.

Serve some Chablis in glasses and you will hear praise.

(From ENCYCLOPEDIA OF PRACTICAL GASTRONOMY, by Ali-Bab, translated by Elizabeth Benson. Copyright © 1974 by McGraw-Hill, Inc. Reprinted by permission of McGraw-Hill Book Company.)

Snail fanciers who always order their favorite delicacy in a restaurant are often reluctant to prepare them for themselves. Since canned snails are inexpensive and easy to finish at home, any cook who is worth his *sel marin* should try them, with the help of the equipment we show you. Try serving them in quantity as a main dish, or in smaller numbers for a first course. All that is needed in the way of serving equipment is, for each person, a pair of tongs, a narrow pick or fork, and a plate with rounded depressions to hold the shells upright. Much of the snail equipment usually offered for sale is ugly—unfortunate, since it comes to the table. We have found a group of attractive and eminently useful utensils for you. Just add good crisp-crusted bread, salad, and wine for a Francophile's delight.

Escargot Tongs 11.42

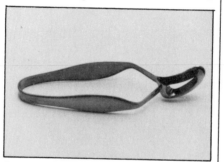

Stainless steel; 5⅞" long; 1¾" wide.
$9.00

The most important piece of equipment for enjoying snails served in their shells is a pair of tongs to hold each smooth, rounded shell securely while the succulent meat is picked out. These tongs, both handsome and well-designed, are made from a single heavy piece of burnished stainless steel, bent to provide tension; they feel good in the hand and look beautiful on the table. The business end is molded into two curved spoonlike projections which hug the slippery shell. Hold the tongs with the curved edges down, press the handles together, causing the clamps to spread, and the tongs will slip easily around the shell; relax your clasp and the snail is held firmly in a viselike grip. Once you have removed the meat, you can drink the remaining butter out of the shell, or pour it into your plate and soak it up with a piece of bread.

We ordered a couple of dozen escargots en pots de chambre to begin with. These are snails baked and served, for the client's convenience, in individual earthenware crocks, instead of being forced back into shells. The snail, of course, has to be taken out of his shell to be prepared for cooking. The shell he is forced back into may not be his own. There is thus not even a sentimental justification for his reincarnation. The frankness of the service en pot does not improve the preparation of the snail, nor does it detract from it, but it does facilitate and accelerate his consumption. (The notion that the shell proves the snail's authenticity, like the head left on a woodcock, is invalid, as even a suburban housewife knows nowadays; you can buy a tin of snail shells in a supermarket and fill them with a mixture of nutted cream cheese and chopped olives.)

"Dietetics," by A. J. Liebling, in The Most of A. J. Liebling, *Simon & Schuster, New York, 1963*

Escargot Fork 11.43

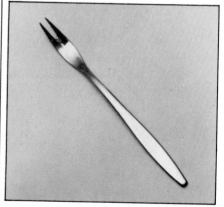

Stainless steel; 5⅝" long.
$4.00

Designed to be used with the tongs above, or by itself if you serve snails in individual pots (11.49, 11.50), this small stainless-steel fork has a satin finish like

Escargot Tongs
Escargot Fork
Escargot Dish
Copper Escargot Dish

Stainless-Steel Escargot Dish
Pair of Escargot Dishes
Stoneware Escargot Dish

that of the tongs. The two tines are very sharp, so they are sure to extract the snail in one piece from the shell. A lobster pick (11.36) will accomplish the same purpose, but for true snail lovers this is the genuine article.

Escargot Dish 11.44

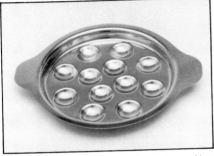

Stainless steel; 8″ diam.; 12 depressions. Also avail. with 6 depressions.
$9.00

Simple and modern, this is a utilitarian snail dish for informal entertaining or for use in rustic surroundings. The 8″ size has 12 depressions for the true aficionado, but the plate is also available with 6 places for first-course servings to those of moderate appetite. Made in Switzerland of high-grade stainless steel with a brushed surface, it has two handles formed in one piece with the plate. No ugly ducklings these: they are clean-lined plates to blend with any decor and keep their good looks forever, presenting many exquisite meals in the process.

Copper Escargot Dish 11.45

Copper with stainless-steel lining, brass handles; 8¼″ diam.; 12 depressions. Also avail. with 6 depressions.
$39.00

For true devotees of the snail, this is the most opulent of plates on which to serve him. The gleaming copper dish is lined with burnished stainless steel (no relining will ever be necessary, as it would be with a tinned surface), and it is fitted with two heavy brass handles. Several of these dishes hung in a decorative row will add distinction to any kitchen. The plate, a little over 8″ in diameter, comes with depressions for 12 snails; if you like these mollusks enough to pay the price of these costly dishes, you will probably want always to serve a dozen of the little beauties per person. The plate also comes with a half-dozen depressions.

Stainless-Steel Escargot Dish 11.46

Stainless steel; 9″ diam.; 12 depressions. Also avail. with 6 depressions.
$17.00 for two

The traditionalist will fall in love with the design of this escargot dish. Its curving lines will be right at home in a French Provincial setting, as well as in Chippendale or Queen Anne surroundings. Formed from a single piece of stainless steel, the dish can be had with a highly polished finish resembling silver, or with a dull burnished gloss. Care must be taken with the brighter finish, as it can be easily scratched both by the snail shells and by stacking after use. This is a large dish, 9″ in diameter, with depressions to hold either 12 or 6 snails. For all its good looks, it is surprisingly inexpensive. If you serve snails only occasionally or if our copper dishes above are too costly for your purse, don't hesitate over buying these: they are far more than a consolation prize.

Pair of Escargot Dishes 11.47

Stainless steel; 8″ diam.; 12 depressions.
$19.00 for two

From the same Jean Couzon who made 11.46, this dish is smaller and shallower, with a simpler design. With its raised beaded edge and highly polished surface it will fit into any English, Federal, or even Louis XVI decor. The finish is highly susceptible to scratching; clean and store these snail dishes with care. For practical types, there is also available a brushed surface—not as pretty, but more utilitarian. Serve a salad and some good bread along with a dozen delectable snails apiece to yourself and a friend—this dish comes only with 12 spaces, and is sold in pairs—for a light supper or a substantial lunch.

Stoneware Escargot Dish 11.48

Stoneware; 7″ diam.; 6 depressions, each 2″ diam., 1¾″ deep.
$5.00

All snails, whether from a California garden or a French vineyard, must be carefully cooked and bathed in seasoned

Continued from preceding page

butter to bring them to their absolute peak of flavor. The shell serves as a natural container for both the snail and its butter, but some people prefer not to have to pry them out of this covering. If you wish to buy your snails in the can and not bother with stuffing them back into the shells nor with subsequently removing them for eating, this is an ideal serving plate. The Bennington Potters, we have seen, make a variety of excellent and attractive stoneware items, both for retail sale and for use in their own Vermont restaurant, once the domain of the late, lamented Dione Lucas, chef extraordinaire. This escargot dish is made by them of the finest stoneware, fired at 2350 F. so that it's absolutely heatproof both during baking and brief trips under your broiler. The attractive pentagon shape holds six deep egg-shaped depressions to encompass plenty of butter in addition to a big fat snail apiece. A warm, rustic unglazed brown outside, our dish has an interior of smooth glossy white for both attractive presentation and ease of cleaning. Also available are dishes in a tawny hue, or in all white, or in white and blue. You'll be able to use these dishes for other purposes besides snails. Hard-cooked or stuffed and garnished eggs can be transported to your picnic in style, and how nice this dish would be to hold for each person an individual plate of sambals, relishes and condiments to accompany curry. After the party's over you can nest the dishes together for storage.

ESCARGOTS EN BROCHETTES— SKEWERED SNAILS

Prepare the snails as in the preceding recipe [Escargots en Coquilles] ...cool in the court bouillon, remove them from the shells, and remove the intestines.

Thread the snails on skewers, alternately with small squares of lean bacon.

Prepare a snail butter as in the preceding recipe. Melt it. Soak the skewers so that everything is well impregnated with the seasoned butter, then roll in some dry, sifted breadcrumbs and broil them under the broiler or on a grill, basting them with the rest of the melted butter.

Serve very hot.

(From ENCYCLOPEDIA OF PRACTICAL GASTRONOMY, by Ali-Bab, translated by Elizabeth Benson. Copyright © 1974 by McGraw-Hill, Inc. Reprinted by permission of McGraw-Hill Book Company.)

Very Small Leach Pots 11.49

Porcelain; 2¼″ diam.; 1½″ deep.
$1.75

Bernard Leach is undoubtedly England's premier potter. A specialist in tenmoku and other fine glazes, those crystalline coatings which originated in Japan centuries ago, Leach, with his apprentices, produces pots, bowls, and casseroles that are works of art. The small, sturdy, hand-thrown pots we show you here are miniature examples of Leach's excellence. We suggest them as individual snail servers—each one is capacious enough for a couple of sauced snails— but they can also be used as egg cups or salt cellars. Or they may be filled to the brim with butter for single servings at a country dinner. It would be nice to assemble a number of these pots in different glazes and finishes and present several of them filled with succulent snails to each guest. A bonus: you could use your oyster forks if you want to keep things in harmonious scale—or see our snail forks, 11.43.

Godet à Escargot 11.50

Porcelain; 1¾″ diam., ⅞″ deep.
$5.50 for six

In French, a *godet* is, among other things, the calyx of a flower, which this tiny pot resembles. The fat, round porcelain body has been treated to a coppery glaze with a pearly finish rather like that of antique lusterware. It is roomy enough for both a generous dab of garlic butter and a chubby snail, and inexpensive enough so that you can purchase dozens of them and serve six or so to each guest. A baking sheet will support a plenitude of these tiny cups for easy heating of your escargots: the flat bottoms are unglazed, so the cups will not slide around on the pan or on the plate on which you place them for service. Again, you will not need tongs if snails are served in this fashion, nor are special forks essential: not necessary, but nice, would be our fork (11.43) beside each helping.

Porcelain Snail-Shell Cup 11.51

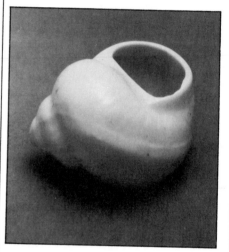

Porcelain; 2″ wide; 1⅜″ high.
$2.00 per doz. ▲

Mimicking the snail shell, this white porcelain cup is quite a bit larger than the original, so you can serve two snails, plus snail butter, in each one if you wish. You will not need a special escargot plate in addition to these servers, as the bottom of each one is flat instead of being rounded like a natural shell. Place a collection of them on a baking sheet for making your snails piping hot, then transfer them to plates for presentation at the table. Snail tongs and forks are required, just as they are when you serve snails in natural shells but, unlike the real thing, the porcelain copy-cats can be popped into your dishwasher for easy cleaning.

The Victorians believed in solid information—
witness this page from The Book of Household
Management, *by the famous Mrs. Beeton.*

Specialty Cookware: Utensils for Egg Cookery

Eggs—you can put them all in one basket, you can use them to thicken a sauce or a soup, serve them for breakfast, lunch, or dinner, whip them into a soufflé, boil and stuff them, mash them, or eat them hard-cooked, shirred, baked, fried, poached, scrambled, or made into an omelet. Eggs are the basis of numberless dishes from pots de crème to many forms of pasta. A French gastronome with a mathematical mind once counted 685 ways to prepare them. Even if your imagination is not quite so prodigious, mastering at least a few of the myriad ways of cooking and serving eggs appeals on two counts—economy and gastronomy.

Samuel Butler once observed that "A hen is only an egg's way of making another egg." A slight to the bird, perhaps, but a tribute to its product. Doctors warn that danger lurks in each cholesterol-laden egg yolk, but nutritionists argue that eggs are one of the most perfect sources of protein known—stuffed with vitamins A, B₂, and D and those other good-for-you ingredients, iron, sodium, phosphorus, potassium, and lecithin. No matter. Americans consume 294 eggs per person a year because they taste good and because they are one of the least expensive protein products around. A lot of hokum attaches to the price of eggs, however. Whether encased in brown shell or white, the contents are identical in nutrition and taste. The same applies to fertilized eggs; although these are touted in health-food stores, the only thing they are richer in is their cost. One thing that can be trusted is the U.S. Department of Agriculture's grading of eggs, if you buy them from a source with fairly fast turnover (eggs deteriorate quickly if not kept cold). They are rated at the time of inspection according to quality, which mostly means freshness. Grades AA and A are the best, as they are the freshest—Grade AA is marketed within strict time limits—and, when poached, boiled, or fried, eggs of these grades will have the yolk centered in the white. Grade B is best used in baking or added to other ingredients, although eggs of this grade are just as nutritious, if not as fresh, as the other grades. Eggs also come in sizes ranging downward from Jumbo through Extra Large, Medium, and Small to Peewee—the eggs of young pullets. Most recipes specifying eggs mean Large ones, weighing 24 ounces per dozen, but two Small eggs (18 ounces per dozen) or even smaller Peewees can be substituted.

THE PERFECT PACKAGE

Mother Nature dotes on the egg. Why else would she have clothed it in that perfect oval container? Try to squeeze a raw egg in your fist; the fragile shell will not yield. This covering is just one of the egg's remarkable qualities. Housed within, the saffron yolk and translucent white await the cook's cue. Understanding their special properties unlocks many of the mysteries of cuisine, haute and otherwise.

Cart-before-the-horse cookery seems to prevail in relation to eggs. Many a cook learns the secret of a successful soufflé before mastering the basics of egg poaching or making a plain, perfect omelet. In no other area of cookery, perhaps, is technique as important to superb results. Fortunately, however, the raw material is so inexpensive, the range of dishes so broad, that no one can be bored during learning. A

OEUFS JEANETTE—STUFFED EGGS JEANETTE

6 large eggs
¼ cup minced parsley
4 cloves garlic—peeled, crushed and finely chopped
¼ cup heavy cream
½ teaspoon salt
¼ teaspoon freshly ground white pepper
1 tablespoon white wine vinegar
1 teaspoon Dijon mustard
½ cup vegetable oil
2 tablespoons unsalted butter

Place eggs in cold water in an enamel or glass pan. Bring to boil, simmer 12 minutes. Cool under cold running water. Cut the eggs in half lengthwise and place the yolks in a small bowl (not aluminum). With a fork, mash yolks until smooth. Mix in parsley, garlic, cream, salt, and pepper to make a smooth paste.

Fill each egg white with yolk mixture, just level with the top. Set aside.

Add the vinegar and mustard to any yolk mixture remaining in the bowl and beat well with a wire whisk.

Now add the oil slowly, almost drop by drop, beating constantly, until you have the consistency of a light mayonnaise. (Or, put the remaining yolk mixture, vinegar, and mustard in a blender container. Add 2 tablespoons oil. Remove center cap of blender cover; put cover on blender. Turn blender on high; immediately start to pour the remaining oil into blender container in a steady stream. Turn off blender when all oil has been added.)

Just before serving, heat butter in a large heavy skillet. When sizzling, add the stuffed eggs, white side down, and sauté on medium heat until lightly brown—2 or 3 minutes. Turn on other side and brown for 2 to 3 minutes more. Arrange on a heated platter and coat with the sauce. Serve immediately.

broad range of techniques is used to transform the egg into any of its various guises. Beaten thoroughly, an egg yolk binds oil or melted butter and flavorings to itself in such an emulsified and seemingly miraculous cold sauce as mayonnaise, such hot sauces as Hollandaise and Béarnaise. Because heat congeals egg quickly, only a gentle application of warmth is needed to thicken an egg-based sauce to a velvety texture—too much heat will cause it to separate and curdle beyond all hope of redemption.

HOW TO SUCCEED IN EGG COOKERY

The methods of egg cookery we describe demand nothing from you but ordinary dexterity, a fair amount of concentration, and the proper equipment. Most kitchens are equipped with the basics, but for those shy of some kinds of equipment, we show frying pans, saucepans, and double boilers in Chapter 6 and mixing and beating bowls in Chapter 5, where you'll also find wire whisks and egg beaters, both manual and electric. In this section our experts have assembled a mighty collection of utensils designed for each of the methods of egg cookery. We also show you some ovenproof dishes of porcelain, stoneware, and glass, intended for eggs but so lovely you're sure to find other uses for them as well. All of them will make the preparation as simple as the egg itself.

"Some hens are very capricious as regards sitting: they will make a great fuss, and keep pining for the nest, and, when they are permitted to take to it, they will sit just long enough to addle the eggs, and then they're off again. The safest way to guard against such annoyance, is to supply the hen with some hard-boiled: if she sits on them a reasonable time, and seems steadily inclined, like a good matron, you may then give her proper eggs, and let her set about the business in earnest."

Isabella Beeton, Beeton's Book of Household Management, *facsimile of the 1861 edition, Farrar, Strauss & Giroux, New York, 1969*

Wire Egg Stand 11.52

Tinned wire; 6½" base diam.; 13" high.
$26.00

This spaced-out table tree, airy as a stabile by Calder, is a breakproof open storage unit for a dozen eggs that you have bought fresh enough to permit them to be kept out of refrigeration until you use them. It's best for a kitchen where you *can* swing a cat, and the cat, or small children, cannot swing *it*. B.I.A. Cordon Bleu imports this stand, which has a stem of coiled wire supporting the two tiers of holders, each fashioned of two wires crossed and bent to the circumference of an egg: 5 eggs go in the middle tier and 7 in the lower, with a single egg on top. The round base is a mesh basket for more eggs, or perhaps for lemons. Why use an egg stand? Even if you normally refrigerate eggs (and you *should* keep your main supply in the refrigerator), you'll want to store some at room temperature ready for use. Their shells will be less likely to crack in boiling, and when their whites are beaten you'll get greater volume. This symmetrical wire sculpture from France is also a natural as a centerpiece at a party —think of it for an Easter brunch, its holders filled by the children with the colored eggs retrieved in the hunt; and it can serve as a lemon-and-lime holder on a bar; and it makes an elegant airborne serving unit, a dandy space saver for your buffet supper.

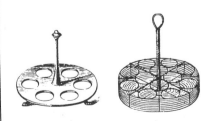

Two nineteenth-century French holders for cooking soft-boiled eggs.

Practic Egg Boiler 11.53

Plastic with glass timer; 5" base diam.; 8" high; holds 6 eggs.
$6.00

At first glance, one suspects a gimcrack item, but another look reveals its usefulness. A graded miniature hour glass filled with cheery pink sand sits atop a plastic rack which holds six eggs. Fill the rack with eggs and set the whole works in an enameled or stainless-steel pot filled with water, boiling or not as you will (see "How to Boil an Egg" for schools of thought). Turn the glass timer over and, as the eggs cook, the sand runs into the bottom portion, which is marked to indicate the minutes the eggs have cooked—anywhere from 3 to 5. Lift the rack from the pot when the timer tells you that the eggs are to your liking and eureka! the perfect soft-boiled egg. Safely cradled in this rack, the eggs can't crack against each other, and the bright red boilable plastic won't overheat and burn your hand. Sand is silent, so keep an eye on the timer.

Automatic Egg Cooker   11.54

Plastic with cast-aluminum basin, aluminum egg rack, Teflon-lined aluminum egg poacher; 7½" diam.; 7¼" high; holds 8 boiled eggs or 4 poached eggs.

$26.95

For those who truly can't boil an egg, this cooker will take the guesswork out of the process. Just pierce the large end of the egg on the needle centered in the middle of the rack, place the egg, small end down, on that rack, measure and add the correct amount of water, and plug it in. No need to pot-watch and no pot to wash—when the light goes out the water has boiled away and the eggs— you can cook 8 at a time—stop cooking. The secret lies in the amount of water you place in the cooker. The lid incorporates a small measuring cup with three markers for very soft, soft, poached, or medium eggs. The first two and the last are for eggs in the shell; the manufacturer says you can also "poach" four eggs, using the Teflon-lined insert, divided into four compartments; the "poached" indicator is for this process. However, to our mind actual poaching must be done *in*, not over, water, and we think this use is of less interest to egg-lovers. Should you have this cooker? Well, a friend swears she had never seen an egg boiled any other way, and assumed everyone owned an egg cooker, "just like a toaster." We don't find it quite so indispensable, but it's a handy gadget nonetheless, especially if yours is a family devoted to having its morning eggs "just so."

French carrier for egg cups, 1886.

HOW TO BOIL AN EGG

Boiling an egg is not always the simple process it is cracked up to be. Lowering a cold egg into boiling water often causes the Humpty Dumpty syndrome—a cracked shell leaking a potful of stringy white and watery yellow. Two variables must be regulated to produce an egg which will delight the autocrat of the breakfast table, or, when cooked longer, travel safely in a picnic hamper: these are water temperature and time.

The shell acts as a cooking container for a boiled egg. While that resilient covering cannot be broken by squeezing it in your hand, it is easily shattered by contact with hot water when its contents are cold. Some cooks play it safe by placing their eggs to be soft-boiled in cold water, bringing it to the boil, turning off the heat, popping on a lid, and timing the cooking from that point. Adventurous types lower their eggs into simmering water and hope for the best. The hot-water beginning is less risky if a sprinkling of salt is added to the boiling water, and if the egg shell is pierced first to minimize the danger of fast expansion and cracking. Room-temperature eggs will survive either method better than refrigerator-cold ones; for that reason we show you a wire egg stand from France that will keep your day's supply handy on a counter.

Within the innocent shell, an egg congeals during cooking into a semiliquid mass or a firm oval, depending on the amount of time it spends in its boiling bath. Timing is vital. A soft-boiled egg needs only 3 to 5 minutes, depending on your taste, to reach the edible stage, while eggs "hard-boiled"—a misnomer—to serve as picnic provender will take anywhere from 8 to 12 minutes in simmering water. Contrary to popular belief, you *can* overcook a hard-boiled egg—such an egg is an ossified lump with a dark aura around the yolk. A quick plunge into cold water right from the pot is also necessary to prevent this discoloration. Very fresh eggs are hostile to peeling, so always age them for a couple of days before hard-cooking them. Mountain dwellers above 5000 feet or so must add a minute or two to the time for soft eggs, several minutes for hard, to produce the same result as sea-level citizens. Because eggs tend to discolor an aluminum pan in which they are boiled, cook them in enamel, glass, or stainless-steel pots.

Gadgetry is rampant in the boiled-egg field. There are innumerable egg timers, egg slicers, egg openers, and special egg cookers. Many such are gewgaws, fragile as the egg itself. Our experts have tested and retested for usefulness and quality the items we show on these pages. Herewith a selection of the best.

Soft-boiled Egg Cutter   11.55

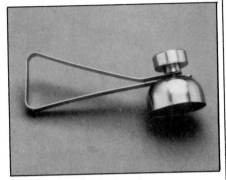

Aluminum; 4" long.
$2.90

Compulsive consumers of soft-boiled eggs like to make neat work of slicing through the shell—not for them the jagged edge left by an ordinary spoon. Having tested various eggshell cutters that work on the scissors principle, our experts have vetoed them all in favor of this doohickey. The small metal cup is topped by a knob—the maker calls it a "spring hammer"—which is attached by a strong, flat spring. Place the cup over the small end of the egg, pull up on the knob twice, and whang! the top of the shell is neatly excised by vibration. No shell fragments to mar the golden liquid of the yolk or to lie disguised in the white, and no burnt fingers. You might even be able to lure your little ones away from their customary bowl of sugar-frosted crunchy-munchies to a healthful soft-boiled egg for breakfast with the promise of using this gadget.

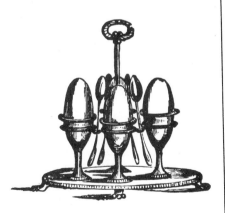

This nineteenth-century egg stand for the breakfast table was recommended in Mrs. Beeton's Every Day Cookery and Housekeeping Book.

EGG SLICERS

Here's the hard-cooked egg, and there's the salad or sandwich to which you'd like to transfer it, neatly sliced. And, of course, you have a knife. But somehow the knife doesn't seem to make the neat slices or sections pictured in the cookbooks, and it takes forever just to carve up half a dozen. For a very small price, mechanical egg slicers and sectioners can do the job in half the time with twice as pretty a result. But buy good ones—nothing is more frustrating than to put your egg in the slicer and find that the one you've bought refuses to cut through the whole egg, leaving the slices limply attached to each other at the bottom—or you might have a completely sliced egg with brown streaks caused by rusty cutting wires marring the white. We've tested all the ones we show. They are efficient and clean, with stainless-steel wires for spotless and smooth slicing.

Egg Sectioner   11.56

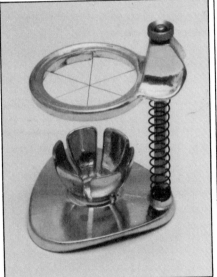

Cast aluminum with wire cutters and spring; 5" high; 3" base diam.
$6.50

A slippery hard-cooked egg can resist all attempts to cut it into sections with a knife—so how to make neat wedges for garnish? With an egg sectioner, of course. Place the peeled egg in the petaled cup, push the metal ring down, and the thin stainless-steel wires intersecting the ring slice that egg into six perfect sections. The cutting mechanism is spring-operated, and the body is of cast aluminum. This gadget won't be in daily use in your kitchen, but you'll bless it when your salad or your hors d'oeuvre tray has a naked look. Wreathe your cold salmon with egg wedges, garnish your Salade Niçoise—the sectioner is fun to use.

A riddle (1792):

As I was walking in a field of wheat,
I picked up something good to eat:
Neither fish, flesh, fowl, nor bone,
I kept it till it ran alone.

Answer: An egg which later became some sort of fowl when it "ran alone."

The Cornucopia, *by Judith Herman and Marguerite Shalett Herman. Harper & Row, New York, 1973*

Plastic-framed Egg Slicer   11.57

Plastic and chrome-plated frame with stainless-steel wires; 4" × 3¼".
$1.39

"So simple a child can do it"—here's a device that deserves that slogan, an egg slicer that appears to have been stolen from a toddler's toy chest. Older brothers and sisters, perhaps even the toddler, will enjoy using it to slice their own eggs for

429

Continued from preceding page

lunch-box sandwiches. A sunny yellow plastic body is fitted with grooves that mesh with the stainless-steel wires set into the attached chrome-plated frame. The body has a double oval depression, so an egg can be sliced either lengthwise or crosswise, an improvement on most such devices. A delightful dime-store item, the best of all the dozens we tested.

Aluminum-framed Egg Slicer 11.58

Cast aluminum with stainless-steel wires; 7½″ long; 3⅛″ diam.

$4.50

For kitchens equipped with nothing but the best, an egg slicer of serious construction to add to the batterie de cuisine. Heavy cast aluminum is molded into a ridged cup and a frame inset with stainless-steel wires. Troughs inside the handles are fitted with a flexible piece of metal which provides the spring action needed for easy and thorough slicing, and a locking mechanism at the base of the handles keeps the utensil shut when not in use. The vaguely triangular shape of the cup and the frame permits both lengthwise and crosswise egg slicing. Decorate a party platter or a smorgåsbord with tidy egg ovals, or stuff them into the kids' sandwiches if you can keep potential lunch-eaters from devouring the slices as you work.

EGG SEPARATORS

Eggs, like Caesar's Gaul, are divided into three parts—the shell, the white, and the yolk. It is sometimes necessary to render each a separate and distinct entity—Sauce Hollandaise needs only yolks, angelfood cake, an airy mass of delicate whites. Fortunately, severance is possible, because each part of the egg has a different shape and consistency.

The white is viscous and fluid, the yolk is a globe encased in a fragile membrane. As you separate them in the usual way, the divided shell is used to contain the yolk as you pour the contents of the egg back and forth between the halves of the shell until the white breaks free and plops into the bowl beneath. We urge tyro cooks to separate each egg over a cup before adding the whites to the beating bowl, as the tiniest speck of yolk, which is fatty, will ruin the beatability of a whole batch of egg whites.

Many chefs, including Japanese cooks, don't bother with the to-and-fro motion of separating an egg by pouring it from one shell half to the other—they simply crack the raw egg into their palm and let the white drip through their fingers into the bowl, a method which works very well, especially for a lot of eggs, and wastes no egg white, although it may not appeal to all. For those who find egg separating by *any* method a nerve-racking procedure, we show the devices that will do the job for them.

Aluminum Egg Separator 11.59

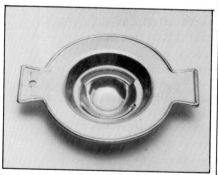

Cast aluminum; 3¾″ diam.

$.79

Utilitarian in aspect, this aluminum egg separator traps the yolk in its cuplike center while the white slides through the slots on either side. The "ears" of the device rest on a cup or small bowl during use and also serve as handles. All human error is eliminated from the task of separating even the most stubborn egg—using this gadget, cooks whose hands shake at the prospect of separating eggs can whip up the same soufflés and meringues as their more accomplished counterparts.

LANGUES DE CHATS—CATS' TONGUES

¼ pound butter
½ cup sugar
Dash of vanilla extract
2 egg whites
⅓ cup all-purpose flour

Grease baking sheets thoroughly and set aside.

Work the butter until soft and fluffy with an electric beater or your hands. Then work in the sugar gradually, along with the vanilla, until you have a creamy homogeneous mixture. Add the egg whites, one at a time, beating them in thoroughly. Fold in the flour with a wooden spatula.

Fit a pastry bag with a plain, small *douille*, or tube, then fill about two-thirds full with the batter. Press batter out on prepared pans in strips about as thick as a cigarette and 3 inches long, leaving 1 inch between to allow for spreading. Before placing in the oven, give the sheet a good bang on your work table to flatten the cookies.

Bake in a preheated 400° F. oven for 12 minutes, or until light brown. Remove from cookie sheets onto cake racks at once, but allow to dry for at least 45 minutes before using.

Cats' Tongues keep well if stored in a tightly covered tin in a cool place. Makes approximately 45.

LEMON CATS' TONGUES: In place of the vanilla, add the grated rind and juice of ½ lemon. Follow the same directions for making and baking.

(From THE OTHER HALF OF THE EGG, by Helen McCully, Jacques Pépin, and William North Jayme. Copyright © 1967 by M. Barrows & Company, Inc. Reprinted by permission of William Morrow & Company, Inc.)

"To prevent house spirits from using the shell for their mischievous pranks . . . to break an egg shell after ye meat is out we are taught in our childhood. . . . and the intent thereof was to prevent witchcraft; lest witches should draw or prick their names therein and veneficiously mischiefe ye persons, they broke ye shell . . . This custome of breaking the bottom of the Eggeshell is (yet) commonly used in the countrey."

Sir Thomas Browne, Pseudodoxia Epidemica, *London, 1686*

Ceramic Egg Separator   11.60

Ceramic; 4″ diam.; 1½″ deep.
$3.00

Endearing, that's what we'd call this egg separator. A plump round object glazed a homey buff, it is winning in its simplicity. A horizontal slot to let the egg white dribble through is slashed midway down the cup, allowing the round yolk to nestle in the flat bottom. The only claim to frills made by this little bowl might be the slight ridges grooved around the upper lip. Withal, it does the same businesslike job of egg separating as does the more practical-looking aluminum separator above.

UTENSILS FOR FRYING EGGS

America's breakfasters dote on the fried egg; every morning, millions of us look upon a plate punctuated by one or more sunny circles accompanied by bacon, ham, or sausage. To a man, we're particular about the style and manner in which our eggs are fried. "Two, looking at you" is an order called out at every lunch counter—translated, it means fry those eggs sunny side up. "Two, over" will get you a plate of fried eggs which have been flipped just before serving.

The fresher the egg, the better its performance in the frying pan. The white of a stale egg is very liquid and will dribble away from the yolk as it is broken into the pan; only a fresh egg has a yolk that will stand up high when the egg is broken. Almost any fat or oil whose flavor you like is suitable for frying. Eggs can be plopped into the same pan in which you have cooked the bacon for a tangy, smoky taste, or a big pat of butter sizzling in the pan will give the egg a rich, country-fresh flavor. Cholesterol watchers prefer polyunsaturated oil or margarine for their ration of eggs, which, like butter, are unfortunately high in that controversial substance as well as in nutrients. For variety, serve a fried egg and toast—actually fried bread—all in one. Cut a circle from the center of a slice of bread, fry it on one side in butter, then turn it over and break an egg into the hole, adding more butter, if it's needed; cook until the egg is just right. Use pumpernickel for a "one-eyed Egyptian," ordinary white bread for a "Cyclops."

High heat may be used to bring the fat to the right temperature for frying your eggs, but it is the enemy of egg tenderness—turn the flame down the instant before the egg is in the pan. Fried eggs cook from the bottom up, of course; if you like the tops set, but not too well done, you can put a lid on the pan (and a few drops of water inside, to create a little steam)—a practical solution to the bane of the broken yolk, a hazard of egg flipping.

A smooth-surfaced pan is the *sine qua non* for a decent fried egg. Cuisinarts (see Chapter 6) makes elegant frying pans with supremely smooth interiors, excellent for the purpose. We do not recommend quick-release (nonstick) finishes such as Teflon for frying eggs unless you keep the pan only for that task. The same nonstick surface which allows you to slip an egg out of the pan with ease also absorbs flavors, so unless you care to risk finding in your egg the slight taste of the fish you fried the night before, use a plain metal pan or a griddle.

EGG RINGS

There are neater ways to fry an egg than to plop it into a pan. True, it will be tasty if it is fresh and properly cooked, ragged edges or no. But there are times when you want a perfect round of white neatly punctuated with a golden globe. All you need to accomplish this feat are some simple metal rings. You arrange the egg rings in the pan or on the griddle and drop in the eggs, which emerge in impeccable rounds, perhaps to top hamburgers or veal cutlets. The rings are also useful for making crumpets (those tasty British cousins of our biscuits), which

Continued from preceding page

are griddle-baked, and you might even want to try your hand at making English muffins in them. While not essential kitchen utensils, egg rings are handy for fried-egg fanatics or compulsively neat egg eaters.

Stainless-Steel Egg Rings   11.61

Stainless steel; 3⅜″ diam.; ½″ deep; handle 2″ long.

$1.00 ▲

Most fried eggs, like the ink blots in a Rorschach test, have an irregular outline—all very well for family breakfasts, but not an asset for fancier dishes such as escalopes de veau à cheval or weiner-schnitzel à la Holstein. You can of course trim each and every fried egg you use for such a purpose with a pair of scissors, but it is much simpler just to plop the eggs into lightly greased individual egg rings on your griddle or in a frying pan. These stainless-steel rings will make perfect 3⅜-inch circles out of even the stalest and most scatter-prone egg. They come in sets of three and the upright handles make it easy to move the rings around or lift them in and out of the pan. Even for a family breakfast, neat round circles centered with a golden eye would be fun to serve.

"It was long supposed that an omelet derived its name somehow from ovum, *an egg, and might mean* oeufs melés. *That etymology has been given up as impracticable by French scholars. . . . The word takes its rise from* lamina, *a leaf or thin sheet, whence the Latin diminutive* Lamella, *in English* Lamel, *which became later* Alumelle, Alumette *and* Aumelette."

Kettner's Book of the Table, *1877*

Chrome-plated Egg Ring   11.62

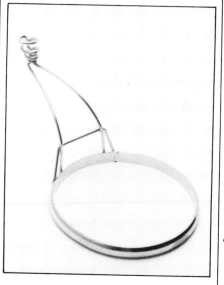

Chrome-plated steel; 4⅛″ diam.; ⅜″ deep; handle 4″ long.

$2.65

As egg rings go, this is the *ne plus ultra.* This chrome-plated steel ring turns out perfect 4½-inch circles, larger than those produced by the rings we show you above. The handle curves away from the ring so it can be kept cool outside the pan. Made of heavy wire, this handle has a curlicue knob on top for a good grip when removing it from the pan. The ring is packaged individually, but you will probably want to buy several so you can cook a number of eggs at a time; or use them, as we suggest, for baking crumpets or English muffins on a griddle.

Mrs. Beeton's advice to the beginning egg-poacher.

UTENSILS FOR OMELETS

What's pale gold, shaped like a tot's football, and stuffed with cheese, chicken livers, fines herbes, tomatoes, onions, shrimp, mushrooms, etc., etc., etc.? An omelet, that's what. Madame Romaine de Lyon, a small and special restaurant in New York City, serves nothing but omelets. There the menu, the size of a telephone book for a small town, rings changes on the theme—everything from a simple cheese omelet to a kingly caviar creation, with 684 combinations in between.

All very well, you say, for the expert cook, but tricky for the tyro. True, a certain amount of dexterity is required to turn out a perfect creamy-centered cylinder. Practice, in this area as in any other, makes perfect.

First, the essential ingredient in omelet making—eggs. You can make an omelet for one or ten, depending on the number of eggs you use and the diameter of the pan in which you cook them. Two eggs make the basic minimum omelet, cooked in a 7-or 8-inch pan. You beat your eggs barely to a froth, preferably with a wire whisk. Over high heat, laze a large lump of butter around the omelet pan with a fork until it is foamy, loosening your wrist for the action ahead. Season the eggs with salt and pepper, give them another whisk, and pour them into the pan as soon as the foam of the butter begins to subside and before it begins to brown the least bit. Now the alchemy between egg, butter,

BILL of FARE

Barr's Dining Rooms.

Eggs.

Fried Eggs,	30
Boiled Eggs,	25
Scrambled Eggs,	25
Scrambled Eggs on Toast,	30
Dropped Eggs,	25
Dropped Eggs on Toast,	30
Poached Eggs,	25
Plain Omelets,	30
Ham Omelets,	35
Sweet Omelets,	30
Jelly Omelets,	35
Oyster Omelets,	35

Families and Parties supplied at their residences with the best Wedding, Pound and Sponge Cake, and the richest assortment of Basket and Fancy Cake, Cream and Water Ices, Meringue Baskets, Jellies, Charlotte de Russe, and Ornamental Pyramids, Mottoes, &c.

Continued from preceding page

and heat begins. Grasp the handle of the pan in your left hand and tilt the pan around briskly to settle the eggs. Take a fork in your right hand and, still shaking the pan vigorously back and forth, stir the eggs quickly and thoroughly with the flat side against the bottom. As the eggs begin to thicken, stop stirring and lift the pan at a 45-degree angle from the stove and push the omelet away from you in a solid mass, folding it over on itself. Switch the handle to your right hand, grab a warmed plate in your left, and roll the omelet out onto it. For a filled omelet, add the goodies just before you fold your eggs over. Southpaws switch hands. Perfectionists run a piece of butter over the finished omelet, still using the fork. All omelet experts serve each omelet the moment it is done.

While any decent skillet will turn out an acceptable omelet, the glory of owning a true omelet pan cannot be denied. The smooth interior and sloping sides of the real article allow even the most uncoordinated cook to produce a reasonable facsimile of Madame Romaine's specialty. But, like everything else, some omelet pans are better than others. One quality is all-important—weight. The ideal omelet pan must be thick-bodied to respond to high heat and diffuse it evenly.

It is a matter of dispute among chefs whether the omelet pan should be used for other chores. Some find this a waste of a good utensil—properly cleaned and cared for, the pan, which after all has a polished, hence sealed, interior, can be used for crêpes or croquettes without impairing its principal mission. We do not show any cast-iron omelet pans because they are porous and absorb the fat, hence the flavors from cooking other food. Using such a pan for both your omelets and liver with onions, say, would obviously not be desirable.

What size to buy? Beginners should master the two-egg omelet before attempting larger ones. For two eggs, a pan with a 7- or 8-inch bottom is right. Advanced omelet makers who can handle 8 to 12 eggs at a clip need a 10- to 12-inch pan and, let us add, a good stove that produces enough heat to cook the omelet quickly but gently. All omelet pans should be preseasoned at home if the manufacturer hasn't done that job for you: Apply a lick of oil on the inside and give the pan a slow warming over a gentle flame, then a brisk rubdown with salt. This makes for an excellent nonstick finish. Thereafter, don't wash your pan with water. A wipe-out with paper towels and a dry-salt scrub for stubborn spots will keep a seasoned pan slick forever. If someone should misguidedly wash your pan, don't despair. Rub it with salt, then repeat the seasoning, and all will be well.

OMELETTE SAVOYARDE

Serves: 4 to 6
Preparation time: 20 minutes
Cooking time: 30 minutes

The open omelette is widely used in Mediterranean country cooking. Here is one that is perfect for a cold day. You may substitute or add anything you like, such as sautéed eggplant cubes, chives or cooked spinach.

INGREDIENTS
1 cup finely cubed potatoes
¾ cup finely cubed bacon or ham
4 tablespoons sweet butter
2 leeks (white part only), cleaned and finely sliced
8 eggs
1 teaspoon salt
Freshly ground white pepper
2 tablespoons grated Gruyère or Swiss cheese
1 tablespoon olive oil

PREPARATION
1. Parboil the potatoes for 10 minutes in boiling salted water and drain.
2. In a heavy 10-inch skillet cook the bacon over low heat until it is almost crisp. Remove it to a side dish and discard all but 2 tablespoons of the fat. Add 2 tablespoons of butter to the pan.
3. When the butter is melted, add the leeks. Cover the pan and cook the leeks over low heat for 10 minutes or until they are very soft. Watch them so they do not brown. When the leeks are done, add the potatoes and cook the mixture for 5 more minutes.
4. In a bowl, beat the eggs with a whisk until frothy and light. Add salt and pepper and the grated cheese.
5. Add the leek and potato mixture and the bacon to the eggs.
6. Heat the remaining butter and oil in the skillet. Pour in the egg mixture and cook until the bottom is set and browned. Place another large skillet, oiled and hot, on top of the first skillet and reverse it. Cook the omelette in the second pan until the bottom is set and lightly browned. Serve immediately.

(From THE SEASONAL KITCHEN, by Perla Meyers. Copyright © 1973 by Perla Meyers. Reprinted by permission of Holt, Rinehart and Winston.)

Sand-cast Aluminum Omelet Pan   11.63

Sand-cast aluminum with walnut handle; 12″ diam.; 2″ deep. Also avail. 8″ or 10″ diam.
$40.00 ▲ $26.00 ▲ $33.00 ▲

The perfect omelet pan is as elusive, we sometimes think, as the Holy Grail, but this American-made one will end the quest. The big, heavy, sand-cast aluminum pan is bright enough to see yourself in and the handsome oval walnut handle allows you a good grip for that "all-in-the-wrists" motion necessary to get an omelet started. The handle has a hanger, so the pan can join your other treasures on the pot rack. As aluminum is famed for its heat absorption, distribution, and retention, this pan, which the maker calls the Omelet Chef, will turn out an omelet firm and golden on the outside, creamy within, using a lower flame than would ordinarily be required. The folding operation is made easier for both expert and novice-class cooks by the shallow sloping sides. As this pan is a beautiful as well as a practical piece of equipment, it would be wise to follow the manufacturer's instructions for cleaning: no soap and water is ever to touch it after it has been properly seasoned. Besides the 12-inch diameter, perfect for 10 to 12 eggs, this prize comes in 8- and 10-inch sizes.

Chef's Steel Omelet Pan 11.64

Dark steel with iron handle; 11″ diam.; 1¾″ deep.

$13.00

You'd best lift weights for a week or so before using this omelet pan, the classic choice of French chefs. Some of us, being of weakling stock, find 4½ pounds of steel a mite difficult to heft. For the muscle-proud, however, it will be a most satisfactory utensil. Made of low-grade, nonporous steel for quick heat response, it has a riveted-on heavy iron handle and the shallow sloping sides of the standard omelet pan. The interior has

been lacquered by the French manufacturer. This coating must be removed with boiling water and a scouring pad before initial use. Season the pan afterward as you would any iron pan—give it a generous oiling with vegetable oil, heat it gradually but well over a stove burner, then let it cool and wipe it clean. Thereafter don't wash it—just scrub off any stubborn spots with salt and a paper towel. A generous 11 inches in diameter, it is meant to make omelets for a party. Even though its virtue is utility rather than beauty, a slot in the handle keeps it handy, hanging on your pot rack.

"Helene had her opinions, she did not for instance like Matisse. She said a Frenchman should not stay unexpectedly to a meal, particularly if he asked the servant beforehand what there was for dinner. She said foreigners had a perfect right to do these things but not a Frenchman and Matisse had once done it. So when Miss Stein said to her, Monsieur Matisse is staying for dinner this evening, she would say, 'In that case I will not make an omelette but fry the eggs. It takes the same amount of butter but it shows less respect, and he will understand.' "

The Autobiography of Alice B. Toklas, by Gertrude Stein

Extra-Heavy Aluminum Omelet Pan 11.65

Heavy-gauge aluminum with plastic handle; 10″ diam.; 1¾″ deep.

$22.50

So far and yet so near. For all the readily visible differences between this pan by Rudolph Stanish and the cast-aluminum one we show you above (11.63), the actual

performance and construction of the two pans are remarkably similar. Both are of heavy, exceptionally thick aluminum, but while 11.63 is of beautiful (if somewhat porous) highly polished sand-cast aluminum, this pan is a workmanlike utensil of dull, solid (thus somewhat heavier) stamped aluminum. Both need to be seasoned with oil and salt (see p. 434 under "Utensils for Omelets"). Both conduct heat—and thus perform—excellently, but with this model you need not fear the pitting which occasionally occurs with sand-cast pans when they are subjected to too much heat. While the sand-cast pan has a lovely walnut handle (with a hole in the end for hanging), this one has a most unlovely, utilitarian black plastic one (with a ring in the end). Both handles protect your hands from the heat. Aside from sheer beauty then, the only major difference between 11.63 and this omelet pan is economic—you can have this one for just over half the price.

Long-handled Steel Omelet Pan 11.66

Dark steel; 10⅜″ diam.; 2½″ deep; handle 20″ long.

$14.50

The exception that proves the rule: The sides of this omelet pan lack the smoothly curving slope of the four classically shaped pans we have just shown you. Instead its slanting sides are sharply angled at their joining with the 10⅜-inch bottom, and the pan is quite deep. That shape, especially the angle, acts as a "stop" to prevent the slippery omelet from landing in the fire rather than on the plate when it is rolled. The pan is attached to a handle 20″ long that keeps the cook at arm's length from an open

Continued from preceding page

fire, or allows omelet-making on the back of a big stove. The same protective lacquer that coats the chef's steel pan is used on this one—it must be boiled and scrubbed off (use a soap-filled scouring pad) before the pan is used for the first time. Season the pan by oiling, heating, and wiping it to give it a non-stick surface and, thereafter, wipe it after use—don't wash. The hole in the black iron handle serves a purpose: the weight of the handle tends to overbalance the pan, so you'd best hang it up to avoid a tangle with the other pans in your cupboard.

Poulard Long-handled Omelet Pan   11.67

Iron; 11" diam.; 2¼" deep; handle 33¼" long.
$14.50

Long, longer, longest—if you thought the 20-inch handle on the pan above was a bit lengthy, this 33¼-inch one is positively extensive. It is very flexible, however, for ease in omelet flipping without using a utensil in the pan. These are the pans used at Mont-St.-Michel in Normandy to cook omelets over an open fire. You may not be able to recreate the monastery and the rushing tides of that romantic spot, but you can add glamor to omelet cookery over your barbecue or firepit with this pan in hand. The pan is deeper than the ordinary omelet pan, and it has a sharp angle where its 8-inch bottom joins the sides rather than the more usual gentle curve, so the folded omelet will not slide out of the pan until

you want it to. The hole in the handle is meant to hang the pan out of harm's way between omelets.

Tansies—omelets made with the herb tansy—were popular from the fifteenth through nineteenth centuries, although the original meaning of the name was lost somewhere along the way. This version is from A Way to Health *by Gervase Markham, 1660: "First then, for making the best Tansie, you shall take a certain number of Eggs, according to the bigness of your Frying-pan: and break them into a dish, abating ever the white of every third Egg: then with a spoon you shall cleanse away the little white Chicken knots, which stick into the Yolks: then with a little cream, beat them exceedingly together: then take of green Wheatblades, Violet leaves, Strawberry leaves, Spinage, Sucory, of each a like quantity, and a few Walnut-tree buds; chop and beat all very well, then strain out the Juice, and mixing it with a little more Cream, put it to the Eggs, and stir all well together, then put in a few Crums of bread, fine grated bread, cinamon, Nutmeg and Salt, then put some sweet butter into the Frying-pan, and so soon as it is dissolved or melted, put in the Tansey, and fry it brown without burning." Here the juices of other plants— "herbs" to the cook of that century— replace the rather pungent and odd flavor of the tansy.*

Recipe quoted in The Seven Centuries Cookbook, *by Maxime McKendry, McGraw-Hill, New York, 1973*

COLD OMELETTES

A cold omelette makes a most beguiling little summer dish. Country people in Italy, Spain, southern France and Greece take them on picnics, but then they are big, thick, substantial, the diameter of a dinner plate and the thickness of six. For an indoor meal I make very small ordinary rolled omelettes in a 6-inch pan, with one large egg to the omelette or three smaller ones for two. When the eggs are nearly but not quite set, put in one of the following fillings: a dozen tiny raw broad beans and a dessertspoon, no more, of fresh cream; a heaped tablespoon of cream cheese mixed with chopped watercress; one small tomato, raw, but skinned and sliced, and a little chopped parsley.

Turn the omelettes out, neatly rolled, on to a flat dish (I use a worn old meat platter with a border of faded pink flowers which looks just right for the purpose. A small point, but not entirely without importance) and strew a sprinkling of chopped parsley or chives over them.

This is just one way of making an all-the-year-round dish into a specifically summer one. And if you have another plate of thin slices from a cold gammon joint, a brown loaf, a pitcher of cider, some creamy butter, a piece of Lancashire cheese—what more do you need for a midday midsummer meal? But don't cook your little omelettes too long in advance.

(From SUMMER COOKING, by Elizabeth David. Copyright © 1955, 1965, 1971 by Elizabeth David. Published by Penguin Books. Reprinted by permission of Elizabeth David.)

OVEN DISHES FOR EGGS

We have been showing you all the ways that eggs can be cooked on top of the stove. But eggs are not just breakfast fare to be poached, scrambled, or fried. Baked or broiled, by themselves or in combination with other ingredients, eggs can be served for lunch, dinner, or dessert.

The utensils for eggs done in the oven differ from those used on top the stove. Ramekins, egg dishes, and soufflé dishes for the oven are usually made of porcelain or pottery, glazed in a range of colors and styles to be handsome as well as practical. They should be of good quality to conduct the heat evenly and slowly, and decorative to blend with your dinnerware and look attractive at the table.

Ramekins resemble small soufflé dishes with high sides, as they are meant to contain not only eggs but a sauce or a purée. They are also excellent for individual soufflés or custards. We like the simple classic ones we show you, little brothers to the full-sized soufflé dishes in the same section further along.

Shirred eggs are known as *oeufs sur le plat* in France. Essentially they are broiled eggs, cooked in egg dishes, the low, round dishes closely related to the gratin pans in Chapter 8. In each small dish you melt a pat of butter. Then you plop in an egg or two and slide the dish in under the broiler until the white is set, the yolk runny, and the whole covered with a glossy film. Perfectly done, shirred eggs become *oeufs au miroir,* looking-glass eggs—a shimmery, shiny delight. For really substantial meals, the eggs can be bedded on any of a number of compatible foods—creamed vegetables, a purée of mushrooms, a slice of ham. One of our peripatetic friends describes a meal she enjoyed in France's three-starred Grand Véfour restaurant—shirred eggs on a sumptuous slab of foie gras, the whole blanketed with not one but two creamy sauces. "An indecent delight," she murmurs.

Eggs cooked in the oven rather than under the broiler are not, technically, shirred. Their texture is more like that of a poached egg, especially if they are baked on top of a purée or covered with cream. Oven cooking is a more time-consuming procedure than doing eggs on top of the stove or shirring them under the broiler: care must be taken that the outside of the egg doesn't toughen before the inside is done. Use good-quality egg dishes or ramekins with heavy bodies to diffuse heat (so you can keep the oven temperature low). Ramekins, or cocottes, are essentially tiny soufflé dishes just big enough for one egg and its friends. Custards—which we'll look into farther along in this section—are eggs married to milk, sugar (usually) and flavorings and then baked. (So-called boiled custards are another story—they're more akin to sauces.) The creamy concoction is usually chilled after cooking. Custard can be simple nursery fare or elegant party food. Served in artless white cups or antique porcelain mugs, custard is a delicious dessert for old and young alike.

The apex of uses of the egg is the soufflé. An astral miracle, the soufflé needs both the thickening qualities of the yolks and the air-retentive ability of the beaten whites to achieve its height and gossamer texture. No wonder special dishes are required: they must be deep and straight-sided to allow the mass to mount to its maximum height, and they must be handsome as well as heatproof—no chance to ladle out the contents into something prettier for service—these dishes *must* go to the table.

Each of these egg baking and broiling techniques demands a different kind of dish. Here we show the best available, from the porcelain factory as well as the potter's wheel.

fully collected and used for baking in bannocks, known as "dumb cakes," as no one was permitted to speak while this was going on.

"Tell me something that you have seen coming from a bird, in either foreign lands or the Arabian lands; it is eaten boiled, fried, roasted; you can put it into the fire; it has neither foot nor hand, neither head nor tail, it is neither living nor dead; tell me what this marvelous thing is."—Ainu riddle.

An Egg at Easter: A Folklore Study, by Venetia Newall. Indiana University Press, Bloomington, Indiana, 1971

Stoneware Egg Dish 11.68

Stoneware; 6⅛" diam.; 1" deep.
$3.00

If we have but one life to live, let us spend it with a cupboardful of Bernard Leach's pottery. We are in love with every object produced by this British craftsman's studio. (For some other examples of his art, see Chapter 7.) This stoneware egg dish, like all the beauties from the Leach workrooms, is sensuous as well as practical. Made of his native Cornish clay, its auburn exterior is left unglazed for maximum heat absorption as well as rugged good looks. The wide unglazed lip meets a slick of celadon-green glaze that coats the shallow, 6⅛-inch interior of the dish. Since the dish is also available with an elegant black-to-rust temmoku glaze or a glaze of cool, mottled gray-brown, choice might be difficult. This, only an inch deep, is really the dish that lets you come closest to the food description *oeufs sur le plat:* it is an ovenproof near-plate with a slight lip. Cook your eggs alone in it, or on a thin bed of puréed spinach; or back them with a thin, thin slice of smoky ham.

In alchemistic belief the egg is the symbol of the four elements: the white of the egg is water, the shell is the earth, the membrane is air and the yolk, fire.

The egg is said to resemble the full moon and thus has been connected to the notion of lunacy. A German belief was that anyone eating eggs would commit seven foolish acts.

Fortunes can be told with egg whites. In Scotland a group would get together and each person would choose an egg. The woman in charge dropped each white of the egg, one at a time, into an ale glass, sealed the brim with her hand and turned it upside down. When all the fortunes had been told (by shapes or positions in the glass) the eggs were care-

Royal Limoges Egg Dish   11.69

Porcelain; 5⅞″ diam.
$10.00

Here is the classic oeufs en cocotte shape in a lovely dish from Limoges. Pluck the pattern from a swatch of Indian crewel, paint it on a plate, and this would be the result. Royal Limoges, porcelain purveyors to the kings of France, makes this elegant piece of china. The glossy white glaze is traced on the inside with flowers and leaves—pink and green, yellow and blue. Two rounded projections form handles. The base is left unglazed for better heat absorption and to keep it firmly seated on the oven rack or service plate. Its 4½-inch interior will only hold one large or two small eggs at breakfast; but don't save it just for that purpose. Bake tomatoes or serve individual helpings of Coquilles St.-Jacques in it. For all its fragile appearance, this dish, like all the other Limoges pieces we show you, is completely ovenproof.

Pillivuyt Egg Dish   11.70

Porcelain; 5″ diam.
$3.50

Here, flanked by two stunning French patterned dishes is plain Jeanne—a pure white porcelain egg dish from Pillivuyt. This simple, classic design will compliment any decor or dinnerware, and the relatively reasonable price will permit you to buy enough dishes to serve shirred eggs to eight (if you can handle that!). The round shape, next of kin to the oval gratin dish (8.16), measures 5″ in diameter, and has typical Pillivuyt shell-patterned handles protruding from the rim. As with the Royal Limoges dish above, the bottom has been left unglazed for better heat absorption. This dish is perfect for a well-prepared egg with a mere snippet of seasoning, but in its simplicity it is also elegant enough for the most complicated of preparations. Use the money you save by buying these (instead of the more expensive dishes we show you) for some foie gras and truffles, and try to duplicate the extravagant recipe of Raymond Oliver (of the Grand Véfour) for shirred eggs with two sauces.

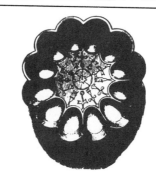

A Roman egg plate.

OEUFS AU PLAT BRESSANE

In each buttered egg dish put a slice of bread fried in butter; over this, pour a tablespoon of heated cream, and then break the eggs very carefully over the bread. Add another 2 tablespoons of the hot cream and cook in a moderate oven for 5 minutes.

If this is to be served as a first dish, one egg is usually enough, as the fried bread makes it fairly filling. Instead of butter, I have sometimes fried the bread in dripping from roast pork, which gives the dish quite a different flavour. If you like garlic, rub the fried bread with a cut clove before putting it into the egg dish.

(From SUMMER COOKING, by Elizabeth David. Copyright © 1955, 1965, 1971 by Elizabeth David. Published by Penguin Books. Reprinted by permission of Elizabeth David.)

Porcelain Egg Dishes and Salt and Pepper Shakers   11.71

Porcelain; 2 dishes, each 6″ diam.; shakers each 2½″ high.
$40.00 set

Dining à deux of a morning, cozy lunches as a couple, intimate fireside suppers—such romantic images are evoked by this pair of elegant egg dishes with their matching salt and pepper shakers. Another patrician product from the Porcelaine de Paris craftsmen, both the dishes and the shakers are in the Pavot pattern —a floral design with an Oriental feeling in rich tones of rust, blue, turquoise, and yellow. Each dish measures 6 inches across—two eggs will rest easy in each, with or without a foundation of vegetables, sauce, or meat. Fittingly, the salt and pepper shakers are egg-shaped and again decorated à Pavot. Sel and Poivre, they announce, as befits a true French product. Newlyweds or old-marrieds would be tickled pink to be made a gift of this set. Extra matching dishes can be purchased for breakfasts that are not à deux.

The ancient Greeks had special dishes for cooking eggs, with cavities corresponding to the size of the eggs. Beginning with a size for a peacock's egg, the spaces diminished to goose-egg proportions, then to a size for a hen's egg.

Arabia Egg Dish   11.72

Stoneware; 8¼″ diam. Also avail. 10″ diam.
$9.50

The Arabia label is beloved by good cooks throughout the world. This fine Finnish firm makes everything from dinnerware to mixing bowls to casseroles. Our egg dish is a member of Liekki family—a special ceramic group twice-fired at extremely high temperatures to be safe both within and atop the stove. Liekki translates as "flame," and the Arabia company guarantees that these dishes will not crack over an open fire if they have first been filled with food or fat. We find this a distinct advantage in egg shirring—nice to be able to melt a big pat of butter over the stove burner before popping in the eggs. Glazed in a handsome dark brown that is almost black, the 7-inch dish has an unglazed base, the better to absorb and distribute the heat. Owning this dish will seduce you into acquiring other pieces in the Arabia line—forewarned is forearmed.

SCRAMBLED EGGS "JAMES BOND"

For four individualists:
12 fresh eggs
Salt and pepper
5-6 oz. of fresh butter
Break the eggs into a bowl. Beat thoroughly with a fork and season well. In a small copper (or heavy-bottomed) saucepan melt four oz. of the butter. When melted, pour in the eggs and cook over a very low heat, whisking continuously with a small egg whisk.

While the eggs are slightly more moist than you would wish for eating, remove pan from heat, add rest of butter and continue whisking for half a minute, adding the while finely chopped chives or fines herbes. Serve on hot buttered toast in individual copper dishes (for appearance only) with pink champagne (Taittinger) and low music.

"New York," essay in Thrilling Cities, *by Ian Fleming. New American Library, New York, 1964*

THE SCRAMBLING AND POACHING OF EGGS

Individuality pervades scrambled-eggery—there are nearly as many methods as there are cooks. The basics are simple: a hot frying pan holds foaming butter or the fat of your choice. A number of eggs beaten together and gently seasoned are poured into the melted fat. A lowered flame—the eggs begin to set slightly—a lick around the pan with spoon or spatula—soft curds begin to form—another lick, more curds—soon a creamy, golden mass.

Yes, but . . . The French complicate and elevate the preparation to epicurean heights. In the top of a double boiler over hot water they beat the eggs to a froth, adding bits of softened butter as the eggs set. The result is a rich, smooth, glossy custard—the ultimate accompaniment to caviar or smoked salmon, a silken-smooth chilled filling for stuffed tomatoes. All scrambled eggs take to just about any addition but milk, which toughens them. If you must increase the quantity of beaten egg, add water. Other flavorful stretchers are chopped ham, minced herbs, grated cheese, diced mushrooms. A small child might dote on a dollop of strawberry jam mixed with his "scrambies"—not likely to appeal to those over the age of puberty, but apt to change the minds of infant egg-haters.

For perfect scrambled eggs, use one of the omelet pans we've shown you, or try the Cuisinart frying pan (6.13), with a slick inside surface, good heat diffusion, and nothing in its makeup to mar the simple, perfect taste of perfectly scrambled eggs.

POACHING

Why don't we show any equipment for poaching? asks the dedicated egg cook. Because all of the so-called egg poachers on the market, however they operate, whatever they do, are not actually poaching at all. A true poached egg is cooked *in* water, not over it, and not in steam—an "egg poacher," with its cuplike insert, actually steams an egg. It will produce a perfect, round result, but one without the melt-in-your-mouth quality of the genuine article.

Every well-equipped kitchen has the necessary tools for turning out a poached egg—a rather deep frying or sauté pan, a wooden spoon, a slotted spoon, and a reasonably dextrous cook. Into the pan pour 2 or 3 inches of water and add a tablespoon of vinegar for each quart of

Continued from preceding page

water. Bring it to the simmer. Break a *very fresh* egg into a cup and slide it gently into the pan while stirring the water around and around in a whirlpool with the wooden spoon. The white will wrap around and enclose the yolk and in four minutes, with the water barely at the simmering point, you lift from the pan with the slotted spoon a tender oval shape with a rich liquid center. You'll find that with practice you can poach several eggs at once. If you are poaching eggs for a crowd, have a bowl of warm water at the ready into which you can slip the cooked eggs to rest until their final appearance atop toast or a robust hash or resting on a flavorful foundation of spinach or creamed mushrooms.

If your poached eggs look a bit ragged, trim the edges with scissors before serving them. And be sure they are well drained on a clean white napkin before you plop them on the toast or whatever—there's nothing worse than a soggy underpinning to a poached egg.

SOUFFLE UTENSILS: THE EGG AND ITS FRIENDS

La Belle France has been generous to the United States. From her we have received the Statue of Liberty, General Lafayette, and the soufflé, into which the simple egg—released from its humble shell, divided into its separate-but-equal parts, and properly treated—bursts like a miracle. A soufflé can be the delicious denouement of a superb dinner, or a satisfying entrée for the dinner itself. The possibilities are endless.

A soufflé uses two of the egg's characteristics—the cohesiveness or thickening power of the yolk and the beatability of the white. A thick sauce made from butter, flour, and liquid—the "thick white sauce" our mothers used to be taught in Domestic Science—is enriched with egg yolks. This is the soufflé base, which takes kindly to the addition of almost any ingredient you can imagine—fish or fowl, fruit or vegetable—a soufflé is accommodating. Beaten to a fare-thee-well, the egg whites trap trillions of tiny bubbles in their stiff airy structure. The beaten whites, folded into the base, expand in oven heat, huffing and puffing into a magnificent explosion. (For beating egg whites, see Chapter 5.)

Constant heat, no drafts, is the secret of success in soufflé baking. In the late, unlamented past, primitive ovens brought forth many a collapsed soufflé and only a skilled and intuitive chef dared attempt the feat. Today, calibrated temperature regulators, standard equipment on the simplest stove (checked, we might add, with a good oven thermometer), make the magic possible for the masses. The soufflé exacts another condition—eat at once. Left lingering on oven rack or table trivet, it punishes the dallier by sinking like a punctured balloon. Thirty minutes in a 375-degree oven will produce a soufflé with a creamy, saucelike center—a Frenchman's delight but fragile. Left in the oven five minutes longer, the soufflé will be sturdier and firmer, more to the American taste.

Equipment befitting its lofty status is no more than a soufflé deserves. To bake—a straight-sided, flat-bottomed container; to beat—a capa-

PHILIP BROWN'S ROMAINE AND CHEESE SOUFFLE

A light, nutritious luncheon or dinner dish, with a surprising crunchiness provided by the inventive inclusion of romaine lettuce.

1 head romaine lettuce
4 tablespoons butter
3 green onions, chopped
4 tablespoons flour
1 cup milk
½ teaspoon Worcestershire sauce
1 teaspoon salt
2 or 3 dashes Tabasco
4 egg yolks
6 egg whites
1 cup shredded cheddar cheese
¾ cup grated Parmesan cheese

Cut the bottom off the head of romaine lettuce and wash thoroughly, then chop coarsely. Cook in boiling water until wilted (4-5 minutes), drain well and chop fine.

In a 9-inch skillet, cook the onions in 1 tablespoon butter until soft but not brown. Add the lettuce and cook, stirring, until moisture has evaporated.

In a large saucepan, melt the remaining 3 tablespoons of butter, add the flour to make a roux and cook the roux, stirring constantly, for 2 or 3 minutes. Heat the milk—not to the boiling point—and add to the roux to make a white sauce. Cook until thickened.

Beat the yolks, one at a time, into the white sauce. Add the cheddar cheese and cook until smooth. Stir in the romaine lettuce and onion mixture and blend well. Add salt, Worcestershire sauce and Tabasco.

Butter a 1½ quart soufflé dish generously. Into the buttered dish sprinkle the grated Parmesan cheese, turning the dish to coat the bottom and sides and then shaking out (and reserving) the excess cheese. Beat the egg whites until they hold soft peaks—but are not dry—and stir about one-third of the beaten egg white into the lettuce mixture. Blend thoroughly, then gently fold in the remaining egg white. Pour into the prepared soufflé dish and smooth the top. Sprinkle the top with the remaining grated Parmesan cheese and place in the oven, which has been preheated to 400°. Immediately reduce the heat to 375° and bake 20 to 30 minutes, until puffed and browned. Do not overcook: the soufflé should be somewhat soft in the middle.

Serve at once.

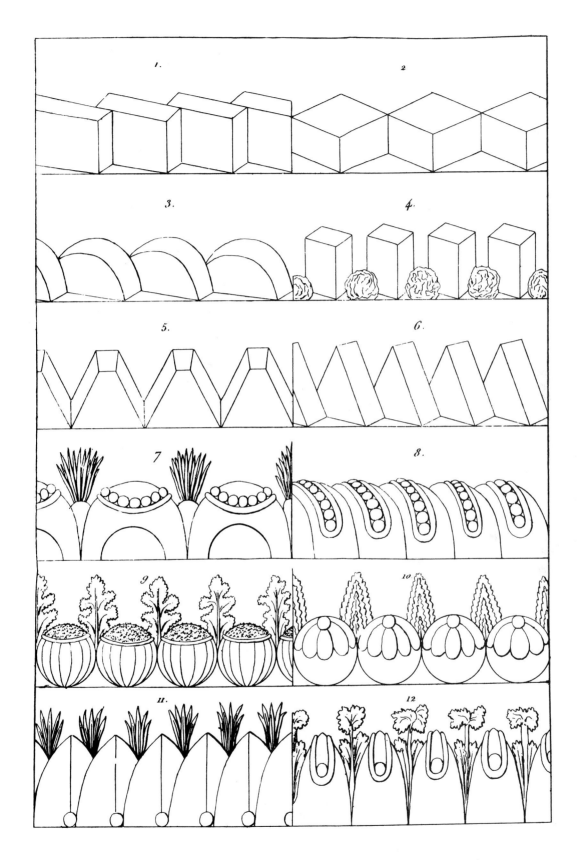

In his Pâtissier Royal, *Carême illustrated his ideas for garnishing cold entrées.*
Here numbers 1 through 6 are shapes to be cut out of aspic;
with number 7 he embarks on garnishes employing eggs and (number 9) tiny onions.

Continued from preceding page

cious bowl and a balloon whisk (see Chapter 5) or an electric mixer (Chapter 5). French chefs beat their whites in a round copper bowl; the chemical interaction of the copper, the egg whites, and the whisk gives an added lift to the whites for greater volume. Those without copper beating bowls can add a pinch of cream of tartar to help keep the whites stiff. But you should accept no substitutes for a classic soufflé dish—the mixing bowl or casserole can't do double duty here. Your recipe will specify the proper size of dish for the particular soufflé. If the soufflé dish you have is a trifle small, a double strip of aluminum foil or brown paper can be tied around it to increase the height while baking; the strip is then removed quickly before serving. The collar should stand at least 3 inches above the rim of the soufflé dish, so you would cut a piece about 8 inches wide and several inches longer than the dish's circumference. Fold it in half lengthwise, then butter and sugar or bread-crumb it, treating it just as you did the dish, then tape it in place until you can tie it securely around the dish with twine.

A soufflé overmatched by a too-large container is a pitiful sight. It may taste just as good without its haughty crown but it won't look nearly as magnificent. So that you won't have to use too large a dish, soufflé dishes are often sold in sets of three or more, convenient for those who dine both à deux and en famille. Handsome is as handsome does—soufflé dishes go right to the table from the oven, so good looks have a function. All the ones we show here are both serviceable and beautiful.

PORCELAINE DE PARIS

As you must realize by now, we are opposed to giving advertising puffs for individual manufacturers. We like a casserole from one firm, a frypan from another, and we are not easily sent into ecstasies by the entire output of any company. But every now and then we find that we are mentioning the same firm over and over again, a company in which manufacture and art are so deftly combined that it is nearly in the realm of the artisan-potters, of whom, as you know, we are enamored. So it was with Nambé (see Chapters 6 and 7), the American company whose aluminum alloy is sand-cast into pots of breathtaking beauty and then polished by artisans to an all-but-silver finish. And so it is with Porcelaine de Paris—"this industry which is also an art," as their catalog rightly maintains.

In the late eighteenth century, when the manufacture of fine china in France started and became concentrated in the environs of Paris, one of the finest firms was that of Jean-Baptiste Locré. Over the years the other porcelain makers left for the provinces, while only Locré remained in the capital, continuing to make superb porcelain according to the old formulas. Thus: Porcelaine de Paris, and thus: a line of exceptionally beautiful ware not only for the table but also for the kitchen. There are plates and teapots and tart pans and soup tureens, serving platters and saucepans and mixing spoons and egg cups; in short, there is an unbelievable range of shapes and functions. But there

TURKEYS' EGGS.

The eggs of certain domestic fowl were more widely used in the nineteenth century than they are now. Mrs. Beeton illustrated various possibilities in her Every Day Cookery and Housekeeping Book.

CORNMEAL SPOON BREAD

2 cups milk
½ teaspoon salt
¾ cup cornmeal
4 tablespoons butter
4 eggs, separated

This is really a heavy soufflé. It is a dish that has maintained a remarkable popularity and is excellent eaten with butter, or with sauce from a fricasseed chicken or such things, or as an accompaniment to game.

Bring the milk and salt to a boil and reduce the heat to simmer. Stir in the cornmeal and continue to stir until it thickens. Add the butter. Remove from the heat and beat in the egg yolks, slightly beaten. Cool slightly and fold in the whites, stiffly beaten. Bake in a buttered 1½-quart casserole or soufflé mold at 375 degrees about 40 minutes.

NOTE: Instead of separating the eggs, you may beat them whole and add to the mush mixture. Place in a buttered baking dish 9 × 9 × 3 inches and bake at 375 degrees 1 hour.

is, in addition, a wide variety of decoration in brilliant colors. Each piece of china is fired, then has a transfer design applied to it, and then is fired again; this is one of the few firms which still uses double firing.

In general, the theme of the decoration is agriculture and horticulture. The designs range from the botanical realism of the Gros Légumes pattern, which shows one mammoth vegetable on each plate, to the stylized blue chrysanthemum of the Ming Bleu. In between there are fruits: sprays of berries in the Fruits Sauvages, and fruits and flowers mixed in various proportions in the Quatre Saisons and Abondance patterns. And there are flowers in different styles: a delicate chain in Fleurs Persanes, a fragile bouquet in Bouquet Vénetien, and chinoiserie in Pavot and Vieux Chine Bleu. It is the policy of the company to use any of the designs on any of their products, within technical limits. This means that you cannot have the mammoth harvest vegetables of the Gros Légumes pattern on your egg cups, but you can have them on your platter or soup tureen or gratin pan.

What we haven't said yet is that these porcelain dishes and pots are not only well-made but beautiful—ravishing—enchanting. A tart pan from Porcelaine de Paris, decorated with a spray of raspberries laid on a creamy white glaze, is expensive, but is worth every penny it costs because it was made by an industry which is, as they say, also an art.

There is a hearty no-nonsense quality about Arabia ware. These soufflé dishes take to the dishwasher, think nothing of the freezer, and can be placed under the broiler without a second thought. Similar in their classic fluted shape to the Pillivuyt soufflé dishes, they are heavier, hardier objects, glazed top to bottom, bases, rims, and all. They range in size from an individual 4-ounce dish to a 2½-quart family size, all of which can be purchased separately. A batch of the smallest size is good to have on hand for first-course soufflés or dessert mousses or custards. The middling sizes are serviceable for a soufflé for two or three, to use as vegetable dishes, or to fill in as casseroles when no lid is required. The largest will hold a dessert soufflé for 6 to 8 appreciative diners—it is quite deep, so no paper collar will be needed. If your dinner china is Royal Crown Derby, you'll probably opt for something a bit more delicate than these sturdy dishes, but for everyday use, they have no peer.

"I must go see Mrs. Medway. Funny how servants cannot bear the police. Her cheese soufflé last night was quite uneatable. Soufflés and pastry always show if one is off balance."

Murder After Hours, *by Agatha Christie*

Pillivuyt Soufflé Dish — 11.73

Porcelain; 8″ diam.; 3″ deep; 2-qt. capacity. Also avail. with capacity of 2.5, 3.5, 5, or 12 oz., or ½, ⅔, ¾, 1, 1½, 2½, or 3 qts.
$9.00 ▲

As chaste as Greek columns, this soufflé dish bears the prestigious Pillivuyt label. The fireproof porcelain body is symmetrically ridged to resemble the pleated collars still used in fine French restaurants to contain the puffy soufflé. The glazed white interior is smooth as a shell—all the better for fast rising. Not a firm for halfway measures, Pillivuyt makes a dozen sizes of this classic dish—everything from a small one of 2½-ounce ca-

pacity, good for individual soufflés, custards, or what-have-you, to an enormous 3-quart dish for party-size portions. All have glazed bases but unglazed rims, which might make cleaning a bit sticky; the purpose is, again, better heat absorption. If they are first filled with food and have dry bottoms, all these dishes can be used on top of the stove as well as in the oven.

Arabia Soufflé Dishes — 11.74

Porcelain; 4 oz. Also avail. with capacities of 8 and 16 oz., 1¼ and 2½ quarts.
$1.50

Porcelain Soufflé Dish — 11.75

Porcelain; 7″ diam.; 3″ deep; 1½-qt. capacity. Also avail. with capacity of 1 or 2 qts.
$8.00

Oo-la-la! These soufflé dishes are as classically French as the traditional Chantilly pattern which decorates them. Delicate fluted bodies abloom with bright blue flowerets in a tangle of green leaves and brown stems come in three graduated sizes, holding 1, 1½, and 2 quarts. The dishes can be purchased individually, but greedy souls will want all three for the cupboard. A practical soul beats beneath the frills. Heatproof porcelain

443

Continued from preceding page

with zero porosity, they can go from oven to table to dishwasher with nary a worry about breakage. The bottoms are marked with a series of grids to prevent cracking if the hot dish is inadvertently placed on a cold or wet surface. The same Chantilly pattern decorates a number of other items from B.I.A. Cordon Bleu, so if these soufflé dishes appeal, save up for the set.

An eighteenth-century gastronome advised: "Make an intermediary of an egg, which comes between the various parts [of foods] to bring about difficult reconciliations."

Individual Porcelain Soufflé Dishes   11.76

Porcelain; set of 4, each 4¾" diam.; 1¾" deep; 8-oz. capacity. Also avail. individually with capacity of ½, 1, 1¼, or 1½ qts.

$40.00

We have occasional dreams of our first encounter with the Café Nicholson's chocolate soufflé—each steamy serving encased in its own paper-lined dish to be sinfully topped with chocolate sauce and a cool, sweet mound of whipped cream. Ambrosia! A reasonable facsimile of that delight can be served in these elegant little soufflé dishes from Porcelaine de Paris. These, in the Fleurs Persanes design, are bedecked with bouquets of green, yellow, orange, and blue flowers on their fluted exteriors, and a bunch of the same posies rests on the bottom to reward those who have eaten the very

last bite. The bottom rims are crenellated and the bases are scored with intermittent concentric circles so air may circulate beneath the dishes when they rest on a baking sheet. As if all this weren't enough, the thoughtful people at Porcelaine de Paris have included two recipes with each box of three dishes—one for an individual orange soufflé, to some minds and palates a close second to chocolate, the other for soufflés au fromage made with nutty Gruyère cheese. Sure to bring delighted cries and return invitations from the lucky hostesses to whom you have borne these as a gift—why not buy a set for the donor, too? And if you've fallen head-over-heels for these small ones, you'll be happy to hear that Porcelaine de Paris makes larger versions for party-sized soufflés—you can have them holding from 1 pint to 1½ quarts.

CRAB SOUFFLE

Serves 4-6

3 tablespoons butter
1 small onion, finely chopped
3 tablespoons flour
3 tablespoons tomato paste
½ cup cream
1 teaspoon salt
½ teaspoon freshly ground pepper
Dash Tabasco
1 teaspoon tarragon
2 tablespoons Cognac
4 egg yolks
6 egg whites
1 pound crab meat
  (leg meat or lump)

Sauté the onion in the butter till soft. Add the flour, stir, and cook a minute or so. Add the tomato paste and cream and stir till smooth. Add the seasonings and cool slightly. Stir in the egg yolks and beat well. Beat the egg whites till firm but not dry, and fold into the mixture. Butter a 1½-quart soufflé dish. Place a layer of crab leg or lump meat on the bottom. Add one-third of the soufflé mixture, then another layer of crab, and finally the remaining soufflé mixture. Bake at 375 degrees approximately 30 to 40 minutes, or until puffy and browned. Serve with a Hollandaise if you like.

(From AMERICAN COOKERY, by James A. Beard, illustrated by Earl Thollander. Copyright© 1972 by James A. Beard. Reprinted by permission of Little, Brown and Company.)

Deep Pillivuyt Soufflé Dish   11.78

Porcelain; 7" diam.; 3⅝" deep; 2-qt. capacity. Also avail. with capacity of 12 oz., ½, ¾, 1, or 1½ qts.
$9.50

A mighty soufflé dish is this by our old friend Pillivuyt. Deeper than most, it's perfect for meatier, or fishier, or cheesier soufflés for the mainstay of your meal. Plop a few poached eggs on a layer of cheese soufflé, cover them with more of the mixture, bake, and serve a delicious, nutritious dish. For elegant fare with the same surprise twist, poach turbans of sole and place them carefully between layers of an airy seafood soufflé. This high-sided 2-quart dish will hold generous helpings for six or more. Made in the classic fluted shape of heavy white porcelain, it is inexpensive for all its good looks and utility.

Stoneware Soufflé Dish   11.79

Stoneware; 5¾″ diam.; 2¾″ deep; ¾-qt. capacity. Also avail. with capacity of 10 oz., 1¼, or 2 qts.
$5.50

The Bennington Potters make this stoneware soufflé dish in many sizes and colors. They range in capacity from 10 ounces to 2 quarts and in color from brown to tawny, white to blue—all come with a smooth, opaque white interior. They do not have the usual border found on most soufflé dishes, but the outside is classically ridged. The general effect is rustic and homey, if slightly self-conscious—one feels that every piece is prayerfully made by some Princeton dropout. The quality, however, *is* outstanding. This is lead-free vitreous stoneware, fired at a kiln temperature of 2350 F., and it will not discolor or crack in the hottest oven or chip in the dishwasher. Damage *can* be done if it is placed over an open flame, however, so reserve it for use in the oven, its proper place.

Ron Garfinkel Soufflé Dish   11.80

Salt-glazed stoneware; 7¼″ diam.; 4¾″ deep; 1¾-qt. capacity.
$15.00

"Please touch" is the feeling we get from this weighty 1¾-quart stoneware soufflé dish. The speckled look of its earthy brown exterior is produced by salt glazing, a decorative technique which is much used by its craftsman maker, Ron Garfinkel. While the piece is being fired, handfuls of coarse salt are thrown into the kiln. The burning of the salt gives the finished piece a mottled look and a pebbly texture. The slightly flared outer rim is underlined with a cobalt-blue streak—very handsome. This is a heavy dish, looking as if it's meant for substantial soufflés made in a country kitchen. We also see it as a baking dish for cassoulet or other peasant fare, a crock aswim with cornichons, or even, blooming with marigolds, holding center stage on a dining table.

Hand-thrown Stoneware Soufflé Dish   11.81

Stoneware; 8½″ diam.; 3″ deep; 2-qt. capacity.
$12.00 to $24.00

The crafts look, beloved by many, finds expression in this stoneware soufflé dish hand-thrown by potter Cynthia Bringle. Marks of potter's tools ridge the matte-finished exterior, while the highly glazed interior is grooved from fingertip pressure as the pot turns and is formed. The base is left in its natural state. A mélange of earth tones—greige, dark gray, sand brown, chocolate, russet—bleeds together gently in the glaze, and as a result no two dishes are alike. This one might be very happy in a kitchen where it would hold nothing but natural foods —kasha casserole, soybean soufflé, a medley of late-summer vegetables and herbs baked gently in a little oil.

STRAWBERRY-ALMOND SOUFFLE

⅓ cup whole blanched almonds
3 packages (10 ounces each) frozen sliced strawberries, defrosted
1½ tablespoons unsalted butter (approximately), at room temperature
2 tablespoons sugar (approximately)
5 egg whites, at room temperature
Pinch salt
¼ teaspoon almond extract

Grind the almonds in a nut grinder, or grate them in a blender at high speed, turning the blender on and off so that grated nuts do not pack down. Reserve almonds in a large bowl and rinse out the blender container.

Purée the strawberries with their syrup in the blender. Push purée through a sieve to remove seeds. Put the strawberry purée in a heavy 2-quart saucepan and cook over moderately high heat about 40 minutes, or until reduced to a very thick jam-like consistency. Measure out ½ cup (which is about what will be left) and combine with almonds. Set aside.

Butter the bottom and sides of a 6-cup soufflé dish or charlotte mold. Dust the buttered surfaces lightly with sugar. Pour off excess sugar and set the dish aside.

Preheat oven to 400° F. Beat the egg whites with the salt until they form stiff peaks. Stir the almond extract into the strawberry-almond mixture. Then gently fold in beaten egg whites.

Pour the mixture into the prepared dish. At this point you can hold the soufflé for up to an hour by covering it with a large, inverted saucepan; or you can bake it immediately.

Set the dish on a shelf in the middle of the oven. After 2 to 3 minutes, reduce heat to 325° F. Bake 15 minutes more, or until puffed and browned on top. Serve at once.

Continued from preceding page

"*Sweetmeats of all kinds, and of all forms, but principally yemas or yolks of eggs prepared with a crust of sugar were strewn on the floor of a large room, at least to the depth of three inches. Into this room, at a given signal, tripped the bride and bridegroom . . . to convey a slight idea of the scene is almost beyond the power of words. In a few minutes the sweetmeats were reduced to a powder, or rather to a mud, the dancers were soiled to the knees with sugar, fruits and yolks of eggs.*"

An Account of the Gypsies of Spain, by George Borrow, London, 1893

Individual Stoneware Souffle Dish   11.82

Stoneware; 5¼" diam.; 2⅜" deep; ½-qt. capacity.

$3.50

Pudgy stoneware bowls clothed in colorful glazes to hold steaming petite marmite, cheese-topped onion soup, meat pies simmering under a flaky crust—all shaped by the Bennington Potters and fired in their kilns. Choose between the speckled blue and tan agateware, reminiscent of Grandmother's kitchen, or the plain slip glaze in tawny, white, or black. Each pint-sized bowl has a slightly indented rim which flares into two tiny handles. The straight sides meet flat bottoms, unglazed on the base. Feel free to put these bowls in the oven or the dishwasher, but never set them over a stovetop heat source. Solid citizens these; their cost is moderate, so buying a set of six or so won't cause bankruptcy.

SOUFFLE A L'ORANGE

Serves 6-8

Vegetable oil
Granulated sugar
1 large navel orange
⅓ cup plus 2 tablespoons sugar
3 tablespoons sifted flour
¾ cup milk
4 egg yolks
2 tablespoons softened butter
5 egg whites
Pinch cream of tartar
4 tablespoons Cointreau
Powdered sugar

Heat oven to 400 F. Oil lightly a 6-cup heat-resistant soufflé dish and roll granulated sugar around in it to coat lightly. Shake out the excess.

Peel the orange with a vegetable peeler, taking care not to include any of the white pith. Chop the peel and crush it with 1 tablespoon sugar in a bowl or with pestle and mortar.

In a saucepan, mix the flour and ⅓ cup sugar. Add a little of the milk to blend. Beat in the remaining milk and the mashed orange peel and sugar. Stir over gentle heat until the mixture thickens and reaches the boiling point. Boil for 30 seconds only. Remove the pan from the heat and allow to cool slightly.

Beat the egg yolks into the sauce one at a time. Beat in 1 tablespoon softened butter and dot top of sauce with the remaining tablespoon of butter.

In a bowl beat the egg whites and cream of tartar until soft peaks are formed. Sprinkle on 1 tablespoon sugar and beat until stiff peaks are held.

Stir the Cointreau into the sauce; then stir in ¼ of the egg whites. Fold in the remaining whites and turn mixture into the prepared soufflé dish, leaving a space of 1¼ inches below the rim.

Put a baking sheet in the center of the oven and put the soufflé on it. Reduce the heat to 375 F. and bake for 20 minutes.

Quickly sprinkle the soufflé top with powdered sugar and bake for 10 to 15 minutes longer. The top should be pleasantly browned.

(From THE GREAT COOKS COOK-BOOK, by The Good Cooking School, Inc. Copyright © 1974 by The Good Cooking School, Inc. Reprinted by permission of Ferguson/Doubleday.)

Glass Souffle Dish   11.83

Heat-resistant glass; 1, 1½, and 2 qt. capacities.

$17.00 set ▲

For culinary voyeurs, a crystalline container for their soufflés—a dish as pure and simple as water from a mountain stream. Made by the Corning glass works, it is fragile in appearance but sturdy in use, safe both in oven and dishwasher—its only enemy is a butterfingered cook with a hard kitchen floor. Remember to reduce oven temperatures ten degrees when cooking in glass—it heats more quickly than porcelain or pottery. The visual is important here. Imagine these soufflé dishes holding an airy puff of cheese, a cloud of chocolate. For that matter, any food with eye appeal can be enjoyed to the fullest—frosty summer soups, celadon-green cucumber or fiery gazpacho; a kaleidoscope of fruits and berries; a verdant salad, fresh and cool. We would relish the view as well as the tang of a cold lemon soufflé brought to table in transparent glass. Keep your sauerkraut or baked beans under wraps in earthenware—these dishes are only for comely comestibles. Bless Corning for packing them in sets of three, holding 1, 1½, and 2 quarts. If you own a set of this manufacturer's glass canisters with accompanying cork mats, you can dump out your sugar or coffee as dinnertime approaches and use them as soufflé dishes in place of these.

Swedish Glass Soufflé Dish   11.84

Heat-resistant glass; 6″ diam.; 4″ deep; 2-qt. capacity.
$16.50

Breathes there a man with soul so dead he wouldn't covet this gorgeous glass soufflé dish from Sweden? No ordinary glass this, but a diamond-hard variety—safe in the oven and, with an asbestos pad beneath, on top of the stove. Then, when all its wonders have been performed, it's perfectly safe in the dishwasher. The sides are fluted in the classic manner, the bottom is flat and peppered with tiny bubbles—a testament to hand-blowing. A chaste lip of clear glass rims the top, giving an added lift to the rising soufflé and making for ease in handling the dish. Fill it with your most enchanting soufflé to dazzle your family and friends—it holds a generous 2 quarts. Strike it lightly—it chimes like a bell. Expense should be no object with a dish this elegant—when you're in the mood to treat yourself, we urge you to make this the treat.

Low Flameproof Soufflé Dish   11.85

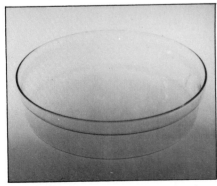

Heat-resistant glass; 8½″ diam.; 2½″ deep; 1¾-qt. capacity.
$22.50

It is hard to imagine this fragile-looking beauty sitting over a flame, but we've seen it and it's so. Related by manufacturer to the preceding glass soufflé dish, it has as its only decoration a slightly protruding lip. It comes equipped with a burner pad which seems too plebeian for such an aristocratic vessel—keep the pad in the kitchen for use atop the stove. At the table bring out the best of the trivets—all the way up to Georgian silver. Only 2½ inches deep, the dish will hold 1¾ quarts of crème brulée or our savory zucchini casserole, as well as any soufflé you fancy.

CUSTARD CUPS

Creamy and cool, the simple custard appears after dinner in many countries. Spaniards call it flan and bake it over a layer of caramel that forms a sauce when it is unmolded; the French know it as crème. An elementary amalgam of eggs, milk, and sugar, custard takes to a great range of flavorings with great success. Choose vanilla or chocolate, orange or almond—each a sublime combination of texture and taste. Custard can be humbly served in the kitchen or elegantly presented as the finale to a fine dinner. It can be made on top of the stove, as in crème anglaise, or baked, like crème caramel, the French version of the Spanish flan. Sometimes a combination of heats is required. Crème brulée is cooked on top of the stove, but needs broiler heat to caramelize its sugar topping before it is chilled and served. If you find your broiler chancy for this delicate operation, you can use a hand-held salamander (see Chapter 8) to form a crusty coating on the crème.

Custard looks well in just about any dish. You can bring custard to the table in one of the beautiful soufflé dishes we show you, or in the individual ramekins in the preceding section. Bavarian creams and other custard-based desserts stiffened additionally with gelatin can be molded into pretty shapes (see the molds farther along in this chapter) and handsomely served unsupported by any container. Pots de crème look best in the petite porcelain pots designed for the purpose. But for the simple baked custards, those freighted with childhood memories, nothing can take the place of the old-fashioned custard cup. We show a selection of the best of these classics.

CREME AU FROMAGE—CHEESE CUSTARD

for four people:

¾ C. grated Gruyère cheese
4 T. heavy cream
2 tsp. butter
6 eggs
salt and pepper

Beat together the eggs, cream, and ⅔ cup of the cheese. Season to taste.

Butter six small molds or ramekins and sprinkle on the rest of the cheese. Pour in the mixture you have just prepared, cover the molds to keep the contents from rising while cooking, and poach them in boiling water for twenty minutes.

Unmold and serve with a tomato hollandaise sauce (hollandaise sauce to which a little tomato purée has been added for color).

(From ENCYCLOPEDIA OF PRACTICAL GASTRONOMY, by Ali-Bab, translated by Elizabeth Benson. Copyright © 1974 by McGraw-Hill, Inc. Reprinted by permission of McGraw-Hill Book Company.)

447

White Porcelain Custard Cup 11.86

Porcelain; 3" diam.; 2¼" deep; 6-oz. capacity.
$1.50

As tots, abed with a germ, we were served custard in just such chaste white pots, innocent as ourselves. Our recovery progressed by creamy spoonfuls. Those days are gone forever, but the custard cup goes on unchanged. The glazed white porcelain body of this cup, smooth within, fluted without, is heavy in the hand, the better to withstand oven heat and careless handling. These are the custard cups found in restaurants from Maine to Monterey. They come in a standard 6-ounce size and can also be had in black, brown, avocado, or olive. Give us sentimentalists old-fashioned white in memory of our bygone childhood.

Brown and Buff Custard Cup 11.87

Stoneware; 3¼" diam.; 2¾" deep; 6-oz. capacity.
$.90

This homely pot suggests other simple desserts—bread and rice puddings, for instance—as well as custards. Copied in Japan from English restaurant ware, the cup is coated with a warm two-tone glaze: shiny dark brown within spills over the lip to meet a basic buff beneath. The stoneware body is resistant to both heat and cold, so the cup is practical for baked custards as well as frozen mousse. You can have a dozen for little more than the cost of the custard-makings.

Louis P. de Gouy, in The Gold Cookbook, *attributes this verse to one Oliver Herpid, not otherwise identified:*

Alas! My child, where is the Pen
That can do justice to the Hen?
Like Royalty she goes her way,
Laying Foundations every day.
Though not for Public Buildings yet—
For Custard, Cake, and Omelette.
No wonder, Child, we prize the hen
Whose egg is mightier than the Pen. . . .

Large Stoneware Custard Cup 11.88

Stoneware; 4" diam.; 2⅜" deep; 10-oz. capacity.
$3.50

Again stoneware, this cup bears the marks of the potter's wheel—the potter being Byron Temple. Glazed in earth tones, gray and sand, and randomly speckled with brown, this is a graceful cup for all its rustic look. Its small, flat, unglazed base supports a flaring bowl with a larger capacity than most custard cups—it holds 10 ounces. The generous size suggests other uses; it could be a tea cup cradled in both hands Japanese-style, or it could be heaped with a small salad, or it might serve a cup of soup, or even, for bears of all sizes, a helping of breakfast porridge. Dishwasher-safe and ovenproof, a set of these would make a nice gift for country cousins.

Pot à Crème Set 11.89

Porcelain; set of 6, each 2¼" diam.; 2¼" deep; 4-oz. capacity; tray 10" × 7½".
$120.00

Pretty little pots sitting on a tray—these look like the service for a dolls' tea party. But big people are meant to use these charming lidded cups from Porcelaine de Paris for that ravishing dessert beloved by children of all ages, pots de crème. This custard, simple to assemble, can be flavored with basic vanilla, earthy chocolate, sophisticated coffee, or classic caramel. Ladled into these little pots, which hold 4 ounces, and then baked in the oven in a simmering water bath, the custard can go from oven to refrigerator to table. Topped with their lids, the pots de crème are saved from developing a skin while cooling. Each fat little pot and domed lid blooms with the Quatre Saisons pattern; a wreath of the same lush fruits and flowers in mauve and yellow, rust, green, and violet trims the porcelain serving tray. Comfortable handles bulge from every cup, and small minarets top each tiny lid. Mound a dollop of whipped cream centered with a candied violet beneath the lids for a sweet surprise. Of all the pot à crème sets we've seen, this porcelain one is the crème de la crème.

An antique egg basket belonging to chef John Clancy.

Steamers and Steaming Baskets

If you like your vegetables virtually au naturel, with all their crunch and color intact, buy a steamer. Unfortunately, this method of cooking has fallen into a bit of disrepute as the province of either health-food addicts or ulcer victims. No matter: we recommend steaming primarily —in fact only—because it produces a delicious result—bright-green beans and crisp carrots, corn on the cob sans waterlogged kernels, and perfect pearls of new potatoes, just to list a few.

Steaming is also the most economical way to cook your vegetables —you need to heat only a small amount of water to create the steam, hence the economy for these energy-critical times—also steam is measurably quicker than boiling. Steam is also the way that preserves the most of food's goodness: why pour all the vitamins you paid for away with the cooking water? It is an accepted fact that vitamins such as C and the B complexes, found in abundance in green and yellow vegetables, are water-soluble—the more liquid used in the cooking process, the more vitamins go down the drain. The small amount of fluid which remains after you steam your vegetables can enrich a gravy or a soup or a sauce.

We Americans tend to think of steaming as primarily useful for vegetable cookery, but other nations are not so limited. Witness couscous, the national dish of Morocco, and, indeed, of other North African lands too. It is prepared in a couscousière, a specialized double steamer whose perforated top section holds the grain—the couscous for which the whole delicious dish is named—as it is bathed in the delectable vapors of the stew of lamb, chicken, or beef, plus many vegetables, bubbling in the pot beneath. And the Chinese discovered centuries ago that a steamed fish, sprinkled with fresh ginger and shreds of scallion, is not just a wonderful sight but a delight to the palate. We Yankees might try steaming our national dish, the hot dog—all the excess fat would end up in the cooking liquid and not on our waistlines.

All steamers, or pots to hold folding steamers, need tight-fitting lids, but the lid must be loose enough to allow some steam to escape so that pressure won't build up perilously. Stainless steel is our favorite material for steamers—no flavor transfer, good enough heat response, and no mess, no fuss in the clean-up. A good steaming pot should be both deep and wide so the steam can circulate around the food. This applies, too, to the perforated inserts of two- or three-piece steaming devices.

A word of caution before using any of the steamers we show—open the pot at a safe distance from any exposed portions of you, and tip the cover away from you as you lift it. Live steam can inflict a severe burn on the unwary.

SteaMarvel 11.90

Stainless steel; 5½″ base diam.; 9¼″ diam. when opened.
$4.00 ▲

Because she was so skeptical, one of our editors was asked to try out the Stea-Marvel at home. A devotee of Julia Child's quarts-of-water method of vegetable cookery, she had been feeling guilty about the amount of fuel required just to cook a pound of beans, but she loved the crisp, colorful results. Told that her steamed green beans would stay bright green and her carrots crunchy, she was still unconvinced as she unfolded the SteaMarvel, plunked it into a soup pot, and defied it to turn her green beans anything but a soggy beige. After even her vegetable-phobe eight-year-old had asked for seconds of the tender, spring-green results of the process, she averred that our experts were right. For a minimal investment this stainless-steel wonder will transform any pot from about 6 to 9¼ inches in diameter into a satisfactory steamer. The 18 perforated, overlapping petals unfold and expand, and they can be fixed at any point to contain small quantities in small pots, larger amounts in large pots. The steamer rests on three legs to hold your edibles above the water, and the metal post in the center is grooved to accommodate a separate handle which is used to lift the entire apparatus from the pot (carefully, remember steam is hot!). No danger of rusting—everything is made of stainless steel. Corn on the cob can be stacked criss-cross fashion and cooked to perfection in only 8 minutes in the SteaMarvel, and you can even improvise a seafood poacher with it, seasoning the liquid below the fish with herbs for added flavor. Clams will not only be less watery if they are literally and not figuratively steamed, but the concentrated broth which remains in the pot is a delicious dividend for the table, or for use in a sauce for fish. After use, the steamer folds neatly into a 5½-inch disc for storing. Which all goes to prove that good things often come in small—and inexpensive—packages.

Cuisinart Steamer 11.91

Stainless steel with aluminum sandwich, compressed-wood handles; pan 10″ diam., 5″ deep; 5-qt. capacity. Insert 9¾″ diam., 3¼″ deep. Also avail. with capacity of 4 or 6½ qts.

$90.00

Devotees of Cuisinart cookware are legion, and no wonder. Heavy and elegant, all the pots and pans of this maker are worth every penny of their Tiffany-type prices. This superb example of the Cuisinart line gives you not only a capacious pot for general use, but its large steamer insert serves a multitude of purposes in addition to the one for which it was intended. The 5-quart pot, like all these French beauties, has a gleaming stainless-steel body and a flat-ground bottom which sandwiches a thick layer of heat-diffusing aluminum between two layers of stainless steel. The stainless-steel perforated insert has a bucket handle which makes it easy to hoist from the pot. Imagine cooking your spaghetti and then lifting this basket insert to drain it—no colander required! The domed lid fits securely, and a handsome woodgrained knob sits atop the lid. The same compressed wood is secured with rivets to the two welded-on metal handles to provide a heatproof layer for the cook's comfort (although those brass rivets do get hot). This is a pot you will treasure for a lifetime.

Three-in-One Steamer 11.92

Stainless steel with aluminum base plate, Bakelite handles; lower pan 8¾″ diam., 4½″ deep, 3¾-qt. capacity; inserts each 8¾″ diam., 3½″ deep, 2½-qt. capacity.

$89.00

Although it comes from the land of the fjords, inspiration for this tiered steamer must have come from the Orient, where thrifty Chinese often use as many steamer baskets as there are foods to be cooked, stacking one atop the other over water boiling in a wok. This type of cooking is known as wet, or direct, steaming because the holes in the bottom of the steaming baskets let steam circulate around the food being cooked—contrast the steam cooking done in a double boiler, where the water vapor heats the outside only of the insert pan, while the food inside remains untouched by steam. This steamer is a triple-decker, with all parts made of stainless steel. The bottom section, holding almost 2 quarts, is a saucepot or stewpan capable of independent duty for a variety of purposes. The middle part is a capacious steamer with holes in the bottom for wet steaming; the 1¼-quart top is another sizable saucepan or casserole when used alone, a double-boiler top when used with the base. Fitted together, the three parts form a 12″ skyscraper for your stove. This can be considered a three-in-one investment: the lid fits all three pieces, and you can buy an extra one if you wish to use the two solid pans simultaneously—perhaps the base topped with the steamer, and the solid top pan serving as a saucepan. An ingenious knob is affixed to the center of this lid: the broad base of the black Bakelite knob is embossed with two arrows—turn them to the marks on the lid and you seal the lid vapor-tight; rotate them away from the marker and you allow steam to escape from the perforations in the lid beneath the knob. You can, like the Chinese, conserve fuel and make a whole meal in this cooker, and at the end of it you can put the whole kit and caboodle into the dishwasher. If shelf space is short, the base and the perforated pan can be hung from a pot rack; their long Bakelite handles have pull-out hanging loops.

SALMON AND SPINACH WITH MUSTARD SAUCE

Developed specifically for the Three-in-One steamer we show you above, this recipe of Carol Guber's is superbly economical of heat and stove space.

Serves 4

4 salmon steaks 1 inch thick
4 thin slices lemon
Salt and freshly ground pepper
1 lb. fresh spinach, washed and drained
4 tbsp. butter
2 tbsp. chopped shallots
2 cups white wine or dry vermouth
2 cups water
2 tbsp. Dijon mustard
1 tbsp. flour

Sprinkle salmon steaks with pepper and place them in the center (perforated) section of a three-part steamer. Place a slice of lemon on each. Set aside.

Place spinach in the top (solid-bottomed) part of steamer and sprinkle with salt to taste. Set aside.

Heat 2 tbsp. of the butter in the bottom pot of the steamer and cook shallots until tender, stirring; don't let them brown. Add wine and water and bring to the boil.

Reduce heat to a lively simmer and place the midsection containing the salmon over the base; cover and steam for 6 minutes.

Place the pot of spinach over the salmon and place the lid over the spinach. Continue to cook until spinach is tender-crisp and fish is just flaky—do not overcook. Remove spinach and fish sections and keep their contents warm.

Turn the heat up under the cooking liquid and boil hard until reduced to 1 cup. In a saucepan melt the remaining 2 tbsp. butter and stir in the flour. Whisk or stir in the reduced liquid and cook until smoothly thickened. Stir in the mustard, correct the seasonings, and serve with the fish and spinach: Make a bed of the spinach on a warmed platter, arrange the salmon steaks and their lemon slices on it, and spoon a little of the sauce over the fish. Pass the remaining sauce separately.

451

Rice Steamer and Mold 11.93

Aluminum; 7" diam., 2½" deep; tube 2½" diam., 2⅜" high; removable cup 3¼" diam., 2½" deep. Also avail. 6¾" or 8¼" diam.

$8.79

A snowy ring of fluffy rice can be centered with a variety of luscious fillings to make even a family dinner look like company's coming. This aluminum mold from Germany does the cooking and the molding of the rice in one operation. The removable cup fits snugly into the center of the mold; it pops out to measure the rice which you will pour into the basket. This basket is punctured with hundreds of tiny holes. After you settle the tight-fitting lid in place you immerse the whole thing in a pot of boiling water for anywhere from 5 to 22 minutes, depending on the kind of rice you are cooking (the manufacturer of the device provides timings for various kinds). Remove the lid, cover the mold with the serving plate, and gently invert the whole thing. Lift off the mold and *voilà!* the perfect circle. The mold comes in three sizes, to feed two people, or three or four, or a family. Our sample, 7" in diameter, will serve three or four.

POTATO AND VEGETABLE STEAMER
(MAIN'S PATENT).

Multipurpose Verzinkerei Pot 11.94

Enameled aluminum with Teflon II lining, plastic handles, chromed wire basket, aluminum lid; 8¾" diam., 4⅝" deep; basket 8¼" diam., 4⅝" deep.

$50.00

This pot is not just another pretty item for your shelf. Behind its sunny pumpkin-enameled exterior, centered with a black and orange bull's-eye, lurks a practical pot with several practical uses. It performs a variety of functions from ordinary stewing and boiling, to deep-frying, to steaming, to acting as a double boiler. All these operations are accomplished via the inserts included with the pot. Place the separate tripod in the pot and add the perforated insert pan, and the pot becomes a steamer. Use the same tripod, top it with the solid pan, and you have a double boiler or improvised bain-marie. The deep, chromed-wire basket turns the basic pot into a deep-fat fryer. The handles of the basket are designed to sit firmly on the rim of the pot while frying and then to latch over the pot's plastic handles so the food can drain. Included is a separate metal handle which fits both the perforated and solid inserts for easy removal. The pot itself is lined with scratch-resistant Teflon II for easy cleaning—a point especially appreciated after frying. A heavy ground-aluminum base on the otherwise enamel-coated bottom makes for excellent heat diffusion. The lid is a simple affair of shiny aluminum with a black heat-resistant plastic knob, and the same plastic forms the handles affixed to the sides of the pot. To prevent the chipping that most enamelware is heir to, the edges where the coating meets the lid have been finely ground. Since this pot will perform all the chores of a cupboardful

of cookware, it makes a wonderful wedding present, or just the right gift for a bachelor whose quarters are storage-shy.

Wearever's Bungalow Cooker 11.95

Aluminum with plastic handles; insert 9½" top diam., 3½" deep, 2-qt. capacity; base 9" diam., 5" deep, 5-qt. capacity.

$11.50

These clever steamers have been around since Grandmother's day, but their joys have been a well-kept secret among the best cooks we know. What makes them different? The holes are pierced in the upper periphery of the top pan and in the under part of its rim instead of peppering the pan's base, so all the juices of the steamed food remain in the upper pot, available for use in sauces or soups, instead of draining into the cooking water. There is ample steam circulation for fast cooking in this pot, which is made of rather lightweight aluminum. The lid is of heavier metal than the two pans, encouraging condensation of vapors rising against it, and it is ridged to fit the grooves on the rim of the upper pan, forming an excellent vapor-tight seal. The lower pot is capacious, holding 5 quarts of liquid; the steamer section holds 2 quarts. In addition to steaming perfectly everything from wild rice and whole grains to vegetables, this pot quickly reheats and revives the stickiest leftover. Last night's spaghetti, for example, recaptures that just-cooked flavor when warmed up in this steamer rather than in the oven, and you won't need to add liquid to restore it to suppleness. As simple and unpretentious as it is, this cooker has unique qualities that make it one of the favorite kitchen tools of our experts.

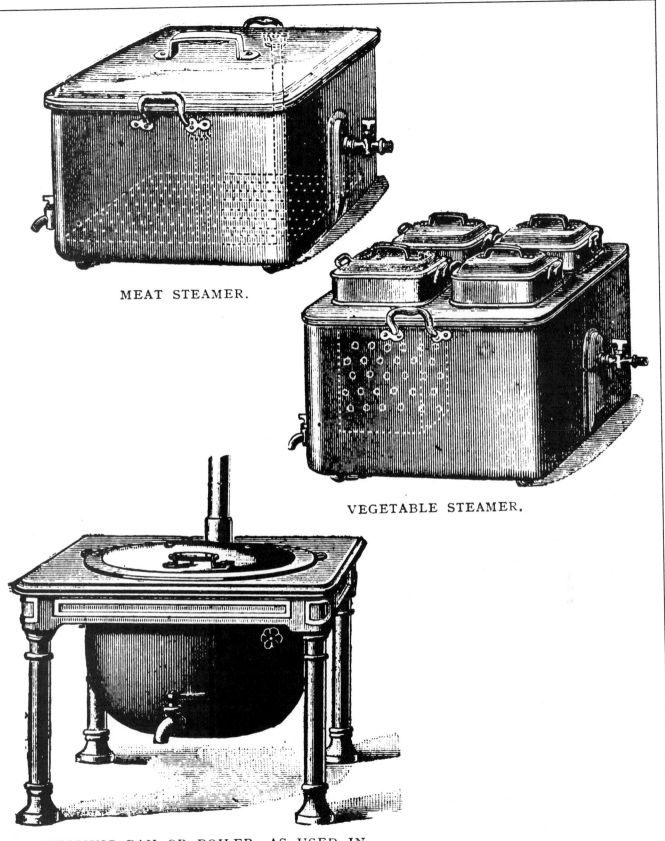

MEAT STEAMER.

VEGETABLE STEAMER.

STEAMING PAN OR BOILER, AS USED IN
LARGE INSTITUTIONS.

*Large-capacity cast-iron steamers offered by a Philadelphia manufacturer in a 1900 catalogue
might have been mistaken for laundry equipment, with their sturdy construction and
elaborate plumbing.*

Fried foods? Horrors, say some health-conscious souls who don't realize that deep-fat frying, done properly in utensils designed for the purpose, results in crisp, greaseless food that is nutritious as well as delicious and completely digestible. A French-fried potato, expertly cooked at home, has as much in common with the soggy sticks served at a greasy-spoon lunch counter as a soufflé has with instant chocolate pudding.

Anyone who has bitten into the crunchy crust of a zeppole at an Italian street festival, or consumed a sugar-dusted beignet soufflé, the peak of perfection for pâte à chou pastry, knows that deep-fat frying is truly an international culinary technique. It is a quick and easy process that produces delectable tempura, the batter-fried shrimp, fish, and vegetables of Japan; Chinese deep-fried dumplings; the Pennsylvania Dutch housewife's funnel cakes. For home bakers, frying solves the problem of what to do with leftover pastry dough—stuff and fry some turnovers, or cut the dough into shapes to sprinkle with sugar after they are browned and crisped. One of our culinary experts reports that rendering a goose of its fat and frying a mess of potatoes in it will make you forget about eating the goose. And you'd better not make any bets about being able to eat just one home-fried potato chip.

No magic formula is required to turn out a greaseless end result when you deep-fry. As a matter of fact, deep-fat frying is one of the simplest methods of cookery: the secret lies in achieving and maintaining the proper temperature. This critical point varies with the cooking fat used—butter is seldom used in this process because it will burn when it reaches about 284 F., while lard can be heated to around 390 F., and most solid shortenings won't smoke or burn much below 400 F. If fat is overheated or is re-used too many times, it "breaks" and deteriorates; this causes a smelly and unwholesome substance, acrolein, to form, and also robs the fat of its ability to "seize" the food and form a crisp, delicious outer layer. This is what has given fried food a bad name which, by rights, is deserved only by the ignorant or careless cook who lets the fat burn.

RECYCLING YOUR FRYING FAT

As the price of cooking oil skyrockets, you may hesitate to use the quart or two required for deep-fat frying. But you can and should recycle your fat: because a coating is formed on the food immediately upon contact with the hot fat, very little exchange of flavors can occur when frying is done correctly—you can fry doughnuts in oil that previously held French-fries or banana fritters. So be thrifty. Strain the oil through a very fine sieve or a piece of cheesecloth and store it airtight for re-use. The French store their strained fat in the fryer itself, but a bottle or a covered canister will do just as nicely. Store it in the refrigerator if you don't plan to use it soon. And one exception to our blithe invitation to re-use your oil: If you deep-fry fish or seafood, save that oil for re-use with similar foods—if your frying has involved only bland foods, you can of course use the fat for any kind of food the next time around.

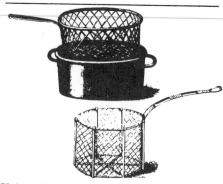

Urbain-Dubois, in his Ecole des Cuisinières, *recommended the frying basket of heavy tinned steel wire as an indispensable item in either the large or small kitchen. The six-sided basket was also used to blanch vegetables and fruits.*

BEIGNETS DE POMME— APPLE BEIGNETS

6 tart cooking apples
½ cup sugar
¼ teaspoon ground cinnamon
½ cup rum

6 to 8 cups peanut oil for deep frying
1 cup confectioners' sugar

FOR THE BATTER:

1¾ cups sifted all-purpose flour
2 tablespoons peanut oil
2 tablespoons butter, melted
¼ teaspoon salt
2 eggs
¼ cup milk

Peel and core the apples and chop them rather coarsely. Put them into a bowl, sprinkle them with the sugar and the cinnamon, pour the rum over them, and let them marinate for 2 hours, turning them several times.

Make the fritter batter by mixing together the flour, oil, melted butter, salt, eggs and milk. Beat thoroughly until very smooth. Let the batter rest for about 2 hours.

Add the apples and their juice to the batter.

Heat the oil to 375° F. on a frying thermometer and drop the apple batter by generous spoonfuls into it. Fry the *beignets* until golden, take them out with a slotted spoon, and drain them on paper towels. Serve the *beignets,* sprinkled with sugar, on a dish lined with a napkin.

(From LA CUISINE, by Raymond Oliver, translated by Nika Standen Hazelton with Jack Van Bibber. Copyright © 1969 by Tudor Publishing Company. Reprinted by permission of Tudor Publishing Company.)

Equipment for Deep-Frying

In addition to a proper pot for deep-frying, it would be wise to acquire a good frying thermometer as well, to make the job of temperature control easier. Get your fat to the correct temperature, never let it smoke, and do not overload the basket with food lest the temperature be reduced disastrously—the main cause of the curse of the soggy crust. (For thermometers, see Chapter 1.)

A deep-fat fryer must be just that—deep. Depth reduces the risk of spattering and insures that every piece of food will be submerged in the cooking fat, which should never be less than 3 inches deep in your pot. The ideal pot has somewhat flaring sides so that it is wider at the top than at the bottom, because the hot food, as it cooks, rises to the surface. You also need a frying basket; in fact, you need a basket more than you need a special pot: with 11.96, for instance, you can transform a pan you already have into a deep-fryer.

We show both top-of-the-stove and electric fryers. Either will do a bang-up job; those powered by thermostatically controlled electricity take the worry out of temperature watching and maintain a steady heat throughout the cooking process so long as you don't overload the pot. Then too, the electric fryers are portable and may be used on porch or patio—anywhere with a source of electric current. All the equipment we show is designed to take the onus off deep-fat frying, that much maligned and misunderstood method of cookery, and to put snap, crackle, and pop into your fritters and French-fries.

Collapsible Multi-Basket 11.96

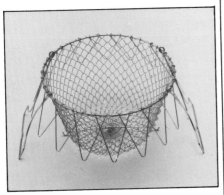

Tinned wire; 8¾″ diam.; 5½″ deep.
$5.00

At first glance this looks like your average lettuce basket, and indeed, it can be very satisfactorily used for shaking your salad greenery dry. But this gadget is also a first cousin of the SteaMarvel above, and like that handy object, it makes the most of what you've already got in your kitchen. While the Stea-Marvel makes any pot a steamer, this basket transforms anything from a large saucepan to a soup pot into a deep-fat fryer. Simply reverse the T-shaped wire handles and hook them into the metal bar which bisects the bottom and you have a basket 5½ inches deep which can be immersed in a potful of boiling oil. The tinned chain-link body is attached at the top to a wire hoop, also tinned. After use, the whole affair collapses quietly into a flat circle 8¾″ across, making for easy storage.

"My mother and her contemporaries were as stubbornly partial to certain utensils in which they cooked their favorite dishes as my father was to the iron 'kittle' in which he insisted dough-nuts must be fried. It made no difference, for example, that the iron spider was heavy and unwieldy, and that its handle was so short and got so hot that an inadvertent touch without a holder would sear the flesh as quickly as the fire itself—all frying had to be done in the spider. Used as it was over a wood fire, the outside was encrusted with burned-on soot, but the inside was as smooth as the softest satin."

Della T. Lutes, The Country Kitchen, Little, Brown, and Company, 1936

Iron Deep-Fat Fryer 11.97

Iron with tinned wire basket; 10½″ diam., 3¼″ deep; basket 6″ diam., 3¾″ deep.
$10.00 ▲

No frills on this simple iron deep-fat fryer from France. Plain and sturdy, it is the classic pot for the purpose. The broad, flat bottom allows a maximum of food to be cooked at one time because it allows for maximal heating, and the flaring sides give the pot the wide top needed for fast-rising fried food. The round, tinned wire basket follows the contours of the pot and is fitted with art-fully bent handles that latch over the high, curved outside handles of the pot so that you can drain your crisp fritters for a moment before placing them on a plate lined with absorbent paper. Be sure to have a pair of extra-thick pot-holders at the ready when frying, as this pot has no heat-resistant surfaces, no cool plastic handles—it's all iron. After use, clean it as you would any piece of cast iron—a simple swipe with paper towels does the job. Super-sanitary types who insist upon washing their iron pots should remember that this material rusts, so it must be dried immediately and thoroughly after washing, ideally by turning it upside down over a very low gas flame.

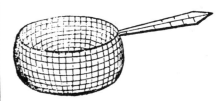

This wire basket, according to an old cookbook, is "the nicest thing to use for frying parsley, or anything small requiring to be fried."

Frying Bassine from France 11.98

Aluminum with cast-aluminum handles, tinned wire basket; 11″ diam., 4¼″ deep; basket 10″ diam., 3⅜″ deep.

$14.60

Aluminum is a very good heat conductor, and conductivity is a useful quality in a deep-fat fryer. Since no acid substances such as wine are used in frying, aluminum can be recommended without reservation. This lightweight bassine from France—a classic French deep-fat fryer—will let you bring the fat to the required high temperature in the shortest amount of time, using the least amount of precious fuel. The broad, flat base is very stable and allows a generous surface for frying large amounts at one time. This is a deep pot, which means minimal spattering in use. The handles on the tinned wire basket are hinged—when they are in the vertical position the basket can be lowered into the hot fat, then, placed horizontally, they fit over raised ridges in the pot's high flat handles so your food can be drained. An added and very French bonus is the tight-fitting lid. The practical French strain their oil and store it in the fryer for the next use—the lid keeps the oil clean and their secret safe. Don't be tempted to cook with the lid on, of course—that would produce a soggy crust rather than a crisp coating.

SWEET-SOUR FISH

INGREDIENTS

1 sea bass (about 2 pounds)
2 scallions
2 slices fresh ginger root
2 tablespoons soy sauce
3 tablespoons wine vinegar
3 tablespoons sugar
1 teaspoon salt
1 tablespoon cornstarch
Oil for deep frying

PREPARATION

Wash and dry the sea bass inside and outside.

Make 3 or 4 diagonal cuts on each side of the bass so that added flavoring will be absorbed by the fish.

Rub both inside and outside of the bass with 1 teaspoon of salt and let stand for 10 minutes.

Wash scallions and cut into ¼″ pieces. Mince the ginger.

Mix 2 tablespoons soy sauce, 3 tablespoons vinegar, 3 tablespoons sugar and 1 tablespoon cornstarch in ½ cup cold water.

COOKING PROCEDURES

Deep fry the fish for about 5-8 minutes or until golden brown. Place in a deep platter.

Stir fry the scallion and ginger in 1 tablespoon oil.

Add the vinegar-soy sauce mixture and bring to boil.

Pour the mixture over the fish and serve hot.

TIPS

The sea bass must be very fresh. It should not weigh more than 2 pounds, as a larger fish is harder to cook this way.

Vary the amount of sugar and vinegar to taste.

(From THE PLEASURES OF CHINESE COOKING, by Grace Zia Chu, illustrated by Grambs Miller. Copyright © 1962 by Grace Zia Chu. Reprinted by permission of Cornerstone Library in association with Simon & Schuster.)

Nesco Electric Deep-Fryer 11.99

Chromed and enameled-steel shell, cast-aluminum well, plastic handles, tinned wire basket; exterior dimensions 10″ × 7½″, 7½″ high; interior 8⅛″ × 5¼″, 6″ deep; basket 7¾″ × 5″, 5¼″ deep.

$49.95

What the beignet soufflé is to the Frenchman, the doughnut is to the American. Naturally American know-how has been applied to the art of deep-fat frying, from the crisp-jacketed clams of the Northeast shore to the tostadas of the Southwest. In this case, it has resulted in a deep-fat fryer powered by electricity, so you need never use your stove. If it puts you in mind of the commercial cookers found in every diner, you are right. Nesco manufactures those larger versions as well as this one for domestic use. The rectangular tinned wire basket, a smaller version of the one in use at your local lunch counter, fits into the heavily insulated, cast-aluminum interior of the fryer, and its contents can be drained by sliding the grooved bar on the basket frame into two specially placed studs within the cooker. The guesswork is taken out of temperature selection by a dial which can be rotated to the proper heat for cooking everything from French-fries to frogs' legs. Or y'all might want to fry up a batch of fish and hush-puppies for a terrace cookout, or even a big platter of tiny cheese fritters for cocktail time. An important feature of this cooker is its quick recovery to frying temperature after the addition of the food. All in all, it is a useful appliance for fry-cookery, American style.

SEB Super Fry 11.100

Stainless steel with plastic lid, handles, and trim; tinned wire basket; 10″ diam., 7½″ deep; basket 9″ diam., 2¾″ deep.

$64.95

Billed by the manufacturer as the amazing Super Fry, this behemoth of an appliance is the antithesis of the simple French deep-fat fryer but still, it *is* French, the culinary equivalent of the

Citroën—complex and luxurious. Made by SEB, it is a giant both in size and function. It will suspend two pounds of French-fries or all four quarters of a chicken at a time in a hot oil bath that is maintained at a constant temperature by the bi-metallic thermostat. This is the only fryer we show (and one of the few that exist) in which the lid must be kept on during the cooking process: no more spattered walls or smelly kitchens—the charcoal filter in the lid traps the oil droplets from the vapor and thus converts the fat-laden vapor to steam. A somewhat soggier product results, we think, but the absence of fumes may make up for that. The tinned wire basket is raised and lowered by a crank handle on the outside of the fryer, so there is no danger of burns to the cook during the process of adding or removing food. For safety from spatters and for those sensitive to the smell of frying food, this is the ideal appliance. It is difficult to clean, but that's not as big a chore as scrubbing down the kitchen walls after frying. The Super Fry comes with an instruction booklet which lists recipes for acacia-flower fritters—fine if you live in Southern California or on the Riviera—and fried sheep's breast as well as the conventional French-fries and fish sticks.

the larger with a diameter of 4″ and the smaller, 3⅛″, hinged together and attached to two long handles. With the "nest" material placed between the baskets, which are held together by the sliding loop on the handles, you then immerse the whole thing in a pot of bubbling oil. The end result will make you look like a kitchen magician, and nowhere is it written that you must tell the secret of your magic.

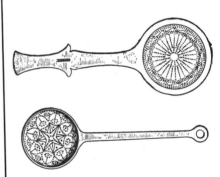

Ancient bronze skimmers found at Pompeii.

SKIMMERS: DEALING WITH THE FAT AND THE FOOD

As deep-fried foods cook, they rise to the surface of the hot oil. Each morsel you immerse will differ slightly in size and weight from the others, so some pieces will be ahead of the rest in turning the desired golden brown. To turn food when one side is done, and to remove each fried fragment from the fat at the peak of perfection, a skimmer is a useful tool. Why not use a slotted spoon? Simple. Such a spoon is too bulky and will lower the temperature of the cooking fat too much when you plunge it in to retrieve your food. Then, too, it will remove a smidgin too much oil with each dip. But a skimmer, with its network of thin wires, has no such drawbacks; used in conjunction with your deep-fat fryer, it will yield maximum returns for a minimum investment. Not a skimmer but a kissin' cousin is our bird's-nest maker, 11.101, which uses wire mesh to form versatile nestlike basketry from julienne potatoes, or noodles, or even bread.

SHRIMP-FILLED POTATO NESTS

Shred the potatoes or cut them into julienne strips. Shape the julienne potatoes into a nest inside of the bird's-nest maker. Plunge it into hot fat heated to 360 F. and fry without loosening the two strainers. When the potatoes start to turn golden, remove the nest from the fryer, drain a moment, and unmold. After a few moments, plunge the potato nest back into the fryer until it turns golden on all sides; keep it below the surface with a skimmer. Drain them on paper towels.

Fill the nests with cold Shrimp with Mustard Mayonnaise (below).

SHRIMP WITH MUSTARD MAYONNAISE

To serve as an hors d'oeuvre, allow about 2 pounds for six

To cook, wash thawed or fresh shrimp under cold water. Place in a large heavy skillet with all the water that clings to them. Place over moderate heat, covered, until the shrimp turn pink. About 3 minutes. Cool immediately under cold water to stop the cooking. Shell and devein.

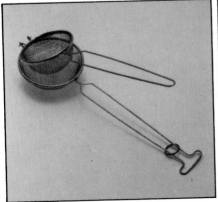

Bird's-Nest Maker   **11.101**

Tinned wire; 14½″ long overall; inside basket 3⅛″ diam., outside basket 4″ diam. Also avail. with outside basket of 3″ or 5″ diam.
$11.50

The proverbial creamed chicken—or any other delicately sauced morsels of meat, fowl, or shellfish—can be elevated to new heights—and *not* up a tree—if it is ensconced in a bird's nest. You won't want to weave your nests of twigs and string in the manner of our feathered friends, but with this gadget you can form an edible replica of a robin's Home Sweet Home out of just about any starchy substance. Julienne-cut potatoes, for example, can be stuffed into the larger strainer, pushed into place and held there with the smaller, and emerge from their bath of hot fat as a biscuit-brown basket. Thin noodles take well to the same treatment: cooked first in milk and sugar, then drained well, they can be fried into golden containers for ice cream or poached fruit. And even a plain slice of bread can be turned into a clever cradle for a poached egg with our bird's-nest maker. The whole apparatus consists of two tinned wire strainers—

Continued from preceding page

MUSTARD MAYONNAISE: To 1½ cups mayonnaise add 3 to 4 tablespoons of Dijon mustard, or to taste. It should be quite vivid. Then add enough heavy cream to bring the mayonnaise to a light consistency.

(Shrimp recipe from THE GREAT COOKS COOKBOOK, by The Good Cooking School, Inc. Copyright © 1974 by The Good Cooking School, Inc. Reprinted by permission of Ferguson/ Doubleday.)

A conscientious elderly gentleman of the late fourteenth century wrote a most complete manual to help his teen-age bride cope with household problems. Among the many delightful recipes he set down is one for marrow: "that is to wit the marrow is put in a pierced spoon, and the pierced spoon with the marrow therein is put in the broth of the pot of meat, and left there for as long as you would leave an unplucked chicken in hot water to warm it up...."

The Goodman of Paris (Le Ménager de Paris), c. 1393. Translated by Eileen Power. George Routledge & Sons, London, 1928

Deep-bowled Skimmer   11.102

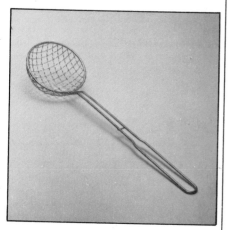

Tinned steel; 16″ long overall; bowl 4⅛″ diam., 1⅞″ deep.
$3.25

This skimmer is known as a dumpling ladle in Germany, where it originates, and there it is used to take dumplings large and small, including spätzle, from a simmering broth. It will also be handy for retrieving anything from croquettes to crullers from your deep-fat fryer. The tinned steel basket has wide-set wires for maximum drainage, and the foot-long handle enables you to remove any "sinkers" from the depths of the pot while it keeps the cook at a safe arm's length from the scalding oil. The handle is angled just before its juncture with the deep, round scoop—again, a good feature when you wish to remove big pieces of food. Simple and sturdy, this is a good utensil for doughnut fans as well as dumpling lovers.

Shallow-bowled Skimmer   11.103

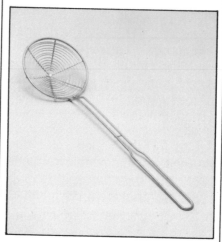

Tinned steel; 16½″ long overall; 4⅝″ diam.
$3.50

Known in its native Germany as a froth ladle and used to skim the scum from soup or stew in the early stages of cooking, this was made by the same Christian Oos who gave us the dumpling ladle above. You can of course use it in the prescribed fashion, but you can also employ it to get a satisfactory grip on your French-fries as they skitter through their hot oil bath. It has an only slightly concave scoop as opposed to the deep wire basket of the dumpling ladle—a more useful shape for potato chips, for example. The disk-shaped scoop is bisected by radiating wires which support finer wire bent round and round in concentric circles; the whole is attached to a foot-long handle at the same angle as the basket of the dumpling ladle. This is a nice companion piece to that skimmer for those who take their deep-fat frying seriously.

Professional Skimmer   11.104

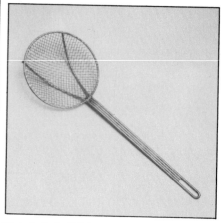

Tinned steel; 20″ long overall; 7″ diam. Also avail. 16″ long, 4″ diam.
$4.75

These are the skimmers found in every professional kitchen from New York City to Nashville. They are truly heavy-duty items built for utility rather than beauty. Fine-mesh tinned-steel scoops are supported by two weighty braces of tinned steel which extend to form the handle, which is reinforced with two more rods of the same steel; all four strips are welded and braced together to form a flat, solid whole. The smaller of the skimmers has a basket 4″ in diameter; its big brother is a sizable 7″ across and both are fairly shallow. In addition to being a fine accessory for deep-fat frying, the larger one would be a useful tool at a clambake—you could lift an entire serving of shellfish from the pot in a single scoop.

Li Liweng suggests this recipe for refined palates: "Guests should be served something special. I often suggest to the little woman that she gather the dew which collects on flowers. When the rice is just cooked, pour a little of the dew on it, and let it stand, covered, for a while. The guests thought that I had served some special grain, but it was only ordinary rice. I kept this a secret for a long time. The dew on wild roses, cassia and citron flowers is best, as these fragrances are not easily distinguished from that of rice. The dew collected from garden roses is too easily identified."

Hsiang Ju Lin and Tsuifeng Lin, Chinese Gastronomy, Pyramid Publications, 1972

Carême, in his Pâtissier Royal, *recommended that fritters be served in elaborate pyramids —attractive, but not likely to help them remain crisp.*

Specialty Cookware: Molds and Ice-Cream Equipment

Do-ahead dishes make life easy for the cook. And when they are beautiful to look at as well, the meal becomes a party. The simplest elements—puddings, pâtés, gelatins, aspics, and ice creams—can be formed into pyramids or palaces, stars or bars, to delight the guest and make the host look like a graduate of the Cordon Bleu.

Molds come in hundreds of sizes and shapes. Some are meant to be used only for chilled ingredients; these are usually of metal joined with tin solder, which melts in contact with more than very moderate heat. All the porcelain molds we show you are ovenproof; molds of other materials should be used only for cold foods, unless the manufacturer has declared his product to be ovenproof. In molds that withstand both heat and cold safely, you may cook your pâté or steam your pudding and then refrigerate it. (Beware, however, of caramel; make it in a separate pan, or risk separating the tin from the base metal of your mold.) These dual-purpose molds are of course usable for cold foods as well: you may pour a gelatin mixture into the same steamed-pudding mold in which you cooked the carrot pudding and produce as beautiful a creation as if you had used a mold designed only for icebox use; similarly, simple pâté molds can be lined with ladyfingers and filled with Bavarian cream for dessert. As a general rule, however, it is best to choose the mold according to the type of food you are preparing. A pâté en croûte won't unmold presentably if it is packed into a pudding shape, and it is just not possible to steam a pudding successfully in a gelatin mold of thin metal and elaborate shaping.

PATE, PUDDING, AND COLD MOLDS

Pâtés are best baked in a special spring-form mold whose sides can be released, leaving the pâté with its covering of crust or fat (or aspic, added after the baking) undamaged. Anyone who has struggled to remove a cooked pâté from an ordinary loaf pan knows that it is far easier to remove the mold from the pâté than the pâté from the mold.

Steamed puddings, beloved in bygone days, are less popular now. We wonder why. They are a delicious dénouement to a winter meal—simple to make and elegant to serve. The cannonball of a Christmas pudding boiled for an entire day by Mrs. Bob Cratchit has been replaced by lighter, fluffier concoctions, rich with eggs and milk, which need only an hour or two in the steamer. A pudding mold, for a modest investment, yields delicious dividends both hot and cold—it can be used for ice cream and gelatin-based salads and desserts as well.

Good molds to form cold foods—ice creams and mousses, gelatins and aspics—are made of metal, which conducts heat and cold quickly, so the contents chill thoroughly and unmold easily. Resist the urge to buy that sweet little mold shaped like a Spanish castle, all battlements and turrets—you're sure to leave part of your mousse in a minaret when unmolding. The simpler and more sculptural the shape of your mold, the less panicky a procedure releasing the contents will be.

Ice cream, America's favorite dessert, deserves better treatment than being dished in raggedy pieces from a cardboard container

Three elaborate hinged pâté molds, from a Hungarian work on the haute cuisine.

PATE DE GIBIER EN CROUTE— GAME PATE IN PASTRY CRUST (COLD)

This pâté may be made with pheasant, duck . . . or chicken. You'll need a 10 or 12 inch pâté form.

PASTRY

3 cups all-purpose flour, sifted
½ teaspoon salt
3 egg yolks
12 table spoons salt butter at room temperature
1 tablespoon pure olive oil
¾ to 1 cup ice water

FILLING

8 ounces thinly sliced fatback
6 ounces lean veal, finely ground
2 raw egg whites
¾ cup light cream
1 teaspoon salt
Freshly cracked white pepper
1 whole duck, pheasant, or chicken (about 3 pounds), completely boned
1 6-ounce slice of lean ham
2 black truffles, coarsely chopped
2 ounces shelled blanched pistachio nuts
½ cup chicken aspic
[any standard recipe]
1 egg yolk beaten with 1 tablespoon of milk

Sift the flour and salt together into a bowl. Make a well in the center and in it put the egg yolks, butter, and olive oil. Blend this together lightly with the fingertips to a smooth paste. Combine it with ice water to make a firm dough. Form into a ball, cover with a cloth, and let it rest 1 hour. Roll out three-quarters of the dough into a round or oval (depending on the shape of your pâté mold) large enough to line the mold with a half-inch overhang. It should be about

⅛ inch thick. Butter a bottomless pâté mold [or use a mold with hinged sides] and place it on a buttered baking sheet. Line the mold with the dough, pressing it firmly against the sides and bottom. Trim the edges evenly, leaving a half-inch overhang.

Preheat the oven to 350° and prepare the filling. Line the inside of the pastry with three-quarters of the fatback. Put the veal in a small metal bowl over a bowl of ice. With a wire whisk, beat in the egg whites. Slowly add the light cream, drop by drop. Season with the salt and pepper. Beat well. Spread half of this mixture on the fatback. Cut the meat of the boned fowl and the slice of ham into thin strips. Lay them in the mold in alternate layers, sprinkling each layer with the chopped truffles and pistachio nuts. Cover the top with the rest of the veal mixture and slices of fatback. Brush the dough on the edge of the mold with cold water.

Roll out the remaining dough and cover the top of the mold with it. Press the edges down on the half-inch border of the bottom pastry and pinch together. Roll out the pastry scraps and cut out decorations such as leaves or flowers. Brush the top of the pâté with the mixed egg yolk beaten with the milk. Stick the decorative pieces of pastry on the top and brush them with the mixture. Make a small hole in the center of the pastry top to let the steam out as the pâté bakes. Bake 1½ hours. If the pastry begins to brown too much, cover it with foil. Remove the pâté from the oven, cool, and chill it. Dissolve the aspic. With a little paper funnel, slowly pour the dissolved aspic through the hole in the pastry to fill up the spaces inside the pâté. Return to the refrigerator to set. Net: 8 servings.

(From THE DIONE LUCAS BOOK OF FRENCH COOKING, by Dione Lucas and Marion Gorman, illustrated by Joseph S. Patti. Copyright © 1947 by Dione Lucas. Reprinted by permission of Little, Brown and Company.)

ROUND MOULD

straight from the supermarket. The owner of an electric ice-cream freezer has a whole new world of flavors to command—and once those late September peaches, or a bucket of wild blueberries, have been converted into a cold, creamy confection, it can be molded into any shape, whimsical or classical, and kept in the freezer for later, and elegant, service.

Here are the tools, then, to make you a Michelangelo of the kitchen: shapes with which you can form stately pleasure domes of aspic, bewitching bunnies in ice cream, or marvels of pastry-wrapped pâté.

. . . AND OTHER THINGS

After we have investigated with you the pâté, pudding, salad, coeur à la crème, butter, and ice-cream molds, we will discuss a selection of the most delectable machines of all, ice-cream makers. We show you both electric-powered and arm-powered types (this last for the nostalgic), as well as a milkshake machine and all the dippers, scoops, and spades that an ice-cream lover could desire. Then—perhaps the ultimate utensil for those with a flock of children or those with a lingering love for ice cream to *lick,* not to spoon up—there is a device for making your own ice-cream cones, fresh and crisp.

Pâté Molds

A pâté by any other name is meat loaf raised to the ultimate degree of culinary interest. It can be as coarse as the chunky country pâtés beloved in the French provinces, or as silken-smooth as pâté de foie gras. Wrapped in bacon, or in snow-white sheets of fresh pork fat, or even baked in a puff of pastry crust, the pâté appears on luncheon main-course plates, at dinner as a first course, or emerges from many a picnic hamper. As well it should. Pâté is a good traveler. Forcemeat baked and sealed away from the air with a layer of fat—in other words, pâté—accompanied explorers to the New World and Crusaders to their holy battles. Archaeologists have discovered traces of meat mixtures that were pâté's forebears in the buried kitchens of ancient Greece.

Perhaps the secret of the popularity of pâtés through the ages is the basic simplicity of the mixture. Strictly speaking, it is nothing more than ground meat and fat, spiced and seasoned, baked to a turn, and cooled. Almost any meats can be used, singly or in combination. Baked in a decorative pot—the classic French terrine—and served directly from the baking dish, a pâté is called a terrine. Some pâtés (or terrines) unite pork and veal; liver stars in others; game and sausage, ham, fish and chicken, all appear in pâté recipes. Studded with pale green pistachio nuts, or layered with thin slices of pink ham, or punctuated with extravagant truffles, the pâté comes to a party. Unmolded and glazed with crystalline aspic, it looks elegant and appetizing on a buffet table; baked in a golden crust, a pâté en croûte introduces a fine dinner or stands alone at lunch.

A simple loaf pan (see Chapter 9) or an oval casserole (Chapter 7)

Continued from preceding page

will serve for baking a simple pâté, but to turn out party-worthy shapes or a pâté en croûte, special pans are needed. We show two of our favorites—one plain, one fancy—to make the baking, cooling, and unmolding of any pâté effortless.

Hinged Pâté Mold 11.105

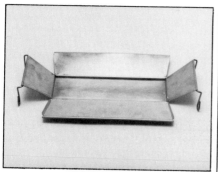

Tinned steel; 10¾" × 4¼"; 3" deep. Also avail. 11¾" or 14" long.

$12.00 ▲

Five shiny pieces of tin, strategically hinged, make this classic pâté mold, of a design similar to those illustrated in cookbooks of the Victorian era. The rectangular mold works in spring-form fashion: heavy wire, threaded through the rolled rims of the end flaps, is bent into clips which fit snugly against the long sides. Released, the clips let the whole affair become as flat as the proverbial pancake, leaving the proud pâté standing free in its pastry crust. If you plan to serve your pâté hot, use egg white as glue to add decorative pastry leaves or other shapes to the basic crust; glaze the crust and the decorations with beaten egg yolk, bake your pâté, unmold, and serve it forth. To serve cold, make sure your top crust has a quarter-size round hole in the middle before baking. When the pâté has cooled and you have unmolded it, pour almost-jelled aspic through the hole to fill up the space between pâté and crust—the pâté has been shrinking as it cools. Refrigerate, and serve when the aspic is firm. If you plan to wrap your pâté in thin slices of fresh pork fat or bacon rather than serving it en croûte, you will find it easier to liberate, with its sticky covering of cold congealed fat, from this presto-chango mold. After it has cooled—possibly weighted on top—in the mold, the surrounding fat will have hardened. Use a sharp knife heated in boiling water to soften the fat around the sides before unhinging the mold, and all will be well. The tinned-steel body of this mold allows for thorough baking and rapid cooling. The long, slim pâté it forms will be ample for a dozen first-course portions.

Pâté en Croûte Mold 11.106

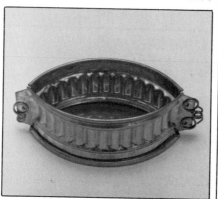

Tinned steel; 8⅝" × 4⅝"; 2⅞" high. Also avail. 7½" or 9¼" long.

$18.50

The miniature fluted temples of pastry-wrapped pâté gracing the serving tables of the finest French restaurants can be duplicated at home with this oval pâté mold. Each side is vertically grooved and horizontally ridged to shape the crust-covered pâté into an elegant little sculpture. The mold is made of three separate pieces of tinned steel, one for the bottom, one for each of the curved sides. Each side fits snugly within the raised lip of the flat bottom, and the sides are held together at either end by separate aluminum clips that look faintly like highly ornamental little clothespins. As the pâté cools, its sides will shrink away from the well-greased metal, making removal of the contents easy even for the least courageous cook. The mold comes in three sizes—the largest would frame a spectacular and savory centerpiece for a good-sized party.

Galantine Mold 11.107

Porcelain; 11¾" × 4½"; 3¾" deep; 2½-qt. capacity.

$35.00

The quintessential mold of cold meat is a galantine, that sublime dish in which the entire boned carcass of a bird holds a Lucullan stuffing of meats and seasonings. Cooked and cooled, glazed and garnished, a galantine is sure to draw raves from your guests. After boning and stuffing the chicken, turkey, pheasant, or capon, wrap it in cheesecloth and poach it. A fish poacher (see "Seafood Tools" in Chapter 11) is excellent for the actual cooking. The galantine must cool in the broth, and then be weighted like a pâté and thoroughly chilled. This mold serves that purpose, turning out a shapely oblong rather than the usual vague meatloaf shape of a galantine *au naturel*. A long heavy rectangle of pure white porcelain, the dish is deep and narrow to form the galantine into a long slim loaf, and it is as beautiful as the garnished galantine it shapes. A fluted handle is placed just so at either end, beneath a border of ridges which limns the rim. The sides flare slightly from a narrow base, which is also underlined with a single ridge. Well proportioned and sturdy, this mold would make an excellent terrine as well, as it is ovenproof.

Carême's presentation of a "bush" of small jellied pâtés.

Hinged Pâté Mold
Pâté en Croûte Mold
Galantine Mold
Hinged Pâté Mold with Patterned Sides
Curved Fish Mold
Three-dimensional Fish Mold

Hinged Pâté Mold with Patterned Sides   11.108

Tinned steel; 12″ X 2¾″; 3¼″ deep; 1¾-qt. capacity. Also avail. 14″ long.

$13.00

This mold is a first cousin to the plain hinged pâté mold we show you (11.105), but consists of three entirely separate pieces. Two pins join the two long-L-shaped side pieces to form an open rectangle. The bottom is a narrow strip of metal, the edges of which have been folded up to form a trough, into which the sides slide. An extension at one end of the bottom hooks up to form a handle, which aids in removing the bottom once your pâté is done. The entire mold is very solidly constructed of heavy tinned steel, with the edges rolled over a thick wire. The sides are indented with a lovely herringbone sort of pattern which is transmitted to any pastry dough baked inside of it, and which also adds strength to the mold, much as hammering lends strength to copper or aluminum pans. We show you the 12-inch size, which has a capacity of 1¾ quarts. Once the mold has been lined with both pastry dough and sheets of pork fat, however, only enough space for about 5 cups of pâté mixture will remain. It is also available in a 14-inch length.

Turkey Mousse: "Seed a large prone turkey, being careful to remove the bones, flesh, fins, gravy, etc. Blow up with a bicycle pump. Mount in becoming style and hang in the front hall."

F. Scott Fitzgerald, The Crack-Up (including The Note-Books), New Directions, New York, 1956

FISH-SHAPED MOLDS

A fish is a beautiful thing—long and slender, armored with glistening scales, it is one of the prettiest shapes in nature. Who would want to mold a mousse that looked like a pork loin or a chicken liver? Pâtés made with those ingredients are best formed into simple rectangles or classic ovals in the molds we have shown you. But when fish stars in your recipe, it deserves to be molded to resemble its original contours. Here, two beauties, to swim across an ocean of aspic or a sea of lettuce chiffonade.

Curved Fish Mold   11.109

Copper with tin lining; 9″ X 4″ wide; 2¼″ deep; 1-qt. capacity.

$13.00

Gleaming copper shaped like a crescent moon has been shaped into a sculptured fish, all arching scales and flaring tail. Framed in fluting, the fish's body curves like a truite au bleu to fit on a round serving platter. The mold, of unusually heavy metal, is tinned within, so no metallic taste will mar your mousse and the copper cannot threaten health with any hint of tarnish. Good for both hot and cold fish dishes, this mold will bake a hot mousse of red snapper (recipe), or mold a cool salmon mousse for a summer luncheon. When not in use, hang it on your kitchen wall by the attached ring to please your eye.

BAKED MOUSSE OF RED SNAPPER

1 lb. fully cleaned fillets of red snapper
2 egg whites
Sea salt
Freshly ground white pepper
Freshly grated nutmeg
1½ cups heavy cream
Butter
8 cooked and cleaned shrimp
Sauce Mornay, Sauce Normande, or
　　other sauce of your choice

Preheat oven to 375 F. Put a saucepan or kettle of water on to boil.

Purée the red snapper fillets in a Cuisinart machine (or put them through a food grinder, then a sieve). Beat in egg whites and salt, pepper, and nutmeg to taste.

Beat the cream lightly, until set but not dry. Fold whipped cream into fish mixture.

Set in the oven a baking pan large enough to hold a 1-quart mold with room to spare.

Butter the mold well. Fill with fish mixture.

Place mold in the baking pan and pour in enough boiling water to rise two-thirds up the sides of the mold. Cook for 30 minutes.

Unmold mousse onto a round platter. Garnish with the shrimps and part of the sauce; pass the remaining sauce.

Three-dimensional Fish Mold   11.110

Stainless steel; 11½″ X 4½″; each half ¾″ deep. Also avail. 8¼″ X 3″ or 13″ X 4¾″.

$22.50

A mousse will emerge from this mold looking as if it were still swimming through the briny. To make it, two heavy sheets of stainless steel have been stamped to form half of the lifelike body of a fish apiece; the halves, held to-

Continued from preceding page

gether with removable clamps, form the whole fish. You oil one half and fill it with a firm forcemeat of fish, lightened with egg white to encourage plumping. Cover with the other half of the mold and bake the whole thing on a rack over steaming water. The contents will expand to fill both sides of the mold and produce a perfect three-dimensional fish. After removing the mold from the oven, invert the whole thing to allow the form of the scales to set well in the second side. Unmold when cool. The mold comes in three sizes—you can have it 8¼, 11½, or 13 inches long. For drama, we see all three making a school of delectable fish mousses floating through a sea of vegetable salad on a pure white platter.

Pudding Molds

"Oh, bring us a figgy pudding" we carol at Christmastime, a paean to the plum pudding served for centuries in merrie old England. That country is the motherland of pudding, served not just for Christmas dinner, but throughout the year. Diet-conscious Americans are devotees of the light dessert and we don't think of steamed pudding as being in this category. Trencherman portions need not be served, however, and a winter meal is very satisfying indeed when topped off by a cozy cranberry or a flavorful fig pudding dripping with a sauce of crème anglaise or eggnog.

In the good old days, a steamed pudding was a weighty affair based on suet and flour. Wrapped in cloth—sometimes a knotted sock—it was boiled or steamed for hours. Today's lighter mixtures combine eggs, milk, and sugar with a variety of fruits or flavorings and need only an hour or two in the steamer. You pour the pudding mixture into a greased and floured mold, cover it tightly, and place it on a rack above boiling water in a large pot with a tight lid. Unmold the finished pudding and bring it hot to the table to be served with a pitcher of heavy cream or a sweet sauce.

If you plan to serve steamed pudding, good molds are essential. They are inexpensive and can be considered a once-in-a-lifetime investment; and, as a bonus, they double as cold molds for blanc-mange or Bavarian cream. All in all, you will find them handy as well as decorative additions to your batterie de cuisine.

Colin Clair, *in his* Kitchen and Table, *quotes from* Misson's Memoirs and Observations in his Travels over England, 1719:

"The Pudding is a dish very difficult to be described, because of the several Sorts there are of it; Flower, Milk, Eggs, Butter, Sugar, Suet, Marrow, Raisins, &c. &c. are the most common ingredients of a Pudding. They bake them in an Oven, they boil them with Meat, they make them fifty several ways: BLESSED BE HE THAT INVENTED PUDDING, for it is a Manna that hits the Palates of all Sorts of People: a Manna, better than that of the Wilderness, because the People are never weary of it. Ah, what an excellent thing is an English Pudding:"

Rosette-patterned Pudding Mold   11.112

Tinned steel; 6¾" diam.; 5¾" deep; 2½-qt. capacity. Also avail. with capacity of 1½ or 2 qts.
$6.50

Similar in shape, design, and function to the preceding one, this tin pudding steamer has a swirling rosette stamped on the bottom for added decorativeness. It, too, is centered with a tube shape; the tube tapers as it rises toward the lid. The lid has an oval handle and two flat metal clamps that fit securely under the outer lip of the mold to form a watertight seal. There is a generous 2½-quart size for those fourteen-for-dinner family Christmases, and the steamer also comes in 1½- and 2-quart sizes for more modest entertainments.

Simple Pudding Mold   11.111

Tinned steel; 7¼" diam.; 5¼" high; 2¼-qt. capacity. Also avail. with diam. of 6¼", 7¾", 8¼".
$5.50   6¼" $5.00▲   7¾" $6.00▲

Christmas puddings as well as frozen desserts will emerge looking as elegant as they taste from this classic pudding steamer. The simple, smooth tin body has a deep bucket shape centered with a slim hollow tube; it produces a pudding or a gelatin dessert shaped somewhat like a small angel-food cake with a pleasantly domed ring shape on top.

Two metal clips hinged to the outside hold the domed lid securely in place so no water will seep into the pudding while it steams, and the lid has a well-attached handle. Although the label reads Made in Germany, this steamed-mold pudding is the same shape as those beloved by generations of English cooks.

Fluted Pudding Mold — 11.113

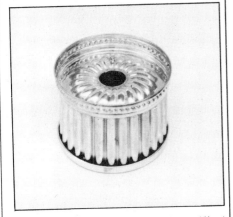

Tinned steel; 6¼" diam.; 3¾" deep; 1½-qt capacity.

$10.00

The proof of the pudding will be in the viewing as well as the eating with this pretty pantheon of a pudding mold. Fluted sides, a slender center tube, and a most graceful rosette design on the bottom make this a mold for a pudding to adorn the most elegant table. Even the rim, which holds the mold above the rack it rests on during steaming, is embossed with a series of bands centered with a pattern of ridges and knobs—it won't appear on your pudding, but it adds to the delicate good looks of the mold itself. A slightly domed lid fits tightly over the top securely enough, but be sure to cover your pudding batter with waxed paper before adding the lid, as there are no latches to fasten the lid to the mold itself and the added covering will tighten the seal. Made of tinned steel, this 1½-quart shape needn't be kept for winter puddings—it will also pretty-up a frozen or gelatin dessert. Both the mold and the lid have small rings, so they may be hung instead of shelved in the storage-shy kitchen or the kitchen in which other handsome utensils are on display.

STEAMED GINGER PUDDING

2¼ cups flour
3½ teaspoons baking powder
¼ teaspoon salt
2 teaspoons ginger
½ teaspoon cinnamon
3 tablespoons butter
⅔ cup firmly packed brown sugar
2 eggs, beaten
⅔ cup milk
1 cup heavy cream, whipped
1 tablespoon syrup drained from a
  jar of preserved ginger

Sift the flour with the baking powder, salt, ginger, and cinnamon. Thoroughly cream together the butter and sugar and stir into them the beaten eggs. Blend in the dry ingredients, a half at a time, alternating with the milk. Pour the batter into a buttered 1-quart baking dish or pudding mold. Cover the container tightly and set it in a deep kettle. Pour around the mold boiling hot water to a depth of two-thirds its height. Cover the kettle and cook the pudding over low heat 1½ hours, replenishing the water as needed to maintain the level. Serve the pudding unmolded and hot, accompanied by whipped cream flavored with the ginger syrup.

(From AMERICAN COOKERY, by James Beard, illustrated by Earl Thollander. Copyright © 1972 by James A. Beard. Reprinted by permission of Little, Brown and Company.)

"Hallo! A great deal of steam! The pudding was out of the copper. A smell like a washing day! That was the cloth. A smell like an eating house and a pastrycook's next door to each other, with a laundress next door to that! That was the pudding! In half a minute Mrs. Cratchit entered,—flushed but smiling proudly,—with the pudding, like a speckled cannon-ball, so hard and firm, blazing in half of half a quartern of ignited brandy, and bedight with Christmas holly stuck into the top."

Dickens, A Christmas Carol

Turk's-Head Mold — 11.114

Tinned steel; 5⅞" diam.; 3¼" deep; 1-qt. capacity. Also avail. 1½ or 2 qts.

$6.00

Stamped on the cover of this mold, in lettering so small that one scarcely sees it, are the words Made in England. Famous for the parliamentary system and for poets, Great Britain is also the home of the steamed pudding, made for generations in molds like this one. This small Turk's-head mold has a pretty fluted dome of tinned steel that fits into the saucer-shaped cover—the base after unmolding. No latches or clamps are required to hold the two parts together because of the vacuum that forms while the pudding steams. A slightly depressed circle at the top of the dome prevents the mold from wobbling when the mold is set on a rack in position for steaming, and a small wire handle on the cover makes it easy to remove the lid when the pudding is done. Ice cream molded in this will assume a beautiful shape, and even the simplest gelatin dessert will have an air of festivity when you turn it out.

Tubeless Fluted Pudding Mold — 11.115

Tinned steel; 5½" diam.; 4¾" deep; 1-qt. capacity.

$18.00

Variation on a theme. This time we show you a classic pudding mold shape without a central tube. Instead, it has been graced with generous fluting. Bernadin de St. Pierre, an eighteenth-century French writer, insisted that the indentations on a melon were meant to make it easier to serve, and the fluting on this heavier-than-usual tinned-steel mold does the same. It is of very solid construction. The cover has two slots along the rim which fit neatly down over two knobs on the edge of the mold, and locks into place with a slight turn. The 1-quart size would make a beautiful blueberry pudding and be equally useful for ice creams or sherbets.

Continued from preceding page

Start with one flavor on the outside and work your way into the interior, chilling as you go.

STEAMED FIG PUDDING

1 cup beef suet
½ pound dried figs, chopped
   (about 1½ cups)
3 cups medium dry coarse breadcrumbs
½ cup milk
3 eggs
1 cup sugar

Fig pudding arrived in the nineteenth century, and was considered not quite as rich as a holiday pudding.

Put the suet and figs together through the fine blade of a food chopper and work them to a paste in a mortar with a pestle or in a bowl with a wooden spoon. Soften the crumbs in the milk and combine them with the paste. Blend in the eggs and sugar, beaten together. Pour the mixture into a pudding mold or a 1-pound coffee tin, cover tightly, and place on a rack over boiling water in a kettle. Cover the kettle and steam the pudding for 3 hours, replenishing the water as needed. Unmold the pudding and serve with Cognac sauce.

Steamed Date Pudding. Substitute pitted dates for figs.

(From AMERICAN COOKERY, by James A. Beard, illustrated by Earl Thollander. Copyright © 1972 by James A. Beard. Reprinted by permission of Little, Brown and Company.)

Charlotte Mold   11.116

Tinned steel; 6″ diam.; 3½″ deep; 1-qt. capacity. Also avail. with capacity of 6 oz., 10 oz., ¾, 1½ or 2 qts.

$11.00 ▲

Ah, what wonders doth the simple charlotte mold perform! Not only will it turn out the fruity baked dessert walled with delicate strips of buttered bread for which it is named, but it will chill and form just about any cold confection from Jello to Bavarian cream. It can also be used for baking things other than puddings. A charlotte mold makes an ideal soufflé dish—its sides are high enough to contain the rising puff without the need of a paper collar, if you match your recipe to your dish. Pure and simple, a charlotte mold is a slightly flared cylinder of tin-washed metal—*tôle étamée*—its only embellishment two heart-shaped handles bracketing its top. The mold shown here also comes with a flat tinned lid that is provided with a plain strip handle. We see it holding a meaty moussaka, molding timbales and gelatin desserts, helping you explore the whole world of puddings —its limits are only those of the cook. It comes in a range of sizes, holding from 6 ounces to 2 quarts. As these molds are reasonably priced, every cook can own an assortment.

"The grateful heart will always inquire— Who was this Charlotte in whose name the apples and other fruits are endowed with a new charm, and become as it were the enchanted apples of a story? . . . She was at one time the most famous of her name in Europe. Napoleon read Goethe's romance of Werther no less than six times, and Charlotte was the heroine of the romance:
   Werther had a love for Charlotte
   Such as words could never utter.
   Would you know how first he met her?
   She was cutting bread and butter."

Kettner's Book of the Table, *1877*

APPLE CHARLOTTE— CHARLOTTE AUX POMMES

10 medium-sized apples
¾ cup butter
½ cup sugar
¼ teaspoon ground cinnamon
1 piece of vanilla bean, 6 inches long
4 tablespoons apricot preserves,
   heated and puréed
12 slices of white bread, crusts removed

Make an apple compote in this way: peel and core the apples, cut them into small pieces, put them in a saucepan with ¼ cup of the butter, and cook them over low heat until they are soft. Stir them frequently to keep them from sticking. Add the sugar, cinnamon and the vanilla bean, halved lengthwise.

Cook slowly for about 15 minutes, until the compote is very thick and reduced. Remove the vanilla bean. Add the apricot-jam purée and mix thoroughly.

Melt the remaining butter and quickly sauté the slices of bread on both sides until golden. Line a 6- to 8-cup charlotte mold with the slices of bread, reserving a few for the top. Spoon the apple compote into the mold and cover the top with the remaining bread slices. Bake the charlotte in a 300 F. oven for 30 minutes. Cool it, chill, and then unmold before serving.

(From LA CUISINE, by Raymond Oliver, translated by Nika Standen Hazelton with Jack Van Bibber. Copyright © 1969 by Tudor Publishing Company. Reprinted by permission of Tudor Publishing Company.)

Open Molds and Ice Cream Molds

Aspic and gelatin desserts, ice cream and blanc-mange—all start life as liquids and end it as solids. The catalyst is cold. Poured into pretty molds, these fluids chill into sumptuous shapes to please the eye as well as the palate. In molds, variety abounds. They come in fanciful baroque designs, all cantilevered plateaus and plazas; in simple fluted patterns for classic tastes; and in shapes to commemorate every holiday from Christmas around the calendar again to Thanksgiving.

Molds for cold shapes are generally made of metal, which cools quickly and thoroughly. The simpler the shape of the mold, the easier it will be to dislodge the contents. A warm, wet towel wrapped around the mold will usually spring your salad or mousse with ease. Alternatively, fill the kitchen sink with lukewarm water and dip the mold in it up to the top edge for a few seconds. Then cover it with a plate or platter, hold on tight, and flip the whole thing over. If the first try fails, repeat. A slick of salad oil over the inside, or a thorough rinsing with ice water before you pour the mixture into the mold, will make unmolding a less than heart-stopping process.

Every housewares department, not to mention every shop that specializes in cookware, stocks a profusion of molds. At one extreme there are disposable ones in heavy aluminum foil, at the other are handsome shapes in metal, porcelain, and copper. We have selected a sampling of the prettiest ones on the basis of both looks and efficiency. Our favorites are also of a quality to last, and they have clearly defined shapes so that what comes out is as appetizing as what goes in.

Antique copper molds are available and beautiful; but this is an instance where copper is more decorative than functional; you don't need copper in a mold for effectiveness in use. Look at Chapter 9 for baking tins that can serve a second function as cold molds.

shape for many dishes made with gelatin—this is one of the prettiest we've seen.

In Thackeray's Pendennis, *an ardent young French chef poetically declares his love by creating a virtually all-white meal to charm the virginal object of his affections, appropriately named Blanche. Among the delicate desserts was "a jelly of marasquin, bland, insinuating, intoxicating as the glance of beauty. This I designated* Ambrosie de Calypso à la Souveraine de mon Coeur. *And when the ice was brought in—an ice of plombière and cherries—how do you think I had shaped them? In the form of two hearts united with an arrow."*

Star-shaped Cold Mold 11.119

Tinned steel; 7″ top diam.; 4¾″ deep; 1-qt. capacity.
$7.50

For a gemlike gelatin dessert or a faceted shimmer of clear aspic, this star mold is perfect. Its design is as crisp as an origami paper sculpture. Made of lightweight tinned steel for quick cooling and easy unmolding, it is deep and high, so a salad or dessert will have see-through sparkle. The mold will hold a quart of liquid and turn it into a glistening edible sculpture worthy to star on any serving table.

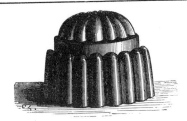

A charlotte russe, from Le Livre de Cuisine *(1874) of Jules Gouffé.*

Aspic Ramekin 11.117

Porcelain; 4″ × 2¾″; 1¾″ deep; 5-oz. capacity.
$2.50

Oeufs mollet, those lightly boiled eggs with a yolk somewhere between soft and hard, can be shelled, encased in sparkling aspic, garnished with garden vegetables, and served as oeufs en gelée—a ravishing first course for a summer meal. These small white oval ramekins are the perfect containers. After the aspic with its delicious burden has set, unmold it on a bed of greens, or serve it as is in this pretty pot. If you are planning to unmold the eggs, decorate the bottom layer of aspic before you place the egg in the cup—use a tiny sprig of tarragon, or tiny shapes cut from olive, pimiento, hard-cooked egg white, or your choice of colorful vegetables. Of simple white porcelain, glazed except for the bases, these ramekins make attractive dishes for a host of other uses, as they are safe in the oven as well as the refrigerator. They can serve as in-dividual terrines for pâté, or to hold a single sauced turban of sole. Versatile, classic, inexpensive.

Fluted Tube Mold 11.118

Tinned steel; 7¼″ diam.; 1½″ deep; ¾-qt. capacity.
$3.75

A fluted ring of tinned steel, a classic with something added, this mold will make almost any aspic or gelatin a joy to the eye of the beholder. Center a rosy ring of tomato aspic with crisp fresh vegetables or a bowl of your own mayonnaise, herb-sprinkled. Think of a homemade cranberry relish molded in this, shimmering on a white platter to accompany your Thanksgiving turkey. Sturdy yet lightweight, the metal will chill its contents quickly and let you unmold with ease. The center tube is welded to a flat metal base which curves into grooved sides. A ring mold is a basic

ABRICOTINE AUX FRAMBOISES— APRICOT ICE CREAM WITH RASPBERRIES

For six people

2 lbs. apricots
1 lb. raspberries
5 T. heavy cream
1 T. gelatine
granulated sugar to taste

Crush the raw apricots and force them through a sieve. Sweeten the pulp quite heavily.

Soften the gelatine in a little cold water, then dissolve by warming it gently. Whip the cream until stiff. Add the gelatine and cream to the apricot pulp and mix well.

Spoon this mixture into an ice cream mold and put the cover on tightly, using a towel between the mold and top so as to seal it well. Put the mold in a bucket filled with crushed ice and rock salt.

Strain the raspberries through a fine sieve; sweeten the pulp and chill it.

Unmold the apricot ice cream, surround it with the chilled raspberry purée, and serve at once.

NOTE: This could also be put in a freezer compartment.

(From ENCYCLOPEDIA OF PRACTICAL GASTRONOMY, by Ali-Bab, translated by Elizabeth Benson. Copyright © 1974 by McGraw-Hill, Inc. Reprinted by permission of McGraw-Hill Book Company.)

Stainless-Steel Rosette Mold 11.120

Stainless steel; 4¼" inside diam.; 3⅜" high; 1-pint capacity. **$20.00**

This is a lovely rosette-shaped ice cream mold. Fill each half of it with softened ice cream. When it firms somewhat, put the two halves of the mold together, attach the clips, and freeze until firm. You might even put a filling of another flavor in the center of each, and create some inner interest. When you are not using these for ice cream, utilize each half to make individual portions of seafood salad or decorative clusters of cottage cheese to garnish a platter of fruit.

Fluted Cold Mold 11.121

Tinned-steel; 5¾" diam.; 2" deep; 3-cup capacity. **$2.75**

This open mold is from the same German manufacturer as the one who supplies the fluted pudding mold we show you (11.115); it is also made of very heavy tinned steel. It is wide and shallow with two concentric circles of bead-like decoration around the bottom. The result is a serviceable and extremely pretty fluted mold for your gelatins, bavarian creams, and mousses. And since there are no narrow crevices, you can be sure that the fantasy with which you fill it will slip out easily, ready to be briefly firmed in the refrigerator, and then garnished and served.

Fluted Ice-Cream Mold 11.122

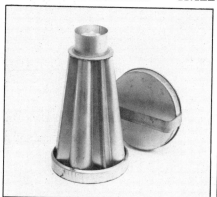

Tinned steel; 5¼" base diam.; 9⅛" high; 1½-qt. capacity. **$25.00**

Looking rather like the art deco pinnacle of a skyscraper, this ice cream mold from France was surely inspired by (if not actually once used for) some of the extravagant *pièces montées* of Carême. Layer it with ice cream, the best you can make or buy, and your guests will want to see you enshrined next to the master. It takes no more effort to fill a decorative mold than a plain one (see 11.123), although more care is required in unmolding. Picture it filled with strawberry ice cream, garnished with whole berries—the results are guaranteed to dazzle. This mold holds a full 1½ quarts, enough to close an elaborate dinner in style.

Peak-shaped Mold 11.123

11.123
Stainless steel; 5" base diam.; 2" top diam.; 7½" high; 1-qt. capacity. **$19.60**

Make a jumbo ice-cream peak in this stainless-steel, one-quart container. The conical shape is graceful and lends itself to all sorts of possibilities. It can form a creamy Matterhorn of vanilla to be avalanched with chocolate sauce before serving; or make a festive Delectable Mountain by layering one flavor atop another. Stud molded plain ice cream with fruits or nuts, decorate it with dragées or jimmies—festive fare. This is a heavy mold which sits firmly on a circle of metal at its rounded narrow end, and on a rimmed tray at the opening. The cylinder is one solid piece of metal—no danger of leaks, and no mark of a seam to mar the perfect surface of your dessert.

Some suggestions by Carême, in his Patissier Royal, *for molded and garnished gelatine desserts.*

'Let's make ice-cream!' Royal shouted.

"Eliza Jane loved ice-cream. She hesitated, and said, 'Well—'

"Almanzo ran after Royal to the ice-house. They dug a block of ice out of the sawdust and put it in a grain sack. They laid the sack on the back porch and pounded it with hatchets till the ice was crushed. Alice came out to watch them while she whipped egg-whites on a platter. She beat them with a fork, till they were too stiff to slip when she tilted the platter.

"Eliza measured milk and cream, and dipped up sugar from the barrel in the pantry. It was not common maple sugar, but white sugar bought from the store. Mother used it only when company came. Eliza Jane dipped six cupfuls, then she smoothed the sugar that was left, and you would hardly have missed any.

"She made a big milk-pail full of yellow custard. They set the pail in a tub and packed the snowy crushed ice around it, with salt, and they covered it all with a blanket. Every few minutes they took off the blanket and uncovered the pail, and stirred the freezing ice-cream. When it was frozen, Alice brought saucers and spoons, and Almanzo brought out a cake and the butcher knife. He cut enormous pieces of cake, while Eliza Jane heaped the saucers. They could eat all the ice-cream and cake they wanted to; no one would stop them."

Laura Ingalls Wilder, Farmer Boy, Harper & Row, New York, 1933

Spumoni Mold 11.124

Aluminum; 3¾″ diam.; 4″ high; 1¾-cup capacity. Also avail. 2½″ diam., 2¼″ high, 5-oz. capacity.

$2.25

This aluminum mold from Italy is meant to make spumoni, that Italian ice-cream, fruit, and nut confection that is molto dolce. It looks like a miniature beehive sitting on a saucerlike tray. You line it with ice cream and freeze until firm; then you fill the center with a mixture of ice cream, almonds, and chopped preserved fruit. Freeze again, then unmold your creation and serve it forth. This comes in two sizes: the individual mold holds just over half a cup of this ambrosia, the larger one, 1¾ cups to be divided among three or four diners with a sweet tooth.

Square Ice-Cream Mold 11.125

Tinned steel; 4¾″ square; 2⅝″ deep; 3-cup capacity. Also avail. with capacity of 1 cup, 2 cups, 1, or 1½ qts.

$7.40

This square mold, as classic a design as the bombe, builds equally elegant ice-cream edifices. Its only decoration is a raised rosette to give the frozen dessert a fluted dome. Made of tinned steel, the mold has overlapping edges similar to envelope flaps, soldered and riveted to the sides so it will be leakproof. It is covered by a square, rimmed lid that protects the contents securely during storage in the freezer. The mold comes in five sizes ranging from individual—1 cup—to a party-size 1½ quarts.

Rectangular Ice-Cream Mold 11.126

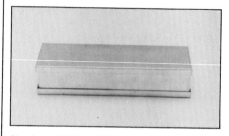

Aluminum; 9¾″ × 3¼″; 2″ deep; 1-qt. capacity.

$8.00

You can assemble your own tri-flavored brick ice cream—vanilla, strawberry, and chocolate—in this rectangular ice-cream mold. It comes in three pieces. The top and bottom are rimmed sheets of aluminum, the center a separate hollow frame of the same metal. This construction makes unmolding a breeze, since both top and bottom are detachable from the sides. Put the sides in place over the bottom, layer the ice cream in, flavor by flavor, cover everything with the top, and freeze—nothing could be simpler than creating this Neapolitan delight. Or interleave any favorite flavors of ice cream with thin slivers of left-over pound cake for a sweet surprise in every slice. Baked Alaska, that magical merger of meringue, ice cream, and cake, starts with a basic rectangle of rock-hard ice cream—begin with this mold which will freeze the core of the dessert in that classic shape. We like this mold for its utility, but also for its clean-lined good looks.

Set of Three Nested Molds 11.127

Aluminum; set of 3; 5¾″, 7″, and 8″ diam.; each 2″ deep.

$11.00

Brides and grooms who have a fitting love and respect for ice cream can have a three-tier wedding "cake" made of their favorite flavors with this set of molds. Similar in size and shape to cake pans, the three aluminum rounds are different in construction. Each has a rimmed top and a rimmed bottom, and the sides consist of an overlapping strip of aluminum that is held in shape by the rims of the bottom and the cover. This makes it extremely easy to unmold your dessert without the use of heat. The largest mold is 8", the medium one 7", and the smallest 5¾" in diameter. They may, of course, be used separately. When they are not shaping frozen treats they nest neatly for storage.

Coeur à la Crème Mold 11.128

Porcelain; 3¼" X 2¾"; 1½" deep. Also avail. 6¾" X 6", 1⅞" deep.

$5.00 ▲

"Where the French, in my opinion, do not compare with the English is in the matter of puddings and sweets. But always, when Monsieur Saint-Hilaire is expected, there is his favorite coeur à la crème. This is a kind of sweet cream cheese, shaped like a heart, and with it was served a large dish of tiny, very ripe fraises des bois which were truly delicious. There was sugar, but without the cream which always accompanies strawberries in England." A young British girl made that entry in her diary on a visit to her French aunt in 1876. Coeur à la crème (recipe), and the molds in which to make it, have not changed in the last century. Small chaste hearts of porcelain with pierced bottoms allow the excess liquid in the sweetened cream cheese to run off as it is chilled. Each container must first be lined with dampened cheesecloth, then filled; the cheese hearts sit in the refrigerator in their porcelain shells on scalloped lips which hold them above the drained liquid as they chill thoroughly. Unmold and unwrap the coeur à la crème, then serve it with

whole fresh berries or, perhaps, a translucent crimson or golden fruit sauce or more cream, thick and fresh. The large heart makes one dessert to serve six diners, but we'd prefer to own a batch of the small molds, as we like the look of each individual heart bedded on a grape leaf and wreathed with strawberries. Wicker baskets are also available to make coeur à la crème—they are satisfactory, but not as sturdy or as sanitary as these china ones.

Paskha, the rich Russian cream-cheese confection served at Easter, was acquired from the Byzantine world. Carême was introduced to it when he served as chef to Alexander I of Russia, and he took the recipe back to France, where he had the idea of molding the mixture in heart forms. Thus were created coeurs à la crème, often served with thick fresh cream or tiny woodland strawberries.

COEURS A LA CREME

The three fresh fruit sauces are for variation from menu to menu. Each will suffice for the six little hearts, and only one sauce is usually served at a time. To make the hearts, you need six 3-inch coeur à la crème wicker baskets or china molds and a length of cheesecloth (see below).

Ice water, baking soda, and
   lemon juice (for cheesecloth)
½ pound cream cheese
⅔ cup confectioners sugar
Scraping of half a vanilla bean
1¼ cups heavy cream, whipped
Optional: 6 large fresh grape
   leaves (for serving)
STRAWBERRY SAUCE
2 cups fresh strawberries
¼ cup Framboise (raspberry brandy)
1 cup seedless black raspberry jam

RASPBERRY SAUCE
2 cups fresh raspberries
1 cup red currant jelly
¼ cup light rum

PEACH SAUCE
3 cups thinly sliced fresh peaches
1 cup strained apricot jam
¼ cup Drambuie

Prepare six 3-inch coeur à la crème wicker baskets or china molds as follows. From a length of 4 thicknesses of cheesecloth, cut 6 squares, each large enough to line a mold plus a 2-inch margin all

around. Mix a bowl of ice water with 1 tablespoon lemon juice and a pinch of baking soda. Soak the cheesecloth squares in this liquid until you are ready to fill the molds. Put the cream cheese in a mixer bowl and beat until it is light and fluffy. Add the confectioners' sugar and vanilla bean scraping and continue beating. Fold the mixture carefully into the whipped cream. Wring the squares of cheesecloth damp-dry and line the little molds, leaving the 2-inch overhang all around. Spoon the cream mixture into the molds and fold the extra cheesecloth over the tops. Stand them on a rack in a jelly roll pan and chill them in the refrigerator at least 2 hours. To serve, unmold and unwrap each cream heart onto a large fresh grape leaf on a crystal dessert plate. Serve with a separate bowl of one of the sauces.

If wicker basket molds are used, serve them on the grape leaf, with each person unwrapping his own.

STRAWBERRY SAUCE. If the strawberries are large, cut them in halves or quarters. Put them in a bowl and sprinkle with the Framboise. Melt the jam over low heat and strain it over the strawberries. Chill at least 1 hour.

RASPBERRY SAUCE. Melt the jelly over low heat. Mix in the rum, and strain. Chill the sauce and raspberries separately at least 1 hour. Mix just before serving.

PEACH SAUCE. Pour the Drambuie over the peaches. Melt the jam over low heat and rub it through a fine wire strainer (if it is too thick, add a little boiling water). Mix the apricot sauce with the peaches, and chill at least 1 hour.

Net: 6 servings

(From THE DIONE LUCAS BOOK OF FRENCH COOKING, by Dione Lucas and Marion Gorman, illustrated by Joseph S. Patti. Copyright © 1947 by Dione Lucas. Reprinted by permission of Little, Brown and Company.)

Nineteenth-century molds for "jellies."

Plastic Gelatin Molds 11.129

Plastic; set of 4, each 3⅜″ diam., 1¾″ deep, 4-oz. capacity.

$2.50

These small molds could be mistaken for sandbox toys, and indeed, a set of them might be the perfect present for a beach-going toddler. Sunny yellow, zinnia orange, sky blue, and chocolate brown, these four plastic molds are safe for small fingers. When not making mud pies, they can be used for more edible ingredients. Set the little ones to work making Jello to chill into these pretty flower shapes, or mold ice cream in them. For good-for-growing-bodies desserts, sweeten orange juice, thicken it with gelatin, and punctuate it with commas of orange slices—there will be no complaints about the vitamins ingested. These molds are so inexpensive that you can buy several sets for the kitchen as well as the toy chest.

Thistle Butter Print 11.130

Hardwood; 3¾″ diam.; 1¼″ thick.

$4.75

Antique stores abound with butter molds of a certain age. These carved wooden blocks were in constant use in the good old days when butter came right from the churn. Today they are collector's items, but the function they performed is still a valid one. This modern butter print echoes the antiques: the hand-carved piece of wood is deeply etched with a thistle flower and its spiky leaves. The thick disc, 3¾ inches in diameter, is buffed to a satin gloss on its working side and on its slightly indented circumference, while the flat top surface is sanded smooth. Dip the model in ice water, then press it on pats of slightly softened butter to make pretty pictures for your table.

Thomas Jefferson's six granddaughters kept little books in which they neatly wrote down the recipes learned at Monticello. The small volume entitled "Creams etc." contains these directions for making cups of chocolate cream, really a junket, which was no easy mat-ter at the time: "Put on your milk, 1 quart to 2 squares of chocolate; boil it away one quarter. Take it off, let it cool and sweeten it. Lay a napkin in a bowl, put three gizzards in the napkin and pass the cream through it four times, as quick as possible, one person rubbing the gizzards with a spoon while another pours. Put in cups and set the cups in cold water half way up their sides. Set the water on the fire, cover it, and put fire on the top. As soon as the water boils take the cups out and set them to cool." The "gizzards" used for this pudding were only the dried inside skins of poultry gizzards, which were removed, washed, and dried as soon as the chicken was killed, and kept in a dry place for storage. They had the same effect on milk as rennet; both caused it to clabber.

Thomas Jefferson's Cook Book, by Marie Kimbal, Garrett and Massie, 1949

Ice-Cream Makers and Serving Accessories

When Marco Polo dined on frozen desserts in the mysterious East, first among Westerners of his age of the world to go there, ice cream and its relations were already several centuries old. Legend has it that Alexander the Great had a weakness for cold confections, though it must have been rarely indulged, as ice was hard to come by in the fourth century B.C.—his frozen desserts are likely to have been based on snow brought to him from the mountains by couriers, just as Roman emperors had their slaves run with Alpine snow to Rome. Woe betide the slow mover—the infamous Nero is said to have executed the general in charge when the snow melted en route.

The exact date when ice cream became the cold creamy sweet we know and love today is lost in the mists of time. From our earliest days as a nation, it has been America's favorite dessert. George Washington owned a "cream machine for making ice," and Thomas Jefferson's French vanilla ice cream (see recipe) is still in use today. Credit an American woman for automating ice-cream making: in 1846, one Nancy Johnson took a wooden bucket, filled it with ice and salt, and fitted within it a metal can equipped with beaters powered by a crank— the first mechanical ice-cream freezer had been born! Unfortunately for Nancy, she didn't patent her invention, and imitations proliferated. Soon ice-cream parlors and soda shoppes bloomed on city streets and in country villages alike—ice cream had become big business.

Today the rich homemade ice cream enjoyed by our forebears is mainly a memory. Packaged in plastic or paper, larded with stabilizers, neutralizers, preservatives, and artificial flavors, ice cream is sold in every supermarket; and only a few fussy manufacturers use the pure and rich ingredients of yore. Gone are the simple Sunday get-togethers on the back porch, with everyone taking a turn cranking the freezer, the children eagerly awaiting their chance to lick the dashers. For those who want to recapture that old-fashioned taste, if not the effort required to produce it, electric ice-cream makers are the answer. They whip air into the cream mixture as it freezes, preventing the formation of ice crystals and producing a frothy, smooth texture. And for those who want to do the whole bit by hand—or rather by arm—we also include an excellent hand-cranked freezer.

We show a variety of the best machines we have tested, in addition to scoops and spades for removing either the homemade or the store-bought variety from the container. If you have made your own ice cream, you will probably want to serve it with flair. Molded into one of the pretty shapes made by the molds in this chapter, it becomes an elegant and luscious dessert—special-occasion food that couldn't be more fun to eat.

ICE-CREAM MAKERS

"I scream, you scream, we all scream for ice cream"—who doesn't remember that childish punning? In all seriousness, the shouts will be louder if the ice cream is made with tender hands at home. Even plain vanilla tastes better when it is made with pure ingredients and left untreated with tetrasodium pyrophosphate or any of the other tongue-twisters which adulterate most commercial ice creams. Then, too, you can make many flavors not found in the supermarket—even the famous Baskin-Robbins thirty-seven varieties don't boast such esoteric flavors as James Beard's Boston brown bread, or what do you say to quince?

Give in to the temptation to buy a big basket of ripe peaches and turn them all into that sublime experience—fresh peach ice cream. Almost any fruit or flavor—even peanut butter—can be combined with cream and sugar and frozen to make a delicious dessert. But a word of caution —don't, in an excess of enthusiasm, make an enormous quantity: ice cream stored for several months develops ice crystals on top and a leaden texture within. On the other hand, it may be quite safe to make quite a lot—we defy you not to consume your own product at once and scream for more.

ICE-CREAM QUALITY AND WHAT IT COSTS

This is one area where making-it-at-home turns out to be more expensive than buying-it-in-the-store. Heavy cream and sugar are expensive, so even if you have bought your fruit at a bargain-basement price, your homemade ice cream is going to be more costly than store-bought. It will also be richer, with less overrun—less air beaten into it—than the commercial kind. If you are going into ice-cream production in a big way, a hydrometer (see Chapter 1) is an asset—with one of these you can measure the amount of sugar in solution—many a batch of ice cream or sherbet has turned into a runny mess because of the anti-freeze effect of too large an amount of sugar. Since all fruit contains natural sugar, the amount to be added can often be a by-guess-and-by-golly affair unless you have a professional testing instrument.

PEAR SHERBET

This pear sherbet of Carol Cutler's is nominated by one of our experts as one of the loveliest desserts of all. She sometimes serves it in poached pear halves, and sometimes when she makes it she adds a very few drops of pear liqueur, a clove, and a strip of lemon peel to the poaching syrup in which the fruit for the sherbet is cooked; this is especially good when the fresh pears are a bit lacking in flavor.

PEAR SHERBET

This is a superb dessert that is surprising for the purity of its flavor. Eating it is like biting into the coolest, freshest pear possible. Flavor like this cannot be bought prepackaged.

8 servings

1¼ cups sugar
1¼ cups water
3 pounds good quality eating pears
½ lemon
3 tablespoons lemon juice
1 egg white

In a flat pan boil the sugar and water together for 10 minutes covered; this will make a light syrup. Meanwhile, peel, core, and quarter the pears and drop them immediately into a bowl of cold water in which you have squeezed the ½ lemon. The lemon will prevent the pears from turning brown.

Remove the pears from the cold water and drop them into the bubbling syrup and cover. Simmer slowly until they are soft and a sharp knife will pierce their pulp easily. This should take 15 to 20 minutes. Turn the pears once during the cooking and baste a few times. Let them cool in the syrup.

Drain the fruit, reserving the syrup. Pass the pears through a food mill. A food mill is better than a blender since it will screen out any thick fibers that may have remained. There should be about 1 quart of purée. Add lemon juice and egg white (very lightly beaten) and mix well. Taste; if you would like a sweeter flavor, add some of the syrup. Put the purée in an ice cream freezer, or in an ice cube tray. Once the sherbet is hard, remove and beat it until it becomes very fluffy. Then refreeze in a serving mold.

(From HAUTE CUISINE FOR YOUR HEART'S DELIGHT, by Carol Cutler. Copyright © 1973 by Carol Cutler. Reprinted by permission of Clarkson N. Potter, Inc.)

Continued from preceding page

If you are making fruit-flavored ice cream, save the pits and the skins when you prepare the fruit and simmer them in the cream you are going to use. The flavor will be intensified and the ice cream will be tinted a delicate shade of the fruit's color. A small amount of brandy or liqueur added to the mixture makes a sophisticated dessert, but be sure to pour it with a light hand, as too much alcohol inhibits the freezing process—you may wish to flame the liqueur before adding it, to dissipate the alcohol while retaining the taste. After your ice cream is made it must be packed in containers and frozen for several hours—this is called seasoning or ripening. Placate the eager children by giving them the dashers to lick and the can to scrape while the ice cream hardens.

THE CRANK VERSUS THE ELECTRIC MOTOR

The hand-cranked ice-cream freezer, which developed Mr. America-class muscles in many a growing arm, is still on the market, but it is less popular since the advent of electric models. A crank freezer is less expensive and is certainly a good bet for country homes where electricity is absent or unreliable. But it is easier on mind and body to let the electric company turn the crank. Electric ice-cream makers come in three varieties—the bucketlike affairs which are first cousins to the hand-cranked models of old; small-capacity types which make ice cream in your freezer, only about a quart at a time; and those that are accessories to the larger multipurpose machines such as food mixers.

The independent ice-cream maker, whether turned by an electric motor or your arm, still requires crushed ice and rock salt in the outer bucket, plus careful timing. A wooden mallet (see "Seafood Tools" in Chapter 11) is a handy tool for ice crushing. Put the ice in a canvas or burlap bag, and be sure to wear rubber gloves when handling the rock salt and ice, as you can "burn" your hands. Once the ice cream has begun to thicken heavily, the ice-cream maker run by electricity must be turned off immediately lest the motor overheat or even burn out. These freezers usually have a large capacity, so you can make several quarts of the same flavor at a time. The freezers that are accessories for larger kitchen machines work on the same principle as independent ones.

THE FREEZER DWELLERS

Modern technology has given us ice-cream makers that are put into the freezer for use. These, of course, need no crushed ice and no rock salt. However, you must have a large separate freezer or a double-door refrigerator-freezer which maintains a very low temperature, ideally zero or below. These are necessarily quite small and will only produce about a quart at a time. Although they do not have Underwriters' Laboratory approval because the cord must pass between the door of the freezer and the frame, we found them to be quite safe in use. Note and follow the manufacturer's instructions concerning safety precautions, such as the use of a grounded outlet.

FRENCH VANILLA ICE CREAM— THOMAS JEFFERSON'S RECIPE

2 bottles good cream [2 pints heavy cream]
6 yolks of eggs
½ lb sugar [1 cup sugar]

Mix the yolks and sugar. Put the cream on a fire in a casserole, first putting in a stick of vanilla. [Omit vanilla bean if using vanilla extract.] When near boiling take it off and pour it gently into the mixture of eggs and sugar. Stir it well. Put it on the fire again, stirring it thoroughly with a spoon to prevent it sticking to the casserole. When near boiling take it off and strain it through a towel [sieve]. [If using vanilla extract, add 2 tsp. at this point.] Put it in the sorbetière, etc. [Freeze according to manufacturer's directions for your ice-cream freezer.]

"There would also be ice cream: This I could hardly believe, for ice cream, real ice cream frozen with ice, was a rarity such as no child born of these days and fairly cradled in a cone could understand. With a lake or pond on every third farm, more or less, and ice to be had for the cutting, only one farmer in a hundred, or less, had an ice house. He who did, and could have ice cream every Sunday, was a Croesus amongst us."

Della T. Lutes, The Country Kitchen, *Little, Brown and Company, 1936*

Ice-cream fanatics will probably want to own both an independent and a freezer-type ice-cream maker. After testing dozens of each variety and having a delicious time doing it, we have singled out the best of each type. And, for those who have never forgotten the delights of malts and milkshakes, we show you a professional-quality milkshake machine to help you use the output of your freezer.

Hand-cranked Ice-Cream Freezer 11.131

Pine tub, tin-plated steel can, tinned cast-iron mixers, beechwood scrapers, and cadmium-plated fixtures; 2-qt. capacity. Also avail. with capacity of 4, 6, 8, 10, 12, or 20 qts.
$34.00

For nostalgia's sake we show this crank-style ice-cream freezer—a throwback to the back-porch variety of our pre-Frigidaire forebears. We hope you can enlist tribes of willing children to provide the power if you choose this one. It is made by the Tiffany of freezer manufacturers, White Mountain, and, like all their products, is of excellent quality. The large outside tub resembles the old oaken bucket of yore, but this one is of maple-stained pine secured with metal hoops. All the metal parts that come in contact with the ice cream are tin-coated, so today's vanilla will not bear the lingering taste of yesterday's peach; and, more important, the steel will resist the rust - encouraging onslaughts of the rock salt you will use. A metal bridge fits across the top of the tub to hold the dashers and the crank, which operates with a three-gear drive for smooth operation. All other fixtures are cadmium-plated. The freezer comes in sizes making from 2 to 20 quarts. We can't imagine anything less than a school or a commune using the larger sizes, but the smaller ones are suitable for a family of eager-beaver ice-cream eaters.

Household Electric Ice-Cream Freezer 11.132

Pine tub, tin-plated steel can, tinned cast-iron mixers, beechwood scrapers, and cadmium-plated fixtures; 4-qt. capacity. Also avail. with capacity of 6 qts.

$65.00 ▲

Put the tin-plated can holding your chilled ice-cream ingredients in place in this handsome maple-finished pine bucket, surround the can with crushed ice and rock salt, affix the motor unit to the top, plug it in, and relax. In 20 minutes you will have either 4 or 6 quarts of the creamiest, smoothest ice cream imaginable and no sweat on your brow. White Mountain has been manu-facturing ice-cream freezers for more than 100 years—this one is the *ne plus ultra* of their line. Like their hand-cranked model above, this freezer is tin-plated in every part which will touch the ice cream. It will operate on either alternating or direct current, and you can, of course, make less than a full batch in either size. For all this beauty and efficiency you will pay a premium price.

Salton Ice-Cream Machine 11.133

Plastic housing with tinned-steel can; 8" diam.; 8" high; 1-qt. capacity.
$20.00 ▲

Salton, the Hotray people, have turned their attention to the opposite end of the temperature spectrum with this ice-cream machine for use inside your freezer. The efficient 55-watt motor, which has a top-mounted fan to prevent overheating, is housed in a plastic dome that is appropriately colored vanilla, chocolate, or strawberry. The motor unit fits onto a round white plastic base that holds the tinned-steel can with its plastic lid and dashers. The entire unit disassembles for easy and thorough cleaning. The 7½-foot cord is covered with a woven wire braid to protect it as it passes through the freezer door, and it is attached to a three-pronged plug which grounds the appliance for maximum safety. (Be sure your wall outlet itself is grounded; if it won't accept the plug of this machine, you can add an inexpensive adapter plug.) Only 8 inches high, the unit fits neatly on the freezer shelf and makes a quart of ice cream with nary a worry about overheating the motor of a conventional freezer, with no ice crushing, and no need for rock salt. The energy-conscious will welcome the fact that only a penny's worth of electricity is used to make each quart of ice cream. However, this object is no beauty and it consumes more freezer space than the French model we show you next. Its advantages are availability and a motor strong enough to keep going until the cream is of a reasonable consistency. Then the dashers lift and the motor shuts off.

STRAWBERRY SORBET

Serves 6-8

2 pints strawberries
3 cups sugar
1 cup hot water
4 tablespoons lemon juice
2-quart electric ice-cream freezer
Freezing salt
2 egg whites

Wash and hull strawberries in that order. Purée in a food mill or force through a wire sieve or strainer. Do not use a blender.

In a heavy pan, dissolve the sugar in hot water. When completely dissolved, bring to a boil over high heat. As it reaches a rolling boil, the temperature will be 216 F. If you have a candy thermometer, use it to test. Take pan off heat immediately and chill syrup over iced water. When cold, mix with strawberry purée and lemon juice and pour into ice-cream freezer.

Pack the space around the container with alternating layers of crushed ice and freezing salt in proportions of three parts ice to one part salt, using 2-cup measures as the unit. Put dasher and lid in place, start the motor and freeze for 20 minutes.

Beat egg whites with a pinch of salt until they hold soft peaks.

Remove cover from freezer and remove dasher. Stir in beaten egg whites and reassemble the ice-cream maker. Freeze for another 20 minutes.

(From THE GREAT COOKS COOKBOOK, by The Good Cooking Scool. Copyright © 1974 by The Good Cooking School, Inc. Reprinted by permission of Ferguson/Doubleday.)

SEB Ice-Cream Maker   11.135

Plastic housing with aluminum can; 8¾" diam.; 4" high; 1-qt. capacity.
$21.95

Trust the French to think of the most beautiful way to make homemade ice cream—this ice-cream maker, which you set inside your freezer, with the cord extending outside to an electric outlet, turns out that frozen confection in elegant circles. One of our testers made batch after batch of one-quart ice-cream rings, unmolded them, and stored them in plastic bags in the freezer. Months of party-perfect desserts then awaited brandied fruit, silken butterscotch, rich chocolate sauce, or any one of a thousand other accompaniments. The motor of this machine is a separate unit which fits in the center of the ring-shaped aluminum freezer unit. The plastic dashers attach to a knob in the center of the motor housing and move around the ring to agitate the mixture during freezing, lifting automatically when the ice cream is done. You then remove the ice cream at your leisure; it will stay safely frozen meanwhile. The whole unit is topped with a bright red plastic lid, and everything comes apart for easy cleaning. This freezer is not as rapid as the Salton machine—it takes an hour or so to produce a quart of ice cream. The beautiful result, however, is worth waiting for.

Milkshake Machine   11.136

Enameled and stainless-steel base with stainless-steel malt cup; base 6¾" × 6½"; 19⅜" high overall; malt cup 4" diam., 7" high, 1-qt. capacity.
$97.50

A milkshake by another name is a malt or a malted milk or a frappé. What you call that cool, calorific drink made basically with milk, ice cream, and flavoring whipped to a froth depends on where you live. For our part, visions of chocolate malts danced through our heads when we received this milkshake machine from Hamilton Beach; suddenly we were kids again, sipping sodas through a straw at the Sweet Shoppe. We covet the machine, but we remember our age and station—and the calorie content of a malt. Well, we can make more sophisticated beverages—daiquiris, whiskey sours, planter's punch—and we'll let the little ones use the machine for the fattening frappés—if they'll give us a sip. This machine is a slim, elegant version of the one down at the ice-cream parlor. A tall, strongly built, enamel and stainless-steel base has mounted on it the mixing spindle and a support for the stainless-steel malt cup which holds a lot—1 quart. Plug it in, attach the cup holding the ingredients, and in a whir you have a scrumptious strawberry, chilly chocolate, or perfect pineapple milkshake, or enough cocktails to delight the most ardent dipsomaniac.

With passionate prose, this turn-of-the century gastronome defends ice cream: "What a wave of grateful coolness the ice and its yet more seductive sister, ice-cream, contribute when the dog-star reigns and cicadas have begun to shrill. Who among the calumniators of sweets would wish them banished in support of a fallacious theory that sweetmeats render woman more capricious, and are injurious to the roses and lilies of her skin?"

George Ellwanger, The Pleasures of the Table, 1902

ICE-CREAM SCOOPS AND SPADES

Many a bent spoon has emerged, frustrated, from a container of rock-hard ice cream to the oaths or wails of the cook. Special scoops are designed to deal with this problem and to give each serving, no matter how firmly frozen, a neat shape. Ice-cream servers can be as simple in construction as a garden trowel, or fairly complicated mechanical affairs with springs, levers, and ratchets. Wherever they fit on that continuum, all the ones our experts have chosen will present your ice cream efficiently and neatly. We recommend that you let frozen desserts soften somewhat before scooping them, however, not because our tools can't cope with even the most concrete confection, but because both ice cream and sherbet taste better when they are not cold enough to freeze your taste buds in their tracks.

Atlas Ice-Cream Scoop 11.139

Stainless steel with phenolic-resin handle; 8½" long; 2⅝" diam.; capacity 12 scoops per qt. Also avail. with capacity of 8, 10, 16, 20, 24, 30, or 40 scoops per qt.
$7.50

If you want professional-looking ice-cream cones or sundaes that look as if they have come from the Sweet Shoppe, a mechanical ice-cream scoop is for you. This one has as its working end a stainless-steel hemisphere fitted with a scraper. Dig the dipper into the ice cream, lift, press the spring-operated lever with your thumb, and the scraper dislodges a perfect sphere of ice cream. A small cog rides smoothly across a ratchet to operate the scraper and perform the magic. The working parts are all stainless steel for smooth and sanitary operation, the handle a comfortable grip affair of black plastic, similar to that on a screwdriver. The dipper comes in eight sizes, shaping from 8 to 40 scoops per quart; each one wears a different color at the base of the grip, for the guidance of the professionals who use this utensil.

Zeroll Dipper 11.137

Cast aluminum; 7½" overall; scoop 2⅛" × 1⅝"; 2½-oz. capacity. Also avail. with capacity of 1½ or 2 oz.

$7.50 ▲

At first glance this ice-cream dipper seems a simple tool, but the secret of its success is hidden from the eye. Encased within the hollow body is a liquid chemical with properties that keep it warm relative to frozen things, so it allows you to shovel out the hardest ice cream in neat oval scoops. The dipper is made of one piece of seamless aluminum with a sealed handle, so the fluid cannot leak out. It comes in three sizes, rated as 12 to 24, which means that it will remove that many scoops from each quart of ice cream; in terms of servings, you can have 1½ ounces, 2 ounces, or 2½ ounces (the size shown here). No effort is needed to operate this scoop—a fact that even the smallest ice-cream lover in your house will appreciate.

Ice-Cream Dipper and Spade Set 11.138

Cast aluminum; spade 8¾" long; dipper 7" long; 2-oz. capacity. Dipper also avail. with capacity of 1½ or 2½ oz.

$6.60 set

Double dippers for serious ice-cream consumers and creators come packaged in a set. The dipper is a slightly smaller version of the Zeroll dipper above, the spade a single sturdy piece of solid aluminum, as simple as a child's sand shovel—you'll see the identical model in your local ice-cream store, where it is used for hand-packing your purchase into a carton. At home you'll find its broad, flat surface handy for filling ice-cream molds or for ladling your soft, newly made ice cream from the freezer can into storage containers for ripening. A delightful, albeit reasonably priced, gift for any ice-cream addict.

477

"Hokey-pokey" was, around the turn of the century, the name for a common kind of ice cream sold in slabs, particularly by street vendors. In Cambridge, England, the hokey-pokey man would arrive with his ice-cream barrow and striped red awning supported on twisted brass poles. Children greeted these vendors with the chanting of:

Hokey-pokey, penny a lump,
The more you eat the more you jump.
Or sometimes they'd sing:
Here's the stuff to make you jump
Hokey-pokey, penny a lump.
The vendors were often said to be Italian, and hokey-pokey may derive from their hawking their wares with the cry "O che poco!" (Oh, how little!).

Cambridgeshire Customs and Folklore, by Enid Porter. Routledge and Kegan Paul, London, 1969

Conical Ice-Cream Scoop 11.140

Stainless steel with plastic handle; 8" long; 2½" diam.; capacity 12 scoops per qt. Also avail. with capacity of 16 scoops per qt.
$11.50
Small peaked mountains of ice cream to sit atop a cone or perch on a piece of cake come from this ice-cream scoop. The conical body is made of heavy stainless steel attached to a round black plastic handle, grooved for a good grip. The lever you press to release the ice cream you have scooped up is fitted with teeth that mesh with a small cog in the top of the scoop—this operates the scraper within the bowl, which has two vent holes so the contents are easily dislodged. This scoop comes in sizes 12

and 16—meaning either 12 or 16 scoops per quart—for large- and medium-sized portions.

Chromed Brass Ice-Cream Scoop 11.141

Chrome-plated brass with stainless-steel spring; 9" long; 2" diam.; capacity 24 scoops per qt. Also avail. with capacity of 12, 16, 20, 30, 36, 40, 50, 60, 65, 70, or 100 scoops per qt.
$13.25
Billed as a food server, this ice-cream scoop from West Germany comes in a dozen sizes. The tiniest will make melon balls or scoop a hundred tiny spheres from a quart of ice cream. The largest is for the gourmand dessert eater, but it can also mold cottage cheese into neat round shapes for luncheon plates or make globes instead of globs of mashed potatoes. Similar in shape and function to the other scoops we've shown you, this one is slightly different in the mechanics. Rather than moving a thumb-operated lever, you work it by squeezing the handles together. This compresses a spring between the handles and causes a small grooved cog to ride across a toothed plate and push the scraper around the bowl. The whole thing is made of solid brass, heavily chrome-plated, with a nonrusting stainless-steel spring. You'll pay a bit more for this excellent quality; whether it's worth it or not will depend upon the requirements of your dessert (or mashed-potato) department.

Thomas Jefferson, a devoted and innovative gastronome, copied down directions for making ice cream [see recipe] while he was in France, and he served it

for the first time in the United States at a state banquet during his Presidency. George Washington is said to have made ice cream, Alexander Hamilton served it, too, and Dolley Madison later made it fashionable.

Ice Cream–Cone Maker 11.142

Cast-aluminum mold with stainless-steel rod and wood handle; mold 2" diam., 2½" high; rod 10" long.
$1.75
Now here's a novel idea for true do-it-yourself ice-cream fans: a cone-maker. Once you've made your own ice-cream, why not make your own cones? For the price of a few boxes of the commercial (and usually stale) kind, you can own this device and turn out fresh cones at will. A long handle screws into a threaded fitting on the inside of the cupcake-shaped aluminum mold; once assembled, you dip the mold into batter, then into a bath of hot, deep fat. A recipe for the batter, along with all the cooking instructions, is printed on the package. Seaside dwellers who find that purchased cones become soggy overnight can make a fresh batch daily with this doohickey. And, in these parlous times, your cones will be cheaper as well as better tasting.

Ice-cream making as a heavenly art: frontispiece of a treatise published in 1768.

We think of cooking at the table as a sophisticated art, practiced in soignée restaurants and in the homes of talented cooks, but it has its origins in the cave man's campfire. No longer a necessity, today it is done to provide pleasure for the guests and kicks for the cook. Let's face it, there's a bit of ham in all of us, and there comes a time when we want to show off our skills. And rather than being sequestered over a hot stove in the kitchen, it's fun to star with style before an admiring audience, whether putting on a pyrotechnical display with flaming liqueurs for a spectacular dessert or cooking sukiyaki from a beautifully arranged tray of ingredients. Whatever the dish, a special heat source is required for cooking at the table.

Braziers and hibachis originated in the Far East, where tableside cookery can be a mannered rite. Fondue is democratic fare from serene Switzerland: there each person pops his own bite of bread into a common pot of melted cheese set over a table burner. In France, elegance prevails in the realm of haute cuisine—crêpes are flamed at the table by a chef or skilled waiter over an alcohol stove, omelets are turned from the pan onto hot plates by an omelet-making artist.

Travel broadens; peripatetic Americans have admired all these methods of cooking at the table and found them adaptable to our informal way of life. Soon the backyard barbecue had moved indoors to the dining room. Fondue pots popped up at family suppers, flaming desserts finished company dinners. American ingenuity improved on the fuels used in other countries. Kerosene and denatured alcohol continued to have their place, but Sterno was safer; butane and propane, although expensive, were cleaner; electricity more dependable.

WHAT TO LOOK FOR

A great variety of burners and stoves are available for tabletop or tableside cookery, so choices must be made. The accomplished omelet cook will want a burner capable of achieving and maintaining a high heat. Fondue lovers need something which will provide constant heat for a long time. For elegant flambées, professionals prefer an alcohol burner under a gleaming copper pan.

It must be kept in mind that tabletop cooking has its hazards. This is one area where quality cookware is not just a luxury but a necessity. While innumerable burners and braziers are available, many of them are so poorly made as to be downright dangerous. An alcohol burner that runs amok just as the host is about to flame the crêpes provides fireworks that are not funny. Buy the best equipment, both burners and pans, and use the proper fuel. Do not, for example, pour lighter fluid into a burner meant for wood alcohol. And be sure to place a large, heavy tray under any burner to protect the table from the heat which will be reflected downward as well as up toward the cooking food. Never, under any circumstances, touch any unprotected metal parts of a burner until you are sure they have cooled down after use. For safety, good looks, and general serviceability, we can recommend the equipment we have assembled here.

FOOD WARMERS

Warmers are close relatives of burners, but their heat output is of

Single-Burner Hot Plate   11.143

Chromed-steel body with machined cast-iron heating plate, plastic knob; 13½" × 8½"; 3" high; heating plate diam. 6".
$40.00 ▲

Hot plates have come a long way from the rickety affairs once used by dwellers in furnished rooms—witness this beauty. A gleaming rectangle of polished chrome is punctuated by a burner plate of smooth, sooty-looking cast iron. A dial, conveniently set into the top of the appliance, controls temperature selection, 12 settings from Warm to Fry. Set it and forget it—a sensor unit centered in the burner plate maintains the proper temperature throughout the cooking. Be sure to use a flat-bottomed pan on this hot plate—the sensor unit must make contact with the pan at all times or the heat will go off. (This means, of course, that we don't recommend this type of unit for omelets or any other dish whose preparation entails lifting the pan from the burner.) This modern miracle is also an energy-saver. The 950-watt burner element heats in seconds and, turned off, will remain warm for an hour. Attractive enough to be centered on the table for fondue cooking if you don't mind the electric cord, the hot plate will cook any top-of-stove food that falls within its heating capability. Think of it on a buffet table holding a polished pot of beef ragôut, or sitting before the host while he flames a pan of dessert crêpes. If you don't wish to leave it sitting on your serving table, the small size of this hot plate makes it easy to store.

course much less. Americans are devotees of hot food and beverages—not for us the tepid soup or gelid goulash. *Too* hot means no taste, however, and often results in a burned tongue, which leaves the sufferer unable to savor anything for days. Warmers, properly used, won't keep your food at boiling temperature, but they will maintain it at a palatable heat for buffet service, or for second helpings, or for those times when dinner, for whatever reason, must be delayed.

CREPE AND FONDUE EQUIPMENT
Crêpe pans and fondue pots should be of the same excellent quality as the burners beneath them, not just for efficiency's sake, but for appearance. This is one area where the equipment shares top billing with the food. As we unpacked the ones we show here, we were delighted with their beauty—you will find them serviceable as well.

HOT PLATES
We tend to relegate the hot plate to the limbo of the make-do appliance—it is what you made the cocoa on in your college dorm, and later what saved the family's bacon while you waited for the stove to be delivered for your new kitchen. Lifesavers—or more properly, mealsavers—in these situations, hot plates also perform a function in tableside cookery.

You won't want to use the battered appliance left over from your student days to cook at the table, but you may find one of the modern beauties on the market perfect for preparing an elegant meal for your family and friends before their eyes. Two-burner models will let you cook the crêpes on one burner and make the sauce on the other. Those with one burner provide a sufficiently gentle heat source for fondue.

Portable and dependable, hot plates are now handsome as well. They are also safer for tabletop cookery than any burner which uses a volatile fuel. Our experts chose the ones we show here as the best and the most beautiful of all the hot plates we tested.

ESCALOPE DE VEAU FLAMBEE—VEAL SCALLOPS FLAMBEED

Per person:
1½ tablespoons peanut oil
1½ tablespoons butter
2 slices of veal (⅜ inch thick), cut from the upper leg and pounded flat
Flour
Salt
Freshly ground white pepper
1 tablespoon minced shallots
2 tablespoons Armagnac
½ cup *crème fraiche**
2 tablespoons white stock
2 tablespoons minced parsley

Heat the oil and the butter in a deep skillet over fairly high heat, dust the veal slices with flour, and sauté them quickly until golden brown on both sides. Season with salt and pepper. Transfer them to a serving dish and keep hot.

Add the shallots to the pan juices and cook them for about 5 minutes, or until they are soft. Return the veal slices to the skillet, add the Armagnac, and flame it. Transfer the veal back to the serving dish and keep hot. Stir the *crème fraiche* into the pan juices, together with the white stock (or good meat juice), and reduce until thick and smooth. Pour the sauce over the veal and sprinkle with chopped parsley.

*Heavy cream may be substituted for *crème fraiche.*

(From LA CUISINE, by Raymond Oliver, translated by Nika Standen Hazelton with Jack Van Bibber. Copyright © 1969 by Tudor Publishing Company. Reprinted by permission of Tudor Publishing Company.)

Table Range   11.144

You could forgo the use of your stovetop entirely with this double-unit hot plate. And, indeed, owners of vacation houses and mobile homes might do just that. A larger version of **11.143**, it has two burner plates, one with a sensor element, one without. Boil the rice on the "burner with a brain," cook the Shrimp Marengo on the simpler element. Breakfast lovers can flip their flapjacks and heat the syrup at the same time; luncheon hostesses will make the crêpes on one burner and cook the filling on the other. Each unit is individually controlled by its own thermostat. Housed in a polished chrome body, this is both lovely to look at and easily cleaned. The 950-watt sensor-equipped burner has 12 temperature settings; the 700-watt burner, without a sensor, has 6.

Chromed-steel body with machined cast-iron heating plates; 20″ × 8½″; 3″ high; heating plates diam. 6″.
$59.50

Buffet Trolley   11.145

Black square iron frame with synthetic-resin boards, stainless-steel burners; 36½″ × 16⅛″; 28″ high.
$270.00

Continued from preceding page

Here is the ultimate. If your life-style involves formal service in the dining room, if you insist on having your food kept warm at tableside, and if you indulge in finishing sauces in the dining room, you will find this a useful extravagance. We daresay you will genuinely enjoy using this buffet trolley equipped with both a double alcohol burner for reheating and flaming, and a built-in food warmer with three candles. The shelves are easy-to-clean synthetic resin in an inoffensive woodgrain pattern, and the frame is of black square iron. Two of the casters lock securely. Suppose your dining room is a distance from the kitchen. A trolley such as this one will allow you to bring your *coulis de tomates* and thin slices of *filet de boeuf* into the dining room and with your guests looking on in delight, to quickly sauté the strips of beef in butter and olive oil in your oval copper pan (see 6.18, 6.19) or your copper flambé pan (11.167), while your garlic-laced tomato sauce keeps warm over the candles (in your copper fait-tout [6.36], perhaps). When all is ready, pour the sauce over the beef, garnish the dish with piquant black olives, fresh parsley, capers and slices of lemon which have been waiting in dishes on the shelves of the trolley. To gild the lily, you might have flamed your beef with cognac before adding the sauce—easy to do with the bottles waiting in another compartment of your trolley. When the assembled guests have been served, the dish can be kept warm—anything this good will require second helpings.

Burners

Burners, braziers, and rechauds are the closest we come to the firepits of our primitive ancestors, but we use them for very sophisticated cookery. Topped with opulent pans of copper and brass, they are props for the cook's performance in the spotlight.

The best-known and still most popular table burners use alcohol. Poured into a container set into a stand, this fuel provides a high-intensity flame for dishes which require it—crêpes and omelets, for example. Denatured alcohol is the most widely used, but wood alcohol is purer and, drop for drop, will burn longer. Alcohol is inexpensive, but it does have an odor and the fuel remaining in the burner must be flamed off or emptied out before you store the equipment.

STERNO
Sterno is alcohol in jellied form. Beloved by campers for its easy portability and its ability to burn in any weather, it is also suitable for use in burners where a great amount of heat is not required, and, as it is spillproof, it is very safe to use. The flame of a Sterno burner cannot be regulated: once lit, it will burn until the can is empty or until the flame is snuffed out with the lid. For these reasons, we do not find it efficient for fondues or flaming dishes, or anything where either long, slow cooking or high heat is required. Sterno is an ideal fuel, however, for chafing dishes and foods that have been cooked earlier in the kitchen and are to be kept warm at the table.

BUTANE AND PROPANE
Two gases of the methane series—butane and propane—are products of modern chemistry. They are more expensive than alcohol but also provide longer-lasting heat and are less dangerous to use than alcohol. Regulated by a thumb-operated control, tabletop butane burners provide as adjustable a heat range as your gas stove.

"This is one of those delicate messes which the gourmand loves to cook for himself in a silver dish held over a spirit-lamp, or in a silver stew-pan; the preparation of the morsel being to him the better part of it."

Annals of the Cleikum Club, *incorporated in* The Cook and Housewife's Manual, *by Margaret Dods (Isobel Christian Johnston),* 1826

BANANES FLAMBEES AU RHUM— BANANAS FLAMBEED WITH RUM

Serves 6

6 large, well-ripened bananas
1 stick sweet butter (4 ounces)
⅓ cup sugar
juice of 1 lime
¼ cup water
⅓ cup good white or dark rum

Although this dish is usually made in the dining room, a couple of steps can be done in advance. Place the bananas in a 400° oven on a cookie sheet and cook for 15 minutes. *The skins should be black and the bananas soft to the touch.* Cut the ends off and make an incision down the entire length of each banana. Set aside. This step can be done 45 minutes to an hour before serving time.

Place the butter, sugar, lime juice, and ¼ cup water in a large copper skillet (a skillet that can be used in the dining room). Cook on medium heat, stirring constantly with a wooden spatula. In about 4 to 5 minutes the mixture should turn to a light caramel color. Remove immediately from the heat. *It will continue to cook and darken off the heat, so be careful not to let the mixture take on too much color before you remove it from the heat.* This step also may be done ahead of time.

At serving time, place the pan with the butter mixture over a heater or flame in the dining room. Add 1 tablespoon of water and mix with a spoon to dilute the basic sauce, which has thickened. Open the bananas and "unwrap" into the skillet. Cook 2 to 3 minutes, basting the bananas with the sauce. When very hot, add the rum. Ignite and keep basting until the flames die out. Turn off the heat and serve immediately.

(From JACQUES PEPIN: A FRENCH CHEF COOKS AT HOME, by Jacques Pépin. Copyright © 1975 by Jacques Pépin. Reprinted by permission of Simon & Schuster.)

MAKING A CHOICE

Plain and fancy, numberless burners are available for every purpose. It is wise to decide on the kind of cooking at the table you're likely to do the most of, and then to choose the very best burner you can find for that type of cooking. If, for example, you have a family of fondue-lovers, buy an alcohol or butane burner with a low, sturdy stand; for flambéing, you can use an alcohol or butane burner, but the frame should be high enough so the cook doesn't have to stoop while he works. We repeat—buy the best-quality burner for the sake of safety as well as appearance. The ones we show have passed our tests on both counts.

Denatured Alcohol-Fired Brazier 11.148

Wrought-iron grill and handles with black sheet-metal base, stainless-steel burner; 11¼" X 7"; 4" high.

$20.00

Table-top cookery brings to mind elaborate extravaganzas—leaping flames, liquer-laced sauces, party food. While not an everyday occurence, it can all take place beautifully and efficiently upon this most sober of alcohol burners. Of black wrought iron, the brazier has a simple, Oriental look. The frame is a series of squared-off rods which hold the pot above the burner. Two very similar metal bars, bent into rectangles, form the handles. The alcohol unit is set into a plain black sheet of metal which detaches from the frame for easy cleaning. Since it comes from Switzerland, motherland of fondue, we find this the ideal unit for that purpose. It is only 4 inches high—guests can watch the pot boil while their food cooks.

Illustration from La Vie Privée des Anciens *by René Joseph Ménard.*

Bernzomatic Propane Camp Stove 11.146

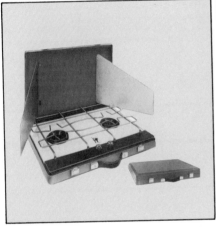

Enameled-steel case with aluminum wind screens, nickeled-steel grate; 14" X 10"; 3½" high when closed.

$61.50

Pools in sylvan settings, gazebos in the garden are often without nearby electric outlets. You needn't settle for a sandwich supper if you've chosen such a site for dinner, however. A camp stove such as this one from Bernzomatic will perform all the functions of your kitchen stovetop. This is a deluxe model of a stove designed for outdoorsmen. The entire unit, only 14 by 10 inches, is encased in a slim steel green-enameled suitcase. You open it to find two burners recessed in a white-enameled top and covered with a sturdy nickeled-steel grate. A pair of aluminum wings unfolds at the sides to protect the flames from passing breezes. A separate canister of propane gas attaches to the stove via a hose and nozzle. No need to panic if the matches have been left behind or have gotten wet—an electronic pushbutton ignites the burners. The campers in your family will want to borrow this lightweight and rust-proof stove for their forest forays.

Ronson Varaflame Table Chef 11.147

Cast-iron base with stainless-steel utensil rings, metallic gray-finished metal butane container with stainless-steel flame bowl, plastic handle; 9¼" base diam.; 5" high.

$45.00

Butane gas is a newcomer to tableside cookery in the home, pioneered by Ronson after the invention of the butane-gas cigarette lighter. Clean and long-lasting, butane won a devoted following among smokers. Having cornered that market, Ronson made use of butane's excellent properties in a cooking unit introduced at the 1964–1965 World's Fair. It was dubbed the Varaflame, a testament to its versatile temperature range. For cooks who swear by their gas stoves, the Varaflame transfers all the virtues of gas cooking from the kitchen to the tabletop. The flame of the burner unit is regulated instantly by a thumb-operated dial, permitting an infinite range of heat settings. A weighty cast-iron stand holds the burner unit, and any pot or pan you wish to use is supported on the snap-out steel rings above. The gas unit is easily refilled with an injector can available at hardware and housewares stores. We find the Varaflame a bit too high for comfortable fondue cookery, but it's ideal for flaming crêpes and other such performances at the dinner table.

OMELETTE SOUFFLEE FLAMBEE

Serves 4-6

8 eggs
½ cup sugar
⅓ cup Cognac or rum
Butter
Granulated sugar
¼ cup Cognac, warmed

Separate the eggs and beat the yolks until light and lemon-colored. Gradually beat in the sugar. Add ⅓ cup Cognac or rum. Heat oven to 375 F. Separately, beat the egg whites until they stand in firm peaks, and fold ⅓ of them into the egg-yolk mixture; then fold in the rest of the whites.

Heat a 10-inch skillet on top of the stove and butter it well. Sprinkle with granulated sugar. Pour the soufflé mixture into the skillet and bake for about 15 minutes. Remove from the oven, sprinkle with granulated sugar, pour the warmed Cognac over it and ignite. Serve at once from the skillet.

(From THE GREAT COOKS COOK-BOOK, by The Good Cooking School Copyright © 1974 by The Good Cooking School, Inc. Reprinted by permission of Ferguson/Doubleday.)

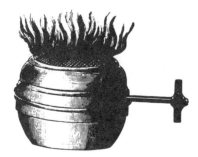

Illustration from the catalogue of a chafing dish manufacturer some time in the 1920's.

"Pablo, as he approached, several times held his nose to the edge of the stew-pan to inhale the appetising exhalations which escaped from it. . . . 'Pablo,' asked the canon, pointing to the chafing-dish, surmounted with its pan, 'what is that silver plate?' 'It belongs to M. Appetite, sir; under this pan is a dish with a double bottom, filled with boiling water, because this great man says the food must be eaten burning hot.' . . . 'Let me see this card,' said the canon, and he read: 'Guinea fowl eggs fried in the fat of quails, relieved with a gravy of crabs. N.B. Eat burning hot, make only one mouthful of each egg, after having softened it well with the gravy. Masticate pianissimo.' "

Eugène Sue's Gluttony, *quoted in M. F. K. Fisher's* Here Let Us Feast

Copper Burner with Fondue Bourguignonne Pan   11.150

Wrought-iron stand with copper tray and burner, copper pan with stainless-steel lining, plastic handle, aluminum spatter shield; tray 9¼" diam.; stand 9" top diam., 4" high; pot 5" top diam., 7" bottom diam., 3½" deep, 3⅛-pt. capacity.

$60.00 ▲

Fondue Bourguignonne is made by heating oil—half olive, half peanut—to shimmering heat and having each diner cook his own cubes of very good beef with a long fork. When done, the meat is dipped into any one of a number of available sauces: Béarnaise, horseradish, mustard, and on to the limits of your imagination. It requires a good stable burner—watch out for boiling oil—and a pot with good

conductivity, shaped with a fairly narrow neck to contain dangerous spatters. We discuss the whole subject here rather than later with the special pots for fondues because the best of the Fondue Bourguignonne pots that we have come across is the one in this set, which has a super burner useful for a myriad of other uses—crêpes and other flambéed delights, for instance. Standing on a polished copper tray, a wrought-iron grill rests on graceful curved legs. It holds a bi-metal burner—beautiful copper on the outside, solid stainless steel on the inside. No wick extends from this burner: instead, a pad of asbestos inside it absorbs great quantities of alcohol, whose flame can be adjusted by the judicious swiveling of the top to expose more or fewer openings. An extra cap serves to extinguish the flame. The fondue pot is also in shining copper lined with stainless steel. This bi-metal construction is used here to great purpose: the copper conducts the heat peerlessly, and the stainless steel can neither melt off (as tin might) nor be sullied by food. The pot has a spatter-shield cover, with cutouts for inserting the forks.

Gourmet Pot Set   11.151

Wrought-iron base with copper burners, copper pot with stainless-steel lining, brass handles, stainless-steel ladle; base 11" × 8¼", 3½" high; pot 9½" diam., 3¼" deep; 3-qt. capacity.

$101.00

A Swiss product, similar to the Fondue Bourguignonne set (11.150) but made for the Oriental fondues, in which many thin slices of meat and vegetables are cooked at once in a large amount of boiling liquid. Made by Spring Brothers, it has a frame that differs from their al-

Copper Burner with Fondue
Bourguignonne Pan
Gourmet Pot Set

Large Alcohol Burner and Grill
Swissmart Alcohol Burner
Sterno Brazier

cohol brazier (11.148) in only one respect—the metal plate has cutouts to hold two wickless alcohol burners, although it can also be used with a single unit. And these alcohol burners are beauties. Copper-clad and capacious, they operate identically to the one in the Fondue Bourguignonne set. The accompanying pot is another splendid example of the Culinox line. Wide yet deep, it has a glossy copper exterior and it is lined with a heavy layer of stainless steel and fitted with sculptured handles of burnished brass. Included with the set is a stainess-steel ladle whose slotted bowl, for separating solids from liquids, is serrated at one edge. A chrysanthemum pot or shabu-shabu, those simple and succulent Eastern fondues for family suppers or informal entertaining will be greeted with as much admiration for the equipment as for the ingredients if it is cooked in this beautiful set.

Large Alcohol Burner and Grill · 11.152

Stainless steel; base 10¼″ bottom diam., 8½″ top diam., 4⅞″ high; grill 14⅝″ × 10¼″.

$133.00

This is the Goliath of alcohol burners. Every part is made of heavy 18/8 stainless steel, and the jumbo heating unit holds two pints of denatured alcohol for a full three hours of cooking. It is cradled in a heavy round frame fitted with two sturdy handles. The burner unit is a larger version of the conventional wickless burners for home use. Air holes are pierced on its upper surface, and the flame is regulated by a metal plate attached to a long handle which opens and

closes the apertures. The heat is extinguished by a metal cap, similarly equipped with a handle, which snuffs out the flame. A separate grill snaps onto the frame of the burner—its ample size will support a restaurant-sized pan. Indeed, the owner of a small café might find this Spring Brothers product a most useful alcohol burner for table-side cooking. The home chef with a small family, or someone who prefers intimate entertaining, will probably invest in something less Brobdingnagian, but for those who think and cook big this is the perfect alcohol burner.

Swissmart Alcohol Burner · 11.153

Matte black enameled-steel base and grill, with stainless-steel burner cover and flame extinguisher; 7″ diam.; 3⅝″ high.

$20.00

A small, lightweight affair, this alcohol burner has a pleasant modern shape. The black steel base is a series of curves, its round body carved with oval cutouts. The stainless-steel burner unit snaps into a well in the solid bottom of this base, while a grill to support a pot fits securely into the notches in its rim. Although the burner unit appears to be the same as the wickless ones we have shown, it burns wood alcohol rather than the denatured kind. While more expensive than denatured alcohol, wood alcohol is purer and burns for a longer time. A half-cup placed in the burner will give 1½ hours of cooking time. Not intended for heavy or constant use, this burner is handsome enough to be placed in the limelight for a fondue party, and inexpensive enough for those for whom such entertaining is a sometime thing.

Sterno Brazier · 11.154

Black iron stand; stainless-steel burner and base; 8¼″ diam.; 3″ high. Also avail. with burner and base of copper-clad stainless steel.

$20.00

While we are not enthusiastic about the use of Sterno for tabletop cooking, we recognize that others find it satisfactory for this purpose. For those who feel that the more volatile fuels such as alcohol are somewhat frightening to use, and butane and propane gases too expensive, Sterno provides an alternative. It is cheap, safe, and easily portable. However, it is not possible to regulate the heat and, as it burns less intensely than other fuels, food takes a longer time to cook. There is a plethora of ugly, cheaply made Sterno braziers on the market. Here, as in all cooking equipment, it pays to buy the best. One of the most beautiful and durable Sterno braziers we tested is this one from Spring Brothers. It has a black iron grill and a stainless-steel base and container for the fuel can; you can, if you wish, have a deluxe model with copper-clad stainless-steel base and container. The can of Sterno is placed in the center well and lighted. When the cooking is done, a metal lid is placed over the can to extinguish the flame. As the units are only 3 inches high, much lower than alcohol or gas braziers, they are handy for fondue cookery or buffet service.

From a manufacturer's catalogue, 1900.

Food Warmers

Soup's on and your husband calls to announce that he'll be an hour late; or a roomful of hungry guests awaits a late arrival while your blanquette de veau cools in the kitchen. Crises such as these can be averted and hot food served to the tardy if the cook invests in a warmer. These can be heated by electricity, like the popular Salton Hotrays, or by the infrared heating units often used in restaurants, or they can be simple affairs in which candles are used for heat, not light. Unlike your oven, warmers won't dry out your dinner.

No warmer is designed for actual cooking, although we admire a foresighted woman who places the ingredients for her ragout in a heavy pot on her Hotray in the morning, dials it to the highest heat, and serves a steaming supper 12 hours later—instant Crock Pot.

Candle warmers are incapable of such feats, because the stubby candles which must be used have a limited life. But they are perfect for keeping dinner in just-cooked condition for an hour or so, and they are beloved by buffet hostesses who can serve their guests palatable seconds and thirds of the spaghetti or boeuf en daube. And it is nice to know that the coffers of the local electric company are not being filled while the candle warmer is in use.

Overhead food warmers are designed to keep food hot for lengthier periods. They use lamps with infrared bulbs which shine on the food and maintain its heat indefinitely—interestingly enough, without raising the temperature of the food's surroundings much if at all. Families whose houses overflow with teenagers on erratic schedules might want to install one permanently in a pantry or a pass-through.

We like the items we show for keeping food warm—for their simplicity, their reliability, and their overall good quality. Where choices were made among them, we opted for the sturdiest and most attractive among a wide selection.

Salton Hotray — 11.155

Shatterproof glass heating surface with aluminum frame, woodgrained vinyl trim, and stained wood handles; 20¼" × 11" overall; heating area 17" × 10".

$38.00 ▲

Say Salton and you think Hotray. This company makes their popular food warmers in every size, from that of a trivet to a table. For general all-purpose use, we suggest this tray-type model. The 17" by 10" heating surface is ample for a large casserole or two small ones; and an extra-warm "sunspot" in one corner will keep the coffee hot. The surface is a sheet of shatterproof glass, impervious to alcohol and stains. It is set into an aluminum frame with a woodgrained trim. Set the dial to the lowest temperature for fragile dishes—eggs, sauces, and such—and turn it up to high for soups and stews. Any food—like many with delicate sauces—which cannot be reheated can be kept in prime condition until serving time—even a fragile poached salmon and its accompanying Hollandaise will keep warm without drying out or curdling. A creamy sauté of chicken with lemon in its sauce (see recipe) could even wait while Mom meets the train. Brides have been presented wth Hotrays for years; if your wedding took place pre-Salton, give yourself a gift which will keep on giving your family good hot meals for years.

Stainless-Steel Candle Warmer — 11.156

Stainless steel; 10½" diam.; 2⅜" high.
$45.00

Supper by candlelight can be kept hot by candle power on this elegant French warmer. A gleaming round of silver, it has a sheen that imitates sterling, but it is actually of practical stainless steel. Beneath a lustrous filigreed plate two stubby candles burn in small metal cups to give gentle heat. Circles of stainless steel attached to a metal rod which projects from one side of the warmer snuff out the flames after use without the necessity of removing the top of the stand. The warmer rests on unobtrusive feet, shaped like tiny metal mushrooms, that keep the heat from the table top. Its classic good looks will be at home on a table set with Baccarat crystal and your best silver, but it will also keep the dinner warm for family suppers in the kitchen.

This nineteenth-century French grill, placed over coals at the side of the hearth, kept foods warm; shown by Urban-Dubois in L'Ecole des Cuisinières.

Butter Warmer 11.157

Stainless steel with copper bottom, rosewood handle; 4¾" diam.; 2" deep; 1-cup capacity.

$14.00

We'll let you in on a secret—the sure way to get the brandy to flame for the Cherries Jubilee is to warm it before you pour it into the pan. Straight from the bottle, it has a disconcerting tendency to fizzle or refuse to light at all while the host peppers the dessert with spent matches. We recommend that you pour the alcohol into a beautiful little pot like this one of copper-bottomed stainless steel and set it on the burner to warm before you sauce the crêpes. A lovely Lilliputian of a pot with a flared rim for spill-proof pouring, it will be right at home with elegant crêpe and flambé pans. The slender oval handle is of rosewood, the better to protect the cook's fingers from hot metal. If you love it as much as we do, you'll find other ways to use this nifty little pot—heating the syrup for the breakfast pancakes, the butter for lobster, or even to warm the baby food.

POULET SAUTE A LA CREME ET A L'ARMAGNAC—CHICKEN SAUTEED WITH CREAM AND ARMAGNAC

For four people, use:
1⅓ C. cream
3 T. butter
3 T. armagnac
5 shallots
1 T. minced onion
4 tsp. olive oil
4 tsp. flour
1 plump chicken with giblets
vegetables as for *pot-au-feu*
lemon juice
salt and pepper

Clean, gut, flame, and cut up the chicken.
   Prepare a broth with the giblets, vegetables, water, salt, and pepper. Boil it down to concentrate it, and strain.

In a big frying pan melt the butter and oil. When this mixture is very hot put in the pieces of chicken, which have been rolled in flour, the shallots, and onion, and brown everything over a hot fire for about ten minutes. Reduce the fire and sauté the chicken for another twenty minutes. Remove the pieces of chicken and keep them hot.
   Deglaze the cooking pan with the strained chicken broth, and add the cream and armagnac. Boil these down to make a fairly thick sauce. Season to taste with lemon juice and add salt and pepper if necessary. Strain the sauce, then put back the pieces of chicken and simmer everything together over a very low fire without letting it boil.
   Serve with rice with mushrooms, or with a purée of truffles.
   For variation, one could substitute, for the armagnac, some *fine champagne* (a type of brandy), and one would add to the sauce some mushrooms dipped in lemon juice and cooked in butter, or some truffles cooked in madeira. In the latter case, one would add to the sauce a little of the truffle cooking liquid, but without letting the madeira flavor become dominant.
   Sautéed chicken with cream and armagnac or with brandy is worthy of the finest tables.

(From ENCYCLOPEDIA OF PRACTICAL GASTRONOMY, by Ali-Bab, translated by Elizabeth Benson. Copyright © 1974 by McGraw-Hill, Inc. Reprinted by permission of McGraw-Hill Book Company.)

"Helene (our cook) used to stay at home with her husband Sunday evening, that is to say she was always willing to come but we often told her not to bother. I like cooking, I am an extremely good five-minute cook, and beside, Gertrude Stein liked from time to time to have me make American dishes. One Sunday evening I was very busy preparing one of these and then I called Gertrude Stein to come in from the atelier for supper. She came in much excited and would not sit down. Here I want to show you something, she said. No I said it has to be eaten hot. No, she said, you have to see this first. Gertrude Stein never likes her food hot and I do like mine hot, we never agree about this. She admits that one can wait to cool it but one cannot heat it once it is on a plate so it is agreed that I have it served as hot as I like. In spite of my protests and the food cooling I had to read. I can still see the little tiny pages of the notebook written forward and back. It was the portrait called Ada, the first in Geography and Plays. I began it and I thought she was making fun of me and I protested, she says I protest now about my autobiography. Finally I read it all and was terribly pleased with it. And then we ate our supper."

Gertrude Stein, The Autobiography of Alice B. Toklas

Oblong Candle Warmer 11.158

Enameled-steel base with stainless-steel grate; 13½" × 6¼"; 2½" high.

$8.50

Some like it hot, the dinner that is, and expect it to be kept that way for second helpings. This candle warmer has a homely, use-me-every-day appearance which might very well make it a fixture on your dining table. A rectangle of steel enameled orange, purple, or black holds a stainless-steel grid with two open squares which serve as slots for grasping when you want to move the grid. Underneath, two short candles are encased in small metal pots. They are extinguished by metal plates which swing back and forth on levers projecting on either side of the warmer. The oblong shape of this warmer makes it useful for warming platters or other large dishes of food—a pan of lasagna, a plateful of fried chicken, even a whole poached fish can be accommodated atop it.

Small Candle Warmer 11.159

Black sheet metal with stainless-steel cover and candle holder; 5½" diam.; 3" high.

$15.00

"Please pass the gravy" is a risky request for second servings. A congealed mass, swimming with greasy globules, is often what is proffered. How nice it is to serve the gravy as hot the second time around as when it came bubbling from the stove! This candle warmer makes it possible. A fat candle sits inside the black metal stand. You can set your bowl of gravy, or Hollandaise, or Béarnaise, for that matter, on the stainless steel grid which covers the top of the stand. Use this candle warmer with the butter warming pan we showed you (11.157). It will keep the butter pourable for serving lobsters, or clams. It will keep the syrup ready for the breakfast waffles.

In the ancient Aztec capital Montezuma enjoyed elaborate feasts which he consumed behind a screen, as no one was allowed to watch the king eat. Among the dishes used for serving him were pottery vessels for holding burning oil. These were placed under pans for food preparation at the table.

Heat Lamp with Carving Board 11.160

Heavy-gauge aluminum base pan, maple cutting board, anodized-aluminum lamp shade, enameled-steel arm, 250-watt infrared bulb; base pan 26" × 18"; cutting board 24" × 16"; jointed lamp arm 25" long.

$181.95

This is what we call a whopper of a warmer. The mammoth cutting board will support an entire seven-rib roast while the host carves, and the heat lamp keeps the meat warm. A 250-watt infrared bulb does the trick. It is set into an anodyzed aluminum shade supported by a reticulated arm that is solidly screwed onto the board itself. The weighty laminated-maple cutting board fits into a heavy-gauge aluminum base pan; there is no reason why you shouldn't set other foods than roasts on it to keep warm. All the wiring is heavy-duty and grease-resistant, and the power cord is attached to a three-pronged grounded plug for safe use. This warmer means business. Large families that eat in shifts will find it useful, and it is a natural for schools and communes.

Infrared Food Warmer 11.161

Stainless-steel and aluminum housing, with infrared heat lamp; 23½" × 8"; 2½" high.

$89.00

This warmer requires permanent installation. Just a shade under two feet long, it resembles a fluorescent lighting fixture, and it is meant to be affixed in the same manner as a light beneath a cabinet or a low ceiling. The warmer is a smaller version of the ones used by restaurants and hotels. The stainless-steel housing holds a long glass heat tube that can keep a whole meal at serving temperature indefinitely. Install it in the pass-through in your country kitchen and keep the dinner warm for returning skiers or surfers; attach it beneath a pantry cupboard, prepare and place beneath it your party fare, and relax with your guests while the food stays hot until you want it. As it never needs to be put away, this warmer poses no storage problem in the kitchen.

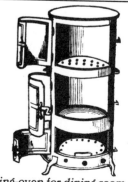

Warming-oven for dining room service. From French Domestic Cookery, *published in New York, 1855.*

Menu de Pique-Nique

(A. Escoffier)

❖ ❖ ❖

Souvenirs d'une Excursion à l'Ile Sainte-Marguerite

Mars 1878

Artichauts aux Épines
Fèves de Marais
Œufs à la Gelée

❖

Petites Langoustes à la Provençale

❖

Bœuf en Daube
Fricassée de Poulet à l'Ancienne
Timbale de Grives des Alpes

❖

Pâté de Foie gras

Salade de Légumes printaniers

❖

Macédoine de Fruits au kirsch
Pâtisseries

❖

Vin vieux de la Gaude
Champagne Veuve Cliquot

❖

Café Turc
Liqueur de Lérina

❖

For your next déjeuner sur l'herbe, *bring along a portable burner to prevent the beef from becoming* en gelée *and the chicken from transforming itself into a* chaud-froid.
Illustration from Almanach des Gourmands *by*
F. G. Dumas, 1904.

Crêpe Pans

Tableside cookery, especially if it involves crêpes, is for showoffs. Once the cook has polished his skills so he can fold a crêpe into quarters with a flick of the wrist or flame a sauce without setting fire to himself or the ceiling, he will want to invest in equipment which does justice to his proficiency. Tabletop cooking is no place for the battered skillet which adequately fries the breakfast eggs, or the beloved, albeit chipped, saucepan which sees nightly service in the kitchen.

First let us define our terms. We refer to two kinds of crêpe pans. In one type you will actually fry the batter into thin pancakes; in the other —usually it is an elegant pan—you will heat the cooked crêpes in a sauce over a burner and serve them forth from it to an admiring audience. The cooking pan is small, the same diameter as a cooked crêpe; the finishing pan is large enough to allow you to heat, sauce, and fold several crêpes at a time.

A good crêpe pan should have many of the virtues of the good omelet pans we show you. It must be heavy and made of a material which will absorb, retain, and distribute heat well. We show only two pans for the actual cooking of the crêpes. One is a classic iron one, meant not for use at the table but for making your crêpes in the kitchen before company comes. The other is for voluptuaries, or those whose expertise allows them to make the crêpes at the table.

Once the crêpes are cooked and neatly stacked on a plate—between sheets of waxed paper, if you like—they will be warmed in sauce or even flambéed over a burner at the table. For this you will want the most beautiful pan you can find. It must also be one which heats quickly and evenly. Look for a nicely balanced utensil—not only does it look better, but it will be much easier to use during the tableside performance.

We have shown you the best of the burners and braziers, and now we present the pans to top them and to do justice to the artistry of the cook and the excellence of the ingredients.

Iron Crêpe Pan 11.162

Heavy iron; 6½″ top diam., 5″ bottom diam.; ¾″ deep. Also avail. 7½″, 8″, or 9½″ top diam.

$10.00 ▲

The pan in which you cook your crêpes should be heavy enough to distribute heat evenly but light enough for the maneuvers—swirling and flipping—that you will perform. It must have a smooth surface so the crêpes won't stick, and shallow sloping sides for effortless flipping. This classic crêpe pan fills the bill. A simple utensil of black iron that turns out 5-inch pancakes, it is the perfect size for dessert crêpes; for main-course crêpes you may want to choose one of the larger sizes. The well-balanced handle—not too long, not too short—gives you good control over the pan. The handle is riveted to the pan and then angles up and away to keep the cook's fingers at a safe distance from the heat. As these pans are inexpensive, you may want to buy two so you can be swirling batter in one while the second side of a flipped crêpe is cooking in the other, cutting in half the time it takes to prepare each batch; you can begin each crêpe in the small pan and finish the cooking in a larger one, or one of the same size. Like any iron pan, this one should be seasoned before it's used and kept clean with oil and an occasional salt scrub thereafter.

Aluminum Crêpe Pan 11.163

Cast aluminum with walnut handle; 8″ diam. Also avail. 10″ or 12″ diam.

$25.00 ▲ $39.00 ▲

Splendid, elegant, opulent, ravishing—all these adjectives come to mind as you hold this consummate crêpe pan from Gourmet Limited in your hand. Its satiny aluminum body and smooth walnut handle have a touch-me, feel-me quality. Pretty is as pretty does—this crêpe pan has muscle as well. Aluminum—the heavier the better—is one of the very best materials to absorb, distribute, and retain the heat. For all its small size—it is only 8 inches in diameter—this is a weighty pan, capable of turning out a perfect golden pancake every time. The handle needs no potholder—made of solid walnut and topped with a metal ring for hanging, it is sanded to a perfect oval for a cool and comfortable grip. This pan should never be subjected to soap and water: once it has been seasoned, a simple swipe with a paper towel and a spot of oil will keep it in tiptop condition. The big brothers to this beauty, the 10- and 12-inch sizes for omelet making, are described in Chapter 11; the one we show you here is perfect for a 2- or 3-egg omelet as well as crêpes. Think of this pan, as costly as it is comely, as a multipurpose investment.

Copper Crêpe Pan   11.164

Medium-gauge copper with tin lining, brass handle; 12″ diam.; 1″ deep. Also avail. 9½″ diam.

$62.75

The cook who likes to star in table-side dramas could have no better prop than this glamorous French copper crêpe pan. Classically lined with glistening tin, it is polished to a fare-thee-well, brass handle and all. The bottom is very flat to make good all-over contact with the burner, and the handle is gracefully curved to protect the cook's fingers from heat. Twelve inches in diameter, it is large enough to cook omelets or to sauce the crêpes for a crowd. It is slightly deeper than most pans made for its purposes, so dishes with a generous amount of sauce can be accommodated. Its sloping sides make this pan ideal for cooking one large pancake such as Apfelpfannkuchen, the giant pancake, stuffed with spiced apples, beloved in Germany—see recipe for German Pancakes. Take care not to use too-high heat with this pan if you do not want to be bothered with frequent retinning. Small amounts of flaming when a fair amount of sauce is in the pan—such as for Crêpes Suzette—won't harm it; but it is not for flambéeing with a large amount of spirits in a dry pan.

CREPES DE MAIS—CORN CREPES

Serves 6

[This is an original recipe developed by Jacques Pépin, following a suggestion by his wife. It is easy to make, quite elegant, and delicate in texture and taste.]

5 medium-size ears of corn, husked, and
    silk removed
4 tablespoons flour
4 eggs
1 teaspoon salt
¼ teaspoon freshly ground pepper
½ cup heavy cream
½ stick (¼ cup) of sweet butter, melted

Bring a pot of salted water to a rolling boil. Drop the husked, cleaned corn into the water and let come to a boil again. Remove corn from water immediately, and let cool until it can be handled. With a sharp knife, cut straight down the middle of each kernel row, slitting each kernel open. Then hold the ear in one hand, the top of the ear resting on the table, and, with a spoon, scrape the pulp out of the opened kernels, extracting all of it as you scrape down the full length of the ear, and all around the ear, row by row. The skin of the kernel that held the pulp will remain attached to the ear; the pulp will be removed. You will have about 1¼ cups of pulp.

Put the pulp in a large bowl and sprinkle with the flour. Mix well with a whisk. Add the eggs, salt and pepper, mixing to blend all ingredients well. Add the cream and combine well. Finally, add the melted butter and mix together once more.

Heat oven to 180 F. Place a crêpe pan or a seasoned heavy iron pan over low to medium heat. When hot, pour 2 tablespoons of the mixture into the pan. This amount is enough for 1 crêpe. If the skillet is large enough to hold 2 crêpes, make 2 at a time, otherwise use several pans. Each crêpe should be about 4″ in diameter. Cook 40 seconds on one side; flip over or turn with a large spatula, and cook 30 seconds on the other side. Keep the finished crêpes hot in oven while you are making the others. Makes about 20 crêpes to serve as a first course or with beef, veal or rabbit stews.

(From THE GOOD COOKS COOKBOOK, by The Good Cooking School, Inc. Copyright © 1974 by The Good Cooking School, Inc. Reprinted by permission of Ferguson/Doubleday.)

Illustration from the catalogue of a chafing dish manufacturer some time in the 1920's.

Culinox Crêpe Pan   11.165

Copper with stainless-steel lining, brass handle; 11″ diam.; ⅞″ deep.

$54.00

Take a peek at the pan from which the captain serves your crêpes flambées next time you dine out and you will probably see a carbon copy of this one. With a copper body lined with stainless-steel—a construction that the maker, Spring Brothers, calls Culinox—it is a crêpe pan for both professional use and the home cook who is a connoisseur. The solid brass handle is a sculptured oval with no sharp edges to hamper your grip. The very low sides are ramrod-straight, giving the pan a clean, modern look, and are topped by a slightly curved rim to protect the copper body from inadvertent spills. For luxurious desserts, sumptuously served, this is the ideal pan in which to sauce and serve the crêpes you have previously made in the kitchen; and, unlike the preceding pan (11.164), which has a tin lining, this one won't be threatened by flames if you use quantities of spirits to flame a dish. Expect to pay more for this beauty—it's worth it—and plan to hang it on your kitchen wall to remind yourself how lucky you are to own it.

In an English cookbook published in 1714 is a recipe for "Thin Cream Pancakes Call'd a Quire of Paper" which closely resemble crêpes. The book is quaintly titled A Collection of Above Three Hundred Receipts in Cookery, Physick and Surgery: For the Use of All Good Wives, Tender Mothers, and Careful Nurses.

GERMAN PANCAKES—DEUTSCHE PFANNKUCHEN

3 to 4 pancakes; 3 to 4 servings

½ cup sifted flour
2 teaspoons sugar
¼ teaspoon salt
4 eggs
½ cup milk
6 tablespoons butter (approximately)

Sift flour, sugar and salt together. Using a rotary beater, whip eggs until light and frothy; beat in milk. Turn flour mixture into beaten egg and, still using beater, whip until you have a smooth batter. Melt 2 tablespoons butter in a 10″ skillet, or a 12″ skillet if you can handle it, and pour in just enough batter to cover bottom with a thin layer. This should take approximately a fourth to a third of batter. As soon as you pour batter, tilt and rotate pan so batter will run over it evenly. Cook over moderate heat until pancakes are golden brown on underside; turn and brown second side. Remove to heated platter.

Continue to fry rest of pancakes in same way until batter is used up. Add 2 tablespoons butter to pan between each pancake. To keep the first pancakes hot while you make the others, arrange them in large open baking dish and place in 250° to 300° oven until you are ready for them. It's a good idea to keep oven door open so they don't bake. Put final topping on rolled pancakes when all have been made.

PANCAKE GARNISHES

1. For a simple dessert or a breakfast entree, sprinkle each crepe with a little cinnamon and sugar. Roll and brush with melted butter.
2. For a more elaborate dessert, add any preserved fruit to crêpe before rolling it. Preiselbeeren, the tiny German cranberries, are excellent for this. After rolling pancakes, brush them with a little melted butter and sprinkle with a little more cinnamon and sugar. Pour a little heated rum, brandy, or any white fruit liqueur, such as kirsch, framboise or quetsch, over rolled pancakes and flambé them.
3. For Apple Pancake (Apfelpfannkuchen), sauté pared apple slices in a little butter until they soften slightly and begin to take on color. Sprinkle with cinnamon and sugar. Prepare pancake batter, and when it has set in pan, add a layer of apples and cover with a thin coating of additional batter. Brown slowly on both sides. Fold in half or roll, brush with melted butter and sprinkle with a little more cinnamon and sugar.

Use 3 medium-sized apples for this amount of batter.
4. For Cherry Pancake (Kirschpfannkuchen), substitute 1 pound cherries—washed, dried, stoned and cut in half—for apple slices.

(From THE GERMAN COOKBOOK, by Mimi Sheraton. Copyright © 1965 by Mimi Sheraton. Reprinted by permission of Random House.)

Copper and Stainless-Steel Crêpe Pan   11.166

Copper exterior with stainless-steel lining and handle; 10″ inside diam.; 1¼″ deep.
$59.00

Not as beautiful as 11.165 but every bit as efficient, this Bi-Metal crêpe pan from Legion will turn out an omelet or a single large pancake as well as heating and saucing smaller crêpes at the table. It is an 11-inch pan of heavy copper lined with another pan, this one of stainless steel; the fused pans, now bordered by a wide lip, have sides that curve and curve again to a flat bottom. There are no angles to impede the folding of an omelet or the flipping of a crêpe. The handle, alas, is the weak point: fairly short and made of stainless steel, it is slightly concave on its upper surface and sharp-edged—no comfortable handhold here. We like the pan, nonetheless, for its beauty and versatility. If you are going to invest in only one crêpe pan, this is a good bet—it's versatile, and there are no worries about retinning.

Flambé Pans

While all the copper crêpe pans with stainless-steel linings we have shown are amenable to housing flames in their interiors, their shapes preclude flambéing larger items such as steaks, fish, or poultry. These main dishes need deeper, more capacious pans. Fresh fruits—pears and peaches, apples and pineapples—sugared and flamed, make easy and elegant desserts, but they, too, require roomy pans. Flambé pans are made for just that purpose. They can take a large amount of heat both outside and inside, and they are deep enough not to overflow as the ingredients are rotated during finishing. We bring to your attention two of the finest we've found. Both are made by Spring Brothers, of Culinox, that felicitous marriage of copper and stainless steel (see 11.165) which has produced some of the most voluptuous pans in our batterie de cuisine.

THE CHAFING DISH

Webster defines a chafing dish as "a pan with a heating apparatus beneath it, to cook food at the table or to keep food hot." We always think of it as the bearer of scrumptious Sunday-night suppers—Welsh rarebit ladled over crusty slices of toast, creamed eggs studded with pink bits of Saturday's ham. Sunday supper need not die: farther along we show you a copper chafing dish that is the experts' choice.

Oval Flambé Pan 11.167

Copper with stainless-steel lining, brass handle; 15¾" × 8¾"; 1½" deep. Also avail. 9", 10⅝", 12⅝", or 14⅛" long.

$52.00 ▲

Once again, copper lined with stainless steel. This pan is related by construction to 11.165, but it is 1½ inches deep. It's also nearly 16 inches long, large enough to flame a party-sized steak au poivre, a whole fish, or Quail Flambé (recipe). A bright brass handle, as comfortable to the touch as it is beautiful to the eye, extends from one of the ends, and there is a wide lip around the edge to support a lid (separately available). We recommend using an oblong rather than round brazier or burner under this weighty pan in order to insure even heat distribution. The manufacturer suggests preheating the utensil before use—simply pass both long sides over the flame before setting it flat on the burner to warm. The quintessential flambé pan for kitchens that boast nothing but the best.

Round Flambé Pan 11.168

Copper with stainless-steel lining, brass handle; 11" diam.; 2½" deep. Also avail. 7⅞", 8⅝", 9½", or 10¼" diam.

$54.00

If your brazier is round rather than rectangular, this flambé pan, a circular (and deeper) version of 11.167, will be more satisfactory. Again, it is of copper over stainless steel—we repeat ourselves for a purpose—nothing is at once so beautiful and so durable as these Culinox pans. The handle is a twin to that of the preceding pan—both are lovely to look at, delightful to hold. Have this pan in the 11-inch version for flambéeing main courses or preparing desserts for a party; the smaller sizes are for making sauces or for smaller-sized flambéed dishes. A full 2½ inches deep in its largest size, the pan is deep enough to hold your food plus sauce with no spillover.

Copper Chafing Dish 11.169

Copper pan with tin lining, wood handles; copper stand with brass legs; copper Sterno container with brass lid and wood handle; 11½" high overall; pan 9" diam., 3" deep; 2-qt. capacity.

$98.00

This proud beauty of a chafing dish is meant to be the centerpiece at a party as well as to serve at Sunday suppers en famille. Gleaming copper from its elegant domed lid to its container for Sterno, it is accented with touches of brass in its three graceful legs and the lid of the burner. Turned wooden handles are attached to the burner unit and to the tin-lined pan. It will hold two quarts of what's-for-dinner on a buffet table and keep it warm for second helpings, or serve for tabletop cooking that doesn't require the high heat of a table range, brazier, or burner. This chafing dish would make a glorious wedding present, or would be a sumptuous gift for your favorite hostess.

In The Pantropheon, *the famous nineteenth-century chef Alexis Soyer describes the culinary practices and equipment of the ancient Greeks and Romans. In this particular vision of Soyer's, a slave is "cleaning and polishing . . . bronze chafing dishes, which are to be used at table to prevent the plates from becoming cold. It is in speaking of this useful invention that Seneca, the philosopher, says, 'daintiness gave birth to this invention, in order that no viand should be chilled, and that everything should be hot enough to please the most pampered palate.' "*

FONDUE POTS

Legend has it that the first fondue was eaten by a shepherd high in the mountains of Switzerland who, bored with his nightly ration of cheese, wine, and bread, combined and heated them in a pot. He must have let out a resounding yodel when he tasted the first bite. The glad word spread and now fondue, while still synonymous with Switzerland, is enjoyed all over the world.

Although the shepherd's cheese fondue is still popular, the concept of cook-it-yourself has broadened to include everything from chicken to chocolate—see the Fondue Bourguignonne set, 11.150. Whatever the fondue ingredients, the same basic method of cooking is followed—morsels of food are speared by the guests on long forks

Continued from preceding page

and dipped into a potful of bubbling sauce. Fondue is food for the affections as well as the appetite. A Swiss custom dictates that he who loses his chunk of crusty bread in the pot of melted cheese must kiss his partner. Dunkers who are known to have steady hands have been seen to develop dropsy over the fondue pot when accompanied by a fetching companion.

Fondue pots must be deep and wide to permit the twirling of several forks in the sauce at once. The classic pot for cheese fondue is of heavy pottery, those for meat are of metal. We prefer enameled cast iron or steel, a combination that possesses the best characteristics of both materials. Like earthenware, it is weighty enough to coddle a cheese mixture and never allow it to curdle or separate, and it is solid enough to diffuse the heat. The cast-iron or steel base will not shatter in use as might pottery over too high a flame, and the enamel coating won't retain the flavor of foods previously cooked in the pot.

We show you two pots, one from France, the other from Switzerland, strictly for fondue.

Enameled Cast-Iron Fondue Pot 11.170

Enameled cast iron; 8″ diam.; 3″ deep; 2-qt. capacity.

$25.95

Le Creuset calls this a saucepan, which it is. It even comes with a lid. They also show it as a fondue pot (without a lid), for which purpose it is admirably suited. Its plump body has a fat, round handle, iced with a slick glaze of brown outside and a cool, clean white within. Made of enameled cast iron, it has a double-thick bottom. Everything about this pot bespeaks good quality. Fill it with a golden cheese fondue (recipe), or dip juicy chunks of fresh fruit into a sauce of sinful melted chocolate for an uncommon dessert. Once it has found a home in your kitchen, we'll wager that you'll find this pot too useful to reserve for fondue alone. Whip a béchamel to smooth perfection in it without a worry about scorch, make potage

St. Germaine with no fear that the peas will char—this pot will be as much at home on your kitchen range as it is atop a brazier.

Brillat-Savarin tasted the fondue in Switzerland, then visited the United States, where he introduced the dish to New England.

FONDUE DE FROMAGE—CHEESE FONDUE (HOT)

This is the classic Swiss recipe. The fondue can also be made with Bock beer in season instead of dry white wine. But of course if you decide to use Bock beer, you should first test it for excellence in the traditional Swiss-German manner. Put on your lederhosen, then pour a small puddle of beer on a varnished wooden stool. Sit on the stool for about 30 minutes and then rise slowly. If the stool rises with you, the Bock beer is of excellent quality and should make a nice flavorful fondue.

4 cups imported Swiss Gruyère cheese, cut into dice
1 large garlic clove
2 cups dry white wine (preferably Neuchatel)
1 teaspoon salt
½ teaspoon freshly cracked white pepper
½ teaspoon freshly grated nutmeg
2 tablespoons all-purpose flour
¼ cup Kirsch
1 long loaf of French bread

Spread the diced Gruyère cheese on a large tray and allow to dry overnight, if possible. Heat a heavy pan. When the pan is hot, rub it out with the clove of garlic, then put into it the cheese, wine, salt, pepper, and nutmeg. Stir over low heat without stopping until the cheese has just melted. Mix the flour into the Kirsch and stir it into the cheese. If the melted cheese is too thick, add a little more white wine. Serve in a chafing dish. Cut the French bread into slices or large cubes, toast them on each side, and serve separately in a basket, with long fondue forks. Net: Serves 8 as a first course, 4 as a main course.

(From THE DIONE LUCAS BOOK OF FRENCH COOKING, by Dione Lucas and Marion Gorman, illustrated by Joseph S. Patti. Copyright © 1947 by Dione Lucas. Reprinted by permission of Little, Brown and Company.)

Enameled-Steel Fondue Pot 11.171

Enameled steel; 7⅛″ diam.; 1½-qt. capacity. Also avail. with a capacity of 1 qt.

$12.00

Not quite as well made perhaps as 11.170, this is nonetheless an endearing fondue pot in a zingy color combination. Of enamel over steel, it sports a butter-yellow interior and a basic-black exterior. It can also be had with the yellow on the outside and the black within, but somehow we don't fancy the look of a pale cheese fondue bubbling in a black-lined pot—others may not share our prejudice. The handle is short and straight and has a pleasant round shape for easy gripping. The rim of the pot is unfinished to help prevent the chipping that can plague some utensils of enamelware. Heavy and sturdy, the pot comes in 1- and 1½-quart sizes. We'd buy both and use one for a cheese fondue, the other for chocolate fondue for dessert, and have a grand party for lovers of both cheese and chocolate, Swiss foods for Swiss pots.

THE NEW
WALDORF
COOK BOOK

By
MRS. ANNIE CLARK

F. TENNYSON NEELY - PUBLISHER - NEW YORK - LONDON

We happen to think that *all* the utensils shown in this catalogue—not just those in this section—are meant for preparing health foods, because high-quality ingredients, properly cooked, are nutritious as well as delicious. But, of course, there have been changes since the good old days, when pure food and water were standard items. And as our environment has become more industrialized, so has the production of the foodstuffs we consume. Many varieties of fruits and vegetables are grown because they are durable enough to withstand mechanized picking and long-distance shipping, not because they taste good or are high in nutrients; and many of the other foods we eat have been dyed, adulterated with additives, or preserved with chemicals. As a result many people have taken up the pure-food cudgels and refuse to buy the prepared foods that proliferate on supermarket shelves. For them the tomato organically grown, for them the fertilized hen's egg, the stoneground flour.

Whether or not this is food faddism or just sensible eating we leave to you and your doctor. The virtues of various diets are touted by their adherents. The macrobiotic regimen that marched under the banner of Zen Buddhism flamed and fizzled; vego-lacto lovers live on. Weight watchers will always be with us in this overabundant society; more diets will appear with the sureness of the seasons.

For every diet, health food or no, there are special tools to make the preparation easier. Many of them will be found in other pages of this catalogue. Bread-bakers will find a grain mill useful (Chapter 4); calorie counters need scales (Chapter 1). Vegetarians require equipment for steaming (Chapter 11), puréeing, and juice extracting (Chapter 4) in order to prepare the staples of their diets. And there are many who find the Oriental method of quick cooking gives the most delicious and healthful results of all.

There are certain utensils designed especially for health-food cookery which have a broader application. Water purifiers remove the pollutants and chemicals from tap water, not only for more hygienic beverages, but for better-tasting coffee and tea. Yogurt makers enable you to culture your own yogurt at home for a fraction of the cost of the supermarket variety, and a device for sprouting seeds makes it possible to produce mung or soy sprouts for your Chinese dishes, alfalfa sprouts for salads, sprouted wheat for your own healthful home-baked bread. We show a small but carefully chosen selection of these machines.

ries, steamed and poached foods figure in their menus rather often. A fish poacher [Chapter 11] can become an indispensable utensil, not only for gently poaching fish to moist perfection, but also for poaching a quantity of smaller items together. In my book Haute Cuisine for Your Heart's Delight I suggest doing the preliminary simmering of boudin blanc (white sausage of chicken and veal) in a fish poacher.

A steamer [see Chapter 11] is another invaluable item to have. A properly steamed potato has a wonderful texture and flavor that does not scream out for the addition of polyunsaturated margarine or the forbidden butter.

If space is lacking for a real steamer for potatoes and other vegetables, one can be easily improvised with a deep pot and a colander or sieve that sits well into the pot. To steam potatoes: put water in the pot, stopping before it reaches the bottom of the colander or sieve. Then line the colander with a dish towel that has been wrung out with cold water, allowing the ends to hang loose. Put the peeled potatoes in the lined colander, then cover completely with the wet towel ends. Place a lid over the colander, bring the water to a boil, and reduce the heat to keep the water boiling briskly but not furiously. Add more boiling water if necessary. The steamed potatoes will be perfection, since the towel prevents the potatoes from possibly turning grey through contact with the metal.

Another item that I feel is a necessity for low-cholesterol meat cooking is a meat thermometer [Chapter 1]. Since roasted meat is not covered with an unctuous sauce, it is critical that it not be overcooked. Roasting your meats just to a rosy degree of doneness will preserve their juiciness.

Good low-cholesterol cooking is not complicated or dull. It simply applies your repertoire of cooking techniques and equipment to a new formula that eliminates cholesterol—producing good food while encouraging good heart health.

LOW-CHOLESTEROL COOKING EQUIPMENT
Carol Cutler

The great penny-saving grace about low-cholesterol cooking is that no special equipment is necessary. What you put into the pan is what counts, not so much the pan itself. Any well-equipped kitchen should have all the sound equipment necessary for turning out exquisite dishes that don't shriek "diet food".

Sound equipment is the key, though: good heavy skillets that cook food evenly and as slowly as you like; tin-lined or enameled pots for cooking with wine sauces; wire whisks and electric beaters for whipping egg whites to impressive but solid volume; good sharp knives for trimming away all the visible fat on meats.

Since people following a low-cholesterol diet usually are also counting calo-

WOODEN FLOUR TUB

Watermate 11.172

Plastic; 9¼" × 6⅜"; 10⅞" high overall; canister 4" diam., 8⅛" deep, 1½-qt. capacity.

$40.00 ▲

Fresh water is the most basic of human needs. Riparian rights have set nation against nation, caused aggression between neighbors and even whole states, and been the subject of many a treaty. Most parts of the eastern and southern United States are blessed with an abundance of water, and the deserts elsewhere are supplied by aqueducts from more fortunate regions. Lakes and streams, rivers and reservoirs supply billions of gallons. As these sources of water have become polluted by the effluents of industries and cities, chemicals have had to be added to drinking water to make it safe to drink. Many people have found the result, while technically safe, unfit for human consumption—at least for the discerning palate. So, like many Europeans, they have taken to buying bottled water for drinking. All well and good, but an expensive pleasure. Alternatively, a permanent purifier can be attached to the home water supply. This is also costly and, since the invention of the Watermate, unnecessary if your requirements are fairly moderate. For a small price the Watermate will remove all the impurities, both chemical and mineral, from 1½ quarts of water instantly. It is a lightweight machine a bit larger than an electric blender. You plug it in—unlike other small water-filtering machines, it is electrical—pour 1½ quarts of tap water into the reservoir, and push the "on" switch. The water is forced through the filter and then bubbles out into the clear plastic receiving jar, ready to be used at once or covered and stored in the refrigerator. Your coffee and tea will taste better, and you may begin to enjoy drinking your allotted eight glasses of water a day. Depending on the kind of water being purified, the filter will need replacement after it has processed from 20 to 100 gallons; a lessened flow is the signal to check the filter.

Slice-a-Slice 11.173

Stainless steel with stainless-steel knife, wood handle; 7½" × 5"; knife 13½" long overall; blade 8¾" long.

$8.95

Diet-conscious Americans are constantly being warned to cut their carbohydrates as well as their overall calorie intake. For most of us that means giving up that lunchtime staple, the sandwich. This deprivation is not really necessary for owners of a Slice-a-Slice. A handy gadget that transforms an ordinary piece of bread into two thin slices, the Slice-a-Slice is useful even for slender members of the population. Use it to prepare bread for homemade melba toast, an entirely different animal from the boxed variety. Tea sandwiches, tart shells formed from bread, and canapés all taste better when you use the thinnest of slices. The tool comes in two parts. The bread holder looks like a grater made of two sheets of stainless steel and firmly based on small rubber feet. The knife is serrated, of stainless steel and very sharp; it is secured with a partial tang to a wooden handle with two brass rivets. The Slice-a-Slice is an asset to the economical, too—a loaf of bread will last twice as long while it is adding only half the calories to your sandwiches.

SEASONING BOX

Yogurt Makers and a Seed Sprouter

At the close of the Neolithic era or thereabouts, people learned to milk the animals they had domesticated and use the liquid for food. Letting it stand, they noticed that it curdled and that the creamy lumps that resulted were good to eat: the interaction of bacteria and warm milk had produced what we know as yogurt. As experience was gained with fermented or clabbered milk, the curds were made into the earliest cheeses. Through subsequent ages, it was discovered that ripening milk in these ways was the ideal method of preserving it in warm climates. Nomads could milk their camels or mares, ferment the milk, and carry the high-protein, easily digested yogurt with them on their travels. In the modern-day Balkan region, the Middle East, and in Central Asia, yogurt, now usually made from cow's milk, and similar preparations became a staple of the diet, as they are to the present day. Indian cuisine relies heavily on cooling yogurt as an accompaniment for hot curries as well as the foundation of many delicious dishes such as Tandoori Chicken (recipe), a spicy oven-roasted bird first marinated in yogurt, perfumed with herbs and spices. Yogurt, under many names,

Continued from preceding page

still accompanies a wide variety of Middle Eastern foods. In many countries chilled yogurt is served as a beverage, too.

Americans have been late to discover the virtues of yogurt. Touted as a diet and/or health food, it enjoyed overnight success a few years ago as we became more conscious of our bodies' appearance and nutrition. The tartness of the natural product was not to everyone's taste, however. To make it more palatable to the masses, yogurt makers added fruit, sugar, and flavoring to their product. Dairy cases throughout the land are now stocked with half-pint containers with such labels as "Dutch apple," "honey and wheat germ," and "peach melba," as well as simple "strawberry," "coffee," and "vanilla". While increasing the popularity of yogurt as a snack food, these additions have also raised the cost and the calorie count.

To get back to the basics, yogurt is a simple food, simply made at home. It can be done without any special equipment by heating milk (or adding warm water to dried milk), adding a little commercial unflavored yogurt or dried yogurt culture as a starter, and letting it stand until it thickens. However, it must be kept constantly at the correct temperature if the culture is to grow properly. Electric yogurt makers take the guesswork out of temperature control, otherwise a matter of devising various heating and insulating methods. And they produce yogurt unsullied by chemicals or high-calorie additives for about one-third the cost of the commercial variety. Anyone who wants preserves or fruit or flavorings with the finished yogurt can add them at serving time.

We recommend an electric appliance for making yogurt to anyone who consumes a container or so a day—at that rate, in no time it will have paid for itself. Those who don't like the taste of plain commercial yogurt might find the flavor and consistency of their own homemade variety more to their liking; they can make it rich or lean, thick or light.

There are dozens of yogurt makers on the market. Our experts tested all of those widely available and found the ones we've chosen produce delicious, creamy yogurt every time with a minimum of fuss and bother and a minimum of expense.

If you enjoy fresh bean sprouts or other sprouted seeds, see the lamentably named Bio Snacky: this performs far better than improvised sprouting equipment, and it is handsome as well.

into the five 6-ounce glass jars, set them into the base, and plug in the machine. Ten hours and one cent's worth of electricity later you remove 30 ounces of firm homemade yogurt. If you like a more liquid yogurt, leave it for only 5 to 6 hours. This appliance does not turn off automatically, but a numbered dial on the clear plastic lid can be set to remind you of the time of day at which the yogurt must be removed. Fruit and flavorings may be added after the yogurt is thoroughly chilled. Use plain yogurt in place of sour cream for low-calorie dips and sauces, or as a tart topping for moussaka or blintzes. It's a nutritious and filling food for babies, too. As this appliance costs only as much as about two dozen containers of commercial yogurt, you'll recoup your investment in a hurry.

TANDOORI CHICKEN— MY VERSION

Serves 6-8

There are two things that I need to point out here. The chickens used for the *tandoor* [oven] in India are usually spring chickens, weighing 2-2½ pounds each. They are cooked whole, with only wings and neck removed, on all sides at once. I find it more convenient to marinate and cook the chicken cut in pieces (it is also easier to serve and to eat this way). I buy the legs and breasts of broiling or frying chickens. (You may have an odd member of the family who just loves wings, and who will need to be placated some other way at some other time.) Also, I should point out again that Indians seem to dislike the chicken skin and always remove it before cooking.

The chicken in this recipe should be marinated for about 24 hours. Assuming that most people like both dark and light meat, I am allocating one whole leg and half a breast for each of 6 people.

1 medium-sized onion, peeled and
    coarsely chopped
6 whole cloves garlic, peeled and
    coarsely chopped
A piece of fresh ginger, about 2 inches
    long and 1 inch wide, peeled and
    coarsely chopped
3 tablespoons lemon juice
8 ounces (1 container) plain yogurt
1 tablespoon ground coriander
1 teaspoon ground cumin
1 teaspoon ground turmeric
1 teaspoon garam masala
¼ teaspoon ground mace
¼ teaspoon ground nutmeg
¼ teaspoon ground cloves

Salton Yogurt Maker   11.174

Plastic with glass jars; 16″ × 3½″, 5″ high; 5 jars, each 3¼″ diam., 3¾″ high, 6-oz. capacity.

$13.00 ▲

"It's simple, sure, and easy," says Salton of the operation of their yogurt maker, and we found it so. The gray and yellow plastic oblong case resembles a toy boat, each white smokestack a yogurt container. It comes with a yellow plastic measuring spoon wearing a thermometer in the handle. This implement gauges the correct amount of starter to be added and tests for the correct temperature of the milk. After the milk has been boiled it must be cooled to the temperature indicated by a mark on the thermometer. At that point you stir the starter or culture into the milk and pour the mixture

¼ teaspoon ground cinnamon
4 tablespoons olive oil (or vegetable oil)
2 teaspoons salt
¼ teaspoon freshly ground black pepper
¼-½ teaspoon cayenne pepper (optional, or use as desired)
½-1 teaspoon orange food coloring (use the Spanish bijol, or Indian powdered food coloring, or American liquid kind; its use is optional)
6 broiler or fryer chicken legs
3 broiler or fryer chicken breasts, halved

GARNISH
1 medium-sized onion
2 lemons
Extra lemon juice (optional)

Make the marinade first. Put the chopped onions, garlic, ginger, and lemon juice in an electric blender, and blend to a smooth paste, about 1 minute at high speed. Place this in a bowl large enough to accommodate the chicken. Add the yogurt, coriander, cumin, turmeric, *garam masala*, mace, nutmeg, cloves, cinnamon, olive oil, salt, black pepper, cayenne, and food coloring. Mix thoroughly.

Skin the chicken legs and breasts. With a sharp knife make 3 diagonal slashes on each breast section, going halfway down to the bone. Make 2 diagonal slashes on each thigh, also going halfway down to the bone. With the point of a sharp knife, make 4 or 5 jabs on each drumstick.

Put the chicken in the marinade and rub the marinade into the slashes with your finger. Cover and leave refrigerated for 24 hours. Turn 4 or 5 times while the chicken is marinating.

About 1½ hours before serving, light your charcoal. It should take 20 to 30 minutes to get red hot. Place the grill on its lowest notch.

Peel the onion for garnishing and slice it paper-thin. Separate the rings and set in a small bowl of ice water, cover, and refrigerate.

When the fire is hot, lift out the chicken pieces and place on the grill. Cook about 7 or 8 minutes on each side, then raise the grill a few notches to cook more slowly for another 15 to 20 minutes on each side. Baste with marinade as you cook.

TO SERVE: Warm a large platter. Place the chicken pieces on it. Drain the water from the onion rings and lay them on top of the chicken. Quarter the lemons lengthwise and place them around the chicken. The chicken tastes very good with extra lemon juice squeezed on it.

This chicken is considered a delicacy and can be served at a banquet with *Pullao* [spiced rice with seafood or lamb], *naans* [leavened bread], a few vegetable dishes, and onions pickled in vinegar.

(From AN INVITATION TO INDIAN COOKING, by Madhur Jaffrey. Copyright © 1973 by Madhur Jaffrey. Reprinted by permission of Alfred A. Knopf, Inc.)

"I had previously bought five yogurt which I poured into an old diaper . . . and I suspended it over a bowl in the pantry to make the famous yaourti tou pouggio [thickened, cheeselike yogurt], and my evening as a hermit was accompanied by the plip-plop of dripping yogurt at regular intervals."

Daniel Spoerri, "A Gastronomic Itinerary," in The Mythological Travels

High-Capacity Yogurt Maker 11.175

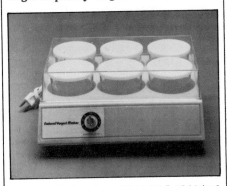

Plastic with glass jars; 11" × 9¼", 5" high; 6 jars, each 2⅞" diam., 3" deep, 8-oz. capacity.

$21.95

This is the *dernier cri* of electric yogurt makers. Clean and modern, with an automatic timer set into its boxy yellow or white base, it makes yogurt production virtually foolproof. The six 8-ounce containers are of clear sturdy glass and are topped with white plastic lids. The instruction booklet is a mine of information on yogurt making. Texture, it tells us, is not determined just by the length of time the yogurt spends in the appliance, but also by the kind of milk used; that made with whole milk will differ from yogurt starting life as milk with the butterfat skimmed off. A dozen recipes for everything from a drink called an Anemic Bloody Mary to a rich and creamy cheesecake are included to set the taste buds tingling and the imagination working for even more uses for your homemade yogurt. It will take the price of four dozen containers of commercial yogurt to pay for this deluxe appliance but it's worth it if you'd like to make 48 ounces with a single filling of the jars.

Bio Snacky Sprouter 11.176

Plastic; 7⅞" diam.; 5⅝" high; 4 trays, each 1½" deep.

$14.95

We like the free fresh wind in our hair and green grass under our feet, but unfortunately, we live eighteen floors above the city streets, where those pleasures are a little hard to come by. So we bought a Bio Snacky Sprouter instead. Now if we can't walk on greenery we can at least look at it and, best of all, eat it. Ignore the cutesy name of this device and think of what the Bio Snacky can do. It will raise a crop of bean sprouts, or cress, or mustard, or all three at once to munching size in a matter of days. It will teach a child the joy of watching his garden grow—with the Bio Snacky your tot can actually see the seeds sprout and unfold their leaves from hour to hour. Tabby can have a treat of home-sprouted catnip; Mom can spice a salad with fresh-picked cress or alfalfa sprouts, and she can easily sprout her own wheat for the ultimate in healthful breads. The sprouter looks like a four-layer cake in Lucite. Three of the trays have corrugated bottoms and small red knobs covering drainage holes. In these trays you will sprinkle the quick-germinating seeds of your choice. You pour water into the top layer; it filters through the drainage holes to moisten the two perforated trays beneath and collects in the bottom bowl. At intervals you repeat the moistening. Between times, the lid seals the sprouter, turning it into a terrarium for safe and speedy germination. Fun for any city-dweller, or for that matter anyone who enjoys fresh, crisp sprouts for eating.

Coffee, the first of the beverages whose appurtenances we'll consider here, is an eye-opener, an ice-breaker, and a warmer-upper. We hazard a guess that there are few kitchen cupboards in America that don't hold coffee in some form, ground or powdered. Like tea, coffee is made by the process of infusion, but it is made in ways so numerous that the mind boggles. If you want to inject a little controversy into a conversation, discuss the relative merits of coffee makers and of coffee-making methods in general. We'd sooner argue the question of virgin birth with a bishop. Percolator or drip, instant or espresso—every method has its ardent supporters.

We remember a sign in a roadside diner that read, "Don't complain about the coffee—you may be old and weak yourself someday." Well, we'd be likely to complain: we'd suffer through the greasy eggs and choke down the limp bacon, but all would be forgiven if we could wash them down with a strong hot cup of coffee. Many a cook's reputation is founded on serving the best cup of coffee in town, and we'd guess that many a lunchroom has survived with little else to recommend it.

WAYS TO MAKE COFFEE

The simplest way to make the best coffee in town is to throw a handful of the ground beans into a potful of boiling water, turn off the heat, cover the pot, and steep it like tea. You usually won't find Mom doing this for the breakfast coffee, but Dad might resort to it on camping trips, and his coffee may taste better than what he's served at home. Next in the quick-and-easy department is the single-pass-through method—the drip method and others using a filter—in which boiling water is poured through finely ground coffee. Percolators are a bit more complicated. Over the heat, they force the water from the bottom of the pot up through a tube to overflow into a basket holding the fairly coarsely ground coffee. It filters through and drips down into the water below, which turns into brewed coffee as the process continues. An espresso machine is to a percolater as a calculator is to an abacus. A tangle of tubes and filters, it uses live steam forced through dark-roast coffee ground to a powder; this process makes coffee so strong that it's virtually an essence, black and delectable. In between these methods of coffee brewing there are numberless variations.

WHAT KIND OF COFFEE?

They have an awful lot of coffee in Brazil, and also in Guatemala and Jamaica, Colombia and Haiti, the Middle East and Africa. The coffee you buy in cans is usually a combination of beans from two or more regions, chosen for a balance of their characteristics—some coffees are winy, some mellow, some suave, some assertive. Purists eschew preground coffee, preferring to buy the beans as freshly roasted as possible and then to pulverize them in their own grinders (see Chapter 4) just before brewing. You'll find these *exigentes* browsing among the barrels at Zabar's, New York City's answer to Fauchon, a cornucopia of culinary delights that is known especially for its fine coffees; every large city (and some small ones) in the land has at least one store where

Coffee cans of an earlier day.

ANITA'S BREAD PUDDING

Straight out of a thrifty Belgian kitchen, this idea for using up the coffee left over from breakfast to make a pudding for dinner.

1 loaf stale French or Italian bread (about 10 ounces)
2½ cups leftover coffee*
1 cup raisins
6 tablespoons (¾ stick) butter or margarine, softened
¾ cup brown sugar
1 teaspoon vanilla extract
2 eggs, slightly beaten
¼ teaspoon cinnamon

Line an 8-inch round cake pan with kitchen parchment. Set aside.

Break up the bread and place in a bowl. Add the coffee and allow to soak for about 20 minutes. At the same time, cover the raisins with water to plump them up. Once plumped, drain. Combine the bread and drained raisins and all remaining ingredients. Mix together with your hands. Pour into the prepared pan and bake in a preheated 375° oven for 1 hour, or until a knife inserted in the center comes out dry—that is, without any batter clinging to it. Turn out on a cake rack. Then reverse onto a serving plate and glaze.

GLAZE: Mix 1 cup sifted confectioners' sugar with 2 tablespoons of water until smooth. Spread over the cake with a metal spatula.

*If you haven't enough coffee, add enough milk to make up the difference.

coffee beans are available, and mail-order companies are other good sources.

If grinding your own beans is the optimum in coffee brewery, using instant coffee is the nadir. Despite the images presented on television of smiling husbands winking at the little woman while she serves him a cup of something purporting to be better than the real thing, it just 'taint so. If you love coffee you'll accept no substitutes; the real thing is as speedy to make as instant, especially if you use our Toddy coffee maker or the whistling SEB coffee pot, and it is twice as good to drink.

Now we ask you a personal question. How good is your coffee? Is it pale and weak, or rancid and bitter? Is it never hot enough or strong enough? Help is on the way. From Chemex to Europiccola, our coffee makers will turn out a brew that is good to the last drop, as a national advertiser has proclaimed for his brand for generations—coffee to make you glad you're alive every morning, to give you a lift during the day, and to finish off the finest dinner.

Chemex Coffee Maker 11.178

Heat-resistant glass with wood grip; 6" base diam.; 9½" high; 2- to 8-cup capacity. Also avail. with capacity of 1 to 3 cups, 2 to 6 cups, 2 to 13 cups, or 6 to 20 cups.

$18.95 ▲

Now we come to Chemex, which some people think of as a generic term for coffee maker. Its homely hourglass shape has been around since the year two, and there are many who don't know there is any other way to make the breakfast brew. We learned of its virtues from a member of our staff who swears by it. Into the top section of the pot she pops a paper filter. Then she measures in the coffee, one heaping tablespoon for each cup and one extra for the pot, if she's making several cups. The boiling water goes from the kettle into a glass measuring cup, then over the grounds. Six minutes or so later, it has all dripped through to the bottom of the pot. Not hot enough, we said. Heat it, she answered, and put the pot on a Flame-Tamer (Chapter 6) on the stove. Well, we had to admit that it was heavenly coffee, even though it was made by the single-pass-through method of which we are not inordinately fond. The Chemex is the plain-Jane of coffee makers, its only frill the heatproof girdle of wood bound with a leather thong that bisects the handblown glass body. The manufacturers might as well stick with a good thing—it would be hard to think of a single way to improve on its design.

Melitta Coffee Maker 11.177

Porcelain; 4¼" base diam.; 5½" deep; 4- to 6-cup capacity. Also avail. with capacity of 2 to 4 cups.

$20.00 ▲

If you like the simple things in life, you probably already own a Melitta coffee maker. It brews coffee by the single-pass-through method, just one step removed from throwing the grounds into a pot of boiling water to steep. We have mixed feelings about the Melitta mode of coffee making. While we appreciate the mellow quality of the coffee it produces, we find the brew never hot enough or strong enough for our taste. But its partisans insist that it produces a tastier, more healthful beverage—more healthful because it's without the oils and sediment that often make for a bitter taste in percolated coffee, for instance. You line the funnel-shaped filter top with one of the paper bags which come with the pot (when you've used them all you can buy another box at any hardware or housewares store). Pour in the boiling water and wait for it to seep through to the pot below. (Tip: Preheating the pot with boiling water will produce a hotter finished cup; or put the pot on an asbestos mat on the stove and turn on low, low heat as soon as the coffee begins to filter into the pot.) Melitta makes many models of their coffee maker, in both glass and porcelain. We like the looks of this chaste white china one—the pot a clean modern shape with a triangular spout and a large, easy-to-hold handle, the filter top similarly designed. This version makes 6 cups, but Melitta makes coffee pots in a range of sizes for households large and small.

The old Union coffee mill.

Bunn Electric Coffee Maker 11.179

Heat resistant glass coffee pot with plastic lid and handle; plastic and vinyl-covered steel power unit housing; 13½″ X 7″; 13¾″ high; 8-cup capacity.

$48.95

Just as there are food fads, there are food appliance fads. Electric coffee makers which operate on the same single pass-through method as the manually operated Melitta and Chemex (11.177, 11.178) are now the rage. If you can't boil water, these are for you—you start with cold water. Though the quality of the brew depends on both the coffee and the water you use, these machines remove much of the guesswork. The Bunn, approved by the Pan-American Coffee Bureau, has the advantage of the multiple-sprayer system which assures that the grounds will become uniformly wet (a feature absent from many similar appliances). Put the coffee into the filter and fit it to the funnel, turn the switch to warm, lift the lid, pour cold water into the top, and, instantly, out comes fresh, hot coffee. The pot sits on an electric warming unit to keep the coffee hot. Neither the plastic unit nor the glass carafe is beautiful, but if the cup of coffee is, you can be happy.

"Coffee is not as necessary to ministers of the reformed faith as to Catholic priests. The latter are not allowed to marry, and coffee is said to induce chastity. . . . I never drink tea, coffee, nor chocolate."

Elizabeth Charlotte, Duchesse d'Orléans (1652–1722)

One-Cup Coffee Maker 11.180

Aluminum with plastic handle; 3¼″ diam.; 1⅞″ high; 1-cup capacity.

$2.00

Somehow there's always one in every crowd who asks for an after-dinner brew different from the one you've prepared. You serve a potful of espresso, they ask for Sanka. You've made 12 cups of decaffeinated coffee, they only drink the "real thing." Well, you can smile sweetly and let them suffer with instant, or you can whip out your one-cup coffee maker and win a friend for life. This gadget reduces single-pass-through coffee brewing to individual service. Basically, it's the coffee maker without the pot. A small aluminum basket holds the ground coffee and rests, by means of a wide lip, on top of the coffee cup. A perforated metal plate fits into the basket and holds down the grounds while you pour the water through. Lift off the entire basket by the plastic handle when the coffee has passed through and place it on the inverted lid to catch the drips. Ummm—that's *real* coffee!

A coffee urn that has become a collector's item.

Neapolitan Filter Pot 11.181

Aluminum with plastic handles; 3¾″ diam.; 8½″ high overall; 4- to 6-serving capacity.

$9.00 ▲

We're working our way up the coffee ladder, you'll notice, to the he-man brews like espresso, strong enough to support a spoon. This coffee maker straddles a middle rung. It doesn't make real espresso but does produce a hair-on-your-chest demi-tasse of café filtre. Its operation reminds us of the two-headed dolls we had as children, the ones whose skirts you flipped to play with Red Riding Hood on one end, the Big Bad Wolf on the other. Well, in this device two polished aluminum containers of equal size, with identical handles of heatproof plastic, are placed end to end and enclose yet another aluminum cylinder, this to hold the coffee in a filter-basket section. You put the cold water in the container without a spout, slip the coffee-basket cylinder into place, spoon the coffee into the basket, screw on the lid of that part, then invert the spouted pot over the whole thing. Set the coffee maker over the heat and, as soon as steam starts pouring from the tiny hole in the side, it's time to invert the pots and allow the hot water to filter through the coffee into the spouted section. There is a separate lid to cover the coffee, if you opt to remove the superstructure at serving time, or to perch atop the whole construction as a jaunty finishing touch.

Bunn Electric Coffee Maker
One-Cup Coffee Maker
Neapolitan Filter Pot
Porcelain Filter Pot
Toddy Coffee Maker
Melior Coffee Maker

"COFFEE: *Imparts wit. Tasty only when it comes from Le Havre. At a formal dinner, should be taken standing. Sipping it unsweetened, very fashionable, suggests you have lived in the Orient.*"

Gustave Flaubert

Porcelain Filter Pot 11.182

Porcelain; 10" high overall; 5¾" high without drip cylinder; 6-cup capacity. Also avail. with capacity of 2,4 or 8 cups.

$16.50

This porcelain pot would be at home in a sultan's seraglio, so long as his spouses were not too numerous. Glazed pristine white, it is a fantasy of curves and arches straight from *The Arabian Nights*. The full moon of a pot wears a comma for a handle and has an undulating spout limned with scallops. Atop the pot sits a porcelain cylinder to hold the ground coffee, bracketed with dimpled handles and wreathed top and bottom with ridges. Next layer above is a perforated insert that distributes the scalding-hot water poured into it over the coffee in the cylinder below, from which it drips through into the pot from which it is served. If you don't drink the coffee at once you can keep this pot warm over a burner covered with an asbestos pad, because it's porcelain. If storage space is short, remember that this pot, minus the filtering apparatus, will do duty for tea-brewing as well. It comes in four sizes, to make from 2 to 8 servings of coffee.

Toddy Coffee Maker 11.183

Glass decanter with plastic attachments; 14¼" high overall; carafe 3¼" diam.; 8" high; 8-cup capacity.

$15.00 ▲

The Toddy makes instant coffee at home, and before you instantly stop reading we should explain that no, it doesn't turn out the feathery or freeze-dried powder that you buy in a jar, but a clear, black, liquid coffee essence. And it does it with cold—you heard me—cold water. Fit the white plastic container onto the glass carafe. Empty one pound of regular-grind coffee into this container after making sure that the filter is in place and the hole at the bottom is plugged with the tiny black stopper. Pour in 8 cups of cold water (a one-pound coffee can holds exactly four cups of fluid). After 10 to 12 hours, pull out the stopper and let the coffee essence drip through into the carafe. A severe case of coffee nerves would result from drinking this brew straight, but an ounce or so of it, measured from the cap into a cup of boiling water, is ambrosia. This coffee concentrate makes the best iced coffee we've ever tasted, and it can be used to flavor your mocha mousse or to turn a pastry cream into a coffee-lover's delight. Put away that behemoth of a percolator which turned out 20 cups of coffee for the Ladies' Aid luncheon; you can make three times that amount of coffee with one batch of essence made by the Toddy and serve it in relays from your best silver coffee pot. Store the concentrate in its carafe in the refrigerator and take a vacation from the daily chore of making the breakfast brew. Even cooks who literally can't boil water will get a reputation for serving the best coffee in town with the help of this one.

Melior Coffee Maker 11.184

Nickel steel with heat-resistant glass interior; 3⅞" diam.; 7⅞" high; 8-cup capacity.

$124.00

Are you ready for yet another method of coffee making? This French pot makes some of the best coffee we've tasted, and in an unorthodox way. A futuristic cylinder with a rodlike handle masquerades as silver, but is really of nickel steel fitted with a Pyrex liner, visible through two oval portholes. The coffee and the boiling water are measured into the pot. Now watch closely as we put on the lid, which has the working parts attached, and press down on the disc of silvery metal that tops the lid. It is attached by a center rod to a perforated metal sandwich with a filter for its filling, and as we press down it slowly and inexorably pushes all the grounds to the bottom of the pot and keeps them there. The coffee is "pressed," as it were, all its strength and goodness infused into the boiling water. You then serve the coffee from the spoutless pot, whose lid has an opening in its edge to accommodate the flow of liquid. We want to emphasize the good looks of this pot—no plastic parts, no obvious trademarks mar its appearance—it is fit to use with your silver service and your Royal Crown Derby cups.

SEB Whistling Coffee Maker   11.185

Stainless steel with plastic lid, handle, and stand; 4¾″ diam.; 9⅛″ high; 6-cup capacity. Also avail. with capacity of 4 or 9 cups.

$18.95

Polly put the kettle on, and when it whistles we'll all have coffee. At least we will if we use this nifty but noisy stainless-steel coffee maker from **SEB**, and we'll have it in only 6 minutes. That's all it takes to brew 6 cups of excellent coffee. Unaccustomed to such speed, we find its whistling alarm more welcome than annoying. The SEB coffee maker uses the pressure-cooker principle. The ground coffee goes into a bitsy basket that screws into an intricate thingamajig, all gaskets and knobs. This in turn fits into the pot, whose bottom half has been filled with cold H_2O. The forgetful are reminded to screw the big black central knob down firmly into the pot in four languages incised on its upper surface. Placed over the heat, the water is forced upward through the grounds into the top chamber, and there's your coffee. Remove it from the heat at once, as the lower chamber is now empty—and drink it promptly, as this is not a pot for rewarming. Of gleaming stainless steel, the pot is equipped with a keep-cool plastic handle and lid, and there is a nice snap-on stand, also of plastic, to protect the table top. The thrifty take note: this pot uses 50 percent less coffee than a conventional percolator. We like it in the 6-cup size, which will also turn out 12 demi-tasse servings, but you can also have it with a larger (9-cup) or a smaller (4-cup) capacity. Now, if you'll excuse us, there goes the whistle . . .

Espresso Makers

Now we've crossed the great divide that separates the beverage you find in your breakfast cup from the coffee you serve in tiny cups with the brandy after dinner. This is espresso, the essence of coffee, a dark, rich delight. Espresso is made by forcing steam rather than water through the ground coffee. It cannot be made in your percolator or your Chemex, even if you buy the extra-strong coffee, roasted until it's almost black, intended only for espresso-making. To produce a cup of the real thing, you need a special pot or machine, one that will drive the steam with enormous pressure through the coffee.

The espresso machines you find in restaurants cost a king's ransom. They are electrified, to produce the live steam needed to make quarts of espresso at a time and to whip milk to a froth for capuccino, the Italian version of café au lait. We show some domestic versions of these professional machines, scaled down in size and price, but still costly items. We love them but do we need them when simpler, less expensive espresso makers are available? The decision is yours—we offer a variety from which to choose.

Junior Espresso Maker   11.186

Cast aluminum with plastic knob and handle; 4″ diam.; 8¼″ high overall; 9-cup capacity. Also avail. with capacity of 3, 6, or 14 (demi-tasse) cups.

$18.00 ▲

We begin humbly with a simple espresso maker from Italy, the birthplace of that inky beverage. This is an octagonal pot in three pieces—the bottom holds the water, the top the finished product; between them is the basket containing the finely ground dark-roast coffee. Screw the top and bottom together after filling the basket and putting water into the base and place it over a low flame. As the water boils, it rises as steam through the coffee and bubbles out of a tube into the upper part of the pot, now transformed into coffee. A safety valve in the lower section insures against the accidental explosion of this pot after the water has been boiled out of the base, but you must be sure to remove it from the heat as soon as the top has filled to avoid ruining the pot. Now—we like the coffee it makes, its simple design and,

above all, its low price. But we aren't fond of the way the aluminum discolors after use, or of the pot-watching necessary to take it off the fire the instant the coffee is done. That said, we admit that we've owned and loved its twin for 10 years. The pot comes in four sizes, from a mini 3 cups to a maxi 14, all demitasse size.

Atomic Espresso Maker 11.187

Cast aluminum with plastic knobs and handles; 5¼" base diam.; 9" high; 6- to 9-cup (demitasse) capacity.

$85.00

This espresso-capuccino maker looks like a prop from a Buck Rogers movie, all silvery tubes and cylinders bedecked with knobs and spouts. Kept on your kitchen counter, it is sure to draw a "what-is-it" from the passing parade. Before we describe how it works, we'd best tell you that its name is not pronounced as in the modifier before *energy*, but ah-tom-EEK, with the accent on the last syllable. Down to business. That long black handle operates the container for the ground coffee—a tug and a twist removes it from the housing above. Unscrew the black knob on that curvy tube and pour in the water. Put the whole kit and caboodle on the stove. When it starts bouncing around it has gotten up a good head of steam and your espresso has espressed. Now you will notice two round red knobs. One of them works a brass pin beneath the coffee container. Pull it before you start the coffee cooking and the brew will come pouring out into the fat little pitcher below when it is done. Push it in and—look, Ma, no drips. Now for that other red knob attached to the skinny spout. That is the capuccino maker. Twist the knob and

steam comes out to foam up the milk for that frothy delight. Two sizes of this make are available—give us the larger one in this case.

Miniature Espresso Maker 11.188

Stainless steel with plastic knob and spouts; base diam. 3⅞"; 8½" high; 3-cup (demi-tasse) capacity.

$35.00

Instead of a silver bibelot, why not present the newlyweds with this miniature marvel of an espresso machine? It's so simple to operate that even the bride whose level of culinary competence is burned toast can serve perfect after-dinner coffee to her mate every time. Everything about this lilliputian electric appliance bespeaks its Italian origin, from its clever shape to its European-type plug (be sure to provide an adapter). The inner workings are connected with a large integral screw attached to the bottom of the pot which threads into a plastic-topped nut perched on the lid. A slim metal straw angles from the lid and ends in two tiny spouts like a reversed V. Just fill it and plug it in—the thermostat turns it off when the coffee is ready. We hate to cavil, but we do wish they had made the cord and plug in espresso brown to match the plastic trim of this utensil, instead of choosing black. On the bright side, we love its neat, shiny stainless-steel body and its foolproof efficiency. As tiny as befits equipment for a just-married's kitchen, it will tuck away neatly between the toaster and the blender.

Europiccola Espresso Machine 11.189

Stove-enameled steel base and stand, with chrome-plated bronze boiler, rubber pad, plastic knobs; 11½" × 8"; 11¾" high; 6- to 8-cup (demi-tasse) capacity.

$275.00 ▲

Take a giant step from the diminutive espresso machine we just showed you and regard this weighty affair. A Rube Goldberg arrangement of levers, cylinders, knobs, and spouts sits on a heavy metal base fitted with a grid-topped well to catch the drips. Two and a half cups of water, enough for 6 to 8 miniature espresso cups of coffee, go into the larger chrome-plated bronze container. Put the coffee, ground almost to powder for the best results, into the small metal filter-equipped cup beneath the lever. After you plug the machine in, push the switch to *massimo* and wait for the steam to rise. Sixty seconds after the water boils, switch the machine to *minimo*. The finished espresso is released by raising and lowering the large lever. With this machine you can make ristretto, the utmost in espresso, by raising the lever only halfway to dilute the coffee essence as little as possible. Steam for foaming the milk to make capuccino pours from a narrow nozzle operated separately by turning a black plastic knob. Two tiny cups of coffee come from the machine with each filling of the coffee filter; we would find this a nuisance if this container weren't so easy to attach and detach. And this arrangement does insure the freshest cup of espresso you can get, freshly brewed every time instead of warmed up. You don't have to be Italian to love espresso, but you'd better have a lot of lira put by if you covet this machine.

Club Espresso Machine 11.190

Stainless-steel body with brass interior, chromed-steel extensions, enameled-steel base and sides, Bakelite knobs and handles, plastic accessories; 13¾" × 11¾"; 13¾" high; 40-cup (demi-tasse) capacity.

$300.00

Cremina Espresso Machine 11.191

Stainless-steel body with brass interior, chromed-steel extensions, enameled-steel base and sides, Bakelite knobs and handles, plastic accessories; 10⅛" × 7⅞"; 13" high; 18-cup (demi-tasse) capacity.

$200.00

Here are the big boys of espresso making, only slightly smaller than the ones used in your local ristorante. The Club is colossal in capacity and cost. It holds more than two quarts of water and turns out 40 little cups of espresso with each filling of water. The Cremina, half the capacity and two-thirds the price of the Club, makes 18 servings. These are professional machines of excellent quality. They operate on the same principle as the Europiccola above: the coffee goes into the filter cup, which must be refilled after making every two cups. Pulling the lever forces the steam through two spouts into serving cups placed on the grid below. Capuccino can be made by foaming the milk with the steam spout—there is one such spout on the Cremina and two on the Club. You can also use these spouts to heat up any beverage by injecting steam into it. Each machine is made of stainless steel with a brass interior and has heatproof Bakelite or plastic handles and knobs. Once you get one of these beauties in your kitchen, you'd better brush up on your pasta-making so you can serve Italian banquets equal to the coffee to follow.

Farber Coffee Urn 11.192

Stainless steel with plastic base and handles; 10¼" diam.; 18¾" high; 18- to 55-cup capacity.

$69.99

Somehow our sensibilities are always offended by that institutional party percolator sitting on our sideboard along with the Wedgwood. But there are times when we must serve more coffee than our silver pot can hold. Our problem was neatly solved when we ran across this electric coffee urn from Farber, the same people who make the pots. While not so ravishing as to send us into transports, it is nonetheless a beauty queen compared to run-of-the-mill urns. Made of gleaming stainless steel, it won't fight with our sterling-silver sugar bowl and cream pitcher, and we're secure in the knowledge that its material won't retain the rancid oils from last month's kaffee-klatsch. We like its lines, a lot more graceful than those of the usual coffee tank—it's really a well-proportioned bowl resting on a footed base, which has a ring of plastic between the metal and your table. Two large, square ring handles dangle from the pot so it can be whisked to the kitchen sans potholders once the party's over. You'll use this pot for lavish entertainments—working as a percolator, it makes and keeps hot from 18 to 55 cups, as occasion requires.

The Cleikum Club, a Scottish culinary confrerie immortalized by Sir Walter Scott in Saint Ronan's Well, *was headed by the fastidious Peregrine Touchwood, known as the Cleikum Nabob. His coffee was made as follows: "Coffee, four years kept, but only one hour roasted, was prepared by the Nabob's own hands—coffee which he himself had brought from Mocha, and now made in a coffee-pot of Parisian invention patronized by Napoleon."*

Quoted in The Scots Kitchen, *by F. Marian McNeill, 1929*

Tea Kettles and Tea Pots

Take tea and see if your headache doesn't disappear, your troubles dissolve in its fragrant steam. Since the first leaves drifted from the bush into the Chinese philosopher's pot of hot water at a date unknown, tea has been used as a panacea for a passel of ailments mental and physical. The ancients believed that it cured everything from consumption to catarrh; modern folk find tea a tranquilizer and a stomach settler, the remedy for a host of ills occasioned by the hectic pace of daily life.

Fact and fancy surround the history and use of tea. Wars have been started in its name (remember the Boston Tea Party?), rituals performed for its presentation. The Japanese tea ceremony is a mannered and mystical ritual that takes years to learn and hours to enact. Gypsy fortune tellers read the future in the random arrangement of leaves left in the drinker's cup. Folk medicine prescribes poultices of tea leaves to draw the swelling from a boil, the pain from a sting.

TEA DEFINED

What is tea? It is an infusion of dried leaves in hot water. Some Americans have rarely seen a real tea leaf, preferring to dunk little white paper bags of pulverized tea by their strings into a cup of boiling water. This method produces shudders in an Englishman or an Oriental who takes his tea brewing seriously. For them, only a pre-warmed pot designed for the purpose plus whole tea leaves, plus fresh water, freshly boiled, will produce a palatable beverage.

Almost anything that grows has been used to make tea, from sassafras roots to lotus blossoms. Commercial tea blends wear poetic labels —Lapsang Souchong, Oolong, Gunpowder, Dragon Well. In each little box of possible thousands is a tea with a different taste. Black teas such as Keemun and Hu Kwa are made from leaves which have been fermented before drying. Green teas, Lu An and Water Nymph, for example, are natural, light in color and full of the bouquet of the living plant. The scented teas, tea leaves blended with petals of jasmine, chrysanthemum, or rose, are gardens in a cup. Teas come from China, Ceylon, India—none grow in our part of the world.

TEA-MAKING EQUIPMENT

Whatever tea suits your taste, treat it with respect if you want to enjoy its full flavor. You will need two pots—one in which to boil the water and one for steeping the tea. Don't improvise and use a coffee pot for tea brewing; its spout, low on the pot, is misplaced for this purpose. The best brewed tea is at the top, so well-designed teapots have spouts set high. Begin with fresh cold water brought to the boil in a clean kettle. Rinse the teapot with boiling or very hot water and add the tea leaves, a spoonful or so to the cup. Then pour in the boiling water and steep it to the desired strength.

The first pot acquired by the new householder is invariably a tea kettle. How else to boil the water for the instant coffee or the Cup-a-Soup? Look at the one you own with a critical eye. Maybe the time has come to retire it to the back burner in favor of a newer, cleaner, or even prettier model. Take a peek inside your kettle. Chances are the interior is pitted from exposure to tap water, or coated with mineral deposits from the same water. If it's impossible to clean your kettle, consider a new one. It may help to keep your new kettle from acquiring pits if you never bring the water to a hard boil; in other words, turn the heat off when the whistling kettle whispers.

Now for the pot. The little tea pot, short and stout, paeaned by the nursery-school set comes in a rainbow of colors and styles to blend with every decor, from Bauhaus to Baroque. After unpacking and admiring hundreds of pots, we chose a triad of the prettiest.

"Tea was extremely expensive in eighteenth-century England. Poor people, unable to afford the heavily taxed luxury, would buy used tea leaves at the back doors of the homes of the rich."

The Kitchen in History, *Molly Harrison, Scribners, New York*

Stainless-Steel Tea Kettle — 11.193

Stainless steel with aluminum-clad bottom, plastic knob; 5½" diam.; 5" high; 2-qt. capacity.

$23.50

We like tea kettles (they're actually water kettles, come to think of it) with removable lids so you can examine and clean the interiors from time to time. This one is a mirror-bright beauty from Finland. It looks like a silver apple with a spout, its handle resembles a ribbon of silver, and in addition to this there is a fat black lozenge of a knob atop its convex lid. The heavy bottom is sprayed with aluminum for improved heat transfer. The absent-minded take note: this, like all the kettles we show, is silent—no warning whistle tells you when the water is hot enough to make the tea. A watched pot is preferable to a burned one, so set your kitchen timer for the estimated span, or keep an eye out for the curling wisps of steam that will tell you that your boiling water is ready. You can do more than just boil water in this compact beauty. It deserves to be called "tea kettle" because you can make tea in it. The spout is set high, and to reach it, fluid must pass through a strainer. Boil water, throw in your tea leaves, let them steep, then serve. All in one.

Specialty Cookware: Coffee, Tea, and Wine Equipment

Copco Tea Kettle 11.194

Enameled steel with wood knob and handle; 7½″ diam.; 5″ high; 2½-qt. capacity.

$19.95 ▲

As nonporous as porcelain, this Copco-ware enameled kettle is as strong as its steel base, and we swoon over its shape. A squat cylinder of indigo blue accented with a flaring spout, it has a smooth wooden handle that collapses for storage. Another round of wood forms a knob on the lid. Glazed in glowing primary colors of red, yellow, or blue, a burnished brown, or a sophisticated bright white, it is lined inside with a slick black coating which resists deposits of rust and other minerals. For the occasional cleaning which you'll do to keep this pot as sweet as the day you bought it, boil a teaspoonful of baking soda in a kettleful of water from time to time.

Gense Glass Tea Kettle 11.195

Heat-resistant glass; 4⅞″ base diam.; 5½″ high; 1-qt. capacity.

$37.50

Thanks to practical Pyrex, we have lost our fear of cooking in glass. But a glass tea kettle? Well, Reijmyre Glasbruk's gone and done it. In their kettle, imported by Gense, you can boil the water and steep the tea too. No guessing about the proper strength, no clock-watching to be sure it's brewed—you can actually see the tea reach the peak of perfection. This kettle is shaped like a miniature milk can, with its lid set into a collar of glass. We love the stalactite of a handle, the swan's neck of a spout—in fact, we admire *everything* about this hand-blown glass tea pot. And we promise never, but never, to forget we've put the kettle on and let it shatter from overheating on the stove. Although chances are excellent that you could get away with setting this pot over direct heat, we counsel prudence: always use an asbestos mat or a Flame-Tamer (Chapter 6) under it.

Chemex Carafe Kettle 11.196

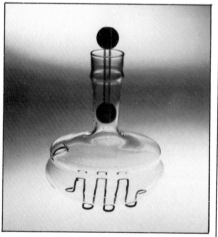

Heat-resistant glass with cork stoppers, painted steel grid; 9¼″ base diam.; 10¾″ high; 2-qt. capacity.

$25.00

Who would ever guess that this exotic glass carafe is a tea kettle? Well, Chemex swears it is and, since they've been making hot-beverage containers for years, we were inclined to believe them. We tested it and found that this bottle will do just as good a job of boiling water as the more familiar tea kettle. We placed the accompanying grid for use on electric burners beneath it, as the manufacturer suggests, and switched on the heat. (We could have set it directly over a gas burner.) When we went to lift the hot water from the stove we looked for the handle. None in sight. Screwing our courage to the sticking point, we grasped the bottle by the neck and found it was cool to the touch. Magic. The secret is the batonlike stopper: two cork spheres are pierced by and joined with a glass tube, so that the steam escapes through a hole in the top ball and the heat bypasses the neck entirely. (You'll remember that glass doesn't conduct heat well, as we pointed out in the history of stovetop cookery in Chapter 6.) The water can then be poured out through this opening or through the curved aperture in one side of the bowl. Don't use this carafe only for boiling plain old water—use it as a server for iced tea, fruit juices, or even soups, hot or cold. No one will suspect that the elegant container in which you serve the sangria can also boil the water for the coffee.

Leach Tea Pot 11.197

Stoneware with cane handle; 3″ base diam.; 5¼″ high; 1-qt. capacity.

$16.00

This tea pot has been designed by Bernard Leach, a British potter who has lived and studied in the Orient, embodies his reverence for the preparation and service of tea. We love its bulbous little dark-brown and rust body holding one quart, its soaring spout, its solid cane handle braided to tiny doughnuts on the pot. We admire the sleek tenmoku glaze and the ribbon of auburn Cornish clay banding the base which ad-

This eighteenth-century brass tea pot was fitted with a handle of cranberry glass to protect the hand from heat while pouring.

Continued from preceding page

vertises its earthy origins. What else can we say? This is the most ravishing pot you could own, of which only the finest tea would be worthy.

British Tea Pot 11.198

Ceramic; 3⅜" base diam; 4½" high; 6-cup capacity. Also avail. with a capacity of 3, 4 or 7 cups.

$6.50

Although we celebrate the beauty of our Leach pot, we also treat ourselves to an occasional cup of tea brewed in our homey British classic. Slicked all over with a dark brown glaze, its silhouette is balanced by a curving spout on one side, a graceful handle on the other. Round and fat, it sits on a broad base. The lid wears a round button knob and a deep collar, so it will stay firmly seated when pouring out the very last drop of tea. This is the pot you will see every afternoon on tea tables across England, where it is known as a "Brown Betty." Find a knitted or quilted cozy for it.

"How did he know there were only two things in the world I could have swallowed, things English and familiar, bread and butter and Tea? I had not known tea could be had in France, though it was tea such as we had not seen, served in a glass, the leaves in a little paper bag tied with a string and soaking in hot water. It was weak but it was hot and I made it sweet and ate four slices of bread and butter."

Rumer Godden, Greengage Summer, *1963*

Hand-thrown Stoneware Tea Pot 11.199

Stoneware; 4¼" base diam.; 7½" high overall; 3-cup capacity.

$15.00

Now try to imagine a tea pot that is tall and straight rather than short and round, one that looks like a milk pitcher or a watering can. If you don't believe that it will brew good tea, ask a Japanese—the rural folk of Japan have been using pots like this for centuries. Hand-thrown by the potter Byron Temple, this pot is winsome despite its strict shape. Maybe it's the cozy arch of the handle, made in one with the pot. Or perhaps it's the unglazed tawny toadstool of a lid, the cap forming the cover, the stem holding it securely to the pot. The glaze, a melange of colors, adds to the lovable look. A cool wash of mottled grey meets two bright bands of brown—one russet, one chocolate—above a thin stripe of unglazed clay. We see it brewing a pot of tansy tea, or even holding a spray of bright brass buttons of tansy flowers on a country kitchen table.

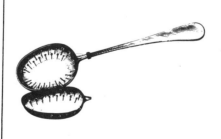

Tea Infuser 11.200

Stainless steel; 1⅜" diam.; 1¾" high; chain 5½" long.

$1.30

We are not fans of the tea bag. But we do admire its good points—there are no limp leaves to float around your tea cup or to be cleaned from the pot, and it makes tea that is never too strong or too weak, because you are watching it steep. Orange Pekoe is not our favorite among teas, however, and that seems to be the one kind most commonly packaged in those little white bags. Imagine our delight when we discovered this gadget. Now we can sip our Lapsang Soochong or Earl Grey without having to strain it through our teeth. A neat little cylinder of stainless steel holds the tea—just the right amount for our 1-quart tea pot. Pricked with tiny holes top and bottom, it has a sturdy little chain with a fishhook at one end to grip the rim of the pot. As it's made of stainless steel, the scent of the jasmine tea which last inhabited this infuser won't perfume your Oolong, and since this metal has no tinny taste of its own, you'll always enjoy pure tea flavor.

British Tea Pot
Hand-thrown Stoneware Tea Pot
Tea Infuser
Dripless Tea Strainer
Stainless-Steel Tea Strainer
Instant Immersion Heater

Dripless Tea Strainer 11.201

Chrome on brass; 2¼" diam.; 2½" high.

$3.25 ▲

Santa left one of these tea strainers in our stocking several years ago and we have blessed him at teatime ever since. A little chromed-brass strainer of the finest mesh pivots on two supports above a Lilliputian saucer. Tilt the strainer above the cup and pour the tea through it. Then set it down and the drips remain in the saucer, not on your tea tray, the leaves in the strainer, not in your cup. You can get a good grip on things with the small hook of a handle. It's an unobtrusive little item, much smaller than the usual tea strainer, so it can be hidden, with those messy leaves, among the silver beauties in your tea service, or even covered with a clean cup. Buy a dozen and give them to all the tea mavens you know.

Stainless-Steel Tea Strainer 11.202

Stainless steel; 6¾" long overall; strainer 2¾" diam., 1" deep.

$3.50

If your silver tea service lacks a strainer, you will want something not too kitcheny-looking to use with it. We nominate this elegant small strainer from Italy, whose bigger brothers are found in Chapter 1, where they are recommended for yeoman service in meal preparation. Reduced to this pigmy version, all the durable and efficient virtues of the larger sizes still exist. In addition, it is just plain good-looking—a cup of satiny mesh framed in a simple round of highly polished stainless steel that is welded to a flared handle similar to those on your flatware. That pretty frame also serves as a lip to seat the strainer firmly on the teacup while pouring. Keep it handy on your pegboard—it hangs from a pretty curved loop atop the bowl.

Instant Immersion Heater 11.203

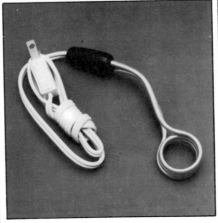

Aluminum coil with Bakelite terminal; 4¾" long.

$1.50 ▲

A busy lawyer we know carries his coffee break in his attaché case. Wherever he may roam, hot beverages are instantly available to him via the instant immersion heater which lies coiled beneath the briefs. He just plugs it into any outlet, dunks the coil into the cup, and even cool coffee-wagon brew is steaming hot in seconds, or he can make his own tea. For those far from hot plate or range top, this heater can warm up the water for tea or coffee, or even the soup for a dieter's bouillon break. Nothing fancy—it is just a simple metal heating coil attached to a red Bakelite terminal (do not get this vital part wet) and a white cord. Office workers find these heaters almost as indispensable as their typewriters.

"Tea à la Française *used to be made somewhat after this fashion. The cup was half-filled with milk, sugar à la discrétion being added. A little silver sieve was next placed over the cup, and from a jug sufficient hot water, in which had been previously left to soak some half-dozen leaf-fragments of green tea, to fill the cup, was poured forth. In fact the visitor was invited to drink a very nasty compound indeed, something like the 'wish' tea with which the school-mistress used to regale her victims—milk and water and 'wish-you-may-get' tea! But they have changed all that across the Channel, and five o'clock tea is one of the most fashionable functions of the day, with the* beau monde: *a favorite invitation of the society* belle *of the* fin de siècle *being:* 'Voulez-vous fivoclocquer avec moi?' "*

Cakes and Ale, *by Edward Spencer, London, Grant Richards, 1897*

Ice Buckets

We've seen ice buckets made from artillery shells, hollow logs, and chamber pots. We've owned handsome ones in silver, and hideous ones in styrofoam. But we prefer ice buckets which maintain a low profile, doing their job of keeping the cubes cold without becoming cutesy conversation pieces.

Americans like their alcoholic beverages to clink in their glasses, and find the warm Scotch and tepid gin beloved by Europeans an abomination. This side of the water, nothing can kill a cocktail party faster than running out of ice. Our newest refrigerators make and dispense cubes automatically, making the sectional ice tray, enemy of the fingernail and the disposition, obsolete. Ice buckets keep those cubes or slivers or balls of ice in pristine shape for hours. Some buckets are insulated with space-age materials, some are simply overgrown Ther-

Continued from preceding page

mos bottles, others layer one container within another. We have chosen the simplest ones, consigning the converted cachepot to outer darkness.

Crystal Ice Bucket 11.204

Crystal with chromed-steel handle; 4¾″ diam.; 4¾″ high.

$37.50

This ice bucket looks like an old-fashioned drinking glass for Gulliver in Lilliput. We loved its looks, but wondered at its practicality. After all, we reasoned, there isn't even a lid to keep the cubes cold, much less any insulation. But we found it efficient in use. For one thing, it will hold one trayful of ice at a time, so two reasonably speedy drinkers will use all the ice before it melts. Then, too, the very heavy glass does a fair job of insulating just by its thickness—and remember that cold air sinks, so the ice, even uncovered, tends to cool itself. And, then, this bucket is pretty, a virtue we find hard to ignore. If you don't tell anyone that the shiny, silvery handle is really chrome, they'll think it is sterling to match your ice tongs. This ice bucket would be a perfect container for a colorful crimson gazpacho for two served on the terrace, once the cocktail hour is over.

"An exclusively feminine department is the water supply. The woman has the water bottles of the household in her charge. These are made out of the woody shell of a mature coconut, with a stopper of twisted palm-leaf. In the morning or near sunset she goes, sometimes a full half-mile, to fill them at the water-hole: here the women forgather, resting and chatting, while one after another fills her water-vessels, cleans them, arranges them in baskets or on large wooden platters, and, just before leaving, gives the cluster a final sprinkling of water to cover it with a suggestive gloss of freshness. The water-hole is the woman's club and centre of gossip, and as such is important, for there is a distinct woman's public opinion and point of view in a Trobriand village, and they have their secrets from the male, just as the male has from the female."

The Sexual Life of Savages, by Bronislaw Malinowski, Harcourt, Brace and World, New York, 1929

Stainless-Steel Ice Bucket 11.205

Stainless steel; 6½″ diam.; 7″ high.

$38.50

Having broken the thermal-glass liner of our last ice bucket by overzealous and undercautious filling, we searched for something more durable. Here is what we found. A handsome modern ice bucket of stainless steel lined with—you guessed it—more stainless steel. Now the worst we can do—and it won't be easy—is dent it. This roomy container is unabashed about its function. It looks like an ice bucket—it *is* an ice bucket, a beautiful one. What else can we say except that it holds at least two trayfuls of ice?

Plexiglas Ice Bucket 11.206

Plexiglas; 6″ high overall; large bucket 8⅝″ inside diam., 5⅛″ deep; small bucket 7⅜″ inside diam., 4¾″ deep; lid 11″ diam.

$50.00

Unlike the stainless-steel container above, this is an ice bucket that looks like a food server or a cheese dish or a storage container. And, indeed, it can serve all these functions in addition to its primary one. It comes in three pieces, all of clear, sturdy Plexiglas. The two slightly squared-off bowls nest one inside the other, leaving air space for insulation around the smaller one. A heavy lid fits tightly over all. When not housing four or more trayfuls of ice, the bowls can be used separately—for salads, summer soups, punch, mixed fruit, or even a big bunch of marguerites or a rainbow collection of beach glass—all would look super in these see-through containers. The lid does double duty as a serving plate—think of wedges of melon, a mound of crudités, a translucent mold of clear aspic shimmering on its transparent surface. Fill the outside bowl with ice, pack the tuna salad in the smaller one within, and take it to the picnic without a worry about spoilage. Back to the kitchen: flip over the larger container and cover the cake, while the smaller serves as a cheese bell. Oh yes, and after all that you can put the pieces back together and use it again, plain and simple, as an ice bucket.

Thermos Carafe   11.207

Chrome-finished steel with plastic base, spout, handle, and lid, glass interior; 5¼" diam.; 9⅞" high; 7-cup capacity.

$27.50

One of our favorite jokes concerns the country bumpkin who insists that the Thermos bottle is the greatest invention since the beginning of the world. Asked why, he says, "Well, you puts in the cold things and they stays cold; you puts in the hot things and they stays hot. Now tell me, how do it know?" Well, we're not too sure, but we do know that it has revolutionized al fresco dining, among other things. This pitcher is a classier version of the plain old Thermos bottle. Of silvery chromed steel in a pretty shape, it has a black plastic handle and pouring spout and a screw-on lid punctuated with a red dot which, positioned over the spout, enables you to pour without removing it. Within, a coppery radiance of thermal glass holds 7 cups of hot soup or cold lemonade for 18 hours without an appreciable change in temperature. When the snow flies and the picnic hamper is retired for the season, use this pitcher to keep the juice cold for the flu sufferer or the cocoa hot for the returning skiers.

Ice Pick   11.208

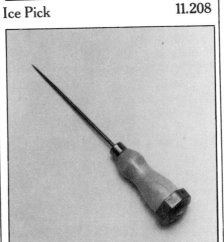

Chromed steel with varnished wood handle; 8" long.

$.98

Frankly, we weren't enamored of any of the ice picks we gathered for evaluation, and this one is, perhaps, only a little better than most. It has a smooth, shaped wooden handle with a weighted metal cap for ice-crushing. The pick itself is fairly sturdy and needle-sharp; it will do a workmanlike job of reducing a solid block of ice to manageable chips. But we don't like the join between the handle and the needle, even though it appears to be securely fastened with a metal collar. Does anyone still make picks like the ones the iceman used in our youth? They were simply a solid piece of steel—needle, handle, and all—with nothing to come apart. We'd like to find one like that again, but in the meantime we'll make do with this.

Old American ice picks.

Wine-serving Equipment

Sometimes old wine needs new bottles. Red wine, as it ages, throws sediment which clouds the clear liquid, and the more antique the vintage, the wiser you will be to decant it into a carafe or a decanter, leaving the sediment safely behind. Oenophiles do this by placing a candle behind the wine bottle, so they can see the instant the sediment starts to leave the bottle—when this happens they stop pouring.

Now suppose the wine you're serving isn't a 1937 Margaux but a 1975 Gallo-by-the-gallon. Those jugs are a trifle difficult to wield at the table, in addition to being somewhat lacking aesthetically. You *could* pour the wine into the orange-juice pitcher, but a beautiful carafe will add more to your table. Middle-aged and young red wines, while they are usually without sediment, need to breathe a bit before serving. They, too, benefit by being decanted before serving.

A wine carafe is generally a simple affair with a flaring mouth, a long, relatively narrow neck, and a bulbous body. As there is no stopper, this vessel is meant for serving, not for storage. A decanter is similar in shape to a carafe, but because it has a stopper, the remainder of the wine can be kept in it from one meal to the next. Whether you choose a carafe or a decanter, stick to clear undecorated glass so the deep maroon of the Burgundy or the pale straw of the Chablis shows to full advantage.

When a festive meal includes Champagne, or when any meal is accompanied by a white wine, you'll need a cooler to keep your bottle at the right degree of chill; and we show you, farther along, our choice among the best available coolers.

WINE ACCESSORIES

All the equipment you really need in order to enjoy wine is a corkscrew and a glass—or better yet, two glasses, since wine tastes even better when it's shared. Even the casual wine drinker will find it useful, however, to own racks to store his wine safely and conveniently; a wine cooler to chill white wines, rosés, and Champagnes; and a decanter or two to show off certain wines to their best advantage.

CORKSCREWS

A poor corkscrew can prove costly when it crumbles the cork of an expensive wine. A good corkscrew, which needn't cost much, should have a coil or worm long enough to fully penetrate even the long corks used for the finest wines—the kind of cork that a poor corkscrew will invariably break. The coil itself should be a true spiral, not a wiggly line, so that even a weak cork will be securely gripped: a poor coil will simply bore a hole into such a cork. In addition, you will find it simpler to use a corkscrew that has some kind of lever mechanism to avoid the awkwardness and occasional accidents that occur when a cork is tugged out of a bottle by sheer force.

WINE COOLERS

Wine can easily be cooled in the refrigerator, but if you want to chill a bottle at the last minute, putting it in ice and water is the simplest solution. This is quicker and safer than using the freezer, where a forgotten bottle may freeze solid. Any big pot will do as a wine cooler, of course, but if you want to keep a wine chilled as you consume it—especially important for Champagne—you will want an attractive wine cooler. Most examples on the market are too shallow and so chill only a part of the wine in a bottle, especially the slim, tapered bottles used for German wines. Ice buckets are even worse, as they are usually short and squat, rather than tall and narrow. Wine coolers made of clear glass are very attractive, but they are also heavy. A plastic wine cooler with a handle is especially practical, since the handle makes it easier to carry a bucket filled with water, ice, and a bottle of wine from the kitchen to the living or dining room.

DECANTERS

Decanting is necessary for old red wines and useful for young ones. The sediment that appears in old red wines is harmless, but it's unattractive when it shows up in your wine glass. The best solution is to stand the wine up for a few hours, to let the sediment fall to the bottom of the bottle, and then to pour it carefully into another container in one continuous motion. If you decant over a light—whether it be a candle, an electric bulb, or a flashlight—you can see when the first wisps of sediment appear, and stop pouring immediately. Any clean glass container will do as a decanter, but for finer wines you may prefer an attractively shaped decanter that will show off your wine on the dining table.

Young red wines are usually uncorked an hour or so before they are to be served, to give them a chance to develop their bouquet and soften their taste. Here again, decanting is the most effective way to let such a wine breathe. You may also want to decant even the least expensive jug wines, simply because it is so awkward to pour wine from a gallon jug into a glass at the table. Even the simplest table setting is enhanced by a carafe of inexpensive red or white wine, which so easily conveys casual generosity.

Whether you use a simple carafe or an elegant decanter, the wine will show better in clear glass, without any design. The container should be big enough to hold the contents of a bottle, and should have a reasonably wide mouth for easy decanting. The carafe or decanter should also have good balance for easy pouring —a fact sometimes forgotten when one holds an empty decanter in a shop. The very wide base of a ship's decanter and the very long, narrow neck of certain modern designs make pouring difficult.

WINE RACKS

Wine bottles should be kept on their sides, so that the cork remains wet and expanded—a dried cork may let in air, which will eventually spoil a wine. The best racks, however simple in design, are those that permit you to expand your wine cellar if you decide to add to your collection. The kind of racks you choose will depend not only on your budget, but also on whether you plan to hide your cellar in a closet or basement, or to use the racks as part of the furnishings of your home, perhaps along a dining-room wall. In the latter case, you might consider putting a shelf on top of your wine racks, which encloses your wines more formally, as well as giving you an additional counter or sideboard.

Crystal Wine Funnel 11.209

Crystal; 3¼" diam.; 6" long overall.

$7.00 ▲

While a funnel is not de rigueur for decanting the younger red wines, it is a distinct help when dealing with older vintages in which a lot of sediment has collected—you can keep your eye on the sediment in the old bottle, not on the neck of the carafe into which you are decanting the wine. A glass funnel like this one will make that tricky process virtually foolproof. A classic bell shape of handblown crystal, the funnel has a spout that angles in a gentle curve designed to pour the wine down the side of the carafe. This insures that no aeration will occur and the wine will not be "bruised" in the pouring. Further, the spout, although super-thick, has a tapering neck so the wine will flow in a tiny stream. A twist of crystal forms a generous handle. Altogether lovely as well as practical, the funnel would be a welcome gift for wine lovers.

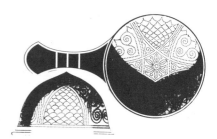

A bronze wine strainer found at Herculaneum.

Crystal Carafe 11.210

Crystal; 5½" base diam.; 9¾" high; 1-qt. capacity. Also avail. with capacity of 18 oz.

$16.50

As simple as a laboratory beaker, this carafe makes the color of the wine itself the main attraction. A lovely globe of glass topped by a narrow soaring neck holds a quart of wine for a party—or buy the smaller one, holding a little over a pint, for intimate dinners à deux. The mouth of the carafe is flared into a small spout for easy pouring, the bottom is heavy and flat for stability. The clean lines of this one blend with any decor, and its price will appeal to any pocketbook.

Rondo Crystal Decanter 11.211

Crystal; 2⅝" base diam.; 8" high; 18-oz. capacity.

$57.50

We love this stoppered crystal decanter from Sweden. As is proper, the wine itself is the star, gleaming in the pretty transparent sphere, flowing through the short neck and wide mouth. A heavy rim of crystal borders the mouth, and as there is no spout, care must be taken not to splash or dribble while pouring from it. The base is very heavy and is incised with the name Kosta for the label-conscious. As it holds only 18 ounces, buy two or more of these decanters for your table, unless you plan to entertain one best friend at a time.

"Claret should be served at the same temperature as Madeira, never with ice; it should remain about forty-eight hours standing, then decanted, care being observed that no sediment enter the decanter."

Practical Cooking and Dinner Giving, *by Mrs. Mary F. Henderson, Harper & Brothers, New York, 1891*

Tall Glass Decanter 11.212

Glass; 3½" diam.; 10⅝" high; 40-oz. capacity. Also avail. with capacity of 11 or 21 oz.

$2.00

A dramatic shape in clear glass, this decanter comes to us from Libbey, the glassmakers, who turn out a host of more humdrum things as well. It is tall and straight with high shoulders, a wide neck, and a flaring mouth. Even though it is made by an American company, it holds an Imperial quart, 40 ounces, the equivalent of two and a half United States pints. When not in use holding the wine, this carafe will look lovely holding a spray of roses or a clutch of tulips. And don't overlook the two smaller sizes, holding 11 and 21 ounces respectively—at our house, at least, we have use for all three.

Classic Italian Decanter 11.213

Glass; 3¾" base diam.; 10" high; 1-liter capacity.

$3.25

Look again at the refined shape preceding this decanter (11.212). Now we show you its inspiration—the classic Italian glass decanter found on the tables of every trattoria and, lately, of every cafe and informal restaurant on these shores. We wouldn't suggest it for your fine burgundies, but when the jug of domestic or Sicilian *vino* is too massive for the table, decant it into this heavy, rustic glass decanter—*salute!*

A French picnic with wine, 1904.

515

Copper Wine Cooler   11.214

Copper with stainless-steel interior, brass loop handles; 8″ diam.; 8″ high.

$92.00

Wine coolers have been made for thousands of years in an endless variety of shapes and materials. Today, with refrigeration readily available, we mostly use coolers to keep single bottles cool once they have been brought to the table. Remember not to chill the wine too much beforehand—it kills flavor. Of the many coolers available, we show one that seems to us to possess all the desirable characteristics. Of handsome copper on the outside and rugged stainless steel within, it is big enough and strong enough to hold your wine plus plenty of ice and water without danger of spills or strain leading to collapse or cracking. The big brass handles make it easy to carry, which is important—full-up, these things get pretty heavy.

From French Domestic Cookery, *Harper & Brothers, New York, 1855.*

CORKSCREWS

The corkscrew is the one essential tool for wine drinkers: it is an impossibility to get the cork out of the bottle with such an instrument as an ice pick, a table fork, or even that all-purpose tool, the bent bobbypin.

The ancient Romans kept their wine in amphorae, large pottery jugs with narrow necks out of which the wine was poured into smaller containers for serving. Beautifully modeled and richly decorated, the amphorae that survived the Empire reside in museums throughout the world. With the discovery that the bark of the cork tree made an effective seal, wine could be aged, stored, transported, and decanted for serving from the same container. But once he learned how to put that cork in, we bet the inventor had the devil's own time getting it out. And so the corkscrew was born.

CORKSCREW CRITERIA

There are literally hundreds of different kinds of corkscrews, all designed to wrest that obdurate cylinder of squeaky cork from the narrow neck of the wine bottle without breaking it, pushing it in rather than pulling it out, or bringing about any of the other calamities that cause either a loss of the user's temper or of the wine itself. The cork in a new wine is fairly sturdy, but as it ages, it becomes more fragile. The same corkscrew that successfully unstops this year's Beaujolais will often make mincemeat of an aged cork stamped Château d' Yquem. All corkscrews should share certain virtues, however. The crux of the matter is the coil or worm—it should be very sharp and kept that way by never being allowed to touch anything but the cork. It must be a thin spiral; thick ones fragment the cork. It should be sturdily attached to the handle so it won't part from it when pressure is applied. It must be long enough to pierce the entire cork, but not so long that the tip comes through the bottom. And it should be made of tinned or chromed steel so, if perchance it does touch the wine, it will not impart any metallic flavor.

We tested dozens of corkscrews. Those we found wanting do not, naturally, appear here. The ones we chose will enable even the fumble-fingered to liberate a cork with the ease of a sommelier.

Waiter's Corkscrew   11.215

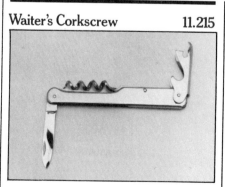

Nickel-plated steel; 4½″ long.

$4.50 ▲

The next time you dine out, watch the waiter as he removes the cork from the wine you've ordered. He uses an implement that looks somewhat like a pocket knife—it is a slender tool with three separate hinged sections, each designed to facilitate prying the most stubborn or fragile cork from the bottle. A small sharp knife blade pops out at one end—this cuts through the metal capsule that encloses the cork and sheathes the top of the bottle. At the opposite end a piece of metal is hinged to the body of the implement. This is a lip rest which fits over the rim of the bottle and acts as a lever when drawing the cork. It also opens bottles and cans. Between these two parts is the business end, the screw-like worm which is long enough to pierce the cork entirely, removing it in one piece from the bottle. This tool is of nickel-plated steel, so no metallic flavor will mar the taste of the wine. No French waiter would be caught dead with any other corkscrew, but he must be hale and hearty, as the power behind the tool is mostly sheer muscle (but leverage helps, too, as we have said). Weak sisters may find it easy to insert the corkscrew, but difficult to draw the cork from the bottle. For them we recommend the winged corkscrew or one of the other devices that follow.

Winged Corkscrew   11.216

Chrome- or brass-plated cast aluminum with chromed-steel worm; 7" long.

$2.50 ▲

For the aforementioned wine lovers who lack muscle we recommend this model, whose cogged wheels and levers do the lifting of the cork for you. It resembles an undersized instrument of torture, but it is a most efficient corkscrew. The plastic-lined cap fits over the exposed cork (use a knife to remove the metal capsule, *not* the tip of the worm). Turning the stirrup-shaped handle on top of the tool sends the worm down through the cork and causes the ratchets on the two arms to mesh with the threads on the interior screw, forcing the arms to a full upright position when the worm is fully inserted in the cork. Then you apply downward pressure on these arms to lift the cork effortlessly out of the bottle. The handle does double duty as a bottle opener. Members of a certain school of wine mavens sneer at this type of corkscrew—perhaps they feel that a little suffering in the opening improves

the character of the wine or the drinker. We find it perfectly acceptable, except for ancient vintages, whose fragile corks might not stand up to the pressure exerted by the opener, or which might suffer because the bottle must be held upright to use this implement. This chromed or brass-plated cast-aluminum corkscrew has a chromed-steel worm. Whichever finish you choose, this works very well.

Wood-enclosed Corkscrew   11.217

Light-finished wood with stainless-steel worm; 7" long.

$1.99

We like the looks of this corkscrew, the worm encased in a handsome housing of varnished wood, two dowels of the same wood sitting on the top. The whole thing has a play-toy look, somewhat like those carved wooden dolls from Scandinavia. Appearances can be deceiving—this corkscrew really works. Tightening the smaller of the dowels sends the worm down into the bottle, a few reverse turns of the larger one pulls the cork out into the wooden cylinder. The worm has the sharpest tip of any we tested. We'd like to give this corkscrew to a wine-loving boat owner we know, as it is immune to rust and, what's more, it floats.

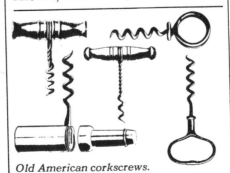

Old American corkscrews.

"*In the Mediterranean during the Greek golden age, many countries produced their own* ordinaires, *but the rich insisted on importing the scarce and expensive vintages of Lesbos and Chios. The great growths appear to have been sweet, and it has been suggested that the most famous wine of antiquity—the Pramnian so frequently mentioned by Homer—may have been as rich as Tokay. Since both Greeks and Romans followed the Egyptian custom of drinking their wines well diluted with water, the finer vintages were often kept until they were as thick and sticky as honey.*"

Food in History, *by Reay Tannahill, Stein and Day, New York, 1973*

Ah So Corkscrew   11.218

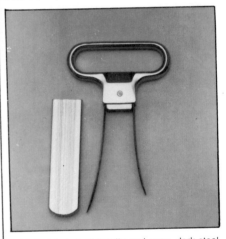

Nickel-plated steel handle and case, dark-steel blades; 4¼" long.

$3.50

If in your *caves* you have stashed a few rare bottles of antique vintage—a St. Estephe '27 or a Romanée-Conti '37—you must necessarily approach the cork with reverence. And caution. Remember that cork is a natural product and suffers from the ravages of age, and take the safest route. Do not pierce the cork but pry it when you are opening an aged treasure. The Ah So corkscrew, despite its smarty-pants name, does this most efficiently. Two flat, flexible blades are sturdily attached to a wide oblong handle. The longer of these pieces is inserted between the cork and the bottle and wiggled gently downward until the shorter piece enters the other side. Gen-

Continued from preceding page

tle tugging while rocking the cork back and forth extricates it "ah so" easily from the bottle. But no method is foolproof—it can happen that the cork will enter the wine instead of leaving the bottle when you use the Ah So. Don't despair—you can use our handy-dandy cork extractor (11.220). Be sure to dry the dark-steel blades of the Ah So carefully before sheathing it in its metal scabbard, or you'll ruin it with rust. If, by some miracle, a portion of your rare Burgundy remains after dinner, the Ah So recorks as well. Just place the cork between the blades, insert them into the bottle, and force the cork back in. The Ah So may be pocket-sized, but it's powerful.

Heavy-Duty Mechanical Corkscrew   11.219

Nickel-plated cast iron with bronze mechanism, wood handle; 11″ long; stands 5″ above countertop, 7¾″ out from counter edge.

$125.00 ▲

Anatomy is not always destiny—this machine does not, repeat not, belong on the workbench, despite its resemblance to a woodworking tool—it is a corkscrew. You might think such an arrangement of levers and clamps a bit of overkill for uncorking the occasional bottle, but we think it the perfect present for the dedicated collector and drinker of good wine. This is the only corkscrew we know about that not only draws the cork from the bottle but ejects it from the worm once it's pulled—no small point for its most faithful users, the proprietors of the auberges of France. There, perma-

nently installed behind the bar, one of these machines will remove a hundred or so corks from the good-but-not-extraordinary wines ordered during a typical lunchtime. How do you use it? Screw the viselike clamp to the edge of the table or the bar. The hollow barrel will then point downward. Fit the mouth of the bottle into the open end, pull down on the big black-handled lever, and the sharp-pointed worm enters the cork; raise the lever and the cork is out of the bottle and, further, has dropped from the worm automatically. Big, heavy, and costly, this ultimate corkscrew can uncork a bottle of wine every ten seconds.

Cork Retriever   11.220

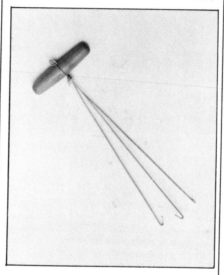

Nickel-plated steel wires with painted-wood handle, plastic ring; 10½″ long.

$2.00

Freud says there are no accidents, but we wonder how he felt when, despite his best efforts, the cork he was pulling slipped down the neck of the bottle into his Bordeaux. Undoubtedly he let go with a few expressions of emotion, just like the rest of us. We were overjoyed when we discovered this nifty tool to save the day and the wine. Long flexible wires, three of them, slip into the bottle easily. Then we grapple for the cork with the three tiny fishhooks at the end of each wire. Once caught, the cork is held firmly by slipping the small plastic ring down the wires until they are close enough together to hold the cork securely. By slowly and carefully pulling on the wooden handle, the cork is removed from the bottle.

Everything Tool   11.221

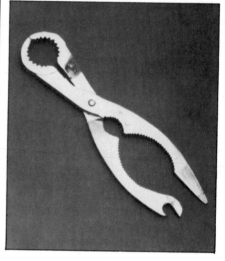

Zinc-plated steel; 7½″ long.

$2.00

A generous friend attached one of these Champagne-cork extractors to a gift bottle of bubbly some years ago, and we wondered at once how we had ever gotten along without it. Unfortunately, it only gets to exercise its major function on rare occasions, but it daily unscrews the top of the ketchup bottle, gets the lid off the peanut butter, and opens the soft drinks. A scissorlike implement, it has three round openings, all of them heavily grooved for a good grip. One is just the right size for the mushroom-shaped cap of a Champagne cork or the stubborn top of the chili sauce; another, smaller one is perfect for dislodging the pesky cap on the bottle of vanilla; and inside the handles two large curves fit around the lid of a pickle or mayonnaise jar. And at the very end of one handle is a bottle opener that works acceptably. We've also used this implement as a nutcracker, and, having mislaid the pliers, once repaired our son's tricycle with it. We don't call it the everything tool for nothing.

Heavy-Duty Mechanical Corkscrew
Cork Retriever
Everything Tool

Champagne-Cork Pliers
Champagne Opener
Hand Corker
Wine Tap

Champagne-Cork Pliers 11.222

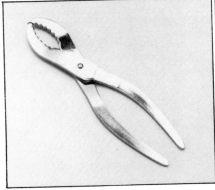

Zinc-plated steel; 6″ long.

$3.50

These are probably the most elegant little pliers ever designed for removing the cork from the most opulent of beverages, Champagne. Of steel plated with zinc, a look-alike here for sterling, they'll look just fine resting next to your Georgian silver wine cooler. While we think they're very pretty, we do have a small complaint about these pliers. Those handsome squared-off handles dig into the user's hand when pressure is exerted on them, so the cork-pulling might be an uncomfortable procedure for some. But don't worry—you're sure to forget the pain with the pop.

Champagne Opener 11.223

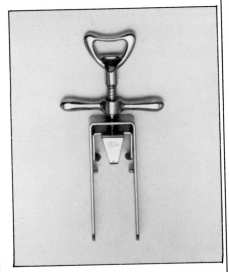

Chrome-plated steel; 8″ long.

$6.00

For some, the simplest approach is not necessarily the best. No wiggling out the Champagne cork by using their God-given thumbs for them, and even the pliers we've described are too straightforward. We'll bet these souls will take to this Champagne opener, though. A weighty chrome-plated affair, it consists of a large screw attached to a three-sided cap lifter bracketed by two heavy steel bars. An oversized wing nut raises and lowers the cap lifter, and a stirruplike handle enables the user to pull it free. And once the bubbly has been poured into the grownups' glasses, that handle can open the cap on the ginger ale to fill the kids'.

"Champagne should either be kept on ice for several hours previous to serving, or it should be half frozen; it is then called Champagne frappé. It is frozen with some difficulty. The ice should be pounded quite fine, then an equal amount of salt mixed with it. A quart bottle of Champagne well surrounded by this mixture should be frozen in two hours, or, rather, frozen to the degree when it may be poured from the bottle."

Practical Cooking and Dinner Giving, *by Mrs. Mary F. Henderson, Harper & Brothers, New York, 1891*

Hand Corker 11.224

Cast aluminum with painted-steel crank, plastic handle; 13″ × 6″. Also avail. in bronze.

$11.00

Wine lovers all, we rarely have a need to recork the wine at our house. However, the less thirsty might hoard a half bottle or so for the next meal. If getting that cork back into the bottle seems an impossibility, turn to this hand corker. A funny-looking hinged affair, the hand corker will put any cork from 18 to 25 mm. in diameter back into the bottle it came from. Just open it up and pop the cork into the groove below the pin. Then close it and grasp the two handles firmly, with the enclosed cork centered over the bottle. A downward push on the black-handled lever forces the pin against the cork and the cork into the bottle. Ingenious, that's what it is. If there are never any half-empty bottles at your house, you're probably real wine lovers. If you try making your own wine, the hand corker will seal all your private-label bottles in a trice. Or, if you have found a perfectly splendid jug wine that comes only in gallons, decant it into smaller bottles—we save those our choicer wines arrived in—and cork it snugly against the day of serving.

Wine Tap 11.225

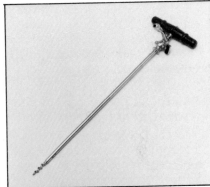

Nickel-plated brass with painted-wood handle; 13¼″ long.

$5.50

Two for dinner, you'd love to drink the Haut Brion '49, but all you have is a magnum. What a pickle! Not if you have a wine tap, it isn't. A nickel-plated brass tube culminates in a tiny corkscrew tip above which are four little holes. You insert this through the cork and into the bottle: the wine is drawn up through the tube and pours out the gargoyle's mouth which forms the spigot. A twist of the simple valve shuts off the flow. When you've had all the wine you want, give a few tugs on the red wooden handle to remove the tap from the bottle, leaving the cork intact, and the wine is sealed for later use. Now we don't call this an indispensable tool for the wine consumer, but it is a useful one and would make an ideal gift for that legendary winebibber who has everything.

Wine-storing Equipment

The spirits of '76 did not include wines. The young nation was awash in hard cider, beer, ale, and rum. In the early nineteenth century, Thomas Jefferson lamented the taxes that made the cost of imported wines prohibitive, fostering a population besotted with rum. Not until the post–World War II years did wine begin to appear on American tables with much frequency. Within a few decades, what was once a connoisseur's predilection became, variously, a hostess' imperative, a businessman's investment, a teenager's party punch, and a bottle of gold for dealers, restaurants, and vintners alike.

A recent, significant development in wine marketing has to do with size. Jug wines, half and full gallons of vins potable (some just barely) are the big sellers for most dealers. More for your money; and, to tell the truth, this class of wines has come up in the world in terms of quality, too—among the rest are wines good enough to hold their own with run-of-the-cellar imports, if not to outstrip them. At the same time, wine glasses holding a healthy 14 or 18 ounces, dwarfing water goblets, are appearing in shops, restaurants, and homes. The cry is more! More! Evoe!

Sweeping along in the rivers of wine, like flotsam in a torrent, are the predictable books and accessories. Wine atlases, guides to wine, corkscrews of every description, wine thermometers (Chapter 1), bottle caddies, and, of course, wine racks. If you limit your consumption to jug wines, skip the racks—you don't need them. However, once you have acquired a few normal-sized bottles of decent wine which you are not planning to down on the spot, storage is a consideration of greater moment than either books or glassware.

WHY RACKS?

A bottle of table wine must be stored horizontally, to keep the cork moist. Otherwise the cork will dry and shrink, air will seep into the bottle, and the delicate fluid will decline faster than the Picture of Dorian Gray. Unlike a box of crackers, the shape of a wine bottle prevents it from lying neatly prone without some kind of support. If you buy wine by the case, you can leave it in the case, turned on its side, and in fact continue to use the case as a makeshift wine rack for future acquisitions-by-the-bottle. Or you may choose to store your wines in a proper wine rack. This could be a compact wire rack to tuck into a cool closet, or it might be a floor-to-ceiling extravaganza, complete with locks and temperature controls. Before deciding on a wine rack, select the spot it is to occupy. Temperature should be a constant 60 to 65 degrees for maximum protection of fine wines, and the location should be away from bright light. This is a description of the classic familial cellar, of course. In tighter quarters, consider a closet, a bedroom, a cool pantry—almost anywhere but the kitchen. Now you are ready to choose wine racks to fit your designated "cellar". Remember that some racks may be placed

Ten-Bottle Iron Wine Rack   11.226

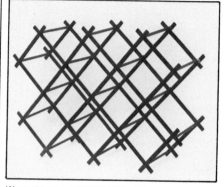

Wrought iron; 23½" X 6⅝"; 15" high; 10-bottle capacity.

$15.00

The familiar design of the collapsible wooden wine rack has here been executed in wrought iron. Diagonal flat strips secured by horizontal supports almost disappear when filled with bottles. While it could be hung on the wall by means of some very secure nails or screws (place one at the apex of each diamond shape), it is basically meant to sit on the little feet formed by the diagonal strips. You can't add to it in any way other than by placing (or hanging) another rack just like it right beside it. The diagonal strips are spaced in such a manner as to cradle the bottles at a suitable slight upward tilt. Though fairly lightweight, it is sturdy. This sensible, practical design will suit Côtes du Rhône and honor your Château Lafite.

Twelve-Bottle Plastic Wine Rack   11.227

Plastic; 15½" X 8"; 12" high; 12-bottle capacity.
$5.98

vertically as well as horizontally, others mounted on a wall, still others expanded from the original module.

CHOOSING RACKS

Ideally, the rack should cradle the wine at a slight upward tilt to keep the sediment more toward the bottom but still keep the cork moist. The rack should be very stable, whether containing a lone defender or filled to capacity. Wine racks that are designed with an open network of crosspieces rather than round cubbyholes are more likely to accommodate magnums or other bottles that deviate from either the slender aristocratic Bordeaux cylinders or the gracefully sturdy Burgundy silhouette. Remove the wine from the rack and let it stand upright for several hours before serving. This is particularly important if you do not plan to decant it.

The colorful and easily assembled units of this wine rack are boxes of light but sturdy plastic, 12 holes front and back, cubbies for your bottles. The holes are 3⅜" in diameter, ample for Bordeaux and most Burgundies but not for bottles of bubbly. If your life presents frequent cause for celebration or if you settle the indecision of whether to serve white or red wine by pouring Champagne with everything, these racks are not for you, even though white, red, brown, yellow, or black modules which can be increased by increments of twelve spaces would do wonders for your decor.

Twelve-Bottle Wood and Metal Wine Rack 11.228

Black-painted steel with stained wood; 16½" × 9⅛"; 12¾" high; 12- to 16-bottle capacity.

$17.50

From our brief dalliance with frivolous plastic we return to solid basic materials. This wine rack is constructed of a trellis of vertical and horizontal steel slats, front and back, joined in the third dimension by strips of wood. The wood

pieces have been given an eighth turn, so head-on they are diamond-shaped. This permits the bottles to be cradled between the slanted sides of every two strips. The metal slats criss-cross in back, and the ends of the wooden blocks are nailed to them. In front, the vertical metal slats are fitted into notches in the wood blocks. Thus, the necks of the bottles rest on the flat of the metal strips in front and are prevented from slipping by the criss-crossed slats in back. The rack can be turned on its side for vertical positioning if your space requires it. Bottles may also be placed across the top as well as in the 12 interior square units, giving this a maximum capacity of 16 bottles. The steel is painted black, the wood stained brown.

Zinc-Plated Wire Shelf Unit, 24"x 15" 11.229

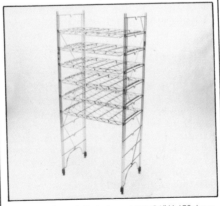

Zinc-plated steel; 5 shelves, each 24" X 15" deep, 5-bottle capacity; 53½" high. Shelves also avail. in widths of 30", 36", 42" or 48", with 7-, 8-, 10-, or 12-bottle capacity, all 15" wide. Uprights also avail. in heights of 63½", 73½", or 88½".

$123.00

Your children have just turned legal age—your commune is switching from fruit juice to a headier grape—you have just inherited several cases of fine wine—your local merchant is offering the buy of the century. Whatever the reason, may your cellars increase. If you expect them to, for these or any other reasons, these commercial zinc-coated steel racks from Metropolitan Wire are the answer to the storage question. The single shelf units are available in lengths to hold from 5 to 12 bottles. With the shelves strung between the uprights, this sturdy unit will accommodate up to 12 cases of wine, depending on the length of the vertical and horizontal elements you choose. The shelves and uprights fit together very tightly.

"Connoisseurs on the subject of wine say much depends upon its treatment before it is served; it is invariably much impaired in flavor through ignorance of proper treatment in the cellar; and that a wine of ordinary grade will be more palatable than one of better quality less carefully managed. They say wine should never be allowed to remain in case, but unpacked, and laid on its side. Above all, wine should be stored where it is least exposed to the changes of temperature."

Practical Cooking and Dinner Giving, *by Mrs. Mary F. Henderson, Harper & Brothers, New York, 1891*

WHISTLE DRINKING CUP

Hammacher Schlemmer Wine Cage   11.230

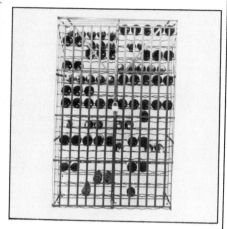

Painted wrought iron; 40" × 22"; 44" high; 200-bottle capacity. Also avail. with capacity of 50, 100, or 300 bottles.

$189.50

You thought you saw one of these in the Tower of London or the Castel Sant' Angelo on your last trip? Only it was equipped with thumbscrews instead of dark-green bottles? Quite possibly. If yours is an extensive wine collection which you want kept safe from unauthorized personnel, place it under lock and key in this wine cage. This armored gazebo, standing up to 64 inches high and 41 inches wide, depending on the size you select, is constructed of wrought iron. Wine bottles cradled on proper metal racks within are highly visible but impossible to remove unless the full-size door is unlocked and swung majestically open. The largest of these "wine jails" will accommodate up to 300 bottles. Smaller versions are available, down to one with a piddling 4-case capacity. Be sure you have a properly cool and sunless area for the wine cage—preferably a cellar or an air-conditioned room.

A basket for moving wine out of the cellar.

Temperature-controlled Wine Vault   11.231

California redwood interior with dark-stained exterior; 53" × 41"; 80" high; 348-bottle capacity. Also avail. with capacity of 174, 624, 852, 1380, or 2028 bottles.

$1675.00

This Hammacher Schlemmer wine closet, without a doubt the largest item in the *Catalogue* and also the most costly, will create a cellar even in a penthouse. Without the wine racks, you might install a pay telephone in it. It is an 80 x 53 x 41-inch box of redwood, with a walnut-finished exterior. Equipped with its own temperature control, it will pamper fine bottles as well as anything this side of Baron Rothschild's caves. The control keeps the wines at a constant cool 53–57 degrees, with proper humidity as well; simply plug it into an ordinary 110–volt A.C. outlet. The door is equipped with a lock to protect up to 29 cases—348 bottles—from all but the keyholding sommelier. A large size is available—it will hold 2028 bottles—as well as a mini-version for 174 bottles, and there are several other sizes in between. It would be pretentious to invest in one of these vaults for Italian Swiss Colony, but if your taste and wine collection run to premiers grands crus, consider it.

"All red wines should be kept dry and warm, especially clarets, which are more easily injured by cold than by heat. Consequently, on account of the rigor of our winters, clarets are better stored in a closet on the second floor (not too near a register) than in a cellar. Champagnes and Rhine wines stand cold better than heat, which frequently causes fermentation. The warmer sherry, Madeira, and all spirits are kept, the better."

Practical Cooking and Dinner Giving, *by Mrs. Mary F. Henderson, Harper & Brothers, New York, 1891*

Bottle Carrier   11.232

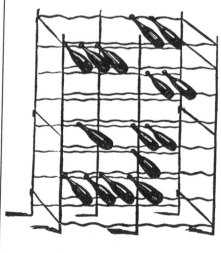

Willow; 9½" square; 8½" high; 4-bottle capacity. Also avail. with capacity of 6 bottles.

$9.99

Strictly fête champêtre or déjeuner sur l'herbe, this wicker caddy is for carrying, not storing. It holds four bottles securely and is comfortable to manage in one hand while you hold the bread and cheese in the other. It would be excellent on a boat. We also suggest it as a nice gift for a skipper or country weekend host or hostess, preferably filled. Its potential extends beyond wine. When the drinking is to be *in situ*, the 9½-inch-square caddy can hold garden tools or cleaning equipment, or how about using it to hold the wild grasses as you harvest them, clippers in hand, for your dried-plant bouquets?

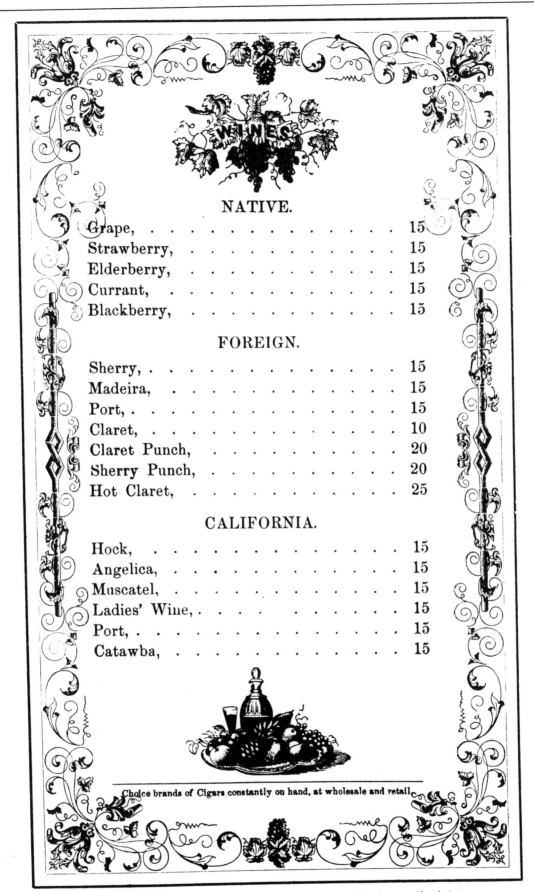

WINES

NATIVE.

Grape,	15
Strawberry,	15
Elderberry,	15
Currant,	15
Blackberry,	15

FOREIGN.

Sherry,	15
Madeira,	15
Port,	15
Claret,	10
Claret Punch,	20
Sherry Punch,	20
Hot Claret,	25

CALIFORNIA.

Hock,	15
Angelica,	15
Muscatel,	15
Ladies' Wine,	15
Port,	15
Catawba,	15

Choice brands of Cigars constantly on hand, at wholesale and retail.

*A wine list dating from the late nineteenth century offers few exotic vintages,
but "Ladies' wine" might give a modern diner pause.*

Since the publication of *The Cooks' Catalogue* in the fall of 1975, our editors have continued to research and test cooking equipment. In this section we show you our selection of new, unique, or unusual developments in this field.

Professional Quality Cheesecloth 76.1

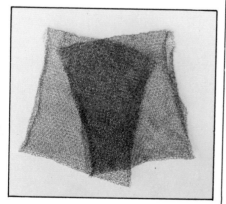

100% cotton, 126" x 36" packaged in a reusable envelope. Source: HOAN Products Ltd., No. BGW 12.

$1.50

Cheesemaking has gone out of fashion, but our pattern of cooking still requires cheesecloth. Tie a whole stuffed fish or galantine in it for poaching, strain stock through several thicknesses to remove impurities, process jellies through it, enclose your bouquet garni in a piece of it. This cheesecloth is pure cotton with smoothly finished edges, and the package provides an ample supply.

Scouring Cloths 76.2

Stainless-steel mesh, 7" x 7". Two cloths per envelope. Source: HOAN Products Ltd., No. BGW 4.

$2.00

The archetype of this material was probably worn in battle during the Hundred Years' War. These professional scouring cloths might serve you for about as long. A sleeve of stainless steel mesh which will not rust, splinter, or ravel, it can be wadded into a ball, spread flat under the hand, or twisted into a thin strip for scrubbing. Restaurants use it. Despite its strength, it is gentle to the fine finishes of your cookware. Having done its duty, it can be restored with a swish under the faucet or a trip to the dishwasher.

Henckels Four Star Chef's Knife 76.3

Friodur high carbon no-stain steel, indestructible polypropylene handle; 13¼" long overall; blade 8" long, 1¾" wide. Also avail. with blade 6" ($21.00), 9" ($29.50), or 10" ($32.00) long; paring blade 3" ($9.90) or 4" ($11.90) long; utility blade 6" ($18.20) long; slicers 8" ($21.70) or 10" ($26.70) long. Source: J.E. Henckels Twinworks.

$27.20

As copper is to pots, so carbon steel is to knives: the preferred material for the function but with a serious drawback in maintenance—both stain and tarnish. Stainless steel often provides the substitute. It is a far better one in knives than in pots. Take this line of high-carbon stainless-steel (Friodur) knives by Henckels. Called Four Star, their hand-honed blades taper to the sharpest edges you are likely to find in a stainless-steel knife. The balance is very good, the black plastic polypropylene handle comfortable (and dishwater-safe, although putting very sharp knives in the dishwasher is not recommended). In addition to the chef's knife we show you, you may select from an assortment of parers and slicers. Most of the leading food authorities in the United States have tested these knives, and the response has been almost uniformly enthusiastic—great handle, wonderful blade, superb balance.

Bialetti Coffee Mill 76.4

Plastic and stainless steel; special ball-grinding mechanism; 6" x 4"; 6⅞" high; container capacity 1¾ cups. Source: Eli Barry Co., Inc.

$40.00

Manufacturers of small electric mills are many, but those who provide the user with the ability to preselect the final texture are few indeed. When it comes to coffee, this is a crucial factor. Some coffee makers call for the fairly coarse "all purpose" grind; others require finer textures down to the silken powder of Turkish. Bialetti joins Braun with a good-looking compact coffee mill which permits you to dial the desired grind on a scale of one to eight. For electric home coffee mills, the "B's" get an "A." Lift off the smoky plastic cover to add the beans. At the flick of a switch they are funneled down into the grinding mechanism. They emerge, custom-ground, in a removable smoky plastic container which holds up to 1¾ cups. The rest of the machine is shiny-white, easy-clean plastic.

Professional Quality Cheesecloth
Scouring Cloths
Henckels Four Star
Chef's Knife
Bialetti Coffee Mill

Aluminum and Stainless-Steel Saucepan
Copper, Aluminum and
Stainless Steel Skillet
Copco Cast-Aluminum Casserole

Aluminum and Stainless-Steel Saucepan 76.5

Pure and alloy aluminum with stainless-steel interior, riveted nickel-plated steel handles; 8″ diam.; 5¼″ high; 4½-qt. capacity (No. 204-½). Saucepan also avail. with capacity of 1½ qts. (No. 201-½, $14.00), 2½ qts. (No. 202-½, $17.00), or 3½ qts. (No. 203-½, $19.80); frypan 7″ (No. 107, $10.70), 8″ (No. 108, $11.80), 10″ (No. 110, $15.50), or 12″ (No. 112, $19.00) diam.; sauté pan with capacity of 1 qt. (No. 401, $13.10) or 2 qts. (No. 402, $16.00); extra-heavy stockpot with capacity of 5 qts. (No. H 505, $28.00); and covers in diam. of 6″ or 8″ (Nos. 906, 908, $3.00, $3.65). Source: ALL-CLAD Metalcrafters, Inc.

$21.50

There is no single ideal material for pots and pans. It all depends on what you want the pan to do for you. We like tin-lined copper and aluminum for their ability to conduct heat, but tin is fragile and aluminum reacts with some foods. Stainless steel won't turn your wine sauce cloudy, but it is not a particularly good conductor. There are various ways of combining metals, allowing the manufacturer to capitalize on the best characteristics of particular metals. The Master Chef line is constructed of alloy aluminum with an interior surface of stainless steel, between which is sandwiched a core of pure aluminum. They are well-designed, professional-looking utensils. They may lack the elegance of the stainless steel sandwich—where the drab aluminum is hidden between two layers of stainless steel—but they do their job of conducting heat more efficiently. The aluminum is not restricted to the bottom; it is the entire outer shell. The riveted nickel-plated steel handles are comfortably contoured, and a hole is provided for hanging, if that is your solution to the problem of storage. The lid is aluminum. The price of the line is extremely low for the quality. In addition to the saucepan we show you, there are frypans, stockpots, and sauteuses. We especially recommend the saucepans.

Copper, Aluminum and Stainless Steel Skillet 76.6

Copper and stainless steel with aluminum core; brass handle; 10″ diam.; 2″ deep (No. 1110). Skillet also avail. 7″ (No. 1107, $23.00), 8″ (No. 1108, $28.50), or 12″ (No. 1112, $44.00) diam.; saucepan with capacity of 1 qt. (No. 1201, $30.00), 2 qts. (No. 1202, $35.00), 3 qts. (No. 1203, $42.00), or 4 qts. (No. 1204, $50.00); crêpe pan 12″ round (No. 1712, $44.00); oval omelet pan 12″ x 8½″ (No. 1612, $52.50); buffet casserole with capacity of 1 qt. (No. 1301, $32.00), 2 qts. (No. 1302, $37.50), 3 qts. (No. 1303, $44.50), or 4 qts. (No. 1304, $52.50); au gratin 8″ (No. 1508, $29.00) or 10″ (No. 1510, $37.50) round, 12″ x 8½″ oval (No. 1512, $50.00); sauté pan with capacity of 1 qt. (No. 1401, $29.00) or 2 qts. (No. 1402, $38.50); and lids in diam. of 6″ or 8″ (Nos. 1906, 1908, $11.00, $16.50). Source: ALL-CLAD Metalcrafters, Inc.

$35.00

Here is a unique combination. Copper outside, a core of pure aluminum, and an easy care, non-reactive interior surface of stainless steel. You have seen copper and stainless together, but when aluminum joins the act, the performance can't be beat. The addition of the aluminum via a patented special roll bonding process creates a pan fully one-eighth of an inch thick which conducts the heat much faster and more efficiently than copper and stainless alone since a thinner section of stainless steel is required. Like the Master Chef aluminum and stainless-steel pans, these have classic, straightforward good looks. The handles are brass. You may select from assorted sizes and shapes in this group, and they are clearly the top of the line.

Copco Cast-Aluminum Casserole 76.7

Cast aluminum; 8″ diam.; 5½″ deep; 2½-qt. capacity. Also avail. with capacity of 5 qts. ($40.00). Source: Copco, Inc.

$30.00

In our discussion of Nambé sand-cast aluminum casseroles in Chapter 7, we commented on their familial resemblance to Magnalite. This new heavy Copco cast-aluminum casserole is the missing link. It is extremely attractive but without the sleek elegance of Nambé. The lid is equipped with a lip which fits it snugly into the pot. Its plump, rounded shape has a flat surface where it counts, on the bottom, making it a marvelous utensil to use on top of an electric stove. The gleaming, polished surfaces are limited to the exterior. Inside, all is dull, serviceable, and utilitarian. We like the design for oven use and would feel extremely happy to carry it right into the dining room and serve the pilaf piping hot.

Heller Loaf Pan 76.8

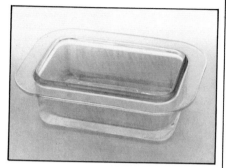

Heat-resistant glass; 5⅝" x 6⅝"; 3" deep; 1¼ qt. capacity. Source: Heller Designs, Inc.

$4.95

We have always loved Alan Heller's sense of design. Which may mean that Mamaroneck, New York, is a lot closer to Milano than you think. Heretofore he offered slick plastic mugs and stackable dishes, strictly for serving and ineligible on these pages. At last he has turned his talent to cookware. A line of oven-proof glass baking dishes and casseroles designed for him by Massimo and Lella Vignelli can grace both kitchen and table with splendid form and function. The loaf/pâté pan has an inch-wide shelf-like lip around its perimeter, giving it weighty balance. The exterior vertical surfaces have been finely fluted, a touch of shimmering texture. All this in ovenproof glass, suitable for microwave as well as conventional baking. Prepare a country pâté, a spoon bread, or a fish pudding, and don't hesitate to serve it from this handsome dish.

Kitchen Twine 76.9

300 ft. packaged in its own dispenser. Source: HOAN Products Ltd., No. BGW 10.

$2.00

Nobody ever misplaces the electric mixer. The potato peeler and the wire whisks are there when you need them. It's the innocuous items, the scissors and twine which, like sleepwalkers, disappear from their places in the kitchen for no apparent reason. Perhaps they just need labels. The chances are excellent that this ball of utility twine will stay put in its KITCHEN container, ready for tying the roast or trussing the turkey.

Fat Separator 76.10

Pyrex glass; 3⅝" diam.; 5" deep; 16 oz. capacity. Comes with cleaning brush. Source: Fat-A-Way. Albany Glassblowing Laboratory.

$8.23 delivered

This piece of equipment confirms the connection between cooking and science. Laboratory glass, thin, clear, a beaker to which has been appended a low-slung spout. A band of metal clasps a handle near the top. It operates on a very simple principle. Because fat rises to the surface, the long spout permits you to draw off the fluid beneath the fat (or impurities in melted fat) for reasonably well degreased stock or gravy (or clarified butter) without tiresome skimming or time-consuming chilling. The side of the beaker is marked in milliliters—up to 500 of them (plus or minus 5%)—for today's international scientific community and tomorrow's American cook. The glass is flameproof and the manufacturer has thoughtfully provided a slender bottle brush for cleaning the tricky spout.

Heller Glass Casserole 76.11

Heat-resistant glass; 9½" diam.; 5½" deep; 2-qt. capacity; lid 9½" diam., 1½" deep. Also avail. with capacity of 1 qt. ($7.95). Source: Heller Designs, Inc.

$9.95

Again, Heller. This casserole dazzles in its multiplicity of uses. With its well-fitted lid in place you have a two-quart casserole. Layer chunks of lamb with a medley of garden vegetables to bake for an informal supper. Uncover it and voilà! a soufflé dish with properly deep, straight sides. The lid itself doubles as a gratin dish (a trifle deep, perhaps) or might be filled with batter for a small cake layer. Like the other ovenproof glass Vignelli designs for Heller, each piece has inch-wide rims and vertical grosgrain fluting, as if the classic French soufflé dish had gone futuristic. The rim, unfortunately, dictates against fitting a collar around the bottom section when using it for soufflés, the only time the design interferes with the function.

Flexible Scraper 76.12

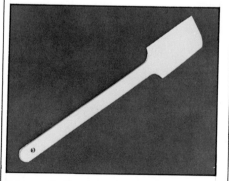

Rubber with fiberglass core; 12½" long overall; blade 3¾" x 2". Source: HOAN Products Ltd., No. BGW 21.

$2.00

When they started using fiberglass sandwich to construct skis, suddenly you could make sleeker turns than you ever thought possible. The ski is flexible, resilient, and responsive to the slightest pressure. So is this scraper. Snow-white rubber has been molded over a fiberglass core. The business end tapers to beveled edges. Only the children who had been used to the lickings of batter left in the bowl by the old-fashioned wood or plastic-handled scraper will be disappointed by this wonderful implement which cleans any bowl or container effortlessly. Every leading food authority who has tried it thinks it's the best.

Dough and Pastry Handlers   76.13

Aluminum with wooden handles; 13" diam. Source: HOAN Products Ltd., No. BGW 3.

$10.00

How many times have you wished you had these? The days when waxed paper and conventional spatulas fail, when pastry for your flan ring winds up looking like the product of a quilting bee, when the *Mörbeteig* cracks as it is fitted into its pan—those days, friends, shall never return. Take a thin, precise circle of aluminum, slice it into a pair of generous semicircles, each fitted with wooden handle. Slip them under your pastry, bring them together, and you can lift the dough—no matter how fragile—neatly into or onto the pan. A triumph.

Baking Weights   76.14

Cast aluminum; ½" approx. diam. Avail. in 2 lbs. 2 oz. (1 kilo) package. Source: Bridge Co.

$6.75

As usual, modern technology has managed to replace the rice and beans which you've been using to weight your blind (unfilled) pâte brisée. These nuggets of cast aluminum have a two-fold advantage: first, they last forever; second, they conduct the heat of the oven to the baking pastry, quickening the process, crisping the surface.

Magic Aire Dehydrator   76.15

Aluminum, fiberglass, acrylite and steel; 21" x 14", 14" high; 8 shelves 19" x 14". Source: Magic Mill.

$179.50

The concept is simple, natural and age-old: drying fresh food to preserve it. We still take certain dried foods for granted. Raisins, apricots, figs, prunes, herbs, mushrooms. Beef jerky and dried fish find their way onto some tables. If the cost of commercial dried foods, the chemical additives often used to process them, or an overly abundant home harvest has you interested in drying your own foods, this is the machine we wholeheartedly recommend. You can't always count on a succession of hot, sunny days, so plug in the roughly TV-set- (or microwave-oven-) size box, array your produce on the eight roomy fiberglass screen trays, attach the magnetized dark lucite cover, set the temperature, and let it go. In anywhere from twelve to one hundred hours, you will have perfectly dehydrated food which can be stored away for future reconstituting or nibbling. The machine operates with what might be a twin for a small space heater—an electric coil and a fan, causing the thermostatically controlled heat to blow continually across the food, a small Sahara sirocco. It works something like the convection oven described in Chapter 8 but with a temperature range of only 80 to 160 degrees. The recommended temperature for drying most foods is 145 degrees. The length of time the process will take depends on the size of the pieces of food. The exterior is white-painted metal; the fiberglass trays can be rinsed or wiped clean. The instruction booklet provides a few recipes to get you started, but basically, as they say, "just add water."

Wigo Electric Coffee Maker   76.16

Heat-resistant glass coffeepot with plastic lid and handle; plastic body; 3¾" base diam.; 4¼" deep; stand 7⅞" x 4¾", 9½" high; 4-cup capacity. Also avail. with capacity of 10 ($39.95, deluxe $59.95) and 12 ($44.95) cups. Source: Zabar's.

$21.95

Can anyone remember what we did before the electric drip coffee maker came on the market for home use? Now, we measure coffee into a filter, water into a container, plug it in and within seconds, the water is heated, and it drips onto the grounds. Coffee, made by the simple pass-through method, fills the pot. We like the neat, bright design of the Wigo,

527

Continued from preceding page

which operates exactly as we have described. The coffee grounds were wet uniformly (failing to accomplish this is one of the drawbacks of some of these machines), and the coffee was kept hot. We advise you to leave the pot on the warming base for a minute or two before serving, so it will be hot enough. The glass pot has straight, simple lines as do the other clear, orange, and white plastic lids, containers and such. The whole forms a compact unit.

Yellow Espresso Maker 76.17

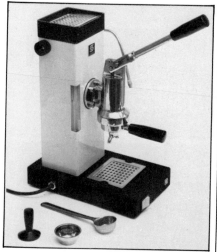

Enameled metal body, black metal base, chromed-steel extensions, plastic knobs, handles, and accessories; 10½" x 6¼"; 14½" high; 12 (espresso) cup capacity. Source: Eli Barry Co., Inc.

$300.00

This may be the least futuristic and the most efficient of the home espresso machines. A vertical yellow enameled metal tower on a black metal base encloses the superbly constructed water heating unit. It will heat 12 (espresso) cups of water. Two handles protrude from the stainless steel cylinder mounted on the front. One holds the bayonet-mounted container for the ground coffee; depressing the other forces the water through the coffee grounds. One or two cups can be dispensed at a time. There is a steam valve for heating milk for capuccino and a window with a colored indicator to show the water level. A grid on the bottom catches the drips while the one on the top of the tower will heat the cups. The machine has a three-prong grounded plug. Press the switch and a small green light is illuminated. When it goes off, the water is hot.

Dripless Tea Ball 76.18

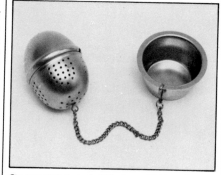

Chrome-plated steel; 1½" diam.; 2" high. Source: HOAN Products Ltd, No. BGW 9.

$2.00

Now we can sip our Lapsang Soochong or Earl Grey without having to strain it and without having our tea infuser drip onto the tablecloth or get in the way on our saucer. A neat little perforated oval of chrome holds the tea. A sturdy little chain leads to its custom-fitted saucer. After your tea has steeped to perfection, remove the tea ball and set it down in its little holder. It will keep the leaves out of your teapot or cup, the drips off your tea tray.

Vinegar Mother 76.19

Oak cask, brass-studded hoops, hand-crafted wooden stand, Italian spigot; 6" diam.; 8¼" long; ½ gallon capacity. Comes with filter screen, funnel and tube for filling. Source: Franjoh Cellars.

$39.95

Any ingredient which contributes as strongly to flavor as vinegar does must be of good quality. All too often the vinegar on hand is an undistinguished commercial brand resulting in unexciting marinades, salad dressing without depth of flavor, or sauces "au vinaigre" lacking proper pungency. If you are advised never to cook with wine you wouldn't drink, consider that the same quality should go into the vinegar you use. It will when you make vinegar at home using the Perpetual Vinegar Cask. A small oaken cask with brass-studded hoops contains a vinegar "mother," the enzymes which will turn the wine into vinegar. Remove the cork and pour in wine through a funnel. The spigot allows you to draw off the vinegar as you need it. Franjoh Cellars of California, which has produced this clever item, includes a supply of red wine (primarily zinfandel) vinegar with it.

Citrus Roulette Super with Cup 76.20

Plastic with stainless-steel skewer; 5" diam.; 7¼" high; 3-cup (7½-deciliter) capacity. Source: HOAN Products Ltd., No. BGW 22.

$10.00

The Zyliss citrus-roulette has one big advantage over other manual squeezers: a 2¾ inch stainless-steel pin which pierces the halved fruit and connects a ridged gripper to the reamer, thus securing the fruit in place. With this pin the halved citrus fruit is centered on the press-cone—no more slipping or irregular pressing of oranges, lemons, or limes. Your hands stay clean as well, because they do not come in contact with the fruit. This cleaver gadget sits atop a smoke-colored plastic measuring cup which holds just over 3 cups. The measurements are marked in deciliters (up to 7½) only, but remember, metric is coming. A non-skid rubber gripper is set into the base of the cup. A snappy design, executed in acid-proof plastic.

Poultry

Professional Equipment in the Home Kitchen

After my retirement from active slavery, I hope to complete many pending projects. Perhaps the last one I attack will be a book on the development of kitchens through the ages. But even today, I can tip off the proverbial kind reader that the kitchen and its equipment have been more influenced by industrial changes and technical developments than by architects, interior designers, and prevailing styles. For instance, when coal replaced wood as the major cooking fuel at the end of the seventeenth century, it meant a complete change in cooking equipment and therefore in the entire kitchen itself.

Count Rumford, an American-born Englishman, invented the first workable cast-iron stove around 1740. This, enclosing the kitchen fire, changed the entire design of the kitchen and even the life style of Americans. The kitchen stove rather than the fireplace became the center of life: it gave out heat and warmth, cooked the food, baked the bread, and was even the main decoration of the entire area. Cooking methods, timing, and pots and pans changed completely.

Dutch ovens, portable cookers—complicated pieces of machinery with fitted equipment—gridirons, baking pans, and pots with flat bottoms—rather than feet to stand in the coals or handles to hang from—dominated the nineteenth century and kept changing the face of both the professional and the home kitchen.

By the middle of that century, another revolutionary change took place: cooking with gas was introduced. Soon many households had gas ovens, and quite a few large professional kitchens, such as that of the Reform Club in London, where Alexis Soyer was chef for a time, employed gas.

The last decade of the nineteenth century introduced electric surface cooking and broiling. Electric broilers first appeared at the Chicago World's Fair of 1893. Eventually infrared and quartz broilers and microwave cooking were to become part of the home and professional kitchen.

BROILERS

There are certain cooking processes—most especially broiling—that cannot be done properly with most household ranges. To broil properly you need an approximate heat yield of 35,000 BTU's per hour—that is British Thermal Units, in which heat output is measured—otherwise, the process becomes a combination of broiling and braising which does not properly seal meat and toughens food. All the professional broiling units achieve these heat levels. There are only a few rare and special domestic units that do the job correctly. Waste King Universal's gas-heated ceramic broiler, for instance, in the 29-inch size, will generate 36,000 BTU's. This unit has to be built in and, as with all these high-intensity broilers, requires a very strong, well-filtered exhaust fan. If you prefer broiling within your stove, try the under-the-griddle broiler in the Chambers range.

PROFESSIONAL RANGES

As far as surface cooking is concerned, the great advantage of the professional ranges is the availability of solid, cast-iron cooking sur-

530

faces—hot tops—which allow a variety of different shapes and sizes of pots and pans to be on the surface at the same time. Also, for prolonged, low-intensity cooking of the type used for stock-making and cooking certain stews, the heat diffusion of a solid top cannot be matched by household-type ranges. The cast-iron top becomes the counterpart of the heaviest pan in terms of its heat transference.

When it comes to ovens, however, the only advantage of those in professional ranges is their size. Otherwise the self-cleaning feature and the precision of the electric home units outweigh the merits of the professional ovens.

Everyone has a favorite amongst the four or five top brands of professional ranges. Mine happens to be Garland, although the difference between that and some of the others is not very large. For instance, I use one with two open burners (much like those on domestic stoves, but with more openings for the burning gas and with a higher BTU output), and a 4-section hot-top unit. The stove is model 283 from the 290 series. This range also has a griddle-broiler, two ovens, and a high shelf. The oven is great when I roast a 7-rib roast or an enormous turkey simultaneously with other items. Plus the fact, of course, that having two ovens next to each other makes quantity baking, or roasting different items at different temperatures, possible. Each of the ovens is 26¼" wide, 22" deep, and 13½" high. At this point, you can get finishes in a variety of colors in these ranges, almost as great as that available in household stoves, as long as you realize the flat hot tops are cooking surfaces and must be black.

PLATE WARMER
If you like to give large buffet parties, there is nothing more convenient than a so-called lowerator which holds dinner plates, bowls, or coffee cups at a comfortably heated temperature. The well of this device contains a calibrated spring, so the dispensing height of the dishes as they rise within reach may be varied by an adjustment at the top of the dispenser. The temperature is controlled by a thermostat, usually preset at 140 F., but adjustable from 100–200 F. To translate this into practical terms, when your guests arrive, the built-in lowerator will hold as many as 50 dinner plates, for instance, and next to it will be located, let's say, your chafing dish or your Corning or Salton food-warming surface. The guest will pick up a warm dinner plate and move on to serve himself, and the next plate will automatically rise to the same height as the first one. The nineteen models of this device, from Shelley Manufacturing Company, Miami, Florida, are available for dish diameters from 4" to 12".

CHARCOAL BROILERS
Charcoal broiling may be hazardous to the health (together with just about any other food or cooking method, if you examine it closely, I guess), but it sure tastes good! There are so many charcoal-broiling units in professional kitchen lines which are available at this point that it would be futile for me to give you advice except, perhaps, to bring these units to your attention.

FRYING EQUIPMENT

Deep-fat fryers are an absolute necessity in the professional kitchen, but unless you are planning to do some real professional testing, or unless you serve fried foods in large quantities, I would advise against buying a professional deep-fryer. If, however, you do plan to buy a fryer, I suggest you look into the Garland Four-Way Gas Cooker, which is a range that includes a very large oven, a griddle top, cooking surfaces, and a fryer. It is of a type also made by South Bend and Vulcan as well as by Garland. A griddle is part of almost any large professional range, so you need not buy a separate unit.

STEAMERS

The technique of steaming is becoming more and more used, and for good reason. I still find the individual household steamers or pressure cookers more practical than any of the professional units.

GLASS WASHERS

Many people spend a considerable amount of time in their home bar, with or without their guests. When you have a cocktail party for 25 or more people, you will need a lot of glasses. By building in a glass washer (for instance, the Hobart Quikk Glassmaster), in a few seconds you can wash with cold water any type of glass and it will be sparkling clean. You just push down the glass and it's automatically sanitized and washed in about 4 seconds.

CONVECTION OVENS

One of the advantages of the convection oven is that the heat is completely evened out by an interior fan which swirls the heat and the air evenly throughout the oven. Supposedly it is faster as well, although I didn't find this noticeable. In my experiments, I did notice much less meat shrinkage. My convection oven's thermostat is adjustable from 150 F. to 550 F. There is a separate on-off switch for the convection fan, in addition to a minute timer. The problem with convection ovens is that most of the professional units are way too large for home kitchens. The smallest unit I found which works well is the Toastmaster Model 3011E. This unit is fine except for the very stupidly designed handle, which can rip your apron off if you're not careful. This can be changed, and we did so in our kitchen. This unit is only 30" wide, 22" deep, and 25" high. For pastries, it is incomparably better than either a professional oven or a conventional household oven. Since that time the Farberware free-standing unit has been introduced and it does a very satisfactory job.

DISHWASHERS

By now, there must be more dishwashers on the market than General Motors has automobile models. As yet, very few homes have tried the Hobart professional dishwasher. Their UM series offers a stainless-steel unit no larger than a standard household unit, only 2 feet in width. You don't need to prerinse; the dual filter system prevents waste recirculation; when you have a large party, it will wash about 300 dishes or 500–600 glasses an hour. The trick is that it has only a 2½-

to 4-minute cycle versus the 15–30 minute cycle of most household dishwashers. However, it does have disadvantages as well.

It needs a special booster unit to get the proper water temperature, and this eats up a lot of electricity and space. The inside racks have uniform divisions; you cannot place dishes and glasses of a variety of shapes and sizes in them at the same time; so it really works for most households only in conjunction with a standard household unit. However, if you give a lot of parties and have extra space in your kitchen, this dishwasher is an invaluable help.

SODA-FOUNTAIN EQUIPMENT

While the country observes the bicentennial of the founding of the nation, some of us will add a mini-celebration; the hundredth anniversary of the discovery of the ice-cream soda. A Mr. R. M. Green accidentally made the heavenly concoction in 1874. At a celebration being held by the Franklin Institute in Philadelphia, he ran out of heavy cream and was unable to serve a phosphate which was made with flavored syrup, soda, and heavy cream. He substituted ice cream. The first time the ice-cream soda was served on purpose in a facility which was specially designed for it was in 1875 at the Philadelphia Centennial. It is curious that people spend thousands of dollars on the most useless gadgets, yet wouldn't think of installing a chilled soda fountain in their kitchens. What you need for it, of course, is a draft arm for soda—and possibly for chilled water—together with a drip pan and tray, plus a carbonator and a compressor. If it sounds complicated—it is. Getting the help of an expert will reduce the problem simply to one of expenditure. By running the water through a purifier, you could have the finest carbonated water short of digging your own Perrier well, and you could make your ice-cream sodas, your spritzers, etc. etc., at will without having to stock up with dozens of bottles.

REFRIGERATORS

What a second-rate French saucier doesn't understand is that since refrigeration has already been invented, there is no longer any need to drown the taste of preparations made with questionably fresh ingredients with various alcohols like Cognac or Sherry. Probably no change in our life style, shopping and storage methods, recipes, and eating habits has been as drastic as that occurring around the turn of the century when iceboxes became part of the everyday household equipment of the western world. In time, refrigerators and freezers revolutionized much of the daily life of the household.

If you can invest money and space on any single object in your kitchen, I would advise you to purchase a two- or four-door professional refrigerator and a separate two-door freezer.

The refrigerator should have a glass front so you can always see what's inside. The common objection that the apparent mess inside will instantly be visible is simply invalid. First of all, you'll make a conscious effort to keep it in order—this is an excellent fringe benefit; and your organizing habit will become so automatic that you're not even aware of it. Furthermore, if the refrigerator is dirty and disorganized, it should be cleaned and put in order. Most of the better manufacturers (Traulsen is one of the best) have dozens of models varying in size and outside finish, but I should perhaps tell you that we have ordered a Koch reach-in refrigerator which has in addition to the standard equipment a so-called food file which is removable and adjustable to hold various sizes of trays and pans; a pull-out wire shelf; a section fitted with a baker's food file for bun pans; and a wire shelf which holds a dozen bottles horizontally. This is most convenient for keeping vodka, aquavit and Sherry permanently chilled.

The essential thing to remember when you consider any of these items is to make sure you will not buy and install equipment you don't really need. Therefore, carefully examine your life and cooking and entertainment style before making wild expenditures. However, if you match your needs with the proper professional equipment, your kitchen will give you much more pleasure and efficiency.

GEORGE LANG

Bibliography

What follows is a selection of books on food—books for cooking, for reading, for reference, or all three. They are listed under the headings of General Cookbooks, American Cooking, Other Cuisines, Specialized Books, Books for Reading and Reference, and United States Department of Agriculture Publications. There is also a short special list of collector's items for bibliophiles. The books range from expensive, lavishly illustrated volumes to U.S. Government pamphlets; from the product of a Japanese publishing house to that of a Junior League committee selling books through a post-office box. There is no attempt to be inclusive—instead the list is a sampling of books of unusual merit and practical value.

GENERAL COOKBOOKS

The Art of Good Cooking, Paula Peck. Simon & Schuster, 1970, $7.50; paperback $2.95. Like Pavlov's bell.

The Complete Galloping Gourmet Cookbook, Graham Kerr. Grosset & Dunlap, 1972, $25.00. Just as entertaining as the television show.

Cooking with Helen McCully Beside You, Helen McCully. Random House, 1970, $7.95. We've cooked with the book and with the real Helen McCully beside us, and either way it's a great pleasure.

The Gourmet Cookbook, The Editors of *Gourmet* magazine. Beautifully bound and illustrated, two volumes containing a wealth of elegant and excellent recipes from soup to nuts.

The James Beard Cookbook, James Beard. Dutton, 1974, $7.50. Also in paperback. A basic cookbook by America's foremost authority.

Joy of Cooking, Irma S. Rombauer and Marion R. Becker. Bobbs-Merrill, 1951, $8.50; New American Library paperback, $3.95. Still the champion all-purpose recipe reference; especially rich in basic culinary information.

Julie Dannenbaum's Creative Cooking School, Julie Dannenbaum. Saturday Review Press, $8.95. Mrs. Dannenbaum is a leading teacher of good cooking in Philadelphia and has a well-deserved national reputation.

The Maurice Moore-Betty Cooking School Book of Fine Cookery, Maurice Moore-Betty. Arbor House, 1973, $8.95. A collection of recipes and techniques from the author's noted school in New York City.

The New York Times Cookbook, Craig Claiborne. Harper & Row, $12.50. For many, their most-used collection of recipes, by the food editor of *The New York Times*.

AMERICAN COOKING

General

American Cookery, James A. Beard. Little, Brown, 1972, $14.95. Massive and authoritative, covering everything American from scrapple to Pacific oysters.

American Food: The Gastronomic Story, Evan Jones. Dutton, 1975, $19.95. Traces our culinary heritage from colonial times to the present, with some five hundred regional and traditional recipes.

The American Heritage Cookbook, Simon & Schuster (American Heritage Publishing Co.), rev. ed. 1969, $6.95. Traditional recipes from the first Thanksgiving turkey to the twentieth century.

Boston Cooking School Cookbook, Fannie Merritt Farmer, Crown, 1973; $8.95, also in paperback. New American Library, 1974. A facsimile edition of the original 1890 edition of the housewife's bible. Its influence can still be felt, but we've come a long way, baby.

Foods of the World series, Time-Life Books. This series of regional recipe and history books blankets the United States, among other lands. Each volume is $7.95.

The New York Times Heritage Cookbook, Jean Hewitt. Putnam, 1972, $12.95. An encyclopedic collection of excellent recipes, organized geographically and covering every regional food and fancy.

Regional American Cooking

Charleston Receipts, Junior League of Charleston. P.O. Box 177, Charleston, S.C.; $4.00. Fine regional receipts.

Colonial Virginia Cookery, Jane Carson. Univ. of Virginia Press, paperback, $4.00. Scholarly history of Virginia food, with many recipes from early American cookbooks.

Fiesta: Favorite Recipes from South Texas, Junior League of Corpus Christi. P.O. Box 837, Corpus Christi, Texas 78403; $5.75. Includes a generous 36 pages of "Tex-Mex" recipes.

Good Earth and Country Cooking, Betty Groff and José Wilson. Stackpole, 1974, $8.95. Family recipes from a popular restaurant in the Pennsylvania Dutch country.

A Good Heart and a Light Hand: A Collection of Traditional Negro Recipes, Ruth L. Gaskin. Simon & Schuster, 1969, $3.95. Besides recipes, includes an affectionate portrait of family and communal life.

Gourmets and Groundhogs, Elaine Light. Author, 119 Church St., Punxsutawney, Pa. 15767; $4.25. Once the groundhog comes out to stay, he gets around the country and the world. Homespun and sophisticated Pennsylvania food.

The New Orleans Cookbook, Rima and Richard Collin. Knopf, 1975, $10. A restaurant critic and his wife present recipes from the city's restaurants and homes, plus some history.

The New Orleans Restaurant Cookbook, Deirdre Stanforth. Doubleday, 1967, $7.95. Only a few restaurants are covered, but there are useful recipes for entertaining.

Private Collections: A Culinary Treasure, Women's Committee, the Walters Art Gallery, Baltimore, Md. 21201; $10.75. Baltimore food; need we say more?

Times-Picayune Creole Cookbook, Dover reprint, 1971, paperback, $3.50. A reprint of the New Orleans newspaper's famous "receipt book." More up-to-date and scientific attempts to record the greatest surviving American regional cuisine lack the flavor of this period piece as well as its encyclopedic sweep.

Talk About Good, Service League of Lafayette, La., P.O. Box 52387, Old Center Station, Lafayette, La. 70501; $5. Recipes from Cajun country.

The West Coast Cookbook, Helen Evans Brown. Ballantine paperback in two volumes, 1974, $1.95 each. A great cook's collection of the best of the West; splendid.

What's Cooking in Kentucky, Irene Hayes. Author, Hueysville, Ky. 41640; $5.95. A postmistress collected these.

OTHER CUISINES

International

Foods of the World series, Time-Life Books. $7.95 each. The most complete collection of the cuisines of the world. While the volumes vary in quality, each is lavishly illustrated and provides worthwhile background on culinary habits of a nation or region. The large-format books are accompanied by small spiral-bound books containing only the recipes from the main volumes, plus some additions.

The Great Cook's Cookbook, The Good Cooking School, Ferguson/Doubleday, 1974, $12.50. Each of eleven different food authorities provides a course, in every sense of the word.

The New York Times International Cook Book, Craig Claiborne. Harper & Row, 1971, $12.50. Recipes from the *Times,* collected by its food editor and presented country by country. Extremely well-indexed.

The Peasant Kitchen, Perla Meyers. Harper & Row, 1975, $12.95. There is a lesson to be learned: how to use humble, homespun ingredients to produce culinary delights.

The Seasonal Kitchen, Perla Meyers. Holt, Rinehart and Winston, 1973, $12.95. Season-by-season use of fresh foods is given the author's very personal touch. Inspired by the cuisines of France, Spain, Austria, and Italy.

Summer Cooking, Elizabeth David. Penguin paperback, 95 cents. A wealth of recipes by the Englishwoman whom some consider to be the world's best food writer.

African

The African Heritage Cookbook, Helen Mendes. Macmillan, 1970, $7.95. Illuminating the culinary secrets of the dark continent.

The Art of West African Cooking, Dinah A. Ayensu. Doubleday, 1972, $6.95. By a diplomat's wife who is also a cooking teacher.

Armenian

The Cuisine of Armenia, Sonia Uvezian. Harper & Row, 1974, $12.50. An authoritative collection, skillfully presented.

Caribbean

The Complete Book of Caribbean Cooking, Elisabeth Lambert Ortiz. M. Evans, 1973, $10.00. No cookbook is exhaustive or ever complete, but this one is as well researched and complete as space (437 pages of text) allows.

Chinese

The Chinese Cookbook, Craig Claiborne and Virginia Lee. Lippincott, 1972, $12.50. Recipes from a noted Chinese cooking teacher, set down in a joint effort with the food editor of *The New York Times.*

Chinese Gastronomy, Hsiang Ju Lin and Tsuifeng Lin, with a preface by Lin Yutang. Pyramid Publications, New York, 1969. Charming and valuable background information, good recipes.

Florence Lin's Chinese Regional Cookbook, Florence Lin. Hawthorn, 1975, $12.95. A respected cooking teacher's techniques for a variety of elegant dishes.

The Good Food of Szechwan, Robert A. Delfs. Kodansha, 1974, $6.95. A well-produced tribute to a spicy regional cuisine of China.

Madame Chu's Chinese Cooking School, Grace Zia Chu. Simon & Schuster, 1975, $9.95. Questions and answers, menus, regional recipes, and recipes from students—she's thought of everything.

Peking Cooking, Kenneth H. C. Lo. Pantheon, 1973, $5.95. The elegant cuisine of the ancient capital, by a Chinese expert living in England.

The Pleasures of Chinese Cooking, Grace Zia Chu. Simon & Schuster, 1962, $7.95; Cornerstone paperback, 1974, $1.50. The original and perhaps still the best book on Chinese cooking for beginners.

The Thousand Recipe Chinese Cookbook, Gloria Bley Miller. Grosset & Dunlap, 1970, $10. A trail-blazer that presents an impressive collection of recipes.

French

The Art of Charcuterie, Jane Grigson. Knopf, 1968, $8.95. The definitive work on how the French make so much of the pig so edible.

The Cordon Bleu Cook Book, Dione Lucas. Little, Brown, 1947, $6.95. Simplicity in fine French food, from a simpler era.

The Dione Lucas Book of French Cooking, Dione Lucas and Marion Gorman. Little, Brown, 1973, $14.95. Excellent recipes from one of the pioneer popularizers of French cooking for Americans.

French Country Cooking and *French Provincial Cooking,* Elizabeth David. Penguin paperbacks, $1.45 and $1.90 respectively. By an Englishwoman who writes as deftly as she cooks. The recipes assume reasonable culinary competence in the reader.

The French Menu Cookbook, Richard Olney. Simon & Schuster, 1970, $10.00. An American's interpretation of French cuisine, written from France.

Jacques Pépin: A French Chef Cooks at Home, Jacques Pépin. Simon & Schuster, 1975, $8.95. A well-known chef tells us how it's done at home. A must for those interested in good home cooking.

The Making of a Cook, Madeline Kamman. Atheneum, 1971, $10.00. By a Frenchwoman who teaches cooking in the United States.

Mastering the Art of French Cooking, Julia Child et al., Knopf, Vol. I, 1961; Vol. II, 1970, $12.50 each. The books that established French cooking in American home kitchens. Extraordinarily detailed; already classics.

Simca's Cuisine, Simone Beck. Knopf, 1972, $8.95. Menus and recipes, with abundantly informative text by Julia Child's French colleague.

Simple French Food, Richard Olney. Atheneum, 1974, $10.00. French cooking at its most economical and practical, geared to the American kitchen.

German

The German Cookbook, Mimi Sheraton. Random House, 1965, $8.95. A splendid survey of German cuisine.

Greek

The Food of Greece, Vilma Liacouras Chantiles. Atheneum, 1974, $12.95. A heartfelt mixture of history, cultural information, and home-tested recipes.

Greek Cooking, Lou Seibert Pappas. Harper & Row, 1975, $7.95. Simple, clear, and straightforward.

Hungarian

The Cuisine of Hungary, George Lang. Atheneum, 1971, $17.50. A Hungarian-born food and restaurant expert devoted years to writing this history and adding his favorite recipes; a wonderful text.

The Hungarian Cookbook, Susan Derecksey. Harper & Row, 1972, $8.95. Fun to read; notes on Hungarian wines, too.

Bibliography

Indian

An Invitation to Indian Cooking, Madhur Jaffrey. Knopf, 1973, $7.95. The only Indian cookbook in English that consistently helps the reader produce food that tastes like what you might eat in an Indian home.

Indonesian

The Complete Book of Indonesian Cooking, Antoinette Dewit and Anita Borghese. Bobbs-Merrill, 1973, $7.95. Call this comprehensive, completeness being impossible.

Italian

The Classic Italian Cookbook: The Art of Italian Cooking and the Italian Art of Eating, Marcella Hazan. Alfred A. Knopf, Inc., 1976, $10.95. The only general Italian cookbook in English worth owning. Wide-ranging and infused with the zeal of a perfectionist infatuated with beautiful Italian food.

The Complete Book of Pasta, Jack Denton Scott. Morrow, 1968, $15.00; Bantam paperback, 95 cents. The right man is worshiping at the right shrine and the results are superb.

Italian Family Cooking, Edward Giobbi. Random House, 1971, $8.95. Wonderful Italian peasant cookery by a sensitive artist. These are the recipes that you will use every day.

Italian Food, Elizabeth David. Knopf, 1958, $6.95; Penguin paperback, $1.50. Demonstrates the enormous variety and excitement of Italian regional cooking.

Leaves from Our Tuscan Kitchen, Janet Ross and Michael Waterfield. Atheneum, 1974, $8.95; Vintage paperback, $2.95. A watered-down version of a classic of the early part of the century that retains some lovely dishes.

The Talisman Italian Cookbook, Ada Boni. Crown, 1955, $3.95. The American version of an Italian standard cookbook —a remarkable survey of what Italians cook at home.

Jewish

The Best of Jewish Cooking, Frucht, Rothschild, and Katz. Dial Press, 1974, $10.00. This started out as a fund-raising project for a New Jersey synagogue and ended up as the only good Jewish cookbook that is both true to religious law and gastronomically sophisticated.

Mediterranean

A Book of Mediterranean Food, Elizabeth David. Penguin paperback, $1.65. The brilliance and pungency of ancient regional cuisines, lovingly and appetizingly conveyed.

Mexican

The Complete Book of Mexican Cooking, Elisabeth Lambert Ortiz. M. Evans, 1967, $7.95. A standard excellent work.

The Cuisines of Mexico, Diana Kennedy. Harper & Row, 1972, $12.50. Culture and cooking go together in this volume, which leaves the Texas border far behind in exploring the variety found in Mexican food.

Middle Eastern

A Book of Middle Eastern Food, Claudia Roden. Knopf, 1972, $10.00. Invaluable information on the region and delicious recipes as a bonus. Provocative and carefully written recipes from all over the Middle East.

Moroccan

Couscous and Other Good Food from Morocco, Paula Wolfert. Harper & Row, 1972, $10.95. Impressive research, well-presented recipes.

Pacific Islands

Trader Vic's Pacific Islands Cookbook, Trader Vic, Doubleday, 1968, $7.95. A jet-set voyage with lots of rum.

Russian

Nothing Beets Borscht: Jane's Russian Cookbook, Jane Blanksteen. Atheneum, 1974, $8.95. A high-school student cooks her way back to her heritage. Amusing text.

Scandinavian

The Great Scandinavian Cook Book, Karin Fredrikson. Crown, 1967, $15.00. A huge and compendious work, a standard in Sweden.

Scottish

Much Entertainment, Virginia Maclean. Liveright, 1973, $10.00. Through Scotland with Dr. Johnson and Boswell. Recipes and marvelous line cuts.

Swiss

The Swiss Cookbook, Nika Standen Hazelton. Atheneum, 1967, $3.95. Essential when entertaining your Swiss banker at home, or helpful for just eating well.

Turkish

The Art of Turkish Cooking, Neset Eren, Doubleday, 1969, $6.95. By virtue of Ottoman rule, Middle Eastern cuisine is Turkish cuisine. Here it is at its source, with both recipes and interesting text.

Viennese

Viennese Pastry Cookbook, Lilly J. Reich. Macmillan, 1970, $10.00. Exquisitely detailed recipes for exquisite delights to set you waltzing.

SPECIALIZED BOOKS

Appetizers

Hors d'oeuvre, etc., Coralie Castle and Barbara Lawrence. 101 Productions, 1973, $3.95. The preliminaries.

The Cocktail Hour: Appetizers and Drinks for Every Occasion, Helen Evans Brown. Ward Ritchie, paperback, 1972, $2.95. One of the great American cooks on a very American subject.

Baking

The Art of Fine Baking, Paula Peck. Simon & Schuster, 1970, $7.50. A stimulating work on classic technique and contemporary adaptations; a good foundation for the aspiring baker.

Beard on Bread, James Beard. Knopf, 1973, $7.95. The master's hand to guide you through your first "perfect" loaf to a collection of excellent examples of the bread baker's art.

The Complete Book of Breads, Bernard Clayton, Jr. Simon & Schuster, 1974, $10.95. A comprehensive collection to delight the bread baker.

The John Clancy Baking Book, John Clancy. Popular Library, 1975, $3.95. John Clancy's illustrated "step-by-step" method perfected at his baking school is presented here.

The Tassajara Bread Book, Edward Espe Brown. Shambhala, $3.95. The bible of the whole-grain, whole-earth bread-baking set; useful to anyone who bakes.

A World of Breads, Dolores Casella. David White, 1966, $8.95. From pumpernickel to pizza to pita; the breads of many nations.

Barbecuing and Outdoor Cookery

Sunset Barbecue Book, Sunset, 1973, $1.95. Straightforward and reliable.

Blender

Good Food with a Blender, Ann Seranne. Morrow, 1974, $8.95. The first and possibly last word on the subject.

Braille & Large-Type Cookbooks

The Braille Cookbook, Hooper and Langar. American Printing House for the Blind, Louisville, Kentucky, 1951. A unique and invaluable aid for the sightless.

The New York Times Large Type Cookbook, Jean Hewitt. Golden Press, 1969, $9.95. You don't have to be nearsighted to love this cookbook. There's one easy-to-read recipe per page and the recipes are interesting, well-written and reliable.

Brides

A Bride's Cookbook, Peggy Harvey. Little, Brown, 1962, $4.95. A long-time favorite; you needn't be married to use it.

Camping

Roughing It Easy, Dian Thomas. Brigham Young University Press, 1974, $7.95, also paper. Wisdom for those who would cook and eat in the wilderness.

Stalking the Wild Asparagus and *Stalking the Blue-Eyed Scallop,* Euell Gibbons. McKay, 1970, $7.95 each. In the countryside and by the sea, food is all around you. These are the guides to locating and preparing dinner after the apocalypse, or on your next hike.

Candymaking

The Art of Making Good Candies at Home, Martin K. Herrmann. Doubleday. More than an art—a science. This may be hard to find, but it's worth seeking out.

Canning, Drying, and Preserving

The Ball Blue Book, the Ball Corporation, Muncie, Indiana, 1975, $1.00. The major manufacturer of canning and preserving jars tells you in detail how to go about filling them.

Home Canning of Fruits and Vegetables, U.S. Department of Agriculture. Send 35 cents to Consumer Information, Public Documents Distribution Center, Pueblo, Colo. 81009. As good as anything in print on the subject.

How to Make Jellies, Jams, and Preserves at Home, U.S. Department of Agriculture. Send 35 cents to Consumer Information, Public Documents Dis-

tribution Center, Pueblo, Colo. 81009. Dependable.

Make Your Summer Garden Last All Year, Patricia Shannon Kulla. Lyceum Books, 1975, $7.95. The latest techniques for drying, storing, and winter growing.

The Pleasures of Preserving and Pickling, Jeanne Lesem. Knopf, 1975, $8.95. Recipes from a long-time United Press food columnist.

A Primer for Pickles, a Reader for Relishes, Ruby and Jack Guthrie. 101 Productions, 1974, paperback $3.95. A family with a long history preserves it.

Putting Foods By, second edition, Ruth Hertzberg, Beatrice Vaughan, and Janet Greene. Stephen Greene Press, 1973, $4.95. The best of old and new ways to preserve food, with recipes for using it.

Children's Cooking

The A to Z No-Cook Cookbook, Felipe Rojas-Lombardi. R-L Creations, 1972, $5.95. A cookbook for kids.

Cuisine Est un Jeu d'Enfants, Michel Oliver. Random House, 1965, $6.95. A useful and entertaining book.

Kids Are Natural Cooks, Parents Nursery School. Authors, 40A Reservoir St., Cambridge, Mass. 02138, 1974, paper $3.75. By parents who know.

Clay-Pot and Crockery-Pot Cookery

The Clay Pot Cookbook, Georgia and Grover Sales. Atheneum, 1974, $8.95. The best recipes thus far published for these cooking vessels.

Crockery Cookery, Mable Hoffman. H.P. Books, 1975, paperback, Bantam, $1.95. More than 200 recipes specifically for slow cooking pots.

Desserts

Maida Heatter's Book of Great Desserts, Maida Heatter. Knopf, 1974, $10.00. Rich and good.

Dinners

Feasts for Two, Paul Rubinstein. Macmillan, 1973, $6.95. On an intimate scale; the best in this specialized category.

Great Dinners from Life, Eleanor Graves. Time-Life, 1974, $14.95. A collection of elaborate menus and recipes that originally appeared in *Life* magazine.

Penny-Wise, Party-Perfect Dinners, The Good Cooking School. Doubleday/

Ferguson, 1975, $5.95. Exactly as expressed in the title of the book.

Eggs

The Other Half of the Egg, Helen McCully, Jacques Pépin, and William North Jayme. Morrow, 1967, $5.95; Barrows paperback, $1.95. What to do with the half of each egg that always seems to be left over; the authors give you 180 possibilities.

Fish

James Beard's Fish Cookery, James Beard. Little, Brown, 1956, $6.95; Paperback Library, 95 cents. Mr. Beard knows his shad and lobster, and he knows how to get the most out of them with the least fuss.

Freezing

The Complete Book of Freezer Cookery, Ann Seranne. Doubleday, $6.95. Clear, concise, and straightforward.

Ice Cream

The Great Ice Cream Book, Paul Dickson. Atheneum, 1972, $7.95. Lickin' good.

Large-Group Cookery and Entertaining

Cooking for Carefree Weekends, Molly Finn and Jeri Laber. Simon & Schuster, 1974, $6.95. A guide, with seasonal menus, for those who go to the country and have to feed six or more for three days.

Country Commune Cooking, Lucy Horton. Coward McCann, 1972, $7.95; paperback, $4.95. Ms. Horton spent a year traveling from one commune to another gathering the best of the youth culture's nonviolent recipes: vegetarian, Oriental, and often for crowds.

Helen Corbett Cooks for Company, Helen Corbett. Houghton Mifflin, 1974, $8.95. Recipes from a woman who has created food and entertainment ideas for Neiman-Marcus and the Greenhouse.

Menus for All Occasions, Julie Dannenbaum. Saturday Review Press, 1974, $9.95. Filled with party-perfect menus.

The Sunset Cook Book for Entertaining. Sunset, 1971, paperback, $1.95. Practical and reliable for easy entertaining.

Leftovers and Economical Cooking

Culinary Classics and Improvisations, Michael Field. Vintage, 1973, $2.95. Dishes designed to be recycled into new delights.

Bibliography

Good Cheap Food, Miriam Ungerer. Signet, 1975, $1.50. Economical dishes, with the author's advice on using up every scrap of food.

Waste Not, Want Not: A Cookbook of Delicious Food from Leftovers, Helen McCully. Random House, 1975, $8.95. An absolute necessity for those interested in learning the techniques for getting the most out of their food budget.

Microwave Ovens

Richard Deacon's Microwave Oven Cookbook, Richard Deacon. H. P. Books, 1974, $6.95. A guide to cooking with one of the waves of the future.

Natural and Health Foods

The Best of Natural Foods Around the World, Elizabeth Alston. McKay, 1973, $6.95. A common-sense approach for the uncommitted.

Diet for a Small Planet, Frances Moore Lappé, and *Recipes for a Small Planet,* Ellen Buchman Ewald. Ballantine paperbacks, $1.95 each. The argument for changing the world's protein imbalance is made persuasively. The first book has a number of recipes, the second, many more. All are designed to provide protein without meat so you can practice what is preached.

The New York Times Natural Foods Cookbook, Jean Hewitt. Avon paperback, $1.95. First-rate.

The Vegetarian Epicure, Anna Thomas. Knopf (Vintage), 1972, paperback, $3.95. An excellent book by a serious student of vegetable cookery.

Zen Macrobiotic Cooking, Michael Abehsera. Avon paperback, 1970, $1.25. If you must cook macrobiotically, this is a comprehensive text.

Pâté

Pâté and Other Marvelous Meat Loaves, Dorothy Ivens. Lippincott, 1972, $7.95. They aren't all French and they aren't all that difficult to make.

Soups

New York Times Bread and Soup Cookbook, Yvonne Young Tarr. Quadrangle, 1972, $9.95. Add dessert for a full meal.

Soups and Stews, Kay Shaw Nelson. Regnery, 1974, $6.95. One-dish main courses with menu suggestions.

Special Diets

Haute Cuisine for Your Heart's Delight, Carol Cutler. Crown, 1973, $6.95. The best of low-cholesterol food for epicures.

Variety Meats

Innards and Other Variety Meats, Jana Allen and Margaret Gin. 101 Productions, 1974, $3.95. Good recipes for parts of the animal too often not eaten.

Vegetables

The Potato Book, Myrna Davis. Doubleday, 1973, $5.95. Everyone who is anyone in the Hamptons, including Truman Capote and Craig Claiborne, pitches in to benefit a Long Island day school. Recipes, lore, and clever drawings.

Nature's Harvest, the Vegetable Cookbook, Arabella Boxer. Regnery, 1974, $10.00. From artichokes to zucchini and everything in between.

A World of Vegetable Cookery, Alex D. Hawkes. Simon & Schuster, 1968, $10.95. One of the best—excellent plant lore, imaginative recipes.

Wines and Cordials

Alexis Lichine's New Encyclopedia of Wines & Spirits, Alexis Lichine. Alfred A. Knopf, 1974, $20.00. Everything you imbibe, from A to Z.

Frank Schoonmaker's Encyclopedia of Wine, Frank Schoonmaker. Hastings House, 1964, revised 1973, $9.95. Prefaced by sections on the history, making serving, and storing of wines. Entries are alphabetical and all-inclusive, from aperitif to digestif and in between.

Making Cordials and Liqueurs at Home, John F. Farrell, Harper & Row, 1974, $6.95. It works, and it saves you money.

The Signet Book of Wine, Alexis Bespaloff. New American Library paperback, 1971, $1.50. A handy guide.

Wine, Hugh Johnson. Simon & Schuster, 1966, revised 1974, $12.95. A pretty book which covers wine by types and regions.

The Wines of America, Leon D. Adams. Houghton Mifflin, 1973, $10.95. There is a lot to know and it's all here.

BOOKS FOR READING AND REFERENCE

Reading

The Alice B. Toklas Cookbook, Alice B. Toklas. Doubleday-Anchor, 1954, paperback, $1.95. Sometimes eccentric, often brilliant repertoire of anecdotes and recipes gathered over a lifetime of acquaintance with the painters, writers, and otherwise famous in France, by Gertrude Stein's lifetime companion.

Delights and Prejudices, James Beard. Atheneum, 1964, $6.95. Beard's autobiography. Delightful reminiscences, delightful recipes.

Book of Household Management, Isabella Beeton, ed. Farrar, Strauss & Giroux, 1969, $15.00. Reprint of the monumental Victorian opus. To read more than to cook from, but it is the best way to understand the culinary pomp and circumstance that England lost along with her empire.

The Cornucopia, Judith Herman and Marguerite Shalett Herman. Harper & Row, 1973, $15.00. "A kitchen entertainment and cook book" with wonderful illustrations. Recipes from 1390 to 1899. Cooks will need scales and courage.

The Delectable Past, Esther B. Aresty. Simon & Schuster, 1964, $6.50. All that's worth remembering.

Food in History, Reay Tannahill. Stein & Day, 1973, $10.00. Mankind has progressed from the stomach outward. Well-researched interpretation of food's role.

Foodbook, James Trager. Grossman, 1970. Food, as history; a popularization crammed with facts and figures.

Horizon's Illustrated History of Eating and Drinking Through the Ages, by the Editors of *Horizon* Magazine. 2 vol., Doubleday, 1968, $16.50. A lavishly illustrated history is in one volume, menus and recipes for your typical Roman banquet or Renaissance feast in the other.

The Physiology of Taste, Brillat-Savarin. Translated by M. F. K. Fisher. Knopf, 1949, $10.00. All about food and man's taste for it—"the bible of all serious eaters."

The Supper of the Lamb, Robert Farrar Capon. Pocket Books, 1970, $0.95. Father Capon's highly personal, original, and fascinating volume on food and cooking.

The Vegetable Passion, Janet Barkas. Scribners, 1975, $8.95. The subject updated.

With Bold Knife and Fork, M. F. K. Fisher. Putnam, 1969, $7.95. A collection of the author's columns published in the *New Yorker.*

All Manner of Food, Michael Field. Knopf, 1970, $8.95. Delightful essays on raw materials, plus recipes by the author of *Michael Field's Cooking School.*

The Barbara Kraus Dictionary of Protein, Barbara Kraus. Harper's Magazine Press, 1975, $8.95. Food value counter.

Beard on Food, James Beard. Knopf, 1974, $10.00. Collected wisdom from

America's food sage; taken from his syndicated column.

The Best of Italian Cooking, Waverley Root. Grosset & Dunlap, 1974, $14.95. Root doesn't cook, but his explanations of foods and dishes are sandwiched between lavish photographs and lavish recipes.

Books for Cooks, Marguerite Patten. Bowker, 1975, $16.95. The master list.

The Book of Spices, Frederic Rosengarten, Jr. Pyramid paperback, 1973, $1.95. Spice history, family trees, and an extensive bibliography.

Calories and Carbohydrates, Barbara Kraus. Signet paperback, 1973. A dictionary of 7500 brand names and basic foods.

The Dictionary of Sodium, Fats, and Cholesterol, Barbara Kraus. Grosset & Dunlap, 1974, $9.95. Know what is in what you eat.

The Encyclopedia of Practical Gastronomy, Ali-Bab, pseud. Translated by Elizabeth Benson from *Gastronomie Pratique, Etudes Culinaires.* McGraw-Hill, 1974, $14.95. A long-awaited translation of a portion of the immense twentieth-century handbook of haute cuisine for the home cook.

The Escoffier Cook Book, A. Escoffier. Crown, 1941, $5.95. The man who simplified the French cuisine of his day provides a dose of theory with multiple recipes and variations to practice on. A masterpiece. Really an expanded chef's memorandum, especially in this creaky translation (the French original is kept in print by Flammarion). Probably to be used by the casual cook for a simple home meal.

French Cheese, Pierre Androuet. Harper's Magazine Press, 1973, $10.00. A master merchant, the best-known in Paris, reviews his nation's varied stock.

Handbook of Practical Cooking for Ladies and Professional Cooks, Pierre Blot. Arno, $12.00. A reproduction of the 1869 manual by the touring French chef who took Reconstruction America by storm.

How to Eat and Drink Your Way Through a French and Italian Menu, James Beard. Atheneum, 1971, $6.95. Also in paperback, $2.95. At last, a lexicon for the restaurant-goer.

La Cuisine, Raymond Oliver. Translated by Nika Standen Hazelton with Jack Van Bibber. Tudor, $27.50. An encyclopedia of techniques, comprehensive and fully illustrated.

Nobody Ever Tells You These Things About Food and Drink, Helen McCully. Holt, Rinehart and Winston, 1967, $6.95; and *Things You Always Wanted to Know About Food and Drink,* Helen McCully, Holt, Rinehart and Winston, 1972, $7.95. Two books by a food expert, with the answers to innumerable basic questions.

Larousse Gastronomique, Prosper Montagné. Crown, 1961, $20.00. Translation of a classic; French cuisine in an 1,100-page nutshell. More for reference than for cooking, although there are those who use it for both.

The Professional Chef, Culinary Institute of America. Cahners, 1974, $24.95. Here you have the commercial recipe for breaded veal cutlets, fifty portions of four ounces each, and hundreds of other dishes you will find in American restaurants.

UNITED STATES DEPARTMENT OF AGRICULTURE PUBLICATIONS

Publications of the United States Department of Agriculture are probably the best overall sources of information on nutrition, food shopping, food preparation, and storage. Many of their booklets are free and those that are not are modestly priced.

You can buy the publications listed below at Government Printing Office bookstores in major cities (see list of addresses below). Many can be requested from your Representative or Senator (see note), and others are most conveniently ordered by mail. Here's a sampling of what's available. The best are starred.

Ordering Information for Free Publications

Up to ten of the following publications can be ordered at a time, without charge, from the Department of Agriculture, Office of Communication, Washington, D.C. 20250. We suggest you also ask for List No. 5, "Popular Publications," which includes a listing of other free publications. The addresses of the Government Printing Office and GPO bookstores are as follows:

Government Printing Office
710 North Capitol Street
Washington, D.C. 20402

Atlanta
Room 100, Federal Building
275 Peachtree Street NE.
Atlanta, Georgia 30303

Birmingham
2121 8th Avenue North
Birmingham, Ala. 35203

Boston
Room G25
John F. Kennedy Federal Building
Sudbury Street
Boston, Massachusetts 02203

Chicago
Room 1463, 14th Floor
Everett McKinley Dirksen Building
219 South Dearborn Street
Chicago, Illinois 60604

Dallas
Room 1C46
Federal Building-U.S. Courthouse
1100 Commerce Street
Dallas, Texas 75202

Denver
Room 1421
Federal Building-U.S. Courthouse
1961 Stout Street
Denver, Colorado 80202

Detroit
Room 229, Federal Building
31 West Lafayette Blvd.
Detroit, Michigan 48226

Kansas City
Room 135, Federal Office Building
601 East 12th Street
Kansas City, Missouri 64106

Los Angeles
Room 1015, Federal Office Building
300 North Los Angeles Street
Los Angeles, California 90012

New York City
Room 110
26 Federal Plaza
New York, New York 10007

Philadelphia
U.S. Post Office & Court House
9th & Chestnut Streets
Philadelphia, Pa. 19107

San Francisco
Room 1023, Federal Office Building
450 Golden Gate Avenue
San Francisco, California 94102

Publications

Family Fare: A Guide to Good Nutrition. A compact booklet, packed with information on shopping, cooking, and food storage in addition to nutrition. G1

How to Buy Beef Roasts. G146
How to Buy Beef Steaks. G145
How to Buy Canned and Frozen Fruits. G191
How to Buy Cheese. G193
How to Buy Dairy Products. G201

Bibliography

How to Buy Dry Beans, Peas, and Lentils. G177

How to Buy Eggs. G144

"Guide for Consumers" series:
Beef and Veal in Family Meals. G118
Breads, Cakes and Pies in Family Meals. G186
Cereals and Pasta in Family Meals. G150
Cheese in Family Meals. G112
Eggs in Family Meals. G103
Fruits in Family Meals. G125
Pork in Family Meals. G160
Milk in Family Meals. G127
Poultry in Family Meals. G110
Vegetables in Family Meals. G105
Nuts in Family Meals. G176
Money-Saving Main Dishes. G43

Ordering Information for the Following Publications

Order the following publications, for most of which a charge is made, from Consumer Information, Public Documents Distribution Center, Pueblo, Colorado 81009. Make your check or money order payable to the Superintendent of Documents. We also suggest that you request the latest copy of the Consumer Information Index for future ordering. The outstanding titles are marked with an asterisk.

Calories and Weight. Pocket guide indicates calories per portion of 563 common foods. 079C $1.00

Food Additives. Describes what they are, how they are regulated. 081C 25 cents

The Food Fad Boom. Questions and answers on the labeling, promotion and nutritional value of organic foods. 083C Free

Food Is More Than Just Something to Eat. Guide to nutrition includes functions of the major nutrients, their importance to good health, where to find them in today's foods. 085C Free

Nutrition Labeling—Terms You Should Know. 086C Free

Antibiotics in the Foods You Eat. Use of antibiotics in food-producing animals, potential hazards, steps being taken to prevent unsafe residue levels. 088C Free

The Food Labeling Revolution. Explains new regulations requiring a food-label information panel. 092C Free

How to Buy Meat for Your Freezer. 094C 35 cents

Keys to Quality. Explains U.S.D.A. grades; lists 15 booklets with more detailed food buying information. 095C Free

Questions and Answers About Canned Foods. 096C Free

Standards for Meat and Poultry Products. Minimum meat and poultry content for 232 food products—e.g. chili, frozen dinners, frankfurters. 098C Free

Your Money's Worth in Foods. Guides for budgeting, menu planning, and shopping for best values. 101C 50 cents

Can Your Kitchen Pass the Food Storage Test? Checklist of food-storage hazards and how to correct them, with emphasis on the proper use of refrigeration. 102C Free

Let's Cook Fish. Selection, storage, preparation, recipes, nutritional importance. 105C $1.25

Seasoning with Herbs and Spices. 106C Free

Soybeans in Family Meals. Recipes and tips for using soybean products in menu planning. 107C 35 cents

What About Metric? Advantages and growing use of the metric system; conversion tables for weight, length, volume and temperature. 244C 80 cents

Note on Ordering

Order the following publications from Superintendent of Documents, Government Printing Office, Washington, D.C. 20402. Make your check or money order payable to the Superintendent of Documents.

Composition of Foods. Also known as "Handbook 8," this is probably the most complete source available of information on nutritional content of raw, processed and prepared foods. Widely used as basis for government and food industry publications. AH8 $2.85

Cheese Varieties and Descriptions. Includes information on cheeses of all types from other countries as well as the U.S. AH54 $1.50

U.S.D.A. Yearbook

Request this from your Representative or Senator. They're given a supply to be distributed free, on request, to constituents:

U.S.D.A. Yearbook, 1974, Shopper's Guide. U.S.D.A. yearbooks are published annually in hard covers. Each deals comprehensively with a particular aspect of the department's work.

A SPECIAL LISTING

Here are thirteen titles, appropriately enough a baker's dozen, of unusual cookbooks of interest to those building a library of gastronomy and to those who just like to read about good food. Look for them in specialized bookshops, or visit New York City's Corner Book Shop, 102 Fourth Avenue, New York, N.Y. 10003; telephone 212-254-7714. This famous shop is noted for out-of-print works, and especially for cookbooks and books on gastronomy. It was founded and is still operated by Eleanor Lowenstein, compiler of the *Bibliography of American Cookery Books 1742–1860,* who provided this list.

Festival Menus 'Round the World, Sula Benet. London, 1957; 195 pp.

Musings of a Chinese Gourmet, F. T. Cheng. London, 1962; 156 pp.

The Derrydale Cook Book of Fish and Game, Louis P. DeGouy. Limited edition, New York, 1937; 2 vols.

Mexican Cook Book, Josefina Velazquez DeLeon. Mexico City, 1971; paper covers; 320 pp.

Long Island Seafood Cook Book, J. George Frederick. New York, 1939; 324 pp.

Caribbean Cookery, Winifred Grey. London, 1962; 256 pp.

Food in England, Dorothy Hartley. London, 1973; 676 pp.

Amana Recipes, Ladies' Auxiliary of the Homestead Welfare Club [Iowa], 1948; 120 pp.

Fit for a King: The Merle Armitage Book of Food, Ramiel McGhee. New York, 1939.

The Scots Kitchen, F. Marian McNeill. London, 1968; 282 pp.

Everyday Siamese Dishes, Sibpan Sonakul. Bangkok, 1966; paper covers; includes glossary; 81 pp.

Traditional Ukrainian Cookery, Savella Stechinshin. Winnipeg, 1967; 495 pp.

The Cooks' Paradise, William Verral. Reprint of 1759 edition, London, 1948; 139 pp.

Availability Information: Items

Catalogue Number	Item Description	Manufacturer or Supplier	Mfr.'s Description
1.1	Foley Stainless-Steel Measuring Cup	Foley	240
1.2	Measuring Cups and Spoons from Foley	Foley	154
1.3	Metal Measuring Spoons from West Germany	Ostrowsky	3106/4
1.4	Measuring Spoon with Slide	Wecolite	9400
1.5	All-in-One Plastic Slide Measure	Wecolite	9402
1.6	Plastic Cup for Weight and Volume	Roth	16-6
1.7	Pyrex Measuring Cups, 1 qt.	Corning	532
1.8	Small Plastic Measuring Cup	Borden	L8N
1.9	Liter Measure from Italy	Zucchi	264
1.10	Porcelain Measuring Pitcher	La Cuisinière	——
1.11	See-Saw Balance Scoop	Roth	16-3
1.12	Compact French Plastic Scale	Terraillon	BA4000
1.13	Danish Wall Scale	Eva	236300
1.14	French Beam Balance	Terraillon	T865
1.15	English Portion-Control Scale	Gemini	0850
1.16	Pelouze Portion-Control Scale	Pelouze	YG425
1.17	Original Pocket Balance	Compass	84
1.18	Mercury Oven Thermometer with Folding Case	Hoan	BGW2
1.19	Taylor Mercury Oven Thermometer	Taylor Instr.	5921
1.20	Taylor Refrigerator-Freezer Thermometer	Taylor Instr.	5923
1.21	Taylor Freezer Thermometer	Taylor Instr.	5925
1.22	Centigrade Freezer Thermometer	Camille Mercier	5076
1.23	Inside-Outside Freezer Thermometer	Taylor Instr.	5922
1.24	H-B Dough Thermometer/Case	Beard Glaser Wolf	BGWHB 16/15
1.25	H-B Meat Thermometer/Case	Beard Glaser Wolf	BGWHB 17/15
1.26	Tiny Instant Thermometer	Taylor Instr.	5982
1.27	Bi-Therm Fahrenheit Centigrade Testing Thermometer	Taylor Instr.	BB2053198
1.28	Thermoelectric Food Thermometer	Orvis	G4721
1.29	Glass Candy Thermometer	Chaney	716
1.30	Large Taylor Candy Thermometer	Taylor Instr.	5907
1.31	H-B Candy or Deep Frying Thermometer/Case	Beard Glaser Wolf	BGWHB 18/15
1.32	Colorful Candy and Fat Thermometer	Chaney	722
1.33	Taylor Deep-Frying Thermometer	Taylor Instr.	5909
1.34	Thermo Spoon	Thermometer Corp.	305
1.35	Thermovins from Germany	Sanbri	TV-B
1.36	Swiss Vinometer	Swissmart	919
1.37	Sunbeam Wall Clock	Sunbeam	81-132
1.38	Egg Timer	Progressus	17
1.39	Terraillon Timer	Teraillon	——
1.40	Time-All	Intermatic, Inc.	E-941
1.41	Salometer	Taylor Instr.	H-4282
1.42	Baumé Hydrometer	Taylor Instr.	22100
1.43	Baumé Hydrometer	Taylor Instr.	H4102
1.44	Restaurant-Size Aluminum Colander	Leyse	5111
1.45	Farberware Stainless-Steel Colander	Farberware	775
1.47	Porcelain Colander or Strainer, 7¼" diam.	Pacific Epicure	2-8
1.48	Spaghetti Strainer or Colander, 5 qt.	Commercial	095
1.49	Stainless-Steel Spaghetti Strainer	Berarducci	A-45
1.50	Wire Spaghetti Drainer	Zucchi	25
1.51	Small Scoop-Strainer or Drainer	Lagostina	1067
1.52	Bowl-shaped Wire Strainer	Bazar de la Cuisine	——
1.53	American Aluminum Strainer 6" diam.	Intedge	C1472L
1.54	Double-Mesh Strainer	Christian Oos	94774
1.55	Shallow Stainless-Steel Strainer, 7½" diam.	Milton Gumpert	134-18
1.56	Stainless-Steel Strainer-Skimmer	Rowoco	195
1.57	Cylindrical Strainer of Stainless Steel, 3½" diam.	Figli Veroli	——
1.58	Tiny Conical Strainer	Williams-Sonoma	——
1.59	Decorative Salad Basket	Hoan	1351/308
1.60	Mouli Metal Spin-Dryer	Hoan	906
1.61	Mouli Plastic Spin-Dryer	Hoan	909
1.62	Danish Salad Dryer	Eva	228520
1.63	Three Brushes from West Germany, natural bristles	Lola	323

Catalogue Number	Item Description	Manufacturer or Supplier	Mfr.'s Description	Catalogue Number	Item Description	Manufacturer or Supplier	Mfr.'s Description
1.64	Three Brushes from West Germany, nylon bristles	Lola	319	2.19	American High-Carbon-Steel Boning Knife, 6"	Harrington	2315-6
1.65	Three Brushes from West Germany, natural bristles and brass needles	Lola	327	2.20	Wüsthof High-Carbon-Steel Boning Knife, 6"	Moss	268
1.66	Visp	Bergquist	30012	2.21	Zanger Boning Knife	Zanger	———
1.67	Huge Pot Brush—Urn Brush	Intedge	B13	2.22	Flexible Henckels Boner	Henckels	32202-5½
1.68	Pot-scrubbing Brush—Pot Brush	Intedge	B5	2.23	Versatile Stainless-Steel Slicer	Zanger	———
1.69	Bottle and Glass Brush—Glass Brush	Intedge	B9	2.24	Henckels Heavy-Duty Slicer, 10"	Henckels	31060-10
1.70	Baby-Bottle Brush	Lola	375	2.25	Flexible-Blade Ham Slicer	Henckels'	227-10
1.71	Narrow Stiff-bristled Brush	Intedge	B6	2.26	Round-tipped Stainless-Steel Slicer, 10"	Forschner	455-10
1.72	Twin Bar Brushes	Intedge	B600N	2.27	Slicer with Hollow Ground Ovals on Edge, 14"	Henckels	314-14
1.73	Bronze and Stainless-Steel Scrubbing Pads	Gottschalk	G30	2.28	Narrow Slicer, 12"	Henckels	324-12
1.74	Bronze and Stainless-Steel Scrubbing Pads	Gottschalk	725	2.30	French Stainless-Steel Bread Knife	Le Roi	64
1.75	Coiled-Plastic Scrubbing Pads	Lola	380	2.31	White-handled Bread Knife from England	Taylor's Eye	7949
1.76	Stainless-Steel Scrubbing Cloth	Wearever	5742	2.32	French Tomato Knife	Rowoco	63
1.77	Griddle Screen	Intedge	223	2.33	Utility Knife with Forked Tip	Zanger	———
1.78	French Pop-up Sponges, package of 3	Hoan	BGW6	2.34	"Ivory"-handled Grapefruit Knife	Taylor's Eye	1707
1.79	Chamois-covered Sponge	Lamalle	1198A	2.35	American Stainless-Steel Grapefruit Knife	Case	PO2565SE
2.1	Henckels Chef's Knife w/Plastic-impregnated Handle, 8"	Henckels	31061-10	2.36	French Frozen Food Knife	Rowoco	105
2.2	Carbon-Steel Chef's Knife from France, 12"	B.I.A.	K968/30	2.37	The Zip-Zap	Zanger	———
2.3	Lighter Stainless-Steel Chef's Knife, 8"	Le Roi	16	2.38	Classic Round Steel, 14"	Intedge	386
2.4	Professional Stainless-Steel Chef's Knife, 10"	Forschner	430-10	2.39	Multi-Cut German Steel	Forschner	650H
2.5	The Largest Chef's Knife of Them All	Forschner	946	2.41	Standard Carborundum Stone, 6x2x1"	Hoan	BGW19
2.6	Henckels Paring Knife, 4"	Henckels	31060-4	2.42	An Elegant Whetstone	Arkansas	BS-D4B
2.7	Henckels Carbon-Steel Paring Knife	Henckels	506-4	2.43	Pocket Steel	Henckels	132
2.8	Superb Stainless-Steel Parer	Zanger	———	2.44	A Pretty Mini-Steel	Forschner	247A
2.9	Petite Paring Knife from France	Rowoco	3102	2.45	The Magnabar XII, 12"	Phelon	———
2.10	Tiny Dishwasher-Safe Parer	Intedge	9101	2.46	Modular Slotted Wooden Rack	Williams-Sonoma	C-148
2.11	All-Purpose Stainless-Steel Cleaver	Henckels	140-6	2.47	One-Row Slotted Wooden Rack, Walnut	Rowoco	521
2.12	Heavy Carbon-Steel Cleaver	Henckels	110-6	2.48	The Butcher Block, 18" x 18" x 12"	Brauner	———
2.13	Superb Stainless-Steel Butcher Knife, 10"	Zanger	———	2.49	Butcher Block Cutting Boards, 18" x 12"	Brauner	888
2.14	Wüsthof Stainless-Steel Butcher Knife, 12"	Moss	154	2.50	End-Grain Cutting Board	Timberline	64-6D6
2.15	Henckels Scimitar Knife	Henckels	32212-10½	2.51	Hard-Rubber Chopping Board, 24" x 18"	Park Rubber	"Gravy Lane"
2.16	Stainless-Steel Skinning Knife, 6½"	Intedge	9636-6½	2.52	Ceramic Cutting Board, White	Corning	P-1620
2.17	Tanqueuer	Le Roi	122	3.1	Swivel Action Peeler	Ekco	3K
2.18	Superb Blooding Knife, 5¼"	Le Roi	3	3.2	French Swivel Action Peeler	Rowoco	183
				3.3	Citrus Shell Cutter	Rowoco	169
				3.4	Zester with Rosewood Handle	Forschner	588

Catalogue Number	Item Description	Manufacturer or Supplier	Mfr.'s Description
3.5	Zester with Plastic Handle	Rowoco	62
3.6	Citrus Peeler	Forschner	589
3.7	French Citrus Peeler	Rowoco	61
3.8	White Mountain Apple Parer	White Mt.	———
3.9	Apple Corer	Rowoco	441
3.10	Apple Corer and Slicer	Intedge	4543
3.11	Zucchini Corer	Rowoco	81
3.12	Double Melon Baller	Forschner	2B
3.13	Gerhard Recknagel Melon Baller	Recknagel	201-20
3.14	Round French Melon Baller	B.I.A.	KE 122
3.15	Oval French Melon Baller	B.I.A.	KE 122A
3.16	Fluted French Melon Baller	B.I.A.	KE 122B
3.17	Tomato Spoon	Ontario	124
3.18	Strawberry Huller	Becker & Becker	09000
3.19	Corn Cutter	Lee Mfg.	202P
3.20	Radish Cutter	Becker & Becker	11210
3.21	Lemon Slicer	Becker & Becker	23800
3.22	Cherry or Olive Pitter	Rowoco	167
3.23	Plum Pitter	Creative	S-1958
3.24	Cherry and Plum Pitter	Edwin Jay	33766
3.25	French Spatula	Le Roi	53
3.26	Serrated Spatula	Rushbrooke	39 #163
3.27	Enormous Italian Spatula	Zucchi	203
3.28	Lighter Italian Spatula	Zucchi	203
3.29	Victorinox Flexible Spatula, 10″	Forschner	162
3.30	Small American Spatula	Burns Mfg.	365R
3.31	Narrow Spatula for Lifting	Forschner	165
3.32	Swedish Sandwich Spatula	Karlsson-Nilsson	1314KN
3.33	American Sandwich Spatula	Burns Mfg.	330
3.34	Stainless-Steel Kitchen Shears	Edwin Jay	33448
3.35	All-Purpose Kitchen Shears	Henckels	43925
3.36	Black-handled Shears	Waldmin & Saam	3503
3.37	Faceted Poultry Shears	Couzon	52863
3.38	Stainless-Steel Poultry Shears	Kretzer	6106
3.39	Eagle Shears	Kretzer	5020
3.41	Curved Steel Shears	Kretzer	5009
3.42	Highly Curved Shears	Kretzer	5013
3.43	French Bowl and Chopper	Rowoco	642
3.44	Mezzaluna I	Ausonia	5131
3.45	Mezzaluna II	Hoan	304
3.46	Chopping Bowl, 3 qt.	Artsam	88/13
3.47	Carbon-Steel Double Crescent Cutter	Bridge	Peugeot
3.48	French Rolling Mincer	Zag-France	Seruite #2
3.49	Double Rolling Mincer	Diogenes-Werk	1101
3.50	Parsley Grinder	Eva	222563
3.51	Swiss Mandoline	Williams-Sonoma	61
3.52	Cabbage Cutter	Schiller & Asmus	K1347
3.53	Cutfix	Lamalle	Cutfix
3.54	Professional Steel Mandoline	Lamalle	583
3.55	White Enamel Slicer	Eva	221730
3.56	Eva Electric Slicing Machine	Eva	225420
3.57	Bosch Electric Slicing Machine	Bosch	———
3.58	French Fry Cutter	Brabantia	1617
3.59	Butter Slicer	Mayer	220
3.60	Butter Curler	Rowoco	70
3.61	Double-Handled Cheese Cutter	Giesser Messer	9610R
3.62	Swiss Cheese Cutter	Swissmart	711
3.63	Single-handled Cheese Cutter	Swissmart	713
3.64	Cheese Chopper	Swissmart	712
3.65	Cheese Scraper and Gouger	Zucchi	41
3.66	Cheese Sampler	Ausonia	1798
3.67	Double-Wire Cheese Cutter	Rowoco	106
3.68	Cheese Slicer	Edwin Jay	34266
3.69	Truffle Slicer	Rowoco	133
3.70	Italian Truffle Cutters	Zucchi	171
3.71	Cutters in Plastic Box	Intedge	715
3.72	Larger Truffle Cutters	Intedge	714
3.73	Large Tin of Truffle Cutters	Intedge	716
3.74	French Gelée Cutters	Matfer	43010
3.75	Alphabet Cutters	Roth	20-C
3.76	Chrome-plated Steel Nutcracker	Edwin Jay	62030
3.77	Double Wooden Nutcracker	Bridge	———
3.78	English Nutcracker	Edwin Jay	61751
3.79	Texas Native Inertia Nutcracker	R.P. Ind.	7141
4.1	Rectangular Carbon-Steel Pounder	Lamalle	1104
4.2	Rectangular Stainless-Steel Pounder	Zucchi	35
4.3	Round Professional Veal Pounder	Rowoco	132
4.4	Stainless-Steel Pounder with Plastic Handle	Ausonia	———
4.5	Brass Pounder	Lamalle	1104A
4.6	Aluminum Meat Tenderizer	Creative	P1960
4.7	Marble Mortar and Pestle	Gaillard	28 cm
4.8	Porcelain Mortar and Pestle, 5⅝″ diam.	Pillivuyt	900113
4.9	Set of Three Porcelain Mortars and Pestles	Continental	1117

Catalogue Number	Item Description	Manufacturer or Supplier	Mfr.'s Description
4.10	Bernard Leach Mortar	Leach	55
4.11	Ash Mortar and Pestle	Pacific Epicure	91-7
4.12	Ironwood Mortar and Pestle	Lamalle	809
4.13	Separate Wooden Pestle	B.I.A.	BEF181
4.14	Magic Mill for Grain	Magic Mill	Magic Mill
4.15	Aluminum Drum Sieve	Wearever Food	5270
4.16	Zucchi Wood and Metal Sieves with Extra Strong Metal Mesh, 12" diam.	Zucchi	1151
4.17	Wood Frame Horsehair Sieve	Sermonetta	———
4.18	Wood-framed Sieve with Nylon Mesh	Zucchi	26
4.20	Wood-framed Coronet Sieve	Zucchi	1152
4.21	Mouli Food Mill, 2 qt.	Mouli	ML-2
4.22	Aluminum Chinois	Wearever Food	4699
4.23	Stainless-Steel Chinois	Zucchi	———
4.24	Stainless-Steel Chinois	Intedge	809S
4.25	Fine-meshed Tinned-Steel Chinois	Intedge	1143
4.26	Chinois with Stand	Bromwell	1-B
4.27	Large Wooden Pestle for a Chinois	Wearever Food	4699R
4.28	Wooden Champignon	Gaillard	———
4.29	Large Wooden Champignon	Michel	———
4.30	Apricot-Wood Champignon	Continental	S118
4.31	Hardwood Champignon	B.I.A.	BEF 175
4.32	Potato Ricer	Levi Peterson	3
4.33	Large Aluminum Onion or Garlic Press	Becker & Becker	08000
4.34	Aluminum Garlic Press	Rowoco	112
4.35	Fisko Flat Stainless-Steel Graters	Kalkus	960/961
4.36	Heavy-Duty Stainless-Steel Grater and Shredder	Intedge	619
4.37	Stainless-Steel Grater and Shredder	Dripcut	SG-200
4.38	French Nutmeg Grater	Hoan	1889
4.39	Large English Nutmeg Grater	Taylor Law	9825
4.41	Two-Piece Round Cheese Grater with Bowl	Edwin Jay	68934
4.42	Plastic Cheese Grater	Scan Plast	C321
4.43	Rotary Grater with Three Cylinders	Mouli	MG-3
4.44	Quick Mill for Cheese	Berarducci	C2-400
4.45	Zyliss Mechanical Grater	Zyliss	132
4.46	Mouli Salad Maker	Mouli	MJ-2
4.47	Mouli Meat Grinder	Roth	10-4
4.48	The Tritacarne Three	Valenti	V200
4.49	Spong Meat Grinder	Schiller & Asmus	SN605
4.50	Hand-operated Meat Grinder with Attachments	Roth	11-1, 11-2
4.51	Perfex Peppermill, 4" high	Rowoco	143
4.52	Peugeot Wooden Peppermill, 3¾" high	Hoan	707
4.53	Stainless-Steel Peppermill	Fraser's	5327
4.54	Wooden Peppermill	Bridge	Grulet
4.55	Salt and Pepper Mill Set	Rowoco	141, 1413
4.56	Pocket Peppermill	Hammacher	———
4.57	Wooden Salt Mill from France	Schiller & Asmus	J477
4.58	Glass Salt Mill	Herring	774S
4.59	Cast-Iron Clamp-on Coffee Mill, 11" high	Schiller & Asmus	MS1
4.60	Wooden Coffee Mill	Bridge	Grulet
4.61	Braun Electric Coffee Mill	Braun	KMM-1
4.62	All-Purpose Quick Mill	Salton	GC-3
4.63	Tomato Juicer and Pulper	Roth	11-6
4.64	Electric Vegetable and Fruit Juice Extractor	Braun	MP-50
4.65	Oster Electric Juicer-Extractor	Oster	362-04
4.66	Presse Viande	Lamalle	696
4.67	Sunkist Citrus Juicer	Friedman	7
4.68	Large Hand-Operated Citrus Juicer	Friedman	932
4.69	Electric Citrus Juicer	Schulte	230
4.70	Stoneware Citrus Reamer, Orange	Bringle	———
4.71	Plastic Citrus Reamer	Creative	3215
4.72	Porcelain Lemon Squeezer	La Cuisiniere	———
4.73	Plastic Lemon Squeezer	Becker & Becker	34000
4.74	Tiny Juice Extractor	Creative	161
4.75	A Special Lemon Squeezer	Edwin Jay	33014
4.76	Single-Speed Blender	Waring	700
4.77	Large Commercial Blender	Waring	CB-6
4.78	Waring Fourteen-Speed Blender and Accessories	Waring	97-56
4.79	Blend and Store Jar	Waring	3-BA-4
4.81	Oster Dual-Range Pulsematic Blender	Oster	861-01
5.1	Cuisinart Food Processor	Cuisinarts	CFP-5
5.2	Robot Coupe	Robot Coupe	Type R2
5.3	Bosch Magic Mixer	Magic Mill	504
5.4	Braun Kitchen Machine	Braun	KM-32 Spec.
5.5	Kitchen Aid K-5A Electric Mixer	Hobart	K-5-A
5.6	Sunbeam Mixmaster	Sunbeam	1-80
5.7	Farberware Hand Mixer	Farberware	277W AORG

Catalogue Number	Item Description	Manufacturer or Supplier	Mfr.'s Description	Catalogue Number	Item Description	Manufacturer or Supplier	Mfr.'s Description
5.9	Ekco Eggbeater	Ekco	689	6.1	Soapstone Griddle, 18¼" x 9¼"	Vermont Marble	22-015
5.11	Flat Whisk	Christian Oos	20801	6.2	Farberware Griddle	Farberware	260SP
5.12	Heavy Wire Stainless-Steel Whisk, 12"	Metropolitan	SC112	6.3	SEB Minute Grill, 10½" x 8¼"	SEB	011340
5.13	Thin Wire Stainless-Steel Whisk, 16"	Metropolitan	SC216	6.4	Copco Grill Pan, 11" diam.	Copco	215
5.14	Heavy Tinned-Steel Wire Whisk, 16"	Metropolitan	516	6.5	Waffle Iron, 10⅜" x 13½"	Farberware	290
5.15	Heavy Stainless-Steel Whisk, 15¾"	Christian Oos	9 1132	6.6	Cast Iron Skillet, 10½" diam.	General Housewares	0008
5.16	Large Wooden-handled Stainless-Steel Whisk	Zucchi	31	6.7	Lightweight Steel Skillet, 12" diam.	Zucchi	——
5.17	Wood-handled Tinned-Steel Whisk, 16"	Pacific Epicure	22-49	6.8	Italian Iron Frypan, 13½" diam.	Zucchi	——
5.18	Wooden-handled Balloon Whisk, 14"	Lamalle	1346	6.9	Copco Skillet, 12" diam.	Copco	107
5.19	Small Wooden-handled Stainless-Steel Whisk, 11¼"	Eva	226029	6.10	Aluminum Frying Pan, 7" diam.	Commercial	1307
5.20	Small Tinned-Steel Rigid Whisk, 8"	Lamalle	1337	6.11	Aluminum Frying Pan with Calphalon, 7" diam.	Commercial	1307HC
5.21	Beechwood Mixing Spoon, 14"	Artsam	MSF14	6.12	Italian Frying Pan, 11" diam.	Paderno	1114-28
5.22	Thin-handled Wooden Spoon, 14"	Artsam	M14	6.13	Cuisinart Frying Pan, 11" diam.	Cuisinarts	22-28
5.23	Stew Spoon, 12"	Lamalle	1206A	6.14	Dansk Aluminum Fry Pan, 7½" diam.	Dansk	AO121
5.24	Boxwood Chocolate Spoon, 11"	Lamalle	1211A	6.15	Glass Frying Pan, 9" diam.	Gense	S-16
5.25	Cherrywood Chocolate Spoon	Lamalle	1211B	6.16	Silver-Lined Frying Pan, 10⅜" diam.	Jensen	8063
5.26	Curved Olivewood Spatula	Lamalle	1185A	6.17	Copper Pan from Portugal, 5½" diam.	Douroamerica	1024
5.27	Beechwood Spatula Set	Bergquist	30008	6.18	Copper Presentation Pan, 10" x 7"	Kamenstein	76
5.28	Boxwood Spatula Set, 18"	B.I.A.	BEF250/50B	6.19	Lamalle Oval Pan, 11⅞" x 7⅞"	Lamalle	272
5.29	Beechwood Spatula Set, 18"	B.I.A.	B210-45	6.20	Lamalle Oval Iron Frypan, 14" x 10"	Lamalle	483
5.30	Copper Egg White Beater Bowl, 12½"	Lamalle	290B	6.22	Farberware Frying Pan, 12" diam.	Farberware	863
5.31	Stainless-Steel Mixing Bowl Set	Regalware	W1844	6.23	Magnalite Chicken Fryer, 12" diam.	General Housewares	4570
5.32	White Ceramic Mixing Bowl, 3 qt.	Jane	530	6.24	Le Creuset Chicken Fryer, 10¼" diam.	Schiller & Asmus	T-2556-27
5.33	Blue-and-White Striped Ceramic Bowl, 1¼ qt.	Green	01-137	6.25	Copco Chicken Fryer, 12" diam.	Copco	147
5.34	Glazed Ceramic Grip-stand Bowl, 3¾ qt.	Green	06110	6.26	Sunbeam Electric Frypan, 11½" diam.	Sunbeam	7-210
5.35	Leach Stoneware Bowl, 1½ qt.	Leach	10	6.27	Copper Sauteuse, 9⅝" diam.	Kitchen Glamor	L303
5.36	Ron Garfinkel Glazed Bowl	Garfinkel	——	6.28	Hammered Copper Sauteuse, 8" diam.	B.I.A.	LEC 3302/20
5.37	3-Piece Pyrex Bowl Set	Corning	95	6.29	Copper Stainless-Steel Sauteuse, 12¼" x 3½"	Legion	B1-1037
5.38	10-Piece Duralex Mixing Bowl Set	Williams-Sonoma	C-140	6.30	Cuisinart Sauté Pan, 5½ qt.	Cuisinarts	33-28H
5.39	Danish Melamine Bowls, 3 qt.	Copco	2506	6.31	Cuisinart Sauté Pan, w/Grip, 2¾ qt.	Cuisinarts	33-22R
5.40	Stoneware Batter Bowl	Bringle	——	6.32	Paderno Stainless Sauteuse, 8" diam.	Paderno	1108-20
5.41	Stoneware Batter Bowl, 1 qt.	Licht-Tomono	5A-S	6.33	Calphalon Sauteuse, 12" diam.	Commercial	5005HC
5.42	Arabia Enamel Bowl	Arabia	4821	6.34	Commercial Aluminum Sauteuse, 9¾" diam.	Commercial	5003
5.43	Handmade Walnut Bowl	Stockdale	——				
5.44	Large Teakwood Bowl, 15"	Verity Southall	22-015				

Catalogue Number	Item Description	Manufacturer or Supplier	Mfr.'s Description	Catalogue Number	Item Description	Manufacturer or Supplier	Mfr.'s Description
6.35	French Hammered Aluminum Sauteuse, 10½″ diam.	Lamalle	5924	6.69	Hammered Aluminum Bain-Marie Pan	Lamalle	594A
6.36	Hammered Copper Fait-Tout, 8¾″ diam.	Lamalle	250	6.70	Copper Buffet Bain-Marie Pan	Friedman	32
6.37	Kitchen Glamor Copper Saucepan, 3 qt.	Kitchen Glamor	M414	6.71	Enormous Double Boiler, 9 qt.	Commercial	87109
6.38	B.I.A. Copper Saucepan, 2½ qt.	B.I.A.	LEC 3301/18	6.72	Farberware Stewpot, 16 qt.	Farberware	846
6.39	Silver-lined Copper Saucepan, 2½ qt.	Jensen	8005	6.73	Large Cuisinart pot, 8½ qt.	Cuisinarts	44-28
6.40	Bi-Metal Saucepan, 2½ qt.	Legion	B1-1012	6.75	Vollrath Stockpot, 12½ qt.	Vollrath	78590
6.41	Banded Aluminum Saucepan, 4 qt.	Hoyang	H0788	6.76	Paderno Stockpot, 10½ qt.	Paderno	1101/40
6.42	Hammered Aluminum Saucepan, 2½ qt.	Lamalle	3062	6.77	Copper and Stainless-Steel Stockpot, 22 qt.	Legion	B1-1092
6.43	Nest of Aluminum Saucepans, set of 4; capacities of ¾, 1¼, 1¾, and 3½ qts.	Le Trefle	15-6101	6.78	Hammered Aluminum Stockpot, 22 qt.	Lamalle	5938
6.44	Tall Aluminum Saucepan, 6½ qt.	Commercial	8706½	6.79	Stockpot by Commercial Aluminum, 11 qt.	Commercial	8711
6.45	Large Shallow Aluminum Saucepan, 8½ qt.	Commercial	8788½	6.80	Steamer Boiler with Basket Insert, 32 qt.	Leyse	5332PC
6.46	Aluminum Saucepan with Calphalon Finish, 1½ qt.	Commercial	8701½-HC	6.81	Stand for Leyse Stockpot	Leyse	32S
6.47	Magnalite Saucepan, 4 qt.	General Housewares	4684	6.82	Wearever Stockpot with Spigot, 25 qt.	Wearever	4252B
6.48	Cast-Aluminum Pan from Dansk, 3 qt.	Dansk	AO113	6.83	Red Enamel Marmite, 10 qt.	Forges de Cousances	Champion
6.50	Windsor Saucepan, 2½ qt.	Legion	TP1501	6.84	SEB Pressure Cooker, 6 qt.	SEB	025420
6.51	Paderno Saucepan, 7 qt.	Paderno	1106-24	6.85	Copco Lid, 12″ diam.	Copco	137
6.52	Finnish Stainless-Steel Saucepan, 3 qt.	OPA Oy	TS205	6.86	Lamalle Copper Lids, Loop Handle, 8¾″ diam.	Lamalle	275
6.53	Farberware Saucepan	Farberware	801-½	6.87	Lamalle Copper Lids, Long Handle, iron, 8¾″ diam.	Lamalle	275A
6.54	Cuisinart Saucepan, 2 qt.	Cuisinarts	11-18	6.88	Lamalle Copper Lids, Long Handle, Brass, 8¾″ diam.	Lamalle	275A
6.55	Le Creuset Saucepan (Mijotin), 1¾ qt.	Schiller & Asmus	2555-20	6.89	Kitchen Glamor Copper Lid with Long Iron Handle, 8″ diam.	Kitchen Glamor	D101-8
6.56	Copco Saucepan, 2 qt.	Copco	124	6.90	Jensen Copper and Silver Lid, 8″ diam.	Jensen	8015
6.57	White Arabia Saucepan	Arabia	9316	6.91	Wearever Aluminum Lid, 11⅞″ diam.	Wearever	4192
6.58	Porcelaine de Paris Saucepan, 1 pt.	Porcelaine de Paris	42080	6.92	Lid from Commercial Aluminum, 12′ diam.	Commercial	314
6.59	Gense Glass Saucepan, 1¼ qt.	Gense	5-13	6.93	Lighter Lid from Commercial Aluminum, 7″ diam.	Commercial	1702-C
6.60	Metal Trivet	Hoan	BGW5	6.94	Legion Stainless-Steel Lid, 12½″ diam.	Legion	S-1406
6.61	Flame-Tamer	Tricolator	——	6.95	Cuisinart Stainless-Steel Lid, 11″ diam.	Cuisinarts	28-C
6.62	Gentle Cooker from France	Zag-France	——	6.96	Cuisinart Universal Cover, 6¼″ diam.	Cuisinarts	12-16-C
6.63	Farberware Double Boiler	Farberware	842	6.97	Porcelaine de Paris Lid, 4½″ diam.	Porcelaine de Paris	42081
6.64	Farberware Double Boiler with Steamer	Farberware	813/831	6.98	Domed Glass Lid, 8″ diam.	General Housewares	C5
6.65	White Enamel Double Boiler, 1½ qt.	General Housewares	11DB15D103	6.100	Paderno Stainless-Steel Lid, 11″ diam.	Paderno	1161/28
6.66	Pyrex Double Boiler	Corning	6283				
6.67	Copper and Ceramic Double Boiler, 2¼ qt.	Williams-Sonoma	6124				
6.68	Aluminum Double Bain-Marie Pan	Lamalle	59Y				

Catalogue Number	Item Description	Manufacturer or Supplier	Mfr.'s Description
6.101	Farberware High-domed Lid, 12″ diam.	Farberware	864
6.102	Farberware Low-domed Lid, 12″ diam.	Farberware	865
6.103	Hammered Copper Lid, 7″ diam.	B.I.A.	LEC3304/18
6.104	Stainless-Steel Implement Set	Lauffer	——
6.105	White Porcelain Tasting Spoon	Hoan	BGW7
6.106	Stainless-Steel Spoon, 11¾″ long	Vollrath	60120
6.107	Aluminum Spoon, 13″ long	Creative	53-12-S
6.109	Perforated Stainless-Steel Spoon, 11¾″ long	Vollrath	61120
6.110	Slotted Stainless-Steel Spoon, 11¾″ long	Vollrath	61110
6.111	Stainless-Steel Skimmer	Vollrath	5884D
6.112	Stainless-Steel Tongs	Edwin Jay	39705
6.113	Flexible Pancake Turner	Intedge	12RS
6.114	Perforated Pancake Turner	Intedge	12RSP
6.115	Extra-long Turner	Lion	344
6.116	Turner with Beveled Edges	Intedge	11RS
6.117	Cast-Aluminum Turner	Creative	1949
6.118	Narrow Perforated Turner	Karlsson & Nilsson	69-921R
6.119	Pot Fork	Creative	16-8
6.120	Stainless-Steel Ladle, 6 oz.	Vollrath	58440
6.121	Large Stainless-Steel Ladle, 1 pt.	Zucchi	704
6.122	Copper Ladle, 4″	Hoan	882
7.1	Leyse Handleless Sauteuse	Leyse	5275PC
7.2	Cuisinart Casserole, 3½ qt.	Cuisinarts	55-24
7.3	Casseruola Bassa I	Lagostina	6½ qts.
7.4	Casseruola Bassa II, 4½ qt.	Paderno	1109-24
7.5	Casseruola Bassa III	Zucchi	ART. 2
7.6	Heavy Iron Kettle	General Housewares	0318
7.7	Copper and Stainless-Steel Casserole, 7 qt.	Legion	B1-1101
7.8	Black Lauffer Casserole, 4 qt.	Lauffer	8 pt. round casserole
7.9	Round Farberware Casserole	Farberware	868
7.10	French Copper Casserole, 3½ qt.	Lamalle	261
7.11	Portuguese Copper Casserole, 1 pt.	Kamenstein	——
7.12	Large French Aluminum Casserole, 8 qt.	Pacific Epicure	13-105
7.13	Italian Aluminum Casserole, 9 qt.	Paderno	6909-24
7.14	Copco Casserole, 2½ qt.	Copco	D2

Catalogue Number	Item Description	Manufacturer or Supplier	Mfr.'s Description
7.15	Round Doufeu, 4 qt.	Schiller & Asmus	C2581-24
7.16	Finnish Casserole with Metal Handles, 3 qt.	OPA Oy	TS202-3qt.
7.17	Round Magnalite Casserole, 6 qt.	General Housewares	4249
7.18	Lauffer Oval Casserole, 2¾ qt.	Lauffer	5½ pt. oval casserole
7.19	Oval Doufeu, 6 qt.	Schiller & Asmus	C2582-16
7.20	Le Creuset Oval Casserole, 3½ qt.	Schiller & Asmus	A2522-25
7.21	Oval Copper Casserole, 3 qt.	Lamalle	258
7.22	Shallow Nambé Casserole, 3 qt.	Nambé	16
7.23	Deep Nambé Casserole, 2 qt.	Nambé	13
7.24	Paderno Stainless-Steel Casserole, 10¼″ long.	Paderno	1120
7.25	Leach Casserole with Handle, 1 qt.	Leach	18
7.26	Leach Casserole with Strapwork Handle, 4 qt.	Leach	54
7.27	Clay Marmite, 5½ qt.	Pacific Epicure	130-4
7.28	Japanese Casserole	Otagiri	51/192A
7.29	Karnes Casserole, 3½ qt.	Karnes	3-4 qt.
7.30	Karnes Casserole, 5 qt.	Karnes	4-5 qt.
7.31	Karnes Bean Pot, 3½ qt.	Karnes	3-4 qt.
7.32	Leach Bean Pot, 2½ qt.	Leach	20
7.33	Bennington Oval Casserole, 4 qt.	Bennington	L1856
7.34	Dansk Casserole	Dansk	2583
7.35	Stangl Double Dish	Stangl	Medium Cooker
7.36	Covered Porcelain Pot, 1¼ qt.	B.I.A.	DES44/6CT
7.37	Glass Casserole, 1¼ qt.	Corning	CG65
7.38	Schlemmertopf, 3 qt.	Reston Lloyd	832
7.39	White Terrine from France, 2 qt.	Hoan	P400
7.40	Mock Pâté en Croûte, 1 qt.	Hoan	PD3
7.41	Brown English Terrine, 1 qt.	Williams-Sonoma	65
7.42	Le Creuset Enameled Terrine, 1 qt.	Schiller & Asmus	MO524-28
7.43	Large Rectangular Terrine, 2½ qt.	Pillivuyt	430324
7.44	Round Mock Pâté en Croûte	Pillivuyt	431952
7.45	English Stoneware Terrine, 1 qt.	Pearson	115
7.46	White Terrine with Blue Flowers	Hoan	BF 300
7.47	Decorated Porcelain Terrine, 1½ pt.	Porcelaine de Paris	40133
7.48	Timbale Milanaise, 1 pt.	Pillivuyt	431949
7.49	Orange Plastic Slow Cooker, 4½ qt.	Rival Mfg.	3300
7.50	English Bean Pot	Pearson	104
7.51	French Bean Pot	Bridge	——

Catalogue Number	Item Description	Manufacturer or Supplier	Mfr.'s Description	Catalogue Number	Item Description	Manufacturer or Supplier	Mfr.'s Description
7.52	Porcelain Marmite, 1½ qt.	Porcelaine de Paris	41200	8.21	Stainless-Steel Turkey Lacers	Kenberry	1124
7.53	Stoneware Marmite or Tureen	Bringle	———	8.22	Fine Turkey Lacers	Recknagel	404
7.54	Individual Marmite	Lamalle	954	8.24	Flat Skewers from Italy, set of 6, 6″	Zucchi	48
7.55	Earthenware Daubière, 6 qt.	Lamalle	8040	8.25	Set of Butcher's Needles	Forschner	1010
7.56	Dansk Buffet Casserole	Dansk	2585	8.26	Butcher's Needle	Intedge	140S
7.57	Individual Covered Casserole	Barker	29021	8.27	German Lardoir	Recknagel	508
7.58	Shallow Royal Limoges Casserole with Lid	Barker	29032	8.28	Italian Lardoir	Zucchi	48
7.59	Oval Royal Limoges Casserole	Barker	29012	8.29	Large Hinged Lardoir	Forschner	1400
7.60	Covered Onion Soup Pot	Cardinal	1404	8.30	Simple Lardoir, 20½″	Intedge	132
7.61	Ron Garfinkel Crock	Garfinkel	Crockette	8.31	Bulb Baster with Injecting Needle	Zim	250
7.62	Tiny Leach Pot	Leach	6	8.32	Aluminum Bulb Baster	Progressus	610
7.63	Karnes Baking Dish	Karnes	Baking Dish	8.33	Glass Bulb Baster	Thermometer Corp. of America	1C
7.64	Rectangular Pyrex Baking Dishes, 1½ qt.	Corning	231	8.34	Nylon Bulb Baster	Chaney	706
7.65	Porcelain Baking Dish with Blue Flowers	Hoan	BF471	8.35	Magnalite Roasting Pan	Gen'l Housewares	4007
7.66	Stangl Baking Dish, 9″ x 6½″	Stangl	Baking Dish	8.36	Deeper Magnalite Roasting Pan	Gen'l Housewares	4115
7.67	Rectangular Porcelaine de Paris Baking Dish, 9½″ x 6½″	Porcelaine de Paris	40332	8.37	French Aluminum Roaster	Lamalle	59/26
7.68	Oval Porcelaine de Paris Baking Dish, 11″ x 6½″	Porcelaine de Paris	47040	8.38	Dansk Roasting Pan	Dansk	725
8.1	Cocambroche Four Rotisserie	Cuisinarts	———	8.39	Wearever Aluminum Roaster	Wearever	4455
8.2	Cocambroche Tambour	Cuisinarts	———	8.40	Professional-Weight Wearever Roaster	Wearever	4423
8.3	Cocambroche Living	Cuisinarts	———	8.41	Enormous Wearever Roaster	Wearever	4433
8.4	Cocambroche Gargantua, with 31½″ Spit	Cuisinarts	———	8.42	Farberware Roasting Pan with Rack	Farberware	766
8.5	Cocambroche Residence	Cuisinarts	———	8.43	Paderno Stainless-Steel Roaster	Paderno	1141-22x30 cm.
8.6	Cocambroche Touraine	Cuisinarts	———	8.44	V-Shaped Roasting Rack	Foley	168
8.7	Farber Broiler-Rotisserie, 15″ x 10″	Farberware	455A	8.45	Deep Oval Enamel Roaster, 14″ x 10″ x 6½″	Gen'l Housewares	B15R
8.8	Aluminum Gratin Set	Lamalle	59N	8.46	Deep Oval Magnalite Roaster, 20″ Long	Gen'l Housewares	4269
8.9	Oval Copper Gratin Pan, 10½″ long	Lamalle	268	8.47	Deep Aluminum Double Roaster	Commercial	1816
8.10	Round Copper Gratin Pan, 8″ diam.	Hoan	894	8.48	Rectangular Aluminum Deep Roaster	Zucchi	15
8.11	Copper and Stainless-Steel Oval Gratin Pan, 15¾″ long	Spring Bros.	460-70/15-¾	8.49	Hoover "Pot-Luck" Roaster, 6 qt.	Hoover	HB001
8.12	Rectangular Nambé Gratin Pan	Nambé	210	8.51	Thermatronic Oven	Thermador	MTR-17
8.13	Cuisinart Round Gratin Pan, 6¼″ diam.	Cuisinarts	27-16	8.52	Amana Radarange Oven	Amana	RR4DW
8.14	Handle for Cuisinart Gratin Pans	Cuisinarts	10	8.53	Litton Microwave Oven	Litton	416
8.15	Copco Oval Gratin Pan	Copco	138	8.54	MicroMite Oven	Welbilt	2000
8.16	Pillivuyt Oval Porcelain Gratin Dish, 12″ long	Hoan	P419/12	8.55	Farber Turbo-Oven	Farberware	460
8.18	Oval Limoges Baking Dish	Barker	29041	8.56	GE Toast-R-Oven	General Electric	T95/3125-012
8.19	Porcelaine de Paris Gratin Dishes	Porcelaine de Paris	40222	8.57	GE Toaster	General Electric	T128/3238-015
8.20	Salamander	Bridge	———	8.58	Toastmaster Toaster	Toastmaster	D114
				9.1	Heavy Aluminum Baking Sheet—Mirror Surface	Leyse	5667
				9.2	Heavy French Baking Sheet, 16″ x 12″	Pacific Epicure	22-168
				9.3	Heavy American Baking Sheet—The Best, 16″ x 14″	Rowoco	823

Catalogue Number	Item Description	Manufacturer or Supplier	Mfr.'s Description
9.4	Lightweight but Good—Black-finished Sheets 15½" x 12"	Grayline	1200
9.5	Professional Perforated Bun Pan	Rowoco	807
9.6	Heavy Jelly-Roll Pan	Commercial	1813B
9.7	Predarkened Jelly-Roll Pan	Rowoco	801
9.8	Black Steel Loaf Pan, 10" x 5"	Stonehearth	Bread Pan 10 x 5 x 3½
9.9	Wearever Seamless Aluminum Pan	Wearever	5433
9.10	Loaf Pan with Folded Ends	Rowoco	812
9.11	Mini-Loaf Pan	Rowoco	827
9.12	Stoneware Loaf Pan, 10" x 4½" x 2¼" deep	Bennington	L1874
9.13	Pyrex Loaf Pans, 8½" x 4½" x 2½" deep	Corning	213
9.14	Pullman Loaf Pan with cover, 13" x 4" x 4" deep	Rowoco	800
9.15	Crinkle-edged Tin Loaf Pan	Jane	342
9.16	Frame with Mini-Loaf Pans	Rowoco	818
9.17	Cast-Iron "Ear of Corn" Pan	General Housewares	1319G
9.18	Skillet for Corn Bread	General Housewares	1320G
9.19	Cast-Iron Popover Pan	General Housewares	1323G
9.20	Large Tinned-Steel Brioche Pan	Lamalle	721
9.21	California Brioche Pan	Marsh	65
9.22	Small Tinned Turk's Head Pan	Rowoco	817
9.23	German Tinned Kugelhopf Mold, 8½" diam.	Hoan	1814/8
9.24	Handmade Stoneware Kugelhopf Mold	Licht-Tomono	4B
9.25	Glass Kugelhopf Molds, 9½" diam.	Jenaer Glaswerk	3057
9.26	Teflon-lined Bundt Pan, 9" diam.	Northland	50423
9.27	Teflon-lined Bundt Pan, 10" diam.	Northland	50325
9.28	Professional Tube Pan	Rowoco	808
9.29	Ceramic Mold for Savarins	Marsh	64
9.30	Three-in-One Springform, 10" diam.	Hoan	1854
9.31	Professional Layer-Cake Pans, 9" diam. 1½" deep	Rowoco	805
9.32	Lockwood's Deep Layer Pan	Rowoco	811
9.33	Square Layer-Cake Pan	Rowoco	818
9.34	Square Pyrex Baking Pan	Corning	222
9.35	Large Shallow Aluminum Pan	Commercial	1813B
9.36	Professional Mary Ann Pan	Rowoco	815
9.37	Fluted German Obsttortenform, 9½" diam.	Hoan	1866
9.38	Obsttortenform with Bundt Fluting	Northland	43427
9.39	"Saddle of Venison" Rehrücken Mold	Koch & Fisher	210-25
9.41	Cast Bunny Mold	Northland	40200
9.42	Cast Lamb Mold	Northland	40100
9.43	Cast Santa Claus Mold	Northland	40300
9.45	Breton Cake Mold Set	Roth	29-9
9.46	Lockwood 12-Cup Muffin Tin	Rowoco	820
9.47	Lockwood 24-Cup Muffin Tin	Rowoco	824
9.48	Jumbo Muffin Tin	Rowoco	826
9.49	Pan for Square Cupcakes	Rowoco	822
9.50	Pan for 12 Miniature Muffins	Taylor Law	1005
9.51	Tin for Mary Ann Miniatures	Rowoco	819
9.52	Pan for Miniature Bundt Cakes	Northland	50623
9.53	Languages de Chat Pan	Zucchi	Lingue Gatto
9.54	French Ladyfinger Pan	Roth	32-3
9.55	French Madeleine Tin	Lamalle	742-A
9.56	Tin for Scallop-shaped Cupcakes, 12 forms	Hoan	TALA1015
9.57	Tiny Scalloped Cake Forms from England	Hoan	TALA1003
9.58	Individual Brioche Molds	Lamalle	783-A
9.59	Six Individual Brioche Tins, 2¼" diam.	Hoan	S73/1
9.60	Miniature Mold with Spiral Fluting	Koch & Fischer	212/3
9.61	Stainless-Steel Baba Molds from Italy	Zucchi	1010
9.62	Individual Savarin Mold	Bazaar de la Cuisine	———
10.1	Professional-Quality Pie Pan, 9" diam., 1¼" deep	Commercial	P3019/¼-A
10.2	Pie Pan with Juice-Saver Rim	Vollrath	62800
10.3	Bennington Pie Plate	Bennington	L1833
10.4	Blue Pottery Pie Plate	Stangl	Deep Pie Dish
10.5	Pyrex Pie Plates, 9" diam.	Corning	208
10.6	Corning Pyroceram Pie Plate	Corning	P309
10.7	Tinned French Flan Ring, 7" diam.	Hoan	7607
10.8	Deep Steel Flan Ring, 8" diam.	Bazaar de la Cuisine	———
10.9	Fluted Flan Ring, 8" diam.	Hoan	7588
10.10	Square Flan Form	Bazaar de la Cuisine	———
10.11	Regular Flan Form	Bridge	Matfer

Catalogue Number	Item Description	Manufacturer or Supplier	Mfr.'s Description	Catalogue Number	Item Description	Manufacturer or Supplier	Mfr.'s Description
10.12	Tinned Loose-bottomed Tart Pans	Lamalle	761A	10.49	Tapered Beechwood Rolling Pin	Hoan	AG1
10.13	Black Steel Loose-bottomed Tart Pan, 10″	Hoan	6426	10.50	Tutové Rolling Pin for Puff Pastry	Bridge	——
10.14	California Ceramic Quiche Mold	Marsh	514	10.51	English Flour Dredger	Hoan	TALA813
10.15	Fluted French Quiche Mold, 7½″ diam.	Pacific Epicure	1-80	10.52	Pair of English Dredgers	Taylor Law	K115
10.16	French Ceramic Fruit Tart Pan, 8¼″ diam.	Porcelaine de Paris	43830	10.53	French Sugar Dredger	B.I.A.	M1220
10.17	Barquette Tin from France, 3⅞″ long	B.I.A.	M1314/180	10.54	American All-Purpose Dredger	Leyse	1024
10.18	Fluted French Barquette Tin, 4″ long	B.I.A.	M1311/100	10.55	Goose-Feather Pastry Brush	Roth	32-9
10.19	Fluted Italian Barquette Tin	Zucchi	1005	10.56	Flat Natural-Bristle Pastry Brush	Thomsen	1500/1
10.20	Fluted Round Tartlet Pan	Lamalle	777	10.57	Round Natural-Bristle Pastry Brush	Thomsen	1508
10.21	Fluted Oval Tartlet Pan	Matfer	MK1307	10.58	Straight-edged Pastry Wheel, 2½″ diam.	Thomsen	1395/24
10.22	Diamond-shaped Tartlet Pan	Matfer	MK1308	10.59	Pastry Jagger	Thomsen	1508
10.23	Tartlet Tins with Loose Bottoms, 4″ and 4½″ diam.	Bridge	——	10.60	Double Pastry Wheel from Italy	Rowoco	139
10.24	Set of Tartlet Molds	Lamalle	F781	10.61	Double Cutter for Circles, 1¾″ rounds	Zucchi	161MM45
10.25	Petit Four Pastry Set	Schiller & Asmus	N350-07	10.62	Six-sided Cooky Cutter	Tomado	1601.300.12
10.26	Tin with Round Tartlet Forms	Roth	28K	10.63	Cutters in Sets of Three, Stars	Roth	19-19
10.27	Tin with Oval Tartlet Forms	Bazaar de la Cuisine	——	10.64	Assorted Cutters	Roth	18-2
10.28	French Cornucopia Form	Hoan	86	10.65	Gingerbread Cutter	Roth	19-47
10.29	Narrow Cone for Lady Locks	Thomsen	#7 Lady Lock Sticks	10.66	Bow-Tie Cutter	Roth	19-48
10.30	Croquembouche Mold	Bridge	——	10.67	Santa Claus Cutter	Handcraft	951
10.31	Stainless-Steel Sifter	Hoan	TALA1609	10.68	Flower-shaped Cutters	Zucchi	167
10.32	Lightweight Aluminum Sifter	Foley	192	10.69	Star-shaped Cutters from Italy	Zucchi	168
10.33	Triple-Screen Sifter	Foley	138	10.70	Biscuit Cutter with Arched Handle, 2″ diam.	Friedman	1440
10.34	Small German Shaking Sifter	Progressus	980	10.71	Doughnut Cutter with Arched Handle	Hoan	373
10.35	Pastry Blender	Roth	171	10.72	Oval Cutter for Puff Paste	Bazaar de la Cuisine	——
10.36	Blending Fork	Rowoco	176	10.73	Oval and Round Puff Paste Cutters, Ovals	Matfer	43009
10.37	Rubber Dough Scraper	B.I.A.	M1102	10.74	Square Vol-au-Vent, Cutter	Cuisinarts	——
10.38	Metal and Wood Dough Scraper	Intedge	6BS	10.75	Vol-au-Vent Machine	Cuisinarts	——
10.39	Wooden-handled Scraper	B.I.A.	ROD18	10.76	Rolling Italian Croissant Cutter	Zucchi	162
10.40	Narrow Rubber Scraper	Schacht	X1054	10.77	Rolling French Croissant Cutter	Roth	30-7
10.41	Large Rubber Scraper	Intedge	P1266	10.78	Circular Wire Rack from Germany	Christian Oos	20315
10.42	Small Rubber Plate Scraper	Schacht	800	10.79	Circular Wire Rack from France	B.I.A.	MG11 76015/28
10.43	Wooden Pastry Board	Artsam	C112	10.80	Heavy-Duty Wire Cake Rack, 24½″ x 16⅜″	Metropolitan	6703
10.44	Marble Pastry Slab	Vermont Marble	PB5	10.81	Rectangular Wire Cake Rack	Christian Oos	23512
10.45	Canvas Pastry Cloth in Frame	Foley	113	10.82	Revolving Decorating Stand	Thomsen	612
10.46	Chocolate Roll Board, 17¾″	Bazaar de la Cuisine	Small Chocolate Roll Board	10.83	English Decorating Syringe	Hoan	TALA9705
10.47	American Ball-Bearing Rolling Pin	Thorpe	Baker's Special	10.84	Aluminum Decorating Syringe	Thomsen	701
10.48	Straight French Rolling Pin	Hoan	AG2				

Catalogue Number	Item Description	Manufacturer or Supplier	Mfr.'s Description	Catalogue Number	Item Description	Manufacturer or Supplier	Mfr.'s Description
10.85	Decorating Pen	Hoan	TALA9672	11.24	Sardine Grill	Lamalle	466S
10.86	French Nylon Pastry Bag, 8″ long	Roth	30-11	11.25	Oyster Knife with Plastic Handle	Birkendahl	——
10.87	Plastic-lined Pastry Bag, 10″ long	Thomsen	——	11.26	Oyster Knife with Wooden Handle	Rowoco	16
10.88	Set of Tubes for Pastry Bags	Thomsen	091	11.27	Carbon-Steel Oyster Knife	Harrington	22
10.89	Set of Decorating Tubes	Thomsen	783	11.28	Clam Knife from Japan	Intedge	21S
10.90	Bismarck Pastry Tube	Thomsen	230	11.29	Unbreakable Clam Knife	Murphy	LGCLS
10.91	Tubes for Flowers and Leaves, Leaf Tube	Thomsen	112	11.30	Clam Opener	Edwin Jay	33693
10.92	Cake-decorating Stencil	Zucchi	11	11.31	Oyster and Clam Knife	Rowoco	14
10.93	Metal Ruler	Fairgate	MS-24	11.32	Bay-Scallop Knife	Murphy	SCALS
10.94	Rolling Pastry Piercer	Zucchi	265	11.33	Sea-Scallop Knife	Murphy	SSDSS
10.95	Cake Tester	Hoan	370	11.34	Crab Knife	Murphy	SSSCM
10.96	Pastry Crimper	Pacific Epicure	22-124	11.35	Lobster Pincers	Couzon	52854
10.97	Pie Bird	Edwin Jay	69329	11.36	Lobster Pick	Couzon	52853
10.98	Banneton for Raising Bread	Williams-Sonoma	C-157	11.37	Lobster Shears	Edwin Jay	33618
10.99	Roll of Parchment Paper	Hoan	BGW11	11.38	Shrimpmaster	Intedge	921
10.100	Parchment Cake-Pan Liners, 8″ diam.	Brown	CP-8	11.39	Shrimp-Ease	Edwin Jay	33704
10.101	Cupcake-Pan Liners, 2⅛″ diam.	Brown	MBC-36A	11.40	Natural Scallop Shells (set of 4)	Mayer	5302
11.1	Stainless-Steel Fish Scaler	American Cutlery	1	11.41	Porcelain Scallop Shell, 5¼″ x 4¾″	Pillivuyt	240312
11.2	Aluminum Fish Scaler	Creative	1966	11.42	Escargot Tongs	Spring Bros.	9035
11.3	All-Purpose Fish Knife	Ontario	32-4⅞″	11.43	Escargot Fork	Spring Bros.	9030
11.4	Small All-Purpose Fish Knife	Rowoco	4	11.44	Escargot Dish, 12 Depressions	Spring Bros.	9530/12
11.5	Heavy Fish Knife	Le Roi	1	11.45	Copper Escargot Dish, 12 Depressions	Spring Bros.	530-7/12
11.6	Fish Shears	American Cutlery	186-10	11.46	Stainless-Steel Escargot Dish, 12 Depressions	Couzon	25262
11.7	Stainless-Steel Fillet of Sole Knife	Le Roi	22	11.47	Pair of Escargot Dishes	Couzon	24262
11.8	High-Carbon Fillet of Sole Knife	Henckels	30032-7	11.48	Stoneware Escargot Dishes	Bennington	L1870
11.9	Rowoco Filleting Knife	Rowoco	6	11.49	Very Small Leach Pots	Leach	46
11.10	Smoked Salmon Knife	Karlsson & Nilsson	738R	11.50	Godet à Escargot	Schiller & Asmus	P2701
11.11	Wooden Mallet	Forschner	2	11.51	Porcelain Snail-Shell Cup	Kessler	AA410
11.12	Bail-handled Fish Poacher, 16″ x 4½″	Lamalle	460A	11.52	Wire Egg Stand	Hoan	315
11.13	Double-handled Fish Poacher, 16″ x 6″	Lamalle	460	11.53	Practic Egg Boiler	Wüster	——
11.14	Stainless-Steel Fish Poacher, 15¾″ x 4¾″	Paderno	1139-40x12	11.54	Automatic Egg Cooker	Oster	581-01
11.15	Oval Fish Poacher or Casserole, 14⅛″ x 7⅞″	Spring Bros.	500-6/14 1/8	11.55	Soft-boiled Egg Cutter	Wüster	——
11.16	Turbot Poacher	Schiller & Asmus	D200	11.56	Egg Sectioner	Ostrowsky	4563
11.17	Seafood Cooker	Gourmet	Slow Cooker	11.57	Plastic-framed Egg Slicer	Kenberry	5086
11.18	Fillet of Sole Dish	Denby	158	11.58	Aluminum-framed Egg Slicer	Creative	4016
11.19	Deep Oval Baking Dish, 15¾″ x 10¼″	Langenthal	LAN 11/40	11.59	Aluminum Egg Separator	Progressus	8
11.20	Stainless-Steel Sole Dish with Lid, 14″ x 3¾″	Spring Bros.	468-6	11.60	Ceramic Egg Separator	La Cuisinière	——
11.21	Fish Grill	Hoan	FG20	11.61	Stainless-Steel Egg Rings	Bergquist	30301
11.22	Fish Grill with Folding Legs, 12″ long	Lamalle	466B	11.62	Chrome-plated Egg Rings	Metropolitan	3804E
11.23	Individual Fish Grill	Christian Oos	570124	11.63	Sand-cast Aluminum Omelet Pan, 12″ diam.	Gourmet	OP-12
				11.64	Chef's Steel Omelet Pan	Hoan	828
				11.65	Extra-Heavy Aluminum Omelet Pan	Bridge	Standish

Catalogue Number	Item Description	Manufacturer or Supplier	Mfr.'s Description
11.66	Long-handled Steel Omelet Pan	B.I.A.	24PEF
11.67	Poulard Long-handled Omelet Pan	Lamalle	486A
11.68	Stoneware Egg Dish	Leach	3
11.69	Royal Limoges Egg Dish	Barker	29043
11.70	Pillivuyt Egg Dish	Hoan	P424
11.71	Porcelain Egg Dishes plus Salt and Pepper Shakers	Porcelaine de Paris	46630
11.72	Arabia Egg Dish	Arabia	A2
11.73	Pillivuyt Soufflé Dish, 2 qt.	Hoan	P8
11.74	Arabia Soufflé Dishes, 4 oz.	Arabia	LAOO
11.75	Porcelain Soufflé Dish, 1½ qt.	B.I.A.	DES28/7
11.76	Individual Porcelain Soufflé Dishes (Set of 4)	Porcelaine de Paris	46570
11.78	Deep Pillivuyt Soufflé Dish, 2 qt.	Pillivuyt	26 11 18
11.79	Stoneware Soufflé Dish, ¾ qt.	Bennington	L1885
11.80	Ron Garfinkel Soufflé Dish	Garfinkel	——
11.81	Hand-thrown Stoneware Soufflé Dish	Bringle	1848
11.82	Individual Stoneware Soufflé Dish	Bennington	L1641
11.83	Glass Soufflé Dish, Set of 3: 1, 1½ and 2 qt. capacities	Corning	CG11
11.84	Swedish Glass Soufflé Dish	Gense	S5
11.85	Low Flameproof Soufflé Dish	Gense	S14
11.86	White Porcelain Custard Cup, 6 oz.	Bridge	849
11.87	Brown and Buff Custard Cup	Cardinal	1395
11.88	Large Stoneware Custard Cup	Temple	37
11.89	Pot à Crème Set	Porcelaine de Paris	42260
11.90	SteaMarvel	Aero	——
11.91	Cuisinart Steamer	Cuisinarts	77-24
11.92	Three-in-One Steamer	Polaris	P520
11.93	Rice Steamer and Mold	Dr. Oetker Ohg	452
11.94	Multipurpose Verzinkerei Pot	Verzinkerei	2065.22
11.95	Wearever's Bungalow Cooker	Wearever	2485
11.96	Collapsible Multi-Basket	Cook Things	M1602
11.97	Iron Deep-Fat Fryer	Hoan	260
11.98	Frying Bassine from France	Lamalle	59/2
11.99	Nesco Electric Deep-Fryer	Nesco	N-140
11.100	SEB Super Fry	SEB	000850
11.101	Bird's-Nest Maker, 4″ diam.	Roth	33-7
11.102	Deep-bowled Skimmer	Christian Oos	21311
11.103	Shallow-bowled Skimmer	Christian Oos	21211
11.104	Professional Skimmer	Metropolitan	1307
11.105	Hinged Pâté Mold, 10¾″ long	Lamalle	756
11.106	Pâté en Croûte Mold, 8⅝″ long	Lamalle	755A
11.107	Galantine Mold	Pillivuyt	28-05-24
11.108	Hinged Pâté Mold with Patterned Sides	Lamalle	8048
11.109	Curved Fish Mold	Bridge	——
11.110	3-D Fish Mold, 11½″ x 4½″	Zucchi	851
11.111	Simple Pudding Mold, 7¼″ diam.	Koch & Fischer	208
11.112	Rosette-Patterned Pudding Mold, 2½ qt.	Hoan	1872
11.113	Fluted Pudding Mold	Saramago	——
11.114	Turk's-Head Mold, 1 qt.	Hoan	1321
11.115	Tubeless Fluted Pudding Mold	Bridge	——
11.116	Charlotte Mold, 1 qt.	Lamalle	729B
11.117	Aspic Ramekin	Lamalle	1002
11.118	Fluted Tube Mold	Matfer	37407
11.119	Star-shaped Cold Mold	Maganza	——
11.120	Stainless-Steel Rosette Mold	Bridge	——
11.121	Fluted Cold Mold	Bridge	——
11.122	Fluted Ice-Cream Mold	Bridge	——
11.123	Peak-shaped Mold	Lamalle	717A
11.124	Spumoni Mold, 3¾″ diam.	Zucchi	1109
11.125	Square Ice-Cream Mold, 3-cup	Bridge	Matfer
11.126	Rectangular Ice-Cream Mold	Zucchi	1100
11.127	Set of 3 Nested Molds	Zucchi	1101
11.128	Coeur à la Crème Mold, 3¼″ x 2¾″	Hoan	P428
11.129	Plastic Gelatin Mold	Creative	2390
11.130	Thistle Butter Print	Rushbrooke	176
11.131	Hand-cranked Ice-Cream Freezer, 2 qt.	White Mt.	643
11.132	Household Electric Ice-Cream Freezer, 4 qt.	White Mt.	692-E
11.133	Salton Ice-Cream Machine	Salton	IC-4
11.135	SEB Ice-Cream Maker	SEB	32001
11.136	Milkshake Maker, Single Spindle Mixer	Friedman	936
11.137	Zeroll Dipper, 2½ oz.	Friedman	313C
11.138	Ice-Cream Dipper & Spade Set, 2 oz.	Roll Dippers	——
11.139	Atlas Ice-Cream Scoop, 12 scoops per qt.	Intedge	321DS
11.140	Conical Ice-Cream Scoop, 12 scoops per qt.	Intedge	320-12
11.141	Chromed Brass Ice-Cream Scoop, 24 scoops per qt.	Intedge	313C

Catalogue Number	Item Description	Manufacturer or Supplier	Mfr.'s Description
11.142	Ice-Cream Cone Maker	Hirco	1219
11.143	Single Unit Hot Plate	Capitol	UL455
11.144	Table Range	Capitol	UL865
11.145	Buffet Trolley	Spring Bros.	895
11.146	Bernzomatic Propane Camp Stove	Bernzomatic	ST820
11.147	Ronson Varaflame Table Chef	Ronson	23401
11.148	Denatured Alcohol-fired Brazier	Spring Bros.	150-6
11.149	Alcohol Burner	Pacific	17-ABC
11.150	Fondue Bourguignonne Set	Spring Bros.	100-7
11.151	Gourmet Pot Set	Spring Bros.	260-7
11.152	Large Alcohol Burner and Grill	Spring Bros.	191-6
11.153	Swissmart Alcohol Burner	Swissmart	247
11.154	Sterno Brazier	Spring Bros.	102-6
11.155	Salton Hot Tray	Salton	H-930
11.156	Stainless-Steel Candle Warmer	Couzon	33340
11.157	Butter Warmer	Polaris	P560
11.158	Oblong Candle Warmer	Brabantia	2624
11.159	Small Candle Warmer	Spring Bros.	350-6
11.160	Heat Lamp with Carving Board	Commercial	916511
11.161	Infrared Food Warmer	Merco	LFW-24
11.162	Iron Crêpe Pan, 6½″	Hoan	180
11.163	Aluminum Crêpe Pan, 8″	Gourmet	CS-8
11.164	Copper Crêpe Pan	Lamalle	282D
11.165	Culinox Crêpe Pan	Spring Bros.	545-70
11.166	Copper and Stainless-Steel Crêpe Pan	Legion	B1-20031
11.167	Oval Flambé Pan, 15¾″ long	Spring Bros.	465-70/15¾
11.168	Round Flambé Pan, 11″ diam.	Spring Bros.	450-70/11
11.169	Copper Chafing Dish	Waldow	01
11.170	Enameled Cast-Iron Fondue Pot	Schiller & Asmus	2507-20
11.171	Enameled-Steel Fondue Pot, 1 qt.	Swissmart	224
11.172	Watermate	Dyneck Corp.	———
11.173	Slice-a-Slice	Mae Mar	700B
11.174	Salton Yogurt Maker	Salton	GM-5
11.175	High-Capacity Yogurt Maker	Electric	NYM-2T
11.176	Bio Snacky Sprouter	Miracle	ME8500
11.177	Melitta Coffee Maker, 4-6 cups	Melitta	CM6-P1
11.178	Chemex Coffee Maker, 2-8 cups	Chemex	CM-3
11.179	Bunn Electric Coffee Maker	Bunn-O-Matic	B8
11.180	One-Cup Coffee Maker	Valenti	V-16
11.181	Neapolitan Filter Pot	Edwin Jay	67407
11.182	Porcelain Filter Pot, 6 cup	Hoan	P418
11.183	Toddy Coffee Maker	Toddy	———
11.184	Melior Coffee Maker	Lamalle	173A
11.185	SEB Whistling Coffee Maker, 6 cups	SEB	027110
11.186	Junior Espresso Maker, 9 cups	Hoan	309
11.187	Atomic Espresso Maker, 9 cups	Pacific Epicure	71-1
11.188	Miniature Espresso Maker	Ramsey	———
11.189	Europiccola Espresso Maker	Ramsey	———
11.190	Club Espresso Machine	Zabar's	———
11.191	Cremina Espresso Machine	Zabar's	———
11.192	Farber Coffee Urn	Farberware	155-A
11.193	Stainless-Steel Tea Kettle	OPA Oy	TS110
11.194	Copco Tea Kettle	Copco	117
11.195	Gense Glass Tea Kettle	Gense	S129
11.196	Chemex Carafe Kettle	Chemex	CCKG
11.197	Leach Tea Pot	Leach	50
11.198	British Tea Pot	Green	76/77-06
11.199	Hand-thrown Stoneware Tea Pot	Temple	33
11.200	Tea Infuser	Irvinware	3499
11.201	Dripless Tea Strainer	Irvinware	92460
11.202	Stainless-Steel Tea Strainer	Rowoco	C193
11.203	Instant Immersion Heater	Progressus	666
11.204	Crystal Ice Bucket	Kosta-Boda	———
11.205	Stainless-Steel Ice Bucket	OPA Oy	TS400
11.206	Plexiglass Ice Bucket	Nordsted	740,700
11.207	Thermos Carafe	Eva	370000
11.208	Ice Pick	Kenberry	6104
11.209	Crystal Wine Funnel	Williams-Sonoma	15
11.210	Crystal Carafe, 1 qt.	Kosta-Boda	———
11.211	Rondo Crystal Decanter	Kosta-Boda	———
11.212	Tall Glass Decanter, 40 oz.	Libbey	795
11.213	Classic Italian Decanter	Bridge	———
11.214	Copper Wine Cooler	Spring Bros.	820-7
11.215	Waiter's Corkscrew	Edwin Jay	52221
11.216	Winged Corkscrew	Rowoco	99C
11.217	Wood-enclosed Corkscrew	Barry	550
11.218	Ah So Corkscrew	Gumpert	25
11.219	Heavy-Duty Mechanical Corkscrew	Hoan	BGW8
11.220	Cork Retriever	Sanbri	AB
11.221	Everything Tool	Cardinal	7942
11.222	Champagne Cork Pliers	Rowoco	140
11.223	Champagne Opener	P.P.L.	3462-A-71

Catalogue Number	Item Description	Manufacturer or Supplier	Mfr.'s Description	Catalogue Number	Item Description	Manufacturer or Supplier	Mfr.'s Description
11.224	Hand Corker	Sanbri	LSS	11.229	Zinc-Plated Wire Shelf Unit, 24″ x 15″	Metropolitan	W1524
11.225	Wine Tap	Sanbri	SC				
11.226	Ten-Bottle Iron Wine Rack	Hoan	112	11.230	Hammacher Schlemmer Wine Cage, 200-bottle	Hammacher	ZDF200
11.227	Twelve Bottle Plastic Wine Rack	Shapecraft	SCW12	11.231	Temperature-controlled Wine Vault, 348-bottle	Hammacher	P11
11.228	Twelve Bottle Wood and Metal Rack	Sherry-Lehmann	88	11.232	Bottle Carrier, 4-bottle	Artsam	13/1

Availability Information: Manufacturers and Distributors

Aero Industrial Co., Inc.
912 Isabel Street
Burbank, Calif. 91506

All-Clad Metalcrafters, Inc.
Canonsburg, Pennsylvania 15317

Alluminio Paderno S.p.A.
20037 Paderno Dugnano
Milan, Italy

Amana Refrigeration, Inc.
Amana, Iowa 52203

American Cutlery & Hardware Co., Inc.
184 Bowery
New York, N.Y. 10012

Arabia, Inc.
8300 N.E. Underground Drive
Kansas City, Mo. 64161

Arkansas Abrasives, Inc.
P.O. Box 1298
Hot Springs, Ark. 71901

Artsam Company, Inc.
84 Eighteenth Street
Brooklyn, N.Y. 11232

Ausonia
Nanutti Beltrame
33085 Maniago
Italy

Ellis Barker Silver Co.
60 Merrimack Street
Amesbury, Mass. 01913

Eli Barry Co., Inc.
River Terminal Development
Port Kearny, New Jersey 07032

Bazaar de la Cuisine
1003 Second Avenue
New York, N.Y. 10022

Beard Glaser Wolf Ltd.
208 Rockingstone Avenue
Larchmont, New York 10538

Becker & Becker, Inc.
50 State Street West
Westport, Conn. 06880

Bennington Potters, Inc.
324 County Street
Bennington, Vt. 05201

Berard Frères
(See Charles F. Lamalle)

Berarducci Brothers Mfg. Co., Inc.
1732 Fifth Avenue
McKeesport, Pa. 15132

Bergquist Imports, Inc.
1412 Highway 33, South
Cloquet, Minn. 55720

Bernzomatic Corp.
740 Driving Park Ave.
Rochester, N.Y. 14613

B.I.A.Cordon Bleu, Inc.
P.O. Box 627
Burlingame, Calif. 94010

Carl & Heinz Birkendahl
565 Solingen
Herberger Strasse 40
West Germany

Borden Chemical, Borden Inc.
1625 West Mund Street
Columbus, Ohio 43223

Boston Warehouse Company
39 Rumford Avenue
Waltham, Mass. 02154

Brabantia
Van Elderen's Metaal Warenfabriek
Brabantia N.V. Aalst N.B.
Nederland

Braun North America
55 Cambridge Parkway
Cambridge, Mass. 02142

J. & D. Brauner Inc.
298 Bowery
New York, N.Y. 10012

Bridge Kitchenware Co., Inc.
212 East 52nd Street
New York, N.Y. 10022

Cynthia Bringle
℅ Penland School of Crafts
Penland, N.C. 28765

Bromwell (Div. of Leigh Products)
Coopersville, Mich. 49404

Brown Company
Service Products Division
Parchment, Michigan 49004

Bunn-O-Matic Corporation
Domestic Division
1400 Stevenson Drive
Springfield, Ill. 62708

Burns Manufacturing Co., Inc.
6710 Commerce Boulevard
Syracuse, N.Y. 13211

Camille Mercier, Ets
6, Rue de L'Helvétie
25500-Morteau, France

Capitol Products Co.
P.O. Box 710
Winsted, Conn. 06098

Cardinal China Company
Cardinal Building
Carteret, N.J. 07008

W. R. Case & Sons Cutlery Co.
Osborne Street
Bradford, Pa. 16701

John L. Chaney Instrument Co.
965 Wells Street
Lake Geneva, Wis. 53147

Chemex Corp.
505 East Street
Pittsfield, Mass. 01201

Commercial Aluminum Cookware Co.
P.O. Box 583
Toledo, Ohio 43693

Compass Instrument & Optical Co.
104 East 25th Street
New York, N.Y. 10010

Contempra Industries, Inc.
371 Essex Road
New Shrewsbury, N.J. 07753

Continental Crafts Co.
145 Portland Street
Cambridge, Mass. 02139

Cook Things
76 Needham Street
Newton Highlands, Mass. 02161

Copco, Inc.
11 East 26th Street
New York, N.Y. 10010

Corning Glass Works
Corning, N.Y. 14830

Jean Couzon
63120 Courpierre
France

Creative House Imports
190 W. Ashland Street
Doylestown, Pa. 18901

Cuisinarts, Inc.
1 Barry Place
Stamford, Conn. 06902

Dansk International Designs Ltd.
Radio Circle Road
Mount Kisco, N.Y. 10549

Denby Ltd., Inc.
41 Madison Avenue
New York, N.Y. 10010

Design Research
48 Brattle Street
Cambridge, Mass. 02138

Diogenes Werk, Herder & Sohn
565 Solingen 11
Kiefernstrasse 2-6
West Germany

Douramerica
Pr. D. Filipa de Lencastre
22-4 Room 64
Porto, Portugal

Dripcut Starline Corp.
P.O. Box S
Goleta, Calif. 93017

Dyneck Corp.
160 Irving Avenue
Port Chester, N.Y. 10573

Ekco Housewares Co.
9234 W. Belmont
Franklin Park, Ill. 60131

Eva Housewares, Inc.
P.O. Box 2687
San Rafael, Calif. 94902

Fairgate Rule Co., Inc.
P.O. Drawer 278
Cold Spring, N.Y. 10516

Farberware
1500 Basset Avenue
Bronx, N.Y. 10461

Foley Manufacturing Company
Housewares Division
3300 N.E. Fifth Street
Minneapolis, Minn. 55418

Forges de Cousances
Cousances-les-Forges
55170 Ancerville
France

R. H. Forschner Co., Inc.
828 Bridgeport Avenue
Shelton, Conn. 06484

Franjoh Cellars
P.O. Box 7462
Stockton, California 95207

Fraser's (Div. WMF of America, Inc.)
85 Price Parkway
Farmingdale, N.Y. 11735

H. Friedman & Sons
16 Cooper Square
New York, N.Y. 10003

Arthur Fuller Associates, Inc.
396 Danbury Road
Wilton, Conn. 06897

Jules Gaillard & Fils
81, Rue de Fauborg St. Denis
Paris Xe, France

Ron Garfinkel
RFD #1, Box 79
Monroe, Maine 04951

Gemini International Corporation
1270 Broadway
New York, N.Y. 10001

General Electric Co.
Housewares Division
1285 Boston Avenue
Bridgeport, Conn. 06602

General Housewares Corporation
P. O. Box 4066
Terre Haute, Indiana 47804

Gense Imports
252 Livingston Street
Northvale, N.J. 07647

Johannes Giesser (Messer) KG
D-7057 Winnenden bei Stuttgart
West Germany

Gottschalk Metal Sponge Sales Corp.
3650 North 10th Street
Philadelphia, Pa. 19140

Gourmet Ltd.
376 E. St. Charles Street
Lombard, Ill. 60148

Grayline Housewares, Inc.
1616 Berkley Street
Elgin, Ill. 60120

T. G. Green Ltd.
(See Boston Warehouse Company)

Milton Gumpert Imports
5269 W. Pico Blvd.
Los Angeles, Calif. 90019

Hammacher Schlemmer
147 East 57th Street
New York, N.Y. 10022

Handcraft from Europe
P. O. Box 372
Sausalito, Calif. 94965

Russell Harrington Cutlery, Inc.
River Street
Southbridge, Mass. 01550

H-B Instrument Company
American & Bristol Streets
Philadelphia, Pa. 19140

Heller Designs, Inc.
460 Ogden Avenue
Mamaroneck, New York 10543

J. A. Henckels Twinworks, Inc.
1 Westchester Plaza
P. O. Box 127
Elmsford, N.Y. 10523

E & M Herring Corporation
(Royal Krona)
225 Fifth Avenue
New York, N.Y. 10010

Hirco Manufacturing Company
4105-07 North Damen Avenue
Chicago, Illinois 60618

Hoan Products Ltd.
615 East Crescent Avenue
Ramsey, N.J. 07446

Hobart Corporation
World Headquarters Building
Troy, Ohio 45374

Hoffritz
(See Edwin Jay, Inc.)

Hoover Company
101 East Maple Street
North Canton, Ohio 44720

Hoyang
(See Nor-Pro)

Intedge
(See International Edge Tool Co.)

Intermatic, Inc.
Intermatic Plaza
Spring Grove, Ill. 60081

International Edge Tool Co., Inc.
565 Eagle Rock Ave., P.O. Box P
Roseland, N.J. 07068

Irvinware, Inc.
24-60 47th Street
Long Island City, N.Y. 11103

Jane Products, Inc.
40 W. 86th Street
New York, N.Y. 10024

Edwin Jay, Inc.
20 Cooper Square
New York, N.Y. 10003

Jenaer Glaswerk
Schott & Zwiesel Glass Inc.
11 East 26th Street
New York, N.Y. 10010

Georg Jensen
225 Fifth Avenue
New York, N.Y. 10010

Kalkus Inc.
571 W. Cermak Road
Cicero, Ill. 60650

Kamenstein, Inc.
190 E. Post Road
White Plains, N.Y. 10601

Karen Karnes
Gatehill Road
Stony Point, N.Y. 10980

Karlsson-Nilsson
P. O. Box 361
S-631 05 Eskilstuna
Sweden

Kenberry Division (Etamco Ind.)
1 Montgomery Street
Belleville, N.J. 07109

Albert Kessler & Co.
1355 Market Street
San Francisco, Calif. 94133

Kitchen Glamor, Inc.
26770 Grand River Avenue
Detroit, Michigan 48240

Koch & Fischer
D-2084 Rellingen 2
Postfach 1170
West Germany

Kosta-Boda USA Ltd.
225 Fifth Avenue
New York, N.Y. 10010

Johan Kretzer
% Norbert Stryer
104-20 Queens Boulevard
Forest Hills, N.Y. 11375

La Cuisinière
867 Madison Avenue
New York, N.Y. 10021

Lagostina S.p.A.
Via IV Novembre 45
28026 Omegna (NO)
Italy

Charles F. Lamalle
1123 Broadway
New York, N.Y. 10010

Langenthal Porzellanfabrik AG
CH-4900 Langenthal
Switzerland

H. E. Lauffer Co., Inc.
Belmont Drive
Somerset, N.J. 08873

Leach Pottery Ltd.
St. Ives, Cornwall
England

Lee Manufacturing Co., Inc.
P.O. Box 20222
Dallas, Texas 75220

Legion Utensils Co., Inc.
21-07 40th Avenue
Long Island City, N.Y. 11101

Le Roi de la Coupe
Coutellerie Chevalerias
La Malaptie-63-Viscomtat
France

Le Trefle
Sté Fse Métaux Ouvrés
Route de Saint-Loup
B.P. 13
70000 Vesoul, France

Levi Peterson Industri AB
(See Scandicrafts, Inc.)

Leyse Aluminum Company
Kewaunee, Wis. 54216

Libbey Glass
P.O. Box 919
Toledo, Ohio 43693

Licht-Tomono, Doris
356 Bowery
New York, N.Y. 10012

Lion General Import
3232 Lurting Avenue
Bronx, N.Y. 10469

Litton Industries
1305 Xenium Lane N.
Minneapolis, Minn. 55440

Lockwood Manufacturing Co.
3170 Wasson Road
Cincinnati, Ohio 45208

Lola Products Corp.
179 Berger Street
Wood-Ridge, N.J. 07075

Mae Mar Industries, Inc.
Div. M. Schwartz Co., Inc.
1667 Meadow Street
Philadelphia, Pa. 19124

Maganza Luigi & Fratelli de Maganza
Viale Argonne 24
20133 Milano
Italy

Magic Mill
Div. of Stratford Squire International
235 West 2nd Street, South
Salt Lake City, Utah 84101

Marsh Industries
1124 East 28th Street
Los Angeles, Calif. 90011

William F. Mayer Co., Inc.
448-52 Nepperhan Avenue
Yonkers, N.Y. 10701

Melitta Inc.
1401 Berlin Road
Cherry Hill, N.J. 08003

Merco Products, Inc.
1298 Bethel Drive
Eugene, Ore. 97402

Metal Box Limited
Bromsgrove Road
Holy Cross, Clent DY9 9QP
West Midlands, England

Metropolitan Wire Goods Corp.
N. Washington & George Avenues
Wilkes-Barre, Pa. 18705

J. Michel & Co.
144 Rue Vendome
69006-Lyons, France

Miracle Exclusives, Inc.
16 West 40th Street
New York, N.Y. 10018

S.I. Moss Co., Inc.
234 Westport Avenue
Norwalk, Conn. 06851

Mouli Manufacturing Co.
1 Montgomery Street
Belleville, N.J. 07109

Robert Murphy Co.
13 Groton-Harvard Road
Ayer, Mass. 01432

Nambé Mills, Inc.
Route 1, Box 202
Santa Fe, N.M. 87501

Nesco
(See Hoover Company)

Nevco
U.S. Industries, Inc.
500 Nepperhan Avenue
Yonkers, N.Y. 10701

Nordsted Design Ltd.
92, Svanemøllevej
DK-2900 Hellerup
Denmark

Norelco
100 East 42nd Street
New York, N.Y. 10017

Nor-Pro, Nordic Products
19232 92nd Avenue West
Edmonds, Washington 98020

Norris Industries
5119 District Blvd.
Los Angeles, Calif. 90040

Northland Aluminum Products, Inc.
Highway 7 at Beltline
Minneapolis, Minn. 55416

Dr. August Oetker
Postfach 85
D-4800 Bielefeld 1
West Germany

Ontario Knife Company
P.O. Box 145
Franklinville, N.Y. 14737

Christian Oos KG
5530 Gerolstein/Eifel
Postfach 1240
West Germany

OPA Oy
(See Scan Furniture)

The Orvis Company
Manchester, Vt. 05254

Oster Corporation
(See Arthur Fuller Associates, Inc.)

S. Ostrowsky
1133 Broadway
New York, N.Y. 10010

Otagiri Mercantile Co., Inc.
20 Hanes Drive
Wayne, N.J. 07470

Pacific Epicure
P.O. Box 38267
Los Angeles, Calif. 90038

Paderno
(See Alluminio Paderno S.p.A.)

Park Rubber Co., Inc.
80 Genesse Street
Lake Zurich, Ill. 60047

Pearson & Co. (Chesterfield) Ltd.
(See Denby Ltd., Inc.)

Pelouze Scales Company
1218 Chicago Avenue
Evanston, Ill. 60202

Phelon Magnagrip Company
East Longmeadow, Mass. 01208

Pillivuyt
18500-Mehun Sur Yevre
France

Polaris Fabrikker A.S.
(See Nor-Pro, Nordic Products)

Porcelaine de Paris
Mrs. Virginia Chapman
Sales Representative
25 Remsen Street
Brooklyn, N.Y. 11201

P.P.L. Industria Levatappi
Pietra Luigi
Via Piemonte 41
20093 Cologno-Monzese-(Milano)
Italy

Progressus Company
40 St. Mary's Place
Freeport, N.Y. 11520

Ramsey Imports
P.O. Box 277
Ramsey, N.J. 07446

Gerhard Stecknagel Stahlwarenfabrik
7541 Straubenhardt 1
Langenalber Strasse 103
West Germany

Regal Ware, Inc.
1675 Reigle Drive
Kewaskum, Wis. 53040

Reston Lloyd Ltd.
Reston International Center
11800 Sunrise Valley Drive
Reston, Va. 22091

Rival Manufacturing Co.
36th & Bennington
Kansas City, Mo. 64128

Robot Coupe
P.O. Box 10131
Jackson, Miss. 39206

Roll Dippers Company
207 Conant Street
Maumee, Ohio 43537

Ronson Corporation
Woodbridge, N.J. 07095

H. Roth & Son
1577 First Avenue
New York, N.Y. 10028

Rowoco
700 Waverly Street
Mamaroneck, N.Y. 10543

R. P. Industries, Inc.
P.O. Drawer 10938
610 West Johnson Street
Raleigh, N.C. 27605

G. Rushbrooke (Smithfield) Ltd.
67-77 Charterhouse Street
London EC1M 6HL
England

Salton, Inc.
1260 Zerega Avenue
Bronx, N.Y. 10462

Sanbri (Sea Mat)
26, Avenue du Raincy
93 250-Villemomble
France

Saramago
Trav Antero Quent Quentas 234
Porto, Portugal

Scandicrafts, Inc.
P.O. Box 665
Camarillo, Calif. 93010

Scan Furniture
11310 Frederick Ave.
Beltsville, Md. 20705

Scan-Plast Industries, Inc.
54 East 54th St.
New York, NY 10022

Schacht Rubber Manufacturing Co.
P.O. Box 770
Huntington, Ind. 46750

Schiller & Asmus, Inc.
1525 Merchandise Mart
Chicago, Ill. 60654

H. Schulte & Co.
4763 Ense-Bremen
Postfach 109
West Germany

SEB of France, Inc.
521 Fifth Avenue
New York, N.Y. 10017

Sermonetta Imports
251 East 77th Street
New York, N.Y. 10021

Shapecraft Corporation
475 Park Avenue, South
New York, N.Y. 10016

Sherry-Lehman, Inc.
679 Madison Avenue
New York, N.Y. 10021

Spring Brothers Company, Inc.
218 Little Falls Road
Cedar Grove, N.J. 07009

Stangl Pottery Company
P.O. Box 2080
Trenton, N.J. 08607

Bob Stockdale
2147 Argon Street
Berkeley, Calif. 94705

Sunbeam Corporation
5400 West Roosevelt Road
Chicago, Ill. 60650

Stone Hearth
40 Park Street
Brooklyn, N.Y. 11206

Swissmart, Inc.
444 Madison Avenue
New York, N.Y. 10022

Taylor Instrument
Consumer Products Division
Suite 408
225 Fifth Avenue
New York, N.Y. 10010

Taylor Law (TALA)
(See Metal Box Ltd.)

Taylor's Eye-Witness Ltd.
Milton Street
Sheffield S3 7WJ
England

Byron Temple Pottery
226 Swan Street
Lambertville, N.J. 08530

Terraillon Corporation
950 South Hoffman Lane
Central Islip, N.Y. 11722

Thermador
(See Norris Industries)

Thermometer Corporation of America
567 East Pleasant Street
Springfield, Ohio 45501

August Thomsen Corporation
36 Sea Cliff Avenue
Glen Cove, N.Y. 11542

Thorpe Rolling Pin Co.
P.O. Box 509
1853 Milldale Road
Cheshire, Conn. 06410

Timberline
Div. of Leeds Engineering Corp.
6041 Variel Avenue
Woodland Hills, Calif. 91364

Toastmaster
Div. of McGraw-Edison Company
Columbia, Mo. 65201

Toddy Products
1206 Brooks Street
Houston, Texas 77009

Tomado Bekaert Group
Bekaert Nederland B.V.
Stationsweg 4 - Postbus 468
Dordrecht, Netherlands

Tricolator Manufacturing Co., Inc.
Bellmore, N.Y. 11710

Gary Valenti
55-72 61st Street
Maspeth, N.Y. 11378

Verity Southall
Div. of Leeds Inc.
6041 Variel Avenue
Woodland Hills, Calif. 91364

Vermont Marble Company
61 Main Street
Proctor, Vt. 05765

Figli Veroli
Via dei Rudero di Torrenova
00100 Roma, Italy

Verzinkerei Zug AG
CH-6301 Zug
Switzerland

The Vollrath Company
(See Arthur Fuller Associates, Inc.)

Waldmin & Saam
(See Milton Gumpert Imports)

Waldow Trading Company
70-72 Adams Street
Brooklyn, N.Y. 11201

Waring Products
Div. of Dynamics Corporation
 of America
Route 44
New Hartford, Conn. 06057

Wear-Ever Aluminum Inc.
Div. of Lincoln Manufacturing Co., Inc.
P.O. Box 1229
Fort Wayne, Ind. 46801

Wecolite Co., Inc.
699 Front Street
Teaneck, N.J. 07666

Paprikás Weiss
1546 Second Avenue
New York, N.Y. 10028

Welbilt Corporation
57-18 Flushing Avenue
Maspeth, N.Y. 11378

White Mountain Freezer, Inc.
Box 231
Winchendon, Mass. 01475

Williams-Sonoma
576 Sutter Street
San Francisco, Calif. 94102

Hans Wüster
8000 Munchen 60
Postfach 349
West Germany

Zabar's
Broadway at 80th Street
New York, N.Y. 10024

Zag-France
47-RIS, Avenue de Clamart
92-Issy-les-Moulineaux
France

Alfred Zanger Company
80 Pearl Street
Thompsonville, Conn. 06082

Zim Manufacturing Co.
2850 West Fulton St.
Chicago, Ill. 60612

Oscar Zucchi
Via S. Antonio all'Esquilino, 15
00185 Roma, Italy

Zyliss W. Reist AG
3000 Bern 23
Scheuermattweg 4
Switzerland

Recipe Index

General Index

566

Mail Order

All objects on this list are available by mail order through Beard Glaser Wolf Ltd., 800 Second Avenue, New York, New York 10017.

Item #	Description		Price
1.2	Measuring Cups and Spoons		$ 9.00
1.3	Metal Measuring Spoons		2.00
1.4	Measuring Spoon with Slide		.60
1.5	All-in-One Plastic Slide Measure		1.25
1.7	Pyrex Measuring Cups	1 cup	1.00
		1 pt.	1.40
		1 qt.	1.80
1.12	Compact French Plastic Scale		17.00
1.14	French Beam Balance		31.00
1.18	Mercury Oven Thermometer		15.00
1.21	Taylor Freezer Thermometer		3.75
1.26	Tiny Instant Thermometer		12.00
1.30	Large Taylor Candy Thermometer		22.50
1.33	Taylor Deep-Frying Thermometer		22.50
1.39	Terraillon Timer		10.50
1.40	Time-All		10.00
1.44	Restaurant-Size Aluminum Colander		33.00
1.45	Farberware Stainless-Steel Colander		14.00
1.53	American Aluminum Strainer	6" diam.	4.00
		8" diam.	4.50
1.55	Shallow Stainless-Steel Strainer	3½" diam.	5.00
		5½" diam.	7.00
		7½" diam.	10.00
1.59	Decorative Salad Basket		11.00
1.63	Three Brushes from West Germany		4.00
1.78	French Pop-Up Sponges package of 3		1.50
2.1	Chef's Knife with Plastic impregnated Handle	6"	18.50
		8"	23.50
		10"	28.50
2.6	Paring Knife	4"	9.50
2.9	Petite Paring Knife from France		3.75
2.11	All-Purpose Stainless-Steel Cleaver		23.50
2.20	High-Carbon Steel Boning Knife	6"	11.50
2.24	Heavy-Duty Slicer	8"	18.50
		10"	22.00
2.27	Slicer with Hollow Ground Ovals on Edge		26.00
2.31	Bread Knife from England		5.00
2.32	French Tomato Knife		2.50
2.35	Stainless-Steel Grapefruit Knife		4.75
2.37	The Zip-Zap		3.00
2.39	Multi-Cut German Steel		50.00
2.45	The Magnabar XII	12"	7.00
		18"	10.00
3.1	Swivel Action Peeler		1.25
3.3	Citrus Shell Cutter		3.00
3.5	Zester		2.00

Item #	Description		Price
3.7	French Citrus Peeler		$ 2.50
3.9	Apple Corer		2.50
3.11	Zucchini Corer		2.00
3.12	Double Melon Baller		2.75
3.18	Strawberry Huller		.75
3.24	Cherry and Plum Pitter		9.50
3.26	Serrated Spatula		8.00
3.35	All-Purpose Kitchen Shears		19.50
3.41	Curved Steel Shears		22.50
3.44	Mezzaluna I		12.00
3.59	Butter Slicer		2.00
3.60	Butter Curler		2.50
3.68	Cheese Slicer		4.50
3.78	English Nutcracker		12.00
4.3	Round Professional Veal Pounder		20.00
4.14	Magic Mill for Grain		300.00
4.21	Mouli Food Mill		13.00
4.34	Aluminum Garlic Press		4.50
4.42	Plastic Cheese Grater		3.25
4.43	Rotary Grater with Three Cylinders		4.50
4.49	Spong Meat Grinder		20.00
4.51	Perfex Peppermill		16.50
4.52	Peugeot Wooden Peppermill		10.00
4.59	Cast-Iron Clamp-on Coffee Mill		18.50
4.61	Braun Electric Coffee Mill		45.00
4.64	Electric Vegetable and Fruit Juice Extractor		60.00
4.65	Oster Electric Juicer-Extractor		80.00
4.74	Tiny Juice Extractor		1.50
4.76	Single-Speed Commercial Blender		50.00
5.1	Cuisinart Food Processor		225.00
5.3	Bosch Magic Mixer		250.00
5.4	Braun Kitchen Machine		200.00
5.5	Kitchen Aid K-5A Electric Mixer		240.00
5.6	Sunbeam Mixmaster		100.00
5.12	Heavy Wire Stainless-Steel Whisk	10"	6.50
		14"	8.00
5.17	Wood-handled Tinned-Steel Whisk	10"	3.75
		12"	4.25
		14"	5.00
5.26	Curved Olivewood Spatula		3.50
5.30	Copper Egg White Beater Bowl		60.00
5.31	Stainless-Steel Mixing Bowl Set		10.00
5.32	White Ceramic Mixing Bowl	40 oz.	4.00
		80 oz.	7.00
5.34	Glazed Ceramic Grip-stand Bowl	2½ qt.	5.00
		4½ qt.	7.00
		6½ qt.	11.00
		12½ qt.	27.50

Item #	Description		Price
5.37	3-Piece Pyrex Bowl Set		$ 6.00
5.38	10-Piece Duralex Mixing Bowl Set		15.00
5.39	Danish Melamine Bowls	1½ qt.	6.50
		2 qt.	7.50
		3 qt.	9.00
		4 qt.	10.50
6.1	Soapstone Griddle	8" x 16"	40.00
6.2	Farberware Griddle		35.00
6.3	SEB Minute Grill		45.00
6.4	Copco Grill Pan		31.00
6.5	Waffle Iron		37.00
6.6	Cast Iron Skillet	8"	5.50
		10½"	7.50
6.9	Copco Skillet	10"	31.00
		12"	36.00
6.13	Cuisinart Frying Pan	8"	26.00
		9½"	33.00
		11"	41.00
6.22	Farberware Frying Pan	8½"	16.00
		10½"	20.00
		12"	24.00
6.23	Magnalite Chicken Fryer	10½"	28.00
		12"	31.00
6.24	LeCreuset Chicken Fryer		37.00
6.25	Copco Chicken Fryer with Cover		56.00
6.28	Hammered Copper Sauteuse		45.00
6.31	Cuisinart Sauté Pan with Cover		33.00
6.36	Hammered Copper Fait-Tout		60.00
6.47	Magnalite Saucepan	1 qt.	19.50
		2 qt.	22.00
		3 qt.	24.50
6.54	Cuisinart Saucepan	1 qt.	22.00
		2 qt.	28.00
		3 qt.	32.00
6.55	Le Creuset Saucepan		24.00
6.56	Copco Saucepan	1 qt.	28.00
		2 qt.	33.00
		3 qt.	38.00
6.60	Metal Trivet		3.00
6.61	Flame-Tamer		5.50
6.64	Farberware Double Boiler with Steamer		33.00
6.66	Pyrex Double Boiler		15.50
6.72	Farberware Stewpot	4 qt.	20.00
		6 qt.	26.00
		8 qt.	29.00
		16 qt.	45.00
6.73	Large Cuisinart pot	5 qt.	56.00
		8½ qt.	70.00
6.80	Steamer Boiler with Basket Insert	32 qt.	65.00
6.85	Copco Lid	10"	16.00
		12"	18.00
6.95	Cuisinart Stainless-Steel Lid	4¾"	5.00
		5½"	6.00
		6¼"	6.50
		7"	7.00
		8"	8.00
		8¾"	9.00
		9½"	10.00
		11"	15.00

Item #	Description		Price
6.98	Domed Glass Lid	8″	$4.50
		9″	5.75
		10½″	6.25
		11¾″	6.75
6.101	Farberware High-domed Lid	12″	13.00
6.102	Farberware Low-domed Lid		
		8½″	8.00
		10½″	9.00
6.104	Stainless-Steel Implement Set		49.00
6.105	White Porcelain Tasting Spoon		6.00
6.113	Flexible Pancake Turner		8.75
6.119	Pot Fork		2.50
7.2	Cuisinart Casserole (covers separately)	3½ qt.	43.00
		5½ qt.	50.00
7.14	Copco Casserole	1½ qt.	25.00
		2½ qt.	37.00
		5 qt.	49.00
		7 qt.	59.00
7.15	Round Doufeu	4 qt.	45.00
		6 qt.	50.00
7.19	Oval Doufeu	4½ qt.	50.00
7.39	White Terrine from France	1 qt.	12.00
		1½ qt.	15.00
		2 qt.	17.00
7.41	Brown English Terrine	1 qt.	20.00
7.42	Le Creuset Enameled Terrine	1 qt.	25.00
7.44	Round Mock Pâté en Croûte		11.00
7.49	Orange Plastic Slow Cooker		34.00
7.64	Rectangular Pyrex Baking Dishes	1½ qt.	2.10
		2 qt.	2.70
		3 qt.	3.10
8.7	Farber Broiler Rotisserie		50.00
8.13	Cuisinart Round Gratin Pan	9½″	28.00
8.14	Handle for Cuisinart Gratin Pans		4.50
8.15	Copco Oval Gratin Pan		26.00
8.16	Pillivuyt Oval Porcelain Gratin Dish	10″	10.00
		12″	12.50
		14″	16.00
8.20	Salamander		8.00
8.31	Bulb Baster with Injecting Needle		2.50
8.38	Dansk Roasting Pan	8″x10¾″	26.00
		10″x12¾″	35.00
8.39	Wearever Aluminum Roaster		16.00
8.44	V-Shaped Roasting Rack		4.50
8.46	Deep Oval Magnalite Roaster	13″	31.50
		15″	36.50
		18″	57.00
8.55	Farber Turbo-Oven		130.00
8.56	GE Toast-R-Oven		50.00
8.58	Toastmaster Toaster		30.00
9.8	Black Steel Loaf Pan	10″	6.50
		12″	11.00
9.13	Pyrex Loaf Pan	1½ qt.	1.70
		2½ qt.	2.10
9.16	Frame with Mini-Loaf Pans		24.00
9.23	German Tinned Kugelhopf Mold	6½″	5.00
		8½″	5.50
		9½″	6.00
9.26	Teflon-lined Bundt Pan		8.00
9.28	Professional Tube Pan		11.00
9.30	Three-in-One Springform		5.00

Item #	Description		Price
9.31	Professional Layer-Cake Pans	9″x1½″	$3.50
		6″x1½″	3.00
9.32	Lockwood's Deep Layer Pan		11.00
9.33	Square Layer-Cake Pan		6.00
9.34	Square Pyrex Baking Pan		2.10
9.46	Lockwood 12-Cup Muffin Tin		12.50
9.47	Lockwood 24-Cup Muffin Tin		16.50
9.55	French Madeleine Tin		5.50
10.5	Pyrex Pie Plate	9″ diam.	1.20
		10″ diam.	1.50
10.7	Tinned French Flan Ring	8″ diam.	2.25
10.11	Regular Flan Form		7.50
10.12	Tinned Loose-bottomed Tart Pan	8″ diam.	2.00
		9½″ diam.	2.50
		11¼″ diam.	3.00
10.15	Fluted French Quiche Mold	10″ diam.	18.00
		11½″ diam.	20.00
10.35	Pastry Blender		1.75
10.36	Blending Fork		1.50
10.38	Metal and Wood Dough Scraper		5.75
10.45	Canvas Pastry Cloth in Frame		5.50
10.47	American Ball-Bearing Rolling Pin		12.50
10.48	Straight French Rolling Pin		4.00
10.49	Tapered Beechwood Rolling Pin		3.50
10.54	American All-Purpose Dredger		2.50
10.56	Flat Natural-Bristle Pastry Brush		1.50
10.59	Pastry Jagger		1.75
10.62	Six-Sided Cooky Cutter		3.00
10.77	Rolling French Croissant Cutter		35.00
10.80	Heavy-Duty Wire Cake Rack	16½″x13″x⅞″	7.00
		24½″x16″x1″	10.00
10.82	Revolving Decorating Stand		26.00
10.84	Aluminum Decorating Syringe		6.50
11.1	Stainless-Steel Fish Scaler		2.75
11.3	All-Purpose Fish Knife		2.50
11.9	Rowoco Filleting Knife		8.00
11.13	Double-handled Fish Poacher	16″	45.00
		18″	55.00
11.14	Stainless-Steel Fish Poacher	16″x5½″x4″	34.00
		17¾″x5¾″x4¼″	40.00
11.21	Fish Grill		17.50
11.31	Oyster and Clam Knife		2.00
11.37	Lobster Shears		5.50
11.51	Porcelain Snail-Shell Cup		2.00
11.61	Stainless-Steel Egg Rings		1.00
11.63	Sand-cast Aluminum Omelet Pan	8″	26.00
		10″	33.00
		12″	40.00
11.73	Pillivuyt Soufflé Dish	6 oz.	1.25
		1 qt.	6.50
		1½ qt.	7.50
		2 qt.	9.00
		3 qt.	14.00
11.83	Glass Soufflé Dish Set of 3		17.00
11.90	SteaMarvel		4.00
11.97	Iron Deep-Fat Fryer		10.00

Item #	Description		Price
11.105	Hinged Pâté Mold		$12.00
11.111	Simple Pudding Mold	6¼″	5.00
		7¾″	6.00
11.116	Charlotte Mold	10 oz.	6.00
		1 qt.	11.00
		2 qt.	16.00
11.128	Coeur à la Crème Mold	3¼″x2¾″	5.00
11.132	Household Electric Ice-Cream Freezer		65.00
11.133	Salton Ice-Cream Machine		20.00
11.137	Zeroll Dipper		7.50
11.143	Single Unit Hot Plate		40.00
11.150	Fondue Bourguignone Set		60.00
11.155	Salton Hot Tray		38.00
11.162	Iron Crêpe Pan	8″	10.00
11.163	Aluminum Crêpe Pan	8″	25.00
		12″	39.00
11.167	Oval Flambé Pan	12⅝″	52.00
11.172	Watermate		40.00
11.174	Salton Yogurt Maker		13.00
11.177	Melitta Coffee Maker	6 cup	20.00
11.178	Chemex Coffee Maker	2-13 cups	18.95
11.181	Neapolitan Filter Pot	4-6 cups	9.00
11.183	Toddy Coffee Maker		15.00
11.186	Junior Espresso Maker		18.00
11.189	Europiccola Espresso Maker		275.00
11.194	Copco Tea Kettle		19.95
11.201	Dripless Tea Strainer		3.25
11.203	Instant Immersion Heater		1.50
11.209	Crystal Wine Funnel		7.00
11.215	Waiter's Corkscrew		4.50
11.216	Winged Corkscrew		2.50
11.219	Heavy-Duty Mechanical Corkscrew		125.00

BGW-1 The Cooks' Catalogue Newsletter
Our Cooks' Catalogue Newsletter—a four page compendium of cooking equipment information, hints, recipes, and items of interest compiled by our staff and contributing editors now being prepared for distribution. Please send $2.00 to cover costs of printing and postage for a one year subscription (four issues).

Mail Order Form

Complete this coupon and mail to: Beard Glaser Wolf Ltd., 800 Second Avenue, New York, N.Y. 10017.

Please send check or money order only. Orders will be filled for any combination of items totaling $7.50 or more, exclusive of tax where required. Please add sales tax that applies to community where your order is being sent. All orders will be shipped within three weeks of receipt.. In case of delay you will be notified by mail.

Gift Giving? Would you like to send some of our items as gifts? For each gift sent, please indicate how card should be signed, or enclose your own card, and tell us when you want it sent.

Item #	Description	Color	Size	Qty	Unit Price	Total
BGW1	Cooks' Catalogue Newsletter				$2.00	

Sub Total

Sales Tax

Postage & Handling

TOTAL

Shipping & Handling

If your order totals:	Add
0 - $7.50	$1.50
$7.51-$15.00	$2.00
$15.01-$25.00	$2.25
$25.01-$40.00	$2.50
$40.01 & over	$2.75

Please Do Not Tape or Staple This Order

Order Blank

Ship To:
(Use this space only if shipping address is different than your address in SOLD TO area below, or if you are sending a gift.)

Mr. Ms.
Mrs. Miss _____

ADDRESS _____

CITY _____

STATE _____ ZIP _____

Sold To:

Mr. Ms.
Mrs. Miss _____

ADDRESS _____

CITY _____

STATE _____ ZIP _____

Note

The equipment and utensils in *The Cooks' Catalogue* were produced by various manufacturers and craftsmen here and abroad. The prices given here are based on market conditions and international currency exchange rates as of September 1976 and are therefore subject to change without notice.

Order Blank

No Envelope Necessary

FOLD, SEAL AND STAMP

USE
LETTER
POSTAGE
HERE

FROM

Name

Address

City _____ State

Zip Code

Beard Glaser Wolf, Ltd.
800 Second Avenue
New York, N.Y. 10017

— THIRD FOLD ON THIS LINE —

— SECOND FOLD ON THIS LINE —

— FIRST FOLD ON THIS LINE —

Important

1. Checks, drafts and money orders may safely be enclosed. Please do not staple or use tape on this envelope.

2. Before sealing please check that your name and address are plainly written, that you have given all necessary information, and that everything you intended to enclose has been included.

3. Kindly include any correspondence or inquiry not connected with this order on a separate sheet of paper complete with name and address.